PUBLIC PAPERS OF THE PRESIDENTS
OF THE
UNITED STATES

William J. Clinton

1995

(IN TWO BOOKS)

BOOK II—JULY 1 TO DECEMBER 31, 1995

UNITED STATES GOVERNMENT PRINTING OFFICE
WASHINGTON : 1996

Published by the
Office of the Federal Register
National Archives and Records Administration

For sale by the
Superintendent of Documents
U.S. Government Printing Office
Washington, DC 20402

Foreword

The period from July through December 1995 was an exceptional time. On fundamental issues—the role of Government, our role in the world, and how we can build a strong American community—our people came together after intense debate to forge new approaches that applied our enduring values to the challenges of new times.

During this period, the American people engaged in a great national debate about how best to balance the budget. I proposed and fought for a plan to balance the budget in a way that reflected our values, by strengthening Medicare, Medicaid, education, and the environment. The congressional majority put forward a plan that I believed did not honor our fundamental values; I vetoed that plan. By year's end, after the congressional majority twice shut down the Government, it was clear that the American people had rallied to our view. We need a smaller Government, but one strong enough to give people the tools to make the most of their own lives.

America also decisively reasserted its role as the world's indispensable nation. On my remarkable trip to Northern Ireland and Ireland—and to Jerusalem, for the funeral of Israeli Prime Minister Yitzhak Rabin—Americans were once again reminded of our unique obligation to lead and to be a force for peace where possible. And in Bosnia, America led the way to bring to an end the bloodiest conflict in Europe since World War II. By committing our troops to help maintain the peace in Bosnia, we recommitted ourselves to being the world's strongest force for peace, freedom, and prosperity.

Perhaps most important, this was a time when we worked to find common ground and bridge the intense divisions of race, religion, and geography that threaten to pull us apart. In a series of speeches, I called on Americans to find common ground. At Georgetown University, I urged a new tone of civility based on the common values that bind us together. In speeches on affirmative action at the National Archives in Washington and in Austin, Texas, I called on all Americans to clean their house of the racism that is still too real among us. And I spoke about the proper role of religion in our lives and communities, arguing that our schools need not be prayer-free zones.

The closing months of 1995 set the course for how our Nation can move confidently toward the 21st century. By holding true to our values—opportunity for all, responsibility from all, and building a strong American community—our Nation passed through this moment of decision stronger than ever before.

Preface

This book contains the papers and speeches of the 42d President of the United States that were issued by the Office of the Press Secretary during the period July 1–December 31, 1995. The material has been compiled and published by the Office of the Federal Register, National Archives and Records Administration.

The material is presented in chronological order, and the dates shown in the headings are the dates of the documents or events. In instances when the release date differs from the date of the document itself, that fact is shown in the textnote. Every effort has been made to ensure accuracy: Remarks are checked against a tape recording, and signed documents are checked against the original. Textnotes and cross references have been provided by the editors for purposes of identification or clarity. Speeches were delivered in Washington, DC, unless indicated. The times noted are local times. All materials that are printed full-text in the book have been indexed in the subject and name indexes, and listed in the document categories list.

The Public Papers of the Presidents series was begun in 1957 in response to a recommendation of the National Historical Publications Commission. An extensive compilation of messages and papers of the Presidents covering the period 1789 to 1897 was assembled by James D. Richardson and published under congressional authority between 1896 and 1899. Since then, various private compilations have been issued, but there was no uniform publication comparable to the Congressional Record or the United States Supreme Court Reports. Many Presidential papers could be found only in the form of mimeographed White House releases or as reported in the press. The Commission therefore recommended the establishment of an official series in which Presidential writings, addresses, and remarks of a public nature could be made available.

The Commission's recommendation was incorporated in regulations of the Administrative Committee of the Federal Register, issued under section 6 of the Federal Register Act (44 U.S.C. 1506), which may be found in title 1, part 10, of the Code of Federal Regulations.

A companion publication to the Public Papers series, the Weekly Compilation of Presidential Documents, was begun in 1965 to provide a broader range of Presidential materials on a more timely basis to meet the needs of the contemporary reader. Beginning with the administration of Jimmy Carter, the Public Papers series expanded its coverage to include additional material as printed in the Weekly Compilation. That coverage provides a listing of the President's daily schedule and meetings, when announced, and other items of general interest issued by the Office of the Press Secretary. Also included are lists of the President's nominations submitted to the Senate, materials released by the Office of the Press Secretary that are not printed full-text in the book, and proclamations, Executive orders, and other Presidential documents released by the Office of the Press Secretary and published in the *Federal Register*. This information appears in the appendixes at the end of the book.

Volumes covering the administrations of Presidents Hoover, Truman, Eisenhower, Kennedy, Johnson, Nixon, Ford, Carter, Reagan, and Bush are also available.

The Public Papers of the Presidents publication program is under the direction of Frances D. McDonald, Director of the Presidential Documents and Legislative Division. The series is produced by the Presidential Documents Unit, Gwen H. Estep, Chief. The Chief Editor of this book was Karen Howard Ashlin, assisted by Scott Andreae, Brad Brooks, Anna Glover, Margaret A. Hemmig, Carolyn W. Hill, Alfred Jones, Rachel Rondell, Cheryl E. Sirofchuck, and Michael J. Sullivan.

The frontispiece and photographs used in the portfolio were supplied by the White House Photo Office. The typography and design of the book were developed by the Government Printing Office under the direction of Michael F. DiMario, Public Printer.

Richard L. Claypoole
Director of the Federal Register

John W. Carlin
Archivist of the United States

Contents

Cabinet

Secretary of State .... Warren M. Christopher

Secretary of the Treasury .... Robert E. Rubin

Secretary of Defense .... William J. Perry

Attorney General .... Janet Reno

Secretary of the Interior .... Bruce Babbitt

Secretary of Agriculture .... Dan Glickman

Secretary of Commerce .... Ronald H. Brown

Secretary of Labor .... Robert B. Reich

Secretary of Health and Human Services .... Donna E. Shalala

Secretary of Housing and Urban
Development .... Henry G. Cisneros

Secretary of Transportation .... Federico Peña

Secretary of Energy .... Hazel Rollins O'Leary

Secretary of Education .... Richard W. Riley

Secretary of Veterans Affairs .... Jesse Brown

United States Representative to the
United Nations .... Madeleine Korbel Albright

Administrator of the Environmental
Protection Agency .... Carol M. Browner

United States Trade Representative .... Michael Kantor

Director of the Office of Management
and Budget .... Alice M. Rivlin

Chief of Staff .... Leon E. Panetta

Counselor to the President .... Thomas F. McLarty III

Chair of the Council of Economic Advisers ..... Joseph E. Stiglitz

Director of National Drug Control Policy .... Lee Patrick Brown

Administrator of the Small Business
Administration .... Philip Lader

Director of Central Intelligence .... John M. Deutch

Administration of William J. Clinton

1995

The President's Radio Address
July 1, 1995

Good morning. On this Fourth of July weekend, I want to talk about one thing that is at the root of all of our independence: going to work. It makes you self-sufficient. It makes you and your family truly independent.

Unfortunately, millions of Americans are not independent because they are dependent on welfare. The vast majority of these Americans dream the same dreams most of us do. They want the same dignity that comes from going to work and the pride that comes from doing right by their children. They want to be independent.

The Congress and I are now working hard on welfare reform to give them that kind of independence. I look forward to Congress passing and my signing into law a bipartisan bill that stands a real chance of ending welfare as we know it.

Though there are very different approaches in the bills now before Congress, we have agreed on much of what we need to do. We agree there must be time limits on welfare, after which all who can must work. And I'm pleased that Congress has now agreed with me that we must enforce child support with the toughest possible laws.

But if we're going to end welfare, we must do more about a crucial element that is missing from the current approach of many in Congress. Instead of providing the child care people need to get off welfare, some in Congress actually are trying to cut child care.

So today I say to Congress, child care must be the central element of our effort to put welfare mothers to work. The bold plan that I support, which has been proposed by Senators Daschle, Breaux, and Mikulski, provides that kind of child care. Our bill presents a genuine opportunity for bipartisan agreement, and I hope we take advantage of it soon. After all, we should want the same thing for people on welfare we want for all Americans, the chance to build strong families and to make the most of their own lives.

The very name of the welfare program says it all: Aid to Families With Dependent Children. Children by nature are dependent. The point of welfare reform must not be to punish children but to help their families become independent. To be independent with dependent children, a person must be able to succeed both as a worker and a parent. That's what most Americans have to do these days.

That's a big reason I worked so hard back in 1993 to cut taxes for working families with children whose incomes were under $28,000, and now they're about $1,000 lower than they used to be. And that's why I'm working hard to include in my middle class bill of rights a tax credit of $500 per child for all the children under 13 in middle class families. And that's why it is pure fantasy to believe we can put a welfare mother to work unless we provide child care for her children. We don't need more latchkey kids. We certainly don't need more neglected children. And we don't want more welfare mothers staying at home, living on welfare just because they can't find child care.

We do want people to be good workers and good parents. And if we want parents on welfare to go to work, we have to make sure they can find good, clean, safe places for their children to go during the day.

Many in Congress want to cut child care just to save money. Well, I want to cut spending, and I want to save money too. But we have to do it the smart way. Cutting child care will make it harder for parents to get off and stay off welfare. It will therefore cost us far more down the road than it will ever save in the near term.

Some people in Congress want to take even more extreme steps that will hurt, not strengthen, families. They don't want welfare reform unless it cuts off all help to children whose mothers are poor, young, and unmarried. I want to discourage teen pregnancy. We have to do that, but not by hurting innocent babies. We should require teen mothers to live at home, stay in school, and turn their lives around so they and their children stay off welfare for good.

Our administration has already put 29 States on the road to ending welfare as we know it with waivers to free them up from cumbersome Federal rules and regulations when they have good ideas to reform welfare. Today I'm pleased to announce that Virginia will receive the newest waiver. Virginia's plan requires people on welfare to go to work. Like the States of Oregon, Missouri, and a few others, it also allows money now spent on welfare and food stamps to go to employers to supplement wages to help create jobs in the private sector. And it helps people get child care. It's a good plan, and I'm proud to be supporting it.

Several months ago, I called on Congress to send me a welfare reform bill by July 4th, Independence Day. I'm disappointed they haven't been able to meet that deadline, but I am hopeful that we'll move forward on a bipartisan welfare reform bill. I don't want filibusters. I don't want vetoes. I don't want gridlock. But I do want real welfare reform that requires work, demands responsibility, and provides the child care people need to move off welfare and to be successful as workers and parents.

It's time to get to work so we can give millions of other Americans a new Independence Day.

Thanks for listening.

NOTE: The address was recorded at 12:38 p.m. on June 30 at the Sheraton Chicago in Chicago, IL, for broadcast at 10:06 a.m. on July 1.

Remarks at the Opening Ceremonies of the Special Olympics World Games in New Haven, Connecticut
July 1, 1995

Let's give her another hand. [*Applause*] Thank you, Loretta Claiborne, for that wonderful introduction. And thank you for the power of your example for young people all across America and throughout the world: I know we're all impressed that you have completed 25 marathons. I'm also pleased that in these games you're representing Team Pennsylvania in one of my favorite sports, bowling. I also want to thank four other very special runners—four members of the United States Special Olympics Team, David Congdon, David McQuarry, Troy Rutter and Daniel Bailey, who came to Washington to the White House this week to run 3 miles with me to highlight the importance of Special Olympics. They were much faster than I was, but they were very gentle and kind that day. I want to congratulate the city of New Haven and the State of Connecticut for the magnificent job that they have done. From the Governor, the Senators, the members of the congressional district, to the mayor, to all the ordinary citizens in this State and this wonderful city where my wife and I met almost 25 years ago: You have done a wonderful, wonderful job.

Ladies and gentlemen, we must also thank the person whose inspiration, leadership, and determination has brought us all here today, the founder of these games, Eunice Shriver. Year after year, decade after decade, her vision grows clearer and her energy seems to increase as she brings more and more and more of us throughout the world into the orbit of her incredible determination to make the Special Olympics all that it can be and to mean all that it can mean for all of us.

We also thank her for making the Special Olympics a family affair. Thank you, Sargent Shriver, for being the creative force behind the worldwide growth of Special Olympics. And thank you, Timothy Shriver, for doing such an outstanding job as president of these 1995 games.

I also want to thank the distinguished former Governor of Connecticut, Lowell Weicker, who has continued to serve his country magnificently as the chairman of these 1995 games. Thank you, Lowell Weicker. Please stand up. Thank you. [*Applause*]

Let me welcome also leaders throughout the world who have come here to cheer for their athletes. We have people from countries all across the globe. I am here to cheer for the Americans. They're here to cheer for their athletes. And we're all here to cheer all of you on. Thank you for coming from all distant corners of the globe.

These world games are being called the games of inclusion. From their beginnings in the United States 27 years ago, the Special Olympics have grown to include more than 144 countries on 6 continents. Large and small nations are represented here, welcomed as equals.

We have seen here people brought together of every race, color, and creed, every faith, in a joyful celebration of peaceful competition, good will, and the triumph of the human spirit. The world could learn a great lesson from all of you standing down here in the Yale Bowl tonight: Everybody counts, and everybody can do something very, very important and good.

You are the living symbol that we can reach across continents, across cultures, across human differences, to unleash the God-given potential that lies within every individual. You have shown us in so many ways that when you are given the chance, you can do extraordinary things. The world community is recognizing this more and more.

We have come so far in such a short time. Here in the United States, it has only been 5 years since we passed the Americans with Disabilities Act, committing ourselves to treating our people on the basis of their abilities, not their disabilities. And the world is moving as well. This week, on its 50th anniversary, the United Nations convened the very first international symposium on intellectual disabilities. There is more to come.

But our work is not yet done. President Kennedy once said that the rights of every man are diminished when the rights of one man are threatened. So tonight I challenge all of you and every citizen of the world watching us to be an olympic champion for inclusion, a champion for equal rights, a champion for dignity, a champion for the triumph of the human spirit in all of us.

That spirit, that spirit, these athletes are about to show all over the globe. So, by all means and with great spirit, let the games begin.

I want all of you to know that you have our love, our support, and our admiration. I hereby declare the 1995 Special Olympics World Games officially open.

NOTE: The President spoke at 9:40 p.m. at the Yale Bowl. In his remarks, he referred to Loretta Claiborne, athlete and Special Olympics board member; Gov. John G. Rowland of Connecticut; and Mayor John DeStefano of New Haven, CT.

Letter to Congressional Leaders on Reauthorization of the Ryan White CARE Act
July 5, 1995

Dear Mr. Speaker: (Dear Mr. Leader:)

I am writing to urge you to lead the Congress in passing the reauthorization of the Ryan White CARE Act before the summer recess. We cannot allow this crucial program to lapse.

There is strong bipartisan support for the Ryan White CARE Act. The initial legislation was approved by overwhelming margins in both houses (95–4 in the Senate and 408–14 in the House) and signed into law by President Bush. Funding for this program has been endorsed from both sides of the aisle throughout the five years of the program and the reauthorization bill in the Senate has 60 co-sponsors. It is a program vital to the lives of Americans living with HIV and AIDS. Its existence has had a dramatic impact on the quality and length of their lives while helping to reduce the cost of their care.

The CARE Act provides direct services to people living with HIV and AIDS through grants to states, cities, community organizations, and local clinics. It emphasizes outpatient care in clinics and other facilities and is designed to relieve the burden on public hospitals and other more expensive inpatient facilities.

It has been a tremendous success in meeting this mandate. By lessening the demand on public hospitals and other facilities, valuable inpatient resources have been freed to care for patients with other diseases, and people with HIV and AIDS have been able to lead more productive lives in their communities. The CARE Act approach serves as a model for delivering more cost-effective health care for people with all diseases.

In 1994, the CARE Act provided care to more than 200,000 uninsured and underinsured people living with HIV or AIDS and early intervention services to another 85,000 people. The Act also funded HIV counseling and testing to nearly 100,000 Americans, provided pharmaceutical assistance to 75,000 individuals, and supported more than 15,000 women and children participating in AIDS-related clinical trials.

Let me share with you the story of one person who has been helped by this program—one person whose experience with the CARE Act is typical of literally hundreds of thousands of other Americans who have benefited from this law. "Debbie" is a 27 year old woman living with AIDS in a rural part of South Carolina. Until recently, few doctors in Debbie's hometown were willing to treat AIDS patients in part because so many were uninsured. With funding from the Ryan White CARE Act, the County Health Department opened a clinic in the town of Orangeburg that operated six days a month with a rotating staff of five physicians and three nurses. The clinic's staff has taught Debbie's mother to care for her daughter at home. When Debbie is too sick to come to the clinic, the staff comes to her. Not only has this prevented more costly hospitalizations, but it provides Debbie and her mother peace of mind. Debbie's Mom calls the clinic's staff her "guardian angels."

The Ryan White CARE Act is a model of compassionate caring for people in need. At a time when AIDS is the leading cause of death of young adults, we cannot let reauthorization of the CARE Act be held up by divisive arguments about how people contracted HIV. Nor should we be deterred by the false argument that people with HIV and AIDS are getting more help than those with other diseases. In fact, total federal spending in FY 1995 for research, treatment prevention, Medicaid, Medicare, and income supplements for AIDS is less than one-third that for cancer and less than one-sixth that for heart disease. (AIDS spending is $6 billion, cancer is $17.5 billion, and heart disease is $38 billion.)

In the United States, an average of 220 Americans are being diagnosed with AIDS every day and an average of 109 Americans are dying of this disease each day. Now is not the time to retreat in our national response to this terrible disease. We must move forward to meet the very real needs of Americans living with HIV and AIDS. We can certainly do more, we cannot do any less.

I hope you will join me in urging the Congress to move forward promptly with a five-year reauthorization of this vital program without complicated amendments so that we can once again show the American people that their government can provide the assistance they deserve.

Sincerely,

BILL CLINTON

NOTE: Identical letters were sent to Newt Gingrich, Speaker of the House of Representatives, and Bob Dole, Senate majority leader.

Letter to Congressional Leaders Transmitting a Report on Most-Favored-Nation Trade Status for Bulgaria
July 5, 1995

Dear Mr. Speaker: *(Dear Mr. President:)*

On June 3, 1993, I determined and reported to the Congress that Bulgaria is in full compliance with the freedom of emigration criteria of sections 402 and 409 of the Trade Act of 1974. This action allowed for the continuation of most-favored-nation (MFN) status for Bulgaria and certain other activities without the requirement of a waiver.

As required by law, I am submitting an updated report to the Congress concerning emigration laws and policies of the Republic of Bulgaria. You will find that the report indicates continued Bulgarian compliance with U.S. and international standards in the area of emigration policy.

Sincerely,

WILLIAM J. CLINTON

NOTE: Identical letters were sent to Newt Gingrich, Speaker of the House of Representatives, and Albert Gore, Jr., President of the Senate.

Remarks at Georgetown University
July 6, 1995

Thank you very much, my good friend Father O'Donovan. You just gave the speech in 5 minutes; there's nothing for me to say. [*Laughter*] I thank you for welcoming me back. I thank the members of our administration who are here: Secretary Riley and Deputy Secretary Kunin, Ambassador Raiser, Director of the USIA Joe Duffy, Chairmen Sheldon Hackney and Jane Alexander, and Penn Kemble, the Deputy Director of the USIA. And I thank my former classmates, some of whom I see out here, and my friends and people around this country who have done so much to try to strengthen the bonds of American citizenship.

Today I want to have more of a conversation than deliver a formal speech, about the great debate now raging in our Nation, not so much over what we should do but over how we should resolve the great questions of our time here in Washington and in communities all across our country. I want to talk about the obligations of citizenship, the obligations imposed on the President and people in power and the obligations imposed on all Americans.

Two days ago we celebrated the 219th birthday of our democracy. The Declaration of Independence was also clearly a declaration of citizenship: " . . . all men are created equal, . . . endowed by their Creator with certain unalienable rights, . . . among these are Life, Liberty, and the pursuit of Happiness." It was also manifestly a declaration of citizenship in a different way. It was a declaration of interdependence: " . . . for the support of this Declaration, with a firm reliance on the protection of Divine Providence, we mutually pledge . . . our lives, our fortunes, and our sacred honor." The distinguished American historian Samuel Eliot Morison, in his "History of the American People," wrote of these words, "These words are more revolutionary than anything written by Robespierre, Marx, or Lenin, more explosive than the atom, a continual challenge to ourselves as well as an inspiration to the oppressed of all the world."

What is the challenge to ourselves at the dawn of the 21st century, and how shall we meet it? First of all, we must remember that the Declaration of Independence was written as a commitment for all Americans at all times, not just in time of war or great national crisis.

My argument to you is pretty straightforward. I believe we face challenges of truly historic dimensions, challenges here at home perhaps greater than any we faced since the beginning of this century we are about to finish and the dawn of the industrial era. But they are not greater challenges in their own way than the ones we faced at our birth, greater challenges than those of slavery and civil war, greater than those of World War I or the Depression or World War II. And they can be solved, though they are profound. What are they?

Most people my age grew up in an America dominated by middle class dreams and middle class values, the life we wanted to live and the kind of people we wanted to be—dreams that inspired those who were born into the middle class; dreams that restrained and directed the lives of those who were much more successful and more powerful; dreams that animated the strivings of those who were poor because of the condition of their birth or because they came here as immigrants; middle class dreams that there would be reward for work and that the future of our children would be better than the lives we enjoyed; middle class values, strong families and faith, safe streets, secure futures.

These things are very much threatened today, threatened by 20 years of stagnant incomes, of harder work by good Americans for the same or lower pay, of increasing inequality of incomes, and increasing insecurity in jobs and retirement and health care. They are threatened by 30 years of social problems of profound implications: of family break-ups, of a rising tide of violence and drugs, of declining birth rates among successful married couples and rising birth rates among young people who are not married. They are threatened by the failure of public institutions to respond, the failure of bureaucracies encrusted in yesterday's prerogatives and not meeting the challenges of today and tomorrow—the schools, the law enforcement agencies, the governments and their economic and other policies. They are threatened by the sheer pace and scope of change, as technology and ideas and money and decisions move across the globe at breathtaking rates, and every great opportunity seems to carry within it the seeds of a great problem.

So that we have anomalies everywhere: Abroad, the cold war ends, but we see the rise and the threat of technology-based destruction—sarin gas exploding in the subway in Japan, the bomb exploding in Oklahoma City. The Soviet Union is no more, and so they worry now in the Baltics about becoming a conduit for drug trafficking, and they worry in Russia about their banks being taken over by organized crime. And here at home, it all seems so confusing—the highest growth rates in a decade, the stock market at an all-time high, almost 7 million more jobs, more millionaires and new businesses than ever before, but most people working harder for less, feeling more insecure.

I saw it just the other day, this cartoon, which you probably can't see, but I'll read it to you. There's a politician—maybe it's supposed to be me—[*laughter*]—up here giving a speech at a banquet, one of those interminable banquets we all attend. And here's a waiter serving one of the attendees. The politician says, "The current recovery has created over 7.8 million jobs." The waiter says, "And I've got three of them." [*Laughter*]

In 1991, as Father O'Donovan said, I came here to Georgetown to talk about these challenges and laid out my philosophy about how we as a people, not just as a government but as a people, ought to meet them. I called it the New Covenant. I will repeat briefly what I said then because I don't believe I can do any better today than I did then in terms of what I honestly believe we ought to be doing.

I think we have to create more opportunity and demand more responsibility. I think we have to give citizens more say and provide them a more responsive, less bureaucratic Government. I think we have to do these things because we are literally a community, an American family that is going up or down together, whether we like it or not. If we're going to have middle class dreams and middle class values, we have to do things as private citizens, and we have to do things in partnership through our public agencies and through our other associations.

In 1994, when the Republicans won a majority in Congress, they offered a different view which they called their "Contract With America." In their view, most of our problems were personal and cultural; the Government tended to make them worse because it was bureaucratic and wedded to the past and more interested in regulating and choking off the free enterprise system and promoting the welfare state; and therefore, what we should do is to balance the budget as soon as possible, cut taxes as much as possible, deregulate business completely if possible, and cut our investments in things like welfare as much as possible.

As you know, I thought there were different things that ought to be done because I believed in partnership. I believed in supporting community initiatives that were working and preventing things before they happened, instead of just punishing bad behavior after it occurred, and trying to empower people to make the most of their own lives. So I believed that there were things we could do here in Washington to help, whether it was family leave, or tougher child support enforcement, or reforming the pension system to save the pensions of over 8 million American workers, or investing more in education, making college more affordable.

What I believe grows largely out of my personal history, and a lot of it happened to me a long time before I came to Georgetown and read in books things that made me convinced that I was basically right. I grew up in a small town in a poor State. When I was born at the end of World War II, my State's per capita income was barely half the national average. I was the first person in my family to go to college. When I was a boy, I lived for a while on a farm without an indoor toilet. It makes a good story, not as good as being born in a log cabin, but it's true. [*Laughter*]

I had a stepfather without a high school diploma and a grandfather, whom I loved above all people almost, who had a sixth-grade education. I lived in a segregated society, and I lived in a family, as has now been well-documented, with problems of alcohol and, later, drug abuse. I learned a lot about what I call the New Covenant, about the importance of responsibility and opportunity.

I lived in a family where everybody worked hard and where kids were expected to study hard. But I also had a lot of opportunity that was given to me by my community. I had good teachers and good schools. And when I needed them, I got scholarships and jobs. I saw what happened to good people who had no opportunity because they happened to be black or because they happened to be poor and white and isolated in the hills and hollows of the mountains of my State.

I saw what happened in my own family to people who were good people but didn't behave responsibly. My stepfather was very responsible toward me but not very responsible toward himself. Anybody who's ever lived in a family with an alcoholic knows that there is nothing you can do for somebody else they are not prepared to do for themselves. And my brother, after all of his struggles with drug addiction, which included even serving some time in jail, I am sometimes more proud of him than I am of what I've done because he has a family and a son and a life, not because of the love and support that we all gave him but because of what he did for himself.

So my whole political philosophy is basically rooted in what I think works. It works for families and communities, and it worked pretty well for our country for a long time. If you look at recent American history, our country has never been perfect because none of us are, but we did always seem to be going in the right direction.

I remember when I was a boy in the fifties and sixties—I remember like it was yesterday when I graduated from high school in 1964, and we had about 3-percent unemployment, about 3- or 4-percent real growth, and very modest inflation. And we all just assumed that the American dream would work out all right if we could ever whip racism. If we could just whip that and make sure all poor people had a chance to work their way into the middle class, we could just almost put this country on automatic. I know that's hard to believe, but that's basically what we thought back then. If we could just somehow lift this awful racial bur-

den off our shoulders and learn how to live together, we could just roll on.

And then in the sixties and the seventies and the eighties, the results got a lot more mixed. Contrary to what a lot of people say now in retrospect, the sixties were not all bad. A lot of good things happened. A lot of people passionately believed that they had a responsibility to help one another achieve the fullest of their God-given potential. And a lot of the important advances in civil rights and in education and in fighting poverty really made a difference. But it was also a time when many people began to have such profound cultural clashes that more and more people dropped out and became more self-indulgent.

Contrary to popular retrospect, a lot of good things happened in the seventies. We made a national commitment as a country to defend our environment. This is a safer, cleaner, healthier place because of what we've done for the last 25 years. We decided in a bipartisan way that the workplace ought to be safer; too many people were dying in the workplace. If any of you have ever spent any time in a factory, seen people walking around without all their fingers, you can appreciate that.

But it was also a time when we became profoundly disillusioned because of Watergate and a lot of other things. We really began to suspect that we couldn't trust our leaders or our institutions. And it was the beginning of the decline of middle class dreams for middle class people. In the sixties, the riots in the cities showed that more and more poor people began to doubt whether they would ever be able to work their way into the middle class. In the seventies, people who were in the middle class began to worry about whether they would ever be able to stay or what that meant. It began 20 years ago.

Then in the eighties, it was also a very mixed bag. It was a time when people exalted greed and short-term profit. It was a time when we built in, by bipartisan conspiracy in this community, the first structural deficit in the history of the United States of America and exploded our debt while we were reducing our investment in our most profound problems, while we spent the tax cuts and behaved just like the rest of the country, worrying about the short run. But it was also a time, let's not forget, where all across the country there was a renewed awareness of the dangers of drugs and drug use began to go down, smoking declined, voluntarism increased. And there was a remarkable explosion of productivity in the industrial sector in America, and the American economy began to go through the changes necessary to be competitive.

In the nineties, everybody knows, I think, that there's been a sort of a sobering increase in personal values of commitment. You see it in the decline in the divorce rate and the increase in healthy habits among many people. You see more commitment expressed in groups and by individuals all across the country. You see it in people reaffirming their commitment to the families in small and large ways: the remarkable husband and wife minister team that I introduced in the State of the Union, the Reverend Cherrys, and their AME Zion Church near here, now one of the two or three biggest churches in America, founded on family outreach; the phenomenal success of this Promise-Keepers organization—you can fill any football stadium in America. It's an astonishing thing, because people want to do the right thing, and they want to get their families and their lives back together. And that's encouraging.

But let us not forget that these profound problems endure. Middle class dreams and middle class values, the things which have shaped our life and our experience and our expectations, are still very, very much at risk.

I will say again: We have all these aggregate indices that the economy has done well: almost 7 million new jobs, the stock market's over 4,500, all the things that you know. But while average income has gone up, median income, the person in the middle, has declined in the last 2 years. A sense of job security has declined with all the downsizing. More and more people are temporary workers. This is the only advanced country in the world where there's a smaller percentage of people under 65 in the work force with health insurance today than 10 years ago.

Millions of American people go home at night from their work and sit down to dinner and look at their children and wonder what they have done wrong, what did they ever do to fail. And they're riddled with worries about it. Millions more who are poor have simply given up on ever being able to work their way into a stable lifestyle. And that, doubtless, is fueling some of the disturbing increase in casual drug use among very young people and the rise in violence among young people. That threatens

middle class values. In almost every major city in America the crime rate is down. Hallelujah! In almost every place in America, the rate of random violence among young people is up, even as the overall crime rate drops.

Government is struggling to change, and I'm proud of the changes we have made. But no one really believes that Government is fully adjusted to the demands of the 21st century and the information age. It clearly must still be less bureaucratic, more empowering, rely more on incentives if we still have to reduce spending and we have to find a way to do it while increasing our investment in the things that will determine our ability to live middle class dreams.

Politics has become more and more fractured, just like the rest of our lives; pluralized. It's exciting in some ways. But as we divide into more and more and more sharply defined organized groups around more and more and more stratified issues, as we communicate more and more with people in extreme rhetoric through mass mailings or sometimes semi-hysterical messages right before election on the telephone or 30-second ads designed far more to inflame than to inform, as we see politicians actually getting language lessons on how to turn their adversaries into aliens, it is difficult to draw the conclusion that our political system is producing the sort of discussion that will give us the kind of results we need.

But our citizens, even though their confidence in the future has been clouded and their doubts about their leaders and their institutions are profound, want something better. You could see it in the way they turned out for the town meetings in 1992. You could see it in the overwhelming, I mean literally overwhelming, response that I have received from people of all political parties to the simple act of having a decent, open conversation with the Speaker of the House in Claremont, New Hampshire. People know we need to do better. And deep down inside, our people know this is a very great country capable of meeting our challenges.

So what are the conclusions I draw from this? First of all, don't kid yourself. There are real reasons for ordinary voters to be angry, frustrated, and downright disoriented. How could our politics not be confusing when people's lives are so confusing and frustrating and seem to be so full of contradictory developments?

Secondly, this is now, as it has ever been, fertile ground for groups that claim a monopoly on middle class values and old-fashioned virtue. And it's easy to blame the Government when people don't feel any positive results. It's easy to blame groups of others when people have to have somebody to blame for their own problems, when they are working as hard as they can and they can't keep up.

But there is real reason for hope, my fellow Americans. This is, after all, the most productive country in the world. We do a better job of dealing with racial and ethnic diversity and trying to find some way to bring out the best in all of our people than any other country with this much diversity in the world.

We have an environment that is cleaner and safer and healthier than it used to be. We still have the lead in many important areas that will determine the shape of societies in the 21st century. There is a real willingness among our people to try bold change. And most important of all, most Americans are still living by middle class values and hanging on to middle class dreams. And everywhere in this country there are examples of people who have taken their future into their own hands, worked with their friends and neighbors, broken through bureaucracy, and solved problems. If there is anything I would say to you, it is that you can find, somewhere in America, somebody who has solved every problem you are worried about.

So there is reason for hope. And I would say, to me the real heroes in this country are the people that are out there making things work and the people who show up for work every day, even though they're barely at and maybe even below the poverty line, but they still work full-time, obey the law, pay their taxes, and raise their kids the best they can. That's what this country is really all about. And so there is really no cause for the kind of hand-wringing and cynicism that dominates too much of the public debate today.

What do we have to do now? First of all, we've got to have this debate that is looming over Washington. We have to have it. It's a good thing. We are debating things now we thought were settled for decades. We are now back to fundamental issues that were debated like this 50, 60, 70 years ago. There is a group who believe that our problems are primarily personal and cultural. Cultural is a—basically a word that means, in this context, there are a whole lot of persons doing the same bad thing. [*Laughter*] And that's what people—and then

if everybody would just sort of straighten up and fly right, why, things would be hunky-dory. And why don't they do it?

Now, I—you can see that with just two reasons—I'll give you two examples. And I made you laugh, but let's be serious. These people are honest and genuine in their beliefs. I will give you two examples that are sort of—stand out, but there are a hundred more that are more modulated: The NRA's position on gun violence, the Brady bill, and the assault weapons ban. Their position is: Guns don't kill people, people do. Find the people who do wrong, throw them in jail, and throw the key away. Punish wrongdoers. Do not infringe upon my right to keep and bear arms, even to keep and bear arsenals or artillery or assault weapons. Do not do that because I have not done anything wrong, and I have no intention of doing anything wrong. Why are you making me wait 5 days to get a handgun? What do you care if I want an AK-47 or an Uzi to go out and engage in some sort of sporting contest to see who's a better shot? I obey the law. I pay my taxes. I don't give you any grief. Why are you on my back? The Constitution says I can do this. Punish wrongdoers. I am sick and tired of my life being inconvenienced for what other people do.

Second example is the one that dominated the headlines in the last couple of days, what Senator Helms said about AIDS: "I'm sick and tired of spending money on research and treatment for a disease that could be ended tomorrow if everybody just straightened up and fly right. I'm tired of it. Why should I spend taxpayer—I've got a budget to balance. We're cutting aid to Africa. We're cutting education. We're cutting Medicare. Why should we spend money on treatment and research for a disease that is a product of people's wrongdoing? Illicit sex and bad drugs, dirty needles—let's just stop it."

Now, at one level, forgetting about those two examples, this argument is self-evidently right. Go back to what I told you about my family. A lot of you are nodding your heads about yours. There is a sense in which there is nothing the Government can do for anybody that will displace the negative impact of personal misconduct. And unless people are willing to work hard and do the best they can and advance themselves and their families, the ability of common action, no matter how well-meaning, won't work.

You look at every social program that's working in every community, and there are lots of them. I was just in New Haven for the opening of the Special Olympics, and I spent a lot of time with the LEAP program up there. It's an incredible program where these college students work with inner-city kids in the cities helping them rebuild their lives. But if the kids don't want to do it and won't behave, there's nothing these college kids can do to help them. So let's give them that. At a certain level, this is self-evidently true.

But what is the problem? These problems are our problems. They're not just single problems. If there's a big crime rate and a whole lot of people getting killed with guns, that affects all the rest of us because some of us are likely to get shot.

Now, I see the Brady bill in a totally different way because I see these problems as community problems. And I think a public response is all right. And I think saying to people who have the line I said, I think we ought to say to people, "Look, it is just not out of line for you to be asked to undergo the minor inconvenience of waiting 5 days to get a handgun, until we can computerize all the records, because, look here, in the last year and a half, there are 40,000 people who had criminal records or mental health histories who didn't get handguns, and they're not out there shooting people because you went through a minor inconvenience. You don't gripe when you go through a metal detector at an airport anymore, because you are very aware of the connection between this minor inconvenience to you and the fact that the plane might blow up, and you don't want that plane to blow up or be hijacked."

Well, look at the level of violence in America. It's the same thing. I don't have a problem with saying, "Look, these assault weapons are primarily designed to kill people. That's their primary purpose. And I'm sorry if you don't have a new one that you can take out in the woods somewhere to a shooting contest, but you'll get over it. Shoot with something else." [*Laughter*] "It's worth it." [*Applause*] I'm glad you're clapping. I'm glad you agree with me, but remember, the other people are good people who honestly believe what they say. That's the importance of this debate. It's the attitudes. We have to—we're having this debate.

The NRA that I knew as a child, the NRA that I knew as a Governor, for years, were the people who did hunter education programs, the people that helped me resolve land boundary disputes when retirees would come to the mountains in the northern part of my State and go into unincorporated areas, and who could and couldn't hunt on whose land. And they actually helped save people's lives, and they solved a lot of problems. I mean, this is a different—these are deeply held world views about working—but the way I look at it is it's like the airport metal detector.

I'll give you another example. It might not be popular in this group. I agree with the Supreme Court decision on requiring people who want to be on high school athletic teams to take drug tests, not because I think all kids are bad, not because I think they all use drugs, but because casual drug use is going up among young people again. It is a privilege to play on the football team. It is a privilege to be in the band. It is a privilege to have access to all these activities. And I say it's like going through the airport metal detector. You ought to be willing to do that to help get the scourge of drugs out of your school and keep kids off drugs. That's what I believe, because I see it as a common problem. So we all have to give up a little and go through a little inconvenience to help solve problems and pull the country together and push it forward. But this is a huge debate.

Look at the AIDS debate. You may think it's a little harder. First of all, the truth is not everybody who has AIDS gets it from sex or drug needles. I've got a picture on my desk at the White House of a little boy named Ricky Ray. He and his family were treated horribly by people who were afraid of AIDS when they first got it through blood transfusions, he and his brother. And he died right after my election. I keep his picture on my table to remember that. Elizabeth Glaser was a good friend of mine. She and the daughter she lost and her wonderful son that survived her, they didn't get AIDS through misconduct. So that's just wrong. I know a fine woman doctor in Texas who got AIDS because she was treating AIDS patients and she got the tiniest pinprick in her finger, a million-to-one, 2-million-to-one chance. But secondly, and more to the point, the gay people who have AIDS are still our sons, our brothers, our cousins, our citizens. They're Americans, too. They're obeying the law and working hard. They're entitled to be treated like everybody else. And the drug users, there's nobody in this country that hates that any more than I do because I've lived with it in my family. But I fail to see why we would want to hasten people's demise because they paid a terrible price for their abuse.

You know, smoking causes lung cancer, but we don't propose to stop treating lung cancer or stop doing research to find a cure. Right? Drunk driving causes a lot of highway deaths, but we don't propose to stop trying to make cars safer. Do we? I don't think so.

So I just disagree with this. Why do we have to make this choice? Why can't we say to people, look, you've got to behave if you want your life to work, but we have common problems, and we are going to have some common responses. I don't understand why it's got to be an either/or thing. That's not the way we live our lives. Why should we conduct our public debates in this way?

And the best example of all to me that our problems are both personal and cultural and economic, political, and social is the whole condition of the middle class economically. I think it requires public and private decisionmaking. Family values, most families have them. But most families are working harder for less so they have less time and less money to spend with their children. Now, that's just a fact. That's not good for family values. And I don't believe exhortation alone can turn it around. It's going to require some common action. I think that what we did with the family leave law supported family values. I think that we can have a welfare reform law that requires parental responsibility, has tough work requirements, but invests in child care and supports family values.

I think we can have a tax system that gives breaks to people to help them raise their kids and educate themselves and their children, and that would support family values. I think we can have an education system that empowers people to make the most of their own lives, and I think that is profoundly supportive of family values. And I do not believe the Government can do it alone. I believe there are other things that have to be done by people themselves and also by employers.

One of our major newspapers had an article yesterday on the front page, or the day before,

saying in the new world economy the employers call all the shots, talking about how more and more workers were temporary workers, more and more people felt insecure. You know, it's all very well to exhort people. But if they're out there really busting it, doing everything they can and falling further behind, and they're not being treated fairly by people who can afford to treat them fairly, then that's something else again, isn't it?

The global economy, automation, the decline of unionization, and the inadequate response of too many employers to these changes have led to a profound weakening of the condition of many American workers. There aren't many companies like NUCOR, a nonunion company, a steel company, where people get a fairly low base hourly wage, but they get a weekly bonus; nobody's ever been laid off; every employee with a college kid, student—a child who's college age, gets about $2,500 a year as a college allowance; and the pay of the executives is tied to the performance of the company and cannot go up by a higher percentage than the pay of the workers goes up.

Now, by contrast, in the 12 years before I took office—this is all in the private sector—the top management of our companies' pay went up by 4 times what their workers' pay went up and 3 times what their profits went up percentagewise. And that trend has largely continued, if anything accelerated, even though we limited the tax subsidy for it in 1993.

So I would say to you that there are some things that mere exhortation to good conduct will not solve, that require other responses that are public or that are private but go beyond just saying these are personal or cultural problems.

I also think that if we want to maintain a public response, there must be a relentless effort to change but not to eviscerate the Government. We have tried weak Government, nonexistent Government, in a complex industrial society where powerful interests that are driven only by short-term considerations call all the shots. We tried it decades and decades ago. It didn't work out very well. It didn't even produce a very good economic policy. It had something to do with the onset of the Depression.

On the other hand, we know that an insensitive, overly bureaucratic, yesterday-oriented, special-interest-dominated Government can be just as big a nightmare. We've done what we could to change that. The Government has 150,000 fewer people working today than it did when I took office. We've gotten rid of thousands of regulations and hundreds of programs. We have a few shining stars like the Small Business Administration, which today has a budget that's 40 percent lower than it did when I took office, that's making twice as many loans, has dramatically increased the loans to women and minorities, has not decreased loans to white males, and hasn't made a loan to a single unqualified person.

We can do these things. I wish I had all day to talk to you about what the Secretary of Education has done in the Education Department to try to make it work better and make common sense and involve parents and promote things like greater choice of schools and the building of charter schools and character education in the schools. It's not an either/or thing. You don't have to choose between being personally right and having common goals.

So that's my side of the argument. That's why I think my New Covenant formulation is better to solve the problems of middle class dreams and middle class values than the Republican contract. But perhaps the most important thing is not whether I'm right or they are, the important thing is how are we going to resolve this and what are citizens going to do. How can we resolve the debate?

I believe—and you've got to decide whether you believe this—I believe that a democracy requires a certain amount of common ground. I do not believe you can solve complex questions like this at the grassroots level or at the national level or anywhere in between if you have too much extremism of rhetoric and excessive partisanship. Times are changing too fast. We need to keep our eyes open. We need to keep our ears open. We need to be flexible. We need to have new solutions based on old values. I just don't think we can get there unless we can establish some common ground.

And that seems to me to impose certain specific responsibilities on citizens and on political leaders. And if I might, just let me say them. They may be painfully self-evident, but I don't think they're irrelevant. Every citizen in this country's got to say, "What do I have to do for myself or my family," or nothing else counts. The truth is that nobody can repeal the laws of the global economy, and people that don't have a certain level of education and skills are

not going to be employable in good jobs with long-term prospects. And that's just a fact. The truth is that if every child in this country had both parents contributing to his or her support and nourishment and emotional stability and education and future, we'd have almost no poor kids, instead of having over 20 percent of our children born in poverty. Those things are true.

The second thing is, more of our citizens have got to say, "What should I do in my community?" You know, it's not just enough to bemoan the rising crime rate or how kids are behaving and whatever. That's just not enough. It is not enough, not when you have example after example after example, from this LEAP program I mentioned, the "I Have A Dream" Program, to the world-famous Habitat for Humanity program, to all these local initiatives, support corporations that are now going around the country revolutionizing slum housing and giving poor working people decent places to live, to the work of the Catholic social missions in Washington, DC, and other places.

It is not enough to say that. People have to ask themselves, "What should I be doing through my church or my community organizations?" People who feel very strongly about one of the most contentious issues in our society, abortion, ought to look at the United Pentecostal Church. They'll adopt any child born, no matter what race, no matter how disabled, no matter what their problems are. There is a positive, constructive outlet for people who are worried about every problem in this country if they will go seek it out. And there is nothing the rest of us can do that will replace that kind of energy.

The fourth thing that I think—the third thing I think citizens have to do that is also important, people have to say, "What is my job as a citizen who is a voter? I am in control here. I run the store. I get to throw this crowd out on a regular basis. That's a big responsibility. We're the board of directors of America. Are we making good decisions? Are we making good decisions? Do we approach these decisions in the right frame of mind? Do we have enough information? Do we know what we're doing?"

I can tell you, the American people are hungry for information. When I announced my balanced budget and we put it on the Internet, one of our people at the White House told me there were a few hours when we were getting 50,000 requests an hour. The American people want to know things.

So I say to every citizen, do you have the information you need? Do you ever have a discussion with somebody that's different from you, not just people who agree with you but somebody who's different? You ever listen to one of those radio programs that has the opposite point of view of yours, even if you have to grind your teeth? [*Laughter*] And what kind of language do you use when you talk to people who are of different political parties with different views? Is it the language of respect or the language of a suspect? How do you deal with people? This is a huge thing. What do you have to do for yourself and your family? What can you do in your community? What can you do as a citizen?

Thomas Jefferson said he had no fear of the most extreme views in America being expressed with the greatest passion as long as reason had a chance—as long as reason had a chance. Citizens have to give reason a chance.

What do the political leaders have to do? I would argue four things: Number one, we need more conversation and less combat; number two, when we differ we ought to offer an alternative; number three, we ought to look relentlessly at the long term and remind the American people that the problems we have developed over a long period of years; and number four, we shouldn't just berate the worst in America, we ought to spend more time celebrating the best.

Those are four things that I think I should do and I think every other leader in this country ought to do. Conversation, not combat, is what I tried to do with the Speaker in New Hampshire, and I want to do more of it with others. I'm willing if they are. I think it would be good for America.

Secondly, differ but present an alternative. That's why I presented a balanced budget. A lot of people said, "This is dumb politics." The Republicans won the Congress by just saying no: No to deficit reduction, and call it a tax increase. Run away from your own health care plan, say they're trying to make the Government take over health care. That may be. But that's because this is a confusing time. It's still not the right thing to do.

Americans don't want "just say no" politics. If they can get the truth, they'll make the right decision 99 times out of 100. And we have to offer an alternative. And so do they. We all

should. When we differ, we should say what we're for, not just what we're against.

The third thing is important, looking for the long term. I was really sad in 1994. I'll be honest with you, on election day I was sad. I kind of felt sorry for myself. I thought, "Gosh, you know, the real problems in this country are these income problems," and "Look what we've done with the family leave law. We cut taxes for families with incomes under $28,000 a year by $1,000 a year. We've done," and I reeled it all off. And I said, "Gosh, I feel terrible." And then I realized, how could they possibly feel anything in 2 years? These income trends are huge, huge trends; huge, sweeping over two decades; fast international forces behind them; trillions of dollars of money moving across international borders working to find the lowest labor cost and pressing down; untold improvements in automation; so fast that you just can't create enough high-wage jobs to overcome the ones that are being depressed in some sectors of the economy. These are a huge deal. How could people have felt that? Nonetheless, our job is not to get reelected; it's to think about the long term because the problems are long-term problems.

I want to read you what President Havel said in his Harvard commencement speech about this—more eloquent than anything I could say: "The main task of the present generation of politicians is not, I think, to ingratiate themselves with the public through the decisions they take or their smiles on television. Their role is something quite different, to assume their share of responsibility for the long-range prospects of our world, and thus, to set an example for the public in whose sight they work. After all, politics is a matter of serving the community, which means that it is morality in practice." I could hardly have said it better.

Fourth, maybe the most important thing is, we should not just condemn the worst, we ought to find the best and celebrate it and then relentlessly promote it as a model to be followed. You know, I kept President Bush's Points of Light Foundation when I became President. And we recognize those people every year because I believe in that. I always—I thought that was one of the best things he did. But I tried to institutionalize it in many ways.

That's what AmeriCorps is all about. The national service program gives young people a chance to earn money for college by working in grassroots community projects all across the country. When I was in New Haven at the LEAP program, I had AmeriCorps volunteers there. I was in Texas the other day walking the streets of an inner city and a girl with a college degree from another State was there working with welfare mothers because she was raised by a welfare mother who taught her to go to school, work hard, and get a college degree, and she did.

We have to find a way to systematically see these things that work sweep across this country with high standards and high expectations and breaking through all this bureaucracy that keeps people from achieving. We can do that. And the President ought to do even more than I have done to celebrate the things that work, and I intend to do it and to do more of it.

Now I believe, obviously, that my New Covenant approach is better than the Republican contract approach to deal with the problems of middle class dreams and middle class values. But when I ran for this job, I said I wanted to restore the American dream and to bring the American people together. I have now come to the conclusion, having watched this drama unfold here and all around our country in the last 2½ years, that I cannot do the first unless we can do the latter. We can't restore the American dream unless we can find some way to bring the American people closer together. Therefore, how we resolve these differences is as important as what specific position we advocate.

I think we have got to move beyond division and resentment to common ground. We've got to go beyond cynicism to a sense of possibility. America is an idea. We're not one race. We're not one ethnic group. We're not one religious group. We do share a common piece of ground here. But you read the Declaration of Independence and the Constitution: This country is an idea. And it is still going now in our 220th year because we all had a sense of possibility. We never thought there was a mountain we couldn't climb, a river we couldn't ford, or a problem we couldn't solve. What's that great line in the wonderful new movie "Apollo 13," "Failure is not an option." You have to believe in possibility. And if you're cynical, you can't believe in possibility.

We need to respect our differences and hear them, but it means instead of having shrill voices of discord, we need a chorus of harmony. In a chorus of harmony you know there are lots of differences, but you can hear all the voices. And that is important.

And we've got to challenge every American in every sector of our society to do their part. We have to challenge in a positive way and hold accountable people who claim to be not responsible for any consequences of their actions that they did not specifically intend, whether it's in government, business, labor, entertainment, the media, religion, or community organizations. None of us can say we're not accountable for our actions because we did not intend those consequences, even if we made some contribution to them.

Two days ago, on July 4th, the people of Oklahoma City raised their flags and their spirits to full mast for the first time since the awful tragedy of April 19th. Governor Keating and Mayor Norick led a celebration in Oklahoma City, which some of you may have seen on television, a celebration of honor and thanks for thousands of Oklahomans and other Americans who showed up and stood united in the face of that awful hatred and loss for what is best in our country.

You know, Oklahoma City took a lot of the meanness out of America. It gave us a chance for more sober reflection. It gave us a chance to come to the same conclusion that Thomas Jefferson did in his first Inaugural. I want to read this to you with only this bit of history. Thomas Jefferson was elected the first time by the House of Representatives in a bitterly contested election in the first outbreak of completely excessive partisanship in American history. In that sense, it was a time not unlike this time. And this is what he said: "Let us unite with our heart and mind. Let us restore to social intercourse that harmony and affection without which liberty and life itself are but dreary things."

We can redeem the promise of America for our children. We can certainly restore the American family for another full century if we commit to each other, as the Founders did, our lives, our fortunes, and our sacred honor. In our hour of greatest peril and greatest division, when we were fighting over the issue which we still have not fully resolved, Abraham Lincoln said, "We are not enemies but friends. We must not be enemies."

My friends, amidst all our differences, let us find a new common ground.

Thank you very much.

NOTE: The President spoke at 11:24 a.m. in Gaston Hall. In his remarks, he referred to Father Leo J. O'Donovan, president, Georgetown University; Molly M. Raiser, Chief of Protocol, Department of State; Gov. Frank Keating of Oklahoma; and Mayor Ronald Norick of Oklahoma City, OK.

Remarks to the National Education Association
July 6, 1995

I want to thank you for your kind introduction and even more for your many years of distinguished leadership for our children, our schools, our parents, and of course, for our teachers. And to all of you delegates, I want to thank you for the support you have given to our administration to help us to get here and to help us honor our commitments to the children, the teachers, and the future of America.

I also want to thank you for the high honor you paid my good friend Secretary Riley by naming him your 1995 Friend of Education. I don't have to tell you that education has no better friend than Secretary Riley. I'm proud to have him in my Cabinet, and I'm proud to have worked with him for nearly 20 years now. He's actually doing what others say we ought to be doing. He's supporting more parental involvement. He's supporting higher standards and results-oriented programs. He's supporting accountability, but he's also supporting grassroots empowerment for teachers, for parents, and for local schools throughout this country. He is really making a difference, and he deserves the support of all Americans and all Members of Congress, without regard for their party.

You know, of course, that the Vice President very much wanted to be with you today. But of course, his mother fell ill and had to have surgery yesterday. I'm happy to report to you that as of this morning Mrs. Gore is doing much better. She is a remarkable woman. Many years ago she was the first woman lawyer in Texarkana, Arkansas, so I've always thought we've sort of had a claim on her, too. I know all of you join Hillary and me in praying for Mrs. Gore and her speedy recovery, and for her husband, Senator Gore, and for Al and Tipper and their entire family.

I'd like to begin this morning by just taking a few minutes to talk about what I said when I spoke at Georgetown University a couple of hours ago. It's something I believe I should be talking about more as President.

When I ran for this office, I said I wanted to do two things: first of all, to restore the American dream and, secondly, to bring the American people together again. What I've learned from the journey we've been on for the last 2½ years is that we cannot restore the American dream unless we do bring the American people together again.

You and I and all Americans must talk about how we treat one another, how we reach the hard decisions we have to make during this time of profound change, how we bridge these great divides in our society. We have got to find a way to reach common ground, a new common ground that honors our diversity but recognizes our shared values and shared interests, drawing strength from both to make the very best of what we can do in America. We have to recognize that there are real reasons why Americans feel that our sense of unity and national purpose is coming apart, why they often feel frustration and anger and confusion.

The challenges of this day are new and profound, as profound as any we have faced in many, many decades. For most people my age and a little younger, two great certainties organized our lives. They've organized the lives of Americans for most of the last half-century: first, the hope of middle class dreams and, second, the strength of middle class values.

Today, more and more Americans are less certain of both. The middle class dream that work will be rewarded and that the future for our children will be better is fading for too many people. More than half of all of our people are working harder to earn less than they did 15 or 20 years ago. And middle class values, the values of hard work, strong families, safe

1057

streets, secure future, those things are under attack, too, as we face threats from violence, the breakdown of families, the fraying of our social fabric, the very pace and scope of changes in this technological information age, where ideas and money and information move across the globe in a fraction of a second.

The question, of course, is what are we going to do about this. That's what I've been working on for 2 years, and that's the fundamental debate now going on in Washington. And we need to have that debate not just here in Washington but all over the country.

We're really back to some pretty elemental principles. Some people argue that our real problems are all social and personal and cultural problems. So they say if everybody would just get up, go to work, behave themselves, obey the law, all of our problems would be solved. Now, on one level they're obviously right. Our problems can never be solved through purely political and community means. I've said all along, we've got to demand more responsibility from America, from all Americans. Unless people are willing to take responsibility for themselves, as every teacher knows, you can't cram information, learning, reasoning, compassion, or good citizenship into the head of someone who won't be open to it.

But at the same time, let's be completely frank. It's also true that nobody in America, no one, especially me, got where he or she is today alone. To believe otherwise is foolish. We all have to play a role, individual citizens in their daily lives, people doing their part to help make their communities stronger, their neighbors safer, politicians in the way they deal with and address our problems. We've all got to do a better job. And I believe we have to recognize that one of the ways we all do more together is through the way our Government works and what it does to help our people meet the demands of change.

This is not an either/or thing. This is not "Are these problems personal and cultural, on the one hand, or social and political, on the other?" That's not the way the world works. It's both. And there is a role, a partnership role, for the Government to help you do what you do and to help all Americans make the most of their own lives.

Education is perhaps the best example of this. It's the work of your lives, but it's also the work of America's future. All of these concerns come together in education because school is where young people can learn the skills they need to pursue middle class dreams, especially now when knowledge is more important than ever to our future. School is also the place where middle class values taught by parents are reinforced by teachers, values like responsibility, honesty, trustworthiness, hard work, caring for one another and our natural environment, and good citizenship.

Government plays an indispensable role in helping to make sure that the schools that you work in are as strong as possible, have the highest standards possible, provide as much opportunity as possible. The dynamic is pretty simple. A good education clearly is key to unlocking the promise of today's economy in the 21st century. Without it, people are at an ever-increasing risk of falling behind.

Today, a male college graduate earns 80 percent more than a male who's just graduated from high school. That gap is double what it was just in 1979. That's why I have been fighting furiously since the day I took office to expand educational opportunity, to give all Americans a chance to grab the key to a prosperous future. As you know well, we have dramatically expanded Head Start. We passed Goals 2000 to set world-class standards for our schools and then to give grassroots reform power to empower, really empower teachers and principals and parents, to give them the flexibility to decide how to meet those standards and how to improve education.

Our national service program, AmeriCorps, gives a helping hand with college for 20,000 people who are helping their country in grassroots programs all across America. The safe and drug-free schools initiative is helping to make schools safe, places where kids can learn again and be free from fear, places where parents can trust their children to be free from crime and drugs. Our direct student loan program makes college more affordable for millions of Americans while actually cutting the cost for taxpayers.

Now, there is one piece of this that is especially important for us to talk about today. As I noted before, you've just honored Dick Riley. I want to commend him for so many things, but in particular for the work the Education Department is doing to teach our children good citizenship and the values we need to stay strong. There is something that we need to remember about that Department of Education that Dick Riley is now heading and heading in the right direction.

Just 18 years ago yesterday, on July 5, 1977, two sons of Minnesota, Vice President Mondale and former Vice President Hubert Humphrey, shared the same stage at another NEA convention. Now, back in 1977, you all know that education policy in America fell under the giant umbrella of the Department of Health, Education, and Welfare, a huge bureaucratic agency responsible for health care policy and welfare responsibility and all the educational responsibilities, whether it was keeping our classrooms up to date, ensuring our public schools had the tools they need to teach our children, maintaining high curriculum standards, giving special-needs schools and special-needs students the support they need. All those things were all lumped into this massive bureaucracy that was Health, Education, and Welfare.

That wasn't in the best interest of public education then. It's certainly not in the best interest of the country today when education is literally the key to our economic future, to restoring middle class dreams, and it's certainly critical to reestablishing the dominance of middle class values.

At that historic meeting, Vice President Humphrey made a passionate plea, and he was a very passionate man, for something the NEA had been fighting for for over 100 years, a Cabinet-level Department of Education. America's children would have only 2 more years to wait. The bill creating the Cabinet-level Department of Education was signed by President Carter in October 1979.

In the last 2½ years, Secretary Riley, a former Governor who labored for 8 years to dramatically improve schools in his native South Carolina, has worked hard to make the Department of Education work better than ever. We need the Department of Education today more than ever before. And we need it even more because Dick Riley has literally reinvented it. It is less bureaucratic. It is smaller. Programs have been consolidated. But he is focusing on the big issues, whether it is the preschool needs of our kids, the standards and the grassroots reform we need in public schools, the need we have for school-to-work transition programs in every State in the country, the need we have for expanded and lower cost and better repayment college loans, or the need he has to cooperate

with the Department of Education to give our working people the right to get the training they need the minute they become unemployed because now so many of them will have to find new jobs with higher skills. That is the record of Dick Riley; that is the record of the Department of Education; and that is why we need it.

As all of you know, during this time when we have increased our investments in education, we have also cut the deficit 3 years in a row for the first time since Harry Truman was President. We're cutting it by more than a trillion dollars over 7 years. We're also cutting the bureaucracy of the National Government over a 6-year period by more than 272,000 positions to make the Federal Government the smallest it's been since President Kennedy was President.

Let me tell you just how dramatic the changes have already been in 2½ years. The Government is already 150,000 people smaller. We have eliminated thousands and thousands of regulations, including regulations in the Department of Education. We have eliminated hundreds of Government programs. And the budget would be balanced today but for the interest we have to pay on just the debt run up the 12 years before I became President.

But we can't stop there. We must continue to cut the deficit until we eliminate it completely and balance the budget. That is why I have proposed a plan to balance the budget in 10 years. While cutting spending to balance the budget, however, under my plan we would continue to invest in our people, especially in education.

We must not sacrifice the future of our children in our zeal to save it. But let me also say to you that I know a lot of people who want to invest more money in our country question whether we actually need a balanced budget. They questioned my wisdom when I proposed a balanced budget. But let me ask you to look at the history of America.

We ran deficits all during the 1970's, but we did it for good economic reasons. That was a period of stagflation, of low growth, a period when it was legitimate to stimulate the economy in a modest way by modest deficits. We never, I reemphasize, never in the history of our Republic had a permanent structural deficit until 1981. After that, a lot of the people who got the tax cuts spent them and there was no way to reach a bipartisan consensus to lower the gap in the deficit. So we quadrupled the debt of this country in 12 years. We're 219 years old, and we've quadrupled the debt in 12 years. Now, we have to change that.

Look what's happened to you. Every year in the 1980's, you had to fight to hold on to the educational advances. Every year when you knew that we needed to be investing more because many parents were able to invest less in terms of money and time in their children's education, you were often disappointed because we were spending more and more and more in interest on the debt.

Next year, interest on the debt will exceed the defense budget. That's how big a problem it is. It makes us poorer. It takes our savings. It makes us more dependent on other economies. And it leaves us less money to invest in education, in infrastructure, in technology, in the things that will grow jobs, raise incomes, increase the middle class, and shrink the under class.

So what we have to do is to balance the budget and increase investment in education. That's why I made the decision to veto the rescission bill that Congress sent me earlier last month. But it's also why I gave them an alternative. I am determined to work with the new Congress to cut the deficit and ultimately to balance the budget. But that rescission bill cut investments in our future, in education, in job training, in the environment, just to fund things that have a far lower value, even though they may be popular in the short term with specific constituencies.

Now that Congress has agreed to restore funding for those investments, I'll be happy to sign a bill. It will cut the deficit, and that's good. But we'll also have $733 million in this year alone in critical investments, including $220 million for safe and drug-free schools, $60 million to help train teachers and pay for education reforms at the grassroots level, $105 million for AmeriCorps.

As we work in the coming months to balance the budget, we have to do it in the same way. You and I know it would be self-defeating to cut our investments in education. Cutting education today would be like cutting defense budgets at the height of the cold war. Our national security depends upon our ability to educate better, not just to spend more money but to reach more people, to perform at a higher level,

to get real results. That's what our security depends upon.

But don't kid yourselves, we've got a real fight on our hands. The congressional budget, which balances the budget in 7 years, cuts education severely, as Keith Geiger just said. My budget, which balances the budget in 10 years, increases education while cutting other spending.

We're also able to go easier on Medicare and Medicaid, to take some real time and promote real health care reform, and to continue to invest in new technologies and research. All we have to do is take 3 more years and cut the size of that big tax cut roughly in half, maybe a little more.

Now, I think 3 years is a pretty small price to pay to save millions and millions of dreams. Let me just give you a few examples of the difference 3 years will make. I want to increase Goals 2000 to about $900 million so that you will be able to work to improve 85,000 schools serving 44 million students. The congressional budget would eliminate Goals 2000, one of the principal engines of grassroots reform, something they say they support.

I want to increase Title I by over $200 million in 1996 to serve 200,000 more children that year. Let me just say something about Title I and your efforts. All the time up here I hear the politicians saying we just throw money at education, and it doesn't get any results, and we spend more money and we don't show more results. Well, as the Secretary of Labor has pointed out, there are public investments in children and private investments in children. We pretty well kept up with our public investments, but our private investments aren't keeping up. More and more of these children are being born in poverty, a higher percentage of them into difficult family circumstances and difficult neighborhood circumstances. And even those who have working parents have parents most of whom are working longer hours for less money. That means that parents have less money and less time to invest in our kids. That's a much bigger burden for you to bear.

Now, the Congress wants to freeze funding and deprive over one million children of the help that you can provide by 2002. I believe the money will make a difference because I know that you can make a difference. You can't make all the difference for what doesn't happen in the family, but you ought to get a lot of credit for trying and for the difference that you do make.

I want to increase the school-to-work program by 60 percent next year so 43 States can help thousands of students learn the skills they need to get and keep high-paying jobs, even when they don't go on to 4-year universities. We're the only major industrialized country that does not have a system for dealing with all of the high school graduates who don't go on to 4-year schools. Now, the Congress wants to cut it to half that amount. I think that's being penny-wise and pound-foolish.

I want to expand AmeriCorps to 50,000 people next year. Congress has proposed to eliminate it completely. I know that's a big mistake. Those 20,000 young people that are out there now, working with each other across the lines of race and region and religion and income are revolutionizing America at the grassroots level, solving problems, serving their communities, being good citizens, doing things that other people just give talks about, and earning money to pay for their education. We ought to keep national service, and we ought to expand it.

We've reformed the college loan system to make college more affordable for up to 20 million Americans. Secretary Riley has done a masterful job, along with his staff, in administering the direct loan program, which actually increases the availability of loans, lowers the cost to students, lowers the paperwork burden to colleges and universities, and cuts the cost to the taxpayers.

Now, the congressional majority wants to cut $10 billion from the student loan program by removing the interest subsidy during the time of the student's education, which will raise costs significantly for up to 7 million students. In the 1980's, the cost of a college education was the only thing that went up more rapidly than the cost of health care among the essential things that families need for the future. I don't think it's a very good idea to cut the college loan program. There are other ways to save the money.

Here's the bottom line. Under my plan, we balance the budget and increase educational investment by $40 billion in proven programs that work. The plan of the Republican majority in Congress balances the budget, but it cuts education by $36 billion, not counting the cuts in student loans.

Now, I'm not for a minute suggesting that balancing the budget is easy. Even under my plan, there will be plenty of pain to go around. We'll have to cut spending in other domestic programs about 20 percent across the board. But the difference between my plan and the congressional plan is the difference between necessary cutbacks and unnecessary, ultimately self-defeating pain. One distinguished business analysis has said that the Republican budget cuts so much so fast that it will actually increase unemployment and bring on a recession and, therefore, delay the time when they can balance the budget.

Now, we do have a responsibility to balance the budget. And I give them a lot of credit for proposing a balanced budget. But we've also got a responsibility to invest in our children and our future. We cannot restore the economy, we cannot rebuild the middle class, we can't recapture middle class dreams or reinforce middle class values if we walk away from our common responsibilities, the education of our people.

If we'll just take 10 years instead of 7, if we cut taxes for the middle class and focus on childrearing and education, and don't have big tax cuts for people who don't really need it because they're well-off and doing very well in this economy, then we can balance the budget and improve education. We can do both, and that's what I want you to fight for.

Our mission, your mission and mine, has got to be to build a bridge to the future that every American can cross. We have to give people the power they need to make the most of their own lives. That is what's behind this, balancing the budget and investing in education means building up America. And it's behind what I called for earlier today at Georgetown, a new common ground in which we come together to solve our problems.

I want our children's generation to inherit an America with as much opportunity as the one I was brought into. The best days of America should be, can be, will be before us if we work together. If people take the kind of responsibility you have taken to make our country better, we will do better. But it's going to take a good attitude. It's going to take good citizenship. It's going to take a willingness to listen to one another to find that common ground.

I have made a commitment that when I differ with the Republican Congress, I will offer an alternative. I have made a commitment that I will have more conversation and less combat, like I did with my conversation with the Speaker up in New Hampshire. I have made a commitment to try to work for the long-term interests of our country, not just for the short-term gain. These are profoundly important things. And I have made a commitment not just to berate the worst in our country but to try to extol, extol the best—people like you that are doing things that work.

What you have to do is to be active and good citizens. Tell these Members of Congress that you will support cutting the deficit, you will support balancing the budget, but investing in our country and having the Federal Government play a role, which in the larger scheme of things is still a modest role but a critical one, is absolutely essential for our future.

You've been working hard out there, and a lot of you work under very difficult circumstances. But there is no more noble, no more important task, especially at this moment when we stand on the threshold of a new century.

I thank you for your service to your country. I thank you for your service to the children and to the future of America. I wish you well. I ask for your good wishes and your strength and your willingness to stand for what you know is right for America.

God bless you all.

NOTE: The President spoke by satellite at 2:20 p.m. from Room 459 in the Old Executive Office Building to the National Education Association (NEA) convention meeting in Minneapolis, MN. In his remarks, he referred to Keith Geiger, NEA president.

Telephone Conversation with Space Shuttle *Atlantis* Astronauts
July 7, 1995

The President. Hello? Captain Gibson?

Commander Robert L. Gibson. Hello, Mr. President. This is Captain Gibson. We're online.

The President. Welcome home, and congratulations. We are very proud of you.

Commander Gibson. [*Inaudible*]—Mr. President. It's a pleasure for us to be back, back on the ground again, and to have had the opportunity to take part in this flight.

The President. Well, the pictures were wonderful, and we all watched you with absolute fascination and incredible support and enthusiasm. This is truly the beginning of a new era of cooperation in space between the United States and Russia. We've built a new relationship between our two countries. We're doing things together. And I think that what you and your team and what the Russians did together symbolizes that more than anything that I could ever say. And I think because of your mission now, the United States and Russia, with our partners in Canada and Japan and Europe, are going to be able to meet the challenge of building the international space station. And I hope

you and all of your team members will take an enormous amount of pride in that.

Commander Gibson. Well, thank you, Mr. President, for those extremely kind words. We certainly will. And I can tell you very honestly that at least all of us on the crew have a lot of very good friends in Russia and among the Russian Cosmonaut Corps and elsewhere in Russia. And I look forward very much to all of us continuing this.

The President. So do I. Before I sign off— I know you're tired and I know you're glad to be home—I want to offer a special congratulations to Norm Thagard on his record-breaking stay on orbit. We're all very proud of that. And I want to invite the entire crew to the White House as soon as you can come, because I want to hear some more about the mission and we need to talk about where we're going from here to keep the United States commitment to space exploration, travel, and to keep our whole program strong and alive.

Astronaut Norman E. Thagard. Mr. President, thanks for the words. This is Norm Thagard. The Russians took good care of me. We're great friends, so I think if what we did on a personal level is any indication, there won't be any problem with us on an intergovernmental level as well. And I'm sitting here looking at my two Russian crewmates, and I couldn't be more pleased with a crew that I've ever had.

The President. The next time we have any problems between American and Russian officials, I'm going to send them into space. I think I now know how to solve all international problems. [*Laughter*]

I thank you very much, and I look forward to seeing all of you. Welcome home.

Commander Gibson. Thank you, Mr. President. We really appreciate your time and your support.

The President. Thank you. Goodbye.

NOTE: The President spoke at 11:27 a.m. from the Oval Office at the White House.

Statement on the National Economy
July 7, 1995

Today's employment report shows that since the start of our administration, the economy has created 7 million jobs, with over 92 percent of them created in the private sector. When I ran for President, I stated that this country must have a strategy to strengthen and restore the American dream and that a core element of this strategy must be to create more and better jobs for hardworking Americans.

Seven million jobs in 30 months is very good news, but still not good enough: millions of families are still working harder than ever just to stay in place. In order to increase incomes for hardworking Americans, we must remain committed to a broadbased economic strategy to reward work, balance the budget, open markets for American goods, invest in education and training, target tax cuts to helping families invest in their futures, and take serious steps to health reform while protecting Medicare.

The President's Radio Address
July 8, 1995

Good morning. Last week I spoke to you about the need for Congress to pass reforms to end welfare as we know it. I want Congress to send me a bill that requires work, demands responsibility, and provides the child care people need to move from welfare to work.

This issue is now before the U.S. Senate. The truth is, Republicans and Democrats alike know what's needed to get this job done. A majority of Senators in both parties agree with me that welfare reform must require everyone who can work to go to work. We agree on the need for the toughest possible child support enforcement. And we agree that no one who can work should be able to stay on welfare forever. So we are close.

Congress could put a bill on my desk, a good bill, within the next few weeks. After a genera-

tion of debate, we have a chance, finally, to do what's right for the taxpayers who pay for a failed welfare system and for the people who are trapped by it. But in recent days we've seen unsettling signs that progress could fall to gridlock. This week, Republican leaders said that a threat from the far right in their own party could keep them from passing a welfare reform bill this year. A handful of Senators are threatening to hold welfare reform hostage to their own political views. They're threatening to block a vote on any bill that doesn't cut off all help to children whose mothers are poor, young, and unmarried.

I believe their position is wrong. Republican and Democratic Governors also strongly oppose Washington telling them to throw children off the rolls simply because their parents are under

18 and unmarried. And the Catholic Church has taken a very strong position on this, fearing that to cut young people under 18 and their children off welfare would lead to more abortions. This approach also would punish the innocent children of unmarried teenagers for the mistakes of their parents. This might cut spending on welfare, but it wouldn't reform welfare to promote work and responsible parenting. That's why so many Republicans and Democrats oppose it.

The threat of the Senators to take this extreme position and block this welfare reform effort is just wrong. We've come a long way in the welfare reform debate in the last few years. Not so very long ago, many liberals opposed requiring all welfare recipients who can work to do so. And not so long ago, most conservatives thought the Government shouldn't spend money on child care to give welfare mothers a chance to go to work and still be good parents. Now we have a broad consensus for both. We should do both, and we shouldn't allow welfare reform to be held prisoner to ideological political debates.

I ran for President to bring new opportunity to the American people and demand more responsibility in return. That's what I call the New Covenant. And welfare reform is a crucial part of this effort. We are now at an historic moment. The failure to pass welfare reform this year would be a disservice to the American people. It shouldn't become another victim to the politics of gridlock. Republicans and Democrats alike have a real responsibility to bring real change to Washington, and a bipartisan majority in the Senate is prepared to vote for a welfare reform bill with time limits and real work requirements and without moralistic dictates that will do more harm than good.

A few days ago, in a speech at Georgetown University, I said our leaders have to stop looking only for political advantage and start looking for common ground. I challenged our leaders to do four things: First, we need more conversation and less combat. So let's settle our differences on welfare reform without resorting to legislative trench warfare designed to stop real reform at any cost. Second, when we do differ, we ought to offer an alternative. When the vast majority of Americans and Members of Congress agree on an issue like welfare reform, a small minority shouldn't be able to get away with "just say no" politics. Third, we ought to look at our problems with a view toward the long term. Moving people from welfare to work will save a lot more money in the long run than throwing children off the rolls. They'll be in trouble, and they'll cost us a lot of money in the long run and a lot of our national life as well. We are never going to end welfare unless people have the training and child care to be good workers and good parents. And finally, we shouldn't just berate the worst in America, we ought to spend more time concentrating on the best. That's what I have done by giving 29 States the freedom from burdensome Federal Government regulations so they can lead the way in helping to find new ways to end welfare.

The only way our country can meet the profound challenges of the 21st century and the global economy is if we all pull together and we all look forward. We don't have a person to waste. That's why welfare reform is so critical. We can't afford to filibuster away our future.

So I say to those in Congress who have joined me in demanding responsibility from people on welfare, you have a responsibility, too. Don't place pride of partisanship ahead of our national pride. Don't pander to the partisan extremes. Let's not let politics stand in the way of making work and responsibility a way of life for the next generation.

Thanks for listening.

NOTE: The President spoke at 10:06 a.m. from the Oval Office at the White House.

Remarks at the Opening of Session I of the Family Re-Union IV Conference in Nashville, Tennessee
July 10, 1995

Thank you very much. I thought it might be nice to stop by here after having done my primary duty, which was delivering the soup to Mrs. Gore. [*Laughter*] I'm delighted to be here, Governor, Mayor, Senator, Members of Congress. To Representative Purcell and the other distinguished members of the Tennessee Legislature who are here, Dr. Erickson, and to all of you, let me say that I came here primarily to listen. And I find that I always learn a lot more when I'm listening than when I'm talking, so I will be quite brief.

I want to say a few things, however. First, I want to thank Al and Tipper Gore for their lifetime of devotion not only to their family but to the families of this State and this Nation, as manifested by this Family Re-union, the fourth such one, something they have done in a careful and sustained way. It's already been mentioned twice that Tipper has worked on the whole issue that we're here to discuss today for many, many years, never in the context of politics but always in the context of what's good for families and what we can do to move the ball forward for our children and for our future. And I think this country owes them a great debt of gratitude. And I'm glad to be here.

Secondly, I'd just like to frame this issue as it appears to me as President and as a parent. I gave a speech at Georgetown a few days ago in which I pointed out that the world in which I grew up, the world after World War II, was basically shaped by two great ideas: the middle class dream, that if you work hard you'll get ahead and your kids can do better than you did; and middle class values, that of family and community and responsibility and trustworthiness, and that both of those things were at some considerable risk today as we move out of the cold war into the global economy and the whole way we live and work is subject to sweeping challenge.

The family is the focus of both middle class dreams and middle class values, for it is the center around which we organize childrearing—our country's most important responsibility—and work. And how we work determines how we live and what will become of us over the long run.

We have seen enormous changes in both work and childrearing in the last several years. We know now that a much higher percentage of our children live in poverty, particularly in the last 10 years, even as we have a percentage of elderly people in poverty going below that of the general population for the first time in history in the last 10 years, a considerable achievement of which we ought to be proud as a country. But still, our children are becoming more and more poor.

We know that a higher percentage of our children are being born out of wedlock. What you may not know, but is worth noting, is that the number of children being born out of wedlock is more or less constant for the last few years. So we not only have too many children being born out of wedlock, we have more and more young couples where both of them are working and having careers who are deferring child bearing and, in many cases, not having children at all. I would argue that is also a very troubling thing in our country—the people in the best position to build strong families and bring up kids in a good way deciding not to do so.

We know that most children live in families where, whether they have one parent or two parents in the home, whoever their parents are in the home are also working. We know that we do less for child care and for supervised care for children as a society than any other advanced country in the world.

We know, too, that most of our parents for the last 20 years have been working a longer work week for the same or lower wages, so that while Representative Purcell here complimented the Governor on his budget because it maintained a commitment to children in terms of public investment, you could make a compelling argument that the private investment in children has been going down because most families have both less time and less money to spend on their children.

And we know that as parents spend less time with their children, by definition the children are spending more time with someone or something else, so that the media has not only exploded in its ramifications in our lives but also has more access to more of our children's time than would have been the case 20 years ago if all these technological developments had occurred when the family and our economy were in a different place. And I think we have to look at all these issues in that context.

Now, it's commonplace to say that most of us believe that there's too much indiscriminate violence, too much indiscriminate sex, and too much sort of callous degradation of women and sometimes of other people in various parts of our media today. I believe that the question is, so what? What we ought to be talking about today is, so what are we all going to do about that? Because our ability to change things, I think, consists most importantly in our ability to affirmative steps.

At this talk at Georgetown, I made a commitment that I would try to set an example for what I thought our political leaders ought to be doing. We ought to have more conversation and less combat. When we criticize, we ought to offer an alternative. We ought to be thinking about the long run; these trends that we're dealing with have been developing over quite a long while now. And we ought to celebrate what is good as well as condemn what we don't like. And I think if we do those four things, then we will be able to make good decisions.

So let me just make two specific suggestions, and then I'd like to get on with listening to other people. First of all, in the spirit of alternatives and celebrating what is good, I'm for balancing the budget, but I'm against getting rid of public television or dramatically cutting it. In our family this is known as the "Leave Big Bird alone" campaign. [*Laughter*] I say that because we are going to have to cut a bunch of stuff, folks, and we are going to have to cut a lot of things. The budget would be in balance today but for the interest we're paying on the debt run up between 1981 and 1993. Next year, interest on the debt will exceed the defense budget. This is a big problem for our families, their incomes, their living standards, their future.

But consider this. Public TV gives, on average, 6 hours of educational programming a day. Sometimes the networks have as little as a half an hour a week. Public television goes to 98 percent of our homes. Forty percent of our people don't have access to cable channels like the Learning Channel or A&E. Fourteen percent, only 14 percent of overall public television channel funding comes from Federal money, but often times in rural places, like Senator Conrad's North Dakota, over half of the money comes from the Corporation for Public Broadcasting. Sixty percent of the viewers have family incomes below $40,000. It costs you a $1.09 a year, per citizen, to fund it. And for every dollar public television and radio get from the Government, they raise $5 or $6 from the private sector. So I think that's my first suggestion.

My second suggestion relates to the presence of Senator Conrad here. If we don't believe in censorship, and we do want to tell parents that they have a responsibility, that television, to use Reverend Jackson's phrase that the Vice President mentioned, may be the third parent, but it can't be the first or the second, and that's up to the parents—if we want to say that, but we know we live in a country where most kids live in families where there's one or two parents there working and where we have less comprehensive child care than any other advanced country in the world, the question is how can we get beyond telling parents to do something that they physically cannot do for several hours a day unless they literally do want to be a home without television or monitor their kids in some other way?

There is one technological fix now being debated in the Congress which I think is very important. It's a little simple thing; I think it's a very big deal. In the telecommunications bill, Senator Conrad offered an amendment which ultimately passed with almost three-quarters of the Senate voting for it. So it's a bipartisan proposal that would permit a so-called V-chip to be put in televisions with cables which would allow parents to decide which—not only which channels their children could not watch but within channels, to block certain programming.

This is not censorship; this is parental responsibility. This is giving parents the same access to technology that is coming into your home to all the people who live there, who turn it on. So I would say when that telecommunications bill is ultimately sent to the President's desk, put the V-chip in it and empower the parents who have to work to do their part to be responsible with media. Those are two specific suggestions that I hope will move this debate forward.

Having said what I meant to say, I would like to now go on, Mr. Vice President, to hear the people who really know something about this. I want to thank you all for your care and concern. And let me echo something the Governor said: There is a huge consensus in this country today that we need to do something that is responsible, that is constructive, that strengthens our families and gives our kids a better future, and that celebrates the fact that this is the media center of the world. And we want it to be that way 10, 20, 50 years from now. But we also want to be that way in a country that is less violent, that has a more wholesome environment for our children to grow up in, where our children are strong and taking advantage of the dominant position the United States enjoys in the world media.

Thank you very much.

NOTE: The President spoke at approximately 9:15 a.m. in Polk Theater at the Tennessee Performing Arts Center to participants in Family Re-Union IV: The Family and. the Media. In his remarks, he referred to the Vice President's mother, Pauline Gore; Gov. Don Sundquist of Tennessee; Mayor Philip Bredesen of Nashville, TN; and Bill Purcell and Marty Erickson, cohosts of the conference.

Remarks at the Closing of Session I of the Family Re-Union IV Conference in Nashville
July 10, 1995

I don't want to end on a downer, but I just want to ask you all to think about the implications of what we are discussing here. And I wish we had time for all the audience to ask their questions and make their comments, but let me just point this out.

Almost every major city in America has had a decline in the crime rate in the last 3 or 4 years, but the rate of random violence among very young people is still going up, notwithstanding the decline in the crime rate. That is just one example. After years of making progress on reducing drug use, the rate of apparently random drug use across racial and income lines among quite young people is now going back up again. The rate of perceived risk or the pointlessness of not doing it seems to be going down.

The ultimate answer may be in programs like the "I Have A Future" program and all these one-on-one programs for all these children. But I would ask you just to remember what one of our psychologists said, which is that most of our young people learn about violence or are affected by it between the ages of 2 and 8. Most of them learn—deal with sex and gender stereotypes between 8 and whenever.

It may be that people between 8 and whenever are more subject to argument at least or counter information or the kind of publicity or you name it on these other issues we can put out. So let's focus at least on the violence. I see no alternative to solving this problem than to reduce the aggregate amount of violence to which these children are subject. And we're going to have to have some help from the media to get that done. I just don't see any alternative to that.

The V-chip is something we ought to do, but if we're going to raise positive role models we also have to reduce the aggregate amount of violence. We must find a systematic way to do it. And in our country, with the first amendment and other things being the way they are, we're going to have to have some voluntary initiatives and some disciplined support from the media in America to get it done.

NOTE: The President spoke at 10:50 a.m. in Polk Theater at the Tennessee Performing Arts Center.

Remarks at the Closing of Session II of the Family Re-Union IV Conference in Nashville
July 10, 1995

I just want to say one thing, if I might. Let me, first of all, start by saying thank you to all of you for being here and for caring enough about this subject to be here and for giving us a chance to discuss this issue in a nonpolitical atmosphere of good citizenship. I thank you for that. I also thank you for what you've done.

But I'd like to comment if I could on what's been said and what has not been said and end with something Mr. Selleck said. First of all, we know that we need to support and get more of the kind of programming reflected on the Nickelodeon, the Disney Channel, "Christy," the Fox Children's Network, and public television, and whoever I left out. We know that, we know we need that.

Secondly, we know we need some guideposts to the future which might be what John Cook talked about or another kind of rating system. And at least some of us would like to see some parents be able to turn some things off now and again, which is why we like the V channel.

Then you get to the next level, which is what the gentleman from the Ad Council talked about. And I agree with—we've got to make sure that no matter how far we go with technology, we save some private space along the way. Then you get to the question of whether we could systematically move the market system a little bit, to take off on Gary's comment.

His is a significant commitment, the Ad Council has made, for two reasons. One is, $8 billion over 8 years is $800 million a year. I'll tell you how much that is; I just sat there and figured it out. In the Presidential elections we spend about $100 million in the general election, telling you how great we are, how terrible our opponents are, and you see a lot of our ads. So if you spend $800 million a year and you do it right, you can make an impact. That's not an insignificant thing, and it should be lauded.

But the other suggestion you made, coming back to what Mr. Selleck said, is that the people who do all this should not be defensive; they should be open. They should realize there are

no simple answers. A few years ago, there was an attempt to do what Oprah Winfrey's doing on her own on a systematic basis through all different kinds of television shows through education. I saw you out there, John. Do you remember when I came out there to Hollywood and they had me give a little speech, because there was an organized effort to try to say, let's take a year and put some positive message about education in all of our programs, our cops and robbers programs, our cowboy programs, our—everything. In this case, it would be the Internet and all that.

And they did it for a year. I don't know that we had any way of measuring what the results were, but I do know what the gentleman from the Ad Council said makes a lot of sense. What I hope will happen is, in the end, that there will be some systematic effort which will not only have more good programs like "Christy" on the air, but which will make everybody think before they put their police show on the air or their you-name-it, whatever show it is: What picture of women am I presenting to America; what message am I sending to these kids about violence; what am I doing?

In other words, if we're going to change the American culture, we have to somehow change the media culture. And we have to do it without finger pointing, but we've got to be honest about it.

I think this Ad Council commitment is a good one, but I think what we need to do—and maybe Gary's right, maybe you have to change the people running the show a little bit—but we need a systematic debate there about what we don't do and what we do do in our regular programming. I really think that's important. I think if we leave that out, we'll leave a big piece of this undone. And I thank you for being willing to deal with that.

Thank you.

NOTE: The President spoke at 12:15 p.m. in Polk Theater at the Tennessee Performing Arts Center. In his remarks, he referred to actor Tom Selleck;

John Cook, executive vice president of corporate affairs, Walt Disney Co.; Gary David Goldberg, television writer and producer; and Oprah Winfrey, television talk show host. A tape was not available for verification of the content of these remarks.

Remarks Honoring the 1995 National Hockey League Champion New Jersey Devils
July 10, 1995

Ladies and gentlemen, welcome to the White House. Governor Whitman, thank you for coming. Governor Byrne, it's good to see you back there. Congressman Menendez. I've been waiting—there are several Members of Congress who are trying to get here, and I was trying to wait for them. But I think we should start, and when they come in, especially if Senator Bradley is the first one, we'll notice them all. [*Laughter*] And we'll be glad to acknowledge them. I thank those who—are they here? Senator Lautenberg, welcome. Senator Bradley, thank you.

I welcome you all here to the White House and congratulate the New Jersey Devils' first Stanley Cup victory in their 13-year history. I identified with you because you were cast as classic underdogs. But your determination and teamwork paid off.

It occurred to me as we were preparing for this that hockey is a lot like what goes on around here. [*Laughter*] You get behind; you get ahead; you never know if you're going to win until the last minute. It's more often a contact sport than it ought to be. The difference is here we don't have a penalty box, and sometimes the referees back there pile on, too. [*Laughter*] But the most important thing is the teamwork.

You know, the Stanley Cup is the oldest professional athletic trophy in North America; it's 102 years old. I'm glad we have it in the White House today again in a place of honor. I noted that it hasn't always enjoyed a place of honor. The Stanley Cup was once forgotten on a road-side, and once it was actually kicked into a frozen canal.

Coach Lemaire has accomplished quite a lot in his first 2 years, I would say. In the first year, the Devils had a record 106 points, 19 more than in any previous year. And of course, this year you won the Stanley Cup. Martin Brodeur has had a busy 2 years after being a rookie of the year last year—I like this nickname—"The Kid" continued to be an outstanding goalie this year. I also want to congratulate Claude Lemieux on his outstanding performance and on being named the Conn-Smythe trophy winner.

Let me congratulate all the players and thank those who have come here. Hockey is becoming an American sport: the teams now are more widely placed across the United States; more and more people understand it and watch it on television; and thanks to television, we are coming to understand it, those of us who live in places where there's never any ice. And I must say, I was very, very impressed and I really got into the Stanley Cup finals this year, so I'm delighted to have all of you here.

I'd like to now ask the NHL commissioner, Gary Bettman, to take the microphone and introduce the team, the players, and do whatever else he would like to do.

Mr. Bettman.

NOTE: The President spoke at 6:07 p.m. in the East Room at the White House. In his remarks, he referred to Gov. Christine T. Whitman and former Gov. Brendon Byrne of New Jersey.

Statement on Budget Rescission Legislation
July 10, 1995

The agreement on the rescissions bill that my administration has reached with Democrats and Republicans in the Congress is a good one, and it ought to be passed now.

I was disappointed when the Senate failed to complete the job before its recent recess. Now that they have returned, I call on Senators to resolve their differences and pass the bill as early as possible.

The bill achieves needed deficit reduction while protecting key investments in children and education and in national service, job training, and the environment. I believe it can be a model for future deficit reduction efforts.

Moreover, the rescissions legislation includes funds I requested that are urgently needed for the Federal Emergency Management Agency's disaster relief activities, for the Federal response to the Oklahoma City bombing, for expanding antiterrorism efforts, and for providing debt relief to Jordan, which is critical to the Middle East peace process.

I urge the Senate to act quickly on this vital legislation.

Message to the Senate Transmitting the Republic of Georgia-United States Investment Treaty
July 10, 1995

To the Senate of the United States:

With a view to receiving the advice and consent of the Senate to ratification, I transmit herewith the Treaty Between the Government of the United States of America and the Government of the Republic of Georgia Concerning the Encouragement and Reciprocal Protection of Investment, with Annex, signed at Washington on March 7, 1994. I transmit also, for the information of the Senate, the report of the Department of State with respect to this Treaty.

The bilateral investment Treaty (BIT) with Georgia was the eighth such treaty between the United States and a newly independent state of the former Soviet Union. The Treaty is designed to protect U.S. investment and assist the Republic of Georgia in its efforts to develop its economy by creating conditions more favorable for U.S. private investment and thus strengthen the development of its private sector.

The Treaty is fully consistent with U.S. policy toward international and domestic investment.

A specific tenet of U.S. policy, reflected in this Treaty, is that U.S. investment abroad and foreign investment in the United States should receive national treatment. Under this Treaty, the Parties also agree to international law standards for expropriation and compensation for expropriation; free transfer of funds related to investments; freedom of investments from performance requirements; fair, equitable, and most-favored-nation treatment; and the investor of investment's freedom to choose to resolve disputes with the host government through international arbitration.

I recommend that the Senate consider this Treaty as soon as possible, and give its advice and consent to ratification of the Treaty, with Annex, at an early date.

WILLIAM J. CLINTON

The White House,
July 10, 1995.

Message to the Senate Transmitting the Latvia-United States Investment Treaty
July 10, 1995

To the Senate of the United States:

With a view to receiving the advice and consent of the Senate to ratification, I transmit herewith the Treaty Between the Government of the United States of America and the Government of the Republic of Latvia Concerning the Encouragement and Reciprocal Protection of Investment, with Annex and Protocol, signed at Washington on January 13, 1995. I transmit also, for the information of the Senate, the report of the Department of State with respect to this Treaty.

The bilateral investment Treaty (BIT) with Latvia will protect U.S. investors and assist Latvia in its efforts to develop its economy by creating conditions more favorable for U.S. private investment and thus strengthening the development of the private sector.

The Treaty is fully consistent with U.S. policy toward international and domestic investment. A specific tenet of U.S. policy, reflected in this Treaty, is that U.S. investment abroad and foreign investment in the United States should receive national treatment. Under this Treaty, the Parties also agree to international law standards for expropriation and compensation for expropriation; free transfer of funds associated with investments; freedom of investments from performance requirements; fair, equitable, and most-favored-nation treatment; and the investor's or investment's freedom to choose to resolve disputes with the host government through international arbitration.

I recommend that the Senate consider this Treaty as soon as possible, and give its advice and consent to ratification of the Treaty, with Annex and Protocol, at an early date.

WILLIAM J. CLINTON

The White House,
July 10, 1995.

Message to the Congress Transmitting the Report of the Corporation for Public Broadcasting
July 10, 1995

To the Congress of the United States:

In accordance with the Communications Act of 1934, as amended (47 U.S.C. 396(i)), I transmit herewith the Annual Report of the Corporation for Public Broadcasting (CPB) for Fiscal Year 1994 and the Inventory of the Federal Funds Distributed to Public Telecommunications Entities by Federal Departments and Agencies: Fiscal Year 1994.

Since 1967, when the Congress created the Corporation, CPB has overseen the growth and development of quality services for millions of Americans.

This year's report, entitled "American Stories," is a departure from previous reports. It profiles people whose lives have been dramatically improved by public broadcasting in their local communities. The results are timely, lively, and intellectually provocative. In short, they're much like public broadcasting.

WILLIAM J. CLINTON

The White House,
July 10, 1995.

Remarks Prior to a Meeting With Congressional Leaders and an Exchange With Reporters
July 11, 1995

Legislative Agenda

The President. Ladies and gentlemen, I want to welcome the congressional leadership back here today. There are many things that we will discuss today. We have a lot of work to do. This summer we are working on finishing the rescission bill, and I very much hope we can succeed in passing the terrorism legislation and welfare reform.

And I hope that we can begin as soon as possible the budget debate. We have major differences over how the budget ought to be balanced, and I think it would be in error to delay it and run the risk of having a crisis in Government. I think the quicker we can begin it and the fuller and more open it can be and the more the American people can hear of it, the better off we'll be.

So those are the things that I hope we can discuss today and I think are very important.

President Boris Yeltsin of Russia

Q. Mr. President, have you heard anything about the condition of Boris Yeltsin?

The President. No.

Q. Any reports on his health?

The President. No. Nothing other than the last time I saw him, he was in good health and seemed to be doing well.

Q. Well, he's been hospitalized this morning for heart problems.

The President. Yes, I know, but I have heard nothing this morning about the condition.

Bosnia

Q. Sir, the Bosnian Serbs are moving into Srebrenica fast, according to the reports. Is it time for NATO air strikes?

The President. We may have something to say on that later today. But let me say I'm concerned about the people who are there, and I'm also concerned about the UNPROFOR troops, the Dutch, who are there. And we may have something later today to say about that.

Vietnam

Q. [*Inaudible*]—the decision on Vietnam, how much more difficult is it for you personally and politically, given your failure to serve in Vietnam?

The President. None.

Q. Does it enter into your decision at all?

The President. No.

Base Closings

Q. Are you going to do base closings——

The President. I don't know yet. We're working very hard on that, worked on it yesterday and last night. We have some more work to do, and I'm waiting for some more information to come back this morning. We spent quite a bit of time on it. It won't be long, but I can't say for sure.

NOTE: The President spoke at 8:30 a.m. in the Cabinet Room at the White House. A tape was not available for verification of the content of these remarks.

Exchange With Reporters Prior to a Meeting With the Congressional Black Caucus
July 11, 1995

Affirmative Action

Q. Mr. President, are you prepared to deliver your affirmative action review next Wednesday, as has been speculated?

The President. What date is that?

Q. The 19th. [*Laughter*]

The President. I believe that's the day we're going to do it.

Q. Have you already reached a conclusion? Are you going to brief these Members today on what your thoughts are dealing with affirmative action?

The President. I'm going to deal with their agenda today. I'm here and I'm listening to them and they're going to go through an agenda and I'm going to respond to it.

President Boris Yeltsin of Russia

Q. Any further word on Boris Yeltsin and how that might impact on U.S.-Russian relations?

The President. No. I got another report after this morning's meeting with congressional leadership, and our latest report is that he seems to be resting well and feeling pretty good and making some decisions from the hospital. That's the latest report I got—is about 30 minutes ago.

NOTE: The exchange began at 10:44 a.m. in the State Dining Room at the White House. A tape was not available for verification of the content of this exchange.

Remarks Announcing the Normalization of Diplomatic Relations With Vietnam
July 11, 1995

Thank you very much. I welcome you all here, those who have been introduced and distinguished Members of Congress and military leaders, veterans, others who are in the audience.

Today I am announcing the normalization of diplomatic relationships with Vietnam.

From the beginning of this administration, any improvement in relationships between America and Vietnam has depended upon making progress on the issue of Americans who were missing in action or held as prisoners of war. Last year, I lifted the trade embargo on Vietnam in response to their cooperation and to enhance our efforts to secure the remains of lost Americans and to determine the fate of those whose remains have not been found.

It has worked. In 17 months, Hanoi has taken important steps to help us resolve many cases. Twenty-nine families have received the remains of their loved ones and at last have been able to give them a proper burial. Hanoi has delivered to us hundreds of pages of documents shedding light on what happened to Americans in Vietnam. And Hanoi has stepped up its cooperation with Laos, where many Americans were lost. We have reduced the number of so-called discrepancy cases, in which we have had reason to believe that Americans were still alive after they were lost, to 55. And we will continue to work to resolve more cases.

Hundreds of dedicated men and women are working on all these cases, often under extreme hardship and real danger in the mountains and jungles of Indochina. On behalf of all Americans, I want to thank them. And I want to pay a special tribute to General John Vessey, who has worked so tirelessly on this issue for Presidents Reagan and Bush and for our administration. He has made a great difference to a great many families. And we as a nation are grateful for his dedication and for his service. Thank you, sir.

I also want to thank the Presidential delegation, led by Deputy Secretary of Veterans Affairs Hershel Gober, Winston Lord, James Wold, who have helped us to make so much progress on this issue. And I am especially grateful to the leaders of the families and the veterans organizations who have worked with the delegation and maintained their extraordinary commitment to finding the answers we seek.

Never before in the history of warfare has such an extensive effort been made to resolve the fate of soldiers who did not return. Let me emphasize, normalization of our relations with Vietnam is not the end of our effort. From the early days of this administration I have said to the families and veterans groups what I say again here: We will keep working until we get all the answers we can. Our strategy is working. Normalization of relations is the next appropriate step. With this new relationship we will be able to make more progress. To that end, I will send another delegation to Vietnam this year. And Vietnam has pledged it will continue to help us find answers. We will hold them to that pledge.

By helping to bring Vietnam into the community of nations, normalization also serves our interest in working for a free and peaceful Vietnam in a stable and peaceful Asia. We will begin to normalize our trade relations with Vietnam, whose economy is now liberalizing and integrating into the economy of the Asia-Pacific region. Our policy will be to implement the appropriate United States Government programs to develop trade with Vietnam consistent with U.S. law.

As you know, many of these programs require certifications regarding human rights and labor rights before they can proceed. We have already begun discussing human rights issues with Vietnam, especially issues regarding religious freedom. Now we can expand and strengthen that dialog. The Secretary of State will go to Vietnam in August where he will discuss all of these issues, beginning with our POW and MIA concerns.

I believe normalization and increased contact between Americans and Vietnamese will advance the cause of freedom in Vietnam, just as it did in Eastern Europe and the former Soviet Union. I strongly believe that engaging the Vietnamese on the broad economic front of economic reform and the broad front of democratic reform will help to honor the sacrifice of those who fought for freedom's sake in Vietnam.

I am proud to be joined in this view by distinguished veterans of the Vietnam war. They served their country bravely. They are of different parties. A generation ago they had different judgments about the war which divided us so deeply. But today they are of a single mind. They agree that the time has come for America to move forward on Vietnam. All Americans should be grateful especially that Senators John McCain, John Kerry, Bob Kerrey, Chuck Robb, and Representative Pete Peterson, along with other Vietnam veterans in the Congress, including Senator Harkin, Congressman Kolbe,

and Congressman Gilchrest, who just left, and others who are out here in the audience have kept up their passionate interest in Vietnam but were able to move beyond the haunting and painful past toward finding common ground for the future. Today they and many other veterans support the normalization of relations, giving the opportunity to Vietnam to fully join the community of nations and being true to what they fought for so many years ago.

Whatever we may think about the political decisions of the Vietnam era, the brave Americans who fought and died there had noble motives. They fought for the freedom and the independence of the Vietnamese people. Today the Vietnamese are independent, and we believe this step will help to extend the reach of freedom in Vietnam and, in so doing, to enable these fine veterans of Vietnam to keep working for that freedom.

This step will also help our own country to move forward on an issue that has separated Americans from one another for too long now. Let the future be our destination. We have so much work ahead of us. This moment offers us the opportunity to bind up our own wounds. They have resisted time for too long. We can now move on to common ground. Whatever divided us before let us consign to the past. Let this moment, in the words of the Scripture, be a time to heal and a time to build.

Thank you all, and God bless America.

NOTE: The President spoke at 2:03 p.m. in the East Room at the White House. In his remarks, he referred to Gen. John W. Vessey, Jr., USA (Ret.), Special Emissary for POW/MIA Affairs; and Deputy Secretary of Veterans Affairs Herschel Gober, Assistant Secretary of State Winston Lord, and Deputy Assistant Secretary of Defense James Wold, members of the Presidential Delegation on POW/MIA Issues.

Message to the Congress Transmitting a Report on Most-Favored-Nation Trade Status for Romania
July 11, 1995

To the Congress of the United States:

On May 19, 1995, I determined and reported to the Congress that Romania is in full compliance with the freedom of emigration criteria of sections 402 and 409 of the Trade Act of 1974. This action allowed for the continuation of most-favored-nation (MFN) status for Romania and certain other activities without the requirement of a waiver.

As required by law, I am submitting an updated Report to Congress concerning emigration laws and policies of Romania. You will find that the report indicates continued Romanian compliance with U.S. and international standards in the area of emigration policy.

WILLIAM J. CLINTON

The White House,
July 11, 1995.

Message to the Senate Transmitting the Trinidad and Tobago-United States Investment Treaty
July 11, 1995

To the Senate of the United States:

With a view to receiving the advice and consent of the Senate to ratification, I transmit herewith the Treaty Between the Government of the United States of America and the Government of the Republic of Trinidad and Tobago Concerning the Encouragement and Reciprocal Protection of Investment, with Annex and Protocol, signed at Washington on September 26, 1994. I transmit also for the information of the Senate, the report of the Department of State with respect to this Treaty.

The bilateral investment Treaty (BIT) with Trinidad and Tobago is the third such treaty between the United States and a member of the Caribbean Community (CARICOM). The Treaty will protect U.S. investment and assist the Republic of Trinidad and Tobago in its efforts to develop its economy by creating conditions more favorable for U.S. private investment and thus strengthen the development of its private sector.

The Treaty is fully consistent with U.S. polity toward international and domestic investment. A specific tenet of U.S. policy, reflected in this Treaty, is that U.S. investment abroad and foreign investment in the United States should receive national treatment. Under this Treaty, the Parties also agree to international law standards for expropriation and compensation for expropriation; free transfer of funds related to investments; freedom of investments from performance requirements; fair, equitable, and most-favored-nation treatment; and the investor or investment's freedom to choose to resolve disputes with the host government through international arbitration.

I recommend that the Senate consider this Treaty as soon as possible, and give its advice and consent to ratification of the Treaty, with Annex and Protocol, at an early date.

WILLIAM J. CLINTON

The White House,
July 11, 1995.

Remarks at James Madison High School in Vienna, Virginia
July 12, 1995

Thank you, Secretary Riley, for the introduction but more for your outstanding leadership of the Department of Education and the work you have done not only to increase the investment of our country in education but also to lift the quality and the standards of education and to deal forthrightly with some of the more difficult but important issues in education that go to the heart of the character of the young people we build in our country. Superintendent Spillane, congratulations on your award and the work you are doing here in this district. Dr. Clark, Ms. Lubetkin, to Danny Murphy—I thought he gave such a good speech I could imagine him on a lot of platforms in the years ahead. [*Laughter*] He did a very fine job. Mayor

Robinson and to the Board of Supervisors Chair Katherine Hanley and to all the religious leaders, parents, students who are here; the teachers; and especially to the James Madison teachers, thank you for coming today.

Last week at my alma mater, Georgetown, I had a chance to do something that I hope to do more often as President, to have a genuine conversation with the American people about the best way for us to move forward as a nation and to resolve some of the great questions that are nagging us today. I believe, as I have said repeatedly, that our Nation faces two great challenges: first of all, to restore the American dream of opportunity and the American tradition of responsibility; and second, to bring our country together amidst all of our diversity in a stronger community so that we can find common ground and move forward together.

In my first 2 years as President, I worked harder on the first question, how to get the economy going, how to deal with the specific problems of the country, how to inspire more responsibility through things like welfare reform and child support enforcement. But I have come to believe that unless we can solve the second problem we'll never really solve the first one. Unless we can find a way to honestly and openly debate our differences and find common ground, to celebrate all the diversity of America and still give people a chance to live in the way they think is right, so that we are stronger for our differences, not weaker, we won't be able to meet the economic and other challenges before us. And therefore, I have decided that I should spend some more time in some conversations about things Americans care a lot about and that they're deeply divided over.

Today I want to talk about a subject that can provoke a fight in nearly any country town or on any city street corner in America, religion. It's a subject that should not drive us apart. And we have a mechanism as old as our Constitution for bringing us together.

This country, after all, was founded by people of profound faith who mentioned Divine Providence and the guidance of God twice in the Declaration of Independence. They were searching for a place to express their faith freely without persecution. We take it for granted today that that's so in this country, but it was not always so. And it certainly has not always been so across the world. Many of the people who were our first settlers came here primarily because they were looking for a place where they could practice their faith without being persecuted by the Government.

Here in Virginia's soil, as the Secretary of Education has said, the oldest and deepest roots of religious liberty can be found. The first amendment was modeled on Thomas Jefferson's Statutes of Religious Liberty for Virginia. He thought so much of it that he asked that on his gravestone it be said not that he was President, not that he had been Vice President or Secretary of State but that he was the founder of the University of Virginia, the author of the Declaration of Independence, and the author of the Statutes of Religious Liberty for the State of Virginia. And of course, no one did more than James Madison to put the entire Bill of Rights in our Constitution and, especially, the first amendment.

Religious freedom is literally our first freedom. It is the first thing mentioned in the Declaration of Independence. And as it opens, it says Congress cannot make a law that either establishes a religion or restricts the free exercise of religion. Now, as with every provision of our Constitution, that law has had to be interpreted over the years, and it has in various ways that some of us agree with and some of us disagree with. But one thing is indisputable: The first amendment has protected our freedom to be religious or not religious, as we choose, with the consequence that in this highly secular age the United States is clearly the most conventionally religious country in the entire world, at least the entire industrialized world. We have more than 250,000 places of worship. More people go to church here every week or to synagogue or to their mosque or other place of worship than in any other country in the world. More peoples believe religion is directly important to their lives than in any other advanced, industrialized country in the world. And it is not an accident. It is something that has always been a part of our life.

I grew up in Arkansas which is, except for West Virginia, probably the State that's most heavily Southern Baptist Protestant in the country. But we had two synagogues and a Greek Orthodox church in my hometown. Not so long ago, in the heart of our agricultural country in eastern Arkansas, one of our universities did a big outreach to students in the Middle East. And before you know it, out there on this flat land where there was no building more than two stories high, there rose a great mosque. And all the farmers from miles around drove in to see what the mosque was like and try to figure out what was going on there. [*Laughter*]

This is a remarkable country. And I have tried to be faithful to that tradition that we have of the first amendment. It's something that's very important to me.

Secretary Riley mentioned when I was at Georgetown—Georgetown is a Jesuit school, a Catholic school. All the Catholics were required to take theology, and those of us who weren't Catholic took a course in the world's religion, which we called Buddhism for Baptists. [*Laughter*] And I began a sort of love affair with the religions that I did not know anything about before that time.

It's a personal thing to me because of my own religious faith and the faith of my family. And I've always felt that in order for me to be free to practice my faith in this country, I had to let other people be as free as possible to practice theirs, and that the Government had an extraordinary obligation to bend over backwards not to do anything to impose any set of views on any group of people or to allow others to do it under the cover of law.

That's why I was very proud—one of the proudest things I've been able to do as President was to sign into law the Religious Freedom Restoration Act in 1993. And it was designed to reverse the decision of the Supreme Court that essentially made it pretty easy for Government, in the pursuit of its legitimate objectives, to restrict the exercise of people's religious liberties. This law basically said—I won't use the legalese—the bottom line was that if the Government is going to restrict anybody's legitimate exercise of religion they have to have an extraordinarily good reason and no other way to achieve their compelling objective other than to do this. You have to bend over backwards to avoid getting in the way of people's legitimate exercise of their religious convictions. That's what that law said.

This is something I've tried to do throughout my career. When I was Governor, for example, we were having—of Arkansas in the eighties—you may remember this—there were religious leaders going to jail in America because they ran child care centers that they refused to have certified by the State because they said it undermined their ministry. We solved that problem

in our State. There were people who were prepared to go to jail over the home schooling issue in the eighties because they said it was part of their religious ministry. We solved that problem in our State.

With the Religious Freedom Restoration Act we made it possible, clearly, in areas that were previously ambiguous for Native Americans, for American Jews, for Muslims to practice the full range of their religious practices when they might have otherwise come in contact with some governmental regulation.

And in a case that was quite important to the evangelicals in our country, I instructed the Justice Department to change our position after the law passed on a tithing case where the family had been tithing to their church and the man declared bankruptcy, and the Government took the position they could go get the money away from the church because he knew he was bankrupt at the time he gave it. And I realized in some ways that was a close question, but I thought we had to stand up for the proposition that people should be able to practice their religious convictions.

Secretary Riley and I, in another context, have also learned as we have gone along in this work that all the religions obviously share a certain devotion to a certain set of values which make a big difference in the schools. I want to commend Secretary Riley for his relentless support of the so-called character education movement in our schools, which is clearly led in many schools that had great troubles to reduce dropout rates, increased performance in schools, better citizenship in ways that didn't promote any particular religious views but at least unapologetically advocated values shared by all major religions.

In this school, one of the reasons I wanted to come here is because I recognize that this work has been done here. There's a course in this school called combating intolerance, which deals not only with racial issues but also with religious differences, and studies times in the past when people have been killed in mass numbers and persecuted because of their religious convictions.

You can make a compelling argument that the tragic war in Bosnia today is more of a religious war than an ethnic war. The truth is, biologically, there is no difference in the Serbs, the Croats, and the Muslims. They are Catholics, Orthodox Christians, and Muslims, and they are so for historic reasons. But it's really more of a religious war than an ethnic war when properly viewed. And I think it's very important that the people in this school are learning that and, in the process, will come back to the distilled essence that every great religion teaches honesty and trustworthiness and responsibility and devotion to family and charity and compassion toward others.

Our sense of our own religion and our respect for others has really helped us to work together for two centuries. It's made a big difference in the way we live and the way we function and our ability to overcome adversity. The Constitution wouldn't be what it is without James Madison's religious values. But it's also, frankly, given us a lot of elbow room. I remember, for example, that Abraham Lincoln was derided by his opponents because he belonged to no organized church. But if you read his writings and you study what happened to him, especially after he came to the White House, he might have had more spiritual depth than any person ever to hold the office that I now have the privilege to occupy.

So we have followed this balance, and it has served us well. Now what I want to talk to you about for a minute is that our Founders understood that religious freedom basically was a coin with two sides. The Constitution protected the free exercise of religion but prohibited the establishment of religion. It's a careful balance that's uniquely American. It is the genius of the first amendment. It does not, as some people have implied, make us a religion-free country. It has made us the most religious country in the world.

It does not convert—let's just take the areas of greatest controversy now. All the fights have come over 200 years over what those two things mean: What does it mean for the Government to establish a religion, and what does it mean for a government to interfere with the free exercise of religion. The Religious Freedom Restoration Act was designed to clarify the second provision, Government interfering with the free exercise of religion and to say you can do that almost never. You can do that almost never.

We have had a lot more fights in the last 30 years over what the Government establishment of religion means. And that's what the whole debate is now over the issue of school prayer, religious practices in the schools, and things of that kind. And I want to talk about

it because our schools are the places where so much of our hearts in America and all of our futures are. And I'd like to begin by just sort of pointing out what's going on today and then discussing it if I could. And again, this is always kind of inflammatory; I want to have a non-inflammatory talk about it. [*Laughter*]

First of all, let me tell you a little about my personal history. Before the Supreme Court's decision in Engel against Vitale, which said that the State of New York could not write a prayer that had to be said in every school in New York every day, school prayer was as common as apple pie in my hometown. And when I was in junior high school, it was my responsibility either to start every day by reading the Bible or get somebody else to do it. Needless to say, I exerted a lot of energy in finding someone else to do it from time to time, being a normal 13-year-old boy. [*Laughter*]

Now, you could say, "Well, it certainly didn't do any harm. It might have done a little good." But remember what I told you. We had two synagogues in my hometown. We also had pretended to be deeply religious, and there were no blacks in my school. They were in a segregated school. And I can tell you that all of us who were in there doing it never gave a second thought most of the time to the fact that we didn't have blacks in our schools and that there were Jews in the classroom who were probably deeply offended by half the stuff we were saying or doing or maybe made to feel inferior.

I say that to make the point that we have not become less religious over the last 30 years by saying that schools cannot impose a particular religion, even if it's a Christian religion and 98 percent of the kids in the schools are Christian and Protestant. I'm not sure the Catholics were always comfortable with what we did either. We had a big Catholic population in my school and in my hometown. But I did that; I have been a part of this debate we are talking about. This is a part of my personal life experience. So I have seen a lot of progress made, and I agreed with the Supreme Court's original decision in *Engel* v. *Vitale.*

Now since then, I've not always agreed with every decision the Supreme Court made in the area of the first amendment. I said the other day I didn't think the decision on the prayer at the commencement, where the rabbi was asked to give the nonsectarian prayer at the commencement—I didn't agree with that because I didn't think it any coercion at all. And I thought that people were not interfered with. And I didn't think it amounted to the establishment of a religious practice by the Government. So I have not always agreed.

But I do believe that on balance, the direction of the first amendment has been very good for America and has made us the most religious country in the world by keeping the Government out of creating religion, supporting particular religions, interfering, and interfering with other people's religious practices.

What is giving rise to so much of this debate today I think is two things. One is the feeling that the schools are special and a lot of kids are in trouble, and a lot of kids are in trouble for nonacademic reasons, and we want our kids to have good values and have a good future.

Let me give you just one example. There is today, being released, a new study of drug use among young people by the group that Joe Califano was associated with, Council for a Drug-Free America, massive poll of young people themselves. It's a fascinating study, and I urge all of you to get it. Joe came in a couple of days ago and briefed me on it. It shows disturbingly that even though serious drug use is down overall in groups in America, casual drug use is coming back up among some of our young people who no longer believe that it's dangerous and have forgotten that it's wrong and are basically living in a world that I think is very destructive.

And I see it all the time. It's coming back up, even though we're investing money and trying to combat it in education and treatment programs and supporting things like the D.A.R.E. program. And we're breaking more drug rings than ever before around the world. It's almost—it's very disturbing because it's fundamentally something that is kind of creeping back in.

But the study shows that there are three major causes for young people not using drugs. One is they believe that their future depends upon their not doing it; they're optimistic about the future. The more optimistic kids are about the future, the less likely they are to use drugs. Second is having a strong, positive relationship with their parents. The closer kids are to their parents and the more tuned in to them they are and the more their parents are good role models, the less likely kids are to use drugs.

You know what the third is? How religious the children are. The more religious the children are, the less likely they are to use drugs.

So what's the big fight over religion in the schools, and what does it mean to us and why are people so upset about it? I think there are basically three reasons. One is, people believe that—most Americans believe that if you're religious, personally religious, you ought to be able to manifest that anywhere at any time, in a public or private place. Second, I think that most Americans are disturbed if they think that our Government is becoming antireligious, instead of adhering to the firm spirit of the first amendment: don't establish, don't interfere with, but respect. And the third thing is people worry about our national character as manifest in the lives of our children. The crime rate is going down in almost every major area in America today, but the rate of violent random crime among very young people is still going up.

So these questions take on a certain urgency today for personal reasons and for larger social reasons. And this old debate that Madison and Jefferson started over 200 years ago is still being spun out today, especially as it relates to what can and cannot be done in our schools, and the whole question, specific question, of school prayer, although I would argue it goes way beyond that.

So let me tell you what I think the law is and what we're trying to do about it, since I like the first amendment, and I think we're better off because of it, and I think that if you have two great pillars—the Government can't establish and the Government can't interfere with—obviously there are going to be a thousand different factual cases that will arise at any given time, and the courts from time to time will make decisions that we don't all agree with. But the question is, are the pillars the right pillars, and do we more or less come out in the right place over the long run?

The Supreme Court is like everybody else. It's imperfect, and so are we. Maybe they're right, and we're wrong. But we are going to have these differences. The fundamental balance that has been struck, it seems to me, has been very good for America. But what is not good today is that people assume that there is a positive antireligious bias in the cumulative impact of these court decisions with which our administration, the Justice Department and the Secretary of Education and the President, strongly disagree. So let me tell you what I think the law is today and what I have instructed the Department of Education and the Department of Justice to do about it.

The first amendment does not—I will say again—does not convert our schools into religion-free zones. If a student is told he can't wear a yarmulke, for example, we have an obligation to tell the school the law says the student can, most definitely, wear a yarmulke to school. If a student is told she cannot bring a Bible to school, we have to tell the school, no, the law guarantees her the right to bring the Bible to school.

There are those who do believe our schools should be value-neutral and that religion has no place inside the schools. But I think that wrongly interprets the idea of the wall between church and state. They are not the walls of the school.

There are those who say that values and morals and religions have no place in public education; I think that is wrong. First of all, the consequences of having no values are not neutral, the violence in our streets—not value neutral. The movies we see aren't value neutral. Television is not value neutral. Too often we see expressions of human degradation, immorality, violence, and debasement of the human soul that have more influence and take more time and occupy more space in the minds of our young people than any of the influences that are felt at school anyway. Our schools, therefore, must be a barricade against this kind of degradation. And we can do it without violating the first amendment.

I am deeply troubled that so many Americans feel that their faith is threatened by the mechanisms that are designed to protect their faith. Over the past decade we have seen a real rise in these kind of cultural tensions in America. Some people even say we have a culture war. There have been books written about culture war, the culture of disbelief, all these sort of trends arguing that many Americans genuinely feel that a lot of our social problems today have arisen in large measure because the country led by the Government has made an assault on religious convictions. That is fueling a lot of this debate today over what can and cannot be done in the schools.

Much of the tension stems from the idea that religion is simply not welcome at all in what Professor Carter at Yale has called the public square. Americans feel that instead of celebrating their love for God in public, they're being forced to hide their faith behind closed doors. That's wrong. Americans should never have to hide their faith. But some Americans have been denied the right to express their religion, and that has to stop. That has happened, and it has to stop. It is crucial that Government does not dictate or demand specific religious views, but equally crucial that Government doesn't prevent the expression of specific religious views.

When the first amendment is invoked as an obstacle to private expression of religion, it is being misused. Religion has a proper place in private and a proper place in public because the public square belongs to all Americans. It's especially important that parents feel confident that their children can practice religion. That's why some families have been frustrated to see their children denied even the most private forms of religious expression in public schools. It is rare, but these things have actually happened.

I know that most schools do a very good job of protecting students' religious rights, but some students in America have been prohibited from reading the Bible silently in study hall. Some student religious groups haven't been allowed to publicize their meetings in the same way that nonreligious groups can. Some students have been prevented even from saying grace before lunch. That is rare, but it has happened and it is wrong. Wherever and whenever the religious rights of children are threatened or suppressed, we must move quickly to correct it. We want to make it easier and more acceptable for people to express and to celebrate their faith.

Now, just because the first amendment sometimes gets the balance a little bit wrong in specific decisions by specific people doesn't mean there's anything wrong with the first amendment. I still believe the first amendment as it is presently written permits the American people to do what they need to do. That's what I believe. Let me give you some examples, and you see if you agree.

First of all, the first amendment does not require students to leave their religion at the schoolhouse door. We wouldn't want students to leave the values they learn from religion, like honesty and sharing and kindness, behind at the schoolhouse door, and reinforcing those values is an important part of every school's mission.

Some school officials and teachers and parents believe that the Constitution forbids any religions expression at all in public schools. That is wrong. Our courts have made it clear that that is wrong. It is also not a good idea. Religion is too important to our history and our heritage for us to keep it out of our schools. Once again, it shouldn't be demanded, but as long as it is not sponsored by school officials and doesn't interfere with other children's rights, it mustn't be denied.

For example, students can pray privately and individually whenever they want. They can say grace themselves before lunch. There are times when they can pray out loud together. Student religious clubs in high schools can and should be treated just like any other extracurricular club. They can advertise their meetings, meet on school grounds, use school facilities just as other clubs can. When students can choose to read a book to themselves, they have every right to read the Bible or any other religious text they want.

Teachers can and certainly should teach about religion and the contributions it has made to our history, our values, our knowledge, to our music and our art in our country and around the world, and to the development of the kind of people we are. Students can also pray to themselves—preferably before tests, as I used to do. [*Laughter*]

Students should feel free to express their religion and their beliefs in homework, through art work, during class presentations, as long as it's relevant to the assignment. If students can distribute flyers or pamphlets that have nothing to do with the school, they can distribute religious flyers and pamphlets on the same basis. If students can wear T-shirts advertising sports teams, rock groups, or politicians, they can also wear T-shirts that promote religion. If certain subjects or activities are objectionable to their students or their parents because of their religious beliefs, then schools may, and sometimes they must, excuse the students from those activities.

Finally, even though the schools can't advocate religious beliefs, as I said earlier, they should teach mainstream values and virtues. The fact that some of these values happen to be religious values does not mean that they cannot be taught in our schools.

All these forms of religious expression and worship are permitted and protected by the first amendment. That doesn't change the fact that some students haven't been allowed to express their beliefs in these ways. What we have to do is to work together to help all Americans understand exactly what the first amendment does. It protects freedom of religion by allowing students to pray, and it protects freedom of religion by preventing schools from telling them how and when and what to pray. The first amendment keeps us all on common ground. We are allowed to believe and worship as we choose without the Government telling any of us what we can and cannot do.

It is in that spirit that I am today directing the Secretary of Education and the Attorney General to provide every school district in America before school starts this fall with a detailed explanation of the religious expression permitted in schools, including all the things that I've talked about today. I hope parents, students, educators, and religious leaders can use this directive as a starting point. I hope it helps them to understand their differences, to protect student's religious rights, and to find common ground. I believe we can find that common ground.

This past April, a broad coalition of religious and legal groups—Christian and Jewish, conservative and liberal, Supreme Court advocates and Supreme Court critics—put themselves on the solution side of this debate. They produced a remarkable document called "Religion in Public Schools: A Joint Statement of Current Law." They put aside their deep differences and said, we all agree on what kind of religious expression the law permits in our schools. My directive borrows heavily and gratefully from their wise and thoughtful statement. This is a subject that could have easily divided the men and women that came together to discuss it. But they moved beyond their differences, and that may be as important as the specific document they produced.

I also want to mention over 200 religious and civic leaders who signed the Williamsburg charter in Virginia in 1988. That charter reaffirms the core principles of the first amendment. We can live together with our deepest differences and all be stronger for it.

The charter signers are impressive in their own right and all the more impressive for their differences of opinion, including Presidents Ford and Carter; Chief Justice Rehnquist and the late Chief Justice Burger; Senator Dole and former Governor Dukakis; Bill Bennett and Lane Kirkland, the president of the AFL–CIO; Norman Lear and Phyllis Schlafly signed it together—*(laughter)*—Coretta Scott King and Reverend James Dobson.

These people were able to stand up publicly because religion is a personal and private thing for Americans which has to have some public expression. That's how it is for me. I'm pretty old-fashioned about these things. I really do believe in the constancy of sin and the constant possibility of forgiveness, the reality of redemption and the promise of a future life. But I'm also a Baptist who believes that salvation is primarily personal and private, that my relationship is directly with God and not through any intermediary. Other people can have different views. And I've spent a good part of my life trying to understand different religious views, celebrate them, and figure out what brings us together.

I will say again, the first amendment is a gift to us. And the Founding Fathers wrote the Constitution in broad ways so that it could grow and change but hold fast to certain principles. They knew—they knew that all people were fallible and would make mistakes from time to time. And as I said, there are times when the Supreme Court makes a decision, if I disagree with it, one of us is wrong. There's another possibility: Both of us could be wrong. [*Laughter*] That's the way it is in human affairs.

But what I want to say to the American people and what I want to say to you is that James Madison and Thomas Jefferson did not intend to drive a stake in the heart of religion and to drive it out of our public life. What they intended to do was to set up a system so that we could bring religion into our public life and into our private life without any of us telling the other what to do.

This is a big deal today. One county in America, Los Angeles County, has over 150 different racial and ethnic groups in it, over 150 different. How many religious views do you suppose are in those groups? How many? Every significant religion in the world is represented in significant numbers in one American county and many smaller religious groups in one American county.

We have got to get this right. We have got to get this right. And we have to keep this balance. This country needs to be a place where religion grows and flourishes.

Don't you believe that if every kid in every difficult neighborhood in America were in a religious institution on the weekends, the synagogue on Saturday, a church on Sunday, a mosque on Friday, don't you really believe that the drug rate, the crime rate, the violence rate, the sense of self-destruction would go way down and the quality of the character of this country would go way up?

But don't you also believe that if for the last 200 years we had had a State governed religion, people would be bored with it, think that it would—[*laughter*]—they would think it had been compromised by politicians, shaved around the edges, imposed on people who didn't really cotton to it, and we wouldn't have 250,000 houses of worship in America? I mean, we wouldn't.

It may be imperfect, the first amendment, but it is the nearest thing ever created in any human society for the promotion of religion and religious values because it left us free to do it. And I strongly believe that the Government has made a lot of mistakes, which we have tried to roll back, in interfering with that around the edges. That's what the Religious Freedom Restoration Act is all about. That's what this directive that Secretary Riley and the Justice Department and I have worked so hard on is all about. That's what our efforts to bring in people of different religious views are all about. And I strongly believe that we have erred when we have rolled it back too much. And I hope that we can have a partnership with our churches in many ways to reach out to the young people who need the values, the hope, the belief, the convictions that comes with faith, and the sense of security in a very uncertain and rapidly changing world.

But keep in mind we have a chance to do it because of the heritage of America and the protection of the first amendment. We have to get it right.

Thank you very much.

NOTE: The President spoke at 10:58 a.m. In his remarks, he referred to Fairfax County School System Superintendent Robert Spillane; Principal Robert Clark; Assistant Principal Linda Lubetkin; Student Council President Danny Murphy; Mayor Charles A. Robinson, Jr., of Vienna, VA; Fairfax County Board of Supervisors Chairman Katherine

Hanley; television producer Norman Lear; conservative spokespersons William J. Bennett, Phyllis Schlafly, and James Dobson; and author Stephen Carter.

Memorandum on Religious Expression in Public Schools
July 12, 1995

Memorandum for the Secretary of Education, the Attorney General

Subject: Religious Expression in Public Schools

Religious freedom is perhaps the most precious of all American liberties—called by many our "first freedom." Many of the first European settlers in North America sought refuge from religious persecution in their native countries. Since that time, people of faith and religious institutions have played a central role in the history of this Nation. In the First Amendment, our Bill of Rights recognizes the twin pillars of religious liberty: the constitutional protection for the free exercise of religion, and the constitutional prohibition on the establishment of religion by the state. Our Nation's founders knew that religion helps to give our people the character without which a democracy cannot survive. Our founders also recognized the need for a space of freedom between government and the people—that the government must not be permitted to coerce the conscience of any individual or group.

In the over 200 years since the First Amendment was included in our Constitution, religion and religious institutions have thrived throughout the United States. In 1993, I was proud to reaffirm the historic place of religion when I signed the Religious Freedom Restoration Act, which restores a high legal standard to protect the exercise of religion from being inappropriately burdened by government action. In the greatest traditions of American citizenship, a broad coalition of individuals and organizations came together to support the fullest protection for religious practice and expression.

Religious Expression in Public Schools

I share the concern and frustration that many Americans feel about situations where the protections accorded by the First Amendment are not recognized or understood. This problem has manifested itself in our Nation's public schools. It appears that some school officials, teachers and parents have assumed that religious expression of any type is either inappropriate, or forbidden altogether, in public schools.

As our courts have reaffirmed, however, nothing in the First Amendment converts our public schools into religion-free zones, or requires all religious expression to be left behind at the schoolhouse door. While the government may not use schools to coerce the consciences of our students, or to convey official endorsement of religion, the government's schools also may not discriminate against private religious expression during the school day.

I have been advised by the Department of Justice and the Department of Education that the First Amendment permits—and protects—a greater degree of religious expression in public schools than many Americans may now understand. The Departments of Justice and Education have advised me that, while application may depend upon specific factual contexts and will require careful consideration in particular cases, the following principles are among those that apply to religious expression in our schools:

Student prayer and religious discussion: The Establishment Clause of the First Amendment does not prohibit purely private religious speech by students. Students therefore have the same right to engage in individual or group prayer and religious discussion during the school day as they do to engage in other comparable activity. For example, students may read their Bibles or other scriptures, say grace before meals, and pray before tests to the same extent they may engage in comparable nondisruptive activities. Local school authorities possess substantial discretion to impose rules of order and other pedagogical restrictions on student activities, but they may not structure or administer such rules to discriminate against religious activity or speech.

Generally, students may pray in a non-disruptive manner when not engaged in school activities or instruction, and subject to the rules that normally pertain in the applicable setting. Specifically, students in informal settings, such as cafeterias and hallways, may pray and discuss their religious views with each other, subject to the same rules of order as apply to other student activities and speech. Students may also speak to, and attempt to persuade, their peers about religious topics just as they do with regard to political topics. School officials, however, should intercede to stop student speech that constitutes harassment aimed at a student or a group of students.

Students may also participate in before or after school events with religious content, such as "see you at the flag pole" gatherings, on the same terms as they may participate in other noncurriculum activities on school premises. School officials may neither discourage nor encourage participation in such an event.

The right to engage in voluntary prayer or religious discussion free from discrimination does not include the right to have a captive audience listen, or to compel other students to participate. Teachers and school administrators should ensure that no student is in any way coerced to participate in religious activity.

Graduation prayer and baccalaureates: Under current Supreme Court decisions, school officials may not mandate or organize prayer at graduation, nor organize religious baccalaureate ceremonies. If a school generally opens its facilities to private groups, it must make its facilities available on the same terms to organizers of privately sponsored religious baccalaureate services. A school may not extend preferential treatment to baccalaureate ceremonies and may in some instances be obliged to disclaim official endorsement of such ceremonies.

Official neutrality regarding religious activity: Teachers and school administrators, when acting in those capacities, are representatives of the state and are prohibited by the establishment clause from soliciting or encouraging religious activity, and from participating in such activity with students. Teachers and administrators also are pro-

hibited from discouraging activity because of its religious content, and from soliciting or encouraging antireligious activity.

Teaching about religion: Public schools may not provide religious instruction, but they may teach *about* religion, including the Bible or other scripture: the history of religion, comparative religion, the Bible (or other scripture)-as-literature, and the role of religion in the history of the United States and other countries all are permissible public school subjects. Similarly, it is permissible to consider religious influences on art, music, literature, and social studies.

Although public schools may teach about religious holidays, including their religious aspects, and may celebrate the secular aspects of holidays, schools may not observe holidays as religious events or promote such observance by students.

Student assignments: Students may express their beliefs about religion in the form of homework, artwork, and other written and oral assignments free of discrimination based on the religious content of their submissions. Such home and classroom work should be judged by ordinary academic standards of substance and relevance, and against other legitimate pedagogical concerns identified by the school.

Religious literature: Students have a right to distribute religious literature to their schoolmates on the same terms as they are permitted to distribute other literature that is unrelated to school curriculum or activities. Schools may impose the same reasonable time, place, and manner or other constitutional restrictions on distribution of religious literature as they do on nonschool literature generally, but they may not single out religious literature for special regulation.

Religious excusals: Subject to applicable State laws, schools enjoy substantial discretion to excuse individual students from lessons that are objectionable to the student or the students' parents on religious or other conscientious grounds. School officials may neither encourage nor discourage students from availing themselves of an excusal option. Under the Religious Freedom Restoration Act, if it is proved that particular lessons substantially burden a student's free exercise of religion and if the school cannot prove a compelling interest in requiring attendance, the school would be legally required to excuse the student.

Released time: Subject to applicable State laws, schools have the discretion to dismiss students to off-premises religious instruction, provided that schools do not encourage or discourage participation or penalize those who do not attend. Schools may not allow religious instruction by outsiders on school premises during the school day.

Teaching values: Though schools must be neutral with respect to religion, they may play an active role with respect to teaching civic values and virtue, and the moral code that holds us together as a community. The fact that some of these values are held also by religions does not make it unlawful to teach them in school.

Student garb: Students may display religious messages on items of clothing to the same extent that they are permitted to display other comparable messages. Religious messages may not be singled out for suppression, but rather are subject to the same rules as generally apply to comparable messages. When wearing particular attire, such as yarmulkes and head scarves, during the school day is part of students' religious practice, under the Religious Freedom Restoration Act schools generally may not prohibit the wearing of such items.

I hereby direct the Secretary of Education, in consultation with the Attorney General, to use appropriate means to ensure that public school districts and school officials in the United States are informed, by the start of the coming school year, of the principles set forth above.

The Equal Access Act

The Equal Access Act is designed to ensure that, consistent with the First Amendment, student religious activities are accorded the same access to public school facilities as are student secular activities. Based on decisions of the Federal courts, as well as its interpretations of the Act, the Department of Justice has advised me of its position that the Act should be interpreted as providing, among other things, that:

General provisions: Student religious groups at public secondary schools have the same right of access to school facilities as is enjoyed by other comparable student groups. Under the Equal Access Act, a school receiving Federal funds that allows one or more student noncurriculum-related clubs to meet on its premises during noninstructional time may not refuse access to student religious groups.

Prayer services and worship exercises covered: A meeting, as defined and protected by the Equal Access Act, may include a prayer service, Bible reading, or other worship exercise.

Equal access to means of publicizing meetings: A school receiving Federal funds must allow student groups meeting under the Act to use the school media—including the public address system, the school newspaper, and the school bulletin board—to announce their meetings on the same terms as other noncurriculum-related student groups are allowed to use the school media. Any policy concerning the use of school media must be applied to all noncurriculum-related student groups in a nondiscriminatory matter. Schools, however, may inform students that certain groups are not school sponsored.

Lunch-time and recess covered: A school creates a limited open forum under the Equal Access Act, triggering equal access rights for religious groups, when it allows students to meet during their lunch periods or other noninstructional time during the school day, as well as when it allows students to meet before and after the school day.

I hereby direct the Secretary of Education, in consultation with the Attorney General, to use appropriate means to ensure that public school districts and school officials in the United States are informed, by the start of the coming school year, of these interpretations of the Equal Access Act.

WILLIAM J. CLINTON

Statement on Environmental Program Reforms To Assist Homeowners
July 12, 1995

I am pleased to announce significant reforms to the Endangered Species Act and Clean Water Act wetlands programs to benefit homeowners. Under these reforms, the vast majority of all American homeowners will never have to worry about endangered species or wetlands requirements.

Specifically, for Endangered Species Act programs, the Department of the Interior will essentially eliminate restrictions on single family homeowners with five or fewer acres of land. Similarly, for wetlands programs, the Army Corps of Engineers will issue a new nationwide permit to allow homeowners to construct or expand their residences without an individual permit. This will apply even if these activities involve filling as much as a half-acre of nontidal wetland.

Finally, I have instructed the heads of each of the relevant departments and agencies to examine all of their programs to determine if there are other actions that they can take to benefit homeowners.

Home ownership and the opportunity for homeowners to use their property without unnecessary restrictions are an essential part of the American dream. We can provide homeowners greater freedom and still protect the environment. This is commonsense, reasonable reform—not a reckless, destructive rollback of health and environmental safeguards, as others are proposing.

Message to the Congress on Economic Sanctions Against Libya
July 12, 1995

To the Congress of the United States:

I hereby report to the Congress on the developments since my last report of January 30, 1995, concerning the national emergency with respect to Libya that was declared in Executive Order No. 12543 of January 7, 1986. This report is submitted pursuant to section 401(c) of the National Emergencies Act, 50 U.S.C. 1641(c); section 204(c) of the International Emergency Economic Powers Act (IEEPA), 50 U.S.C. 1703(c); and section 505(c) of the International Security and Development Cooperation Act of 1985, 22 U.S.C. 2349aa–9(c).

1. On December 22, 1994, I renewed for another year the national emergency with respect to Libya pursuant to IEEPA. This renewal extended the current comprehensive financial and trade embargo against Libya in effect since 1986. Under these sanctions, all trade with Libya is prohibited, and all assets owned or controlled by the Libyan government in the United States or in the possession or control of U.S. persons are blocked.

2. There has been one amendment to the Libyan Sanctions Regulations, 31 C.F.R. Part 550 (the "Regulations"), administered by the Office of Foreign Assets Control (FAC) of the Department of the Treasury, since my last report on January 30, 1995. The amendment (60 *Fed. Reg.* 8300, February 14, 1995) added 144 entities to appendix A, Organizations Determined to Be Within the Term "Government of Libya" (Specially Designated Nationals ("SDNs") of Libya). The amendment also added 19 individuals to appendix B, Individuals Determined to Be Specially Designated Nationals of the Government of Libya. A copy of the amendment is attached to this report.

Pursuant to section 550.304(a) of the Regulations, FAC has determined that these entities and individuals designated as SDNs are owned or controlled by, or acting or purporting to act directly or indirectly on behalf of, the Government of Libya, or are agencies, instrumentalities or entities of that government. By virtue of this determination, all property and interests in property of these entities or persons that are in the United States or in the possession or control of U.S. persons are blocked. Further, U.S. persons are prohibited from engaging in transactions with these individuals or entities unless the transactions are licensed by FAC. The designations were made in consultation with the Department of State and announced by FAC in notices issued on January 10 and January 24, 1995.

3. During the current 6-month period, FAC made numerous decisions with respect to applications for licenses to engage in transactions under the Regulations, issuing 119 licensing determinations—both approvals and denials. Consistent with FAC's ongoing scrutiny of banking transactions, the largest category of license approvals (83) concerned requests by Libyan and non-Libyan persons or entities to unblock bank accounts initially blocked because of an apparent Government of Libya interest. The largest category of denials (14) was for banking transactions in which FAC found a Government of Libya interest. One license was issued authorizing intellectual property protection in Libya and another for travel to Libya to visit close family members.

In addition, FAC issued one determination with respect to applications from attorneys to receive fees and reimbursement of expenses for provision of legal services to the Government of Libya in connection with wrongful death civil actions arising from the Pan Am 103 bombing. Civil suits have been filed in the U.S. District Court for the District of Columbia and in the Southern District of New York. Representation of the Government of Libya when named as a defendant in or otherwise made a party to domestic U.S. legal proceedings is authorized by section 550.517(b)(2) of the Regulations under certain conditions.

4. During the current 6-month period, FAC continued to emphasize to the international banking community in the United States the importance of identifying and blocking payments made by or on behalf of Libya. The FAC worked closely with the banks to implement new interdiction software systems to identify such payments. As a result, during the reporting period, more than 171 transactions involving Libya, totaling more than $6.5 million, were blocked. As of May 25, 27 of these transactions had been licensed to be released, leaving a net amount of more than $5.2 million blocked.

Since my last report, FAC collected 37 civil monetary penalties totaling more than $354,700 for violations of the U.S. sanctions against Libya. Eleven of the violations involved the failure of banks to block funds transfers to Libyan-owned or -controlled banks. Two other penalties were received from companies for originating funds transfers to Libyan-owned or -controlled banks. Two corporations paid penalties for export violations. Twenty-two additional penalties were paid by U.S. citizens engaging in Libyan oilfield-related transactions while another 54 cases of similar violations are in active penalty processing.

Various enforcement actions carried over from previous reporting periods have continued to be aggressively pursued. The FAC has continued its efforts under the "Operation Roadblock" initiative. This ongoing program seeks to identify U.S. persons who travel to and/or work in Libya in violation of U.S. law.

Several new investigations of potentially significant violations of the Libyan sanctions have been initiated by FAC and cooperating U.S. law enforcement agencies, primarily the U.S. Customs Service. Many of these cases are believed to involve complex conspiracies to circumvent the various prohibitions of the Libyan sanctions, as well as the utilization of international diversionary shipping routes to and from Libya. The FAC has continued to work closely with the Departments of State and Justice to identify U.S. persons who enter into contracts or agreements with the Government of Libya, or other third-country parties, to lobby United States Government officials or to engage in public relations work on behalf of the Government of Libya without FAC authorization. In addition, during the period FAC attended several bilateral and multilateral meetings with foreign sanctions authorities, as well as with private foreign institutions, to consult on issues of mutual interest and to encourage strict adherence to the U.N.-mandated sanctions.

5. The expenses incurred by the Federal Government in the 6-month period from January 7 through July 6, 1995, that are directly attributable to the exercise of powers and authorities conferred by the declaration of the Libyan national emergency are estimated at approximately $830,000.00. Personnel costs were largely centered in the Department of the Treasury (particularly in the Office of Foreign Assets Control, the Office of the General Counsel, and the U.S. Customs Service), the Department of State, and the Department of Commerce.

6. The policies and actions of the Government of Libya continue to pose an unusual and extraordinary threat to the national security and foreign policy of the United States. In adopting UNSCR 883 in November 1993, the Security

Council determined that the continued failure of the Government of Libya to demonstrate by concrete actions its renunciation of terrorism, and in particular its continued failure to respond fully and effectively to the requests and decisions of the Security Council in UNSCRs 731 and 748, concerning the bombing of the Pan Am 103 and UTA 772 flights, constituted a threat to international peace and security. The United States continues to believe that still stronger international measures than those mandated by UNSCR 883, possibly including a worldwide oil embargo, should be imposed if Libya continues to defy the will of the international community as expressed in UNSCR 731. We remain determined to ensure that the perpetrators of the terrorist acts against Pan Am 103 and UTA 772 are brought to justice. The families of the victims in the murderous Lockerbie bombing and other acts of Libyan terrorism deserve nothing less. I shall continue to exercise the powers at my disposal to apply economic sanctions against Libya fully and effectively, so long as those measures are appropriate, and will continue to report periodically to the Congress on significant developments as required by law.

WILLIAM J. CLINTON

The White House,
July 12, 1995.

Remarks on Welfare Reform and an Exchange With Reporters
July 13, 1995

The President. Good morning. I want to thank Senator Daschle, Senator Moynihan, Senator Mikulski, Senator Breaux, Senator Harkin for coming. Governor Carper; Mayor Archer; a county executive from Madison, Wisconsin, Rick Phelps; and the majority leader of the Tennessee House of Representatives, Bill Purcell, for joining members of our administration here.

We have just had a good talk about welfare reform and the growing consensus around the approach taken by the bill offered by Senators Daschle and Mikulski and Breaux on welfare reform.

The American people have made it abundantly clear that they want us to fix the welfare system. It doesn't work for the people who are stuck on it, and it doesn't work for the taxpayers.

Welfare reform furthers both of the primary objectives of our administration. If it works, it will further the American dream of opportunity, and it will further the American value of responsibility. Our goal should be to help people be successful and independent workers and to build strong families.

We ought to be able to do this. We've come a long way in this debate. There's a broad consensus, for example, on tougher child support enforcement requirements. And not so very long ago, liberals opposed work requirements; they don't anymore. Not so very long ago, conservatives opposed spending money to provide child care when people move from welfare to work; most conservatives out in the country don't any more.

In America, where people live with this issue, there is a great deal of consensus about what we ought to do. And we ought to build on that consensus here in Washington. The reason we can't is that some people on the far right are blocking any action on welfare reform—and the Senate especially now—that doesn't cut off children and parents if the parents are young, poor, and unmarried. I think that is a terrible mistake. We shouldn't punish babies for their parents' mistakes. We ought to be building strong families and independent workers.

I'm not the only person who feels this way. Yesterday, I had a meeting with the Catholic bishops, who deeply oppose the extreme position of these far right Senators, and they're helping to lead the fight against it. They think it's cruel, and they believe it will even lead to more abortions.

I also think that people in the State legislatures and the Governors' offices throughout the country should think about the approach that is being offered on the other side. We believe it could constitute a huge, unfunded burden on State and local governments, people actually dealing with the welfare reform issue in the years ahead.

Now, there is an alternative. This shouldn't be hard. We basically all agree on what ought to be in a welfare reform proposal. It isn't getting done because a few Senators with an extreme position have decided that it is in their political interest to block any welfare legislation. The United States Senate should not practice "just say no" politics on welfare reform. We can fix this problem.

Every week that goes by, thousands of welfare mothers stay on welfare instead of going to work simply because they can't afford child care. Every week we don't make our child support laws as tough as we possibly can, we leave 800,000 people on welfare who could be off welfare if they got the child support to which they are legally entitled. Every day without welfare reform drains our economic strength, saps our community spirit, and prevents Americans from being able to live up to their full potential.

We need to work together and get this job done. This coalition is growing. We're going to continue to work. We need help. We cannot pass welfare reform without Republicans and Democrats working together. It is time to move away from the extreme position toward the common ground of sensible welfare reform.

I thank all these people who are here for supporting that.

Bosnia

Q. Mr. President, is it time for the U.N. troops to get out of Bosnia and for the U.S. to lift the arms embargo, as Senator Dole and others are proposing?

The President. Well, first of all, let me comment on the events of the last few days. I am very disturbed about what has happened in Srebrenica. We are very concerned about the fate of the refugees. And we have been working hard for the last couple of days to determine what options there are to deal with the immediate humanitarian problems. And we intend to do everything we can on that. And that is the first and foremost thing.

The truth is that the Bosnian Serbs should do what they did the last time this crisis arose, they should withdraw. And the United Nations should go back in there and reestablish the safe area, and the people should be able to go home. But we have to deal with the humanitarian crisis.

Now on the second issue, let me remind you of what my position has always been and what it still is today. The Europeans have tried to take the lead, under the umbrella of the United Nations, in minimizing the loss of life in Bosnia, in keeping the conflict from spreading, and in urging a diplomatic resolution of the war. They are still committed to do that.

I believe if the Rapid Reaction Force idea, which the French and the British have pushed, had been fully implemented before this occurred, this problem could have been minimized.

I still do not believe that it is in the interest of the United States to collapse and force the Europeans out of their willingness to put ground troops on the ground in Bosnia to try to minimize the loss of life and limit the spread. If the United Nations mission does collapse, then I believe that together the allies should all vote on the arms embargo. That is the best way to keep the NATO position unified, to keep the world position unified, and to avoid overly Americanizing the dealings in Bosnia, should the U.N. mission collapse.

I'm quite concerned about that. The Europeans have been willing to try to solve what is clearly the toughest problem they face on their own continent in the aftermath of the cold war. I have tried to be supportive of that. There are serious problems now with this. Unless we can restore the integrity of the U.N. mission, obviously its days will be numbered.

But let's not forget that it has accomplished a dramatic reduction in the loss of life since 1992, and the conflict has not spread. This is a serious challenge to the U.N. mission. It must either be resolved, or there will have to be some changes there.

Cigarette Smoking

Q. Mr. President, on another welfare issue that's headed for your desk, what are you going to do about this tobacco issue that is headed for your decision?

The President. Well, I haven't—let me say this—I have not received a recommendation from the FDA. I saw the news reports today, and they struck me as somewhat premature inasmuch as I have not yet received either a recommendation or, as the news reports indicated, requests for my own guidance on that yet.

But we have had some discussions, and I can tell you this: My concern is apparently what the FDA's concern is, and that is the impact of cigarette smoking, particularly on our young people, and the fact that cigarette smoking seems to be going up among our young people and certainly among certain groups of them. And I think we ought to do more about that than is being done, and I'm willing to do that. But I want to see exactly what their recommendation is.

Base Closings

Q. Mr. President, how do you answer the charge that the White House has injected politics into the base closing process?

The President. First of all, it is absolutely false. I intend to answer it in the letter that I write today, but since you gave me a chance to do it, I'll answer it.

Let's look at the facts here. Where is the politics? This Base Closing Commission made far more changes in the Pentagon plan than either any of the three previous base closing commissions, far more. They've been under a lot of political pressure. I understand that. I don't disagree with all the changes they made.

They acknowledge—secondly, under the law they are supposed to take into account economic impact. Based on their report—which I have read, and I urge all of you to read it if you haven't; before you make any judgments about where there was political influence, I urge all of you to read it—they took 23 bases or realignments off that the Pentagon recommended off the list and then put 9 more on, 3 of which happen to be in California, with the biggest job loss by far in San Antonio at Kelly Air Force Base, rejecting the Defense Department's recommendation that instead of closing these 2 big Air Force depots, they take an across-the-board cut in all 5 of them. That's what they did. Apparently, in all of their deliberations, the only place where they took economic impact into account was at the Red River Depot on the border of Texas and my home State. It is clear that— I think they have a case there. It would have almost doubled unemployment in that community.

But let's look at the facts on this politics. This is about economics. In the report itself, they acknowledge that at Kelly Air Force Base 60 percent of the employees are Hispanic, 45 percent of the Hispanics employed in the entire area work there, that it will have a devastating impact, and they were willing to shut down about 16,000 jobs, when there was another alternative that saved at least as much money, according to the Pentagon, or nearly as much, according to them.

Secondly, in California, here are the facts. I have not seen these anywhere. I have not seen these anywhere. The law requires economic impact to be taken into account. Here are the facts. When this Base Closing Commission process started, California had 13 percent of the population, 15 percent of the people in military, 20 percent of the defense budget. In the first 3 base closings they sustained 52 percent of the direct job losses. We're not talking about indirect jobs; we're not talking about speculation—52 percent.

In this recommendation the Pentagon hit them pretty hard, recommended closing Long Beach, a big facility. This Base Closing Commission, not satisfied with that, made a decision that they had to add back a lot of other jobs. So they decided to take almost all the jobs they took out, out of one place, San Antonio, Texas, and by closing 3 California bases, taking the California job loss in this round to almost 50 percent.

Now, you tell me that my concern over that economic situation, when their unemployment rate is 8.5 percent, they have borne over 50 percent of the burden of the job loss, is political. My concern in San Antonio, Texas, where one decision could virtually wipe out the Hispanic middle class, is political, when there was another alternative that the Pentagon said was better for national security. I am tired of these arguments about politics. My political concern is the political economy of America and what happens to the people in these communities and are they being treated fairly.

Now, I do not disagree with every recommendation the Base Closing Commission made, but this is an outrage. And there has been a calculated, deliberate attempt to turn this into a political thing and to obscure the real economic impact of their recommendations in San Antonio and California, which were made solely so they could put back a lot of other things.

Now, let's not——

Q. Why do you think they did that?

Q. Have you accepted their recommendations?

Q. What is the reason that they did that?

The President. I don't know. I'm not imputing motives to them. I'm just saying it's very interesting to me that there has been almost no analysis of anything. This whole thing immediately became—well, this is a big political story about California. This is an economic story, and it's a national security story. And there has been no analysis of what got put back and why, and what got taken off and why.

And I have been doing my best to deal with what is in the national interest. There are two considerations here. We have to reduce our base capacity. That's the most important thing. We have twice as much base capacity as we need, more or less, for the size of the military force we have. That is a national security interest. And that is my first and most important duty. But secondly, under the law, economic impact was supposed to be taken into account. And as nearly as I can determine, it wasn't anywhere—never in these determinations, with the possible exception of the Red River Depot, based on my reading of the report.

Now, the question is, is there a way to accept these recommendations, because even though I think they're far—they're not as good as what the Pentagon recommended and they do a lot more economic harm for very little extra security gain—is there a way to accept them and minimize the economic loss in the areas where I think it is plainly excessive. And that is what

we have been working on. That is what I've been working hard on. But I just want you to know that I deeply resent the suggestion that this is somehow a political deal.

I have not seen anything written anywhere that the State of California lost 52 percent of the jobs in the first three base closings and that this commission took them back up to nearly 50 percent in this one, even though they only have 15 percent of the soldiers and their unemployment rate is 50 percent above the national average. I haven't seen anywhere what this was likely to do to the Hispanic middle class and to the people of San Antonio, Texas, unless we can save a lot of those jobs there so that a lot of other things could be put back in 10 or 11 places around the country.

And I think that you folks need to look at the real impact of this. I am trying to do my job to reduce the capacity of the bases in the country consistent with the national interest and still be faithful to the statute requiring us to deal with the economic impact on these communities.

Thank you.

NOTE: The President spoke at 10:08 a.m. in the Rose Garden at the White House. In his remarks, he referred to Gov. Tom Carper of Delaware and Mayor Dennis Archer of Detroit, MI.

Statement on the Appointment of the Chairman of the Commission on the Roles and Capabilities of the United States Intelligence Community
July 13, 1995

I am announcing today my intention to appoint Harold Brown to chair the congressionally mandated Commission on the Roles and Capabilities of the United States Intelligence Community. This appointment fills the post held by Les Aspin. Like Les, Harold Brown brings a rich combination of experience, creativity, and vision to this crucial job.

I would also like to take this opportunity to thank former Senator Warren Rudman, who so ably served as Acting Chairman in the interim and who will again assume the position of Vice Chairman. He and Tony Harrington, as Acting

Vice Chairman, have done an excellent job keeping up the momentum of the Commission's work. They and the rest of the Commission are conducting a thorough assessment of the kind of intelligence community we will need to address the security challenges of the future.

Harold Brown is a counselor at the Center for Strategic and International Studies. Prior to this post, he has served as Secretary of Defense from 1977 to 1981. He also served as Director of Defense Research and Engineering from 1961 to 1965, and Secretary of the Air Force from 1965 to 1969. In addition, he was president of the California Institute of Technology from 1969 to 1977, and he was chairman of the Johns Hopkins Foreign Policy Institute from 1984 to 1992.

Letter to Congressional Leaders Transmitting the Report of the Arms Control and Disarmament Agency
July 13, 1995

Dear Mr. Speaker: (*Dear Mr. Chairman:*)

I am pleased to transmit the 1994 Annual Report of the United States Arms Control and Disarmament Agency (ACDA).

The ACDA was established in 1961 in part because Dean Rusk, Secretary of State at that time, believed the President needed access to unfiltered arms control analysis.

After a comprehensive review in 1993 and a second review in early 1995, it is clear to me that Secretary Rusk was correct: sound arms control and nonproliferation policy requires an independent, specialized, and technically competent arms control and nonproliferation agency.

In the absence of such an agency, neither I nor any future President could count on receiving independent arms control advice, unfiltered by other policy considerations. A President would thus at times have to make the most consequential national security decisions without the benefit of vigorous advocacy of the arms control point of view.

Moreover, I have found that ACDA's unique combination of single-mission technical expertise with its painstakingly developed capability for multilateral negotiation and implementation of the most intricate arms control and nonproliferation agreements could not be sustained with equal effectiveness outside of a dedicated arms control agency.

The ACDA's first major success was the establishment of the Nuclear Non-Proliferation Treaty. Twenty-five years later, its most recent major success is its long-term effort culminating in permanent and unconditional extension of that same Treaty. On both counts, America and the world are far more secure because of the ability and dedication of ACDA's leadership and professional staff.

I have therefore decided that ACDA will remain independent and continue its central role in U.S. arms control and nonproliferation policy.

Whether the issue is nuclear nonproliferation, nuclear missile reduction, chemical weapons elimination, or any of the other growing arms control and nonproliferation challenges America faces, ACDA is an essential national security asset.

In that spirit, I commend this report to you.

Sincerely,

WILLIAM J. CLINTON

NOTE: Identical letters were sent to Newt Gingrich, Speaker of the House of Representatives, and Jesse Helms, chairman, Senate Committee on Foreign Relations.

Message to the Congress Transmitting the Report of the Defense Base Closure and Realignment Commission
July 13, 1995

To the Congress of the United States:

I transmit herewith the report containing the recommendations of the Defense Base Closure and Realignment Commission (BRAC) pursuant to section 2903 of Public Law 101–510, 104 Stat. 1810, as amended.

I hereby certify that I approve all the recommendations contained in the Commission's report.

In a July 8, 1995, letter to Deputy Secretary of Defense White (attached), Chairman Dixon confirmed that the Commission's recommendations permit the Department of Defense to privatize the work loads of the McClellan and Kelly facilities in place or elsewhere in their respective communities. The ability of the Defense Department to do this mitigates the economic impact on those communities, while helping the Air Force avoid the disruption in readiness that would result from relocation, as well as preserve the important defense work forces there.

As I transmit this report to the Congress, I want to emphasize that the Commission's agreement that the Secretary enjoys full authority and discretion to transfer work load from these two installations to the private sector, in place, locally or otherwise, is an integral part of the report. Should the Congress approve this package but then subsequently take action in other legislation to restrict privatization options at McClellan or Kelly, I would regard that action as a breach of Public Law 101–510 in the same manner as if the Congress were to attempt to reverse by legislation any other material direction of this or any other BRAC.

WILLIAM J. CLINTON

The White House,
July 13, 1995.

Remarks at the Central Intelligence Agency in Langley, Virginia
July 14, 1995

Thank you so much. Director Deutch and Mrs. Deutch, Deputy Director and Mrs. Tenet, Members of Congress, members of the Aspin Commission who are here, men and women of the intelligence community: I can't help thinking here at the Central Intelligence Agency that if we were giving intelligence awards today they would go to the people back there under the trees. [*Laughter*] Congratulations to all of you for your adaptation of the natural environment to the task at hand.

Before I begin my remarks today I'd like to take care of an important piece of business. Just a month ago it was with regret but great gratitude for his 32 years of service to our country that I accepted the resignation of Admiral Bill Studeman as the Deputy Director of Central Intelligence. Today it is with great pleasure that I award him the President's National Security Medal. Admiral Studeman, Mrs. Studeman, please come up.

This is the highest award a member of our intelligence community, military or civilian, can receive. And no one deserves it more and the honor it represents. Most of you are well aware of Bill's extraordinary and exemplary career in the Navy, at the National Security Agency, and then here at the CIA. Let me say that as Deputy Director of Central Intelligence, he served two Presidents and three DCI's. For two extended periods he took on the responsibilities of Acting Director. He provided continuity and leadership to this community at a time of change and great challenge. Here, in Congress, and throughout the executive branch, he earned a reputation for integrity, competence, and reliability of the highest order. He has dedicated his professional life to making the American people safer and more secure. And today it is only fitting among those who know best the contributions he has made to our country to award him this medal as a small measure of thanks for a job well done and a life well lived.

Thank you, Admiral.

You know, as the Studemans make their way back to their chairs, I have to tell you that even though I have a lot of important things to say, I am loathe to make this speech in this heat. Once in the middle of a campaign for Governor I went up to a place in northeast Arkansas to make a speech for a county judge who was determined that I had to come to celebrate this road that he had built with funds that I gave him. He neglected to tell me that the road ended in the middle of a rice field. [*Laughter*] The only people that are laughing are the people that understand what this means. In the summertime in a rice field, there is nothing but heat and mosquitos. And a swarm of mosquitos came up in the middle of his introduction, literally hundreds of thousands of mosquitos. It was so bad that people were slapping at their cheeks and their legs and blood was streaming down people's faces and cheeks. And this judge was one of the rare people that mosquitoes would never bite. I had been Governor for 10 years; these people knew me better than he did. He took 6 minutes to introduce me. It seemed like it was 6 years. [*Laughter*] And I finally was introduced, and I gave the following speech: Folks, I have a good speech, if you want to hear it, come to the air-conditioned building down there. If we don't get out of here, we'll all die. If you reelect me, I'll kill every mosquito in the county. [*Laughter*] I have to tell you that after that I never received less than two-thirds of the vote in that county. [*Laughter*]

So I'm loath to give this speech. But I will cut it down and say what I have to say to you because it's very important that I say these things and very important that America know that you're here and what you're doing.

Fifty-four years ago, in the weeks that led up to Pearl Harbor, there was a wide range of intelligence suggesting a Japanese attack that made its way to Washington. But there was no clear clearinghouse to collect the information and to get it to the decisionmakers. That is what led President Truman to establish a central intelligence organization.

In the years since, the men and women of the CIA and its sister agencies have done more than most Americans will or can ever know to keep our Nation strong and secure and to advance the cause of democracy and freedom around the world.

Today, because the cold war is over, some say that we should and can step back from the world and that we don't need intelligence as much as we used to, that we ought to severely cut the intelligence budget. A few have even urged us to scrap the central intelligence service. I think these views are profoundly wrong. I believe making deep cuts in intelligence during peacetime is comparable to canceling your health insurance when you're feeling fine.

We are living at a moment of hope. Our Nation is at peace; our economy is growing all right. All around the world, democracy and free markets are on the march. But none of these developments are inevitable or irreversible, and every single study of human psychology or the human spirit, every single religious tract tells us that there will be troubles, wars, and rumors of war until the end of time.

Now instead of a single enemy, we face a host of scattered and dangerous challenges, but they are quite profound and difficult to understand. There are ethnic and regional tensions that threaten to flare into full-scale war in more than 30 nations. Two dozen countries are trying to get their hands on nuclear, chemical, and biological weapons. As these terrible tools of destruction spread, so too spreads the potential for terrorism and for criminals to acquire them. And drug trafficking, organized crime, and environmental decay threaten the stability of new and emerging democracies and threaten our well-being here at home.

In the struggle against these forces, you, the men and women of our intelligence community, serve on the front lines. By necessity, a lot of your work is hidden from the headlines. But in recent months alone, you warned us when Iraq massed its troops against the Kuwaiti border. You provided vital support to our peacekeeping and humanitarian missions in Haiti and Rwanda. You helped to strike a blow at a Colombian drug cartel. You uncovered bribes that would have cheated American companies out of billions of dollars. Your work has saved lives and promoted America's prosperity. I am here today first and foremost to thank you and your families for the work and sacrifices you have made for the security of the United States of America.

I want to work with you to maintain the information and the intelligence advantage we have and to meet the demands of a new era. Today our Government is deluged with more and more information from more and more sources. What once was secret can now be available to anybody with cable TV or access to the Internet. It moves around the world at record speed. And in order to justify spending billions of dollars in this kind of environment on intelligence and to maintain our edge, you have to deliver timely, unique information that focuses on real threats to the security of our people on the basis of information not otherwise available.

That means we have to rethink what we collect and how we organize the intelligence community to collect it. We must be selective. We can't possibly have in a world with so many diverse threats and tight budgets the resources to collect everything. You need and deserve clear priorities from me and our national security team.

Earlier this year I set out in a Presidential decision directive what we most want you to focus on, priorities that will remain under constant review but still are clear enough at the present time. First, the intelligence needs of our military during an operation. If we have to stand down Iraqi aggression in the Gulf or stand for democracy in Haiti, our military commanders must have prompt, thorough intelligence to fully inform their decisions and maximize the security of our troops. Second, political, economic, and military intelligence about countries hostile to the United States. We must also compile all source information on major political and economic powers with weapons of mass destruction who are potentially hostile to us. Third, intelligence about specific transnational threats to our security, such as weapons proliferation, terrorism, drug trafficking, organized crime, illicit trade practices, and environmental issues of great gravity.

This work must be done today, and it is vital to our security. But it cannot be immune to the tough budget climate in which we are all living. That's why I'm pleased that more than every before, our intelligence agencies are cooperating to work efficiently and to eliminate duplication. You are already implementing on or ahead of schedule 33 streamlining recommendations set out by Vice President Gore and former DCI Woolsey as well as changes proposed by Director Deutch. Acting apart, our agencies waste resources and squander opportunities to make our country more secure. But acting together, they bring a powerful force to bear on threats to our security.

Let me also say that I believe there is no zero sum choice to be made between the technological and human dimensions of intelligence. We need both, and we will have both. We've used satellites and signals to identify troop movements, to point agents in the right direction, to tap into secret important conversations. Today, some of your extraordinary in-house innovations are available for broader use, and I am interested in learning more about them: imagery technology, developed for the cold war, now being used in aid to natural disaster relief; imagery technology with great hope for the fight against breast cancer. We have to keep moving on this kind of technological frontier.

But no matter how good our technology, we'll always rely on human intelligence to tell us what an adversary has in mind. We'll always need gifted, motivated case officers at the heart of the clandestine service. We'll always need good analysts to make a clean and clear picture out of the fragments of what our spies and satellites put on the table.

And if we're going to continue to attract and keep the best people, we have to do a better job of rewarding work. I think the best way to do that is for the community leadership to demonstrate to you that excellence of performance, equal opportunity, and personal accountability are the only standards that will count when it comes to promotion. And that is what Director Deutch has pledged to do.

Let me say that I know the Ames scandal has colored a lot of what is the current debate over the future of the CIA. I imagine most of you who work here think that the Ames scandal has colored what the average American thinks about the CIA, although my guess is that you're probably overestimating that and underestimating the common sense and balance of an average American citizen. It's important that we don't minimize the damage that Ames did or the changes that need to be made to prevent future scandals. But Aldridge Ames was a terrible exception to a proud tradition of service, a tradition that is reflected in the 59 stars that shine on the CIA's memorial wall in honor of those who gave their lives to serve our country.

So we owe it to all of you in the intelligence community and to the American people to make sure we act on the lessons of his treason but also to remind the American people that the people who work for the Central Intelligence Agency are patriotic Americans who have made a decision that they are going to devote their careers to keeping this country safe and strong. And I thank you for that.

As soon as Ames was brought to justice, I ordered a comprehensive reexamination in both internal and external studies of our counterintelligence operations. As a result, we changed the way intelligence community does its business. Each agency now requires more attention and continuous training in counterintelligence and evaluates its employees more thoroughly and frequently.

Above all, we are insisting that those involved in an operation take responsibility for its integrity. That requires careful advanced planning that integrates counterintelligence into everything you do from day one. This isn't just about safes and locks, it's about designing operations that minimize the possibility of a security breakdown.

Director Deutch and I want to ensure that these new policies are carried out carefully so that we can avoid creating a climate of suspicion that embitters rather than empowers you. As we guard against a repeat of the Ames episode, we have to be careful not to produce a culture so risk averse that case officers refuse to take chances and analysts are afraid to speak their minds. You must not be paralyzed by the fear of failure.

This administration will continue to support bold and aggressive actions by the intelligence community consistent with the laws of the land, consistent with our interests, and consistent with our values. I applaud Director Deutch's plan, for example, to issue new rules on dealing with foreign agents suspected of human rights abuses. We owe you clear guidance on this issue. And as a country, we have to resolve it in the right way.

Finally, we owe the American public and Congress a full role in the debate over the future of intelligence. For over 40 years, bipartisan support for the work you perform has been central to your success. That support and the confidence of the American people were built on the unique oversight and consultative role Congress plays in intelligence. That's why Director Deutch and I will take with the utmost seriousness the concerns and suggestions of both the Congress and the Aspin commission.

Every morning I start my day with an intelligence report. The intelligence I receive informs just about every foreign policy decision we make. It's easy to take it for granted, but we couldn't do without it. Unique intelligence makes it less likely that our forces will be sent into battle, less likely that American lives will have to put at risk. It gives us a chance to prevent crises instead of forcing us to manage them.

So let me say to all the men and women of our intelligence community, I know and you know the challenges we face today will not be easy, but we know that you are already working every day to increase the security of every American. You are making a difference. Now we have to work together, and I have to support you so that we can meet the challenge of doing this work even better with even more public support and confidence in its integrity and long-term impact. That is my commitment to you as you renew your commitment to America in a world fraught with danger but filled with promise that you will help us to seize.

Thank you very much, and God bless you all.

NOTE: The President spoke at 11:45 a.m. In his remarks, he referred to Director of Central Intelligence John M. Deutch and his wife, Patricia; Deputy Director of Central Intelligence George J. Tenet and his wife, Stephanie; and former Director of Central Intelligence Adm. William O. Studeman, USN (Ret.), and his wife, Diane.

Statement on the 30th Anniversary of the Older Americans Act
July 14, 1995

Today I am pleased to mark the 30th anniversary of the Older Americans Act, an act which has allowed millions of elderly Americans to live with dignity, safety, and independence.

When President Johnson signed this bill into law 30 years ago, he characterized the best intentions of a Nation when he said:

"The Older Americans Act clearly affirms our Nation's sense of responsibility toward the well-being of all of our older citizens. But even more, the results of this act will help us to expand our opportunities for enriching the lives of all of our citizens in this country, now and in the years to come."

Indeed, we should be proud of our Nation's compact with older Americans and the public private partnership that is embodied in the Older Americans Act. This compact has included community-based services such as Meals on Wheels, transportation, ombudsman services, and other efforts to prevent abuse of the elderly.

As the Congress considers reauthorization of the Older Americans Act this year, my administration is committed to keeping the act whole and preserving the core principles which have guided its success: grassroots support, citizen input, bottom-up planning, and coordination of services. Programs like the Title V Senior Community Service Employment Program have been instrumental in helping us all benefit from the accumulated experience and judgment of older Americans. I will fight to keep these programs strong and to maintain the active role of the national aging network in assisting elderly Americans.

While we commemorate an important anniversary today, every American should be proud that we have greatly improved the way our people live their lives as they grow older, providing new hope for entire lifetimes of purpose and dignity. We must remember that with this kind of opportunity in a democracy goes continued responsibility. Our job today is to preserve this progress not only for our current seniors in their lifetimes but for all generations of Americans to come.

The President's Radio Address
July 15, 1995

Good morning. My job here is to make America work well for all of you who work hard. I ran for President to restore the American dream of opportunity for all, the American value of responsibility from all, and to bring the American people together as a community, not to permit us to continue to be divided and weakened. To do this we need a Government that empowers our people to make the most of their own lives but is smaller and less bureaucratic and less burdensome than it has been.

So we've got to cut regulations that impose unnecessary redtape or they just plain don't make sense. And we have to change the way regulators regulate, if that is abusive or it doesn't make sense. But as we cut, we have to remember that we have a responsibility to protect our citizens from things that threaten their safety and their health. Those are goals we all support, and we can accomplish them in a reasonable, responsible, bipartisan way.

Our administration is taking the lead. We've already reduced Government positions by 150,000, cut hundreds of Government programs, eliminated 16,000 pages of regulations. We've cut the Small Business Administration regulations by 50 percent, the Department of Education regulations by 40 percent, the time it takes to fill out the EPA regulations by 25 percent. We're changing the way we enforce the regulations. We want less hassle. We want more compliance and less citations and fines. In other words, we've got to get out the worst problems of big Government and still keep protecting the public health and safety.

Right now, Republicans in the Congress are pushing a very different approach to regulation. I believe it poses a real danger to the health and safety of our families. They call it regulatory reform, but I don't think it's reform at all. It will force Government agencies to jump through all kinds of hoops, waste time, risk lives whenever the agency acts to protect people's health and safety. It will slow down, tangle up, and seriously hinder our ability to look out for the welfare of American families.

It will create just the kind of bureaucratic burdens that Republicans for years have said they hate. It will be more time for rulemaking, more opportunities for special interests to stop the public interest, and many, many more lawsuits. I want a Government that's leaner and faster, that has a real partnership between the private sector and the Government. They want more bureaucracy, slower rulemaking, and a worsening of the adversarial relationship between Government and business that shifts the burden and the balance of power.

If the Republican Congress' bill had become law years ago—listen to this—it would have taken longer than it did to get airbags in cars; schoolbuses might not have ever had to install those sideview mirrors that help drivers see children crossing in front. The longer we waited to do these things, the more lives it would have cost.

Now, let me tell you what the world would look like in the future under these extreme proposals. You've probably heard about the cryptosporidium bacteria that contaminated drinking water in Milwaukee. It made 400,000 people sick; it killed 100 Americans. It will be very difficult to prevent that kind of danger from finding its way into our water and to control it when it does if these rules take effect.

If the new system Congress proposes takes effect it will take much longer to impose new safety standards to prevent commuter airline crashes, like the five that happened last year. We've proposed standards in that area, and they're being resisted. And it will be far less certain that we can use microscopes to examine meat and stop contaminated meat from being sold.

You may think that's amazing, but listen to this story. If we lived in a world like the one Congress is suggesting, there would be more tragedies like what happened to Eric Mueller. In 1993, Eric was a 13-year-old young man in California, the president of his class, the captain of his soccer team, an honor student. One day, like millions of other kids, he ordered a hamburger at a fast food restaurant. But he died a few days later because he was poisoned by an invisible bacteria, *E. coli*, that contaminated the hamburger. Dozens of others also died. And just last week, five more people in Tennessee, including an 11-year-old boy, got sick again because of *E. coli*.

How did this happen? Because the Federal Government has been inspecting meat the same old way since the turn of the century. Believe it or not, inspectors basically use the same methods to inspect meat that dogs use. They touch it and smell it to see if it's safe, instead of using microscopes and high technology. That's crazy, and for the last 2 years we have been working hard to change that, to reform the meat inspection rules so that Americans can be confident they're protected.

And believe it or not, while we're working to bring meat inspection into the 20th century, some special interests are trying to stop it, in spite of the fact that people have died from *E. coli*, and this Congress is willing to help them. We're trying to make our drinking water cleaner, but this Congress is willing to adopt a regulatory system that would let polluters delay and sometimes even control the rules that affect them.

In the last 6 months, we've seen these so-called regulatory reform bills actually being written by lobbyists for the regulated industries. The Congress even brought the lobbyists into the hearings to explain what the bills did. After all, they had to; the lobbyists had written the bills. I don't think that's right. I know it's not in the best interest of the American people, and it ought to be stopped.

No one has done more than our administration to streamline and reform a regulatory system. You'll never catch me defending a dumb regulation or an abusive Government regulator. The 16,000 pages of Federal regulations we have cut are enough to stretch 5 miles. We say to small business, if you have a problem and you fix it, you can forget the fine.

I want to sign a real regulatory reform bill. And there is a good alternative sponsored by Senator Glenn and Senator Chafee. It provides a good starting point and—listen to this—it includes a 45-day waiting period in which Congress can review and reject any Government regulation that doesn't make sense. Now, isn't that a lot better than letting the interest groups actually delay these regulations forever, even though we need them for our health and safety?

I want Democrats and Republicans in Congress to show the American people that we can reform without rolling back. We can cut redtape, reduce paperwork, make life easier for business without endangering our families or our workers. We do have a responsibility to cut regulation, but we also have a responsibility to protect our families and our future. We can and must do both.

Thanks for listening.

NOTE: The address was recorded at 3:24 p.m. on July 14 in the Roosevelt Room at the White House for broadcast at 10:06 a.m. on July 15.

Message to the Congress Transmitting the Revision to the United States Arctic Research Plan
July 14, 1995

To the Congress of the United States:

Pursuant to the provisions of the Arctic Research and Policy Act of 1984, as amended (15 U.S.C. 4108(a)), I transmit herewith the fourth biennial revision (1996–2000) to the United States Arctic Research Plan.

WILLIAM J. CLINTON

The White House,

July 14, 1995.

NOTE: This message was released by the Office of the Press Secretary on July 17.

Remarks at the Unveiling Ceremony for the Official Portraits of President George Bush and Barbara Bush
July 17, 1995

Thank you. Thank you very much, Mr. Breeden, for your kind remarks and for your essential work on behalf of the White House and the history of this country.

We're delighted to be here with President and Mrs. Bush today and Vice President and Mrs. Quayle, all the Members and former Members of Congress, the members of the Bush administration, and the friends of George and Barbara Bush and especially the family members. We welcome you all here to the White House.

It's impossible to live in this wonderful old place without becoming incredibly attached to it, to the history of our country and to what each and every one of these rooms represent. In a way, I think every family who has ever lived here has become more and more a part of our country's history, just for the privilege of sleeping under this roof at night. And so perhaps the most important thing I can say to President and Mrs. Bush today is, welcome home. We're glad to have you back.

I want to say, too, that we thought that we ought to have this ceremony in the East Room. This has always been the people's room. In the 19th century, it used to get so crowded at receptions that one of the windows over here was turned into a door so people could get out if they couldn't bear the crowds anymore. There are so many here today, perhaps we should have

done it again. But we thought the air-conditioning made it advisable for us to all stay put.

Many of you know that it was in this room that Abigail Adams used to dry the family laundry when the room was nothing more than a brick shell. You may not know that the great explorer Meriwether Lewis set up camp here, surrounded by canvas tarps, books, and hunting rifles in the day when he was Thomas Jefferson's secretary. John Quincy Adams frequently would come here to watch the Sunrise after he finished his early morning swim in the Potomac. That also is something we're considering taking up if the heat wave doesn't break.

The portraits that we add here today celebrate another chapter to our rich history and particularly to the rich history of the East Room where they will remain for a few days before they are properly hung. I managed to get a glimpse of these portraits, and I must admit that I think the artist did a wonderful job, and we're all in his debt. But I also want to say, President Bush, if I look half as good as you do when I leave office, I'll be a happy man. [*Laughter*]

I want to again compliment Herbert Abrams, the artist. He also painted the portrait of President Carter. So once again, President Bush has set another outstanding example of bipartisanship.

These portraits, as has already been said, will be seen by millions of Americans who visit here, reminding them of what these two great Americans stood for and for what they have done to strengthen our country. The portraits in the White House are more than likenesses. They tell the story of the promise of one American life and, in so doing, the promise of all American life. They offer a lesson, an example, a challenge for every American to live up to the responsibilities of citizenship.

As Americans look for ways to come together to deal with the challenges we face today, they can do well in looking at the lives of President and Mrs. Bush. They have been guided by the basic American values and virtues of honesty, compassion, civility, responsibility, and optimism. They have passed these values on to their family and on to our American family as well. And for that we should all be profoundly grateful.

Mrs. Bush's portrait will hang adjacent to the Vermeil Room on the ground floor corridor, taking her place in history in the line of America's First Ladies. One role of the First Lady is to open the doors to the White House. Mrs. Bush will be in the hearts of Americans forever for the gracious way in which she opened so many doors, not just to this house but to a world of endless possibility through reading. Her campaign for literacy exemplified our country's great spirit of voluntarism and our primary concern for the potential of every individual American. Her life of helping others has brought recognition to all those Americans, especially to American women, who have seen unmet needs in their communities and reached out to meet them. We cannot thank her enough.

President Bush's portrait will hang out here in the Grand Foyer, across from the portrait of President Franklin Roosevelt, the Commander in Chief he served in World War II. It will stand as a reminder of George Bush's basic integrity and decency and of his entire adult lifetime devoted to public service. Most of all, it will stand as a testimony to a leader who helped Americans move forward toward common ground on many fronts. We see this clearly in the causes George Bush led us in as President, causes that aimed at improving the lives not just of Republicans but of all Americans.

He made education a national priority when he hosted the education summit in 1989, something I will never forget and always be especially personally grateful for, because he understood that a solid education is essential to every Amer-

ican's ability to meet the challenges of the 21st century.

He led us to a new dedication to service and extolled the real heroes in America, the ordinary Americans who every day go about solving the problems of this country in courageous, brave, and quiet manners. The Points of Light initiative held up the best in America, reminded us of what we can do when we truly work together. And I can say that it was the one thing he did that he personally asked me to continue when I took this office, and I was honored to do it because it was so important. And it remains important to the United States today.

He signed the Americans with Disabilities Act, something that has now acquired broad support among people of all parties and all walks of life and which has made a real difference to the quality of life of Americans who are now making larger contributions to the rest of us. And he supported and signed the Clean Air Act, which is terribly important today in preserving the quality of American life.

He also led our Nation and the world in the Gulf War alliance, in an example of contributions and cooperations in the aftermath of the cold war that I believe will long be followed.

Finally, since he has left this office, he has continued to be an active and aggressive citizen for what he believed in. He worked here to help us to pass NAFTA, something for which I am profoundly grateful. And just the other day, he earned the gratitude of all Americans who believe in law and order and believe in civil citizenship when he defended the honor and reputation of law-abiding law enforcement officers and Government employees. For all these things, all Americans should be grateful to George Bush.

For President and Mrs. Bush, love of country and service to it have always meant the same thing. We honor them both today for their leadership, their character, and their concern for their fellow citizens.

On November 2, 1800, the day after his very first night in the White House, John Adams wrote to his wife, "I pray Heaven to bestow the best of blessings on this house and on all that shall hereafter inhabit it. May none but honest and wise men ever rule under this roof." In the case of George Bush, John Adams' prayers were surely met.

It is my great honor and pleasure now to unveil the official portraits of President and Mrs. Bush.

NOTE: The President spoke at 10:19 a.m. in the East Room at the White House. In his remarks, he referred to Robert L. Breeden, chairman of the board, White House Historical Association.

Message to the Congress Reporting on Sanctions Against the Federal Republic of Yugoslavia (Serbia and Montenegro)
July 18, 1995

To the Congress of the United States:

On May 30, 1992, in Executive Order No. 12808, the President declared a national emergency to deal with the threat to the national security, foreign policy, and economy of the United States arising from actions and policies of the Governments of Serbia and Montenegro, acting under the name of the Socialist Federal Republic of Yugoslavia or the Federal Republic of Yugoslavia, in their involvement in and support for groups attempting to seize territory in Croatia and the Republic of Bosnia and Herzegovina by force and violence utilizing, in part, the forces of the so-called Yugoslav National Army (57 *FR* 23299, June 2, 1992). I expanded the national emergency in Executive Order No. 12934 of October 25, 1994, to address the actions and policies of the Bosnian Serb forces and the authorities in the territory of the Republic of Bosnia and Herzegovina that they control. The present report is submitted pursuant to 50 U.S.C. 1641(c) and 1703(c). It discusses Administration actions and expenses directly related to the exercise of powers and authorities conferred by the declaration of a national emergency in Executive Order No. 12808 and Executive Order No. 12934 and to expanded sanctions against the Federal Republic of Yugoslavia (Serbia and Montenegro) (the "FRY (S/M)") and the Bosnian Serbs contained in Executive Order No. 12810 of June 5, 1992 (57 *FR* 24347, June 9, 1992), Executive Order No. 12831 of January 15, 1993 (58 *FR* 5253, Jan. 21, 1993), Executive Order No. 12846 of April 25, 1993 (58 *FR* 25771, April 27, 1993), and Executive Order No. 12934 of October 25, 1994 (59 *FR* 54117, October 27, 1994).

1. Executive Order No. 12808 blocked all property and interests in property of the Governments of Serbia and Montenegro, or held in the name of the former Government of the Socialist Federal Republic of Yugoslavia or the Government of the Federal Republic of Yugoslavia, then or thereafter located in the United States or within the possession or control of U.S. persons, including their overseas branches.

Subsequently, Executive Order No. 12810 expanded U.S. actions to implement in the United States the United Nations sanctions against the FRY (S/M) adopted in United Nations Security Council ("UNSC") Resolution 757 of May 30, 1992. In addition to reaffirming the blocking of FRY (S/M) Government property, this order prohibited transactions with respect to the FRY (S/M) involving imports, exports, dealing in FRY-origin property, air and sea transportation, contract performance, funds transfers, activity promoting importation or exportation or dealings in property, and official sports, scientific, technical, or other cultural representation of, or sponsorship by, the FRY (S/M) in the United States.

Executive Order No. 12810 exempted from trade restrictions (1) transshipments through the FRY (S/M), and (2) activities related to the United Nations Protection Force ("UNPROFOR"), the Conference on Yugoslavia, or the European Community Monitor Mission.

On January 15, 1993, President Bush issued Executive Order No. 12831 to implement new sanctions contained in U.N. Security Council Resolution 787 of November 16, 1992. The order revoked the exemption for transshipments through the FRY (S/M) contained in Executive Order No. 12810, prohibited transactions within the United States or by a U.S. person relating to FRY (S/M) vessels and vessels in which a majority or controlling interest is held by a person or entity in, or operating from, the FRY (S/M), and stated that all such vessels shall be considered as vessels of the FRY (S/M), regardless of the flag under which they sail.

On April 25, 1993, I issued Executive Order No. 12846 to implement in the United States the sanctions adopted in UNSC Resolution 820 of April 17, 1993. That resolution called on the Bosnian Serbs to accept the Vance-Owen peace plan for the Republic of Bosnia and Herzegovina and, if they failed to do so by April 26, called on member states to take additional measures to tighten the embargo against the FRY (S/M) and Serbian controlled areas of the Republic of Bosnia and Herzegovina and the United Nations Protected Areas in Croatia. Effective April 26, 1993, the order blocked all property and interests in property of commercial, industrial, or public utility undertakings or entities organized or located in the FRY (S/M), including property and interests in property of entities (wherever organized or located) owned or controlled by such undertakings or entities, that are or thereafter come within the possession or control of U.S. persons.

On October 25, 1994, in view of UNSC Resolution 942 of September 23, 1994, I issued Executive Order No. 12934 in order to take additional steps with respect to the crisis in the former Yugoslavia. (59 *FR* 54117, October 27, 1994.) Executive Order No. 12934 expands the scope of the national emergency declared in Executive Order No. 12808 to address the unusual and extraordinary threat to the national security, foreign policy, and economy of the United States posed by the actions and policies of the Bosnian Serb forces and the authorities in the territory in the Republic of Bosnia and Herzegovina that they control, including their refusal to accept the proposed territorial settlement of the conflict in the Republic of Bosnia and Herzegovina.

The Executive order blocks all property and interests in property that are in the United States, that hereafter come within the United States, or that are or hereafter come within the possession or control of United States persons (including their overseas branches) of: (1) the Bosnian Serb military and paramilitary forces and the authorities in areas of the Republic of Bosnia and Herzegovina under the control of those forces; (2) any entity, including any commercial, industrial, or public utility undertaking, organized or located in those areas of the Republic of Bosnia and Herzegovina under the control of Bosnian Serb forces; (3) any entity, wherever organized or located, which is owned or controlled directly or indirectly by any person in, or resident in, those areas of the Republic of Bosnia and Herzegovina under the control of Bosnian Serb forces; and (4) any person acting for or on behalf of any person within the scope of the above definitions.

The Executive order also prohibits the provision or exportation of services to those areas of the Republic of Bosnia and Herzegovina under the control of Bosnian Serb forces, or to any person for the purpose of any business carried on in those areas, either from the United States or by a U.S. person. The order also prohibits the entry of any U.S.-flagged vessel, other than a U.S. naval vessel, into the riverine ports of those areas of the Republic of Bosnia and Herzegovina under the control of Bosnia Serb forces. Finally, any transaction by any U.S. person that evades or avoids, or has the purpose of evading or avoiding, or attempts to violate any of the prohibitions set forth in the order is prohibited. Executive Order No. 12934 became effective at 11:59 p.m., e.d.t., on October 25, 1994.

2. The declaration of the national emergency on May 30, 1992, was made pursuant to the authority vested in the President by the Constitution and laws of the United States, including the International Emergency Economic Powers Act (50 U.S.C. 1701 et seq.), the National Emergencies Act (50 U.S.C. 1601 et seq.), and section 301 of title 3 of the United States Code. The emergency declaration was reported to the Congress on May 30, 1992, pursuant to section 204(b) of the International Emergency Economic Powers Act (50 U.S.C. 1703(b)) and the expansion of that National Emergency under the same authorities was reported to the Congress on October 25, 1994. The additional sanctions set forth in related Executive orders were imposed pursuant to the authority vested in the President by the Constitution and laws of the United States, including the statutes cited above, section 1114 of the Federal Aviation Act (49 U.S.C. App. 1514), and section 5 of the United Nations Participation Act (22 U.S.C. 287c).

3. There have been no amendments to the Federal Republic of Yugoslavia (Serbia and Montenegro) Sanctions Regulations (the "Regulations"), 31 C.F.R. Part 585, since the last report. The Treasury Department had previously published 853 names in the Federal Register on November 17, 1994 (59 *FR* 59460), as part of a comprehensive listing of all blocked persons and specially designated nationals ("SDNs") of the FRY (S/M). This list identified individuals

and entities determined by the Department of the Treasury to be owned or controlled by or acting for or on behalf of the Government of the FRY (S/M), persons in the FRY (S/M), or entities located or organized in or controlled from the FRY (S/M). All prohibitions in the Regulations pertaining to the Government of the FRY (S/M) apply to the entities and individuals identified. U.S. persons, on notice of the status of such blocked persons and specially designated nationals, are prohibited from entering into transactions with them, or transactions in which they have an interest, unless otherwise exempted or authorized pursuant to the Regulations.

On February 22, 1995, pursuant to Executive Order 12934 and the Regulations, Treasury identified 85 individuals as leaders of the Bosnian Serb forces or civilian authorities in the territories in the Republic of Bosnia and Herzegovina that they control. Also on February 22, Treasury designated 19 individuals and 23 companies as SDNs of the FRY (S/M). These designations include FRY (S/M)-connected companies around the world that are being directed from Cyprus, two Cypriot-owned firms that have had a central role in helping establish and sustain sanctions-evading FRY (S/M) front companies in Cyprus, and the head of the FRY (S/M)'s Central Bank who is also the architect of the FRY (S/M) economic program.

Additionally, on March 13, 1995, Treasury named 32 firms and eight individuals that are part of the Karic Brothers' family network of companies as SDNs of the FRY (S/M). Their enterprises span the globe and are especially active in former East Bloc countries. These additions and amendments, published in the Federal Register on April 18, 1995 (60 *FR* 19448), bring the current total of Blocked Entities and SDNs of the FRY (S/M) to 938 and the total number of individuals identified as leaders of the Bosnian Serb military or paramilitary forces or civilian authorities in the territories in the Republic of Bosnia and Herzegovina that they control to 85. A copy of the notice is attached.

Treasury's blocking authority as applied to FRY (S/M) subsidiaries and vessels in the United States has been challenged in court. In *Milena Ship Management Company, Ltd. v. Newcomb,* 804 F.Supp. 846, 855, and 859 (E.D.L.A. 1992) *aff'd,* 995 F.2d 620 (5th Cir. 1993), *cert.* denied, 114 S.Ct. 877 (1994), involving five ships owned or controlled by FRY (S/M) entities blocked in various U.S. ports, the

blocking authority as applied to these vessels was upheld. In *IPT Company, Inc. v. United States Department of the Treasury,* No. 92 CIV 5542 (S.D.N.Y. 1994), the district court also upheld the blocking authority as applied to the property of a Yugoslav subsidiary located in the United States. The latter case is currently on appeal to the Second Circuit.

4. Over the past 6 months, the Departments of State and Treasury have worked closely with European Union (the "EU") member states and other U.N. member nations to coordinate implementation of the U.N. sanctions against the FRY (S/M). This has included visits by assessment teams formed under the auspices of the United States, the EU, and the Organization for Security and Cooperation in Europe (the "OSCE") to states bordering on Serbia and Montenegro; continued deployment of OSCE sanctions assistance missions ("SAMs") to Albania, Bulgaria, Croatia, the former Yugoslav Republic of Macedonia, Hungary, Romania, and Ukraine to assist in monitoring land and Danube River traffic; support for the International Conference on the Former Yugoslavia ("ICFY") monitoring missions along the Serbia-Montenegro-Bosnia border; bilateral contacts between the United States and other countries for the purpose of tightening financial and trade restrictions on the FRY (S/M); and ongoing multilateral meetings by financial sanctions enforcement authorities from various countries to coordinate enforcement efforts and to exchange technical information.

5. In accordance with licensing policy and the Regulations, FAC has exercised its authority to license certain specific transactions with respect to the FRY (S/M) that are consistent with U.S. foreign policy and the Security Council sanctions. During the reporting period, FAC has issued 109 specific licenses regarding transactions pertaining to the FRY (S/M) or assets it owns or controls, bringing the total as of April 25, 1995, to 930. Specific licenses have been issued (1) for payment to U.S. or third-country secured creditors, under certain narrowly-defined circumstances, for pre-embargo import and export transactions; (2) for legal representation or advice to the Government of the FRY (S/M) or FRY (S/M)-located or controlled entities; (3) for the liquidation or protection of tangible assets of subsidiaries of FRY (S/M)-located or controlled firms located in the U.S.; (4) for limited transactions related to FRY (S/M) diplomatic representation in Washington and New York; (5)

for patent, trademark and copyright protection in the FRY (S/M) not involving payment to the FRY (S/M) Government; (6) for certain communications, news media, and travel-related transactions; (7) for the payment of crews' wages, vessel maintenance, and emergency supplies for FRY (S/M) controlled ships blocked in the United States; (8) for the removal from the FRY (S/M), or protection within the FRY (S/M), of certain property owned and controlled by U.S. entities; (9) to assist the United Nations in its relief operations and the activities of the U.N. Protection Force; and (10) for payment from funds outside the United States where a third country has licensed the transaction in accordance with U.N. sanctions. Pursuant to U.S. regulations implementing UNSC Resolutions, specific licenses have also been issued to authorize exportation of food, medicine, and supplies intended for humanitarian purposes in the FRY (S/M).

During the past 6 months, FAC has continued to oversee the liquidation of tangible assets of the 15 U.S. subsidiaries of entities organized in the FRY (S/M). Subsequent to the issuance of Executive Order No. 12846, all operating licenses issued for these U.S.-located Serbian or Montenegrin subsidiaries or joint ventures were revoked, and the net proceeds of the liquidation of their assets placed in blocked accounts.

In order to reduce the drain on blocked assets caused by continuing to rent commercial space, FAC arranged to have the blocked personalty, files, and records of the two Serbian banking institutions in New York moved to secure storage. The personalty is being liquidated, with the net proceeds placed in blocked accounts.

Following the sale of the M/V Kapetan Martinovic in January 1995, five Yugoslav-owned vessels remain blocked in the United States. Approval of the UNSC's Serbian sanctions Committee was sought and obtained for the sale of the M/V Kapetan Martinovic (and the M/V Bor, which was sold in June 1994) based on U.S. assurances that the sale would comply with four basic conditions, which assure that both U.S. and U.N. sanctions objectives with respect to the FRY (S/M) are met: (1) the sale will be for fair market value; (2) the sale will result in a complete divestiture of any interest of the FRY (S/M) (or of commercial interests located in or controlled from the FRY (S/M)) in the vessel; (3) the sale would result in no economic benefit to the FRY (S/M) (or commer-

cial interests located in or controlled from the FRY (S/M)); and (4) the net proceeds of the sale (the gross proceeds less the costs of sale normally paid by the seller) will be placed in a blocked account in the United States. Negotiations for the sale of the M/V Bar, now blocked in New Orleans, are underway and are likely to be concluded prior to my next report.

Other than the M/V Bar, the four remaining Yugoslav-owned vessels are beneficially owned by Jugooceanija Plovidba of Kotor, Montenegro, and managed by Milena Ship Management Co. Ltd. in Malta. These vessels have many unpaid U.S. creditors for services and supplies furnished during the time they have been blocked in the United States; moreover, the owner appears to have insufficient resources to provide for the future upkeep and maintenance needs of these vessels and their crews. The United States is notifying the UNSC's Serbian Sanctions Committee of the United States's intention to license some or all of these remaining four vessels upon the owner's request.

With the FAC-licensed sales of the M/V Kapetan Martinovic and the M/V Bor, those vessels were removed from the list of blocked FRY entities and merchant vessels maintained by FAC. The new owners of several formerly Yugoslav-owned vessels, which have been sold in other countries, have petitioned FAC to remove those vessels from the list. FAC, in coordination with the Department of State, is currently reviewing the sale terms and conditions for those vessels to ascertain whether they comply with U.N. sanctions objectives and UNSC's Serbian Sanctions Committee practice.

During the past 6 months, U.S. financial institutions have continued to block funds transfers in which there is an interest of the Government of the FRY (S/M) or an entity or undertaking located in or controlled from the FRY (S/M), and to stop prohibited transfers to persons in the FRY (S/M). Such interdicted transfers have accounted for $125.6 million since the issuance of Executive Order No. 12808, including some $9.3 million during the past 6 months.

To ensure compliance with the terms of the licenses that have been issued under the program, stringent reporting requirements are imposed. More than 279 submissions have been reviewed by FAC since the last report, and more than 125 compliance cases are currently open.

6. Since the issuance of Executive Order No. 12810, FAC has worked closely with the U.S.

Customs Service to ensure both that prohibited imports and exports (including those in which the Government of the FRY (S/M) or Bosnian Serb authorities have an interest) are identified and interdicted, and that permitted imports and exports move to their intended destination without undue delay. Violations and suspected violations of the embargo are being investigated and appropriate enforcement actions are being taken. There are currently 37 cases under active investigation. Since the last report, FAC has collected nine civil penalties totaling nearly $20,000. Of these, five were paid by U.S. financial institutions for violative funds transfers involving the Government of the FRY (S/M), persons in the FRY (S/M), or entities located or organized in or controlled from the FRY (S/M). Three U.S. companies and one air carrier have also paid penalties related to exports or unlicensed payments to the Government of the FRY (S/M) or persons in the FRY (S/M) or other violations of the Regulations.

7. The expenses incurred by the Federal Government in the 6-month period from November 30, 1994, through May 29, 1995, that are directly attributable to the authorities conferred by the declaration of a national emergency with respect to the FRY (S/M) and the Bosnian Serb forces and authorities are estimated at about $3.5 million, most of which represent wage and salary costs for Federal personnel. Personnel

costs were largely centered in the Department of the Treasury (particularly in FAC and its Chief Counsel's Office, and the U.S. Customs Service), the Department of State, the National Security Council, the U.S. Coast Guard, and the Department of Commerce.

8. The actions and policies of the Government of the FRY (S/M), in its involvement in and support for groups attempting to seize and hold territory in the Republics of Croatia and Bosnia and Herzegovina by force and violence, and the actions and policies of the Bosnian Serb forces and the authorities in the areas of Bosnia and Herzegovina under their control, continue to pose an unusual and extraordinary threat to the national security, foreign policy, and economy of the United States. The United States remains committed to a multilateral resolution of the conflict through implementation of the United Nations Security Council resolutions.

I shall continue to exercise the powers at my disposal to apply economic sanctions against the FRY (S/M) and the Bosnian Serb forces, civil authorities, and entities, as long as these measures are appropriate, and will continue to report periodically to the Congress on significant developments pursuant to 50 U.S.C. 1703(c).

WILLIAM J. CLINTON

The White House,
July 18, 1995.

Statement on the Departments of Veterans Affairs and Housing and Urban Development Appropriations Legislation
July 18, 1995

The 1996 VA–HUD appropriations bill passed today by the House Appropriations Committee is unacceptable.

By abolishing AmeriCorps it would eliminate opportunities for thousands of young people to serve their communities through the national service program. By dramatically slashing resources for the Environmental Protection Agency and imposing severe restrictions on that agency, the bill would decimate the Government's ability to protect the American people from air and water pollution. By cutting assistance for the Nation's homeless in half, it would punish

some of the weakest and most vulnerable in our society.

We need to balance the budget, and we need to cut spending to do it. But there is a right way and a wrong way. A bill so contrary to the priorities and concerns of the American people clearly represents the wrong way.

I will not stand by as the Republican majority tries to impose this extreme agenda on the Nation. If this bill is presented to me in its current form, I will veto it. I call on the Congress to correct the appropriations bills now under consideration before they reach my desk, not after.

Remarks on Affirmative Action at the National Archives and Records Administration
July 19, 1995

Thank you very much. To the Members of Congress who are here, members of the Cabinet and the administration, my fellow Americans: In recent weeks I have begun a conversation with the American people about our fate and our duty to prepare our Nation not only to meet the new century but to live and lead in a world transformed to a degree seldom seen in all of our history. Much of this change is good, but it is not all good and all of us are affected by it. Therefore, we must reach beyond our fears and our divisions to a new time of great and common purpose.

Our challenge is twofold: first, to restore the American dream of opportunity and the American value of responsibility and, second, to bring our country together amid all our diversity into a stronger community, so that we can find common ground and move forward as one.

More than ever these two endeavors are inseparable. I am absolutely convinced we cannot restore economic opportunity or solve our social problems unless we find a way to bring the American people together. To bring our people together we must openly and honestly deal with the issues that divide us. Today I want to discuss one of those issues, affirmative action.

It is, in a way, ironic that this issue should be divisive today, because affirmative action began 25 years ago by a Republican President with bipartisan support. It began simply as a means to an end of enduring national purpose: equal opportunity for all Americans.

So let us today trace the roots of affirmative action in our never-ending search for equal opportunity. Let us determine what it is and what it isn't. Let us see where it's worked and where it hasn't and ask ourselves what we need to do now. Along the way, let us remember always that finding common ground as we move toward the 21st century depends fundamentally on our shared commitment to equal opportunity for all Americans. It is a moral imperative, a constitutional mandate, and a legal necessity.

There could be no better place for this discussion than the National Archives, for within these walls are America's bedrocks of our common ground, the Declaration of Independence, the Constitution, the Bill of Rights. No paper is as lasting as the words these documents contain, so we put them in these special cases to protect the parchment from the elements. No building is as solid as the principles these documents embody, but we sure tried to build one with these metal doors 11 inches thick to keep them safe, for these documents are America's only crown jewels. But the best place of all to hold these words and these principles is the one place in which they can never fade and never grow old, in the stronger chambers of our hearts.

Beyond all else, our country is a set of convictions: "We hold these truths to be self-evident, that all men are created equal, that they are endowed by their Creator with certain unalienable Rights, that among these are Life, Liberty, and the pursuit of Happiness." Our whole history can be seen first as an effort to preserve these rights and then as an effort to make them real in the lives of all our citizens.

We know that from the beginning there was a great gap between the plain meaning of our creed and the meaner reality of our daily lives. Back then, only white male property owners could vote. Black slaves were not even counted as whole people, and Native Americans were regarded as little more than an obstacle to our great national progress. No wonder Thomas Jefferson, reflecting on slavery, said he trembled to think God is just.

On the 200th anniversary of our great Constitution, Justice Thurgood Marshall, the grandson of a slave, said, "The Government our Founders devised was defective from the start, requiring several amendments, a civil war, and momentous social transformation to attain the system of constitutional government and its respect for the individual freedoms and human rights we hold as fundamental today."

Emancipation, women's suffrage, civil rights, voting rights, equal rights, the struggle for the rights of the disabled, all these and other struggles are milestones on America's often rocky but fundamentally righteous journey to close the gap between the ideals enshrined in these treasures here in the National Archives and the reality of our daily lives.

I first came to this very spot where I'm standing today 32 years ago this month. I was a 16-year-old delegate to the American Legion Boys Nation. Now, that summer was a high-water mark for our national journey. That was the summer that President Kennedy ordered Alabama National Guardsmen to enforce a court order to allow two young blacks to enter the University of Alabama. As he told our Nation, "Every American ought to have the right to be treated as he would wish to be treated, as one would wish his children to be treated."

Later that same summer, on the steps of the Lincoln Memorial, Martin Luther King told Americans of his dream that one day the sons of former slaves and the sons of former slave-owners would sit down together at the table of brotherhood, that one day his four little children would be judged not by the color of their skin but by the content of their character. His words captured the hearts and steeled the wills of millions of Americans. Some of them sang with him in the hot sun that day. Millions more like me listened and wept in the privacy of their homes.

It's hard to believe where we were just three decades ago. When I came up here to Boys Nation and we had this mock congressional session, I was one of only three or four southerners who would even vote for the civil rights plank. That's largely because of my family. My grandfather had a grade school education and ran a grocery store across the street from the cemetery in Hope, Arkansas, where my parents and my grandparents are buried. Most of his customers were black, were poor, and were working people. As a child in that store, I saw that people of different races could treat each other with respect and dignity. But I also saw that the black neighborhood across the street was the only one in town where the streets weren't paved. And when I returned to that neighborhood in the late sixties to see a woman who had cared for me as a toddler, the streets still weren't paved. A lot of you know that I am an ardent movie-goer. As a child, I never went to a movie where I could sit next to a black American. They were always sitting upstairs.

In the 1960's, believe it or not, there were still a few courthouse squares in my State where the restrooms were marked "white" and "colored." I graduated from a segregated high school 7 years after President Eisenhower integrated Little Rock Central High School. And when President Kennedy barely carried my home State in 1960, the poll tax system was still alive and well there.

Even though my grandparents were in a minority, being poor Southern whites who were pro-civil rights, I think most other people knew better than to think the way they did. And those who were smart enough to act differently discovered a lesson that we ought to remember today: Discrimination is not just morally wrong, it hurts everybody.

In 1960, Atlanta, Georgia, in reaction to all the things that were going on all across the South, adopted the motto, "The city too busy to hate." And however imperfectly over the years, they tried to live by it. I am convinced that Atlanta's success—it now is home to more foreign corporations than any other American city, and one year from today it will begin to host the Olympics—that that success all began when people got too busy to hate.

The lesson we learned was a hard one. When we allow people to pit us against one another or spend energy denying opportunity based on our differences, everyone is held back. But when we give all Americans a chance to develop and use their talents, to be full partners in our common enterprise, then everybody is pushed forward.

My experiences with discrimination are rooted in the South and in the legacy slavery left. I also lived with a working mother and a working grandmother when women's work was far rarer and far more circumscribed than it is today. But we all know there are millions of other stories, those of Hispanics, Asian-Americans, Native Americans, people with disabilities, others against whom fingers have been pointed. Many of you have your own stories, and that's why you're here today, people who were denied the right to develop and to use their full human potential. And their progress, too, is a part of our journey to make the reality of America consistent with the principles just behind me here.

Thirty years ago in this city, you didn't see many people of color or women making their way to work in the morning in business clothes or serving in substantial numbers in powerful positions in Congress or at the White House or making executive decisions every day in businesses. In fact, even the employment want ads were divided, men on one side and women on the other. It was extraordinary then to see women or people of color as television news anchors or, believe it or not, even in college sports. There were far fewer women and minorities as job supervisors or firefighters or police officers or doctors or lawyers or college professors or in many other jobs that offer stability and honor and integrity to family life.

A lot has changed, and it did not happen as some sort of random evolutionary drift. It took hard work and sacrifices and countless acts of courage and conscience by millions of Americans. It took the political courage and statesmanship of Democrats and Republicans alike, the vigilance and compassion of courts and advocates in and out of Government committed to the Constitution and to equal protection and to equal opportunity. It took the leadership of people in business who knew that in the end we would all be better. It took the leadership of people in labor unions who knew that working people had to be reconciled.

Some people, like Congressman Lewis there, put their lives on the line. Other people lost their lives. And millions of Americans changed their own lives and put hate behind them. As a result, today all our lives are better. Women have become a major force in business and political life and far more able to contribute to their families' incomes. A true and growing black middle class has emerged. Higher education has literally been revolutionized, with women and racial and ethnic minorities attending once overwhelmingly white and sometimes all-male schools. In communities across our Nation, police departments now better reflect the makeup of those whom they protect. A generation of professionals now serve as role models for young women and minority youth. Hispanics and newer immigrant populations are succeeding in making America stronger.

For an example of where the best of our future lies, just think about our space program and the stunning hookup with the Russian space station this month. Let's remember that that program, the world's finest, began with heroes like Alan Shepard and Senator John Glenn. But today it's had American heroes like Sally Ride, Ellen Ochoa, Leroy Chiao, Guy Bluford, and other outstanding, completely qualified women and minorities.

How did this happen? Fundamentally, because we opened our hearts and minds and changed our ways. But not without pressure, the pressure of court decisions, legislation, executive action, and the power of examples in the public and private sector. Along the way, we learned that laws alone do not change society, that old habits and thinking patterns are deeply ingrained and die hard, that more is required to really open the doors of opportunity. Our search to find ways to move more quickly to equal opportunity led to the development of what we now call affirmative action.

The purpose of affirmative action is to give our Nation a way to finally address the systemic exclusion of individuals of talent on the basis of their gender or race, from opportunities to develop, perform, achieve, and contribute. Affirmative action is an effort to develop a systematic approach to open the doors of education, employment, and business development opportunities to qualified individuals who happen to be members of groups that have experienced longstanding and persistent discrimination.

It is a policy that grew out of many years of trying to navigate between two unacceptable pasts. One was to say simply that we declared discrimination illegal and that's enough. We saw that that way still relegated blacks with college degrees to jobs as railroad porters and kept women with degrees under a glass ceiling with a lower paycheck.

The other path was simply to try to impose change by leveling draconian penalties on employers who didn't meet certain imposed, ultimately arbitrary, and sometimes unachievable quotas. That, too, was rejected out of a sense of fairness.

So a middle ground was developed that would change an inequitable status quo gradually but firmly, by building the pool of qualified applicants for college, for contracts, for jobs, and giving more people the chance to learn, work, and earn. When affirmative action is done right, it is flexible, it is fair, and it works.

I know some people are honestly concerned about the times affirmative action doesn't work, when it's done in the wrong way. And I know there are times when some employers don't use it in the right way. They may cut corners and treat a flexible goal as a quota. They may give opportunities to people who are unqualified instead of those who deserve it. They may, in so doing, allow a different kind of discrimination. When this happens, it is also wrong. But it isn't affirmative action, and it is not legal.

So when our administration finds cases of that sort, we will enforce the law aggressively. The Justice Department files hundreds of cases every year attacking discrimination in employment, including suits on behalf of white males. Most of these suits, however, affect women and minorities for a simple reason, because the vast majority of discrimination in America is still discrimination against them. But the law does require fairness for everyone, and we are determined to see that that is exactly what the law delivers.

Let me be clear about what affirmative action must not mean and what I won't allow it to be. It does not mean and I don't favor the unjustified preference of the unqualified over the qualified of any race or gender. It doesn't mean and I don't favor numerical quotas. It doesn't mean and I don't favor rejection or selection of any employee or student solely on the basis of race or gender without regard to merit.

Like many business executives and public servants, I owe it to you to say that my views on this subject are, more than anything else, the product of my personal experience. I have had experience with affirmative action, nearly 20 years of it now, and I know it works.

When I was attorney general of my home State, I hired a record number of women and African-American lawyers, every one clearly qualified and exceptionally hardworking. As Governor, I appointed more women to my Cabinet and State boards than any other Governor in the State's history and more African-Americans than all the Governors in the State's history combined. And no one ever questioned their qualifications or performance, and our State was better and stronger because of their service.

As President, I am proud to have the most diverse administration in history in my Cabinet, my agencies, and my staff. And I must say, I have been surprised at the criticism I have received from some quarters in my determination to achieve this.

In the last 2½ years, the most outstanding example of affirmative action in the United States, the Pentagon, has opened 260,000 positions for women who serve in our Armed Forces. I have appointed more women and minorities to the Federal bench than any other President, more than the last two combined. And yet, far more of our judicial appointments have received the highest rating from the American Bar Association than any other administration since those ratings have been given.

In our administration, many Government agencies are doing more business with qualified firms run by minorities and women. The Small Business Administration has reduced its budget by 40 percent, doubled its loan outputs, dramatically increased the number of loans to women and minority small business people, without reducing the number of loans to white business owners who happen to be male, and without changing the loan standards for a single, solitary application. Quality and diversity can go hand-in-hand, and they must.

Let me say that affirmative action has also done more than just open the doors of opportunity to individual Americans. Most economists who study it agree that affirmative action has also been an important part of closing gaps in economic opportunity in our society, thereby strengthening the entire economy.

A group of distinguished business leaders told me just a couple of days ago that their companies are stronger and their profits are larger because of the diversity and the excellence of their work forces achieved through intelligent and fair affirmative action programs. And they said, "We have gone far beyond anything the Government might require us to do because managing diversity and individual opportunity and being fair to everybody is the key to our future economic success in the global marketplace."

Now, there are those who say, my fellow Americans, that even good affirmative action programs are no longer needed, that it should be enough to resort to the courts or the Equal Employment Opportunity Commission in cases of actual, provable, individual discrimination because there is no longer any systematic discrimination in our society. In deciding how to answer that, let us consider the facts.

The unemployment rate for African-Americans remains about twice that of whites. The Hispanic rate is still much higher. Women have narrowed the earnings gap, but still make only 72 percent as much as men do for comparable jobs. The average income for an Hispanic woman with a college degree is still less than the average income of a white man with a high school diploma.

According to the recently completed glass ceiling report, sponsored by Republican Members of Congress, in the Nation's largest companies only six-tenths of one percent of senior management positions are held by African-

Americans, four-tenths of a percent by Hispanic-Americans, three-tenths of a percent by Asian-Americans. Women hold between 3 and 5 percent of these positions. White males make up 43 percent of our work force but hold 95 percent of these jobs.

Just last week, the Chicago Federal Reserve Bank reported that black home loan applicants are more than twice as likely to be denied credit as whites with the same qualifications and that Hispanic applicants are more than 1½ times as likely to be denied loans as whites with the same qualifications.

Last year alone the Federal Government received more than 90,000 complaints of employment discrimination based on race, ethnicity, or gender; less than 3 percent were for reverse discrimination.

Evidence abounds in other ways of the persistence of the kind of bigotry that can affect the way we think, even if we're not conscious of it, in hiring and promotion and business and educational decisions.

Crimes and violence based on hate against Asians, Hispanics, African-Americans, and other minorities are still with us. And I'm sorry to say that the worst and most recent evidence of this involves a recent report of Federal law enforcement officials in Tennessee attending an event literally overflowing with racism, a sickening reminder of just how pervasive these kinds of attitudes still are.

By the way, I want to tell you that I am committed to finding the truth about what happened there and to taking appropriate action. And I want to say that if anybody who works in Federal law enforcement thinks that that kind of behavior is acceptable, they ought to think about working someplace else.

Now, let's get to the other side of the argument. If affirmative action has worked and if there is evidence that discrimination still exists on a wide scale in ways that are conscious and unconscious, then why should we get rid of it as many people are urging? Some question the effectiveness or the fairness of particular affirmative action programs. I say to all of you, those are fair questions, and they prompted the review of our affirmative action programs about which I will talk in a few moments.

Some question the fundamental purpose of the effort. There are people who honestly believe that affirmative action always amounts to group preferences over individual merit, that affirmative action always leads to reverse discrimination, that ultimately, therefore, it demeans those who benefit from it and discriminates against those who are not helped by it.

I just have to tell you that all of you have to decide how you feel about that, and all of our fellow country men and women have to decide as well. But I believe if there are no quotas, if we give no opportunities to unqualified people, if we have no reverse discrimination, and if, when the problem ends, the program ends, that criticism is wrong. That's what I believe. But we should have this debate, and everyone should ask the question.

Now let's deal with what I really think is behind so much of this debate today. There are a lot of people who oppose affirmative action today who supported it for a very long time. I believe they are responding to the sea change in the experiences that most Americans have in the world in which we live. If you say now you're against affirmative action because the Government is using its power or the private sector is using its power to help minorities at the expense of the majority, that gives you a way of explaining away the economic distress that a majority of Americans honestly feel. It gives you a way of turning their resentment against the minorities or against a particular Government program, instead of having an honest debate about how we all got into the fix we're in and what we're all going to do together to get out of it.

That explanation, the affirmative action explanation, for the fix we're in is just wrong. It is just wrong. Affirmative action did not cause the great economic problems of the American middle class. And because most minorities or women are either members of that middle class or people who are poor who are struggling to get into it, we must also admit that affirmative action alone won't solve the problems of minorities and women who seek to be a part of the American dream. To do that, we have to have an economic strategy that reverses the decline in wages and the growth of poverty among working people. Without that, women, minorities, and white males will all be in trouble in the future.

But it is wrong to use the anxieties of the middle class to divert the American people from the real causes of their economic distress, the sweeping historic changes taking all the globe in its path and the specific policies or lack of them in our own country which have aggravated those challenges. It is simply wrong to play politics with the issue of affirmative action and divide our country at a time when, if we're really going to change things, we have to be united.

I must say, I think it is ironic that some of those, not all but some of those who call for an end to affirmative action also advocate policies which will make the real economic problems of the anxious middle class even worse. They talk about opportunity and being for equal opportunity for everyone, and then they reduce investment in equal opportunity on an evenhanded basis. For example, if the real goal is economic opportunity for all Americans, why in the world would we reduce our investment in education from Head Start to affordable college loans? Why don't we make college loans available to every American instead?

If the real goal is empowering all middle class Americans and empowering poor people to work their way into the middle class without regard to race or gender, why in the world would the people who advocate that turn around and raise taxes on our poorest working families, or reduce the money available for education and training when they lose their jobs or they're living on poverty wages, or increase the cost of housing for lower income working people with children? Why would we do that? If we're going to empower America, we have to do more than talk about it. We have to do it. And we surely have learned that we cannot empower all Americans by a simple strategy of taking opportunity away from some Americans.

So to those who use this as a political strategy to divide us, we must say no. We must say no. But to those who raise legitimate questions about the way affirmative action works or who raise the larger question about the genuine problems and anxieties of all the American people and their sense of being left behind and treated unfairly, we must say yes, you are entitled to answers to your questions. We must say yes to that.

Now, that's why I ordered this review of all of our affirmative action programs, a review designed to look at the facts, not the politics, of affirmative action. This review concluded that affirmative action remains a useful tool for widening economic and educational opportunity. The model used by the military, the Army in particular—and I'm delighted to have the Commanding General of the Army here today be-

cause he set such a fine example—has been especially successful because it emphasizes education and training, ensuring that it has a wide pool of qualified candidates for every level of promotion. That approach has given us the most racially diverse and best qualified military in our history. There are more opportunities for women and minorities there than ever before. And now there are over 50 generals and admirals who are Hispanic, Asian, or African-Americans.

We found that the Education Department targeted on—had programs targeted on under-represented minorities that do a great deal of good with the tiniest of investments. We found that these programs comprised 40 cents of every $1,000 in the Education Department's budget.

Now, college presidents will tell you that the education their schools offer actually benefit from diversity, colleges where young people get the education and make the personal and professional contacts that will shape their lives. If their colleges look like the world they're going to live and work in and they learn from all different kinds of people things that they can't learn in books, our systems of higher education are stronger.

Still, I believe every child needs the chance to go to college, every child. That means every child has to have a chance to get affordable and repayable college loans, Pell grants for poor kids and a chance to do things like join AmeriCorps and work their way through school. Every child is entitled to that. That is not an argument against affirmative action, it's an argument for more opportunity for more Americans until everyone is reached.

As I said a moment ago, the review found that the Small Business Administration last year increased loans to minorities by over two-thirds, loans to women by over 80 percent, did not decrease loans to white men, and not a single loan went to an unqualified person. People who never had a chance before to be part of the American system of free enterprise now have it. No one was hurt in the process. That made America stronger.

This review also found that the Executive order on employment practices of large Federal contractors also has helped to bring more fairness and inclusion into the work force.

Since President Nixon was here in my job, America has used goals and timetables to preserve opportunity and to prevent discrimination, to urge businesses to set higher expectations for themselves and to realize those expectations. But we did not and we will not use rigid quotas to mandate outcomes.

We also looked at the way we award procurement contracts under the programs known as set-asides. There's no question that these programs have helped to build up firms owned by minorities and women who historically had been excluded from the old-boy networks in these areas. It has helped a new generation of entrepreneurs to flourish, opening new paths to self-reliance and an economic growth in which all of us ultimately share. Because of the set-asides, businesses ready to compete have had a chance to compete, a chance they would not have otherwise had.

But as with any Government program, set-asides can be misapplied, misused, even intentionally abused. There are critics who exploit that fact as an excuse to abolish all these programs, regardless of their effects. I believe they are wrong, but I also believe, based on our factual review, we clearly need some reform.

So first, we should crack down on those who take advantage of everyone else through fraud and abuse. We must crack down on fronts and passthroughs, people who pretend to be eligible for these programs and aren't. That is wrong. We also, in offering new businesses a leg up, must make sure that the set-asides go to businesses that need them most. We must really look and make sure that our standard for eligibility is fair and defensible. We have to tighten the requirement to move businesses out of programs once they've had a fair opportunity to compete. The graduation requirement must mean something: It must mean graduation. There should be no permanent set-aside for any company.

Second, we must and we will comply with the Supreme Court's *Adarand* decision of last month. Now, in particular, that means focusing set-aside programs on particular regions and business sectors where the problems of discrimination or exclusion are provable and are clearly requiring affirmative action. I have directed the Attorney General and the agencies to move forward with compliance with *Adarand* expeditiously.

But I also want to emphasize that the *Adarand* decision did not dismantle affirmative action and did not dismantle set-asides. In fact, while setting stricter standards to mandate reform of affirmative action, it actually reaffirmed the need for affirmative action and reaffirmed the continuing existence of systematic discrimination in the United States. What the Supreme Court ordered the Federal Government to do was to meet the same more rigorous standard for affirmative action programs that State and local governments were ordered to meet several years ago. And the best set-aside programs under that standard have been challenged and have survived.

Third, beyond discrimination we need to do more to help disadvantaged people and distressed communities, no matter what their race or gender. There are places in our country where the free enterprise system simply doesn't reach; it simply isn't working to provide jobs and opportunity. Disproportionately, these areas in urban and rural America are highly populated by racial minorities, but not entirely. To make this initiative work, I believe the Government must become a better partner for people in places in urban and rural America that are caught in a cycle of poverty. And I believe we have to find ways to get the private sector to assume their rightful role as a driver of economic growth.

It has always amazed me that we have given incentives to our business people to help to develop poor economies in other parts of the world, our neighbors in the Caribbean, our neighbors in other parts of the world—I have supported this when not subject to their own abuses—but we ignore the biggest source of economic growth available to the American economy, the poor economies isolated within the United States of America.

There are those who say, "Well, even if we made the jobs available, people wouldn't work. They haven't tried. " Most of the people in disadvantaged communities work today, and most of them who don't work have a very strong desire to do so. In central Harlem, 14 people apply for every single minimum-wage job opening. Think how many more would apply if there were good jobs with a good future. Our job has to connect disadvantaged people and disadvantaged communities to economic opportunity so that everybody who wants to work can do so.

We've been working at this through our empowerment zones and community develop banks, through the initiatives of Secretary Cisneros of the Housing and Urban Development Department, and many other things that we have tried to do to put capital where it is needed. And now I have asked Vice President Gore to develop a proposal to use our contracting to support businesses that locate themselves in these distressed areas or hire a large percentage of their workers from these areas, not to supplement what we're doing in affirmative action—not to substitute for it but to supplement it, to go beyond it, to do something that will help to deal with the economic crisis of America. We want to make our procurement system more responsive to people in these areas who need help.

My fellow Americans, affirmative action has to be made consistent with our highest ideals of personal responsibility and merit and our urgent need to find common ground and to prepare all Americans to compete in the global economy of the next century.

Today, I am directing all our agencies to comply with the Supreme Court's *Adarand* decision and also to apply the four standards of fairness to all our affirmative action programs that I have already articulated: No quotas in theory or practice; no illegal discrimination of any kind, including reverse discrimination; no preference for people who are not qualified for any job or other opportunity; and as soon as a program has succeeded, it must be retired. Any program that doesn't meet these four principles must be eliminated or reformed to meet them.

But let me be clear: Affirmative action has been good for America.Affirmative action has not always been perfect, and affirmative action should not go on forever. It should be changed now to take care of those things that are wrong, and it should be retired when its job is done. I am resolved that that day will come. But the evidence suggests, indeed, screams that that day has not come.

The job of ending discrimination in this country is not over. That should not be surprising. We had slavery for centuries before the passage of the 13th, 14th, and 15th amendments. We waited another 100 years for the civil rights legislation. Women have had the vote less than 100 years. We have always had difficulty with these things, as most societies do. But we are making more progress than many people.

Based on the evidence, the job is not done. So here is what I think we should do. We should reaffirm the principle of affirmative ac-

tion and fix the practices. We should have a simple slogan: Mend it, but don't end it.

Let me ask all Americans, whether they agree or disagree with what I have said today, to see this issue in the larger context of our times. President Lincoln said, "We cannot escape our history." We cannot escape our future, either. And that future must be one in which every American has the chance to live up to his or her God-given capacities.

The new technology, the instant communications, the explosion of global commerce have created enormous opportunities and enormous anxieties for Americans. In the last 2½ years, we have seen 7 million new jobs, more millionaires and new businesses than ever before, high corporate profits, and a booming stock market. Yet most Americans are working harder for the same or lower pay, and they feel more insecurity about their jobs, their retirement, their health care, and their children's education. Too many of our children are clearly exposed to poverty and welfare, violence and drugs.

These are the great challenges for our whole country on the homefront at the dawn of the 21st century. We've got to find the wisdom and the will to create family-wage jobs for all the people who want to work, to open the door of college to all Americans, to strengthen families and reduce the awful problems to which our children are exposed, to move poor Americans from welfare to work.

This is the work of our administration, to give people the tools they need to make the most of their own lives, to give families and communities the tools they need to solve their own problems. But let us not forget affirmative action didn't cause these problems. It won't solve them. And getting rid of affirmative action certainly won't solve them.

If properly done, affirmative action can help us come together, go forward, and grow together. It is in our moral, legal, and practical interest to see that every person can make the most of his own life. In the fight for the future, we need all hands on deck, and some of those hands still need a helping hand.

In our national community we're all different; we're all the same. We want liberty and freedom. We want the embrace of family and community. We want to make the most of our own lives, and we're determined to give our children a better one. Today there are voices of division who would say forget all that. Don't you dare.

Remember we're still closing the gap between our Founders' ideals and our reality. But every step along the way has made us richer, stronger, and better. And the best is yet to come.

Thank you very much, and God bless you.

NOTE: The President spoke at 11:40 a.m. in the Rotunda. In his remarks, he referred to Gen. Dennis J. Reimer, USA, Chief of Staff, Army.

Memorandum on Affirmative Action
July 19, 1995

Memorandum for Heads of Executive Departments and Agencies

Subject: Evaluation of Affirmative Action Programs

This Administration is committed to expanding the economy, to strengthening programs that support children and families, and to vigorous, effective enforcement of laws prohibiting discrimination. These commitments reflect bedrock values—equality, opportunity, and fair play—which extend to all Americans, regardless of race, ethnicity, or gender.

While our Nation has made enormous strides toward eliminating inequality and barriers to opportunity, the job is not complete. As the United States Supreme Court recognized only one month ago in *Adarand Constructors, Inc. v. Peña.* "[t]he unhappy persistence of both the practice and the lingering effects of racial discrimination against minority groups in this country is an unfortunate reality, and government is not disqualified from acting in response to it." This Administration will continue to support affirmative measures that promote opportunities in employment, education, and government contracting for Americans subject to discrimination or its continuing effects. In every instance, we will seek reasonable ways to achieve the objectives of inclusion and antidiscrimination without specific reliance on group membership. But where our legitimate objectives cannot be achieved through such means, the Federal Government will continue to support lawful consideration of race, ethnicity, and gender under programs that are flexible, realistic, subject to reevaluation, and fair.

Accordingly, in all programs you administer that use race, ethnicity, or gender as a consideration to expand opportunity or provide benefits to members of groups that have suffered discrimination, I ask you to take steps to ensure adherence to the following policy principles. The policy principles are that any program must be eliminated or reformed if it:

(a) creates a quota;
(b) creates preferences for unqualified individuals;
(c) creates reverse discrimination; or
(d) continues even after its equal opportunity purposes have been achieved.

In addition, the Supreme Court's recent decision in *Adarand Constructors, Inc. v. Peña* requires strict scrutiny of the justifications for, and provisions of, a broad range of existing race-based affirmative action programs. You recently received a detailed legal analysis of *Adarand* from the Department of Justice. Consistent with that guidance, I am today instructing each of you to undertake, in consultation with and pursuant to the overall direction of the Attorney General, an evaluation of programs you administer that use race or ethnicity in decision making. With regard to programs that affect more than one agency, the Attorney General shall determine, after consultations, which agency shall take the lead in performing this analysis.

Using all of the tools at your disposal, you should develop any information that is necessary to evaluate whether your programs are narrowly tailored to serve a compelling interest, as required under *Adarand*'s strict scrutiny standard. Any program that does not meet the constitutional standard must be reformed or eliminated.

WILLIAM J. CLINTON

Teleconference Remarks and a Question-and-Answer Session With the National Council of La Raza
July 19, 1995

The President. Thank you, Irma Flores-Gonzalez, for that warm introduction, and thank you, ladies and gentlemen, for your warm welcome.

I'm glad to see so many of my friends out there, and I want to say a special hello to your president, Raul Yzaguirre, and Irma's predecessor, Dr. Audrey Alvarado. The First Lady sends her regrets at not being able to be with you today. I hope you won't be too disappointed that I'm going to be her stand-in. I'm also sorry I can't be with you in person, as I was last year in Miami.

Just a little over an hour ago, at the National Archives here in Washington, I announced the results of our administration's review of Federal affirmative action programs and my convictions about what we ought to do with affirmative action. I made it clear that an essential part of our search for common ground in the exercise of our freedom is an unwavering commitment to genuine equal opportunity for all Americans. Affirmative action is simply a tool in the pursuit of that enduring national interest, equal opportunity.

Hispanics are making huge strides in ways we cannot have even imagined just a generation ago. I don't want any Hispanic child in America to feel that his or her race is an impediment to full achievement. Every child has a right to the American dream, and all of us have a responsibility to nourish that dream.

But until this country has achieved equality of opportunity, until we have stamped out discrimination, we will still need the remedy of affirmative action. It must be done the right way: It must be flexible, it must be fair, and it must work. Let me be clear: Our administration is against quotas, we're against guaranteed results, but we do need to guarantee genuine equality of opportunity for all Americans.

We want to support the programs that are working, and we want to get rid of the ones that aren't. If you ask me in a sentence what we need to do, I'd say we need to mend but not to end affirmative action. We ought to stay with our principles and fix whatever practices we need to fix.

Our study showed that, indeed, affirmative action has been an effective tool in expanding opportunity for those who have suffered discrimination in the Army, in education, in small business loans, in employment by Federal contractors, in the set-aside programs. We have seen again and again that when affirmative action is done in the right way, it has helped more minorities and women to pursue the American dream, people like Paul Gutierrez in Omaha, who owns Midwest Maintenance; Ernest Gonzalez of West Babylon, New York, who owns a chemical distribution company; Santos Garza of Bethesda, Maryland, who owns a security company.

After 25 years of experience, we know that these programs can work, but we also know that there have been some problems with them. So it is time to take a good look at what's working and what isn't. That's why I announced the series of steps that we'll take to change and to improve our approach to affirmative action. First, we want to crack down on those who take advantage of other people who deserve the program through their own fraud and abuse. We'll still offer new businesses a leg up, but we're going to make sure the set-asides go to the businesses that need them most.

Second, we're going to comply with the Supreme Court's decision in the *Adarand* case last month. That means focusing set-asides to regions and business sectors where the serious problems of discrimination are clear and provable. I have directed the Attorney General and the agencies to move forward with this expeditiously. The *Adarand* decision did require us to improve the way in which we do affirmative action, but I want all of you to understand, it did not dismantle set-asides. In fact, a huge majority of the Supreme Court, seven of the nine Justices, reaffirmed the need for good affirmative action because of the continuing evidence of discrimination in our national life.

The stricter standards of *Adarand* have been met by State and local governments who were ordered several years ago to adhere to these standards. And the best State and local set-asides that have been challenged have met the standards and survived the challenge.

The third thing we need to do is to help disadvantaged people and distressed communities wherever they are and regardless of their race or gender. That's what we tried to do in the empowerment zone program. And that's why I've asked Vice President Gore to develop a proposal to use our contracting in the Government to support businesses that locate themselves in truly distressed areas or that hire many of their workers from these areas.

The truth is that there are whole pockets of America that have been left behind in the free enterprise system. And we need to give people incentives to invest in those areas and those people, not as a substitute for affirmative action but as a supplement to it. We need to do this. Most of these areas will be disproportionately minority, but not all of them will be. I am convinced we have got to focus on getting people who are in these isolated areas, whether they're in rural or urban areas, the benefits of the American dream. We cannot grow the American economy in the 21st century if we continue to have pockets of abject poverty where people are dying to go to work.

I have also directed all our agencies to apply four standards of fairness to all our affirmative action programs: first, no quotas or any inflexible numerical straitjackets in theory or in practice; second, no illegal discrimination of any kind, including reverse discrimination; third, no preferential treatment for people who are not qualified; and finally, when a program has met its goal it must be retired. Any program that doesn't meet these four principles must be eliminated or reformed.

Affirmative action has been good for America. That doesn't mean it's always been perfect. It doesn't mean it should go on forever. It should be retired when its job is done, and I am resolved that that day will come. But you and I know that job is not done yet, and we do not need to abandon affirmative action.

It is my firm belief that our diversity can be America's greatest strength in the 21st century. We're going into an information age. We have to be prepared to compete and win in the global economy, with all of its different cultures. And we are so well positioned in this country, with well over 150 different racial and ethnic groups, with opening opportunities to women as well as men. But we have to say

to ourselves honestly, we are not where we need to be. And we're going to need everyone pulling together if our country is going to move into the 21st century in good shape. So we can't back away from our commitment to expand equal opportunity and to require responsibility from every single American.

You know, I ran for President to do two things: first, to restore the American dream of opportunity and the American value of responsibility and, second, to bring the American people together again, so that we could move into the next century together. I have learned in the past 2½ years that we can't do one without the other. We can't solve our economic problems or our social problems unless we do them together and unless we come together. We all have to bring the American people together.

That's really the bottom line of this debate about affirmative action. You and I and all Americans have to sit down and find a way to bridge the great divides in our society. We have to find a way to honor our diversity in the context of our shared values, our shared interests, and our shared commitments to both equal opportunity and to high standards of qualification and performance. If we do this, we'll be stronger; we'll be better prepared as a nation to meet the challenges that lie ahead.

By the year 2010, Latinos will be the largest minority group in our country. Your voices and your talents are absolutely critical to lead us into the new century. You're already doing that in many ways, in daily life and in public service.

We should all be grateful for the work that all of you do, but I want to mention one of your number in particular, New Mexico Congressman Bill Richardson. He did a great job in Haiti. He did a great job in North Korea. And I know how proud all of you are—and I can hear by your applause—at the work he did, the brilliant work he did to help to bring home the two Americans who were wrongfully imprisoned in Iraq. He is a great American, and every American should be grateful to him for what he did.

Just last week at the Southwest Voter Registration and Education Dinner, Vice President Gore announced my intention to honor another great American, Willie Velasquez, with the Presidential Medal of Freedom. I am honored to honor the memory of a man who gave all of us so much. For too long, Latinos were deprived of the chance to serve in the highest levels of government. This was a loss for your community and a loss for our Nation. We are a rich country but not so rich that we can afford to waste the talents of so many of our best people. Willie Velasquez knew this. His memory and legacy are alive in every corner of our administration.

And as we continue to move forward together, you know that we have more to do. But there are already more than 2 times as many Hispanic appointees in our administration than in the previous two administrations. In addition to Henry Cisneros at HUD and Federico Peña at the Department of Transportation, there are so many others who are contributing to our country and our future.

Let me just make one other point in closing, and then I know you have a question or two. You have to help us as a country make sure that this affirmative action program is not used as one more way to divide middle class and working poor Americans.

The real problem that is driving this new debate on affirmative action is a problem you know well. The ground is moving under America. Look at the last 2½ years. I have instituted a new economic strategy that has helped to bring us 7 million jobs. We have an enormous increase in the number of new businesses, the highest on record. We have more new millionaires than ever before. The stock market is at an all time high. Corporate profits are high. But you know what? More than half the American people are working harder today for the same or lower wages they were making 2½ years ago. More than half of our people still feel insecure about their jobs, their health care, their retirements, their ability to educate their children. Now, these are things that we have to face.

I know Secretary Dick Riley has already talked with you about the need to strengthen our commitment to education. But before I go on that, I want you to focus on this. A lot of this heat on affirmative action is being generated by people who want to blame minorities, who want to blame women's groups, and who want to blame the Federal Government and this administration for the economic distress of the middle class. It's been building for decades, and we have a strategy to do something about it. Affirmative action—it did not cause the economic problems of middle class America. And affirmative action alone will not solve all the economic problems of women and racial minorities in this country.

So what we have to do is to say, let's look at affirmative action on its own merits. Let's realize we're all stronger when we grow together. But let's also recognize that we have to have a strategy to lift this country up. Don't let the people who are pursuing policies that will drive us down and drive us apart prevail by preying on the legitimate anxieties of middle class Americans to get this country moving for them again.

That all begins with a commitment, a renewed commitment to education. This issue is so important to all of us here that I just want to take one minute to echo and amplify what Secretary Riley said to you. Affirmative action without a commitment to education won't work. School is where young people learn the skills to pursue middle class dreams. It's where middle class values are taught and where parents can know that the teachers will reinforce things like responsibility and honesty and trustworthiness and hard work and caring for one another and for our natural environment, where good citizenship can be taught and where it can be modeled.

A good education has always been key to unlocking the promise of tomorrow. And today, more than ever, those without it are being left behind. That's why under our plan we can balance the budget and increase educational investment by $40 billion in proven programs that work, from expanding Head Start to more affordable and repayable college loans.

The plan of the Republican majority in Congress will balance the budget, all right, but it cuts education by $36 billion, right at the time when we need to be doing more to prepare our young people to take their productive places in the global economy. It does not make sense. It also doesn't make sense for them to cut funds on the fight on crime, cut our investments in safe and drug-free schools. There are a lot of things that don't make sense.

So, as we work in the coming months to balance the budget, I hope you'll help me do it in the right way. If we take a little longer and we don't give huge tax cuts to people who don't really need it, we can invest in middle class Americans and in poor Americans who were determined to work their way into the middle class.

You and I know it would be self-defeating to cut our investments in education. Cutting education today would be like cutting defense budgets at the height of the cold war. Our national security depends upon our ability to educate all of our people, to give them the tools they need to make the most of their own lives.

Our mission, yours and mine together, must be to build a bridge to the future so that every American can cross it. We have to give every Latino and every other American the power they all need to make the most of their own lives and to give their children better lives. That's what's behind my approach to affirmative action. That's what's behind my commitment to education. That's what's behind my economic strategy. I want our children's generation to inherit an America with as much new opportunity as the one into which I was brought into. If people take the kind of responsibility you have taken to make our country better and we do the right things here, we will be better.

I thank you for your service to your community. I thank you for your service to your country. I ask you to stay at it, stand up for the proposition that all of us are going forward together.

Thank you, and God bless you all.

[A participant asked how the administration planned to address the concerns of Hispanic women in the work force.]

The President. Thank you.

First of all, I'd like to talk a little bit about our survey. In our Working Women Count Campaign, conducted by Secretary Reich at the Department of Labor with the able assistance of Hermalinda Pompa of the Women's Bureau, we circulated a questionnaire to working women. Two hundred and fifty thousand Hispanic women replied. They told us they were interested in pay and benefits, in having the ability to both work and to care for their children, and in making sure that women could be valued and treated properly and fairly in the workplace.

We are determined to do what we can to advance this cause. First of all, we want to make sure Hispanic women understand the rights and opportunities to which they're entitled as working Americans. And we have translated into Spanish, for example, information on the family leave law, information on the sexual harassment laws, information on pregnancy and other employment discrimination practices. I think that is very important.

But secondly, and even more important, we have to pursue an economic agenda that will help Hispanic women. We, first of all, have to raise the minimum wage. There are 300,000 Hispanic women in this country who would make an average of more than $1,800 a year more than they're making now and put another $1 billion into the American economy if we raised the minimum wage. And if we don't raise the minimum wage, next year, in terms of its real buying power, the minimum wage will fall to a 40-year low.

One of the real big fights we're having up here in Washington today is the fight between my vision of a smart-work, high-wage future and the alternative vision of a high-profit but hard-work and low-wage future. I think it's clear which one is in the best interest of the American people. We ought to start with raising the minimum wage.

The second thing we need to do is to pass the "GI bill" of rights for America's workers, which includes consolidating all the various Government training programs into one big pool and then giving people who are unemployed or under-employed the right to a voucher worth $2,600 a year for 2 years, which they can take to the local community college or anyplace else if they want to get retraining and education after they have left high school and when they're in the work force. That is a very important proposal we have made that has achieved—gotten too little attention. I think we have a chance to pass it, and we ought to do so.

The third thing that we ought to do in my opinion is to concentrate tax relief on middle income families and on childrearing and education costs. That will help Hispanic women enormously.

The fourth thing we need to do is to pass the welfare reform bill that has been proposed in the United States Senate by Senator Barbara Mikulski, Senator Daschle, and Senator Breaux, which focuses on giving people who are on welfare the child care they need so that they can be able to go to work, they can be required to work, and we can end welfare as we know it by helping people be good parents.

So these are just some of the things that I think we ought to do, and I hope you'll help me implement it. We have to win this budget fight. All this is going to play out in the context of the budget fight. Our budget fight is good for growing Americans. It's good for children. It's good for middle class people. It's good for people who want to work their way out of poverty. And we have to win it.

[A participant explained that he was satisfied with the President's commitment to affirmative action but was concerned that there were not enough Hispanic-Americans in the administration. He then asked how the President planned to become more actively involved with the Hispanic-American community.]

The President. Well, first of all, let's deal with the facts as they exist. Our administration has appointed more Hispanics than any administration in history, more than twice as many as either of the previous two, and several hundred. We also have major domestic policy considerations in the hands of Secretary Cisneros and Secretary Peña.

I've also had the privilege, as you know, to have the regular counsel of the head of the EEOC, Gil Casellas; Norma Cantu at the Department of Education; Maria Echaveste at the Department of Labor; Nelson Diaz at HUD; George Muñoz at Treasury, Aida Alvarez at HUD, Fernando Torres-Gil at HHS, Katherine Archuleta at Transportation and Joaq Otero at Labor, among others.

And at the White House, as you know, we have lost some people, but we still have an awful lot of talented Latinos on our staff. In fact, one of them made history this afternoon. Carolyn Curiel personally helped me craft my affirmative action speech. She had more to do with drafting it than anybody else. And she is the first person of color and, more importantly, the first Latino in the history of our country to write speeches for the President. And it may be that the one she wrote today will go down as one of the two or three most important I have ever delivered. In the White House, as you know, she's joined by Rick Hernandez, Janet Maguida, Ray Martinez, Liz Montoya, Suzanne Ramos, Suzanna Valdez, Vicki Rivas-Vazquez, Araceli Ruano, and others.

Now, I want to answer your two questions here. Number one, I am always looking for more good people for important appointments to boards and commissions and other things. But I want to point out again, if you look at my record on judges, I have appointed more than 3 times as many Hispanic judges in the

first 2 years of my Presidency as Presidents Reagan, Bush, and Carter combined did in the first 2 years of their Presidency. And in only 2 years, I have appointed more judges than any other administration in history. So I think my record is pretty good on that. I do want to continue to do better. And I do believe that there is more we can do.

Now, on the consultation issue, I really think that's one I really need to put back on you because my perception is that we have reached out and we have consulted and we have had a lot of good meetings that were more than just briefings but were really asking for input. If you don't believe that's true, then what I think you ought to do is make a proposal to me and let me see if I can accommodate it so that we can give you and all the people you represent and the people that you work so hard for and do such a wonderful job for the feeling that they do have an open door and a listening ear at the White House, because in the end that is maybe the most important thing.

I have to keep working on these appointments because that empowers people who, in turn, send ripples all across the country. A lot of these judges, for example, will serve for 20 or 30 or more years and will make decisions that will together affect millions and millions of people in positive ways.

But while I am here, your feeling of access and involvement and participation in this administration is perhaps the single most important thing that I can give you. So I want to say again, I would like to invite you to make a proposal about how you think we should do it, what the right way to do it is. I will do my best to accommodate it and, in any case, we will make sure that people feel that we are moving this issue forward.

[A participant expressed concern about the anti-immigration movement in America and asked how the President planned to help change such feelings of animosity toward the Hispanic community.]

The President. Well, first of all, let me say that I think there is a rising tide of—it's sort of the same—I view the immigration issue rather like the affirmative action issue. In the case of affirmative action, I think there were legitimate questions raised about the way the programs work and whether they need reform.

There were even some who asked honestly whether affirmative action was the right or wrong thing for America. And then there were a whole lot of people that were using affirmative action to drive a political wedge in this country as a false excuse for the problems of the American middle class and the economic anxieties broadly felt by Americans.

I think the immigration issue has sort of flared up again, in my judgment, driven by two factors. One is the general economic anxiety of Americans and the feeling that we are at an all-time high in the number of immigrants we let in every year and that that may be depressing wages and causing economic difficulties.

But I think the far more important problem is the sense that this country has been very undisciplined in its handling of illegal immigration in ways that have cost the taxpayers an awful lot of money and undermined our sense that our laws matter. And so, I think we need to have the same attitude about immigration that I have about affirmative action.

This is a country of immigrants. The fact that we have so many immigrants in this country and that they come from so many different places, from so many different racial, ethnic, and religious backgrounds is a mother lode of opportunity for us. The fact that Hispanics are fast-moving to become our largest minority population is a godsend, given the fact that for the next 20 to 30 to 50 years our greatest opportunity for growth and trade will be in Mexico, Central and South America, and in the Caribbean. So I see this as a positive force.

And I think we have to do several things. Let me just mention some of the things we are trying to do. I think we have to examine our immigration policies in a factual, calm, nonpolitical way just as we try to do with affirmative action. I think we need to do whatever we can to reduce the burden of illegal immigration without unduly hurting innocent children.

As you know, I opposed Proposition 187 in California. I was unsuccessful, but I did my best. And I did it because I thought it was unfair to children and counterproductive and self-defeating. On the other hand, I noticed that the post-election polls showed that significant percentages of Hispanic-Americans voted for it, not a majority but a significant percentage. And I think the reason is that a lot of people don't like having people who deliberately violate our laws spend our tax money. I think that is a very—it is very hard to defend that practice, and I don't intend to defend it.

So I have tried to keep America open as an immigration-friendly society while toughening our ability to enforce our own immigration laws and to deport people who are here illegally, especially those who come in contact with the criminal justice system. I also believe, however, it's very important that legal immigrants be encouraged to pursue their citizenship and that we do what we can to accelerate it.

I would like to look at this note here. We naturalized in 1994 half a million people. That's a 50 percent increase over 1992. And we're trying to break that record this year. I have directed the INS to get an extra almost $10 million to help to process people for naturalization. We're trying to get volunteers. We're doing everything we can in that regard. And I have repeatedly spoken out against immigrant bashing and negative feelings.

So I think that what we need to do is to have a sensible approach to immigration. It needs to be open. It needs to be nondogmatic and nonbigoted. We need to be firm but reasonable in the way we deal with the problem of illegal immigration. And we need to try to get as many of our immigrants who want to do so to become citizens as quickly as possible so that the American people will all see that this is a part of the process of American history which is a good one for our country.

Q. Mr. President, we thank you very much. And you'll have our proposal on Monday. And we're here to help you with advice if you need us. Thank you very much.

The President. I always need it. I thank you. For the members of the Hispanic community who gave me advice and had input on the affirmative action speech, let me thank you especially. This was a very important day for America. I hope that what I said and the way it was said will reach the hearts and minds of the vast majority of the American people. I believed it very deeply. And I thank all of you who have had any input on that directly or indirectly.

Thank you very much.

NOTE: The President spoke at 2:16 p.m. by satellite from Room 459 of the Old Executive Office

Building to the convention meeting in Dallas, TX. In his remarks, he referred to Irma Flores-Gonzalez, chairman of the board, National Council of La Raza; and the late Willie Velasquez, founder, Southwest Voter Registration and Education Project.

Teleconference Remarks and a Question-and-Answer Session With the National Conference of State Legislatures
July 20, 1995

The President. Thank you, Jane Campbell, for your gracious introduction and for all the great work you've done as president of the NCSL. I saw your mother yesterday morning at my affirmative action speech, and I wonder who you're going to produce in your family to start tomorrow off right for me. I'm very glad to see you again.

I want to wish your incoming president, Jim Lack, the best of luck in the coming year. I think he can expect interesting times as well.

Let me express my thanks to your NCSL vice president, Mike Box; your former president, Bob Connor; two of your assembly chairs, my good friend Dan Blue, and Representative Bill Purcell, with whom I enjoyed working at the Vice President's family conference in Nashville recently. It's great to be here with all of you, even if I'm only here by satellite.

You know, the image that is bringing me to you traveled from Washington to a satellite about 22,000 miles away in space, and then back down to Milwaukee, a total of 44,000 miles. Back when I was a Governor, there were times when I felt that Washington was that far away. And it's been very important to me, as you said, to try to make you feel that we're not 44,000 miles away, that we're not living on a different planet, that we can stay in touch with you and that we can work together.

For 12 years I lived with State government, and I saw how it can be the laboratory of our democracy. I know how you drive us forward as a nation with your innovation, your will to experiment responsibly, and your common sense. You are the inspiration for so much of what we're trying to do up here. And I thank you very much for that.

America's State legislators have had a very productive year. I noticed that in Utah, West Virginia, New Mexico, and Montana, statutes were enacted that permit employers to establish medical savings accounts for health care. Delaware and Ohio have led the way with truly meaningful welfare reform legislation that is focused on protecting our children and moving people from welfare to work, something I've been laboring with for 15 years now. And I understand that those of you from Iowa saw fit to put diaper-changing tables in all the Statehouse restrooms. Now if that is not a sincere commitment to family values, I don't know what is.

For many of you, your work for the year is done. But in Washington, as you know, we've still got a very long way to go. When I ran for President as the Governor of my State, I did it for two reasons. First, I thought that, on the verge of the 21st century, we were in danger of losing the American dream of opportunity for all and in danger of losing our sense of responsibility with all the social problems that were tearing our country apart. So I wanted to restore opportunity and a sense of responsibility.

But I also wanted to bring the American people together as a community. Politics has been used too long to divide us when what we really need to do is to rise above partisanship to find common ground. In order to do that, Washington needs to inspire the trust of more people throughout the country with a Government that empowers people to make the most of their own lives, empowers communities to solve their own problems, and is far less bureaucratic and less proscriptive.

Now, in the last 2½ years, I believe we've produced some real achievements. The economy is up; inflation is low; trade is expanding; interest rates and unemployment are down. The facts speak for themselves. In the last 2 years, we have cut the deficit by a third, and we're in the process of reducing it for 3 years in a row for the first time since Harry Truman was President. We have put in place more than 80 new trade agreements, including NAFTA and the GATT world trade agreement and an historic pact to finally, finally open Japan's markets to American cars and American auto parts.

These efforts have added about 7 million new jobs to our economy, and almost all of them have been in the private sector. To give you an idea of what that means, it's like creating a job for every person in Delaware, Idaho, Maine, Mississippi, Montana, and Wyoming combined. In 1993, our country established more new businesses than ever before, and in 1994 Americans broke that record again.

One of the best pieces of evidence that this country is turning around is right in the room here. The report NCSL issued for this conference, the report the New York Times put on its front page on Sunday, says that the finances of the State are, and I quote, "the best they have been since the 1980's." Last year employment grew in all 50 States and independent forecasters expect the same thing to happen again this year.

I have only one thing to say to that. As good as this is, you ain't seen nothing yet if we stay on the same course. We couldn't have done all this without a strong commitment to changing the way the Government does the people's business here in Washington, because the old Federal ways and the old Federal bureaucracy were not going to permit the kind of changes that we have to make as a country to get to the 21st century.

Our Federal work force is well on its way to being the smallest it's been since John Kennedy was President. It will be in just another year or two. Already, we've cut well over 100,000 positions from the Government; hundreds of programs have been abolished. Just last month, we got rid of 16,000 pages in the Federal Code of Regulations. Fifty percent of the regulations at the Small Business Administration are on their way to being history. We've reduced that budget by 40 percent and doubled the number of small business loans.

Forty percent of the Education Department's regulations are being scrapped. And as you know, that will directly help a lot of you. The time it takes to fill out EPA regulations has been cut by 25 percent. And we're now telling small businesses around America, if you call the EPA and you ask for help on a problem, you cannot be fined for 6 months while you try to work it out.

Reinventing Government means reinventing the way the Federal Government does business with you as well. Our job has been to bring together all levels of government to cooperate, to find common ground, to actually work together to solve our Nation's problems, instead of just talking about them. We have worked very hard to forge a genuine partnership between the States and the National Government.

I learned about the importance of this partnership a long time ago. When I was the Governor in Little Rock, the legislature and the Governor's offices were close together, just one floor apart in the capitol. We saw each other all the time. Legislators dropped by my office at any time of the day or night during the legislative sessions. Many legislators even came to the Governor's morning planning meetings. There was a spirit of teamwork, a tremendous amount of goodwill, and an awful lot of good came out of it.

As you know, unfortunately, we too often don't work that way in Washington. I am doing my best to build on that tradition to go beyond partisanship to finding common ground and actually solving a lot of these issues.

I've also tried to give you more say in your own affairs. We have now given 29 States a total of 33 waivers from Federal rules to enact their own welfare reform proposals. In the last 2½ years, more States have received waivers than in the previous 12 years of the previous two administrations combined. We have also given 10 States waivers to carry out major health care reform initiatives.

I did sign, as Jane said, the Unfunded Mandates Act, which restricts Congress from passing new mandates on State and local governments without paying for them. From now on, Congress will not be able to take you out for a 10-course dinner and then stick you with the check.

We have proposed setting up performance partnerships with you. Under this initiative, you would have a real say in how Federal programs are run in your State. But in exchange for more flexibility and more freedom to innovate, you would also be more accountable for the results.

The list goes on. OSHA and the EPA no longer play cops and robbers with you as they used to. We're moving away from punishment to compliance as a goal. FEMA used to be a disaster, but all of you who had to use it in the last 2½ years know that it is a genuine disaster agency now, helping States all across our country to respond quickly and efficiently and compassionately to crises.

Even though we've made strides, I know we still have a lot to do. That's why I have submitted my balanced budget plan, which I believe is important because of the way it balances the budget and because of the things that it still does in the budget both for the American people and with the American States.

All of you have to balance your budget, and you know it's important. The United States never had a structural deficit until about 12 years ago. Before, when we ran deficits, it was just because of economic conditions. But from 1981 until the day I took office, we quadrupled the debt of this country. And we were in a position where we were going to have deficits forever and ever, with all the economic weakness that that implies.

I know what you have to do and the tough choices you have to make. I used to do it every year for 12 years. We are now at an historic moment, because for the first time in a long time, the leaders of both parties in Washington agree that we must balance the budget. The Congress has a budget plan that I have differences with, but at least we share this common goal. And I am confident we are going to be able to work together to balance the budget and to help all Americans achieve the objectives of a balanced budget, a stronger economy, and a brighter future for ourselves and our children.

But in the meanwhile, we need to be honest and open about our differences, and there are real differences. The biggest difference is the difference between necessary cuts and unacceptable and ultimately self-defeating pain. Our balanced budget plan cuts spending by more than $1 trillion. It cuts non-defense discretionary spending by an average of 20 percent across the board, except for education. The congressional plan wants to make deep cuts in education and training, while I want to increase our investment in education, because that is essential to our ability to meet the challenges of the next century.

Let me say also that I am very concerned about the direction that the House Appropriations Committee seems to be going with regard to the bill which includes funding for key education and training initiatives. The bill they've

come up with would eliminate the Goals 2000 program. It would drastically cut back the school-to-work initiatives that we have used to help all of you establish systems in your own State to move everybody who doesn't go on to 4-year colleges into a continuing education program.

And let me stop and say that when I became President, I knew that the United States was the only advanced economy in the world that had no system for the young people who did not go on to 4-year universities. We all have our community colleges; we all have our vocational schools; we all are blessed with private sector employers that try to provide people on-the-job training. But we had no system on a State-by-State basis in all 50 States for keeping up with those young people who don't go to the 4-year schools and making sure that they can make the transition from school to work in a job with a chance to have a growing, not a shrinking income. So I think it's a mistake to walk away from the school-to-work program.

They also want to effectively gut the safe and drug-free schools and communities program. I know that a lot of you have schools that need more help with security measures, that need more help with drug prevention measures, and that you cannot provide this money on your own. The safe and drug-free schools program has enabled all the schools of our country to access the resources they need to try to have the schools be safe and drug-free. This House proposed budget would also deny Pell grants to 300,000 students who want to attend college. And it would cut job training for hundreds of thousands of Americans just when we need to help our people build the skills to meet the demands of the 21st century.

If Congress sends me this bill in its present form, I will have to veto it because it will weaken our economy and it will undermine the good that we can do by balancing the budget. The congressional plan will also cut Medicare in a way that could impose huge costs on the elderly. We have to reduce the rate at which Medicare costs are increasing. We can reform the Medicare program, but we have to make sure that it will be intact for Americans who need it.

Congress also has a plan that will give very large tax cuts that will primarily go to people who are better off. I think the tax cuts are too large and will require cuts in Medicare, Medicaid, and education that are too large. But if we simply cut taxes for people who really need it, cutting taxes for middle class people so that they can invest that money in their children and in their education, we can afford a sizable tax cut, balance the budget, and continue to invest in our fundamental needs.

The congressional plan would balance the budget in 7 years. I believe that that is too fast. We have had a deficit since 1969. We have had a huge structural deficit for 12 years. We've already cut the deficit for 3 years in a row. I think it is better to take a little more time so that we can continue to invest in education, protect Medicare, protect our relationships and our partnerships with you, and invest in the things that will grow our economy. If we can balance the budget in 10 years without doing that kind of harm, we ought to take more time and do it right.

So I say, let's balance the budget, but let's balance the budget in 10 years, not 7 years. We cannot expect to undo these decades of fiscal damages overnight. And we must continue to make investments here at the national level, in education, in investments in science and technology and the environment, and obviously, in Medicare and Medicaid.

How we balance the budget is as important as balancing it. Just 3 extra years will preserve the dreams of millions of Americans, and it will strengthen our economy. We get all the economic benefits of balancing the budget and the economic benefits of opening the doors of college education to all with affordable and repayable loans; continuing to increase the impact of Head Start for our young people; and being able to create a genuine big training program for unemployed and underemployed people, so that we can get rid of all these many, many dozens of Federal training programs and still have enough money to put in this block so that people who lose their jobs or are underemployed can have access to training which they can take to the local community college or any other place of their choice.

Now, to me, this choice is clear, and I hope you will agree. I was gratified to learn that yesterday, your Federal budget and taxation committee passed a resolution calling for a balanced Federal budget within 10 years. That will enable us to maintain our partnership.

The congressional budget would also do something else. I believe it would put an unfair burden on every one of you. Anybody who's worked in State government in the 1980's learned a very painful lesson. Washington's budget decisions all throughout the eighties gave us too many problems and too few resources. States were stuck with a horrible combination of more mandates and less funding. I know there are people in this room who worked night and day to see to it that the citizens of your State were taken care of, but it wasn't easy. There was an awful lot of unnecessary pain. And I don't see any reason on Earth why we ought to go through that again. But that is exactly what could happen with the congressional budget.

It sounds good. It calls for block grants for Medicaid and food stamps. But I have to tell you, I have real doubts that these block grants would be able to keep pace with the demands that you are going to face in your individual States. And in the real world, remember that economies change, populations rise, needs evolve. As those things happen you could be locked into a grant that could lock you into a real bind. And no matter how great a job you've done getting your own fiscal house in order, no matter how hard you've worked to prepare your State for the next century, you'll have to respond. And that could mean putting the working families of your State, the children of your State, the elderly of your State either in dire straits at the moment that we need to be doing everything we can to help them to make the most of their own lives, or forcing you to raise taxes when that might not be in the economic interests of your State or your people.

Should the States have more responsibility? Of course, they should. I'm doing my best to give you more. Should you deliver primary services? You always have. Should we in Washington do more than we have to free you up? Absolutely, we should. But we ought to do it in partnership. Simply moving the bureaucracy from one place to another or shifting the problems from one level to another is nothing more than a shell game. Giving you the responsibility without the resources could be disastrous. We can do better than that. We can get rid of this deficit. We can give our people the tools they need to make the most of their own God-given talents, and we can give our States more flexibility.

The budget process is entering a crucial stage now. If there was ever a time for you to add your voices, the time is now. We need to get to work, and we need to do it in a bipartisan fashion. I have the feeling that even today at the State level there is less partisanship, less ideological argument, and more willingness to roll up your sleeves and get down to work than there is too often here in Washington.

You can help us with that. We need an infusion of that. We can solve the problems of this country. We can give you more flexibility, balance the budget, still invest in our people as we need. But to do it, we have to look beyond the hot air and the harsh talk and try to find common ground.

Thank you very much, and God bless you.

Representative Jane Campbell. Thank you, Mr. President. It is now my pleasure to call upon two of our colleagues to pose questions to President Clinton. The first is NCSL's incoming president, Senator Lack of New York.

Senator Lack.

Senator James Lack. Good morning, Mr. President.

The President. Good morning, Senator.

Senator Lack. As I assume the presidency of NCSL I certainly look forward to continuing the relationship between our organization and you and your administration and would like to take this opportunity to extend an invitation to you to join with us next year at our conference in St. Louis if you can.

The President. Thank you.

Senator Lack. Mr. President, you alluded to block grants. State legislators, for many years, have supported the flexibility provided by block grants and performance partnerships. However, the worst scenario we could imagine would be to receive block grants that really aren't block grants. Will you support us in keeping block grant legislation free of mandates and other proscriptive elements?

The President. Well, first of all, I agree with you that if we're going to have a block grant program, it ought to be as free as possible of proscriptive mandates, consistent with the larger objectives of the program. The community development block grant program that I used as a Governor, that presumably many of you still take full advantage of at the State level, worked pretty well in that regard.

And I am generally in favor of pushing more and more decisionmaking away from the Federal Government down to the States and, where appropriate, not only to local government but to private citizens as well. For example, I have proposed this "GI bill" for America's workers, which would take these 70 Labor Department job training programs and just get rid of them, put it into a block, and when someone is unemployed, they can apply and get a voucher worth $2,600 a year for up to 2 years to take to your local community college or wherever else they want to get the training.

We have given, as I said in my remarks, welfare reform waivers to 29 States, and we have more pending. I am opposed to Washington's micromanagement, whether it comes from the right or the left. And I have been very concerned that in the welfare reform debate we were going to wind up under the guise of giving the States more responsibility, essentially putting more details on the States and putting the States in an economic bind.

Right now, the welfare reform bill is stalled in the Senate because some of those mostly on the extreme conservative end of the Senate believe that it doesn't contain enough mandates to, for example, prohibit any funds going to teenage mothers who have children out of wedlock and to their children.

I believe that what we ought to do, consistent with the very few things we know—I've worked on welfare reform for 15 years—we know a few things. We know that most people on welfare will go to work if they're given a chance to do it. We know that the absence of child care is a big problem, a barrier. And we know that the States will figure all this out if they have the tools to do it right. So what I want to do in the welfare reform debate is to give you the maximum amount of flexibility, consistent with some simple objectives. I do think the only place we need Federal rules and welfare reform—and you and I, I think, have talked about this before—is in the area of child support enforcement because so many of those cases cross State lines.

So I'm going to do my best to get you a welfare reform proposal which gives more flexibility to the States and doesn't have a lot of ideological proscriptions one any or the other and just focuses on one or two big things that need to be done. I think that is the right way to do it.

Let me just say one other thing, though, about these block grants. Block grants are very good if they can be used by you for the purpose for which they're intended and they don't have some trap down the road. So for example, with the community development block grant, the dollar amount I got was held constant for a decade. So in real terms, it got smaller and smaller and smaller. But since I didn't have a dependent population that had to have it every year we were able to work and make the most of it, use it to create jobs in my State without causing any problems anywhere else.

Now, if we turn food stamps into a block grant, what are we going to do the first time we don't have all 50 States growing? The food stamp program, because it goes to people in need, worked very well in the 1980's when, first of all, we had the so-called bicoastal economy. The coasts were doing well, and the heartland was doing terribly. Then when the heartland and the Middle West and the South came back, the coast got in trouble; the food stamp program worked as an economic stabilizer as well as a personal safety net, moving back and forth across the States to help deal with the problems of those States. I think that there's a real potential for problems for you in that.

And I feel the same way about Medicaid. If you have a Medicaid block grant with—particularly with all the other problems you've got, what are we going to do the first time that there's a terrible but uneven recession in America?

And in the case of the welfare program, if there were an AFDC block grant with no local participation requirement, look what that could do to you. What are you going to do if you get cut across the board, Medicaid cuts, education cuts, welfare cuts, and you've got a welfare block grant with no local participation requirement, and then that money becomes the target of every lobby group in your State legislature that needs it? What's going to happen to the poor children in your State?

So what I think we need to do is to be very practical about this, not ideological; use the block grants where they'll work, and give you as much flexibility as possible to be creative. The Federal Government should be defining the objectives we want to achieve, and unless we have absolute, clear, unambiguous evidence that some condition or another is a precondition of achieving that objective, we ought to give you the maximum amount of creativity. That's what I tried to do with this waiver process, and that's the direction I think we ought to take.

Representative Campbell. Thank you, Mr. President. Our second questioner is Representative Dan Blue of North Carolina, chair of our Assembly on Federal Issues.

Representative Blue.

Representative Daniel Blue. Thank you, Madam President. Good morning, Mr. President.

The President. Good morning, Dan.

Representative Blue. Mr. President, you alluded briefly to welfare reform. State legislators have welcomed the current debate on the welfare system. We, like you, believe that it is in need of substantial reform. However, NCSL believes that any welfare reform legislation must contain some kind of contingency or rainy-day fund to assist States during periods of emergency. And we wonder whether you would share with us your position on this issue.

The President. Well, I clearly agree with you. If we're going to the block grant proposals, there have to be some protections for the times when the economy goes down in the country as a whole and the times when the economy goes down in some parts of the country but not in others. I have tried to say all along that one of the big risks with these block grants is that some States are going to come up short in the next recession, and all States could.

And one of the things that really concerns me—I'm very excited about the fact that there's a lot of energy here in Washington and a lot of energy for reform throughout the country. We've got a lot of new people in Government with a lot of really determined ideas about what to do to change. And even when they disagree with me, I think it's an exciting thing to have this kind of debate. But we must have memory, also, and we must have some way of calling on our common experience.

I am gratified that the productivity of the American private sector and the economic policies that we have established, the kind of work that many of you do in economic development in your own State, have given us now a couple of years of nationwide economic growth. But I want to reemphasize, if you go back over the last 20 years in our history, this period is atypical. In most of the last 20 years, we've had some regions doing well while others were doing poorly.

And we need to make sure that we don't have States left holding the bag if their own economies hit a log down the road. Now, I have spoken to State legislators now throughout the country, in Florida and Indiana and other places, and I can tell you that—I mean, Florida and Iowa and other places, excuse me—and I can tell you that I've talked privately with Republicans and Democrats alike, who ask me to fight for protections like the contingency fund and even the State match. Particularly in the fast-growing States, they're worried about this. So I will support you on that. I will stand with you on that.

I think that what you need to do here is to make sure when each one of these issues is being debated in Congress that you understand both the up sides and the down sides, because when Congress proposes these kind of block grants they may be in philosophical agreement with you at one level, that you should have more say over your own affairs, but keep in mind also, there's a big desire to meet these very, very tough deficit reduction targets that they have set for themselves. So if they are using you to save money, it only works for you

if the increased flexibility and the diminished paperwork and hassle and the increased creativity you can bring to the task means you can do the same work for less money as well or better than you were doing it before. And it only works if these economic changes have been taken into account.

So I'm with you on it. I'll work with you. We can get this done. I will say again, for all of my differences with the Congress, we have got to balance the budget. We are going to do that. We are going to reach an agreement on it. But we need to do it in a way that enables you to do your job and that promotes the objectives of a balanced budget: more jobs, higher incomes, a more stable future for our children.

Thank you very much.

NOTE: The President spoke at 11:16 a.m. by satellite from Room 459 of the Old Executive Office Building to the convention meeting in Milwaukee, WI.

Remarks to Federal Law Enforcement Officials
July 20, 1995

Thank you very much, Eljay. If you want to see which job has more stress, this is the print on his introduction, and this is the print on my card. [*Laughter*]

Let me say, first of all, I came here to express my appreciation to all of you for continuing these regular meetings and increasing our ability to do the work of law enforcement by this kind of coordination. I think it is terribly important, and I thank you for doing it.

Because so many issues involving Federal law enforcement have been in the public's mind in the last several weeks, I would like to say a few things and then just sit here and visit with you and listen to you for a while. Let me begin by saying that we all know that this country still has too much violence, too many drugs, too many gangs, that the culture of violence is still causing enormous difficulty in our country.

There was a profoundly moving story in one of our newspapers today about a 16-year-old boy who just shot a 12-year-old boy dead be-

cause he thought he'd been treated with disrespect. And this comes just a few days after a national survey in which two-thirds of young gang members said they thought it was acceptable to shoot a person just because they treated you with disrespect.

This is the environment that we have to change in America today, the paranoia, the division, the willingness to resort to that kind of destructive behavior. And that's why I've been so disturbed about the recent attempts to attack police officers, in general, for doing their jobs. People may disagree with certain laws, like the ban on assault weapons, but that doesn't give them a right to disobey the law. People have no right to assault or kill police officers simply for doing their duty.

Now, I want to talk just a minute about the Waco hearings and especially what happened yesterday. We know that law enforcement people made mistakes at Waco. Our administration said that in 1993. We had an exhaustive review, and when the results came in, we took appropriate action. Changes were made; people were dismissed. That's the way our system is supposed to work, in an open and accountable way. Congressional hearings were held in 1993 and in 1994. And if Congress wants to have further hearings today, that is their right, and it is entirely appropriate. We have to hope some more good things will come out and we can learn how to better do our jobs.

But I think it's important to get the facts here quite clear. Yesterday's testimony was a sad and painful reminder of the depravity that took place inside that compound and the facts which confronted the President, the Attorney General, and the Federal law enforcement officials at the time. Here was a man who was molesting young girls and paddling children with boat oars, a man who was laying up supplies and illegal weapons for Armageddon, a man who was instructing women and children about how to commit suicide, a man who took the trust of young children and twisted it, who told people that if they wanted to do the will of God they had to be willing to kill for God.

Those are the facts. There is no moral equivalency between the disgusting acts which took place inside that compound in Waco and the efforts that law enforcement officers made to enforce the law and protect the lives of innocent people. There is no moral equivalency. That is the point that has to be hammered home over and over. It is irresponsible for people in elected positions to suggest that the police are some sort of armed bureaucracy acting on private grudges and hidden agendas. That is wrong. It's inaccurate, and people who suggest that ought to be ashamed of themselves.

People in law enforcement make mistakes. There are all kinds of people in law enforce-

ment, just like there are all kinds of people in any endeavor, and all people, the last time I checked, were imperfect. When people make mistakes, they ought to be held accountable and appropriate action ought to be taken.

I said yesterday, I am appalled by what happened at that gathering in Tennessee. We're going to find the facts. We're going to take appropriate action. But that is a very different thing from suggesting that there is some sort of equivalency between what the law enforcement officers tried to do at Waco and the kind of things that were going on in that compound. And this country needs to be able to make that distinction and not to forget it.

In Oklahoma City, after the terrible bombing, Americans were wearing a T-shirt—I've got a copy of it here that was given to me, and I'd never seen this before. But this T-shirt shows all the different things that Federal law enforcement officials do and mentions all the different agencies and has the following quote on it, "A society that makes war against its police had better learn to make friends with criminals." That's a fact.

We need to be accountable. We need to get all the facts out. If we make a mistake, we need to correct it. But we must not make war against police. And we must not confuse making mistakes with the moral equivalency of what decent people are doing to protect the citizens of this country with the awful things that happened in that compound at Waco.

Thank you.

NOTE: The President spoke at 12:12 p.m. in the Blair House. In his remarks, he referred to Eljay Bowron, Director, U.S. Secret Service.

Remarks to the American Legion Girls Nation
July 21, 1995

Thank you. Well, good afternoon. I'm delighted to see you all. I'm sorry we're beginning a little late, but I think all of you know that we have been working very hard for the last few days on the crisis in Bosnia. So I'd like to say a few words about that and then make

the remarks that I wanted to make to the delegates to Girls Nation.

As you know, there are meetings now going on in London in which the United States is working with our allies to reach a common position which would permit the United Nations mission to continue but would empower the international community to stand up against the outrages that have occurred in the last few days.

We're all concerned about those events, and we welcome the statement by Foreign Secretary Rifkind that an attack by the Bosnian Serbs on the United Nations safe area of Gorazde will be met by a substantial and decisive response. For the United States, the most important word is "decisive."

The conference has also agreed that the U.N. mission should be strengthened and that access to the city of Sarajevo should be ensured by the rapid reaction force that the British and French and others are attempting to establish and that we have strongly supported. There is more work to be done, and the United States is determined to do everything that we can not only to deal with the problems of Gorazde and Sarajevo but also to find a peaceful end to this war.

The meetings so far, from my point of view, are proceeding well. There seems to be a real sense of resolve to come together in common purpose, and I am encouraged. We will have more reports later.

Now, let me welcome all of you here. As all you know, I hope—or some of you doubtless know, I was here as a delegate to Boys Nation on this month, 32 years ago. This is a very different time but a very challenging time for our country. And I'd like to make, if I might, just a few observations about the world that will be your future.

At the end of the cold war and the dawn of the next century, our country is in so many ways better positioned for the future than any other country in the world. And I believe that the chances are very strong that the young people of America will have, by far, the most exciting lives, the most full of possibility, and the most free of the fear of war and destruction of any generation of Americans ever.

But this is a difficult time as well. And let me just sort of put out the two sides of the coin. If you look at it, the positive side is our economy is strong. We have seen 7 million new jobs in the last 2½ years, very low inflation, low unemployment. The stock market's at an all-time high. Business profits are high. The last 2 years in America, in each year we have had the largest number of new businesses formed of any year in our history and a record number of Americans becoming millionaires, through their own efforts, through their own efforts, suc-

ceeding in our system. In almost every major area of our country where the crime rate has been high, there has been a substantial drop in the crime rate. That is the good news.

On the other hand, it is also true that in spite of all this economic good news, more than half the American people are working harder today for the same or lower incomes they were making 2½ years ago, so that this opportunity is only coming to part of our people. It is also true that even though the crime rate is down overall in the United States and in many of our major cities, young people are still subject to extraordinary rates of violence and crime, that drug usage is still way too high, and that an increasingly high percentage of our children are born into poverty in a welfare culture.

So the question for you is: How are we going to solve the problems and keep the opportunities? What kind of country do you want to live in? If you look beyond our borders, it's the same thing. The United States now is living in a world where we and the Russians are dismantling our nuclear weapons, where—you know, when I was your age we were still worrying about whether we had nuclear fallout shelters in case there was a bomb dropped. We don't have to worry about that now.

We're seeing peace progress being made everyplace from South Africa to Northern Ireland to the Middle East, democracy restored in Haiti, a lot of good things going on. But what you see in Bosnia and what you see in Rwanda and Burundi is an example of the continuing power of division, division by race, by religion, by ethnic group, to tear people apart and destroy lives.

What you saw in Oklahoma City, what we see when a bus of children or innocent tourists is blown up in the Middle East, what you saw in the subway in Japan where sarin gas was released and killed people, is the new threat to our security from terrorism. And the freer and the more open the world gets, the more vulnerable free people everywhere will be to the organized forces of destruction. So the question is how to reap the benefits of freedom and the end of the cold war and openness and still fight the organized forces of destruction.

My vision for this country is that in the 21st century, in your great lifetimes, we will be a high-opportunity society; a high-growth, high-wage, smart-work society, making real progress on our social problems; that people will be empowered to make the most of their own lives and the most of their God-given abilities; and communities and families will have the ability to solve their own problems. That is the kind of America that I want to see in a world where peace and freedom and progress are always moving in the right direction.

There will never be an end to problems as long as we're on this Earth, but we need to be going in the right direction and taking advantage of these opportunities. And I am convinced that in our country at this time, when we're changing so much, there is sort of a common-sense consensus about what we ought to do that has been damaged by excessive partisanship and excessive reliance on harsh rhetoric and extreme positions to divide the American people for the political advantage of those who seek to reap it.

And in a time like this of really profound change, we all have to try to imagine the future we want and then ask how are we going to get there and what do we have to do to pull together to get there. That's essentially what we're trying to do here.

So that, for example, I find myself—I agree with the Republican majority in Congress that we ought to balance the budget. We can't afford to have a permanent deficit. But I disagree that we ought to do it in ways that will imperil the Medicare system, undermine our ability to guarantee all the young people in this country the right to go to college and get the education that they need, or undermine our ability to protect our environment and our natural heritage

and our future. So we have to get through those disagreements.

The main thing I want you to know is that this is an exciting time. On balance, it's a good time. I believe that your adult years will be lived out in America's best period in history if, but only if, we find a way to live together and work together and bridge our divisions and focus on the challenges before us.

And that really will be the great issue of your time. We're going to change regardless. The question is, what kind of change will it be? And are we going to see a country like ours, which is so diverse—well over 150 different racial and ethnic and religious groups in the United States—are we going to see that country come together and take advantage of that, or are we going to suffer from some of the same problems we've seen paralyzing the rest of the world and leading to the deaths of innocent people?

On balance, I am quite optimistic. But this is a very serious time for the United States and a very important time for you to be here. So I hope you will keep that in the back of your mind as you spend all this time here and then when you go back home next year.

Welcome, and God bless you all. Thank you.

NOTE: The President spoke at 2:21 p.m. in the East Room at the White House. In his remarks, he referred to Secretary of State for Defense Malcolm Rifkind of the United Kingdom.

Statement on Budget Rescission Legislation
July 21, 1995

The rescission bill that the Senate approved, and that I will be pleased to sign, shows how we can work together to produce good legislation.

From the start of this rescission process, I agreed with Congress on the need to cut spending. The question was, how should we do it?

I vetoed the original rescission bill because it would have cut spending the wrong way by targeting education and training, environmental protection, and other key national priorities. I then worked with Republicans and Democrats

alike to produce a better bill. I am pleased that this bill cuts $16 billion in spending while protecting our key investments in education and training, the environment, and other priorities.

Like the earlier version, this bill also provides much-needed supplemental funds that I have sought for disaster relief activities of the Federal Emergency Management Agency, the Federal responses to the bombing in Oklahoma City, increased antiterrorism efforts, and debt relief to Jordan to facilitate progress toward a Middle East peace settlement.

To be sure, I do not support every provision of this bill. For instance, I still do not believe that this bill should contain any of the provisions relating to timber. But the final bill does contain changes in the language that preserve our ability to implement the current forest plans and their standards and to protect other resources such as clean water and fisheries. Therefore, after signing the rescission bill into law, I will direct the Secretary of Agriculture, the Secretary of the Interior, and all other Federal agencies to carry out timber salvage activities consistent with the spirit and intent of our forest plans and all existing environmental laws.

I am pleased that bipartisan leaders of Congress worked with me to produce a good bill. Working together, we can continue to produce good legislation for the American people.

The President's Radio Address
July 22, 1995

Good morning. Over a month ago, Speaker Newt Gingrich and I met with a group of senior citizens in Claremont, New Hampshire. That sunlit event had a special spirit. We showed that the great debate now occurring in our country can and should be conducted with civility and a sense of common ground. Many Americans of both parties have told me since then that this is exactly the way they want their leaders to work together. And that's what I'm committed to doing.

Perhaps the most visible example of that spirit of New Hampshire came when the Speaker and I shook hands on the question of political reform, something that has divided the two parties and the Congress and the country for too long. The first question we answered was from a retired steelworker named Frank McConnell. He said that politics had become polluted by special interests and that too often the voice of the people was shut out. He said that bickering between the parties had blocked reform for too long, and he proposed that we create a blue-ribbon, bipartisan commission to write reforms to curb the power of special interests. There, in front of the entire country, the Speaker and I agreed to create this commission.

A bipartisan commission could cut the knot that is strangling change. This panel would follow the approach that has worked on other critical issues. It would be comprised of distinguished citizens and would recommend broad changes in the rules which cover lobbyists and in how we finance political campaigns. Most important of all, the Congress would have to vote within a strict deadline, up or down, on the package as a whole, no loopholes, no amendments.

I'm happy to report that in addition to myself and Speaker Gingrich, this very idea has been strongly endorsed for some time by Senate majority leader Bob Dole, who just last February said again that this was the way we ought to approach this question.

It's clearer than ever that we need political reform. The American people believe their political system is too influenced by narrow interests, that our Government serves the powerful but not hard-working families. Even before the '94 elections, the special interests prevented passage of both campaign finance reform and lobby reform legislation that I had strongly asked the Congress to pass. When a minority in the Senate killed lobbying reform in 1994, lobbyists were standing right outside the Senate chamber cheering.

Since the New Congress came in, I'm sad to say, it's gotten worse, for even more power has been given to the lobbyists. Now this new majority lets lobbyists for polluters write legislation rolling back environmental and public health protections. They've brought them in to explain the legislation. They even gave them a room off the House floor to write the amendments and the statements the Members would have to give explaining the bills that the lobbyists had written for them.

Since things have gotten in this state, it was a real moment of hope when the Speaker and I shook hands on reform in New Hampshire. Just 5 days later, I sent Speaker Gingrich a letter laying out in detail my ideas for how to move forward. Now, 5 weeks later, I must say

I'm very disappointed by what has happened since or, more accurately, what hasn't happened. The Speaker announced that he would send me his proposal, but he never has.

I think the people of this country want us to move forward with political reform. Speaker Gingrich and I shook hands on it. We have an obligation to get this done and not walk away. If we're going to restore a spirit of civility to American politics, a handshake has to mean in 1995 what it meant when I was growing up: We have to be as good as our word.

Today, to move this process forward, I'm announcing that two distinguished Americans have agreed to work with me to get the commission idea underway. They're the kind of people I will appoint as its members. John Gardner's name is synonymous with integrity. He's a Republican Cabinet Secretary to a Democratic President, the founder of the citizens' lobby Common Cause, a wise and effective man. Doris Kearns Goodwin is a political scientist and a Pulitzer Prize winning author. She understands through her knowledge of history and today's political situation how politics affects the lives of ordinary people.

I have asked John Gardner and Doris Kearns Goodwin to meet with Speaker Gingrich as soon as possible and the other congressional leaders, to get them going on this idea so that we can make this commission a reality and keep our commitment to the Frank McConnells and all the other Americans who want us to improve the way our political system works.

John Gardner and Doris Kearns Goodwin will help us to get this movement going. And now I call on Speaker Gingrich and the other congressional leaders to come forward and do their part. The Speaker and I made a deal, and it's time to keep it. There's no excuse for further delay.

We already have signs of bipartisan agreement. On Monday, the Senate begins to debate on legislation to require lobbyists to disclose who they are, what they're paid, and what bills they're trying to influence. And the Senate will vote on legislation to ban lobbyists from providing lawmakers meals or gifts or travel. If a judge took a paid vacation from a lawyer in his courtroom, he'd be disbarred. But if a lobbyist pays for a trip to a sunny climate, right now it's perfectly legal. And it happens all the time.

Congress should send me the strongest possible ban on lobbyist gifts, such as the bill introduced by Democratic Senators Carl Levin and Paul Wellstone and Republican Senator Bill Cohen. Congress should not send me a bill that's more loophole than law. I hope the action I'm taking today will help lead to real political reform. We have to do everything we can to show the American people that their Government works for them and not the special interests.

Thanks for listening.

NOTE: The President spoke at 10:06 a.m. from the Oval Office at the White House.

Remarks to the American Legion Boys Nation
July 24, 1995

Thank you very much. To all the delegates of Boys Nation, I'm delighted to be here, as you know, with many members of our administration who are involved in the setting of economic policy for our country; delighted to see Mr. William Detweiler, the national commander of the American Legion, here; along with your other leaders, Ray Smith; Ron Engel; Jack Mercier, who has been with Boys Nation for 31 years and I believe was there—that would make 32 years—when I was there in 1963; George Blume and others.

Let me say, as I'm sure you know, I am especially delighted to welcome all of you here to the White House. I don't have to tell you what an important event this is for me every year and how much I look forward to it. But this is an especially important time for all of you to be here. The world in which you will live, the world which I am sure many of you will help to lead, can be America's greatest time. But it is a world being transformed to a degree seldom seen in all American history. Much of this change is good. But it's not all good.

If you look at what is happening in America, we have more new businesses being formed, more Americans becoming millionaires, more people finding success than at any period in our history. But most Americans are still working harder for the same or lower pay they were making a few years ago, with greater levels of personal insecurity about their ability to take care of their parents if they get sick, their ability to educate their children, their ability to hold on to their own health care.

If you look at what's going on, most of our social problems are being addressed very well in many places. In most major cities the crime rate is down, but the rate of random violence and crime among our youngest teenagers is going up, and there are still too many problems with crime and violence, with drugs and gangs.

If you look around the world, the cold war is over and peace and freedom and democracy and world trade are all increasing. But still there are serious problems with what I call the organized forces of destruction: ethnic, religious, racial hatreds leading to awful wars, the proliferation of weapons of mass destruction in tiny amounts, as you saw when the terrible bomb exploded in Oklahoma City or the gas was released in the Japanese subway. So we have both a great deal of good and a great deal of troubling change going on in the world today and in our country.

In recent weeks I have addressed those challenges in the face here at home, first, to restore the American dream of opportunity and the American value of responsibility and, second, to bring our country together in a stronger community so that we can move forward together. I believe those two goals are inseparable. I believe the only way we can restore economic opportunity and solve our social problems is to unite our people more.

I can tell you that it would have been unthinkable when I was here in 1963—we had a lot of problems in 1963; we had severe racial problems still; the country was still largely segregated—but it would have been unthinkable if someone had told us in 1963 that 30 years from now the country would be as deeply divided as it is today and that people would have lost faith in their institutions and would have the level of cynicism and skepticism that they have today.

My vision for your future is a very positive one. I want this country to be a high-opportunity, smart-work country with good jobs and safe streets, with a clean environment and excellent education and health care, a country in which diverse people live and work together, in which communities and families can solve their own problems and in which people are given the chance as individuals to live up to the fullest of their God-given potential in a world that is steadily moving toward more peace and freedom.

When I say we have to restore the American dream of opportunity and the American value of responsibility, when I say we have to rebuild America's sense of community, that is simply a strategy to reach that vision, a strategy rooted in an obligation Americans have always accepted, the obligation to give each successive generation a better life than the preceding one had. That is an obligation from which I benefited and one from which millions of others have benefited as well.

Exactly 32 years ago, on July 24, 1963, I came here as a delegate to Boys Nation when John Kennedy was President. I would never have made it here and gone from that day to this one without the benefit of the shared beliefs and convictions and opportunities that made up the America of my youth. I lived in a family where everyone worked hard and where children were expected to study hard. I also had a lot of opportunity given to me by my community. I had good teachers, good schools, and when I needed them, scholarships and jobs to make my education possible.

I saw what happened, too, when good people had no opportunity. There were a lot of good people I grew up with who had no opportunity because they were of a different race or because they happened to be poor and white and isolated in poor communities in the hills and hollows of my State. I have lived my public life believing that everybody ought to have the chances that I had and that if everybody did and we all worked together, this country would be able to go on indefinitely as the world's best hope for freedom and opportunity. My philosophy is rooted in these beliefs, and the experience of the United States bears out that they are the right ones.

I imagine the same is true in your lives. I'm sure a lot of you have been amazed at how very different your backgrounds are and yet how much you seem to have in common. Our Nation's work must reflect what you have in common. And our Nation's budget, which we're debating here with such intensity now, must also reflect those common values and our shared vision for the future.

The priorities of American families and their household budgets aren't all that much different than the priorities of our larger American family and our Nation's budget. The way we spend our money as individuals, as a family, and as a nation says an awful lot about who we are, what our values are, and what our vision for the future really is. We are at an historic moment, as I have said. For the first time in a long time, the leaders of both major parties agree on one thing we have to do consistent with our values, and that is to balance the Federal budget and relieve our children and our grandchildren from the burden of a permanently increasing Federal debt.

You know, we never had a structural or permanent deficit in our country until about 1981. But from 1981 until the day I took office, the national debt was quadrupled. When I came here I was committed to getting that deficit off our backs. In the first 2 years of our administration, we cut the deficit by a third, and we are now reducing it for 3 years in a row for the first time since Harry Truman was President of the United States just after World War II.

But it is still such a problem, what happened in the previous 12 years, that the budget would be balanced today, today, except for the interest payments we make on the debt run up between 1981 and the day I became President. And this debt is so great that next year interest on the debt could be larger than the defense budget. This is a very significant problem, and there is more to do.

Therefore, it is good news that both the Congress and I have offered plans to balance the budget. Both plans involve significant spending cuts which will not be easy to meet. Both plans protect our ability to maintain a strong defense and the world's finest military. Beyond those similarities, however, there are profound differences, differences that go to the heart of our ability to find common ground, to rebuild the American community around the old-fashioned values that I talked about just a moment ago. The commitment to our future I believe that we all have must be defined in large measure today in how this budget contest is played out.

The congressional budget balances a budget in 7 years. My budget does it in 10. The con-

gressional budget cuts taxes by about $250 billion over 7 years. Our budget cuts taxes but by slightly less than half that amount. Why? Because our budget, by making those changes, enables us to increase investment in education and training by about $40 billion over the next 7 years, to help make sure all Americans have a chance to develop the fullest of their abilities and to compete and win in the global economy.

This is very important. About half of all the students in college today everywhere in America have some form of financial assistance. It is critically important to maintain it. It is critically important that everybody who wants to go to school has a chance to go and has a chance to finish. And it's a big part of what our national security will mean in the global economy.

Our budget strengthens health care coverage, especially for seniors through Medicare, and provides families some help in caring for their elderly parents who don't go into nursing homes. Our budget protects the food we eat, the air we breathe, the water we drink. It rewards work, concentrating tax policies on helping working families to raise their children and to educate both their children and themselves, because we know more and more adults will have to go back for job training over the course of their work lives. And it preserves our investments in science and technology, so that our workers and our businesses can compete the world over in a rapidly changing technological era.

Our budget achieves all the economic benefits of balancing the budget. It gives you lower interest rates, higher investment in private dollars. It reduces the amount we'll have to pay on the debt for interest in the years ahead. But it maintains these other priorities, which I believe are essential to rebuilding the American community and finding common ground.

These priorities are not Democratic or Republican priorities. They are commonsense, national decisions that have served us very, very well over the last generation. They have stood the test of time. They have marked our character as a nation, and they mark the road to the future we should take.

Now, some in Congress say we need to retreat from the common ground we have so carefully built on education, on Medicare, on the environment, on science and technology to balance the budget in 7 years with these big tax cuts. They say we need to slash Federal aid to the schools and to increase the cost of student loans. They say it is all right to make the elderly pay up to thousands more for their Medicare benefits and to dramatically reduce our ability to protect the environment to meet the 7-year time period with the big tax cuts. They say all this is necessary to balance the budget. But many would use the balanced budget as an excuse to do these things which they wish to do anyway.

I have shown we can balance the budget without retreating from our common ground on education, on health care, on the environment. So I invite Senators and Members of Congress from both parties to join me in balancing the budget while protecting our common ground. I will work hard to get their support. But if they refuse, I must continue to act, alone if necessary, to protect the common ground that brought every single one of you into this White House today. I will do that. [*Applause*] Thank you very much.

Let me say again, there is no question that we have to balance the budget. And the majority in Congress deserve credit for proposing a plan to do that. But we do not have to do it in 7 years. We do not have to do it with massive tax cuts to people who don't really need it.

The haste of their schedule and the scope of their tax cuts are luxuries, and this is not a time for luxuries. Think again about your family's budget. If you can't afford luxuries right now, you don't sacrifice necessities to have them. Take education. I think it's a necessity. From the birth of the land-grant colleges during the Civil War to the creation of the GI bill 51 years ago this summer, we have understood that when we invest in the education of our people, it makes the whole country stronger.

We have understood that, regardless of party, right through the first 2 years of our administration. In 1993 and in 1994, we had bipartisan support for the most remarkable education agenda in the last 30 years. We had higher standards for our schools. We had more affordable college loans with better repayment terms. We had a national service initiative, AmeriCorps, that now gives 20,000 young people a chance to serve in their communities and earn money for their college educations.

We had a dramatic expansion of Head Start, a program that has enjoyed bipartisan support for decades now. We expanded the age at which children were eligible, improved the quality of the program, and increased the numbers of kids in Head Start to make it more likely that more Americans will have a chance to be sitting where you're sitting today. But now, as a part of this balanced budget program, many in Congress are willing to cut 50,000 people out of the Head Start program and block its expansion.

Another example is the commitment to educate and train all Americans. We know the global economy demands more skills and information than ever before. We know—we know that the middle class in America today, including many of your parents, are either going up or going down economically, are either increasing their security or feeling more insecure, based directly on the level of skills they have. We know that. We know that is a reality for the lives of Americans all across this country.

So what did we propose? We proposed to do everything we could to increase the access of people to college and to increase the training available to adults. But again, many in Congress would cut the Pell grant program by 300,000 slots a year. That's 300,000 poor people who won't get college degrees to become middle class people, maybe even rich people, and pay back far more to the Treasury in taxes than they ever took out in the Pell grants.

And the job training in some ways is the most troubling of all. I have proposed that we consolidate all the Government's training programs into one big scholarship program for adult workers who are unemployed or are underemployed, giving them a voucher worth up to $2,600 a year to go back for 2 years to get further training so they can increase their abilities to earn a good living. We should not reduce this. We should increase this. We shouldn't reduce it. People are in trouble out there today in this country because they don't have the education and skills they need to maintain family-wage jobs in a global economy. These are very important. We don't have to get rid of this to balance the budget.

The same is true about health care. Thirty years ago, we decided as a people that we would at least protect the elderly of this country from the fortunes of not having adequate health care. We did it with Medicare. We did this as an extension of the compassion we feel in our own families, for the elderly in our individual families.

Medicare has worked well. It has low administrative costs. It has covered all people over 65. I might add that we are the only advanced country in the world that doesn't have some form of universal health coverage for everybody. But at least we do it for senior citizens. It's a basic American value. We help take care of people who raised us up and took care of us.

Before Medicare, half of the elderly people in this country had no health insurance whatever. Now, 97 percent of the senior citizens in America have access to health care. Of course, we have to reduce the rate of inflation in the Medicare program. I have said that from the first speech I gave to the Congress as President. But we can do this by reforming Medicare, not by ruining it. We can still maintain protections for every senior citizen in America, instead of deciding that some will do fine and others will get the shaft.

Some in Congress want to cut $270 billion from the Medicare program, about the same amount they want to cut taxes. Their proposal would require our seniors—maybe some of your grandparents—to pay as much as $5,600 more a couple in out-of-pocket costs. So we cut spending in one way and offload the burden to others. That does not reflect the values of most American families. Maybe some people can afford to pay some more because they're upper income, but most seniors in this country hardly have enough to live on as it is.

If you look at the attack on the environment, you see another example. The environment has been a bipartisan issue in America. The Environmental Protection Agency was established under the Presidency of Richard Nixon, a Republican President. We have shared a common commitment to the environment. Perhaps our country's most outstanding environmental President was our first environmental President, Theodore Roosevelt, again, a Republican. This has never been a partisan issue.

We have agreed for a long time as a people that the stewardship of our natural environment is a big part of maintaining the American dream. With the first Earth Day, 25 years ago, Americans came together to say no to dirty air, toxic food, polluted water and say yes to leaving our children a nation as unspoiled as their dreams. We recognize together that our business in creating jobs was not undermined, and in fact could be enhanced, by protecting the environment.

We all know that in the last two decades there have been some rigid regulations and some unreasonable enforcement that have limited the effect of our laws and alienated people from the whole cause of environmental protection. So we should change the way our regulators do their work. We have worked very hard to do that. Right now, we have in motion an initiative that will reduce by 25 percent the amount of time people in the business community spend complying with the environmental laws.

Right now we are putting in place a small business program that says to every small business person in America, if you're worried about violating an environmental law, if you will call us and ask for help, you cannot be fined for 6 months. We will work with you because you asked for help. We're not interested in fining people; we're interested in protecting the environment. But that is very different from just walking away from our commitment to protect the environment.

Some in Congress want to slash funding for enforcement by almost 50 percent. It could put at risk the safety of the water we drink. It would increase the chances of raw sewage washing up on our beaches. It would excuse some polluters from having to clean up their mess. That is not our vision.

Believe it or not, some of these restrictions would actually undermine the ability of the United States to enforce the Clean Air Act. The Clean Air Act was last signed by President Bush, my Republican predecessor, who said it was his proudest legislative achievement. This has always been a bipartisan thing. It is now being put at risk in this budget debate. And I believe it undermines our ability to find common ground.

Others say we should cut science and technology, the most powerful engine we have to boost our economy.

Finally, there are even proposals that would undermine our ability to make work more attractive than welfare. I have worked now for 15 years, long before I became President, to move people from welfare to work. I have learned that most people on welfare want to go to work and that one of the things that we permitted to happen over the years was to build in too many disincentives to work. So that's why I've supported welfare reform proposals that would move people from welfare to work. We have given 30 States permission to get out from under Federal rules and regulations, to come up with new and innovative ways to move people from welfare to work, including letting States take welfare checks and give them to employers as income supplements so they would actually hire people to go to work.

One of the things we have to do is to make sure we don't tax people back into poverty. And when people are out there working on low wages, what we did in 1993 was to say, if you're out there working 40 hours a week and you have children in your house, you should not be in poverty. The tax system shouldn't put you in poverty. We will lower your taxes. If necessary, we will give you a tax refund so that if you'll work 40 hours a week, you can raise your kids outside of poverty. There are even some people who want to erode that tax cut so that we can cut taxes for people who don't really need it in this budget program.

There are a lot of things being done here which will violate and undermine our chances to achieve common ground. And they do not fall into the traditional partisan differences. Most of these things have been supported by Republicans and Democrats. The tax provision for working families was called by President Ronald Reagan the most important pro-family, anti-poverty initiative in the last 30 years. Now there are people in Congress who are trying to erode it. And it is wrong. And it undermines our ability to make common ground.

The 7-year timetable and the huge tax cut, these are luxuries. To make room for them, some in Congress would slash necessities. I say, let's take 10 years instead of 7; let's have a modest tax cut targeted toward what people really need, which is help in raising and educating their children and knowing they can always get new education and training themselves; and let's keep on investing in the things that are our necessities. These things will create millions more American dreams if we continue them.

We can cut taxes. We can balance the budget. But we have to do it in a way that maintains what has been for decades and what clearly is now the common ground on which we can go forward together.

Your parents recognized that it was unacceptable to destroy the environment and created the environmental movement. My parents saw the pain of their parents and insisted that we create Medicare. Every generation has done something to build up and create the fabric that is what we know as the American dream. We now have to create a system of lifetime education and training that all can have access

to, and we now have to deal with these social problems that have been too long ignored. We can do it in a way that permits us still to balance the budget and lift that burden from your future. So I say to the Congress, come back to common ground. We can do this.

The Congress has recently passed the so-called rescission bill. You may not know what that means, but basically it's a downpayment on our balanced budget. It cuts from the budget that we are presently spending in this year.

This rescission bill, when they first sent it to me, caused me to veto it because it had unacceptable cuts in education, training, and the environment. When we went back to the table to work together, Congress came up with a revised bill that reflects our shared values. It permits us to cut $16 billion from this year's budget; to maintain our commitment to education, health care, and the environment; to invest in helping those people in California who still are suffering from the earthquake; to deal with the terrible tragedy in Oklahoma City; to keep our commitment to the Middle East peace process and a number of other things and still cut even more spending to continue our work toward balancing the budget.

Now we share, I hope and believe, a basic commitment that each generation must take account of the accumulated wisdom of generations that have gone before as well as our new ideas. When we ignore the evidence of what has plainly worked, in the attempt to fix what is plainly wrong, we pay a terrible price. We mustn't throw over, in a moment of partisan zeal, the common sense and bipartisan conclusions of our fathers and mothers, derived from lifetimes of experience with problems that we will only have to suffer through again if we ignore that experience.

So I ask you as you come together in this wonderful Boys Nation experience, and you debate these issues. Imagine what you want your country to look like. Ask yourself what your vision of the future is like. Write it down on a piece of paper. What do you want America to look like in 20 years? What is your vision, and how will we achieve it? And what things do we have to do together? What things ought we to be for, whether we're Republicans or Democrats, whether we live in the Northeast or the far West, whether we're men or women, and without regard to our racial or religious background? What are those things that we can say, "This is what we want America to look like."?

That, my friends, is where we must find our common ground. And that is what I am determined to protect in this great debate to balance the budget.

Thank you very much.

NOTE: The President spoke at 12:11 p.m. in the East Room at the White House. In his remarks, he referred to Ray Smith, chairman, American Legion National Americanism Commission, and Ron Engel, director; Jack Mercier, director of activities; and George Blume, legislative director, Boys Nation.

Remarks at the Posthumous Commissioning Ceremony for Johnson C. Whittaker
July 24, 1995

To the members of the Whittaker family, Secretary West, General Davis, General Gorden, General Griffith, Senator Hollings, Senator Thurmond, Congressmen Spratt and Clyburn, ladies and gentlemen, welcome to all of you.

Today is a good day for the United States. Today we honor the memory of a great American, Johnson Chesnut Whittaker. Born into slavery, he was appointed to West Point in 1876 at the age of 17. Life at West Point was harsh for all cadets, but for the few African-Americans like Johnson Whittaker, it was doubly difficult. He was ostracized by his white peers. Few spoke to him except to issues orders and commands.

From the beginning, the odds were against him. Then in April of 1880, Johnson Whittaker was assaulted in his barracks. Three masked men tied him to his bed and left him battered, bleeding, and unconscious. His superiors charged that Whittaker had mutilated himself and faked unconsciousness to gain attention. After a lengthy court-martial, he was convicted and sentenced to dismissal from the Army.

The court-martial was overturned by President Chester Arthur. But on that very day, the Secretary of War dismissed Johnson Whittaker from West Point. The grounds for dismissal: He had allegedly failed an oral examination in philosophy.

Johnson Whittaker was a rare individual, a pathfinder, a man who through courage, example, and perseverance, paved the way for future generations of African-American military leaders: General Chappie James, Lieutenant General Benjamin O. Davis—who is with us today—General Colin Powell, and so many others. In part because Whittaker and others like him took those first brave steps, America's Armed Forces today serve as a model for equal opportunity to our entire country and indeed to the world.

Johnson Whittaker did more than open doors in our military; he left to his descendants a remarkable legacy of determination and a sense of duty. Two of his sons served as Army officers during World War I. One returned home and served the citizens of his State as president of South Carolina State University. A grandson flew with the famed Tuskegee Airmen during the Second World War. His granddaughter, Cecil Whittaker Pequette, who is here with us today, gave voice to her community as a founder of the Detroit Tribune. And today his great-grandsons, one a lawyer, the other a surgeon, also carry on the Whittaker tradition.

During his 4 years at West Point, Cadet Whittaker found his greatest source of comfort and strength in the Bible. Today, fading words on the inside cover of that fragile volume reveal a young man whose essential goodness still offers a lesson to all of us: "Try never to injure another by word, by act, or by look even," he wrote in his second year at the academy. "Forgive as soon as you are injured, and forget as soon as you forgive." On the following New Year's Day, Johnson Whittaker resolved, and wrote in his Bible, "never to commit an act at which my kind mother would have to blush, to do right at all times, under whatever circumstances and at whatever cost."

We cannot undo history. But today, finally, we can pay tribute to a great American, and we can acknowledge a great injustice. I would like to do two things today: first, to present to Mrs. Cecil Whittaker Pequette what may have been her grandfather's most prized possession, that old Bible that soothed his loneliness and was confiscated and kept all these years as a part of his court-martial record. And second, I am honored to present the Whittaker family with the bars that Second Lieutenant Johnson Chesnut Whittaker earned but was denied.

May God bless his memory, and may all of us honor his service to the United States of America.

Major, please read the commission.

NOTE: The President spoke at 1:38 p.m. in the Roosevelt Room at the White House. In his remarks, he referred to Secretary of the Army Togo D. West, Jr.; Lt. Gen. Benjamin O. Davis, Jr., USAF (Ret.); Maj. Gen. Fred A. Gorden, Commanding General, U.S. Army Military District of Washington; and Gen. Ronald H. Griffith, Vice Chief of Staff, U.S. Army.

Statement on the Terrorist Attack in Tel Aviv, Israel
July 24, 1995

On behalf of all Americans, I offer my deepest condolences to the Government and people of Israel at this tragic moment. Our thoughts and prayers are with the victims of this terrorist atrocity and their loved ones.

We join with all those working for peace in expressing our outrage and condemning in the strongest possible manner this brutal act. Those responsible are seeking to deny to Israelis and Palestinians alike the realization of a new and better life of peace and hope. But they shall not be allowed to succeed. Their vision is of the past, not of the future, of hatred, not the reconciliation which Israeli and Palestinian peacemakers are striving to achieve.

Peace requires courage. The people of Israel have demonstrated enormous resolve and determination in pursuing the path of peace. Through times of suffering as well as rejoicing, the Government and people of the United States stand with them.

Statement on House of Representatives Action on Appropriations Legislation
July 24, 1995

I proposed a reasonable plan to balance the budget while investing more in education and training. Republicans want to balance the budget through cuts that hurt working families while providing a huge tax cut that goes largely to people who don't need it. They are cutting deeply into Medicare and Medicaid, and they are cutting the very education and training programs that our working families need.

Nowhere are the differences between my approach and theirs more clear than the extreme bill passed by the House Appropriations Committee today. That measure slashes critical resources for education, training, and jobs for our people. If Congress sends me this bill in its present form, I will have to veto it.

I want to invest in our people, not turn back the clock on them. There has always been a strong bipartisan consensus for investment in quality education, training, health, and worker protections. These harsh, partisan, and unwise cuts undermine that consensus as well as the future income and living standards of working families and their children.

In addition, I believe abortion should be safe, legal, and rare. But this bill effectively ends the family planning program that Republicans and Democrats have long agreed is needed to help prevent the need for abortion. Furthermore, it changes existing law to allow States to deny poor women access to abortions under Medicaid even if they are victims of rape or incest. That is wrong.

I once again urge the Congress to begin the work of making commonsense corrections in this and other appropriations bills. I will not allow our people to be sacrificed for the sake of political ideology.

Remarks on the 30th Anniversary of the Passage of Medicare
July 25, 1995

Thank you very much, Mr. Vice President, for your introduction and your leadership. Senator Kennedy and Congressman Dingell, thank you for your incredible inspiration to the country and to me. Mr. Glover, thank you, and thank you for your speech. To Congressman Gephardt and Senator Daschle, I want all of you to know that they lead well and they are doing well for our country. To my friend Arthur Flemming and his family and Mother Johnson and her family and to all of you seniors who are here, I am honored to be here, and I have loved listening to these stories and these speeches and hearing this commitment.

I am honored to stand in the tradition of the Presidents who fought for Medicare. I believe that President Roosevelt and President Truman and President Kennedy and President Johnson were right. And I think those who opposed them were wrong.

If you really think about Medicare and Medicaid, which was also passed at the same time, they've given all of us stories. I loved hearing the Vice President talk about his wonderful mother.

All of you know that since I've been President I have lost my mother and my fine stepfather, but what you may not know is that my stepfather had a heart attack 10 years before he died, in the middle of one of my inaugural speeches for Governor. And when he woke up from his surgery, his quadruple bypass, I told him it was not that good a speech. [*Laughter*] But because he was a senior citizen covered by health care, he had 10 more good years. And my mother had a very difficult fight with cancer, which she lost. But because she was a senior citizen covered by good health care, she lived to see her son become President of the United States.

I ran for President because I wanted to broaden that sense of security and opportunity for our people. I wanted middle class Americans to have family-wage jobs and be able to educate their children and have the same health security we had given to senior citizens, as Congressman Dingell said.

And the same crowd that killed Harry Truman's plan for health care, the same crowd that fought against Medicare, were successful in derailing what we tried to do last year. But they did it in a brilliant way, because by last year Medicare had become so much of our common ground as Americans, so much a part of the fabric of our daily lives, that no one anymore thought about these Members of Congress having anything to do with it. It was just a part of our daily lives, just like getting up in the morning and seeing the Sun shine. And so these people, the same crowd that fought it tooth and nail 30 years ago, came up with this brilliant argument that because I said, when they denied it, the Medicare Trust Fund was in trouble and we had to reform health care, that I wanted to see the Government mess with their Medicare.

And we had people all over America coming up to me or the First Lady or to Senator Kennedy, saying, "Don't let the Government mess with my Medicare." People had actually forgotten where it came from, as if it sort of dropped out of the sky. Well, I got the message of the 1994 election, and I'm not going to let the Government mess with your Medicare.

I really thought Medicare had passed beyond the partisan and political divide into the generational life of our country. The people who passed it did it for their parents' generation and knew that they would have it when they came along and knew that, in so doing, they would relieve a burden from their children, who could then focus on building good lives for themselves and their children. It was sort of a part of the social compact of the American family.

Now the Vice President's father, who's been mentioned several times and is a particular favorite of mine, said that the absence of health care for the elderly was, I quote, "a disgrace in a country such as ours." We got rid of the disgrace, and along with Social Security, as Secretary Shalala has said, we at least have finished that part of our country's work.

We still have a lot of work to do. But the answer to the problems of the great American middle class, the answer to the problem of curing the American deficit, the answer to the problem of dealing with the challenge of educating a new generation of Americans for a new, highly competitive economy—surely the answer to those problems is not break down the one thing we have done right completely, which is to keep faith with our elderly people.

I want to talk just a little bit about what this could mean to you. As I said, in 1965, the legislation which created Medicare also created Medicaid. A lot of Americans think it's just a program for poor people. Well, it did provide desperately needed care for poor children and their mothers, but it also provided more care for older and disabled Americans, especially long-term care. Two-thirds of the Medicaid budget goes for older Americans and disabled citizens. Without Medicaid, middle class families struggling to pay their own bills and raise and educate their children could face nursing home bills for their parents averaging $38,000 a year. I remember what those nursing homes looked like before Medicaid. Some of you do, too.

We need to celebrate and recommit ourselves to this. And we need to ask ourselves, what is the future? We are at an historic moment. For the first time in a long time there is a willingness to try to bring the budget into balance, a willingness to try to secure the Medicare Trust Fund. But I know we can do both while maintaining our generational commitment. I know we can do both without returning Medicare to the area of American partisan politics and to nightmares for the elderly people and their children in this country. We can do it.

As Mr. Gephardt said, the congressional majority appears to be choosing for the first time ever to use the benefits we provide under Medicare, paid for by a dedicated payroll tax, as a piggybank to fund huge tax cuts for people who don't really need them. But we showed that you could have a balanced budget plan, with no new Medicare costs for older Americans, that stabilized the Medicare Trust Fund.

We know that. They instead would cut $270 billion from Medicare and raise Medicare premiums and out-of-pocket costs an average of $5,600 per couple over 7 years, even for people who don't have enough money to get by as it is. They want to use this to pay for a $245 billion tax cut.

If they would just reduce the size of the tax cut, target the middle class families and their basic needs, string out the time which we take to balance the budget, we would not need one penny, not a red cent of the Medicare beneficiary cuts they've proposed. Don't you let anybody tell you that we have to do that to stabilize the trust fund or to balance the budget. We do have to stabilize the trust fund. We should balance the budget. But we don't have to raise the roof on the beneficiaries to do it. We do not have to break our generational commitment to do it. Do not let anybody tell you that. It is simply not true.

This plan kind of sounds good in the rabid antigovernment atmosphere in which we live today—their plan does. The majority's plan in Congress would provide older Americans with a voucher for a set amount each year. They almost make it sound like you can make a profit out of it. It supposedly would cover enough to buy medical insurance. The problem is that private health care costs are projected to increase 40 percent more than the value of the voucher. So if you're over 65 and you're healthy as a horse, this might be a good deal for you. But what if you get sicker as you get older? If the vouchers are inadequate, the elderly must make up the difference out of their own pockets.

There's no clear provision that would give a larger voucher for a patient like my mother, who developed cancer, as opposed to one the same age who was healthy, not even a clear provision to give a larger one to seniors who are fortunate enough to live into their eighties. That's the fastest growing group of elderly people in America, in percentage terms, people in their eighties. But to be healthy in your eighties you just naturally use the health care system more. There's no clear provision to take care of that, no clear provision to stop companies from simply turning seniors down because of their medical condition or cutting them off when they get sick.

In the past, various experts have suggested that Medicare budget cuts will inflict harm and financial suffering on the elderly, but as the grisly details of the plan become known, it becomes clearer and clearer that we could actually see a denial of medical care to those who need it. That was the very thing Medicare was designed to do away with.

You know, my mother was a nurse-anesthetist. I can remember what it was like before there was any Medicare or Medicaid. I remember people that would actually come to our house with a bushel basket full of peaches, for example, trying to pay in kind for the medical service my mother had rendered. And I remember that the old folks weren't healthy enough to go pick peaches. I remember these things, and we should not forget. We can change without wrecking, and we need to be awfully careful before we buy a pig in a poke.

It is easy to see how, in all but the direst of emergencies, millions of older Americans would actually just give up the medical attention to which they are entitled and which they need. Let me just give you some examples of what could happen. These are real examples of what could happen.

Suppose a 75-year-old woman has exhausted her savings and is too sick to work, but her voucher isn't enough to permit her to afford any health insurance plan anymore. She'd have to reach into her own pocket, but she doesn't have any money there. She can't get to the hospital unless it's a dire emergency because she's got to pay a $750 deductible for that. So she can't get to the doctor's office because she can't pay the extra premium there. So the woman is stuck, and no care.

Or suppose you have a 75-year-old man who gets a voucher that just about covers the cost of his health insurance, and in 3 years his voucher only goes up 5 percent a year, but the health insurance premium goes up 10 percent a year. So after 3 years, the gap is so wide he can't afford to pay. He doesn't have the money. He dropped his Medigap coverage because he was persuaded this voucher system would work. So he's stuck, no care.

A 70-year-old man with open-heart surgery recovered enough to go home and be treated by a visiting nurse, but under the plan of the congressional majority, he must now pay $1,400 in copayments for that visiting nurse. He can't afford that, so he stays in the hospital at 3 or 4 times the cost to the taxpayers. But after

a while, Medicare stops paying for that, too. So he's stuck.

Now, these are things that can happen. Those who want to keep what they have now will have to pay significantly more. Every person on Medicare will pay $1,650 more over 7 years. The average person who receives care in home—something we need more of, not less of—will pay $1,700 more in the year 2002 alone for the same health care. Remember, these are people who already pay over 20 percent of their income for health care.

So I ask you, can the elderly really afford $1,650 more for premiums to cover their doctor bills? Can the elderly really afford $1,700 more for the same home health care in one year alone? Will vouchers cover them against sudden premium increases if they get sick? That's what health insurance is supposed to do, you know, cover you when you get sick, not when you're healthy. Will the medical costs stay sufficiently under control to permit these vouchers to cover the full cost of care? No expert thinks so.

Is it fair to make older Americans give up their doctors and be forced into managed care, instead of giving the option to them to go into a managed care network? Is it really necessary, to balance the budget and to stabilize the Medicare Trust Fund, to do what the congressional majority proposes? The answer to every single one of these questions is no. No.

Those who want to gamble with Medicare are asking Americans to bet their lives. And why should they bet their lives? Not to balance the budget, not to strengthen the Medicare Trust Fund, but simply to pay for a big tax cut for people who don't need it. It's a bad deal. We ought not to do it. It will break up America's common ground. And you can help to stop it.

If the Congress and the majority really wants to balance the budget and reform the Medicare Trust Fund, let me ask them to join with me in a real commitment to health care reform that can be achievable, even by their standards. Senator Kennedy has already introduced a bill with Senator Kassebaum that goes part of the way. Let us require insurance plans to cover those with preexisting conditions. Let us make a commitment to preventive and long-term care. Let us encourage home care as an alternative to nursing homes and give folks a little help to have their parents there. Let us let workers take their insurance coverage with them when they change jobs and crack down on fraud and abuse and give people the option to choose a managed care option if they want it; don't force people to take something they don't want.

If we really want to work together, there ought to be four basic principles that everybody, without regard to party, signs off on. We have to make sure that good, affordable health care is available to all older Americans. That's what we do now; let's don't stop it. We must not cut Medicare to pay for a bigger tax cut than can be justified, that goes to people who don't really need it, a lot of whom don't even want it. We ought not to do that. We must be committed to reducing medical cost inflation and stabilizing the Medicare Trust Fund through genuine reforms, not by destroying Medicare and hurting the people who are on it. We must not balance the budget by cutting Medicare to older Americans. We do not have to do any of these things.

This is a time of great and exciting change, I know that. But you know, the conservatives are supposed to be in charge around here, and conservatism means—if nothing else—if it ain't broke, don't fix it. And do no harm. That's the first principle.

My fellow Americans, this is a big fight, but it's not just for the seniors in this audience and in this country. It's for all their children. Most senior citizens have children that are working harder for the same or lower pay they were making 5 or 10 years ago. They have their own insecurities and their own problems. They need their jobs and their incomes and their children's

education and their own health care stabilized. We don't need to do something that makes their lives worse, either. And it's for all their children, the people on Medicare's grandchildren. They deserve a chance to have a good education, to be sent to college. Their parents should not wake up in the middle of the night torn between their own parent's health care and their children's education.

This is not just a senior citizens issue. We need to increase opportunity and security for all Americans. And the worst thing we could do is to tear down Medicare. That would increase insecurity, not just for the elderly but for all Americans. It would cloud the future of this country.

We have come a very long way by pulling together. Do not let this budget debate tear this country apart. Do not turn back on Medicare. Stand up and say, if you want to do something to balance the budget and stabilize the Medicare Trust Fund in a way that helps the elderly people of this country, we will stand with you. But if you want the Government to mess with my Medicare, the answer is, no.

Thank you, and God bless you.

NOTE: The President spoke at 11:06 a.m. in the Caucus Room of the Cannon House Office Building. In his remarks, he referred to Eugene Glover, national president, and Genevieve Johnson, DC chapter president, National Council of Senior Citizens; and Arthur Flemming, chair, Save Our Security. He also referred to his mother, Virginia Kelley; and his father-in-law, Hugh Rodham.

Remarks to the Americans with Disabilities Act Roundtable
July 26, 1995

Thank you very much. Secretary Rubin, Attorney General Reno, to the distinguished members of this panel, Senator Harkin and Congressman Hoyer, Chairman Coelho, Dr. Hitt, Gil Casellas, Marca Bristo, the members of the administration who are here—I see Reed Hundt and Patsy Fleming out there—I thank all of you for being here to celebrate this fifth anniversary of the Americans with Disabilities Act.

Five years ago, when the ADA became law, we became the first nation in the world to com-

mit ourselves to equal rights and equal opportunities for all citizens with disabilities. Because of the ADA, our country is stronger today. Our fellow citizens are being judged by their ability to contribute, not by their disabilities. Now all of you and millions of others all across this country have an opportunity they never had before to make the most of their own lives.

That opportunity is critical to what we have to do as a nation to meet the great challenges we face and to move forward into the next century. In many ways, the ADA is the perfect example of what I mean when I talk about our job is to create more opportunity and demand more responsibility from all of our citizens.

The ADA has meant more opportunity for 49 million Americans with disabilities to do their part to make us a stronger and better country. It has meant that more people can go to work and participate in community life and do things that most Americans take for granted, like helping to take care of their families or getting a good education or registering and voting. It's also a perfect example of what I have meant in recent weeks when I have urged the American people to come together to find common ground in order to move forward together as a nation.

That was true across party lines. Members of both parties, including three who are here today, Senator Harkin, Representative Hoyer, and former Congressman Tony Coelho, fought for the ADA in the Congress. And President Bush signed it into law. The ADA became law because Americans, like so many of you, worked together in the best interest of everyone, putting party behind country. There was a realization that the best way to keep our country moving forward was to allow every American, regardless of whether he or she used a wheelchair, was blind, had a mental disability, or was HIV-positive, to live up to his or her God-given potential.

And today, even as we celebrate the rights gained under the ADA, the budget cuts proposed by the congressional majority would sharply reduce the services and the supports that enable people to effectively exercise the rights granted by the ADA. Under the proposed cuts, States would be forced to drop 1.4 million people with disabilities from Medicaid rolls, and 4 million disabled Americans on Medicare would have to pay more every year for the same health care. They also have proposed eliminating funds for training special education teachers.

Now, we have to join together to maintain our commitment and our common ground. I will vigorously implement and enforce the ADA through the Cabinet and the administration. We will not allow Americans with disabilities to be kept from realizing their dreams by closed doors or narrowed minds.

We should also celebrate, all of us, this fifth anniversary of the Americans with Disabilities Act in the best way possible: By all, each of us, rededicating ourselves to creating a society of equal access and equal rights for all. That is the best kind of affirmative action for all the American people.

Thank you very much.

NOTE: The President spoke at 10:22 a.m. in the Cash Room at the Treasury Department. In his remarks, he referred to Tony Coelho, Chair, President's Committee on Employment of People With Disabilities; R. Scott Hitt, Chair, Presidential Advisory Council on HIV/AIDS; Gilbert F. Casellas, Chairman, Equal Employment Opportunity Commission; Marca Bristo, Chair, National Council on Disability; Reed F. Hundt, Chair, Federal Communications Commission; and Patricia S. Fleming, Director of National AIDS Policy.

Remarks to the White House Community Empowerment Conference
July 26, 1995

Thank you very much, Mr. Vice President; to all the mayors and other distinguished visitors who are here; to the Members of Congress and all those who have worked on the empowerment zone program here in our administration. And I'd like to say a special word of thanks to the Vice President and all of his staff, and to Secretary Cisneros and Andrew Cuomo. They have literally worked themselves to exhaustion to make sure that this program is a success.

We told you when we started this that this would not be some one-shot deal and there would be no followup. And I think it's fair to say we have kept our word. And from the looks of this crowd, you have kept your word. And I thank you for that.

I also want to say a special word of thanks to Congressman Rangel and to the other Members of Congress here who were very active in passing the empowerment zone legislation as a part of the budget plan in 1993.

I can't say how much I appreciate the work the Vice President's done on this community empowerment board, because it's one thing to talk about all this and quite another to do it. And your presence here proves that you also are committed to doing it.

As I have said many times in many places, I think this country has two great challenges. The first is to restore the American dream of opportunity for all Americans and the American value of responsibility from all Americans. And the second is to rebuild our sense of community, our sense that we are working together, not at odds with one another, toward the same goals. The more I work at this job the more I become convinced that we can't achieve solutions to our economic or our social problems unless we do a better job of working together and reaching across the divides. That is, by definition, what you all had to do to be selected to be part of the empowerment zone program in the first place.

In the past few weeks, I have tried to talk to the American people more about how we can find common ground even in very controversial issues. I gave a speech at Georgetown laying it out, and then I went to the Vice President and Mrs. Gore's Family Conference and talked about how we could find common ground on the controversial issue of the role of the media in our family lives and community lives. And as if that weren't controversial enough, I then went out to James Madison University— James Madison High School here and talked about where I thought our common ground was on the issue of religion in public education in America. And then, of course, I had the opportunity just a few days ago to talk at the National Archives on the important subject of affirmative action.

Today, I want to say to you that I think that the empowerment zone concept embodies everything we have to do as Americans, everything. To make it work, we have to create economic opportunity, solve social problems, and pull people together who have been apart. It is the embodiment of what we want to do.

The second point I want to make at the very beginning is, I think it is good for the rest of America and is a good model for the rest of America, because if you look at it, one of the things that troubles me about the debate we are having now on balancing the budget is that the congressional majority wants to balance the budget but admits that if their plan is implemented, our economy will have anemic growth for 7 years in a row. I want to balance the budget because I think it will explode economic growth. I think it will lower interest rates and free up money and cause more people to borrow money and invest in our communities.

And why do we have slow growth? Why is the cover of Business Week magazine, the current issue, about how wages aren't going up? Why does survey after survey after survey reveal when we tell the American people that we have lowered the deficit and provided 7 million new jobs to this economy, voters say, "I don't believe you. Don't bother me with the facts, I don't believe you." Why is that? Because people think, "Well, if that had happened, I would somehow feel more secure in my own life."

So we have to increase the rate of economic activity in America. And how can we do that? Well, we can do it by expanding trade, and I've tried to do that. But we also can do it by finding underutilized assets in America. That's what the empowerment zones are all about. The greatest residual economic asset left in the United States, the new economic frontier in America, are old-fashioned Americans who've been left behind in the rush to the 21st century. And if we can tap into that, then all Americans will benefit. All Americans will see increases in their incomes as the economy grows more rapidly.

So this is not just a program for Baltimore or Philadelphia, Cleveland, Detroit, Chicago, New York, the Kentucky Highlands, South Texas, the Mississippi Delta, you name it—Los Angeles, wherever else I left out that's here. I'm sorry. [*Laughter*] You will help everybody. If economic activity rises in the Philadelphia/East Camden, New Jersey area, it will be felt in western Pennsylvania. It will also be felt in the Western part of the United States. This is a very important issue. And if you prove that this strategy works, then other people will do it, and it will spread like wildfire throughout the country.

When I talked the other day about affirmative action, I said that I thought we ought to mend it, not end it. I thought that it was important but that everybody should realize something. The people who didn't think they were for it should understand that if we got rid of it, it wouldn't solve the economic problems of America. And the people who were for it should realize that if we keep it, it won't solve their economic problems either, unless we find ways to grow this economy and bring the American people together and deal frankly and forthrightly with our challenges. That's what this is all about. It's about bringing opportunity back.

Government has got to become a real meaningful partner again for people in urban America and rural America who are trapped in cycles of poverty. I know it can be done from my own experience. I was thinking today as I was walking over with the Vice President, when I was reelected Governor of Arkansas in 1982, we had an unemployment rate that was 10 percent or higher in the State. In the Mississippi Delta portion of our State, we had several counties with over 20 percent unemployment—several, not just one or two.

The first thing I did as a Governor-elect was go to a town that had had a Singer sewing machine plant there since the 1920's and shake hands with over 600 people as they walked off the job for the last time. It was a very sobering experience. And we tried everything we could to restructure our economy and to get it going.

At length, I noticed something. After working for about 2 years, I noticed that in isolated pockets in the poorest part of America, the Mississippi Delta, there would be a town here and a town there that for reasons no one could explain by economic, social, or racial makeup, had lower unemployment rates and higher growth rates, had schools where the races went to school together and there was no white flight, no big movement toward private schools, had functioning public institutions. No one could explain it, so I decided I'd figure out why on my own. And the answer wasn't complicated. People found a way to work together in those counties. In those communities, people found a way to take advantage of the opportunities they had instead of just bellyaching about the problems they had.

One of these little towns was in the middle of a county with an astronomical unemployment rate. And they had about a 5 percent unemployment rate, because every time a plant closed they sent a team of 50 people to the State and they used our WATS lines all night long, day-in and day-out, until they called hundreds and hundreds and hundreds of people to come look at their little town and put their people back to work.

That simple experience was the beginning for me of this whole empowerment zone idea. And so we set up a process in the 11 poorest counties in our State to try to do what we've attempted to do here. Today, our State's unemployment rate is just a little above 4 percent. It took a long time to turn around, but it happened. And if you have the patience and the roots deep enough to make the commitment necessary to turn your communities around, you can turn America around by setting an example and proving this works. You can do it.

This sort of locally driven, positive approach was not invented by me or anybody else. It came out of the grassroots of America. It was endorsed when I was a young man by Robert Kennedy when he went into the poorest areas of our country and when he supported what became known as the Bedford-Stuyvesant Corporation. Republicans have embraced it, who have had experience with it. I applaud Jack Kemp for his remarks in the last several days, saying that instead of using issues like affirmative action to divide us, we should be searching for ways like empowerment zones to fight poverty and create opportunity for all Americans. We need more of that kind of talk from people without regard to their political parties. And I applaud him for doing it.

I was interested the other day in a comment that Speaker Gingrich made about affirmative action, which was encouraging to me. As you know, there are those who say that we should get rid of affirmative action because they think there's no need for it or it's inevitably biased. I don't agree with that. I think that we have to continue with these efforts, even though we have to improve them until there is no more need for them. But I also was encouraged, even though I didn't agree with what the Speaker said about affirmative action—because he said he didn't like it—he also admitted that just getting rid of it was no answer. And I thought that was hopeful. He said that he didn't want to end affirmative action until they found something to replace it.

Well, I don't think we should end it until we don't need it anymore. But I do think we should do some more things. Discrimination is, as I said before, only one of the things that traps people. The general conditions of the economy, the terrible social problems we face, they take away more American dreams every day. And that is something Americans share in common.

When Mr. Gingrich said that he thought we ought to design a program to lend a helping hand, I say that's exactly what we're trying to do with the empowerment zones, with the Community Development Act, with the improvements for the community reinvestment program, with the community development financial institutions, with all the other empowerment initiatives of this administration. So I say, based on what Jack Kemp said and based on what the Speaker said, I want to invite the leaders of the Republican Party to join me in a comprehensive approach to solving these problems, because every Republican in America will be better off if we can revitalize our inner cities and our forgotten rural areas and so will every Democrat and so will every independent.

This should not be a partisan issue. If you look at the problems that have plagued us, whatever our race or gender or background, urban or rural, north, south, east, or west, if we could address them, this country would have about half the problems we've got today. You know it, and I know it. So I hope that this conference, this gathering, and these hopeful comments that have been made by two different Republicans in the last couple of weeks means that we may have a chance to come together here and work together at the national level the way I see Republicans and Democrats working together at the city level and in the urban areas where these empowerment zones have prevailed because of the partnerships we've created. I wish we could follow your example here in Washington, and I'm going to do my best to get that done.

Now, let me say that when you look at where we ought to go beyond affirmative action and beyond what we're doing with the empowerment zones, as a part of our affirmative action review, it occurred to me that while we shouldn't replace affirmative action, we should reform it, and we should also supplement it, because it was clear that no amount of affirmative action could create economic opportunity where there was none. We give everybody an equal opportunity at a shrinking pie, that's not a nice prospect. What we want is for everybody to have an equal opportunity at an expanding pie.

And that is why I have proposed to set aside Government contracts for businesses that lay down roots in poor communities, to locate there and hire people there. I think we ought to have contracts that can bring money and opportunities to poor neighborhoods every day. Businesses make profits; employees get paychecks; workers take their paychecks home to their families and lift their children out of poverty, buy groceries from local merchants, support their local community organizations and stronger community police forces to make the streets safer, to make the schools better. Opportunities that can go to people without regard to their race or gender if they meet a simple condition: they live in a place with genuine need.

I believe this can make a real difference to America, not to get rid of affirmative action but to create real opportunity for all Americans. And I hope you will support this. I have asked the Vice President to examine this challenge and to take it on, as he has so many others, and to come up with what I have to do to get this done, whether I have to send a bill to Congress or fashion an Executive order or do a combination of both.

But I think this can make a real difference. And it is utterly consistent with the empowerment zone strategy. It emphasizes the three things that make the empowerment zone work: the values of family and work and responsibility, a sense of investment in our people and our opportunities, and a partnership across all the lines that too often divide us.

I am very, very hopeful about that, and I believe it can reinforce some of the other things we're doing. If you look at this values issue, I think we need some values incentives that are tough. That's why we think that people on welfare who can work ought to be required to work. That's why we're trying to get the toughest possible child support enforcement. That's why the crime bill had tougher penalties.

But I also think if you want to promote values, empowerment works there. People ought to have the incentives. That's what the Family and Medical Leave Act was all about. That's what child care and a welfare reform program is all about. That's what the crime prevention aspects of the crime bill were all about. And I think it's interesting to point out, as they're under assault today, that it was the law enforcement communities of America, the people in uniform and the prosecutors and the former prosecutors, like Mayor Rendell, who told us that we had to have crime prevention programs and something for our children to say yes to as well as to say no to. I have walked the streets of Baltimore with Mayor Schmoke, who was a former prosecutor, and seen examples of that.

So if we're going to promote values, let's think of empowerment as well as restraint. We need to do both. When we think of investment, we ought to think of empowerment. Head Start is an empowerment program. The college loan program is an empowerment program. The national service program is an empowerment program. The Goals 2000 program, no matter what the attacks on it, is the biggest piece of local incentive, local reform legislation for public schools passed by the Federal Congress in the 30 years we've been acting in the education area.

We need to think of these things as empowerment, not Federal prescriptions. If you think about our community investments, the crime bill was about community empowerment. That's what 100,000 police officers does. That's what the whole community policing program is about.

So I hope that you can help us to develop a language and an attitude and a frame of mind for discussing our common problems as a country so that Americans, even Americans who don't live within your jurisdiction and have the particular benefits of the empowerment zone, will see this as a way of not only solving our economic problems, dealing with our social problems, but empowering people and bringing them together. That is the issue for America at this point in our history. That is the issue.

We cannot maintain the American dream if we go another 20 years when we are very successful by some measures. I mean, consider the last 2½ years. I came to this job committed to restoring the middle class, and I did everything I knew to do. We lowered the deficit. We increased investment in education, in technology, in research and development. We expanded trade frontiers. We have 7 million more jobs. We have a record number of millionaires. We have an all-time high stock market. We have more new businesses than ever before in the history of the country in each of the last 2 years. And most people are still working harder for lower pay than they were making the day I was sworn in as President.

We have to change that. And the only way we can change it is if we realize that we have to get beyond these big ideological debates and

roll up our sleeves and reach out to each other and create opportunity for everybody just like you're trying to do. And we should talk about all of these initiatives in terms of what it does to enable people and families and communities to solve their own problems and make the most of their own lives.

That could be the enduring legacy of this administration and very much worth all the efforts that the Vice President and Secretary Cisneros and others have put into this and very much worth the very heated fight that these Members of Congress here present waged for this program over 2 years ago.

So I ask you to think about all that. I want this to work in your community. I know you do, too. I know you will evaluate these empowerment zones based on whether they do bring people together and they create jobs and opportunity for your people. But I want you never to forget that you may be creating the way that we do business as Americans in the 21st century. And if you can do it, if you can bring people together across all the lines that divide them around the concept of commitment to opportunity for everybody, we'll be a long way down the road toward ensuring the viability of the American dream in the 21st century.

So I ask you to think about that. And when we have these debates up here in Washington about what to fund and what to cut, about how to balance the budget—not whether to balance the budget—you ask yourself: Are they funding the empowerment programs where there's very little bureaucracy in Washington and a whole lot of things happening out in the country? Don't we need some more of the community development banks like we established in Los Angeles? Don't we need to protect a sensible community reinvestment act when we know that credit still does not go evenhandedly to all who are qualified? Don't we need to keep the Small Business Administration functioning when they proved they could double the loan output and lower their budget and increase dramatically loans to women and minorities without lowering their quality standards? Don't we need, in short, to continue on the empowerment agenda when we make our decisions about what to cut and what to fund?

We need to be in a position to help you not just now, but next year and the year after that and the year after that, long into the future. So I ask you to think about that as well.

And again, I say this need not be a partisan issue. You have to ask yourself—we've been pretty successful as a country in identifying the things on which our security hinged and building a consensus for them. I mean, for 50 years we maintained a remarkable—almost 50 years—a remarkable bipartisan consensus that we would spend more than any other country in the world on maintaining a strong national defense, not only for ourselves but for others, so that communism would not prevail and there would never be an incentive to launch a nuclear war. And we fought like crazy about other things, but we created this umbrella that permitted us to grow and go forward as a country. We had a general national consensus created almost 50 years ago that we would be an engine of expanding opportunity throughout the world because that would help us to grow here at home and it would stabilize people throughout the world, to give them hope and help them promote democracy.

So what is it that threatens our security as Americans today? The kids that are being lost every day on our street, the schools that aren't functioning, the number of the people who work hard and are never rewarded, rising levels of anxiety among our families. We ought to be able to find ways to have the kind of consensus on that reflected by the process that brought you here.

So I tell you, you want to do something for your country? Make your empowerment zone work. And make sure everybody in America knows it and knows that's the way we ought to do America's business, not just where you live but here where the American people all have a stake in the future.

Thank you very much.

NOTE: The President spoke at 12:23 p.m. in Room 450 of the Old Executive Office Building. In his remarks, he referred to Mayor Edward Rendell of Philadelphia, PA, and Mayor Kurt Schmoke of Baltimore, MD.

Remarks on Presenting the Congressional Space Medal of Honor to James A. Lovell, Jr., and an Exchange With Reporters
July 26, 1995

The President. I am delighted to be here with all these distinguished Members of Congress. I hope I don't miss any. I have Senators Mikulski, Burns, Heflin, Glenn; Members of the House, Congressmen Hall, Sensenbrenner, Cramer, Chapman, and Mineta. I also want to thank Dr. Jack Gibbons, my science adviser, for being here and for his support of the space program and, of course, Dan Goldin, the Administrator of NASA, who told me just a few moments before coming out here that he worked on the engine as a young scientist that brought Jim Lovell home safely. So he's—[*applause*]—we thank you for that. And of course, we're delighted to have Pete Conrad, a former astronaut and a Space Medal recipient here, and Tom Hanks and his son, Colin, are here. They're here not only because of "Apollo 13" but because when they make the sequel to "Forrest Gump," now he won't have to have a computer-generated President. [*Laughter*]

Most of America is now familiar with the five words spoken by Gene Kranz when he was Flight Commander of *Apollo 13* because of the wonderful movie that so many of us have seen: Failure is not an option. That was the creed for the *Apollo 13* crew and for the dedicated people of Mission Control and throughout NASA during those difficult days of April 1970.

Everyone connected with the mission understood that it was imperative to work together and to remain diligent in the face of enormous obstacles. The words "failure is not an option" have meaning far beyond that one extraordinary mission. In many ways, they have become, for millions of Americans seeing that movie, a statement of the national purpose we all need as we move toward a new century and a new and uncharted time here on Earth.

The space program was born of competition with the Soviet Union, but it sowed the seeds for peaceful cooperation today. We enjoy with the Russians today a remarkable partnership, which we saw recently in that astonishing rendezvous between the shuttle and the *Mir*. By replacing warheads with space capsules atop the Saturn V rocket, we launched more than a space program; we launched the beginning of the end of the cold war.

Although we face great challenges today, I think we all know deep down inside that if we can muster the same determination, dedication, commitment, and sense of partnership that we saw in the story of the heroes of *Apollo 13*, we will get the job done.

I am so honored to have Captain and Mrs. Lovell with us today. And to Jim Lovell: And now all America knows more clearly than they have for 25 years that while you may have lost the Moon, as the phrase goes, you gained something perhaps far more important, the abiding respect and gratitude of the American people. And you gained another important foothold in the long struggle here in the United States to maintain our space program and to make it a part of our definition of what it means to be an American and to fight for the future.

What you did up there and what you have accomplished in your life here on Earth continues to be an inspiration to all your fellow Americans. And therefore, I am honored to present to you, in the presence of two former recipients, the Congressional Space Medal of Honor. I thank Peter Conrad and my good friend Senator John Glenn for being here and for their contributions to the space program and to the welfare of the United States.

And I'd like to say, thank you, again, Captain Lovell, on behalf of all Americans. I'd like to ask my military aide now to read the citation.

[*At this point, Lt. Comdr. June E. Ryan, USCG, read the citation.*]

Captain Lovell. Mr. President and distinguished guests, you know, I humbly accept this medal as Commander of *Apollo 13*, but with the understanding, really, that it was the efforts and the intuition and the teamwork of my crewmates, Jack Swigert and Fred Haise, and the hundreds of people within NASA and the contractor group that really worked hard to make this team effort and the success of *Apollo 13* to come back to be a successful recovery.

And so, thank you very much. I really do appreciate this.

Bosnia

Q. Mr. President, do you think that the Senate vote on the arms lift is a repudiation of your policies?

The President. No, I think it is an expression of the concern the Senate has for the inability of the United Nations mission in the past to do what it said it was going to do and to protect the people of Bosnia from the aggression of the Serbs.

And I think the—first of all, I think in the adoption of the amendment by Senator Nunn and in several other ways the resolution is better than it was. Secondly, I noted from the comments that there are many people who voted in the majority who are still willing to work with us.

I do not believe the strong course for the United States and the strong course for the people of Bosnia is to unilaterally lift the arms embargo, collapse the U.N. mission, and increase the chances of injecting American troops there. I don't believe that. I think the strong course is to have a powerful use of air power and to support the rapid reaction force that the French and the British are putting on the ground that they have proved will attack back if they're attacked.

I have worked for 10 days to get NATO the ability to act through the United Nations to really use that air power to raise the price of aggression for the Bosnian Serbs. That is the only thing that has worked in the last 2½ years, and it has worked when we have done it.

And I will say that in London over the weekend and then yesterday at NATO we have made substantial progress. We have a commitment now to a much tougher air posture. That is the only thing that we know based on our own experience that has a chance of working and pushing this whole process back to the conference table and stopping the aggression.

So I think the Congress wants something done. I do, too. I do not believe a unilateral lift of the embargo is the right way to go. I believe that there is clear evidence from the speeches that were made, the amendments that were adopted, the votes that were cast, that we're going to be able to work together and continue to push for a strong position. But I don't favor a unilateral lift. I think what we're doing with the use of air power is by far the better course, as long as the allies will do what they say they're going to do. And I believe now, after 10 days of hard work, we have got that done.

Q. [Inaudible]—Boutros Boutros-Ghali will that make it easier for you to coordinate Washington policy?

The President. Because he has delegated the authority? Absolutely. And I applaud that. That was the right decision for him to take, and it shows that he, too, is concerned that the United Nations cannot express a commitment to protect the security of people and then walk away from it. I applaud the statement that he made and the action he took today.

Q. Do you wish maybe he had said it a little sooner than just the exact time of the vote?

The President. Well, of course, but you know, the whole world can't calibrate their activities based on what we're doing here at a given moment. I think that the United Nations is working their way through this. And keep in mind, they've had people on the ground. They haven't wanted to have their hostages taken and then been made vulnerable to being killed or tortured or imprisoned for long periods of time. But if the United Nations guarantees the security of certain areas and certain standards of conduct, then we have to stand behind the guarantees.

I think President Chirac and Prime Minister Major, in putting together this rapid reaction force, and then the work that I was able to do to get them to come back to a clear line of authority to use aggressive air—that is the strong approach. That is the approach that we know from experience has a chance to work, to raise the price of aggression.

The other course has a lot of downsides, and we don't know if it will work. We know this will work if we do it. And I am determined to see that we follow through.

Thank you.

NOTE: The President spoke at 3:45 p.m. in the Oval Office at the White House. In his remarks, he referred to actor Tom Hanks; United Nations Secretary-General Boutros Boutros-Ghali; President Jacques Chirac of France; and Prime Minister John Major of the United Kingdom.

Statement on Proposed Foreign Relations Legislation
July 26, 1995

Congress is now considering legislation—S. 908, "The Foreign Relations Revitalization Act of 1995"—that would undermine the President's authority to conduct our Nation's foreign policy and deny us the resources we need to lead in the world. If this legislation comes to my desk in its present form, I will veto it.

S. 908 attacks the President's constitutional authority to conduct America's foreign policy. No President, Democrat or Republican, could accept these restrictions because they threaten the President's ability to protect and promote American interests around the world.

The legislation would ban or severely restrict diplomatic relations with key countries. Indeed, had it been in effect a few months ago, it would have prevented us from concluding the agreement with North Korea to dismantle its nuclear program. The legislation would handcuff our ability to take part in and lead United Nations operations, limiting our choice each time a crisis arose to acting alone or not at all. The legislation would abolish three important agencies, the Arms Control and Disarmament Agency, the Agency for International Development, and the U.S. Information Agency. Each is already making serious and successful efforts to streamline its operations, as part of my administration's reinventing Government program. Eliminating them entirely would undermine our effectiveness, not enhance it.

In short, the legislation would put Congress in the business of micromanaging our Nation's foreign policy, a business it should not be in.

This legislation combined with S. 961, "The Foreign Aid Reduction Act of 1995," would also slash our international affairs budget, which already is only a little over 1.3 percent of our total Federal budget. We use these funds to fight the spread of nuclear weapons and technology; to combat terrorists, drug traffickers, and international criminals; to create American jobs by opening new markets for our exports; and to support the forces of peace, democracy, and human rights around the world who look to America for leadership.

The proposed cuts in the international affairs budget are dangerous and shortsighted. We know from experience that it is a lot less costly, in terms of money spent and lives lost, to rely on development aid and diplomacy now than it is to send in our troops later. There is a price to be paid for American leadership. But the return on our investment, in terms of increased security and greater prosperity for the American people, more than makes up for the cost. What America cannot afford are the foreign affairs budget cuts proposed in these bills.

As I have made clear before, I want to work with Congress to get an international affairs bill I can sign, a bill that protects the President's authority to conduct foreign policy, maintains vital resources, and reflects a bipartisan spirit that serves America's interests. The legislation Congress is considering fails each of those tests. If it is sent to me as it now stands, I will veto it.

Statement on Senate Action on Appropriations Legislation
July 26, 1995

Yesterday's action by a Senate appropriations subcommittee removing funding for the Office of National Drug Control Policy would seriously undermine the Nation's battle against drug abuse and drug-related crime.

Removal of all funding for this office would severely curtail my ability to sustain a coordinated strategy among some 50 Federal agencies involved in drug control, including supply and demand, enforcement, interdiction, eradication, education, treatment, and prevention. Just when this coordinated effort is showing sustained success, the subcommittee is proposing we go back to the days when the Nation did not have a coordinated drug control strategy.

The Republican majority is already proposing severe cuts in antidrug programs—a 60 percent cut in safe and drug-free schools, which teaches 39 million children about the dangers of drugs; a 26 percent cut in prevention and treatment services aimed at reducing the number of potential criminals; and a 50 percent cut in international antidrug cooperation programs, a cut that could prevent the continued arrests of the world's top drug kingpins.

Members of Congress cannot tie our hands by cutting effective antidrug programs, kill the very office that coordinates our national antidrug strategy, and then expect to be taken seriously when they criticize the administration for not doing more. It's time instead for the Congress to support our antidrug initiatives.

Lee Brown, Director of the ONDCP, is doing an extraordinary job focusing the Nation's attention on the need to fight drugs at all levels. He has helped me develop a comprehensive, effective, balanced antidrug strategy and has worked to reduce duplication among those agencies who play a role in our counternarcotics efforts.

As this bill is now constructed, I will not sign it. I urge the full Appropriations Committee and the Senate to restore the funding of this office that is so critical to our battle against drugs.

Remarks on Signing Emergency Supplemental Appropriations and Rescissions Legislation and an Exchange With Reporters
July 27, 1995

Good morning. Before I sign this bill I'd like to thank the congressional leadership from both parties for sticking with this project through thick and thin. Right before we came in, one of the Senators said this is the only bill he'd ever seen that was passed 16 different times.

But I want to thank everyone who worked on this and say a special word of thanks to the Appropriations Committee members and especially to the Senate and House Appropriations Committee chairs who are here today, who burned the midnight oil to get this done.

The bill I am here to sign is proof that we can put party politics aside and do things that are good for our country. We're never going to agree on everything, and we shouldn't. That's the way our system works. But there is so much we do agree upon that if we deal with our disagreements openly and honestly, we plainly can make progress.

On balance I am very pleased with this bill. The timber provisions are not exactly what I wanted, but they are better than they were, and I believe we can and should carry out the timber salvage plans and that we can do it consistent with our forest plan and with existing environmental laws.

The budget cutting in this bill is exactly the kind of thing we should be doing. Together we are making a down payment on a balanced budget, cutting $16 billion in spending from this year's budget, cutting unnecessary spending but maintaining our commitment to education, to health care, to the environment. At the same time, the Congress has voted for funds that will help the people of California finish the work that has to be done to recover from the earthquake; that will help the people in Oklahoma City to deal with the financial aspects, at least, of the terrible tragedy they endured; that will help us to step up the fight against terrorism; and that will enable us to keep our commitment to the Middle East peace process.

This is how we should work together. We agree we should balance the budget. We disagree on how. But this shows that we can work through those disagreements. Everyone here, just about, was raised with the old saying that where there's a will there's a way. If we have the will to balance the budget, we know we can find the way because of what happened on the rescission bill.

Let me again say a word of thanks to the Members who are here. To Chairman Hatfield and Chairman Livingston and to Senator Lott and to Senator Ford, I thank you very, very much. And it's an honor and a pleasure to be able to sign this legislation that you've provided to the American people.

Thank you.

[*At this point, the President signed the bill.*]

Bosnia

Q. Mr. President, are you going to veto the Bosnia arms bill?

The President. Hasn't passed yet.

Q. Mr. President, do you think it's time for the allies to make a similar agreement with the U.N. to defend Bihac?

The President. Well, you know what we did at NATO. We agreed that since NATO and the United Nations had said that Bihac and Sarajevo should both be protected, we urged that our NATO planners begin working on the plans for that. And of course, that's what I believe the United Nations should do.

Now that we understand what has to be done to compensate the UNPROFOR forces, the United Nations must never again be caught in a position where it makes a commitment, as it did in Srebrenica, and then does not attempt to keep that commitment.

So, I certainly believe that should be done. But I was very pleased, I must say, by Secretary-General Boutros-Ghali's actions yesterday, and I hope that this indicates that the United Nations is going to keep its commitments. And the United States is certainly determined to see that it does so.

And I think the vote in the Senate should be taken as a message, simply a message to do that. The United States Senate, both the 69 people who voted for the resolution and the 29 people who voted against it, all believe that the United Nations must move aggressively to protect the people of Bosnia from what they have endured.

Q. Mr. President, because of so many hollow allied threats in the past, why should the Bosnian Serbs be scared of this latest allied threat of massive airstrikes?

The President. Well, they ought to be able to tell from what's going on here in the United States that if the U.N. fails the next time, that there will be a different course.

NOTE: The President spoke at 9:08 a.m. in the Roosevelt Room at the White House. H.R. 1944, approved July 27, was assigned Public Law No. 104–19.

Remarks in a Telephone Conversation With Mayor Ronald Norick of Oklahoma City, Oklahoma
July 27, 1995

The President. Mayor?

Mayor Norick. Yes.

The President. How are you? Good morning.

Mayor Norick. Good morning, Mr. President. How are you doing this morning?

The President. I'm doing fine. How are you managing your heat wave down there?

Mayor Norick. Well, it's typical for Oklahoma, so we don't mind it too bad. But I appreciate your call, and I especially appreciate the reason for your call.

The President. Well, as you know, I signed the rescission bill today, and because of your efforts and the efforts of many other people, the bill includes $39 million in funding to restore and revitalize the area that was affected by the bombing. And we tried to give you significant flexibility so that you could use these funds in a way that would spur economic recovery and have the biggest impact.

So I wanted to tell you that we signed it today, and we thank you for your efforts. And I hope that they'll be very helpful to you.

Mayor Norick. They will be extremely helpful. We have a—the group from NEA have been in here for the last week assisting us, and we've come up with our first plan for the area revitalization, have been meeting with a number of the business owners. They're obviously very excited about the interest that not only the White House but that HUD, that Cisneros has taken, and also the city, making sure their area is rebuilt.

Also I want to let you know that Councilman Schwartz, who has been instrumental from our end also is here with me. On the short notice, we were the only two that happened to be within a 3- or 4-minute drive time of city hall, and really do appreciate all the efforts that you've been able to make toward our city. And I know from your earlier conversations that should we need any additional help in any other areas, that that door is open. And we will not abuse that opportunity, should it arise.

The President. Well, I know that Secretary Cisneros will be in regular touch with you, and he'll also try to keep me in touch. But if you need us, let us know. And you tell Councilman Schwartz I said hello as well.

Councilman Mark Schwartz. Thank you, Mr. President.

Mayor Norick. Okay. Well, thank you, Mr. President. And I appreciate very much your call. And I especially appreciate your signature. If you've got an extra pen, send it down here. *[Laughter]*

The President. As a matter of fact, I saved one for you. I'll send it to you.

Mayor Norick. I would love to have it. It would be something that will be a real keepsake for our community, and I'm sure when we finally get the memorial done and all of that it would be a wonderful item to put in our memorial.

The President. Thank you, sir.

Mayor Norick. Thank you.

The President. Have a good day. Good-bye.

NOTE: The President spoke at 10:15 a.m. from the Oval Office at the White House. A tape was not available for verification of the content of these remarks.

Remarks Welcoming President Kim Yong-sam of South Korea
July 27, 1995

President and Mrs. Kim, members of the Korea delegation, welcome to the United States and welcome to Washington. Let me extend a special greeting to the many Korean-Americans who contribute so much to America's strength and diversity: Thank you, too, for being here today.

The Republic of Korea and the United States are joined by a history of shared sacrifice and by a future of common purpose. Today President Kim and I will pay tribute to that past and continue our work toward that future.

Mr. President, your great personal sacrifice and single-mindedness of purpose help return democracy to your country for the first time in three decades. Since your election 2½ years ago, South Korea has matched its incredible economic success with remarkable political progress. And in so many areas, from regional security to expanded trade, from peacekeeping to diplomacy, you have strengthened the partnership between our two nations.

Today I reaffirm America's pledge to stand by that partnership. Our forces will remain in Korea as long as the Korean people want them there. Ultimately, the North-South dialog and the future of the Korean Peninsula are in the hands of the Korean people. But you will always have the support of the United States.

Together we have made great progress. With Japan, we secured an agreement from North Korea to end its dangerous nuclear program. With other Northeast Asian nations we are strengthening our security alliance, so that a region too often torn apart by war knows a future of peace. We are taking historic steps to make trade and investment more free throughout the Asia-Pacific region so that all our people know a future of prosperity. South Korea is and must remain a vital leader in all these efforts, and all of this will be on our agenda today.

Today President Kim and I will also commemorate the foundation of our partnership when we dedicate the Korean War Veterans Memorial. The monument pays tribute to the Americans who fought side by side with South Koreans in defense of their land. And it stands as evidence of an unshakable alliance between our two nations, an alliance today that is stronger than ever.

Mr. President, we're glad to have you with us. Welcome back to the White House; welcome back to America.

NOTE: The President spoke at 10:46 a.m. on the South Lawn at the White House.

The President's News Conference With President Kim Yong-sam of South Korea
July 27, 1995

President Clinton. On this day, as we remember the sacrifice of those who built the great alliance between the United States and Korea, President Kim has come back to the White House to look forward. In our discussions, we focused on the clear and common goals that our nations have pursued together for decades: to strengthen our alliance, to stand together against threats to our shared ideals and interests, and to increase the safety and prosperity of our peoples. Over the past 3 years, President Kim and I have worked closely together to advance these goals. And in him I have found an ally whose courage is matched only by his commitment to freedom.

Our talks centered on the critical strategic challenges facing Korea and the United States. Forty-two years have passed since the Korean war ended, but for the people of South Korea the threat is present every day. Through all these years, America's commitment to South Korea has not wavered. And today I reaffirmed our Nation's pledge to keep American forces in Korea as long as they are needed and the Korean people want them to remain.

President Kim and I discussed the strategy our nations, along with Japan, are using to confront a new, but no less terrible, threat to his people, North Korea's dangerous nuclear program. Already, thanks to our efforts, North Korea has frozen its existing program under international inspection. Today President Kim reaffirmed his strong support for the framework and for the understanding reached in Kuala Lumpur that confirmed South Korea's central role in helping the North acquire less dangerous light-water reactors.

I also told President Kim that the United States regards North Korea's commitment to resume dialog with the South as an integral component of the framework. President Kim expressed to me his determination to enter into meaningful dialog with the North, and the United States stands ready to support his efforts.

As North Korea fulfills its nuclear commitments and addresses other concerns, it can look forward to better relations with the community of nations.

I emphasized to President Kim, however, that until South and North Korea negotiate a peace agreement, the armistice regime will remain in place.

President Kim and I also touched on a number of regional and global security issues: efforts to ensure stability in Northeast Asia, Korea's commitment to peacekeeping, and our commitment to work together on issues facing the United Nations Security Council.

Finally, we reviewed a wide range of economic issues, including APEC, and we talked about efforts to expand our bilateral trade. Korea is already our country's sixth largest export market.

One hour from now, the President and I will look to the past as we dedicate the new Korean War Veterans Memorial on The Mall. This monument is a long overdue reminder of what Americans, fighting alongside the people of South Korea, sacrificed in the defense of freedom. Today's meetings remind us that the people of South Korea have built a nation truly worthy of that sacrifice, the eleventh largest economy in the world and a thriving, vital, vibrant democracy. It is a country America is proud to claim as an equal partner and ally, a reminder that the strength of democracy and the power of a free people to pursue their own dreams are the strongest forces on Earth.

Let me now invite President Kim to make opening remarks.

President Kim. Today President Clinton and I exchanged wide-ranging views and opinions on the situation on the Korean Peninsula and in Northeast Asia and agreed to further strengthen cooperation between our two countries to preserve the peace and stability of the region.

President Clinton reaffirmed the United States firm commitment to the security of the Republic of Korea, and I supported the U.S. policy of foreign deployment, of U.S. troops to maintain peace in East Asia. President Clinton and I reconfirmed that maintaining and strengthening a firm, joint Korean-U.S. defense posture is essential to safeguarding the peace and stability not only of the Korean Peninsula but also of the Northeast Asian region.

We share the view that improvement of relations between the United States and North Korea should proceed in harmony and parallel with the improvement of relations between the Republic of Korea and North Korea. We also agreed that our two countries will cooperate closely with each other in encouraging North Korea to open its doors in order to ease tensions on the Korean Peninsula and promote peace in Northeast Asia.

With regard to this issue, I noted that the issue of establishing a permanent peace regime on the Korean Peninsula should be pursued through dialog between South and North Korea, under the principle that the issues should be resolved between the parties directly concerned. President Clinton expressed the U.S. total support and resolve to cooperate with the Republic of Korea regarding this issue.

Korean Government supports the results of the Geneva agreement and Kuala Lumpur agreement. And President Clinton and I affirmed that the Governments of our two countries, while maintaining close coordination with regard to the implementation of the U.S.-North Korean agreement, will continue to provide the support needed by the Korean Peninsula Energy Development Organization.

President Clinton and I express satisfaction over the fact that the economic and trade relations between our two countries have entered a mature phase in terms of the size of our bilateral trade, the trade balance, and bilateral investments and should continue to develop further on a well-balanced basis. At the same time, we reaffirmed that our two nations will further expand mutually beneficial bilateral cooperation under the new international economic conditions being created by the inauguration of the World Trade Organization. We also agreed that any bilateral trade issues arising out of increasing volumes of trade between two countries will be resolved smoothly through working-level consultations.

President Clinton and I concurred that our two countries need to further improve bilateral relations, both in terms of quality and quantity, so that in the forthcoming Asia-Pacific era of the 21st century, our two nations can assume leading roles in enhancing cooperation and the development of the Asia-Pacific region.

In this context, President Clinton and I agreed to coordinate closely with each other to ensure that the upcoming APEC summit conference in November of this year in Osaka will be a success. Furthermore, we agreed that our two countries will bolster multipronged collaboration in the United Nations and other international organizations.

We are fully satisfied with the results of our talk, which we believe will provide added momentum to the efforts to develop the five-decade-old Korean-U.S. relations forged in blood further into a future-oriented partnership between allies for the next half a century.

I would like to express my appreciation once again to President Clinton and the U.S. Government for their warm hospitality and kindness extended to me and my delegation.

Thank you.

President Clinton. Thank you.

Bosnia

Q. Mr. President, your administration said that if the Congress voted to lift the arms embargo on Bosnia that that would almost guarantee that U.S. ground troops would have to be sent in. The Senate voted that way yesterday by a margin that suggests you couldn't sustain a veto. The House looks like it's going down the same road. How close are we now to having to send U.S. ground troops in? And do you feel this is a vote of no confidence in your foreign policy?

President Clinton. I think it's a vote of no confidence in the fact that the United Nations did not move to do anything when Srebrenica fell after Srebrenica had been declared a safe area and the fact that the war seems to be dragging on without resolution. But I also wouldn't be so sure we couldn't sustain a veto. I think that depends entirely on the vigor and the strength of the response of the U.N. forces in Bosnia and their NATO allies.

And we are working hard in that regard. I have been very encouraged by what Secretary-General Boutros-Ghali said yesterday, and I have been very impressed by the determination of President Chirac and Prime Minister Major to set up this rapid reaction force and to fight back if attacked, not simply to be taken hostage.

So we're going to see what will happen in the days ahead. But I wouldn't be so presumptive about what would happen in the Congress. I noted that the French Prime Minister, Mr. Juppe, said not very long ago that if—just a few hours ago—that if, in fact, the Congress took this action and it became U.S. policy, that

they would withdraw from Bosnia and that would require us to send our troops in to help them get out, which is exactly what I said. And if we do it alone, if we unilaterally lift the arms embargo, that means that the rest of the world will consider that we are responsible for what happens from then on, solely. And I think that we need to consider that.

Mr. President.

North Korea

Q. Looking back to the attitude of North Korea in the past, despite the fact that the Kuala Lumpur agreement is there for us, still we can expect more difficulties coming from the North Korean behavior in the future. Have the two Presidents, through the meeting this time in Washington, had a chance to discuss how to secure Korea's central role in the process of dealing with North Korea?

President Kim. Yes. In fact, we had a chance to mention this issue in my statement of the press conference today, and also yesterday in my congressional speech, I mentioned this issue as well. We entirely support the result of the Kuala Lumpur agreement. Concerning the question, our position is that between the United States and Republic of Korea, we have had very full and complete agreement on our joint position towards North Korea, and we are in full and thorough accordance with each other and how to deal with North Korea.

I think that if we do our best in trying to persuade North Korea that it is in their interest to faithfully implement the contents of the agreement, I think that, in fact, we can see a good result. And I firmly believe that we can achieve that goal.

Together with that agreement, I think the fact that the KEDO had its executive meeting, which has confirmed Korea's central role in the nuclear light-water project, in addition to President Clinton's letter given to me, which was a letter of assurance that Korea's central role will be guaranteed, I think, enough for us to believe that we would not be faced with major problems in the future negotiations. So in our position, there is no change at all.

Bosnia

Q. Mr. President, there is a perception that U.S. leadership, prestige, has really suffered under this devastating debacle of Bosnia. You wanted to bomb—more than 2½ years ago—

heavy bombing to stop—that peacekeeping per se, despite the humanitarian side, is a misnomer. What do you think are the lessons of Bosnia? And do you think that the U.S. leadership has gone down the drain?

President Clinton. No. Keep in mind, when I became President, a decision had been made—a decision, by the way, that I couldn't criticize—that in the aftermath of the cold war, the Europeans should take the lead in dealing with the first major security crisis on the European Continent at the end of the cold war and that they would do that under the umbrella of the United Nations, that our role would be to support that with airlifts of humanitarian goods and then later with enforcing a no-fly zone and then later with enforcing the peace agreements that the United Nations had made through the use of air power. That happened when I was President.

And we also would support this effort to some extent from the sea as well and through enforcing the embargo and through putting our troops in the Former Yugoslav Republic of Macedonia. That was the agreement.

And I still believe that, on balance, it was working better than the other alternatives, considering there was no peace to keep a lot. The death rate went down breathtakingly from 1992 to 1994, and there was a long period of time there where we had a chance to make a peace.

Then what happened—and as you know, I believe that a multilateral lift of the arms embargo early on would have helped us to make a quicker peace. I still believe that that would have happened. What happened was, along toward the end of last year—well, there was an agreement for a cease-fire. Then it expired. Since it expired, the Bosnian Serbs concluded that the United Nations would not keep its commitments to the safe areas if it took peacekeepers as hostages and that under the rules of engagement in which the peacekeepers were there, and given their fairly lightly armed nature, they could be easily taken as hostages. Now, that happened.

That, I think, when that happened and the threat of hostage-taking and the effect of hostage-taking caused Srebrenica to fall without a terrific response in terms of air punishment, that collapsed the support for the United Nations. And all of us, including the United States and NATO, who had supported it suffered in prestige, if you will, not because we didn't win but

because the U.N. didn't do what it said it was going to do. You can't go about the world saying you're going to do something and then not do it.

So I—that's why I spent all that time, leading up to the London conference and, since then, working with NATO to say, look, we have to reestablish the fact that we will have a strong—not just close air support but a strong air response to raise the price of Serbian aggression. Secondly, I strongly support the decision of the French and the British to establish this Rapid Reaction Force so that they just can't be taking hostages at will.

But I would remind you that this was—the question of whether a lot of people still say, "Well, America ought to fix it." But we don't have troops on the ground now. And this distribution of responsibility all grew out of a decision made prior to my Presidency—which I am not criticizing, I say again—to try to say that, okay, here's a problem in Europe, the Europeans ought to take the lead, they would put people on the ground. We have had troops since I have been President, I would remind you, in Somalia, in Rwanda, in Haiti. We have not been loath to do our job. But we have tried to support the base commitment of the Europeans there. And it has not worked. No one can say it has worked.

So I decided we're either going to do what we said we were going to do with the U.N. or we'll have to do something else. This is the last chance for UNPROFOR to survive. But I do believe if it can be made to work, it has a greater chance of securing a peace and minimizing death of the Bosnians. That's what I believe. And I also believe it would be a very great thing for Europe if the Europeans can take the lead in resolving the first post-cold-war security crisis on the European Continent.

Inter-Korean Summit

Q. When does the Korean President expect to hold inter-Korean summit meeting? And to Mr. Clinton, what is your—[*inaudible*]—plan to hold the South and North Korean summit?

President Kim. Actually, this is not an appropriate stage to discuss this issue because in North Korea there isn't still an official leadership of succession. Of course, we know that there isn't any other alternative to the leadership than Kim Jong Il. However, we don't know when this inter-Korean summit meeting can take place, and I think it is not desirable for use to discuss this issue now. I really didn't have the opportunity to discuss this one in depth with President Clinton specifically on the possibility of an inter-Korean summit meeting.

President Clinton. But, sir, I think the important point for me to make, on behalf of the United States, to the people of Korea is that it is still our position that the armistice will remain in effect until the Korean people themselves reach an agreement for a permanent peace. And in that, our position is 100 percent behind the position taken by the President and the Government of South Korea.

Yes. Go ahead, Brit [Brit Hume, ABC News].

United Nations Peacekeeping

Q. Mr. President, has this difficult experience that the United States has had in getting the U.N. to do, as you put it, what it has said it would do, shaken your confidence in the U.N. as an institution through which the United States and with which the United States can work toward its various foreign policy aims?

President Clinton. No. But I think what it has done—let me—I would say there should be two lessons that we draw out of this as Americans. Number one, the United Nations cannot go to a place with a limited peacekeeping mission if there is no peace to keep, without considering what it's going to do if it can't fulfill its original mission. That's really been the fundamental problem here. The rules of engagement for the forces there have made them very vulnerable to be taken hostages and, therefore, to become the instrument in the last few months of Serbian aggression, Bosnian-Serbian aggression.

The second lesson I would ask the American people, all of us, to think about is, that if we determine that in various parts of the world at the end of the cold war it is appropriate for other countries to take the lead, and they have troops on the ground and people at immediate risk and we don't, then we have to be willing to accept the fact that we may not be able to dictate the ultimate outcome of the situation.

The difficulty for the United States is this: We are still the world's only superpower; people want us to fix things or at least say we're absolutely not involved in them. And here's a case where we decided to let someone else take the lead in a, to be fair to them, very difficult problem, but to be involved in a supporting role. And that, to some extent, has put our own prestige, the prestige of NATO, and the prestige of the United Nations all at risk. And because we don't have the large segment of troops on the ground, our ability to dictate the course of events has been more limited.

Now, having said all that, keep in mind, we are trying to work our way through, in this post-cold-war era, sort of an uncharted field in which the United States can lead the world, can be, in effect, the repository of last resort, of responsible power, but still give others the chance and responsibility to take the lead where they can.

So I think we have learned the hazards of that policy. And I think that the kinds of problems we have had here have led us to learn things that we won't repeat. But I would caution the American people that that does not mean they should give up on the U.N. The U.N. is doing dozens of things today that you will not be able to show on the news tonight, Brit, for the precise reason that they are working and they won't rise on the radar screen.

So it's important that we not throw out the baby with the bathwater here. We need to learn what went wrong in Bosnia, why it didn't work, what the limits of our partnership are. But we shouldn't give up on the United Nations, because it still has great capacity to do important things.

Thank you very much.

NOTE: The President's 100th news conference began at 1:12 p.m. in Room 450 of the Old Executive Office Building. President Kim spoke in Korean, and his remarks were translated by an interpreter.

Remarks at the Dedication Ceremony for the Korean War Veterans Memorial
July 27, 1995

Thank you. Thank you very much, President Kim, for your fine remarks on behalf of all the people of Korea and for your leadership and for your defense of democracy in your country, proving that these sacrifices of the Americans and others were not in vain.

Thank you to all the distinguished guests who are here. I'd like to say also a special word of thanks for those who are responsible for this memorial, for those who designed and built it and conceived it, and those who operate it. It is a magnificent reminder of what is best about the United States, and I thank you all for your contribution.

I also believe that everyone in this crowd, indeed everyone in this country, owes a special debt of gratitude to General Davis and to his predecessor, General Stilwell, for their 8-year dream to make this day a reality. General Davis served our country with great distinction in World War II and went on to win the Congressional Medal of Honor in Korea. But he had 8 more long years of combat to make this day happen. And all of us who are here owe it to him to say thank you for all of that service.

Today, we are surrounded by monuments to some of the greatest figures in our history while we gather at this, our newest national memorial, to remember and honor the Americans who fought for freedom in Korea. In 1950, our Nation was weary of war, but 1.5 million Americans left their family and friends and their homes to help to defend freedom for a determined ally halfway around the world or, as the monument says, a place they had never been and a people they had never met.

Together with men and women from 20 other nations, all of whom are represented here today, they joined the first mission of the United Nations to preserve peace by fighting shoulder to shoulder with the brave people of South Korea to defend their independence, to safeguard other Asian nations from attack, and to protect the freedom that remains our greatest gift.

The Korean war veterans endured terrible hardships—deathly cold, weeks and months crammed in foxholes and bunkers, an enemy of overwhelming numbers, the threat of brutal imprisonment and torture—defending the perimeter at Pusan, braving the tides at Inchon, confronting the world's fastest fighter jets in Mig Alley, enduring hand-to-hand combat on Heartbreak Ridge and Pork Chop Hill, fighting the way back from Chosin Reservoir. They set a standard of courage that may be equaled but will never be surpassed in the annals of American combat.

If I might recount the deeds of just two men, so as to bring to life today, so many years later, the dimensions of this conflict. One from my home State, 26-year-old Lloyd Burke was trying to lead his company to high ground outside of Seoul. Pinned down by enemy fire, he wiped out three enemy bunkers in a lone assault. Handgrenades were thrown at him, so he caught them and threw them back. Later, he knocked out two enemy mortars and a machine gun position. Despite being wounded, he led his men in a final charge and took the hill. For his extraordinary courage and leadership, Lloyd Burke was awarded the Congressional Medal of Honor.

Corporal Ronald Rosser was a forward observer in the hills near Pangil-ri when his platoon came under fire from two directions. With just a carbine and a grenade, he charged the enemy position and knocked out two bunkers and cleared a trench. Twice he ran out of ammunition and twice he crossed through enemy fire to resume his attack. Later, even though he was wounded, Ronald Rosser repeatedly dodged enemy fire to bring other injured soldiers to safety. And for his exceptional bravery, he, too, was awarded the Medal of Honor.

These two great Americans, Lloyd Burke and Ronald Rosser, are with us here today. I ask them to stand and be recognized on behalf of all the veterans of the Korean war.

In this impressive monument, we can see the figures and faces that recall their heroism. In steel and granite, in water and earth, the creators of this memorial have brought to life the courage and sacrifice of those who served in all branches of the Armed Forces from every racial and ethnic group and background in America. They represent, once more, the enduring American truth: From many we are one.

Tens of thousands of Americans died in Korea. Our South Korean allies lost hundreds of thousands of soldiers and civilians. Our other U.N. allies suffered grievous casualties. Thousands of Americans who were lost in Korea to this day have never been accounted for. Today, I urge the leaders of North Korea to work with us to resolve those cases.

President Kim and I are working together to open the door to better relations between our nations and North Korea. Clarifying these MIA cases is an important step. We have not forgotten our debt to them or to their families, and we will never stop working for the day when they can be brought home.

This memorial also commemorates those who made the ultimate sacrifice so that we might live free. And I ask you on this hot, summer day to pause for a moment of silence in honor of those from the United States, our U.N. allies, and from our friends in the Republic of Korea who lost their lives in the Korean war.

[At this point, a moment of silence was observed.]

Amen.

On this day, 42 years ago, President Dwight Eisenhower called the end of hostilities an armistice on a single battleground, not peace in the world. It's fair to say that when the guns fell silent then, no one knew for sure what our forces in Korea had done for the future of our Nation or the future of world freedom. The larger conflict of the cold war had only begun. It would take four decades more to win.

In a struggle so long and consuming, perhaps it's not surprising that too many lost sight of the importance of Korea. But now we know with the benefit of history that those of you who served and the families who stood behind you laid the foundations for one of the greatest triumphs in the history of human freedom. By sending a clear message that America had not defeated fascism to see communism prevail, you put the free world on the road to victory in the cold war. That is your enduring contribution. And all free people everywhere should recognize it today.

And look what you achieved in Korea. Today, Korea is thriving and prosperous. From the unbelievable poverty and ruin at the aftermath of the war, this brave, industrious, strong country has risen to become the 11th largest economy in the entire world, with a strong democratic leader in President Kim. In Asia, peace and stability are more firmly rooted than at any time since World War II. And all around the world, freedom and democracy are now on the march.

So to all the veterans here today, and to all throughout our land who are watching, let us all say, when darkness threatened, you kept the torch of liberty alight. You kept the flame burning so that others all across the world could share it. You showed the truth inscribed on the wall: that freedom is not free.

We honor you today because you did answer the call to defend a country you never knew and a people you never met. They are good people. It's a good country. And the world is better because of you.

God bless you, and God bless America.

NOTE: The President spoke at approximately 3:20 p.m. on The Mall. In his remarks, he referred to Gen. Raymond G. Davis, USMC (Ret.), chairman, and Gen. Richard G. Stilwell, USA (Ret.), former chairman, Korean War Veterans Memorial Advisory Board.

Statement on Senate Action on the Reauthorization of the Ryan White CARE Act
July 27, 1995

I am very pleased to see the Senate moving ahead in a strong bipartisan manner on approval of the reauthorization of the Ryan White CARE Act. This vital program provides primary care to hundreds of thousands of Americans living with HIV and AIDS. As I said in a letter to Majority Leader Dole and Speaker Gingrich, it is imperative that we move quickly to approve this important legislation. Senator Kassebaum deserves high praise for her important leadership on this issue and, in particular, her work to protect the lives of newborn infants from HIV.

Message to the Congress Reporting on Terrorists Who Threaten the Middle East Peace Process
July 27, 1995

To the Congress of the United States:

I hereby report to the Congress on the developments concerning the national emergency with respect to organizations that threaten to disrupt the Middle East peace process that was declared in Executive Order No. 12947 of January 23, 1995. This report is submitted pursuant to section 401(c) of the National Emergencies Act, 50 U.S.C. 1641(c); section 204(c) of the International Emergency Economic Powers Act (IEEPA), 50 U.S.C. 1703(c); and section 505(c) of the International Security and Development Cooperation Act of 1985, 22 U.S.C. 2349aa–9(c).

1. On January 23, 1995, I signed Executive Order No. 12947, "Prohibiting Transactions with Terrorists Who Threaten to Disrupt the Middle East Process" (the "order") (60 *Fed. Reg.* 5079, January 25, 1995). The order blocks all property subject to U.S. jurisdiction in which there is any interest of 12 terrorist organizations that threaten the Middle East peace process as identified in an Annex to the order. The order also blocks the property and interests in property subject to U.S. jurisdiction of persons designated by the Secretary of State, in coordination with the Secretary of the Treasury and the Attorney General, who are found (1) to have committed, or to pose a significant risk of committing, acts of violence that have the purpose or effect of disrupting the Middle East peace process, or (2) to assist in, sponsor, or provide financial, material, or technological support for, or services in support of, such acts of violence. In addition, the order blocks all property and interests in property subject to U.S. jurisdiction in which there is any interest of persons determined by the Secretary of the Treasury, in coordination with the Secretary of State and the Attorney General, to be owned or controlled by, or to act for or on behalf of, any other person des-

ignated pursuant to the order (collectively "Specially Designated Terrorists" or "SDTs").

The order further prohibits any transaction or dealing by a United States person or within the United States in property or interests in property of SDTs, including the making or receiving of any contribution of funds, goods, or services to or for the benefit of such persons. This prohibition includes donations that are intended to relieve human suffering.

Designations of persons blocked pursuant to the order are effective upon the date of determination by the Secretary of State or his delegate, or the Director of the Office of Foreign Assets Control (FAC) acting under authority delegated by the Secretary of the Treasury. Public notice of blocking is effective upon the date of filing with the *Federal Register*, or upon prior actual notice.

2. On January 25, 1995, FAC issued a notice listing persons blocked pursuant to Executive Order No. 12947 who have been designated by the President as terrorist organizations threatening the Middle East peace process or who have been found to be owned or controlled by, or to be acting for or on behalf of, these terrorist organizations (60 *Fed. Reg.* 5084, January 25, 1995). The notice identifies 31 entities that act for or on behalf of the 12 Middle East terrorist organizations listed in the Annex to Executive Order No. 12947, as well as 18 individuals who are leaders or representatives of these groups. In addition the notice provides 9 name variations or pseudonyms used by the 18 individuals identified. The FAC, in coordination with the Secretary of State and the Attorney General, will continue to expand the list of terrorist organizations as additional information is developed. A copy of the notice is attached to this report.

3. The expenses incurred by the Federal Government in the 6-month period from January 23 through July 21, 1995, that are directly attrib-

utable to the exercise of powers and authorities conferred by the declaration of the national emergency with respect to organizations that disrupt the Middle East peace process are estimated at approximately $55,000. Personnel costs were largely centered in the Department of the Treasury (particularly in the Office of Foreign Assets Control, the Office of the General Counsel, and the U.S. Customs Service), the Department of State, and the Department of Justice.

4. Executive Order No. 12947 provides this Administration with a new tool for combatting fundraising in this country on behalf of organizations that use terror to undermine the Middle East peace process. The order makes it harder for such groups to finance these criminal activities by cutting off their access to sources of support in the United States and to U.S. financial facilities. It is also intended to reach charitable contributions to designated organizations to preclude diversion of such donations to terrorist activities.

In addition, I have sent to the Congress new comprehensive counterterrorism legislation that would strengthen our ability to prevent terrorist acts, identify those who carry them out, and bring them to justice. The combination of Executive Order No. 12947 and the proposed legislation demonstrate the United States' determination to confront and combat those who would seek to destroy the Middle East peace process, and our commitment to the global fight against terrorism.

I shall continue to exercise the powers at my disposal to apply economic sanctions against extremists seeking to destroy the hopes of peaceful coexistence between Arabs and Israelis as long as these measures are appropriate, and will continue to report periodically to the Congress on significant developments pursuant to 50 U.S.C. 1703(c).

WILLIAM J. CLINTON

The White House,
July 27, 1995.

Remarks at a State Dinner for President Kim Yong-sam of South Korea
July 27, 1995

Let me welcome President and Mrs. Kim, the members of the delegation from the Republic of Korea. To all of our distinguished guests, Hillary and I are delighted to have you here in the White House. I have especially enjoyed this day that I have spent with President Kim, a man whose extraordinary resilience is matched only by his commitment to democracy.

Mr. President, this is our fourth meeting. And if you'll permit me just a personal note, I am struck by how much we have in common. We were both elected to office at an early age. You won a seat in your National Assembly when you were just 25. You entered the Blue House just a month after I came to the White House. Or to put it in another way, we have both spent the past 20,000 hours or so dealing with our respective Congresses and fielding hard questions from the press. [*Laughter*] I'm happy to say that President Kim is also an enthusiastic jogger who permitted me to jog with him in Korea. And even in this heat, Mr. President,

after this meal, we may have to run an extra mile together tomorrow. [*Laughter*]

Mr. President, for all the things we have in common, I must also comment on something that sets you apart from most other leaders in the world today, and that is the extraordinary hardship you endured and the courage you displayed to bring democracy to your country. Your many years in opposition were marked by jail terms, years of house arrest, an assassination attempt, and a 23-day hunger strike that almost took your life. As you once put it, a short life of integrity is better than a long life in disgrace.

But you persisted, and you prevailed. At your inauguration you said, "Deep in my heart I have a vision of a new Korea, a freer and more mature democracy. At last we have established a government by the people and of the people of this land." Now under your leadership, Korea is taking its rightful place in the world as both a thriving economy and a dynamic democracy.

Mr. President, the bonds between our people, forged in the fires of war upon your land, have only grown stronger with time. We are united now by a history of shared sacrifice and a future of common purpose. These are our common goals: lasting peace, security, and reconciliation on the Korean Peninsula; a stable and prosperous Asia-Pacific region; a rising tide of democracy around the world. Working together, the Republic of Korea and the United States can help to achieve them.

Mr. President, when I visited you 2 years ago, you presented me with a beautiful work of calligraphy with your favorite saying: *Taedo Mumun*, Righteousness overcomes all obstacles. Mr. President, tonight, in the presence of so many people from your country, so many Korean-Americans, your wonderful wife, and your two daughters who live in our country, I ask everyone in this room to raise a glass to a man who, through his own righteousness, has overcome all obstacles: Kim Yong-sam. To you, Mr. President, and to the enduring friendship between our two great nations.

NOTE: The President spoke at 8:30 p.m. in the State Dining Room at the White House. In his remarks, he referred to President Kim's wife, Kim Myoung Soon, and his daughters, Lee Hye Young and Song Hye Kyung.

Remarks to the Presidential Advisory Council on HIV/AIDS and an Exchange With Reporters
July 28, 1995

The President. Good morning, and welcome. I'd like to begin by thanking Patsy Fleming for the work that she's done with me and with you and for our country on this issue and by thanking all of you for your service on this advisory council. We need your advice, your wisdom, your enthusiasm, your energy, and America needs your service. And I thank you for it very much.

As you know, I have been strongly committed to an increasing Federal response to the AIDS crisis. In spite of the fact that we have cut and eliminated hundreds and hundreds of programs since I have been President, we've increased overall AIDS funding by 40 percent and funding for the Ryan White CARE Act by over 80 percent since I've been President.

I was very, very pleased to see yesterday how overwhelmingly the Senate voted to reauthorize the Ryan White CARE Act. I've got a budget before them which would increase our funding considerably more. I hope that will pass. But the United States Senate made an important statement yesterday, almost unanimously. And I think we should all appreciate that and be grateful for it.

This terrible plague has cost our country 270,000 American lives and over 100 every day. There are some encouraging signs on the research front, as all of you know. Scientists have discovered ways to block the transmission of HIV from mothers to children. New classes of drugs are being developed to actually repair damaged immune systems, which is very, very hopeful. These scientific advances give us all reason to hope and should redouble our determination, even in this season of balanced budgeting, to reinvest even more and more of our Nation's wealth into medical research in AIDS and medical research of all kinds.

This is not the time to slow down or retreat. It is not the time to give in. AIDS is a challenge that all of us face. That's what the United States Senate said yesterday. It really is a part of our common ground. I think we can attack this disease without attacking each other. And apparently, sensible, good, farsighted Americans in both parties agree.

When we begin to pit one disease against another, or one group of people against another in this country, we all wind up behind. And I felt much better about the future of our country, at least on this point, when I saw how the United States Senate conducted itself yesterday. Now, our task is to continue to marshal all the forces we've got to lift the visibility of this issue.

When I spoke about this matter in my speech at Georgetown just a few weeks ago, I said that this was one area where we had to find common ground. This morning, I think we got a chance to do it. And with your help, we'll continue to make progress on it.

Thank you very much.

Bosnia

Q. Is the United States orchestrating the transfer of arms to the Bosnian Muslims through Arab or Middle Eastern countries or anywhere else?

The President. No.

The Economy

Q. Mr. President, have you managed to achieve the economic soft landing?

The President. Well, I think the economy is coming back up, if that's what you mean. We had a slow second quarter, we knew we did. But the general thrust of the economy looks strong again. The fundamental problem is now that we had a slow second quarter—if you're going to have a long, long period of growth, you're going to have uneven periods within that.

The fundamental problem is, we've created 7 million jobs, and most Americans haven't got-

ten a raise. Most Americans still feel economically insecure in their own circumstances because their incomes haven't gone up, because they don't think their jobs are secure, because they're worried about their family's health care. And we need an agenda in this country that I have been pushing for 2 years now that not only creates jobs but also raises incomes and increases the security of families.

That is the fundamental problem. But it starts with having a good economic policy. So we wouldn't even be where we are if we didn't have the 7 million jobs and a lower unemployment rate with low inflation. So I'm proud of what we've accomplished. But it's only half the job.

Thank you.

NOTE: The President spoke at 11:26 a.m. in the Roosevelt Room at the White House. In his remarks, he referred to Patricia S. Fleming, Director of National AIDS Policy.

Remarks to the American Federation of Teachers
July 28, 1995

I must say I enjoyed the class being a little rowdy this afternoon. [*Laughter*] I thank you for your welcome. I thank you for your support. Most important of all, I thank you for the work you do every day. Thank you, Al Shanker, for the introduction and for being here and for being a consistent and clear voice for opportunity and excellence in education. Thank you, Ed McElroy; thank you, Sandy Feldman; thanks to all of my friends in the AFT. And thank you for bringing these children up on the stage today to remind us what this is all about.

You know, if you go in any classroom in America you see the infinite promise of our country in a beautiful essay or a difficult math problem solved or just an act of kindness from one child to another. And you come face to face with the terrible challenges confronting this country, in children who are old beyond their years because of what they've had to endure, too tired or hurt or closed off from each other and the world to learn.

You also know that what happens to your students in the classroom depends a lot on what happens to them before they get there and after they leave. And I must say in that connection, I've often thought it ironic that some of the people that bewail the loss of family values in our country are all too eager to criticize teachers for the problems in our schools, when the truth is that oftentimes the school is the only coherent, consistent direction, family-oriented, value time that a lot of our kids get.

It is true that this administration has worked hard to be a friend to education. Secretary Riley, Deputy Secretary Kunin, and all the fine people at the Department of Education I think have done an excellent job in working with you and in broadening their reach; working with Secretary Reich and the people in the Labor Department; working with the private sector all over the country, trying to build a grassroots consensus for what is best about education in our country, trying to build this country up instead of using education as yet one more issue to divide the American people and to distract us from our real problems.

Today I want to talk to you really seriously about what happens to the kids in this country, mostly before and after school in the context of this big family values debate we're having again this year. I don't regret the fact that we're having it, and I believe the debate has been too polarized between the opposite sides that I believe have a lot to say to each other. And if you want any evidence of that, read your own bill of rights and responsibilities. I just got a great copy of it. It's two sides of the debate raging today about family values.

There are those who see family problems and children's problems as primarily matters of personal and social morality. And they believe that all the Government has to do is to encourage good behavior like praying in school or sexual abstinence, or to punish bad behavior like criminal conduct or the unwillingness to move from welfare to work, even when a job's available.

Then there are others who see family problems primarily as a result of the unbelievable economic and social difficulties facing Americans today. And they believe the role of Government is to develop policies that help all of us make the most of our own abilities and to reward people who are working hard and playing by the rules.

But on a lot of issues, these two sides really aren't as far apart as they may seem. Again, I say, read your own bill of rights and responsibilities and you see both sides of that argument coming at you.

A moral problem can quickly become an economic problem. The epidemic rates of teen pregnancy in our country, for example, mean that an awful lot of kids who are born into poverty and never escape it, and an awful lot of parents who don't escape it because they don't have education and child care. On the other hand, an economic problem can rapidly become a moral problem.

Parents, on the whole, are working harder today than they were 25 years ago—literally, more hours at work for about the same or lower wages than they were making 15 years ago. That means you don't have much time for your kids, to teach them the things that they can only learn from their families. So economic problems can spill over into the family area as well and have a moral dimension. So I argue to you that what we really need is an American family val-

ues agenda, kind of like the bill of rights and responsibilities you've articulated for the schools, that basically takes the best of both of these approaches and, more importantly, lifts this debate up, gets it beyond partisan strategies to divide the American people for short-term gain, because too often these issues are raised in that way. If we really want family values, we've really got to value families.

Think about the bewildering array of problems faced by families today. Young couples, both of them working, they have a child, they desperately want one of the parents to stay home for a few weeks with the child—good solid family values. Will they lose one of the jobs if that happens?

You've got people who look out their windows at playgrounds and wonder if they can let their children play on them because they'll be violating family values if their kids aren't safe. You have fathers cooking dinners for children right before they go to work all night. And then they have to sleep all day while mother goes to work. So it never quite gets worked out that both the family parents get to work with the children the way they wish. This happens all the time.

I never will forget, I used to—every election in Arkansas when I was Governor, I used to make the earliest factory gate in my State—the Campbell's Soup plant in Fayetteville, Arkansas. People started going to work at 4:30 in the morning. And I figured that I'd get some votes just for being fool enough for showing up at 4:30. [*Laughter*] And sure enough, I did. [*Laughter*] I never will forget, one day—and I'd go there, stay there from 4:30 to 5:30, and shake hands with everybody that showed up. I never will forget it—at a quarter to 5 one day, a pickup pulled up and the door opens, the light came on inside the pickup, and there was a fine-looking young man and his fine-looking young wife and three little babies sitting between them in the pickup. And she had to be at work, punched in, at 5 every morning. Then he had to be at work at 7. And they had to figure out somebody that had day care by a quarter to 7 in the morning so that he could drop those kids off and get there.

Now, we talk about family values—that is the typical experience—it's earlier in the morning, but most families in this country are working their fingers to the bone doing the best they can up against very difficult odds. And we need to talk about this in terms of the real experience of real people.

There are a whole lot of families that are spending their money trying to take care of their elderly parents and keep them out of nursing homes, and so they don't think they'll be able to send their kids to college. That also stretches family values.

There are a lot of children who are losing hope. And a recent study was published on rising rates of casual drug use among young people, pointing out that the ones who tend to get into drugs early are young people who have either no strong religious values or no real hope for their own personal future or no strong relationship with their own parents.

So there really are serious issues here, but we need to see it in the real world. How many teachers do we know who have students of exceptional promise that they're afraid will never live up to the promise because of the economic handicaps on the family of the student.

So I say this to make the following point: Families do not eat and breathe and sleep political slogans; they do not. Most families couldn't tell you for the life of them whether I'm up or down in the polls this week, and they couldn't care less. They just know whether they're up or down in their real life struggle this week. And that's what we ought to think about.

If you add all these family stories together, you see that America is kind of a good news-bad news story. This is remarkable—in the last 2½ years—when I came here and I campaigned to you for President, I said, if you vote for me, I will do my best to revive the middle class in this country, to give poor people a chance to get into the middle class, and to pave the way for a brighter future for all of our people. I will emphasize creating more opportunity, I will insist on more responsibility to the American people, and I'll try to bring the people together without regard to race or region or religion or other things that divide us.

And in the last 2½ years, we've put into effect an aggressive economic program, an aggressive education program, an aggressive trade program, an aggressive anticrime program. We have today 7 million more jobs, a lower unemployment rate, a lower inflation rate. The crime rate is down in virtually every major urban area of the country. We are moving on our problems. But with a record business profits, a record stock market, a record number of new businesses, a record

number of new millionaires, most Americans are working harder for the same amount of money they were making 2½ years ago, feeling somewhat more insecure on the job, a little bit uncertain about their retirement and their family's health care, and worried sick they won't be able to educate their kids.

How did this happen? We're moving into a global economy, an information society. A smaller percentage of the work force are protected by organizations like yours. And there is more uncertainty out there. So I believe we do need to ask ourselves, if we believe that the stability of our society and the strength of our country and the future of our children depend upon our families, then what are our family values? And how are we going to reward good family conduct? How are we going to stabilize life for families who are willing to do the right thing? How are we going to attack the real problems? How are we going to avoid this kind of phony debate?

And I'll just give you a short agenda here. I'm going to give you a test on this at the end of this. [*Laughter*] Here are 14 things we could do to help families. Brief.

One, help people care for their elderly parents and, for sure, don't make it harder. Two, reform the health insurance system so that at least people don't lost their health insurance if they change jobs or if somebody's sick in their family. Three, keep the family and medical leave law and make sure everybody in America knows what it is and knows how to take advantage of it.

Four, have tougher national standards for child support enforcement. Five, figure out who's been successful in preventing teen pregnancy and organize a national campaign to do the same thing in every community in the country. Six, build on what works to prevent drug abuse and drug use, and do it. Don't just talk about—invest money, time, and effort in consistent commitment to drug abuse prevention.

Seven, if you want to cut health care costs and increase life expectancy, do something to stop all these kids who are beginning to smoke at early ages. It's killing them. Eight, expose our children to less violence by enforcing the Brady law and keeping the ban on assault weapons and passing the ban on cop-killer bullets.

Nine, if you're concerned about violence and children and the role the media is contributing to it, instead of giving a speech about it, do something about it. When Congress passes a telecommunications law that's going to make a bunch of money for a bunch of people, and it will be all right if it creates a lot of jobs and helps us get more information, tell them to put in the law the simple provision to give everybody that's got a cable hookup a V-chip so that the parents can decide what comes across to the television to the kids. And by the way, don't get rid of public broadcasting. At least parents have an alternative.

Ten, do something about family incomes for people who are doing the right thing. Raise the minimum wage to $5.00 an hour. Eleven, if you want to give a tax cut, give a family-oriented tax cut to help people raise their children and educate their children. That's the kind of tax cut we ought to have in this country.

Twelve, remember that adults need education, too. And take all these Government programs that were enacted with the best of intentions over a long period of time and consolidate them, and instead, when somebody loses their job or they're working for a minimum wage and they want to get a new training program, send them a check to take to the local community college so they can get a decent education that will lead them to a job.

Thirteen—don't get nervous, I'm saving you for last. [*Laughter*] Thirteen, every list of civic values ever given to kids in school that I have ever seen says, teach young people respect for themselves, respect for other people, respect for our country, and respect for our natural environment. Thirteen, do no harm—stop this crazy effort to dismantle all the environmental and public health protection in the United States Congress today.

Fourteen, education: Don't cut it. Don't cut Head Start. Don't take a million kids out of Chapter 1. Don't get rid of Goals 2000, which gives teachers the chance to really do something significant. Do not increase the cost of a college loan; that is the dumbest thing I ever heard of in my life. It is not necessary to cut education to balance the budget. It is only necessary to cut education to balance the budget if you're determined to do it in 7 years instead of 10, with a tax cut nobody can justify with a deficit this high and an education deficit at the same time. Put the money into education and into our future. The wealthiest Americans support this approach; they know it's the right thing to do.

So I want to amplify on a couple of these, not all 14, but I want to say them again. Help people care for their elderly parents. Reform the health insurance system so fathers and mothers don't lose the health insurance for themselves and their kids if somebody in the family has been sick or they change jobs. Keep the enforcement of the family and medical leave law; don't support the Congress taking out all the funds for enforcement. More people need to know about it, not fewer. Not a single business has gone broke since we protected family and medical leave in 1993.

Tougher child support enforcement; prevent teen pregnancy; reduce drug abuse among young people; prevent teens from starting smoking; handgun and assault weapons, keep those bills in there on the Brady bill and the assault weapons bill, and pass the cop-killer bullet ban; raise the minimum wage; have a reform of the family tax system so we give the tax breaks to people raising their kids and educating them; put the V-chip in the cable TV if you want to do something about culture and violence; pass the "GI bill" for America's workers, give people who are unemployed a check, not a list of 70 programs they'll find at the local community college; protect the environment; and do not cut education. Now, that is an agenda that we can live with—I think I left out the minimum wage, but I won't forget it when we get to the budget.

Now, let me tell you, Sunday—Saturday or Sunday, sometime over the weekend, will be the exact day of the 30th anniversary of Medicare. We need to reform Medicare. We can't have medical costs going up at 2 and 3 and 4 times the rate of inflation. But let's not forget, before Medicare, fewer than half the elderly people in this country had any health insurance, and 97 percent of them do.

And if any of you have been through what I have—and I imagine most of your have been. If you had, as I had, your mother and your father-in-law desperately ill for long periods of time, you think, my goodness, what would we do without Medicare? And I realize how much better off I am than most Americans, and it would have bankrupted me. What would most Americans do? What would the elderly do?

So can we slow the rate of increase? Sure we can. But to pick an arbitrary number just because we've got to balance the budget in 7 years instead of 10 and have this huge tax cut that, by the way, is about the amount of money we're going to save out of Medicare. That's wrong.

Instead, we ought to reform the system. And we could save money over the long run by taking a little of that money and helping States to set up opportunities for people like you to help your parents stay out of nursing homes as well as to pay for them when they go in. That is the better way to approach that problem. And I'd like to see us do it.

I mentioned family and medical leave. I couldn't believe it when I saw there were people in the Congress who wanted to strip the Government of the ability to enforce the law. Nobody has gone broke doing this. Nobody has. I want to tell you, the most moving personal encounters I think I've had, except with children, since I've been President, have come from adults who have taken advantage of the family and medical leave law.

Here is a letter my wife got this week. I want to read this to you. This is a law some people in Congress say we shouldn't enforce anymore: "Dear Mrs. Clinton, I am writing to let you know that 2 months ago my husband died of congestive heart failure after a prolonged period of several years of illness. Because my husband signed into law the Family and Medical Leave Act, I was able to transport him to doctor appointments and hospital visits. The act enabled me to keep my job and bring him comfort at the end of his life. I will be eternally grateful." Signed, Lynn Wade Tomko, of Highland Ranch, Colorado.

There's a lot of people out there like that. And every one of you deserves it. Every one of you.

Now, there is a bipartisan bill on health insurance reform. There's a bipartisan bill in the Congress right now, a bipartisan bill, saying at least if we can't give everybody health insurance, if we can't do that, at least we ought to be able to say when parents change jobs they and their children don't lose their health care, coverage shouldn't be tied to whether somebody in their family's been sick once or twice. And people who work for small businesses ought to be able to get—in every State in the country, they ought to be able to go into a pool that is big so they can buy insurance on the same rates that people like us who work for government or big units do. Simple, basic things. And there ought to be a longer period of time where

people keep their health insurance if they lose their jobs.

On the child support enforcement, all the Governors, even the most pro-State's rights Governors, have understood and supported our efforts to have national standards of child support enforcement. Why? Because over a third of all the child support orders that are delinquent are for people who have crossed State lines. So we need a national approach to this. The welfare reform bill I have sent to Congress has that. We have to have this.

Here are the things that it has, and ask yourself if you think it's reasonable: employer reporting of new hires to catch deadbeat dads who move from job to job; uniform interstate child support laws; computerized collection of speeding up payments; streamlined efforts to identify the father in every case when the child is born; and tough new penalties, like professional license revocation for people who repeatedly refuse to pay their child support—or driver's license.

Let me tell you, I don't think most Americans—we estimate that if everybody paid the child support they owe, there would be 800,000 fewer people in this country off of welfare. You have no idea how much money you're paying as taxpayers to support children that their parents could legally be supporting and have the money to support. You don't have any idea. It's a lot of money, money that could be going into Head Start, money that could be going into Goals 2000, money that could be going into college loans. It's not right.

I could go on and on. I'm going to have more to say about the drug abuse prevention and the teen pregnancy issues later on. I will say this—we'd be down the road a little bit if the Senate hadn't played politics with Dr. Henry Foster's nomination. But I'm going to bring him back in some way and get him to help us on this because it's so important, it's a big issue.

On the drug issue, everybody talks about being tough on drugs. But you've got to do four things if you want to make a difference. You have got to work with foreign governments to cut drugs off at the source. We are busting a lot of big gangs, and we're making some real progress. And we're getting more help from foreign governments than the United States has enjoyed in many years. We've worked hard at it, and a lot of people in other countries risk their lives every day to keep your kids free of cocaine and crack. And you need to know that.

We say, why don't they do more? A lot of them put their lives on the line every day to do it. And more than ever before, we're making progress on it. We also have to break the cycle of drugs and crime by providing treatment to people who need it. It works; it does work. It doesn't always work, but two-thirds of the time, the treatment works. Now, would you rather spend a little money to have it work two-thirds of the time, or put 100 percent of those people behind bars at a greater cost to you? It does work.

We also have to punish people properly who break the law. But finally, we've got to do something to try to keep our kids off of drugs in the first place. And therefore, I think it is a mistake for the Congress to eliminate the money we're giving to your schools to promote safe and drug-free schools. Those are good programs and we shouldn't get rid of it.

I'm going to say more in the next several days about this issue of teenage smoking. But you just think about the number of people every year in America we lose because of smoking-related illnesses. And you realize that having a whole lot of young kids get into that pipeline is pretty significant. And all the evidence is that if people don't start smoking until they're adults, that even if they smoke a little, they don't become really hooked. They don't do it a lot. They quit after a little while, and they go on and live normal lives. This is a big deal.

Most people who have serious problems with smoking started when they were children. It is now illegal to sell children cigarettes, but it happens all the time. And we have to do more to stop it. That's a family values issue—cut the cost of health care, help us meet our budget targets, keep people healthier longer, and make for more alert, effective students in your classrooms.s

I just want to mention one or two other issues. Let me just say, about the minimum wage, you all clapped and I realize you agree with me—[laughter]—but a lot of Americans, every time we raise the minimum wage, there's this great hue and cry about how we're going to lose jobs, and it has never happened. And 40 percent of the people on minimum wage are women who are the sole support of their kids. And if we don't raise the minimum wage next year, it will reach in real dollar terms a 40-year low. That's the problem in America. We should be having a high-opportunity, smart-work, high-wage future, not a hard-work, low-wage future. There is no percentage in it for us to support those kind of low wages.

Let me just say a couple of words about some specific things in the education area. I wouldn't be up here if people hadn't helped me get an education. I had college loans, I had scholarships. I had six jobs—never more than three at once. [Laughter] All of that was opportunity and responsibility. The same kinds of things that are in your bill of rights and responsibility.

We know now there is a greater difference in the ability of people to earn more successively and to live out the American dream based on their level of education than ever in the entire history of the country. We know that. We know, too, that in the 1980's the only item in a family's budget that went up faster than the cost of health care was the cost of college education. We know that. Now, our administration has done two things that I'm real proud of.

First of all, we started the AmeriCorps program, which gives people a chance to serve their local communities and earn money to go to college. I thought it was sort of a Republican-like program, you know—it was a grassroots program. There's no bureaucracy; we fund preexisting local projects in a highly competitive way. It's an empowerment program. You can't even get any money from the Government unless you work yourself to death for trying to help people solve their problems. Sounds to me like the kind of thing they're always talking about. [Laughter] Sometimes I wonder if a Republican President had proposed it, I don't think it would be a target in this budget cycle. But why would you get rid of that?

More importantly, we found—I found before I became President—when I was Governor, I met young people who were dropping out of college because they thought that the careers for which they were being trained, including many of them who wanted to be school teachers—they thought they would not be able to earn enough to meet their college loan repayment obligations.

And so, we did something remarkable, Secretary Riley, Deputy Secretary Kunin, the Education Department, we discovered that if we set up a system for the Federal Government to make direct loans, that we could loan the money at lower cost to the students and give them four different options to repay the loans so that you could—if you chose one option, you would always repay it at a certain percentage of your salary, whatever it was. So there would never be a time when repaying a loan would be a deterrent to taking it out in the first place or finishing your college education or serving the public as a teacher or a police officer or a nurse or doing something else that might not pay all the money in the world but was immensely rewarding and immensely important to the rest of society.

This direct loan program is reducing the cost to the Government, reducing the deficit, increasing the number of people who can have college loans and improving their repayment terms. It's also much less hassle for the college administrators. Who doesn't like it? The middlemen who were cut out. What are they doing? They're up in the Congress right now trying to get rid of it. Who wants to get rid of it? Not the kids who have got them, not the college administrators who administer them, not the people who are worried about the budget but the special interests that have too much influence in this Congress say, "We lost our money; we want it back. We don't care what happens to these kids." That is wrong, and you ought to stand up against it.

Now, we don't have to have a partisan, divisive fight about family values. And we don't have to argue whether we need improvements in personal conduct or political policies and economic policies. The truth is, we need a whole bunch of both. And nobody is smart enough to do everything we need to do politically and economically, and nobody will ever be good

enough so that they won't be able to stand a little improvement. So this is a bogus debate.

What we must not do is let one group take one side of this debate and use it as an excuse to divide the American people and walk away from our real responsibilities to the real families that are working their hearts out to do the best they can by their children in this country. That's what we must not do.

So, let us stand together in fighting for the cause of education, the right kind of education, your kind of education—opportunity and high standards of excellence and accountability—the things you have stood for for years and years and years. That is a very important part of our Nation's family values agenda.

And let us stand together to do things about the time that the kids have to spend before they come to you and after they leave you. This does not have to be a big divide. All we have to do is to find the common ground that is already out there in every neighborhood, in every community, in every city, town, and rural area in this country. All we have to do is bring what people know in their hearts to be true in the heartland here to the halls of Government. If we do that, we can really have a family values agenda.

Thank you, and God bless you all.

NOTE: The President spoke at 1:33 p.m. at the Sheraton Washington Hotel. In his remarks, he referred to Albert Shanker, president, and Edward McElroy, secretary-treasurer, American Federation of Teachers; and Sandra Feldman, president, United Federation of Teachers.

Message to the Congress on Trade with Maldives and Moldova
July 28, 1995

To the Congress of the United States:
The Generalized System of Preferences (GSP) program offers duty-free treatment to specified products that are imported from designated beneficiary developing countries. The program is authorized by title V of the Trade Act of 1974, as amended.

Pursuant to title V, I have determined that Maldives should be suspended from the GSP program because it is not making sufficient progress in protecting basic labor rights. I also have decided to designate Moldova as a beneficiary developing country for purposes of the

GSP program because I have determined that Moldova satisfies the statutory criteria.

This notice is submitted in accordance with the requirements of section 502(a)(1) and 502(a)(2) of the Trade Act of 1974.

WILLIAM J. CLINTON

The White House,

July 28, 1995.

NOTE: The related proclamation is listed in Appendix D at the end of this volume.

Message to the Congress on Continuation of the National Emergency With Respect to Iraq
July 28, 1995

To the Congress of the United States:

Section 202(d) of the National Emergencies Act (50 U.S.C. 1622(d)) provides for the automatic termination of a national emergency unless, prior to the anniversary date of its declaration, the President publishes in the *Federal Register* and transmits to the Congress a notice stating that the emergency is to continue in effect beyond the anniversary date. In accordance with this provision, I have sent the enclosed notice, stating that the Iraqi emergency is to continue in effect beyond August 2, 1995, to the *Federal Register* for publication.

The crisis between the United States and Iraq that led to the declaration on August 2, 1990, of a national emergency has not been resolved. The Government of Iraq continues to engage in activities inimical to stability in the Middle East and hostile to United States interest in the region. Such Iraqi actions pose a continuing unusual and extraordinary threat to the national security and vital foreign policy interests of the United States. For these reasons, I have determined that it is necessary to maintain in force the broad authorities necessary to apply economic pressure on the Government of Iraq.

WILLIAM J. CLINTON

The White House,

July 28, 1995.

NOTE: The notice is listed in Appendix D at the end of this volume.

Statement on Signing the Emergency Supplemental Appropriations and Rescissions Legislation
July 28, 1995

Pursuant to my signature yesterday, I have approved H.R. 1944, the Emergency Supplemental Appropriations for Additional Disaster Assistance, for Anti-terrorism Initiatives, for Assistance in the Recovery from the Tragedy that Occurred at Oklahoma City, and Rescissions Act, 1995. This legislation shows how we can work together to produce good legislation.

I hereby designate as an emergency all funds in this Act so designated by the Congress that I have not previously designated pursuant to section 251(b)(2)(D)(i) of the Balanced Budget and Emergency Deficit Control Act of 1985, as amended.

I am pleased that bipartisan leaders of Congress worked with me to produce a good bill. Working together, we can continue to produce good legislation for the American people.

WILLIAM J. CLINTON

The White House,

July 28, 1995.

NOTE: H.R. 1944, approved July 27, was assigned Public Law No. 104–19. An original was not available for verification of the content of this statement.

Radio Address by the President and Hillary Clinton on Medicare
July 29, 1995

The President. Good morning. This morning I'm speaking to you from the Oval Office with the First Lady. And we're joined by families from all across our country, grandparents, parents, and children, including Hillary's mother and my stepfather. We want to talk with you this morning about the respect and dignity we owe to older Americans and the security we owe to their families.

This weekend we're celebrating the 30th anniversary of the passage of Medicare. Guaranteed health care for older and disabled Americans is now so much a part of our lives that it's easy to forget how growing old once meant growing poor in our country. In 1965, over one-third of older Americans were poor, and half of them were uninsured.

I remember because my mother was a nurse-anesthetist, and older people without insurance would sometimes come to our house, offering to mow our lawn or bringing a bushel of peaches to pay for her services. These Americans had worked hard their whole lives, they didn't have any health insurance, and they were in danger of losing their health.

Vice President Gore's father, Senator Al Gore, Sr., was in the Senate back in 1965 when he said that this was a disgrace in a country such as ours. Senator Gore helped to create Medicare to put an end to that disgrace. And since then, Medicare has lifted millions of seniors out of poverty and provided insurance for almost every older American.

Mrs. Clinton. We need to remember that Medicare is not just important for older men and women, it is a compact across generations. Medicare means that we don't have to choose between doing right by our parents and giving our children the opportunities they deserve.

A friend of ours told me a story about how, before Medicare, her mother would take a part of her paycheck each week and put it in an envelope to pay for an aging parent's health care bills. That meant the family had less money

for putting food on the table or sending their children to college or saving for their own retirement. That's the way it was for families before Medicare and the way it could be again for all families, especially those of us with both responsibilities for parents and children.

Parents ought to be able to save for their children's college and protect their parents' health, and Medicare means they can. It certainly has been there for our family and for the Vice President's.

You may know that the President and I have both lost parents in the last 2½ years. We've sat in those hospital waiting rooms. We've been in those intensive care units. And we've also experienced in the past week with the Vice President the joy of having his mother come out of the hospital. For all our worries, the one thing we didn't have to worry about was a mountain of health care bills. Medicare was there.

That is the story for millions of Americans, people like Arthur Flemming and Genevieve Johnson, who are here with us. Mr. Flemming helped start Medicare 30 years ago, and Mrs. Johnson was among the first people to benefit from it. Today, both are in their nineties and receive Medicare, and both have worked tirelessly to make sure Medicare will be there for their grandchildren, too. And I think it's because they know what life is like for most older Americans. The median income for women over 65 in our country is $8,500 a year.

The President. To preserve Medicare for all of our grandchildren we do have to strengthen the Medicare trust fund, which holds the money we all pay in to cover hospital, nursing homes, and home health bills. I've been working to reform Medicare since I took office, and frankly, the trust fund is in better shape than it was when I did take office. But real reform is about making the situation better, not worse. Real reform means fixing the trust fund without putting beneficiaries in a fix.

I also believe we have to balance the budget. But I know we can do that and strengthen the trust fund without rolling back 30 years of progress against poverty and fear for older Americans. That's what my balanced budget will do. It will eliminate the deficit, secure the Medicare trust fund, and still protect older Americans from one penny in new Medicare costs. Times are tough enough without forcing families to pay more to keep the health care they have right now.

The congressional majority sees it differently. They are now willing to join me in shoring up the trust fund, but they want to do it in a way I don't agree with, that goes way too far, because they insist on such a huge tax cut that also make older couples pay $5,600 more out of their pockets over the next few years. For people who don't have that kind of money, the message will be simple: Fend for yourselves. Many people just won't be able to do it.

As I said before, we often take for granted the security that comes from Medicare. But according to a new study by the Department of Health and Human Services, the congressional majority would push 500,000—a half a million—older Americans into poverty by increasing the cost of health care. And these cuts would force their families to make choices between generations that no family should have to make.

We do need to protect Medicare from going bankrupt, but we don't have to bankrupt older Americans to do it. None of the cuts driving families into poverty would go into the trust fund. They would simply pay for a huge tax cut for people who don't really need it. That's unnecessary, and it's wrong. Medicare is too important to all families to become a piggy bank for tax cuts for just a few. It's especially important today because so many families are working harder and earning the same or less than they did 10 years ago.

For all Americans, Medicare must remain a source of certainty and security. For our parents, but also for our children, I pledge to do my part to keep Medicare strong.

Thanks for listening.

NOTE: The President spoke at 10:06 a.m. from the Oval Office at the White House.

Question-and-Answer Session With Senior Citizens on Medicare
July 29, 1995

The President. Yes, Sarah [Sarah McClendon, McClendon News].

Q. What's your strategy? What's going to be the Democrats' strategy? We can't live with this present condition like this. We can't do it. People are dying every day because they don't have preventive health care. And what's going to be the strategy of the Democrats to overcome this?

The President. Well, first of all, we're going to try to win as many of the fights as we can as they come up. You know, yesterday we won a really important victory in the House of Representatives where, really, the first time since the new majority took over, over 50 Republicans bolted and voted to protect the environment, a very important issue in States like Florida and other States around the country. The House had a bill before it that would literally strip the Federal Government of its power to protect the environment. So that—and 50 Republicans joined with almost all the Democrats and said, no, we're not going to do that.

So I think that we've got a chance now, a real chance to build a sensible, common-sense, common ground majority. And that's what we're going to try to do. I don't know that these Medicare cuts can pass the Congress. And I'm certainly going to do what I can to defeat them. That's our first strategy.

The second thing, to follow up on what you said, is that we believe that if we're going to slow the rate of growth in Medicare spending dramatically, without imposing great new costs on seniors and making the system work, we ought to take a little of that money we're going to save and put it into preventive care, to try to help people take care of their parents or their grandparents outside of institutions, outside of nursing home care. I think it would save money over the long run. It wouldn't cost a lot of money to start, and we'd sure find out over the next 2 or 3 years.

And in my budget, we take some of that money to put into home health care. We've put some of that money into respite care for people with Alzheimer's. We do some other things with it, and we'll be able to monitor over the next 2 or 3 years whether it saves money or not. I think it will, and it doesn't have anything to do with stabilizing the trust fund. So that's our strategy.

And I'm encouraged by yesterday's vote on the environment that there may be some Republicans willing to brave the pressure, the enormous pressure they've been under to toe the line, to do what's right for America. So I'm encouraged.

Q. Mr. President——

Q. Larry, let's go do the discussion first and then we'll——

The President. Larry, what were you going to say?

Q. I'm sorry.

The President. I want to hear from all of you first, and then we'll take the press questions.

[*At this point, Mayor Norman Abramowitz of Tamarac, FL, asked the President to continue the fight to protect Medicare and Medicaid and asked if he would address the concerns of the younger generation and their desire for change.*]

The President. Well, you tell—first of all, tell them I won't give up the fight. We've just begun the fight. But I think, to be fair, the young people of our country are worried about their own future. And it's an amazing time in our country. We've got—just since I've been President, we've brought the deficit down, we've got 7 million new jobs, we've got a record high stock market, we've got a record number of new businesses. But a lot of people, including a lot of young people, are working harder for less. They feel more and more powerless. And so a lot of them think, well, maybe the answer is to turn against everything we've done in the past, turn against programs like Medicare, turn against the elderly, walk away from everything that's been done.

And the problem with that is, all they will do is make themselves and their parents and their own future worse. We have to properly analyze what's the matter, and we have to get the kind of change we want. We do need to raise incomes as well as create jobs, just like

we need to stabilize the Medicare trust fund. People are living longer and longer, so there are more people drawing Medicare. And the older you are, on balance, the more you use the health care system. So the cost per person goes up as people get over 80, let's say. But the answer is to fix it in a way that won't break it and that won't bankrupt the seniors of this country.

And I think it's—you know, I'm glad you mentioned Medicaid. A lot of people think Medicaid is exclusively a program for young, poor people on welfare. And two-thirds of Medicaid money goes to the elderly and disabled. That's what funds the parents of middle class America who have to go into nursing homes, for example. And if you look at the nature of the Medicaid cuts, we're going to see a lot of middle class Americans who will no longer be able to afford to send their kids to college because they'll be paying for their parents in nursing homes if they can afford to do that.

So, the answer—I think you ought to tell these young people, we are in a period of change. And we have to change our Government policies to be prepared for the 21st century. But the answer is to enable everybody to make the most of their own lives, not to pit one generation against another or one group of Americans against another. That is a dead loser for this country. That is a really foolish thing to do. It helps a lot of politicians win elections when they can pit people against one another, but it doesn't help the country much. And we have never progressed doing it. You look back in the whole history of America, we have never taken one step forward by pitting one group of Americans against another one, and we never will.

[*A participant described a recent illness she suffered and explained that she had been very concerned that Medicare would not cover the expenses. She stated that she was fortunate that she had daughters to help provide care for her but that the average older person could not afford the expense of a serious illness and the nursing care required.*]

The President. But you know, your story illustrates a point that the mayor just made. I mean, first of all, for about 10 years now, the elderly in our country have had a lower poverty rate than very young people. And that's a wonderful thing. And two things did it, the cost of living on Social Security and Medicare. That's what did it.

Now, if we put another half a million older Americans in poverty with this program, is that going to lift any little children out of poverty? No. Is that going to help that young worker? No. All you're going to do is take more money out of the incomes of middle class working people who are working harder for less.

So the answer is to raise their incomes and increase their security. The answer is not to make this swap. And who would get the benefit of this, this tax cut? I want to emphasize again, this money is not necessary to fix the Medicare trust fund. They don't have to make this much savings.

And an enormous amount of this huge tax cut is going to people who don't even need it, and many of them, frankly, don't want it. Many of them do not want it. I've had a lot of upper income people tell me that they do not want—they want to balance the budget, take care of Medicare, invest in education, get this country going. So I—this is a battle we have to win.

Yes, ma'am. Go ahead.

[*A participant described a letter the President sent her about Medicare.*]

The President. Bless you.

Q. And I know you want it because you wouldn't have done it. You wouldn't have done this today. You didn't have to sit here.

The President. Thank you.

Go ahead.

[*A participant stated that if Medicare and Medicaid were cut, a great number of disabled and elderly people would fall below the poverty line.*]

Hillary Clinton. One of the concerns we have—and I think one of the reasons the President wanted to do this, to go back to Sarah's question, is there's a lot of misinformation out there. And I think, Mayor, that's what some of the young people are responding to. And we're now seeing ads being run that are trying to scare people and trying to say that, you know, if we don't do what the majority in Congress wants to do, then there won't be any Medicare—a lot of real scare tactics. And I think we have to get the information out to people.

For example, there's a difference, as you know, between Part A and Part B of Medicare. And what the President has proposed in his budget will improve the Trust Fund. But the beneficiary cuts and the additional costs that the majority in Congress want older people to have to pay out of their own pockets have nothing to do with the Trust Fund.

The President. Nothing to do with the Trust Fund.

Mrs. Clinton. See, this is one of those shell games. Remember when you'd walk down the street and you'd see how fast people could do all that, and I never could figure it out—well, it's going on again. But it's going on in a much more serious way, trying to really keep the balls moving so fast that they think that they'll fool people, and not just fool older people but fool the children and grandchildren, so that people will think, well, all they're trying to do is to fix the Medicare Trust Fund, and so if people have to pay more—not remembering that 75 percent of the people on Medicare make less than $25,000 a year—so where are they going to get the $2,000, the $5,000 to pay more? And it has nothing to do with the Part B cuts, with the Part A Trust Fund.

So that's one thing that we have to keep explaining to people. And I think the truth, as is often the case, is one of our most effective arguments.

The President. A lot of people, like a lot of young people, don't know. They'll see these ads, and they think, well, they're trying to fix the Trust Fund. But I just want to remind—look, we need to do a little history here. When—1993, when I gave the State of the Union Address and I became President, I said, look, we've got to fix the Trust Fund. In 1994, I said, we have to fix the Trust Fund. When I presented health care reform, I said, we have to fix the Trust Fund. A lot of these same people, now, who are alarmed about the Trust Fund said, "There's no real problem, there's no health care crisis, what's he talking about?"

Then when a report comes out this year and it shows we've actually improved things for the Trust Fund but we still have to fix it, they say, "Oh, we have to fix the Trust Fund, and that's why we need to load all these costs on the seniors." But the costs—I want to say again what the First Lady said—the costs being loaded on the individual seniors do not go against the Trust Fund. They're being used to finance an excessively large tax cut and to balance the budget at the arbitrary date of 7 years.

And, you know, it is just not fair. I have never seen a time when the seniors of this country were not willing to bear their fair share, were not willing to make their own contributions. You know as well as I do, modest changes have been made in Medicare and Social Security over the years. That's not what this is about. This is about just what Mr. Flemming said; it's about taking the heart out of this program, to drastically change the way the Government's priorities are. And it is wrong. And you and your children, your grandchildren, in some cases your great-grandchildren, you've got to stand up against it.

[*A participant stated that she resented claims that the President and the Vice President were scaring older people.*]

The President. I'm not trying to scare anybody. But I am trying to arouse——

Q. I'm defending you——

The President. I am trying to arouse the citizens of this country. I've seen scare tactics. I've had them used against me and what I was trying to do. I saw a couple hundred million dollars worth of scare tactics last year when I was trying to secure your health care future. So I know all about scare tactics. I'm not trying to scare you, but I think it's wrong for people to go around with this little plan to mess with your Medicare and try to keep the details of it secret until the 11th hour, then pop it through and have it all gone. And I think we need to—this is like a covey of quail. We need to flush it—[*laughter*]—get it out there and see what's going on here.

Go ahead, what were you going to say, ma'am?

[*A participant said that she was concerned that Medicare cuts could affect the number of older women who get mammograms.*]

Mrs. Clinton. Well, I'm glad you raised that because we've got the experts back there who run this program, and we know that one of the barriers to older women getting regular mammograms is cost. And if we make the cost of Medicare even more expensive for older people in general, but particularly women, then the preventive health care that they need—which will save us all money if people take care of themselves and get those tests—will be lost as well.

And I want to say one other thing because I think this is part of the—sort of the scare tactics as well that are being used. A lot of people say, "Well, families should take care of each other and families should be there for each other and the Government shouldn't do it." The majority leader has said, you know, he doesn't want any part of Medicare; it shouldn't be a program in any free country, and everybody should take care of themselves.

Well, I think everybody in this room certainly and most people I know around the country do everything they can to help their parents. Your daughters came to take care of you, and you're grateful that they could. And we will continue to do that, financially, emotionally, in every way we can. But there are two, I think, realities we have to look at. There are a lot of older people who don't have those children and those grandchildren. There are a lot of older people who have outlived their children, who don't live anywhere near their children or their grandchildren, who are in no position to be able to get any help. What we are going to do with them, particularly all these older women who are on their own?

And the second thing is that because a lot of young people are struggling very hard for themselves I have no doubt they would make the sacrifice if they had to, but with the cost of medical care, my goodness, we will drive more young people into poverty if they have to spend all of their assets to try to help take care of their parents and their grandparents. That's why what we're talking about here is something that doesn't just affect older Americans. It affects every single American, no matter what our age. And I hope that people will understand that more.

[*A participant suggested that the President should express his plan to reform Medicare very clearly to avoid confusion about the differences between his proposal and the Republican proposal.*]

The President. That's what the First Lady said. These personal costs that are going to be loaded on the individual seniors under their plan do not make a contribution to stabilizing the Trust Fund. They are not necessary to stabilize the Trust Fund, and we don't have to do it.

I know we've got to break up. We'll hear from one more person.

[*A participant expressed concern about the impact on minorities living in poverty if Medicaid were no longer an entitlement, especially in view of cutbacks in assistance at the local level.*]

The President. It's a mistake. Let me just say this. Just look at the—you know, of course, the main Medicaid benefit to seniors is nursing home care. And you know, most States have more people in nursing homes under Medicaid than Medicare, way more.

But let's just talk about the next generation. Let's talk about the children. We've all got a big stake in seeing how well they do. Medicaid is the program that provides health insurance to really poor children in this country. Now, you tell me what's going to happen if you block-grant Medicaid and you don't require the States to come up with their portion. And the next time the State legislature meets in Florida—let's take Florida, a State I know quite a bit about. You know, Hillary and I have—her family live there, two of her brothers. Let's just take Florida. And it's a fast-growing State. And they come in and we have a legislature, and the people say, we don't have enough money for the schools. And they're telling the truth, because it's fast-growing. And then they say, we've got all these new communities, and we don't have enough money for the water systems we need or the sewer systems we need. And they'll be telling the truth. Or we don't have enough money for the road systems we need. And they'll be telling the truth.

Now, then let's say the seniors have a strong enough lobby to come in and save the money for the nursing homes. What happens? They'll cut off all the aid to the poor children. And then what happens if you take the health care away from the poor children? Then all of us will be paying for them when they're either really sick or they don't develop mentally and physically as they should 5, 10, 15 years down the road.

This is not a good idea. This is a bad idea. Not all change is good. We've got to have the right kind of change. And you're absolutely right. And I hope you will fight for it. And I will fight for it. And we just need to tell the American people about it. We can prevail.

Thank you. You guys have been great.

Q. Mr. President, just to give you a chance to respond to, undoubtedly, what the Republican response will be. They say that you have not offered a really detailed proposal of your own for changes with Medicare——

The President. Have they? Have they? What I have done—I have done what's important. I have said, we are not going to accept the beneficiary increases that they are. I have said that we can fix the Medicare Trust Fund without requiring the kind of cost increases on these folks that they are recommending to pay for their tax cut. That is a huge change.

Secondly, I have said that we don't have to do as much on the provider side into the health care system as they want to do, because I want to balance the budget in 10 years instead of 7. So, any set of options I adopt, they will have to adopt more severe options, which is why they want to go into the August recess with their plan a secret and why they allegedly apparently have plans to come back here and drop this thing out right before the fiscal year begins and allow about 2 days debate on it and then roll it through.

Now, I have proved—when I had responsibility for the budget, I did that. We made the Medicare Trust Fund better, with no help, I might add, from them. Not a single vote. We made it better. They denied that there was a problem with the Trust Fund. Then when they won the majority in the Congress, what happened? All of a sudden they discovered this problem in the Trust Fund, and they used it as a pretext to raise costs on Medicare beneficiaries so much so they could pay for the big tax cut they promised and meet the 7-year balanced budget deadline they promised.

If you want to talk about—am I willing to work with them on Medicare reform to fix the Medicare Trust Fund? Absolutely, I am. Why did I present a balanced budget and alternative? So I could reach out my hand in good faith to work with them. So far that has not been an option. So far they have been proceeding down their own course. All I'm saying is, I am serving notice that I will not support what they are attempting to do to the seniors.

Now, we can fix the Medicare Trust Fund. It doesn't have anything to do with what we've been talking about here today.

NOTE: The President spoke at 10:12 a.m. in the Oval Office at the White House. In his remarks, he referred to Arthur Flemming, chair, Save Our Security.

Statement on the Death of Major Richard J. Meadows
July 29, 1995

I mourn the passing today of Major Richard J. Meadows, USA (Ret.), whose dedicated and exceptional service is cherished by everyone who knew of his extraordinary courage and selfless service.

I recently had asked General Wayne Downing, the commander-in-chief of the U.S. Special Operations Command, to present the Presidential Citizens Medal to Major Meadows. I am gratified to know that Major Meadows' wife, Pamela; his son, Mark, a U.S. Army captain; and daughter, Michele, will receive this award tonight at a gathering of those involved in the Sontay raid at Hurlburt Field. Although this will now be a posthumous honor, I am pleased that Major Meadows knew of this honor before he died.

To Major Meadows' family and friends and to the Special Operations community, I extend my heartfelt condolences. We will all remember him as a soldier's soldier and one of America's finest unsung heroes.

Remarks to the National Governors' Association in Burlington, Vermont
July 31, 1995

Thank you very much, Governor Dean. And thank you for the gift of those proceedings. I discovered two things looking through that book very quickly, which will be interesting perhaps to some of you. One is that the first Governors' conference—one thing I knew and one I didn't—the first Governors' conference was called by President Theodore Roosevelt to bring all the Governors together to develop a plan to conserve our Nation's resources. It was an environmental Governors' conference.

The second thing was that they really set the tone of bipartisanship which has endured through all these years—something I didn't know—I saw that the two special guests at the Governors' conference were William Jennings Bryan and Andrew Carnegie. So they were spanning the waterfront even then.

I really look forward to this, but I kind of got my feelings hurt. I understand Senator Dole came in here and told you that my cholesterol was higher than his. [*Laughter*] I came to Vermont determined to get my cholesterol down with low-fat Ben & Jerry's Cherry Garcia. [*Laughter*] I do want you to know that my standing heart rate, however—pulse rate—is much lower than Senator Dole's. But that's really not his fault; I don't have to deal with Phil Gramm every day. [*Laughter*] I think on matters of health, age, and political anxiety, we have come to a draw.

I thank you very much for having me here. I love looking around the table and seeing old friends and new faces. I thank Governor Dean for his leadership of the Governors' conference. And Governor Thompson, I wish you well, and I thank you for the work that we have done together over so many years. I thank all the State officials from Vermont who came out to the airport to say hello and the mayor here of Burlington. I know that your former Governor, Madeleine Kunin, is here, the Deputy Secretary of Education. She has done a very great job for us, and I thank her for that.

I want to talk to you today primarily about welfare reform. But I'd like to put it in the context of the other things that we are attempting to do in Washington. I see Senator Leahy and Congressman Sanders back there; Senator Jeffords may be here. I think I'm taking him back to Washington in a couple of hours.

I ran for President because I was genuinely concerned about whether our country was ready for the 21st century, because of the slow rate of job growth, 20 years of stagnant incomes, 30 years of social problems. I knew that we were still better than any other country in the world at so many things, but we seemed to be coming apart when, clearly, we've always done better when we went forward together as a nation.

I have this vision of what our country will look like 20 or 30 or 40 years from now. I want America to be a high-opportunity, smart-work country, not a hard-work, low-wage country. I want America to be a country with strong families and strong communities, where people have the ability to make the most of their own lives and families and communities have the ability to solve their own problems, where we have good schools and a clean environment and decent health care and safe streets.

I think the strategy to achieve that is clear. We have to create more opportunity and demand more responsibility from our people, and we have to do it together. I have concluded, having worked at this job now for 2½ years, that we cannot achieve the specific strategies of creating opportunity or providing for more responsibility unless we find a way to do more together.

In the last 2½ years, as Governor Dean said, I have spent most of my time working on trying to make sure we had a sound economic policy, to bring the deficit down and increase trade and investment in technology and research and development and education, to open up new educational opportunities, and to work with you to achieve standards of excellence with less direction from the National Government.

We also have tried to put some more specific responsibilities into the programs that benefit the American people. That's what the national service program was all about. We'll help you go to college, but you need to serve your country at the grassroots level. We reformed the college loan program to cut the cost and make the repayment terms better, but we toughened dramatically the collection of delinquent college loans so that the taxpayers wouldn't be out more money. We passed the family leave law, but we've also tried to strengthen child support enforcement, as so many of you have.

I want to help people on welfare, but I also want to reward people who, on their own, are off of welfare, on modest incomes, which is why we have dramatically expanded the earned-income tax credit, the program that President Reagan said was the most pro-family, pro-work initiative undertaken by the United States in the last generation. Now, this year, families with children with incomes of under $28,000 will pay about $1,300 less in income tax than they would have if the laws hadn't been changed in 1993.

We also tried to change the way the Government works. It's smaller than it used to be. There are 150,000 fewer people working for the Federal Government than there were the day I became President. We have dramatically reduced Government regulations in many areas. We're on the way to reducing the regulatory burden of the Department of Education by 40 percent, the Small Business Administration by 50 percent. We are reducing this year the time it takes to comply with the EPA rules and regulations by 25 percent and establishing a program in which anybody, any small business person who calls the EPA and honestly asks for help in dealing with a problem cannot be fined as a result of any discovery arising from the phone call while the person is trying to meet the requirements of Federal law.

We have also tried to solve problems that have been ignored. We reformed the pension system in the country to save 8½ million troubled pensions and stabilize 40 million more. Secretary Cisneros has formed an unbelievable partnership to expand home ownership with no new tax dollars, which will get us by the end of this decade more than two-thirds of Americans in their own homes for the first time in the history of the Republic.

The results of all this are overwhelmingly positive but still somewhat troubling. On the economic front, we have 7 million more jobs, 1½ million more small businesses—the largest rate of small business formation in history—2.4 million new homeowners, record stock markets, low inflation, record profits. And yet—and a record number of new millionaires, which is something to be proud of in this country, people who've worked their way into becoming millionaires; they didn't inherit the money. But still, the median income is about where it was 2½ years ago, which means most wage-earning Americans are still working harder for the same or lower wages. And the level of anxiety is quite high.

On the social front, you see the same things. The number of people on food stamps is down. The number of people on welfare is down. The divorce rate is down. The crime rate is down in almost every major metropolitan area in the country. The rate of serious drug use is down. But the rate of random violence among very young people is up. The continuing, gnawing sense of insecurity is up. The rate of casual marijuana smoking among very young people is up, even as serious drug use goes down.

So, what we have is a sense in America that we're kind of drifting apart. And this future that I visualize, that I think all of you share, is being rapidly embraced by tens of millions of Americans and achieved with stunning success. But we are still being held back in fulfilling our real destiny as a country because so many people are kind of shut off from that American dream.

I am convinced that the American people want us to go forward together. I am convinced that there really is a common ground out there on most of these issues that seem so divisive when we read about them in the newspaper or see them on the evening news. I think if just ordinary Americans could get in a room like this and sit around a table, two-thirds of them or more would come to the same answer on most of these questions. And I believe that we cannot bring the country together and move the country forward unless we deal with some issues that we still haven't faced.

I've tried to find a way to talk about really controversial issues in a way that would promote a discussion instead of another word combat. I've given talks in the last few days about family and media, about affirmative action, about the relationship of religion and prayer to schools in the hope that we could have genuine conversations about these things.

But I am convinced that almost more than any other issue in American life, this welfare issue sort of stands as a symbol of what divides us, because most Americans know that there are people who are trapped in a cycle of dependency that takes their tax dollars but doesn't achieve the goals designed that they have, which is to have people on welfare become successful parents and successful workers and to have parents who can pay, pay for their children so the taxpayers don't have to do it. I am convinced that unless we do this, and until we do it, there will still be a sort of wedge that will be very hard to get out of the spirit and the life of America.

There is here—maybe more than on any other issue that we're dealing with that's controversial—a huge common ground in America, maybe not in Washington yet, but out in the country there is a common ground. Not so very long ago there were liberals who opposed requiring all people on welfare to go to work.

But now, almost nobody does. And as far as I know, every Democrat in both Houses of Congress has signed on to one version of a bill or another that would do exactly that.

Not so long ago there were conservatives who thought the Government shouldn't spend money on child care to give welfare mothers a chance to go to work. But now nearly everybody recognizes that the single most significant failure of the Welfare Reform Act of '88, which I worked very hard on and which I missed, was that when we decided we couldn't fund it all, we should have put more money into child care even if it meant less money in job training, because there were States that had programs for that, and that you can't expect someone to leave their children and go to work if they have to worry about the safety of the children or if they'll actually fall behind economically for doing it because they don't have child care. We now have a broad consensus on that.

When Governor Thompson and Governor Dean and others came to the White House to the Welfare Reform Conference in January, I was very moved at the broad consensus that while we needed more State flexibility, in one area we had to have more national action and that was on standards for child support enforcement, for the simple reason that over a third of all delinquent child support cases are multi-State cases and there is no practical way to resolve that in the absence of having some national standards. If everybody who could pay their child support and who is under an order to do it, did it, we could lift 800,000 people off the welfare rolls tomorrow. That is still our greatest short-term opportunity, and we all need to do what we can to seize it.

There's also a pretty good consensus on what we shouldn't do. I think most Americans believe that while we should promote work and we should fight premature and certainly fight out-of-wedlock pregnancy, it is a mistake to deny people benefits—children benefits—because their parents are under age and unmarried, just for example. And I think most Americans are concerned that the long-term trend in America, that's now about 10 years long, toward dramatic decline in the abortion rate might turn around and go up again, at least among some classes of people, if we pass that kind of rule everywhere in the country.

So I think there is a common ground to be had on welfare reform. I proposed a welfare reform bill in 1994 which I thought achieved the objectives we all needed. I thought it would do what the States need to do. I though it would set up time limits. It would have requirements for responsible behavior for young people, requiring them to stay at home and stay in school. It would have supported the efforts of States through greater investments in child care and would have given much greater flexibility. It didn't pass.

In the State of the Union this year I asked the new Congress to join me in passing a welfare reform bill. It still hasn't passed because, unfortunately, in 1995 there have been ideological and political in-fights that have stalled progress on welfare reform and have prevented the majority, particularly in the Senate, from taking a position on it.

Some of the people on the extreme right wing of the Republican majority have held this issue hostage because they want to force the States to implement requirements that would deny benefits to young, unmarried mothers and their children. But I believe it's better to require young people to stay at home, stay in school, and turn their lives around, because the objective is to make good workers, good parents, good citizens, and successful children. That's what we're all trying to do.

So I'm against giving the States more mandates and less money, whether the mandates come from the right or the left. I'm also opposed to the efforts in Congress now to cut child care because, I say again, the biggest mistake we made in the Welfare Reform Act of '88 was not doing more in child care. We would have had far greater success if we had invested more money then in child care for people on welfare.

Now, I believe that it would be a mistake—if we cut child care and do all this other stuff, we could have more latchkey children, we could have more neglected children. And there are all kinds of new studies coming out again saying that the worst thing in the world we can do is not to take the first 4 years of a child's life and make sure that those years are spent in personal contact with caring adults, where children can develop the kind of capacities they need. So this is a very big issue if your objective for welfare reform is independence, work, good parenting, and successful children.

Now, you know I believe all this. That's why we worked so hard to grant all these waivers,

more in 2½ years than in the past 12 years combined. But I also have to tell you that I'm opposed to welfare reform that is really just a mask for congressional budget cutting, which would send you a check with no incentives or requirements on States to maintain your own funding support for poor children and child care and work.

And I do believe honestly that there is a danger that some States will get involved in a race to the bottom, but not, as some have implied, because I don't have confidence in you, not because I think you want to do that, not because I think you would do it in any way if you could avoid it, but because I have been a Governor for 12 years in all different kinds of times and I know what kinds of decisions you are about to face if the range of alternatives I see coming toward you develop.

I know, with the big cuts now being talked about in Congress in Medicaid, in other health and human services areas, in education, in the environment, that you will have a lot of pressure in the first legislative session after this budget comes down. And I know that somewhere down the road, in the next few years, we'll have another recession again.

And it's all right to have a fund set aside for the high-growth States. I like that; it's a good idea. But what happens when we're not all growing like we are now and we were last year? What happens the next time a recession comes down? How would you deal with the interplay in your own legislature if you just get a block grant for welfare, with no requirement to do anything on your own, and the people representing the good folks in nursing homes show up and the people representing the teachers show up and the people representing the colleges and universities show up and the people representing the cities and counties who've lost money they used to get for environmental investments show up?

I don't know what your experience is, but my experience is that the poor children's lobby is a poor match for most of those forces in most State legislatures in the country, not because anybody wants to do the wrong thing but because those people are deserving, too, and they will have a very strong case to make. They will have a very strong case to make.

So I believe we ought to have a continuing partnership, not for the Federal Government to tell you how to do welfare reform but because any money we wind up saving through today's neglect will cost us a ton more in tomorrow's consequences. And this partnership permits you to say, at least as a first line of defense, we must do this for the poor children of our State.

I also believe there is a better way to deal with this. And I'd like to say today, I come to you with essentially two messages, one I hope we will all do with Congress and one that we can do without regard to Congress.

First, we do need to pass a welfare reform bill that demands work and responsibilities and gives you the tools you need to succeed: tough child support enforcement, time limits in work requirements, child care, requiring young mothers to live at home and stay in school, and greater State flexibility.

The work plan proposed by Senators Daschle, Breaux, and Mikulski ends the current welfare system as we know it and replaces it with a work-based system. I will say again, the biggest shortcoming, I believe, of the bill that I helped write, the Family Support Act of 1988—on your behalf or your predecessors—was that we did not do enough in the child care area. The work first bill gives States the resources to provide child care for people who go to work and stay there. It rewards States for moving people from welfare to work, not simply for cutting people off welfare rolls. It is in that sense real welfare reform.

I know a lot of you think it has too many prescriptions, and I want to give you the maximum amount of flexibility, but it certainly is a good place to start to work on bipartisan efforts to solve this problem. And I will say again, to get the job done, we've got to have a bipartisan effort to do it.

I want to compliment Senator Dole for what he said here today. I made a personal plea to Senator Dole not very long ago to try to find a way to make a break from those who were trying to hold the Republican conference in the Senate hostage on this welfare reform issue so that we could work together. And today, if I understand his remarks—and I've read the best account of them I can—he proposed getting rid of ideological strings in requirements on States and giving States more say in their programs. And that is a very good start for us to work together.

Some of you may agree with him instead of me on that, but as I understand it, he also proposes a flat block grant with no requirement

for States maintaining their present level of effort or no maintenance of effort requirement of any kind. As I said, maybe it's just because I have been a Governor, I think this is a very bad idea. I don't think we should do this, because this program, after all, is called Aid to Families with Dependent Children, not aid to States with terrible budget problems created by Congress. [*Laughter*]

But while we have differences, Senator Dole's speech today, given what's been going on up there, offers real hope that the Congress can go beyond partisan and ideological bickering and pass a strong bipartisan welfare reform bill. The American people have waited for it long enough. We ought to do it. I am ready to go to work on it. And I consider this a very positive opening step.

I hope, again I will say, that you will consider the great strengths of the Daschle-Breaux-Mikulski bill, which I also believe is a very positive opening step and shows you where the entire Democratic caucus in the Senate is. They presently all support that.

My second message to you is, we don't have to wait for Congress to go a long way toward ending welfare as we know it; we can build on what we've already done. Already you are and we are collecting child support at record levels. Earlier this year, I signed an Executive order to crack down on Federal employee delinquency in child support, and it is beginning to be felt. Already in the last 2½ years, our administration has approved waivers for 29 States to reform welfare your way. The first experiment we approved was for Governor Dean to make it clear that welfare in Vermont would become a second chance, not a way of life. Governor Thompson's aggressive efforts in Wisconsin, which have been widely noted, send the same strong message.

Now, we can and we should do more, and we shouldn't just wait around for the congressional process to work its way through. We can do more based on what States already know will work to promote work and to protect children. Therefore today I am directing the Secretary of Health and Human Services to approve reforms for any State on a fast track that incorporate one or more of the following five strategies.

First, requiring people on welfare to work and providing adequate child care to permit them to do it. Delaware recently got an approval to do this; so have several other States. Why not all 50?

Second, limiting welfare to a set number of years and cutting people off if they turn down jobs. Florida got approval to limit welfare, provide a job for those who can't find one, and cut off those who refuse to work; so did 14 other States. Why not all 50?

Third, requiring fathers to pay child support or go to work to pay off what they owe. Michigan got approval to do this; so did 13 other States. Taxpayers should not pay what fathers owe and can pay. Why not all 50 States?

Fourth, requiring underage mothers to live at home and stay in school. Teen motherhood should not lead to premature independence unless the home is a destructive and dangerous environment. The baby should not bring the right and the money to leave school, stop working, set up a new household, and lengthen the period of dependence, instead of shortening it. Vermont got approval to stop doing this; so did five other States. Why not all 50?

And finally, permitting States to pay the cash value of welfare and food stamps to private employers as wage subsidies when they hire people to leave welfare and go to work. Oregon just got approval to do this; so did Ohio and Mississippi. Arizona and Virginia can do it as well. Why not all 50 States? This so-called privatizing of welfare reform helps businesses to create jobs, saves taxpayers money, moves people from welfare to work, and recognizes that in the real world of this deficit we're not going to be able to have a lot of public service jobs to people who can't go to work when their time limits run out. I think this has real promise.

So I say to you today, if you pass laws like these or come up with plans like these that require people on welfare to work, that cut off benefits after a time certain for those who won't work, that make teen mothers stay at home and stay in school, that make parents pay child support or go to work to earn the money to do it or that use welfare benefits as a wage supplement for private employers who give jobs to people on welfare, if you do that, you sign them, you send them to me, and we will approve them within 30 days. Then we will have real welfare reform even as Congress considers it.

To further support your actions, I am directing the Office of Management and Budget to approve a change in Federal regulations so that States can impose tougher sanctions on people who refuse to work. Right now, when a State reduces someone's welfare check for failing to hold up their end of the bargain, the person's food stamp benefit goes up. So it turns out not to be much of a sanction. We're going to change that. If your welfare check goes down for refusal to work, your food stamp payment won't go up anymore.

Finally, as another downpayment on our commitment to our partnership with you on welfare reform, today our administration has reached agreement on welfare reform experiments for West Virginia, Utah, Texas, and California. Massachusetts has a sweeping proposal on which agreement has been reached on every issue but one—as I understand it, we're getting much closer there. The West Virginia proposal helps two-parent families go to work. Utah provides greater work incentives but tougher sanctions for those who turn down work. California has adopted the New Jersey system of the family cap. Texas has a very interesting proposal to require parents on welfare to prove that their children have been immunized to continue to draw the benefits.

And I would say, just in response to this, this will now, obviously, bring us to 32 States, and I think soon to be 33 States, with these kinds of experiments. We also are announcing food stamps experiments today as applied for by Delaware and Virginia.

All of these are designed to promote work and responsibility without being stifled by Washington's one-size-fits-all rule. But I think we need to accelerate this process. I don't like the so-called Mother-may-I aspect of the waiver system, either. That's why I say, if you act in these five areas, under the law you have to file an application for an experiment, but it will be approved within 30 days.

And I want to identify other areas like this. This Texas immunization idea is very important. We have lower immunization rates than any advanced country in the world. We are moving hard at the national level to make sure that the vaccines are affordable. Texas was the first State to use national service workers, AmeriCorps volunteers, in the summer of '93, to immunize over 100,000 children. And since then they've immunized another 50,000. But if you were to require it of people on public assistance, it would have a big impact on getting those numbers up, I believe. So, as we begin to get more information about this and other things, we will be issuing other reforms that if you just ask for them, we'll say yes within 30 days. This is very important.

Now, let me be clear. Congress still does need to pass national legislation. Why? Because I don't think you ought to have to file for permission every time you do something that we already know has worked and that other States are doing. Because we do need national child support standards, time limits, work requirements, and protections for children. And we do need more national support for child care.

I hope these efforts that I'm announcing today will spur the Congress to act. But we don't have to wait for them, and we shouldn't. We can do much more. If every State did the five things that I mentioned here today, every State, we would change welfare fundamentally and for the better. And we ought to begin it, and we shouldn't wait for Congress to pass a law.

There is common ground on welfare. We want something that's good for children, that's good for the welfare recipients, that's good for the taxpayers, and that's good for America. We have got to grow the middle class and shrink the under class in this country. We cannot permit this country to split apart. We cannot permit these income trends which are developing to continue. We have to change it. You will not recognize this country in another generation if we have 50 years, instead of 20 years, in which half of the middle class never gets a raise and most of the poor people are young folks and their little kids. We have to change it. And we can do it.

But we have to remember what we're trying to do. We're trying to make the people on welfare really successful as workers and parents. And most important, we're trying to make sure this new generation of children does better.

A few months ago I was down in Dallas, visiting one of our AmeriCorps projects. And I saw two pictures that illustrate why I think this issue is so important. One, I was walking with a young woman who was my tour guide on this project. She was a teen mother, had a child out of wedlock, thought she had done the wrong thing, went back and got her GED, and was in the AmeriCorps program because she wanted to work in this poor community to help them and earn money to go to college. But the second person I met was the real reason we ought to be working for welfare reform. I met a young woman who was very well-spoken. She told me she had just graduated from a university in the Southeast. But she was working on this anyway, even though she really didn't have to go on to college anymore. And I said, "Why are you doing this?" She said, "Because I was born into a family of a welfare mother. But I had a chance to get a good education; I got a college degree. And I want these young people to come out like I did."

Now, that's the kind of citizen we want in this country. Those are the kind of people that will turn these disturbing trends around. Those are the kind of people that will enable us to come together and go forward into the future.

We owe them that. And we can do it. You and I can do it now. Congress can do it this year. And every one of us ought to do our part.

Thank you, and God bless you.

NOTE: The President spoke at 2:45 p.m. by satellite at the Sheraton Burlington Hotel. In his remarks, he referred to Gov. Howard Dean of Vermont, chair, and Gov. Tommy Thompson of Wisconsin, vice-chair, National Governors' Association; and Mayor Peter C. Brownell of Burlington, VT.

Statement on Oil and Gas Drilling on the Outer Continental Shelf
July 31, 1995

The Government today has reached an agreement protecting sensitive coastal areas off Florida and Alaska from oil drilling, which has been prohibited since 1988, through Democratic and Republican Presidencies.

Concern for our coasts is part of the common ground we share as Americans, not only in the areas protected today but in places as different as California, Massachusetts, Oregon, New Jersey, and Washington. Once sensitive areas are damaged—beaches, the fishing industry, tourism—our natural heritage suffers greatly.

This settlement is good for the environment, good for taxpayers, good for the economy, and fair to the oil companies.

I am pleased that Secretary Babbitt and Attorney General Reno reached this agreement with the oil companies. We celebrate today with the citizens of Florida and Alaska, and I pledge continued protection of our coasts.

Remarks on Congressional Action on Appropriations Legislation and an Exchange With Reporters
August 1, 1995

The President. Good morning. Looking over the last few days, it is clear that this Congress is on the wrong track. I began the year hoping to make bipartisan progress on balancing the budget, on reducing paperwork, reforming regulation and welfare. And therefore, I was very pleased last week when a bipartisan majority voted to reject the extreme anti-environment provisions adopted in the House committee. That was the right thing to do.

But then the lobbyists for the polluters went to work. They got the leadership of the House of Representatives to call the bill back up. And last night, in a remarkable exercise of special interest power, the House voted to gut environmental and public health protections. It was a stealth attack on our environment in the guise of a budget bill.

The bill would effectively end Federal enforcement of the Clean Water Act and the Clean Air Act, a bill that my Republican predecessor said was his proudest legislative achievement. It allows poisons in our drinking water, raw sewage on our beaches, oil refineries to pollute, and limits a community's right to know what chemicals are toxic which are released in their neighborhoods. It would be bad for our children, our health, and our environment.

This is Washington special interest politics at its most effective and at its worst. Even before the 17 special interest provisions were added, the bill had already dramatically undercut environmental protection by cutting environmental enforcement in half.

You don't need to damage the environment to balance the budget. Our budget demonstrates that, and the budget the American people get out of this session of Congress ought to demonstrate that. In the past few days, a battalion of lobbyists has swarmed Capitol Hill, exerting

enormous pressure to save these loopholes. I said I would use the power of my office to help people, not polluters. I believe we can protect the environment and grow the economy.

So on this so-called environmental bill, my message to the American people should be very, very clear: Don't worry. We'll make common-sense reforms. But the minute this polluter's protection act hits my desk, I will veto it.

One of the most interesting things that has achieved not too much notice in the last few days is that while Congress has been taking care of the special interests, it's also taking care of itself. It is way behind schedule on virtually every budget bill, in the hope, apparently, of enforcing a choice at the end of this fiscal year between shutting the Government down and adopting extreme budget cuts which will be bad for our country, bad for our economy, and bad for our future. Apparently, they don't even plan on letting the American people see their planned Medicare cuts until the last possible minute. But one bill, wouldn't you know it, is right on schedule, the bill that funds the Congress, its staff, and its operations.

I don't think Congress should take care of its own business before it takes care of the people's business. If the congressional leadership follows through on its plan to send me its own funding bill before it finishes work on the rest of the budget, I will be compelled to veto it.

I want to work with Congress to pass a balanced budget that protects the health and the security of the American people, a balanced budget that strengthens our economy and raises the incomes of our people and the future prospects of our children. But we have to remember in order to do this that all the special interests have to be subordinated to the broader public interest. That is not happening now, but we can still get things back on track. That's what I want to do, and I still ask, again, the Congress to work with me to do it.

Helen [Helen Thomas, United Press International].

Opposition From Congress

Q. Mr. President, your policies and your judgment calls appear to be under siege on Capitol Hill, Waco, Whitewater, Bosnia, social programs, and so forth. How debilitating has this been on you personally, on your administration, on the country? And obviously, you're whistling in the dark if you think you're going to have common ground.

The President. I disagree. It's not been debilitating; it's been invigorating. And I wouldn't be so surprised. There are two significant things that—I would say big issues—that have become clear in the last few days. One is you can see who's in control in this Congress, who's in control of the people that compelled this unusual revolt on the environmental issues. You see the story on the NRA today: No gun control measures will be voted out of committee or on the floor of the House. I'm sure glad we got the Brady bill and the assault weapons ban first, and I still think we ought to have a ban on the cop-killer bullets. You see—we're investigating—this Congress is investigating the AARP and letting the NRA run one of its own investigations. So you see who's in control. That's the first thing you see.

The second thing you see is more hopeful. There were, after all, 50 Republicans who broke ranks in the House and said that they would put the environment ahead of party. Senator Dole yesterday said that—in Vermont at the Governors' conference—that he wanted to pass a welfare reform bill free of the extremist provisions which the members of his caucus, some of them, had demanded that he put on a welfare reform bill. And so we may be moving toward finding common ground in welfare reform.

So you see two things. You see who's in control, and it's not good. You see some people feeling uncomfortable about it, and we may be able to make some progress. And so I don't think we know what the outcome will be.

Waco Hearings

Q. There's a report today that Mack McLarty said in a memo that there would be no significant action on Waco without White House approval. When did you know of the plan to tear-gas the compound, and did you personally approve it?

The President. Mr. Mikva has said in the letter exactly what my role in that was, and it's consistent with what I've said all along. And I don't have anything new to add to that.

Bosnia

Q. Mr. President, have you made a final decision that there will be no retaliation for the shoot-down of Captain O'Grady? And if so, why not?

The President. I have no comment on that.

Political Reform Commission

Q. Mr. President, speaking of special interests, do you feel that the Speaker is dragging his feet on the bipartisan campaign finance reform commission? And what else are you willing to do to make sure that that happens?

The President. Dragging his feet is an apt, but inadequate, description of what has happened. [*Laughter*] I mean, we shook hands on that in New Hampshire. I thought it was a fairly simple deal. The man said—the gentleman who asked us the question, he said "Why don't you guys do a base closing commission." We said okay. Five days later I wrote a letter to the Speaker. I didn't get an answer. Five weeks later, I wrote—I said, again, okay, here are two people that are the kind of people that I would put on this commission, and I'd like for them to get with someone you designate, and we'll set it up—Doris Kearns Goodwin and John Gardner. Those are pretty respectable Americans. So far, they have not gotten any response or had any success either.

So we're going to keep trying. I mean, I think that it is wrong to say you're going to do something and not do it. So I hope we can do it.

Q. Have you met with them—have you met with the two of them already, Goodwin and——

The President. I have not, but we've obviously been in touch with them. And we're trying to— we're going to keep pushing until we get an answer one way or the other. If the Speaker does not want to do this, he ought to say that he has no intention of doing it. But we shouldn't just let it hang out here. What we ought to do is to do it.

Whitewater Hearings

Q. Mr. President, is there anything you or the First Lady could do to end all of the hearings on the continuing interest in the Whitewater business, especially in the aftermath of the Vince Foster suicide? For example, there's a proposal in Newsweek magazine by Joe Klein that Mrs. Clinton volunteer to testify before the committees to explain her role.

The President. I don't know what in the world we could do. I mean there's basically been this big—you know, I don't have anything new to add. We've answered all the questions. There has been a $3.6 million RTC investigation which basically says that what we said was there all the time. You know, no one questions—no serious person questions all the reports on whether Vince Foster committed suicide or not. I don't know what to do. I think these hearings will proceed and our people will cooperate, and we'll just see what happens.

Yes, Bill [Bill Plante, CBS News].

Bosnia

Q. Mr. President, we know that you just met with the leadership to try and make your veto of the Bosnia arms embargo lifting stick. But in the event that it doesn't, and not knowing as we speak what the size of the margin is going to be, what's the next step? What else would you look to do?

The President. Well, whatever the vote is, we still might sustain a veto. But I was encouraged by a few people who told me that they had decided on reflection that it was not the thing to do now. The Rapid Reaction Force, after all, is showing some strength there. And I would remind you that the only thing that has ever worked in the last 2½ years is when the Bosnian Serbs thought the United Nations would permit NATO and the Americans who are working with NATO to use air power to stop the aggression so that there would have to be a negotiated settlement. And in the last several days, the last couple of weeks in Gorazde, you know, we've gotten five convoys through; there has been no assault on it.

And I think that this new strategy will work if we can hammer out a negotiated settlement and there's a new effort there. So I believe that is the best strategy. I've said it all along, and I haven't changed my position. I'm going to try to see that position prevail.

Whitewater and Waco Hearings

Q. Mr. President, on both the ongoing hearings, Waco and Whitewater, are you convinced and can you say for the record that everything that is going to come out is out, vis-a-vis where you stand in the White House and your policy decisions on both?

The President. As far as I know—we have not added anything new to what was already known, but as far as I know we have been totally forthcoming and have said everything there is to be said on it.

Telecommunications Reform

Q. Mr. President, can you tell us, first of all, why you want to veto the telecommunications bill? I understand that you're concerned about concentration of media power. And in regard to that, can you comment on the merger yesterday between ABC and Walt Disney and the proposed merger that may happen today between CBS and Westinghouse and whether you see this concentration of power happening?

The President. Well, I think first of all, you have to take—on these mergers, under our law and as a matter of economics, you have to take them case by case and analyze them. And all I know about the proposed mergers is what I read this morning when I woke up. So I can't comment on that.

I do think it would be an error to set up a situation in the United States where one person could own half the television stations in the country or half of the media outlets. And we don't have a fairness doctrine anymore, and we don't have—particularly if we took the Federal Government out of—all the Federal agencies out of any kind of maintenance of competition or maintenance of competitive environment, by taking the Justice Department out of it, for example.

I would remind you that we have the most successful telecommunications operations in the world partly because we have had the proper balance between a highly competitive environment and an openness to new forces and new technologies and new entries in it from all around the world.

I want very badly to sign a telecommunications bill. We tried to pass one, this administration did, during the last session of Congress. One of the interest groups affected by this great drama that's unfolding in the telecommunications area prevented, through its supporters in the Senate, prevented the bill from passing in the last session of Congress. I hope we can get it, but we want to get it right.

The Vice President has done a lot of work on this over the years. He and I have talked about this at great length. And we have negotiated in good faith with the Congress to try to get it right. We want very much to sign a bill. We believe it will be good for the American economy and good for the American consumers if it's the right kind of bill. So we'll keep working on it.

Thank you.

NOTE: The President spoke at 11:17 a.m. in the Briefing Room at the White House.

Teleconference Remarks to the Fraternal Order of Police
August 1, 1995

Thank you very much, Dewey. I'm going to miss those introductions. I want to thank you for your 8 years of strong leadership as the national president of the Fraternal Order of Police. It gives me great pleasure to present you a Presidential commendation for your distinguished service to the Nation, which I believe the Attorney General will personally deliver to you tomorrow.

I also want to thank the other departing board members for all the hard work that you have done to help us strengthen law enforcement around the country. I understand that the elections to succeed all of you folks are on Thursday, so let me say as a fellow candidate, I want to wish the other candidates the best of luck and offer every one of them my heartfelt sympathy. I know how tough the last couple of days before an election can be; I've been there.

Your new president will lead the FOP into a better, safer world for law enforcement; a better, safer world because of the hard work of people like Dewey Stokes; a better, safer world because of the partnership our administration has been privileged to forge with you and with men and women in law enforcement all across our great country.

In the years before I came to Washington, it was clear that those of you who put your lives on the line to protect the rest of us were simply not getting the tools you needed to get the job done. The facts spoke for themselves. Crime was going up, but the number of police was staying the same or falling in so many cities and rural areas. It was a dangerous ratio.

I also had a lot of personal experience as a guide. As attorney general and then as a Governor, I went to too many funerals for police officers who were friends of mine killed in the line of duty. When I became President, I knew we all had to do more. So I came to Washington with a clear agenda: more police, guns out of the hands of criminals, an emphasis on community policing and other strategies to build stronger neighborhoods and to stop crimes before they happen. Working together, we have turned that agenda into law.

You and I and others who are on our side broke 6 years of gridlock and passed a crime bill that was written with the help of police officers all across America. We knew we needed more police officers, so we're putting 100,000 more police on the street. Already we've boosted your ranks by awarding more than 20,000 new police officers to over half the departments in the United States. We knew we had to get deadly assault weapons out of our lives, so we banned 19 types of assault weapons, weapons that target police officers and children. At the same time, we protected about 650 hunting and sporting weapons specifically.

We knew too many criminals were getting too many chances to do harm, so now we have "three strikes and you're out," and it's being enforced around the country. We knew there had to be zero tolerance for killing a law enforcement officer, so now in Federal law, we have the death penalty for anyone who murders a police officer. We also passed the Brady bill, which languished in Congress for 7 years. Last year alone, this commonsense law prevented more than 40,000 felons and fugitives from purchasing handguns.

And in June, I announced my support of legislation to ban armor-piercing bullets. Our current laws control ammunition based on what it's made of, and that's not good enough. Too many lethal bullets still slip through the cracks. This legislation will change that. It will see to it that we judge ammunition not on the basis of what's in it but on the harm it can do. If it can rip through a bulletproof vest like a knife through butter, then it should be history, no matter what it's made of.

These measures are helping you bring safety and security back to the lives of millions of Americans and helping you to be somewhat safer while you're doing that very difficult job.

And you have made a phenomenal amount of progress. Crime is down in major cities all around the country. Last Sunday, the New York Times reported that the dramatic drop in crime in New York City is a direct result of sensible gun laws, increased police presence, and a focus on hot spots, on the areas with high crime rates. A study the Justice Department sponsored in Kansas City yielded similar results: target an area, get rid of the guns, intimidate the criminals, the crime goes down. We are making progress.

But you and I both know we've got a lot more to do, because even as the overall crime rates drop, the rate of random violence among young people is still going up—dramatically in many places. As a parent, I am sick and tired of seeing stories like the one I read recently about a 16-year-old boy who shot a 12-year-old boy dead because he thought he'd been treated with disrespect by the younger boy. This story came just days after a national survey in which an unbelievable two-thirds of young gang members said they thought it was actually acceptable to shoot someone if they treated you with disrespect.

As long as there are stories like this, as long as young people are more likely to be both the victims and the perpetrators of crime, as long as casual drug use among our children is rising even as overall hard drug use goes down, as long as there are children who have never been taught the difference between right and wrong, we'll all have more work to do.

And that's why I'm troubled by so much of what's going on here in Washington. We have to balance the budget, all right, but there are some in Congress who would do it by tipping the balance against law enforcement. They would replace our efforts to put 100,000 new police officers on the street with a block grant that doesn't require a single new officer to be hired. They want to cut 23 million students out of our safe and drug-free schools initiative— out of the programs that so many of you bring to our schools every day all across America. And literally, they want to shut down the National Office of Drug Control Policy.

We can't give up on the war on drugs. And we can't back off of our support for law enforcement. And the truth is, we don't need to sacrifice these national priorities to balance the budget. We can continue to implement the crime bill and balance the budget. The only thing we'd have to do is to give up on an unnecessarily huge tax cut and to take a little longer to balance the budget. Now that luxury seems a small price to pay for necessities like balancing the budget and strengthening law enforcement at the same time.

And believe it or not, there are still some in Congress who want to repeal the Brady bill and lift the ban on assault weapons. Let me be clear: These attempts to roll back the clock are misguided. We cannot turn back in the fight against crime. There are still too many streets in America where our children are afraid to stand at a bus stop, too many neighborhoods where our seniors are fearful of going to the grocery store, too many communities where families are scared to head outside for a walk on a warm summer evening.

So those in Congress who would attempt to repeal the Brady bill or the assault weapons ban or our pledge to put 100,000 new police officers on the street, let me say one more time: You're going nowhere fast. If you do succumb to the political pressure from extremist groups to repeal any of these measures, I will veto them in a heartbeat.

On these issues I have a simple pledge. I won't let any bill pass my desk that hurts you or the people you protect. That's a good American standard. We all ought to judge our conduct by it.

You know, this has been a difficult period for law enforcement. You seem to be under assault from many fronts. Like people from every walk of life, police officers sometimes do make mistakes and have to deal with the consequences. But unlike other citizens, you also put your lives on the line for the rest of us every day. I'm reminded of a T-shirt that people in Oklahoma City made after the terrible bombing there. It read, "A society that makes war against its police had better learn to make friends with criminals." That's the fact.

I'm sorry I can't be with you in person today, but I want you to have no doubt I am still standing shoulder to shoulder with you in the battle against crime and violence. It threatens us all every day, every night, and you're trying

to do something about it. As long as you are, I'll be with you for as long as I'm here.

Thank you, and God bless you all.

NOTE: The President spoke at 12:45 p.m. by satellite from Room 459 of the Old Executive Office Building to the FOP conference in Virginia Beach, VA.

Statement on Proposed Telecommunications Reform Legislation
August 1, 1995

My administration is committed to enactment of a telecommunications reform bill in this Congress. Such legislation is needed to stimulate investment, promote competition, provide open access to information networks, strengthen and improve universal service, and provide for flexible regulations for this important industry. Consumers should receive the benefits of lower prices, better quality, and greater choices in their telephone and cable services, and they should continue to benefit from a diversity of voices and viewpoints in radio, television, and the print media.

Unfortunately, H.R. 1555, as reported by the Commerce Committee and amended by the managers' amendment, does not reach any of these goals. Instead of promoting investment and competition, it promotes mergers and concentration of power. Instead of promoting open access and diversity of content and viewpoints, it would allow fewer people to control greater numbers of television, radio, and newspaper outlets in every community.

H.R. 1555 with the managers' amendment would:

—allow a single owner to acquire television stations that can reach 50 percent of the Nation;

—allow the acquisition of an unlimited number of radio stations in every community and across the Nation;

—repeal the newspaper/broadcast and broadcast/cable cross-ownership bans that currently exist;

—permit the Bell Operating Companies to offer long distance service before there is real competition in local service, with less-than-minimum structural safeguards and without requiring a determination by the Department of Justice that entry will not impede competition;

—allow an excessive number of in-region buyouts between telephone companies and cable operators, substituting consolidation for competition and leaving consumers in rural areas and small towns with no rate protection in most cases and no foreseeable expectation of competition;

—deregulate cable programming services and equipment rates before cable operators face real competition and without providing any consumer protection provision after deregulation;

—preempt the States from implementing certain rate regulation schemes and opening their local phone markets to certain types of competition as they choose; and

—not include the V-chip proposal the Senate adopted.

The cumulative effect of these provisions would be to harm competition and to weaken the benefits to the public. If H.R. 1555 with the managers' amendment is sent to me without deletion or revision of a significant number of these provisions I will be compelled to veto it in the best interests of the public and our national economic well-being.

Memorandum on Timber Salvage Legislation
August 1, 1995

Memorandum for the Secretary of the Interior; the Secretary of Agriculture; the Secretary of Commerce; the Administrator, Environmental Protection Agency

Subject: Implementing Timber-Related Provisions to Public Law 104–19

On July 27th, I signed the rescission bill (Public Law 104–19), which provides much-needed supplemental funds for disaster relief and other programs. It also makes necessary cuts in spending, important to the overall balanced budget plan, while protecting key investments in education and training, the environment, and other priorities.

While I am pleased that we were able to work with the Congress to produce this piece of legislation, I do not support every provision, most particularly the provision concerning timber salvage. In fact, I am concerned that the timber salvage provisions may even lead to litigation that could slow down our forest management program. Nonetheless, changes made prior to enactment of Public Law 104–19 preserve our ability to implement the current forest plans' standards and guidelines, and provides sufficient discretion for the Administration to protect other resources such as clean water and fisheries.

With these changes, I intend to carry out the objectives of the relevant timber-related activities authorized by Public Law 104–19. I am also firmly committed to doing so in ways that, to the maximum extent allowed, follow our current environmental laws and programs. Public Law 104–19 gives us the discretion to apply current environmental standards to the timber salvage program, and we will do so. With this in mind, I am directing each of you, and the heads of other appropriate agencies, to move forward expeditiously to implement these timber-related provisions in an environmentally sound manner, in accordance with my Pacific Northwest Forest Plan, other existing forest and land management policies and plans, and existing environmental laws, except those procedural actions expressly prohibited by Public Law 104–19.

I am optimistic that our actions will be effective, in large part, due to the progress the agencies have already made to accelerate dramatically the process for complying with our existing legal responsibilities to protect the environment. To ensure this effective coordination, I am directing that you enter into a Memorandum of Agreement by August 7, 1995, to make explicit the new streamlining procedures, coordination, and consultation actions that I have previously directed you to develop and that you have implemented under existing environmental laws. I expect that you will continue to adhere to these procedures and actions as we fulfill the objectives of Public Law 104–19.

WILLIAM J. CLINTON

Message to the Congress Reporting on the National Emergency With Respect to Iraq
August 1, 1995

To the Congress of the United States:

I hereby report to the Congress on the developments since my last report of February 8, 1995, concerning the national emergency with respect to Iraq that was declared in Executive Order No. 12722 of August 2, 1990. This report is submitted pursuant to section 401(c) of the National Emergencies Act, 50 U.S.C. 1641(c), and section 204(c) of the International Emergency Economic Powers Act, 50 U.S.C. 1703(c).

Executive Order No. 12722 ordered the immediate blocking of all property and interests in property of the Government of Iraq (including the Central Bank of Iraq) then or thereafter located in the United States or within the possession or control of a U.S. person. That order also prohibited the importation into the United States of goods and services of Iraqi origin as well as the exportation of goods, services, and technology from the United States to Iraq. The order prohibited travel-related transactions to or from Iraq and the performance of any contract in support of any industrial, commercial, or governmental project in Iraq. United States persons were also prohibited from granting or extending credit or loans to the Government of Iraq.

The foregoing prohibitions (as well as the blocking of Government of Iraq property) were continued and augmented on August 9, 1990, by Executive Order No. 12724, which was issued in order to align the sanctions imposed by the United States with United Nations Security Council Resolution 661 of August 6, 1990.

Executive Order No. 12817 was issued on October 21, 1992, to implement in the United States measures adopted in United Nations Security Council Resolution 778 of October 2, 1992. Resolution 778 requires U.N. Member States to transfer to a U.N. escrow account any funds (up to $200 million apiece) representing Iraqi-oil sale proceeds paid by purchasers after the imposition of U.N. sanctions on Iraq, to finance Iraq's obligations for U.N. activities with respect to Iraq, such as expenses to verify Iraqi weapons destruction, and to provide humanitarian assistance in Iraq on a nonpartisan basis. A portion of the escrowed funds also funds the activities of the U.N. Compensation Commission in Geneva, which handles claims from victims of the Iraqi invasion and occupation of Kuwait. Member States also may make voluntary contributions to the account. The funds placed in the escrow account are to be returned, with interest, to the Member States that transferred them to the United Nations, as funds are received from future sales of Iraqi oil authorized by the U.N. Security Council. No Member State is required to fund more than half of the total transfers or contributions to the escrow account.

This report discusses only matters concerning the national emergency with respect to Iraq that was declared in Executive Order No. 12722 and matters relating to Executive Orders No. 12724 and 12817 (the "Executive orders"). The report covers events from February 2, 1995, through August 1, 1995.

1. During the reporting period, there were no amendments to the Iraqi Sanctions Regulations.

2. The Department of the Treasury's office of Foreign Assets Control ("FAC") continues its involvement in lawsuits seeking to prevent the unauthorized transfer of blocked Iraqi assets. In *Consarc Corporation v. Iraqi-ministry of Industry and Minerals,* a briefing schedule has been set for disposition of FAC's December 16, 1994, appeal of the district court's order of October 17, 1994, transferring blocked property.

Investigations of possible violations of the Iraqi sanctions continue to be pursued and appropriate enforcement actions taken. There are currently 43 enforcement actions pending, including nine cases referred by FAC to the U.S. Customs Service for joint investigation. Additional FAC civil penalty notices were prepared during the reporting period for violations of the International Emergency Economic Powers Act and Iraqi sanction Regulations with respect to transactions involving Iraq. Three penalties totaling $8,905 were collected from two banks for funds transfers in violation of the prohibitions against transactions involving Iraq.

3. Investigation also continues into the roles played by various individuals and firms outside Iraq in the Iraqi government procurement network. These investigations may lead to additions to FAC's listing of individuals and organizations determined to be Specially Designated Nationals ("SDNs") of the Government of Iraq.

4. Pursuant to Executive Order No. 12817 implementing United Nations Security Council Resolution 778, on October 26, 1992, FAC directed the Federal Reserve Bank of New York to establish a blocked account for receipt for certain post-August 6, 1990, Iraqi-oil sales proceeds, and to hold, invest, and transfer these funds as required by the Order. On March 21, 1995, following payments by the Governments of Canada ($1,780,749.14), the European Community ($399,695.21), Kuwait ($2,500,000.00), Norway ($261,758.10), and Switzerland ($40,000.00), respectively, to the special United Nations-controlled account, entitled "United Nations Security Council Resolution 778 Escrow Account," the Federal Reserve Bank of New York was directed to transfer a corresponding amount of $4,982,202.45 from the blocked account it holds to the United Nations-controlled account. Similarly, on April 5, 1995, following the payment of $5,846,238.99 by the European Community, the Federal Reserve Bank of New York was directed to transfer a corresponding amount of $5,846,238.99 to the United Nations-

controlled account. Again, on May 23, 1995, following the payment of $3,337,941.75 by the European Community, $571,428.00 by the Government of the Netherlands and $1,200,519.05 by the Government of the United Kingdom, the Federal Reserve Bank of New York was directed to transfer a corresponding amount of $5,109,888.80 to the United Nations-controlled account. Finally, on June 19, 1995, following the payment of $915,584.96 by the European Community and $736,923.12 by the Government of the United Kingdom, the Federal Reserve Bank of New York was directed to transfer a corresponding amount of $1,652,508.08 to the United Nations-controlled account. Cumulative transfers from the blocked Federal Reserve Bank of New York account since issuance of Executive Order No. 12817 have amounted to $175,133,026.20 of the up to $200 million that the United States is obligated to match from blocked Iraqi oil payments, pursuant to United Nations Security Council Resolution 778.

5. The Office of Foreign Assets Control has issued a total of 590 specific licenses regarding transactions pertaining to Iraq or Iraqi assets since August 1990. Licenses have been issued for transactions such as the filing of legal actions against Iraqi governmental entities, legal representation of Iraq, and the exportation to Iraq of donated medicine, medical supplies, food intended for humanitarian relief purposes, the execution of powers of attorney relating to the administration of personal assets and decedents' estates in Iraq, the protection of preexistent intellectual property rights in Iraq and travel to Iraq for the purposes of visiting Americans detained there. Since my last report, 57 specific licenses have been issued.

6. The expenses incurred by the Federal Government in the 6 month period from February 2, 1995, through August 1, 1995, which are directly attributable to the exercise of powers and authorities conferred by the declaration of a national emergency with respect to Iraq are reported to be about $4.9 million, most of which represents wage and salary costs for Federal personnel. Personnel costs were largely centered in the Department of the Treasury (particularly in the office of Foreign Assets Control, the U.S. Customs Service, the Office of the Under Secretary for Enforcement, and the Office of the General Counsel), the Department of State (particularly the Bureau of Economic and Business Affairs, the Bureau of Near Eastern Affairs, the Bureau of International Organization Affairs, the Bureau of Political-Military Affairs, the U.S. Mission to the United Nations, and the Office of the Legal Adviser) and the Department of Transportation (particularly the U.S. Coast Guard).

7. The United States imposed economic sanctions on Iraq in response to Iraq's illegal invasion and occupation of Kuwait, a clear act of brutal aggression. The United States, together with the international community, is maintaining economic sanctions against Iraq because the Iraqi regime has failed to comply fully with United Nations Security Council resolutions. Security Council resolutions on Iraq call for the elimination of Iraqi weapons of mass destruction, Iraqi recognition of Kuwait and the inviolability of the Iraq-Kuwait boundary, the release of Kuwaiti and other third-country nationals, compensation for victims of Iraqi aggression, long-term monitoring of weapons of mass destruction capabilities, the return of Kuwaiti assets stolen during Iraq's illegal occupation of Kuwait, renunciation of terrorism, an end to internal Iraqi repression of its own civilian population, and the facilitation of access of international relief organizations to all those in need in all parts of Iraq. More than 5 years after the invasion, a pattern of defiance persists: a refusal to account for missing Kuwaiti detainees; failure to return Kuwaiti property worth millions of dollars, including military equipment that was used by Iraq in its movement of troops to the Kuwait border in October 1994; sponsorship of assassinations in Lebanon and in northern Iraq; incomplete declarations to weapons inspectors; and ongoing widespread human rights violations. As a result, the U.N. sanctions remain in place; the United States will continue to enforce those sanctions under domestic authority.

The Baghdad government continues to violate basic human rights of its own citizens through systematic repression of minorities and denial of humanitarian assistance. The Government of Iraq has repeatedly said it will not be bound by United Nations Security Council Resolution 688. For more than 4 years, Baghdad has maintained a blockade of food, medicine, and other humanitarian supplies against northern Iraq. The Iraqi military routinely harasses residents of the north and has attempted to "Arabize" the Kurdish, Turcomen, and Assyrian areas in the north. Iraq has not relented in its artillery attacks against civilian population centers in the south or in its burning and draining operations in the southern marshes, which have forced thousands to flee to neighboring States. In April 1995, the U.N. Security Council adopted resolution 986 authorizing Iraq to export limited quantities of oil (up to $1 billion per quarter) under U.N. supervision in order to finance the purchase of food, medicine, and other humanitarian supplies. The resolution includes arrangements to ensure equitable distribution of such assistance to all the people of Iraq. The resolution also provides for the payment of compensation to victims of Iraqi aggression and for the funding of other U.N. activities with respect to Iraq. Resolution 986 was carefully crafted to address the issues raised by Iraq to justify its refusal to implement similar humanitarian resolutions adopted in 1991 (Resolutions 706 and 712), such as oil export routes and questions of national sovereignty. Nevertheless, Iraq refused to implement this hu-

manitarian measure. This only reinforces our view that Saddam Hussein is unconcerned about the hardships suffered by the Iraqi people.

The policies and actions of the Saddam Hussein regime continue to pose an unusual and extraordinary threat to the national security and foreign policy of the United States as well as to regional peace and security. The U.N. resolutions require that the Security Council be assured of Iraq's peaceful intentions in judging its compliance with sanctions. Because of Iraq's failure to comply fully with these resolutions, the United States will continue to apply economic sanctions to deter it from threatening peace and stability in the region.

WILLIAM J. CLINTON

The White House,
August 1, 1995.

Remarks on Education and an Exchange With Reporters
August 3, 1995

The President. Good afternoon. I'm glad to be here today with the Vice President and Secretary Reich, Secretary Riley, Deputy Secretary Kunin, Congressman Owens, Congresswoman Pelosi, and all these distinguished education leaders.

The Secretary of Education is going to present me his draft report on the condition of education today. And since the House is about to vote on the education funding bill, I thought it was appropriate to make a brief statement.

This is a critical time for American education for at least two reasons. First of all, everybody knows that the level of education and skills of our work force will determine their ability to get and keep good jobs and to have a secure future. Secondly, the number of children in our schools is once again rising. Today, one in four Americans is in school. The need for skills development is greater than ever, and the number of people who need it is larger than ever.

I have made a proposal on education which shows that you can balance the budget and fully fund education and training in a way that is good for the economy. It's good for the econ-

omy to balance the budget; it's good for the economy to invest in education. And it is what we owe to our young people and to older people who need further education and training to get better jobs.

Our balanced budget actually increases education $41 billion over the next 7 years. The bill being voted on today in the House does exactly the reverse. It dramatically cuts education—$36 billion. It would take 180,000 children off Head Start. It would end funding for Goals 2000, which raises standards and shrinks class size, which is terribly important. It would cut one million children who are poor out of the benefits of the Title I program. It would cut 300,000 low-income students out of Pell grants for college. It would target almost 600,000 unemployed and underemployed adults who won't be able to get job-training programs, mostly in their local community colleges, throughout this country. This is wrong. It is simply wrong.

Before this Congress, education and training have been matters of bipartisan common ground. President Bush often talked about how proud he was of increasing Head Start. This is the first time, as far as I know, in the history of the Head Start program when the Congress is poised to reduce the number of children in Head Start.

The school-to-work program is being cut. It's terribly important. There are a lot of young people who don't go to 4-year colleges who need the opportunity to get further training after high school and good jobs. And of course, what is being done to the college programs and the job training programs are simply unacceptable.

So from preschoolers to adults, this bill is a body blow to their future and a body blow to our efforts to create a high-opportunity, high-wage economy, not a hard-work, low-wage economy. This is a decision today that will affect the incomes of the American people.

The biggest problem we've still got is that we've got good economic performance, but more than half of our people are having stagnant wages. This will make the problem worse. Under the guise of balancing the budget, we are consigning millions more Americans to a more limited future. It is wrong, and I certainly hope it is defeated today.

Bosnia and Croatia

Q. Mr. President, does it help to have Croatian forces engaging the Bosnian Serbs on the western edge?

The President. Well, we have—what we have cautioned the Croatians about is widening the war. We don't want to see a widening of the war. We understand their desire to relieve the pressure on Bihac. And of course, that is a commitment the United Nations has made as well.

So we hope that whatever is done can be done without leading to a wider war. One of the prime objectives of the United States has been to try to confine the conflict to its present dimensions.

Teenage Smoking

Q. Mr. President, do you think that smoking among youth is——

The President. I think that smoking among youths should be diminished, and the Government has a responsibility there. I'm looking at what our options are, and we'll have an announcement on it before too long.

Q. So you support that idea?

Q. Is that a yes?

The President. I think—I told you what I— I think it's a terrible problem. We've got to do something about it. It's going up when it ought to be going down. If you want to lower health care costs, increase life expectancy, and broaden the quality of life for people, reducing teenage smoking is one good way to start. There's hardly anything we could do that would have a bigger impact. The question is, exactly what should we do? I've gotten some recommendations on it, and we'll have a position shortly. I just don't have an announcement to make today.

NOTE: The President spoke at 12:15 p.m. in the Cabinet Room at the White House.

Statement on Proposed Welfare Reform Legislation
August 3, 1995

I strongly support the Work First bill proposed by Senators Daschle, Breaux, and Mikulski. Instead of maintaining the current welfare system, which undermines our basic values of work, responsibility, and family, this plan sends people to work so they can earn a paycheck, not a welfare check. It provides the child care people need to move from welfare to work and to enable them to stay off welfare in the first place. It holds State bureaucracies accountable for real results and rewards States for putting people to work, not just cutting people off. It saves money by moving people to work, not by shipping the States more problems and less money. The Work First plan is real reform, and it should be the basis for a strong bipartisan bill.

It is time for Congress to reach across party lines and pass real welfare reform. The American people have waited long enough.

Statement on Hurricane Erin
August 3, 1995

For several days now, we have been watching and waiting as Hurricane Erin approached the Florida coast, not knowing what to expect but preparing for the worst. We thank God that this storm did not pack the catastrophic punch that others have in the past. However, it did cause considerable damage.

Our hearts and prayers go out to all who have been impacted by the hurricane. We pray for a quick recovery. To help that process get underway, I have tonight signed an emergency declaration for the State of Florida and have asked James Lee Witt, the Director of the Federal Emergency Management Agency, to coordinate all efforts to save lives and protect the health, safety, and property of those affected.

There are already FEMA trucks loaded with plastic sheeting, chainsaws, generators, and other tools headed for the impacted area. Director Witt will go to Florida first thing in the morning, inspect the damage, and report back to me.

I have spoken with Governor Chiles and asked him to convey to the people of Florida our commitment to this recovery effort. I am proud of the work Governor Chiles and all of the State and local emergency workers did in preparing for this storm. As a former Governor, I know how important emergency preparedness is in saving lives and protecting property. I applaud their efforts and salute the courage and strength of all Floridians dealing with the damage caused by the hurricane.

Letter to Congressional Leaders Reporting on Iraq's Compiance With United Nations Security Council Resolutions
August 3, 1995

Dear Mr. Speaker: *(Dear Mr. President:)*

Consistent with the Authorization for Use of Military Force Against Iraq Resolution (Public Law 102–1), and as part of my effort to keep the Congress fully informed, I am reporting on the status of efforts to obtain Iraq's compliance with the resolutions adopted by the U.N. Security Council.

Since its recognition of Kuwait last November, Iraq has done little to comply with its numerous remaining obligations under Council resolutions. At the most recent review of Iraq sanctions on July 11, 1995, the Security Council unanimously decided to maintain the sanctions regime on Iraq without change. We shall continue to insist that the sanctions be maintained until Iraq complies with all relevant provisions of U.N. Security Council resolutions.

Iraq remains out of compliance with its obligations regarding weapons of mass destruction (WMD), according to recent reports from the U.N. Special Commission on Iraq (UNSCOM). Iraq's recent admission that it had an offensive biological weapons program has received much

attention. This admission should come as no surprise, the evidence of this program having been known for some time. Now we must see if Iraq discloses the details of this program, as required. If history is any indicator, we can expect Iraq to conceal information about details of the program until confronted with irrefutable evidence by UNSCOM.

The Iraqi regime recently said it would not be forthcoming on its biological weapons program until UNSCOM "closed the file" in the missile and chemical weapons areas. This type of quid pro quo is unacceptable. The Council's resolutions are unconditional. Iraq cannot trade compliance in one for a "clean slate" in another. The fact that issues remain to be addressed in these various areas can be directly attributed to a pattern of Iraqi obfuscation. Moreover, the nature of UNSCOM's mandate is such that files can never be pronounced "closed." The UNSCOM must be able to investigate new leads as they arise in any area.

In addition to failing to comply with the WMD provisions of Security Council resolutions, the regime remains in violation of numerous other Security Council requirements. The regime has failed to be forthcoming with information on hundreds of Kuwaitis and some third-country nationals missing since the Iraqi occupation.

Iraq has also not returned to Kuwait the millions of dollars worth of Kuwaiti property looted during the occupation. This includes a vast store of military equipment. Earlier this year, Iraq dumped a large amount of military equipment on the Kuwaiti border in an attempt to convince the Council it was making a good-faith effort to comply. None of the equipment returned was operational. It had all been stripped bare of anything of value. Some of the material returned had not even originated in Kuwait; it was captured from Iran during the Iran-Iraq War. Some vehicles and items still bore hastily painted-over portraits of the Ayatollah Khomeini and contained Iranian identity papers. None of the top-of-the-line military equipment looted from Kuwait has been returned.

The Council on April 14 unanimously adopted Resolution 986, an effective means to provide relief for the hardship that ordinary Iraqis are suffering as a result of Saddam Hussein's failure to comply with Council requirements. Nonetheless, on June 1, Secretary General Boutros-Ghali informed the Security Council that Iraq had officially refused to implement this resolution. The sanctions regime does not prevent the shipment of food or medicine to Iraq. However, Saddam Hussein continues to squander Iraq's resources on his repressive security apparatus and personal palaces, while using the suffering of ordinary Iraqis as a propaganda tool to press for the lifting of sanctions. Resolution 986 undermines his self-serving excuses for neglecting the legitimate needs of the Iraqi people.

The no-fly zones over northern and southern Iraq continue to deter Iraq from using its aircraft against its population. However, the Iraqi government persists in its brutal campaign against its perceived enemies throughout the country. Iraqi forces periodically shell villages in the south and the north with artillery. In the south, Iraq's repression of the Shi'a population, and specifically the Marsh Arabs, continues, as does a policy of deliberate environmental devastation. The threat to the traditional way of life of Iraq's Marsh Arabs remains critical. In the last few years, the population of the marsh region has fallen sharply as Iraqi military

operations have forcibly dispersed residents to other areas and thousands of Shi'a refugees have sought refuge in Iran.

The human rights situation in Iraq remains unchanged. As previously reported by the Special Rapporteur of the U.N. Commission on Human Rights (UNHRC), Max van der Stoel, the Iraqi military's repression against civilian populations continues, as do political killings, mass executions, and state-sponsored terrorism. Clearly, the Government of Iraq has not complied with the provisions of UNSC Resolution 688 demanding that it cease repression of its own people.

The Special Rapporteur has asserted that the Government of Iraq has engaged in war crimes and crimes against humanity, and may have committed violations of the 1948 Genocide Convention. The Special Rapporteur continues to call on the Government of Iraq to permit the stationing of human rights monitors inside Iraq to improve the flow of information and to provide independent verification of reports of human rights abuses. We continue to support Mr. van der Stoel's work and his call for monitors.

The Multinational Interception Force (MIF) continues to play a vital role in enforcing U.N. economic sanctions against Iraq. The Gulf states of Saudi Arabia, Qatar, Bahrain, the United Arab Emirates, and Kuwait have cooperated with the MIF by accepting ships intercepted for attempting to smuggle commodities from Iraq and in taking action against their cargoes in accordance with relevant U.N. Security Council resolutions, including Resolutions 665 and 778. In addition, the United States has provided information to the Governments of Panama, Honduras, St. Vincent and the Grenadines, and the United Arab Emirates concerning sanctions violations committed by vessels under their flags. Two of these governments have initiated deflagging proceedings, with Panama formally deflagging one vessel.

For more than 3 years, the story has not changed; the Baghdad regime flouts the sanctions, demonstrates disdain for the United Nations, and engages in actions that we believe constitute continuing contraventions of Security Council Resolutions 686, 687, and 688.

We are monitoring closely the plight of the civilian population throughout Iraq. Our bilateral assistance program in the north will continue, to the extent possible. We also will continue to make every effort, given the practical constraints, to assist the populations in southern and central Iraq through support for the continuation of U.N. humanitarian programs. Finally, we will continue to explore with our allies and Security Council partners means to compel Iraq to cooperate on humanitarian and human rights issues.

Security Council Resolution 687 affirmed that Iraq is liable under international law for compensating the victims of its unlawful invasion and occupation of Kuwait. The U.N. Compensation Commission (UNCC) has received about 2.6 million claims worldwide, with an asserted value of approximately $176 billion. The United States has submitted approximately 3,300 claims, with an asserted value of about $1.8 billion.

To date, the UNCC Governing Council has approved some 355,000 individual awards, worth about $1.39 billion. About 620 awards totaling over $11.8 million have been issued to U.S. claimants.

The UNCC has been able to pay only the first small awards for serious personal injury or death ($2.7 million). Unfortunately, the remainder of the awards cannot be paid at this time, because the U.N. Compensation Fund lacks sufficient funding. The awards are supposed to be financed by a deduction from the proceeds of future Iraqi oil sales, once such sales are permitted to resume. However, Iraq's refusal to meet the Security Council's terms for a resumption of oil sales has left the UNCC without adequate financial resources to pay the awards. Iraq's intransigence means that the victims of its aggression remain uncompensated for their losses 4 years after the end of the Gulf War.

In sum, Iraq is still a threat to regional peace and security. Thus, I continue to be determined to see Iraq comply fully with all its obligations under the UNSC resolutions. I will oppose any relaxation of sanctions until Iraq demonstrates its overall compliance with the relevant resolutions. Iraq should adopt democratic processes, respect human rights, treat its people equitably, and adhere to basic norms of international behavior.

I appreciate the support of the Congress for our efforts, and will continue to keep the Congress informed about this important issue.

Sincerely,

WILLIAM J. CLINTON

NOTE: Identical letters were sent to Newt Gingrich, Speaker of the House of Representatives, and Albert Gore, Jr., President of the Senate.

Message to the Congress Transmitting the National Urban Policy Report
August 3, 1995

To the Congress of the United States:

I transmit herewith my Administration's National Urban Policy Report, "Empowerment: A New Covenant With America's Communities," as required by 42 U.S.C. 4503(a). The Report provides a framework for empowering America's disadvantaged citizens and poor communities to build a brighter future for themselves, for their families and neighbors, and for America. The Report is organized around four principles:

First, it links families to work. It brings tax, education and training, housing, welfare, public safety, transportation, and capital access policies together to help families make the transition to self-sufficiency and independence. This linkage is critical to the transformation of our communities.

Second, it leverages private investment in our urban communities. It works with the market and the private sector to build upon the natural assets and competitive advantages of urban communities.

Third, it is locally driven. The days of made in Washington solutions, dictated by a distant Government, are gone. Instead, solutions must be locally crafted, and implemented by entrepreneurial public entities, private actors, and a growing network of community-based firms and organizations.

Fourth, it relies on traditional values—hard work, family, responsibility. The problems of so many inner-city neighborhoods—family break-up, teen pregnancy, abandonment, crime, drug use—will be solved only if individuals, families, and communities determine to help themselves.

These principles reflect an emerging consensus in the decades-long debate over urban policy. These principles are neither Democratic nor Republican: they are American. They will enable local communities, individuals and families, businesses, churches, community-based organizations, and civic groups to join together to seize the opportunities and to solve the problems in their own lives. They will put the private sector back to work for all families in all communities. I therefore invite the Congress to work with us on a bipartisan basis to implement an empowerment agenda for America's communities and families.

In a sense, poor communities represent an untapped economic opportunity for our whole country. While we work together to open foreign markets abroad to American-made goods and services, we also need to work together to open the economic frontiers of poor communities here at home. By enabling people and communities in genuine need to take greater responsibility for working harder and smarter together, we can unleash the greatest underused source of growth and renewal in each of the local regions that make up our national economy and civic life. This will be good for cities and suburbs, towns and villages, and rural and urban

America. This will be good for families. This will be good for the country.

We have undertaken initiatives that seek to achieve these goals. Some seek to empower local communities to help themselves, including Empowerment Zones, Community Development banks, the Community Opportunity Fund, community policing, and enabling local schools and communities to best meet world-class standards. And some seek to empower individuals and families to help themselves, including our expansion of the earned-income tax cut for low- and moderate-income working families, and our proposals for injecting choice and competition into public and assisted housing and for a new G.I. Bill for America's Workers.

I am determined to end Federal budget deficits, and my balanced budget proposal shows that we can balance the budget without abandoning the investments that are vital to the security and prosperity of the country, now and in the future. I am confident that, working together, we can build common ground on an empowerment agenda while putting our fiscal house in order. I will do everything in my power to make sure this happens.

WILLIAM J. CLINTON

The White House,
August 3, 1995.

Remarks on Political Reform and an Exchange With Reporters
August 4, 1995

The President. Good afternoon. I have just finished a very productive and stimulating meeting with two outstanding Americans, John Gardner and Doris Kearns Goodwin. In the best tradition of our citizenship, they have set aside their very busy lives and concerns and work to take some time to come to Washington to try to help make political reform a reality.

We discussed how the trust of the American people has been eroded by what they see in Washington, by how the lobbyists hold sway more today then ever before. And the American people don't like it. The hardworking American families of this country know that they did not pay for the kind of influence that they see exercised too often in today's Congress.

When Congress treats telecommunications reform, for example, merely as a joust among would-be monopolists, ordinary consumers lose out. When the NRA hijacks a congressional hearing process, crime victims and police officers lose out. And everybody knows that last week's vote in the House to dramatically undermine our ability to enforce our environmental laws would not have happened if real campaign finance reform and real lobbying reform had been on the books.

For too long these issues have been mired in partisan in-fighting and paralyzed by special interests. We have an obligation to act when we can to move beyond partisanship. I had hoped we had reached such a point several weeks ago in New Hampshire when I shook hands with Speaker Gingrich on a proposal made to us by an ordinary American in the audience that we create a political reform commission that would work more or less like the base closing commission to make recommendations on campaign finance reform and lobbying reform.

Shortly after I returned from New Hampshire, I sent the Speaker a letter putting forward my ideas on how to do that. That moment of optimism gave way to 5 weeks of silence. When I asked John Gardner and Doris Kearns Goodwin to help me make this happen, I certainly hoped that the respect and eminence that they bring to this process would help move things forward. If there were a commission, these are the kinds of people I would appoint to it.

We continue to hope that the Speaker will live up to his handshake and move forward on this commission. But we shouldn't wait, and Congress shouldn't either.

Today I am announcing that I will use the power of my office to bring the sunlight of full disclosure to the lobbying process in Washington. Right now lobbyists can operate in secret. They can lawfully conceal who they work for, what loopholes or contracts or regulations they are seeking to pass, or what actions they are seeking to stop. And lobbying of the executive branch isn't disclosed at all.

Last week, an overwhelming bipartisan majority in the United States Senate voted for lobbying reform. But the House leadership has made it clear that they will not even schedule a vote on this measure for quite a long while. Delay, debate, and division: that's the same old thing. They won't put lobbyists in their proper place in our governmental structure.

So today I have decided to act on my own within my executive authority. I am requesting the Attorney General to prepare an Executive order that would bar executive branch employees from meeting with any lobbyist who does not fully disclose his or her activities to the public. In other words, if lobbyists want to contact the executive branch, fine, they can. That's an important part of our work here. But they can do it only if they tell the public who they are, what they're working on, how much they're spending, and what policy they are pushing or trying to block. We will, in other words, follow the strict and meaningful standards of the Senate bill. From now on, the executive branch

will operate as if the Senate bill had become law.

I have now acted on lobby reform. Now there is no excuse for congressional delay. The Senate has done its work. I urge the House to finish the job. This is really a moment for real bipartisan progress on political reform. In recent days, strong and often growing bipartisan majorities in the United States Senate have voted to preserve, first of all, public funding of Presidential campaigns—something John Gardner here did so much to create—to schedule a vote on campaign finance reform over the objection of the Senate majority leader and to pass a tough gift and lobby reform program in the Senate.

This bipartisan impulse is our best hope for true and lasting reform. But to get there it will have to spread to the House, which has been moving back into the past, not going forward into the future. That is our challenge today.

From the reform victories of the turn of the century progressives to the changes that followed Watergate, moments of national renewal have always called forth people of good will, regardless of party, who were willing to do what it takes to change things for the better. This is part of our national history, and it must be part of our common ground.

I call on Congress to join us here to pass lobby reform and campaign finance reform, to do it in a bipartisan way, and to restore the public trust. In the meanwhile, I am going to establish lobby reform in the executive branch by enacting by Executive order the bill passed by the United States Senate.

I'd like now to invite John Gardner and Doris Kearns Goodwin to say a few words.

[At this point, John W. Gardner, founder of Common Cause, and historian Doris Kearns Goodwin made brief remarks.]

Speaker of the House Newt Gingrich

Q. Mr. President, the Speaker today said that the reason he hasn't responded to the handshake is because his priority now is saving Medicare and that you're not doing anything to save Medicare and why not focus in on that as an issue instead of political and campaign finance reform.

The President. First of all, it takes no energy at all. He doesn't have to do anything in the Congress right now. All he has to do is to do what he said he'd do when he shook hands with me. Let's set up a commission. He can make his appointments, Senator Dole can make his appointments, I'll make my appointments, and Senator Daschle and Congressman Gephardt can make their appointments, and then let the commission go do its work. That is not a persuasive reason. There is nothing to do. That takes about 2 or 3 hours of staff time and about 30 minutes of his time.

So—and let's say this. Our administration has made the Medicare Trust Fund better. Their Medicare cuts are not necessary either to fix the Trust Fund or to balance the budget. Over half of their Medicare cuts—or roughly half of them—are increased costs to beneficiaries of Medicare which will not put one red cent into the Medicare Trust Fund. That is not what this is about.

We have shown you can balance the budget without hurting people on Medicare. And that's what I think the Speaker and the majority in the House and the Senate ought to say they want to do. And when they say that, we can resolve further problems with the Medicare Trust Fund. I have shown I'm willing to deal with that. I proposed some savings to help deal with that. This is not about the Medicare Trust Fund. This is about whether these beneficiaries are going to be soaked for no good reason.

Campaign Finance Reform

Q. Mr. President, why not take the same kind of unilateral action on campaign finance reform as you seem to be doing on lobbying reform, say, with respect to soft money donations to the party? And does the party understand fully, sir, your feelings about them selling access to you to big money donors?

The President. Yes, and we changed that. And we can change that. And I have no problem changing that. That is wrong.

I think—by the way, I think that the President and that any other person in public office ought to meet with his or her supporters, including financial supporters. I think that's important. I would do that anyway. I have always done that; from the time I was attorney general of my State I have done that. But it is wrong to raise money on the promise of guaranteed specific kinds of access. That is wrong, and we stopped that.

Now, the difference is, I can do this lobby reform and hold the executive branch to a higher standard and challenge the Congress to follow suit in a way that does not in any way under-mine the public interest. But if I hold the Democrats to a standard which in effect paralyzes them financially, in comparison to the Republicans, I will be punishing the very public interest that I seek to advance because it will make it less likely that there will be competitive elections.

The American people's only chance to make the right choices is when there are genuine competitive elections. I would love nothing better—if I could get an agreement with the Republican Party we could shut this whole thing down tomorrow. We could, by mutual agreement, at least change the party rules on campaign finance reform. And if they would do it, we could do it and we wouldn't have to wait for Congress to act.

Telecommunications Reform

Q. You mentioned the telecommunications bill, sir. Have the changes that have been made to it today made it any more acceptable to you?

The President. Well, I want to wait and see what happens. I know that they acted to try to stop one person from being able to own television stations, newspapers, radios, and cable networks in the same market. That was a very important step forward. I congratulate the House on that. Did the V-chip amendment pass? They're working on that. That's also very important to me.

As you know, I issued a letter on the House bill, which was changed markedly after it came out of committee—that's a very unusual procedure—setting forth the concerns that I have, the Vice President shares, our administration has. We'll just have to review the bill when it gets in its final form.

Bosnia and Croatia

Q. What about the war in Croatia? Are you concerned that that could spread into an all-out war in the Balkans?

The President. Yes—well, I'm concerned that it could spread the war in Bosnia and in the Croatia-Serbia area.

Let me just back up and say the Croatian offensive originally was launched in response to the Serb attack on Bihac, one of the protected areas. And it has largely, apparently, relieved a lot of pressure on Bihac. But because it is so comprehensive, it runs the risk of a wider war. And that is what we have cautioned against in our contacts with the Croats.

Q. So, Mr. President, you're saying that the actual offensive is justified?

The President. I explained that the original Croatian action, which we were told by the Croatian Government they would feel compelled to take, was animated by the Serbian attack on Bihac. But we have asked them to exercise real restraint because we are very concerned about a wider war.

Thank you.

NOTE: The President spoke at 2:15 p.m. in the Oval Office at the White House.

Statement on the 30th Anniversary of the Voting Rights Act
August 4, 1995

This Sunday, August 6, 1995, marks the 30th anniversary of the Voting Rights Act, guaranteeing the right to vote to all Americans, regardless of race. Passed by a bipartisan majority in Congress and signed by President Lyndon Johnson after years of struggle, the Voting Rights Act has correctly been recognized as the single most important civil rights law our Nation has ever adopted. It was accomplished through the sacrifice of thousands of Americans of all colors who courageously faced down a terrible injustice.

At the time the Voting Rights Act was enacted, people of color in many parts of the country were denied the right to exercise the most fundamental right of American democracy—the right to vote. African-American voter registration was practically non-existent in many areas due to an organized system of disenfranchisement, often backed by brutal intimidation, designed to fence people out of the political process.

In the 30 years since the enactment of the Voting Rights Act, minority registration rates have soared and thousands of people who once could not get elected simply because of the color of their skin are serving in Congress, State houses, and city halls throughout the country.

More important than those results, however, has been the effect of opening our democracy to all Americans. The Voting Rights Act guarantees that no American need ever again be afraid to register to vote, no American need ever again fear the walk to the polling place, no American need ever again fear that their vote is not wanted or will not count.

In signing the law, President Johnson said, "This act flows from a clear and simple wrong. Its only purpose is to right that wrong . . . The wrong is one which no American, in his heart, can justify. The right is one which no American, true to our principles, can deny."

On this 30th anniversary, my administration reaffirms its commitment to the full enforcement of the Voting Rights Act. We must continue to protect the right of every American to fully participate in the electoral process. I challenge Americans of all races and colors to rededicate ourselves to exercising our precious right to vote. Voting is the oxygen of democracy, and millions of Americans have given their last breath to keep that right alive. So, even as we celebrate 30 years of righting a terrible wrong, we must keep working to make sure that 30 years from now, every American over the age of 18 is a voting American.

Statement on Signing the Emergency Supplemental Appropriations and Rescissions Legislation
August 4, 1995

On July 27, 1995, I approved H.R. 1944, the Emergency Supplemental Appropriations for Additional Disaster Assistance, for Anti-terrorism Initiatives, for Assistance in the Recovery from the Tragedy that Occurred at Oklahoma City, and Rescissions Act, 1995. This legislation shows how we can work together to produce good legislation.

From the start of this rescission process, I agreed with the Congress on the need to cut spending. The question was, how should we do it?

I vetoed the original rescission bill because it would have cut spending the wrong way, by targeting education and training, environmental protection, and other key national priorities. I then worked with Republicans and Democrats alike to produce a better bill. I am pleased that this bill cuts nearly $16 billion in spending while protecting our key investments in education and training, the environment, and other priorities.

Like the earlier version, this bill also provides much-needed supplemental funds that I have sought for disaster relief activities of the Federal Emergency Management Agency, the Federal response to the bombing in Oklahoma City, increased anti-terrorism efforts, and debt relief to Jordan to facilitate progress toward a Middle East peace settlement.

To be sure, I do not support every provision of this bill. For instance, I still do not believe that this bill should contain any of the provisions relating to timber. But the final bill does contain changes in the language that preserve our ability to implement the current forest plans and their standards, and protect other resources such as clean water and fisheries. In addition, I am pleased that the Congress amended the bill to limit its special authorities for timber sales to end on December 31, 1996. Therefore, I have directed the Secretaries of the Interior, Agriculture, Commerce, the Administrator of the Environmental Protection Agency, and other Federal agencies to carry out timber salvage activities consistent with our forest plans and existing environmental laws.

In addition, though this bill includes a rescission of summer youth jobs funding for the summer of 1996, the Administration continues to support the program and will work with the Congress in the FY 1996 appropriations process to ensure that the program for the summer of 1996 is funded.

I have designated as an emergency all funds in this Act so designated by the Congress that I had not previously designated pursuant to section 251(b)(2)(D)(i) of the Balanced Budget and Emergency Deficit Control Act of 1985, as amended.

I am pleased that bipartisan leaders of Congress worked with me to produce a good bill. Working together, we can continue to produce good legislation for the American people.

WILLIAM J. CLINTON

The White House,
August 4, 1995.

NOTE: H.R. 1944, approved July 27, was assigned Public Law No. 104–19.

Statement on Signing the District of Columbia Emergency Highway Relief Act
August 4, 1995

Today I am pleased to sign into law H.R. 2017, the District of Columbia Emergency Highway Relief Act, a law to enable our Nation's capital city to advance critically needed highway construction projects. By temporarily waiving the District's cost-sharing requirements for these projects, this legislation assists the District during its period of fiscal crisis in a very practical and important way without imposing any additional cost on the American taxpayer.

Recognizing the importance of maintaining the District's highways for its residents, commuters from throughout the national capital area, and thousands of tourists from around the Nation and the world, this Administration initiated legislation to secure a similar temporary waiver for the District. With bipartisan and intergovernmental support, and through the dedicated efforts of members of the congressional delegation from this region, this legislation was expeditiously passed by both houses of Congress.

The District will be held accountable for the funds advanced for highway construction under this bill. The District is required to repay its share and must establish a dedicated highway fund to ensure it is able to make this repayment and to meet its matching share requirement in the future.

This legislation will enable the District to begin rebuilding its infrastructure almost immediately, as projects that were stalled for months due to a lack of funds can now quickly resume, creating many new jobs and safer streets for all who come to our Nation's capital.

WILLIAM J. CLINTON

The White House,
August 4, 1995.

NOTE: H.R. 2017, approved August 4, was assigned Public Law No. 104–21.

Message to the Congress Transmitting the District of Columbia Financial Authority Budget
August 4, 1995

To the Congress of the United States:

In accordance with section 106(a) of the District of Columbia Financial Responsibility and Management Assistance Authority Act of 1995, I am transmitting the District of Columbia Financial Responsibility and Management Assistance Authority's operating budget for FY 1996.

The Authority's request for its FY 1996 operating budget is $3.5 million. This budget was developed based on an estimated staffing level of 35 full-time employees. After reviewing the budgets and staffing levels of other control boards, the Authority believes this staffing level is the minimum necessary to carry out its wide range of fiscal, management, and legal responsibilities.

This transmittal does not represent an endorsement of the budget's contents.

WILLIAM J. CLINTON

The White House,
August 4, 1995.

Message to the Congress Transmitting the Energy Policy Report
August 4, 1995

To the Congress of the United States:

Throughout this century, energy has played a prominent role in American progress. The rise of the great industrial enterprises, the ascendence of the automobile, the emergence of environmental awareness, and the advent of the truly global economy all relate to the way that society produces and uses energy. As we face the opportunities and challenges of the next century, energy will continue to exert a powerful influence on our Nation's prosperity, security, and environment.

Energy policies that promote efficiency, domestic energy production, scientific and technological advances, and American exports help sustain a strong domestic economy. The need to protect the environment motivates our continual search for more innovative, economic, and clean ways to produce and use energy. And although oil crises have receded into memory, their potential for harming our economy and national security remains.

Our Administration has actively pursued a national energy policy since January 1993. We have engaged in an active dialogue with thousands of individuals, companies, and organizations. Informed by that dialogue, we have committed the resources of the Department of Energy and other agencies to ensure that our policy benefits energy consumers, producers, the environment, and the average citizen.

This report to the Congress, required by section 801 of the Department of Energy Organization Act, highlights our Nation's energy policy. The report underscores our commitment to implement a sustainable energy strategy—one that meets the needs of today while expanding the opportunities for America's future. By implementing a sustainable strategy, our energy policy will provide clean and secure energy for a competitive economy into the 21st century.

WILLIAM J. CLINTON

The White House,
August 4, 1995.

Message to the Congress Transmitting the Bulgaria-United States Nuclear Cooperation Agreement
August 4, 1995

To the Congress of the United States:

I am pleased to transmit to the Congress, pursuant to sections 123 b. and 123 d. of the Atomic Energy Act of 1954, as amended (42 U.S.C. 2153 (b), (d)), the text of a proposed Agreement Between the Government of the United States of America and the Government of the Republic of Bulgaria for Cooperation in the Field of Peaceful Uses of Nuclear Energy with accompanying annex and agreed minute. I am also pleased to transmit my written approval, authorization, and determination concerning the agreement, and the memorandum of the Director of the United States Arms Control and Disarmament Agency with the Nuclear Proliferation Assessment Statement concerning the agreement. The joint memorandum submitted to me by the Secretary of State and the Secretary of Energy, which includes a summary of the provisions of the agreement and various other attachments, including agency views, is also enclosed.

The proposed agreement with the Republic of Bulgaria has been negotiated in accordance with the Atomic Energy Act of 1954, as amended by the Nuclear Non-Proliferation Act of 1978 and as otherwise amended. In my judgment, the proposed agreement meets all statutory requirements and will advance the non-proliferation and other foreign policy interests of the United States. It provides a comprehensive framework for peaceful nuclear cooperation between the United States and Bulgaria under appropriate conditions and controls reflecting our strong common commitment to nuclear non-proliferation goals.

Bulgaria has consistently supported international efforts to prevent the spread of nuclear weapons. It was an original signatory of the Non-Proliferation Treaty (NPT) and has strongly supported the Treaty. As a subscriber to the Nuclear Supplier Group (NSG) Guidelines, it is committed to implementing a responsible nuclear export policy. It played a constructive role in the NSG effort to develop additional guidelines for the export of nuclear-related dual-use commodities. In 1990 it initiated a policy of requiring full-scope International Atomic Energy Agency (IAEA) safeguards as a condition of significant new nuclear supply to other nonnuclear weapon states.

I believe that peaceful nuclear cooperation with Bulgaria under the proposed agreement will be fully consistent with, and supportive of, our policy of responding positively and constructively to the process of democratization and economic reform in Eastern Europe. Cooperation under the agreement will also provide opportunities for U.S. business on terms that fully protect vital U.S. national security interests.

I have considered the views and recommendations of the interested agencies in reviewing the proposed agreement and have determined that its performance will promote, and will not constitute an unreasonable risk to, the common defense and security. Accordingly, I have approved the agreement and authorized its execution and urge that the Congress give it favorable consideration.

Because this agreement meets all applicable requirements of the Atomic Energy Act, as amended, for agreements for peaceful nuclear cooperation, I am transmitting it to the Congress without exempting it from any requirement contained in section 123 a. of that Act. This transmission shall constitute a submittal for purposes of both sections 123 b. and 123 d. of the Atomic Energy Act. The Administration is prepared to begin immediately the consultations with the Senate Foreign Relations and House Foreign Affairs Committees as provided in section 123 b. Upon completion of the 30-day continuous session period provided for in section 123 b.,

the 60-day continuous session period provided for in section 123 d. shall commence.

WILLIAM J. CLINTON

The White House,
August 4, 1995.

The President's Radio Address
August 5, 1995

Good morning. Today I'm at the Children's Inn at the National Institutes of Health in Bethesda, Maryland, with young patients and their families, some of whom are guests of the inn. For them, the Children's Inn is home while their children get well. The inn is built on a simple premise that even with the best doctors, medicine, and technology, no treatment is complete unless it includes the family.

Children know that better than anyone, that it's their mothers and fathers who carry them through the tough times. And that's true for all of us. But we all know, too, that our families all across America are going through tough times today. Right now, our families are feeling real pressure. Too many are working harder for less. Too many are afraid of losing their jobs or their retirement or their health care. Too many live in fear that their children are exposed to violence and drugs.

We have to do what we can to strengthen our families and to help them through these changing times. That's what we did with the very first law I signed as President, which took effect 2 years ago today. It's called the Family and Medical Leave Act. It could be called the working family protection act. Under this law, if you get sick, if your child gets sick, or your parent needs medical care, you can take time away from work without losing your job. Sometimes this time off can be the most important time in a family's life. It can also be the toughest time. But it would be a lot tougher if the family couldn't face it together.

If you know a family who's needed to use this leave, you know why it's so important. I know some of these families, and three of them are here today. Kenny Weaver, a Texas petroleum worker, took guaranteed leave to be with his daughter, Melissa. Diane Atwood of Little

Rock, Arkansas, needed leave to fight her own battle with Hodgkin's disease. J.C. Shardo of Atlanta needed to take a leave when her brother Swartz needed her by his side when he became ill. Because of this law, families in crisis can be together, and the breadwinners need not fear they'll lose their jobs.

The family and medical leave law is good for our families and it's good for our businesses because it allows our people to be both good parents or good children or good siblings and good workers. It supports family stability and family responsibility.

I want to make sure that if you're eligible for guaranteed leave, you know about it. As many as 50 million Americans are eligible, and as many as 3 million people a year may need to use it. If you work in the public sector or in the private sector for an employer who employs 50 or more people, you qualify to apply for a leave of 12 weeks for family or medical reasons.

The U.S. Labor Department has backed the claims of thousands of workers who were denied leave or fired when they tried to use this law. That's illegal. We'll protect your rights and the rights of your family. This law shows that we, as a nation, can value families through the choices we make together.

We've got a lot of other family choices to make in the weeks and months ahead. This week the Senate finally will take up welfare reform, which is also all about helping people become good workers and good parents. We've reached agreement on requiring teen mothers to live at home and stay in school, requiring parents to pay the child support they owe or work off what they owe. Now we need a bipartisan agreement that requires people on welfare to work but makes sure they get the child care they need to stay off welfare for good and to be good parents.

Family values are a big part of our national budget. Two years ago, our national budget reduced the deficit; that's good family values. But we increased the number of children in Head Start, we provided for immunizing all our children under 2, we made college loans more affordable and easier to repay, we increased tax relief for working parents, and we increased job training. We need to build on that family agenda, not tear it down.

The congressional majority seems to be determined to cut back on programs that advance our family values. How can you talk about family values in one breath and, in the next, take Head Start away from 50,000 poor children or cut back college loans and grants for students who need and deserve them or cut back worker training for people who are unemployed? But all that happened in the House of Representatives this week. They call it change. I say it shortchanges America's families in the fight for the future. This vote is antifamily, and I won't let it stand.

It's not too late to build a legacy—to build on the legacy of family leave. We ought to invest in education, invest in our families, raise the minimum wage, target tax relief to raising children and educating them, protect the Medicare of our seniors, and protect the right of people to keep their health insurance if they change jobs or if someone in the family gets sick. These are the kind of things that are worthy of the legacy of family leave. We have to work hard so that we know that our families will be better off, so that we can make tomorrow better than today for every family.

Thanks for listening.

NOTE: The President spoke at 10:06 a.m. from the Children's Inn at the National Institutes of Health in Bethesda, MD.

Interview with Bob Edwards and Mara Liasson of National Public Radio
August 7, 1995

Bosnia and Croatia

Mr. Edwards. Well, Croatia is back into it, and we wonder how the Croat offensive affects the prospects of a U.N. withdrawal and the accompanying commitment of U.S. ground troops.

The President. Well, my guess is that if the Croat offensive concludes successfully in the Krajina area, as it appears to be doing, and that is the extent of it, that it will not increase the chances of the U.N. withdrawing. But it does change the kind of balance of play in the area. And when you put that with the new resolve of NATO and the willingness of the U.N. to let NATO use air power and the establishment of the Rapid Reaction Force, two things we worked very hard for in the last few weeks, it may create some new opportunities to work toward a resolution of this.

Now, we're concerned, and we've told the Croatians we're concerned about anything that would spread the war, that would widen the war. But if the offensive concludes with the reestablishment of the dominance, the Croatia in the Krajina area, then I think it will not increase the chances of U.N. withdrawal.

Mr. Edwards. In the absence of direct U.S. involvement, why should the American people care about this conflict?

The President. The American people should care, first of all, because if the war spreads in the Balkans to other areas it could destabilize many, many countries in which we have a vital interest and bring America into the fray. Secondly, we should care because an awful lot of human damage has been done there, and a lot of people's human rights have been violated, and we should try to minimize the loss of life and human suffering. Thirdly, we should care because it's the first real security crisis in Europe after the end of the cold war, and it is important that we, working with our European allies through the United Nations and through NATO, do as much as humanly possible to do, given the fact that when you have these kind of intra-ethnic conflicts within countries, to some extent, any outside power is going to be limited in stopping the killing until there is a greater willingness to make peace. But we have to do our best to try to minimize the carnage, to try to keep it from spreading, and to try to demonstrate a consistent and determined and long-lasting commitment by our allies through the United Nations and through NATO to resolve this.

Ms. Liasson. Mr. President, there are tens of thousands of Krajina Serbs now who are being ethnically cleaned, and they're fleeing over the border into Bosnia. Can you tell us how that influx of Serbs into Bosnia will affect the conflict there? And also, what can you tell us about Croatian President Franjo Tudjman's intentions? Does he want to maintain the Bosnia Croat Federation, or do you think he wants an ethnically pure state of his own?

The President. Well, first, let's remember what gave rise to this offensive. There was a Bosnian Serb attack supported by the Krajina Serbs on the Bihac area of Bosnia, which is a Muslim area or at least a government area now. And President Tudjman ordered a counterattack to try to relieve Bihac and, in the process, to try to secure the areas within Croatia under control of his government.

I believe that he wants to see the Croats and the Muslims stay in their confederation within Bosnia. And you know, the United States took the lead in brokering that confederation. I think that it's very important because it ended, in effect, one-half of the civil war within Bosnia. So I felt good about that. And I think it will endure. I believe that confederation will endure.

What impact the Krajina Serbs going over into Bosnian territory will have is, frankly, impossible to determine at this time. If they become members of the Bosnian Serb army, then it could have a destabilizing impact. But no one knows for sure. That's why I say that circumstances have changed there in a way that might give us the opportunity to make some new efforts at a diplomatic settlement, and I'm going to be talking with our allies over the next few days to discuss that.

Ms. Liasson. But before the Croat offensive started, you warned the Croatians not to target civilians and not to target U.N. peacekeepers. They seem to have ignored both of those warnings. Do you have any control over the Croats?

The President. No, but I think we have—I think we and the Germans have some influence with the Croats. And I think what appears to have happened is they had more success than they had, I think, perhaps even imagined they might in the battle. And so they kept going until they had recovered that portion of their territory which had been previously under the dominance of the Krajina Serbs.

I do believe that President Tudjman will be reluctant to do anything that will knowingly spread the war and totally destabilize the situation in ways that undermine his interest and the interest of the Bosnian Croat Confederation within Bosnia. So, as I said, I'm hopeful that this will turn out to be something that will give us an avenue to a quicker diplomatic resolution, not a road to a longer war.

Mr. Edwards. This is the most important foreign policy problem of your Presidency, and you are seen as indecisive. Senator Dole has tried to take advantage of that. Is this frustrating to you in a situation such as Bosnia, where no action might actually be the best action?

The President. Well, first of all, I disagree that it's the most important foreign policy problem. It's the foreign policy problem that's the longest lasting and therefore the most publicized. But the most important things we have done, I think, you'd have to start out with our continued efforts with Russia and the other republics of the former Soviet Union to denuclearize; our efforts to stem the proliferation of weapons of mass destruction, which have been very successful and which the United States has led; our efforts at peace in the Middle East. All those things, it seems to me, over the long run, in terms of America's vital interest, are more important.

The Bosnian situation is heartbreaking. And it is potentially very important to our security interests should it spread, which is why I have sent troops to the Former Yugoslav Republic of Macedonia to try to make sure that it doesn't spread. But is it frustrating? Sure it is, because most of the people who criticize don't have a better alternative. And many of them who criticize don't have any alternative.

The United States, before I became President, made a decision not to send troops in the U.N. peacekeeping mission in Bosnia. Frankly, at the time, it's my understanding that our European allies agreed with that. They wanted to take the lead in dealing with this big security problem, the first one of the postcold-war era. The U.N., in any case, was not supposed to be trying to determine the outcome of the war but simply trying to minimize the violence and get the humanitarian aid through.

Now we have spent as much or more money as any country in supporting the peace process in Bosnia, in supporting the humanitarian aid and the airlift, and trying to keep the war out of the air, and doing all the things that we have done from our ships and from our bases, to fly literally tens of thousands of flights. We have also been responsible for taking the lead in establishing the alliance between the Bosnian Government and the Croatians. We took the lead in asserting the need for NATO to use its air power. In 1994, we had a pretty good year there because of this aggressive action on our part. And it fell apart when the United Nations decided not to let NATO use its power whenever a U.N. soldier had been taken hostage.

Now we have changed the ground rules on the ground with the Rapid Reaction Force, and we've got a new set of command and control rules for NATO. So we seem to be making some progress. There have been several convoys go in and out of Gorazde, for example, without being attacked.

I believe we have done all we could to work with our allies, and I think we have exercised all the influence we could, considering the fact that they have soldiers on the ground and we don't. And I do not believe that under these circumstances we should have put ground troops on the ground in the U.N. mission. So I think history will reflect that, given the options, none of which were very pleasant in a very difficult situation, that we have done the right things and that they were better than the alternatives available to us.

Ms. Liasson. Mr. President, recently you said the reason why the United States and NATO and the U.N. have all lost prestige in Bosnia is because they went around saying they were going to do something and then they didn't do it. In retrospect, would it have been better not to have said that you were going to lift the arms embargo and then help the Muslims with air strikes? Do you think you raised expectations there that couldn't be met?

The President. No because when I ran for President I made it clear that I would support a lifting of the arms embargo multilaterally. I never said I would lift it unilaterally. I was, frankly, surprised, given the record we had of Serbian aggression when I became President,

that our allies would not agree to lift the arms embargo multilaterally. But they felt it would put their own troops too much at risk, and they believed that it would not do what I thought, which was to induce the Bosnian Serbs to make a quick peace.

Let me say that air strikes cannot win a war, but they can raise the price of aggression. And if you believe as I do, that territorial disputes between the sides now could be resolved without the legitimate interests of any ethnic group being eroded, I think that's a very important reason for using air strikes to increase the price of aggression.

But it didn't happen in '93, so in '94, we got a different kind of agreement to use air power, our own air power, in return for not lifting the arms embargo on the Bosnian Government. And it worked. The Serbs and the Bosnian Government brought their heavy weapons into collection points. The cafe areas were largely free from shelling and military activity. And the whole thing only came apart when, number one, no peace was reached in 1994 and, number two, when military activity started in the central part of the country spread to these safe areas and the U.N. would not permit NATO to strike back.

So that's what I would say. If you say for sure you're going to do something, you simply have to do it. And if you don't do it, you suffer. And that's what happened to the U.N. and the NATO. And because the United States is a part of those organizations and has a leading role in NATO, it hurt us as well. And that's why I told our allies I would try one more time to have NATO play a role in this, one more time to try to support them with their Rapid Reaction Force. But the United States could not be part of any endeavor that made commitments which were not kept. We have to keep commitments once we make them.

Ms. Liasson. You've talked, though, about the limits of the U.S. being able to dictate the outcome of something when we don't have troops on the ground. Does that mean that the U.S. can only lead if it's willing to commit troops in situations like this?

The President. As I said, we have exercised a leadership role in pushing the air power and leading the humanitarian air lift and putting our troops on the border and in getting the Croatians and the Bosnian Muslims to agree to a confederation. So in that sense, we have. But our ability to exercise a leadership role when the British, the French, the Dutch, and the others who have troops on the ground believe that what we want to do will endanger their troops but not ours, since we're not there, is necessarily limited. But that is, after all, part of what we, I think, should be working toward in the post-cold-war world.

The United States, obviously, will have to make a decision whether we think we should run every show and totally dominate every crisis. But if we want to do that, we do have to be willing to have troops on the ground where others have troops on the ground. I believe that we have exercised a great deal of leadership, and I think it's been consistent with our interest in not having troops there in this U.N. mission. I could not have countenanced putting American troops in the position where they could be fired upon and taken as hostages without firing back. I don't believe in that. I don't think that's what the United States is all about. And I do not believe the United States should be there trying to win this war on the ground, as a combatant. I don't believe in that. So I have said that I would not send troops there unless it's necessary to take our allies out.

Teenage Smoking

Mr. Edwards. You're wrestling with a difficult decision on tobacco. Why not let the FDA regulate tobacco? Polls show a lot of support for regulating smoking among teenagers.

The President. Well, I don't know that it's such a difficult decision. We're working through what our options are, and I've talked with Dr. Kessler at the FDA. He has asked me to do that, and we've been involved with him and discussed that.

But this country has to do something about the problem of teenage smoking. It's going back up. We know that a significant percentage of young people who start to smoke will smoke consistently throughout their lives, and that if they do, a significant percentage of them will die from diseases directly related to their smoking. We know that if we wanted to lower the cost of health care and increase the life expectancy of our people and improve the health of the American people, there's almost nothing you could do that would have a bigger impact than dramatically reducing the number of young people who stop smoking or who never start smoking. So we have to have a vigorous response

to that, and I expect to have an announcement on that in the next several days—not too far away.

Ms. Liasson. Is it possible to regulate tobacco as a drug and not spark years of litigation?

The President. Well, that's one of the things that bothers me. You know, I think we need a tough and mandatory type program, but I don't want to see us in a position where we act like we're going to do something but we wind up in years and years and years of costly litigation while kids continue to be bombarded with advertisements plainly designed to get them to smoke, with all kinds of promotional activities while they can still buy cigarettes in vending machines, while there's no real comprehensive national law against their buying cigarettes. And meanwhile, these lawsuits drag on.

So I'm concerned about that. And that's one of the reasons I think that Dr. Kessler and the FDA have wanted to have a series of conversations with the White House because everybody involved in this, at least from our point of view, wants to focus on the whole problem of children smoking and how to stop it and to stop it from starting.

Mr. Edwards. You say mandatory, you're not going to have any kind of voluntary program for the industry?

The President. Well, I believe we have to have some means of knowing that whatever we all agree to, whatever people say they're going to do is done. And I think we need some strength there. So we'll just—I'm looking at what my options are, and I expect to have an announcement in the near future. You won't be waiting long to know how we're going to resolve this. But there will be a strong commitment here to doing something about children smoking.

Ms. Liasson. Are you saying the tobacco industry can't be trusted to comply with some kind of a voluntary deal?

The President. I've already talked a lot about this. I'll have more to say in the next few days.

Relief for Middle Class

Mr. Edwards. You've spoken a lot about the squeeze on the American middle class, although the economy is good, incomes are not keeping up, people are working harder for less, and they've been anxious about their futures. Without control of Congress, what can you do to relieve some of that anxiety?

The President. Well, one thing that I can do is to keep trying to grow the economy and to keep following policies that will lead to balanced and fair growth. That's what we were trying to do with the Japanese trade action, for example. I have been responsible for a greater expansion of trade than any other administration, I think, than any other President, with NAFTA and GATT and 80 separate trade agreements. But I also want fair trade. I want trade that will strengthen the jobs and the incomes of America's workers, which is why I took the action I did with Japan with regard to auto parts and autos.

We also can make sure that the laws we have on the books are enforced in a way that tend to support good jobs and good wages. That's why I don't favor, for example, a repeal of the Davis-Bacon law or some other laws that are on the Government's books which at least say when we're doing business we want to try to support a high-wage, high-opportunity society.

But there are things that I think this Congress can do and some other things I think they shouldn't do. And I'll just—let me just give you three examples very quickly. Two things I think they should do. I think they ought to raise the minimum wage. The minimum wage has had bipartisan support in the past, and I think has broad bipartisan support among the American people. If this Congress does not raise the minimum wage, as I have asked it to do, we'll have the lowest minimum wage we've had in 40 years in terms of real purchasing power next year. That's not my idea of the kind of country I'm trying to create for the 21st century. I don't want a hard-work, low-wage America. I want a high-opportunity, high-growth America.

The second thing they could do is to pass the bill I have proposed which has bipartisan support to create a "GI bill" for America's workers. And our proposal is to take the 70 or so separate training programs the Government has now, collapse them, put them in a big pot of cash, and give workers who are unemployed or who are underemployed a voucher which they can take to their local community college worth $2,500 or so a year for up to 2 years to get the training and education they need. This would go around the Federal Government, the State government, and the local government. This is just something we could give to unemployed Americans, people that lose their jobs and need to acquire new skills. Almost every American now is within driving distance of a community college or other fine training institute. They'd make the decisions, and all they'd have to do is prove they spent the money at the appropriate place. They could pass that.

The third thing that Congress should do is to do no harm—do no harm. They are on a path now which will dramatically increase the middle class squeeze. By cutting all this education money, they are cutting off the future for millions of Americans. By cutting all the Medicare and Medicaid money, what they are doing is to make sure that more and more middle class people who are middle-aged will have to spend much higher percentages of their incomes supporting their elderly parents and therefore will have less to spend on themselves and in educating their own children. And none of that is necessary to balance the budget. I have given them an alternative.

So they should raise the minimum wage, pass the "GI bill" for America's workers, and do no harm on education and health care. Those things will help us.

But you know, we've never had a period like this before, really, where we've got 7 million new jobs; 2½ million new homeowners; 1½ million new businesses, the largest number in American history in this period of time; very high stock market—about 4,700—rapid growth of corporate profits; and stagnant wages for half the American workers. We've got to turn that around. And these things will help.

1996 Election

Ms. Liasson. Mr. President, you did a pretty good job in 1992 figuring out what the election was going to be about, what was on people's minds. What do you think the election of 1996 is going to be about? What are the three or four top issues that you think Americans care most about right now?

The President. Well, in 1996, I think the election will be—there will be economic issues still at the forefront, more in terms of family security. That is, I think that people will see the economy as a two-step process, not a one-step process. And I hope maybe I can communicate that more clearly. That is, what we started doing—reducing the deficit, expanding trade, increasing investment in technology, promoting defense conversion, all those things—they produce a lot of jobs, but now we have to raise incomes and a sense of family security. So I think there will be a whole cluster of family security issues that are economic and that deal with the whole issue of opportunity.

Then I believe there will be some significant debates about social issues and what kind of responsibilities we have individually and to each other in this society. If we don't get welfare reform legislation through, that will be an issue. If there's a continuing effort to undermine law enforcement as there has been now in the Congress—the leaders of Congress told me, for example, after Oklahoma City they would have the antiterrorism bill on my desk by Memorial Day; that's late May. Here we are almost to mid-August and no sign of the bill. I think that will be an issue because Americans are still concerned about their security.

And then the third set of issues will be about—so the opportunity issues, responsibility issues, and then I think there will be a set of issues that have to do with how we're going to move together into the 21st century. How are we going to handle our diversity? What's the responsible way to handle our immigration problems, which are considerable?

So those are the kinds of things that I think will dominate this election. It's basically, this is one more jumping off stage, the last one we'll have before the next century. And I hope that it will be dominated by two competing visions of what America will look like in the next century and how we will live and how we will work together.

Mr. Edwards. But the strongest sentiment we're hearing from voters seem to reject both visions. They seem to be looking for a third party, a third force to put their faith in. What is that——

The President. I don't know that they reject both visions. I think they consistently accept my vision when they hear it. It's almost impossible for people to know what's going on out there given the nature of communications today. There's a lot of information, but it's always on something new day-in and day-out. And it tends to emphasize conflict over achievement. And so I think what we need is an election to see that.

And also, a lot of people are kind of frustrated with their own lives and don't see the connection between governmental action on the one hand and improvements in their circumstances on the other. All of this is to be expected in a time of transition and difficulty. But I basically think the prognosis for America's future is quite bright. And if somebody wants to run as a third party candidate they ought to, but that's like— that's "the buyer's remorse" and "the grass is always greener on the other side," and all of that. You know, you hear all of that.

But I believe that the '96 election will really give me an opportunity I have not had since I've been here to get out and talk about what we've done that we promised to do, what difference it's made for America, and what still needs to be done. I think the third category should be the most important thing, what are we going to do tomorrow? But I'm not at all pessimistic about where America is or where this administration is. We've done a lot of things that were very important. We've kept up very high percentages of our commitments. We've had a great deal of success with the efforts that we've made, and I look forward to having a chance to discuss that. But meanwhile, I'm going to try to delay the onset of the political season as long as possible and just keep doing my job.

Mr. Edwards. But how can you say that the American people share your vision? A majority did not elect you and then came the '94 election that——

The President. Yes, but that doesn't mean— the American people didn't ratify the contract on America. What they ratified—there were two things. A lot of the people who voted in '92 were disillusioned and didn't vote because they'd been fed a steady diet of bad news and because their own circumstances hadn't improved. And we said this many new jobs came into the economy and the deficit was reduced by 50 percent for 3 years in a row for the first time since Harry Truman was President. Huge numbers of voters said, "I just don't believe it; I just don't believe it," because their lives weren't better, and they didn't hear about it in their regular communications. They were anxiety ridden; they were frustrated; they were angry. The Republicans said, "Vote for us, we've got a plan, and the first item is balancing the budget." All the research after the election showed that that's what people knew.

Now, there are two plans to balance the budget. I believe two-thirds of the American people agree with my way. I think they'd rather take a little longer, have a smaller tax cut and protect the incomes of elderly Americans on Medicare, protect our investments in education from Head Start to affordable college loans and not gut the environment. That's what I believe. I believe the American people want a high-wage, high-growth, high-opportunity future, with safe streets and a clean environment, where people have a chance to make the most of their own lives. I believe that's what they really want. And I think they believe we ought to work together toward that.

And my referendum will come in '96, and we'll just see. But there's a lot—if you look at the research, I think there is a lot of common ground in America. I believe the American people, left to their own devices, would come to commonsense, progressive conclusions on a lot of these issues. And I think the political system basically seeks to divide them in little slices and wedges to advance the causes of whoever's doing the dividing. But that's not really what the American people want, which is why they often say, "I'd like a third way," because they're sick of partisan bickering in Washington and people who are trying to advance their short-term interest at the expense of the long-term public interest in this country.

Federal Budget

Ms. Liasson. I wanted to ask you about some partisan bickering that's coming up pretty soon, which is the big battle over the budget in the fall. Now, you've said you didn't want to pile up a stack of vetoes, you've threatened quite a few of them. But Republicans say they don't believe that you're going to make good on all these threats, especially if it means that agencies will close or if the Government can't borrow the money to send out benefit checks. Are you willing to see the Government shut down if that's what it takes to protect your priorities?

The President. Well, first of all, let's look at what they're threatening to do. And the American people need to know it as unprecedented. They are responsible. If the Government gets shut down, it will be their responsibility. They will have to vote or not vote to lift the debt ceiling. They will have to vote or not vote for continuing resolutions to let this Government go on. I will have no role in that; that is their responsibility.

My responsibility was fulfilled when I offered them an alternative balanced budget and a willingness to discuss it. So far, none of them have been willing to discuss anything. They have not been willing to discuss this. They seem deter-

mined—for example, they seemed absolutely determined to raise the cost of Medicare in copayments, in premiums and deductibles to seniors with incomes of $25,000 a year or less. They seem determined to raise the cost of going to college. They seem determined to cut kids off Head Start. They seem determined to gut the environmental laws of this country when none of that is necessary to balance the budget, and they haven't even discussed it with me.

So what I'm going to do is—and these veto threats that I've been issuing, they're really sort of veto notices. I'm just trying to be as forthright and honest and forthcoming as I can with people who so far have not expressed any interest in having any dialog with me. It's a funny way to do business. But if you ask me am I going to blink at the end and basically, to avoid shutting down the Government, risk shutting down America 10 or 15 years from now because of the costs we're taking, the answer to that is, no, I am not going to blink at the end. As awful as it is, it would be better to shut the Government down for a few days than to shut the country down a few years from now because we took a radical and unwarranted road here that the American people never voted for, don't believe in.

So I think it's easy to over-read the results of the '94 election. I think you could convincingly argue that the NRA put the House of Representatives in Republican hands if you look at the number of short races, close races that were turned there. But the other voters that were voting for the Republicans and the other voters that were staying home weren't ratifying a repeal on the assault weapons ban or a repeal of the Brady bill.

So I don't think you can make these kind of connections. I'm just going to stand up and fight for what I believe in but be willing to work with them. But if they don't ever want to work with me and they keep trying to push this country off the brink, I cannot in good conscience let America gut its commitment to education from Head Start for poor children to affordable college loans for college students, when I know that that is the key to our economic future. And I know it's the only way to expand middle class incomes over the long run. I cannot in good conscience let a budget go through which essentially undermines our ability to provide for clean air, clean water, and pure food when I know good and well the American people never voted for that in 1994.

And I certainly have no intention of destroying Medicare under the guise of saving it when I know we can fix the Medicare Trust Fund, which does not have anything to do—the Medicare Trust Fund that the Republicans are always talking about is in some trouble, less trouble than when I took office. I pushed the insolvency date out 2 or 3 years already, and I know we can fix that and never touch the premiums, the copays, and the deductibles. And they know it, too. They know this has nothing to do with fixing the Medicare Trust Fund.

So we ought to get together like civilized human beings and good Americans and do what's best for the American people. The one time I thought we were going to do it was when I had the meeting with the Speaker up in New Hampshire and that fellow asked us a nice question, and we shook hands on it. We said, yes, we'd appoint a commission like a base closing commission to look into political reform. And 5 days after I got back I sent a letter to the Speaker suggesting that we ought to appoint this commission in the same way the base closing commission was appointed. Five weeks later I still hadn't gotten an answer to my letter. I still haven't gotten an answer to my letter. It's been 7 or 8 weeks now. So I appointed two distinguished Americans, John Gardner and Doris Kearns Goodwin, to go try to work this out. They haven't seen the Speaker either.

So this is a different world up here. The American people don't understand this. I think most Americans are still conservative and old-fashioned in the best sense. They think when

you shake hands, especially when you do it in broad daylight in front of the whole country, you ought to do what you say you're going to do. And I intend to do it. That's just the way I am. It's the way I was brought up. I don't understand this. I don't understand people that don't talk to one another and don't try to see one another's point of view and that don't try to reach common accord. So that door over there is going to stay open all the way, but I will not be—I will not be blackmailed into selling the American people's future down the drain to avoid a train wreck. Better a train wreck for a day or 3 or 4, better political damage to Bill Clinton than damaging the future of millions and millions and millions of Americans. I'm just not going to do it.

Mr. Edwards. Thank you, Mr. President.

The President. Thank you.

China

Ms. Liasson. Mr. President, just one quick yes or no question. Should Mrs. Clinton go to China if Harry Wu is still held?

The President. Well, no decision has yet been made on that, and we're just going to follow events as they develop and try to make a good decision. It's an important conference. The United States will be represented, but no decision has been made yet about whether she will go.

NOTE: The interview began at 1:48 p.m. in the Oval Office at the White House, and it was recorded for broadcast on August 9. The final question referred to Harry Wu, human rights activist imprisoned in China.

Remarks on Environmental Protection in Baltimore, Maryland
August 8, 1995

Thank you very much. As you can tell, the Vice President really has no strong convictions about this issue. [*Laughter*] That's the darnedest stump speech I've heard in a long time. I thought for a minute he was a write-in candidate for mayor here. [*Laughter*] It was a great speech, and thank you for what you said.

Thank you, Doris McGuigan, and thank you to all of your allies here for reminding us what's

really behind all these issues. One of the biggest problems we have in Washington, even though it's very close to Baltimore—one of the biggest problems we have is having people there remember that the decisions they make there affect how you live here and then making sure that people who live here understand the impact of the decisions that are made there. You have helped us, every one of you—Doris, for what you've done and all of you, for coming out here today—you have helped us to reestablish that critical link between the American people and their Government, so you can decide what you're for and what you're against and how it's going to affect your children and your future. Thank you, Lieutenant Governor Kathleen Kennedy Townsend, for coming. Thank you, Congressman Gilchrest, for your outstanding support of the environment. And I want to thank all of my friends who are State officials and city officials. And Senator Miller, thank you for coming. And I want to say a special word of appreciation, too, to the first person who spoke, our EPA Administrator, Carol Browner, who has done a magnificent job in her work.

I want to deliver a pretty simple message today. Every office I have ever held of the public trust, from being attorney general of my State to being Governor to being President, required me to swear an oath to protect the people I was elected to serve, to give people the security they need to live up to the most of their God-given potential. Central to that security is the right to know that the air we breathe and the food we eat and the water we drink will be safe and the right to know if there's any risk to those things.

This basic security really is in jeopardy today. There are people who want to strip away decades of public health protection. I intend to fight them every step of the way. As I said, the battle over environmental protection is being fought in Washington, but here in communities like this one all across America, big and small, you see what is really at stake. Most hard-working families have enough on their minds without having to worry about an environmental hazard in their neighborhood.

Most people have enough trouble just trying to educate their kids and pay their bills and keep body and soul together and deal with all the changes in the global economy and how they bear down on community after community and business after business and job after job. Most people have enough to deal with without having to worry about their food, their air, and their water. But at least they have a right to know what is in it and whether something else is about to be put in it. That's what this Community Right-to-Know Act was all about. You heard the Vice President say it was passed almost a decade ago now, signed by President

Reagan, strengthened by President Bush, strongly supported by this administration.

This is an issue that's very personal with me. I've dealt with the whole issue of right-to-know around chemicals for nearly 20 years now, since I was a young attorney general and a train loaded with chemicals in car after car blew up in a small southern town in the southern part of my State where a relative of mine was the sheriff. And it was just a God's miracle that we didn't have hundreds and hundreds of people killed in this little town. And the first thing that occurred to everybody is: Who knew what about what was on the train? Who knew what about how safely it was being carried? Who knew what about what kind of precaution should have been taken when the train pulled into the station?

That was almost 20 years ago, and I have seen this issue catch on now like wildfire as people in American communities all across our country have demanded the right to have some basic control over their own lives and their futures. The right-to-know law now requires manufacturers to tell the public how much they pollute. And if you want to know what's coming out of the smokestacks across the water, for example, all you have to do now is call your local library or the EPA and the information is there for you.

The Community Right-to-Know Act does not tell companies what they can and can't produce. It doesn't require massive bureaucracy. It doesn't affect every company, just those in certain industries. It's carefully focused on a list of 650 specific dangerous toxins. About 300 of those have been added since this administration came into office, I might add. And over 100 of them are known to cause cancer. This law works, as you have heard.

You have had particular success here because you've had such a good grassroots community effort with your 74 percent reduction. But you need to know that nationwide, every place in the country since the Community Right-to-Know Act has been on the books reported reductions in toxic emissions, or about 43 percent for the whole country. Now, that is a law worth passing—no new bureaucracy, just power to the people through basic knowledge.

This has kept millions of pounds of chemicals out of our lives. It's helped people to stay healthy and live longer. And as you have already heard, it's also helped to spur innovation to help businesses work smarter and cleaner and become more profitable, not less profitable.

Our environmental progress, from the community right-to-know law to the Clean Air Act to so many others, has been the source of bipartisan pride, as has been mentioned. Therefore, it has been something of a surprise to many of us—and I think some in the Republican Party as well as most of us in the Democratic Party—to see what is happening in the Congress now, to see this dramatic departure from the bipartisan efforts of the last 25 years.

The House voted to gut environmental and public health protections last week under the pressure of lobbyists for those who have a vested financial interest in seeing that happen. The budget bill they passed would cut environmental enforcement by 50 percent. It would virtually bring to a halt the Federal enforcement of the Clean Water Act and toxic waste cleanups— a terrible mistake, a terrible mistake.

In a brazen display of the power of these special interest groups, the House added 18 separate loopholes, giveaways, and stop-in-your-tracks orders, stripping away very specific public safeguards to benefit very specific interest groups. One provision allows oil refineries to spew benzene, a cancer-causing chemical, without stringent safeguards. Another would allow factories to dump 15 million pounds of toxic chemicals into our Nation's rivers, lakes, and streams next year alone—one year. Another permits cement kilns and other incinerators to burn cancer-causing chemicals without effective control. The House majority also voted to gut community right-to-know, literally rolling back protections that are already on the books.

And if you ask them why they did this, they say, "Oh, well, we regret it, but there are all these crazy Federal regulators that are bringing to a halt the American economy." The problem is, there is no evidence that environmental protection has hurt our economy at all—none. And furthermore, this administration and this EPA Administrator have done more than anybody in 25 years to try to streamline regulation, reduce the burden of excessive regulation, get rid of dumb rules that don't make sense. Carol Browner has committed to reduce by 25 percent the amount of time businesses have to spend filling out forms, but not to destroy the standards, the rules, the regulation, and the community empowerment that are keeping our environment clean. And I am telling you, we can fix

bureaucratic problems, but we cannot fix, we cannot fix, the environmental damage that would be done if they tore up the progress of the last 25 years.

If the environmental laws have been so terrible for this country, you tell me how our economy has produced 7 million jobs in the last 2½ years, 1½ million new businesses, 2½ million new homeowners. Why is the stock market at 4,700 if the environment is so bad? We've got some problems. We have stagnant middle class incomes. We've got to get more money for people who are out there doing America's work. But the economy is doing well, and the people who own these businesses are doing well. And our country is moving forward in every single measure except raising middle class incomes. That is the problem. But the environment is not causing that, and there is no evidence for this. This is a big mistake. It is a terrible mistake. And I will not let our country make it. There is no evidence to support it.

I think all of you know, and I have already said, that the minute these antienvironmental measures hit my desk they will be dead. But I intend to do more than that. I want to use the authority of my office to ensure the right of parents to know what chemicals their children are being exposed to. I want more communities to be able to proudly introduce people like Doris and say we've reduced our chemical emissions by 74 percent. That's what I want. I want to see more people doing their own work for their own people and their own future. So just before I left for Baltimore, I signed an Executive order which says any manufacturer who wants to do business with the Federal Government must tell its neighbors what dangerous chemicals it puts into the air, the earth, and the water. No disclosure; no contract. [*Applause*] Thank you. And I am directing our agencies to take the next steps to act quickly and openly to continue to strengthen community right-to-know, if appropriate, to extend it to more industries and thousands more communities, to require companies to disclose more complete information.

Let me say this: There is an orderly process for this now. It is an orderly, open, fair process where we say what we're thinking about doing through the EPA. Then all the interests affected—people like you all across America and the industries, too, and the businesses—they get to come in and say what they feel. And if there are mistakes or if the Government is going too far, if everybody admits something doesn't need to be done, it can all be changed. That is the orderly way this should be done. And that is precisely what Congress—at least some in Congress—are trying to stop us from doing, this orderly, neighborly, open, honest process in which we arrive at these kind of standards.

I want to continue to strengthen the right-to-know through that kind of open and fair process. But I want you to know something else. If Congress passes a law to block this kind of process in future right-to-know issues, then I will issue another Executive order to finish that job as well.

The message here is clear. Congress can go right on with its plan to undermine America's antipollution laws, but it will go nowhere fast. Community right-to-know is here to stay. I want more neighborhoods like this one all across America. And I want America to see you tonight on the evening news and hear about you tomorrow in the newspapers and on the radio stations so people know what they can do if they work together with the law.

Let me just say there is more here than a single law at stake. Democracies always have depended upon the free flow of information to ordinary citizens. Our democracy in this age, which has been heralded the information age, is being regaled constantly with the dreams of all the television channels we're going to be able to get, all the different radio stations, all the different magazines we can read. We are going to be awash in information. Wouldn't it be tragic if, in the information age, the single most significant thing to come out of this Congress was blocking information that you need to know about the most basic health and safety requirements of your families, your children, and your community? That's not my idea of the 21st century information society. I want you to know more, not less. And I think you do, too.

And if you need any evidence of that, just look what happened when the former Soviet Union and the whole Communist empire in Eastern Europe broke up. We saw some of the awfullest environmental problems anywhere in the world because there was development there

without democracy, because today's economics took the place of the health and safety of their people and, in the end, helped to undermine their economy. If we needed any other evidence, that alone ought to be enough.

So I just want to close by asking you when you walk away from here to think about what your ordinary day is like. Think about the information that keeps you and your family safe and healthy. Think about what your child might see that might change his or her behavior: a stop sign, a label that tells you what's in the food you buy for your family, the warning on a pack of cigarettes. This and other things are simple things that we take for granted because their cost is minimal. But their value is priceless. The silent threat posed by pollution is as real and dangerous as the threat of a speeding car to a walking child. We've known for a long time that what we can't see can hurt us.

Our health and safety laws, they're our line of defense against these dangers. We're not about to abandon them, not about to abandon them, because of people like you. You know, there's a couple of lines in the Bible that say, if your child asks for bread, would you give him a stone; if he asked for fish, would you give him a serpent; if he asked for an egg would you give him a scorpion? Today we must ask, if our child asked about the future, will we give him or her dirty air, poison water; would we keep them from knowing what chemicals are being released into their neighborhoods and keep their parents from protecting them? We all know what the answer is. It's no.

It seems simple here in this wonderful neighborhood. Why don't you help us make it simple in Washington, DC?

Thank you very much.

NOTE: The President spoke at 1:10 p.m. at Fort Armistead Park. In his remarks, he referred to Doris McGuigan, environmental activist in the Brooklyn-Curtis Bay community of Baltimore, and Thomas V. (Mike) Miller, Jr., president of the Maryland Senate. The Executive order on Federal acquisition and community right-to-know and the related memorandum are listed in Appendix D at the end of this volume.

Statement on Welfare Reform
August 8, 1995

Six months ago, I convened a Presidential conference on welfare at the Blair House. Democrats and Republicans from the Congress to the State houses came to Washington to forge a bipartisan agreement on welfare.

At the conference we agreed on the need for child support to be a part of any welfare reform legislation. Now, the bill passed in the House and the legislation in the Senate includes comprehensive child support reform.

Since the conference, we have agreed to drop any inclusion of orphanages in welfare reform. Since the conference, we have agreed to require teen moms to live at home and stay in school as a condition to receiving welfare. Since the conference, we have agreed that all recipients must sign a work contract as a condition upon receiving benefits.

In addition to the progress we have made on a bipartisan basis of what welfare reform legislation must include, I have signed a sweeping Executive order concerning child support collection from delinquent parents. My administration is collecting a record amount of child support, making responsibility a way of life, not an option.

This year alone I have approved a dozen welfare reform experiments. The experiments have included new proposals, among them: requiring people to work for their benefits, requiring teen moms to stay at home and in school, requiring welfare recipients to be held to a time limit, requiring delinquent parents to pay child support, and requiring people on welfare to sign a contract which would hold them accountable to finding a job. The State experiments now total 32 States reaching 7 million individuals.

It is time to put partisanship and politics aside and to get the job done. The American people deserve real welfare reform and have been kept waiting long enough. We need a bipartisan bill that ends welfare and replaces it with work. I hope the Senate will place welfare at the top of its agenda in September and take swift action.

While Congress continues to debate welfare, I will proceed with the far-reaching welfare reforms I initiated with the States over the last 2 years. We will continue to move people from welfare to work. We will continue to require teen moms to stay in school and live at home as a condition of their benefits. I call on this Congress to join me in a bipartisan endeavor, with politics aside and the national interest at the center of our efforts.

Remarks to the Progressive National Baptist Convention in Charlotte, North Carolina
August 9, 1995

Thank you. Mr. President Smith, I'm glad you explained that whole thing because here I was about to speak—I'd let enough time go by between Gardner Taylor and me that you could maybe forget some of my—*[laughter]*—and then you said, "We're going to wait until after he speaks to sing 'Oh Happy Day.'" *[Laughter]* But I think I understand it.

To all the vice presidents and your convention secretary and Reverend Booth and many of my friends who are here, Reverend Otis Moss, Reverend Charles Adams, Reverend Billy Kyles, and Reverend Shepard. To my wonderful friend Reverend Gardner Taylor, thank you for what you said. I intend to tell the story of the hound dog and the hare. *[Laughter]* Where appropriate, I will give you credit. *[Laughter]* To Governor Jim Hunt—ladies and gentlemen, Jim Hunt may be the most popular Governor in America. He's certainly one of the two or three finest Governors in America and a great friend of mine. We're glad to have him here. In 1979—that was a long time ago—when I had no gray hair and he had much less—*[laughter]*—he nominated me to be the vice chairman of the Democratic Governors Association. No one knew who I was. I was 33 years old. And if it hadn't been for that, I might not be here today. Now, that may get him in a lot of trouble down here for all I know, but I will always be grateful to Jim Hunt for the role he had in my life and the role he's had in the life of this State and Nation.

I have looked forward to coming here. I feel at home. Most people down here don't speak with an accent; I like that. [*Laughter*] And since I'm at home, I want to talk about something I have been trying to deal with all across America lately, and that is, how are we going to find the common ground we need to walk the road we have to walk together? How can we rise above our differences and march into the future together?

You've set a good example here. I understand this is the first-ever joint meeting between the Progressive Baptist Convention and the Alliance of Baptists. This will have a lot of subsidiary good benefits. For example, it's doing those white folks up there a world of good to sing in a choir like that. [*Laughter and applause*] That may be a racially insensitive, politically incorrect remark, but having spent countless hours of my life in Baptist church choirs, I do know what I am talking about. [*Laughter*] I can't believe I said that. [*Laughter*] "A happy heart doeth good like medicine." [*Laughter*]

I do believe as strongly as I can say that we have to fight for common ground instead of fight to tear each other apart. And I say that not because I have suffered my share of slings and arrows as President in the absence of common ground—it's just an honor to show up for work every day. St. Paul said that God put a thorn in his flesh so he would not be exalted in his own eyes. If that is the test, I feel downright humble today. [*Laughter*]

Whether we like it or not, we are all in this together. Whether we like it or not, we are an American family, and we behave like a good family or a bad family or a little bit of both, but we are a family. We have to get together. That's why I made the speech I did on affirmative action. Let's don't get away from something that's helping us until we don't need it anymore. I thought it was important to tell the American people that everything is not equal in terms of opportunity in our country today, even though the laws have changed, and also important to remind people about what affirmative action is and isn't. It's not about quotas. It's not about

unqualified people getting anything. It's not about reverse discrimination. All of that is illegal and will not be tolerated wherever we can find it.

We ought to shift more efforts to help people just because they're poor, without regard to their race or gender. But we need to recognize that we have to have ways to make sure we're going forward together. The future really should be America's best time. Here we are living in this global society where information goes around the world in a split second. We flip on CNN; we know what they're doing in some country we couldn't find on a map 6 months ago. It's great.

But if we're going to be a global village, what country is in a better position to do well than the one that is the most racially, ethnically, religiously diverse, with the most powerful private sector in the world, the United States. If we can find a way to get along together and to work together and solve our problems together, our best days are before us. That is what is at issue here.

And we know that affirmative action won't amount to anything if we don't deal with our big problems. We don't want to be part of a lot of Americans fighting over a shrinking pie. We don't want to be one of these families with a whole lot of heirs and the estate's going down. We want to be a family where everybody has a brighter future. So that means we have to deal with the economic problems of the American family, the social problems of the American family. And it means we have to be candid in saying that we can't make up for the shortcomings of our individual families or churches or communities unless they do their part.

And that's what I want to talk to you about today. There's been a lot of talk for 15 or 20 years now about family values. What are the family values of the American family, and what do they compel us to do right now, today, this day, and tomorrow when we get up in the morning and God gives us another day of life? What do they say we ought to do? Are we going to use this discussion of family values this year and next to lift up or to tear down, to unite or to divide? Is it going to be a weapon of words to harden the hearts of some Americans against another, or is it going to be a way of asking ourselves what's this family all about?

Some folks like this family values issue because they get to preach at other people. They get to preach against violence and premature sex and teen pregnancy, and they get to preach against the media promoting such things. They get to preach against drugs and crime. They get to tell people, "Behave." Now, that's not all bad. But is it enough?

Some folks like this issue because, frankly, they are working hard to keep their own families together, to keep body and soul together, to pay their bills, raise their kids, take care of their parents, and they'd like a little help from their Government or their community or from their church.

But raising a family—what's it about? Isn't it fundamentally—think about your own family. Isn't raising a family fundamentally about the obligations we owe to other people in the family? Isn't it fundamentally about the responsibility we have to fulfill those obligations and then to behave in such a way that we can make the most of our own lives? And if we're going to talk about the family values of America, shouldn't we talk about it like that? Isn't that what the American family ought to be about, the obligations we owe to other members of the family, the responsibilities we have to fulfill those obligations, and the responsibility we have to conduct our lives so that we can live up to the fullest of our God-given capacities?

Now, that means that we can stand some good preaching, but we've got to be good Samaritans, too. It also means that when we look at our neighbor and we see that sty in his or her eye, we've got to make sure the beam's out of ours.

But these problems—the point I'm trying to make is that all these problems we face as an American family or in our individual family, they have a moral aspect which needs some preaching and behaving, and they have a communal aspect which may need a little help from Samaritans.

You look at the teen pregnancy problem. People obviously have to make a decision not to do that. We can't make that decision for them. They have to make that decision and people have to be—[applause]—that's a matter of personal ethics and discipline and values. And we're just kidding ourselves if we pretend that there's some picture-pretty social program that will solve this.

On the other hand, when people do want to behave, they're entitled to a little help from their friends, from their Samaritans. If a young girl has a child and wants to get off welfare and wants to go to school or go to work, then there has to be some child care. So you need— if you want to fight the crime problem, you've got to punish those who do wrong, but you also have to take these kids who are in severe, severely difficult circumstances, at great risk of doing wrong, and give them something to say yes to, something to be hopeful about.

You know, a couple of years ago when we passed the crime bill, which had the toughest punishments in history, we put more money into prevention programs than ever before. And the people who opposed us ridiculed us in the name of something called midnight basketball. As far as I know, nobody has ever been arrested playing midnight basketball for dealing dope on a basketball court with an adult supervisor there.

So who are we trying to kid here? Let's take it the other way. Look at an economic problem. It can also become a moral problem. The fact is most families in the American family are working families. Most poor people in America are now living in working families. And most people are working longer hours today than they were 10 years ago for the same or lower wages. Now, that's a fact. Now, you say, that's an economic fact. Well, it can become a moral fact if people who are working harder for less have less time and energy, not to mention money, to invest in their children and their education, to keep their kids out of trouble, to do what they want to do.

I never will forget a few years ago, every time I ran for office at home in Arkansas, I used to make it a point to go to the earliest factory gate in my State—Campbell Soup factory in northwest Arkansas. People started going to work there at 4:30, and I figured if I'd show up between 4:30 and a quarter to 5 and shake hands with everybody on that shift, somebody would say, "Well, if that guy's fool enough to do this, we ought to give him a vote." [*Laughter*] And it worked. [*Laughter*] And so I did it. But I never will forget, one day I was there quarter to 5 in the morning; pickup truck pulls up outside the factory; the door opens; a light comes on inside the pickup truck. There's this really attractive young couple there. The young wife is going to work; the husband is driving off. They have three little kids in that pickup truck, in the front seat. And I said, "Now what are you going to do?" He said, "Well, my wife has to be at work, she has to check in, by

5 o'clock every morning. And I have to be at work by 7. So I have to find somebody who will take my children at 6:30, which most child care people won't. So I've got to now go back home, make breakfast for these kids, get them there, and then drop them off at the child care center. Then I've got to show up at 7."

Now, that's maybe an extreme example but not an atypical example of the way most families live today. Isn't that right? Most people are working today. So I would argue to you that that's an economic issue that has become a moral issue. How can our society succeed unless people can be good parents and good workers? And if we have to choose one or the other, who's going to fall between the cracks? The kids. We live in a world where we must not make people choose. We have to succeed at both.

Now, for 2½ years that's what I have been working at. That's why I want to bring this deficit down and balance the budget. That's why I tried to create jobs with investments and special incentives for people to put money into poor areas and expanding trade so we could sell more of our stuff around the world. That's why I tried to increase education from Head Start to kids, to more affordable college loans and scholarships and national service for kids to go to college. That's why we're putting money into the fight against crime and the war against drugs, for education and training and treatment and also to try to crack down on people who are importing these drugs into our country. That's why we're doing that. That's why we passed the family and medical leave law, the symbol of being a successful parent and a successful worker. Why should you lose your job if your kid gets sick? Why should you do that— and you've got to go home and take care of them? Why we want to immunize all the children in this country under the age of 2 and why we bailed out a very sick pension system in America and saved 8½ million people's retirements and protected 40 million other people's retirement up the road—because those are all family values to me.

And we have, as a result, 7 million jobs, 2½ million new homeowners, 1½ million new businesses, the largest number of new millionaires in a 2-year period in history. Unemployment's down. Inflation's down. African-American unemployment's below 10 percent for the first time since the Vietnam war. And people are not working at fighting. In almost every major area of this country, the crime rate is down. And divorce is down. The country is beginning to come back together.

If that's true, why aren't we happy? Because many people are still, in fact, less secure. And many of our families are less secure, because underneath those statistics, the rising tide is not lifting all boats. And a huge number of people are being left out of this nice picture. And it's going to affect all the rest of us, just like any other family.

You know, I'm really proud of my little brother, but he once had a terrible drug problem, and it affected all the rest of us. We didn't get off scot-free because we didn't find a way to solve this problem. It wasn't his problem; it was our problem. That's the way it is with America. It's our problem.

When companies—their profits are up and they're still downsizing and laying people off, that's our problem. That's our problem. When we see people losing their health care even though they still got jobs—the only place—we're the only rich country in the world where that's happening—that's our problem. When people are faced with dealing with their parents or educating their children, that would be our problem, not just their problem. What's happening with crime and drugs is that the overall statistics are going down, but the rate of random, violent crime associated by very young teenagers is going way up. And people feel that, and it scares them. And it's our problem. The rate of random, careless, casual drug use is going up, even though a lot of the statistics are going down. Young, young teenagers are in big trouble in this country.

Now, we've got to decide how to deal with it. If all we do is preach, we can play on our anxiety and our anger and we can divide one from another and we can fight over a shrinking economic pie. And it may be a wonderfully successful electoral strategy, but it won't solve anything. We go through another set of elections where nothing gets better. People vent their steam and express their fears and their anger, but nothing ever changes.

So you see it today. People say, "Well, the American family would be all right if it weren't for the immigrants or if it weren't for the people on welfare or if it weren't for the affirmative action program giving all the money to people who aren't qualified or if it weren't for the Government throwing all our money away.

Now, what I want to say to you is the same thing I said about affirmative action. We have problems in immigration. We've got no business spending money on illegal immigrants. We should not—people who wait for years to get into this country lawfully should not be leaped over by people who just cross over because they can get in. That's not right. And our administration has put more effort into sealing our borders and sending illegal immigrants back and people that come into the criminal justice system who aren't here legally than anybody has in a long time.

It is true that people shouldn't be on welfare if they can also be working. That's also true. And we have done more than any administration in history to move people from welfare to work. It's also true that, as I said before, we have to make some changes in the affirmative action program so we can keep it and make it work right. That's all true.

And finally, it's true that there is waste in Government. But our administration has cut more out than anybody has in over 20 years. The point I want to make is, if you do all that, it still won't solve the problems unless you deal with these fundamental problems of the American family: What are the fundamental economic problems? What are the fundamental social problems? And how can we deal with them together? That's what our job is. We need to start acting like family members, do our part and ask what our obligations are.

So let me say—the other day I tried to do this at the American Federation of Teachers convention. I'm going to try again. Here's what I think the family values of America in 1995 ought to be and what we can do about them in Government. And then you ask yourself, what can you do about them?

Number one, if you were running a family right, you wouldn't saddle your kids with unnecessary debt. In other words, if you borrow money, you're borrowing it to buy a house, finance an education, build a new business, but you wouldn't borrow it to go out to eat on the weekend. That's what this country's been doing. We ought to balance the budget. It's the right thing to do.

But if you're running a family right, you'd first and foremost try to take care of your children. Now, our children—[*applause*]—our chil-

dren don't need to balance the budget on their backs. We don't have to cut Head Start or college loans and make it more expensive to educate the children to balance the budget. We can do them both.

The third thing that you want your family to do is to take care of your parents. I mean, after all, they raised you, right? And in the American family, we decided a long time ago we would take care of our parents from middle class and lower middle class people and even through pretty well-to-do people, largely through Medicare and Medicaid. Medicare pays for hospital care, and then if you buy into the second part of it, it pays for doctor visits, a number of other things. And Medicaid pays for people who have to go into nursing homes. That's about two-thirds of the cost; that's how we pay for it.

Now, we don't have to balance the budget by exploding the cost of Medicare to ordinary people. You know, 75 percent of the people on Medicare are living on incomes of under $25,000. We don't have to increase their premiums, their copays, their deductibles to make it so they don't have enough money to live on. We don't have to make their children pay even more than they're already paying in the payroll tax. All the children are paying for Medicare now; they're paying for it in the payroll tax. We don't have to make them pay more, which means that they will have—how are they going to educate their kids if they have to pay twice through Medicare?

So I'm telling you, do we have to make some changes in Medicare? Yeah, we do. Why? Because we're living longer, and more of us are getting older. But do we have to absolutely bankrupt the elderly people in this country to balance the budget? No, we don't. And we shouldn't do it. It violates our family values.

What's the fourth thing we've got to do? I already said it. In the world we're living in today, most people do not have an option, they have to work. We spent a lot of time and energy trying to get people from welfare to work. Most people are trying to find work. Most people on welfare want to go to work. Most people in jobs are trying to keep the one they've got or get a better one. Isn't that right? That's the normal thing in life. So the problem most people have is, how am I going to keep my job or get a better one and be a good parent? How can I do the right thing by our children? So what should we do?

We should keep the family and medical leave law, for one thing. It's a good law. We should make it possible for everybody who works 40 hours a week and has a child in the home not to be in poverty. If people leave welfare and they show up for work every day and they've got kids in the house, what kind of message does it send to them if they're in poverty? It's not the right message. So in 1993, we changed the tax law, and we said, we're going to give a tax credit, a working family tax credit. Today, for every family of four in America with an income of $28,000 a year or less, the tax bill is $1,000 lower than it was before I took office because we don't believe people who work 40 hours a week and have kids should be in poverty. We should increase that program. The last thing we should do is do what some people want to do and cut back on that program. We should reward people who are doing their best at working and parenting.

We ought to change the health care system. We're the only country in the world where working families are losing health care every year. We ought to change the rules so that if you change jobs, you don't lose your health care. If you have somebody in your family get sick, you cannot be cut off. And people ought to get a little help to keep their parents out of nursing homes as well as help pay for them when they get in them. We can do that and still balance the budget.

And the last thing we ought to do, I believe strongly, is raise the minimum wage. It's too low. If we don't raise the minimum wage next year, in terms of its ability to buy things, it will be at a 40-year low, a 40-year low. I don't know about you, but my idea of the 21st century is an exciting, high-tech deal where there are all these gadgets that I don't even know how to work, but my daughter and all my grandchildren, they'll be working them like crazy and doing well. My idea of the 21st century is not a hard-work, low-wage dead-end society. Let's raise the minimum wage. We can go forward together. That's what family members do. That's our obligation to people who are out there doing that kind of work the rest of us don't want to do. That's part of our family obligations.

The next thing we ought to do is when we cut taxes we ought to make it support families. My tax cut program gives people a tax cut for raising kids and for educating their children and themselves, families, pro-family. And we ought to say we know some people are going to lose their jobs in all this downsizing. It's always happened, and now it seems to be happening a little more. But when people lose their jobs, if they're working people, the least we can do is guarantee them a right to immediately—not to wait until their unemployment runs out—immediately, immediately get more education. And I have proposed a "GI bill" for America's workers that would allow any unemployed person in the country that loses a job to get a voucher worth $2,500 or so a year and take it to the local community college for up to 2 years to get education and training. That's a family value. That's a family value.

Just a couple of other things. I believe—you know, in our family, we were raised—I was raised in the South. You can tell by the way I talk, especially after I'm around you for a while and get in a good humor. [*Laughter*] We were raised to love the land, to love the water, to believe that we had to live in harmony with it, to cut the trees in a way that there'd still be trees a generation from now, to till the land in a way that there would still be topsoil for our grandchildren. That's what we were raised to do. And I believe part of our family values should be teaching our people to preserve our environment. And I don't understand this new obsession in Washington with ripping out all the protections for the environment and for the public health and safety, for clean food, clean water, clean air. I don't understand that. I don't understand that.

And the last thing I want to say is, it seems to me that the American family has got to be focusing on social problems we have that affect our children especially, especially. What are our obligations there? And on these I need your help because there's only so much the Government can do, although there are things the Government can do.

We were, most of us, raised to know what the seven deadly sins were. Remember that? Pride, lust, gluttony, sloth, avarice, anger, envy. Anger and gluttony, those are the two I have to work on all the time. [*Laughter*] We've all got our little list, don't we? But I would like to point out that there are four things that are threatening our children that could be deadly sins to them: violence; the problem of teen pregnancy, for the young fathers as well as the young mothers; smoking, something people don't often think about, I want to talk about that a little bit; and drugs.

And I want to say we have to think about the children. Families are fundamentally the device through which we perpetuate ourselves. They're really about children. They're organized to raise children. And nobody in all of human history has ever come up with an appropriate, adequate substitute. Jesus said, "Let the little children come to me and do not hinder them, for to such belongs the kingdom of heaven."

When they come, what do you do? Luke 11, "If a child asks for bread, would you give him a stone? If he asks for a fish, would you give him a serpent? If he asks for an egg, would you give him a scorpion?" That's what the kids of this country are being given, a whole lot of them.

Look at violence. Every 2 hours in this country a child dies of a gunshot wound. Last year in Washington we had a 13-year-old honor student just standing at the bus stop shot down because he just happened to be in the middle of two gangs that were fighting. Homicide is the leading cause of death among African-American males between the ages of 15 and 24. The number of people arrested for murder is going down among those older than 25 but going up for juveniles and young adults. The number of juveniles—juveniles—arrested for murder increased 168 percent between 1984 and 1993.

In one of our newspapers the other day there was this incredible story about a 16-year-old boy who shot a 12-year-old boy dead because he thought he was showing him disrespect. All this boy's friends, the 12-year-old boy's friends, said that's the way he treated everybody, he was a jokester. The 16-year-old felt insecure. They had one incident; nothing happened. They had another incident; he pulled out the gun and shot him when he was running away and then stood over his body and emptied the gun into his body.

Now, this happened just a couple of days after there was this great national survey, a very fascinating survey of young gang members in which two-thirds of these young men honestly said, quite openly, they thought it was all right to shoot somebody who disrespected you. If that's all right, I'd be plumb out of bullets; the whole country would be. [*Laughter*] We're laughing, but this is deadly serious. How many of us—how many times were we raised with,

"When you get mad, count to 10 before you open your mouth." Don't you say that? Don't you do that? That's how we were raised up. Who's telling these kids to count to 10?

What's happening out there? How can two-thirds of the kids who belong to these gangs think it's okay to shoot somebody for some word they say? Whatever happened to,"Sticks and stones can break my bones, but words will never hurt me"? Whatever happened to people being told to define themselves from the inside out, not from the outside in? Whatever happened to all that?

I'm doing what I can. Look, when we passed that crime bill last year a lot of Members of Congress literally gave up their seats in Congress and gave up their careers to vote for that crime bill, because it banned assault weapons. And they were taken out. I'm telling you, the NRA took them out in the last election. And they did it for your children. Most of these people came from rural districts where their voters didn't understand and they could be stampeded because they didn't know anybody with an assault weapon. And they figured if somebody bought one and wanted to take it to a shooting contest they ought to have a right to. And they were spooked, and a lot of them voted against these good Members of Congress. But they did it for our kids who are living in these cities where these kids are being gunned down. They said, "If it costs me my career to get the Uzis out of the high school, I'll give it up."

Now, that was a great thing. That was an important thing. And that bill gave some money to community groups for crime prevention programs and for job programs and for things to give these kids something to say yes to. We're doing what we can, but you know and I know we can put 100,000 more police on the street, we can ban assault weapons, we can have the Brady bill, we can have these funds for community programs—and I hope we can save them, by the way, in this Congress—but the parents still have to be there, or if they're not there, the churches, somebody has got to be there to teach these kids right from wrong. Somebody has got to say, "I don't care what they call you, it is better to live to be 70 years old and have children and grandchildren and have a useful full life. What difference does it make what they call you?" Somebody has to be there to do that. And we've all got to do that together.

Yes, there are some other things we can do. The other day—we're in a big argument in Washington now—I think we're going to win this one because it's not partisan—about the influence that our culture has, you know, are kids exposed to too much violence in the movies and principally on television, because that's how most people watch it? And I think the answer is, yes, they are. Of course they are.

But the answer to this is not simply to condemn but to ask the people who are making these movies to help us and to ask the people who are showing them to us to help us. And now, with all the wonders of technology, we know that everybody who has cable TV can get something called the V-chip which would allow every family to determine which channels or even programs within channels they don't want their little children to watch. Kids get numb to violence. If by the time you're 6 or 7 years old, you've seen thousands and thousands and thousands of people shot down on the street, it numbs you. So we ought to pass this law and require the V-chip and give families the right to program for their children. It's a family right.

But in the end, we have to do this together. And if we don't deal with this, all the rest of this stuff is just like whistling "Dixie" because you can't bring one of these kids back. In this life, you cannot see them again once they're dead. So we must—this is something we must commit to do together. And this ought not to be a partisan issue. It ought not to be a racial issue. It ought not to be a regional issue. We have to do something about the rapid growth in violence among our very young people.

The second thing I want to talk about a minute is teen pregnancy. Every year a million young girls between the ages of 15 and 19 become pregnant. Some of them are married, but most of them aren't. Eighty percent of the children born to unwed teenagers who dropped out of school, 80 percent of them live in poverty. It is literally true that if teenagers who are unmarried didn't have babies and all babies were born into families where at least one person both had a job and a high-school education, you would cut the poverty rate by more than 50 percent in America. The new poor in America are young mothers and their little children.

In the last 2½ years, we're worked hard on this. And our welfare reform program sends a clear signal to young people. I believe if people are going to draw welfare when they are young and unmarried, we should say, this is not so you can go out and set up your own household and perpetuate this. Unless you have a bad situation at home, you ought to have to live at home and stay in school or stay at work to take the check.

And I think we should hold fathers more accountable. There's a lot of child abuse in teen pregnancy. At least half the babies born to teenage girls are fathered by men who are 20 or older. That's child abuse. That's not right. It's not right. And even young men—even young men—there was a young man in our hometown in Arkansas before I moved here who made a mistake and fathered a child. He was a young man in school. But you know, that kid got up every day before school and went to work and every day after school went back to work and gave all that money to the child. We need more people doing that. That's the kind of thing that we have got to have happen. We need to be, all of us, for very, very tough child support enforcement. We cannot tolerate people who won't take care of their own children. Eight-hundred thousand people could move off welfare if we just enforced the child support laws of the United States of America. And we need to be for that.

But I will say again, I can't solve this problem with a Government fix. This is about how people behave and whether they get personal, personal, one-on-one kinds of reassurance. I am working to get all the leaders of all sectors of our society involved in this fight. But what I want to say is we know there are things that work. The Teen Health Connection here working with low-income teenagers right here in Charlotte has made a real difference. Dr. Henry Foster's "I Have A Future" program has made a real difference.

And I want to say, by the way, I thank you for standing behind Henry Foster. He is a good man, and I'm glad you've got him coming here. And I'm going to do my best to keep him involved in this struggle because he has proved— I saw those young people. I saw those kids from the housing projects in Nashville, Tennessee. A lot of them didn't have a nickel to their names, and they got on a bus and they left their lives, they left what they were doing, and they rode to Washington to tell the United States Senate they ought not to let politics keep Henry Foster from becoming Surgeon General, because he had changed their lives. He had ended the epidemic of teen pregnancy and violence and had given them a chance to start a better future. That's what we need more of.

The same thing is true of drugs. Let me just give you this. In the latest survey of drug use among 8th, 10th, and 12th graders, 43 percent of high school seniors had used an illegal drug by the time they reached their senior year. Marijuana, LSD, inhalants like glue and aerosol—that stuff people did when I was barely out of high school—all these things are coming back. And the feeling that these drugs are dangerous is going down in these surveys. Same people, two-thirds of them who say we can go out and shoot somebody that disrespects us say, "Oh, this stuff's not dangerous."

Now, we are now doing more than a National Government's ever done to fight drugs, based on cutting off the source in foreign governments. You probably saw in the press this week another drug kingpin busted in Colombia. We work hard on that, and we are making real progress on that. But you also have to do things here at home. You've got to punish the real serious offenders here at home. But you have to have some sort of treatment, education, and prevention programs as well. Therefore, I am opposed to these efforts in the Congress to balance the budget by cutting 23 million students out of the safe schools and drug-free schools program.

You know, I bet a lot of you had your children come home and tell you how much they liked their D.A.R.E. officer in the school talking about staying off drugs. A lot of these police officers that are going into these schools are the best role models a lot of these young kids have. And we need to support this sort of thing. We don't need to walk away from it. And you have to help. You have got to make sure that every single solitary school in this country has a good safe and drug-free schools program. You have got to do that. Whatever we do in Washington, you have got to do that.

The last thing I want to talk about is smoking. And I want to tell you why I want to talk about it. I know that tobacco is very important to the economy of this fine State. And I've worked hard to help the economy of this and every other State. And there are a lot of wonderful people in this country who make a living as tobacco farmers, and their families have for a couple of hundred years. That's important to understand.

But we cannot pretend that we're ignoring the evidence. One of the greatest threats to the health of our children is teenage smoking, and it's rising. Listen to this, every single day 3,000 young people become regular smokers and nearly 1,000 of them will die prematurely as a result. For more than a decade, even as adult smoking was dropping, the smoking rate among high school seniors did not go down. That was bad enough. But since 1991, the percentage of teenage smokers has risen steadily and rapidly. There's been a 30 percent increase in the 8th graders who smoke, a 22 percent increase in the number of 10th graders who smoke, and by the age of 16, the average teenage smoker is smoking every day and will not stop. If you wanted to do something to reduce the cost of health care, help over the long run to balance the budget, and increase the health care of America, having no teenagers smoke would be the cheapest, easiest, quickest thing you could ever do to change the whole dynamic of health care in America.

Now, again I will tell you, it's just like the drugs and the gangs; the number of teenagers who believe smoking is dangerous is dropping dramatically. There's a lot more peer approval. This also is a recipe for disaster. There are some things we can do at the governmental level, and we'll be talking about that in the near future. But what I want to say to you is this is just another example of where, no matter what you do with the law, people have to change inside, and somebody has to help them change inside. And we have to do it in an organized, disciplined way.

James Baldwin once said, "Children have never been very good at listening to their elders." As a parent, that's comforting to know. [*Laughter*] "But," he said, "they have never failed to imitate them."

So, I say to you what I said at the beginning. We are on the verge of the 21st century. It should be America's century. The best days of this country should be before us. If we recognize that we're a family and we're going forward, up, or down together, we will go up and forward together.

But we have to ask ourselves, what are our family values and what do we in the American family value and what are we going to do about it? Today, I've tried to tell you what I intend to do about it. And I ask you to say, what are you going to do about it, and how are you going to continue to work?

I want to say a special word of thanks to our host pastor, Reverend Diggs, because I know that he has worked in this community to try to make a difference on these issues. And so many of you have.

You've got this alliance of these two groups here meeting today. We need this kind of alliance on these problems, the kind of problems that our children are facing at the grassroots level. They know no racial barrier; they know no income barrier even; they certainly know no regional barrier. We have got to get over this using family values to drive a stake between us as American people and let it lift us up. We have got to do that.

And I ask you to leave here determined to do what you can to be good preachers and good Samaritans and good examples, to make the family of America a place where family values lifts us up, pulls us together, and takes us into the future. We can walk and not faint. We can run and not grow weary. And if we do not lose heart, we shall reap.

God bless you all, and thank you.

NOTE: The President spoke at 12:48 p.m. at the Charlotte Convention Center. In his remarks, he referred to Rev. Bennett W. Smith, Sr., president, and Rev. Gardner C. Taylor, former president, Progressive National Baptist Convention, Inc.; and Gov. James A. Hunt, Jr., of North Carolina.

Remarks in a Roundtable Discussion at the Teen Health Connection in Charlotte
August 9, 1995

The President. I want to explain to all of you why I came here, and then I want you to talk to me a little bit. I spend an enormous amount of my time, as you might imagine, trying to do things that I believe will help our country meet the challenges we face today so that young people will have a better future. And it's obvious to me that even if I do the best job I could possibly do and have a good economic policy, even if we do everything we can at the national level with the passing of an anticrime bill or a welfare reform bill, even if I keep the country strong in terms of its national security relationship with other countries, unless young people have good, healthy, constructive lives at the grassroots level, the things that I do will not succeed in getting you the future you deserve.

And I've been talking a lot in the last few weeks about how we can bring the American people together to get over all these partisan and other racial and income and regional divisions in our country and try to bring people together to solve problems. And every time I get a chance I tell people, look, there's not a problem in this country that hasn't been solved by somebody somewhere. And so I pledged a few weeks ago and I started doing this, that

as I traveled around the country, in addition to giving speeches and talking to people—in fact, I just talked to this big Baptist convention—I would actually go visit places where people were solving problems and helping other people live their lives, to try to highlight it so people in other parts of the country would see it and say, "Hey, I could do that, too. Hey, my kids can be better off, too. We can do this." So that's really why I'm here.

So I want to give you the chance to educate me about what you're doing and what you think, maybe what else others like me could do to help you more. And I want, through that, to give you the chance to educate the country about what you're doing, so that people in other places that may not have a facility like this will take heart and maybe do the same thing. That's why I'm here. And however you all want to handle it, I'll be glad to—I just want to listen.

[*At this point, moderator Barbara Zeigler, founder and executive director of Teen Health Connection, invited participants to speak, and several patients shared their experiences with the center, explaining how it had helped them physically and emotionally.*]

The President. Do most of these young people that come in here have no health insurance?

Dr. John Johnston. A number has Medicaid and a number on a sliding pay scale, which means that there's a minimal amount that they pay.

The President. But most of them don't have private health insurance?

Dr. Johnston. No, it is—no, sir.

The President. So, they're either Medicaid eligible or they just pay whatever they can?

Dr. Johnston. Right.

Q. Mr. President, I also wanted to thank you for what you did for the foster children and for welfare because if it wasn't for what you did, most of us wouldn't be able to come here, wouldn't be able to have Medicaid.

The President. I'm glad you said that because that's one of the big issues. We're trying to save that program in this Congress. And the proposals for the cuts in Medicaid—most people think of Medicaid as just some sort of vague welfare program, so they think we can just cut any amount of money out of it and be all right. But two-thirds of the Medicaid money in our country goes to take care of older people and disabled people who live in nursing homes or other care facilities. And the other third goes to people like you, to children.

I don't know—if we cut this Medicaid program too much it's going to be very hard for facilities like this to succeed. And just to point out, there's no telling how much money you're saving. In addition to giving all these kids a better life, there's no telling how much money you save in the health care system because, otherwise every time somebody gets sick, as you just said, they're going to show up at the emergency room whether it's an appropriate emergency room procedure or not. And if you have something—if you have a diabetic condition, you have no choice. I mean, if you don't have a regular health connection—I use your—[*inaudible*]—but if you don't have a regular health connection, you're in deep trouble if you get sick. You've got to show up.

But what else? What else does this place do for all of you? Anybody else want to talk?

[*A participant stated that teens could depend on the Teen Health Connection for emotional and physical help.*]

The President. It's kind of like a community facility, though, isn't it?

[*The participant explained how support from the program had helped her adjust to her foster home.*]

The President. What about the parents? What's your experience with this program?

[*Parents explained how the program benefited their children by providing a place to talk about problems confidentially.*]

The President. How much growth have you had?

Ms. Zeigler. More than triple since we opened.

The President. So now how many young people are you serving?

[*Ms. Zeigler stated that there were over 3,500 patients in the program and they hoped to open new locations in the future.*]

The President. Especially if you're going to give them this kind of personal attention.

Ms. Zeigler. Well, and that's always a problem because you're torn between the need to meet the needs and particularly with managed care coming in, you know, just get moving and get your kids in and out. But if you're really going to do good—[*inaudible*].

The President. Do all your young people live in Charlotte?

Ms. Zeigler. Yes. We do have a few that will come in from South Carolina, a few from other counties.

The President. But by and large, they're all from here.

Ms. Zeigler. Yes, by and large, they're all from here.

The President. And how many uninsured young people are in this county?

Ms. Zeigler. Well, 20 percent of our youth is in poverty in Charlotte. I'm not sure of the exact numbers that are uninsured. But I could——

The President. But it's a big number? It's more than 3,500.

Ms. Zeigler. Oh, yes. I mean, it's about 14,000. There are 14,000 that are uninsured that are on Medicaid. But there have been many more others that actually have——

The President. Who weren't on Medicaid but don't have comprehensive health insurance.

Ms. Zeigler. Yes, that don't have health insurance. And there's a lot of people who may live in a two-parent family, but they are right above getting Medicaid but are not working in a situation where they're provided with comprehensive health care. So those are also the families that use the emergency room, which is good because the physicians are there—very, very costly to the community. And it doesn't give continuity that you see here.

The President. One of the things I think we have to think about, again—that's why it's important we don't just say we're going to cut Medicaid a certain amount of money without knowing what we're getting in return. We can't just sort of jump off a big old cliff without knowing what the consequences are. If we're going to go to managed care, in my opinion, we ought to have facilities like this. There ought to be some sort of managed care formula so you can meet all the needs of these young people. You can estimate, for example, if you have a diabetic condition, how many times a year you might need to be in here and what are the kinds of things that could happen, because the idea of managed care is that they would get a certain amount of money, instead of being able to bill Medicaid every time. Let's say you sign up, and this is going to be your primary medical place, and they get a flat amount of money. But it's hard to know.

I see your teen pregnancy prevention posters back there, you know. I see your AIDS posters back there. I know all of you talked about the kind of psychological support and emotional support; I mean, I don't know how you put a dollar figure on that. So I think we have to be very careful because what we really need is these community comprehensive health facilities for young people all across America. And as you point out, they are very cost-effective, but you've still got to be able to show up every morning and turn the lights on.

Ms. Zeigler. And they're people-effective, and I think they make a difference.

Dr. Johnston. I think we've been lucky that we have a community that is supporting us and involved in efforts. And those in the community—you say that is cost-effective, but is also expensive when you're dealing with kids that have more problems that we see than you would normally see. You really need to put your resources together to meet those problems. It pays off, but you're going to have a hard time always convincing people that are pulling out their checkbook that that's the case.

The President. You guys want to say anything about the center?

[A participant who recently moved to Charlotte explained how supportive the center was and how comfortable he felt talking to Dr. Johnston. Another participant explained how a sliding scale payment plan helped him pay his medical bills and still attend college.]

The President. I'm glad you like to talk to him, even if he doesn't say what you agree with. Guys like us, you know, when we get old with gray hair we're supposed to say things you don't agree with. That's our job. *[Laughter]*

But this is very encouraging. Last year when we tried to get health insurance for everybody and we didn't succeed—that's the system every other country has. If we're not going to have that system, then the only way we can do right by the children of this country is literally to make a facility like this available to every child in America. There is no other alternative. You either have to have everybody having a health insurance policy or you have to have a community comprehensive health facility like this where Medicaid covers the poor kids, kids with low enough incomes, and everybody else is on some kind of sliding scale but nobody gets turned away. Those are the only two ways known to humankind to serve all the young people. And every young person needs to be able to get health care.

What about you, Anthony?

[Anthony Lattimore described how counselors helped him confront family problems and encouraged him to make responsible decisions.]

The President. That's really important. You know one of the biggest problems we have all over America with young people today is trying to make sure that all of our young people stop and think before they make decisions or say or do things that they'll later regret. I mean it's a general problem. And it's a bigger problem today than ever before, not only because a lot of young people have difficulties at home but also because we live in a world where things happen so fast. This whole—young people like you, many of you exposed to television where you see whole life stories in a 30-minute program or you see all these—there are a lot of things that have happened that have changed the way we think. And I think every young person needs somebody, to talk to somebody that basically gives you permission and gives you the ability and the strength to stop, look, and listen before you make a decision that you may regret.

Q. I mainly come here to talk to the counselor because I have a lot of friends who are—[*inaudible*]—and I come here to talk to the counselor, Melissa. And I tell her my problems because I sometimes can't tell them to my mom. But I tell her mostly about things going on in my life, and she listens. She can tell me what I should do and what she thinks I'm going to do.

The President. Let me ask you something. Do you think most young people who come here feel more comfortable, for example, talking to the counselors here than they would at the school they attend?

Q. Yes.

The President. And why do you think that is?

Q. Because at school they can—I wouldn't talk to the school counselor because they're friends with the staff and—well, over here I can really—I trust them over here.

The President. So if something was bothering you that had to do with school, you think if you shared it with a counselor they might violate your confidence and make it hard for you to feel like you were making any progress.

[*Participants explained that information shared with employees of the center was kept completely confidential and parents were not informed without the patient's consent.*]

The President. They really treat you—you have a lot of responsibility and a lot of say-so.

[*A participant explained that Teen Health Connection counselors were more accessible than the counselors at her school.*]

The President. Robert.

[*Robert Goulding described how center employees helped him improve in school and find a job. Dr. Johnson, Teen Health Connection medical director, then explained the center's confidentiality policy.*]

The President. Do you want to tell me anything?

[*A participant explained how center employees encouraged him to do well in school.*]

The President. How often do you come? Are you scheduled to come on a regular basis, or

do you kind of come when you feel the need to?

Q. I usually come—[*inaudible*]—my physical's every year. Once a year for physicals.

The President. And if you feel you need to come but you don't have a scheduled appointment, do you call in advance and tell them you want to come or do you just show up?

Q. Yes, you call and make an appointment with the doctor.

[*Ms. Zeigler explained the importance of encouraging patients to be responsible and treating them with respect.*]

The President. When you have a council, a teen council in place, what do they do?

[*Ms. Zeigler discussed the many suggestions that the teen advisory board made to improve the center and urged parents to listen to their children's ideas.*]

The President. I've never learned anything when I was talking. Or rarely. Once in a while I get a new idea when I'm talking. It's usually when I'm listening, I'm learning.

[*A participant explained that Medicaid allowed her to continue receiving medical care.*]

The President. Let me ask you something. What are your other funding sources besides Medicare and the payments people make on a sliding scale?

[*Ms. Zeigler explained that the center obtained about 62 percent of its funding through grants and fundraising.*]

The President. And 38 percent in either Medicaid or copay?

Q. Right. It's a hard show to pull off, but as you can—[*inaudible*]—and I think unless anybody else has——

The President. It's so cost-effective. You know, it's a funny thing to say—you can't put a dollar value to it. You can put a dollar value to how much more it would cost if Prince had to go to the emergency room to deal with diabetes, but you can't put a dollar value to what all the things you really tell me you care about there, the way people make you feel that you can talk to somebody. But I know this, that a whole lot more of you will have successful lives as a result of this clinic.

And the rest of us, you know, if you don't make it, it's not good for us either. That's the point you were making. And we pay a terrible price for that. This has been very encouraging, and I thank you for taking time to talk to me.

Thank you, Barbara. Thank you, Doctor.

Ms. Zeigler. Mr. President, staff, and everyone who has made this possible, we have just been thrilled to have you here.

The President. I'll be talking about this place all over the country. You may have to put on a show for some other people. [*Laughter*] I may run some other people down here.

Q. I know that you have a teenage daughter, right? I just wondered if you could help the foster care—[*inaudible*]—and we do need help because everyone's real short on cash, everyone is, when it comes to——

The President. What you said to me is important. I'm going to go back and look at this proposed budget and see how it deals with all the foster care issues because it is real important to me, not only because I have a teenage daughter whom I stayed up past midnight talking with last night about all the things that were on her mind but also because we really need to make this foster care system in our country work better. And as you know, most kids on foster care don't even have—a lot of them at least don't have the option of even maintaining contact with a parent, don't even know who their parents are.

There are a lot of real problems with the way the foster care system works in this country. So, you made an impression. I'll go back and——

Q. I'm a foster child myself, and I know how she feels. [*Inaudible*]—I'm in the program now 6½ years, and you know, I know what it is being a foster child. I know who my mother is. I know who my father is.

The President. Did you ever want to be put up for adoption?

Q. At one time I thought about it. Then I realized well—[*inaudible*]—sometimes I thought about it. I wondered how my mom would—[*inaudible*]—she was the one—I've always forgiven my mama what she did. I mean, but there are some children in foster care now who, you know, "I'm not going to forgive my mama this because she left me out." It doesn't matter. She took you in her womb for 9½ months. [*Inaudible*]—I have never gone from the past. Yes, sure I was—I got in foster care when I was about 12 years old.

The President. You're 18 now?

Q. I'm 19 now. I think it was 12. I'm 19 now. I start college September 5th. I'm going to—scot-free. I don't have to pay for one book. And it was because I've had a lot of backup. Especially my father, you know. Rick Massey, he's my foster father. But he is, you know—diabetes. He's stuck up for me. He's helped me through a lot. And some of these, you know, now in foster care, they think that the foster parent don't care about them, but, you know——

The President. A lot of them do.

Q. Yeah, a lot of them do. If that child would sit down with their foster parents and see all the things that they have to go through—they don't realize, you know, he or she is trying to help them. And I've received a lot of help, especially in my medical condition.

The President. Kimberly, what do you think I need to worry most about in terms of health of foster kids?

[*Kimberly Taylor voiced her concern about cuts in funding since many foster children were dependent on that funding for adequate medical care.*]

The President. If the foster parents are going to take the responsibility to try to do a good job, then at least the rest of us can take the responsibility for health care. That's what you're saying, right?

Ms. Zeigler. That's really——

The President. I like it.

Q. [*Inaudible*]—wrap this up.

The President. I'm having a great time. Whenever I start to have a good time, I'm always supposed to go somewhere.

Ms. Zeigler. We thank you.

Q. Thank you, sir.

Ms. Zeigler. This has been a wonderful opportunity to showcase teen health care.

The President. You guys are great. I feel better about my country.

Ms. Zeigler. As we grow old, we're going to have good people, young people taking care of us. And thank you again for giving us this opportunity to showcase Teen Health Connection and to listen to some of our most important citizens.

The President. Thank you.

NOTE: The President spoke at 2:20 p.m. at the Teen Health Connection. In his remarks, he referred to patient Prince Wright.

Memorandum on the President's Oklahoma City Scholarship Fund
August 9, 1995

Memorandum for the Heads of Executive Departments and Agencies

Subject: The President's OKC Scholarship Fund

The tragic bombing of the Alfred P. Murrah Building in Oklahoma City took 168 lives and permanently damaged many more. The families of the dead and injured, even witnesses and rescue workers, had their lives changed by that irrational and despicable act of violence.

In the aftermath of this national tragedy, however, we can be proud of the abiding strength and resilience demonstrated by the American people. The days and weeks that followed the explosion witnessed an outpouring of love and support for the victims and their families as Americans of every age, region, and background rallied to assist them.

A number of Federal agencies and public charities established funds to provide emergency assistance for the bombing victims and their families. However, in addition to the provision of relief for the immediate needs of the victims, I am concerned about providing for the education of the children whose parent or parents died or were severely disabled as a result of the bombing. Consequently, I have asked the Federal Employee Education and Assistance Fund (the "FEEA"), a private charity, to establish the President's OKC Scholarship Fund (the "Scholarship Fund"), which will be administered as part of its existing Oklahoma Fund, solely for the provision of educational needs of those children.

The Scholarship Fund will accept donations from all sources and 100 percent of all contributions will be distributed for the benefit of the eligible children. The FEEA will establish an Advisory Board to help direct financial assistance from the Scholarship Fund, to advise the FEEA concerning eligibility criteria, and to provide such information and advice as the Board of Directors of the FEEA may require. As set forth in a Memorandum of Understanding Between the Director of the Office of Personnel Management (OPM) and the FEEA, either I or my designee will recommend persons for appointment to the Advisory Board.

Those who wish to contribute to the Scholarship Fund should send donations to the FEEA; checks should be earmarked "The President's OKC Scholarship Fund." The FEEA's mailing address is: Suite 200, 8441 West Bowles, Littleton, Colorado 80123.

The Federal family has again come together in the aftermath of the Oklahoma City bombing, with contributions of money, clothing, annual leave, and even blood. I hope we will be just as generous in supporting the education of the innocent children whose parents were killed or disabled in this terrible act.

I urge each of you to support the Scholarship Fund and encourage your employees to do likewise.

WILLIAM J. CLINTON

Remarks to the Black Enterprise Magazine 25th Anniversary Gala
August 9, 1995

Thank you, Earl. I'm delighted to be with you, and I appreciate your introduction. It is I who should be thanking you tonight and many of those who are there with you for your incredible effort over so many years and especially for your valuable input and support on the affirmative action policy.

I also want to say hello to my Secretary of Commerce, Ron Brown. [*Applause*] I'm glad you applauded him. He certainly is one of the finest Secretaries of Commerce this country ever had. He has done more to promote jobs and businesses for all Americans than anybody has in a long time. I want to say hello to Dr. Earl Richardson, the president of Morgan State. To

Tom Labrecque of Chase Manhattan Bank, thank you for being there and for your work. Reverend Jackson, I'm sorry I missed your prayer. I need it more than anybody who's there. [*Laughter*] I'm sorry I missed it. Mayor Schmoke, Governor Wilder, I enjoyed being with you a few days ago. And to my longtime friend Maynard Jackson, and to all the Graves family and all my friends who are gathered there tonight to honor your achievements, Earl, I want to send my best wishes.

I also know that I speak for all of you when we offer our best wishes to someone who had planned to be with you tonight—our prayers and best wishes are with David Dinkins. We wish him well, and we know he's going to be all right.

Earl, I want to add my congratulations to you and to Black Enterprise for 25 years of leadership in African-American business. This evening celebrates initiative, achievement, and opportunity. Initiative has always been the American genius, and Earl, you have set a singular example of that kind of genius. And because of your example, countless African-Americans have been empowered to take advantage of opportunity, to achieve. A life of accomplishment has exponential impact, and you, Earl Graves, have proved that.

A quarter century ago, you and Black Enterprise began to fill a large void for African-Americans who needed a source for information, encouragement, and guidance, to become entrepreneurs and to succeed in business. And over the years Black Enterprise has helped dreams to become reality. I know it will continue to do so for more African-Americans for many, many more years to come.

It's fitting that this anniversary is being celebrated with another important initiative by Earl Graves and that is to build up business education at one of our Nation's finest historically black universities, Morgan State. That's an investment that will pay great dividends for the next generation and beyond and I hope one that will encourage others to follow Earl's lead and to do their part to help expand opportunities in business and education for African-Americans. When we do that, all of America benefits.

I declared the last week in September Minority Enterprise Development Week to call attention to an important avenue to economic empowerment in America. But the fact is, we should be celebrating and promoting business growth in minority communities every day of the year. This business growth is essential for our continued prosperity, and it's the right way to create wealth, to encourage self-sufficiency, to generate jobs, and to build our people up and to build our communities up.

Our administration is working hard to strengthen all our Nation's businesses. We've opened new domestic and international markets, due in no small part to the hard work of Ron Brown and all those at the Commerce Department who have helped to expand the opportunities for American businesses. We've reduced the cost of borrowing for business start-ups and for expansions. While the Small Business Administration has cut its budget by 40 percent, it has doubled its loan output and increased its loan output to minority businesses and women by almost 80 percent.

Now, all this is making an impact. Overall, new businesses are growing as never before. And since 1992, nearly 100,000 new African-American businesses have been created in the United States. By 1997, according to the Census Bureau, there will be 717,000 African-American businesses in America, the result of the largest increase in any 5-year period. That's an accomplishment to be proud of, and I would tell you that if we get another 4 years to work on the economy, the number may be bigger than that.

Last month, as Earl said, I reaffirmed America's need for affirmative action, including set-asides for minority business owners in Federal contract procurement. I did it because I believe our country still needs this tool to address the limits of opportunity which still exist in our society, based on gender and race. I did it because I believe we'll be stronger if every American has a chance to live up to his or her God-given abilities.

We must have a mission, a national mission at the end of this century to restore the American dream of opportunity and the American value of responsibility. We must have a mission to do this together. We've got a big decision to make about whether we're going forward together or not. Whether we like it or not, we're all in the future together. We are a national family, whether we like it or not. And we're going forward, like a good family, together, or if we squabble and get divided and get sidetracked, we'll be held back, like a not very good family, together. We are a part of America's greater national community. All of you have to be part of that mission. I am committed to doing everything I can to build a good partnership with you, to move our country forward.

We've come a good ways in the 25 years since Black Enterprise was born, but there is still a lot to be done. Too many people still don't have the chance to reach their God-given potential, and affirmative action is just one part of a larger strategy to expand opportunities for all Americans, in education and business and all our workplaces. That larger strategy has to begin with Head Start for poor children. It has to include lower costs and better, more available college loans for the children of working families as well as poor families. It has to include adequate job training for people when they lose their jobs or when they're underemployed. It has to include creating business opportunities where none existed before.

That's what our empowerment zones are for. That's what the community development financial institutions are for. That's what stronger enforcement of the Community Reinvestment Act is for. We have to invest in our cities and the people who live there. We have to invest in our rural areas and the people who live there. We have to invest in our workers and in our working families.

That's why I believe we need a real family values agenda, which includes raising the minimum wage, targeting tax relief to the raising of children and the educating of children, protecting Medicare for our seniors, and protecting the right of people to keep their own health insurance if they change jobs or someone in the family gets sick.

We can balance the budget, and we should. Progressives, minorities, Democrats, those of us who care about public investment, we don't have a stake in a permanent Government deficit. That just gives more and more money every year to the people who hold the debt and less and less to the people who need the investment. But we have to balance this budget in a way that allows us to grow together, without gutting our responsibilities to our parents in health care, without gutting our responsibilities to our children in education, without undermining our responsibilities to maintain a social safety net and provide for a clean environment and a healthy and safe environment as well.

We have to follow the right kind of strategy to balance the budget, grow the economy, and help all Americans, together. Only when we

work together can we restore economic opportunity, solve our social problems, compete and win in the global economy of the 21st century, only when we do it together.

We do not have a person to waste. That is the big decision that all of us have to face. Captains of industry, leaders in education, mentors to a new generation: that's what many of you are. You have a big role in this strategy for America's future. Every time you help a young person get an education, help someone get started in business, provide an example by being a successful person yourself who took on the challenge and responsibility of entrepreneurship and made it, every time you do one of those things, you're making a difference and helping to move us forward.

I want you to think about what's at stake. Here in Washington, the old debate about what was liberal or conservative is really not what's going on. You know, I have cut the deficit more, reduced the size of Government more, eliminated more governmental regulations and governmental programs than my two Republican predecessors. I've also invested more in education, expanded trade, tried to help poor areas and minority businesses, tried to empower families with things like family and medical leave and affordable college loans and national service, things that have traditionally been called liberal. I'm trying to move people from welfare to work but only if they can support their children and help them to grow up and be successful.

We've got to do things in a different way. But the debate we're having here is the most profound debate we've had in a hundred years. And every one of you has got to make up your mind to be a part of it because the old conservative things that I just mentioned, they're hardly on the radar screen here.

We're debating here with a new generation of so-called conservatives who, I think, have some radical ideas. They believe that, except for defense, any tax cut, any tax cut, is better than any Government program. They believe that some of the things we'd like to do through Government are nice enough but not worth imposing any, any, requirement or sacrifice or contribution on Americans who aren't going to directly benefit. They believe in a future that really would unleash us all from each other, minimize our responsibilities to each other, and run the risk of giving us a country with a whole lot of wealthy people but vastly more poor and a declining middle class.

I believe in a high-opportunity, high-growth future where we grow the middle class and shrink the under class, where we support entrepreneurs but we also believe that we have an obligation to help everybody make the most of their own lives. And to do it, we need strong neighborhoods with safe streets and good health care systems and good schools and clean environments. And we need a commitment to help people through education and through efforts to deal with our very difficult and thorny social problems.

In other words, I believe we really are a family. I think we have certain obligations to one another that we have a responsibility to fulfill. And I don't believe any of us are going to be the kind of people we want to be, and I don't think our children will have the kind of future we want them to have, unless we make up our mind that there are some things we have to do together.

If you look at the 21st century, and you say, what's it going to be like—there will be a global economy, information will speed around the world quickly, goods will cross national borders, the world will get smaller—you have to say that the United States, because of the strength of our economic system and because we are the most diverse, big, rich country on Earth—racially, religiously, ethnically—that we're in better shape for the 21st century than any other great country, that our best days are still ahead of us. But we have to answer the debate now going on in Washington properly for that to be true.

We haven't had a debate like this since the industrial revolution changed America and Theodore Roosevelt and Woodrow Wilson had to answer questions like, "How are we going to keep a private economy but have real competition in things like oil and steel?" They had to ask questions like, "How are we going to let people work but stop these 9- and 10-year-old kids from working 10 hours a day, 6 days a week, in coal mines and factories?" We reached the right kind of decisions then, and we preserved the free enterprise system and broadened freedom and opportunity throughout the 20th century steadily. We even survived the Great Depression and conquered the oppressors in World War II because of the power of our country.

Well, now we're moving into a dramatically different kind of economy. The way we work and live is changing dramatically. And we are literally having the debates again in Washington that we had a hundred years ago. You have got to be a part of that. You know that believing that we work together and grow together is not inconsistent with believing in enterprise and individual effort and personal responsibility and hard work. You know that.

That is the lesson America must emblazon in its heart and its mind if the 21st century is going to be our golden age. I think it will be because of people like Earl Graves, because of efforts like Black Enterprise, because of all the African-American entrepreneurs who have made a difference in our Nation, knowing that whenever they succeed, they're helping us all to come closer together, closer to the dream of equal opportunity for all Americans, without which we will never, never have the progress we all want and need for our children in the next century.

Thank you, Earl. Thank you all, and God bless you.

NOTE: The President spoke at 9:10 p.m. by satellite from the Diplomatic Reception Room at the White House to the gala in New York City. In his remarks, he referred to Rev. Jesse L. Jackson of the Rainbow Coalition; Mayor Kurt Schmoke of Baltimore, MD; former Governor of Virginia L. Douglas Wilder; Maynard Jackson, former mayor of Atlanta, GA; and David Dinkins, former mayor of New York City.

Remarks Prior to a Roundtable Discussion on Teenage Smoking
August 10, 1995

Well, good morning. Ladies and gentlemen, today I have brought together medical experts and children who have taken a pledge against smoking to talk about our common commitment to ending youth smoking. This issue is critical to our efforts to improve the health of our Nation. According to the Center for Disease Control, of the 2 million Americans who will die in 1995, over 400,000 of them will have conditions related to smoking.

Later today, I will announce my strategy for combating this problem based on one simple idea: We should do everything we possibly can to keep tobacco out of the hands of our young people in the United States.

Now I'd like to call on Shana Bailey, who is a 12-year-old from Florida who's part of a successful program that teaches students how and why they should stay smoke-free.

NOTE: The President spoke at 10:18 a.m. in the Oval Office at the White House.

The President's News Conference
August 10, 1995

Teenage Smoking

The President. Good afternoon. Today I am announcing broad executive action to protect the young people of the United States from the awful dangers of tobacco.

Over the years, we have learned more and more about the dangers of addictive substances to our young people. In the sixties and seventies we came to realize the threat drugs posed to young Americans. In the eighties we came to grips with the awful problem of drunk driving among young people. It is time to take a third step to free our teenagers from addiction and dependency.

Adults are capable of making their own decisions about whether to smoke. But we all know that children are especially susceptible to the deadly temptation of tobacco and its skillful marketing. Today, and every day this year, 3,000 young people will begin to smoke. One thousand of them ultimately will die of cancer, emphysema, heart disease, and other diseases caused by smoking. That's more than a million vulnerable young people a year being hooked on nicotine that ultimately could kill them.

Therefore, by executive authority, I will restrict sharply the advertising, promotion, distribution, and marketing of cigarettes to teenagers. I do this on the basis of the best available scientific evidence, the findings of the American Medical Association, the American Cancer Society, the American Heart Association, the American Lung Association, the Centers for Disease Control. Fourteen months of study by the Food and Drug Administration confirms what we all know: Cigarettes and smokeless tobacco are harmful, highly addictive, and aggressively marketed to our young people. The evidence is overwhelming, and the threat is immediate.

Our children face a health crisis that is getting worse. One-third more 8th-graders and one-quarter more 10th-graders are smoking today than 4 years ago. One out of five high school seniors is a daily smoker. We need to act, and we must act now, before another generation of Americans is condemned to fight a difficult and grueling personal battle with an addiction that will cost millions of them their lives.

Adults make their own decisions about whether or not to smoke. Relatively few people start to smoke past their teens. Many adults have quit; many have tried and failed. But we all know that teenagers are especially susceptible to pressures, pressure to the manipulation of mass media advertising, the pressure of the seduction of skilled marketing campaigns aimed at exploiting their insecurities and uncertainties about life.

When Joe Camel tells young children that smoking is cool, when billboards tell teens that smoking will lead to true romance, when Virginia Slims tells adolescents that cigarettes may make them thin and glamorous, then our children need our wisdom, our guidance, and our experience. We are their parents, and it is up to us to protect them.

So today I am authorizing the Food and Drug Administration to initiate a broad series of steps all designed to stop sales and marketing of cigarettes and smokeless tobacco to children. As a result, the following steps will be taken. First, young people will have to prove their age with an I.D. card to buy cigarettes. Second, cigarette vending machines which circumvent any ban on sales to kids will be prohibited. Third, schools and playgrounds will be free of tobacco advertising on billboards in their neighborhoods. Fourth, images such as Joe Camel will not appear on billboards or in ads in publications that reach substantial numbers of children and teens. Fifth, teens won't be targeted by any marketing gimmicks, ranging from single cigarette sales to T-shirts, gym bags, and sponsorship of sporting events. And finally, the tobacco industry must fund and implement an annual $150 million campaign aimed at stopping teens from smoking through educational efforts.

Now, these are all commonsense steps. They don't ban smoking; they don't bar advertising. We do not, in other words, seek to address activities that seek to sell cigarettes only to adults. We are stepping in to protect those who need our help, our vulnerable young people. And the evidence of increasing smoking in the last few years is plain and compelling.

Now, nobody much likes Government regulation. And I would prefer it if we could have done this in some other way. The only other way I can think of is if Congress were to write these restrictions into law. They could do that. And if they do, this rule could become unnecessary. But it is wrong to believe that we can take a voluntary approach to this problem. And absent congressional action, and in the presence of a massive marketing and lobbying campaign by cigarette companies aimed at our children, clearly, I have no alternative but to do everything I can to bring this assault to a halt.

The issue has touched all of us in personal ways. We all know friends or family members whose lives were shortened because of their involvement with tobacco. The Vice President's sister, a heavy smoker who started as a teen, died of lung cancer. It is that kind of pain that I seek to spare other families and young children. Less smoking means less cancer, less illness, longer lives, a stronger America. Acting together we can make a difference. With this concerted plan targeted at those practices that especially prey upon our children, we can save lives, and we will.

To those who produce and market cigarettes, I say today, take responsibility for your actions. Sell your products only to adults. Draw the line on children. Show by your deeds as well as your words that you recognize that it is wrong

as well as illegal to hook one million children a year on tobacco.

Terry [Terence Hunt, Associated Press].

Q. Mr. President, with your decision on tobacco you're taking on one of the biggest cash crops in a region where you've already got major political problems. Are you writing off the South for next year's elections? And isn't this is a blow to other Democratic candidates in tobacco States?

The President. Well, first of all, the most important thing is that there is an epidemic among our children. You've got a third more 8th-graders, a quarter more 10th-graders smoking than there were 10 years ago. Whatever the political consequences, a thousand kids a day are beginning a habit which will probably shorten their lives. I mean, that is the issue. And I believe that is the issue everywhere.

I believe there are tobacco farmers in the States which grow tobacco, who have been involved in it a hundred years or more—their families—who don't want their kids to start smoking. We're not talking about whether they have a right to grow tobacco or reap the paltry 4½ cents, which is all they get out of a pack of cigarettes. We're talking about whether we are going to do what we know is the right thing to do to save the lives of America's children. And I think it is more important than any political consequence.

Helen [Helen Thomas, United Press International].

Bosnia

Q. Mr. President, the war in Bosnia is widening. How long is the world, particularly the Europeans who have been there in the past, how long are they going to stand—we all are going to stand by and watch this barbarism on both sides? And what are your new initiatives to end this suffering?

The President. Well, first of all, let me briefly review what our objectives are. Our objectives are to minimize suffering, to stop the war from spreading, to preserve the integrity of a Bosnian state. We have promoted the Muslim-Croat Federation. We have plainly succeeded in limiting the war. And except when the United Nations and NATO had not done what they said they would do, we have saved lives.

This is an important moment in Bosnia, and it could be a moment of real promise. Because of the military actions of the last few days, the situation on the ground has changed. There is some uncertainty and instability. It could go either way. But I think it's a time when we should try to make a move to make peace.

Now, since the fall of Srebrenica and Zepa, we have tried to do two things: first of all, to strengthen the presence of the United Nations through the Rapid Reaction Force of the French, the British, and the Dutch, which we are supporting; and through getting a clearer chain of command and a stronger, broader use of authority for NATO to have air power where necessary where the protected areas are threatened.

The second thing we want to do is to see whether or not some diplomatic solution can be brought to bear that would be fair and decent and just and that would take advantage of this moment where people are reassessing their various positions. And that's what Mr. Lake is doing in Europe. We are consulting with all of our allies, and we're going to do the very best we can. I think we need to try to make a decent and good peace here because, ultimately, that's the answer to all the questions you ask.

Q. [*Inaudible*]—you have new ideas?

The President. Well, we're exploring some ideas with the Europeans. I will say again what I said from the first day I came here: I do not believe it is right to impose peace on people. I don't think in the end you get a lasting peace. So the United States does not seek to impose peace. But we're exploring some different ideas. We don't have a set map; we don't have a set position. We have some ideas that the new events may make possible, and we're discussing it with our allies.

Brit [Brit Hume, ABC News].

Teenage Smoking

Q. Mr. President, in view of the powerful evidence of the dangers of smoking which you cited, wouldn't it have been more logical to impose an outright ban instead of a regulatory partial step which has the effect of getting the Federal Government into the business of regulating the size of print in advertising?

The President. Well, first I don't know that the Federal Government will regulate the size of print; we regulate the warning labels. And of course, there is a proposal here on advertising to try to deal with restricting access to billboard advertising and others.

But I think it would be wrong to ban cigarettes outright because, number one, it's not illegal for adults to use them. Tens of millions of adults do use them, and I think it would be as ineffective as prohibition was. But I think to focus on our children is the right thing to do. Purchasing of cigarettes by young people, children, is supposed to be illegal in all 50 States, but they do it regularly. These fine young people here were with me this morning, and one of them talked about how he bought cigarette pack after cigarette pack after cigarette pack out of vending machines to try to demonstrate to his local legislators that the laws were a sham. These will not make the laws a sham. This will enable us to save young people's lives.

China

Q. Mr. President, has there been any progress in getting China to free human rights activist, Harry Wu? And related to that, will Mrs. Clinton be going to China in September to attend the U.N. Conference on Women?

The President. On the first question, we're obviously very concerned about Harry Wu and following his case very closely. And I think the situation is in a position where the less that is said about it right now, the better. But it's a very important issue to the United States, and I think to people throughout the world.

No decision has yet been made about whether the First Lady will go to China. But I think it's important for the American people to understand that this conference on women is a United Nations-sponsored conference that they decided to hold in China. It is a very important thing in its own right, and the United States will be represented there with a very strong delegation, whether she goes or not. And I think it's important that we be represented there.

Yes, Wolf [Wolf Blitzer, CNN].

Iraq

Q. Mr. President, the situation in Iraq seems to be somewhat fluid right now with the defection of two of Saddam Hussein's daughters, two of his sons-in-law, his oldest grandchild to Jordan. And King Hussein's granting political asylum to all of these people. First of all, can you assess what is happening in Baghdad right now? And have you offered additional assurances to Jordan that the United States will provide security if there is a threat from Iraq?

The President. Well, as soon as the defections occurred, King Hussein contacted us, and I called him back as quickly as I could on Tuesday evening and we had a long talk about it. I think what these defections demonstrate is just how difficult things are within Iraq now and how out of touch Saddam Hussein has become with reality, how difficult things are for his people. I also think this evidence supports the strong and firm position the United States has taken of not lifting the sanctions until Iraq fully complies with all the United Nations resolutions. I think that is—it's clear that we have done the right thing.

Now, with regard to your second question, King Hussein's decision, located where he is, to grant asylum to those individuals was clearly an act of real courage. And I have assured ·him and told him that we would stand behind Jordan. We owe it to the people who are our partners in peace in the Middle East to stand behind them, and we have already made it clear that if Iraq threatens its neighbors or violates United Nations resolutions, we would take appropriate action. I think we have to do so in this case.

Q. Any contingency steps being taken?

The President. Well, I think you saw when Kuwait was threatened a few months ago, we are quite well-organized, and we have thought through what our—various scenarios there and how we might move. But beyond that, I don't want to say. And I don't want to raise a red flag. I'm just saying we know that Saddam Hussein has been unpredictable in the past, we know this must be a very unsettling development, and it should be clear that the United States considers Jordan our ally and entitled to our protection if their security is threatened as a result of this incident.

Teenage Smoking

Q. Mr. President, given the fact that there's been a 20-year war against drugs, which are illegal for everybody, which has produced, at best, mixed results, and given the fact that anybody who has kids know that the more you prohibit something, the more attractive it often becomes, what makes you think that you think you can do any better in the war against cigarettes than we've done against drugs?

The President. Well, first of all, let me say that—let me take on your premise here. There have been sustained periods of years in our country and in recent history when drug use has gone down in all categories of drugs, among all ages of people without regard to race or income. Unfortunately, today the picture is somewhat mixed because casual drug use among young people seems to be going up in areas where they feel a certain level of hopelessness. And we intend to reassert our efforts there.

But it's simply not true that cultural changes and legal bars together cannot work to reduce consumption. With regard to cigarettes, we have seen cultural changes leading to reduction in consumption. But what we see among young people is adults quitting and young people increasing their usage. If you make it clearly illegal, more inaccessible, you reduce the lure of advertising and then you have an affirmative campaign, a positive campaign, so that you don't just say no, you give young people information and make it the smart, the cool, the hip thing to do to take care of yourself and keep yourself healthy and alive. I believe there is every evidence from what has happened in drugs and in many other areas that we will see a dramatic decline in smoking among young people. I think we can do that.

And I think you see—there have been a lot of cultural changes to that effect in other areas. You see some States that have done it right have big increase in the use of seatbelts. Drunk driving goes down dramatically in some areas with the combination of the right sort of enforcement and the right sort of publicity. So I believe—I just don't accept your premise. I think we'll have a big dent in this problem.

Appropriations Legislation

Q. Mr. President, the House has cut $20 billion in discretionary spending for next year. Will they have to return some of those cuts to avoid you vetoing some of their appropriations bills?

The President. Yes. [*Laughter*]

Whitewater Hearings

Q. Mr. President, on Whitewater, you've said in the past that as far as you know everything as far as major evidence that is going to come out is out. We now face the prospect though of hearings going into 1996. Do you view this as pure politics? Do you worry about the overall shadow it has cast, merely the appearance of wrongdoing over the White House?

The President. I don't have anything new to add to what I've already said about that. I will reiterate, when I started this whole episode I said I would cooperate fully; I have cooperated fully. There is nothing else for me to do. I have to spend my energies and time being President, and that's what I'm doing my best to do.

Yes, Mara [Mara Liasson, National Public Radio].

Political Reform and Ross Perot

Q. Mr. President, what message do you want Senator Dodd and Mr. McLarty to take to Ross Perot when they go down there this weekend? And also, do you feel that Ross Perot's contribution to the issue of political reform is significant enough that you would consider appointing him to the bipartisan commission, should it get established?

The President. The answer to the second question—let me answer that first—the answer to the second question is, yes, I would consider doing that, but first, the Speaker has got to answer my letter or see John Gardner or Doris Kearns Goodwin or do something to respond to the handshake we made in New Hampshire. Of all the strange things that happen in Washington—and I know people think that all the rules are different here than they are for anybody anywhere else in America—but even here, when you shake hands with somebody in broad daylight and say you're going to do something, you ought to at least act like your going to do it. [*Laughter*] Where I come from, you know, if kids did that, their mamas wouldn't let them have dinner before—they got spanked, when I was growing up I mean, this is an amazing thing. So, yes, I would.

The second part of the question was what will their message be. Their message will be: Number one, that the things that Ross Perot and Bill Clinton advocated in '92 had a lot of overlap, and we have made significant progress in implementing 80 percent of the things that Ross Perot campaigned for in 1992; two, a lot of the things that we haven't done are because of obstruction in Congress, and I mention only two, the line-item veto and political reform; and third, our budget is more consistent with the budget priorities outlined by Ross Perot and his campaign in 1992, that is, balance the budget but increase investment in education, research, and development, technology, and defense conversion.

So, we've got a record message. We've got a present conflict message. We've got a message to ask them to come help us to support meaningful political reform and the right kind of balanced budget.

Tobacco Industry

Q. Mr. President, you noted in your speech in Charlotte yesterday that children follow what we do more than what we say. And I wonder what you think the message is when, on the one hand, the Government cracks down on teen smoking, on the other hand, it spends perhaps $25 million a year subsidizing the growth of tobacco, and when you yourself continue to smoke those big old cigars. [*Laughter*]

The President. Well first of all, as you know, I'm allergic to cigars, so I don't smoke many anymore. But I smoke a handful a year probably, and I probably shouldn't. And I try not to do it in any way that sets a bad example. But I plead guilty to that.

On the tobacco program, if it is self-financing—and I have always supported the tobacco program. It is essentially a self financing program. The question is, do you want this tobacco grown by family farmers, or do you want it grown by big corporations if it's a self-financing program? I would not favor a large taxpayer outlay for it. But a self-financing program, essentially which is what that is, has been designed to preserve the structure of family farms and the culture of the family farms rather than let the big tobacco companies grow it themselves and turn all those folks into hired hands. I have thought, since it was going to be grown one way or the other, the family farm structure was a better one. I don't think that sends a signal that we think young people ought to smoke cigarettes.

Drug Cartels

Q. [*Inaudible*]—the Colombian Government has captured some of the top leaders of both cartels, and there's been friction between your government and the Samper government when he came in. My first question is, do you think they are doing everything they can? And the second question is, how worried are you that as the Colombian cartel wanes in influence, Mexican cartels will pick up the breach?

The President. Well, first of all, I want to support the statements made by the DEA Director in my administration, Tom Considine. We have worked very hard with the Colombians and with others in South America, and you see the results in the last several months. We have had more major drug dealers arrested than in any previous similar time in our history, I believe. And we're on the verge of breaking this Cali cartel. It's been great cooperation; we've worked hard. It's making a difference.

Secondly, as long as the raw crops can be grown and processed and distributed, we will have a constant battle, as long as there's demand in the United States, to keep any vacuum from being filled. And we are exploring today what the problems created by our successes might be, that is, if we continue to break down existing cartels, who will take up the slack and how can we prevent it.

Teenage Smoking

Q. Mr. President, last week you said that you did not want to advance a tobacco strategy that would get caught up in the courts and prevent any kind of action from taking place for years. Now you seem to have embarked on that strategy. Tobacco companies have already today filed suit against your proposals. Why did you determine a voluntary effort in concert with the tobacco companies would not work? And is there any hope for some sort of compromise, some sort of either compromise with the tobacco companies or congressional action before you implement these regulations?

The President. Well, first of all, I had hoped that the tobacco companies would agree to support these restrictions and to put them in law. And it's still not too late for that. The FDA—Dr. Kessler has announced today a rulemaking procedure on the assumption of jurisdiction and on the specifics that I just outlined. If the tobacco companies accept those and this Congress will write them into law, then you will not have a long regulatory proceeding. But you will have immediate, immediate, effects. That is, if they would rather have a law than Federal regulation, the FDA Director, Dr. Kessler, and I would rather have an immediate impact on teen smoking, not 2 years of litigation and then start the work. So it is not too late for that.

But I am against a voluntary plan. I'm against it for several reasons. First of all, there would be no way to enforce it. Secondly, the history of voluntary agreements with the tobacco industry is not good, to put it mildly. And thirdly, even if they tried to adhere to it, I don't believe they could legally do so.

Let me just give you one example. Suppose you were in the vending machine business and you sued the tobacco companies for deciding together that they were going to not let your vending machines go anywhere. Without a legal requirement there's a good chance that could be held in a court of law to be a restraint of trade. So I think even if they tried to do it, they couldn't do it.

So we have to have a mandatory system. But I would just as soon have an act of Congress. Dr. Kessler agrees because we've got an epidemic of teen smoking, and far better to start right now as soon as we can pass a law than wait until we wade through all this litigation.

Airline Safety

Q. Mr. President, there was a scary breakdown yesterday in the air traffic control system in the Western United States, and we've had similar incidents in past months and recent years. Can you tell the American people that the FAA is doing everything possible to preserve the safety of the flying public, or do you see that new measures need to be taken?

The President. I can tell you that I have asked that question repeatedly since I have been President, and I have worked very hard on making sure that we are moving to do everything we can constantly to make sure that the air traffic control system is as safe as possible.

We also, as you know, have ordered some new measures to be taken to promote airline security, which the Secretary of Transportation announced just in the last couple of days. And I do want to emphasize to the American people because I know there's been a lot of discussion about it, there was no specific incident that prompted me to make the decision to try to increase security around airports. But the overall conditions, it seemed to me, dictated that we do that.

And I think that this country has been very strong against terrorism through military action, imposing sanctions, stopping sanctions from being lifted, stopping terrorist incidents before they occur, arresting terrorists shortly after they commit acts. This is a part of our ongoing effort to protect the American people from that.

And parenthetically, I would like to say I certainly wish the Congress would pass the antiterrorism legislation which was promised to me on Memorial Day. That would also help us in this regard.

Teenage Drinking

Q. In going after teenage smoking, Mr. President, did you consider including alcohol abuse as part of that? I know you mentioned drunk driving in your opening remarks, but alcohol among young people is thought to be as much of a problem as smoking is.

The President. First of all, it is far less accessible. It's harder to get. What we have advocated there, and I hope the Congress will adopt, is a national zero tolerance for alcohol among young drivers. If we go to zero tolerance among young drivers, I think it will make a difference. Now, I noted last week—and I would like to give the State credit for it—one State adopted zero tolerance this last week. We are now up to 27 States that have done it on their own. But I think zero tolerance is the best thing to do.

Sarah [Sarah McClendon, McClendon News].

Opposition From Congress

Q. Mr. President, there's a move on Capitol Hill among some right-wing Senators—Faircloth of North Carolina—and also joined by—and D'Amato, of course, New York—and several left-wing Democrats, real liberal left-wing Democrats to try to get you out of office this month. They're going to try to do that by embarrassing you so that you will resign. Would you resign your office under any circumstances? [*Laughter*]

The President. Well, if you promise to run off with me, I might. [*Laughter*] But otherwise I can't think of any reason. [*Laughter*]

1996 Election

Q. Mr. President, continuing on the political mien, if we might. [*Laughter*] A year from now the Republican Presidential convention opens. Looking at the electoral vote now, it seems to be a lot of political experts say that you're in trouble in the South, in trouble in the West, it's really going to be an uphill battle for reelection. How do you assess your position at this time?

The President. Well, first of all, I don't think my position at this time amounts to anything because the world will turn around. At this time, when I started running for President—I hadn't even declared for President this time 4 years ago, and everybody said the incumbent President could not be defeated. So I don't think

anyone knows, and I think all this is idle speculation.

I will tell you this: I have done my best to do what I said I would do when I ran. This is the second anniversary of our economic plan. We passed our reconciliation bill on this day 2 years ago. Theirs is still not passed. And the people who are now in charge of the Congress said that it would be the end of the world; we would have a terrible recession; it would bankrupt the country; it would be awful. And 2 years later, we have 7 million jobs, 2½ million new homeowners, 1½ million new small businesses, a record, a record number of new self-made millionaires, a very high stock market, very low inflation.

Now, this is the first time in history we've had this kind of surge that hasn't also raised the incomes of ordinary people because of the new realities which we face. So now, economic policy must be seen as a two-step, not a one-step process. We've got to grow the economy and raise incomes. That's why I want to raise the minimum wage. That's why I want to give every unemployed worker or underemployed worker the right to 2 years of education at the local community college. That's why I'm trying to have a tax cut that's focused on childrearing and education, to raise incomes.

But I believe when the record of this administration is made, in every area, whether it's this or in fighting crime or protecting the environment or educating our people or trying to prepare the world for the end of the post-coldwar era and a new era of cooperation, I believe the American people will listen, and then they'll make their own judgments about it. But I don't think anybody can know what's going to happen a year and a half from now.

Teenage Smoking

Q. Mr. President, are you sure you wouldn't like to pledge today not to smoke cigars anymore to set an example? [*Laughter*]

The President. Well, you mean should I go from five or six down to zero a year? Maybe so. But I don't think that's the point. The point I want to make is, number one, cigars and pipes were not found by the FDA to be part of this. Did you know that?

Number two, the issue is, for me—I try to set a good example. I try never to do it when people see. I admitted that I did do it when Captain O'Grady was found because I was so happy. It was a form of celebration. But I don't think you should let that become the issue. The issue is whether the children are smoking cigarettes in this country.

Nuclear Testing by France

Q. Mr. President, on the French nuclear testing, the French are now saying they will agree to a zero threshold for nuclear tests in the Nuclear Test Ban Treaty. Will the U.S. concur? Do you think the French should cancel their tests? And very importantly, has the U.S. agreed to share technology with the French so that they can develop their own computer simulations and not have to test?

The President. I applaud the French statement today. It will make it much easier for us to get a comprehensive test ban. I do not think they should resume testing, but they know that. That's a difference between us and them and most of the rest of the world and them. And we will have a statement about our own policy in the very near future, but I don't want to make it today.

Press Secretary Mike McCurry. Let's make this one the last question.

Teenage Smoking

Q. Mr. President, the steps that you outlined today are tailored very carefully to curb the sale of tobacco to young people. My question is, if they're implemented, will the FDA retain power that would allow them at a future date to ban or curb sale of tobacco to adults?

The President. Well, of course, that's what the tobacco companies are worried about, I guess. Our belief is that this is a pediatric disease. This is a problem for children, that when tobacco is lawful, it would be wrong for a Government agency to try to in any way restrict the access of adults to it if it is lawful. So the answer is, I don't know what the law would be because, in this case, I'm not the lawyer for the agency. I can't give you a lawful answer. I can tell you that the policy of this Government is that the focus should be on our children, their health and their welfare. That is the focus.

If there is a worry underlying the question you asked, there is an answer to that worry: Put it in the law. Let's have the tobacco companies come in. Let's talk to the Members of Congress from the tobacco-growing States. Let's pass it into law. Pass these restrictions. Put them into law. Do it now. Then we won't have all

these lawsuits, and we will begin immediately, right now, to protect the children of this country. That is the answer.

Yes, Deborah [Deborah Mathis, Gannett News Service].

Whitewater Hearings

Q. Mr. President, there has been a parade of you and your wife's friends, associates, aides, former aides on Capitol Hill lately in both the Senate and House Whitewater hearings. How does it make you feel to see so many of your old friends and associates being grilled, in effect? And have you been keeping track of the hearings, and if so, how?

The President. The answer to the second question is, not really, Occasionally I see a clip or something, but I don't watch television very much, except late at night for a few minutes before I to go bed. So I haven't had a chance to keep up with it. My impression is that they have all acquitted themselves quite well, and I've been proud of them. But I don't have anything to say on the underlying substance beyond what I've already said.

Teenage Smoking

Q. Mr. President, on the FDA rule again, a coalition of advertisers is filing suit today saying that for a legal product, your rule would go far beyond any precedent in restricting first amendment rights. Is there any precedent that you could cite that would be equivalent in its reach into the first amendment? And if not, are you not concerned about that aspect?

The President. First of all, nobody who's ever held this office loved the first amendment any more than I do. And no one has ever felt both edges of it any more than I have. I believe in the first amendment. That's what my speech about religious freedom was about the other day. I believe in it.

But I would remind you of just a few basic facts. It is illegal for children to smoke cigarettes. How then can it be legal for people to advertise to children to get them to smoke cigarettes? And does anybody seriously doubt that a lot of this advertisement is designed to reach children so we get new customers for the tobacco companies as the old customers disappear? It cannot be a violation of the freedom of speech in this country to say that you cannot advertise to entice people to do something which they cannot legally do. So I just don't buy the first amendment argument, it's just not true.

And by the way, that is why—to go back to an earlier question—the FDA ran the risk of having a rather complex rule to make it clear that there should be some freedom left, some considerable freedom left to advertise to adults. Yes, ma'am.

China

Q. Mr. President, your administration has said on many occasions that you're going to adhere to the one-China policy. However, the two sides of Taiwan's fate obviously have different views on what this one China is. And you are the one who made the decision to allow President Teng-hui to come to the United States, and China is very, very unhappy now. So I wonder, how are you going to balance between a democratic Taiwan willing to risk everything to seek international recognition and, on the other hand, the very, very important strategic interests between the United States and China?

The President. First of all, we're going to balance them by continuing to adhere to the one-China policy. It is the policy of the United States; it has been for years; it continues to be.

Secondly, we are going to do everything we can to make sure that our policy is clearly understood in China and in Taiwan. I made the decision personally to permit President Li from Taiwan to come into this country not as the head of state, not as the head of a government that we had recognized but because he wanted to come. I'm sure there were political aspects to this, but he asked whether he could come to his college reunion, whether he could give speeches, whether he could travel in our United States. He is a law-abiding person. We had no grounds on which to deny him.

In the American culture there is a constitutional right to travel and a constitutional right to speak. And as a man who has almost never missed any of his high school or college reunions, I just felt I ought to give him the same opportunity. It was not an abrogation of our one-China policy in any way. It was a recognition of something that's special in our culture about the rights we accord individuals who obey our laws and comport themselves appropriately.

Welfare Reform

Q. Mr. President, as you know, the welfare reform bill has been delayed in the Senate. I wonder how optimistic you are that welfare reform can pass this year and to what extent welfare reform has been wrapped up in Republican Presidential politics.

The President. Well, it plainly has been wrapped up to some extent in Republican Presidential politics, and that's bad because 85 percent of the American people want it. As I think Senator Dole acknowledged a day or so ago, I made a personal appeal to him to try to work with me to get a welfare reform bill out and to do it this year.

What do we want out of welfare reform? We want work. We want time limits. We want responsible parenting. Those are the three things we want. Can we get there from where we are? I think we can. I think that Senator Dole has moved somewhat away from the extreme right of his party. Senator Daschle, Senator Mikulski, and Senator Breaux have offered a bill which has united the Democrats in moving away from the conventional wisdom toward welfare reform. And what we need to do over this break is that folks need to get together and figure out how we can put these approaches together and come out with a bill which promotes work, which promotes time limits, which promotes responsible parenting. I cannot believe we can't reach an agreement here.

Meanwhile, I will keep trying to get more States involved. You know, I have 32 States now that I've given permission to get out from under the Federal rules to promote welfare reform. And I would remind you I have offered all 50 States within 30 days the right to require young teen mothers to stay at home and stay in school to get checks, to put time limits and work requirements on welfare reform, and to allow the States to convert the welfare benefits and the food stamp benefits into wage supplements to get private employers to hire people in the private sector. Every State in the country could do that within the next 30 days. They just call us and send a request; we do it.

So we'll keep working, but we need the legislation, especially because we have to have national standards for tough child support enforcement that we cannot implement without the law.

I think our time is—one more question. Yes, go ahead.

Legislative Priorities

Q. Before the tobacco regulations came up this news conference was billed as your chance to give a farewell message to Congress. If you could send them a postcard from Jackson next week—[*laughter*]—what would you list as your top three or four priorities?

The President. We need to pass a decent budget that balances the budget but doesn't do it on the backs of elderly people who don't have enough to live on by exploding their Medicare costs; it doesn't walk away from our commitment to education, the education of our young people from Head Start to more affordable college loans through national service; that doesn't undermine our common commitment to the environment. We can find common ground on this budget that brings the American people together and moves us forward.

The second thing I would say is, we need to pass welfare reform. We need to pass welfare reform—work, time limits, responsible parenting.

The third thing I would say is, let's get to work on the unfinished agenda here, pass the antiterrorism bill, the line-item veto, appoint the political reform commission. Let's get after it. Let's do the things that we all are for, we keep saying we're for. Let's deliver for the American people.

Let me say in closing that my family and I are leaving on Tuesday for Wyoming, and I want you to enjoy your vacation.

Thank you, and God bless you. Thank you.

NOTE: The President's 101st news conference began at 1:32 p.m. in the East Room at the White House.

Interview With Tabitha Soren of MTV
August 11, 1995

Teenage Smoking

Ms. Soren. Mr. President, minors buy one billion packs of cigarettes a year. How are you going to make not smoking and quitting smoking cool and attractive to young people?

The President. Well, I think we have to do several things. I think, first of all, the Government's responsibility is to make sure that the young people understand that it's addictive and dangerous and can kill them and that about one-third of the young people who start smoking every day—about 1,000 people a day, young people, start smoking who will have their lives shortened because of it. The second thing I think you have to do is make it less accessible. Then the third thing we have to do is make it less attractive, that is, we need to change the advertising and limit the ability of advertising to be a lure.

We had a young teenager in here who was part of an antismoking group yesterday who said to me—I was so touched—she said, "We look at these TV ads," she said, "these girls smoking, they're always tall; they're always thin; they always have long hair; they're always pretty." She said, "It's just like when the boys who are young

see a movie star holding a gun." And it was shocking what she said.

And then what we want the tobacco companies to do is to spend some money on an affirmative strategy to put out positive messages—over MTV, for example—about how it's cool not to smoke instead of to smoke. So I think you make it less accessible, less attractive, and then put out a positive message. And of course, we need a lot of help. We need people like you to do programs like this, and every parent in this country needs to talk to their children—all the parents need to talk to their children about it, because we now have done 14 months careful research and we know how damaging this is, and we know that the tobacco companies know how damaging it is from their own files. We've got to do something about it.

Ms. Soren. Do you worry about making smoking more enticing by making it more forbidden to young people?

The President. I think that's always a concern; there could be some of that. But the staggering magnitude of the damage that it's doing is so great, I think if young people really understand how dangerous it really is and all the things that can happen to them and how it can affect their future, I don't think it will be more glamorous.

Ms. Soren. You know, though, what kids are going to say. In a time where they're growing up and sex is associated with AIDS, alcohol with drunk driving, going out late at night you could be shot, it's very violent, smoking during your adolescence almost seems like a lesser evil.

The President. I know it does, but in some ways it's the thing that puts the most at risk over the long run. And we have to do something about the other things, too. I've fought very hard to get the assault weapons out of the hands of gang members, to pass the Brady bill, to put more police officers on the street. The crime rate is going down in almost every—almost every big city in this country, the crime rate is going down. We have to—we're doing a better job trying to keep big shipments of drugs out of the country. We're working hard on that.

But this is a serious problem. On alcohol, it's less accessible than cigarettes. It's still a problem, but I want a zero tolerance drunk driving law for young people in every State in the country or here in the Congress. But the cigarettes—the magnitude of the damage caused is greater than all of that right now. And we just have to focus on it.

I know it—because there normally is a period of several years between the time you start and keep smoking and the time you face the consequences, and when you're young you think you're going to live forever, I know that it's going to be harder to get young people to focus on that. But we have to. There's a lot of destructive behavior in America we need to attack at the same time, and I just think that we can get these numbers way, way down.

You gave the number—a billion packs of cigarettes or a billion cigarettes a year—we can get that way down. And when we do, we'll get the life expectancy of these young people and their quality of life way up.

Ms. Soren. Did you ever experiment with cigarettes as a teen? Did you go through that phase?

The President. I didn't. But I'm surprised I didn't, but I didn't. The reason I didn't is because my mother was a heavy smoker. She smoked a couple of packs of cigarettes a day until my daughter got her to quit for her 8th birthday. When my daughter turned 8, her grandmother gave her that for a present. So

I had a bad feeling about it from childhood. But it was only because of that. I'm sure I would have done it otherwise.

Ms. Soren. Why were you savvy enough to have a bad feeling about it? You didn't like the smell of the house, or you didn't like——

The President. Yes, I didn't like the smell in the house. And I thought it was—it struck me as a bad habit, kind of a nervous habit, a reliance. And I had a feeling that it was not good for her health.

Ms. Soren. What would you say to Chelsea if you saw her fall under peer pressure of some of her friends and start smoking or if you found ashes in her bedroom in an ashtray or something?

The President. I would talk to her about it and tell her I thought it was a bad idea. She's the most militant person in our house, though.

Ms. Soren. Yes, it doesn't sound like you're worried.

The President. She and Hillary are always on me. You know, as I confessed yesterday, I still, once in a great while, maybe five, six, seven times a year, will smoke a cigar when I'm outside. They think that's awful—at all. And I've got to do better with it. But if they see me chewing one on the golf course or something, they're on me. So my family is doing a better job with it than I am.

Ms. Soren. Some kids I talk to said that nothing but an outright ban on cigarettes would deter them. So why not a ban? Because cigarettes are just as deadly, if not more so, for adults.

The President. They are, but they're not illegal. You have to go through all the same problems we went through with prohibition with liquor. It would have significant economic dislocations for a large number of Americans. And I think as a practical matter, because so many adults are, in effect, hooked on it, it would be very, very difficult to enforce.

What I want to do is to phase it out over time by getting—if young people stop using cigarettes—if we could get young people, the usage down to zero, then eventually it will phase out. That would be my goal. I think we just have to start with our young people.

Ms. Soren. Do you consider tobacco companies evil?

The President. I wouldn't go that far. I don't think that. And I certainly don't consider the tobacco farmers evil. I think they're good people. Most of them—a lot of them come from families that have been doing it 100, sometimes 200 years.

I think some of these companies have known for a long time, according to their own documents, that nicotine was both addictive and destructive. And they have—insofar as they have pretended that they did not know that, that is wrong.

I think some of these companies have said, we don't want teenagers to smoke, but they have consciously directed their advertising strategies to make it appealing to young people and not just Joe Camel, which was obvious, but a lot of other things as well. I think those things are wrong.

And what I want the tobacco companies to do is stop doing the wrong thing and start doing the right thing. I think they ought to come in here and support this—these restrictions. I think they ought to ask Congress to enact them into law now. If they don't want the FDA to regulate them, let's enact the law now. And I think that we ought to start the very next day on this campaign together. If the tobacco companies really don't want kids to smoke, we can do this together.

Ms. Soren. Are you going to try to bring back the cigarette tax? California has had a lot of success with that in their State.

The President. Well, this Congress would not adopt that. I have had a number of people who've come from tobacco countries suggest that some of the cigarette tax ought to be devoted to helping the farmers who want to convert their farmland to other purposes, to some sort of buy-out program.

But I think that right now what we ought to do is—the bulk of the cigarette tax is available to the States, and a lot of the States now are passing cigarette taxes to help to pay for the health care bills of people who are suffering from tobacco-related illnesses. And I don't want to see the Congress and the Federal Government crowd that out. So when I proposed a tobacco tax before, it was to pay for health care. That's not going to happen this year.

Ms. Soren. Right now, advertising is written off as a business expense, and that means the public pays in some fashion for all advertising, including cigarette advertising. Would you consider getting rid of the tax deduction for cigarette advertising?

The President. You're the first person who's ever suggested it to me. I'd never though of that. That's an interesting idea.

Ms. Soren. So I'll give you a few minutes to absorb it, and I'll come back.

The President. That's an interesting idea. I've never thought of that.

Ms. Soren. Because I think a lot of people would be offended by the idea of paying for an unhealthy product to advertise and garner more smokers through it. But I'll let you dwell on it.

Not only do you want to regulate tobacco products, but you're also in favor of regulating how they're marketed. And I was wondering, how far do you plan to go? When a musician sits down to talk with me and they're smoking a cigarette, should I not air that footage on MTV? Should I ask Keith Richards to put out his cigarette before he does an interview with me? Should this go for all television? Because of lot of young people watch MTV.

The President. I think that's a decision for you to make. I think you should ask him to put it out because I think there are a lot of young people——

Ms. Soren. It is Keith Richards.

The President. I know. [*Laughter*] And I know he's an icon—for me, too.

Ms. Soren. I don't know if he—his heart might stop if he doesn't have a cigarette.

The President. That's the great thing about their endurance, you know.

But that's a decision that each network, each interviewer, they'll have to make. Let me just say this: I believe very strongly in the first amendment and the right to free speech, free association, and freedom of religion. I believe in a very broad interpretation of it. But I believe that we should be restricting advertising directed at children because it's illegal to sell cigarettes to children. So, therefore, if it's illegal to sell cigarettes to children, it can't be illegal to stop the advertising directed at children. So that's what my focus is.

In terms of the interviews and everything, I would hope every American adult, even those who smoke, would think, as I had to when I became President and I had this occasional bad habit of having my cigar once in a while, I would hope they would think about not doing it in public, not doing it around children, not setting a bad example. I think we adults have a responsibility to try to set a good standard for our young people and to basically say everybody's got a lot of problems, but being self-destructive is not a way to deal with them.

Ms. Soren. Mr. President, I want to say this as politely as I can, but I think a lot of our viewers are going to be wondering why should they listen to you about this issue?

The President. Well, they don't have to listen to me about this issue. What we're going to do is change the law. But I'll tell you why they should listen to me or to anybody else. I would say that if they wanted to listen to me, don't listen to me, look at the medical research, look at the evidence. This is about their lives, not mine. I've lived most of my life. Their lives are ahead of them. And the reason they should listen to me is that the evidence is on my side, not just because I'm President. We know that nicotine in cigarettes and smokeless tobacco is addictive, is destructive, and will shorten the lives of one out of three people who start smoking on a regular basis. We know that.

So what they should do is say, "Okay, here's the evidence; now, what kind of life do I want to live?" Ultimately, it's going to be their decision, because even if the law keeps cigarettes away from them in the near-term, soon they'll turn 18, and they'll be able to do whatever they want to do. They have to make these decisions. But I think—my job, what I'm trying to do here every day and with the economy, with saving the college loan program, with trying to preserve the environment from this awful assault that the Congress is making on it, is to give the young people of our country a good country to grow up into and a good life to look forward to. Then they have to make a decision about how to live that life.

And what those of us who are older are supposed to do is to say here's what we think will maximize your choices. Here's what we think will give you the chance to live up to the fullest of your abilities. And that's what I hope they'll listen to, because the evidence is on my side. I'm not just preaching here, I have all this evidence.

Ms. Soren. Right. Right. It's not like you don't have enough things to do already.

The President. But this is a big deal. Look, look. Everything I try to do here, if you look at—let's just take trying to save the college loan program from attack and trying to preserve the environmental protections we have in this country. Why would I do that? Because I want my

child and our grandchildren and all the young people coming up to enjoy a good life. That still requires all these individuals who are watching us to make decisions about how they're going to live. And being addicted to tobacco is not a smart thing to do if you want to have a long, full, good life. It's a huge roll of the dice.

I never will forget a few years ago having to speak at the funeral of a very close friend of mine, a man that had literally no other vices. He was one of the most perfect human beings I ever knew. But he smoked a couple of packs of cigarettes a day, and he died of lung cancer 2½ years after he had his last cigarette because it takes that long to clean out your lungs.

Ms. Soren. Wow.

The President. And he was younger than me. I never got over it. I never will get over it.

Abortion

Ms. Soren. While I have you, there are a couple of other issues I wanted to ask you about that are important to young voters, in addition to smoking and their health, which you sort of rattled off very quickly.

First, though, the woman best known as Jane Roe, whose struggle to obtain an abortion led to the Supreme Court's *Roe* v. *Wade* decision, has come out against anything but first trimester abortions. How big a blow do you feel this is to the pro-choice movement?

The President. Well, as I understand it, she's gone through a number of changes in her life and had a serious religious conversion and believes that abortion is wrong now. The rule of *Roe* v. *Wade* is it permits everybody in America to make that same decision. That is, I think there are too many abortions in America. I have always believed that abortion should be rare but that they should be safe and legal until the third trimester when the child can live outside the mother's womb. If somebody hasn't made the decision by then, unless the life of the mother's in danger, I think they should be illegal, and they were in my State.

But I think that leaving the decision to the woman and her doctor and whoever else she wishes to consult, I think on balance is still the right decision in our country. And that makes it possible for people like this woman to make up her own mind and to have her own convictions and then try to persuade other people that she's right. It leaves her free to say, "My religious conviction is what is right for all of you; I hope you will follow me." People can do that.

And we have a very vibrant, as you know, pro-life movement in this country of people trying to convince other people of that all the time. But we don't say to people who disagree that we're going to criminalize your conduct until the child can live outside the mother's womb. And I think, on balance, that is the right position for our country, and I would stick with it.

Ms. Soren. Since abortion is under such attack in Congress, do you think that you should be doing more to support the pro-choice movement?

The President. Well, I don't know what else I can do. I'm doing—I think I'm doing everything I can. I certainly have made it absolutely clear where I stand. I have resisted the attempts in the Congress to take away the rights of choice to women in the service, to women who work for the Federal Government.

There is a wholesale assault on the right to choose going on in the Congress now in all kinds of little, indirect ways. And I hope we can beat it back because I think it's—I don't think that's the right thing to do. I don't think the law here is the way to resolve all these problems.

Opposition in Congress

Ms. Soren. You've used executive actions in the first 2 years of your Presidency for issues like abortion. And in recent months, with the Republican majority, you've turned to them more frequently, the regulation of teenage smoking being the most recent one. Do you feel like you're subverting the will of Congress by tackling issues this way?

The President. No. I think that I probably should have been doing more of this all along. But in the first 2 years, I had to pour all of my energies into trying to do something to bring the deficit down, to invest more in education, to try to expand trade, and get the economy going again. And we were able to do that, but the voters still gave the Congress to the Republicans. And now it frees me up, in a way, to— most of my efforts, to try to keep them from undoing the gains we have made from wrecking an economic strategy or wrecking the education program or wrecking the environment.

But I can now do things like use my executive authority, for example, to promote welfare reform in all 50 States, to do the other things that we talked about. So I think I probably should have been doing more of it all along.

President's Legal Defense Fund

Ms. Soren. Today lawyers for the legal defense fund are announcing how much money they've raised. Does that make you feel awkward to have them up there saying, "We've collected this money for the President to defend him?"

The President. No. I mean, it's a little—I wish it weren't necessary. But I'm not a wealthy person and my adversaries decided that they would try to embroil me in all kinds of legal things, and I can't afford to take any time off to think about it. So they're dealing with it the best they can in a legal and appropriate way. And I did not want to go to a few wealthy people and ask them to spend a ton of money to pay all my legal bills. So we resolved that the most appropriate thing to do would be to raise funds in a legal defense fund that had the same financial restrictions that running for Federal office does. And so that's what we've tried to do.

Bosnia

Ms. Soren. Senator Dole and Senator Helms have proposed asking for $100 million in arms aid for Bosnia. Do you support this legislation?

The President. Not now because the arms embargo is on. My position is that the United States should not, by ourselves, violate the U.N. rule against selling arms into Bosnia because it applies to all Yugoslavia, that instead, what we ought to do is have that U.N. mission there work to stop aggression against Bosnia by letting NATO use its air power and by strengthening the U.N. mission on the ground.

What happened in Srebrenica was awful. But it happened in large measure because the United Nations would not permit the United States and the other NATO allies to take strong action from the air against the Serbs. Now that there's been a real change on the ground and the Serbs have been rolled back in the western part of Bosnia and in Croatia by the Croats, I hope we have a chance to make a decent peace there.

I would not be against—if the U.N. mission fails, I would be for selling arms to the Bosnians or making it possible for the Bosnians to buy arms, but only when we get everybody to lift the arms embargo at the U.N.

But let me just say this in closing. We have an embargo against Saddam Hussein in Iraq, and you see what happened. We put a lot of pressure on it; we now have some defectors coming over, weakening his power. If we say, "We're going to ignore you, and we're going to sell arms to the Bosnians," then what's to prevent other countries from saying, "Okay, we'll ignore the U.N. embargo in Iraq, and we'll bolster Saddam Hussein?"

Rap Music

Ms. Soren. I just have two more quick questions. Do you think it's a good thing that Time-Warner wants to sell Interscope Records? Do you know anything about that?

The President. No.

Death of Jerry Garcia

Ms. Soren. I wanted to ask you if you were—well, Jerry Garcia has affected millions of Americans.

The President. Me, too.

Q. Were you a fan? Have you ever been to a Grateful Dead show? And why do you think he affected so many people of different backgrounds and generations?

The President. Well, first of all, he was just a great talent. I mean, he was really—he was a genius. And I was really pleased to see the Grateful Dead have one more great run around the country, you know, in the last couple of years and see all these young teenagers gravitating to a group that all of us liked 20 or more years ago. He had a great gift. And he even wound up putting out that line of ties. He had great ties. I would go around wearing Jerry Garcia ties and giving them away to people. So I was very sad when he died.

But he also had a terrible problem that was a legacy of the life he lived and the demons he dealt with. And I would hope that all of us who loved his music and valued his contributions would also reflect on the consequences of, again, really self-destructive behavior. I mean, the lesson of Jerry Garcia's life is that he made a great contribution and he really was a—he had at least two generations of Deadheads, you know.

Ms. Soren. Is Chelsea a fan at all? Has she ever gone to a show?

The President. Yes, very much. But she and I were talking—we had a long talk about it the other day, right before I left to come to the office. She called me on the phone. She's out of town, and she called me on the phone, and we were talking about it. And she was talking about all the kids in her school who are great fans of Jerry Garcia, and we had a long talk about it.

But I would hope that as we mourn him and sort of feel grateful for what he did, we also—young people should say, "I'm not going to die that way. I'm not going to die in a clinic with a drug addiction. I'm not going to do it." You don't have to have a destructive lifestyle to be a genius and make a contribution. You don't have to do that.

Cigarette Advertising

Ms. Soren. Any thoughts on the advertising, cigarette advertising being a tax deduction?

The President. I'll look into it. It's an interesting idea. Nobody ever even raised it to me before. Maybe you should be here making public policy. That's great.

Ms. Soren. I don't think so. I think I'm quite busy. I wouldn't want your job.

The President. Thanks.

NOTE: The interview began at 11 a.m. in the Oval Office at the White House. In his remarks, the President referred to rock musicians Keith Richards of the Rolling Stones and the late Jerry Garcia of the Grateful Dead; Norma McCorvey, plaintiff in the *Roe* v. *Wade* case; and President Saddam Hussein of Iraq.

Remarks Announcing Comprehensive Nuclear Weapons Test Ban Negotiations
August 11, 1995

Good afternoon. Today I am announcing my decision to negotiate a true zero yield comprehensive test ban. This is an historic milestone in our efforts to reduce the nuclear threat to build a safer world. The United States will now insist on a test ban that prohibits any nuclear weapons test explosion or any other nuclear explosion. I am convinced this decision will speed the negotiations so that we can achieve our goal of signing a comprehensive test ban next year.

As a central part of this decision, I am establishing concrete, specific safeguards that define the conditions under which the United States will enter into a comprehensive test ban. These safeguards will strengthen our commitments in the areas of intelligence monitoring and verification, stockpile stewardship, maintenance of our nuclear laboratories, and test readiness.

They also specify the circumstances under which I would be prepared, in consultation with Congress, to exercise our supreme national interest rights under a comprehensive test ban to conduct necessary testing if the safety or reliability of our nuclear deterrent could no longer be certified.

As a part of this arrangement, I am today directing the establishment of a new annual reporting and certification requirement that will ensure that our nuclear weapons remain safe and reliable under a comprehensive test ban.

I appreciate the time, the energy, and the wisdom that the Secretaries of State, Defense, and Energy; the Chairman of the Joint Chiefs of Staff; the Directors of Central Intelligence and the Arms Control and Disarmament Agency have all devoted to the review of this crucial

national security issue over the last several months.

American leaders since Presidents Eisenhower and Kennedy have believed a comprehensive test ban would be a major stride toward stopping the proliferation of nuclear weapons. Now, as then, such a treaty would greatly strengthen the security of the United States and nations throughout the world. But now, unlike then, such a treaty is within our reach.

It would build upon the successes we have achieved so far: Securing a permanent extension of the Nuclear Non-proliferation Treaty; freezing North Korea's nuclear program; cutting existing nuclear arsenals by putting the START I Treaty into force; persuading Ukraine, Belarus, and Kazakhstan to give up their nuclear weapons and to reach agreements with Russia that now mean that both our nations no longer target our missiles at each other.

A comprehensive test ban is the right step as we continue pulling back from the nuclear precipice, a precipice which we began to live with 50 years ago this week. It moves us one step closer to the day when no nuclear weapons are detonated anywhere on the face of the Earth.

Thank you very much.

NOTE: The President spoke at 1:05 p.m., in the Briefing Room at the White House.

Statement on Comprehensive Nuclear Weapons Test Ban Negotiations
August 11, 1995

One of my administration's highest priorities is to negotiate a comprehensive test ban treaty (CTBT) to reduce the danger posed by nuclear weapons proliferation. To advance that goal and secure the strongest possible treaty, I am announcing today my decision to seek a zero yield CTBT. A zero yield CTBT would ban any nuclear weapon test explosion or any other nuclear explosion immediately upon entry into force. I hope it will lead to an early consensus among all states at the negotiating table.

Achieving a CTBT was a goal of both Presidents Eisenhower and Kennedy. Now, as then, such a treaty would greatly strengthen U.S. and

global security and create another barrier to nuclear proliferation and nuclear weapons development. At the conclusion of the Nuclear Non-Proliferation Treaty Review Conference in May, all parties to that treaty agreed to work to complete a CTBT no later than 1996. Today, I want to reaffirm our commitment to do everything possible to conclude the CTBT negotiations as soon as possible so that a treaty can be signed next year.

As part of our national security strategy, the United States must and will retain strategic nuclear forces sufficient to deter any future hostile foreign leadership with access to strategic nuclear forces from acting against our vital interests and to convince it that seeking a nuclear advantage would be futile. In this regard, I consider the maintenance of a safe and reliable nuclear stockpile to be a supreme national interest of the United States.

I am assured by the Secretary of Energy and the Directors of our nuclear weapons labs that we can meet the challenge of maintaining our nuclear deterrent under a CTBT through a Science Based Stockpile Stewardship program without nuclear testing. I directed the implementation of such a program almost 2 years ago, and it is being developed with the support of the Secretary of Defense and the Chairman of the Joint Chiefs of Staff. This program will now be tied to a new certification procedure. In order for this program to succeed, both the administration and the Congress must provide sustained bipartisan support for the stockpile stewardship program over the next decade and beyond. I am committed to working with the Congress to ensure this support.

While I am optimistic that the stockpile stewardship program will be successful, as President I cannot dismiss the possibility, however unlikely, that the program will fall short of its objectives. Therefore, in addition to the new annual certification procedure for our nuclear weapons stockpile, I am also establishing concrete, specific safeguards that define the conditions under which the United States can enter into a CTBT.

In the event that I were informed by the Secretary of Defense and Secretary of Energy—advised by the Nuclear Weapons Council, the Directors of DOE's nuclear weapons laboratories, and the Commander of U.S. Strategic Command—that a high level of confidence in the safety or reliability of a nuclear weapons type which the two Secretaries consider to be critical to our nuclear deterrent could no longer be certified, I would be prepared, in consultation with Congress, to exercise our "supreme national interests" rights under the CTBT in order to conduct whatever testing might be required. Exercising this right, however, is a decision I believe I or any future President will not have to make. The nuclear weapons in the United States arsenal are safe and reliable, and I am determined our stockpile stewardship program will ensure they remain so in the absence of nuclear testing.

I recognize that our present monitoring systems will not detect with high confidence very low yield tests. Therefore, I am committed to pursuing a comprehensive research and development program to improve our treaty monitoring capabilities and operations.

Thirty-two years ago, President Kennedy called the completion of the Limited Test Ban Treaty in Moscow a "shaft of light cut into the darkness" of the cold war. With it, he said, the Nation could "step back from the shadows of war and seek out the way of peace." We did, and the world is a safer place because of it. I believe that we are ready to take the next step and lead the world to a comprehensive test ban. This would be a fitting tribute to all those, Republicans and Democrats, who have worked for a CTBT over the past four decades.

NOTE: A fact sheet on arms control and nonproliferation and a fact sheet on comprehensive test ban treaty safeguards were attached to the statement.

Statement on Vetoing Legislation To Lift the Arms Embargo Against Bosnia
August 11, 1995

I am announcing today my decision to veto legislation that would unilaterally lift the arms embargo against Bosnia and Herzegovina.

I know that Members of Congress share my goals of reducing the violence in Bosnia and working to end the war. But their vote to unilaterally lift the arms embargo is the wrong step at the wrong time. The American people should understand the consequences of such action for our Nation and for the people of Bosnia.

- First, our allies have made clear that they will withdraw their troops from Bosnia if the United States unilaterally lifts the arms embargo. The United States, as the leader of the NATO Alliance, would be obliged to send thousands of American ground troops to assist in that difficult operation.

- Second, lifting the embargo now could cause the fighting in Bosnia to escalate. The Serbs will not delay their assaults while the Bosnian Government receives new arms and training. Getting humanitarian aid to civilians will only get harder.
- Third, unilaterally lifting the embargo will lead to unilateral American responsibility. If the Bosnian Government suffered reverses on the battlefield, we, and not the Europeans, would be expected to fill the void with military and humanitarian aid.
- Fourth, intensified fighting in Bosnia would risk provoking a wider war in the heart of Europe.
- Fifth, for this bill to become law now would undercut the new diplomatic effort we are currently engaged in, and withdrawal of the United Nations mission would virtually eliminate chances for a peaceful, negotiated settlement in the foreseeable future.
- Finally, unilateral lift would create serious divisions between the United States and its key allies, with potential long-lasting damage to the NATO Alliance.

This is an important moment in Bosnia. Events in the past few weeks have opened new possibilities for negotiations. We will test these new realities, and we are now engaged with our allies and others in using these opportunities to settle this terrible war by agreement. This is not the time for the United States to pull the plug on the U.N. mission.

There is no question that we must take strong action in Bosnia. In recent weeks, the war has intensified. The Serbs have brutally assaulted three of the United Nations safe areas. Witnesses report widespread atrocities: summary executions, systematic rape, and renewed ethnic cleansing in Bosnia. Tens of thousands of inno-

cent women and children have fled their homes. And now the Croatian army offensive has created new dangers and dramatically increased the need for humanitarian aid to deal with displaced citizens in the region. But these events also create opportunities.

Along with our allies we have taken a series of strong steps to strengthen the United Nations mission, to prevent further attacks on safe areas, and to protect innocent civilians:

- NATO has decided it will counter an assault on the remaining safe areas with sustained and decisive use of air power. Our response will be broad, swift, and severe, going far beyond the narrow attacks of the past.
- For the first time, military commanders on the ground in Bosnia have been given operational control over such actions, paving the way for fast and effective NATO response.
- And well-armed British and French troops are working to ensure access to Sarajevo for convoys carrying food, medicine, and other vital supplies.

Despite these actions, many in Congress are ready to close the books on the U.N. mission. But I am not—not as long as that mission is willing and able to be a force for peace once again.

I recognize that there is no risk-free way ahead in Bosnia. But unilaterally lifting the arms embargo will have the opposite effects of what its supporters intend. It would intensify the fighting, jeopardize diplomacy, and make the outcome of the war in Bosnia an American responsibility.

Instead, we must work with our allies to protect innocent civilians, to strengthen the United Nations mission, to bring NATO's military power to bear if our warnings are defied, and to aggressively pursue the only path that will end the conflict, one that leads to a negotiated peace.

Message to the Senate Returning Without Approval the Bosnia and Herzegovina Self-Defense Act of 1995
August 11, 1995

To the Senate of the United States:

I am returning herewith without my approval S. 21, the "Bosnia and Herzegovina Self-Defense Act of 1995." I share the Congress' frustration with the situation in Bosnia and am also appalled by the human suffering that is occurring there. I am keenly aware that Members of Congress are deeply torn about what should be done to try to bring this terrible conflict to an end. My Administration will continue to do its utmost with our allies to guide developments toward a comprehensive political settlement acceptable to all the parties. S. 21, however, would hinder rather than support those efforts. It would, quite simply, undermine the chances for peace in Bosnia, lead to a wider war, and undercut the authority of the United Nations (U.N.) Security Council to impose effective measures to deal with threats to the peace. It would also attempt to regulate by statute matters for which the President is responsible under the Constitution.

S. 21 is designed to lead to the unilateral lifting by the United States of the international arms embargo imposed on the Government of Bosnia and Herzegovina. Although the United States has supported the lifting of the embargo by action of the U.N. Security Council, I nonetheless am firmly convinced that a unilateral lifting of the embargo would be a serious mistake. It would undermine renewed efforts to achieve a negotiated settlement in Bosnia and could lead to an escalation of the conflict there, including the almost certain Americanization of the conflict.

The allies of the United States in the U.N. Protection Force for Bosnia (UNPROFOR) have made it clear that a unilateral lifting of the arms embargo by the United States would result in their rapid withdrawal from UNPROFOR, leading to its collapse. The United States, as the leader of NATO, would have an obligation under these circumstances to assist in that withdrawal, thereby putting thousands of U.S. troops at risk. At the least, such unilateral action by the United States would drive our allies out of Bosnia and involve the United States more deeply, while making the conflict much more dangerous.

The consequences of UNPROFOR's departure because of a unilateral lifting of the arms embargo must be faced squarely. *First,* the United States would immediately be part of a costly NATO operation to withdraw UNPROFOR. *Second,* after that operation is complete, the fighting in Bosnia would intensify. It is unlikely the Bosnian Serbs would stand by waiting while the Bosnian government received new arms and training. *Third,* under assault, the Bosnian government would look to the United States to provide arms and air support, and, if that failed, more active military support. Unilateral lift of the embargo would lead to unilateral American responsibility. *Fourth,* intensified fighting would risk a wider conflict in the Balkans with far-reaching implications for regional peace. UNPROFOR's withdrawal would set back fresh prospects for a peaceful, negotiated solution for the foreseeable future. *Finally,* unilateral U.S. action under these circumstances would create serious divisions between the United States and its key allies, with potential long-lasting damage to these important relationships and to NATO.

S. 21 would undermine the progress we have made with our allies and the United Nations in recent weeks to strengthen the protection of the safe areas in Bosnia and improve the provision of humanitarian assistance. NATO has agreed to the substantial and decisive use of air power to protect Gorazde, Sarajevo, and the other safe areas. The U.N. Secretary General has delegated his authority to the military commanders on the ground to approve the use of air power. The British and French, with our support, are deploying a Rapid Reaction Force to help open land routes to Sarajevo for convoys carrying vital supplies, strengthening UNPROFOR's ability to carry out its mission. These measures will help provide a prompt and effective response to Serb attacks on the safe areas. This new protection would disappear if UNPROFOR withdraws in response to the unilateral lifting of the embargo.

Events over the past several weeks have also created some new opportunities to seek a negotiated peace. We are actively engaged in discussions with our allies and others on these prospects. Unilaterally lifting the arms embargo now would jeopardize these ongoing efforts.

Unilaterally disregarding the U.N. Security Council's decision to impose an arms embargo throughout the former Yugoslavia also would have a detrimental effect on the ability of the Security Council to act effectively in crisis situations, such as the trade and weapons embargoes against Iraq or Serbia. If we decide for ourselves to violate the arms embargo, other states would cite our action as a pretext to ignore other Security Council decisions when it suits their interests.

S. 21 also would direct that the executive branch take specific actions in the Security Council and, if unsuccessful there, in the General Assembly. There is no justification for bringing the issue before the General Assembly, which has no authority to reconsider and reverse decisions of the Security Council, and it could be highly damaging to vital U.S. interests to imply otherwise. If the General Assembly could exercise such binding authority without the protection of the veto right held in the Security Council, any number of issues could be resolved against the interests of the United States and our allies.

Finally, the requirements of S. 21 would impermissibly intrude on the core constitutional responsibilities of the President for the conduct of foreign affairs, and would compromise the ability of the President to protect vital U.S. national security interests abroad. It purports, unconstitutionally, to instruct the President on the content and timing of U.S. diplomatic positions before international bodies, in derogation of the President's exclusive constitutional authority to control such foreign policy matters. It also attempts to require the President to approve the export of arms to a foreign country where a conflict is in progress, even though this may well draw the United States more deeply into that conflict. These encroachments on the President's constitutional power over, and responsibility for, the conduct of foreign affairs, are unacceptable.

Accordingly, I am disapproving S. 21 and returning it to the Senate.

WILLIAM J. CLINTON

The White House,
August 11, 1995.

The President's Radio Address
August 12, 1995

Good morning. This week I directed the Food and Drug Administration to propose stiff restrictions on the advertising, marketing, and sales of cigarettes to children, after a 14-month FDA study, an exhaustive study which found tobacco addictive, harmful, and readily available to young Americans. I did so because sometimes we must act sternly and boldly to fulfill our most fundamental moral obligation: Our duty as adults to ensure that our children grow up healthy and strong.

The grim fact is that every single day in America 3,000 new teenagers light up for the first time. Most are destined to become addicted, and a thousand of them will die before their time from diseases caused by tobacco.

Teenagers don't just happen to smoke. They're the victims of billions of dollars of marketing and promotional campaigns designed by top psychologists and advertising experts. These campaigns have one inevitable consequence: To start children on a lifetime habit of addiction to tobacco. And if you don't start smoking as a teen, chances are very good you'll never start at all. Somebody has to stop this. That's why I decided to act.

The way the cigarette companies reach children is especially effective. They sponsor auto races or tennis matches. The subtle message is that smoking can't be that bad for you if it's so intimately involved with sports. Well, our plan stops companies from sponsoring events in cigarette brand names.

Stores sell cigarettes in kiddie packs of a handful of cigarettes, or even sometimes just one cigarette, so teenagers with very little money can buy smokes out of their pocket change. My plan bans that, too. Billboards and ads in teen magazines show rugged men and glamorous women lighting up and blissful couples sharing their cigarettes. The message is: Smoking is sexy; it'll make you more attractive; it'll make you happier. My plan will ban those manipulative visual images, too.

Let's be clear: Cigarettes are a legal product, but cigarettes sales to minors are illegal in all 50 States. But lots of children smoke in all 50 States, getting these small packs or getting the cigarettes out of vending machines or sometimes just buying them across the counter. And the advertising has a lot to do with it. So let's end the hypocrisy of pretending that while sales to teens are illegal, marketing to teens is legal. Let's stop pretending that a cartoon camel in a funny costume is trying to sell to adults, not children.

Cigarette companies say they want to reduce teen smoking, but their lawyers rush to the courthouse to seek an order blocking our actions. Well, that's their right. But it is my duty to safeguard the health and the safety of our children. And I won't back down.

Now I'd like to turn the microphone over to a brave man, Victor Crawford. For years Mr. Crawford was a lobbyist for the top tobacco companies. He smoked, and tragically, he's now fighting his own battle against cancer. I think his comments on the tactics of tobacco advertising may be especially helpful.

Mr. Crawford.

Victor Crawford. Thank you, President Clinton, for giving me this chance to talk to the young people of America. And from the bottom of my heart, I thank you for the wonderful things you're doing to protect them from smoking. This was an issue you could have easily avoided, but instead you did the right thing and took the leadership position.

Kids, cigarettes are bad for you, and they're killers. I know. I used to work for the industry that makes them. I was part of a well-organized machine that depends on young people like you

believing that cigarettes are okay. Some of the smartest people in America work at just one thing, figuring out how to get you to smoke. As tobacco kills off people like me, they need kids like you to replace me.

As the President has described already, anything goes, any marketing gimmick, any trick to make you want to smoke. They talk about peer pressure; how do you think that peer pressure starts? We did it through our advertising.

For several years I protected the cigarette industry from anybody who wanted to restrict smoking. I fooled a lot of people, and kids, I fooled myself, too. I smoked heavily, and I started when I was 13 years old. And now in my throat and in my lungs where the smoke used to be, there's a cancer that I know is killing me. It's too late for me, but it's not too late for you. Use your brain. Don't let anybody fool you. Don't smoke.

And Mr. President, on behalf of millions of other people like me, I thank you very much for the steps you are taking to stop cigarette companies from fooling the people into smoking and being a true leader that this country needs. Thank you.

The President. Mr. Crawford, thank you. Your courage in speaking out has inspired me, and it will help all of us to save the lives of countless young people in the future. Better than almost anyone in America, you know the powerful forces that are trying to preserve the status quo. But no one, no one, should risk our children's future for their own personal gain. And your personal struggle, Mr. Crawford, and that of millions of other Americans who suffer from smoking's consequences, show why we must act and act now for our children, our families, and our American family.

Thanks for listening.

NOTE: The President spoke at 10:06 a.m. from the Oval Office at the White House.

Statement on the Death of Mickey Mantle
August 13, 1995

When I was growing up in the 1950's, millions of young people like me loved watching Mickey

Mantle lead the Yankees. As a ballplayer, Mickey inspired generations of fans with his power and grit. As a man, he faced up to his responsibilities and alerted generations to come to the dangers of alcohol abuse. He will be remembered for excellence on the baseball field and the honor and redemption he brought to the end of his life.

Message on the Observance of Indian Independence Day, 1995
August 15, 1995

Greetings to all those celebrating Indian Independence Day.

Our two nations share a commitment to democracy and a reverence for freedom that has nurtured our warm friendship. India's ongoing economic transformation offers the people of India great hope for fulfilling their aspirations, and we stand beside them. The United States looks forward to realizing a full range of new personal, political, and economic ties with India in the future.

Please accept my best wishes for a joyous celebration and for peace, prosperity, and the continued blessings of liberty in the future.

BILL CLINTON

Letter to Congressional Leaders on Continuation of Export Control Regulations
August 15, 1995

Dear Mr. Speaker: (Dear Mr. President:)
On August 19, 1994, in light of the expiration of the Export Administration Act of 1979, as amended (50 U.S.C. App. 2401 *et seq.*) I issued Executive Order No. 12924, declaring a national emergency and continuing the system of export regulation under the International Emergency Economic Powers Act (50 U.S.C. 1701 *et seq.*). Under section 202(d) of the National Emergencies Act (50 U.S.C. 1622(d)), the national emergency terminates on the anniversary date of its declaration unless the President publishes in the *Federal Register* and transmit to the Congress a notice of its continuation.

I am hereby advising the Congress that I have extended the national emergency declared in Executive Order No. 12924. Attached is a copy of the notice of extension.

Sincerely,

WILLIAM J. CLINTON

NOTE: Identical letters were sent to Newt Gingrich, Speaker of the House of Representatives, and Albert Gore, Jr., President of the Senate. This letter was released by the Office of the Press Secretary on August 16. The notice is listed in Appendix D at the end of this volume.

Statement on Senator Bill Bradley's Decision Not To Seek Reelection
August 16, 1995

Senator Bill Bradley's decision not to seek a fourth term in the U.S. Senate is a loss to the people of New Jersey and all Americans.

I will miss his leadership in our efforts to deal with the critical issues of race, crime, and violence and America's opportunity and responsibility in the post-cold-war era. I am also grateful for his leadership and support in moving the Democratic Party in a new direction to bring economic opportunity to all Americans by reducing the deficit, investing in our people for the future, and creating more trade opportunities for American products around the world, while we continue our traditional mission to protect the environment and the health, safety, and welfare of our elderly and our children.

In every aspect of his career—as an Olympian, as a professional basketball player, as a Senator—Bill Bradley has performed admirably. New Jersey and America are better for his service. Hillary and I wish the best for him and for Ernestine and their daughter, Theresa Anne.

Statement on Welfare Reform
August 17, 1995

In the past 2½ years, as part of my continuing effort to make Government better reflect the values of the American people, my administration has granted more State welfare reform experiments than in the past 12 years combined. Today, 33 States are experimenting in requiring welfare recipients to work for their benefits, requiring teen moms to live at home and stay in school, requiring delinquent parents to pay child support, and requiring recipients to be held to a time limit.

I am offering States a new, simpler way to achieve welfare reform. My fast-track dem- onstration initiative will let States build on strategies we already know are moving people from welfare to work. We must replace our broken welfare system with one that reflects the fundamental American values of work, responsibility, and family. When Congress returns, they should immediately put welfare reform at the top of their agenda and send me a tough, bipartisan bill that builds upon our progress. In the meantime, I will continue to do everything in my power to move welfare reform forward in the States and in Washington.

Letter to Congressional Leaders Transmitting a Report on the Partnership For Peace
August 17, 1995

Dear Mr. Chairman: (*Dear Claiborne:*) (*Dear Lee:*)

In accordance with Section 514(a) of Public Law 103–236 (22 U.S.C. 1928(a)), I am submitting to you this report on implementation of the Partnership for Peace (PFP) initiative.

The ongoing adaptation of Europe's security structures to post-Cold War realities remains one of our highest foreign policy priorities. A central element of this adaptation is the extension of NATO's zone of stability and security to include Europe's emerging democracies. Over the past year and a half the Partnership for Peace has made a significant contribution to this goal by forging new cooperative ties between the Alliance and its partners. This U.S. initiative has united NATO Allies with former adversaries and traditionally neutral states in a partnership based on respect for democratic principles, peaceful resolution of disputes, and practical cooperation. Consistent with our broad, inclusive approach to European security, the Partnership embraces 26 partner states, including Russia.

For all Partners, PFP will be an enduring instrument for forging stronger ties with NATO. For those Partners interested in joining NATO, PFP will be the path to membership.

Already, through joint training exercises and other PFP activities, PFP is helping interested Partners improve the ability of their forces to work alongside NATO's for possible future joint missions. As you will see from the attached report, NATO and its partners have made impressive progress in broadening and deepening the Partnership over the past year. We are working with our Allies and Partners to build on the Partnership's early momentum, in the shared conviction that cooperation and common action are among the best means to achieving lasting peace and security throughout the Euro-Atlantic area.

Sincerely,

WILLIAM J. CLINTON

NOTE: Identical letters were sent to Jesse Helms, chairman, and Claiborne Pell, ranking member, Senate Committee on Foreign Relations; and Benjamin A. Gilman, chairman, and Lee H. Hamilton, ranking member, House Committee on International Relations.

The President's Radio Address
August 19, 1995

Good morning. As I speak to you this morning, I can look out on Grand Teton National Park in the Rocky Mountains where my family and I are enjoying our summer vacation. We're looking forward to exploring both Grand Teton and Yellowstone National Parks over the next several days. The beauty of these mountains is absolutely breathtaking, and their tranquillity is good for the soul.

We could all use a lot more peace and quiet in our lives and in our society these days. So today I want to talk about our progress in reducing the violent crime that has shattered the lives of too many Americans for too long.

Just a year ago this week, we ended 6 years of partisan stalemate in Washington by pushing a tough, sweeping crime bill through the Congress. Narrow interest groups on the left and the right didn't want the bill to pass, and you can be sure the criminals didn't, either. But every major law enforcement organization in America fought hard for the crime bill, and so did I, because it puts Government firmly on the side of the people who abide by the law, not the criminals who break it.

Already the crime bill is making a difference. So far, we have awarded community policing grants to put 24,000 new police officers on the street. And we paid for it with the money saved by reducing the size of the Federal bureaucracy to its lowest level since John Kennedy was President. Already there are 150,000 fewer people working for the U.S. Government than there were the day I became President.

The assault weapons ban and the Brady bill have stopped thousands of criminals from getting their hands on deadly weapons. We're giving States more help in building prisons to keep serious offenders behind bars longer. And we're giving communities funds for prevention, to give our young people something to say yes to as well as something to say no to.

Although it's far too early to declare victory, aggressive efforts like these and aggressive efforts by local police departments to expand community policing and crack down on drugs and gangs have helped to reduce the murder rate this year in Chicago, New York, New Orleans, and several other major cities. In fact, the crime rate is down overall in almost every area in America.

The crime bill has also given prosecutors tough new penalties to use against violent criminals. The death penalty can now be imposed for nearly 60 Federal crimes, such as killing a law enforcement officer and using weapons of mass destruction resulting in death. Prosecutors are using this statute to seek the death penalty in indictments in the Oklahoma City bombing just now.

And just this week, a violent career criminal in Iowa named Thomas Farmer was sentenced to life imprisonment because the crime bill says to repeat offenders, when you commit a third violent crime you'll be put away and put away for good, "three strikes and you're out."

Until this week, Thomas Farmer had been a textbook case of what's wrong with our criminal justice system. He committed one violent crime after another and each time was paroled long before his sentence was up. In 1970, he murdered a doctor and drew a 20-year sentence, but he was paroled a few years later, even after he tried to escape. In 1979, he was sentenced to 25 years for armed robbery. Two years later, he murdered a fellow inmate and was sentenced to an additional 10 years, but the State paroled him yet again. And last fall he went on a crime spree, robbing two supermarkets and threatening to kill an employee who was taking too long to open the store safe.

No wonder law-abiding Americans are fed up with a system that lets too many career criminals get out of jail free. If Thomas Farmer had been convicted in State court again, he might have been out on the street again in less than 3 years. But our "three strikes and you're out" law slammed that revolving door shut. Thomas Farmer has made a life of violent crime; now he will pay for the rest of his life behind bars where he belongs.

Thomas Farmer was the very first career criminal we put away under the "three strikes and you're out." But he will not be the last. Federal prosecutors already have another 16 "three strikes" cases pending around the country, including three convictions that are awaiting sentencing now.

One year ago, we overcame deep partisan differences and bitter partisan opposition to make "three strikes and you're out" the law of the land. Now it's time for Members of Congress to do that again, to put aside demands for ideological purity and give the American people the reforms they want, the reforms they need, the reforms they need in welfare, the reforms they need in other areas of our Government. And

these reforms clearly include the antiterrorism legislation I sent to Congress after the Oklahoma City bombing.

It's hard to imagine what more must happen to convince Congress to pass that bill. Yet partisan politics has blocked it in the House of Representatives. I call on the House to pass that antiterrorism bill when they return so we can continue to make all Americans safer.

Because of the crime bill passed a year ago, the people of Iowa are safer today, and a career criminal who haunted them for decades is off the streets for good. I'll keep doing everything in my power to ensure that those who commit crimes are caught, those who are caught are convicted, those who are convicted are punished, and those who have made a life of crime spend the rest of their lives behind bars.

The American people deserve a justice system that reflects our values and a Government that fulfills its first responsibility, to keep Americans safe.

Thanks for listening.

NOTE: The address was recorded at 7:21 p.m. on August 18 at the Rockefeller residence in Jackson Hole, WY, for broadcast at 10:06 a.m. on August 19.

Remarks on the Death of American Diplomats in Bosnia-Herzegovina and an Exchange With Reporters in Jackson Hole, Wyoming
August 19, 1995

The President. Good morning. As all of you know by now, we lost some fine Americans in Bosnia in a terrible accident a few hours ago, working for the cause of peace there. I have spoken with Dick Holbrooke and with General Clark in Sarajevo and, of course, with Secretary of State Christopher and Deputy Secretary Talbott. I have received a full account of what occurred. I am convinced that it was a tragic accident.

I am very grateful for the service that these fine men have rendered to their country and to the world. And I am encouraged by the determination of their colleagues to continue on. Within a matter of moments from now, Secretary Holbrooke and General Clark will continue with a scheduled meeting with President

Izetbegovic to press for the cause of peace. I expect them then to come home with their comrades and, after a few days, to return to press the peace mission again vigorously.

This is a sad and tragic day for the families of the men who were killed, and Hillary and I, and I'm sure all Americans, send our prayers and our thoughts to them and our profound gratitude for their service. I think the American people would have been very proud of the response of their colleagues today in the wake of this incident. And I am very grateful for the continued determination of Secretary Holbrooke and General Clark to continue on the peace mission.

Q. Mr. President, as far as you're concerned, there's no need to stop the U.S. efforts to seek a diplomatic solution; this won't in any way affect that?

The President. No, I hope it will intensify it. The men who gave their lives—these were immensely talented, patriotic Americans who were profoundly concerned with what the war in Bosnia has done to the people there and what it means for the values of decency and freedom and peace. And I would think that the thing that they would want us most to do is to press ahead, and that is what we intend to do.

Q. You're convinced there was no foul play involved?

The President. Based on everything we know from the—I have now—I talked to Secretary Holbrooke and General Clark, who were virtual eye witnesses, and they say there's no evidence of that.

NOTE: The President spoke at 10:10 a.m. at the Teton Pine Golf Club. In his remarks, he referred to American diplomats Robert Frasure, Joseph J. Kruzel, and Samuel Nelson Drew, who died when their military vehicle crashed en route to Sarajevo; Richard Holbrooke, Assistant Secretary of State for European and Canadian Affairs; and Lt. Gen. Wesley K. Clark, USA, Director, Strategic Plans and Policy, Joint Staff.

Statement on the Death of American Diplomats in Bosnia-Herzegovina
August 19, 1995

I am deeply saddened by the deaths today of three dedicated Americans serving the cause of peace, near Sarajevo, Bosnia-Herzegovina. We have confirmed reports that Ambassador Robert Frasure, Deputy Assistant Secretary of State for European and Canadian Affairs; Dr. Joseph J. Kruzel, Deputy Assistant Secretary of Defense for European and NATO Policy; and Air Force Colonel Samuel Nelson Drew, a member of the National Security Council staff, were killed this morning in a crash of their military vehicle on the way to Sarajevo. Two other members of the delegation were injured. These men were part of an American team searching for an end to the conflict there. That effort will continue.

In addition, one French soldier was killed and two were injured; the three were part of the team escorting the delegation.

I also want to thank the Government of France and the United Nations Protection Force (UNPROFOR) for their extraordinary efforts to care for the casualties.

My heartfelt sympathy is extended to the Frasure, Kruzel, and Drew families. In honor of their sacrifice, I have directed that our Nation's flags be lowered. Their loved ones were engaged in the greatest cause of all—the search for peace. As the Scripture tells us, "Blessed are the peacemakers, for they shall be called the children of God."

NOTE: The related proclamation is listed in Appendix D at the end of this volume.

Remarks at a Memorial Service in Arlington, Virginia, for the American Diplomats Who Died in Bosnia-Herzegovina
August 23, 1995

My fellow Americans, distinguished members of the diplomatic corps; most importantly, to the family, the friends, the colleagues, the loved ones of Robert Frasure, Joseph Kruzel, and Nelson Drew: Today we gather to honor three peacemakers who gave their lives seeking for others the blessings we Americans hold dear and too often take for granted, the opportunity to work and to dream, to raise our children to live and to love in a land of peace.

When I named Robert Frasure Special Envoy to the Former Yugoslavia, a key United States representative in seeking solutions to modern diplomacy's most difficult challenge—ending the bloodshed and bringing peace in the Balkans— he had already made diplomacy the steady dedication of a lifetime. He earned, justifiably, a reputation as a man for all crises, and many, many people around this world from Ethiopia to Estonia have better lives because of his superb work.

Joseph Kruzel put his mind to the test of creating lasting security in a world that has known too much war. Besides his outstanding work in Bosnia, he led the Pentagon's efforts on critical issues of NATO enlargement and the re-integration of Eastern Europe into the West after the cold war. His service to our country spanned 28 years, from an Air Force officer in Vietnam to work on SALT I to being a major force in bringing the nations of Europe into the Partnership For Peace. The world is a more secure place because of his dedication.

Colonel Nelson Drew was a soldier, a scholar, a teacher, and a gentleman. He was trained to fight war. But in more than 20 years of service as an Air Force officer, he gave his heart and soul to the search for peace. He was largely responsible for investing the military and diplomatic initiatives of our Nation in Bosnia with a coherent design. And he was universally respected for his knowledge, his negotiating skills, his strategic thinking about the future of NATO and Europe after the cold war. The White House and the Nation are better for his service.

Bob, Joe, and Nelson each represented the finest qualities of American citizenship. For their service and their sacrifice in the cause of peace and freedom, it is my honor on this day to award them each the President's Citizens Medal.

Let me say to Katharina Frasure and Sarah and Virginia; to Gail Kruzel and John and Sarah; to Sandy Drew and Samantha and Philip; and to all your other family members here, the American people mourn your loss and share your grief. America is profoundly grateful for the work your husbands and fathers did to make the world a better place.

I hope you will always remember, along with the personal memories you shared with me just a few moments ago, the pride they took in their calling and the passion they brought to the search for peace. And I hope that always, always, you will be very proud.

They were extraordinary Americans who made reason their weapon, freedom their cause, and peace their goal. Bob, Joe, and Nelson were in Bosnia because they were moved by the terrible injustice and suffering there. And they were there because they believed it could and must be changed. The sorrow we feel here reminds us of the suffering Bob, Joe, and Nelson sought to ease there.

So as we praise these men—Robert Frasure, Joseph Kruzel, and Nelson Drew, quiet American heroes who gave their lives so that others might know a future of hope and a land at peace—let us resolve to carry on their struggle with the strength, determination, and caring they brought to their families, their work, and their very grateful Nation.

May God bless their memories and lift up their souls.

NOTE: The President spoke at 1:10 p.m. in Memorial Chapel at Fort Myer.

Statement on the Death of Alfred Eisenstadt
August 24, 1995

We join today to mourn the death of the dean of photojournalism. From the pages of Life magazine to art galleries throughout the world, Alfred Eisenstadt, one of the most talented photojournalists of our time, has chronicled our country's history through his work.

His legacy will continue through his photographs for Americans and people across the globe to enjoy. Hillary and I extend our deepest personal sympathies to his companion Lu Lu Kaye as well as to his family and friends.

Letter to Congressional Leaders Transmitting a Report on Haiti
August 24, 1995

Dear Mr. Speaker: *(Dear Mr. President:)*

As required by section 107 of Public Law 104–6, I transmit herewith the report on the cumulative incremental cost of all United States activities in Haiti subsequent to September 30, 1993.

Sincerely,

WILLIAM J. CLINTON

NOTE: Identical letters were sent to Newt Gingrich, Speaker of the House of Representatives, and Albert Gore, Jr., President of the Senate.

Statement on Fire Suppression Assistance for New York State
August 24, 1995

Tonight in Suffolk County, New York, firefighters and other emergency workers are heroically fighting several dangerous fires that have forced the evacuation of hundreds of people, including residents of two nursing homes among other facilities.

In order to help the State and county governments sustain these efforts without worry of financial hardships, I have tonight authorized fire suppression grants which will allow the Federal Emergency Management Agency to reimburse the State for most of the costs associated with the emergency operations.

I have also directed the mobilization of the resources of the U.S. Forest Service to provide direct assistance in fighting the fires, including all necessary equipment and teams of particular expertise in fighting wild land fires. They are on their way. I have directed FEMA Director James Lee Witt and Assistant Secretary of Agriculture Jim Lyons to go to New York tonight to manage the Federal firefighting effort. Fires are frightening, and I know that the residents of these areas are going through difficult times. Our hearts and our prayers are with them, and we commend the efforts of all of those people on Long Island who are valiantly working to contain these blazes.

NOTE: The President also recorded this statement at 9 p.m. outside the press filing center in Jackson Hole, WY, for later broadcast in New York State.

Remarks on the 79th Anniversary of the National Park Service in Yellowstone National Park, Wyoming
August 25, 1995

Hi, folks. Well, I'm sorry about the rain, but I want to tell you that Hillary and Chelsea and I are having a wonderful time here. I want to thank the Park Superintendent, Mike Findley, and all the people who work at Yellowstone for making our visit so nice, even with the rain.

I wanted to make a couple of points today: 79 years ago today the Congress established the National Park Service to organize and preserve our natural heritage and to preserve our common environment. Last year at the 369 national parks, 270 million visitors came. That is an astonishing number.

Yellowstone is the symbol of our national parks because it's the oldest one and the first one in the history of the world. And I came here today basically to make two or three points: First of all, I am committed to preserving these parks. There was an effort in Congress—[applause]—there was an effort in Congress to cut the budget in a way that could have forced the closure of 200 of these parks. That's wrong.

There are some people who say we ought to just sell some of our natural treasures off to the highest bidder. And that's wrong.

But I do think we need some reforms, and let me just mention two or three. Number one, I support keeping the fees that you pay when you come to the national parks in the parks. That's one of the things that we want to do so that the money can be used to preserve the parks.

Secondly, we want to allow the national parks more flexibility to go out and raise money from private citizens to preserve, not to destroy, our natural heritage. And that's in the plan that we have given to Congress, and we hope that they will adopt it.

And finally, we want to see the people who do business in our parks give a fairer share of that business back to the parks for the preser- vation of the people in the future, like the people who run this hotel do. And Mr. Findley's worked hard on that. We want more of that in the future.

The last thing I want to say is this: We have a big stake in what you see around you here at Yellowstone. It's a part of what I call our common ground. And we should not do any- thing this year, anything, to weaken our ability to protect the quality of our land, our water, our food, the diversity of our wildlife, and the sanctity of our natural treasures. We can balance the budget without doing any of that, and that's the commitment all of us ought to make today on this anniversary of the National Park Service.

Thank you, and God bless you all.

NOTE: The President spoke at 1 p.m. at Old Faith- ful Lodge.

The President's Radio Address
August 26, 1995

Good morning. There's an old Native Amer- ican saying that goes: In all our deliberations we must take into account the well-being of the seventh generation to follow. The wisdom of those words has come alive to me during my family's Wyoming vacation.

During the past week and a half, Chelsea, Hillary, and I have been vacationing in two of our Nation's most spectacular national treasures, Grand Teton and Yellowstone National Parks. We've been hiking, horseback riding, rafting on the Snake River. We've seen Old Faithful, the canyon falls, and the young wolves that are being reintroduced into Yellowstone. We've seen buffalo, moose, elk, eagles, osprey, red hawks. No bears yet, but we're still looking. We've seen breathtaking mountains, lakes, streams, and meadows. And all of this belongs to you, the American people, for all time to come.

I've also seen lots of Americans, young, old, and in-between, from all over our country in these parks. Mostly I've seen families, hard- working families who can afford these wonders of the world because these parks belong to them. So I'm more grateful than ever that those who came before us saw fit to preserve this land for the enjoyment of future generations of Americans. That was the intent of Congress when it established the National Park Service 79 years ago today. I can think of few things that mean more to the national life of our coun- try than our national parks.

Last year, more than 270 million visitors made their way to places like Yellowstone, Grand Teton, and Grand Canyon National Parks, and to urban treasures like Golden Gate in Califor- nia, Cuyahoga in Ohio, and Gateway in New York. They came to big parks and to smaller ones, like the one in my hometown, Hot Springs National Park.

Our 369 national parks aren't simply aestheti- cally pleasing; they're also important to the economies of their communities. For example, in 1994, visitors to Yellowstone, the world's first national park, pumped more than $643 million into the local economy, creating more than 12,000 jobs. Visitors to Big Bend National Park, along the Texas-Mexican border, spent more than $77 million while creating 1,544 local jobs.

But while the parks have been good for local economies, many of them have fallen into dis- repair. So if we want them to be there for our children in the 21st century we've got to turn this around. But there's a right way and a wrong way to do it. The wrong way is to say that this is an investment no longer worth making, to close the parks and sell them off to the highest bidder. Some people want to do that, but it wouldn't be in faith with the kind of commonsense values that have made our country great and the kind of common ground we've had over our national parks throughout the 20th century.

That's why I strongly oppose the budget cuts that were proposed earlier this year by the congressional majority. They could have forced the closing of more than 200 national parks and recreation areas. The right way to help our parks is through the kind of sensible reforms our administration has proposed.

First, we have to put our parks on sound financial footing by keeping park fees that the citizens pay in the parks. Most visitors to our national parks believe their fees are used for park improvements, but they aren't. That will change under our reforms. Many visitors tell us they want their money to stay in the parks and they'd even pay a little more if they knew that was the case. Well, that's what we propose to do, keep the fees in the parks.

The second thing we want to do is to make it easier for our parks to form partnerships with people in the private sector who want to invest money to preserve our natural heritage, not to destroy it.

And thirdly, we want to change the out-of-date contracting policies that keep the concession fees paid by businesses operating in the parks unreasonably low. We've got to change that because those who make a profit from the private businesses in our parks should pay a fair amount for the privilege, so that they can make a profit and help us to maintain our parks.

I'm also concerned about activities on land that belongs to the American people which are being used for profit in ways that could damage our national parks. For example, just 2½ miles from Yellowstone Park there's a proposal to build a big gold mine. Before that mine can be approved, it must meet the highest standards in an environmental impact statement. And yesterday I declared a 2-year moratorium on any new mining claims in the area near the northeast corner of Yellowstone Park.

Unfortunately, we're still burdened with an 1872 mining law which allows these claims to be staked and mined while giving virtually noth-

ing back to the American people who make it possible. We have to do everything we can to protect parks like Yellowstone. They're more priceless than gold.

Finally, if we want to maintain our national heritage for our children and our grandchildren, we have to do more than preserve our national parks; we've got to preserve our environment. Right now we face a lot of pressure to pollute the environment and to go back on our commitment to keeping it safe and clean and healthy. The House recently voted to gut environmental and public health protections in the name of regulatory reform. Some in the Senate tried to do the same. They were willing to put at risk the safety of our air, our food, our drinking water, the water we fish and swim in, for short-term financial gains for a few.

The budget bill the House passed would cut environmental enforcement by 50 percent, virtually bringing to a halt Federal enforcement of the Clean Water Act, the Clean Air Act, and it would stop toxic waste clean-ups. This would be a terrible mistake, and I'm determined to fight it with vetoes, if necessary.

For a long time now, the American people have stood together on common ground to preserve our environment. At the beginning of this century, Theodore Roosevelt, a Republican, began a fervent call for conservation. In 1905, he said, "There can be nothing in the world more beautiful than a Yosemite, the groves of giant sequoias and redwoods, the canyon of the Colorado, the canyon of Yellowstone, its three Tetons. And our people should see to it that they are preserved for their children and their children's children forever."

Well, I second that emotion. And after spending the last week in Wyoming, I have an even deeper commitment to fulfilling it. So let's end this century by meeting the challenge Teddy Roosevelt set for us at the beginning. We've made a lot of progress in the protection of our environment and our national heritage. But the future can be even brighter. Do we need reforms? Yes. Should we reverse course? Not on your life. It's up to us.

Thanks for listening.

NOTE: The address was recorded at 9:40 p.m. on August 25 at the Rockefeller residence in Jackson Hole, WY, for broadcast at 10:06 a.m. on August 26.

Remarks on the 75th Anniversary of Women's Suffrage in Jackson Hole, Wyoming
August 26, 1995

Thank you very much. Thank you very much, I think, Hillary. [*Laughter*] In my own defense, I brought these boots home about 10 years ago, and the shine has kind of come off of them now. [*Laughter*] They don't wake anybody at night anymore.

I want to thank Rosemary Shockley and all the representatives and guests of the women's organizations who are here who put this wonderful event together. I want to thank the wonderful people who work for the Grand Teton and Yellowstone National Parks for making this an incredible vacation for our family. We have had a wonderful couple of days.

Yesterday we were up in Yellowstone, and I remarked that I had had a lot of incredible things happen to me in my life, but in spite of that, if anybody had ever told me that within the space of about 8 minutes I would be feeding bison to wolves and then would be hailed on in August—[*laughter*]—or as one of the park rangers said, this is "hail on the Chief"—[*laughter*]—I would never have believed it. So this has been an incredible thing for me, and I'm so profoundly grateful to everybody here in Wyoming who has made our vacation so wonderful.

I'm glad to be here for this occasion. I was thinking how amazing it is that a State like Wyoming would be the first place, the first democracy anywhere in the world to give women the right to vote. And maybe it was because the men were more secure here than they were other places at the time. [*Laughter*] But for whatever reason, it was a very good thing.

I have always been interested in these issues because, as Hillary said, I was born to a working mother in the 1940's and raised by a working grandmother in the 1940's. So my mother and my grandmother were both working 50 years or so ago, just 25 years after women were given the right to vote in the country as a whole.

I'd like to say a word, if I might, at the beginning about this world conference on women. I'm glad the First Lady is going to lead our delegation. And you heard her describe the delegation. They come from all walks of life, from different political parties and religions, and they disagree about a lot of things. But they do agree that if you look at the world and imagine what the future is going to be like and if you believe as I do that more and more the fate of Americans—even in landlocked States like Wyoming and Arkansas, where I grew up and lived until I became President—will be caught up in the fate of what happens to people all around the world, we must have a common agreement that we need a united front for treating women all over the world with dignity and respect and giving them opportunities in the family and education and in the workplace.

We can't imagine what it's like in America because of the progress being made in this country by women, but there are still places where women babies are more likely to be— little girl babies are more likely to be killed just because they are little girls. There are countries in the world today that have a huge imbalance in the number of males and females because the little girls are killed at birth because they're not thought to have sufficient value.

There are still countries in the world that try to force women not to have children, and that's something we can't imagine in this country, where that's the most profound right that women have in the family. There are still countries in the world where a young bride can be burned if her family can't come up with the dowry or won't come up with a little more. There are still places in the world that are held in abject poverty because women who are entrepreneurial and creative and willing to work don't have a chance even to borrow what would be a pittance in America to start a little business to ply their trades and work their skills.

And all of this will affect us because we're going to live in a global economy. And if we want to trade with the rest of the world and promote democracy and freedom with the rest of the world, then, obviously, we need to be working with people who are trying to unleash the potential of every citizen in their country. And we believe that's the only thing that works here in America.

One of the most troubling things to me about our politics today in America is that everything gets turned into just another version of the same old political fight, and all these issues seem to be torn like Silly Putty into extremes. So now there's this huge effort in America to try to convince the American people that this conference is somehow anti-family and that we're sending some sort of radical delegation there. Why? Not because it's true, but because it furthers the almost addictive, almost narcotic drive among some elements in our society to take every single issue and use it as a cause for division among our people when we need to be more united.

This conference is going to talk about education and domestic violence and grassroots economics, employment, health care, political participation. It's going to talk about a lot of things we take for granted here in this country that we think if everybody had access to it around the world we'd be a lot better off. And however anyone might try to paint this conference, the truth is it is true-blue to families, to supporting them, to conserving them, to valuing them.

And I want you to know that I think America will have some things to learn from this conference as well. And we don't intend to walk away from it when it's over. I'm going to establish an interagency council on women to make sure that all the effort and the good ideas actually get implemented when we come back home.

I have declared this day Women's Equality Day because there is so much to celebrate and so much still to do. All around the country, as I'm sure you know, there are events commemorating this important anniversary, but no place has a better claim to it than Wyoming, for all the reasons that Hillary said.

The suffragists left us a living legacy and a continuing challenge. The legacy is full citizenship for our mothers, our sisters, our daughters. The continuing challenge is to honor that legacy by using these privileges to lead our Nation in the right direction.

The vote for women came at the end of an enormous philosophical war. Some of the things said kind of remind me about what people are saying about this conference on women now. It was bloodless, but it was highly costly. It literally consumed the lives of thousands of American women who were dedicated to gaining the right to vote. The dividends that were won we are still reaping today.

But remember what the opponents said about that. The opponents said that allowing women the vote would mean a disaster for our Nation; it would destroy our families; it would end all distinctions between the sexes. [*Laughter*] Happily, they were wrong on all counts. [*Laughter*] But the arguments then and the arguments you hear about this conference on women today, they illustrate one of Clinton's laws of politics, which is that the American people have one peculiarity: they're all for change in general, but a lot of them are against it in particular. [*Laughter*]

I remember back in 1993 when I was trying to get Congress to enact my deficit reduction program that would also have lowered taxes on working families with children and increased our investment in education and technology, and the people who wouldn't vote for it said it would mean the end of the American economy. It would bring on a great recession. It would just be a disaster. It would be the end of everything good and true about America. A bunch of those folks are running for President today. [*Laughter*]

So it turned out that the results of that program were that we reduced the deficit from $290 billion to $160 billion. We got about halfway home toward our goal of balancing the budget before anything is done this year. We got 7 million new jobs, 2½ million new homeowners, 1½ million new small businesses, the largest number in American history, the stock market at 4,700, and things are rocking along pretty good. And they still say it was just the worst thing that ever happened. Everybody is for change in general, but it's difficult to get people to do the particular things to achieve those changes. I think that's important to remember.

Somehow, by some magic of harmony with this beautiful nature behind me and a sense of self-confidence and fairness, men who were in the decisionmaking process in Wyoming found the self-confidence and the innate fairness, without regard to their other partisan or philosophical differences, to say it doesn't make sense to have half our folks not have the right to vote. And that's a great tribute to the people of Wyoming. It led directly to the passage of the 19th amendment, without which none of these other things would have happened.

And of course, as Hillary already said as she introduced the survivors here of that remarkable slate of women who swept the elections in Jackson in 1920—I thought that was an incredible thing, and I liked it a lot until I read that one of the women actually defeated her own husband. [*Laughter*] Those guys have even more self-confidence than I do when it came to that. [*Laughter*]

If you think about it, it's interesting, women have always had great symbolic importance in our country's democracy. Our greatest symbols for justice and liberty are women. Think about it, a woman holding the scales of justice, blindfolded; the Statue of Liberty holding a torch. One promises fairness; the other, freedom.

We are a country that, more than anything else, is still around after all this time because we kept expanding the boundaries of fairness and freedom, because we never listened to not only the naysayers among us but also the naysayers in our own spirits, for each of us, inside, every day wakes up with the scales balanced between hope and fear. And somehow we've always found the magic balance to go forward for fairness and freedom.

Susan B. Anthony, Elizabeth Cady Stanton, Lucretia Mott, Esther Morris, Carrie Chapman Catt, they helped to achieve that. Mother Jones fought to end child labor. Sojourner Truth fought to end discrimination and to establish social justice. My friend Rosa Parks set in motion the civil rights movement by simply refusing to sit in the wrong place on a bus. A lot of ordinary women all over this country, decade after decade after decade, have worked to advance the cause of fairness and freedom.

When we look back on them from the vantage point of the present, it's hard to imagine that as recently as 1920 American women couldn't vote. The suffragists had a lot of vision. They knew that the vote would be an opening, a door through which women could help to direct our Government to where it should be and with which women could stand behind issues that would make their families stronger and their children's lives better.

When you look back, it seems remarkable that all this has happened in the last 75 years. Now, more and more women are completing higher and higher levels of education, entering fields which were closed to them not so long ago. Every time I visit a Federal facility, every time I go to these national parks, I marvel at how many of the park rangers are women.

We just celebrated, Hillary and I did, a milestone in the progress to erect a memorial in Washington to the women who are veterans of our wars. And I was so proud to be able to say at this ceremony that in the 2½ years I

have been President, we have opened more than 250,000 positions in the United States military to women that were closed just 2½ years ago.

In the last 3 years, the Small Business Administration in our administration has cut its budget by 40 percent, almost doubled its loan volume, and increased loans to women entrepreneurs by 85 percent. We're not at 50 percent yet, but I have six women in my Cabinet, twice the number of any previous administration, and over one-third of our Presidential appointees and about one-third of the new Federal judges appointed in the last 2½ years are women. Women are beginning to participate more fully throughout this country in the life of America. And so far as I know, the sky is not falling anywhere. [*Laughter*]

We also have to recognize that the people who were against the right to vote for women were wrong when they said this would abolish all differences between the sexes. And some of the differences that still exist are not such good ones. We know that women are still, in peculiar ways, more vulnerable to violence, and we have established a violence against women section in the Department of Justice which is doing exemplary work. And the former Attorney General of Iowa, Bonnie Campbell, heads that, and she is also going to the women's conference.

We have tried to do a lot of work to see that our national medical research focuses more on the health concerns of women. I was stunned when I started running for President, I never knew before how women had been systematically left out of a lot of the research efforts in the health area, particularly areas relating to cancer. And so we have done a lot of work to make sure that in medical research and treatment, with heart disease, cancer, AIDS, and other diseases, women are more fully represented in the testing protocols and the research to make sure that we do what we ought to do.

Hillary has launched a national campaign to try to increase the use of mammograms which will help in the early detection and the saving of thousands of lives. And I hope it will be ever more successful.

As you look ahead, I ask you to think about what is the agenda for women and for families, for more than any other people in our society, women have always carried on the struggle to find both personal fulfillment and still fulfill the social obligation of maintaining strong families and giving our children a better chance. And I think now that's what we want for all Americans.

If you look at the American economy today, the truth is that most people don't have the option not to work. For those who do, I applaud them for any decision they choose to make because the most important thing in our society is still raising children and doing a good job of it. That is still the first and most important job of our society.

But if you look at this world toward which we are moving, the 21st century, the way we work and live is changing dramatically. And we are in a big, huge debate today, not just in Washington but in every State in the country, about how we're going to reestablish common ground, how can we agree on the basic things we have to do to enable our people to succeed, first and foremost, in raising their children, secondly, in being successful in the workplace, and thirdly, in preserving our freedom and our way of life. Those will be the great challenges, the new family values challenges for the 21st century. And we have to ask and answer those questions.

If I might, let me just suggest a few things that I think are quite important if we are going to extol family values and give women a chance to live up to the fullest of their God-given capacities as we move into this next century.

First of all, we've got to say, it is the policy of the United States of America for people to be able to succeed as parents and as workers. It is the policy of the United States for people to be able to succeed. In that sense, perhaps the most important law I've signed since becoming President is the first one, the family and medical leave law. The people—again everybody was for change in general but against it in particular. People got up and gave the awfullest speeches you ever heard about that law. They said it would mean the end of the free enterprise system, businesses would go bankrupt, stores would be boarded up everywhere.

We have no instance, not a single one, of a business going bankrupt because of the family and medical leave law. But there are a whole lot of people out there who can take a little time off from work when their children are sick—sometimes their children are dying—without losing their job. And that's a good thing. There are women who can take time off from work to deal with their own illnesses without

losing their health insurance and thereby losing their ability to work, because of that law. So I think that's a part of our family values agenda.

If you look at the family values agenda, you have to say in the world toward which we are moving the level of education people have determines their income and their capacity to earn more than ever before in American history. So I think giving every child a good start in school and guaranteeing everybody the right to go to college with an affordable college loan, preserving programs like the national service program that allows people to work their way through college, giving every unemployed person in the country the right to what I call a "GI bill" for America's workers, a voucher that they can take to the nearest community college so that they can get retrained when they lose their jobs, these are family value issues that will profoundly affect the women of our country and their ability to do well in the future.

I think immunizing all the children in this country is a pretty important family values issue. I think we ought to keep going until we've got the job done. I think we ought to recognize that, yes, we have to slow the rate of inflation in Medicare and Medicaid, but we shouldn't forget that if we want our working people to be able to educate their children, then we ought not to cut Medicare and Medicaid so much that they will undermine the ability of middle class people to have their parents get the care they need and undermine senior citizens' ability to get that kind of care.

Let me make it clear: I believe balancing the budget is a family values issue. I think it—this year—this year, we would have a surplus in the budget but for the interest run up on the debt accumulated in the 12 years before I showed up in Washington. This is a big issue.

Next year, interest on the debt will be bigger than the defense budget. We're worried about getting an adequate budget for the parks here. We're worried about getting an adequate budget for education. No American has a stake in a permanent deficit. That also is a family values issue; lifting the burden of this awful debt off of our children is a family values issue. But we can do it without breaking Medicare and bankrupting the ability of middle class families to know that their parents can get the health care they need while they educate their children. We can do both, but we must do both. It's not an either-or choice.

I think maintaining what you see behind me is a family values issue, and making it available for all the American people. And I think being willing to honestly confront some of the most difficult conflicts in our society where short-term economic gain will cause a heavy price over the long run is also an important part of our maturing as a country.

And let me just mention one issue, a difficult one. Everybody told me that I—all my political advisers told me I had taken leave of my senses when I said it was time to stop walking away from the terrible health consequences of teen-age smoking. But I believe the United States is right to say this is a children's disease. Kids are being addicted, 3,000 kids a day start smoking, 1,000 of them, 1,000 of them, will have their lives shortened as a result of it. I think that is a family values issue, and we should take it and face it together.

So if we're going to do this, it is important that we remember the kind of self-confidence that was demonstrated in Wyoming when women got the right to vote. It is important that men and women, with all their differences, political and otherwise, have the level of self-confidence to sit down and say, America is still a great big family. Like every great big family, there's a whole lot of differences, and there's always going to be a whole lot of argument, and we're always going to be looking at some of our family members cross-eyed, like we do our second cousin that we wish wouldn't show up to the reunion. [*Laughter*] But there are limits to the extent to which we can demonize one another. We've got to treat each other with respect and work through these things.

And if we really want the day when women will become full partners in the decisionmaking process in America—and we believe that's a good thing, and we want to face these issues which will determine whether we go into the 21st century with the American dream alive and well and the American community strong and together—we have got to have that level of self-confidence. We have got to remember that every time, every time we have faced the choice between going forward with freedom or fairness, two things symbolized by women, we have had to deal with the demon of insecurity in our country and even inside.

And we have heard all these proclamations, all these Chicken Little proclamations that every change we make—that we knew we ought to make would cause the sky to fall. And we're still around after almost 220 years because somehow, someway when it came time to make the decision, we decided Chicken Little was wrong.

Blind justice was right; the Statue of Liberty was right; and the kind of self-confidence displayed by the people of Wyoming when they led the world in giving women the right to vote was right. It was right then, and it still is.

Thank you, and God bless you.

NOTE: The President spoke at approximately 11:30 a.m. at Jackson Lake Lodge on the 75th anniversary of the ratification of the 19th amendment to the Constitution. In his remarks, he referred to Rosemary Shockley, president, League of Women Voters of Wyoming.

Statement on the United States District Court Decision on the Child Support Recovery Act
August 28, 1995

On July 26, 1995, the United States District Court for the District of Arizona struck down the Child Support Recovery Act as an unconstitutional exercise of congressional power. I respectfully disagree with this decision. I asked the Justice Department to review this case, and the Department has filed a motion asking the court to reconsider its decision.

The Child Support Recovery Act gives us the power to punish deadbeat parents who cross State lines to avoid paying child support. It is essential for Federal law enforcement to have this authority because the States cannot bring these criminals to justice, especially the hardcore group of parents who flagrantly move from State to State to evade their obligations.

A child should be able to expect the most basic support from those who chose to bring that child into the world. Parental responsibility does not end at the State line. The taxpayers of America should be able to expect that the burden of caring for these children will be placed on the shoulders of the parents, where it rightfully belongs.

Message on the Observance of Labor Day, 1995
August 28, 1995

Each year at this time we pause to reflect on the value of labor and the accomplishments of the American worker. This country's success depends on the efforts of its citizens to open the door to a better future. Work is the engine that drives our economy forward, moves struggling families upward into the middle class, and creates opportunities for our children. We must continually strive to create more opportunity for work for those who are willing to take the responsibility to make better lives for themselves and their families. Our labors ensure that the blessings of life, liberty, and the pursuit of happiness will benefit generations to come.

Let us give thanks to those who came before us and who strived to improve working conditions and create fair labor laws. They risked their livelihoods and often their very lives to ensure that children could go to school instead of to work in mines and factories, that laborers could work without risking injury, and that Americans who toiled throughout the week would be rewarded with a decent living and could spend more time raising their families. These reformers brought dignity to the workplace and integrity to our society.

Today, we recognize that management and labor face common challenges and a shared destiny in the global economy. We must continue our efforts to create further job growth and new opportunities, enabling more of our citizens to realize the American Dream. As we celebrate Labor Day, we can find strength and renewed inspiration in the Dream—the idea that we can be good workers as well as good parents and that, through our individual efforts, we can build better lives for our children.

Best wishes to all for a memorable and meaningful holiday.

BILL CLINTON

Letter to Congressional Leaders Reporting on the Cyprus Conflict
August 28, 1995

Dear Mr. Speaker: (*Dear Mr. Chairman:*)

In accordance with Public Law 95–384 (22 U.S.C. 2373(c)), I submit to you this report on progress toward a negotiated settlement of the Cyprus question. The previous report covered progress through May 31, 1995. The current report covers the period June 1, 1995, through July 31, 1995.

Throughout the period, my representatives continued efforts to urge meaningful negotiations among the parties and to encourage them to take steps to create a healthy environment for talks and progress on overall settlement issues.

In July, Assistant Secretary of State for European Affairs Richard Holbrooke met with U.S. Presidential Emissary for Cyprus Richard I. Beattie and U.S. ambassadors to the region, as well as private individuals and members of Congress, to consider the current Cyprus situation.

There is general agreement that the recent decision by the European Union (EU) to begin discussion of Cyprus' accession to the EU could provide added motivation to the parties to achieve a settlement. Special Cyprus Coordinator James A. Williams visited a number of EU member countries during this period to consult on ways to take advantage of this opportunity to move the peace process forward.

Sincerely,

WILLIAM J. CLINTON

NOTE: Identical letters were sent to Newt Gingrich, Speaker of the House of Representatives, and Jesse Helms, chairman, Senate Committee on Foreign Relations. This letter was released by the Office of the Press Secretary on August 29.

Statement on the First Anniversary of the Cease-Fire in Northern Ireland
August 30, 1995

Tomorrow marks the first anniversary of the Irish Republican Army's cease-fire in Northern Ireland, joined 6 weeks later by the Combined Loyalist Military Command. These historic decisions opened a door that had been closed to the people of Northern Ireland for too long— the gateway to peace. On this anniversary, I urge the parties to build on the important work of the past year to secure a just and lasting settlement to a conflict that has cost so many lives.

We owe much of the progress to the courage and determination of Prime Minister Major and Taoiseach Bruton and their continued willingness to take risks for peace. I also salute the people of Northern Ireland for their extraordinary perseverance and their dedication to the cause of peace. They have endured violence with so much dignity, and now the future that they have long deserved is within reach.

I am looking forward to visiting a peaceful Northern Ireland later this year and paying personal tribute to those who have worked so hard to bring about this new day. I welcome the progress made in recent months toward reducing barriers, alleviating tension, and promoting reconciliation. Much, however, remains to be done. To advance the goal of peace, I urge both republicans and loyalists to do their part and seriously address the issue of decommissioning paramilitary weapons. This is an essential step toward banishing once and for all the specter of violence that has haunted Ireland. I urge the parties to sit down together soon to discuss their aspirations for the future as well as their fears and differences. As I have said before, I would be pleased if talks were underway by the time of my visit.

As we look back on a year in which the bombs and guns have been silenced, I hope all the parties will reaffirm their commitment to build a peace in Northern Ireland for generations. The United States stands ready to support the people of Northern Ireland and the British and Irish Governments in that effort.

Remarks on Arrival in Honolulu, Hawaii
August 31, 1995

Thank you very much. Sergeant May, thank you for that introduction, and more importantly, thank you for your service. Governor Cayetano, Senator Inouye, Mayor Harris, General Lorber, Admiral Macke, members of the armed service, distinguished guests, honored veterans, Senator Akaka, Congressman Abercrombie, ladies and gentlemen: It is wonderful for our family and for me personally to be back in Hawaii. It is a great honor to be here to celebrate the 50th anniversary of the end of World War II.

We come to celebrate the courage and determination of the Americans who brought us victory in that war. But as we do, our thoughts and prayers must also be with the men and women of our Armed Forces who are putting their bravery and their professionalism on the line in Bosnia.

I want to restate to you and to all the American people why our forces and their NATO allies are engaged in the military operation there. The massacre of civilians in Sarajevo on

Monday, caused by a Bosnian Serb shell, was an outrageous act in a terrible war and a challenge to the commitments which NATO had made to oppose such actions by force if necessary. The United States took the lead in gaining those commitments by NATO, and we must help NATO to keep them.

The NATO bombing campaign and the related artillery campaign against the Bosnian Serb military in which our forces are taking part skillfully is the right response to the savagery in Sarajevo. The campaign will make clear to the Bosnian Serbs that they have nothing to gain and everything to lose by continuing to attack Sarajevo and other safe areas and by continuing to slaughter innocent civilians. NATO is delivering that message loud and clear. And I hope all of you are proud of the role that the members of the United States Armed Forces are playing in delivering that message.

The war in Bosnia must end, but not on the battlefield, rather at the negotiating table. Just 2 weeks ago, we lost three of our finest American diplomatic representatives in a tragic accident in Bosnia as they were working for a negotiated peace. Today our negotiating team continues its work as well. And in the skies above Bosnia, our pilots and crews and their colleagues from other NATO countries are risking their lives for the same peace. We are proud of those who fly and those who are seeking to negotiate the peace.

Ladies and gentlemen, it is only fitting that we begin to commemorate this 50th anniversary of the end of World War II here at Hickam Air Force Base, for it was here, right here, that the guns of war shattered the peace of our land and drew America into the fight for freedom.

Looking out at the active duty troops who are with us today, representatives of the greatest fighting force in the world, standing watch for freedom all over the world, it is hard to imagine just how far our Nation had to come to win World War II. Just before 8 o'clock on December the 7th, 1941, when the first wave of enemy bombers swooped down upon our planes, parked wingtip to wingtip on this tarmac, all 231 aircraft at Hickam were either destroyed or damaged. At Pearl Harbor, as all of us know all too well, the pride of the Pacific's fleet lay in ruins.

But just a few hours later, just a few hours later, in the depth of our darkest hour, a handful of Army and Navy planes that were still able

to fly took to the skies from Hickam in search of the enemy fleet. The long journey to reclaim freedom for the Pacific and for the world began with that first mission from this very field. And it ended 50 years ago this week when the forces of freedom finally triumphed over tyranny.

In the days ahead, we will commemorate that victory, honor its heroes, and remember their sacrifice. But we will also celebrate more than the end of war; we will pay tribute to the triumph of peace. Through war in World War II, our people came together as never before. But after the war, they used their newfound sense of unity and common purpose at home and a sense of mission abroad to build for all of us 50 years of security, prosperity, and opportunity.

Today, we turn toward a new century, in a very different set of economic and political and social challenges. We now must draw on the legacy of those who won World War II and built peace and prosperity afterward to do our job to fulfill the spirit of that most remarkable of American generations. They understood the duty they owed to one another, to their communities, to their Nation, and to the world. After they won the war, they advanced the peace, the values, the liberties, and the opportunities that they fought and died to win.

Here on this island of peace that knows all too well the horror of war, let us vow to carry forward their legacy. The World War II generation taught us that when the American people find strength in their diversity and unity in a common purpose, when we stop arguing about our differences and start embracing what we have in common, nothing, nothing, can stop us. And so I say to you, if we apply the lessons that the World War II generation handed down to us to the challenges of the 21st century, nothing will stop us.

Thank you, and God bless you, and God bless America.

Thank you very much. And now, as we proceed with the program, I would like to introduce and call forward for some remarks my friend and colleague, your distinguished Governor, Governor Ben Cayetano.

NOTE: The President spoke at 12:17 p.m. at Hickam Air Force Base. In his remarks, he referred to Robert May, World War II veteran and founder of the 11th Bomb Group Association; Gov. Benjamin J. Cayetano of Hawaii; Gen. John

Lorber, USAF, Commander, Pacific Air Forces; Adm. Richard C. Macke, USN, Commander in Chief, U.S. Pacific Command; and Mayor Jeremy Harris of Honolulu.

Memorandum on Micro-Enterprise Programs
August 26, 1995

Memorandum for the Secretary of the Treasury

Subject: Micro-Enterprise Programs

I hereby direct you to take all appropriate actions to coordinate all micro-enterprise programs administered by the Federal agencies and departments. This should be accomplished through an interagency coordinating body chaired by the Administrator of the Community Development Financial Institutions (CDFI) Fund.

I also direct you to take the necessary steps for the establishment of a presidential awards program designed to honor outstanding micro-enterprise lenders, consistent with the mission of the CDFI Fund.

In discharging these responsibilities, you are directed to consult with the heads of other Executive departments and agencies as may be appropriate.

WILLIAM J. CLINTON

NOTE: This memorandum was released by the Office of the Press Secretary on September 1.

Letter to Congressional Leaders on the Alternative Plan for Federal Pay Adjustment
August 31, 1995

Dear Mr. Speaker: *(Dear Mr. President:)*

The law requires that the President transmit to the Congress an alternative plan for Federal pay adjustments if he views the pay adjustments that would take effect under the law as inappropriate. Therefore, to ensure that substantially larger increases do not take effect automatically, I am transmitting an alternative plan for the 1996 pay adjustments.

Under section 5303(a) of title 5, United States Code, the rates of basic pay would rise by 2.4 percent, effective in January 1996. In addition, pursuant to section 5304 of title 5, General Schedule employees also would receive an increase in their locality-based comparability payments that would cost 2.7 percent of payroll. When combined with the 2.4 percent basic pay increase, the locality-based payments would produce a total payroll increase of about 5.1 percent that would cost $3.9 billion in 1996—$2 billion more than the 2.4 percent pay increase I proposed in my 1996 Budget and which is included in my Balanced Budget Plan.

Sections 5303(b) and 5304a of title 5, however, provide me the authority to implement an alternate pay adjustment plan if I view the pay adjustments that would otherwise take effect as inappropriate due to "national emergency or serious economic conditions affecting the general welfare." As you know, Presidents have used such authority many times over the past 15 years.

In evaluating "an economic condition affecting the general welfare," the statute directs me to consider such economic measures as the Index of Leading Economic Indicators, the Gross National Product, the unemployment rate, the budget deficit, the Consumer Price Index, the Producer Price Index, the Employment Cost Index, and the Implicit Price Deflator for Personal Consumption Expenditures. I have reviewed these and other pertinent measures of our economy.

The budget discipline that my Administration has put in place has contributed to sustained economic growth and low inflation. To continue this discipline and its favorable impact on economic conditions, I have determined that an alternative pay adjustment of 2.4 percent is appropriate for the 1996 pay raises under sections 5303 and 5304. This raise matches the 2.4 percent basic pay increase that I proposed for military members in my fiscal 1996 Budget and that the Congress likely will include in the 1996 Defense Authorization bill.

Because many Federal civilian employees do not receive locality pay, I will put the bulk of the 2.4 percent adjustment into the general increase under section 5303, thus giving all employees a meaningful raise. I will apply the remainder to increasing the locality-based comparability payments under section 5304.

Accordingly, I have determined that the following alternate pay plan is appropriate:

(1) Under the authority of section 5303(b) of title 5, United States Code, the pay rates for each statutory pay system shall be increased by 2 percent, effective on the first day of the first applicable pay period beginning on or after January 1, 1996.

(2) Under the authority of section 5304a of title 5, United States Code, locality-based comparability payments in the amounts set forth on the attached table shall be effective on the first day of the first applicable pay period beginning on or after January 1, 1996. When compared with the pay-ments currently in effect, these comparability payments will increase the General Schedule payroll by about 0.4 percent.

Finally, the law requires that I include in this report an assessment of the impact that my decisions will have on the Government's ability to recruit and retain well-qualified employees. While I regret that our fiscal situation does not permit granting Federal employees a pay increase greater than 2.4 percent, I do not believe this will have any material impact on the quality of our work force. In accordance with the Federal Workforce Restructuring Act of 1994, I am committed to reducing Government employment substantially; consequently, hiring and attrition are very low. In addition, the Government has at hand many pay tools, such as recruitment bonuses, retention allowances, and special salary rates, to maintain the high quality work force that serves our Nation so very well.

Sincerely,

WILLIAM J. CLINTON

NOTE: Identical letters were sent to Newt Gingrich, Speaker of the House of Representatives, and Albert Gore, Jr., President of the Senate. The locality based comparability payment table was attached to the President's letter. This letter was released by the Office of the Press Secretary on September 1.

Remarks at the Joint Service Review at Wheeler Army Airfield in Honolulu
September 1, 1995

Thank you, General Weyand, for your wonderful remarks and, even more importantly, for your lifetime of service to the United States.

Governor Cayetano; Secretary Perry; Admiral Macke; Secretary Brown; General Shalikashvili; distinguished guests, especially our friends and as good a friends the veterans of the United States have ever had, Bob and Dolores Hope; the honored veterans of World War II; your families, your friends; ladies and gentlemen: As we gather to celebrate the end of a war that engulfed the world, I ask your leave to say a few words about recent developments in the prospects for peace in troubled Bosnia. Just a couple of hours ago, we were able to announce that the Foreign Ministers of Bosnia, Croatia, and Serbia have agreed to meet late next week in Geneva to try to reach agreement on the basic principles of a settlement for peace.

This is a positive step forward, but much remains to be done. Our own negotiating team will continue its work to bring the parties together. And as I said yesterday, no one should doubt NATO's resolve to prevent the further slaughter of innocent civilians in Sarajevo and the other safe areas in Bosnia.

I know that every American shares my pride in the skill and professionalism, the bravery, and the success of our pilots and crews and their NATO colleagues in the last few days. They are a shining example of the point that General Weyand just made.

Ladies and gentlemen, in this remarkable place, so much like Paradise, we recall when war made the idyllic Pacific hell on Earth. And we celebrate the generation of Americans who won that war and ensured the triumph of freedom over tyranny. Never before had the fight for freedom stretched across such a vast expanse of land and sea. And never before had the energies of the American people been so fully required or so fully joined.

At war, our people found a sense of mission in the world and shared purpose at home that became the bedrock for half a century of peace and prosperity. The World War II generation truly saved the world. Our security, our prosperity, our standing among other nations, all these are the legacy of the men and women, the heroes before us who we honor today.

Of course, today we can hardly imagine history taking a different turn. But when the Japanese Zeroes rounded those mountains and cut to pieces hundreds of aircraft here at Hickam and Kaneohe, when they then devastated the Pacific Fleet at Pearl Harbor, there was nothing inevitable about America's victory. As Asia fell to tyranny and fascism held sway from the Russian heartland all the way to the English Channel, free people everywhere must have stood in some doubt.

In the Philippines, our forces fought valiantly, making their final stand in Bataan and Corregidor. To this very day you can feel the memory of courage that hangs over the rock of Corregidor, as I had the privilege of doing last November when we commemorated the Pacific war in the Philippines. But the brave Filipino and American defenders could not hold out. After determined resistance, months of sickness and hunger, a massive artillery bombardment turned the sky to lead, and freedom's foothold there was lost.

President Roosevelt likened that time to the winter at Valley Forge, when our troops ran on courage and determination. Then, the enemy believed Americans would not sacrifice and fight on remote islands they had never heard of. But they were wrong.

Enlistment offices were flooded by American volunteers from our greatest cities and our smallest towns. Industry turned to military production. American consumption turned to rationing. And Americans turned to one another and found unity in the fight for freedom. Everyone pitched in, and together all across the country and all across the world, Americans got the job done.

Here in the Pacific, the long journey back to freedom began aboard the aircraft carrier *Hornet*. Four months after Pearl Harbor, an overloaded bomber lumbered down its flight deck. The crew wondered then if it would fall into the sea. But slowly, it took flight. Fifteen other airplanes followed on a daring one-way trip to Tokyo and on to China. Colonel Jimmy Doolittle's famous bombing raid sent a clear message: America had not given up, and America was on the offensive.

Two months later, our combat pilots and code-breakers, including Japanese-American intelligence officers, labored valiantly but in silence throughout the entire war. These people came together at a place called Midway. There, in 5 minutes of furious air attack, a single bomber squadron rallied the enemy fleet and changed the course of the war.

But still, soldiers, sailors, aviators, and Marines confronted terrors they had never imagined: in the disease-ridden swamps of Guadalcanal; in the water that ran red with the blood of Marines coming ashore at Tarawa; in the frozen wastelands of Kiska and Attu; in the planes flying the treacherous route over the Hump; in submarines rocked by depth charges. But always they pushed forward: into the skies over the Marianas, with barely enough fuel or daylight to fulfill the mission; in the seas off Leyte in the greatest naval battle of all time; from beachhead to beachhead on Guam, Saipan, and Tinian; and through the gunfire on Mount Suribachi, where the flag raising over Iwo Jima gave America its most stirring symbol of our common purpose and impending victory.

From beginning to end, the Americans who fought the Pacific war bestowed a glory upon our Nation with acts of heroism that will never be surpassed. On the very first day of the war, during the attack on Kaneohe Naval Base 40 miles from here, Lieutenant John Finn manned a machine gun out in the open. Constant bombing and strafing left him badly wounded. He went for first aid only when he was ordered to do so. And then, though he could hardly move, he helped to rearm returning American planes.

Three and a half years later on Okinawa, the last and bloodiest battle, an 18-year-old Navy corpsman named Robert Bush was giving plasma to a wounded officer. Artillery, machine gun, and mortar fire rained all around him, and he stands here today. Under ferocious attack he stood his ground, he emptied his pistol and then a carbine to repel the assault. He was blinded in one eye, but he continued holding the plasma, and he refused treatment for himself until the wounded officer was evacuated.

For their extraordinary service, John Finn and Robert Bush received the Congressional Medal of Honor. Today we recognize them and the other Medal of Honor winners who are here with us today. We ask them all to stand. [*Applause*] And now I would like to ask all the veterans of the Pacific war to stand and those who cannot stand, to raise their arms and be recognized so that we can express our appreciation to each of them. Please, gentlemen. [*Applause*]

To all of you and to your comrades who are watching at home on television and to the families of the more than 50,000 Americans who never came home from the Pacific, our Nation is forever grateful. We will never forget your fight for our freedom.

After the war and all you had endured, it was only natural that the World War II generation would turn your energies from the frontlines to the homefront. But thankfully, you did not turn your back on the world. Instead you helped to rebuild the devastated nations of Europe and Japan. And because you chose reconciliation over revenge, those who once were our enemies now are thriving democracies and strong friends.

Let me welcome all of those from other nations who have come here. And let me say especially how much the American people appreciate the recent powerful words of the Japanese Prime Minister, Mr. Murayama, when he expressed his nation's regret for its past aggression and its gratitude for the hand of reconciliation that this, the World War II generation, extended 50 years ago.

We owe the World War II generation our thanks because they also understood our Nation had a special role to play in continuing to preserve the peace and extending the reach of freedom. They forged the international institutions, the economic institutions, the United Nations, and NATO, that brought 50 years of security and prosperity to our Nation, to Europe, and to Japan. They kept our Armed Forces strong so that tyranny could never again run rampant, and they persevered in the cold war until the forces of freedom prevailed yet again.

Today, we continue to stand watch for freedom and to advance the cause of democracy across the Pacific, across the Atlantic, all around the globe. To meet that obligation and to preserve our own liberty, we must reaffirm our pledge to these fine men and women behind me and their counterparts throughout the world who bear today the responsibility that World War II's veterans shouldered so magnificently 50 years ago. So I say to you, you will always be the best trained, the best equipped, the best prepared fighting force in the world.

You represent the best of our country, our best hope for the future. And we know that for you and your children and your grandchildren, we must remain the strongest nation on Earth so that we can defeat the forces of darkness in our time and in the future, just as the veterans here defeated the force of tyranny 50 years ago.

Fifty years ago today, aboard a ship in Tokyo Bay, a Navy radioman penned this letter to his young son in Abilene, Texas. "When you grow a little older," he wrote, "you may think war to be a great adventure. Take it from me, it's the most horrible thing ever done by man."

Veterans of the Pacific, because you were willing to undergo the most horrible thing ever done by man, freedom is the order of the day in most of the world 50 years later.

Now it is for us to be true to your legacy of courage and devotion, to follow your lead in finding strength in America's diversity and unity in America's purpose. You worked together, and you never gave up. We must now preserve the liberty you won for us.

We say to you from the bottom of our heart, God bless you, and God bless America.

NOTE: The President spoke at 9:30 a.m. at the reviewing stand. In his remarks, he referred to Gen. Fred Weyand, USA (Ret.), former Army Chief of Staff; and entertainer Bob Hope and his wife, Dolores.

Remarks to the Troops at Wheeler Army Airfield in Honolulu
September 1, 1995

Audience member. Go Razorbacks!

The President. That's good. Promote that man. [*Laughter*]

Let me say, first of all, I thank you for the magnificent job that you did today. It was thrilling to all the veterans who are here and all their family members, and thrilling to the people in the United States who saw it on television. I thank you for your service and your devotion to your country. I hope you realize just how historic these few days are. I hope every one of you has the opportunity to get out and meet some of these World War II veterans who were here 50 years before you and whose legacy you have carried on so greatly.

I just want you to know that I, as the President and Commander in Chief and as an American citizen, am profoundly grateful to you for your service to this country, proud of what you represent, and I'm determined to do everything I can to support you, to see that we can, together, do our job to preserve our freedom and expand democracy. You are terrific.

Thank you. God bless you all.

NOTE: The President spoke at 11:43 a.m. on the lanai of the consolidated mess.

Letter to Congressional Leaders Reporting on the Deployment of United States Aircraft to Bosnia-Herzegovina
September 1, 1995

Dear Mr. Speaker: (Dear Mr. President:)

I last reported to the Congress on May 24, 1995, concerning U.S. support for the United Nations and North Atlantic Treaty Organization (NATO) efforts in the former Yugoslavia. I am today reporting on the use of U.S. combat and support aircraft commencing on August 29, 1995 (EDT), in a series of NATO air strikes against Bosnian Serb Army (BSA) forces in Bosnia-Herzegovina that were threatening the U.N.-declared safe areas of Sarajevo, Tuzla, and Gorazde. The NATO air strikes were launched following an August 28, 1995, BSA mortar attack on Sarajevo that killed 37 people and injured over 80. This tragic and inexcusable act was the latest in a series of BSA attacks on unarmed civilians in the safe areas.

By way of background, and as I am sure you are aware, the situation in eastern Bosnia-Herzegovina, and in particular the safe areas in the so-called "eastern enclaves," changed dramatically in the month of July. On July 11, 1995, the safe area of Srebrenica fell to the BSA following repeated BSA attacks. As a result of the fall of Srebrenica, over 40,000 persons were forced from their homes. Similarly, on July 26, 1995, the safe area of Zepa fell to attacking

BSA forces with over 8,000 persons displaced. As a result of these actions by the BSA, intensive discussions took place between U.N. and NATO authorities to address what could be done to enhance protection of the remaining safe areas of Sarajevo, Tuzla, Bihac, and Gorazde.

Under United Nations Security Council Resolution (UNSCR) 824 of May 6, 1993, certain portions of Bosnia-Herzegovina, including the city of Sarajevo, were established as safe areas that should be "free from armed attacks and from any other hostile act." Additionally, under UNSCR 836 of June 4, 1993, member states and regional organizations are authorized, in close coordination with the United Nations, to take all necessary measures, through the use of air power, to support the United Nations Protection Forces (UNPROFOR) in the performance of its mandate related to the safe areas. This mandate includes deterring attacks and replying to bombardments on the safe areas. Consistent with these and other resolutions, and in light of the recent events described above, the United Nations requested and NATO initiated air strikes on August 29, 1995. The air strikes were fully coordinated with the simultaneous artillery attacks by the Rapid Reaction Force.

On July 25, 1995, and August 1, 1995, the North Atlantic Council (NAC) approved a number of measures designed to meet further BSA attacks on the remaining safe areas with a "firm, rapid and decisive response." Specifically, the NAC agreed that a "direct attack (e.g., ground, shelling, or aircraft)" against any of the remaining safe areas would initiate air operations as determined by the common judgment of NATO and U.N. military commanders. The NATO air strikes commencing on August 29, 1995, are pursuant to the NAC's decision of August 1, 1995, and are an appropriate and necessary response to BSA actions. The NATO and U.N. operations are intended to reduce the threat to the Sarajevo safe area and to deter further attacks there or in any other safe area. These operations will continue until NATO and U.N. commanders determine that they have achieved their aims.

During the first day of operations, some 300 sorties were flown against 23 targets in the vicinity of Sarajevo, Tuzla, Gorazde, and Mostar. The aircraft struck a variety of BSA targets, including heavy weapons emplacements, command and control facilities, communications sites, air defense sites, and ammunition facilities. Initial reports suggest that the strikes were successful in damaging or destroying a number of BSA targets. No U.S. aircraft were destroyed during the strikes nor were any U.S. personnel killed,

wounded, or captured. At the same time that the air strikes were being conducted, the U.N.'s Rapid Reaction Force fired over 600 artillery and mortar rounds at BSA heavy weapons systems and ammunition storage sites around Sarajevo.

I authorized these actions in conjunction with our NATO allies to implement the relevant U.N. Security Council resolutions and NATO decisions. As I have reported in the past and as our current diplomatic actions clearly indicate, our efforts in the former Yugoslavia are intended to assist the parties to reach a negotiated settlement to the conflict. I have directed the participation of U.S. forces in this effort pursuant to my constitutional authority to conduct the foreign relations of the United States and as Commander in Chief and Chief Executive.

I am providing this report as part of my efforts to keep the Congress fully informed about developments in the former Yugoslavia, consistent with the War Powers Resolution. I am grateful for the continuing support that the Congress has provided, and I look forward to continued cooperation in this endeavor.

Sincerely,

WILLIAM J. CLINTON

NOTE: Identical letters were sent to Newt Gingrich, Speaker of the House of Representatives, and Strom Thurmond, President pro tempore of the Senate. This letter was released by the Office of the Press Secretary on September 2.

Remarks at the National Cemetery of the Pacific in Honolulu
September 2, 1995

Thank you very much, General Wilson, for your outstanding remarks, and even more for your service to our country. Reverend Perkins, Rabbi Goldfarb, Reverend Fujitani, Secretary Brown, General Shalikashvili, Secretary Perry, Members of Congress, Governor, Mayor, representatives of the Allied Nations who are here, and most of all, to the honored veterans of World War II: Today we commemorate this day 50 years ago, when the most destructive conflict in all human history came to an end. On this island, where America's peace was first shattered and then restored, we commemorate the tri-

umph of freedom over tyranny. We remember the extraordinary sacrifice that victory required. We honor the extraordinary generation of Americans who came together to meet the challenge of war and then, as General Wilson has said, worked together to seize the promise of peace.

World War II lasted 2,194 days. It stretched from Pearl Harbor to St. Petersburg, from the beaches of Normandy to the shores of Iwo Jima. It destroyed whole cities. It ravaged countrysides. It cost in total the lives of 55 million people: soldiers killed in battle, civilians and prisoners felled by disease and starvation, children buried in the rubble of bombed buildings, millions wiped out in the gas chambers. It cost the lives of all kinds of people.

And victory was won by the courage and character of citizen soldiers, citizens we remember for their bravery from Britain to Russia, from all the islands in the Pacific, island by island, and the battles that were won.

We remember all these Medal of Honor winners who are here among us today and humbly express to them our profound gratitude. We know that the heroism of millions of other men and women in uniform was never adequately recognized. We know that things happened here in the Pacific which bred a certain spirit and character and determination which infused the lives of those who served us when they came back home.

The war in the Pacific enjoyed the service, among others, of five men who became President of the United States, from the extraordinary heroism of President Kennedy and the legendary *PT–109* to President Bush who was shot down and rescued over the Pacific 51 years ago this very day.

We must never forget both the tragedy and the triumph of that time because it holds lessons for all time. We learned in World War II the forces of darkness give no quarter; they must be confronted and defeated. We learned that the blessings of freedom are never easy or free, they must always be defended.

We learned, too, something remarkable about America. This century, marked by so much progress and too much bloodshed, witnessed humanity's capacity for the best and the worst in life, is now known as the American Century.

For America, World War II was the pivot point of that century, the moment when we understood more than at any other time the core of the American spirit, the ties that bind us together, and the duty we owe to one another. Americans found in World War II unity in a shared mission, strength in a common purpose. More than ever, in World War II, our United States were truly united.

On December 7, 1941, James Daniels, the young Navy pilot born and raised on a farm in Missouri, was stationed aboard the U.S.S. *Enterprise*. As the ship steamed back toward Pearl Harbor, a general alarm sounded. He ran to his plane. He took to the skies to fly what would be the very first American combat mission of the war, because of what had happened at Pearl

Harbor. On that first mission, he searched in vain for the enemy fleet. He said, "I had no briefing, no map. I didn't know what the heck was going on." At nightfall, all he saw were the remains of our sinking fleet.

At that time, things looked pretty bleak for the United States, and a lot of people doubted that our democracy was up to the job. We had a standing Army of less than 200,000 men. Seventeen countries had larger armies than the United States on December 7, 1941. Our soldiers, believe it or not, trained with wooden rifles.

But our enemies sold short the strength and will of the American people, the grocery clerks and farmers, the students and salesmen, the short-order cooks and the factory workers, the whites, the blacks, the Hispanics, the Asian-Americans who served, including Japanese-Americans, the Native Americans, including the famous Navajo code-talkers. Most of them didn't know a lot about each other and even less of the world beyond our borders. But they had a core of shared traits bred in the American bone, determination, optimism, an unshakable dedication to freedom, and a faith that right would prevail. They merged their disparate voices into a harmonious chorus of defiance. President Roosevelt called them the incalculable force of American democracy, a free people united by a common purpose.

At home, they built democracy's arsenal, hundreds of thousands of planes, ships, tanks, and trucks. They planted the victory gardens. They collected scrap metal. They bought the war bonds. They rationed the gas. They learned to do with less in every part of their lives so those in uniform could conduct the war. And abroad, in the rain-drenched jungles and on rocky ridges, under the seas, over the waves, in the clouds, Americans fought on the frontlines of fear.

We know, and others have said today, that tens of thousands lost their lives, leaving their loved ones with only memories: parents who would never again see the pride of their lives, wives who would never again embrace their husbands, children whose fathers would never again take them swimming or see them graduate or know the adults they would become.

Here, in the peace of these sacred grounds where thousands of these brave Americans lie at rest, let us now join briefly in a moment of silence for those who gave their dreams for our freedom.

[*At this point, a moment of silence was observed.*]

Amen.

Fifty years ago today, on the deck of the aircraft carrier *Missouri* in Tokyo Bay, freedom finally prevailed. On this anniversary of V–J Day, we celebrate the end of the war but also the beginning of a new American era of peace and progress. At the end of the war, there were 12 million Americans in uniform, and 7 million were still overseas. We brought them home where they applied the lessons learned in war to the promise of peace. In peace, as in war, they understood that developing and uniting the energy and genius of every American is the best way to fulfill our country's potential.

Before the war, in the darkness of the Great Depression, millions of you veterans who are here today and your family members could only have dreamed of going on to college, could only have dreamed of building a better life than your parents had and of passing an even better one on to your children. But after the war, you seized the opportunities a grateful nation offered. You took advantage of the GI bill of rights. You became graduates. You bought your first home. And we know by the lives you've lived and the hopes you've passed on you took responsibility to make real your American dreams.

From Pearl Harbor to V–J Day, 16 million American women worked assembly lines; 300,000 more wore uniforms, drove trucks in combat zones, trained troops, nursed them back to health. After the war, America would begin to integrate this extraordinary force into the economy and into our Nation's military and change the face of America forever.

From Pearl Harbor to V–J Day, thousands of African-Americans distinguished themselves in military service, as Tuskegee Airmen and Triple Nickel paratroopers, Sherman tank drivers, and Navy Seabees. And slowly, after the war, America would begin to act on a truth so long denied, that if people of different races could serve as brothers abroad in uniform, they could surely live as neighbors at home.

In peace, the World War II generation gave America the security, the prosperity, and the progress the rest of us have known and cherished for half a century. You understood that you could together make the world a better place and that you could not permit America again to withdraw from the world, from former enemies and allies who were in ruins, from the looming threat of the cold war.

You gave us the Marshall plan. You chose reconciliation over revenge and helped to turn former enemies into close allies today. When the terrible new tyranny of communism arose, you held it in check until the power of democracy, the failure of repression, and the heroic determination of people to be free won the cold war. The seeds of democracy you planted and nurtured flower today in every corner of the globe.

From the cliffs of Normandy to the beautiful waters of Hawaii, we have celebrated over the last year and a half the extraordinary achievements of the generation that brought us victory in World War II. It is only fitting that here, in the middle of the ocean whose name means peace, the place where World War II began and ended for America, that we mark the war's end and honor the men and women who saved our world.

We owe it to the World War II generation to remember, but we owe them more. For just as freedom has its price, it also has its purpose, to enable all people to live up to their God-given potential and to continue the march of human progress. We, who are the heirs of their legacy, must always be the guardian of their dreams.

It falls now to us to stand against those who sow the seeds of war and to stand with those who take the risks of peace; to create a new prosperity for ourselves and for others; to help our people to prepare for the challenges of a new century; to strengthen our families, our faith, our communities; to give all Americans the opportunity to make the most of their lives.

In order to succeed, we must remain true to the spirit of that brilliant time. A time when our people cared for each other and sacrificed for others, when our Nation stood united in purpose and mighty in spirit as never before, a time when Americans forged the strength of their diversity into a community for victory and progress.

I told you earlier about Jim Daniels, who flew that first flight after Pearl Harbor. After Pearl Harbor, Jim took command of a 37-plane squadron. He logged 55 combat missions in the Pacific. The pilots under his wing came from as many different backgrounds as there are States in the Union, country boys who'd never seen a paved road, city dwellers who couldn't swim, well-to-do's and ne'er-do-well's. The only thing they had in common was that when they started flight school, they all didn't know how to fly. Jim Daniels remembers that, and I quote, "It didn't matter. We had a job to do, and we had to do it together."

On August 15th, 1945, the very last day of World War II, Jim Daniels was in the air again. It was a picture-perfect South Pacific morning. Then the word crackled over the radio: The enemy had surrendered; come on down. And so Jim Daniels, the American who flew on the first day and on the last day of our Nation's war, turned toward home. Today, Jim Daniels and his wife of 55 years, Helen, are here with us today. I'd like to ask them to stand. Mr. and Mrs. Daniels. [*Applause*] Bless you.

And I would like to ask all the veterans of World War II who are here today to stand and be recognized or to wave and be recognized. Please stand up. [*Applause*]

On August 15th, 1945, when Jim Daniels brought his plane down he descended through the clouds, along with all the other Americans in uniform, not toward a dark night of uncertainty but toward a bright future of hope, blessed by peace, graced by prosperity, a future in which more Americans than ever before would have the opportunity to live the lives God meant for them to have. It was a future won by a remarkable generation who found unity in war and built us a half century of progress in peace.

Now, my fellow Americans, we stand at the dawn of a new century, and their challenge has become ours. Their spirit must be ours as well. We pledge to carry on their work. And we vow to remember Jim Daniels' words, "We have a job to do, and we have to do it together." For us, as for them, the future depends upon it.

May God bless the Americans who brought us to this day, and may God bless America. Thank you.

NOTE: The President spoke at 9:21 a.m. In his remarks, he referred to Gen. Lewis H. Wilson, USMC (Ret.), former Commandant of the U.S. Marine Corps; and Rev. Kenneth D. Perkins, Rabbi Morris Goldfarb, and Rev. Yoshiaki Fujitani, who gave the invocations.

The President's Radio Address
September 2, 1995

Good morning. On this Labor Day weekend, I am paying tribute to some of the most important labor ever performed on behalf of the American people. Hillary and I are in Hawaii, where we have gathered with veterans of World War II to honor the bravery and sacrifice of an extraordinary generation of Americans.

Fifty years ago today, freedom triumphed over tyranny because those brave men and women, along with their colleagues from the allied nations, won a victory for freedom in the great struggle of World War II. America and the entire world will forever be in their debt.

So when the veterans of World War II came home, America was ready to pay its debt to our soldiers. Even before the war ended, President Roosevelt had already signed the GI bill into law. The GI bill opened the doors to college for veterans and helped them to get a start on life with a new home. And because our Nation provided that kind of opportunity for the World War II veterans, the opportunity to build good lives for themselves and their families, they in turn were able to play an enormous part in making our Nation the strongest and most prosperous on Earth.

Today, our challenge is to build on the foundation they laid, to keep our Nation strong and to give all Americans the opportunity to make the most of their own lives as we move into the 21st century.

A central part of that challenge is our effort to balance the Federal budget to relieve future generations of Americans of the crushing debt burden imposed almost entirely in the 12 years before I took office. During that 12-year period, our national debt quadrupled. In 1993, in our administration's economic program, we passed the bill that cut the deficit from $290 billion a year all the way down to $160 billion in just 3 years. In fact, our budget would be balanced today but for the debt run up in the 12 years before I became President.

Well, now we all have to go the rest of the way to balance that budget. But how we do it will say a lot about the values we have as a people and how we understand what's in our interest as we move to the next century. I have a good plan to balance the budget. But it will also give every American the opportunity to build a good life for himself or herself and to build better futures for their families.

Our plan will give our children the best possible education. It will keep our streets safer. It will take care of our elderly. It will maintain the purity and clarity of our environment. And it will maintain the strength of our Armed Forces.

Our plan also will keep faith with the men and women who have put their lives on the line to protect the freedoms that we now hold dear. For over 50 years, all Americans who joined our military have known that they are making a bargain with America and that in return for their service to our country our country will stand by them. The young men and women who serve today in our military give us some of the best years of their lives. And one of the things we tell them is that the longer they serve our country, the more our country will owe them when their service is done.

Amazingly, there are those today who believe that in order to balance the budget it's all right to break our commitment to a group of more than 800,000 men and women who've already served for at least 15 years. Now when these people joined the armed services, they were told that their retirement pay would be based on whatever salary they were earning the day they retired. But now in the name of balancing the budget, some propose that we scale back their retirement pay in a way that will mean cuts for retired military personnel of as much as $200 a month.

But I disagree. I believe that after asking so much of these men and women, our country should keep its commitment to them and find a better path to balance the budget. I have a plan to balance the budget that doesn't break our commitment to those who serve us in uniform. I think that kind of broken commitment is unconscionable. And as long as I'm President, we're not going to break our word to the members of our Armed Forces or our veterans.

For the last 50 years, our Nation has kept commitments to veterans who fought and won World War II, those whom we honor here in Hawaii and all across America this weekend, and to the veterans who followed them. That's a big reason that we now have the finest military in the world, outstanding and brave men and women who understand the duty they owe to one another, their communities, to our country, and to the world. I think we have an obligation to them. You know, they give up a lot to serve us, a lot in time and money. But one of the things they get in return is a commitment on retirement, a reward for the work—the important work they do.

So on this Labor Day weekend when we honor the work of all Americans, let us, all of us, recommit ourselves to the legacy of World War II, to the men and women in uniform today, and to our obligations to them.

Hillary and I wish all of you a wonderful Labor Day weekend. Thanks for listening.

NOTE: The address was recorded at 7:25 p.m. on September 1 at Wheeler Army Airfield in Honolulu, HI, for broadcast at 10:06 a.m. on September 2.

Remarks at a Wreath-Laying Ceremony Aboard the U.S.S. *Carl Vinson* in Pearl Harbor, Hawaii
September 2, 1995

Thank you very much. Thank you, Admiral Fluckey, for your kind words and far more for your astonishing service to our country. Secretary Dalton, Secretary Perry, Secretary Brown, Admiral Boorda, Admiral Macke, Admiral Zlatoper, Admiral Moorer, Admiral Moore, Captain Baucom, to all the distinguished veterans who are here from the United States Navy, the Marine Corps, the Coast Guard, and the merchant marine; to the crew of the U.S.S. *Carl Vinson*: It's good to be back. I was on board in San Francisco in August of 1993, and now I have two of these caps which I can proudly wear around the United States.

Fifty years ago today, on the other side of this Pacific Ocean, the war ended. It was a war that erupted in smoke and horror aboard the battleship *Arizona* and concluded with peace and honor aboard the battleship *Missouri*. Today we gather to offer a commemoration and to renew a commitment. We commemorate the men and women of the Navy, the Marine Corps, and their sister services who gave everything they had to the cause of freedom. And we commit ourselves to their legacy by meeting the great demands of this age with the same determination and fortitude.

More than 2,000 years ago, Pericles gave a funeral oration in which he said it was the actions of his fallen soldiers and not his own words that would stand as their memorial. Today we say the same about our own beloved war dead, and you, their brothers and sisters still living who served alongside them. Your deeds in the Pacific will forever remain the greatest tribute to the American naval services.

Millions of sailors, aviators, submariners, and marines joined in the effort against Japan. They steered and stoked and flew and fought aboard thousands of ships and planes and boats. They were transported ashore by the Coast Guard, sustained by the merchant marine, supported by the WAVE's, and healed by the Medical Corps. You who served lived in a world of gray steel and saltwater, coarse sand and endless skies, violent rain and hard wind, white coral and precious red blood. Long days and endless nights passed between hard battles. But the frontline was usually no further away than the bow of your ship.

The Pacific journey started where we stand today in Pearl Harbor, our darkest dawn. Here in the span of an hour, as they put out fires and struggled to save their ship, farm boys became sailors and teenagers grew into men. They fought in a war unlike any previous war, waged in places most Americans had never heard of, in disease-filled jungles and on an ocean we once thought too huge to fight across.

It was a war of battles dominated by aircraft carriers, first at Coral Sea, then at Midway when a superior Japanese force was undone by American code-breaking and the courage of our pilots who dove into impossible odds to sink the enemy carriers.

It was a war where, for the very first time, sailors, soldiers, aviators, and leathernecks all worked together. At Guadalcanal, the Navy, the Marines, and the Army began to turn the tide in freedom's favor. Before they were done, sunken ships had transformed the sea floor into a steel carpet. The surrounding waters actually were renamed "Iron Bottom Sound." In the Gilberts, the Marshalls, the Marianas, the Carolines, amphibious forces shot to shore with a prayer and the cover of their comrades in the air and at sea.

It was a war that required unparalleled courage: at Leyte, where PT boats took on cruisers, where battleships damaged at Pearl Harbor returned to break the back of the Japanese fleet; at Iwo Jima, where more than 6,800 marines gave their lives to have our flag snap in the wind atop Mount Suribachi; and finally, on Okinawa, the war's final and bloodiest struggle.

In the Pacific, no two battles were the same, but each was fought for freedom. In the Pacific, our leaders were colorful and could not have been less alike, but they all shared a certain American greatness: Nimitz and Halsey, Spruance and Holland Smith, and Admiral Arleigh Burke, who honored me with his presence at dinner in Washington just a few weeks ago. And of course, behind them all was President Roosevelt, who had been Assistant Secretary of the Navy in World War I and who remained the guardian and inspiration to the Navy from his first day to his last as President.

In the Pacific, each ship was an outpost of liberty. In the Pacific, every American demonstrated that, as Admiral Nimitz said, they had uncommon valor as a common virtue.

In the Pacific, we won a war we had to win, but at a terrible cost of tens of thousands of lives never lived fully out. That sacrifice touches all of us today. But those of you here, more than anyone, who lost a shipmate or a friend, someone with whom you refueled a plane or scraped a railing or reloaded an overheated 40-millimeter gun, you endured. And the basic American values of courage, optimism, responsibility, and freedom all triumphed. And all of us are in your debt.

I would like to ask all the veterans of the Pacific war who are here to stand or, if you cannot stand, to wave your hand and be recognized. Please stand up. [*Applause*]

We also owe you a very great deal because of what you did with your remarkable victory. You did not leave your ideals at the war's edge; you brought them home. You carried them to college on the GI bill and into work. And together, you created the most prosperous nation on Earth. You extended our vision across the globe to rebuild our allies and our former adversaries, to win the cold war, to advance the cause of peace and freedom.

So to all of you who brought us from the *Arizona* to the *Missouri*, all of us who followed will always remember your commitment, your deeds, and your sacrifice. They are as constant as the tides and as vast as this great Pacific Ocean.

May God bless you, and God bless America.

NOTE: The President spoke at 11:30 a.m. on the flight deck. In his remarks, he referred to Rear Adm. Eugene Fluckey, USN (Ret.), Congressional Medal of Honor recipient; Adm. Jeremy M. Boorda, USN, Chief of Naval Operations; Adm. Ronald J. Zlatoper, USN, Commander in Chief, U.S. Pacific Fleet; Adm. Thomas H. Moorer, USN (Ret.), former Chairman, Joint Chiefs of Staff; Rear Adm. Edward Moore, Jr., USN, Commander, Cruiser Destroyer Group Three; and Capt. Larry C. Baucom, USN, Commanding Officer, U.S.S. *Carl Vinson.*

Remarks at a Stamp Unveiling Ceremony Aboard the U.S.S. *Carl Vinson* in Pearl Harbor
September 2, 1995

Postmaster General Runyon, let me begin by thanking you for the outstanding job you have done in promoting this project. I have enjoyed very much participating with you in it. Secretary Dalton, Secretary Brown, and distinguished military leaders who are here, Mrs. Howard and Mr. Carter, who assisted us in the unveiling, I am delighted to unveil this fifth and final set of stamps honoring the men and women who brought our Nation victory in World War II.

Again, let me congratulate the Postal Service on producing these stamps. They will for a long time remind all of our people of the spirit that animated our triumph and the common cause that united us 50 years ago. They also remind us that in World War II, as never before in our history up to that time, the many who make up our Nation came together as one. Old divisions melted away as our people turned to the job of liberating the world and then to the task of creating a better future at home.

We are fortunate to have with us today in this unveiling two individuals whose service exemplifies the best of this changed America that emerged from World War II and the best of our changed military.

Herbert Carter was a member of the famed Tuskegee Airmen. He flew 77 combat missions over North Africa and Italy. He has a chest full of medals and a record of real bravery and achievement. His accomplishments and those of thousands of other African-Americans who served our Nation so valiantly helped to open the way to the day when all Americans will be judged by the content of their character and not by the color of their skin.

Rita Howard joined the Navy Nurse Corps in 1941. At war's end, she was serving on board of the hospital ship U.S.S. *Refuge,* mending the wounds and lifting the spirits of newly freed POW's. Because of her and hundreds of thousands of women like her who wore the uniform and millions more who helped build democracy's arsenal, the role of women in our Nation was changed forever. And, I might add, the role of women in our military has been changed forever. Their achievements cleared the way for women to reach their full potential whether in boardrooms or on board bombers.

The generation that fought World War II came home and built America into the richest, freest nation in history. They returned to their towns and cities and built careers and communities. Some, like Herbert Carter and Rita Howard, remained in uniform, safeguarding our liberties and ensuring that tyranny never again threatened our shores. Together, they built a half a century of progress and security for which we must all be eternally grateful.

I hope all Americans will remember the debt they owe to Herbert Carter, to Rita Howard, to the millions of others they see embodied in these fine stamps. And I hope all of us will be inspired to carry forward their work of continuing to make our Nation safe and strong and free.

Thank you very much.

NOTE: The President spoke at approximately 12:40 p.m.

Remarks at a World War II Commemorative Service in Honolulu, Hawaii
September 3, 1995

Thank you, Bishop, for your remarks, your service, your introduction. To all of the distinguished people who have participated in this magnificent program today, let me say that after Captain Lovell spoke and Colonel Washington sang and the Bishop made his remarks, I'm not sure there's much else to say. [*Laughter*] And I'm certain that the rest of us have been warmed by this ceremony beyond belief.

But I do believe—I think there are two brief things that ought to be said. One is we ought to express our appreciation to this magnificent choir for the music they have given us today. [*Applause*] And secondly, inasmuch as this is the last of a long and magnificent series of events commemorating the 50th anniversary of the end of World War II, I would like to ask General Mick Kicklighter and any other members of the World War II Commemorative Commission who are here to stand and receive our gratitude for a job very well done. [*Applause*]

Let me ask you as we close what you believe people will say about World War II 100 or 200 or 300 years from today. I believe the lesson will be that people, when given a choice, will not choose to live under empire; that citizens, when given a choice, will not choose to live under dictators; that people, when given the opportunity to let the better angels of their natures rise to the top, will not embrace theories of political or racial or ethnic or religious superiority; that in the end, we know that Thomas Jefferson was right: God created us all equal, with the rights to life, liberty, and the pursuit of happiness, and whatever differences there are among us, we have more in common.

That was the ultimate lesson of the magnificent remarks that Captain Lovell made. And it better be the ultimate lesson we learn from the tragedy of World War II. As we move into the 21st century, as the world gets smaller and smaller, as the fragile resources we have that sustains life and permit progress have to be maintained and enhanced, we must remember that.

That was a lesson that some people knew even in World War II. And I'd like to close with a reading from this little book, "The Soldier's and Sailor's Prayer Book," that a lot of our veterans carried with them in battle in World War II. This is a prayer written by the famous American poet Stephen Vincent Benét that became known as the President's prayer because President Franklin Roosevelt prayed it on Flag Day, June 14th, 1942. I hope this is what people remember as the lesson of World War II one and two hundred years from now:

"God of the free, grant us brotherhood and hope and union, not only for the space of this bitter war but for the days to come, which shall and must unite all the children of Earth. We are, all of us, children of Earth. Grant us that simple knowledge: If our brothers are oppressed, then we are oppressed. If they hunger, then we hunger. If their freedom is taken away, our freedom is not secure. Grant us the common faith that man shall know bread and peace; that he shall know justice and righteousness, freedom, and security; an equal opportunity and an equal chance to do his best not only in our own land but throughout the world. And in that faith, let us march toward the clean world our hands can make."

Amen, and God bless America.

NOTE: The President spoke at 11:18 a.m. at the Waikiki Band Shell. In his remarks, he referred to Bishop James Matthew, World War II veteran and bishop of the United Methodist Church; Capt. James A. Lovell, Jr., former astronaut; and Lt. Col. D.C. Washington, vocalist.

Remarks at the Dedication of California State University at Monterey Bay in Monterey, California
September 4, 1995

Thank you so much. It's a gorgeous day. It's a wonderful reception. I thank you. I can't imagine anybody in America who's having a better time on Labor Day than I am right now, and I thank you.

Senator Boxer and Lieutenant Governor Davis, Congressman Mineta, Secretary West, Chancellor Munitz, President Peter Smith, my longtime friend from the time he was the lieutenant governor of Vermont and I was the Governor of Arkansas. We worked on education together. You've got a good person here; you're very lucky to have him. And my good friend Congressman Sam Farr who has worked like a demon for this project and talks to me about it incessantly. You think I came out here because of Leon, but the truth is I showed up today because I couldn't bear to watch Sam Farr cry if I hadn't come. [*Laughter*] And let me say to Beatrice, I'm glad your daddy is here. If you were my daughter, I'd have been very proud of you here today. You were great. You were terrific. Thank you. Stand up there. Give him a hand. [*Applause*] Thank you, sir. Thank you.

I want to thank all the others who made this possible, the other distinguished platform guests. And to Milrose Basco, thank you for singing the national anthem. You were terrific. I thank the Watsonville Community Band, the Bethel Missionary Church Choir, the Western Stage of Hartnell College, El Teatro del Campesino, everyone who kept you occupied and entertained in the beginning. I thank the members of the general assembly who worked hard to make this possible.

You know, I was listening to Leon talk about the time he introduced me in Rome. That's really true, he translated my remarks in Rome. We were in the town square there—thousands and thousands of those handsome, robust Romans were around—Leon and I standing before the cheering crowd. They were chattering away in Italian. The attractive, young mayor of Rome was to my left. I leaned over, and I said, "What are they saying, Mayor?" He said, "Do you really want to know?" [*Laughter*] I said, "Yes." He said, "They're saying, who's that guy up there with Leon Panetta?" [*Laughter*] This fall I'm going to take him to Ireland and give him a dose of his own medicine. [*Laughter*]

We were in there a few moments ago, and I was meeting some of the folks that helped to make this project possible. One lady went through the line and shook my hand, and she said, "Mr. President, follow your heart, and do what Leon tells you to." I want to say if she had told me to do what Sylvia tells me to, I'd come nearer to doing it. [*Laughter*]

One of the reasons that I felt so strongly—the first time I had a talk with Leon Panetta and I asked him to become head of the Office of Management and Budget, which, in many ways, in a time when we're downsizing the Government and when we have to cut so much and still try to save enough money to invest in things like education, it was really important to me to have someone who not only understood the value of a dollar and how the budget worked but someone I thought had good, basic American values and knew what it would take to build the community of America for the 21st century. That's why I asked Leon Panetta to do that job. And I have to tell you, when you pick somebody you don't know for a position, you don't know real well, it's very difficult to know whether you're making the right decision. You always kind of look for clues, you know. And I'm now old enough and been in enough jobs that I've hired thousands of people to do different things. And I have to tell you, one of the things that made the biggest impression on me, probably because of my own experience, was the partnership that Leon and Sylvia had working for this congressional district over so many years. That's the kind of thing we need more of in our country today, and it made a big impression. And I thank you.

I've got a lot to say today, and you may not remember much of it. If you don't remember anything else, remember this: This country will be the greatest country in the world in the 21st century, just as it has been in the 20th century, if, but only if, we take all the challenges that are before us and approach them in the same way that you approached the challenge that you faced when Fort Ord closed and you made this the 21st campus for the 21st century in California.

We are at a period of historic change, the way we work, the way we live, the way we relate to each other, the way we relate to others beyond our borders, the way we think about our lives, the way we think about the relationship of the economy to the environment, the way we think about the relationship of managers to workers, the way we think about our respective obligations to raise our children well and to succeed in the workplace at the same time. These things are undergoing a profound change, greater than anything we have seen in our country since the beginning of the 20th century when we moved from being primarily an agricultural and rural country into being an industrial and more urban country. We are out of the cold war. We have moved into a global economy. We are transforming our economy, even manufacturing and agriculture, into a more information-based, technology-based economy. Things are changing rapidly. And what we know and what we can learn more than ever before will determine what we can earn and, in some cases, whether we can earn.

This is a period of very, very profound change. And when you face these kind of challenges, it matters not only what particular decisions you make but how you do it. And what has always made America great is, when the chips were down and when we have a lot of challenges, we overlook our differences, we embrace what we have in common, we work together, and we work for tomorrow. That is what I have been trying to say to the American people since the day I announced for President in October '91. This is a new and different time. We've got to work together, and we've got to work for tomorrow.

You know, I just had the profound honor of representing all of you as the President to commemorate the 50th anniversary of the end of World War II. It was moving to me in many ways. But I would ask you to remember what happened to this country. If you look back in history now, you think, well, we couldn't have lost. But in the war in the Pacific, we lost all our early battles, and we had to come back. In the war in Europe, before we got in, Great Britain hardly won a battle for 2 years, and they had to come back. When we began, there were 17 countries in the world with bigger armies than the United States had. And we had to put it all together. It looked so inevitable in the light of history, but it wasn't. It happened because free people beat dictators. People who chose to live together beat empires. People who willfully found common ground and bridged their differences joined hands and moved forward. That's how we did that. And don't you ever forget it. And that's what we have to do now if we want this country to be what we expect it to be in the 21st century.

It's amazing how long it took us after the war to learn the lessons of the war in the peace. We honored our veterans. We gave them the GI bill. They had a chance to go to college, they had a chance to buy a home because we recognized our obligations to each other and to the future. We built the greatest economy the world had ever known in the aftermath of the Second World War. We rebuilt our former enemies, Germany and Japan. We rebuilt our allies in Europe who were devastated. We expanded the benefits of global commerce to Latin America, to Asia, and to other places. We did a good job in that because we worked together and we worked for tomorrow. We won the cold war because we were strong and resolute and because eventually people's hunger for freedom brought down the Iron Curtain, because we worked together and we worked for tomorrow.

Now, if you look at what we have to do today in this period of profound change—I will say again, a period of change as great as we have faced in 100 years—we have to change the whole way our National Government works. It has to be smaller. It has to be less bureaucratic. It has to be more oriented toward results and releasing the energies of people and establishing these kinds of partnerships and less oriented toward just telling people exactly what they have to do.

We have got to balance the Federal budget. You know, I say this to all the people who like Government programs that can promote education, as I do. This country never had a permanent deficit in all of our history until 1981. We had deficits when we needed them. When the economy was slow, we'd spend a little more money and juice it up. Then when the economy got good, we'd balance the budget and clear our debts and go on. Or we'd borrow money when we wanted to invest in something, just the way you borrow money if you start a business or build a home or buy an automobile. But we didn't borrow money just to go out to dinner at night. We weren't borrowing money all the time until 1981. And after having been a country now for 219 years now, almost 219 years, we quadrupled our debt in only 12 years.

That's bad for you and me. Our budget would be balanced today if it weren't for the interest run up in the 12 years before I became President and that we have to pay on that debt. It would be balanced today. And next year, unless we have real luck with the interest rates, next year interest on the debt will exceed the defense budget. Now, that's not good. That's not a good thing. Nobody in this audience, I don't care if you're a Democrat or a Republican or an independent or whatever your politics are, you don't want that little baby that was held up to me in the audience a few moments ago to grow up into a world where everybody pays taxes just to pay interest on the debt. Nobody's got any money to invest in this kind of project a generation from now. So we have to do that.

We have to reassert the values that made this country great, that helped us in the war and afterward. We have to have policies and practices that strengthen our families and our communities and that reward personal responsibility. And above all, we have got to equip our people to meet the challenges of the 21st century. Our parents built America and passed it on to my generation. And we dare not let this time pass without making sure that we have given the next generation a chance to live the American dream.

I will say again, there is nothing we have to do at the national level as a people that we cannot do if we follow the directions that you have laid out here: common sense, common ground, higher ground. Think about what we've got in common. Think about possibilities, not problems. Believe in the future.

Colonel Hank Hendrickson, who was once Fort Ord's commander and is now the vice president of administration for this fine institution, says, and I quote, "On the same ground where we once taught 18-year-old soldiers to fight and survive in a war environment, we are now teaching 18-year-old students to compete and flourish in the global economy." That's what you have done together, and that's what America must do together.

I am proud of the contribution that your National Government could make. I think we owed it to you, with the economic development grants, the environmental cleanup, the help for the displaced workers, the young AmeriCorps volunteers who were working to help people here. I am proud of all that. But that $240 million was an investment in your future, and you earned it. You contributed to our victory in the cold war. Your Nation could not leave you out in the cold. It was the right thing to do. But you made it possible by all the things that you did here.

So I ask everybody who is cynical about America's future to just look around. You want to know what to do, you want to know how we ought to do our business in Washington, how should we decide how to balance the budget, look around. We ought to behave the way you did. You couldn't run a family, a business, a university, a church, a civic organization, you couldn't run anything in this country the way people try to run politics in Washington— [*laughter and applause*]—where talking is more important than doing. The night's sound bite on the evening news, if you want to be on it, you know you have to have conflict, not cooperation. If you have cooperation, people will go to sleep, and you won't get on the news. You have to exaggerate every difference and make it 10 times bigger than it is. And you have to be willing to sacrifice every good in the moment for the next election. No one could run anything that way.

So we have an obligation now to do what you do, to do what you did here. The large buildings to my left and right were battery headquarters for artillery units. One is the library, the other is a multimedia center. I don't know whether a Republican or a Democrat turned them into that. I just know it's good for the country because you're going to be better educated. That's the way we ought to run the country.

The old airfield will become an airport for business planes. And when people land and give their numbers, they won't have to talk about politics, they'll just be permitted to land and do their business. Not only that, the golf courses are going to be operated for the public.

This is happening throughout California, you know. And Alameda County, where I'm going later, machinists who once welded Bradley fighting vehicles together are now going to be building electric cars for the 21st century. Up in Sacramento, Packard Bell has already hired almost 5,000 people, including 500 jobs they brought back from overseas, to assemble personal computers at a former Army depot. We can do this, folks. It's not complicated; it's just hard. It's hard. It requires a lot of effort, but it's not complicated.

All across America on this Labor Day, our people are beginning to convert from the cold war economy to the new economy of the 21st century. And we are trying to do what we can to help. We brought the deficit down from $290 billion a year when I took office to $160 billion this year. Interest rates are down. Trade and exports are up. Investment in education and technology and research are all up. We've got 7 million new jobs, 2½ million new homeowners, 1½ million new small businesses, a record in this time period.

California lagged behind because California rose so much on the economy of the cold war. So when the cold war was over, you got hurt worse than other States. Then you had to deal with earthquakes and fires and—you know, God just wanted to test you and see how strong you were. Leon's a Catholic; he tells me it's a character-builder. [*Laughter*] He's advising me on this every day.

But California is coming back. The unemployment rate is down, but much more importantly, people here are building for the long run. That's what this is. This is a decision. This thing we celebrate today is a decision that you made for yourselves, your children, and your grandchildren. It's a decision you made for the 21st century. It's a decision you made by working together to prepare for tomorrow. It's not very complicated. That's what your country needs to do. And that's what I'm determined that we will do.

Now I want to emphasize one of our greatest challenges on this Labor Day when we reward work. One of our greatest challenges is that the global economy works so differently from the economy we've lived in that everybody's work is no longer being rewarded. If you had told me—I thought I understood this economy. I was a Governor for a dozen years. I worked on base closings and defense conversion, everything like that, with committees like the one that made this possible. I thought I really understood this economy. But if you had told me on the day I became President that in 30 months we'd have over 7 million jobs, the stock market would be at 4,700, corporate profits would be at a record high, we'd have 2½ million new homeowners, we'd have the largest number of new small businesses recorded in any 2-year period since the end of World War II, but the median wage would go down one percent, I wouldn't have believed it. And most of you wouldn't either.

But technology is changing so fast, so many jobs are in competition in the global economy, and money can move across national borders like that—and nothing any person in public life can do will stop that—that the working people of this country that are bringing our economy back have not gotten their fair share of our prosperity. And that is our biggest challenge on this Labor Day.

What is the answer? The answer, first of all, is not to close our borders; it's to continue to expand trade because trade-related jobs pay about 20 percent more than jobs that have nothing to do with the global economy. We can't turn away from that. But we have to be for fair as well as free trade. And that's why I'm so proud of the agreement we negotiated with the Japanese over automobiles and auto parts. We want more trade but on terms that are fair to all Americans.

The other thing we have to do is to do more of what you're doing. We must, we must, see that all of our young people finish high school and that everybody, everybody, has access to education after high school. We've got to open the doors of college education to all Americans. Our administration has worked hard to make more affordable college loans available to all the young people in this country. Millions of people now can borrow money to go to college at lower cost on better repayment terms. We have worked hard to try to increase our investment in education from Head Start through college.

I have two proposals now before the Congress in our balanced budget plan that I pray will pass. One would give American middle class people a tax deduction for the cost of all education after high school without regard to the age of the people who get it. The other would collapse about 70 different Government training programs into a big pot of money. And whenever anybody is unemployed or underemployed or on welfare, they could get a voucher worth $2,600 a year to take to the nearest community education institution like this one. Don't go through a program; go to your local institution. That's something we could do to provide a "GI bill" in our time for America's working people. Those two things would lift the incomes of the American people.

I also think we ought to raise the minimum wage. Let me tell you, if we don't raise the minimum wage this year, on January 1st of next year, our minimum wage in terms of what the money will buy will be at a 40-year low. I want a high-wage, high-growth, high-opportunity, not a hard-work, low-wage 21st century. And I think you do, too. And that's what we ought to do.

Now, I believe that the reason wages are stagnant for so many people is that we haven't done enough to educate our people. We haven't done enough to try to raise the incomes of our people. The Government can't do all that, however. The people in the private sector have a responsibility, too. The best American companies are out there today sharing their profits with their workers and making sure that they're well-treated. And all American companies on this Labor Day should be challenged to follow the example of the best American companies. The people of this country are our most important resource.

In the next year or so, all of you are going to have to decide what you think the answer to this wage problem is. There are people who will tell you that the answer to the—the real reason middle class wages are stagnant is that welfare people are taking all your tax money away or that we have too many immigrants or that affirmative action is destroying opportunities for the middle class.

Well, let me tell you, in each of those areas, we have problems. But that's not the real reason for the middle class economic anxieties. We ought to move more people from welfare to work because they'd be better off and their kids

would be better off and our country would be stronger. But the welfare rolls are going down as the job rolls go up. It's only 5 percent of our budget. I want desperately to have more welfare reform. I've done more in the last 2 years than was done in the previous 12 years to move people from welfare to work. And I will continue to do that. But if we want to raise wages of middle class people, we have to have good jobs, good educations, and a competitive economic policy.

If you look at the immigration issue, there are problems. We have too many illegal immigrants in the country. We've done what we could to close the borders and to send people back. But you know what? This is a nation of immigrants. Most of us do not have ancestors who were born here. So I've tried to deal with this issue in a responsible way. Former Congresswoman Barbara Jordan of Texas, a great American, headed a commission for us and said, here's how you can relieve the problems of immigration in America and still make us a nation of immigrants.

When I was in Hawaii—let me just tell you one story. When I was in Hawaii for the 50th anniversary of World War II, the commission asked me if I would spend the afternoon playing golf with six veterans of World War II. And I did, and we just sort of lolled around. We didn't even finish the round. We had the best time in the world talking.

Let me tell you, one of those men was a Japanese-American who came to this country on his own as a boy because he dreamed of coming to America. When the war broke out, they put him in an internment camp. He still volunteered to serve his country. By the grace of God, the war ended about 3 days before he would have been on an island fighting against two of his own brothers who were in uniform for Japan. When the bomb was dropped in Japan, it injured his house and his mother, and his youngest brother subsequently died of radiation poisoning.

There's not another country in the world that could tell that story. Why? Because people from all over the world wanted to be part of what is America. And we should never forget that. We'll have times when we can have higher immigration quotas and times when we should have smaller ones because of the economy and how much it takes to absorb people. But we should never, ever, ever permit ourselves to get into a position where we forget that almost everybody here came from somewhere else and that America is a set of ideas and values and convictions that make us strong.

I feel the same way about this affirmative action issue. I have lived with this for 20 years now. And let me tell you, there are problems with the affirmative action programs of the Federal Government. I've already abolished one that I thought was excessive, and I was glad to do it. And we're reforming a lot of them. But let me tell you that we are a better, stronger country because we have made a conscious effort to give people without regard to their race or gender an opportunity to live up to their God-given capacities. We are a better, stronger country.

I'm against quotas. I'm against reverse discrimination. I'm against giving anybody unqualified anything they're not qualified for. But I am for making a conscious effort to bring the American people together. If you doubt it, look at our military. We have the best military in the world. Nobody doubts it. It's the most successfully integrated institution in the United States of America, and nobody unqualified gets anything. But there was a conscious effort made to do that. Last year, a quarter of a million new roles were opened to American women in military services, and they're doing every one of them very well. And that's just one example.

So I say to you, let's look at this, let's fix the problems in America, but let's do it with common sense. Let's look for common ground. Let's do it the way you built this great institution. Let's do it in a way that will grow our economy.

So, when we come back to Washington, we've got some tough decisions to make. I've got a plan to balance the budget. The Congress has two different plans in the House and Senate. We have to cut Government spending. I'm all for that. But we ought not to cut education. We ought to increase our investment in education as we balance the budget.

We ought to cut taxes, but we shouldn't cut taxes so much and give such tax cuts to people who don't need them that we have to cut Medicare and Medicaid and hurt our obligations to the elderly people in this country who depend upon them for health care.

We ought to cut the size of Government, and we ought to cut regulation. Let me tell you, we have already reduced the size of your Federal Government by 150,000 people. It will be reduced by 270,000 people if not another law is passed by what's already been done. We have reduced thousands of regulations. We ought to do more of that. But we should not cripple the ability of the American people through their Government to assure safe food, clean air, clean water, and a decent environment, because we all have a stake in that.

I want all of you to follow this very closely. When I go back to Washington and the Congress takes up its business, this will be no ordinary time. For the first time, both parties are committed to balancing the Federal budget. The question is, how will we do it, and what will the priorities be? And that will determine what kind of country we're going to be.

I believe we've got to work together and work for tomorrow. I do not want any more of the politics of partisan polarization. I believe the American people are pretty much like all of you sitting around here today. You are celebrating an incredible achievement that you know is a good, right, decent thing. And you are here as Americans.

Now, there'll be plenty of things for us to disagree on, but at this moment our national security in the 21st century depends upon our agreeing to invest in our people and to grow our economy and to pull our country together as we balance this budget. So the decisions made in the next 60 to 90 days will determine what kind of country we're going to be into the 21st century. And I ask every one of you, without regard to your party or your philosophy, to implore your Representatives to reach for that common higher ground, to work together, and to work for tomorrow.

Just think about it. By Christmas, if we do our job right, we could have passed a balanced budget, provided for that tax deduction for education expenses, overhauled welfare, expanded educational opportunities, strengthened instead of undermined health care security, and put our people on the road to raising their incomes as they work harder.

We can do that. But we've got to do what you did here. We have got to work together, and we've got to work for tomorrow. Wish us well, insist on it, and help us get it done.

Thank you, and God bless you all.

NOTE: The President spoke at 12:02 p.m. at the Campus Center. In his remarks, he referred to

Lt. Gov. Gray Davis of California; Chancellor Barry Munitz, California State University; and Beatrice Gonzales-Ramirez, student, California State University at Monterey Bay.

Remarks at the Alameda County Labor Day Picnic in Pleasanton, California
September 4, 1995

The President. Thank you. Can you hear me in the back? Good. Ladies and gentlemen, I am so glad to be here to share Labor Day with you, to count our blessings and to embrace our challenges. But let me just begin by thanking you for that wonderful welcome. I feel right at home, and I'm proud to be with the working families in this country.

I also want to say how very pleased I am to be here with all the distinguished labor leaders and public officials who are here behind me from the State of California—some from our administration—to be here with President Donahue. You know, this is his birthday. He has to celebrate his birthday on Labor Day. He gets a two-fer today, so we ought to say happy birthday, Tom.

I'm delighted to be here with Jack Henning, who still gives one of the best speeches I ever heard; with John Sweeney and Lenore Miller and Chuck Mack and George Kourpias and all the other labor leaders who are here. I thank Judy Goff and Owen Marron for having me here. And I want to say a special word of thanks to the people who represent you in Congress, two of the finest people in the entire United States Congress, Congressman Ron Dellums and Senator Barbara Boxer. They are great people.

You know, we are going through a sea change in American life. You know it, and I know it. What I want to tell you is I believe that when the history of this time is written and people look back on how you and other ordinary Americans lived, they will say that this period represented the biggest challenge and the biggest change to the way we live and work and raise our families of any period since 100 years ago, when we changed from being a primarily agricultural and rural society to being an industrial society and a more urban one.

All of you know the facts. We've ended the cold war. We're moving into a global economy. We have more and more competition and more and more technology. We have more opportunities and more fears. And there are a lot of good things that are going on today, but there are a lot of troubling things as well.

And I came here to tell you that in the next 90 days in Washington, DC, we're going to make some decisions that will say a lot about what kind of people we are and where we're going. And I believe—I believe that if we decide to work together and work for the future, the 21st century and the global economy will be America's time. But we have to make that decision.

I want a high-wage, high-growth, high-opportunity future, not a hard-work, low-wage, insecure future for the working families of the United States of America.

I've worked as hard as I know how to bring the economy back. But let me ask you this: You all know what the problem is. If I had told you 30 months ago, the day I became President, that the following things would happen— just listen to this as a good news, bad news story. In our country we have over 7 million new jobs. We have 2½ million new homeowners. We have 1½ million new small businesses. We have reduced the deficit from $290 billion to $160 billion a year. We have done it while increasing our investment in education and training and technology and research to generate new jobs. We have doubled the loans of the Small Business Administration to try to create more small business opportunities.

We have done all these things. In California, as hard hit as you were by all the defense cuts, the jobs that were lost in the previous 4 years have been replaced and then some. And we're overcoming the impacts of earthquakes and fires and defense cuts. And California's coming back. But you know what? In spite of all of that, the median wage has dropped one percent. That means most working people are working harder for the same or lower wages that they were making not just 2 years ago but 10 and 15 years ago. That is the great challenge of this time.

Are we going to be a smart-work, high-opportunity, high-wage country, or a hard-work, low-wage country where the middle class is dividing? And that is the thing that ought to inform every decision we make. I think I know what we have to do, and I want you to stand with me because you know what we have to do.

The first thing we ought to do—the very first thing we ought to do is to say we are going to do no harm; we're going to stop trying to undo the protections in the American law for working men and women. We're going to stop trying to weaken workplace safety. Let's work in partnership with managers to make it a safer workplace in America, not walk away from our obligations to the safety, health, and welfare of the American workers.

Then, what is our affirmative agenda? Number one, don't cut education and training; spend more on it. And for those who say we have to do that to balance the budget, I say, that is wrong. My balanced budget plan gives the working families of America a tax deduction for the cost of all education after high school. Our balanced budget plan would give working people who lose their jobs the right to a voucher worth $2,600 a year for 2 years to take to the nearest community college or other education and training institution to get a better start in life. Increase our investment in education; don't cut it.

The second thing we ought to do is to have fair as well as free trade. That's what the fight with the Japanese over autos and auto parts was all about. I'm all for more trade, but it's got to be fair. It's got to be fair to American workers. We can now compete with anybody in the world and win if we're given a fair chance to do so.

The third thing we ought to do is raise the minimum wage. Let me tell you, there is no evidence to support the claim that opponents of the minimum wage always make, that it costs jobs. But we know one thing for sure: On January 1, 1996, if we do not raise the minimum wage this year, it will drop in terms of what the money will buy to a 40-year low. Two-thirds of the people making minimum wage are adults. Forty percent of the people making the minimum wage are the sole support of their families. We have children growing up on it. It is wrong

to expect people to work for $4.25 an hour. Let us raise the minimum wage and do it now.

In California, we have a lot of other things to do. We have to maintain the defense conversion programs that our administration has put in place. We should not cut the attempts to build people's future. I have worked as hard as I could to make sure that you knew that the defense contractors and the people that worked on the military bases, who won the cold war for this country, would not be left out in the cold when the defense budget was cut. And we have to keep working on that.

Let me give you an example of the kind of thing I'm talking about. Today, it is my honor to announce that our Department of Transportation is going to give to Cal-Start, a consortium of California companies, $3.4 million to help them start building electric cars for the future of America.

Men and women who used to weld Bradley fighting vehicles together for our national defense will now build family vehicles that will use smart technology, help the environment, and give people good jobs for a good future for their families. That's the kind of thing we ought to be doing more of in this country. They will be made at what used to be the Alameda Naval Air Station. This is the kind of thing that I want our Government to do, to work with you in partnership for the future.

And just today, right before I came out of here, the head of Amerigon, Lon Bell, and George Kourpias, the head of the Machinist Union, signed an agreement that commits both sides, management and labor, to teamwork and a true partnership on the shop floor, working together, working for tomorrow. America ought to follow that model. We need more of it.

Folks, this is happening all over California. Earlier today, in Monterey, I dedicated the new campus of Cal State on the grounds of Fort Ord. They had—instead of a place that is a shell, an empty shell, they're now going to have a vital university. They had 4,000 applications for the first 600 places open there. And within just a few years, they'll have thousands and thousands of people there, creating more jobs than were there when Fort Ord was running at full steam. That is the future of America, working together, working for tomorrow.

In Sacramento, Packard Bell has already hired about 5,000 people, including 500 people where they've moved jobs from overseas back to the

United States to northern California to assemble personal computers at a former Army depot, with more jobs there than were lost at the height of the defense production. That is the future of California and the future of America.

Let me just say one more thing on this Labor Day. In the last 2½ years, we had 7 million new jobs, 2½ million new homeowners, 1½ million new businesses, record corporate profits, the stock market's gone to 4,700. I think it is time for American businesses to follow the lead of our best employers and share more of those profits with their working people. The Government can't do that; business has to do that.

Thirty years ago, in the biggest companies in this country, the average executive made about 12 times what the average shop worker did. Today it's 120 times. It's time for the working people——

Audience members. Boo-o-o!

The President. All right, let me tell you. I'm all for people becoming millionaires. We've had more self-made millionaires since I've been President than any comparable period in American history. And I like that. That's the American idea. But the people of this country that make it go are the average working families. And they deserve their fair share of their own productivity and competitiveness. And it's time to do it.

So when I leave you today, I'm going back to Washington for the critical struggles over the budget in the next 90 days. And I will say again, this is the period of biggest change we've had in 100 years. We are going to shape the future. Are we going forward together, looking toward tomorrow, or are we going to be divided? Are we going to have a high-wage, high-growth, high-opportunity future for your children, or a hard-work, low-wage future for half of the working people in this country? Those are the questions.

Yes, we have to balance the budget, but let's do it in a way that increases our investment in education, technology, research, and the good jobs of tomorrow. Let's don't walk away from it.

Yes, middle class people ought to have tax relief for education and childrearing. But let's don't cut taxes so much just to find tax cuts for people who don't need it and, in turn, turn around and raise the cost of Medicare, raise the cost of nursing home care on ordinary elderly people and their middle-class children who

cannot afford it. That is wrong. We should not do that.

Yes, we ought to reform regulation and reduce cumbersome bureaucracy. You know something—this is something you ought to tell tomorrow when you're talking to people—our administration has reduced the size of Government, the number of regulations, and the number of Government programs more in 2 years than the previous two administrations did in 12. But I did not reduce worker protections and our commitment to clean water, clean air, and safe food. That is nuts. We should not do that. It is not good for America.

So as Congress comes back to work, as you send Ron Dellums and Barbara Boxer and Dianne Feinstein back to their labors, let me tell you, folks, send a message to everybody. This country, it got where it is today because we pulled together and we worked together and we worked for tomorrow.

I just got back from Hawaii, celebrating the 50th anniversary of the end of World War II. I met with veterans from all different races and all different backgrounds who forgot all their differences and worked together. And that's why we won. And when they came home, the GI bill gave them all the chance to go to college and to own their own homes and to educate their children. And that's why America won the cold war and did so well.

This idea, this crazy idea that somehow we can go into the 21st century by weakening our middle class, by dividing our people against each other, by convincing hard-working middle class people that the reason they don't have a good income is because of welfare or affirmative action or immigration—all of which need improvement, and we've done more on that than the guys did before as well—but that's not what's holding your wage down. What's holding your wage down is the inability to get a fair deal in a competitive global economy because we need more investment in education, more investment in training, more investment in high-wage jobs. And you know that in your heart of hearts.

This country never got anywhere being divided against one another. So let's go forward together for a better future.

God bless you all, and thank you.

NOTE: The President spoke at 3:30 p.m. at the Alameda County Fairgrounds. In his remarks, he referred to Tom Donahue, president, AFL–CIO; Jack Henning, secretary-treasurer, California Labor Federation, AFL–CIO; John Sweeney, president, Service Employees International Union, AFL–CIO; Lenore Miller, president, Retail, Wholesale and Department Store Union, AFL–CIO; Chuck Mack, secretary-treasurer, Local 70, and president, Joint Council, International Brotherhood of Teamsters; George J. Kourpias, president, International Association of Machinists and Aerospace Workers, AFL–CIO; Judy Goff, president, and Owen Marron, secretary-treasurer, Central Labor Council of Alameda County, AFL–CIO; and Lon E. Bell, president, Amerigon.

Statement on the Agreement Between Greece and the Former Yugoslav Republic of Macedonia
September 4, 1995

I welcome the decision by Prime Minister Papandreou and President Gligorov to send their Foreign Ministers to New York next week to complete an agreement on steps to establish friendly relations between their two countries. This courageous and visionary decision by both leaders is an extremely important step that will support current efforts to bring peace and stability to the Balkans. It is the result of months of intensive diplomatic efforts by Cyrus Vance, the United Nations mediator, and by the President's Envoy, Matthew Nimetz, as well as meetings today in Athens and Skopje by the negotiating team lead by Assistant Secretary of State Richard Holbrooke.

In this context, I also welcome Greece's strong support for the U.S. peace initiative in the Balkans and its steadfast support as a NATO ally. Greece is an important partner in the ongoing negotiations and in the critical military decisions being taken within NATO. We will continue to consult closely with the Greek Government in the coming weeks.

President Gligorov is dedicated to assuring that his new nation takes its rightful place in the international community. The imminent completion of an agreement with Greece demonstrates that significant progress has been made. I consider today's announcement a major step toward peace and stability in the Balkans. It is my fervent hope that it will encourage the leaders of Bosnia, Croatia, and Serbia to take further steps of their own toward peace.

Presidential Determination No. 95–39—Memorandum on Assistance to Rwanda
September 1, 1995

Memorandum for the Administrator, U.S. Agency for International Development

Subject: Determination to Allow DFA to be used to Support Administration of Justice Activities in Rwanda

Pursuant to the authority vested in me by Section 614(a)(1) of the Foreign Assistance Act of 1961, as amended (FAA), I hereby determine that it is important to the security interests of the United States to furnish up to $4 million of fiscal year 1995 funds made available for Chapter 10 of Part I of the FAA and, in addition, up to $3 million of prior year funds, for assistance to Rwanda to support the establishment of the rule of law and promote the impartial administration of justice, without regard to any limitations contained in Section 660 of the FAA.

You are hereby authorized and directed to report this determination to Congress and to publish it in the *Federal Register*.

WILLIAM J. CLINTON

NOTE: This memorandum was released by the Office of the Press Secretary on September 5, but it was not received for publication in the *Federal Register*.

Remarks and a Question-and-Answer Session With Students at Abraham Lincoln Middle School in Selma, California
September 5, 1995

The President. Good morning. Is this the first day of school?

Students. Yes.

The President. Well, that's good. I mean, I think it's good. You might not think it's so good. I think it's great. I want to take a little time today to speak with you. I know you've been briefed a little bit about what I want to talk about, but I want to speak just for a few minutes. And then I'd like to answer questions or hear from you.

I think it's very important—you're in this school named for Abraham Lincoln, who most of us believe was our greatest President—it's very important that at your age you understand some things about the history of our country and that you understand what the time you're living in is all about.

In every time in history there are a few basic things that are really, really important, and if you want to make the most of your life you have to know what those basic important things are. So I thought what I would do today is just take a few minutes and talk about three or four of those times, bring us up to date now, and tell you what I think is most important about this time, and then let you say whatever you want to say or ask whatever questions you'd like to ask.

When Abraham Lincoln was President, as you know, we had the great Civil War. And we had only been a nation for less than 100 years. We were still a relatively small country in terms of population, and we were famous for being a democracy in a world where most countries were not democracies. Most people did not get to vote for or against people at election time and to pick their own leaders.

And the Civil War was really about two things: First of all, it was about whether the country would stay together as one country or split between North and South and, secondly, about whether we would continue to have slav-ery, even though our Constitution said that all people were created equal and that people were equal in the eyes of God. So because the Civil War came out the way it did, we stayed one country and we abolished slavery and we began the long and unending task of trying to live in a nation that didn't discriminate against people based on their race. That was a very, very important thing.

And because those two things happened, we then became a very powerful economic country. And the country became more and more industrialized so that by the beginning of this century that we're about to end, the beginning of the 20th century, we'd become quite a powerful economic country with quite a large industrial base.

Then World War I broke out, and we became involved in a war in another continent for the first time ever. And we tried to help our friends in Europe defeat the attempts of the Germans to take over all of Europe and to establish an empire and make people live against their own will.

After World War I, because our country had never been—we'd never been involved much with other countries before. We didn't much want to be involved in other countries. When George Washington, our first President, left office, he said we should be very careful about getting too involved with other nations and their affairs. So the American people, after World War I, which was over in 1918, went back to their own business and basically withdrew from the world.

Unfortunately, they couldn't withdraw from the world because by then, our economic well-being was caught up with the economic well-being of other people in other parts of the world. And there was a Great Depression in the 1920's, not only in this country but throughout the world, that led directly to the rise of Adolph Hitler in Germany, whom I'm sure you've all read about, and the Nazi power there, and led to the start of World War II.

I have just come from Hawaii, where we ended over a year's worth of celebrations of the 50th anniversary of the end of World War II, which ended in 1945, the year before I was born. World War II was about defeating Hitler, who wanted to establish an empire, along with the Italian dictator, all over Europe and in Russia. And the Japanese empire, they wanted to control everything in the Pacific—nondemocratic and running other countries.

When they were defeated, our country then was the most powerful country in the world. The year I was born, 40 percent of all the wealth in the world was generated in America with only 6 percent of the people in the world, because all the other big countries had been devastated by the war.

So then for the first time ever, really, in our whole history in 1945, America was forced to lead the rest of the world and to be involved in the rest of the world. And we had two reasons for doing so. One is we had to build an economic system that would avoid having another Great Depression, that would enable everybody to make a living and work hard and raise their children and have a good life in our country and in other countries.

The second was that as soon as the war was over, World War II was over, the Soviet Union presented a whole new threat, what was known as the cold war. And the cold war basically involved the United States and its allies, basically Britain and France and the other democracies and now Japan and Germany, standing against the expansion of communism which then dominated the Soviet Union, most of Eastern Europe, China, and North Korea, ultimately, and then some other smaller countries around the world and also involved our being divided because we had nuclear weapons and they did, too. And we knew that if either side exploded the nuclear weapons it could lead to a war that would end the human race because the bombs had the power to kill so many people.

But from the end of World War II in 1945 until just a few years ago, we had this cold war until communism failed, the Soviet Union collapsed, Russia became an independent country and a democracy and all these other countries that had been governed by communism now have different forms of government, most of them are democracies in one way or another.

China is still a nondemocratic country, but essentially the cold war ended when the Soviet Union collapsed.

And so for 4 or 5 years, we've been moving into a new world in which we're reducing the number of nuclear weapons, so that by the time you are grown and you have your own children, I hope no one will be afraid of the prospect of two countries going to war with each other and killing millions and millions and millions of people with nuclear weapons.

But we also have a new economy now where, for example, all the agricultural products sold in this valley depend in no small measure on what happens in the world economy. Can they export these products? Can they be competitive? Are they going to be facing imports from other countries?

So as you look to the future, I hope—if we do our job right, people my age, from the President on down—I hope you won't have to worry about a world in which you and your families could be destroyed by nuclear warfare. I hope you will never again have to face the prospect of dictatorships controlling hundreds of millions of people with aggressive attitudes that might force you to go into war.

So as you look ahead into the 21st century, I hope that most of what you will be concerned about is a competition not based on bombs or guns but based on our minds and our ability to work. And I hope that you will be living in a country that will be the most successful country in the world, because we will find a way, without the pressure of war, to bring us together, to all get along together in spite of all of our differences.

So if you look ahead from where we are now to, let's say, when you are in your early twenties, I think the world will have two great challenges. One is the challenge presented by the global economy and the technology and information revolution: How can all Americans who are willing to work hard make a good living, get a good job, establish a family, and raise their own children? It's a big problem today. Some people are doing well, but other people are working hard, and they aren't doing very well.

The second is, how are we all going to get along in this world where we're of so many different races and religions and we have so many different opinions on everything. How can we get along? How can we find common ground and work together? I'm sure you see on the news at night the problems in Bosnia or you see what happened in Rwanda or Burundi in Africa where people of different tribes or ethnic groups or religious groups—they don't threaten you in the sense that nobody is threatening to drop a bomb on you, but they're killing each other rapidly. And even in this country there is a lot of tension still among people with different or religious convictions or ethnic backgrounds.

So I think the two big things you'll have to deal with are how are you going to do well, you and all the people of your generation? How are you going to do well in the global economy? How are we going to guarantee that the American dream, which is that if you work hard and obey the law and do what you're supposed to do, will give you the opportunity to live up to your own dreams? And the second thing is, how are we going to deal with a world in which, while there are two great powers threatening to bomb each other out of existence, there are a whole lot of people who basically think that the differences between people are more important than what we have in common, and they're willing to fight and kill and die for that?

When you see a bus blown up in Israel because nobody wants peace in the Middle East— because some people don't want peace in the Middle East—that's an example of that. And that's what I—those are the two great challenges I think you will face.

There's only one you can do anything about right now, and that is your own future, how you're going to do well in this global economy. And there's one thing you need to know. In the world in which we're living, in the world toward which you're moving, education is more important today than ever before.

Fifteen years ago, just for example, a high school graduate made about 40 percent less than a college graduate in their first year of work. Today the difference is 80 percent. The gap has doubled, because in a global economy, based on information and technology, education really matters.

I come from a farming State that's not the same kind of agriculture you have here in the valley, but even the farmers I know, most of them now bring in their crops based on their ability to use sophisticated computer software, and I'm sure it's the same here.

So while education has always been an important part of the American dream, today it is an essential part of your future, because if you look at people your parents' and your grandparents' age, for the first time in the last 15 years, for the first time, our middle class in America has basically been splitting apart between people who are doing pretty well in this new economy and people who aren't doing so well, good people who are working harder but never getting a raise and don't have a stable income. And almost exclusively—not entirely, but almost entirely—the issue is education. People that have higher levels of education are doing pretty well. People that don't aren't doing as well.

And that's why, since I've been President, I've done everything I could not only to put more money into education but also to provide more opportunities for young people like you to go on to college or to get training after high school if you don't go to college, to give more poor little kids the chance to be in a Head Start program so they can get started to school in a good way. Because education now is more than just giving you an individual opportunity. Your whole country's future and this world's that we're living in and the one you're going to live in depends on our ability to educate our people.

The other thing I would say is there is something you can do about the second problem, which is all these racial and religious and ethnic tensions that you see all over the world. The United States, of all the big countries in the world, is really the most ethnically diverse. We have—I mean, look around this room. Los Angeles County has people from over 150 different racial and ethnic groups. And if we can learn to get along, to respect each other's differences and to work together, then it means that the United States will have a huge advantage in the 21st century as other people find it impossible to bury the hatchet and to reach across their different religious and racial and ethnic lines. If we can do it, we're going to have a huge advantage.

So anything you can do as a student, as a young person dealing with other young people to learn to really respect people who are different from you and understand them—it's okay to disagree with them, but to find a way to work together with them, that will really help your country. And it will also give you a better future.

Anyway, that's a short history of the last 130 years of America—140 years—and where I think we are and where I think we're going. I really believe that there's a very good chance that you will live in the best period in American history, that you will live in the most exciting period in American history, that you will have more opportunities to do more things than any group of people ever has. But it depends upon our dealing with those two challenges: We've got to learn to get along with people that are different from us and work together, and we have to educate everybody. If we do that, we're going to be fine.

Anybody have any questions, comments?

Student. Did you always set high education goals for yourself?

The President. Yes, always. I was—I lived with my grandparents until I was four because my— or from the time I was two until the time I was four, because my father was killed in an automobile accident just before I was born. So my mother went back to nursing school so she could get some training and could support me. And my grandmother and grandfather, who didn't have a lot of—my grandfather only finished the sixth grade, but they really drilled into me from the time I was small that I should do well in school. And they taught me to count. They even had me reading little books when I was 3 and 4 years old. So it was a big thing in my family. And my mother was also very strongly in favor of education and so it was always a big issue in our family. And I always understood that it would help me personally.

But when I got out of—let me—what I want to emphasize is the difference between then and now, my time and your time. When I got out of high school, our country's unemployment rate was about 3½ percent or something like that. And I literally didn't know anybody who wanted a job that didn't have one—nobody. And everybody I knew who worked had a good chance of getting a raise year-in and year-out. So that people with very high levels of education, they might do better, they might make more money, but all Americans really had a pretty stable situation economically when I got out of high school.

That's just not true anymore. So that it's not just a question if you want to be President or Governor or the superintendent or the principal that you need to have high educational aspirations. Every one of you is smarter than you think you are. Your mind will absorb more; you can learn more; you can develop more than

you think. And it's very important now. And it's very different than it used to be. Now, it's got to be a—learning has to be something for everyone now.

But yes, I did; even when I was a little boy I was raised to believe that I had to learn as much as I could and that, even though I came from a family with no money or no particular standing, that it didn't matter. If I worked hard and learned a lot, I could do whatever I wanted to do. That's what my family raised me to believe. It turned out they were right.

Student. What did you want to be when you were young?

The President. Well, when I was—I'm not sure I thought about it that much when I was your age. But when I was in high school I was basically interested in three things. I was interested in music, and I was very serious about it. I was interested in medicine, and I considered studying to become a doctor. And I was interested in what I'm doing now; I was interested in public service.

And when I grew up, it was a noble thing to want to be an elected official. I see all these surveys now where parents don't want their children to go into politics, and people think it's a bad thing to do. I don't believe that. The political system which gave Mr. Dooley a chance to serve in Congress and gave Ms. Eastin the chance to be the education superintendent and gave me a chance to be a Governor and then a President is what's kept this country going for 200 years.

So when I was raised, just like I was raised to believe and have high education aspirations, I was raised to respect the political system that we have and to believe in it. And I still feel that way. So those are the three things I was really interested in when I was in high school.

And finally, I just decided that I wanted to do what I'm doing now because I enjoyed it more and because I thought I was better at it. I think, generally, you need to find something you really like to do with your life and something you think you can become good at and do it. It doesn't mean you'll always win at what you're doing or you'll always be successful. I've lost two political races in my life. And I have not always achieved everything I've tried to do in the public offices I've held. But I think that generally you'll be happier if you do something that you're interested in and that you think you can be good at, even if it's extremely difficult.

And I remember when I went to college, sometimes, I made the worst grades in what were supposed to be the easiest courses, and then sometimes the hardest courses I did better in just because I cared more about it and I would throw myself into them.

So that—I don't have any advice for you except to find out what you really—what you like, what you care about and then do it without reservation—whatever it is.

Student. Mr. President, I'm very overwhelmed by your visit this morning. But how was it like meeting President Kennedy?

The President. It was—well, for me, it was an incredible experience. And it was interesting. In 1963, when I went there to the White House, I was 16 years old. I had been out of Arkansas, I think, twice in my life—out of my home State. I think I'd only been out of the State twice. And I got this trip to Washington with these other—a hundred of us, who were young boys who were at this—in this program I was in. This was the American Legion Boys Nation program.

And I really wanted to meet President Kennedy because I admired him and I liked him and I agreed with what he was trying to do. And I liked him because he was highly controversial in my home State and throughout the South because he was trying to finish the work of the Civil War. He was trying to pass all of the civil rights legislation. He was trying to eliminate racial discrimination. And he was taking a lot of heat for it. And a lot of people in my part of the country weren't for him because of it. But I was for him because of it, because I believed in what he was doing. So it was not only a great thing for me to meet the President, but I thought that he was really looking out for our future, and I thought I would live in a better America because he was President. So I was very excited about it.

And I remember the day it occurred. I didn't know if the President was going to shake hands with all of the 100 boys, but because I was from Arkansas, I was at the top of the alphabet—[*laughter*]—and because I was above average in size, I could sort of elbow my way up to the front of the line. [*Laughter*] So I made sure I got to shake his hand. Although he was quite nice; he stayed around. I think he shook most people's hands that day.

But it was a wonderful thing, you know. That's a great thing about this country. I mean, I just—here I was coming from a modest-sized town, and one day I was shaking hands with the President, kind of like this. That's one of the great things about democracy. You know, your families' votes count just as much as mine does.

Anybody else?

Student. What are your plans after you leave office?

The President. I don't know. I haven't thought about it much. Once in a while I think about it, but I haven't—you know, if I stay healthy, and I've been blessed with pretty good health, I hope I can continue to do some things that are useful for my country. I'm not much on just laying around. I like to work, and I like to do things. So I'll try to find something very useful to do that will help America and help the causes that I believe in in this country and around the world. But I haven't really thought about it much. It takes all my concentration to do my job.

Did you have your hand up?

Student. What do you think the most important thing you've done while you've been in office is?

The President. I think the most important thing I've done in office is to basically make the Presidency a place where problems are dealt with again. You know, in other words, instead of just being—what I've tried to do is to use the office of the Presidency to actually tackle the problems of the country and not just to make speeches and talk and try to stay popular. And I've done a lot of controversial things. And I know I've made some mistakes, but I have actually used the power of the Presidency to take on things that have not been taken on.

For example—I'll just give you some examples. When I became President, the debt of our country had gone up by 4 times in only 12 years. We literally quadrupled the national debt from 1981 to 1993. And it was unconscionable. But it's not easy to reduce it. But we reduced our annual deficit from $290 billion a year to $160 billion this year in only 3 years. And it was the first time since right after World War II that our country had reduced deficit spending 3 years in a row.

There was a crime bill that had been languishing around for 6 years in the Congress to try to help local communities fight crime more. We passed it—puts 100,000 more police officers on the street, stiffens punishment, provides some prevention programs for local communities to give kids something to say yes to, instead of things to say no to.

There's a bill that had been banging around in Congress for 7 years called the family and medical leave law, which we passed, which gives most working people in this country the right to take a little time off if they have a sick child or a sick parent without losing their jobs.

We had—I passed a number of other bills through the Congress. Trade legislation—very—the NAFTA bill, which helped the valley in its farm exports, was very controversial. We passed that. We passed the Brady bill, a bill that was very controversial. It had been banging around for 6 or 7 years in the Congress that nobody wanted to—no President would really take it on—that requires people who buy handguns to have a background check before they can get a handgun to see if they've got a criminal record or a mental health history. And we passed the bill.

Just the other day, we announced a campaign to try to reduce smoking by young people, because we know 3,000 young people start smoking cigarettes every day in America. And 1,000 of those 3,000 young people will have their lives shortened because of it, because of lung cancer or heart disease or strokes. But nobody had ever done anything about it before in the White House because they didn't want to make the tobacco lobby mad, because they've got a lot of money and they're powerful.

Every job I've ever had in public life I've tried to do things. And what I've tried to do is to change the attitude about what we can do. I want you to believe that your country can work and that you can have a good future and that you can solve your problems. That's what I want you to believe. I don't believe in cynicism. I don't like people who are cynical or skeptical. I like people who get up every day and think they can make something happen.

So, I mean, if you ask somebody else what the most important thing I've done, they'd probably say, our economic program turned the economy around, created 7 million jobs, and got economic growth going again. But I think—but I believe the most important thing we've done is to prove that we can do things again, that you can actually take these problems on and make a difference and look to the future.

We made the college loan program more affordable for millions of young people. But to do it, we had to take on powerful banking interests that are now trying to get their money back because we took some money away from the middlemen in the college loan program so we could lower costs for people like you to go to college.

We just did a lot of things. And I think the most important thing I've done is to try to force the Government, and hopefully the American people, to keep looking toward the future and to say, "Okay, here are these problems. Let's take them on. Let's move into the future."

Even the major effort I tried that failed, to try to provide health insurance for all American families, even though I failed to do it, a lot of the things that I advocated are now happening anyway. And I think that the President is supposed to be someone who tries to bring the American people together around good values and high hopes and then to get people looking toward the future, you know, work together and work for tomorrow. And I think that largely I have achieved that. And that's what I intend to continue to do.

Student. Since you've been President, what's the hardest decision that you've had to make?

The President. That's a very good question. Interestingly enough—let me tell you, first of all, interestingly enough, the hardest decisions are often not the ones that you would think. They're often not the ones that are most controversial.

Let me just mention two. One Mr. Dooley was involved in. I think the—I'll mention two that were very hard for me.

One was right after I became President I was told by the Republican leaders in the Congress that they would not vote for my budget; none of them would vote for it, no matter what I did to it; that they wanted a partisan issue and that if I tried to bring the deficit down, if it didn't work, they would blame me, and if it did, they would say, well, I raised taxes in '93 to bring down the deficit. So I had to pass an economic program—I had to put together an economic program that would bring our country's deficit down by $500 billion only by members of my own party. And we had to make all kinds of decisions about what it would take to do that, including some things that I didn't necessarily agree with.

And that was very hard for me because I went to Washington determined to work with Democrats and Republicans. And I was shocked to find out how partisan it was. And it was very hard for me—I mean, I was shocked to find out people say, "Well, I'm just not going to work with you because you're in the other party. I'm just not going to do it. We have to oppose you. That's the political thing to do." It turned out that they were right. It helped them politically. But that was very hard for me to accept and very hard for me to deal with and then to figure out what to do to pass the program, but we did it.

And because we reduced the deficit and reduced interest rates and invested more in education at the same time and gave California and other States some money to deal with the impact of base closing and defense cutbacks, we got the economy going again. But it was hard. It was really, really hard.

And the other thing that was—sort of the hardest thing to do was to decide what to do—how to deal with Bosnia. For a long time it was very difficult because I think the United States has to work within the United Nations and within the rules set within the United Nations for a problem like Bosnia. But it's hard for us when we're the strongest country in the world, when other countries are—don't do what we think they should do. And we have no way to make them do it because we didn't have soldiers there. But that was very hard for me.

Now I have to tell you I agree with what we're doing in Bosnia. I strongly—you may know this from the news, but NATO planes are striking the Bosnian Serb targets again today in Bosnia because they refused to take all their heavy weapons away from Sarajevo and stop shelling the city. And we strongly supported that.

So now we're working together, and I agree with the policy. But that was very hard for me. Now that the cold war is over, it's very important that other countries all take some responsibility for dealing with problems in their area and that we work with them. But it's hard when you're trying to work with somebody and what they want to do is not what you want to do. That's tough.

Now, the controversial things I've done were not so hard for me. For example, when I sent our troops into Haiti to remove the dictators it was—the only difficult thing there was understanding how to do it in a way that would minimize the likelihood that any Americans would die. But whether we should do it or not seemed the right thing to me.

The most unpopular thing or the thing I've done that had the least popular support—I don't know if it had the most opposition; it had the least popular support—was to help Mexico when it was about to go bankrupt several months ago. A lot of—nobody—there was a poll on the day I made the decision that said the American people were against it 81 to 15. They thought I was doing the wrong thing to try to help Mexico. But I thought I was doing the right thing because I knew if Mexico collapsed, we'd have a lot more illegal immigration problems. I knew that they wouldn't be able to buy any of our products. I knew that there was a serious chance that there would be an economic collapse in other countries in Latin America. So basically, I had more information than most Americans did, so even though I was making a very controversial and unpopular decision, it turned out to be an easy one for me.

So sometimes the controversial decisions are not the hardest ones.

Anybody else?

Teacher. I think we're—I'm trying to keep an eyeball on the time, and I think—unless you'd like to take one last question.

The President. Yes, let me take one more. Go ahead.

Student. Did you ever think about being President when you were young?

The President. I did, but I didn't really— I did. I guess when I met President Kennedy I thought about it. But it wasn't—it wasn't that I really thought it would happen. I mean, I thought—Abraham Lincoln said when he was a young man, he said this—this is something you should think about, whatever it is you want to do—he said, "I will work and get ready, and perhaps my chance will come." That's what Abraham Lincoln said. And since you're here in the school named for him, that's a very good thing for you to think about in your own life, whatever your ambition and hope is.

I didn't really decide to actually run for President or think about it seriously until the 1980's. I thought about running in 1988 and decided not to, and then I decided to run in 1992 and was fortunate to be elected. But I thought about it in terms—I thought in general terms. I aspired, actually, to be a Senator from Arkansas when I was a young man. And it turned out I never got a chance. I never served in the

Congress. I was a Governor, and then I got to be President.

But I think every young person, if you're interested in public life, you think, well, maybe that could happen. But I don't think that I focused on it in the same way I did when I started running, for example. It's just something you say, well, Lincoln said it best, I'll work, get ready; perhaps my chance will come.

Teacher. Thank you. Eleanor, our student body president, has something in her desk that she'd like to give to you, some things from our school.

Eleanor, why don't you come on up.

[At this point, a gift was presented to the President.]

The President. I like that. Thank you. Thank you. This is great.

Well, I've had a wonderful time. Lindsey asked a question. Let me close by saying this. If you do anything in life where you make decisions, you're going to make some that don't turn out right, or some where, maybe even if you didn't make a mistake, the consequences, the unforeseeable consequences turn out to be very bad. So sometimes the decisions that are the most difficult on the front end don't have those kind of consequences.

The budget had happy consequences. But the worst days as President are days when things happen that you set in motion that are bad. The other day, three of our peacekeepers, three of our negotiators died in Bosnia in an accident, in a complete accident. But they were all men about my age with children about my daughter's age and about your age. And you feel terrible about that. When our soldiers were killed in

Somalia, it was the darkest day of my Presidency for me.

I say that to make this point in closing: Anything you do with your life, some of the things you do, they're just not going to work out like you meant for them to. You're going to make mistakes, or bad things will happen that you have no control over. And the important thing is that you keep going. You have to believe in yourself, believe in your dreams, believe in the life you want to live, and keep going, because we're all human and things are not always going to work out.

But I can tell you that now I have been to 30 years' worth of high school reunions. I've never missed a high school reunion. We have one every 5 years. And the saddest people in my high school class are not the people who have failed but the people who didn't try to do what they wanted to do.

So I leave you with the thought. You just figure out what it is you want to do and go for it. And if you don't make it, you'll still be better than if you hadn't tried in the first place. You've just got to get up every day and keep living and keep believing that your life can be good.

Don't forget what I told you: You live in a time in which education is more important than in any time in the whole history of the United States. So it's important to make the most of this time in school, because there is no alternative because of the world we live in. Besides that, you'll have more fun in your life.

Thank you. Goodbye.

NOTE: The President spoke at 11:10 a.m. In his remarks, he referred to Delaine Eastin, State school superintendent of public instruction.

Remarks to the Community at Abraham Lincoln Middle School in Selma
September 5, 1995

Thank you very much. It is wonderful to be here today. I want to thank Cal Dooley for his kind remarks and for his remarkable leadership in the Congress. He does a terrific job for all of you. I thank Delaine Eastin for her commitment to education and for being here with me today. I want to thank your school

principal, Lucile King, who on next-to-no notice allowed me to come in here and share some time with some of your students. I thank Eleanor Brown who did a fine job speaking here. I said, "Eleanor"—before she came up, I said, "Eleanor, are you having a good time, or are you nervous?" She said, "I'm a little nervous."

So I said, "Well, just pretend you're talking to a few people." And she did a fine job, didn't she? Let's give her another hand. [*Applause*] I thought she did a great job. I also want thank the Selma High Marine Corps ROTC, who posted the colors, the high school choir, and the Black Bear Brigade Band, who played very well when I came up here today, I thought.

I'd also like to thank the mayor and the members of the City Council and the school board who met me. One of the school board members gave me this Save the Children tie to wear in the speech. And the mayor told me, as the sign said, that this is the raisin capital of the world. And I said, "Well, the only thing I can say is, I don't know about raising them, but I have probably consumed more raisins than any President who ever held this office. And I've enjoyed every one of them.

Ladies and gentlemen, and to all the young people who are here, I want to talk about education today. This is back-to-school day. But before I do, I have to say just a few words about the situation in Bosnia. You may know that this morning our pilots and crews and their NATO allies resumed the bombing of Bosnian Serb military positions. I support that; it's appropriate; its necessary, because the Bosnian Serbs failed to comply with the conditions set over the weekend to withdraw their heavy weapons from Sarajevo. We have to follow through on our commitment to protect Sarajevo and those other safe areas. We cannot allow more innocent civilians and children to die there. This war has to end by negotiation, not on the battlefield.

I'm glad to be here in the number one agricultural region in our Nation. The Central Valley's orange groves and pistachio trees and the acres of vineyards and cotton and corn and the people who grow the raisins are critical not only to your State's economy but to our Nation's economy.

I wanted to come here to this community today because I think that all of you symbolize, in what you're doing here, what we have to do as a country. We've got to take responsibility for ourselves and our children. We've got to work together, and we've got to work for the future.

All of you know that education for individual Americans has always been the key to the American dream. I have a simple message today: At the end of the cold war, at the beginning of this period of global economy, of the informa-

tion age, the technology age, education is more important today to individual Americans, to families, to communities, and to our future than it has ever been in the entire history of the United States, and we have to act on that fundamental truth as a people.

Thirty months ago, I set out to change the economic direction of our country, to bring the economy of America back and to help the economy of California recover. Thirty months later, we have over 7 million more jobs, 2½ million more homeowners, over 1½ million more small businesses. The jobs you lost in the difficult 4 years before I took office have been replaced, and you're beginning to come back in California.

But there is one fundamental problem left in America economically, and that is for the last 15 years more than half of the hourly wage earners in America are working a longer work week for the same or lower wages. And there is a simple, clear reason for that. In the global economy, no matter how hard people work, if you don't have the skills that will command high incomes, it is difficult to earn those incomes. We have simply got to make a commitment as a nation to revolutionizing the availability and quality of education, starting with the youngest preschoolers and going through adults who need it to get better jobs or when they're unemployed. And we have to do it together. It is the fundamental fact of our time.

When Congress comes back from its recession—excuse me, recession—whatever that—recess—[*laughter*]—school—it's a school day—the recess. When Congress comes back from their recess tomorrow, we will have 90 days of decisions about the budget, 90 days to choose what direction we're going to take. There's some good news for these children in the audience about decisions that have already been made. For the first time in over a dozen years, we now have a bipartisan commitment to balance the Federal budget and remove the burden of debt from our children and our grandchildren. That is a very good thing to do.

The question is, how are we going to balance the budget? I have given Congress a plan which recognizes both these fundamental truths: that we have to balance the budget and that we have to provide for education and invest in our young people's future. They are working on a plan that balances the budget, but by their own estimate only produces weak economic growth, in part because it cuts education. In California you have had enough of cutting education. We need to invest more in education, and we can do that.

I hope as strongly as I can say that you're going to see the most productive 90 days we've seen in a long time in Congress. We can balance the budget. We can end welfare as we know it. And we can invest in education and protect the medical care of our elderly and protect our ability to have a safe and clean food supply and environment. We can do all this in a balanced way if we'll work for common ground with common sense. That's what we have to do.

There are some who say that there should be no compromise this autumn, but I say that good people of good will want us to find common ground, want us to find honorable compromise, want us to balance the budget and keep faith with the children of America and their educational needs.

You know, I believe that the overwhelming majority of Americans of both parties are committed to an agenda of balancing the budget and investing in education. When I became President and we increased our investment in Head Start and added 50,000 more poor children to the Head Start rolls, it had bipartisan support. When we passed the Goals 2000 program to give schools the chance to reform themselves and to get more computers and other technology in the classroom and to have smaller class sizes and higher standards, it had overwhelming bipartisan support. When we began to help the States of this country to set up programs for young people who graduate from high school but don't go to 4-year colleges and still need further education to get good jobs and good wages, a school-to-work program, it had bipartisan support. When we established the safe and drug-free schools program to support the message to our young people that if you want to learn, you have a right to learn in safety and you have to learn without drugs, it had bipartisan support. When we expanded the availability of college loans and scholarships for lower income students and college loans for all students, we lowered the cost and improved the repayment terms, it had bipartisan support. There are young people here with AmeriCorps who are working in the communities of the valley and earning money to go to college. That program was created with bipartisan support.

Education is not supposed to be a partisan political football, and it should not be when the Congress returns tomorrow. We ought to all stay on the side of education.

I will be urging the Congress to adopt two new education ideas which will help the working families in this valley to provide for their future. Number one, there's going to be a tax cut; the question is, who's going to get it and what's it going to be for? I believe we ought to give a tax cut for working families to have the cost of their education tax deductible after high school: college education, training for technicians, unemployed people. That's the kind of tax cut I think we ought to have.

The other thing I hope they will do is to recognize that adults need education, too. I have urged the Congress to create a fund which would give to every person who loses a job in the United States the right to get a $2,600 voucher for a year for 2 years to take to the nearest community college, junior college, or other educational institution to get retrained if they lose their jobs and they need a brighter future.

One other thing I'd like to say: I want to thank the young people who were in that class with me today practicing citizenship, asking me tough questions, some of which I had never been asked before by anyone. I want to thank them for being an example of what I want for all of our young people.

One of the things that I feel very strongly about is that our schools have to teach good citizenship and good basic character and values: fairness and honesty, respect for self and others, responsibility. Those things are too often absent in our schools today.

And I'm proud to announce that through our Department of Education we have been supporting the spread of character education, basic principles of citizenship and personal character all across America. And today we are releasing four grants to four States, including the State of California, to make sure that we do everything we can to help our principals, our teachers, and our parents inculcate the values and character of good citizenship into our young people throughout this country.

So I ask you, my fellow Americans, without regard to your political party or your philosophy, to stand firm on this central principle. Tell the Congress and the President you want the budget balanced but you want us to invest in education and the future. We don't want to be penny-wise and pound-foolish. We don't want to weaken our economy by balancing the budget. We want to strengthen our children's future by getting the burden of debt off of them. There is a plan that balances the budget and increases investment in education, and that's what we should do.

We don't need—we don't need—to take 45,000 children out of the Head Start program. We don't need to deny every State in the country the right to benefit from smaller classes and more technology and educational excellence in the Goals 2000 program. We sure don't need to stop helping the schools who need it with the safe and drug-free schools program. We don't need to stop helping people who want to go on to good jobs with higher skills but aren't going to higher education and 4-year schools. We need the school-to-work program. And we sure don't need to make college loans and college scholarships less available.

Look what's happened in California. We need more college scholarships. We need more college loans. We need more affordable education and higher education.

I have promised the Congress that I would never disagree with them without offering an alternative. I have given a balanced budget plan which increases investment in education. And

on Thursday, I will talk more about how we can save even more money in this budget to put into reducing the deficit, balancing the budget, and investing in education.

But before you leave here today, I want to ask every adult American in this audience—you look at these children. You know they're our future. You know we're living in a global economy. You know that what you earn depends on what you can learn. You know it's more important to our whole country than every before. What do you want this country to look like in the 21st century? If you want a high-wage, high-growth, high-opportunity society, if you want every American, no matter how humble their background, to have a chance to live the American dream, if you don't like the fact that too many of our people are trapped in a hard-work, low-wage future, then we can change it only if we decide to both balance the budget and invest in the education of our people. That is our commitment. I ask all of you to make it.

God bless you, and thank you very much.

NOTE: The President spoke at 12:10 p.m. In his remarks, he referred to student body president Eleanor Brown and Mayor Ralph P. Garcia of Selma, CA.

Message to the Senate Transmitting the Philippines-United States Extradition Treaty
September 5, 1995

To the Senate of the United States:

With a view to receiving the advice and consent of the Senate to ratification, I transmit herewith the Extradition Treaty Between the Government of the United States of America and the Government of the Republic of the Philippines, signed at Manila on November 13, 1994.

In addition, I transmit for the information of the Senate, the report of the Department of State with respect to the Treaty. As the report explains, the Treaty will not require implementing legislation.

Together with the Treaty Between the Government of the United States of America and the Government of the Republic of the Philippines on Mutual Legal Assistance in Criminal Matters, also signed November 13, 1994, this Treaty will, upon entry into force, enhance cooperation between the law enforcement communities of both countries. It will thereby make a significant contribution to international law enforcement efforts.

The provisions in this Treaty follow generally the form and content of extradition treaties recently concluded by the United States.

I recommend that the Senate give early and favorable consideration to the Treaty and give its advice and consent to ratification.

WILLIAM J. CLINTON

The White House,

September 5, 1995.

Message to the Senate Transmitting the Philippines-United States Legal Assistance Treaty
September 5, 1995

To the Senate of the United States:

With a view to receiving the advice and consent of the Senate to ratification, I transmit herewith the Treaty Between the Government of the United States of America and the Government of the Republic of the Philippines on Mutual Legal Assistance in Criminal Matters, signed at Manila on November 13, 1994. I transmit also, for the information of the Senate, the report of the Department of State with respect to the Treaty.

The Treaty is one of a series of modern mutual legal assistance treaties being negotiated by the United States in order to counter criminal activity more effectively. The Treaty will enhance our ability to investigate and prosecute a wide variety of crimes, including drug trafficking and terrorism offenses. The Treaty is self-executing.

The Treaty provides for a broad range of cooperation in criminal matters. Mutual assistance available under the Treaty includes: taking of testimony or statements of persons; providing documents, records, and items of evidence; serving documents; locating or identifying persons or items; transferring persons in custody for testimony or other purposes; executing requests for searches and seizures; assisting in proceedings related to forfeiture of assets, restitution, and collection of fines; and any other form of assistance not prohibited by the laws of the Requested State.

I recommend that the Senate give early and favorable consideration to the Treaty and give its advice and consent to ratification.

WILLIAM J. CLINTON

The White House,
September 5, 1995.

Message to the Senate Transmitting the International Convention for the Protection of New Varieties of Plants
September 5, 1995

To the Senate of the United States:

I transmit herewith for Senate advice and consent to ratification the International Convention for the Protection of New Varieties of Plants of December 2, 1961, as Revised at Geneva on November 10, 1972, on October 23, 1978, and on March 19, 1991, and signed by the United States on October 25, 1991 (hereinafter "the 1991 Act of the UPOV Convention"). I transmit for the information of the Senate, the report of the Department of State with respect to the Convention.

Ratification of the Convention is in the best interests of the United States. It demonstrates a domestic commitment to effective protection for intellectual property in the important field of plant breeding. It is also consistent with United States foreign policy of encouraging other countries to provide adequate and effective intellectual property protection, including that for plant varieties.

I recommend, therefore, that the Senate give early and favorable consideration to the 1991 Act of the UPOV Convention and give its advice and consent to ratification subject to a reservation under Article 35(2), which allows parties to the existing Convention (the 1978 Act) to retain their present patent systems for certain varieties of plants.

WILLIAM J. CLINTON

The White House,
September 5, 1995.

Remarks Prior to a Meeting With Mayors and County Officials and an Exchange With Reporters
September 6, 1995

The President. Good morning. We're about to start a meeting with a bipartisan group of mayors and county officials who represent a much larger number of their counterparts all across America and who are quite concerned about the consequences of the proposed budget and the budget cuts to the people they represent.

They have declared September 7th a national day for budget awareness, and they're going back to the people they represent to explain to them exactly what the consequences will be in terms of either human harm or lost services or higher taxes at the local level. They will be joining to educate their citizens about the potential damage that could be done to our country's future if the particulars of the budgets now being debated in the House and Senate are adopted pretty much as they have passed, especially in the House.

Later today I will meet with a group of CEO's who are concerned about what these cuts will mean to our educational improvement programs and especially to Goals 2000, which has helped us to help States and local school districts throughout the country to improve the quality of education, to bring more technology into the classroom, to get smaller class sizes, to promote education reforms.

Business executives all across America, especially in a bipartisan way, both Republicans and Democrats, have supported Goals 2000 very strongly, and so they'll be coming in to discuss this. This is back-to-school time in our country, and it seems to me that we need to focus on the values of education and the values of our community and on what we really mean by America's family values.

It seems to me that we are departing from what has been the experience of our country now for many years in terms of having a bipartisan commitment to a lot of the things that now some in Congress seem more than willing to abandon, including our commitment to education. As I said yesterday in California, there is an alternative, a way to balance this budget. It's not that we shouldn't balance the budget; we should balance the budget. I strongly support it. We ought to do that, I believe we're going to do that, but we don't have to do it in a Draconian way that hurts the American people.

If you just take the education issue, for example, the proposed budget in Congress by the Republican majority would cut education by $36 billion. It means more overcrowded classrooms. It means fewer teachers. It means fewer computers for the students. It means 45,000 kids cut off of Head Start by 1996. It means the elimination of the Goals 2000 program. It means cutting over a million of our poorest children off from extra educational help. It means cutting 23 million students out of the safe and drug-free schools program, something that clearly ought to be at the forefront of any family values agenda in our country. It means taking 50,000 young Americans out of national service, out of the AmeriCorps program and other service programs that help them to pay their way to college. It means denying millions of students access to college educations because of weakening of the Pell grant program and the elimination of the direct loan program or the severe limitation of it.

So I would say that what we need to do now at back-to-school time is to get educated; all Americans need to be educated about the details of the budget debate. The question is not whether we're going to balance the budget. I have a plan to balance the budget, but it doesn't cut education by $36 billion. There are ways to balance the budget and still permit these local officials to do the work that they have to do and maintain a partnership. And the ways are fairly clear, and we can achieve it.

I know there are those who say that we ought to just shut the Government down and that there is a mandate essentially to dismantle the partnership that has existed between our National Government and local government and the citizens of this country. I don't agree with that. I think we need common sense, common ground. I think we need to appeal to our better instincts. And I think it would be a great mistake for the people of our country to miss this back-to-school opportunity to become educated about what's really at stake here and to be involved in it. And I thank these mayors and county officials for showing up here today and for the work they're about to do in this next week.

Budget Debate

Q. Mr. President, what are you going to do about Senator Dole saying that this is going to be the autumn of discontent, of no compromises?

The President. Well, I am going to stick with my position. Now, it's been several months since I offered an——

Come on in, Mayor Rendell. Sit down. [*Laughter*]

Mayor Edward Rendell. Sorry. Blame it on Amtrak, although Amtrak usually does a great job. [*Laughter*] And we shouldn't be cutting its funding. But they were late today.

The Vice President. We know a cameo entrance when we—[*Laughter*]

The President. That's right. Actually he arrived at 6:30 this morning and was—[*Laughter*].

There will be a lot of things said and a lot of maneuvers made, I suppose, in the next 90 days. I think the important thing is that we balance the budget without destroying our commitment to education, without wrecking Medicare and Medicaid and undermining the security and stability that our elderly people are entitled to have, and without undermining the fabric of the country and the strength of the economy.

I mean, you know, we even have one economic study claiming that the congressional majority's budget would provoke a long-term reces-

sion. I mean, presumably, we are balancing the budget to help the American economy, to take the burden of debt off of our children and our grandchildren. That's why I want to do it. I want to do it because I think it'll help the economy, not to give the American people a low-grade infection for 7 years. And so I believe that we need to look at the facts. And I'm going to do my best to avoid a lot of this political rhetoric and a lot of these charges back and forth.

And the thing that has impressed me about the mayors and the county officials that are here is that they really are going to spend a week looking at the facts, trying to make sure that their citizens look at the facts. That's what I want the American people to do. But I'm going to bend over backwards not to get into a lot of political word wars and just keep looking at the facts. And we can——

Q. Lots of luck. [*Laughter*]

The President. Yeah? Thank you. Thank you. [*Laughter*] Let me just say this. I will—I like that so much I will never again criticize editorializing by news—[*laughter*]—that was a wonderful comment. [*Laughter*]

Q. Mr. President, will you be able to avoid this train wreck, however, that you've been talking about, and how can you do that?

The President. Well, I hope so. But I mean, I think, frankly, that's up to Congress. I have been—it's up to the leaders of Congress whether we have a train wreck. I have now had my position out there clear and crystal clear and in great detail for months. That's what they said they wanted me to do, and I did it. I offered them an alternative balanced budget. I offered the opportunity of negotiations. I said what I thought we had to do, that we shouldn't wreck the fabric of health care for seniors. We shouldn't wreck the educational commitments of our country. We shouldn't totally overlook the impact of these budget cuts on the people who actually had to do the work of America, the mayors, the county officials, the Governors of our country, and that we could do this. And I committed to a balanced budget, and I offered it.

So I have done all I can do now. The rest of it is largely up to them, but we should not have a train wreck. There's no reason for a train wreck. You know, we've already done a lot of their work for them. When I became President, we had a $290 billion deficit. Now it's down to $160 billion. We've cut it nearly in half in 3 years, and we did it without any train wrecks. We did it in a more rapid way in the last Congress than had been the case for the previous 10 or 12 years, so we can get a lot of this work done if we'll just do it. There just needs to be a little less talk and a little more action, a little more common sense, a little more working together.

NOTE: The President spoke at 10:15 a.m. in the Cabinet Room at the White House. Edward Rendell was mayor of Philadelphia, PA.

Remarks Prior to a Meeting With Business Leaders Supporting Goals 2000 and an Exchange With Reporters
September 6, 1995

The President. Good afternoon. As you can see, I'm about to have a meeting here with some distinguished American business executives who support the idea that our most important agenda here in Government is to advance the cause of education, and they have in particular been good supporters of the Goals 2000 program in which 48 of our 50 States are now participating and which is the most grassroots-oriented reform program the United States Department of Education has ever promoted for improving the quality of education through reforms at the State, school district, and school level to provide more technology, to raise standards, to have smaller classes, to do a whole range of things that will make education better.

There is a way to balance the budget without destroying the Goals 2000 program. The proposed congressional majority budget would get rid of Goals 2000, and it would deprive 44 million students of the opportunities that they would otherwise have to be in more grassroots reform efforts.

This Goals 2000 project is the result of the recommendations we've gotten over the years from business leaders, as well as educators and, frankly, the result of all of the work that Secretary Riley and I did for more than a decade in our previous jobs. And I very much hope it can be saved, and it is not necessary to balance the budget to back up on the education commitment. I think the partnership we've enjoyed, both the bipartisan partnership between Republicans and Democrats and the partnership between business and government that we've enjoyed in this education reform effort should not be destroyed, because it doesn't have to be to balance the budget.

I'd like to ask Mr. Joe Gorman to make a couple of remarks about the program, and then we'll go on with our meeting.

Joe?

[At this point, Joseph Gorman, chairman and chief executive officer, TRW, Inc., made brief remarks supporting Goals 2000.]

Q. Mr. President, are you also going to discuss with the CEO's the stagnant wages over the last two decades that you always keep talking about?

The President. Every time I talk to business leaders I talk about that. But let me just say, as I've said on Labor Day, there are a lot of alternative explanations being offered for this, but one of the clear lessons not only for our country but for every wealthy country is that is we want to continue to raise incomes in a global economy, we have to raise the level of education of the work force. We've got to do it.

There are some other things we can do and that I hope we will do and some things they can do and that many of them are doing. But if we don't raise the educational level of the American work force and if we don't set up a system of real reform for excellence in our public schools and then lifetime education afterward, nothing they or we do will achieve that goal.

So I will say again, the purpose of balancing the budget is to remove the burden of debt off of our children and grandchildren and to free up more capital for private investment so that the economy will grow. The purpose of balancing the budget is not to shut the economy down by undermining our fundamental commitment to education. So the question is, how can we meet both objectives?

I've presented a plan which does that, there are lots of ways to get it done, and that's what I think we're all agreed on, again without regard to party.

United Nations Conference on Women

Q. Have you heard from the First Lady, sir?

The President. Yeah, I had a nice talk with her. I've talked to her twice since she left for China. I talked to her after her speech. I told her I thought she had done a great job on the speech. I liked it very much, and she seemed very pleased with it. And she said that the women, the many thousands of women who were there gave it a very good response.

We had a very—we had kind of a brief conversation; the connection wasn't the greatest because I was in an airplane.

Q. Was there any concern about the treatment of Secretary Shalala?

The President. Secretary Shalala spoke for herself on that. I thought what she said was just great. She'll do just fine. [*Laughter*]

Q. Any public relations——

Q. Was there any concern that the First Lady's remarks might have any impact on the U.S.-Chinese relations?

The President. No, I don't think so. You know, she said—what she said was what we have both said many, many times on the issues that affect China, and much of her speech pertained to conditions in other countries, not China, and some of it related to conditions in our country as well. So I thought it was a balanced speech. There was no attempt to single any country out. She stood up for the rights and the potential and against the abuse of women everywhere in the world.

I thought that's what made the speech powerful, that there was no attempt to have a particular political agenda or single any country out. It was a very strong speech.

Q. They know who they are.

The President. I was proud of her.

NOTE: The President spoke at 2 p.m. in the Oval Office at the White House. A tape was not available for verification of the content of these remarks.

Letter to Congressional Leaders on Welfare Reform
September 6, 1995

Dear Mr. Leader:

I am glad the Senate has finally come to this important debate on welfare reform. The American people have waited a long time for this. We owe it to the people who sent us here not to let this opportunity slip away by doing the wrong thing or by failing to act at all.

Over the last two and a half years, my Administration has aggressively pursued welfare reform at every turn. We proposed sweeping welfare reform legislation to impose time limits and work requirements and promote the values of work, responsibility, and family. We have put tough child support enforcement at the center of the national welfare reform debate: My Administration collected a record level of child support in 1993—$9 billion—and I signed a far-reaching Executive Order to crack down on federal employees who owe child support.

We have put the country on the road to ending welfare as we know it, by approving welfare reform experiments in a record 34 states. Through these experiments, 7 million recipients around the country are now being required to work, pay child support, live at home and stay in school, sign a personal responsibility contract, or earn a paycheck from a business that uses money that was spent on food stamp and welfare benefits to subsidize private sector jobs. Today, my Administration is granting two more waivers to expand successful state experiments in Ohio, which rewards teen mothers who stay in school and sanctions those who don't, and in Florida, which requires welfare recipients to go to work as a condition of their benefits and provides child care when they do.

I am confident that what we're doing to reform welfare around the country is helping to instill the values all Americans share. Now we need to pass a welfare reform bill that ends the current welfare system altogether and replaces it with one that puts work, responsibility, and family first.

That is why I strongly support and urge you to pass the welfare reform bill sponsored by Senators Daschle, Breaux, and Mikulski that is before the Senate today. Instead of maintaining the current broken system which undermines our basic values, the Daschle-Breaux-Mikulski plan demands responsibility and requires people to work. The Work First bill will cut the budget by moving people to work, not by asking states to handle more problems with less money and shipping state and local taxpayers the bill.

I support the Work First plan because welfare reform is first and foremost about work. We should impose time limits and tough work requirements, and make sure that people get the child care they need to go to work. We should reward states for putting people to work, not for cutting people off. We will only end welfare as we know it if we succeed in moving people from welfare to work.

Welfare reform is also about family. That means the toughest possible child support enforcement, because people who bring children into this world should take responsibility for them, not just walk away. It also means requiring teen mothers to live at home, stay in school,

and turn their lives around—not punishing children for the mistakes of their parents.

Finally, welfare reform must be about responsibility. States have a responsibility to maintain their own efforts to move people from welfare to work, so that we can have a race to independence, not a race to the bottom. Individuals have a responsibility to work in return for the help they receive. The days of something for nothing are over. It is time to make welfare a second chance, and responsibility a way of life.

We have a ways to go in this welfare reform debate, but we have made progress. I have always sought to make welfare reform a bipartisan issue. The dignity of work, the bond of family, and the virtue of responsibility are not Republican values or Democratic values. They are American values—and no child in America should ever have to grow up without them. We can work toward a welfare reform agreement together, as long as we remember the values this debate is really about.

The attached Statement of Administration Policy spells out my views on the pending legislation in further detail.

Sincerely,

BILL CLINTON

NOTE: Identical letters were sent to Bob Dole, Senate majority leader, and Thomas A. Daschle, Senate Democratic leader.

Message to the Congress Transmitting the Report on Federal Advisory Committees
September 6, 1995

To the Congress of the United States:

As provided by the Federal Advisory Committee Act, as amended (Public Law 92–463; 5 U.S.C. App. 2, 6(c)), I am submitting my second Annual Report on Federal Advisory Committees covering fiscal year 1994.

This report highlights continuing efforts by my Administration to reduce and manage Federal advisory committees. Since the issuance of Executive Order No. 12838, as one of my first acts as President, we have reduced the overall number of discretionary advisory committees by

335 to achieve a net total of 466 chartered groups by the end of fiscal year 1994. This reflects a net reduction of 42 percent over the 801 discretionary committees in existence at the beginning of my Administration—substantially exceeding the one-third target required by the Executive order.

In addition, agencies have taken steps to enhance their management and oversight of advisory committees to ensure these committees get down to the public's business, complete it, and then go out of business. I am also pleased to report that the total aggregate cost of supporting advisory committees, including the 429 specifically mandated by the Congress, has been reduced by $10.5 million or by over 7 percent.

On October 5, 1994, my Administration instituted a permanent process for conducting an annual comprehensive review of all advisory committees through Office of Management and Budget (OMB) Circular A–135, "Management of Federal Advisory Committees." Under this planning process, agencies are required to review all advisory committees, terminate those no longer necessary, and plan for any future committee needs.

On July 21, 1994, my Administration forwarded for your consideration a proposal to eliminate 31 statutory advisory committees that were no longer necessary. The proposal, introduced by then Chairman Glenn of the Senate Committee on Governmental Affairs as S. 2463, outlined an additional $2.4 million in annual savings possible through the termination of these statutory committees. I urge the Congress to pursue this legislation—adding to it if possible—and to also follow our example by instituting a review process for statutory advisory committees to ensure they are performing a necessary mission and have not outlived their usefulness.

My Administration also supports changes to the Federal Advisory Committee Act to facilitate communications between Federal, State, local, and tribal governments. These changes are needed to support this Administration's efforts to expand the role of these stakeholders in governmental policy deliberations. We believe these actions will help promote better communications and consensus building in a less adversarial environment.

I am also directing the Administrator of General Services to undertake a review of possible actions to more thoroughly involve the Nation's citizens in the development of Federal decisions affecting their lives. This review should focus on the value of citizen involvement as an essential element of our efforts to reinvent Government, as a strategic resource that must be maximized, and as an integral part of our democratic heritage. This effort may result in a legislative proposal to promote citizen participation at all levels of government consistent with the great challenges confronting us.

We continue to stand ready to work with the Congress to assure the appropriate use of advisory committees and to achieve the purposes for which this law was enacted.

WILLIAM J. CLINTON

The White House,
September 6, 1995.

Message to the Senate Transmitting the Hungary-United States Legal Assistance Treaty
September 6, 1995

To the Senate of the United States:

With a view to receiving the advice and consent of the Senate to ratification, I transmit herewith the Treaty Between the Government of the United States of America and the Government of the Republic of Hungary on Mutual Legal Assistance in Criminal Matters, signed at Budapest on December 1, 1994. I transmit also, for the information of the Senate, the report of the Department of State with respect to the Treaty.

The Treaty is one of a series of modern mutual legal assistance treaties that the United States is negotiating in order to counter criminal activities more effectively. The Treaty should be an effective tool to assist in the prosecution of a wide variety of modern criminals, including members of drug cartels, "white-collar" criminals, and terrorists. The Treaty is self-executing.

The Treaty provides for a broad range of cooperation in criminal matters. Mutual assistance available under the Treaty includes: (1) taking testimony or statements of persons; (2) providing documents, records, and articles of evidence; (3) serving documents; (4) locating or identifying persons or items; (5) transferring persons in custody for testimony or other purposes; (6) executing requests for searches and seizures; (7) assisting in forfeiture proceedings; and (8) rendering any other form of assistance not prohibited by the laws of the Requested State.

I recommend that the Senate give early and favorable consideration to the Treaty and give its advice and consent to ratification.

WILLIAM J. CLINTON

The White House,

September 6, 1995.

Message to the Senate Transmitting the Austria-United States Legal Assistance Treaty
September 6, 1995

To the Senate of the United States:

With a view to receiving the advice and consent of the Senate to ratification, I transmit herewith the Treaty Between the Government of the United States of America and the Government of the Republic of Austria on Mutual Legal Assistance in Criminal Matters, signed at Vienna on February 23, 1995. I transmit also, for the information of the Senate, the report of the Department of State with respect to the Treaty.

The Treaty is one of a series of modern mutual legal assistance treaties being negotiated by the United States in order to counter criminal activity more effectively. The Treaty will enhance our ability to investigate and prosecute a wide variety of offenses, including drug trafficking, violent crimes, and "white-collar" crimes. The Treaty is self-executing.

The Treaty provides for a broad range of cooperation in criminal matters. Mutual assistance available under the Treaty includes: (1) taking the testimony or statements of persons; (2) providing documents, records, and articles of evidence; (3) serving documents; (4) locating or identifying persons or items; (5) transferring persons in custody for testimony or other purposes; (6) executing requests for searches and seizures; (7) assisting in forfeiture proceedings; and (8) rendering any other form of assistance not prohibited by the laws of the Requested State.

I recommend that the Senate give early and favorable consideration to the Treaty and give its advice and consent to ratification.

WILLIAM J. CLINTON

The White House,
September 6, 1995.

Message to the Senate Transmitting the Albania-United States Investment Treaty
September 6, 1995

To the Senate of the United States:

With a view to receiving the advice and consent of the Senate to ratification, I transmit herewith the Treaty Between the Government of the United States of America and the Government of the Republic of Albania Concerning the Encouragement and Reciprocal Protection of Investment, with Annex and Protocol, signed at Washington on January 11, 1995. I transmit also, for the information of the Senate, the re-

port of the Department of State with respect to this Treaty.

The Bilateral Investment Treaty (BIT) with Albania will protect U.S. investment and assist the Republic of Albania in its efforts to develop its economy by creating conditions more favorable for U.S. private investment and thus strengthen the development of its private sector. The Treaty is fully consistent with U.S. policy toward international and domestic investment. A specific tenet of U.S. policy, reflected in this

Treaty, is that U.S. investment abroad and foreign investment in the United States should receive national treatment. Under this Treaty, the Parties also agree to international law standards for expropriation and compensation for expropriation; free transfer of funds related to investments; freedom of investments from performance requirements; fair, equitable, and most-favored-nation treatment; and the investor's or investment's freedom to choose to resolve disputes with the host government through international arbitration.

I recommend that the Senate consider this Treaty as soon as possible, and give its advice and consent to ratification of the Treaty, with Annex and Protocol, at an early date.

WILLIAM J. CLINTON

The White House,
September 6, 1995.

Message to the Congress Transmitting a Report on United States Government Activities in the United Nations
September 6, 1995

To the Congress of the United States:

I am pleased to transmit herewith a report of the activities of the United States Government in the United Nations and its affiliated agencies during the calendar year 1994. The report is required by the United Nations Participation Act (Public Law 264, 79th Congress; 22 U.S.C. 287b).

WILLIAM J. CLINTON

The White House,
September 6, 1995.

Remarks on the National Performance Review
September 7, 1995

Thank you very much. I have to tell you that those of you here who have the privilege of being seated probably missed what almost became the newest example of our reinvented, full-service Government. Just as the Vice President was becoming most eloquent about how we were providing a full-service, high-quality Government, the people who were suffering in the sun standing in the back almost got a shower along with their press conference when the garden spray came on there. [*Laughter*] I saw them moving closer and closer and closer; I thought, well, maybe they can't hear. And then I finally realized they were about to get a shower. [*Laughter*] You come back tomorrow, we'll start with a shower.

Let me begin by saying a special word of thanks to the Vice President for the absolutely extraordinary energy and discipline and dedication and quality of effort that he has put in over 2½ years now. This has been an exceptional achievement. There's nothing quite like it in the history of modern American Government, and it would not have happened had it not been for his leadership. And I am profoundly grateful to him for it.

I also want to join in thanking the supporters we've had among the Members of Congress, the people in our administration who have had to implement a lot of these recommendations. It's a lot easier to talk about than to do, and they have had a difficult job to do. And I thank the Cabinet especially and the agency heads for the embrace that they have given this.

I want to say a special word of thanks to the reinventing Government staff and especially to the Federal employees and to their representatives. They have worked very, very hard at this difficult job, and they have done it remarkably well.

Finally, I'd like to thank David Osborne and Tom Peters and Philip Howard for the books they have written and the inspiration they have provided. The Vice President and I and many of our team have read them all with great care and have done our best to be faithful to the ideas and principles which they have espoused.

When we were running for office, the Vice President and I, back in 1992, we said that, if elected, we would do our best to give this country a Government that was smaller and less bureaucratic, that had a lower cost but a higher quality of service, that devolved more power to States and localities and to entrepreneurs in the private sector, that was less regulatory and more oriented toward incentives, that had more common sense and sought more common ground. We have surely not succeeded in everything we have tried to do, and I am certain that there are areas where people could say we have erred. But we have certainly been faithful to the effort and we have made, I think, a great deal of progress in keeping the commitments that we made.

I wanted to do this because I thought it was important for more than one reason. First of all, it was important because we had a huge Government deficit, we had quadrupled our debt in 12 years, and we still needed to invest more money in certain critical areas of our national life, in the education and training of our people, in research and development, in new technologies, in helping people to convert from a cold war economy to the 21st century global economy. So it was important; we needed to do it.

Secondly, we needed to do it because the level of anxiety and alienation about people's relationship to the Federal Government needed to be mended. We needed to make the Government work better.

Thirdly, we needed to do it because of this historic era in which we live. We, after all, have moved through a rapid transition now at the end of the cold war and at the end of the traditional industrial economy into a global economy with new challenges, new conflicts characterized by a high rate of change; rapid movement of money, technology, and capital; and revolutions in information and technology. In that environment, the model that we use to deliver Government services and to fill public needs was simply no longer relevant to the present and less so to the future. And so we began to try not only to cut the size of the Government, to cut the number of programs, to cut the number of regulations but to change the way the Government works and to develop

new partnerships and to devolve responsibilities to others who could more properly make the decisions.

There are so many examples of that that are not properly part of this particular report now but that have been driven by the philosophy of the Vice President's reinventing Government. We've given every State in the country now the opportunity to reform it's own welfare system without waiting for legislation to pass. It's a dramatic thing. There's nothing like it in the history of modern American Government. And the philosophy of doing it grew out of the work we have done with reinventing Government.

When the Pentagon reformed its procurement procedures, America laughed when the Vice President cracked the ashtray on the David Letterman show, but the taxpayers are better off and the national defense is more secure because the money we're saving there can go into making our people safer and more secure and fulfilling the objectives of the United States all around the world.

And there are many, many other things. The Secretary of the Interior is not here, but he's done his best now to try to resolve some of the thorniest conflicts between the Federal Government and various groups in the western part of our country by pushing more of these decisions down to local councils of people who can make them a long way from Washington but very close to where everyone has to live with the consequences. And there's so many examples of this in every Department of every leader in the Government here present. And I thank them all for that.

Fundamentally, this is a question, though, about our values. If you go back and read the Declaration of Independence and the Constitution, you understand that the American people from our beginnings meant for the Government to do those things which the Government needs to do because they can't be done otherwise; meant for the Government to be an instrument of the public interest.

And we have a moral obligation to make sure that we do this right, that we take the money earned by the hard efforts of the American people and use it in ways that further the public interest. If we can't justify doing that, we can't justify being here, and we can't justify taking the money. And we have a moral obligation to prepare the future for our children and our grandchildren.

Now, this reinventing Government effort is much more important today in many ways than it was on the day I became President because of the choices facing us now in the great budget debate in the Congress. It is much more important now. If we are going to go forward and balance the budget, if we're going to cut spending even more, we have to be even more careful about how we spend the people's money and what we do with the time of public servants and the power that public servants have.

I believe very strongly that we have to balance the budget. I think we have to do it to take the burden of debt off of future generations. I think we have to do it to keep interest rates down and to free up capital for investment now so that we can achieve higher rates of growth. But I think that we have to do it in a way that will achieve our objectives.

And what are our objectives? Our objectives are to grow the American economy, to strengthen the American society, to free up investment so that the American people can live up to the fullest of their potential. That means that we cannot balance the budget in a way that will drive us into a prolonged recession, that will cut off our nose to spite our face, that will be a penny-wise and pound-foolish, that will aggravate the wage stagnation and the other problems that people have in this country today, which means we have to have the money that is left to invest in ways that really serve the American people and serve their larger purposes.

We've reduced the annual deficit from $290 billion the year I took office down to $160 billion this year. The total reduction is about a trillion dollars over a 7-year period. We have to finish the job, but we have to do it in a way that honors the purpose of a balanced budget, which is to strengthen the future of America. We have to decide, in other words, what is important for us today and what's important for our future.

Of course, the Federal Government was too large and needed to be cut back. Of course, there is still waste and duplication. Of course, there are still regulations that don't make a lick of sense, and they needed to be changed, and they still need to be changed. But we have to keep in mind there are still public purposes that as far as we know today cannot be fully discharged without the involvement of America's National Government: the health care of elderly citizens; protection of our environment; the safety of our food; the needs of the people whose triumph we celebrated in Hawaii last weekend who won the Second World War for us and paved the way for the last 50 years of the American Century, giving the poor a chance to work their way into the middle class and giving our children and now increasingly our adults access to the best possible education opportunities. Those are the values and priorities of the people of this country. They have to be reflected in the budget as well.

The Vice President's report that I received today has over 180 specific cuts in Government that will save over $70 billion in the next 5 years. One by one, these are not the kind of cuts that make headlines and, I guess, I don't expect them to make too many headlines tomorrow. But when you put them all together, as Everett Dirksen said once, "a billion here and a billion there, and pretty soon you're talking about real money." [*Laughter*]

These are kinds of cuts that will allow us to balance the budget without cutting the single most important investment we can make in our future: education. That's why I was able to give to the Congress a balanced budget plan that increases education. By contrast, the proposals of the congressional majority spend $76 billion less on education and training than I do in the next 7 years. They make deep cuts in education at a time when it's more important than ever before. That's why so many people estimate that that budget could actually slow the rate of economic growth over the next 7 years instead of increase it, which is the whole purpose of balancing the budget, to grow and strengthen the economy.

If the congressional proposal is passed, fewer children will go to Head Start, fewer schools will be able to teach their children to stay away from drugs and gangs or have the resources to use the best possible technology or have smaller classes or set up the charter schools when the existing system is not working. There won't be as many young people who get scholarships to go on to college, and the cost of the college loan program to ordinary students will go up dramatically in ways that will reduce the number of people going to college at precisely the time we need to see them increasing.

Now, that is really what this choice is all about. There was—I thought that chart was showing when it blew down, but you can see here that we have to make these kind of choices. Should we balance the budget by reducing education spending by $76 billion, or should we cut $70 billion in Government waste and duplication? Do we want fewer people to go to college? Do we want larger classes in our schools? Do we want to scale back our efforts to keep our schools safer and drug-free? Do we want to say that having the highest standards for what we teach our children is not a proper objective for the education budget? I don't think we do.

And the point I want to make to you all is we do not have to do this. The sacrifice of all these people in Government to promote this reinventing Government project must not be in vain. We must take the money that is left and spend it properly. We must take the money that is left and spend it properly.

Let me give you some examples of the cuts in Appendix C of the Vice President's report. Like I said, a lot of them don't sound very interesting, but after you add them up, you got some real money there: $118 million by closing 200 weather stations with the National Weather Service, because computers do the job better and cheaper; $14 million in the Small Business Administration by consolidating their loan-processing operations. Let me just point out, the SBA, in the last 2 years, has cut their budget by 40 percent and doubled their loan volume. Don't tell me that we can't make Government work better—doubled their loan volume and cut their budget.

Secretary Cisneros has proposed a remarkable plan for the Department of Housing and Urban Development. They have three basic responsibilities: public housing, affordable housing, and economic development. Instead of running 60 programs to do three things, now they've proposed to run three programs to do three things and save $825 million in administrative costs alone, not money that would otherwise go to Mayor Rice out in Seattle or the other local leaders around our country but administrative costs. It is wrong, in a time when you have to balance the budget, for us to take one red cent in administrative costs that does not have to be taken when the money ought to be put on the streets of America to benefit the American people. And I thank you for that, Secretary.

The clean coal technology project was implemented to develop a way to burn coal cleanly, as cleanly as it could possibly be burned. Well, they did it. The project was started to do that

job. It did the job, but nobody ever closed it down. Now, we're going to do that, not because it failed but because it succeeded.

The Naval Petroleum Reserve in Elk Hills, California, was created during World War I because America's new battleships needed oil. Well, I think World War I is over, and I know that the strategic need for the Navy to have its own oil fields has long since passed.

By eliminating the clean coal technology program, privatizing Elk Hills, and doing a lot of other cuts like this in the energy area, the Energy Department will save $23 billion over the next 5 years. That's a great tribute to the Energy Department's recommendations, and it's the right thing to do.

Believe it or not, the National Oceanic and Atmospheric Administration has a corps of 400 officers who command a fleet of less than 10 old ships. I think that we can be adequately protected by the Army, the Navy, the Air Force, the Marines, and the Coast Guard. So we're going to stop paying for those 10 old ships and use the money for better purposes.

Well, you get the picture. These are commonsense things. We've been working on this hard for 2 years, and we still keep finding these opportunities, and we will continue to do it.

How do people know this will work? How do they know that the savings on paper will become savings in the bank? Well, we have got a track record on that. The Vice President's first report predicted we could save $108 billion in 5 years by reinventing Government. After 2 years, $58 billion is already in the bank. That much has been implemented and saved, in law, in fact—more than half the savings promised in less than half the time.

Two years ago, we said we could shrink the size of Government by 252,000 positions. With the help of Congress offering us humane and decent buyout proposals, the Federal Government today has 160,000 people fewer on the payroll than it did on the day I took office. We are well ahead of schedule on the 252,000.

At the same time, the people who are left are doing their jobs better, and they ought to get credit for it. Last May, Business Week—not an arm of the administration—Business Week magazine ran an article about the best customer service in America on the telephone. They rank companies, great companies like L.L. Bean, Federal Express, and Disney World, people who, for different reasons, need to be very effective on the telephone. But do you know who they said provides the most courteous, knowledgeable, and efficient telephone customer service in the country? The Social Security Administration of the United States Government. I am very proud of that, and you should be, too.

The operators at Social Security are some of the thousands of people who are proving the skeptics wrong, people who think Government can never do anything right. Because of their hard work, we know we can balance the budget without cutting education and risking our children's future. But I will say again, we have to make some decisions.

When I became President—I just want to mention one other—I asked the Secretary of State and the Secretary of Commerce to work together to make sure we started promoting America's economic interest overseas. I have had 100 business people in the last 2 years tell me that for the first time in their entire business lives, every time they go to another country, the State Department is working for them. I have never talked to a business person who has extensive dealings overseas who doesn't tell me that the Commerce Department is more effective in promoting the interests of American businesses and American jobs around the world than at any time in the past. That is also part of reinventing Government. We want you to get more for your money, not just reduce the size of Government.

This can happen, but we need to continue to do this. This has to be a continuous process. Our goal, the Vice President's and mine, is to build this into the culture of Government so that no future administration can fail to embrace this. Our goal is to make this a part of the daily lives, the breathing, the working habits of every manager in the Government, every Federal employee, everybody. We want them to think about it because, believe me, there are

still things that go on every day in the Government that the President can't know about, the Vice President can't know about, but that will affect the lives and the interests and the feelings of the American people.

But we are making a difference. Now we have to decide in this budget debate how we're going to cut, how we're going to balance the budget. This is just like the productivity changes that many large American companies underwent throughout the 1980's. I know we can keep doing this. I know we can do more than even we think we can do. I know we can.

But this is the sort of thing we ought to be doing. And it would be a great mistake if in the next 90 days, in the desire to balance the budget, which I share fully and which we started and which has taken us from a $290 billion deficit to $160 billion deficit, we became penny-wise and pound-foolish. And we forgot that one of the reasons we're doing this is to make sure that the money left can advance the cause of America's economic interest and the basic values of the American people to give every citizen the chance to live up to his or her God-given capacity, to keep the American dream alive, and to give us a chance to come together in a prosperous, secure, and exciting future. That is ultimately, ultimately, the great benefit of this whole effort.

So I ask you to continue to support it and, as we come to this budget debate, to say, we do not, we do not have to make the wrong choices for the right objective. We can balance the budget and we can do it in the right way and reinventing Government proves it.

Thank you very much.

NOTE: The President spoke at 11:15 a.m. in the Rose Garden at the White House. In his remarks, he referred to Mayor Norman Rice of Seattle, WA.

Remarks at a Clinton/Gore '96 Dinner
September 7, 1995

Thank you very much. Thank you all for your wonderful welcome. What a way to come back from vacation. I want to thank Fred Baron and

Larry Stewart so much for the work they did to help bring us all together tonight. I want to thank all of you for being here and for the contributions you have made to our campaign. Many of you are old friends of mine, and I'm glad to see you again. Some of you I have never seen before, and I hope I have a chance to shake a few more hands before I leave tonight.

I thank Terry McAuliffe and his fine staff, all of them, for the work they have done, and I want to thank my good friend John Breaux, not the least—so many reasons I have to thank him for—for finally giving me credit for where he got that joke. [*Laughter*] Pretty funny, don't you think?

I told him another story he didn't tell tonight, which illustrates another point about what's going on in Washington today, which is that one of my laws of American politics which people—everybody tends to be for change in general but against it in particular. So it's important to know what the fine print is in these contracts.

The same minister he talked about was having trouble getting his congregation to exercise, so he worked his heart out on a sermon that he thought would finally inflame his congregation. And he was going on and on and pumping, and they were saying "Amen" and ginning. And finally he got to the punch line, and he said, "I want everybody in this congregation who wants to go to Heaven to stand up." Everybody leapt to their feet, except this one old lady on the front row that hadn't missed a Sunday in church in 45 years. And he was crestfallen. He said, "Well, Sister Jones, don't you want to go to Heaven when you die?" And then she jumped up. She said, "I'm sorry, Preacher, I thought you was trying to get up a load to go right now." [*Laughter*] It's very important to get the fine print of these contracts.

I want to tell you, I've had a wonderful experience with the American people in the last few weeks. My family and I had the opportunity to go to Wyoming, as I'm sure you know, on vacation, and we got to spend a lot of time in Grand Teton and Yellowstone National Parks. And I had the opportunity there as President to defend the national parks and the importance of preserving and maintaining them in this budget battle. I wish every young person in our country could go to one.

I also had an opportunity to talk to a lot of Westerners who, you know, think that one of their hands would fall off if they ever voted for a Democrat, because they're so used to, you know, disliking the Federal Government, and they've got us identified with them. You

know, it's interesting, the Republicans, if they hate the Government so much, why do you supposed they've devoted a whole generation to trying to take it all over? [*Laughter*] They lost the White House for 2½ years, and they missed it so much they can't bear to give it up. [*Laughter*]

But anyway, I talked to a lot of people, then I went to Hawaii and represented our country at the last of the many wonderful occasions commemorating the 50th anniversary of World War II. And I got an incredible sense of the diversity of this great country, meeting again, as—I'm always overwhelmed by this incredible generation of Americans that literally saved our way of life and paved the way for all the prosperity and the security and the victory we had in the cold war.

My State had one of those Japanese internment camps in World War II, and I met a couple—it's an incredible story—that met and got married in the internment camp in Arkansas. And the man had volunteered to join the service, and they sent him to Mississippi to train, and he said he got hungry for Japanese food. And they said the only place you can get anything is internment camp in Arkansas. [*Laughter*] So he went over and met his wife there, he said, "We're the only two Japanese-Americans who actually are glad those camps were set up. We had our marriage there."

I met another Japanese-American who came here on his own, was thrown into a camp, volunteered to join the military, got out, and by the grace of God, the war ended the day before he was about to be sent to an island where he would have been in combat against two of his brothers who were in uniform for the Japanese. But the atomic bomb had ended the war, damaged his own home, injured his mother, and killed one of his other brothers.

This is an incredible country. We come from all different backgrounds and all different walks of life. And we've come a long way in the last 50 years.

When I ran for President in 1992, I did it because I thought we were not making the changes we needed to make to get ready for the 21st century. I did it because I thought that we had not seriously come to grips with the economic and social challenges of the time. And I said I would try to change the economic direction and the social direction of the country, to try to move us forward and bring us together.

And virtually everything I've talked about doing, except the fight we lost on health care, we've succeeded on.

The deficit was $290 billion a year when I took office; it's going to be $160 billion this year. It's come down for 3 years in a row for the first time since Harry Truman was President. For 6 years, there had—[*applause*]—thank you—for 6 years, the American people watched Congress condemn the crime problem in America and do nothing about it and just fight over this crime bill. We passed the crime bill. It puts 100,000 more police on the street, has prevention programs to give our kids something to say yes to, has stiffer punishment for serious offenses, and contained the assault weapons ban that was so controversial. A lot of Members of our party laid down their seats in Congress for that because their voters were told they were going to lose their guns. Next November they'll see they didn't lose their guns, but there are a bunch of criminals that don't have Uzis in the schools and on the streets, and they did the right thing, and we were glad to do it.

I was concerned, before it became fashionable up here, about the problems of welfare, because I think the welfare system is bad for everybody that's involved in it the way it is. It perpetrates dependency, but it doesn't liberate anybody. But it's a pretty bad way to live.

And when the Congress did not act on welfare reform under our Executive order, we just gave States the authority to do what they wanted by getting out of under the existing Federal rules. Now, 34 States have adopted their own reforms that we've approved.

The other party and their Presidents often condemned Federal power and said they wanted more passed back to State and local government, but we gave States and localities more authority to change their welfare systems and their health care systems in 2½ years than they did in 12 years. And those are important things to do.

For 7 years, Congress and the President argued about a simple little law that 175 other countries had to guarantee people that they wouldn't lose their jobs if they had to take a little time off work when their families needed it, if they got sick or their children got sick or their parents got sick, the family and medical leave law. It was the first law I signed as President. We just celebrated the second anniversary of that law at the National Institutes of Health with a lot of parents who have children with

cancer who are struggling along. But those parents at least still have their jobs now because of that law, and not a single, solitary business in America has gone broke because of it. But the other guys said that they would.

So I'm proud of the fact that the United States has been a leader in the cause of peace, from the Middle East to Northern Ireland to Southern Africa to Haiti. I met a woman tonight whose got a young son in uniform in Haiti. And I'll tell you, that's an amazing story that has never fully been told. It's the most totally integrated, planned, and executed military operation in the history of this country which, thank God, did not require us to fire a shot. But it had an enormous positive impact, the ability of the United States to be a force for peace and democracy and freedom throughout our hemisphere. And I'm very, very proud of all the young men and women who engaged in it. And I am very proud of all the young people in uniform who are part of the NATO operation in Bosnia, which is going to give us a chance to make a decent, honorable peace there and stop the slaughter of innocent civilians.

And as John Breaux said, the economic consequences of what we've tried to do have been, I think, quite impressive. We now have well over 7 million new jobs in 30 months; 2½ million new American homeowners; new small businesses starting in America at a rate of 750,000 a year, by far the highest rate on an annual basis since the end of World War II when we started keeping such statistics; the combined rates of unemployment and inflation are at about a nearly 30-year low; the stock market has hit 4,700, profits at an all-time high. I'm pretty pleased by that.

We've had more new self-made millionaires in America in each of the first 2 years I was President than at any time in the history of the United States. We are clearly, clearly, the most entrepreneurial, flexible, open, forward-looking major country in the world right now. And we have the right kind of partnership between business and Government. Our Commerce Department, our State Department have worked hard to help sell American products overseas. We've expanded trade by more than at any time in modern history. These things are going well.

So you might ask yourself: If that's all true, how come they won in the election last November? And I think there are some important answers to that question as we look ahead to '96. And I'd like to talk about it very briefly.

Number one, they talk better than our guys do sometimes. [*Laughter*] They talk about hating the Government. We reduced it. There are 160,000 fewer people working for the Federal Government today than there were the day I became President. We're going to have the smallest Federal Government since Kennedy was President if they don't do anything in this year. We have abolished thousands of pages of Federal regulations. We have abolished hundreds of Government programs. We've begun to make Government work again.

The Small Business Administration cut its budget by 40 percent and doubled the loan volume. Business Week wrote an article a couple of months ago about evaluating all these major companies that have to use the telephone, for who had the best quality telephone service, L.L. Bean and Federal Express and all these companies that really depend on phone service. You know who they said had the best, most courteous, most enlightening telephone service in the United States? The Social Security Administration of the United States Government—Business Week—not an arm of the Democratic Party—Business Week.

So they did that. They talk better. They wave the contract. It sounded like a good idea. But more importantly, a lot of people hadn't felt the positive benefits of the things we've done. There's a time lag between when you do something in Government and when people feel it. But more profoundly than that, there is a lot of unease and uncertainty in our country because we're going through a period of change as profound as the change we went through when we became an industrial society out of an agricultural society. That is the fundamental lesson of this time. And that is why your voice and your work and your convictions are so important. This is a time of historic importance for citizenship.

I've really spent a lot of time trying to come to grips with all the things that are going on in this country and in ordinary people's lives. I read a significant percentage of the mail I get from ordinary citizens. I set up a separate zip code when I became President for the people that I went to grade school and junior high and high school with, most of whom are ordinary, hard-working, middle class people to write me letters so I could know what they were going through.

And I'm telling you, I believe that the period we're living through is the most profound period of change since roughly the time between 1895 and 1916 when we decided how we were going to respond to the fact that we were a great industrial power. And we had to define what the role of Government was going to be and what the purpose of our common existence as Americans was going to be.

We started out with dealing with the antitrust laws, because we decided we needed competition, not monopoly in America. Theodore Roosevelt told us we had to preserve our natural resources. We couldn't just develop it all and leave nothing for our children and our grandchildren and posterity. We had child labor laws because it wasn't right to make kids work in factories and mines 6 days a week, 10, 12, 14 hours a day. And finally, in 1916 the Congress even adopted an income tax so that there would be some proportionally fair way to raise the money that had to be spent to further the public interest.

That 20-year period was a very tumultuous time. And people's lives were changing a lot, and they were trying to come to grips with it. The elections were kind of close and sometimes inconsistent because we were working our way through that. That's what's happening now. The cold war is over. We're moving into a global economy where most of the conflicts will not be as cataclysmic as the threat of one nation bombing another into oblivion. I'm proud of the fact that there are no Russian missiles pointed at this country for the first time since the dawn of the nuclear age, since our administration came in.

But don't be fooled. We still have problems. We thwarted terrorist attempts to set off a bomb in the Lincoln Tunnel, to blow up a plane going across the Pacific. We dealt with the World Trade Center, as well as the problem in Oklahoma City. You see what happened to the Japanese when they had that religious fanatic explode the—or break open the little vial of sarin gas in the subway, or whenever a car bomb blows up in Israel—all this is a part of the new security threat as groups, distinct groups, begin to break apart from the whole and the consensus that binds us together as civilized people.

Economically, you see this incredible thing. We've got 7 million new jobs. But if I had told you 30 months ago on the day I was inaugurated, I said, here's what's going to happen in 30 months: We'll have 7 million jobs, 2½ new homeowners, 1½ new businesses, the stock market will be at 4,700, corporate profits will be at an all-time high, and the median wage will drop one percent. So that after 2½ years most hourly wage earners will be working a longer work week for a lower wage, once you adjust for inflation. You might not have believed that, but it happened.

So the bedrock middle class people of this country worry whether the American dream is supposed to work. They keep reading these great numbers, and they say, "What about me? I don't feel more secure. I don't feel more prosperous. I'm concerned."

I say this to you not to be down. I'm actually very hopeful about the future. If you wanted to bet on the future of any major country in the world today for 50 years from now, you'd have to bet on the United States, because of our economic strength, because of our diversity, because of our creativity.

But we have two great challenges and alternative explanations at work in Washington today about how best to meet those challenges. We have to face the future together, because we're going to live in a global society, which means we have to get along with people who are different from we are—from ourselves—different in terms of their religious views, different in terms of their racial backgrounds, different in terms of their ethnic heritage, different in terms of their politics. We've got to find a way to get along, because teamwork wins in the global economy, not division.

The second thing we have to find a way to do is to always be thinking about the future. How are we going to grow the middle class and shrink the under class and keep the American dream alive?

Now, one explanation that we hear all the time is that all we have to do is destroy the Federal Government, and everything will be hunky-dory. All we have to do to make middle class people's wages grow again, if they happen to be white and male, is to get rid of affirmative action or get tough on welfare or immigration.

Let me tell you something—again this is the difference in talking and doing. Our administration has done more than the last two to reform

affirmative action, to fix it, number one; to change welfare; and to take on the problems of illegal immigration and the whole problem of immigration generally. We are trying to do the things that ought to be done. But let's not forget what's really happening to the middle class is the global economy, the technology revolution, the downward pressure on wages of people who can't command high incomes because of their education and skill.

So if we really want to turn it around, yes, we have to reform the systems of Government and all of that, but let's not kid ourselves. Average people need protection. Great institutions of power in the private sector need accountability. And we need to recognize that we have got to work together and work for the future if you really want to raise incomes and have a good future for the United States. That's my theory.

And when you see this fight we're going to have over the budget here, which I hope will end in reasoned, principled compromise on common ground and higher ground, but which cannot, cannot, result in just abandoning the ordinary citizens of this country, when we need to guarantee that their parents and little kids will have health care; we need to make sure that everybody will have access to education to make the most of their own lives; we need to make sure that the environment and clean air and clean water and public health generally are protected—we're going to have a debate. And I believe the answer is, we've got to work together and work for the future.

The alternative vision is, "What we need to do is keep everybody torn up and upset and hating the Federal Government and blaming somebody else for their problems." Now, those are the two big paradigms here. And if you go back to the period between 1895 and 1916, you will see exactly the same thing. But you shouldn't be upset about it. You should be glad that you were given the opportunity to be an American citizen at a once-in-a-hundred-years time of change because it means you are going to have a chance to shape the future for another hundred years. You have an opportunity to decide what kind of world your children and your grandchildren and their children will grow up in. And the next 90 days in this budget, not because of how much money is spent on program X, Y, or Z but because it will say what kind of people we are. That will help to define it.

Several of you have told me tonight that you were in Camden Yards in Baltimore with me last night when Cal Ripken broke Lou Gehrig's record. Why was everybody so happy about that? Everybody loves seeing somebody who was successful that no one could resent. Why? Because here's a guy who showed up for work every day, right? [*Laughter*] Showed up for work every day and did it well, and had a good time doing it, but displayed the kind of constancy and teamwork that we all respect.

Did you ever ask yourself, why is it that in our citizenship, in our voting habits, we reward the kind of behavior that we would not tolerate on a baseball team or in a business or a community organization or a church or a family? You think of any operation you are a part of, what makes it work? People who are interested in unity, not division; people who are looking to the future; people who are optimistic and upbeat; and people, if they spent all their time— anybody in any of these operations spent their time trying to divide people in the group against one another, you would run them off. You would get rid of them. Here, we elect them. [*Laughter*] Now, why is that? Why is that?

Because every one of us wakes up every day with a little scale inside: hope on one side; fear on the other. And sometimes we vote based on how the scales are balanced. And we're all for change, but you know, the average person is just trying to keep body and soul together, trying to do what Cal Ripken does, showing up for work every day. One reason that's so popular is most of the people that were in that baseball stadium last night are the same kind of people. They show up for work every day. They work when they don't feel good. They work when the weather's bad. They work to earn money to do right by their children. They are the people that keep this country going. But they see the play which plays itself out in Washington indirectly, not directly. You have to bring it home directly. You can do it because you, every one of you, in a different way, touches the lives of those kinds of people.

And it's not that I'm going to be right on every issue. But I'll tell you what, I'm on their side. And I'm thinking about their future and their children's future and their grandchildren's future. And I know that in a time of change, what makes a country work is the same thing that makes a team work, a business work, a church work, a family work. You've got to pull together, and you've got to work for tomorrow. And you've got to think about everybody, everybody.

So every issue you're interested in, that's how I am going to evaluate it. How is it going to affect the ordinary person? How is it going to affect these families that are struggling to hold body and soul together? How is it going to affect the dreams people have of the future? That's really what we ought to be doing. And I say to you, you should be very, very happy. You should think it is a privilege that you happen to be alive and at the peak of your influence and energy at a time when your country needs your energy, your knowledge, your experience, your ability, and your determination. This only happens about once every 100 years.

And we are the longest lasting democracy in history because every time it's happened to us before, we did the right thing. We got started right. We fought the Civil War, and it came out right. We stayed together, and we got rid of slavery. We went through this vast economic change, the first big one. Then we dealt with the Depression, World War II, and the cold war. Now we're going through our second vast economic change. So I say, sign up, saddle up, throw your shoulders back, smile, have good time, and we will prevail.

Thank you, and God bless you.

NOTE: The President spoke at 6:55 p.m. in the Mayflower Hotel. In his remarks, he referred to fundraisers Frederick M. Baron and Larry Stewart; Terence McAuliffe, national finance chairman, Clinton/Gore '96; and Senator John Breaux, chairman of the next majority trust, Democratic Senate Campaign Committee.

Remarks at a Breakfast With Religious Leaders
September 8, 1995

Thank you very much, and welcome to the White House. I thank the Vice President for his wonderful introduction. I earnestly hope someday he won't have to close his eye when he reads the—[*laughter*]. Thank you. I cannot tell you all the wonderful contributions he's made to our country and to me and my family, but I can say that when my term in this job is over, one of the things that I will get credit for, even among people who disagree with nearly everything I do, is that I made a good decision when I picked a Vice President, and he then became clearly the most influential person ever to be in the Vice President's office in the history of this—[*applause*].

I have come to very much look forward to this breakfast. As I think most of you know, this is the third such breakfast we have had with leaders of faith from all walks of life, from all over our country, at about this time when we come back from vacation, our children go back to school, and we here in Washington have to go back to work. That itself is an act of faith sometimes. [*Laughter*] And a lot of you know that I have been very interested in the role of faith in public life and in the life of public persons for many years, since long before I became President.

Two years ago, I spoke about the profound impact on me of Stephen Carter's book, "The Culture of Disbelief," and I don't know whether Mr. Carter's forgiven me or not, yet. It's changed his life a little bit anyway since we talked about that. But Carter made an important point, that we simply, in this, the most religious of all countries and a country that in our Constitution protects the right of everyone to believe or not as he or she sees fit, we have to make room for something that important in the public square. And we have to do it in a way that recognizes that most American of rights, the right to differ.

After that experience I had reading the book and then having this breakfast and working on all this, we redoubled our efforts in this administration on the Religious Freedom Restoration Act and on implementing and on its implications and on trying to live up to the spirit as well as the letter of the law in many ways that a lot of you are familiar with. And that is also what led me to give the speech I gave about the role of religion in education at James Madison High School in Virginia a few months ago, and then, following up on that, to have the Secretary of Education Dick Riley issue the guidelines that were just going out to all of our schools on the relationship of religion and public schools.

That was a very important thing for a lot of our schoolchildren and educators around this country and for a lot of people in this room and those whom you represent. We made it clear that under our law, schools are not religion-free zones; we simply, under the Constitution, prohibit the power of Government through the schools to advance particular religious beliefs. But students can still pray individually or together, silently or aloud. Religious clubs have a right to meet, just like any other clubs, and to do what they wish to do. Flyers can be distributed. Homework and other assignments can even be used to express religious convictions by students. Religion can be a part of the curriculum of public education as long as particular views are not advocated.

I think this is a very important thing. There are those who say that they think more should be done, and I think that part of it is they feel that, unless our young people, particularly those who may not be subject to religious influences, understand the basic values behind the great religions that our country permits to flourish and encourages to flourish, they might not grow up to be the kind of citizens they ought to be. So we've also done a lot of work on what has popularly been called character education in our country, trying to emphasize to our schools and to encourage them to teach the basic values of good citizenship, values that make a good life.

Secretary Riley has been extremely supportive and a strong advocate of what he calls the moral code that holds us together. In teaching that in our schools, teaching our students to be honest and trustworthy, reliable, to have respect for themselves, for others, for property, and for our natural environment, to be good citizens, and also to do the things that I advocated a few months ago when I spoke at my alma mater, Georgetown University, to treat one another with civility and tolerance and to exercise personal responsibility. After all, if we all did what we were supposed to, we wouldn't have to spend so much time talking to other people— [*laughter*]—and neither would anybody else.

And this character education movement, I predict to you, will do quite well in this country. There will be more and more and more deliberate efforts to teach these values in our public schools. There is evidence already that in the schools that have a thoroughgoing, comprehensive, disciplined commitment to this, the dropout rate is down, and the student performance is up. That's because you basically can't live without values. You've got some. It's just a question of what they are. And it's important to be explicit about them, and you can do that within the framework of the first amendment.

So if any of you are more interested in that, we can get you the information on what the Department of Education is doing. I just announced in California a couple of days ago that we have actually put out modest grants to four States to help school districts in those States develop comprehensive character education programs.

Let me say, the freshest evidence that this is important is a recent study, a very, very large study of young people and drug use that Joe Califano brought to my attention about 3 weeks ago that said that the three major determinants in whether young people use drugs or not was whether they had a strong relationship with their parents, whether they tended to believe in the future and be optimistic about it, and whether they had a connection to a church. Those three things were the three repeating constants in what is otherwise an incredible kaleidoscope of different life circumstances that lead young people either to use drugs or to refrain from using them. So I think that is important.

The Vice President talked about the night we had—I might say, it made a special night for us because he and I went to Baltimore with his son and my daughter, and each of them brought a friend. So we got to see this great event through the eyes of children. And the thing that struck me about it was that everybody was so happy and nobody resented Mr. Ripken's success. Not a person. I don't think a person in the country. Why? Because it was about more than talent, success, and making several million

dollars a year. It was about showing up for work every day—[*laughter*]—and sticking with your team. It wasn't about who got the best contract, who made the best deal. It was about keeping your end of the bargain.

And I think one of the reasons that people were so ecstatic about it is that it was an exceptional example of what most people try to do in their own lives every day. When I got home from California the night the record was tied, it was about midnight. And before I went to bed—I don't know about you, but when I get off an airplane and come in the house, I can't just plop down and go to sleep. So I turned on the television, and I saw the late local news. And there was a feature on the local news in Virginia of a bus driver who had not missed a day's work in 18 years. And here was this bus driver, he never would have been on television before, and they were doing a feature on him.

And the local reporter was riding a bus with him. And he was meeting the people that he picked up every day and let off every day and talking about how his daddy told him he was supposed to work, that he didn't think there was anything unusual. Why? Why wouldn't you go 18 years and never miss a day's work? And I thought, that man would have never been on television if it hadn't been for Cal Ripken breaking Lou Gehrig's record. There was a reaffirmation of the idea of responsibility, personal responsibility, the dignity of work, the devotion— that guy's team were the people that carry the folks around every day. Pretty important team. And I think it sort of reinforced to me this idea that in spite of all the differences in this country, there really are a lot of things that bind us together, that we believe very deeply.

I appreciate what the Vice President said about the First Lady. I wish she could be here today. She's getting home sometime tonight. But I think that that speech she gave resonated so powerfully across the world because it was elemental, basic, true, profound in the simplicity of the things that we all know, things that we all know we should do, things we all know we shouldn't do and shouldn't permit if we can stop. And it was a very powerful thing because it brought people together.

Now, I think that's very important today in America because of the kind of things that are going on. And I just want to talk very briefly about that and the work we're about to undertake here.

In many ways, the big trends in America look good. Economically we have 7 million more jobs, 2½ million more homeowners. We're creating new businesses at a rate of 750,000 a year, by far the highest rate in American history. We have low inflation, high growth. By any standard, this is about the best combined economic picture in 20 years. African-American unemployment rate below 10 percent for the first time since the Vietnam war. A lot of the social indicators are encouraging. In almost every major city in America, the crime rate is down, the welfare rolls are down, the food stamp rolls are down.

A lot of the cultural things are encouraging. The divorce rate is down. The abortion rate is down. There are signs that people are beginning to get together even in troubled places. The United States has been honored to be a force for peace in the last 3 years in Northern Ireland and South Africa and the Middle East, in Haiti. We even see signs of hope in Bosnia. Today representatives of Bosnia, Croatia, and Serbia are meeting as a part of the peace initiative the United States has pushed so hard in Europe, and we pray for their success. They need to quit killing each other; it's not that much land involved. And there is nothing in their different religious faiths that dictates that kind of bloodletting.

So there is a lot to be hopeful about, a lot of common ground to celebrate. But if you look at it, you'd never know that to listen to what we do here. And I think there is a reason for that—there are two reasons for that. One is the culture around here and the way we do business or the way it's been done for years—I haven't been here too long, but I'm still learning about it—and the larger reasons of what's going on in the world today.

But let me deal with the basic, fundamental issues here. What worked for the bus driver and for Cal Ripken? Showing up for work, having the right attitude, working on the team, working for tomorrow, that's what works. What works in a church? Working together, working for the future around shared values. What works in a family? What works at a business? Not surprisingly, people don't like what they see in Washington if they don't see people working together and working for the future, if all they ever see is what are they fighting about today?

What is the new partisan difference that is all of a sudden all the rage?

I think we all have a common interest in balancing the budget, and I'm glad to see both parties' leadership now committed to doing that. For 2 years, we had a lonely battle here. We took the deficit from $290 billion down to $160 billion. It was a one-party operation. And when that happens, you have to make decisions that in the details are so controversial, it's unsettling to people. When both parties work together, they can do it better. So I think it's great; we're going to balance the budget.

Then the question is how should we do it, because it's not just a matter of debits and credits, it's also a matter of values and responsibilities. How you do this defines who you are. And I would argue to you that this is a much more important process today than it would have been a generation ago for reasons I will explain in just a moment.

But if you believe that, then we have to ask: What are the values? How are we going to provide for our children's future, especially for their education? What do we owe the elderly in this country in terms of health care? Seventy-five percent of the people who are eligible for Medicare live on $24,000 a year or less. What do we owe to them? What do we owe to people like those veterans of World War II that we honored in Hawaii just a few days ago, who literally made the world that we are all living off of now, who set in motion the circumstances that permitted all of us in the age groups represented here to flourish? What do we owe to the poor and to the homeless?

What do we owe? How do our obligations here—can they be fulfilled, anyway? What kind of Government do we have to have to make this stuff work? Yesterday, the Vice President announced his 2-year report on our reinventing Government project. There are 160,000 fewer people working for the Government now than were when I became President. About 400 programs have been eliminated, many thousands of pages of regulations have been scrapped. But we've also worked very hard on improving the quality of Government.

Business Week magazine evaluated all the business units in America that depend heavily on being successful on the phone, great companies like L.L. Bean and Federal Express. And they said that the Federal Government Social Security Administration had the most effective, information-laden, courteous phone service of any major organization in America, which I thought was a remarkable thing, because we're in pretty high cotton there with those other companies. [Laughter]

But what do we owe to the country in terms of the kind of Government we have and the way it performs? What are our obligations and responsibilities? How do all these compare with tax cuts that have been proposed? What do those tax cuts reflect in terms of our values? There are many different proposals, and they're all different. What do we get out of a balanced budget? I'll tell you. We get the opportunity to lift the burden of debt off of our children and grandchildren. We get lower interest rates. We free up the money that's available to be borrowed by people in the private sector to create new jobs. We get more growth if we do it right.

But if we're penny-wise and pound-foolish, if we don't think about our larger values, if we don't also take care of educating our people and lifting up our children, even the poorest of them, then we could wind up with a budget that doesn't do all of those things. Prosperity really has to grow out of having good, shared values. We're lucky; we're big; we're diverse; we've got a lot of resources. But we still have to do the right things.

If you look at the gentleman who was a bus driver, God gave him a good constitution. But a lot of healthy people don't show up for work every day for 18 years. Mr. Ripken is 6'4" and weighs 220 pounds, and not many people have a body like that. But there are a lot of people with bodies like that, that miss a lot of baseball games because they don't take care of it. They don't always do the right things.

So we have to do the right things. And that's very important. And it can't just be a mechanical thing. It can't just be a political thing. It can't be just who's got the political power and who's got the influence to get this or that deal done. This is an historic obligation we have. And we have to do it in a way that reflects common sense and that reaches common ground that's higher ground. That's what I've tried to say when I talked about the New Covenant in the last 3 years. It's not just a matter of contracts and deals. This is a—we're going through a period of great change. And we have to reach deep down inside for the right things to do that will bring us together.

Let me say that I—if ever there was a case of preaching to the saved, that's what I'm doing today. [Laughter] In more ways than one. A lot of you are involved in ministries that do this. You not only build the edifice of your churches, you serve the needs of your people. And that's what we have to do in America. And we cannot allow the usual partisan, divisive atmosphere which characterizes our national politics and which does make, frankly—to defend all the players here, many of whom have been here a lot longer than I have in Washington—they think that having these kind of differences and articulate them in a way that's most favorable to their constituents is the only way to communicate them across the vast distance that exists from Washington, DC, into the homes of the nearly 260 million Americans who live here, because it's not like being the pastor of a church or the Governor of a small State or the mayor of a city. They are so far from where their folks are, the way of doing things here tends to put a greater premium on words than deeds, a greater premium on positioning and division than production and teamwork and accomplishment. But that doesn't make it right. And it doesn't make it acceptable for this time.

So I'm trying to bring a new spirit here. I'm trying to deal with a lot of hot-button issues that need to be dealt with in the right spirit.

The welfare system needs to be reformed because the people that are on welfare hate it. Nobody wants to be dependent. So we should end welfare as we know it, but we ought to be mindful of the fact that we're doing it because our country will be better off if people are successful workers and successful parents. We don't need a permanently dependent system.

I'm trying to deal with the issue of crime in a responsible way that punishes criminals more but also seeks to prevent crime by giving our young people some things that they can say yes to as well as say no to.

We're trying to deal with the issue of immigration in a way that says that it's wrong for people to immigrate here illegally. They may need to do it. It may be a good thing for their family, but from our point of view, since we've got folks lined up willing to wait for years, we have to try to enforce the immigration laws and control our borders and be disciplined about this. And when we look at the volume of legal immigration, we have to look at it in terms of our ability to maintain a decent standard of living for our own people and to imagine what it's going to be like over a 10-year period. But I think to try to blame immigrants for our problems is a mistake. We're all a nation of immigrants. Nearly everybody came from somewhere else.

And of course, you all pretty well know what I think about the affirmative action issue. There are some problems in the way these programs have been implemented. They ought to be fixed. There are some of them that don't work right, and they ought to be fixed. And nobody has a stake in America in promoting reverse discrimination or quotas or giving somebody something they're not qualified to receive.

But we should make a conscious effort to include all Americans in the bounty of America. Conscious effort is not the same thing as giving preference to unqualified people. A conscious effort is animated by the belief that God put within everybody the capacity to rise to higher levels, and we need everybody to become what we ought to be. So let's fix what doesn't work. But let's don't pretend that it's a bad thing to try to get the most out of everybody and to make effort. That's what I believe.

Let me tell you why I think this is all more important now than it is normally. Two years ago, I recommended a book by a nonreligious leader, Stephen Carter. Today I'll recommend another one. I've been reading this. This is a fascinating book by a man named Benjamin Barber, whom I had the privilege to know, called "Jihad Versus McWorld."

Now, let me tell you what the essential argument here is. Let me tell you why I believe it's important. Mr. Barber is arguing that democracy and the ability to hold people together and have reliable, predictable, good lives for people who work hard and do the right thing is being threatened today, first of all, by the globalization of the economy, which has a lot of benefits for those of us who have good educations and can benefit from it, with the movement of money and technology all across the world. But it's elevating consumerism to even higher and higher levels and promoting short-term gains. You watch this money—we watch it every day, billions and trillions of dollars moving across the globe in the split of an eye just because of an event here, an event there, an event the other place. It's very hard in those conditions to preserve even in the wealthy, powerful countries the conditions of stable, ordinary life.

Therefore, you see what happens in America. We have 7 million new jobs; we have all these things that are happening that are good, but most hourly wage earners are working harder for the same or less money than they were making 10 years ago. And a lot of people feel insecure in their jobs because the economy is changing so much and they have no confidence that if they lose the job they have they can get another one that is just as good or better.

So we're living in this global economy where there are a whole lot of winners. But a lot of people who think they do just what Cal Ripken and the Virginia bus driver do think they may still lose, and that's a big problem for America. If people think they're willing to show up every day, they're working hard, they're doing right by their kids, they wouldn't break the law, they wouldn't cheat the Government out of a nickel on their taxes, they wouldn't begin to do anything wrong, and they still may not make it, that's a problem for America.

The other word, "jihad," as you know, refers to holy war, the Arabic concept—Muslim concept of the holy war. It's not an anti-Muslim book, by the way. Islam is a beautiful religion with great values. What it refers to is, as people face a world that they cannot control, when they think that democracy is not going to work for them, that they can't keep the family of the United States or the family of France or Germany or Russia or Estonia or you name it, together, they are vulnerable—because their nerves are raw and they have no sense of certainty—to extreme manifestations of people who claim to have revealed truth, so that the likelihood of having more conflicts rooted in ethnic, racial, or religious differences increases perversely as the world becomes more economically integrated. And he argues, I believe correctly, that it is even more important today for the United States of America to succeed, even more important today for democracy to work, even more important today for the basic values that we just talked about to be able to be made real in the lives of ordinary citizens.

And that's why what we're doing with this budget debate is so important and why we have to do it right. If we don't balance the budget, we're going to hurt America's future. If we do it in the wrong way, we're going to hurt America's future.

About once in 100 years this sort of thing happens. We are going through a level of change in the way we work and live that is comparable to the change we went through when we moved from being an agrarian society to an industrial, more urbanized society. And it took our country from roughly the end of the 1890's until about 1916 to sort through all that. I mean, it's a continuing process. But we basically had to decide what is the responsibility that we have as a country? What does the Government have to do? How will we deal with this?

Now we're moving out of that age to a more information-based, technology-based age. We're moving from the cold war to the global economy. We're moving from the possibility of nuclear war between superpowers to the possibility that terrorists can carry around biological weapons that kill people in Japanese subways or make homemade bombs that blow up the World Trade Center or the Federal building in Oklahoma.

Believe me, it's better that we don't have to worry as much about everybody being wiped out. Let's not kid ourselves. But it's important to realize that our great country, this family of America, has forces beyond it economically that are pulling at our ability to hold everybody together, and in reaction to the insecurity that is caused and the uncertainty that is caused, there are forces internally in every great democracy forcing people to be divided among themselves. That's why I said the other day, do we have to fix welfare? Yes. Affirmative action? Yes. Immigration problems? Yes. Is that the cause of the anxiety of the middle class in America? No, not really. That's not the real cause. That's not an excuse not to fix them; we do. But we need to know what the real cause is.

And when you're living in a time like this when people are torn from pillar to post, having those basic values to fall back on, knowing that there is a church with a larger ministry is important. But also be humbled enough to know that in a time like this, when you're moving into a future you can't fully predict, nobody has all the answers, that's important, too.

I don't want to embarrass him, but not very long ago, I was home in Arkansas, and my pastor, Rex Horne, who's here, gave a fascinating sermon in which he was talking about how Jesus treated different kinds of people. And he pointed out how humble Christ was in dealing with the leper, the hated Zaccheus, the woman caught in adultery. He reminded us of the stories of the Prodigal Son and the Good Samaritan in the Bible. And then he said, you know, the only people Jesus was really hard on and acted like He was arrogant to—[*laughter*]—were the Pharisees and the Sadducees and the religious hypocrites who appeared to have all the revealed truth, and the people he ran out of the temple because they got church and state mixed up, too. They tried to take over the temple. [*Laughter*] Right?

Now, this is an important lesson, and it had a huge impact on me, on my level of humility. We all need a good dose of humility. This is—it is not given to any of us to fully understand the future, but we do know we're moving into a different time with no precedent. And Mr. Barber, he may not be right about everything, but he's got a fix on it, and it's worth thinking about. And I ask all of you to think about that and to think of your work—when you see the people in your churches and your synagogues, in your mosques, who have problems in their lives, ask yourselves, are these problems the kind of problems that would happen at any age in time, or are they aggravated by this different period of change through which we're going, and how can we move together to respond to it?

So I say to you, I hope you will pray for all of us here in these next 90 days, without regard to our party or our religion, because we have a hard and difficult job to do. We have to act. We have to succeed, but we have to do it in the right way for America to move into the next century with the American dream alive and well and with the ability to keep the kind of character and strength that we celebrated this week not only in the achievement of Cal Ripken but in the achievement of the bus driver and all the people that were cheering because they shared something that we desperately need to elevate and preserve as long as this country exists.

Thank you, and God bless you.

NOTE: The President spoke at 10:33 a.m. in the State Dining Room at the White House. In his remarks, he referred to Joseph A. Califano, Jr., director, Center on Addiction and Substance Abuse, Columbia University.

Statement on the Agreed Basic Principles for a Settlement in Bosnia-Herzegovina
September 8, 1995

Today's successful meeting in Geneva of the Foreign Ministers of Bosnia, Croatia, and the Federal Republic of Yugoslavia is an important milestone on the road to peace in the former Yugoslavia. As a result of intensive mediation by Ambassador Holbrooke and his team—supported by our Contact Group partners in the European Union and Russia—the three Foreign Ministers have endorsed a set of Agreed Basic Principles that will serve as the framework for a political settlement to the conflict in Bosnia. The Foreign Ministers of Croatia and the Federal Republic of Yugoslavia have also agreed to work actively toward a peaceful solution in Eastern Slavonia, the Serb-controlled area of the Republic of Croatia also known as U.N. Sector East.

The Agreed Basic Principles commit all three governments to support a settlement consistent with the goals we have long sought in Bosnia. Most importantly, for the first time, all three have agreed that Bosnia-Herzegovina will continue as a single state, with its present borders and with continuing international recognition. Consistent with the Contact Group plan, under the terms of a settlement, all three agree that Bosnia-Herzegovina will consist of two entities: the Federation, established under last year's Washington Agreements, and the Serb Republic.

The 51:49 parameter of the Contact Group's territorial proposal will be the basis for a settlement, subject to any adjustments that the parties make by mutual agreement. The two entities will have the right to establish relationships with neighboring states, but these must be consistent with the sovereignty and territorial integrity of Bosnia-Herzegovina. The parties have pledged to adhere to international human rights standards, to ensure freedom of movement and the right of displaced persons to return to their homes and to collaborate on joint economic projects that will promote transportation links and communication among all of Bosnia's peoples. These are important principles around which we now can move toward intensive negotiations for a full peace agreement.

I want to congratulate the three Foreign Ministers, Secretary of State Christopher, National Security Adviser Anthony Lake, Ambassador Holbrooke and his team, and our Russian and other European partners for today's impressive achievement. Much work remains to be done in translating these principles into a final peace agreement. All the parties will need to display the same flexibility and statesmanship that made today's agreement possible if we are to turn away from war and achieve our common goal of a durable peace in the Balkans.

Message to the Congress Transmitting a Budget Deferral
September 8, 1995

To the Congress of the United States:
In accordance with the Congressional Budget and Impoundment Control Act of 1974, I herewith report one revised deferral of budgetary resources, totaling $1.2 billion.

The deferral affects the International Security Assistance program.

WILLIAM J. CLINTON

The White House,

September 8, 1995.

NOTE: The report detailing the deferral was published in the *Federal Register* on September 19.

The President's Radio Address
September 9, 1995

Good morning. As a candidate for President, I pledged to end welfare as we know it. And as President, I've been doing everything in my power to keep that pledge.

Earlier, for more than 15 years, first as Governor of Arkansas and later when I became President, I have always felt it was critically important to fix our broken welfare system. It doesn't honor our values of work and family and personal responsibility. Well, it's been a long time coming, but finally the Senate is taking up this issue.

Meanwhile, over the last 2½ years, while I've been urging Congress to act, my administration has worked as hard as we can to change the welfare system by executive action in a way that honors the values most Americans hold dear: work, responsibility, and family. We've put tough child support enforcement at the center of the national debate. Our administration collected a record level of child support in 1994—$10 billion. And I signed a tough Executive order to crack down on Federal employees who owe child support.

We've also cut through Federal redtape to speed up welfare reform all around the country by approving experiments in a record 34 States. Just through these experiments, 7 million recipients of welfare around the country are now being required to work, pay child support, live at home, and stay in school or earn a paycheck from a business that pays them with money that used to be spent on food stamps and welfare. Now, I have told all 50 States they can have these welfare reforms immediately, within 30 days, just by asking.

Next week, it's the Senate's turn to do its part. The current system must be replaced. Instead of requiring people to work, now it penalizes people who go to work. Instead of strengthening families, now it gives teenagers a separate check to leave home, leave school, and set up their own households. Instead of demanding responsibility, it lets too many parents who owe child support just walk away without paying. That's not right, and it's time to change it.

But we should do this the right way, not the wrong way. Real reform, first and foremost, must be about work. We should impose time limits and tough work requirements while making sure that parents get the child care they need to go to work. We should reward States for putting people to work, not for cutting people off. We will only succeed if we move people from welfare to work.

But real welfare reform is also about family. That means putting in place the toughest possible child support enforcement. It means requiring teen mothers to live at home, to stay in school, to turn their lives around. But it doesn't mean punishing children for the mistakes of their parents.

And finally, welfare reform must be about responsibility. States have a responsibility to maintain their own efforts to move people from welfare to work. That way we can have a race to independence, not a race to the bottom. And individuals have a responsibility to work in return for the help they receive. It's time to make welfare a second chance, not a way of life. It's time to make responsibility a way of life.

Let me be clear: Some differences still remain between the congressional proposals and me. But we must find common ground, and soon. Look how far we've come already. Not long ago, some conservatives were talking about putting young people in orphanages. And not long ago, many liberals opposed requiring welfare recipients to work. But we've reached consensus on these issues. Now we need to go the final mile.

We've stood at the brink of welfare reform before. But for too long, American people have been frustrated by demands for ideological purity, by politicians who put their personal ambitions first. Millions of people who are trapped in the system and millions more taxpayers who pay the tab have suffered as a result. We can't let that happen again.

This is a time to deliver for the American people, not to pander to extremists who have held us back for too long. We can't let welfare reform die at the hands of ideological extremism or Presidential politics or budget politics. If welfare reform gets caught up in the whirlpool of the budget debate, we run the risk that it might drown.

This is an historic moment. For 30 years, under both Democratic and Republican leadership, we've been saddled with a broken welfare system. Now we've got a real chance to reach common ground and higher ground. The Senators owe it to the people who sent them to Washington not to let this opportunity slip away by doing the wrong thing or by failing to act at all. The American people have waited long enough.

Next week, let's end the old system that fosters dependence, and let's give the American people a new one based on independence, work, responsibility, and family.

Thanks for listening.

NOTE: The President spoke at 10:06 a.m. from the Oval Office at the White House.

Statement on the Death of Jamie Whitten
September 9, 1995

It is with deep regret that I learned today of the death of former Congressman and Chairman of the House Appropriations Committee Jamie Whitten. Congressman Whitten served Mississippi and our country in Congress for 53 years, longer than any other person in the history of this Republic. He was literally an institution himself within one of the most important of our democratic institutions.

Throughout his long service and especially as chairman of the House Appropriations Committee from the 96th Congress through the 100th Congress, Congressman Whitten dedicated himself to the concerns of the hard-working people of this country. He worked tirelessly on behalf of America's farmers, especially our family farmers, and he never gave up working to build more opportunity for all Americans willing to make the most of their own lives.

The people of the United States and of Mississippi will miss Jamie Whitten. Hillary and I send our sympathies to his family and loved ones.

Roundtable Discussion With Students on Student Loans at Southern Illinois University in Carbondale, Illinois
September 11, 1995

The President. Is everybody in? For the members of the press corps that came in with me, as you know, I have been doing these roundtable discussions with students and faculty members and others in colleges around the country. And this is the kickoff of a back-to-school week we're doing this year to emphasize the choices that have to be made in Washington in the next 60 days that will affect education. And so I came here to Southern Illinois University.

One of the big issues is what's going to happen to the student loan program and, particularly, the direct loan program which our administration started. So I thought that we should start by having Pam Britton, who is in charge of financial aid here at SIU, talk a little bit about how it works—the direct loan program—and what you're doing here.

So, Pam, why don't you lead it off.

[At this point, Ms. Britton welcomed the President and asked the participating students to introduce themselves. Following the introductions, Ms. Britton explained the importance of the student loan program at Southern Illinois University.]

The President. Thank you. Let me explain—how many of you come from schools that have the direct loan program? You know the old guaranteed student loan program basically gave banks a 90 percent guarantee if they made a student loan to a student and the student didn't repay. And they got a handsome commission and fee on it. Under the direct loan program, the Government makes the loan directly through a Government institution like a lot of the other Government mortgage institutions. And what we found is that, number one, as Pam said, the loans are going out much faster, much, much faster. There is less paperwork for the college administrators, less paperwork for the students. If the students get the loans on time, then they don't have to go borrow money, what you talked about, short-term loans.

In addition to that, believe it or not, they are less expensive because the fee doesn't get paid. So the Government actually spends less money on them. And best of all, for students that have to borrow a lot of money, unlike the old guaranteed student loan program, there are four different repayment options, including an option to pay the money back as a percentage of your income, so that, for example, if you decide to take a job that you find very rewarding but doesn't pay very much money and you have a big loan, you still can't ever go broke doing it. There's no incentive ever to drop out of school because you can pay the money back as a percentage of your income.

This was a major part of my administration's economic proposal in 1993, and we got it through. And ever since then it's been under assault by the bankers who made the money under the old loan program. It is true that they're worse off. I mean, they lost a lot of business. But the students are better off, the administrators are better off, the Federal Treasury's better off, and the country's better off because now we're going to have more people borrowing money and going to school. But the bankers aren't better off, and they've persuaded the House of Representatives to get rid of the program, go back to the old system. And now it's under assault in the Senate; they'll be voting this week.

So one of the reasons I wanted to come here is to try to galvanize people like you all across the country to ask our Congress to stand up to the special interests that, you know, want their money back and to keep this program, which is working better for you.

I mean, ultimately, the purpose of the loan program is to educate more young people, to make loans—and not-so-young people going back to college, because a lot of people my age are now going back, and they can't do it without student aid.

So I want to hear all of your stories, but Pam told me she had sort of a testimonial—the experience that SIU has had with the direct loan program, and I must say, I hear that everywhere.

I met a young couple in Florida the other day who were both graduated from medical school with $140,000 in student loans between them, and they told us that if it weren't for the direct loan program, which permits them to repay as a percentage of their income—because, see, they're all going to become interns; they won't make a lot of money when they get right out of medical school. They said they would be spending over half of their monthly income repaying their loans. They wouldn't have enough money, literally, to pay for food and rent but for the direct loan program.

So, Pam, why don't you take over for now. Let's go around and listen to the other students.

Ms. Britton. Okay. One of our student participants would like to begin by speaking to direct loan issues at her institution. Noemi?

Noemi Rivera-Morales. Mr. President, Ms. Britton, fellow students, good morning. *Buenos dias.*

The President. Buenos dias.

[*Ms. Rivera-Morales recounted her past difficulties in receiving her loan disbursement under the Pell grant program, but stated that this year she had received her loan within a week of applying to the direct loan program.*]

The President. So it was one week?

Ms. Rivera-Morales. One week. With a holiday in between.

The President. With a holiday in between. So much for Government inefficiency.

[*Ms. Rivera-Morales explained that the efficiency of the direct loan program had increased the amount of money given yearly to students at the university from $16 million to $28 million.*]

The President. From 16 to 28?

[*Ms. Rivera-Morales stated that she was fearful that future cuts in spending would prevent some people from attending college.*]

The President. So am I. That's why I'm here.

Ms. Britton. We are concerned about direct loans, but we're also concerned about the Pell grant program here at SIU as well as other undergraduate grants. And Duane would like to speak to that.

[*Duane Sherman explained that without the help of Federal grant programs he and many other students would not be able to attend college. He also stated that the education students receive enables them to become productive, tax-paying citizens who are able to compete in a global society*].

The President. I agree with that. You know, I think most taxpayers resent it if they think their money is going to people who don't need it, people who get tax breaks who are very well off or people who won't work, who won't try to help themselves. The student loan and the student scholarship program, by definition, go only to people who are trying to help themselves.

We have increased the maximum amount of the Pell grant and propose to do it some more and to have some smaller Pell grants, between $400 to $600 a year, to help people who maybe have a little money but don't have enough.

One of the big arguments that I'm in now with the Republican Congress is that both of us agree we should balance the budget, but I think it better to take a little longer, have a smaller tax cut, and increase our investment in education. So the difference between our two proposals is there would be 360,000 fewer people getting Pell grants under their proposal than mine, and the maximum grant would be considerably smaller, and the smaller grants would be cut out under their proposal.

Again, I would say that it seems to me that the main thing we ought to be doing today is try to help people who are willing to help themselves, trying to empower people to make the most of their own lives. And they say that's what they believe in, but it's just inconsistent. You do not have to cut education to balance the budget; you don't have to do it. And it's sort of cutting off our nose to spite our face. I mean, the whole argument for balancing the budget is that it's going to strengthen the economy. And you know, I mean, that's the argument for doing it, right? And if we do it right, it will. Obviously, if we don't keep borrowing money every year just to pay the same bills, it will lower interest rates and free up money for people to borrow money and start businesses or expand businesses and create jobs. But if the way to balance the budget is to make the

American people less well-educated, all it will do is to continue to drive wages down in this global economy where most people are working harder for less money anyway.

I consider this decision on education basically one of the three most important decisions that will be made in the Congress in the next 60 to 90 days over this budget. Is it worth it to balance the budget in the way they want to do it if to do it you have to cut education, if there is a better way to balance the budget? I think the answer is, no, take the better way. But that is the big—I mean, Duane just sort of laid it out, what the choices are for you, and you can multiply that by millions and you can see the future of America.

Who's going next?

Ms. Britton. We have some concern related to graduate students, and Mary wanted to speak to especially——

The President. Mary, I read about you. [*Laughter*]

[*Mary Armstrong explained how important subsidized loans were to her education. She said that if they were reduced due to budget cuts, she would have a difficult time paying for her education because the profession she has chosen will not pay a very high salary. She then added that the student loan program was an investment in the future.*]

The President. Good for you.

Ms. Britton. We have one last student that is prepared to give just an indication of their personal experience, Rick Collie.

[*Mr. Collie explained how the Federal loan program had helped him to go to college and become a successful and productive citizen.*]

The President. A great story. You know, Mary, one of the proposals on the student loan program has been to start charging students interest on the loan while they're in school and then to maybe—and also start charging them the so-called grace period, you know, the 6 months after school you can go look for a job and finally try to find placements.

If that happened and the direct loan program were abolished or made unavailable to huge numbers of students, the combined impact of that, on the average for graduate students, would be an increase in the debt of about $9,300 without the option to pay it back as a percent of your income, which for graduate students—which for graduate students in the nonprofessional areas would be a disaster—I mean, like the lawyers and the doctors and the accountants, you know, you might argue—well, even the accountants, a lot of them are not going to make much money in the beginning. But I mean, the——

Q. I couldn't do it.

The President. It's a serious problem. I really do believe if enough of your voices are heard between now and whenever we finally adopt this budget, which will probably be sometime in October or November, in that range—they're not going to do it by September 30th, which is the deadline and they won't make it this year—but I just think it's very important to get this story out there.

And Rick, I'll just use you as an example. When I ran for President, I was in my fifth term as Governor of my State; I was having a good time. A lot of my State looks like southern Illinois, which is probably why I did so well here when I ran. But I just realized that unless somebody did something to change the direction of the country, we were going to face—we had already faced by 1992 almost 20 years of stagnant wages for hourly wage earners. Now we have—since '73, the average male worker in America today, once you adjust for inflation, is making about 10 percent less than he did in 1973 working a slightly longer workweek.

Almost all of the economic gains have gone to those people like me in the upper 20 percent of the society. So my goal has been as President not only to create more jobs but to raise the incomes again, to give working families some sense of stability. It's the biggest economic problem in the country.

Most people who do what they do, like Mary said, most people do what they do knowing they're never going to be rich. That's not the point. The point is that people ought to know that if they work hard and are diligent that at least they'll do a little better year-in and year-out—not that you're going to get rich but that you'll be able to have a family and raise children and have a stable life. And so that's a very serious concern.

And if you look at the last 2 years of our administration—now, this wage thing has been going on for 20 years. So you just can't turn it around like that. So in the last 2½ years, we have—to show you how pervasive it is—

since the day I became President, we've got 7 million more jobs, 2½ million more home-owners, 1½ million more—actually, probably like 2 million more small businesses now—the most rapid growth of small business in American history. The stock market is at a record high. Corporate profits are high. Inflation is low. The combined rate of employment and inflation is at a 25-year low. But the median income, the person in the middle—not the average because the average gets jerked up by the people at the top—the median, the person in the middle has dropped one percent.

And why is that? There are only—there are two or three things we can do about it. The first thing we have to do is to try to change the mix of jobs in America, to try to get more higher wage jobs with a longer term future. But you can't do that overnight. The second thing we have to do is to raise the educational level of the American people because the people who are being just hammered out there in this country today are people who don't have at least 2 years of community college education. Basically people that have 2 years or more tend to do pretty well in this economy, tend to be able to hold their own and then sort of move forward. And it strengthens the American economy. That's what this issue is about.

So if we balance the budget—and I'm all for that. We've cut the deficit from $290 billion a year to $160 billion a year since I've been President. I think it's nuts just to run a permanent debt. But if we cut it by cutting education, then we will compound the most important economic problem we have which is that people are working harder for less. So what we need is more people like you, not fewer.

Mr. Collie. The student loan program allowed me to free up my distress and bills that were due and things I had to pay, and I could focus on my education. And I graduated with honors.

The President. Don't you believe, though, if we dramatically raised the cost of higher education that fewer people would go and more would drop out?

Students. Absolutely. Most definitely.

The President. We have evidence of that, by the way. I just was in California over Labor Day where—California had the worst recession of all the States in the last few years because they had the huge impact of the defense cuts because they had most of the defense industry when we built it up. And there were other reasons as well.

And one of the decisions they made in California was when times got tough, they would cut education and raise the cost. And the California system of public education was generally believed to be the finest ever created by any society anywhere. They have 21 colleges in the State university system. And then I think they have another 9 or 10 in the University of California system.

And it used to be free, and—they had to put some fees on it. But they raised the cost so much in the last few years that enrollment is down 19 percent. Well, if you've got a high unemployment rate and stagnant incomes, the last thing you want to do is drive down college enrollment, right? You want to drive up college enrollment. So, I don't want our country to do that.

So, it's not just all of you, there are millions of people out there like you, millions. And the whole future of the country depends in part on—in other words, it doesn't matter what I do in terms of economic policy or how much I try to change the job mix in America unless the people in America have the education to do the jobs of the 21st century.

To me, this is self-evident. You cannot imagine how important this event is today. I'm telling you, this is one of the two or three most important decisions we're going to make in the next 60 to 90 days, and it will color the whole future that you will have.

Q. Mr. President, I was lucky enough to get in under this program. I have a son who is a junior in college who was lucky enough to get in. I have a son in Maine who has a five-year-old child who had a liver transplant at the age of 6 months. Rex wants desperately to go to school, but he doesn't fit into this program.

Ms. Britton. You talked about the higher cost of education. We might want to hear from our Knox College private——

The President. I'll look into that. Go ahead.

[*A student explained that he was able to attend Knox College due to Federal money and a work-study program at the Knox College youth center.*]

The President. That's good.

Q. And while I was working there, I learned the skills that enabled me to acquire a job with the National Football League this summer in terms of enterprise computing.

The President. Really?

[*The student said that he now had a full-time position with the NFL because of the experience he received through the work-study program. He also emphasized the importance of a graduate degree in the job market. Another student then explained the importance of loan programs to students from low-income families.*]

Ms. Britton. And at the graduate level, Vanika is on the special fellowship——

[*Vanika Mock spoke about the importance of a grace period for students who must repay a large amount in student loans after graduating from college.*]

The President. You've got to have a job first.

[*Ms. Mock explained that in order for her to pursue a career as a teacher, her loan would have to continue.*]

The President. So you could pay it back as a percentage of your income?

[*Ms. Mock said that was the only solution for people who wanted to work in a profession that they enjoy but which would not pay a lot of money.*]

The President. And, of course, most of the jobs will be in service job growth, too.

Brian, were you going to say something?

[*Brian Szuda commented on the importance of the grace period in loan repayment for people who were unable to find jobs immediately after graduation.*]

Ms. Britton. I know Michelle's been trying to say something here.

The President. I'm sorry, Michelle.

[*Michelle Birch explained how difficult it would be for her to attend college without help from Federal loans and subsidized day care for her son. She stated that in order to stay off of welfare she would need to continue receiving this assistance.*]

The President. That's the argument we're having in Washington now over welfare reform.

Ms. Birch. I know.

The President. I told them that I would gladly support programs that would save money on spending and welfare reform and put limits on how long people could stay, if you would give more for child care and if we keep the student aid programs. Because basically, welfare reform is about education and work and child care; it's not very complicated.

You know, I have spent since 1980, when most of you were real children, I have spent a lot of time with people on welfare. And I found that people with the deepest desire to change the system are people who have been on it.

I've almost never met anybody that didn't want to get off, and also who all have the best ideas. I'm glad to hear you say that. Good for you. I'm proud of you.

[*Ms. Birch stated that she had a strong desire to succeed in life because she was raised by a family who instilled those values in her.*]

Ms. Britton. We're running short of time, and I want to give Ramon and Allison an opportunity to say at least one thing.

The President. You guys are great.

[*Ramon Blakley explained how Federal loans help students from low-income families.*]

The President. That's why I'm with you.

Allison Crabtree. I guess I have a question more than anything. I was talking with one of your aides beforehand about the proposals by the new Congress to limit the growth of the direct lending program, and that's been so beneficial, I know, on my campus. It's so much more of an efficient program. And as I was talking to my Congressman this last weekend, he was informing me that what it does bottom-line is it takes more of the money that you put into the student loan programs at the Federal level into the hands of students as opposed to administrators, such as banks and private lending institutions.

The President. You got it.

Ms. Crabtree. So I was wondering how you felt about the possibility it will be capped off?

The President. I think it's a terrible idea. But capping is not as terrible as getting rid of it altogether, though. The House of Representatives wants to get rid of it altogether. I mean, not the Congressmen that are here, they all fought it, but the majority. This is not complicated. Banks used to make a lot of money doing this, and they want their money back. This is not a complicated thing.

They want—and, interestingly enough, they pulled an incredible gimmick. They basically

got—the new majority in the Congress got the people who run their budget office to pull an incredible gimmick. They said that in calculating the cost of the direct loan program, as compared with the cost of the old student loan program, the guaranteed loan program, we had to calculate the administrative costs of the direct loan program and put it in, but we couldn't count anything of the administrative costs that we paid for the guaranteed loan program to try to make the direct loan program look more expensive than the guaranteed program when everybody knows it's cheaper. It is bizarre. I mean, that's the kind of stuff that's going on up there.

And it's just classic—it's a special interest grab that overlooks the fact that the stories that all of you have told are good stories for America's future.

Let me just say one other thing. I will say this: A lot of these guaranteed loan providers have gotten quicker and cheaper and more responsive because of the competition. So what we wanted to do—I've never wanted to deprive a student or an institution of the right to use a guaranteed student loan provider. Because if we did that, the Government might get sort of fat and sassy, too, and unresponsive, if you see what I mean.

In other words, my goal always was to set up a competition where people could choose a direct loan program because of its obvious strengths, where the others would have to do more to try to compete, and where, if the direct loan program started to fail people down the road because they thought they had a monopoly, there were other options available as well.

That's what my goal is. My goal is to have 100 percent open option for the colleges and universities of the country. But the worst thing to do would really be terrible if it were abolished, and I think it would be a mistake to cap it.

Ms. Britton. That's probably a good note for us to end on. We'd like to have you for the rest of the afternoon; but there's a few thousand people out there who would also like to hear you.

The President. You know, I'll give a better speech because I was in here with you. I mean, really, you know. One of the problems we have in Washington is that people like you, the people who basically are out here making this country go are—normally tend to be so busy keeping body and soul together and doing what you want that you're not organized. The people that are organized and can hire lobbyists and have influence up there, you're not them.

So that's one of the biggest problems in decisionmaking. And that's why I try to do everything I can to get out in the country and give people like you, by my presence here, a chance to have your voice heard up there because there's more of you than them. You're just not there. You're here. And I hope we can save this program.

Yes, Brian, what were you going to say?

[Mr. Szuda stated that many students were able to relax and concentrate on their classes because of the efficiency of the direct loan program.]

The President. Didn't you say you had a national defense loan?

Q. Yes.

The President. I did, too. And you're the first person in your family to go to college?

Q. No.

Q. I am. I'm the first in my family.

[A student showed the President an example of the application form for the direct loan program.]

The President. A one-pager.

Q. One page, that's it. That's it. The margin of error is extremely small.

Q. I've got that myself.

[Several students explained the less efficient application process for a Pell grant.]

The President. Let me just point out one other thing——

Q. It's just a long—a long period of time. You need a crystal ball just to find out where the problem is—[*laughter*]

The President. I'll tell you something else——

Q. It's just——

Q. Let the President talk. [*Laughter*]

The President. No, no. The loan default—another thing, because of this you need to know the loan default rate. If you look at it from the point of view of the taxpayers who want their money back—I mean, I paid my college loan back. I felt morally obligated to. And I think I feel like you, that one of the reasons I never resented the taxes I pay is that my country helped me get an education; I figured I ought to give it back so other people could get one.

But what I was going to say is, one thing the taxpayers need to know is that we have cut the loan default rate in half since I've been President—the loss to the taxpayer. And part of it is because the system is different. If you're running a bank, right, and you loan me 10 grand and you've got a 90 percent guarantee from the Government, and I don't pay you back, if you don't lift your finger to get $9,000. If you hire a lawyer you've already spent more than $1,000, right? So the whole thing—that's another thing—the whole system is organized to maximize default.

Our system is organized to make it easy for everybody and to be tough on getting the money back. I mean, it's very different.

Q. Here is another point. [*Laughter*]

The President. I'd better take her back to Washington with me. [*Laughter*]

[Several students described past problems with receiving loans.]

The President. This has been unbelievable. I don't want to leave you guys. You're great. Thank you.

Ms. Britton. We thank you very much for all you do for us.

The President. Thank you.

NOTE. The President spoke at 10:51 a.m. in Pulliam Hall.

Remarks to the Community in Carbondale
September 11, 1995

Thank you, Jason. Thank you, Ted Sanders. I want to thank Senator Paul Simon and Senator Carol Moseley-Braun for being here and Representatives Jerry Costello, Glenn Poshard, and

Dick Durbin, the SIU Carbondale president, John Guyon, and I want to welcome all of the colleges and universities that are connected to us by satellite all around the country. Mayor

Dillard, I thank you for being here, and I want to compliment the Saluki Marching Band and the pep band. Thank you for your music. Great job. I know that we have a lot of schoolchildren here, but I've got an especially large number of invitations from one middle school that marched here as a group, the Lincoln Middle School. There they are over there. Thank you very much. [*Applause*] I also want to thank all the national service AmeriCorps members who are here and who are working in southern Illinois.

Ladies and gentlemen, I am glad to be back here at SIU, a place which has a very warm place in my heart. I spoke here in 1991 just before I declared as a candidate for President of the United States. It was a memorable evening. I've been back here since then. This is the first time I've been as President, and I am very, very glad to be back here. I've had a wonderful day, and I thank you for making me feel so welcome.

I came here today to talk to you about the future of education in America, the role of the student aid programs in that future, and the decisions that will be made about the national budget in the next 60 to 90 days that will affect your future and the future of all Americans.

One hundred and thirty-seven years ago this week in Jonesboro, just down the road here about 20 miles, Abraham Lincoln and Stephen Douglas held one of their famous debates. According to a newspaper report at the time, interest in the event was not what it should have been. When the candidates arrived in town, they were met, and I quote, "by two yoke of steers and a Stephen Douglas banner hanging bottom-upwards." [*Laughter*] Well, I didn't see any cattle on my way in, and all of the banners I've seen today are rightside-up, and there seems to be a good deal of interest. So I thank you for that, and I'm glad to see you.

It's appropriate that we're here talking about the student loan issue because, as I'm sure all of you know, about halfway between here and Jonesboro is Senator Paul Simon's hometown of Makanda. Senator Simon is retiring from the Senate this year, but I want everybody in this audience to know that more than anyone else in the United States Congress, he was instrumental in supporting our efforts to pass the direct loan program in 1993, and no one has done more to make the dream of a college education

a reality for all American students than Paul Simon of Illinois.

The Lincoln-Douglas debates were historic because they occurred at an historic time over an historic issue. The issue then was slavery and whether our country would remain united or be divided, and everyone knew the whole future of the country depended on how it was resolved.

Today at the dawn of a new century, we are in the midst of another period of historic change. The issue today is the end of the cold war and traditional industrial society and the growth of the global economy, the information and technology age and whether we can preserve the American dream for all Americans in this new world. And the whole future of the country depends upon how we answer that great issue, just as it did in 1858.

How do we keep the American dream alive in a world where jobs and capital, technology and ideas can travel across borders as fast as the satellite signal that right now is beaming this speech to colleges and universities all around this country? How do we make sure in this age of information where what you can learn determines what you can earn—how can we make sure that there's really opportunity for all people in this country without regard to where they live or what their racial or economic background is?

How can we make sure that your country gives you the chance to make the most of your own life, a gift that was given to me and most other people my age that helped us to make the most of our own lives?

This is a period of intense change, with a lot of wonderful things going on. I honestly believe that the young people in this audience will grow up into an America that will have its best days. I think the future is still going to be better than the past but if, only if, we meet the challenges of this time.

Let's face it, folks, these changes that are going on are awfully good for people who have an education, people who can be in the forefront of the change. They're pretty tough on millions and millions and millions of hard-working families that are being discarded by big companies as they downsize, forgotten by economic units for which they worked for 10, 20, sometimes 30 years; people who don't have a very good education and can no longer get the kind of jobs they used to or if they get a job never,

ever, ever seem to get a raise; not so good for the million Americans who are working every year who lose their health insurance. Why? Because all these changes are uprooting people, uprooting companies, uprooting ties that used to bind. We know, we know, that unless we can better educate our people, too many of them will be left behind in the global economy of the 21st century. We know today that for 20 years most Americans earning hourly wages have been working harder and harder for the same or lower wages—for 20 years. And we know that if we want to preserve the American dream for all of you, we have got to turn that around. And we know how to do it.

At the end of World War II when the GI's came home 50 years ago, the GI bill gave people who fought in the war a chance to go to college and the chance to buy their own home. And it made us the strongest economic power in the world by educating our people. In the 1950's, when we got into a race with the then-Soviet Union into space, national defense education loans and other investments in higher education gave a whole new generation of Americans a chance to go to college and broaden their horizons. And it made a real difference.

I was the first person in my family to go to college. I had scholarships and loans, a job in college, and six jobs in law school. I paid all my loans back, but if it hadn't been for those loans, I might never have been given the opportunities that brought me to the point where I am today. And I am grateful to the people in my country who gave me that chance.

Now when I became President, my goal was to get this economy ready for the 21st century and to open opportunity for you, to create more jobs and to set the conditions which will allow us to raise incomes and raise the stability of American families. And in 1993, we passed an economic program that reduced the deficit from $290 billion a year to $160 billion, that cut taxes on the lowest income of our working people and made 90 percent of our small businesses eligible for lower taxes, and that invested more money in education, research and development, and the technologies of the future to create more high-wage jobs.

And in 2½ years, we've got 7 million more jobs, 2½ million more homeowners, nearly 2 million more small businesses. But average incomes have still not gone up. You cannot turn around 20 years of trends in 2 years. But I am telling you, folks, there is no way to do it unless we continue to increase the number of Americans of all ages who are going on to colleges, from the community colleges to the 4-year colleges to the graduate schools of America.

Listen to this: In 1980, a worker with a college education earned 36 percent more than a worker with only a high school degree—1980. Today, 15 years later, that 36 percent gap has grown to 74 percent. The difference in earnings between high school graduates and college graduates has more than doubled in only 15 years. Every year of higher education today increases earnings by 6 to 12 percent and, in many cases, guarantees the right to get a job in the first place, something which is increasingly rare for people who don't have a good education.

The unmistakable faultline in America over who makes it and who doesn't today, more than ever before, is education. So as we go back to school and the Congress goes back to work, the question is, will your country continue to help those who want to help themselves? Will your country do what it ought to do now, which is what it did for me when I was your age? Will your country meet the challenges of the 21st century, or will we cut off our nose to spite our face by cutting back on educational aid at the time when we need to invest more in it?

Let me be clear on this. In this great debate to balance the budget, I am on the side of balancing the budget. Our country has no business running a permanent deficit. We never had a permanent deficit before 1981. We quadrupled the debt of the country in the 12 years before I became President. We have taken the deficit down from $290 billion a year down to $160 billion a year in only 3 years. It is important that we continue to work to balance the budget.

It is important because if we can get a balanced budget, we will spend less of your taxes on debt and we can spend more of it on education, the environment, and the elderly. It is important because, if we have less debt, people in private business will be able to borrow money at lower interest rates to create more jobs. It's important to balance the budget. But you want to do it to strengthen the economy and strengthen the incomes of the American people. Therefore, I say we should not balance the budget by cutting education, because we do not have to cut education to balance the budget.

We have worked hard in the last 2½ years to expand scholarships like Pell grants for deserving students, and we have worked very, very hard on the direct loan initiative. I see the students from Indiana University out here holding up their sign. This year I learned at this campus you went to the direct loan program and 11,000 students got direct college loans. And they didn't have to spend so many hours filling out forms or a day waiting in line for the loan at the bursar's office this year because the program works.

The direct loan program gets rid of redtape, bypasses banks and middlemen, sends the student loan directly to the school where the student gets it in a hurry. I talked to a student just a few moments ago who told me that the difference in this year and last year was a difference in 4 months and 1 week in getting the student loan. This program is better for the students, better for the schools, and believe it or not, it costs the taxpayers less money. It has been a good investment for America, and I thank, especially, Paul Simon and all these other Members of Congress for supporting the direct loan program.

For many of you, perhaps the most important feature of the direct loan program is that you can now pay back your loans as a percentage of the income of the job you have when you leave college. This is very important because a lot of people go to school to get jobs that will not make them wealthy but that will be very important for society. They want to be teachers or nurses or social workers or do something else that's profoundly important to our country. And they borrow money that is so great that if they had to make the loan payment back on traditional terms, they couldn't do it. But if they can make the loan payment back as a percentage of their income, then there will never be a disincentive to go to school. There will never be a disincentive to staying in school. No one will ever have to drop out of school just because they think their loans are getting too big. We should keep the direct loan program and keep the scholarship programs going.

I also favor retaining the policy that does not charge students for interest on their loans while they're in school and gives a 6-month grace period after school before you begin making those repayments. You have to have a job before you can repay the loans.

But make no mistake: With the opportunity of the loan comes the responsibility to repay it. I was appalled when I became President and I realized the size of the college loans default. I was absolutely appalled that there were that many people that would take money from their Government for a college education and not repay it. And I am proud to say we have cut the loan default rate in half in our administration, and we're going to cut it some more.

I just want to mention a couple of other things. One of my proudest moments as President was having the opportunity to sign the bill that created AmeriCorps, our national service initiative. AmeriCorps is giving thousands and thousands of young people the chance to earn and save up money for college while serving their communities.

In Carbondale, we have AmeriCorps members working in the local elementary schools, 20,000 this year, up to 50,000 next year could be serving their country if the Congress will continue to fund the AmeriCorps program. It is a great investment, and it's making America stronger.

There are two other proposals that I have made that I hope this coming Congress will adopt. Since there will be a tax cut, the question is: What are we going to cut taxes for, and who will get it? I favor as my number one priority giving a tax deduction to hard-working American families for the cost of education after high school, for their children or for themselves.

The second proposal that I have asked the Congress to adopt is one which would basically reflect the new reality of unemployment in our country. Thirty years ago when a person went on unemployment, the chances were 8 in 10 that person would be called back to the same job, that unemployment was a matter of the business cycle, and the unemployment check, therefore, just tided people over until they were called back to the same job.

Today, just 30 years later, the chances are when you're laid off, 8 in 10, that you won't be called back to the old job and you've got to find a new one. Therefore, I have recommended that the Congress consolidate about 70 separate training programs in the Government and just create a fund that will give a voucher to an unemployed American for $2,600 a year for up to 2 years to take to the nearest community college or other community education institution to get the training that he or she needs to get back in the work force and on the road to progress.

Under all these reforms I've just mentioned, if we stick with them by the year 2002, as many as 20 million more Americans will be able to get less expensive and more flexible college loans. We will be able to award over 3 million more Pell grant scholarships. And if we maintain our commitment, we're on target to increase the number of Americans who are going to college by over one million by the end of this decade, and we need it, all of us need it, for the strength of the United States. That means better jobs, higher incomes, a stronger America.

All this progress is now threatened by the budget debate now going on in Congress. The congressional majority proposes to balance the budget a little faster than I do and to give a tax cut much larger than the one I propose. Much of it goes to people who are already doing very well and don't really need the money.

To do this, they have been willing to cut education and training by $36 billion below the present budget, which is $76 billion less than I propose to spend while we balance the budget, too. They've proposed to get rid of AmeriCorps. They've proposed to get rid of the direct lending program and go back to the old system, which was more cumbersome, which will cost the students more money, which will lead to fewer people taking advantage of the loan program, which will mean more headaches to the colleges and universities, but the banks will make their money back. That's all that will happen.

They propose to make changes in the interest payments on college loans so that the cost of college loans could be raised by as much as $3,000 for undergraduates and over $9,000 for graduate students. I'm not even talking now about the risks to the education programs that help kids get ready for college. Under these proposals, there will be 50,000 fewer children in the Head Start program. All the public schools in our country that are participating in our Goals 2000 program will lose their money. The safe and drug-free schools program will be denied to millions and millions of American children.

Two million American children would face roadblocks on the road to college between now and the end of this decade, the beginning of the next century, if the proposals of the Republican Congress become the law of the land. That

is penny-wise and pound-foolish. We shouldn't cut education to balance the budget. We don't have to do it, and we shouldn't do it.

Folks, before I came out here, I spent a fascinating hour or so talking to 11 students from the various States that are represented here, from Indiana and Kentucky and Tennessee. And I met some people from Missouri here earlier, as well as from Illinois, students, people who are starting their own lives. They're behind me today. Every one of them could not have pursued his or her education without the benefit of student financial aid.

I'd like to ask the people who were with me before I came out here to stand up and be recognized. Would you all stand up? [*Applause*] They range in age from 21 to 51. One is a community college student. One is in graduate school. They go to public and private universities. They have different life stories. One has worked her way off welfare and into a position in college leadership. One was an Upward Bound student who is going to be very upward bound, who will become a doctor. All these people are America. They are what this is all about, not the organized forces that lobby in Washington. These 11 people—I am doing my best to represent them and their future in your Capital. That is what this is all about, your future.

I only wish that every American, every American, could have heard these 11 people tell their stories, talk about the loan programs, the scholarship programs; talk about how our direct loan program works; talk about what it means to have hope and a new life and to be working like crazy to make that life; understand that we're not talking about welfare here; we're not talking about giving people something they don't need; we're not talking about giving anybody something for nothing. We're talking about helping people to make the most of their own lives.

And if you don't believe that it will hurt America to walk away from student financial aid, let me just ask you to consider this: In the last 4 years, in the State of California, the State that was hit hardest by the recession because they lost so many defense-related jobs, higher education was cut by 19 percent, and over a 2-year period, enrollment dropped by over 10 percent. We need to be increasing enrollment in this country, not decreasing it. We need more people in all of these community colleges and colleges and universities and all these programs that are critical to our future, not fewer people.

The American dream depends upon our ability to not only create new jobs but to raise wages and enable our people to compete and win in the global economy of the 21st century. I have been in factory after factory after factory since I've been President. We are now the most productive economy in the world. It is wrong for our economy to be growing and the American people's incomes to be stuck. And education is the way out. I am determined to see that you get it.

Let me just say this in closing. Education in my lifetime has never been a partisan issue. When I asked the Congress to create the national service program, Democrats and Republicans supported it. When I asked the Congress to expand Head Start, Democrats and Republicans supported it. When I asked the Congress

to invest in all of these other educational programs, just 2 years ago, Democrats and Republicans supported it. Never before has this been a partisan issue.

Do not be fooled by the smokescreen of balancing the budget. We are all for balancing the budget. You do not have to balance the budget by cutting college aid. You do not have to balance the budget by shortcutting the future of America. We can do better than that. Help me. Stand up. Write your Members of Congress. Tell them to balance the budget and increase investment in education and America's future.

Thank you, and God bless you all.

NOTE: The President spoke at 11:58 a.m. on the Pulliam Hall lawn. In his remarks, he referred to Jason Ervin, student, and Ted Sanders, chancellor, Southern Illinois University; and Mayor Neill Dillard of Carbondale.

Remarks on the First Anniversary of AmeriCorps and an Exchange With Reporters
September 12, 1995

The President. I am glad to be here today with Senator Pell, Congressman Reed, Congressman Kennedy, Eli Segal, Senator Wofford, and the remarkable representative group of leaders from the State of Rhode Island, including leaders of the majority of the institutions of higher education there; business leaders, Mr. Fish, Mr. Romney, thank you for coming from Massachusetts; and young AmeriCorps volunteers; and of course, Senator Wofford. And Nick Lowry has been a great supporter of AmeriCorps from its beginning.

We are here to mark AmeriCorps' first year of accomplishment and to find ways to make it better in the second year when 25,000 Americans will be out serving their country and earning some money for their higher education.

AmeriCorps members have helped children to do better in school. They've helped to close crack houses. They've helped communities team up with police to keep themselves safe. They've cleaned mountain trails and urban waterways. And from Oklahoma City to south Florida, from the banks of the Mississippi to the streets of Los Angeles, whenever our people were faced

with disaster in these last couple of years, AmeriCorps members have been there to help.

AmeriCorps has truly brought out the best in America. Behind this success is a partnership that cuts across every line and sector in our country, where young people and others who work in the communities, leaders in business, education, community service, and public service, work together to make lives better for ordinary Americans.

AmeriCorps members help our Nation as they help themselves. They earn money to help pay for college. And of course, some colleges are going even further. The Rhode Island colleges and universities here represented and those who are not here will be matching AmeriCorps scholarships and college loan repayments. And I want to thank all of them.

Meanwhile, CEO's like Mitt Romney of Bain Capital in Boston, have urged others to follow their examples of support for AmeriCorps participation. Foundations like the Ford Foundation, which has contributed $3 million as a challenge pool to community foundations, have also helped to stretch our Federal investment.

An investment in AmeriCorps goes far. A team of noted conservative economists found recently that every dollar of Federal money invested returns at least $1.60 to $2.60, and maybe even more, for the taxpayers in public benefits. And of course, that doesn't calculate the long-term benefit of the increased education of the young people who participate in AmeriCorps. AmeriCorps is about personal responsibility and community, about giving young people positive avenues to opportunity.

Now, the majority in Congress threatens to cut college scholarships and college loans and AmeriCorps. But in AmeriCorps we have a program that lifts our values and solves our problems; it helps send civic-minded, hard-working young people to college. That's the kind of thing America should do to build up and not tear down.

Tens of thousands of young Americans are lining up to serve their country in AmeriCorps. And I don't want Congress to close the door on them. I want the Republican majority to learn what the rest of our country now knows. Without regard to party, AmeriCorps works. If the congressional majority really wants to build more personal responsibility and expand opportunity only for those who are willing to help themselves, if they really want to rebuild a sense of community in America, then their principles and our common future should be put above politics. AmeriCorps should grow. It should not die.

I want to reemphasize that it is not necessary to balance the budget to destroy AmeriCorps or even to cut it in half. It is absolutely not necessary. This is a good program, and I think we'll be around next year to celebrate the second anniversary and look toward the third year, thanks to people like all of you around this room. I thank you very, very much.

Q. Mr. President, do you think that the Republicans want to end the program simply because it's so closely associated with you and because it has been one of your head programs?

The President. I don't think they'd be that small. I think that would be an incredibly small thing to do. I don't think they'd be that small. You know, I don't speculate on people's motives. But I believe that some people in the Congress really don't believe that any spending program is as good as any tax cut. That's what I think. And I believe that any new thing that's been done—I happen to have been President the last

2 years—I think any new thing that's been done is in their mind an easy thing to eliminate if you want to balance the budget. But it is not necessary. We have given them a balanced budget plan. They don't have to cut this to balance the budget. This is a tiny, tiny budget item that does an enormous amount of good.

Q. They say that—[*inaudible*]—to the GAO report, I think, that's out now that shows that the amount of money that's actually spent per volunteer is a lot more than the $4,000 that the White House says——

The President. Well, we have, you know, we have a lot of evidence that refutes that. I don't—and I'll be glad to give it to you; Mr. Segal can. But it's clear that this is an enormously popular program. The one thing the GAO didn't do is to consider all the people that are kicking into the program; they leverage the private money. And there's no calculation given to the extra economic benefit to the country from all these young people that are going on to school. But even on its own terms, I don't think it's right economically.

This has been a good deal for America. And there's not a community—yesterday I was in Carbondale, Illinois, in the American heartland, a small town with a good-sized university, where the young AmeriCorps volunteers are working in the elementary school there. All these people are working people, and a phenomenal percentage of them are working poor people who live in this community. And they'd like to see their AmeriCorps volunteers stay. And they'd like to see them going on to school there. And I think we're going to give them the chance to do that.

Q. Mr. President, how optimistic are you of keeping the program alive?

The President. Very.

Q. I mean, are you finding a consensus among other Members of Congress to keep it going?

The President. First of all, there are a lot of Republicans that down deep in their heart want this program to live. And after all, we created this program with bipartisan support. I went out of my way in 1993 to say that I did not want any educational initiative created if we didn't have bipartisan support for it. I did not want this to be a partisan issue. And I have not made it a partisan issue.

And I just believe that we have to be more discriminating about what we eliminate. To go back to the question you asked, I honestly believe that, particularly in the House of Representatives, there are 100 to 150 Members that I believe that, except for the national defense, any tax cut is better than any spending program. But I think that's wrong. And we don't have to—we do not have to eliminate this to balance the budget. And I think I'll be able to make that point as we get into these budget negotiations. And I think—I think the program will survive because it's a good, decent program, it's an effective program, and it has bipartisan support.

Budget Debate

Q. Are you willing to sign on to the Republican spending limits without accepting their priorities as a possible compromise on the budget?

The President. Well, I don't know that that's a compromise. I have an alternative; they have an alternative. I picked up some kind of reading between the lines of some of the comments of the leadership and other prominent Members of Congress in the last couple of weeks, the

possibility of some movement that might enable us to get together. I don't want a train wreck. I want a balanced budget in a fixed number of years that has great credibility in the marketplace, and I believe we'll get it. I'm very hopeful.

Q. And will you sign a continuing resolution in the meantime?

The President. Oh, I hope we'll get a good continuing resolution. That's quite important. It's important that we not just walk away from our responsibilities.

Thank you.

NOTE: The President spoke at 1:22 p.m. in the Cabinet Room at the White House. In his remarks, he referred to Larry Fish, chairman and chief executive officer, Citizens Financial Group, and New York Jets football player Nick Lowry. A tape was not available for verification of the content of these remarks.

Teleconference Remarks on Education and an Exchange With Reporters
September 12, 1995

The President. Can you all hear me?

School Superintendents. Yes, yes.

The President. That's great. Well, I'm on the phone here with Secretary Riley. And I want to thank all you superintendents for joining me today on this conference call to discuss the importance of continuing our national commitment to education. All of you know better than I that America has just started back to school.

Over the last week I have met with chief executive officers from major corporations such as IBM and TRW, with mayors and county executives from large and small cities, and yesterday with college students from 10 different universities in 5 States. And I have just come from a meeting with some of our young national service corps, AmeriCorps, participants, along with college presidents and business leaders who support their involvement. And everywhere I go, when I deal with people who are working with Americans who are struggling to make the most of their own lives or trying to help our country adjust to the global economy, I hear the same message: It is wrong for our economy to be growing with so many hardworking Americans'

incomes not growing. And everywhere I hear the same response: The answer is to give people a better education, to give our young people the tools they need to learn and to give all Americans a chance to build better lives.

That's why I presented to Congress a balanced budget, which shows that we can get rid of the deficit and still invest more in education and training, to put our young people and our future first. That's why we have committed ourselves to a greater investment in Head Start, to the Goals 2000 program that many of you are very familiar with, to decreasing class sizes through programs like Title I, to the safe and drug-free schools program.

These are not bureaucratic programs. These are programs that relate to the future of our children, the strength of our economy, and therefore the future of all the rest of us in America.

I know that it is easy to cut these programs here in Washington. We are a long way from the schools and the grassroots. You're a long way from the human consequences of those cuts. But these things actually mean something where all of you live and work. And that's what I want you to talk about.

For example, four schools in Portland, Oregon, helping 9th and 10th graders to reach higher standards in math and science, will lose their funding, just at the time when we know our young people are taking more advanced courses, doing more homework, and trying harder to measure up to global standards of excellence. Four hundred and fifty teaching assistants and other staff who help children with basic reading, writing, and math skills will have to be laid off in Miami. There are examples like this all across the country. That's why we've had such incredibly strong bipartisan business support for our education budget.

Joe Gorman, the chief executive officer of TRW, said last week that, and I quote, "Goals 2000 is critically important. Far more than dollars are involved. It provides incentives to States to change themselves within their educational systems." Lou Gerstner, the CEO of IBM, said, "Goals 2000 is the fragile beginning of the establishment of a culture of measuring standards and accountability in our country. We have to go way beyond Goals 2000, but if we lose Goals 2000 it is," and I quote, "an incredibly negative setback for our country."

So I think that we've got good, bipartisan support in the grassroots for continuing to invest in education. We are only helping people who are willing to help themselves. We are not giving anything to people who don't need it, and we are not giving things to people who won't use it. We're just making an investment in America's future. And I hope that together all of us can succeed in securing both a balanced budget and an education budget that will be good for America's future.

I'd like to ask Secretary Riley to say a few words, and then I'd like to hear from all of you. Mr. Secretary.

[At this point, Secretary of Education Richard W. Riley described the progress made in education and the need for greater investment.]

The President. Thank you, Mr. Secretary. Now I'd like to call on the superintendents to speak. And I'd like to emphasize one more time something that—the American taxpayers always say that they don't want us giving anybody something for nothing. They don't want us giving people things they don't need. And they're right about that.

But we're talking here about a student population that we now know is working harder, doing more homework, investing more in their own future, and understanding more about education. And as I said, I was—just yesterday, I was at Southern Illinois University. And I met with 11 recipients of student aid. And every one of them was a working person struggling to get a good education to make their own lives better and this country stronger. So that's what we're talking about here. And it's a good expenditure of our tax dollars.

I'd like to begin by calling on the Superintendent of the Dade County, Florida, schools, Octavio Visiedo. And sir, you're the first up. Just say whatever's on you mind.

[Mr. Visiedo discussed the recent layoff of paraprofessionals in Dade County and emphasized its impact on students who recently immigrated.]

The President. Thank you very much. I'd like to now ask the Superintendent of the Portland, Oregon, schools to speak, Jack Bierwirth. Mr. Bierwirth.

[Mr. Bierwirth discussed the Head Start program, Goals 2000, and the need for national education standards.]

The President. I thank you for saying that. I want to emphasize, because there's been a little bit of controversy about Goals 2000, that I think the genius of the program is that, under Secretary Riley's leadership, we have done more to give more flexibility to local school districts and individual schools to creatively pursue their own solutions for excellence while trying to develop national standards so that parents could know what their children should know and whether they're learning it. And it seems to me that was a very good bargain for the American people and one we ought not to back off of now.

Mr. Bierwirth. And it's beginning to pay off very well out here.

The President. That's the thing. It's just beginning to work. And I really appreciate you saying that.

I'd like to call on Dr. Gerry House, the superintendent of the Memphis school systems. Dr. House.

[Dr. House discussed the impact of funding cuts on child nutrition and the safe and drug-free schools program and described the Memphis school system's antismoking campaign.]

The President. Well, thank you very much, and thank you for telling us about your smoke-free program. I appreciate that, and I hope you are very successful with it.

I think I'd like to make just two points here. One is—one the Secretary of Education made me clearly aware of, and that is that we're fixing to have another big increase in school students, what Secretary Riley called the "baby boom echo." And that means that these reductions in the School Lunch Program will be much more severe than they might look on paper because we have calculated—in our budget we asked for money based on the increase in student population we know we're going to have. And a disproportionate number of these young people, of course, do come from low-income families and often don't get the kind of nourishment they need.

The other point I want to make is that the safe and drug-free schools program passed as a bipartisan program. This was not, when it was started, a partisan issue. This was a bipartisan issue. And one of the things that the Republicans have always said is that we needed to do more to change people's behavior as it relates to drugs and violence, that we can't just concentrate on drug treatment, we can't just concentrate on punishing people, we can't just concentrate on trying to interdict drugs when they come in this country. We have to do more to change people's behavior.

This program works on changing people's behavior and, therefore, to undermine it and not give the schools the resources they need to deal with this terrific problem, it seems to me to run counter to the position that they've taken consistently, at least since I've been here in Washington for the last 2½ years.

So I appreciate what you said, and I hope we can do well by both those programs before this is over.

I'd like to call on the superintendent from Milwaukee now, Robert Jasna, to say whatever he would like to say.

[Mr. Jasna discussed the impact of funding cuts on the safe and drug-free schools program, the school-to-work program, and class size.]

The President. Thank you very much, Mr. Jasna. As you know, a lot of—this conversation is being held not only in the presence of representatives of the national media here but for regional media around the country. So I think

I should make two points about the very important comment you've made.

First of all, the school-to-work program, which you discussed, is basically the effort of the local school districts around the country supported by Federal and sometimes by State funds to train people both academically and vocationally while they're in school, both in the school and in the workplace, and to continue that training after they leave high school so they have a chance to get a good job with a growing income.

In the United States, because we don't have a comprehensive system of training people who don't go on to colleges, we often find that the earnings of people without a college education are dropping dramatically and have been for 20 years now.

The school-to-work program is an attempt to build in a flexible American way the kind of systems that the Germans, for example, have had for many years, which have led to rising incomes for a lot of their workers without university degrees but with very good education and very good training.

So this would hit a huge percentage of young American workers who have the chance to escape the declining earnings that have plagued non-college-educated Americans for 20 years now.

And on the class size issue, I just want to mention one thing to hammer this home. There has been an enormous amount of educational research in the last 10 years especially demonstrating that if you can get class sizes down to under 20 to 1, especially—you mentioned you had class sizes of 15 to 1—that kids with serious learning problems can dramatically improve with that kind of student-teacher ratio.

So if you have to double it, there's no question that the learning capacity of our system or our teaching capacity will go way down. And I really appreciate both the points you made.

Mr. Jasna. Thank you.

The President. I'd like to now call on a long-time friend of mine, the superintendent of the Philadelphia schools, David Hornbeck. David, are you there?

[Mr. Hornbeck discussed the impact of funding cuts on Goals 2000, the Head Start program, and AmeriCorps.]

The President. Thank you, David, and thank you for what you said about Goals 2000. I think one of the problems we've had with Goals 2000

is that only the educators have understood it. You know, it doesn't ring any bells in the public mind. And I think when people understand it's about high expectations, high standards, and grassroots reform, it will help us to continue the work.

On AmeriCorps, let me say one of the things that came out today. Today we had representatives of most of the colleges and universities in Rhode Island and business leaders from Rhode Island and Boston that are supporting it, and we also had a man who worked as President Ford's Commissioner of Education who had evaluated the program. And they said that one of the attacks on AmeriCorps was that if young people got paid for their college education for volunteering in their communities, it would run volunteers off, and that quite to the contrary, the average AmeriCorps volunteer had generated 12 more volunteers. And you say in Philadelphia it's up to 20 in the schools, so that's a wonderful statement, and I thank you for your good work and for what you said today.

Now I want to call on a gentleman who was here just a few days ago to visit with me about some of these issues, Albert Thompson, the superintendent of the Buffalo, New York, schools. Mr. Thompson.

[*Mr. Thompson discussed the impact of Chapter I cuts on several groups of students. Secretary Riley concluded the remarks by indicating that the proposed cuts would represent a retreat from support of education.*]

The President. Thank you very much, Mr. Secretary.

Let me just close by thanking all of you for the work you're doing out there every day and through you, your principals and your teachers, and the parents that are helping you. You know, this issue—I wanted to do this call today to make it clear that this issue is not just another money issue; this is about the future of this country. And these programs we're talking about, every one has been enacted or expanded with bipartisan support. And the direction that I have taken since I've been President, working with Secretary Riley, rooted in our experience as Governors with people like you, has been to focus on high expectations, high standards, and high accountability and rewarding the assumption of personal responsibility by students.

These are the things that the American people know we need to do. And everybody knows we

can't turn around the stagnation of American incomes unless we dramatically increase the output but also the investment in American education.

So I think that you know that history is on your side, that right is on your side. We're just going to have to keep working here so that we can prevail in Washington and make sure that here in Washington people understand the consequences of what they do out there where you live. And you have gone a long way to help us make that case today, and we're very, very grateful to you.

Thank you.

School Superintendents. Thank you, Mr. President. Thank you.

The President. Thank you all. Goodbye.

[*At this point, the teleconference ended, and the President took questions from reporters.*]

Education Budget

Q. Mr. President, do you think you're going to be able to save these programs? It looks like there's a real wall there.

The President. Yes, I do, because I think— I think that—keep in mind, if you look at the educational programs that I started here, like Goals 2000, the safe and drug-free schools program, the school-to-work program, the AmeriCorps program, or if you look at the ones we've expanded, like Head Start, or the ones we've reformed, like the Chapter I program, without exception, these programs had bipartisan support, not only out in the country but in the Congress.

Now the Congress is basically operating within a budget resolution which has an arbitrary timeframe of 7 years and an arbitrary tax cut of $250 billion and, I think, a very modest estimate of revenue growth or economic growth for America, 2.3 percent, which is less than we've grown for the last 25 years. Presumably, they believe that if we balance the budget we'll grow faster, not slower. In other words, I don't think they want to balance the budget to give America a low-grade economic infection.

So I believe when we start to talk about these things and we pull out what has historically been there, which is the bipartisan support for education plus what everyone understands, which is that we've now got 20 years of stagnant incomes in this country and the only way to turn it around is to raise the educational level, I think we have an excellent chance of saving these programs because they work; they're good; they're grassroots oriented; they're not Federal bureaucracies.

Q. Mr. President, if you're to avoid the train wreck that you—[*inaudible*]—earlier, some in Congress have suggested that a budget summit of some kind may be the only way to work out these very stark differences between you and the Republican leadership. Is that something that you'd be willing to agree to?

The President. Well, I think the discussion of the summit is premature at this time. I do believe, as I said earlier today, I've seen in some of the comments of some of the Republican leaders the prospect that we might be able to bridge these differences. I'm willing to reach across the bridge, but it takes two people to reach across a bridge to meet in the middle somewhere. So I think we can do it. We're just going to have to work at it.

But the first thing we ought to do, and what I'm trying to do here today and what I'm trying to do this whole week with this back-to-school theme, is to try to lift this issue beyond politics, beyond partisan politics and beyond Washington politics. That is, why are we balancing the budget? Because we want to lift debt off our children, and we want to reduce borrowing now so we'll have more money available in the private sector to generate jobs and incomes. That's why we're doing it.

Why did they propose a tax cut? Why do I propose a tax cut, even though we're very different? Because we think it will make family

life better; it will make childrearing stronger; it will make the economy stronger; it will make America a more solid, stronger country.

If those are our objectives, then we have to pursue balancing the budget and reducing taxes in a way consistent with our objectives, not a partisan deal, not a political deal. Education, if you take it out of the equation, the objectives will fail. That's the point I'm trying to make. That's the point I want us to focus on. And it is not necessary to make these education cuts to balance the budget. I think we've got a real chance to make that case, and I'm very, very hopeful.

Bomb Plot in Austin, Texas

Q. Mr. President, word is starting to come out about the aborted bomb plot against the IRS center in Austin, Texas. Have you been briefed on that, sir?

The President. No.

Thank you.

Budget Debate

Q. Do you think you're going to get a continuing resolution while this debate goes on?

The President. I certainly hope so. I think that's the responsible thing to do. And I think that—my guess is that there's a good chance that will occur.

Thank you.

NOTE: The President spoke at 2:25 p.m. from the Roosevelt Room at the White House.

Remarks on the Legislative Agenda and an Exchange With Reporters
September 12, 1995

The President. Let me—first of all, I want to welcome the leadership of the Congress here and thank them for coming down to the White House for the meeting today. I'm looking forward to having a chance to discuss a number of things, including the present situation in Bosnia, the status of the welfare reform legislation, the budget—progress toward a balanced budget, and a number of other issues, including the lobby reform measure passed by the Senate and the line-item veto and anything else that

might be on the minds of the congressional Members who are here.

I have said before, I will say again, I'm very hopeful that we can achieve common ground on this budget. This is a truly historic moment. We do have some different priorities, but I think we can reach an agreement if we work at it. It seems clear now that such cannot be the case by the time this fiscal year ends on October 1st, so I'm hopeful that we can, for a limited period of time, pass a continuing resolution. It would be a straightforward resolution, appropriate for the reduction of spending to meet the overall budget targets, and I look forward to working on that.

I believe that the American people want us to work together and get something done, and I think most of us want the same thing, so that's what we're going to talk about.

Bosnia

Q. President Clinton, can you give us a—[*inaudible*]—the way you see the situation in Bosnia right now and what you plan to talk about?

The President. Well, I think the agreement signed in Geneva by the three parties is very, very hopeful—the Bosnian Government, the Croatian Government, the Serbian Government. I think the negotiations should continue. I'm sending Ambassador Holbrooke back there tonight. In terms of the bombing, that's really up to the Serbs. The U.N. Security Council resolution is clear, and the conditions laid out by our committee on the ground are clear, and we'll just have to see what happens there.

Q. Mr. President, Russia is comparing the bombings to genocide. Other than the traditional ties to the Serbs, what do you think is behind Yeltsin's sterner and sterner opposition to bombings?

The President. Well, I think you have to ask them that. Let's just make it clear—if you look at the facts of the bombing attacks, they are clearly not that. First of all, they were authorized by the United Nations; secondly, they came only after extreme provocation, after the killings, the shelling—resulting from the shelling of Sarajevo, the killing of innocent civilians; and thirdly, they have been very, very carefully targeted and carried out with great discipline and skill by the United States pilots and the NATO allies. There has been no genocide there. There has been an extraordinary amount of care and discipline but firmness and strength. They were appropriately done. And I want to say in the presence of these Members here how much I appreciate the comments that Senator Dole and others have made on that.

The United States, I think, is united in being opposed to resumption of the killing of innocent civilians in protected areas. They said we wouldn't do it, we wouldn't tolerate it, and we can't.

Thank you.

NOTE: The President spoke at 5:42 p.m. in the Cabinet Room at the White House, prior to a meeting with congressional leaders. A tape was not available for verification of the content of these remarks.

Statement on the Commission on Immigration Reform
September 12, 1995

I reiterate my earlier congratulation to the Commission on Immigration Reform for its hard work on legal immigration reform. The Commission has provided the Congress and the Nation with an excellent framework to achieve gradual reductions in the level of legal immigration. This is a goal and objective I share.

The Commission's first report on illegal immigration endorsed many of the activities my ad-

ministration has initiated. This report on legal immigration also shares many of my principles to guide reform. Our legal immigration system must be based on principles that are pro-family, pro-work, and pro-naturalization. I anticipate working with Congress in a spirit of bipartisanship to craft the specific legislation that will put these principles in practice.

Memorandum on Career Transition Assistance for Federal Employees
September 12, 1995

Memorandum for the Heads of Executive Departments and Agencies

Subject: Career Transition Assistance for Federal Employees

Our highly trained and dedicated Federal work force is one of the Federal Government's most valuable resources. In order to help Federal employees who have dedicated their careers to public service find new job opportunities as Federal organizations undergo downsizing and restructuring, the executive branch must implement programs that provide Federal employees with career transition assistance. The Office of Personnel Management (OPM) Interagency Advisory Group has recommended that appropriate career transition assistance services be provided to Federal employees who either have been or are likely to be separated from Federal service due to a reduction in force. The goal of such services is to assist employees in taking charge of their own careers by providing them with the support they need to find other job offers, either with government or in the private sector.

I hereby direct the head of each executive department or agency (hereafter collectively "agency" or "agencies"), to the greatest extent practicable and in accordance with the guidance and any necessary regulations to be provided by OPM pursuant to this memorandum, to establish a program to provide career transition assistance to the agency's surplus and displaced employees. Such a program shall be developed in partnership with labor and management and shall include:

(1) collaborating with State, local, and other Federal employers, as appropriate, to make career transition services available to all of the agency's surplus or displaced employees;

(2) establishing policies for retraining displaced employees, as appropriate, for new career opportunities, either in government or with the private sector;

(3) establishing policies that require the selection of a well-qualified surplus or displaced internal agency employee who applies for a vacant position in the commuting area, before selecting any other candidate from either within or outside the agency; and

(4) establishing policies that require the selection of a well-qualified displaced employee from another agency who applies for a vacant position in the commuting area before selecting any other candidate from outside the agency.

I direct the Director of the OPM, in consultation with the Interagency Advisory Group, to: (a) prescribe minimum criteria for and monitor the effectiveness of agency career transition programs and (b) provide guidance and any necessary regulations for the agencies on the implementation of this memorandum. The OPM shall work with the Interagency Advisory Group to facilitate interagency cooperation in providing career transition services. The OPM shall work with agencies to maximize the use of existing automated job information and skills-based recruiting systems and develop new systems, as necessary.

Nothing in this memorandum shall affect the Priority Placement Program operated by the Department of Defense.

Independent agencies are requested to adhere to this memorandum to the extent permitted by law.

This memorandum is for the internal management of the executive branch and is not intended to, and does not, create any right or benefit, substantive or procedural, enforceable by a party against the United States, its agencies or instrumentalities, its officers or employees, or any other person.

WILLIAM J. CLINTON

Remarks to the National Family Partnership in Elkridge, Maryland
September 13, 1995

The President. Thank you very much. Terrell did a great job, didn't he? Let's give him another hand. Didn't he do a great job? [*Applause*] When Terrell was going up to speak, the Governor said, "He seems so calm." And I said, "Well, after all, it's his crowd." [*Laughter*]

I am honored to be here with your Governor; with the Attorney General, Janet Reno; and with our Nation's drug czar, Dr. Lee Brown; with the National Family Partnership chair, Carol Reeves; with the members of the family who did a lot to inspire what we're doing here today, Myrna Camarena, who is Enrique Camarena's sister and a DEA agent; Dora Camarena, Enrique's mother; and Rick Evans, the executive director of the National Family Partnership; and of course, along with the Governor and all the other State officials who are here, Congressman Cardin. And to your principal, your superintendent, the school board members, and all the others who are here, I'm delighted to be in this wonderful school. And I thank all of you who work here and who send your children here for making this such a successful place. I'd also like to thank all the law enforcement officers who've come here from all around the country.

Let me tell you why we're here; we're here to do two things: First of all, as the Attorney General has said, to observe the first anniversary of the enactment of the crime bill into law and to celebrate its accomplishments and, secondly, to reaffirm the elemental proposition that if we don't do something to keep our young people drug-free, we will never solve the crime problem, and that that begins first and foremost with an act of personal responsibility on the part of every American, personal responsibility on the part of the students, on the part of parents and educators and others, for self, for family, for community, and for country.

Lee Brown has done an outstanding job in working with our high schools to reduce drugs and violence. Yesterday, he kicked off our national back-to-school "stay drug-free" public service announcement campaign, enlisting the involvement of prominent sports figures and other entertainers to tape radio and TV spots urging young people to stay drug-free and urging parents to stay involved. He's also passing

out this wonderful little bumper sticker that I think could go very well with your red ribbon campaign. It says, "Stay drug-free; you have the power"—you have the power.

A year ago, when the crime bill was enacted, those of us who supported it, I believe, exercised our personal responsibility to the young people of America to do everything we could to ensure their safety and to provide alternatives to crime and violence. It was one of the proudest accomplishments of my tenure as your President.

We broke 6 long years of partisan, rhetorical, political gridlock to put in place a crime bill that was both tough and smart, that actually holds out the promise of saving lives and increasing the quality of life and the safety of the American people. We put 100,000 more police on the street; made "three strikes and your out" the law of the land; banned assault weapons from our neighborhoods, our streets, and our schools; finally elected to do something about the terrible problem of violence against women, much of it, unfortunately, domestic violence, and we gave our young people some things to say yes to as well as to say no to, because these police officers said we had to have more prevention in education programs in our schools if we wanted a safe America for the next generation.

Today, there are those who in the name of a balanced budget would go back on all this progress. They are the same people who said we would never put 100,000 police officers on the street. They said we couldn't even put 20,000 on in 6 years, over 25,000 in one year. We're going to. We're on time. We're ahead of schedule. We're below cost. We are keeping our commitments to the American people. So those who want to turn away from measures that have lowered the crime rate in almost every major urban and rural area in this country, I say, not if I can stop it—not if I can stop it.

Let me be clear—the Governor mentioned it—this is not about balancing the budget. I am for balancing the budget. When I became the President, we had quadrupled the debt in 12 years and a bipartisan agreement to make out like it didn't matter. We had a $290 billion a year deficit. That deficit today is $160 billion. We've cut it nearly in half in only 3 years. I am for balancing the budget.

But the purpose of balancing the budget is to lift the burden of debt from these young people in this audience, to free up money in America to be borrowed by private business people to invest, to create jobs, to strengthen our economy, to improve the quality of life in the future. We cannot do that if we decide to balance the budget in ways that will undermine our economy or our quality of life. And that is why I have said repeatedly, we do not have to cut education, and we must not cut our efforts to reduce the crime rate, to reduce violence, and to give our children a safer, more secure future. It is not necessary to balance the budget, and it undermines the very purpose of doing it. We must not take that course.

I just want to say one other thing. What we have done on the crime bill has worked because of the exercise of personal responsibility by other people in the criminal justice system. In Washington, we can give these fine police chiefs here and the people with whom they work the tools, but they have to use the tools, and citizens have to help them. Therefore, everyone in America who is a good citizen can justifiably claim some responsibility for the fact that the crime rate for all serious offenses, including murder, rape, robbery, and aggravated assault, is down in almost every area in the United States. That is an American achievement, and we need to keep working until we bring it down to an acceptable level, where it ought to be.

But just as we have made progress in certain areas, there are clouds still hanging over our future. And I want to talk about two of them today because they affect these young people in this audience.

Last week, the Justice Department issued a report which showed that while overall crime is down, violent crime committed by juveniles, people under the age of 18, is still at an all-time high. Juvenile violence has now become the number one crime problem in the United States of America. We cannot rest, we cannot rest in our official positions, we cannot rest as citizens, we cannot rest as parents until we do something to change that.

I am so sick and tired of picking up the newspaper and reading stories about honor students standing at bus stops being shot down by careless drive-by shooters. I am so tired of reading stories about a 16-year-old boy shooting a 12-year-old boy and killing him because he thought he was treated with disrespect. Whatever happened to," Sticks and stones can break my bones"? What ever happened to,"Count to 10 before you talk, much less act"?

I couldn't believe it, the other day there was a survey of teenage gang members in which two-thirds of them said they felt justified in shooting someone who treated them with disrespect. If the President took that position, we'd be out of bullets in the country. [*Laughter*]

Who ever heard of this kind of behavior? It's funny, but it's not. It's not funny. We have to take responsibility for the way the young people of this country look at the world, how they define right and wrong, how they define their dignity. The greatest human beings who have ever lived in the whole history of humanity were consistently abused by others, and they were great because they did not lash out. What is this madness that our children are being taught, that it is all right to take violent action against other people if they say something you don't like? We must do something about it.

The second thing that bothers me, besides juvenile violence, was revealed in a report yesterday released by our Government through the Department of Health and Human Services, which showed that while drug use is down among people between the ages of 18 and 34 and cocaine use is down, marijuana use is going up again among young people between the ages of 12 and 17, nearly doubling in just 3½ years from 4 percent to 7 percent who say they've used marijuana in the last month.

That's because apparently more and more young people don't think it's bad for you. Well, it's wrong; it's illegal; it's dangerous. It's a horrible first step, and we have got to turn that number around. And that's one big reason I am here today with young people who know it and who are prepared to say it.

I have believed in and participated in the National Family Partnership's red ribbon campaign for a long time. When I was the Governor of my State, Hillary and I were always actively involved every year about this time. We were always proud to do it. And I believe every year I was Governor, we ranked in the top three States in America in the number of our young people participating. And since we only had 2.4 million people, I was pretty proud of that.

What you are doing is important because the red ribbon chairs, the red ribbon parents, and most important, the red ribbon students are doing what no law, no government can do. They are assuming responsibility for their behavior, the behavior of their children, and in so doing, for their own futures. The red ribbon is the symbol now in America of our children's pledge to lead drug-free lives. The young people here are doing the right thing. Saying no to drugs is saying yes to life.

In addition to the pledge by the students and the display of red ribbon, the red ribbon campaign also focuses on educating our young people about the dangers of drug use and mobilizing every community to develop its own solution. And I want to emphasize that. Every community in America needs its own plan, based on its own resources and its own problems, to deal with this issue. There is no cookie-cutter plan coming out of Washington that will solve all these problems. Every community needs people like you to chart the future and to hold up these young people as models.

That's why I want to thank those of you in the National Family Partnership for choosing this day to kick off your Red Ribbon Campaign. It's a wonderful day. We're celebrating the first anniversary of the crime bill, its results, and a declining crime rate, the exercise of responsibility by adults in positions of authority. But more importantly, we're celebrating the future by the exercise of responsibility by these young people.

We have to do something to make their future less violent. As the Attorney General said, the Justice Department in its youth violence initiative is going to help 10 communities establish partnerships between police departments and courts and schools, hospitals and civic leaders to reduce violence.

In Maryland, in Baltimore, 24 community police officers will form curfew enforcements and juvenile violence crime teams to work with the schools to lower violence against young people, not to punish children but to demand responsibility from them and their parents.

In Inglewood, California, the police department has made street terrorism a crime and intensified their community efforts to increase penalties for gang members who practice it. We cannot tolerate terrorism of any kind in our country. Why should we go to all the trouble to keep these terrorists from coming into the country if we're going to let homegrown kinds terrorize our children on their own streets?

In Birmingham, police officers are working with schools to make sure that they get rid of guns in schools. No one should ever fear being shot in or around their schools. Similar efforts will be supported in Bridgeport, Connecticut; Cleveland; Milwaukee; Richmond; San Antonio; Seattle; and Salinas, California.

But nothing we will do will work unless all of us who are adults take the time to teach our children what it means to be a good person and a good citizen. Our Secretary of Education has called this character education, trying to encourage our schools to teach basic values that make for a good life, like honesty and trustworthiness and respect for self, others, property, and our environment. These values make a difference. And that is what this red ribbon campaign is all about.

I'd like now to ask the young people who are up here on the stage with me and all the young people in the audience who want to do it, to stand up and repeat the red ribbon pledge for the United States of America, so everybody in the country can hear it today. Stand up and I will say it, and you repeat after me:

I pledge to lead a healthy, drug-free lifestyle. I will say no to alcohol. I will say no to other drugs. I will help my friends say no. I pledge to stand up for what I know is right and remain drug-free and proud.

[The participants repeated the pledge line by line after the President.]

The President. Thank you very much.

Now, I want to invite the students, starting here, as I finish, to come up here and sign this pledge with me. But as I do, I want every adult in this audience to think about this. We're proud of these children who made this pledge. Most of us who know something about this problem are sitting here thinking, gosh, I wish every child in America would make this pledge.

We expect these children to keep their word. Well, if we do, why don't we set an example by keeping our word to them, to make this the safest possible country with the healthiest possible future for them by doing what we know works to reduce crime and to give them a chance to keep the pledge they just made.

Thank you, and God bless you all.

NOTE: The President spoke at 11:35 a.m. at the Mayfield Woods Middle School. In his remarks, he referred to student Terrell Brice; Gov. Parris Glendening of Maryland; and Myrna and Dora Camarena, sister and mother of Drug Enforce- ment Administration Special Agent Enrique Camarena Salazar, who was killed while conducting an undercover investigation of drug traffickers in Mexico.

Statement on the Normalization Agreement Between Greece and the Former Yugoslav Republic of Macedonia
September 13, 1995

I welcome the agreement signed by the Foreign Ministers of Greece and the Former Yugoslav Republic of Macedonia in New York today normalizing their relations. The agreement is very much in the interest of both nations and will significantly strengthen regional stability while aiding our efforts to negotiate a wider peace in the Balkans.

Both Prime Minister Papandreou and President Gligorov deserve congratulations for demonstrating the courage and determination needed to reach an agreement that was fair to both sides. I hope both governments will now proceed to establish friendly and enduring bilateral relations while taking steps to resolve their remaining differences, including over the name issue.

I also wish to thank U.N. Special Representative Cyrus Vance and U.S. Special Envoy Matthew Nimetz for their tireless efforts in helping to mediate the dispute.

In view of the significant progress represented by this agreement, I wrote to President Gligorov earlier in the week inviting his government to establish diplomatic relations with the United States. I am pleased to announce that I have received his positive response and can confirm that diplomatic relations now exist between our two countries.

I look forward to meeting with the negotiators and representatives of the two countries tomorrow to congratulate them personally on this important achievement.

Remarks Prior to Discussions With Representatives From Greece and the Former Yugoslav Republic of Macedonia and an Exchange With Reporters
September 14, 1995

Normalization Agreement

The President. First of all, let me say that I am delighted to be joined here by the Foreign Minister of the Former Yugoslav Republic of Macedonia and the Ambassador to Greece to formally congratulate these two countries on the agreement they signed yesterday in New York, agreeing to normalize their relations.

I want to say a special word of thanks to a great American, Cy Vance, who is here, who represented the United Nations; and my Special Envoy, Matt Nimetz, for the remarkable role they played in bringing these two countries together.

As you know, the United States has had troops stationed, since I became President, in the Former Yugoslav Republic of Macedonia to try to help to prevent the spread of the Balkan war. And for these two countries to work out their longstanding differences and look forward to relationships of permanent peace and commerce and accord with one another is an enormous step forward in our attempts to find a comprehensive peace in the Balkans.

Now, I also want to tell you that we have some reason to hope that we are making progress, thanks to the determination of NATO and the United Nations, in securing Bosnian Serb compliance with the conditions the U.N.

and NATO have set forward for the cessation of the bombing campaign. And we are working on that, will continue to work on it hard today. And obviously, if there are any developments, we will announce them.

Bosnia

Q. Do you have Russian acquiescence to place troops around Sarajevo?

The President. Well, let me say, first of all, we are working on the details of the agreement. When they are worked out, we will then say what they are and answer all the questions.

Q. But sir, is there an agreement for the Serbs to pull their artillery from the positions around Sarajevo?

The President. That is what we are attempting to secure at this moment. We are working through that. There's been some progress in the last—there's been some reason to hope for progress in the last several hours, beginning last night our time. But we're not prepared to make a final announcement yet. When we are, we will, and we'll answer all the questions.

Medicare

Q. The Speaker of the House today said that the Democratic position on Medicare is to scare 85-year-olds, and he called the party morally bankrupt.

The President. Well, you know, I think it's questionable to use words like "morally bankrupt," but let's look at the facts. For 2 years, I said the Medicare Trust Fund was in trouble,

and Mr. Gingrich and others mocked me and denied that it was in trouble. All by ourselves, with no help from them, we added 3 years to the life of the Trust Fund. We have proposed legislation which would add 10 years to the life of the Trust Fund and will get Medicare out of trouble.

I don't want to use a term like "morally bankrupt," but I think it is morally questionable at least to propose vast Medicare cuts which would increase the cost of Medicare to elderly people living on under $24,000 a year and claim that it's going to the Trust Fund when they know not one red cent of the money being paid by seniors will go to the Trust Fund. It will go to fund a tax cut that is too big. And they should tell the truth to the American people that they want to charge the providers more money and put that in the Trust Fund. They want to charge the elderly people of this country more money and put that into the tax cut.

Now, that is the truth. And if we're going to talk about what morality requires, morality requires them to tell the truth to the American people.

NOTE: The President spoke at 10:45 a.m. in the Oval Office at the White House. Following his remarks, the President met with Greek Ambassador to the United States Loukas Tsilas and Foreign Minister Stevo Crvenkovski of the Former Yugoslav Republic of Macedonia. A tape was not available for verification of the content of these remarks.

Remarks on the Agreement To End Air Strikes in Bosnia and an Exchange With Reporters
September 15, 1995

The President. Good morning. I welcome the agreement by the Bosnian Serbs to comply with a condition set by NATO and the United Nations for ending the NATO air strikes.

American pilots and crews and their NATO colleagues have been carrying out those strikes to prevent further slaughter of innocent civilians in the Sarajevo area and in the other safe areas of Bosnia. Now, the Bosnian Serbs have stated that they will end all offensive operations within the Sarajevo exclusion zone, withdraw their

heavy weapons from the zone within 6 days, and allow road and air access to Sarajevo within 24 hours. NATO and the U.N., therefore, have suspended air operations temporarily and will carefully monitor the Serb compliance with these commitments.

The suspension is appropriate. But let me emphasize, if the Bosnian Serbs do not comply with their commitments, the air strikes will resume.

Today's developments are a direct result of NATO's steadfastness in protecting the safe areas and the close cooperation between the U.N. and NATO. They also reflect the intense diplomatic efforts by Assistant Secretary of State Richard Holbrooke and the U.S. negotiating team as well as those of our European and Russian partners.

Now the Bosnian Serbs must carry out their commitments and then turn their energies toward a political settlement that will end this terrible conflict for good. They should have no doubt that NATO will resume the air strikes if they fail to keep their commitments, if they strike again at Sarajevo or the other safe areas.

Today's actions, however, following last week's successful meeting in Geneva of the Foreign Ministers of Bosnia, Croatia, and Serbia, are important steps along the path to peace in Bosnia. A lot of work remains to be done, but we are absolutely determined to press forward to reach a settlement to this conflict, not on the battlefield but at the negotiating table. We can and we must end Bosnia's long nightmare.

Q. Mr. President, what do you think is the possibility of transforming this into a permanent peace in Bosnia?

The President. I think there's a good possibility if the parties themselves wish to do it. And Ambassador Holbrooke and his team are working hard. We're getting good support from Europe and from Russia. I think we have a chance.

Q. Since you last spoke in so formal a setting, even so formal a setting as this, a lot has happened, including the biggest military operation in NATO's history, something that you certainly urged, intense activity by your diplomats. And

you have seemed almost shy about coming out and talking about it. Is that just an abundance of caution, or why is that, sir? [*Laughter*]

The President. Not an abundance of caution, but what I have wanted to do, first of all, is let our actions speak for themselves. I thought it was important to have our actions speak for themselves.

I also think it is important that even though the United States has provided a great deal of the energy and leadership in this effort, in this, the first difficult security crisis in Europe after the cold war, I think it is important that the NATO forces and the United Nations be seen to be united and working together, and we are. And so that explains how we have tried to handle this publicly.

Q. In talking with Mr. Mladic and Mr. Karadzic and in really getting them to sign an agreement, is there a contradiction because they are convicted war criminals or accused war criminals——

The President. Accused.

Q. ——accused war criminals? And do you think they can now enter sort of the world of nations just like any other leader?

The President. First of all, those decisions will all have to be made down the line by the community of nations. The most important thing is that the work continue now to make a comprehensive peace.

NOTE: The President spoke at 10:04 a.m. in the Briefing Room at the White House. In his remarks, he referred to Bosnian Serb leaders Radovan Karadzic and Gen. Ratko Mladic.

Remarks Honoring the 1995 NCAA Champion California State University at Fullerton Baseball Team
September 15, 1995

Thank you very much. Thank you. Please be seated. Dr. Gordon, Coach Garrido, Assistant Coach George Horton, Congressman Royce, to my friend Roger Johnson and to all the members of this championship team: Now, I knew that Cal State-Fullerton had won the national baseball championship because I keep up with it. But some of the less schooled people here

in the White House, when they heard that Cal State was coming today and it was about baseball, they thought that someone had given Cal Ripken a whole State. [*Laughter*] And when they said that, I said, "Well, I hope he'll share it with me next year." [*Laughter*] Think about that.

Coach Garrido, Coach Horton, to all the student athletes who are here, I want to congratulate you on a remarkable baseball season and on your national championship.

Baseball is both a team sport and a collection of individual players. Most important of all, it's a team sport, but I think it's worth noting that four of these players were selected to the College World Series All Tournament Team: Brian Loyd, the catcher; the third-baseman, Tony Martinez; Ted Silva, the pitcher; and the series MVP and the college player of the year, the outfielder, Mark Kotsay.

I also want to compliment the coach and the players on complete honesty and full disclosure. They told me when I was in there that one of their pitchers, Tim Dixon, who had a perfect season, 13 and 0, played last year at the University of Arkansas at Little Rock. I'm glad we can make some contribution to some national champion this year, since we didn't quite make it in basketball.

You have been called college baseball's dream team: an 18-game season ending winning streak, the world series sweep, the best-ever season record for the school of 57 wins and 9 losses. You know, a lot of your success, I'm sure, has the same roots as the remarkable success that we celebrated just a few days ago when I joined a lot of other Americans in Camden Yards, and others watching all across America, when we saw Cal Ripken break Lou Gehrig's record.

It really takes a commitment to hard work and dedication and teamwork and basically doing it every day. One of the things that I like about baseball is that there are a lot of games in the season. Sometimes, being in politics, I wish we had more than one game every 4 years. But it's very important in baseball to have that daily discipline, that daily awareness, that daily readiness, that steadiness that so many Americans bring to other aspects of their lives.

And I think that America has kind of fallen back in love with baseball again the last few weeks, and I hope it gets a lot more attention. And I hope the qualities required for real success and excellence in baseball will become more and more appreciated by all of our people, because they're qualities that we can all use in our everyday lives, no matter what else we do.

So I want to join your Congressman and the entire State of California in expressing to all you young men my pride in you and your achievement. Congratulations for a job well-done. And I hope you will take the spirit and the values that brought you to the national championship with you throughout the rest of your lives, no matter what you do.

Good luck, and God bless you.

NOTE: The President spoke at 10:04 a.m. in the Rose Garden at the White House. In his remarks, he referred to Milton A. Gordon, president, and Augie Garrido, baseball coach, California State University at Fullerton; and Roger Johnson, Administrator of General Services.

Remarks to Representatives of Senior Citizens Organizations
September 15, 1995

Thank you very much. I'm delighted to see all of you. I'm glad to see you with your buttons and your—apparently, with your spirits intact. That's good. [*Laughter*]

As all of you know, we're having this huge debate in Washington today about the future of this country. I want to try to put this struggle over Medicare and Medicaid into some kind of proper context so that you can take it not only to the Members of Congress and to your own members but out to the American people at large.

There is an enormous consensus in our country, with which I agree, that we ought to pass a budget this time that will bring our books into balance by a date certain. I agree with that. We got into a bad habit, this country did, before I showed up here, in the eighties and the early nineties, of running a permanent deficit, not to invest, to grow the economy, to create jobs, but just because every year we preferred to spend more money than we were taking in. And it wasn't good for the country. We're on the verge of paying more in interest next year than we pay for defense, for example. And every year we keep doing that, we spend more and more on interest, and we have less and less to spend on everything else.

But why do we wish to do that? What are the values implicit in that choice? We do it because we want to free our children and our grandchildren from the burden of unnecessary debt. We do it because we don't want to have a country where the Government is taking all the money and the money will be free to be borrowed by private businesses to create jobs and to grow the economy. We do it because we think morally we'll be a stronger country if we don't just borrow money for the sake of borrowing it.

But our objectives will be undermined if we forget about the other obligations we have. That's why I've said, you know, we ought to balance the budget, but why would we cut education and thereby hurt the economy and hurt the future of the very children we're trying to help? Why would we undermine our ability to protect the environment and public health and thereby erode the very quality of life we say we're strengthening by balancing the budget?

And the same thing is true here. We have historically recognized significant obligations to the health care of people who are entitled to be taken care of through the Medicare program or, through no fault of their own, have to be given some assistance. It's a part of who we are; it's a part of what kind of country we are.

And that's what this fight over Medicare and Medicaid is all about. What are our obligations to each other? How are we going to fulfill them? This is a compact between the generations, a compact we have honored now for three decades. It has made America a stronger, better, more humane place. It has made family life more secure not only for seniors, not only for Americans with disabilities but for their family members, their hard-working family members who knew that they got a little help so that they could all fulfill their responsibilities. These are the values I would argue that we want to advance as we try to balance the budget. We don't want to undermine them. We want to do this in a way that will bring the American people together, not tear the American people apart. That is what I am working to do here.

It is truly ironic that this whole Medicare fight is being played out against the background of the trouble that the Trust Fund is in. Where did you hear that first? From me, right? And in 1993 and 1994, when I said the Medicare Trust Fund is in trouble, we have to do something to lengthen its life, we have to do the responsible thing and keep it strong, and I proposed solutions to keep it strong, some of those who are for cutting Medicare $270,000 billion today said that I was raising a red herring, that it wasn't really in trouble, and why were we even worried about this. How quickly they forget.

But thanks to the responsible people in the Congress in the last 2 years, we extended the life of the Medicare Trust Fund by 3 years. And in my balanced budget proposal, we extend the life of the Medicare Trust Fund by more than a decade from this day forward, making it in better shape than it's been in 9 of the last 15 years. That is what we have proposed to do and to do it without imposing new costs on seniors.

Now, the congressional Republicans have outlined their plan to balance the budget, which includes a $270 billion Medicare cut, 3 times the size of any previous cut, and a $180 billion Medicaid cut. Together that's nearly half a trillion dollars taken out of the health care system over the next 7 years. I doubt seriously that the health care system can afford that. And that again affects all of us, not just people on Medicare, not just people on Medicaid. Almost half a trillion dollars.

Their plan would increase premiums and other costs for senior citizens. It would reduce doctor choice. It would force many doctors to stop serving seniors altogether. It threatens to put rural hospitals and urban hospitals out of business. Brick by brick, it would dismantle Medicare as we know it.

Now, here's the point. If all this were necessary, really necessary to save Medicare, maybe we'd all be willing to do it. But it isn't. And that is the point that has been missing from all this public debate, the point I tried so hard to make yesterday, the point you know but, I have to tell you, most of your fellow Americans, even members of your various groups who are on Medicare, do not know: The proposed reductions in the congressional or Republican congressional plan in Medicare spending on providers do go into the Trust Fund; the proposed increased costs on seniors do not go into the Trust Fund as a matter of law.

So all this conversation we have heard about saving the Trust Fund—give them their due, when they're talking about holding back money from Part A to the hospitals and the doctors, they're telling the truth; that will go into the Trust Fund. But the extra cost to seniors, by law, will not go into the Trust Fund. You know it and I know it and everyone in America should know it. Every nickel that will be taken from the seniors will go into the General Fund where it will be used to carry out this 7-year plan, which includes a very large tax cut. So this is a plan to take more from people on Medicare, three-quarters of whom live on less than $24,000 a year, and put it into a tax cut, more than half of which will go to Americans who plainly don't need it.

Now that has to be driven home. That is a fact. And it is a fact I almost never hear discussed. This is not about saving the Trust Fund. If we were really about to see the Trust Fund go broke and there were no other options, we would all be saying, "Let's get in a room and roll up our sleeves and figure out what it is we have to do to save the best of this program," wouldn't we? Every one of us would be; none of you would be here raising sand about that. And you'd also want to say to the hospitals, "We want to keep you open," to the doctors, "We want to keep you going. We don't want to bankrupt anybody. Let's see how we can have a fair plan of shared sacrifice."

But by law, the money coming out of the seniors does not go to that Trust Fund. And it is a grave disservice to the American people not to just tell everybody that, not to say, "Hey, we'd like to fix the Trust Fund, and here's what the providers are going to have to sacrifice." Then you could look at the President's plan and their plan and you could compare. I think my plan asks about all of the providers they can come up with, and it adds 10 years to the life of the Trust Fund. Unless we can dramatically lower medical inflation, I think it asks about all we can right now. But it's good that it adds a long time to the Trust Fund.

But the money we're asking for from seniors—not us, but the congressional Republican plan—the money they ask for from the seniors won't go into that Trust Fund. And no one must be allowed to believe that it does. This is going into the balanced budget plan to pay for the tax cut.

I am also for a tax cut. I believe we ought to help working families raise their children and educate themselves and their children and give tax reductions for those purposes. But I do not favor funding them by raising the price of Medicare on the poorest elderly people when, as all of you know, the average senior citizen today is paying the same percentage of his or her income for health care in 1995 that they were paying in 1965 before Medicare came in. So it isn't true to say the seniors of this country haven't done their part to try to keep Medicare going. We've seen increased costs with inflation.

So I ask you to hammer this point home. This should not be a debate between things that the seniors and the disabled people of this country can't afford to pay and a system we can't afford to let go broke. That is not the choice. You know it; I know it; America must know it before these decisions are made. Fine, let's save the Trust Fund. We're going to do it. I've been working on it for 2½ years. We've made it better. But let us not pretend that it is necessary to do what is being done either to balance the budget or to save the Trust Fund. These fees on seniors are going up to meet that particular plan with that very large tax cut. And everyone must know that.

A lot of these most painful cuts have been hidden altogether. In this congressional plan, deep within the fine print of the Medicare plan are cuts to be revealed later. What is it called— automatic look-back. [*Laughter*] We've all done that once or twice in one or two ways.

Now, think about this: What about the Medicaid program? You hardly hear anything about Medicaid. People say, "Oh, that's that welfare program." One-third of Medicaid does go to help poor women and their poor children on Medicaid. Over two-thirds of it goes to the elderly and the disabled. All of you know that as well. America must know that. If we reduce projected Medicaid spending by $180 billion and if States were to follow through with across-the-board cuts, our best estimates are that by the year 2000, there would be 300,000 people who would be either removed from or not be able to get into nursing homes and 4 million poor children who would not have access to medical care. Hundreds of thousands of families would have a much harder time caring for a member of their family in their home or helping their family members in some other way.

This is very important. If you don't do it across the board—you say, oh, we're going to take care of the people in nursing homes, the seniors—that's even more disabled people who are cut off. That's even more seniors in their homes who aren't helped. That's even more children who are in the streets without any health care. This is not a free ride.

Do we need to lower the rate of inflation in Medicaid? You bet we do. I proposed a plan to do that. It doesn't reduce spending by near as much as theirs does because I don't know that we can do that. I honestly believe these things are going to happen. And we need to consider the consequences of them. I don't want to do something that could close our rural and urban hospitals, that could make the lives of poor children even more difficult, that could be terrible for not only the disabled and the elderly who would be affected by it but for all their family members. You think about how many middle class working people are not going to be able to save to send their kids to college because now they'll have to be taking care of their parents who would have been eligible for public assistance.

I am not saying that we shouldn't balance the budget and that we don't have to slow the rate of increase. But look at the proposals we made in this administration. We made sensible, disciplined proposals that won't be easy to meet, but can be met and are directly related to saving the Medicare Trust Fund and to bringing the cost inflation down in health care and to balancing the budget, without asking the seniors of this country to pay for a tax cut for people who don't need it or where the size of it is too big.

And I'm telling you, you can have the right kind of tax cut, you can have a healthy Medicare Trust Fund, you can have reductions in cost inflation in Medicare and Medicaid without these draconian consequences. That's what you have to tell the American people. If these were the only choices, it'd be tough enough. But this is an easy choice once you know the alternatives. If these health care cuts come to my desk, of this size, I would have no choice but to veto it.

But let me say this. What always, always becomes the news every day is what the new fight is, what the new conflict is. We ought to be here to build a bridge. I can't believe anyone would willingly, willingly damage the seniors of this country, the Americans with disabilities, the children of this country as much as I believe this proposal will damage them, especially to pay for a tax cut that is too large, when we can have a targeted tax cut for education and childrearing for middle class families without doing any of this, when we can balance the budget without doing any of this, when we can save the Medicare Trust Fund without doing any of this. [*Applause*]

I'm glad you cheered and I'm glad you clapped, but there is a bridge to be built here. We can get all Americans on the solution side of this problem. We can get Republicans and Democrats on the solution side of this problem. It is not too late. We have a few weeks here. But first, the American people must know the facts. So I implore you—most of you know so much about this you just assume other people do, too. And it is a very powerful thing to tell an average American working family that deeply believes in this country that we've got to do what it takes to save Medicare. That's a powerful thing. Well, we do. But this is not what it takes to save Medicare, this proposal that we're opposed to.

So I ask you, stand up for what you believe. Fight for what you believe. Know that I'll be there for you if it comes to crunch time. And if I have to use the veto pen, I will. But go out there and build a bridge. Start it with the facts, the evidence, the truth. Ask people to come to grips with the truth. And ask them what our obligations are to one another. Ask them why we're balancing the budget and don't we have to balance the budget consistent with our desire for strong families, for honoring the people who have made this country what it is today, and for building a better future for our children, whether they're rich or poor.

That, I think, ought to be the message. If so, we'll wind up building that bridge and making this country stronger.

Thank you, and God bless you all.

NOTE. The President spoke at 3:41 p.m. in Room 450 of the Old Executive Office Building.

The President's Radio Address
September 16, 1995

Good morning. Last week I spoke with you about what I believe must be done to reform our Nation's broken welfare system. I said that real welfare reform should reflect the values all of us as Americans share: work, personal responsibility, and family. And I challenged the Senate to put aside its partisan differences to stand up to ideological extremism and to find common ground and higher ground.

Ever since the 1992 campaign, I've been appealing to Americans to join me in an effort to end welfare as we know it. Since I became President, I've been working to reform welfare State by State while pushing for national action in Congress.

Our administration has freed 34 States from Federal rules to enable them to move people from welfare to work. We've offered all 50 States the opportunity to set time limits on welfare, require people to work or stay in school, give private employers incentives to work. And it's working. The welfare rolls are down, the food stamp rolls are down across America. But we still need national action in Congress.

The votes taken this week by the United States Senate under the leadership of a bipartisan coalition of Democrats and moderate Republicans give us hope that a conclusion to this effort may only be days or weeks away.

After months of sometimes bitter debate, we are now within striking distance of transforming the welfare system in four fundamental ways: First, people on welfare will have to work in return for the help they receive. Second, no one who can work will be able to stay on welfare forever. Third, we will begin to make work possible by providing child care for mothers of young children. And fourth, we will put in place the toughest child support enforcement measures ever.

It wasn't always this way. Not long ago, some in Congress wanted to punish children for the mistakes of their parents, and some still do. Others wanted to pretend that States could require mothers to work without the child care they need.

But this week, an overwhelming bipartisan majority in the Senate rejected that course and began to insist that welfare reform should be about moving people from welfare to work, not simply cutting them off. Senators in both parties agreed to provide resources for child care.

They agreed that States have a responsibility to maintain their own efforts to move people from welfare to work and to care for poor children and that States should have access to a contingency fund to protect against an economic downturn that would put people out of work and on welfare through no fault of their own. They also agreed on a revolutionary work performance bonus that I have urged that for the first time ever will reward States for placing welfare recipients into private sector jobs.

They agreed that instead of just cutting off young unwed mothers, we should require them to live at home, stay in school, and turn their lives around. And if their homes are unsuitable, this bill provides incentives for States to establish second-chance homes, a part of our national effort to reduce teen pregnancy and give young people a better start in life.

All these things have long been critical elements of my approach to welfare reform, from my service as Governor to my work as President. For 15 years I have worked on this problem. I know these things will make a real difference in moving people from welfare to work.

Soon, both the House and the Senate will have endorsed all the tough child support enforcement provisions I supported last year, including saying to parents who owe child support, "If you can pay up and you don't, we'll take your driver's license away."

Despite the progress we've made, our work isn't done yet. We'll be working hard on this bill over the next few weeks to make sure the right incentives are there to move people from welfare to work, to make sure children are protected, and that States not only share the problem but have the resources they need to get the job done. And we'll be working hard to build on the bipartisan progress we made this week. We must not let it fall apart when the House and Senate meet to resolve their differences.

Still, there are some on the far right who say they don't want welfare reform at all unless it meets all their ideological litmus tests. These extremists want to cut off all help to children whose mothers are poor, young, and unmarried, even though the Catholic Church and many Republicans have warned that this would lead to more abortions. These same people want Washington to impose mandates, like a family cap, even though Republican and Democratic Governors alike agree that these decisions should be left to the States.

By an overwhelming bipartisan majority, the Senate showed wisdom and courage in rejecting those litmus tests this week. I challenged the conference committee of House and Senate Members to do the same. One of the primary reasons I ran for President was to reform welfare. I've done my best to do it without congressional action, but with the right kind of congressional action, we can do the job right. We can advance work and personal responsibility and family.

Finally, we're on the verge of coming to grips with one of the most fundamental social problems of our time, moving people from welfare to work. Now we must finish the job, and we can't let ideological extremism and politics as usual get in the way. Make no mistake: If Congress walks away from this bipartisan progress, they will kill welfare reform.

But we've worked too hard, too long, to let partisan extremism kill this effort. Welfare reform will not work and cannot pass unless it's a truly bipartisan effort. And it will only become law if it truly reflects the spirit of our great Nation and the values of all Americans.

There's an important lesson in what took place this week. If we can find common ground on the issue of welfare reform, surely we can find it in our efforts to solve our other problems, especially in our effort to balance the budget in a way that will strengthen families and prepare our citizens to meet the challenges and opportunities of the 21st century. Let's do welfare reform, then let's do the budget and do it right.

Thanks for listening.

NOTE: The President spoke at 10:06 a.m. from the Oval Office at the White House.

Presidential Determination No. 95–42—Memorandum on Travel to Lebanon
September 15, 1995

Memorandum for the Secretary of Transportation

Subject: Partial Resumption of Travel to Lebanon

By virtue of the authority vested in me by 49 U.S.C. 40106(b), I hereby determine that the prohibition of transportation services to Lebanon established by Presidential Determination 85–14 of July 1, 1985, as amended by Presidential Determination 92–41 of August 17, 1992, is hereby further amended to permit U.S. air carriers, solely through interline arrangements, to engage in foreign air transportation to and from Lebanon of:

a) passengers who are not U.S. citizens; and
b) U.S. citizen passengers who have received written approval from the Department of State for travel to Lebanon;

and their accompanying baggage.

All other prohibitions set forth in the above-referenced Presidential Determinations, including the prohibition on direct operations to Lebanon by U.S. air carriers, remain in effect.

You are directed to implement this determination as soon as is practical, with due regard to the safety of travelers going to and from Lebanon.

You are further directed to publish this determination in the *Federal Register*.

WILLIAM J. CLINTON

NOTE: This memorandum was released by the Office of the Press Secretary on September 18, but it was not received for publication in the *Federal Register*.

Remarks Prior to a Meeting With Community Leaders in Philadelphia, Pennsylvania
September 18, 1995

First of all, let me say to all of you how much I appreciate your taking the time to come here and discuss this with me today. To all who have spoken, I appreciate the kind remarks you had about the efforts of the administration.

I think the time and effort we have put in on this is not so much rooted in the political party I happen to belong to as the fact that I happen to have been a Governor for a dozen years, and I have closed defense bases. And I have also worked for a decade on trying to restructure the economy of a State that was devastated in the first big recession of the early eighties. And if you look at the challenge to America of creating jobs and raising incomes that we faced here in 1993, when I became President, it is obvious that—it was obvious to me then; it's more obvious to me now—that general policies that may generate an enormous amount of economic opportunity will still leave great pockets of problems, rooted primarily in America today in two things: one is the general distress of isolated urban and rural areas, and second and to the point here, the aggravated impact in some areas of the defense cutbacks in terms of base closings and the defense contracts being cut.

So in 1993, we developed a plan to try to accelerate the rate by which we could turn over these facilities to localities so we could begin more quickly to generate jobs. And then, in 1994, we gave, I think, some of the property here at the Philadelphia Naval Yard. And now what I'm interested in doing is finding out what the remaining problems are, what I can do to accelerate it.

I do believe that we have, as the mayor said, committed over $100 million to this project. That's not counting the approximately $170 million in loan guarantees we were prepared to come forward with through NARAD if this shipbuilding project goes forward. I think that is an appropriate thing for our country to do for a naval yard that built and repaired ships for this country throughout virtually its entire history and for the workers who have given their entire lives to this work.

I would like to emphasize that we have also had a very strong interest in maintaining and enhancing the shipbuilding capacity of the United States. I believe that the international economics have changed on that. I think we have opportunities we simply did not have 10 years ago. I have seen, because of our efforts and also because of the international market and because of the increasing productivity of American workers, I have seen a major facility saved in southern California; I have seen new contracts from around the world come to the Gulf Coast and to the Atlantic Coast. And so, again, I think that this project is really worth pressing.

I think trying to maintain these kinds of jobs for the people here is not an unrealistic expectation in the world as it exists today and the future as far as we can foresee it. So I would encourage you to do that.

One last thing I'd like to say is that we really want to help you do what you want to do. My strong belief is that the Federal Government works best, in economic areas and quite often in social policy, when we are giving help, giving encouragement, being a partner, but the ultimate decisions are being made by people at the grassroots level.

I just visited a part of Philadelphia that's in your empowerment zone today, and the same philosophy for me holds there. In our education reforms we've tried to do that. Tomorrow, Governor, we're going to announce the next round of grants for the school-to-work project, which is developing training programs for people who don't go to 4-year colleges. And Pennsylvania will get about $6.5 million in that. Again, projects designed by Pennsylvanians for your State, not something that somebody in Washington decided that you ought to be doing.

I also would like to say a special word of thanks to Dr. Singerman for leaving the Ben Franklin Partnership and coming to work for us. Now, if you don't like what we're doing, you can blame him instead of me. [*Laughter*] And you can literally say that he knows better—[*laughter*]—because of his long experience with you. We thank you.

And the last thing I'd like to say is, again, I want to say a special word of thanks to the Members of Congress here and to you, Senator Specter, for the work you have done to try to give us a chance to develop a bipartisan economic policy, to get the people in this country through the economic transition period that we now see underway.

And lastly, let me just say there can be light at the end of the tunnel. I was in northern California a few days ago. There is an airbase there that was closed—an Army base—a few years ago that now has far more employees than it did on the day that it closed. We are on the verge of doing that in three or four other places—and the same or higher quality jobs, not just more jobs.

We can do this here, and we can do it more quickly if we can figure out how to serve you better and, obviously, if we could get one big project early, a magnet project. All these big developments always work better if you can get somebody to anchor it early.

So I want to be there; I want to help. And I thank you for all that you've done so far. Thank you.

NOTE: The President spoke at 5:23 p.m. at the Wyndham Franklin Plaza Hotel. In his remarks, he referred to Phillip A. Singerman, nominee to be Assistant Secretary of Commerce for Economic Development.

Remarks at a Fundraiser in Philadelphia
September 18, 1995

Thank you very much. Ladies and gentlemen, thank you for being here tonight and for all your support. I want to thank, obviously, Tom Leonard and Ken Jarin and Alan Kessler and Bill Batoff and Lynn Barrick and everyone else who worked so hard on this. Mr. Mayor, we're delighted to be back in your city. I thank my good friends from Pittsburgh for being here and from throughout the State, the State legislators and others, and of course, the four distinguished Members of the House of Representatives who are here, without whom a lot of the accomplishments the Vice President just reeled off would not have occurred.

I'd also like to say a special word of thanks to two Pennsylvanians—one of who is here and one of whom is not—to my good friend Harris Wofford for helping me to give birth to national service and for now, his willingness to lead the fight to preserve national service and to increase it; and to Marjorie Margolies-Mezvinsky for her wonderful leadership in Beijing, China. I thank you.

I came up here, and the Vice President had just concluded and introduced me. I said, "Al, whatever I say now, I'm going to be behind. Why don't you just keep on talking; it sounds pretty good." I'd forgotten we did half the stuff he talked about.

I say that only half in jest. You know, when I asked Al Gore to become the nominee for Vice President on our Democratic ticket, I did it after we had a long set of talks, and we agreed that we were going into an uncertain time when we had to make difficult decisions rooted in what was best for the United States over a 10- or a 20- or a 30-year period, that might not be popular in the short run, that might not even be able to be easily explained in the short run. We knew that.

And we and our wonderful spouses made a commitment to an administration that would always look toward the future, that would always embrace new ideas, that would have the highest standards of excellence, but most important of all, would seek to find common ground in the things we all believe in: the preservation of the American dream, bringing Americans together around work and responsibility and family and community, leading the world into a new era of peace and prosperity, and giving our children the opportunity to have a better future in the 21st century. And I am very grateful for that.

One of the reasons I like dealing with people like your mayor is that they're open to new ideas and to changing things. And thanks to the Vice President, we've done a lot of those things he talked about. It may take 10 more years, but some day America will develop what we call in our administration a clean car, one that will get triple or quadruple the mileage that automobiles get today and produce less air pollution and contribute less to the global warming that we all now see all the scientists in the world saying is a problem. There may not be a single vote in it, but our children will live in a better world because Al Gore made a partnership with the auto companies for a clean car and a cleaner future. That is the sort of thing that we have tried to do.

When we started this work on reinventing Government, I said, you know, there's never been a single incident when a President or an administration generated any popular support for changing the way the Government works. But we are going into a new age, and we can no longer have a top-down bureaucracy that is too heavy with management, that delivers too few services, and is too oriented toward yesterday's top-down regulation. It may not be any sort of political benefit in it, but 10 years from now, our country will be better off because we have downsized the Government, because we have abolished regulations, because we have forged new partnerships with people to do the right things because they want to do the right things, not because someone in Washington is figuring out 900 different ways to tell them how to do it.

These are the kinds of things that we have tried to do. And I say that simply to make this point, that I really have appreciated the kind of partnership that the mayor discussed that the Vice President and I have enjoyed. We've done a lot of things that no other administration has done. And we have been told we were politically crazy for doing it. We were advised not to liberate Haiti, but we did it and it worked out all right.

We were advised that if I became the first sitting President to take on the NRA over the issues of the Brady bill and the assault weapons ban that it would be a terrible political mistake. And it turned out to be a terrible political mistake for a lot of brave Members of the House of Representatives who laid down their seats in Congress so that we could keep Uzis out of schools and off the street and keep kids from being shot down in drive-by shootings, but it was the right thing to do.

And let me tell you, we were told that we had no business becoming the first administra-

tion to ever take on the powerful tobacco companies in our campaign to reduce teenage smoking. But 3,000 kids start smoking every day, and 1,000 of them will have their lives shortened as a result. And who cares what the political consequences are? It is the right thing to do. And that is the kind of thing we are trying to do.

I say that to make this general point about why it is so important that you're here today. This is an incredible country that we have been given, and we happen to have been given the responsibility to live in this country at a remarkable moment in history.

When I ran for President in 1991 and 1992, I did so believing that the end of the cold war and the dawn of this new global economy presented us with challenges which would require us to change the way we conducted our business, both personally as families and communities and as a country, and that we had to break out of a lot of the established ideas that both parties had advanced. And I wanted to do that. I did not imagine, even though I thought I understood it well, the absolute scope and sweep and depth of those changes.

And I come here tonight to tell you that I believe we are living through the period of most profound change in the way we live and work as Americans that we have experienced in 100 years.

It was about 100 years ago when we basically became an industrial and more urbanized country, shifting from an agricultural and rural country. And we had to decide what that meant about how we were going to treat each other. For when we became an industrial country, a lot of people were getting fabulously wealthy, and it was a time of incredible opportunity. But a lot of the ties that bound people together were uprooted; families were uprooted; whole communities began to disappear. People came to great urban centers looking for opportunities. Immigrants came here from other countries looking for opportunities. And those that found them were doing very well. But we also saw children working 10, 12, 14 hours a day, 6 days a week in the mines and the factories of this country. We saw an absolute disregard for the preservation of our natural resources.

And for about 20 years we had this raging debate, and we decided that the National Government should promote genuine competition, if it meant breaking up monopolies; should protect children from the abuses of child labor that were then present; should attempt to preserve our natural resources; and should, in common, promote the personal well-being and the development of our people. Those decisions were made about 100 years ago, from roughly 1895 to about 1916.

And what happened after that was the most dramatic, breathtaking period of economic and social progress in the United States ever experienced by any country. Yes, we had to get through the Great Depression; yes, we had to win a great world war; yes, we had to make good on the promise of the Civil War and the amendments thereafter to liberate ourselves from legalized racial discrimination. But it all happened because we decided that we were going to be one country, that we were going to live up to the promise of the Constitution and our best values in a new time.

We are now going through all that all over again. When you hear these radical debates in Washington, you hear people say things you think are half crazy. You should not be surprised; it is because we are being kind of uprooted again, for we are moving from an industrial economy to one based on information and technology, even manufacturing more based on information and technology. We are moving from a cold war arrangement among the nations, where we're divided into two armed camps of nation-states looking across the Iron Curtain at each other, into a global economy where the borders of all nations are becoming more porous as money and technology and trade flee around the world at rapid paces; where we're becoming more integrated economically, but in every country there are pressures for disintegration as the global economy makes it more difficult for families and communities to keep going and as radical political groups tend to arise capturing the benefits of the frustration of ordinary people. And you see it all across the globe.

We don't now fear a bomb dropping on us from the Soviet Union. I am proud to say that since I've been President, for the first time since the dawn of the nuclear age there are no Russian missiles pointed at the people of the United States. And you should be proud of that.

But we do see the development of organized terrorism all around the world, whether it is someone blowing up the Federal building in Oklahoma City or someone blowing up a school bus of innocent people in Israel or someone breaking open a vial of poison sarin gas in a subway in Tokyo.

So we're living now in a world that is in transition, that is full of incredible possibilities, exhilarating hope, and troubling change. It is against that background that this election in 1996 must occur. It is our duty to preserve the American dream for our children. It is our duty to bring the American people together around our common values of work and family and responsibility and community. It is our duty to lead the world to a new era of peace and prosperity. And we ought to be happy about doing our duty.

We also have to understand that in a period like this, it is hard for a lot of people to sort out what's going on and that we cannot worry about what is popular in the short run. We have to do what we think is right 10 or 20 or 30 years from now. There is no political roadmap. We must create the future consistent with our values, not based on what we think is popular in the moment.

So I say to you, I have loved the opportunity to serve as your President. I have been frustrated from time to time when there was no clear answer. And in the end, I have tried to do what I thought was right. The Vice President's account of our record would indicate that, more often than not, it's come out all right.

But we have to look to the future. What is our job in the future? Let's look at the economy. Let's just begin with that. If I had told you 30 months ago that in the space of 2½ years we would have 7½ million new jobs, 2½ million new homeowners, 2 million new small businesses, a record number of new self-made millionaires in America, the stock market would go over 4,700, we'd have record corporate profits, the African-American unemployment rate would drop below 10 percent for the first time in more than two decades but the median wage of Americans, the guy in the middle, would drop in the midst of all this, it would have seemed impossible. But that's exactly what happened.

Why? Because only some of us are doing well in this global economy; because we live in a world where what you earn depends on what you can learn; because there are some people who are caught in the transition from a defense to a domestic economy. That's why we had the meeting about what's going to happen at the Philadelphia shipyard today, because there are some places that have been ignored in all this entrepreneurial explosion and no one is investing in our best economic opportunity, which is all the working people of America who live in poor communities. That's why we have the empowerment zone program. But it's not surprising when you hear all this fabulous economic news and you realize it hasn't reached everybody. So it is our duty to see that it reaches everybody.

If you look at our social situation, believe it or not, in almost every major area in America the crime rate is down, the murder rate is down, the welfare rolls are down, the food stamp rolls are down, divorce is down, and abortion is down. Almost everywhere we are coming back to our roots. But we still know it's way too high. And we're afraid of losing our children because juvenile crime is up, people under 18 are committing more crime, because casual marijuana use among young children is up, because they don't know if they've got a future.

So what we have to do is to say, "Hey, look at what's going on good in this country. We can do it. We can make it." And we have to have the discipline and courage to spread those good things to everybody in this society. I honestly believe if we do our job in this period of transition, our best days are before us. But we have to remember what we're trying to do.

Now, if you look at the budget debate in that context, to me, what we ought to do becomes easier, and it's not so partisan or political. Should we balance the budget? You bet we should. This country never had a permanent deficit unrelated to economy slowdowns until 1981. It was only 12 years ago—or 12 years before I became President—that there was a political decision made or not made, that it was easy to cut taxes and increase spending and then too hard to do anything about it, so we just run a deficit from now to kingdom come.

Always before, the country borrowed money for two reasons: One is, there was an economic slowdown and we needed to pump things up. And that was a good thing to do. The other is, we needed to borrow money as a nation the way you borrow money as a family or a business, the same way you'd borrow money to buy a home or start a business. We didn't borrow money to go out to dinner on until 12 years before I became President. And in only 12 years, we quadrupled the debt of the country.

The Democratic Party should work with the Republican Party to get rid of this. It is a bad precedent. We're spending more and more money on interest on the debt. It we don't balance the budget next year, we'll spend more on interest than we do on defense. This year, the budget would be in balance but for the interest we pay on the debt run up in the 12 years before I took office. And we've taken the deficit from $290 billion to $160 billion a year, and we ought to go all the way until we get the job done. America should invest in the future, not squander the present. And we should all be for that.

But we should do it consistent with our values. Why are we going to do it? Because we want America to be stronger in the 21st century. We want our kids to have the American dream like we had. What does that mean for how you balance the budget? It means, number one, don't cut education, don't cut technology, don't cut defense conversion, don't cut research and development. All together, it's a small part of our budget.

But if we want to grow the economy and give children a chance, why would we reduce the number of people on Head Start? Why would we reduce the number of schools in the safe and drug-free schools program or the number of schools that can teach character education to kids who may not get it anywhere else or the number of schools who can put computers in their classes or have smaller classes for poor kids so they can get the kind of instructions they need or the number of people who can get low-interest college loans on better repayment terms or scholarships? No, we should balance the budget, and we can have a tax cut. But we can't balance the budget in 7 years with a tax cut that the Congress proposes without cutting education. And cutting education would be like cutting the defense budget at the height of the cold war. It's our national security. We ought not to do it. We ought to avoid that.

And I say—not because it's money but because of the way the money is being invested now—high standards, high expectations, high accountability, that's what we're doing now, grassroots reform. It is different than it used to be. It's not just throwing money at the problem.

The same thing about Medicare. Our administration warned 2 years ago that the Trust Fund which finances hospital care for Medicare was close to running out of money. We warned that. And we said, here's a plan to give it more life. And the people now in the majority in Congress said we were wrong, said we were crazy, said we didn't know what we were doing. And so without any help, we added 3 years to the life of the Medicare Trust Fund. Then, in health care reform, we proposed to do some more. And they said, "Oh, you can't cut Medicare by that much. You'll wreck the system." Now that they're in the majority, they've proposed to cut it more than twice as much as we ever did.

Now, do we have to slow the rate of health care inflation to preserve Medicare for future generations? Yes, we do. Yes, we do. We absolutely should. Do seniors who have the ability to pay a little bit more have a responsibility to do it because they have very high incomes? I think you can make that case.

But here is what is going on, folks. Under the guise of bailing out the Medicare Trust Fund, people in Congress are trying to require elderly people who make less than $24,000 a year—don't forget, three-quarters of all the people on Medicare in this country make less than $24,000 a year—they want them to pay more in their own premiums. And what they don't tell you is, not a single penny of that money goes into the Trust Fund. The premium money goes to pay for things like doctor bills, and that's paid for out of the general budget. So what they're saying is, we want to charge elderly people with incomes of less than $24,000 a year more so we can pay for this tax cut and balance the budget in 7 years.

I say, let's save Medicare. But let's don't take money away from older people with less than $24,000 to give it to people like me who have not even asked for a tax cut but do want their budget balanced. Let's do it consistent with America's values and what we owe to the people of this country who have made us what we are.

The Vice President talked about the environment. You know, my family and I just took a vacation in Yellowstone and Grand Teton National Parks. And every day, we benefit from what our country has done for public health and the environment that we don't even think about, cleaner air, clean water, safe food. Now there are those who say, "Well, we shouldn't even have the Government involved in this." The House of Representatives actually defeated an amendment twice to say, "Well, at least give

us the money to go ahead and regulate things like arsenic in water." They defeated once an amendment that said, "At least give us the chance to keep things like cryptosporidium out of municipal water supplies." That's what killed all those people in Milwaukee about a year ago.

Now, folks, Al Gore, since he's been Vice President, running our reinventing Government project, has helped us to eliminate 16,000 pages of Federal regulations. We have cut regulations at the Small Business Administration in half. We cut the budget of the Small Business Administration by 40 percent and doubled the loan volume, doubled the loan volume. We kept the loan volume the same to white males and dramatically increased it to females and minorities and never changed the standards. We're committed to less regulation. We've cut the regulations at the Department of Education on school districts by 40 percent. We're cutting the time people have to fool with the EPA by 25 percent. We want to get rid of regulation, but somebody has to show up every day to make sure that your children have clean water, clean air, and safe food. We should not cut that to balance the budget.

You heard the Vice President talking about crime. The crime bill we adopted was rooted in the advice we got from prosecutors and police officers. It was bipartisan. Mayor Rendell came down with Mayor Guiliani from New York several times to lobby for the crime bill. It has punishment. We just convicted the second "three strikes and you're out" felon, five serious felonies. For once, the guy is going to jail for life so he can't hurt anybody anymore. We have more police officers on the street, and we have more prevention to give our children something to say yes to.

There are those who say, "Well, let's just get rid of it. Send a check to the States." I say, we had a solemn commitment to 100,000 police. This is a small part of the bill. We paid for it entirely by personnel cuts in the Federal Government. That is not the way to balance the budget.

I could give you a lot of examples. I just want to give you one more, because to me it represents the most important thing of all. In the world toward which we're moving, it's going to be harder and harder to keep families together. More and more parents are working, more and more two-parent families are working. The most important job of any society is still to raise children in an appropriate way. We therefore have no more important obligation than to enable people to succeed as parents and as workers. I think we would all admit that. That's why the family leave law was so important.

Another thing that we did in that budget last year was to cut taxes on 15 million American working families with over 50 million Americans, almost 20 percent of our people, through something called the earned-income tax credit, the family tax credit. You heard the Vice President talking about it. Eventually, it will lower taxes for families of four with incomes of under $30,000 or $31,000 a year. For families of four with incomes of $11,000 a year, they can get up to $3,000 back. Why? Because we believe no one should be taxed into poverty.

If you want people to move from welfare to work, if you believe in family, work, and responsibility, then people who are willing to go out there and work full-time and still do the best they can with their kids and they're making all they can make, should not be taxed into poverty. The tax system should lift them up, not tear them down.

Now, in this budget fight, there are those who believe that they should get rid of this earned-income tax credit or cut it in half or cut it by a third. How in the world can we justify raising taxes on low-income working people, lowering taxes on folks like me, and then telling them, "Don't you be on welfare. You get out there and work. You do your part." This is not about money. This is about who we are. What are our obligations to one another? How are we going to give our kids the American dream? I'm telling you, I will say again: This is a very great country. We wouldn't be around here after almost 220 years if this were not a great country and if more than half the time we didn't make the right decisions.

We have a set of 100-year decisions to make, 100-year decisions. You know that, deep in your bones, you know how much change we're going through. But what works is what has always worked for us. When we look to the future, when we work together, when we try to give people the ability to make the most of their own lives, when we try to be a force for peace and freedom throughout the world, we do just fine.

So I say to you, this is not an ordinary election. And this election cannot be won by sound bites. And this election cannot be run on the politics of resentment. This election must be won by the mind and the heart and the vision of Americans looking down the road to the next generation and saying, I want the 21st century to be an American century, too. I want the American dream to be alive and well.

When I was born, in my home State the per capita income was 56 percent of the national average. I was the first person in my family ever to go to college. I was raised by a grandfather with a 6th-grade education. I became President of the United States not because of my hard work and my innate goodness but because I had the help of a country that cared about the old-fashioned things and wanted every single American to have access to them.

So I say to you, if we do this election right, if we make these 100-year decisions right, the best is yet to be.

Thank you, and God bless you all.

NOTE: The President spoke at 9:05 p.m. at the Wyndham Franklin Plaza Hotel. In his remarks, he referred to Philadelphia Democratic fundraisers Thomas A. Leonard, Kenneth M. Jarin, Alan C. Kessler, William Batoff, and Lynn Barrick; Mayor Edward Rendell of Philadelphia; and Mayor Rudolph Guiliani of New York City.

Statement on the Death of Helen McLarty
September 18, 1995

Hillary and I were deeply saddened to learn of the death of a wonderful woman and good family friend, Helen McLarty.

I have known Helen McLarty my entire life. She was an exemplary citizen and a devoted wife and mother. Like my own mother, she fought a long battle against cancer with courage and perseverance. Throughout her illness, she was a constant source of strength to all of those around her.

In addition to the love and support she gave to her family, Helen McLarty was a remarkable citizen whose contributions to her community—as the first woman to serve on the Arkansas Industrial Development Commission and as a partner with her husband in building the McLarty Companies into one of the region's largest transportation firms—will not be forgotten.

Our thoughts and prayers are with Helen's sons, Mack and Bud McLarty, her grandchildren, and the rest of her family and friends during this difficult time.

Message to the Congress Reporting on the National Emergency with Respect to Iran
September 18, 1995

To the Congress of the United States:

I hereby report to the Congress on developments concerning the national emergency with respect to Iran that was declared in Executive Order No. 12957 of March 15, 1995, and matters relating to Executive Order No. 12959 of May 6, 1995. This report is submitted pursuant to section 204(c) of the International Emergency Economic Powers Act, 50 U.S.C. 1703(c) (IEEPA), and section 505(c) of the International Security and Development Cooperation Act of 1985, 22 U.S.C. 2349aa–9(c). This report discusses only matters concerning the national emergency with respect to Iran that was declared in Executive Order No. 12957 and matters relating to Executive Order No. 12959.

1. On March 15, 1995, I issued Executive Order No. 12957 (60 *Fed. Reg.* 14615, March 17, 1995) to declare a national emergency with respect to Iran pursuant to IEEPA, and to prohibit the financing, management, or supervision by United States persons of the development of Iranian petroleum resources. This action was in response to actions and policies of the Government of Iran, including support for international terrorism, efforts to undermine the Middle East peace process, and the acquisition of weapons of mass destruction and the means to deliver them. A copy of the order was provided to the Congress by message dated March 15, 1995.

Following the imposition of these restrictions with regard to the development of Iranian petroleum resources, Iran continued to engage in activities that represent a threat to the peace and security of all nations, including Iran's continuing support for international terrorism, its support for acts that undermine the Middle East peace process, and its intensified efforts to acquire weapons of mass destruction. On May 6, 1995, I issued Executive Order No. 12959 to further respond to the Iranian threat to the national security, foreign policy, and economy of the United States.

Executive Order No. 12959 (60 *Fed. Reg.* 24757, May 9, 1995) (1) prohibits exportation from the United States to Iran or to the Government of Iran of goods, technology, or services; (2) prohibits the reexportation of certain U.S. goods and technology to Iran from third countries; (3) prohibits transactions such as brokering and other dealing by United States persons in goods and services of Iranian origin or owned or controlled by the Government of Iran; (4) prohibits new investments by United States persons in Iran or in property owned or controlled by the Government of Iran; (5) prohibits U.S. companies and other United States persons from approving, facilitating, or financing performance by a foreign subsidiary or other entity owned or controlled by a United States person of transactions that a United States person is prohibited from performing; (6) continues the 1987 prohibition on the importation into the United States of goods and services of Iranian origin; (7) prohibits any transaction by any United States person or within the United States that evades or avoids or attempts to violate any prohibition of the order; and (8) allowed U.S. companies a 30-day period in which to perform trade transactions pursuant to contracts predating the Executive order.

In Executive Order No. 12959, I directed the Secretary of the Treasury to authorize through licensing certain transactions, including transactions by United States persons related to the Iran-United States Claims Tribunal in The Hague, established pursuant to the Algiers Accords, and other international obligations and United States Government functions. Such transactions also include the export of agricultural commodities pursuant to preexisting contracts consistent with section 5712(c) of title 7, United States Code. I also directed the Secretary of the Treasury, in consultation with the Secretary of State, to consider authorizing United States persons through specific licensing to participate in market-based swaps of crude oil from the Caspian Sea area for Iranian crude oil in support of energy projects in Azerbaijan, Kazakhstan, and Turkmenistan.

Executive Order No. 12959 revokes sections 1 and 2 of Executive Order No. 12613 of October 29, 1987, and sections 1 and 2 of Executive Order No. 12957 of March 15, 1995, to the extent they are inconsistent with it. A copy of Executive Order No. 12959 was transmitted to the President of the Senate and Speaker of the House by letter dated May 6, 1995.

2. In its implementation of the sanctions imposed against Iran pursuant to Executive Order No. 12959, the Office of Foreign Assets Control (FAC) of the Department of the Treasury has issued 12 general licenses and 2 general notices authorizing various transactions otherwise prohibited by the Executive order or providing statements of licensing policy. In order to ensure the widest dissemination of the general licenses and general notices in advance of promulgation of amended regulations, FAC published them in the *Federal Register* on August 10, 1995 (60 *Fed. Reg.* 40881). In addition, FAC disseminated this information by its traditional methods such as electronic bulletin boards, FAX, and mail. Copies of these general licenses and general notices are attached to this report.

General License No. 1 described those transactions which were authorized in connection with the June 6, 1995 delayed effective date contained in Executive Order No. 12959 for trade transactions related to pre-May 7 trade contracts. General License No. 2 authorized payments to or from Iran under certain circumstances and certain dollar clearing transactions involving Iran by U.S. financial institutions. General Licenses No. 3 authorized the exportation of certain services by U.S. financial institutions with respect to accounts held for persons in Iran, the Government of Iran, or entities owned or controlled by the Government of Iran. General License No. 3 also contained an annex identifying 13 Iranian banks and 62 of their branches, agencies, representative offices, regional offices, and subsidiaries as owned or controlled by the Government of Iran. General License No. 4 authorized (1) domestic transactions involving Iranian-origin goods already within the United States except for transactions involving the Government of Iran or an entity owned or controlled by the Government of Iran, and (2) transactions by United States persons necessary to effect the disposition of Iranian-origin goods or services located or to be performed outside the United States, provided that they were acquired by that United States person in transactions not prohibited by the order or by 31 C.F.R. Part 560, that such disposition does not result in the importation of these goods or services into the United States, and that such transactions are completed prior to August 6, 1995. General License No. 5 authorized the importation into the United States of information and informational materials, confirmed the exemption of such information from the ban on exportation from the United States, and set forth a licensing policy for the exportation of equipment necessary to establish news wire feeds or other transmissions of information. General License No. 6 authorized the importation into the United States and the exportation to Iran of diplomatic pouches and their contents. General License No. 7 provided a statement of licensing policy for consideration, on a case-by-case basis, to authorize the establishment and operation of news organization offices in Iran by U.S. organizations whose primary purpose is the gathering and dissemination of news to the general public. General License No. 8 authorized transactions in connection with the exportation of agricultural commodities pursuant to pre-May 7 trade contracts provided that the terms of such contract require delivery of the commodity prior to February 2, 1996. General License No. 9 authorized import, export, and service transactions necessary to the conduct of official business by the missions of the Government of Iran to international organizations and the Iranian Interests Section of the Embassy of Pakistan in the United States. General License No. 10 provided a statement of licensing policy with respect to transactions incident to the resolution of disputes between the United

States or U.S. nationals and the Government of Iran in international tribunals and domestic courts in the United States and abroad. General License No. 11 authorized the exportation of household goods and personal effects for persons departing from the United States to relocate in Iran. General License No. 12 authorized the provision of certain legal services to the Government of Iran or to a person in Iran and the receipt of payment therefor under certain circumstances.

General Notice No. 1 described information required in connection with an application for a specific license to complete the performance of pre-May 7 trade contracts prior to August 6, 1995 (except with respect to agricultural commodities as provided by General License No. 8). General Notice No. 2 indicated that the Department of the Treasury had authorized the U.S. agencies of Iranian banks to complete, through December 29, 1995, transactions for U.S. exporters involving letters of credit, which they issued, confirmed, or advised prior to June 6, 1995, provided that the underlying export was completed in accordance with the terms of General License No. 1 or a specific license issued to the exporter by FAC. General Notice No. 2 also noted that the U.S. agencies of the Iranian banks were authorized to offer discounted advance payments on deferred payment letters of credit, which they issued, confirmed, or advised, provided that the same criteria are met.

3. The Iranian Transactions Regulations, 31 CFR Part 560 (the "ITR"), have been comprehensively amended to implement the provisions of Executive Orders No. 12957 and No. 12959. The amended ITR were issued by FAC on September 11, 1995 (60 *Fed Reg.* 47061–74) and incorporate, with some modifications, the General Licenses cited above. A copy of the amended regulations is attached to this report.

4. In consultation with the Department of State, FAC reviewed applications for specific licenses to permit continued performance of trade contracts entered into prior to May 7, 1995. It issued more than 100 such licenses allowing performance to continue up to August 6, 1995.

5. The expenses incurred by the Federal Government in the 6-month period from March 15 through September 14, 1995, that are directly attributable to the exercise of powers and authorities conferred by the declaration of a national emergency with respect to Iran are approximately $875,000, most of which represents wage and salary costs for Federal personnel. Personnel costs were largely centered in the Department of the Treasury (particularly in the Office of Foreign Assets Control, the Customs Service, the Office of the Under Secretary for Enforcement, and the Office of the General Counsel), the Department of State (particularly the Bureau of Economic and Business Affairs, the Bureau of Near Eastern Affairs, the Bureau of Politico-Military Affairs, and the Office of the Legal Adviser), and the Department of Commerce (the Bureau of Export Administration and the General Counsel's Office).

6. The situation reviewed above continues to involve important diplomatic, financial, and legal interests of the United States and its nationals and presents an extraordinary and unusual threat to the national security, foreign policy, and economy of the United States. The declaration of the national emergency with respect to Iran contained in Executive Order No. 12957 and the comprehensive economic sanctions imposed by Executive Order No. 12959 underscore the United States Government's opposition to the actions and policies of the Government of Iran, particularly its support of international terrorism and its efforts to acquire weapons of mass destruction and the means to deliver them. The Iranian Transactions Regulations issued pursuant to Executive Orders No. 12957 and No. 12959 continue to advance important objectives in promoting the nonproliferation and antiterrorism policies of the United States. I shall exercise the powers at my disposal to deal with these problems and will report periodically to the Congress on significant developments.

WILLIAM J. CLINTON

The White House,
September 18, 1995.

Message to the Congress Reporting on the National Emergency With Respect to Angola (UNITA)
September 18, 1995

To the Congress of the United States:

I hereby report to the Congress on the developments since March 26, 1995, concerning the national emergency with respect to Angola that was declared in Executive Order No. 12865 of September 26, 1993. This report is submitted pursuant to section 401(c) of the National Emergencies Act, (50 U.S.C. 1641(c), and section 204(c) of the International Emergency Economic Powers Act, 50 U.S.C. 1703(c).

On September 26, 1993, I declared a national emergency with respect to Angola, invoking the authority, *inter alia,* of the International Emergency Economic Powers Act (50 U.S.C. 1701 *et seq.*) and the United Nations Participation Act of 1945 (22 U.S.C. 287c). Consistent with United Nations Security Council Resolution 864, dated September 15, 1993, the order prohibited the sale or supply by United States persons or from the United States, or using U.S.-registered vessels or aircraft, of arms and related materiel of all types, including weapons and ammunition, military vehicles, equipment and spare parts, and petroleum and petroleum products to the territory of Angola other than through designated points of entry. The order also prohibited such sale or supply to the National Union for the Total Independence of Angola ("UNITA"). United States persons are prohibited from activities that promote or are calculated to promote such sales or supplies, or from attempted violations, or from evasion or avoidance or transactions that have the purpose of evasion or avoidance, of the stated prohibitions. The order authorized the Secretary of the Treasury, in consultation with the Secretary of State, to take such actions, including the promulgation of rules and regulations, as might be necessary to carry out the purposes of the order.

1. On December 10, 1993, the Treasury Department's Office of Foreign Assets Control ("FAC") issued the UNITA (Angola) Sanctions Regulations (the "Regulations") (58 *Fed. Reg.* 64904) to implement the President's declaration of a national emergency and imposition of sanctions against Angola (UNITA). There have been no amendments to the Regulations since my report of March 27, 1995.

The Regulations prohibit the sale or supply by United States persons or from the United States, or using U.S.-registered vessels or aircraft, of arms and related materiel of all types, including weapons and ammunition, military vehicles, equipment and space parts, and petroleum and petroleum products to UNITA or to the territory of Angola other than through designated points. United States persons are also prohibited from activities that promote or are calculated to promote such sales or supplies to UNITA or Angola, or from any transaction by any United States persons that evades or avoids, or has the purpose of evading or avoiding, or attempts to violate, any of the prohibitions set forth in the Executive order. Also prohibited are transactions by United States persons, or involving the use of U.S.-registered vessels or aircraft, relating to transportation to Angola or UNITA of goods the exportation of which is prohibited.

The Government of Angola has designated the following points of entry as points in Angola to which the articles otherwise prohibited by the Regulations may be shipped: *Airports:* Luanda and Katumbela, Benguela Province; *Ports:* Luanda and Lobito, Benguela Province; and Namibe, Namibe Province; and *Entry Points:* Malongo, Cabinda Province. Although no specific license is required by the Department of the Treasury for shipments to these designated points of entry (unless the item is destined for UNITA), any such exports remain subject to the licensing requirements of the Departments of State and/or Commerce.

2. The FAC has worked closely with the U.S. financial community to assure a heightened awareness of the sanctions against UNITA—through the dissemination of publications, seminars, and notices to electronic bulletin boards. This educational effort has resulted in frequent calls from banks to assure that they are not routing funds in violation of these prohibitions. United States exporters have also been notified of the sanctions through a variety of media, including special fliers and computer bulletin board information initiated by FAC and posted through the Department of Commerce and the

Government Printing Office. There have been no license applications under the program.

3. The expenses incurred by the Federal Government in the 6-month period from March 25, 1995, through September 25, 1995, that are directly attributable to the exercise of powers and authorities conferred by the declaration of a national emergency with respect to Angola (UNITA) are reported to be about $170,000, most of which represents wage and salary costs for Federal personnel. Personnel costs were largely centered in the Department of the Treasury (particularly in the Office of Foreign Assets Control, the Customs Service, the Office of the Under Secretary for Enforcement, and the Office of the General Counsel) and the Department of State (particularly the Office of Southern African Affairs).

I will continue to report periodically to the Congress on significant developments, pursuant to 50 U.S.C. 1703(c).

WILLIAM J. CLINTON

The White House,
September 18, 1995.

Message to the Congress on Continuation of the National Emergency With Respect to UNITA
September 18, 1995

To the Congress of the United States:

Section 202(d) of the National Emergencies Act (50 U.S.C. 1622(d)) provides for the automatic termination of a national emergency unless, prior to the anniversary date of its declaration, the President publishes in the *Federal Register* and transmits to the Congress a notice stating that the emergency is to continue in effect beyond the anniversary date. In accordance with this provision, I have sent the enclosed notice, stating that the emergency declared with respect to the National Union for the Total Independence of Angola ("UNITA") is to continue in effect beyond September 26, 1995, to the *Federal Register* for publication.

The circumstances that led to the declaration on September 26, 1993, of a national emergency have not been resolved. United Nations Security Council Resolution 864 (1993) continues to oblige all Member States to maintain sanctions. Discontinuation of the sanctions would have a prejudicial effect on the Angolan peace process. For these reasons, I have determined that it is necessary to maintain in force the broad authorities necessary to apply economic pressure to UNITA.

WILLIAM J. CLINTON

The White House,
September 18, 1995.

NOTE: The notice is listed in Appendix D at the end of this volume.

Letter to the Chair of the Federal Communications Commission on the Children's Television Act of 1990
September 18, 1995

Dear Chairman Hundt:

The Children's Television Act of 1990 recognizes the power and value of television's influence on our nation's children. The Act sets forth a reasonable exchange—it requires commercial broadcasters to honor their public trust by offering programming that enhances children's learning. The dissemination of true educational programming across the public airwaves is a priceless gift to our children.

The American public had every reason to believe that when the Children's Television Act was signed into law, programming specifically designed to benefit children would become an important part of the choices on every broadcast channel. The American public has been disappointed, and American children have lost countless opportunities to learn and to be challenged intellectually.

I urge you again to review the purpose of the Children's Television Act and the broadcast programming our children are offered today. To paraphrase former FCC Commissioner Newton Minow, if we can't figure out how the public interest standard relates to children, the youngest of whom can't read or write, and all of whom are dependent in every way on adults, then we will never figure out the meaning of the public interest standard.

I believe the public interest should require broadcasters to air at least three hours per week, and preferably more, of quality children's programming at reasonable times of the day. The FCC and the broadcast industry have an unequaled opportunity to redefine how television can serve the public interest, especially with respect to our children. I urge you to do so.

Sincerely,

BILL CLINTON

NOTE: This letter was released by the Office of the Press Secretary on September 19.

Remarks to the Community in Jacksonville, Florida
September 19, 1995

Thank you so much. Wow! Sheriff Glover, I don't ever want to be on the ballot against you. I'm glad to be here.

Thank you, Congresswoman Corrine Brown, for your friendship and your support, and thank you for your support of the crime bill, which has made our streets safer and made the children's future here more secure. Thank you, Governor Chiles, for being my friend and adviser and for your leadership. And thank you, Lieutenant Governor MacKay, for your long support and your leadership here. Mayor Delaney, we are delighted to be here in this great and growing community. I want to thank you and the State's attorney, Harry Shorstein, and all the other local officials here.

And I want to say, as President, it's a particular honor for me to be here in Jacksonville not only because this is a vibrant, growing city that did get a professional football team—[*applause*]. Don't be discouraged by the rough starts. I've had a lot of rough starts in my life. The opera is not over.

I want to also say a special word of thanks to the people of Jacksonville for the remarkable contribution that has been made by this community over so many years to the national defense of the United States. We are grateful for that, and we continue to be grateful for that.

I want to say a special word of appreciation, too, to Florida's own, our Attorney General,

Janet Reno, for the wonderful job that she has done as the Attorney General of the United States. And the Director of our COPS program, who is also here on my far left, Joe Brann, from California, who has come to Washington as a chief of police to work with us to get these police officers out in the United States. I thank them for being here, and I thank them for their leadership.

I want to thank all the schools that are represented here. I have a list. I may miss some, but I think we're joined by Kite Elementary School, Lake Forest Elementary, Moncrease Elementary, Ribalt Middle School, Raines and Ribalt High School, and the Edward Waters College choir, thank you.

I'd also like to thank one more person, Police Officer Larisa Crenshaw, who walked down the street with me today, because she and these other officers in uniform behind me, they're what we're here to talk about. I thank her, and I thank these people for being willing to serve your community in law enforcement.

You know, when I ran for President in 1992, I had a vision of what I wanted America to look like as we enter the 21st century. I want this to be a high-opportunity country for all Americans, where entrepreneurs can flourish, where people who work hard can be in the middle class, where we shrink the under class and give everybody who is willing to do what it takes to make the most of their own lives a chance to do it. I wanted us to have strong families and strong communities with good education systems, good health care, a clean environment. But I knew that in order to do that we first had to tackle the problems of crime and drugs. Without safe streets, safe schools, and safe homes, America will never be what it ought to be.

We've worked hard for the last 2½ years to bring the deficit down, to invest more in education, to deal with all of these issues I talked about. And we've got more jobs and less crime in America than we had 2½ years ago. And I think that's pretty good evidence that our strategy is working to move this country forward.

On the issue of crime, I was astonished when I got to Washington, having been a Governor for 12 years—if there was one issue that had nothing to do with partisan politics all my life, it was crime. I never met a Republican or a Democrat that wanted to be a victim of crime. I couldn't imagine that there would ever be any partisan issue there. When I was a Governor, when I was attorney general, we all worked together on issues affecting public safety. And I can see that's what you do here in Jacksonville. When I got to Washington, I discovered that even though the violent crime rate had tripled from the 1960's to the 1990's, they had been fighting partisan battles over the crime bill for 6 long years—hot air in Washington, more crime on the streets.

In 1994, we ended the hot air and the partisan bickering and passed the crime bill, and crime is going down on the streets of America. The crime bill featured more police, helped the States to build more prisons, stronger punishment for people who deserve it but also more prevention to give our young people something to say yes to as well as something to say no to, the chance to avoid getting into trouble in the first place.

We made "three strikes and you're out" the law of the land. What that means is that people who are serious career criminals now will go to jail for the rest of their careers so they can't get out and continue to do violence and to victimize people. We banned deadly assault weapons from our streets and from our schools, while protecting hundreds of sporting weapons for law-abiding hunters and sports men and women in this country. It was a good balance and the right one to strike.

We created an office to combat the problems of violence against women, in the home and on the street, a special problem in the United States and one the First Lady talked about when she went to China and represented us so well there just a few days ago.

The most important thing we did was to give the communities of this country the ability to hire 100,000 police officers to do what these 31 police officers behind me are going to do, to walk up and down the streets of America, like Marvin Street, to talk to neighbors, to talk to people, to get them involved in keeping their communities safe and free of crime.

We give the communities the resources they need to put the police officers on the street, and people like Sheriff Glover all over America take responsibility to train and deploy those officers. Then the officers help ordinary citizens, like the folks I just visited with, walking up and down the street, to find the commitment to do their part in fighting against crime.

If we're going to make our streets safe, if we're going to do what we have to do to give our children a chance at a future, we have got to have the help of grassroots citizens who are willing to work with police officers. If we can get them on the streets, you've got to help them do their jobs. In the 6 months since community police officers started patrolling this neighborhood, in 6 months, violent and property crimes have dropped by more than 8 percent in just 6 months. And they're just beginning.

What I want you to know is that, just like Sheriff Glover said that Jacksonville could do anything, America can do this. We do not have to put up with the high rates of crime we have. We do not have to put up with the high rates of drug abuse among our children we have. We can do something about it. You have evidence on this street, in this neighborhood. We can do something about it.

All over America today, the crime rate is down, the murder rate is down. We see people making progress to take control of their own lives, their families, their neighborhoods, their schools, and get this country going in the right direction.

But let me tell you, there are also troubling signs on the horizon. And I'll just give you two. While drug use is down among people between the ages of 18 and 34, casual drug use, marijuana, among teenagers is going back up again. While the crime rate is down all over America and the murder rate is down, violent crime among teenagers is going up again.

The Justice Department issued a report the other day which showed that while the overall crime rate is down, violent crime among juveniles is going up, and a majority of members of gangs say that they think they are justified in shooting someone who treats them with disrespect. We actually had a case in another city not very long ago where a 16-year-old boy shot a 12-year-old boy who was sort of the neighborhood comic. And he thought the 12-year-old boy was treating him with disrespect.

Whatever happened to "Count to 10 before you do something you might later regret"? Whatever happened to kids being taught that sticks and stones can break your bones, but words can never hurt you? Whatever happened to people defining self-respect based on what they believe about themselves, not what somebody else says about them? Shoot, if the President followed that rule, he wouldn't have any respect. [*Laughter*]

You think about it. It's a big problem. Look at what happened in Los Angeles over the weekend. A family took one wrong turn and because they were in the wrong place, gang members felt they had the right to shoot at them and take their lives, kill an innocent child.

So what I want to tell you is, this is a moment of great hope. We know we can lower the crime rate. We know we can lower the murder rate. We know we can reduce drug abuse and drug dealing in our neighborhood. We know we can take our streets back. We know how to do it. Your sheriff has proved that he can do it, working with you, if you will help him. We know how to do this. This is one of the most important things that has happened to America in the last 20 years. We don't believe we are helpless in the face of crime anymore. We know we can turn it around. But we also know that the job is not yet done.

Therefore, to go back to what the Congresswoman said at the beginning, we fought through one partisan political battle to get this crime bill. I heard people say on the floor of Congress that the crime bill was a fraud, that it wouldn't help to lower the crime rate, that we would never get 20,000 police on the street in 6 years, and we were promising 100,000 in 6 years. Well, in one year, we're over 25,000, and we're going to make it on time, ahead of the budget, ahead of the schedule.

And we now have a consensus among the American people. I believe that we ought to keep on lowering the crime rate. I don't believe—I haven't heard the first person write me a letter and say, "Dear Mr. President, I don't like the fact that the crime rate is going down. Please stop what you're doing." [*Laughter*] I haven't gotten one letter saying that.

Now, in Washington the Congress is trying to balance the budget. I support that. We ought to balance the budget. We never had a permanent deficit until the 12 years before I became President. We have taken the deficit from $290 billion a year when I took office to $160 billion this year, more than 40 percent reduction. And I want to finish the job.

We can balance the budget, and we should. But what I want to tell you is, we do not have to destroy our commitment to the education of our young people, to the training of unemployed people, to the economic future of America. We do not have to have dramatic increases in the health care costs of elderly people when 75 percent of them are living on less than $24,000 a year. We do not have to sacrifice the environmental and public health and safety protections that give us clean air, clean water, and safe food. We do not have to do any of this to balance the budget.

I have given the Congress a balanced budget plan which does not do any of these things. And we certainly, we certainly do not have to come off of our commitment to put 100,000 police officers on the street and have more and more stories like the ones I heard walking up and down Marvin Street today. We owe it to America to balance the budget and to reduce the crime rate until Americans are safe in their streets, safe in their homes, safe in their schools.

So I ask you, because you are fortunate enough to live in this growing and vibrant community, because you are fortunate enough to have elected leaders that work together across party lines and know that crime is an American problem and a human problem, because you are fortunate enough to have a sheriff who has proved to you that community policing works, because you are fortunate enough to have experienced a drop in the crime rate, I ask you to join with me and say to the United States Congress, this is not about partisan politics. We are lowering the crime rate in America. If we have more jobs and lower crime, America is going to be a better place. So let's continue to do that. Let's continue to do that.

And let us say: Balance the budget, yes. But do it and still send us our police officers, because we want our children to have a healthy, safe, strong, drug-free, crime-free, violence-free future. And now we know we can do it. Let's don't stop. Let's keep on until the job's done.

Thank you, and God bless you all.

NOTE: The President spoke at 9:47 a.m. at the Carvill Park Community Center. In his remarks, he referred to Sheriff Nathaniel Glover of Duval County; Gov. Lawton Chiles and Lt. Gov. Buddy MacKay of Florida; Mayor John A. Delaney of Jacksonville; and Joseph Brann, Director, Community Oriented Policing Services (COPS), Department of Justice.

Remarks on Departure From Jacksonville
September 19, 1995

Thank you very much. Thank you for coming out. Thank you for waiting in the hot sun. Thank you, Governor Chiles. Thank you, Lieutenant Governor MacKay. I thank your State's attorney for being here, and Congresswoman Corrine Brown, I thank you for being here. It's wonderful to see all of you.

You heard Governor Chiles say that we have just been with Sheriff Glover in one of the neighborhoods here in Jacksonville. I want to say two or three things about being in this community. First of all, congratulations on your football team. I'm glad you got one. And I know the season got off to a rough start. But I've had a few seasons like that; it's not over. Just stay in a good humor about it.

I also want to thank the people of Jacksonville for the dramatic contribution that you have made over so many years to the national defense of the United States, so many people here serving in our military, supporting it, and we're very grateful to you for that.

And I'm sure you know that in the recent rounds of military reorganizations and base closings, Jacksonville is one of the communities in the United States that will actually gain several thousand jobs over the next few years because of the work you have done and the quality of support you have given to our military. So I thank you for that.

I want to make, if I might, just a couple of remarks; then I want to get out in the crowd and just say hello to all of you. I ran for President in 1991 and 1992 because I was afraid that our country was going in the wrong direction; that we had forgotten the basic values that make us strong, our devotion to work and family

and responsibility and community; and that we were not changing to meet the demands of the 21st century.

The economy is different. You all know it. We have different challenges in holding our country together. And I made up my mind that if the people gave me a chance to serve, I was going to try to get the economy going again so we could grow the middle class and shrink the under class; I would try to make the fighting of crime a major priority so we could reduce the crime rate in America and make our streets and our schools and our homes safer; I would try to change the way the Government works, to be a genuine partner with people in their lives. And that's what we've been here celebrating today.

Florida is creating jobs at 3 times the rate it was when I became President. We have lowered the deficit. We have increased investment. We have a plan for a balanced budget. We're moving forward economically. The crime rate is down. The murder rate is down. All across America we are proving that we can lower the rate of crime in America if we work together and put more police officers on the street under the plan that was enacted in the 1994 crime bill. I'm proud of that. People used to tell me we will never lower the crime rate. They were wrong. We can do it, and we can do it all over America.

We're now trying to reform the welfare system. I just want to say a word about that. I've worked with Governor Chiles on this for years. I'm all for reforming welfare if what we mean by reforming welfare is moving people from welfare to work and giving them a chance to be good parents and good workers. I am not for punishing poor children just because they were born poor. We ought to be reforming welfare in a way that liberates people. I'm all for having tough standards and tough requirements on people to go to school and go to work if they've got a chance to do it and to take care of their children. So when you watch this welfare reform debate in Washington ask yourself, is this going to produce good workers and good parents? Is this going to make families stronger and children better? That is the test.

So I want to say to all of you, now I'm going on down to south Florida and then I'm going on across the country to Colorado, and I'm going to be talking with Americans all across the country about the debate in Washington about balancing the budget. And I want to say to all of you, Florida has a lot of interest in that debate. Every American should want the budget balanced. We never had a permanent deficit until the 12 years before I became President, and we've taken that deficit from $290 billion a year down to $160 billion in just 3 years. I'm proud of that. We should keep doing that.

But we also have responsibilities. You see it here in Jacksonville. We have responsibilities to

the national defense. We have responsibilities to the children and the schools. We have responsibilities to lower the crime rate. We have responsibilities to the elderly who depend on Medicare and Medicaid for their health care. And I say to you, we can balance the budget without undermining the national defense, without cutting our commitment to put 100,000 police on the street, without cutting the number of children in Head Start and the number of young people who are getting college loans, and without burdening older people. Seventy-five percent of the people in this country who get the benefits of Medicare and Medicaid live on less than $24,000 a year. We can fix Medicare without burdening them.

That is my commitment: Fix the Medicare system. You don't have to stick it to the older people in this country who barely have enough money to live on. So let's balance the budget and do it right so we can grow the economy, reduce the crime rate, and bring this country together. That is my commitment, and I think it's yours.

Thank you, and God bless you all.

NOTE: The President spoke at 10:55 a.m. at Jacksonville International Airport.

Remarks in a Roundtable Discussion With Senior Citizens in North Miami Beach, Florida
September 19, 1995

The President. Thank you for taking a little time to meet with me and the Governor today. I wanted to just say a few words. First of all, let me thank Governor Chiles for being here. You know, when he was a Senator, he was the chairman of the Budget Committee, so he knows a lot about what we're going through in Washington.

Gov. Lawton Chiles. These people knew me when I had the Aging Committee, before I had the pleasure to know you. [*Laughter*]

The President. That's right. Before you were aging. [*Laughter*]

I'd like to just talk for a couple of minutes and then spend the rest of the time listening to you, trying to answer your questions or at least hearing your concerns about this. You all

know we're in a major debate in Washington about balancing the budget, and we're trying to balance the budget. I think that's a good thing to do. Our country never had a permanent deficit in our Government accounts until the 12 years before I became President, and I've tried to change that.

When I became President, the annual deficit was $290 billion a year; we've now got it down to $160 billion a year. That's a huge decrease in only 3 years, and I'm proud of that. But we have to ask ourselves now that we're going to go all the way and balance this budget, why are we doing it, and how are we going to do it in a way that reflects our basic values as Americans, our sense of personal responsibility, our sense of family responsibility, our responsibility to our communities? And maybe most important, what are the obligations we owe to each other across generational lines and across income lines in America? How can we balance the budget in a way that permits us to honor these values and these obligations?

We want to balance the budget because we'd like to take this debt off of our children and grandchildren, because we would like not to spend so much money every year paying off interest on the debt so we'd have more money to invest in things like education and health care and the economy, but we have to do it in the right way.

Now, I have offered the Congress a balanced budget that increases our investment in education, because I think we owe the next generation quite a lot—in a global economy they'll need more education and because so many of our children, particularly poorer children, need the tools to work themselves into the middle class. I have offered a balanced budget that continues our fundamental obligations to clean air, clean water, safe food, public health, and the environment. And I have offered a balanced budget that deals with the need to slow the rate of growth in medical expenses so that health care does not consume the entire budget and does not take more and more of our income and more and more of your income.

Now, in addition to that, there is this issue with the Medicare Trust Fund, which the congressional majority, the Republican majority, has made a great deal of. But I'd like to talk a little about the Medicare Trust Fund and what its relationship is to the budget, and then we can hear from you.

The Congress has proposed to balance the budget in 7 years and to pay for a $250 billion tax cut and to cut Medicare by about $270 billion over that 7-year period and to cut Medicaid by about $180 billion over that 7-year period.

My proposals, which balance the budget in 10 years with a much smaller tax cut, have a Medicare reduction that's less than half of theirs and a Medicaid reduction that's about a third of theirs. Now, if you hear them talk, they will say two things. They will say, first of all, "We're not cutting anything; we're just slowing the rate of inflation in these programs." And secondly, they'll say, "We have to cut Medicare because it's necessary for the Trust Fund." So I would like to deal with both of those issues if I might.

First of all, on the Trust Fund, there's a legitimate issue with the Trust Fund. Our administration brought it up in '93 and in '94 in the health care debate. And many of the same people who are saying we have to cut Medicare by $270 billion today were denying that we could have any reductions at all just last year and denying that there was big problem with the Trust Fund. But there is a problem with the Trust Fund. And so our obligation, not only to the people on Medicare today but to the people we want to have Medicare in the future, our obligation is to fix the Trust Fund.

The actuaries say that we need to put about $90 billion into fixing the Trust Fund. That is, if we put $90 billion in, we will secure it for another decade, and during that decade, we'll have time to figure out what we're going to do when all the baby boomers retire and they get on Medicare because then there will be a lot more people on Medicare.

But neither proposal really deals with that. We're just talking about how to add a few more years, 10, 11, 12 years to the Trust Fund. My proposal takes it out 11 years from today. And that's better than we're been doing in most of the last 15 years. My proposal does it by recognizing that the Trust Fund essentially provides hospital care and other services and is paid for essentially by asking the providers to take less money in the future and by cracking down on fraud and abuse.

And by the way, we have a study which says that Medicare fraud and abuse is about 10 percent of our total cost. And we have the United States Attorney here for this part of Florida, and he can tell you what we're trying to do in Florida. But we have doubled the prosecutions on fraud and abuse, we have assigned 3 times as many FBI agents to try to crack down on fraud and abuse as any previous administration, and we've brought in more money from people who are skimming the system illegally than ever before. So there is a lot of money there. And we can do that.

Their proposal would ask the beneficiaries of the system to pay more, dramatically more. And it's important that you realize that in their Medicare cuts, about half of them will be absorbed by providers or by improvements in fraud and abuse, but about half of them will come from beneficiaries. And none of that money goes into the Trust Fund. So let's get that on the table. This has nothing to do with the Trust Fund.

And the only way you can get money from beneficiaries is either to charge more or give fewer services or serve fewer people. And that all goes into the budget.

Now, on Medicaid, 30 percent of Medicaid goes to care for poor women and their poor children, but 70 percent of it goes to pay for health care for the elderly and the disabled. So this dramatic Medicaid cut, since the elderly people who get that are disproportionately low income, will have to either be paid for by their children or it means that we're going to serve fewer people. There will be fewer people in nursing homes, fewer people getting in-home services and things of that kind.

You just simply can't decree that the rate of medical inflation will go down to the level they say it will, because we have more and more older people coming onto the system all the time and, thank goodness, living longer and living better.

So what we need to do is to find the right way to balance the budget, in a way that preserves the Medicare Trust Fund and extends it for at least a decade but does not, does not, cripple the health care system for today's elderly and those who will be coming on in the next decade. Seventy-five percent of the people on Medicare live on less than $24,000 a year.

So I say to all of you, we need to be open to changes in the system—we can't continue to let it grow at 10 percent a year—but we need to do it in a way that recognizes our obligations across generational lines and across income lines. And we have to be very careful before we approve of a system that would cost our seniors a huge amount more or cause them to have to give up medical services in order to fund tax cuts that go to people like me who don't really need it—and haven't asked for it, to be fair, haven't asked for it.

So my point is we can have a tax cut if we target it toward raising children and educating people and middle income people who need it. We can have a balanced budget and we can fix the Medicare Trust Fund and we can do all of that without imposing undue burdens on Medicare and Medicaid recipients who simply cannot afford it. And that's the trick. That is what our obligation ought to be.

And I believe that a proposal that would basically reduce future spending in health care by $450 billion, almost half a trillion dollars, you're either going to—you're going to do one of two things: You're going to either close a lot of hospitals in rural areas and urban areas and teaching hospitals and take a lot of doctors out of the system who won't serve anymore, or you're going to hurt the beneficiaries either by charging them more than they can afford or simply by not serving a lot of elderly people anymore.

So that's the point I've been trying to make going around America. We all have an obligation to fix the Trust Fund, but the proposals in Congress go way beyond that. About half the money in Medicare will go to fix the Trust Fund; the other half goes to their balanced budget tax cut plan. And there's no way around it; that's just the fact. And I just don't think that's right.

Governor, do you want to say anything?

[*At this point, Governor Chiles explained that Florida would be greatly affected by proposed Medicare and Medicaid cuts because its population is rapidly increasing.*]

The President. I guess the two things I want to hammer home are these: The trustees on which the Republican Congress have relied in saying that the Medicare Trust Fund is in trouble recommend an expenditure of between $90 billion and $100 billion to bail out the Trust Fund over the next 7 years. That's in Medicare. That's not $270 billion; that's between $90 billion and $100 billion. I have proposed at around $120 billion, to ask the providers to do some things that will save money in both Part A and Part B of Medicare. But the premium costs to elderly people that go into Part B are all going into that general budget to fund the balanced budget tax cut plan.

The second point I want to make about Medicaid is, 4 percent inflation sounds like a lot, because we now have inflation down at an all-time low for the last 30, 40 years in America, down to about 2 percent and medical inflation down to 4 and 4½ percent.

The problem is, if you live in a State where—let's say you kept medical inflation to 4½ percent for 7 years, let's just say you could do it. That's 4½ percent per person, and that includes young people as well as older people, and that assumes no population growth. So if you're Florida and you have population growth and most of your health care goes to elderly people, we know that the older you get, the more health care you access, so the inflation will always be more there.

So that's why these numbers simply won't work and will have to be modified and why we must reduce the size of these cuts in order to achieve a balanced budget in a way that reflects our obligations across generational lines and across income lines. You just need to remember those two big points, and everything else flows from that.

Now, you know more about this than I do, so I'd like to stop now and hear from you and let you say whatever you'd like to say or ask whatever questions you'd like to ask in whatever order you want to proceed.

Who would like to go first?

Governor Chiles. Let the ladies go.

The President. Doctor, you want to go first?

[*A Dade County doctor discussed the decline of nonprofit hospitals and gave an example of a patient who received inadequate followup care due to the practices of for-profit hospitals.*]

The President. Now, does this person—is this person in an HMO or not?

[*The doctor said that she was not sure whether the patient was in a Health Maintenance Organization but thought perhaps the same company owned both the hospital and the HMO. She continued to cite examples of practices that she felt amounted to fraud in the health care system.*]

The President. Let me just point out that, if I might, I'd like to ask—our U.S. Attorney is here, and I'd like to ask him to—Kendall Coffey—just to talk very briefly about what we're doing in this here in Florida because this is one area where I hope we can get bipartisan agreement with the Congress.

There is a lot of money to be saved in fraud and abuse. And our friends in the press corps who are covering this, you know, they hear this in every Government program, and people tend to get cynical. But in the Medicare/ Medicaid program, it's expanded so fast and diversified so much, and we have so much—things like Alzheimer's that you were talking about—there is genuinely a lot of fraud and abuse. And I think if we could get an agreement—there are some good things, by the way, in their plan that I like about dealing with this. And if we can get an agreement on about how much money we could save, this could help us to go some way toward resolving our differences.

So, Mr. Coffey, maybe you could talk a little bit about what you're doing here in Florida to deal with this fraud and abuse problem.

[*Mr. Coffey described Federal and State efforts to crack down on medical fraud and Medicare fraud in particular.*]

The President. The one thing I want to say is I think we are finally organized to handle this now so that when people like you believe you know about this, it's very important that you make a referral to the U.S. attorney's office, because I think a lot of people all across America have these feelings that things aren't right, but they don't know that anyone would ever prosecute it or look into it. We now are organized to handle these problems, and it's very important that not only those of you here but those who will hear about this meeting all across America will call their United States attorneys and let them know when they think there is some evidence of a problem.

Q. Thank you.

The President. Who else would like to go? Yes, sir.

[*A participant voiced his distrust of doctors and hospitals and his concern that they often overcharge for services and asked what the Federal Government could do to regulate them.*]

The President. Well, I think there are two things we can do, two things we have to do at the same time. One is to increase our capacity to investigate fraud and abuse, and that's what we've done. As I said, we've got 3 times as many FBI agents as ever before. We've already doubled the number of prosecutions. We're bringing in more funds. We're moving on that. And then we need help—organized seniors groups can help us a lot by telling us what you think is wrong. You may not always be right, but we won't know unless you give us leads.

The second thing we have to do is to simply slow the rate at which we're putting new money into the system. Now, in this area, there is pretty much bipartisan agreement on at least rough numbers of how much we should slow the rate of money which we're putting into Part A of the Medicare system. And so we have some— we've got agreement. We know if we slow the rate of growth into the provider pool—that's the Trust Fund, the Part A part—that we will force certain discipline on the system and will help to save it money and help to lengthen the Trust Fund. So I think that we're agreed on that—you know, not to the last dollar, but generally those are the two things that can be done about it.

I don't think that the answer to the fact that the system is consuming too much money, however, is to ask the seniors on fixed incomes to pay a whole lot more for the same health care.

Q. That's what worries us.

The President. That's what—what we've tried to do is to strike a proper balance. And my plan is to make full disclosure—is to try to continue the system we've had, but to fix the percentage of Medicare premiums that the seniors have to pay. So if the overall cost goes up, your out-of-pocket costs will go up, because the percentage will be a percentage of the bigger number. That way, we share the responsibility and there's some incentive not to overuse the system. But the main problem is the one that you have outlined.

Who else would like to go next. Yes, sir?

[A participant explained that Medicare and Social Security not only benefit the elderly but also younger people who are no longer burdened with the high cost of taking care of their elderly parents.]

The President. Governor Chiles and I were talking about that on the way in. I don't think people—that whole aspect of it hasn't been thought through. The extent to which, particularly if you look on the Medicaid budget, people who have to go into nursing homes and people who get help with in-home care, a lot of the elderly people themselves have low incomes, but their children have—a lot of them are basically getting by on middle class incomes. And their incomes would also be dramatically lowered if they had to basically go back to try to take care of their parents and their grandparents who were also less independent than they have previously been. I think it's a very important point, and thank you for making it.

Q. It is.

Q. Can we get this across to the congressional majority?

Governor Chiles. Now, that's a different ball game. You'll have to help us.

The President. I think if you can make those points, that this could be, in effect, an indirect middle class tax increase if they overdo it, then it would register, I think, on people, because

it certainly would be. I mean, basically it would be an indirect tax increase on young people who are fortunate enough to still have their parents and grandparents living. And I'm saying, of course, it's just like everything else, some could afford to pay it, some couldn't, which is why I like the universal nature of Social Security and Medicare, because it basically empowers and gives dignity to the lives of people. It also strengthens families' ability to take care of their children. So you don't have people choosing between their children and their parents. That was a very important point.

[A participant thanked the President for his support of Medicare and asked the Holy Spirit to guide him in his efforts.]

The President. Bless you. If we had a little more of the Holy Spirit, we could probably come close to—[laughter]

[A participant voiced her concerns about older people who could not afford medical care and about doctors who would no longer take elderly patients. She said that while this was not the case where there were many HMO's, there were other problems with HMO's, such as fraud and excessive profits.]

The President. I think we're going to have to do a lot more work on that because, you know, some of them are wildly popular and are doing a good job. Some of them have taken their management savings, for example, and given people who've joined them free prescription drug benefits—something that Medicare doesn't provide—which is a godsend for people who need it. So we shouldn't condemn the whole industry. I mean, some of them have done a wonderful job. But it also provides a vehicle through which people who care only about making a quick buck can justify just about any way to, in my opinion, to abuse people.

What were you going to say?

[A participant explained the fraudulent practices of some HMO's and what is being done to prevent further abuse.]

The President. Let me say, you know, I think we are getting close to agreement on the question of whether people should have more HMO choices available to them on Medicare and Medicaid but should not be forced into it.

And I'm adamantly opposed to that, any kind of forced—but even if you do that, then you have a problem that we have to be very vigilant about, that Governor Chiles talked about, because the healthiest people which used to go into HMO's and get the best deals, and then the HMO's could then decline to take people who might need, say, the drug benefit. And then 3 years from now, we could be spending even more money on the program than we are now because we let the people that don't cost much go into HMO's and get the regular fee and then everybody else will be out there, we'll have to spend even more on them.

So if this is not a—the HMO, it's a good option in many cases, if it's a well-run HMO. But it's certainly not a be-all and end-all to the problem of medical costs.

[A participant voiced her support for Medicaid but stated that reforms must be made to ensure that the system would benefit those in need and that all programs should be monitored. Another participant then stated that, despite the belief of some people, elderly persons were not being selfish in their need for assistance. She also noted that the talents and capabilities of nurses were going unused in many hospitals.]

The President. Well, as you know, I strongly support that. And I was interested in a comment you made—I hadn't thought to make this point today, but I think it's worth making—when you said that a lot of seniors have children in their fifties who can't get health insurance.

We are—I tried to do something about that, as you know, unsuccessfully. We are losing now—a million Americans a year are losing their health insurance—non-seniors, under 65. This is happening in no other country in the world with an advanced economy. No other country would tolerate this.

Q. Outrageous.

The President. We lose one million a year. Now, we would lose more but for the Medicaid program. The Medicaid program not only helps seniors who need institutionalized care or who need in-home care, it helps some low-income people who are working poor people, who are not on welfare but are working poor, who are not on welfare but still have low incomes from other sources. And many States have tried to do what Governor Chiles has tried to do here, which is to achieve some savings in the Medicaid program by having a decent selection of HMO's and take the money and put it into

providing subsidized insurance to the working poor.

All of that will go totally out the window if we reduce Medicaid spending by the amount we're talking about, so that instead of just being the only country in the world that doesn't provide health insurance for people under 65, the only country in the world with an advanced economy losing a million people a year—that number, that one million number will go up quite a lot. We will then begin to lose even more people who are younger.

So this is—that's another way in which this whole issue is an intergenerational thing. I will say again, I believe we can slow the rate of growth in Medicaid spending and Medicare spending. We have already done that in the last 2½ years. But I do not believe that you can just jerk $450 billion out of the system and pretend that there will be no adverse consequences. That is the point I want to make.

Go ahead. What were you going to say?

[A participant praised the ombudsmen appointed by Governor Chiles to investigate complaints against nursing homes in Florida and stated the need for more control of physicians' fees for particular services.]

The President. Thank you. We have a big crowd of people downstairs, and it's kind of hot for them, so we probably ought to go down there. I want to thank you for sharing this time with me. And I want to assure that I will take your concerns back to Washington, and the things that I can do something about by myself, I will do it. And I hope that this forum will serve to inform this debate that will occur in Congress over the next month or two.

And I hope all of you will speak out. And I hope you will make many points, but first of all, be clear on how much fraud and abuse you think is in the system, because I think that will help to focus people on that. And secondly, remind people of the point you made, that this is not just about elderly people. This is about our intergenerational way of life in America, how we live, how our families function. That's a very important point.

Q. Well, a lot of the older people are taking care of their little grandchildren.

Q. Right now they are, yes, unfortunately.

The President. I bet they are.

Q. Sure they are. And we've got to keep the older people well for the children.

The President. Thank you all. You were great. Thank you.

NOTE: The President spoke at 1:40 p.m. at Point East Senior Center.

Remarks to Senior Citizens in North Miami Beach
September 19, 1995

The President. Thank you. Wow. Thank you so very much, Governor Chiles and Lieutenant Governor MacKay and Attorney General Butterworth and members of the legislature and Mayor, other local leaders, and especially Ginger, thank you for that wonderful introduction and that wonderful comment about the joys of old age. [*Laughter*] The last year has brought me prematurely closer to those joys—[*laughter*]—as I have worked along in Washington.

I did come here today to talk about Medicare and Medicaid, but I'd like to put them, if I might, into a little bit of context about what's going on in our country today for all the American people. We are, all of us, privileged to be living through one of the most interesting periods in our country's history, where the way we work and the way we live is changing very, very rapidly.

I think that you could argue that since we got started as a country, we've had about four periods of really profound change: obviously, leading up to and then after the Civil War and then when we changed our economy from a rural to an industrial economy between about 1895 and about 1916 and then the Great Depression and World War II and the cold war and now, coming out of that.

I believe this is the most profound period of change we have faced in 100 years in the way we live and the way we work. And whenever those kinds of things happen, we have to think anew about what our basic values are, what kind of people we are, what our obligations to one another are across the generations and across incomes and in different ways of making a living, and we have to chart a course for our country's future.

For me, that means that we have to have a period that is governed by new ideas rooted in old-fashioned values. This is still a country, fundamentally, that's about individual liberty and individual responsibility, devotion to family and devotion to community, rooted in the idea that

we all ought to work if we can and we all have responsibilities, not only to ourselves but to each other, and that we also have a responsibility to be a beacon of hope to the rest of the world. And that is what we have tried to do.

We've tried to change the economic policy of the country in a way that would bring the deficit down but invest more in education and technology, and it seems to be working. We've got 7.3 million new jobs. Florida is growing jobs at 3 times the rate it was growing them before our administration came in. And we've reduced the deficit from $290 billion a year to $160 billion a year in only 3 years. So we need new ideas and a new direction.

We have found a way to do this while increasing our investment in the education of our children, something I know all of you care deeply about and something that is more important than ever before. We know we've got to cut some things. Your Government is much smaller than it was the day I became President. We've reduced the size of the Federal Government by 160,000, and by the time I finish this term, we'll have the smallest Federal Government we've had since President Kennedy was the President of the United States, trying to give you a more entrepreneurial, less bureaucratic, less cumbersome Government, but still one that could fulfill our fundamental values.

Today, even as we speak, the Congress, in the Senate at least, is debating the very important subject of welfare reform, something I've worked on for 15 years, almost as long as I've worked on issues affecting senior citizens in America. What we all want, I think, is for people on welfare to be able to live the way the rest of America lives. We want people to be able to succeed as workers and as parents. We want the values of family and work and responsibility to triumph. We don't want anybody to be trapped, generation after generation, on welfare. And we know it would be good for the rest of us as well if they were liberated and became taxpayers instead of tax drawers. We know that.

Since I've been President, waiting for the Congress to act, I've done what I thought I could to move people from welfare to work and help them succeed as parents. Florida is one of 34 States now that have received permission to get out from under old-fashioned Federal rules to put people to work. And in just one of Governor Chiles's experiments in the last year, the Florida Family Transition Program, they've moved over 800 people from welfare to work. It's one thing to talk about it, quite another thing to do it. And so, congratulations, Governor, for doing it.

Now, this bill that they're debating in the Senate today has broad bipartisan support because it will help to move people from welfare to work, and it will help families to stick together. And I want to say more about that in the context of Medicare and Medicaid in a moment.

So if welfare reform remains a bipartisan effort to promote work, protect children, and collect child support from people who ought to pay it, we will have welfare reform this year, and it will be a very great thing. But if the Congress gives into extremist pressure and walks away from this bipartisan American common ground, they will kill welfare reform. So I ask you to do what you can without regard to your party to encourage your Senators and your Members of Congress to give this country a welfare reform bill that is pro-family, pro-work, pro-responsibility and pro-child. We can do that, and we ought to do it.

Now, what's all that got to do with Medicare and Medicaid? Everything. Why? Because now we have also a bipartisan consensus in Washington for balancing the Federal budget, something that hasn't been done since 1969, although the deficits in the seventies were pretty small and basically related to economic slowdowns. So there is a broad bipartisan agreement that we ought to do it. I believe we ought to do it. And I'm glad to help supporters in the Congress from both parties who want to do that. We had to have a one-party effort to take the deficit from $290 to $160, and we need everybody's help to go all the way. And I'm for that.

But how we decide to balance the budget will tell us a lot about what kind of people we are, what our values are, what we're going to take into the next century, what we're going

to say to our young people about what they can look forward to as they grow up into productive adults and then they grow into old age. It will say a lot about what we think our obligations are across generational and income lines.

One of the things that has dismayed me about this discussion of Medicare and Medicaid has been the suggestion that anybody that doesn't support the congressional plan is somehow a wealthy older person who is insufficiently sensitive to the needs of the younger generation. That is a load of bull. I can tell you that in all my experience in public life, and I have been working on these issues for 20 years now, the thing that has always humbled me—and my State, Arkansas, had, when I was serving, in every year the second or the third highest percentage of people over 65 in the country—the thing that always amazed me was how much the seniors in my State wanted to take care of their children and their grandchildren, how much they supported efforts to improve education, how much they supported efforts to strengthen the economy, how much they were not interested only in their own issues.

And so I say to you, if you say you don't like this plan in Congress, that doesn't mean that the rest of us think you're either rich or greedy. You have a right to see that there is decency and honor and obligation across generational and income lines as we balance the budget. We have to do it in a fair and decent and honorable way.

Now, here's the problem. It is true that medical costs in the budget have become a bigger and bigger and bigger part of the Federal budget. It is true that medical inflation is going up faster than the inflation rate as a whole. It is also true that we're all living longer. So we've got a higher percentage of Americans on Medicare and elderly people on Medicaid. Praise the Lord, we're all living longer. That's a good thing. I hope it extends to Presidents. [*Laughter*]

It's also true that the system itself, through fraud, abuse, and other problems, has had a higher rate of inflation so that, unfortunately, both the Government and people on Medicare have been paying more every year for the same health care in ways that are unacceptable. And that if we want to balance the budget, we need to slow the rate of growth in health care spending.

It's also true that the Medicare Trust Fund has to be protected. Now, let me talk a little about that. You pay Medicare. You know—if you're involved in Medicare, you know how it works. You know how it works. There's a Part A which is basically hospital and related services paid for by a payroll tax, and that goes to providers and essentially that is in the Trust Fund. And there's a Trust Fund. There's a Part B that deals with all kinds of other services, primarily physician services, medical equipment, and other things, which are paid for out of general tax revenues and contributions by seniors directly—payments.

Here is what I want to say to you about this Medicare issue: We have proposed a balanced budget—I have—that slows the rate of medical inflation and payments to providers to fix the Trust Fund for another 10 years. And we have proposed to do it exactly like the people who are in charge of the Trust Fund, the trustees, say we need to do. And it doesn't cost seniors anything more than they are otherwise going to pay in the ordinary course of medical inflation.

The Congress, the majority in Congress, have proposed Medicare cuts that are more than twice that much. And less than half of them are going into the Trust Fund. The rest are going to pay for the 7-year balanced budget and the tax cut.

So I say, I will work with anybody, anytime, anywhere, to fix the problems of the Medicare Trust Fund. But it is wrong to take more money from people whose average income is way below $20,000 to pay for a 7-year balanced budget and cuts in other areas and a big tax cut for people who don't need it. That is not right. So let's fix the Trust Fund, but let's don't dishonor our obligations across generational and income lines by pretending that we're fixing the Trust Fund when we're taking money from seniors to pay for a tax cut that is too large. That is not right.

Audience member. Hear! Hear! Tell 'em!

The President. Let's look at the Medicaid problem. Medicaid has nowhere near the political support in the country now that Medicare does because most people think it's a welfare program. And they think, if it's a welfare program, we can probably cut it some.

I have proposed to slow the rate of spending in Medicaid. Their cuts are 3 times as great as mine. The problem is that 70 percent, almost, of Medicaid spending goes to elderly people and disabled people for nursing home care and in-

home care. And if these cuts are as large as they are said to be—and for hospital care for low-income people—if these cuts are as large as they are said to be, then we will have people who through no fault of their own, who don't have any money, who either won't be able to get in nursing homes, won't be able to get in-home care, and millions of kids who won't be able to get hospital care.

If you take $450 billion out of the system over the next 7 years, I question whether we can keep our urban and rural hospitals open, whether the great teaching centers—making us the finest medical country in the world in terms of the quality of health care—will be able to do well. And there is a limit to how much seniors can afford to pay. Seventy-five percent of the people over 65 in this country live on less than $24,000 a year.

I came here to say to you, we're going to make some changes in this program. We need to save the Trust Fund, but don't you be fooled into thinking it costs $270 billion to save the Trust Fund. It costs less than half of that. And the rest of that money is going to go right into the general treasury and be used to pay for a 7-year budget and a tax cut that's too big. And I don't think that is an appropriate thing to do. And I don't think you think it is an appropriate thing to do.

I am not promising pie in the sky. Everybody here knows that the average senior on Medicare is paying the same percentage of income out of pocket for health care as you were paying before Medicare came in in the first place, because medical inflation has gone up so much. You all know that there's a lot of fraud and abuse in the system. And by the way, both parties agree on that, and I think we'll reach an agreement on it. And I want you to know what I'm trying to do about that. We have doubled, doubled, prosecutions for fraud and abuse since I've been President. We have tripled, tripled, the number of FBI agents working on health care fraud since I've been President.

We need your help. The United States Attorney for this district, Kendall Coffey, is here. He gave a report to the group upstairs about what he's trying to do here. We need senior groups all over America to help us to uncover fraud and abuse. A congressional study said as much as 10 percent of the money may go into fraud and abuse. If that's true, we can put that into savings, and it doesn't have to come out of anybody's pocket, except people who shouldn't be spending the money in the first place.

We are going to have to make some changes. We do have an obligation to preserve Medicare for you, for the people who come behind you, for your children, and for your grandchildren. It's a program that works. But we also have an obligation to make sure that Medicare and Medicaid do their job for America's seniors and do their job for the poor children of this country.

It isn't popular to speak up for the poor children today. It isn't popular—sort of the fashion is to say, well, if they're poor, whatever they get they deserve. The Bible says the poor will always be with us. And all those little poor children, they're going to be grown up some day. And if they don't have decent health care and decent nutrition and good role models and people who care about them, do you think they're going to be good citizens who can take care of my generation when we get old? So just because they're poor, and they're on Medicaid, too, we shouldn't forget about them. We shouldn't act like we have no responsibility to them. It's not their fault what families they were born into. It's not their fault what their family circumstances are.

So what I want you to do is this: I want you in one voice to say to all of us, "We don't care if you're Republicans or Democrats; go balance the budget, go fix the Medicare Trust Fund, make the changes you have to make to do that, but do not take money from elderly people that barely have enough to live on, that have made their contributions all their lives, and give it to people who aren't even asking for a tax cut and don't need it. Don't do that. That doesn't make any sense. It defies common sense. Slow the rate of growth in that Medicaid program, but don't do it so much that we can't take people into nursing homes. Don't do it so much we can't deliver home care to people who need it and that's cheaper. Don't do it so much that we have to turn away poor children who will be scarred forever if we don't take decent minimal care for them. That's not necessary. We don't have to do that to balance

the budget." Send a voice that I know is in your heart.

I have been—as I said, I have been working on issues of health care, consumer rights for seniors for 20 years. I had my first long-term care conference as an attorney general almost 20 years ago. And I know that the senior population in this country is generous and forward-looking. But I also know that the only way we can continue to have a growing, healthy, strong senior population that is generous and forward-looking is to be decent and honorable and fair.

It is fair and decent to fix the Trust Fund. It is right to do what we can to crack down on fraud and abuse and to slow the rate of medical inflation and to slow the rate of medical inflation in the Medicaid and the Medicare program. But it is not right to pay for an arbitrary balanced budget and a very large tax cut, a lot of which goes to people who don't need it and, to be fair to them, have not even asked for it, to turn around and run the risk of putting Medicare out of the reach of seniors, putting Medicaid out of the reach of seniors, and undermining our solemn obligation to honor one another across the generations. That's what we need to do.

We can get into the 21st century with a growing economy, a balanced budget, a stable future, but only if we do it consistent with our fundamental values. What is proposed up there is not consistent with our values and doesn't make common sense. But we can make common sense, balance the budget, save the Trust Fund, and leave Medicare and Medicaid in good shape for you and the people that come behind you.

So tell the Congress and everybody else in Washington to throw away the partisan, political, extremist ideology and the rhetoric and get down to work on doing America's job for America's future.

Thank you, and God bless you all.

NOTE: The President spoke at 2:47 p.m. at Point East Senior Center. In his remarks, he referred to Robert Butterworth, Florida attorney general, and Ginger Grossman, who introduced the President.

Remarks at a Fundraiser in North Miami Beach
September 19, 1995

The President. Thank you. This is the quietest this has been all night. [*Laughter*]

Audience member. Four more years, Mr. President!

The President. Thank you. I want to thank Governor Chiles and Lieutenant Governor MacKay and your attorney general and the other State officials, the State legislators and local officials and others who are here. Mostly, I just want to thank all of you for coming here to support our candidacy.

This has been a wonderful day in Florida for me. I started the morning in Jacksonville with the sheriff there, looking at some police officers who were hired under our crime bill who have already contributed to lowering the crime rate on the streets of Jacksonville. And then I flew down to North Miami Beach and had a wonderful meeting with some senior citizens about Medicare and Medicaid. And then I came on here.

I know that this is sort of a festive occasion. You're all packed in like sardines in a can, and we're all standing up instead of sitting down. And I won't keep you here very long, but I want you to understand that as profoundly grateful as we are to you for your contributions to this campaign and to all of you who did so much to organize this event, it is even more important that you make a personal commitment tonight to do what you can to make sure that we carry the State of Florida next November.

And the Vice President was talking to you about some of the things that are important. This administration has been good for Florida. We've tried to be good to Florida, and our general policies have helped the economy in Florida. We have also fought against those things that we thought would hurt you. We have represented your State in our Cabinet. We have tried to be sensitive to your concerns. We are trying to work through this budget process in a way that will be fair to the incredible diversity and richness and growth that is Florida.

I feel deeply, personally committed to you because of the fact that I have family members here, my wife's brothers, Hugh and Tony, and their wives, Maria and Nicole. And now I have a little nephew whom I was just holding up-

stairs. He doesn't think I'm too charismatic. He goes to sleep every time I pick him up. And because our campaign—my campaign really got started here in December of 1991 at the Florida Democratic caucus—first election I ever won in the Presidential campaign.

But more importantly, we all got a big stake in the future, and a great deal of how we live for the next 20 years will be determined by the outcome of this Presidential election. So let me try just in a couple of minutes, after which the Vice President and I will come down and try to finish shaking hands with everybody and visit and laugh, just ask you to take a couple of minutes to be serious about what is at stake here.

When I ran for President in 1992 and I asked Al Gore to join with me to form what is clearly the most unique partnership between a President and a Vice President in American history—Al Gore is clearly the most influential, effective, important Vice President in the history of the United States of America—we basically agreed that we were in a time of profound change and that we needed a clear vision of the future. We needed a commitment to new ideas. We needed a commitment to old-fashioned American values. We needed a commitment to seeking common ground to going beyond the kind of partisan politics that is eating Washington, DC, alive. And maybe most important of all, we needed to be willing to do what is right for the future of this country, even if it's unpopular in the short run. And that is exactly what we have tried to do in Washington for the last 2½ years.

My vision is that in the 21st century this country will be a high-opportunity place, where we are growing entrepreneurs and growing the middle class and shrinking the under class, where we have good schools and good health care systems and safe streets and a clean environment, where people have the opportunity to make the most of their own lives and families and communities have a chance to solve their own problems and America is a force for freedom and prosperity and peace throughout the world. That is my vision.

To achieve that, we need old-fashioned values: freedom and responsibility, work and family, community, excellence, accountability, and a real devotion to the American dream and a willingness to stand up for this country. But to get there we need some new ideas. We can't keep doing business as usual. That's the only reason I ran for President in 1992.

We are going through a period of change as profound as anything that's happened in this country in a hundred years. This is like when we moved from being a rural agricultural country into being an industrial urbanized country. Now we're going from being an industrial economy to a high-technology, information-based economy. We're going from the cold war relationships in our global foreign policy to a global economy, where we're becoming integrated economically and there are all kinds of pressures for disintegration, disintegration of families, of communities, of national economic policy, and the growth of extremism all over the world, political and religious and ethnic extremism. You know it. You see it when a bus blows up in Israel. You see it when radicals run for office or stop elections in other secular Islamic countries. You see it when the sarin gas explodes in the subway in Japan or when, God forbid, the Federal building blows up in Oklahoma City.

So this is a confusing world. There's a lot of wonderful things happening and a lot of troubling things happening. We cannot continue to do things the way we always did.

Our administration has a clear economic policy for this global economy, reduce the deficit but increase our investment in people, in education, in technology, in research, in things that will grow the economy. Look at the places that are left behind. Help the places who need help because of defense cutbacks. Help the places who need incentives for people to invest in inner cities and rural areas. And don't forget that the people come first.

What are the results? In 2½ years, the good news is, 7 million jobs, 2½ million homeowners, 2 million new businesses, a record number of self-made millionaires, the stock market's at 4,700, corporate profits at an all-time high. But guess what? The median income has dropped one percent. Why? Because we still have a lot of people who can't do very well in this new global economy. And I'm telling you, go back to our values. Everything we do, everything we

do, has to be directed toward helping people who are willing to work hard and do their best to be good workers, good parents, and successful in this global economy. That's what we have to do.

Look at our social problems. Believe it or not—you couldn't tell it maybe from the daily press, but in this country in the last 2 years, the crime rate is down, the murder rate is down, the people on welfare's numbers are down, the food stamp rolls are down, the divorce rate is down, even the abortion rate is down. But we still have some terrible problems. Why? Because young people feel like nobody's looking out for their future. The juvenile crime rate is up. Casual drug use among people under 18 is up. And so we have to find ways to work together.

That's what our crime bill was all about that the people in Congress are trying to undo. We put 100,000 police on the street, not just to catch criminals but to prevent crime and to give our young people some role models and some people they could relate to, people who would be standing up for their future and telling them there are things you ought to be saying yes to as well as saying no to crime and violence and drugs. And we need to do more of that, not less. We need a different approach that recognizes that we have to do both things.

Today, finally, the Senate moved away from partisan extremism and 87 people voted in the Senate, 87 of 100, for a welfare reform bill that has the elements that I've been advocating now for 2½ years. It encourages work. It provides child care for people on welfare so they can go to work without worrying their hearts out about their kids. And it is very tough in collecting child support that is owed by people; even if they cross State lines, you ought not to be able to run away from the obligation to take care of your own children. That's what we did today.

The point I want to make about all this is that we need to try new and different approaches. And when we do, we can get results. When we fall back into these old patterns of turning everything in Washington into a partisan fight, all it does is turn the American people off and doesn't do a single, solitary thing to move the American people into the future.

Now we have a chance with this budget to find real common ground. I want to balance the budget. The leaders of the Democratic Party want to balance the budget. I have presented a balanced budget plan. But the question is, can we balance the budget consistent with our values and with these new ideas? Why are we balancing the budget? To take the debt off these kids here, to free up money to be borrowed at lower interest rates, to create jobs, to stop spending your tax money paying interest on the debt and start spending it educating our children or taking care of our health needs or fighting crime. That's why we want to balance the budget.

Therefore, I say to you, I don't have to take a back seat to them in balancing the budget. When I took office—I've only been in Washington 2½ years, and most of them had been here forever and a day, and we cut the deficit from $290 billion to $160 billion in 3 years. I want to do it.

But I do not believe that the way to cut the deficit is to cut the number of children in Head Start, cut the number of young people in national service, increase the cost of student loans. That is wrong. That is cutting off our nose to spite our face. Cutting the education budget today would be like cutting the defense budget at the height of the cold war. In the global economy, education is our national security weapon, and we dare not cut it.

Al Gore has done a lot to give this country a different kind of Government. You heard him say we've cut the size of the Government, we've abolished 16,000 pages of regulation. Carol Browner from Florida, running the EPA, has cut by 25 percent the paperwork burdens of the EPA. But I'll be darned if I think the way to move into the global economy is to wreck the environment or the public health of this country in the name of balancing the budget. That is not necessary, and it is not right.

I've already said, I was up in Jacksonville with the magnificent sheriff there talking about the crime bill today. There are those who say in the name of balancing the budget, they want to stop the effort to put 100,000 police on the street and send less money in the form of a blank check to local governments. I say we know how to lower the crime rate; there is no constituency in America for raising the crime rate. Why in the wide world would we seek to balance the budget in ways that will raise the crime rate when we know how to lower it? Let's keep lowering the crime rate, put the police on the street, put the prevention programs out there, put the prison programs out there. Let's don't

wreck the crime bill. Let's keep bringing the crime rate down.

I'll give you just two other ideas that are out there to balance the budget. One of the most important things we did that we got next to no credit for in 1993 was cutting the taxes of 15 million working families with 50 million Americans in them, including 10 times as many people in Florida as paid a tax increase. The reason for this was very simple in my mind. I really believed the biggest problem in America today is the stagnant wages of middle class people who are working harder for less. I really want people to go to work off welfare. I believe if you tell people you want them to work, work has to pay.

Most parents today have to work. We have no higher duty than to make sure that people who work and have children can be both successful at work and successful in the raising of their children, our most important job.

So what do we do? We expanded the family tax credit to give all those people a tax cut so there would never be an incentive to be on welfare. What do they want to do in Washington? They want to raise taxes on the lowest income working people and give everybody else a tax cut. It doesn't make sense; that is not the way to balance the budget.

And finally, let's talk about Medicare and Medicaid. The discussion has appalled me in Washington. The people who are proposing $450 billion worth of cuts in Medicare and Medicaid act like if you're not for their plan, you don't want to save the Medicare Trust Fund; if you're not for their plan, you must be some greedy, wealthy older person who just doesn't want to pay your fair share.

Let me tell you something, folks. One of the most important decisions we have to make as we change this economy is what our obligations to each other are. Lawton Chiles said we needed a country that's a community, not a crowd. Are we going to be a community or a crowd? Are we going to define ourselves by what we can do together, or what we can do cut alone as a bunch of isolated individuals?

Now, the truth is that most elderly people in this country are more than willing to do what's right, have already done what's right all their lives, and care a great deal about the welfare of their children and their grandchildren and the future of this country. And it is a bum rap to say that those of us who have questions about whether we should just jerk $450 billion out of Medicare and Medicaid don't want to balance the budget and don't care about our country. That is not true, and it is not necessary to balance the budget.

I want you to tell people that. When you hear people say we've got to cut all this money out of Medicare because of the Trust Fund, you just remember one thing: Not one red cent that senior citizens pay in medical bills will go into that Trust Fund, not a penny. It's all going to fund the budget program and the tax cut. Don't ever forget it.

So I say to you, let's balance the budget, but let's do it in a way that reflects our shared values and what we owe to each other. We can balance the budget without cutting education. We can balance the budget without endangering the environment. We can balance the budget without letting the crime rate go up again. And we can certainly balance the budget, slow the rate of health care inflation, fix the Medicare Trust Fund without soaking the elderly people of this country, 75 percent of whom are struggling to get by today on less than $24,000 a year. We can do these things.

The last thing I want to tell you is—I thought about it today a lot because I was up in Jacksonville—if you are President of the United States at a time when everything is kind of going haywire and changing, you cannot always do what is popular and be right. Sometimes you have to do what's going to be right in 10 or 20 years. That's what you have to do.

Now, I am well aware that I hurt myself terribly in north Florida when I became the first President in the history of the United States, while he was in office as opposed to after he left, to say to the National Rifle Association, "You are wrong about the Brady bill. You are wrong about assault weapons. We need to make our children safer." I'm aware of that.

And believe you me, I am aware that every political adviser I had said, "Look at the States you won last time. You're crazy if you take on the tobacco companies over teenage smoking." But I tell you, folks, 3,000 children a day begin to smoke, and 1,000 of them every day will shorten their lives because of doing that. And I say who cares what the political consequences are if we save 1,000 lives a day from now on. It is worth doing. It is worth doing.

When I sent the United States military to liberate Haiti from its dictators, everybody said I was crazy; there was no political support for it in the country; it was impossible. But I said the United States was promised by those military dictators that they would go. They gave their word to us, and we must keep our word for freedom's sake. We did, and we were right. Unpopular, yes. Right, yes. You have to do what's right over the long run.

I'll give you a more mundane example. When the Vice President and I decided to invest massive amounts of his time and the most talented people we could find to work in the White House to reinvent the Government, my political advisers said, "This is nuts. No President has ever made a single vote on management. No one will ever believe the Government runs well anyway. No one will ever believe the Government gets smaller anyway."

Well, let me tell you something, folks, that may all be true, but we cannot do what we need to do for the United States in the new information age unless we have a smaller, less bureaucratic, more efficient, less costly, better Government. So it's going to be the smallest it's been since John Kennedy, and it's going to put out twice as much output, and we're going to have more examples like the Small Business Administration where we cut the budget by 40 percent and doubled the loan volume to create small business in America. You're going to have a lot of that. There may not be any votes in it, but it's the right thing for America.

When I stuck up for the elemental principle that we should reform affirmative action because there were some problems with it but that there was still discrimination in this country and we ought to reach out and try to make sure everybody was considered without regard to their gender or their racial or ethnic background, not given quotas, not given reverse discrimination, but at least given consideration for equal opportunity, I was told, "This is dumb politics. Look at the polls. You're crazy." All I know is, look around this room, we're going up or down together, folks. Our ethnic diversity is the greatest resource we have if we use it in a sensible way. So we should amend affirmative action but not end it.

The Vice President said something I'm really proud of. He will tell you, we were told by expert after expert after expert about politics that the First Lady should not go to China. They said, "Oh, it's a no-win deal. If you go over there, people that are concerned about human rights will attack her and attack you. And whatever you say, if you say anything strong, well, you'll put our relationship haywire. It's a lose-lose deal." But you know what? Somebody needs to speak up on behalf of the United States for the principles of freedom and liberty and decent treatment for women here at home and throughout the world. What happens to women and little girls throughout the world will have a great deal to do with the world we live in. And I'm proud of what she did, and we did the right thing to send her there.

Well, you get the idea. So what I want you to do is to go out of here and say, "Look, you may not agree with everything Bill Clinton and Al Gore do." [*Laughter*] "I don't agree with everything Bill Clinton and Al Gore do. They make mistakes. But you've got to give them

one thing: They've got a clear vision of what they want America to look like, they've got new ideas and old values, they are committed to working with Democrats and Republicans to find common ground based on those values, and they're doing what's right for the next generation, even if it is politically unpopular. And in a time of change, that's what we've got to do."

I want you to take that out to every person in Florida. We need to win Florida. But more importantly, America needs to stay on the right course: more jobs, higher incomes, safer streets, a cleaner environment, an opportunity to lead in a world that is safer and better, and to come together. If we do that, the best is yet to be.

Thank you, and God bless you.

NOTE: The President spoke at 7:35 p.m. at the Sheraton Bal Harbour.

Statement on House of Representatives Action To Reauthorize the Ryan White CARE Act
September 19, 1995

I congratulate the Members of the House of Representatives on their overwhelming vote to approve a 5-year reauthorization of the Ryan White CARE Act. This legislation will assure that Americans who are living with HIV and AIDS will continue to receive the life-sustaining

services that they need. The Ryan White CARE Act is a lifeline to thousands of Americans who otherwise have nowhere to turn. I hope the House and Senate can quickly work out their differences on this legislation and send me a final bill as soon as possible.

Remarks and a Question-and-Answer Session at the Little Sisters of the Poor Home for the Aged in Denver, Colorado
September 20, 1995

The President. The reason I wanted to come here today is because by coming I hope to honor the work that this home has done and also to point out how dramatically our Nation has been able to improve care for elderly people in the last several years because of the commitments we have made through the Medicare and Medicaid program.

And as you know, there's a big debate in Washington going on now about balancing the budget and what we have to do to balance the budget. And the health care programs have been

the fastest growing part of our budget, just as they've been the fastest growing part of a lot of families' budgets—the cost of health care. So I strongly believe we should balance the budget, and I believe we have to lower the rate of growth in health care spending. But the real question is, how do you do it?

And the Medicaid program I think is particularly important because 70 percent of the people who receive the benefits are elderly and disabled people who live in places like this. And the program is funded between 50 and 80 percent, depending on the State, by the Federal Government, and the State government makes up the rest. And it's administered by the Governors. Governor Romer is here, and he and I worked together for years when we were both Governors on this.

But one of the congressional proposals we believe—he and I believe—would cut the Medicaid spending by so much that it would endanger the ability of our country to care for every eligible person and to maintain the high quality of care. You know, when President Reagan— this has been a bipartisan issue, I should add, until this very moment. In 1987, President Reagan signed a law that many of us who were Governors strongly supported, upgrading the standards of care in residential facilities. You remember that.

Before that, as many as 40 percent of the people, elderly people in residential facilities in this country, were over-medicated, were often unnecessarily physically restrained. It was a very different situation, not here, but in other places in these for-profit homes. And since then, there's been this dramatic improvement in care. Now, the Congress did make some mistakes, and we've largely corrected them, I think, in the last 3 years, in trying to make sure that the program grew at a manageable rate.

But with more people living longer and more and more people becoming eligible for Medicaid, for this kind of care, I think it is very, very important that we recognize that we have two fundamental moral obligations here.

I think we're obligated to balance this budget to take the debt off our children and grandchildren, but we're obligated to do it in a way that represents—that reflects our responsibility to our parents and grandparents. And in doing the right thing by America across the generations, it's not always easy, but it's clearly one of our most important obligations.

And of course, as all of you know, the families—if we were to have a budget in place in the National Government which would make hundreds of thousands of people over the next 7 years ineligible for support in nursing homes and millions of people ineligible for help for home care, it would have a drastic impact not only on the senior citizens but on their children.

So I wanted to come here just to highlight to America not only the magnificent work being done here by Mother Patricia and others but to talk about what's being done all over America

and how we have to find a way to balance the budget without wrecking the system that makes this kind of thing possible.

I think it must be very rewarding for all of you to know that not only that this place exists for you, but there are places like this all over America where people can live in dignity and security and have not only their health care but their emotional needs met.

So that's why we're here. And I'd like to— perhaps the Governor would like to say something, but I'd like to spend whatever time I can listening to you talk a bit.

[*At this point, Gov. Roy Romer of Colorado advocated a national floor for Medicare and Medicaid so States would provide the same minimum standard of care.*]

The President. I should say, just to explain what the Governor said, yesterday the House of Representatives seemed to be embracing— the majority of the House of Representatives seemed to be embracing a plan where the Federal Government would just send every State a check for the next 7 years and cut what we project to spend on Medicaid by about a third, give them a third less and tell them to do whatever they wanted to with the money, which means that now we have a more or less uniform system. That is, States can provide more services, if they like, to seniors or to poor children under Medicaid, but there is a floor below which they can't go, which means that as more and more families move across the country and live in different places, it means that their parents and grandparents can live anywhere they want with them, be in any kind of facility and know that at least within some limits, they'll be treated equally across the country. That's the point the Governor is trying to make.

[*A participant described the service her organization performed for seniors to ensure their independence and dignity and stated that Medicaid was essential. She then explained that she became involved because she was inspired by Mother Patricia Friel, administrator, Little Sisters of the Poor Home for the Aged.*]

The President. She's an inspiration to me. I think I might—[*laughter*]—I'm interested in living to be 90 now. Before I got here this morning, I didn't know. [*Laughter*]

Let me say that our best estimates are—the proposal that I made would basically slow the rate of growth of spending and require some real discipline on the part of the States. But it is about a third as costly as the congressional proposal. We estimate the congressional proposal could keep, within 7 years, 300,000 people who are now eligible out of nursing homes and over a million people who are now eligible from getting home health services.

And of course, obviously, with people—the fastest growing group of people in America today by percentage are people over 80. And more and more of them are able to live at home because we're learning so much more about what it takes to stay healthy, stay fit. As you know—you're working with them—it would be, I think, a terrible mistake, indeed, even a terrible economic mistake to do anything that would undermine our ability to support home care.

[*A participant explained that helping senior citizens to remain independent was more cost-effective and allowed them their dignity.*]

The President. Since you made that point, I'd like to, if I might, just interject one thing that I've not seen in any coverage of this anywhere. And I'm not faulting the press; I think it's something that none of us have really thought to emphasize. But, Roy, a lot of these programs where some of the people are on Medicaid and some aren't depend on the Medicaid money, in effect, to subsidize the service of the others. So the number of people who could be losing the benefits of this could be far greater than the number of people in Medicaid because of that.

As you also know, Medicaid for the last several years has provided help to low-income elderly people to help them buy into Part B of Medicare. So also, another thing that will happen, I believe, is that we could be getting very false savings by all of a sudden having elderly people drop out of Part B of Medicare, and it looks like we're spending less money on Medicare, so they don't get regular care, and then we wind up aggravating a problem we already have, which is spending too much money on intensive care when people are desperately ill and maybe nothing can be done.

I'm glad you brought that up because I hadn't thought to mention that to anyone in this whole debate. But I know it to be true from my own experience as a Governor. We had lots and lots of programs where Medicare—we put in a little

money, let's say, for half the people, and the other half of the people, maybe they could come up with a little something, but they really basically got to be served at a discount because Medicaid was there.

What about you?

[*A participant described how a cutback in Medicaid would affect her family and asked if the working class would be the only group affected by the changes.*]

The President. The answer is, I think, to be perfectly accurate, I think there is—a small part of the savings would come from charging wealthy retirees and their families significantly more for a part of Medicare. And in that sense, in an atmosphere of cutbacks, that was a part of the plan that I offered last year when I was trying to get universal health care coverage. But the vast, vast majority of the burden will be borne by the middle class and by lower income elderly people and their families, because they tend to rely—first of all, you have to be of a certain income level to be eligible for Medicaid. And secondly, in Medicare—75 percent of the people on Medicare have family incomes of under $24,000.

And again, I think this becomes a moral question. If the whole thing were going broke and we couldn't do it, we would all have to look at whatever options were available, where what we need to do is to fix and reform these systems in a disciplined way so they'll be there from now on. And we can do that without causing the kind of havoc that's going to be visited on average people's lives, I think.

One of the reasons I wanted you all to be here is I want people to understand that this is a thing that has family impact.

[*Governor Romer explained that Colorado calculations showed the congressional proposal would increase costs to the State by $40 to $50 million at a time when the State had planned to increase education expenses by the same amount, forcing the State to choose between education and health care.*]

The President. In other words, the Congress is taking the position that they'll just give this arbitrary cut to the States, and they are sure they'll be able to just manage the program better. But the truth is, they'll be making decisions just like you will be. Children will be making decisions between their parents and their own kids, between their health care and their parents and the education of their children. States will be making decisions between the health care of their elderly citizens and the education of their children in a much more extreme way than in our experience.

And again, I would say, if it were absolutely necessary to either save Medicare or Medicaid or to balance the budget, it would be one thing. But it is not necessary. There are many options to balance the budget and preserve what you are celebrating here around this circle this morning.

Would you like to say anything?

[*A participant suggested that the money being spent on Medicaid and Medicare be invested.*]

The President. You mean invested by the Government?

Q. Yes.

The President. Well, one of the things that they propose to do, that they're trying to do, the Congress is trying to do, is to allow people to invest some of their money that would otherwise go into Medicare and Medicaid into a medical savings account.

The problem with doing it that way—I'll answer your two questions—and I've thought of both things. I think a medical savings account, by taking some of the money that would have gone into Medicare-Medicaid, giving it to citizens, letting them invest it in a medical savings account, the good thing about that is that you might be able to get a higher rate of return than the Government gets a—I mean, we invest essentially in Government securities. The problem is that it only works if you happen to be a healthy elderly person, if you see what I mean. In other words, if you have a period of long-term health where you're investing and earning, you do great. If you get sick in a hurry, where you have to draw down, you'll be in the hole, which is why we have programs for the whole society. So the medical savings account may be something that we ought to explore and experiment with, but it will always, I'm convinced, be sort of an add-on, a marginal support for what needs to be a fundamental program.

The problem with the Government investing in mutual funds is—knock on wood, I hate to say this since the stock market has gone up so much since I've been President—is that it's fine if we get a higher rate of return than we get from Government securities, but the prob-

lem is you have to be taking money out on a regular basis, as you know, to fund a health care program, and sometimes the stock market's going up and sometimes it's going down and when the time came for our quarterly withdrawal if there had been a 50-point drop the day before in the stock market, we could be really in deep trouble, which is why we've always relied on the basic steady but lower rate of return from Government securities when we invest in them.

Q. Can you do half-and-half?

The President. Well, I don't know. The problem is—another problem is, because we've been running a deficit, is that we have to have the money to basically, in effect, to finance our own deficit. It may be an option, but I think that's something—that's one thing that States will be able to look at if they have some more flexibility here.

But the problem is, when you make those investments in mutual funds, the thing that really makes it go is if you believe there is a long-term trend in the stock market, you have to have the flexibility, just like an individual investor, of when to withdraw. In other words, the investor decides when to withdraw. So if you lose money, you say, "Oh, it's awful, but thank goodness I don't have to cash my stocks in. I think there will be a turn." Even after October '87, the people who could ride it through if they could wait a year or two, were making a profit again. But the Government, we'd have to withdraw these funds on a regular basis to pay our bills, so that is the risk inherent in that.

Q. Well, according to the trustees' report, though, if we go with your plan, we'll be out of money like 2005, and the Republican plan would be 2015.

The President. The trustees haven't said that yet. It depends on what the Republicans do. If the Republicans have all of their Medicare cuts coming out of doctors and hospitals, they could stretch it to 2015, but the general conclusion of the health care community is that if they did that, they would be closing large numbers of health care facilities, and a huge number of doctors would simply opt out of the program. So that's why they've got a problem. They actually adopt—right now, they adopt cuts in the hospital program—the Part A—about the same size as ours. But they have this $90-billion amorphous amount of money that they can't say how they're going to save yet. So they can't go any further than we do unless they take more money away from the hospitals and doctors.

My problem is that—let me just back up and say, my problem in this whole thing is, when we put our budget together, we asked the following questions to the best of our ability. We asked the substantive questions. How much can we take out of Medicaid over the next 7 years without having doctors opt out or closing hospitals that need to stay open or really damaging the elderly in the country? How much can we cut Medicare over the next 7 years without really hurting the hospitals and the medical delivery system that depends on it? Let's squeeze it as hard as we can. That's what we did.

What they did was to say, "We promised to balance the budget and give a $250-billion tax cut to the American people. How much do we have to cut Medicare and Medicaid to meet that number?" It seems to me that once you commit to an end of balancing the budget, then you have to say, how can you balance the budget consistent with how much money you can take out of the health care system?

What they said is, "Here is our target date. Here's how much of a tax cut we're going to give. Therefore, we're going to take $450 billion out of the health care system." And I think that, frankly, they have no idea whether they can do that. They don't know what the system will bear. And I think it's far better to be more disciplined about it and take a little bit longer and know that you're not going to upset this complex of relationships here that have developed. If you do that, you can always experiment with the medical savings accounts; you could always experiment with alternative investments; you could always do these things. But you have to realize that these people, they have to get up and run this place tomorrow.

Q. That's right.

The President. And the hospital downtown, they have to get up and run those places. I mean, their lives go on. And some decision we make in Washington may or may not be consistent with the reality of what it takes to run the place. That's what we're trying to struggle with there.

[The participant described the percentage of the budget which should not be cut and then asked why cuts could not come from the remaining percentage, like tobacco subsidies.]

The President. Well, one thing, there is a lot cut out of that, a great deal being cut out of that. And a lot of that is——

Q. How about more?

The President. But a lot of what's left is education and infrastructure and the things that grow the economy. Again, you have to understand, I think the issue is: What are our objectives here? If our objectives are to balance the budget, secure the financial integrity of Medicare so that it's there from now on, and invest enough in Medicaid and Medicare to make sure that the fundamental mission can be achieved as we slow the rate of inflation growth, and then the rest of your money we should spend to provide the national defense and to grow the economy and to help people help themselves. Then we should put all that together and come out with a plan to balance the budget as quickly and as well as we can.

But they did it backwards. They said, "We promise to balance it in 7 years and to give a $250 billion tax cut—this is how much we have to cut this other stuff—and to increase investment in defense to build new weapons systems."

And I just believe that—believe me, we are looking at all possible alternatives. I have already passed—the first 2 years of my Presidency with the previous Congress, they took the deficit from $290 billion to $160 billion; they added 3 years to the life of the Medicare Trust Fund; they voted to reduce the Government to its smallest size since John Kennedy was President. I mean, it is the first time in decades that we have actually reduced that other part of the budget, dramatically.

But that other part of the budget also includes things that will really shape our children's future: research and development, investment in technology, medical research, a whole range of things. It's now a much smaller part of our budget than it used to be. Most of what we spend money on today is Medicare, Medicaid, Social Security, and defense.

Now, the other thing you should know if it weren't for—to make the point further about how much we've been cutting—if it weren't for the interest on the debt we pay today for the debt run up between 1981 and the day I became President in 1993, the budget would be in balance today. So there really is an argument for trying to bring this budget into balance so you stop wasting so much money on interest and start freeing it up. And we are doing our best to cut these other things.

For example, the tobacco program—and you know I'm the first sitting President ever to take on this issue to try to limit teenage smoking, and I'm in a big struggle with tobacco companies. But you should know that the tobacco program itself is self-financing. There is no direct Government subsidy to tobacco farmers. They pay a fee, and then it rotates back there. So it's a self-financing program. The only expenditure the Government has, I think, is for whatever administrative costs the Department of Agriculture has to administer the program, which is not—it's a very small amount of money.

And believe me, I tried to raise the cigarette tax to help pay for health care last year, so I'm open to that. But there's just not much money there.

[*A participant expressed concern about fraud and abuse on the part of the providers.*]

The President. That's correct. There has been a substantial amount of fraud and abuse on the part of providers. And the General Accounting Office of the Congress has estimated that it may be as much as, in some years, 10 percent of the total cost, which is a lot of money. So, to try to address that, we have tripled the number of FBI agents that are working on health care fraud and we have doubled the number of prosecutions of serious Medicare and Medicaid fraud. And that's beginning to make a big difference.

And that's one of the ways that we proposed to meet the inflation targets. If you can take that out of the system, you can continue to give homes like this one an adequate return through Medicaid to do the work that they have to do. That's what we're—but you're absolutely right; in terms of the recipients, there is no question of fraud. You never have any questions about Medicare and Medicaid eligibility the way you do the Food Stamp Program, for example, which, by the way, we're also doing a better job of—food stamp rolls are down, and we're getting a hold of that.

But since you're eligible here by age in Medicare, or by age and income in Medicaid, it's a much clearer situation. And you're right, it's very hard to abuse the program,

[*A participant explained how excessive regulations interfered with quality respite care.*]

The President. You mean you can't just do that, having met the standards of running this operation?

[*The participant explained that eliminating unnecessary regulations would help to ensure that senior citizens received good respite care while their families were away.*]

The President. You know, no one has ever mentioned this to me before. This is very interesting, and I'm somewhat embarrassed to say it's never occurred to me before. It's a great idea.

Let me ask you, if you wouldn't mind, would you be willing just to put on paper for me the kinds of things that you think ought to be changed, that you think would facilitate you doing this kind of thing? I'd be happy to see what I could do, because we are really working hard—we have already abolished 16,000 pages of Federal regulation. And we're trying to do a lot more, because I think a lot of things are over-regulated and they focus too much on input rather than evaluating the results. If you get good results—as a matter of fact, this is—I don't know why we shouldn't do it in this context, but we are now picking 50 big companies in the country for a new experiment on clean air. And if they tell us that they will meet the clean air requirements of the law and be tested on a regular basis, we'll let them throw the rulebook away for figuring out how to do it. In other words, if they can figure out how to do it cheaply and more efficiently than all the rules and regulations, they can just ignore them, because all we care about is whether the air is clean.

So those are the kinds of things that I think we ought to be looking at. So if you would send me that suggestion I would be very, very happy to—if you could also send a copy to the Governor, because some of those things may be things that are within the State's ability to deal with rather than the Federal Government.

[*A participant described the respite care program offered by the Little Sisters of the Poor.*]

Governor Romer. Do you have a program for Governors? [*Laughter*]

The President. You know, Roy and I would like a little respite care here. [*Laughter*]

We'll be back in a month.

[*Mother Patricia Friel asked for concluding remarks. A participant described her life at the home and indicated that it would not have been possible without Medicare and Medicaid.*]

The President. Would you like to say anything before we go?

[*A participant described the impact of Medicare and Medicaid on her life.*]

The President. I don't know what we'd do if it weren't for people like you who would work until you're 74. Bless you. Thank you.

[*Archbishop Francis Stafford of the Denver archdiocese thanked the President and the participants.*]

The President. Let me also tell you just one thing. We're going to do our best in the next 2 months not to play politics with your lives. I mean, not to unduly aggravate the differences, not to—I'm going to do my best to get an agreement here that will give the country the confidence that we can balance our books and go on into our future but that also will give you the confidence that you can educate your son and not worry about your mother. I believe it can be done.

But I believe we have to look realistically, and we have to do it from the bottom up. We have to know what is possible, and that's why I wanted to meet here today. And we're going to explore every conceivable alternative. But in the end, we need to—places like this need to do well, and programs like yours, helping people stay home and running respite care, they need to do well, because we're all going to be—this country is going to get older, and people are going to live longer, and that is a good thing. It is a good thing, not a bad thing. We just have to find a way to manage it, and it's a new thing.

Governor Romer. Mr. President, you're not going to have a chance to see this whole facility. I've just been staring at this floor. I don't know——

The President. Amazing, isn't it?

[*Governor Romer and Mother Friel made brief concluding remarks.*]

The President. Thank you very much.

NOTE: The President spoke at 9:43 a.m. in the first floor lounge.

Remarks to the Community at the Little Sisters of the Poor Home for the Aged in Denver
September 20, 1995

Thank you very much. Thank you very much, Marie Schroeder, for that robust introduction. [*Laughter*] And quite to the point. I was almost lost in my notes there for a moment—[*laughter*]—there it was, time to be here.

Mother Patricia, Mother Provincial Margaret, Archbishop Stafford, and my long-time friend Governor Romer, I thank you all for being here today, and I thank you for your wonderful welcome. I want to say a special word of thanks to Helen Cooper and to her daughter and son-in-law, and to Reynalda Garcia and to her two daughters, for spending some time with me just a few moments ago to discuss the care that they receive in this wonderful home and the role that Medicare—I mean Medicaid plays in that. I want to thank all of you for giving me the chance to come here. And I'd like to begin by a special word of appreciation to the Little

Sisters of the Poor who run this wonderful facility and who in their lives, with just a little bit of help from the Government here in the form of Medicaid, illustrate an ethic of service that few Americans can hope to match but all Americans should seek to emulate. I thank them for that.

I have come here to talk about a Government program called Medicaid, what it means to families like yours all across the country and what role it should play in our efforts to balance the national budget.

We are all now living through a period of remarkable change in our country's history. Everybody knows it. You have only to follow either the events in the news or perhaps even the events in the lives of your own families to know that we are changing the way we work and the way we live more dramatically than at any time in the last 100 years.

About 100 years ago, we began a transition from an agricultural and rural society to a more urban and industrial society. Now we are in the midst of a transition from that urban industrial society to a society that runs primarily on dramatic increases in technology and in information and one in which all the countries in the world are increasingly united together after the cold war in a global economy but one that is not free of difficulty, as you know.

The more we seem to be integrated economically, the more we often seem to be splitting apart in other ways. And we see the rise, for example, of extremism and groups of hatred rooted in religious or ethnic or racial differences all across the world. We see it when a bus blows up in Israel or when a fanatic breaks open poison gas in a Japanese subway or when, unfortunately, the Federal building was blown up in Oklahoma City.

So in this period of change, it is not surprising that one of the things that we have to do is to be open to new ideas about what we have to do to change the way we do business in America so that we can adapt to this new age. But it is also important to remember that every period of change is a challenge, in my mind, issued ultimately by God, to make the adjustments we need to make change our friend while maintaining true to our basic values. And that's really what this debate in Washington about the balanced budget is all about.

We ought to balance the budget. We never had a permanent, built-in deficit in our country until 1981. We quadrupled the debt of America in the 12 years from 1981 until the day I became President. We built in this huge deficit. We wanted lower taxes and we wanted higher spending, and we took both and forgot about the consequences to our children, our grandchildren, and the future. It is so bad today that interest on the debt next year could exceed the defense budget. And interest payments today are so great that the budget would be in balance today but for the debt run up in the 12 years before I became President.

On the other hand, if we're going to balance the budget, we have to say, why are we doing this? What's America all about? What have you given to us that we have to give to our children and grandchildren? A reverence for work and family, for personal responsibility, and responsibility to the community, a devotion to excellence and to service.

Yesterday I was in Florida with the Governor of Florida, who is a friend of Governor Romer's and mine, and he said, "America has always been and must always be a community, not a crowd." He said, "A crowd is a collection of people who are all on their own, the survival of the fittest. Power gets more; weakness gets less. A community is a group of people that recognizes that they have responsibilities to each other, responsibilities to each other."

The generation that lives in this home conquered the Great Depression and World War II, launched the cold war to stand freedom against democracy, saved the world, and gave us the most prosperous country the world has ever known. We have obligations to the generation of elderly Americans who did that, our parents and our grandparents. We have obligations to our future, to our children and their children to balance the budget.

The great question in Washington is, can we meet both obligations? And if so, how? I believe we can, and I am determined to do it. I believe that the future of this country contains our greatest day if we can still stand for freedom and responsibility, if we can still stand for work and family, if we can honor our children and our parents, and if we can all recognize, without regard to our income or personal circumstances, we're in one community and we have certain obligations to each other. That is really what this debate on the balanced budget is all about.

I believe that we should balance the budget. When I became President, our annual deficit was $290 billion; now it's down to $160 billion. Some of you may actually remember that the last time the deficit went down 3 years in a row was when Harry Truman was President of the United States. I am proud of the fact that we're emulating Mr. Truman's record. And I want to go all the way and bring this budget into balance.

One of the biggest problems with bringing the budget into balance is that inflation in health care has been going up faster than economic growth, not only for the Government but for a lot of you who are out there on your own private budgets. Inflation in health care has been one of the fastest growing areas of a family's budget. And if we don't do something to lower that rate of inflation, we can never bring the budget into balance unless we're prepared to just stop investing in education or stop investing in the new technologies and the new sciences that may offer us the answer to a lot of the world's problems or walk away from some of our other obligations.

So we have to slow the rate of medical inflation. I've worked hard on that. For 2½ years, we have made the Medicare Trust Fund more solvent, we have corrected some of the abuses that were in the Medicaid program, but we have really faced the fact that we still have fundamental responsibilities to help people who depend upon Medicare and Medicaid to live.

Now, there is—the great contest in Washington today is basically over how much we should cut health care, how much we should cut education, how much we should cut the environment, how much we should cut taxes, to balance the budget.

The congressional proposal, which came out yesterday, I believe, on Medicaid, I believe endangers the Medicaid program that makes it possible for places like this wonderful home to exist. And I do not believe it is necessary to balance the budget. So I came here today to tell you two things: One is, we need to slow the rate of medical inflation in every program, including the ones that benefit you, and we can. But two is, we don't have to wreck the program and throw families into abject insecurity to balance the budget. It is not necessary.

I have given the Congress a balanced budget plan which will preserve the integrity of Medicare and Medicaid and enable us to serve the senior citizens of the United States. And that is important.

Let me tell you about Medicaid. Two-thirds of the Medicaid program goes to benefit senior citizens and people with disabilities. Seven in 10 Americans in nursing homes get help from Medicaid to pay their bills. Forty-three percent of the residents in this nursing home get that sort of support. Medicare can be the difference between quality care in a quality facility and an uncertain future. In the United States as a whole, the average cost of nursing home care is $38,000 a year. Three quarters of our senior citizens live on incomes below $24,000 a year. You don't have to be a mathematical genius to know that someone has to step into the breach. There has to be a system to honor the people in this country who have done their part for America and need this kind of help.

The plan proposed by Congress would take away the guarantee that Medicare would be there to help, would instead cut future spending by about a third and send a check to all the States. That's what Governor Romer was talking about. Marie Schroeder was able to come here from another State to be near her son because Medicaid is a national program, run State-by-State, but it has certain basic guarantees in it. If it becomes a State-by-State program, a lot of people who live in States that may have good care, may literally be robbed of the chance to go visit and live with their children because they live in States that don't.

A lot of middle class families, who have the security of knowing that their parents are okay, can help their children to finance their college education. If they lose that security, they may not be able to help their kids go to college. This is a huge issue. We must do this right.

The plan proposed in Congress, we estimate, could mean that up to 300,000 American senior citizens who today are eligible to go into nursing homes won't be eligible in just a few years. And over a million who get services in their own homes, who get to go to senior centers and other things to support in-home care, won't be able to get those services, not to mention the 30 percent of the program that goes to help the very poorest children in the United States today.

It isn't fashionable anymore to speak up for the poor, but the truth is, those kids are our future. And at least in this country, as poor as you are, at least you can go to a doctor because of Medicaid, and these kids can get off to a good start in life. But there's not much of a political lobby for poor children. So if we become a crowd instead of a community, a lot of them are going to get left behind. So that's what I want to emphasize to you. We can slow the rate of growth in Medicaid without wrecking the program.

Today, if you have to go into a nursing home and you need help from Medicaid, by law you can get it. And you don't have to force your spouse, for example, to sell your possessions. Under this new plan, States would be permitted to force someone, for example, whose husband has to go into a nursing home to actually sell her car and her house before they could get any help from the Government. I don't think that's right. I don't think that's right.

1405

I also don't think it's right to totally abandon a commitment to national standards of quality. Now, just a few moments ago, Mother Patricia was telling me about some Federal rules and regulations that she thought ought to be changed. And we have done more to deregulate the Government in sensible ways than any previous administration in the last 30 years. We've abolished 16,000 pages of Federal regulations, and we're working on thousands more.

But before we had national standards for residential care in 1987—which was, by the way, up until then, totally a bipartisan thing; it was signed by President Reagan—before that, up to 40 percent of people in nursing homes were overmedicated and overrestrained. And you don't see that anymore.

You know, unfortunately, not everybody can get into a facility run by the Little Sisters of the Poor. I wish they could. I wish everybody in America could do that. So we do need some standards to protect people, to make sure it's not just a money deal. That would all be gone.

The other thing I'd like to say is, a lot of our poorest elderly people are able to use their Medicaid money under national law to pay for their Part B premiums under Medicare so they can get doctor care and in-home services and medical equipment. This would do away with that, which means a lot of our poorest elderly people wouldn't be buying into Part B of Medicare. It's a good way to save money on Medicare. People say, "Oh, my goodness, Medicare is not as expensive as it used to be," but it will be very expensive for this country not only in the diminished dignity of seniors who have it now but in their increasing health care costs when they can't be regularly treated in a preventive, sensible way. It's a mistake; I'm against doing away with that. It's unnecessary, and we shouldn't do it.

Again, let me say to you, I have proposed reducing the rate of inflation in Medicare and asking the Medicare providers to take less so that we can keep the Trust Fund strong for another 11 years. I have proposed reducing the rate of inflation in Medicaid and forcing economies in the program but only about a third as much as the Congress proposes.

The reason they have proposed this huge number is they said no matter what, we're going to balance the budget in 7 years, not 8, 9, or 10, and no matter what, we're going to give a tax cut of $250 billion, a lot of which will go to people like me who don't need it and haven't asked for it.

And the point I want to make to you is not that we don't have to make any changes in these programs, not that we don't have to slow the rate of medical inflation but that we have to do it in a way that is consistent with our ethical obligation to honor our parents and grandparents and to honor the idea that we have obligations across generational lines and our obligation to help middle class people free up their incomes so they can educate their children while their parents live in dignity. That this the objective here.

So I say to you, I hope all of you will join me, without regard to your political party, in this national effort to balance the budget in a way that is consistent with our values. We're going through a time of big change. And the reason this country is still around after more than 200 years is that when we have gone through periods of huge change, we have recognized that we needed teamwork more than conflict. We have recognized that no one had all the answers, that no one was the repository of infinite wisdom—that belongs upstairs—and that we are going into a future that we have to do our best to shape not for the moment, for what's popular in the moment, but what will work 10, 20, 30 years from now. And we need to do it as a team. We need to do it as a community, not a crowd.

We need to do it in ways that will fulfill both our objectives of balancing the budget and honoring our obligations to our parents and to our children. Now, we can do that. But we cannot do that if we are excessively ideological, excessively partisan and arbitrary in saying we care a lot about this program but not as much about the program as we do having a $250 billion tax cut in a 7-year time frame. We can do this, but we need to do it in good faith.

So I ask all of you, in your prayers and in your pleas and in your letters, to reach out to the Congress in a spirit of cooperation and say we all want to help, but Medicaid does a lot of good for the senior citizens of this country. Medicaid enables this country to be what it is today. Medicaid supports private, charitable work. Medicaid in this nursing home is the embodiment of the lesson in the Catholic Bishops' letter that the quality of life in a society is the sum of both the personal choices made by individual citizens and families and the big choices made by the society as a whole. And they have to fit together.

So I say to you, this should be an exciting time to be an American. Whatever your age, you are living through a truly historic era. But we have to do this right. And to do it right means we have to do it consistent with our basic fundamental values. If we don't stray from them, we can embrace all the new ideas in the world and come out on the other side of the divide with a stronger, better America.

But if we forget for a moment what we owe either to our parents or to our children, then we will be making a grave mistake. I'm betting on America. I'm betting that the best is yet to come. But we have a difficult, invigorating, tough 60 or 90 days ahead of us in which you and people like you all across America can have a profound influence on the decisions we make

and on whether we preserve this very, very important partnership which has brought dignity to the lives of millions and millions and millions of Americans.

Thank you very much.

While you're all standing up, I now have one more announcement to make. Ethel Hoag, who is sitting right over there in that pink chair, is 94 years young today. This is her birthday. I believe we should end this wonderful meeting by singing "Happy Birthday" to Ethel Hoag.

NOTE: The President spoke at 10:40 a.m. In his remarks, he referred to Mother Provincial Margaret Halloran, Chicago Province, Little Sisters of the Poor; Cecile Cooper and Daniel Ely, daughter and son-in-law of home resident Helen Cooper; and Ramona Sena and Evangeline Landford, daughters of home resident Reynalda Garcia.

Remarks at Pueblo Community College in Pueblo, Colorado
September 20, 1995

The President. Thank you so much.

Audience members. I love you——

The President. I love hearing it. Thank you very much.

Ladies and gentlemen, let me begin by thanking you all for making me feel so very welcome. Thank you, Dr. May, for opening your fine institution and for bringing all your students and a lot of the folks from the surrounding area here. Thank you, Governor Romer, for your leadership and your friendship. Ladies and gentlemen, I had the privilege of being a Governor of my home State for 12 years before I was elected President. I was never part of the Washington scene, but I knew quite a lot about what it took to be a Governor. And by the time I left office, most of us thought Roy Romer was probably the best Governor in the United States of America and was doing more for education than anybody else. Thank you, Diana, for your introduction and for the power of your example. You and your family are the best of what this country is all about. And I came here to talk about your future and the future of all the students here and, in fact, this entire country.

I'm glad to be back in Pueblo. Anyplace where I can wear my cowboy boots and feel comfortable and has an Arkansas River is all right as far as I'm concerned. I also believe in community colleges. When I was a Governor I helped start several. I saw it open the doors of opportunity to people of all ages and all backgrounds. They are truly the community colleges, the most open and democratic and opportunity-filled institutions in the United States today. And I know I am at a good one today, and I'm proud to be here.

You know, our country has come a long way in over 200 years because we believed that we could always make the future better, and we believed we had an obligation to try. Pueblo was established in 1862, and one of the county commission's first acts was to collect money for a school. They knew that education could be better than gold, way back in 1862, and in 1995 it is more important than ever before.

I am here because the future of your education and those who come behind you is going to be affected by decisions which will be made in Washington, DC, in the next 2 to 3 months. All of you know that we are in a period of great change in our country. I believe that this period will be written up by the historians as a period of most profound change in 100 years, since the time we became an industrial society from a rural and agricultural one. Today, we are becoming a global economy, an information-based, technology-based society. We know that, and we know we have to make some changes so that we will be able to benefit from all these things that are going on in the world.

We know that one of the things we have to do is to provide lifetime learning for all of our people, to give everybody the opportunity to do well. And I've worked hard at that. I want to get more kids off to a good start at school. That's why we expanded Head Start. I want higher standards—[*applause*]—I want higher standards and smaller classes and more computers and other opportunities for our school students. That's what Governor Romer and I worked on Goals 2000 for.

I want more opportunities for young people who don't go on to the 4-year schools to get good jobs with good prospects for the future. That's what the school-to-work program that your president talked about is all about. I want more scholarships, more opportunities for community services, and more affordable loan programs for young people to go to college and for people who aren't so young to be able to go back to college. It's important.

Make no mistake about it, my fellow Americans, every dollar we spend investing in education has a big economic payoff not just for the people who benefit from it. Every year of education after high school today generates between 6 and 12 percent of higher income for the people who get it. But it's more important than that. It gives more dignity, more meaning, more possibility to people's lives, and it makes our Nation stronger. We know we must do this.

I want to ask you today to think about all the things you know are going on in your Nation's Capital and the big argument we're having over the budget in terms of this fundamental fact: We're living in a global economy; what we can learn determines what we can earn. We have an obligation to pass on to the next generation a stronger, better America. We also have an obligation to balance the budget. That is part of passing on to the next generation a stronger, better America.

And so I ask you to consider this: How should we do that? That's the big question, not whether we should but how we should. I think we need

new ideas and our old-fashioned values. We need to make decisions about this budget rooted in our devotion to freedom and responsibility; to work and to family; to giving young people a chance to do better; to fulfilling our obligations to the elderly, the disabled, and to poor children; to finding common ground instead of cheap and easy political rhetoric; and to doing the right thing for the future even if it's unpopular in the moment. We have to create the right kind of future for the United States of America.

We need to balance the budget. Your country never had a permanent structural deficit before 1981. In the 12 years before I moved to Washington as your President we quadrupled the national debt over the previous 200. There's no excuse for that. It's so bad now that the budget of your country would be balanced today if it weren't for the interest we pay on the debt run up in the 12 years before I took office. And we have cut the deficit of your country from $290 billion a year down to $160 billion in just 3 years. And it's the first time in 45 years that we've been able to do that.

So the question now is, how do we go all the way? How do we balance the budget consistent with our obligations and our values? I believe that we should balance the budget in the same way I've been reducing the deficit—by cutting other things and increasing our investment in education, because that will make us a stronger country as well.

You know, almost half the people at this community college have Pell grants. I want to see more people have access to Pell grants, so more people with modest incomes can go on to college. Next year the University of Southern Colorado will join so many others around the country in participating in our direct student loan program, and this fine community college has applied to participate in it. Let me tell you what it does. The direct student loan program enables the Government to get rid of all the redtape, the banks, and the middlemen and all the excessive costs from the student loan program, to send money directly to a school to give to the students at lower costs with better repayment terms, receiving the money more quickly.

Every school I have talked to that has participated in this program loves it because it's a lower cost for the school, lower cost for the students, and there are many more options to repay. One of the most important things about this direct loan program is that a young person can repay his or her loans based on a percentage of the income they earn when they go to work. So you never need to fear that you can't afford to borrow money because you may not have a lot of money when you get out.

I believe in the direct loan program. I believe in the Pell grant program. I believe in the AmeriCorps program, the national service program which enables people to earn money for college. Here in Colorado, you have young people working to keep kids out of gangs, to teach adults to read, to renovate vacant houses for working families, to clean up parks for children to play in, and in return, earning some money to go to school.

And I also believe that we can balance the budget and have the right kind of tax cut. But I favor a smaller, more targeted tax cut for middle income American families to educate themselves and their children and to raise their children. Let's value childrearing and education. If we're going to have a tax cut, let's finance more people going on to school.

The last thing I want to say is that I think we ought to have special educational opportunities for people who lose their jobs through no fault of their own. When I was—30 years ago when I was in college, 8 in 10 people who were laid off from work were called back to the same old job as soon as the economy got better. Today, 8 in 10 people who are laid off from work are not called back to the same old job because the economy is changing.

So I have asked this Congress to take about 70 different training programs the Government has, put it into a pool of money, and just simply give a voucher to a person who loses a job, worth up to $2,600 a year, to take to the local community college to get trained for a better life, a new start, a stronger beginning.

If we do this and balance the budget, over the next 7 years, 20 million more people will be eligible for lower cost, better repayment college loans. Three million more people will get the Pell grant scholarships that enable so many of you to be here. If we keep this commitment, we can have over 1.1 million people going on to college by the end of this decade, and we can do all that and balance the budget. The question is, will we?

The debate we're having in Washington today—I want to emphasize again—is not over whether to balance the budget, it's over how to balance the budget consistent with the fun-

damental values of this country. A majority of people in the Congress have a plan that reflects very different value choices. If their plan prevails, we won't be able to help as many poor kids get off to a good start in school. We won't even be able to keep helping as many as we are now. We won't be able to help as many schools to achieve those smaller classes and higher standards and more computers in the classrooms. And we certainly will see it become harder and more expensive to finance a college education, which means not as many people will go. There will be no more AmeriCorps, no national service program. There will be over 4 million fewer people getting Pell grants over the next 7 years. The direct lending program that this school wants to get into is going to be either severely limited or abolished, and the application that you have to give all your people here a better chance to go on and succeed will never see the light of day.

Now we learn that some in the Senate even want to charge colleges to process the Government loans. The president of the University of Kansas was quoted today as saying, "That's like charging people who run grocery stores to handle food stamps." Can you believe that? They actually want to start making the community college pay just to have people here with college loans. They want to raise the interest charged to working families who take out loans to send their children to college. They also, believe it or not, want to do some other things which will dramatically undermine the ability of people to go to college and all told—listen to this— all told, will cost over $7 billion for students, their families, and their schools over the next 7 years.

Now, this is not about money. This is not about balancing the budget. This is about what kind of country we're going to be and what our obligations to each other are. They have made three value choices in Congress. They say we have to balance the budget in 7 years, even if we could increase education and still balance it in 8, 9, or 10 years.

Then they say we have to give a huge tax cut of $250 billion, half of it going to upper income people like me who don't need it and don't want it. But they're determined to give it anyway, even if they take it away from you and your education and your children's future. And they say that we're going to take some of this student loan money away from the students and give it back to the banks and the middlemen, even though it raises the cost of going to college, provides more paperwork headaches for the schools, delays the loans getting to the students, and robs you of the option of repaying based on a percentage of your earnings. They say these interest groups didn't like it when they lost the money. We're cutting education, but we're going to give them some of their money back.

Now, those are value judgments. This is not just about money. Our solemn obligation is to reward people who are willing to work to make the most of their own lives, to make sure that the enthusiasm these young people have shown us today becomes mirrored in brilliant, successful, happy lives that make America a stronger place and guarantees that their children will have an even better America to grow up in. That's what this is all about.

So I challenge Congress to work with me to find common ground, to balance the budget without raising the cost of going to college to pay for a tax cut. It is not necessary, and it is not right. It is not consistent with basic American values. We can balance the budget, cut taxes for middle class people who need it to educate and raise their children, and still increase our investment in education. Let us do this the right way and advance what America really stands for. That's what this is all about.

I saw a very moving picture in the newspaper here today of the trip that President Kennedy made in 1962. He came here to honor the citizens who had built Pueblo 100 years before, and he said this: "I hope that those of us who hold positions of public responsibility in 1962 are as farseeing about the needs of the country in 1982 and 1992 as those men and women." Well, President Kennedy's generation was. They went to the Moon. They explored new frontiers of science and technology. They ensured that we would win the cold war. They advanced the cause of education and economic growth and world peace.

In this day and age, the popular thing to do would be just to go along with all of this, because the popular thing is to tell you that your Government is the cause of all your problems; all Government is bad and all tax cuts are good. I know that would be popular. But friends, almost all the money the Government spends today is on medical care for the elderly and the disabled, Social Security, the national defense, interest on the debt, and education and other investments in our future. I want to cut it some more. I want to get rid of the things we don't need. I want to balance the budget. But the popular view is not right.

Your Government is you. And we better invest in your education and your future. Twenty, thirty, forty years from now, the people who are sitting here on this great lawn will appreciate it if they know we balanced the budget and secured our financial future in a way that protected the educational future, the economic well-being, and the fundamental values of the United States of America. Let us resolve to do that and to do it together.

Thank you, and God bless you all.

NOTE: The President spoke at 2:33 p.m. on the College Center lawn. In his remarks, he referred to Joe May, president, Pueblo Community College, and student Diana Gurule.

Statement on the Decision To End Airstrikes in Bosnia
September 20, 1995

The U.N. and NATO commanders are in agreement that the Serbs have completed the required withdrawal of heavy weapons from the exclusion zone. The Sarajevo airport has been opened. U.N. and humanitarian traffic is moving along the main routes into the city. Therefore, the commanders have concluded that the NATO airstrikes can be discontinued. I welcome this development. The NATO air campaign in Bosnia was successful.

But let me also repeat what I have said before: Renewed attacks on Sarajevo or the other safe areas, or any Serb noncompliance with their other commitments, will trigger a resumption of NATO airstrikes.

The results of NATO's and the U.N.'s actions will help us achieve a peaceful settlement in

Bosnia. They show, once again, that firmness pays off. We all are proud of the American and allied air crews who conducted the NATO operation with such bravery and skill.

All parties should now turn from the battlefield to the bargaining table and complete a political settlement. Ambassador Holbrooke and his team have made additional progress since the Geneva meeting 12 days ago. The time has come to end the fighting for good and begin the task of reconciliation and reconstruction in the Balkans.

Message on the Observance of Rosh Hashana
September 20, 1995

Warm greetings to all who are celebrating Rosh Hashana, marking a new year of both promise and renewal.

On this solemn occasion each year, the powerful call of the shofar is sounded, summoning Jews around the world to a spiritual reawakening. The message of Rosh Hashana—remembrance and redemption for the new year—serves as a timeless lesson for all of us as we seek a closer relationship with God and work to find deeper meaning in our lives.

This sacred holiday is also a time for self-examination and an opportunity to celebrate God's ongoing creation. Let all who are rejoicing in this season of hope also strengthen their resolve to work for a better, brighter future.

Best wishes for a joyous Rosh Hashana and for a new year of peace.

BILL CLINTON

Remarks at a Clinton/Gore '96 Dinner in Denver, Colorado
September 20, 1995

Thank you very much, Mr. Vice President; you certainly convinced me. [*Laughter*] Folks, I hope I live long enough to see Al Gore look at this seal when he won't have to close his eye to read, "President of the United States of America." [*Applause*] Thank you. You have no idea how good a speech that was. Sunny must have waked him up down there at dinner or something because the Vice President and I were in Philadelphia 2 nights ago; I flew to Miami; he flew back to Washington. But the next night when we were speaking in Miami, he was in Miami. Now here we are in Denver. I flew to Denver last night; he flew back to Washington—[*laughter*]—and then got up this morning and flew to New Mexico and then came here. He is a bionic person. He actually has a little computer chip at the base of his spine that was about to play out. [*Laughter*] And I don't know how he got through this tonight, but I'm grateful to him for doing it. [*Laughter*]

Let me say that I am honored to be here with Wellington Webb and with Wilma. I admire his leadership, and I admire their partnership. That has a pretty high place in our family's deliberation; I like that. I've enjoyed working with Mayor Webb on many things, and we've got a lot of things to work on in the future for the benefit of the people of Denver, and I look forward to that.

I always love the time that I have to spend with Roy Romer, who, as all of you know, is a longtime friend of mine. He and Bea and Hillary and I have known each other a long time because we both were fortunate enough to serve as Governors for a long time. And I said today down in Pueblo, I want to say again—by the time I left the governorship in 1992 to become President it was the consensus of the Governors of the United States in both parties that Roy Romer was the best and most innovative Governor in the entire country.

I also want to thank all of you who sold the tickets and who raised the money and those of you who gave it and came here. Tonight I want to talk to you a little bit about—the Vice President has talked about what we have done—I want to talk about what we're going to do and what matters to our country. And I want to ask you when you leave here not to think that your job is done.

I am profoundly grateful for the support, for the work that Terry McAuliffe and Laura Hartigan and our people have done and all the people here in Colorado and the folks who have come from Arizona and other places all across America. I thank you for that. But I would remind you that this is just a beginning. Every one of you was given at your seats a little article about our administration, written by a person I've never even met, but it's pretty favorable. [*Laughter*] And you can read the other stuff every day—[*laughter*]—and a summary of the things that the Vice President just talked about. I hope you'll take it home with you. I hope you'll give it to your friends. I hope you'll use it. I hope you'll begin to speak about why this election is important, because I believe that what we have done and what it is we still have to do as a people, make this coming election one of the most important elections of this century.

I also want to say one very serious word about the Vice President. You know, all those things he said we've done he told the truth about, but what he didn't say is a lot of them would not have happened if he hadn't been the Vice President. And I think even the people who don't like me and don't agree with a lot of our policies cannot dispute that because of his role in reinventing Government, in telecommunications policy, in the environment, and in foreign policy, he is the most influential Vice President in the history of the United States of America.

Now, one of the things that wasn't on his David Letterman's list of the 10 best reasons to be Vice President that should have been is, working with Bill Clinton. I know so much more about so many things than he does, I have an interesting job, and when it goes wrong, he takes the heat. [*Laughter*] But nonetheless, it's been an incredible partnership.

First thing I want to tell you is that this is one of those sort of get-off-the-dime elections. You know how people always say they want you to be brave and courageous and they want this, that, and the other thing, but they don't, really?

[*Laughter*] You know? It's fine if you do it, but not them. Or, one of Clinton's laws of politics is, everybody is for change in general, but against it in particular.

I heard a story the other day that a friend of mine—actually, my senior Senator—told me about our neighbors in Louisiana, when Huey Long was preaching his "share the wealth" gospel in the Great Depression. And he was out in a country crossroads speaking to a bunch of farmers in their overalls. And he saw one he knew out there, and he was trying to make the point that half the people in the country were starving and out of work, people in Louisiana were in terrible shape. And he saw this old farmer, and he said, "Now, Brother Jones, if you had three Cadillacs, wouldn't you give one of them up so that we could drive these country roads and collect all these kids up and take them to school during the week and to church on Sunday?" He said, "Of course I would." He said, "Brother Jones, if you had $1 million, wouldn't you give up half of it so we could build a house for every family in this county and put a roof over their heads, give them three good meals a day?" He said, "You bet I would." He said, "And Brother Jones, if you had three hogs—" He said, "Now, wait a minute, Governor, I've got three hogs." [*Laughter*] So everybody's for change in general.

Or my favorite story—I've got to quit this, but—[*laughter*]—my favorite story is the minister who gave very boring sermons, and finally he decided he would, if he never gave another one, finally give a passionate sermon that would move his congregation to give up all their inhibitions and stand up and shout and reaffirm their faith. And he worked and worked and worked, and he was doing a brilliant job. And he got to the climax of the sermon and he says, "I want everybody who wants to go to Heaven to stand up." And the whole congregation leapt to their feet, except one old lady on the front row that hadn't missed a Sunday in 40 years. And he was crestfallen. And he said, "Miss Jones, don't you want to go to Heaven when you die?" And she leapt up, and she said, "I'm sorry, Preacher, I thought you were trying to get up a load to go right now." [*Laughter*] So we're all for this in general but not in particular.

Now, what is the point of all of this? What is the point of all this? We are living, I believe—when historians look back at this time, they will say that we are living now through a period of change so profound that its only parallel really is what happened 100 years ago when we became an industrial and urbanized society, moving out of a rural agricultural society. We are now becoming not an industrial society but a society rooted in information and technology, even in manufacturing where the permutations of the uses of information and technology are staggering, unending, and rapidly increasing all the time.

We are moving from a bipolar world of nation-states roughly organized by the cold war into a post-cold-war era where there is remarkable global economic integration but very frightening forces of disintegration all across the globe, mostly organized forces of religious or racial or ethnic bigotry that can access technology to do terrible damage, whether it's a bomb blowing up a bus in Israel or a fanatic breaking open a vial of sarin gas in a subway station in Tokyo or a disturbed young man blowing up the Federal building in Oklahoma City with a bomb, the instructions for making which you can now find over the Internet if you're plugged into one of the fanatic programs.

On balance, this is a very exciting world we are moving into, and most of the people in this room, we're going to do great. And it's the most exciting time you can imagine. But it's also a time that is full of challenge.

Whenever people have to change, as I just tried to illustrate from my little stories, there is always a sort of inbred reluctance. We can't get to where we need to go, we can't make the 21st century America's century, we can't keep the American dream alive for all our people unless we're willing to embrace new ideas and new approaches. But we also have to be faithful to our basic values.

To go back to the remarks that Governor Romer made earlier tonight, that really is what this debate in Washington is all about today. How can we change and do what we need to do and be true to our basic values: freedom and responsibility, work and family and community, the obligation to find common ground and to work together, the obligation to do some things that may be unpopular in the present because they will be right for our kids 20 and 30 years from now? How can we help families to stick together? How can we help parents to raise their children in the right way? How can we give communities the capacity to solve their own problems and seize their own opportunities? How can we both help people who are trying to help themselves but hold people accountable who are doing things that are destructive of where we all want to go? That, it seems to me, is the great question of the day.

Now, you heard what the Vice President said. Our economic policies have brought a lot of good. We didn't do it alone, but we were a good partner with the private sector. And I want us to do more. Some of you here tonight are into communications. I want us to have a telecommunications reform in this country that will unleash enormous competitive impulses and create tens of thousands of new jobs. But I don't want to do it at the expense of ordinary people; I want us to have a fair and balanced approach to this. And let me explain why.

If I had told you on the day I was inaugurated—just consider this—now, if I told you on the day I was inaugurated, 30 months from now here's what will happen: We'll have 7½ million jobs, 2½ million new homeowners, 2 million new small businesses, the largest number of new entrepreneurs than at any time in our history; we will have the largest number of new self-made millionaires in American history—hallelujah—the stock market will be at 4,700; but the wage of the guy in the middle in America will have dropped one percent, you would think, "Nah, no way, can't have happened." But that's exactly what's happened.

In other words, in the midst of what by any standard is a very strong economic recovery, the 25 percent increase in exports and all the other things the Vice President said and with the jobs being created, on balance, paying way above average wages, the median wage, the wage of the person in the middle, is still slipping.

Why is that? Because all these forces toward global integration work to press disintegration on families and communities who aren't prepared to compete and win in that world. That means if our value is to keep the American dream alive for everybody who's willing to work hard, we have to ask ourselves, now what do we have to do, not only to keep the economic recovery going but to spread its benefits to all those people that are out there doing the right thing and still can't keep up?

If I had told you 30 months ago that the crime rate would be down in this country, the murder rate would be down, the welfare rolls would be down, the food stamp rolls would be down—even some of our deeper social issues that don't go directly to Government actions—the divorce rate is down, the number of abortions in America is down, we seem to be coming back to a more traditional way of coming to grips with our problems, you would say, "That's very good." And a lot of our policies did contribute to some of that. We're collecting more child support as well. We are collecting more delinquencies on student loans. We are holding people more accountable for their actions. That's all great. How could this happen and at the same time we are facing, as the mayor and I talked about tonight, an explosion in crime among juveniles between the ages of 12 and 17? Drug use among people between the ages of 18 and 34 is down in America, but casual drug use among people between the ages of 12 and 17 is up. There are a lot of reasons for this, folks. And I may be stepping on somebody's toes tonight, but a lot of these kids are out there raising themselves. A lot of the schools are turning them out too early. And a lot of them see people their own age being manipulated in horrible ways. And as I said, this may not be popular. I don't have any comment on whether those Calvin Klein ads were legal or illegal, but those kids were my daughter's age that were in those ads, and they were outrageous. It was wrong.

And it is wrong to manipulate. It is wrong to manipulate these children, to use them for commercial benefit. It's hard enough to grow up in this world as it is without confusing people further. It's hard enough to give kids a chance to grow and to learn and to adjust to how they ought to relate to other people without their being either ignored or manipulated.

So I say to you, we ought to be happy about these good things that are happening. I am ecstatic. But we cannot lose a whole generation of our children. And if they don't happen to be in our families, and they happen to be poor and they happen to live a long way from us, we still better be concerned about them.

Yesterday when I was with Governor Romer's and my friend Lawton Chiles, the Governor of Florida, who used to be the chairman of the Senate Budget Committee and was always trying to get us to do something about the deficit, he said an interesting thing. He said America has to decide whether we are a community or a crowd. He said a crowd is just a bunch of people that just do the best they can and the strongest win and the weakest lose. And most folks just get pushed around. A community recognizes that we do better if we go up together and that we have obligations to one another and that when we change, as we are now, we have to ask ourselves all over again, what are those obligations going to be, and how will they be defined in this new age?

Now, that's what this budget debate is all about. Make no mistake about it, this is not about money; it's about values. The money is almost incidental to the decisions that are being made to affect people's lives.

But I ask you to consider this: The issue is not whether we should balance the budget. The Vice President told you the truth. We have effected a great change in the Democratic Party. People used to say, "Well, the Democrats are the party of Government and big spending." It was always overstated. The truth is that in every year of the Reagan and Bush years except one, in every year but one, the Congress spent less money than the President asked them to. A lot of the Democrats won't believe that, but it's the truth. I went back and checked myself. [*Laughter*]

We said to the Democratic Party in Congress, we said, we shouldn't be running a permanent deficit. We never had a permanent deficit in this country until 1981. Oh, yes, we ran a little deficit in the 1970's because we had all that stagflation, and it was a bad economy. But we never committed ourselves to the proposition that we ought to just spend more than we take in forever and a day until 1981. And in 12 years, we quadrupled the debt of this country. The budget of this country would be balanced today but for the interest we have to pay on the debt run up in the 12 years before I moved to Washington as your President. Now, that's the truth.

So, now we've got both parties saying, "Let's balance the budget. Hallelujah, it's the right thing to do." But how we do it in a period of great change will make all the difference. So I say to you, let's look at these things. What are our obligations to the next generation to build the American dream? What are our obligations to our parents who built this country, defeated the Depression, won World War II, set up the cold war, prevailed there, gave us the greatest period of prosperity the world had ever known? What are our obligations across the lines of generations and incomes? And how are we going to change to build the kind of economy that will permit everybody to benefit from the explosion of opportunity that is the information age?

The first thing we have to recognize is, we'll never get everybody's income up until we educate everyone. The plain, hard fact is that in the world we are moving toward, people in rich countries with low levels of education are going to be pounded. We know that. Therefore, we ought to help more kids get started right. Therefore, we ought to help our schools have smaller classes and higher standards and greater accountability and more computers and whatever else they need. Therefore, we ought to help people move from school to work. If they're not going to a 4-year college, at least give them the kind of training they need to get a good job with growing prospects. And therefore, we certainly ought to help our young people do things like national service or get Pell grants or get more affordable college loans with better repayment terms so they can go on to college and make the best of their own lives. This is huge deal.

So I say to you, we do not have to destroy the education budget of this country to balance the budget. Therefore, we shouldn't do it. Now, the congressional plan reflects a different value judgment. Their value judgment is, "We said we'd do it in 7 years, and we didn't know how. But we're going to do it in 7 years, not 8, 9, or 10, even though if we took a little longer, we could protect education. And we said we were going to give a $250 billion tax cut, and we're going to do it if we have to bust a gut doing it, even though half the money will go to people who are doing real well now who haven't asked for it and most of them don't want it, we're going to do it anyway. And if it means we have to cut education, if we have to kick kids out of Head Start, or we raise the cost of college loans or do other things that are bad for America, well, it's just too bad. We've got to have 7 years and $250 billion."

I say we ought to do what's right for the children of this country. We owe it to them. And we know, we know, that America will not be the place that we grew up in if we have another 30 years where half the people work harder every year for lower wages. Now, we know that. You don't have to be brilliant; we know that. So we ought to do it.

There are those who say that the free enterprise system is being hobbled by all these terrible rules for clean air and clean water. In the Congress this year in one House, they voted to say we couldn't enforce the Clean Air Act. It wouldn't be so good for Denver. They voted to say that we couldn't enforce the rules to keep cryptosporidium out of municipal water supplies. That's what killed all those people in Milwaukee. It wouldn't be so hot if it got in your water supply.

They voted to say for a while, until we defeated them, that we couldn't even implement the regulations for safe meat to stop more *E. coli* outbreaks like those that killed those kids in those fast food places a couple of years ago. We're still inspecting meat the way dogs do. [*Laughter*] That's the truth. We smell it and look at it. [*Laughter*] Your Government has never modernized the technology that's there available. Now we're going to do it. Our administration has worked for 2 years to do it. Mike Espy, when he was Secretary of Agriculture, started it. And they tried to delay it, because it was going to add the teeniest—I mean the teeniest—amount to the cost of a hamburger. If it keeps a kid alive, it's worth it.

Some of them have suggested we ought to close a couple of hundred national parks. You know, Hillary and Chelsea and I went to Grand Tetons and Yellowstone this summer, and we spent our time in the national parks. We got to feed the wolves that we're trying to reintroduce into Yellowstone. We got to see things that were priceless.

But you know what was unique about it? Anybody in America in a car could get in for $10. Anybody in America in a car could get in for $10. We've got some folks wanting to build a gold mine 3 miles from Yellowstone. And you know, when you mine gold or any other mineral, you have a lot of waste product, and it's acidic, and if it gets into the water, it will ruin the water quality. And up there where they want to mine it, they only have about 2 months of frost-free days a year, so you've got a lot of variation in the temperature. They want to build sort of a hard plastic bag, 70 football fields long and 6 or 7 or 8 stories high, and put it between 2 mountains and say, "Well, we're just sure nothing will happen to Yellowstone in the next 20 or 30 or 40 years."

This is the sort of mentality—this is not about money. Eighty percent of that gold will go to jewelry, not to some great scientific purpose. What's Yellowstone worth? What's our natural heritage worth? What's clean air and clean water worth?

Now, Al Gore—we have worked very hard to take some of the crazy regulations out of the EPA. Next year, the average person complying with the EPA regulations will spend 25 percent less time than they used to. If a small business person calls the EPA and asks for help now, they cannot be fined—listen to this—they cannot be fined for 6 months because they're trying to do the right thing.

We have tried to change the burdensome things. But I'm telling you, there is no value to put on the preservation of our natural heritage, and it is not necessary to balance the budget to destroy it. It will only undermine the future of America if we do that, and we must not do it.

You heard what the Vice President said about the crime bill. Some people say that we should cut spending on the crime bill—which we paid for by eliminating 100,000 Federal employees—we ought to cut spending on the crime bill, not require 100,000 new police officers, and send a block grant to local governments and hope it gets spent right.

I never thought there was a constituency for raising the crime rate until this happened. [*Laughter*] The one thing any law enforcement officer in America will tell you is if you put more police into community policing and they walk the streets or they drive around the same blocks all the time and they know their neighbors, you can actually lower the crime rate.

This is a big deal. If you told anybody 5 years ago we could lower the crime rate, most Americans would say, "Nah, not a chance," you know, "We're just going in the wrong direction, people don't have enough respect for each other. There's too much violence, too much guns, too much this, too much that." Well, it's not true.

We passed the Brady bill, and tens of thousands of people now, tens of thousands of people with criminal histories or dangerous mental health histories have not gotten guns who would have gotten it otherwise. It has worked. And those police officers, they're working. We're lowering the crime rate. You cannot convince me that we have to raise the crime rate to balance the budget. It is not true. That is a value judgment. That is a value—you're laughing, but you

know, you've got to be like Abe Lincoln, you're laughing because you're too old to cry. [*Laughter*] This is true.

And I could give you so many other examples. Ronald Reagan said the best antipoverty program put in in the last 30 years was the program the Vice President talked about, the earned-income tax credit. It's a family tax credit. And I increased it dramatically, or at least I asked the Congress to and they did, because I had a simple idea. I said, "Look, everybody wants to reform welfare, but if we're going to reform welfare, we ought to make work pay."

And most people who are parents in this country today have to work, so we ought to want people to succeed as parents and workers. Therefore, we should use the tax system to lift people out of poverty if they're working 40 hours a week and they've got kids in their home. And by the way, it's had an ancillary economic benefit because, as the Vice President said, those folks spend all the money they make, and it's helped to jump the economy; it's helped to support our economy. But it's been—basically, it wasn't a money deal, it wasn't all that much money. It was about family and work and fairness and responsibility. And it worked.

So there are people now in the Congress who say that the best way to pay for our tax cut is to cut back on the earned-income tax credit and thereby raise the taxes of the working poor. Now, I didn't think there was any constituency in America for making welfare more attractive than work again. But that would be the necessary impact of this. We don't have to do it to balance the budget, and we shouldn't. It's not about money; it's about our values.

The last thing I want to say is, there's a lot of talk about Medicare and Medicaid. I understand there was some talk in the local paper about it today. And some people say, "Now, the acid test about whether you really want to balance the budget is just how much you want to cut Medicare and Medicaid. That shows whether you're really macho on balancing the budget."

Well, I want to say this: When I became President, the Medicare Trust Fund was in trouble. Now, you hear the leaders of the Congress telling you how much trouble it's in now. It's still in trouble, but it's in 3 years less trouble than it was when I became President when they denied it and wouldn't help us. And we fixed it because we knew something had to be done about this. And something does.

Why? Because medical costs are going up faster than the rate of inflation, and we can't keep going. But I want you to understand, we can fix the Medicare Trust Fund and we can slow the rate of medical inflation without having huge increases on elderly people on Medicare—and keep in mind, three out of four of them live on less than $24,000 a year—without foreclosing 300,000 opportunities for people to be in nursing homes and over a million opportunities for people to have home health care under the Medicaid program. We can do that.

I have proposed substantial reductions in Medicare and Medicaid that don't do that, that don't run the risk of hurting your city hospitals here or closing these rural hospitals in the Plains States. We can do this if we recognize our fundamental obligation, if we say, how are we going to balance the budget in a way that promotes our values?

So I want to ask you all to do what you can to help, with all the people who represent you in Congress, without regard to their party. Tell them you want them to balance the budget. Tell them you expect them to balance the budget. We're doing it to lift this terrible burden of debt off our children and to free up money to be invested in the private economy to grow more jobs. But we cannot do it in a way that undermines the very fabric of what it means to be an American. That is the issue in the budget debate.

I just want to make two other points. One is, we've got to keep trying to find common ground. There's too much in our politics today driving people to the extremes, trying to use every issue as a wedge issue. This welfare issue—it's very important to reform welfare. You know why? Because it isn't good for the children and their parents to be trapped on it and because it undermines our country when everybody can't live up to the fullest of their own abilities. But it is not busting the bank. It's only costing you about 2 or 3 percent of all the money that the Government spends.

We need to do it because of the values involved. And therefore, it is important that we do it in a way that brings us together, not drives us apart. We shouldn't punish little babies for the mistakes of their parents. We shouldn't do anything that doesn't support the two objectives we have: We want these people to be good

parents, and we want these people to be successful in the workplace. That should be our objective. And everything about welfare reform should be seen through that prism. I believe in being tough, holding people accountable, requiring them to work if they can, but not at the expense of raising their children successfully in the right way.

Let me give you another example. This affirmative action issue, there are a lot of people who say this ought to be a big issue in the Presidential campaign because they believe that they can convince white voters who've got stagnant wages that the real reason is somebody did something for minorities or for women under affirmative action.

Well, let me tell you, I conducted a huge review of all the affirmative action programs of the United States Government. And there are some problems with some. We've already abolished one. Some more may be abolished. Several more will have to be amended. But we are still not a country where people have equal opportunities without regard to their gender or their race. And until we are, it is okay to take account of that in trying to make sure that everybody has a fair chance.

I'm against quotas. I'm against reverse discrimination. We have brought reverse discrimination suits in our administration. But I say we should not end affirmative action until we have gotten the job done, and we should not use this issue to divide the American people when we should be united over it.

I feel the same way about immigration. There are people who want to make a big political issue out of that to divide us. We have had unprecedented levels of immigration and unprecedented problems with illegal immigration in the last 10 years. I have—instead of making a political issue out of it, I appointed Barbara Jordan, the distinguished former Congresswoman from Texas, to look at the issue and say what is right for America. And we have done far more than was done in the previous years to try to limit illegal immigration, and she has recommended and I have supported a reduction in the annual quota for immigration because we went way high after the cold war to try to help people adjust to the end of the cold war. And if we're going to lift wages, if we're going to expect people on welfare to go to work in those kinds of jobs that will be available, we have to make sure that we have a decent tight labor market. And so I'm in favor of that.

But let's not forget, except for the Native Americans in this audience tonight, we all came from somewhere else. We are a nation of immigrants, and we should not use immigration to divide us. Our diversity is our strength in America, not our weakness.

And the last thing I want to say is this: I have no earthly idea what is popular or not or what will be on election day, because one of the things you have to reconcile yourself to in a period of great change is unpredictability. And we have to do things in Washington that look terribly unpopular in the moment because we think they're right for America 10 or 20 or 30 years from now.

I'll give you a mundane example. When we decided to invest the Vice President's prestige and some of the most talented staff people in this reinventing Government thing, all the political advice I got was, "This is nuts. No President has ever made a single vote on managing the Government." All I know is that they're having a terrible disaster now in the Virgin Islands and Puerto Rico. And our Emergency Management Agency used to be a disaster, but now they're down there helping people. And that was worth doing. And that's one example of what we've done.

You heard the Vice President—they told me that I had absolutely slipped my lid when I made the decision to do what we did in Haiti. Everybody said, "This is crazy. Nobody is for it. Nobody understands it." But I knew that those military dictators who were murdering people down there had promised us—they had given us their word on our soil that they would get out and let the elected President of Haiti return, and that if we didn't enforce their word to us, then the United States would not be able to be a force for peace and freedom and democracy in our own hemisphere. And nobody would respect us if we let them get away with lying to us. And what we did was right and decent, and it did not cost the life of a single American. It was the right thing to do.

I can say this in Colorado; I know what I'm talking about here. All the political advice I had was not to do the Brady bill. And once we did the Brady bill, "For goodness sake, don't ban assault weapons, because the NRA will convince all the country people with a gun that you're coming after their rifle." And that hap-

pened, folks. If you get them in a quiet room, the leaders of the Republican House will tell you they probably have a majority today because we banned assault weapons. And I knew it was bad politics. You know why? If you took a poll in Colorado, two-thirds of the people would have agreed with the Democrats to banning the assault weapons. But the people who didn't were all going to vote against them. The people that agreed with them found some other reason to vote against them.

You want to know why people never take on organized interest groups? That's why. And if you want people in public life to do it, you need to stick with them when they do. But do you know why we did it? You know why we did it? You know why we did it? Because I went to city after city after city—I sat in Philadelphia, I sat in Chicago—I'll never forget this in my life—and I talked to all these people who were running emergency rooms in Chicago telling me that the mortality rate of children with gunshot wounds was 3 times what it was 15 years ago because they have 3 times as many bullets in them when they're brought into the hospital. And I say, if it gets the Uzis out of the high schools and off the streets and give some more kids a chance, it's worth the risk to do it. But we ought to do it.

We've got another broadside today in Washington over this fight we're in to try to discourage teenage smoking. And all the experts said this is politically nuts because, while most people agree with you, those that don't will take you out, and those that do will find some other reason to oppose you. But you know what? We studied this problem for 14 months, and there were two inescapable conclusions. All previous voluntary agreements had failed. The tobacco companies knew that the product was addictive, was dangerous, and they were directing their efforts at children. And the second, and most important thing, was 3,000 kids a day start smoking and a thousand of them are going to die sooner because of it.

And if it saves a thousand kids a day, in the end who cares what the consequences are? In the 21st century that could make a huge difference to the children of America and to the kind of country we have and the kind of people we have and what we're attuned to.

Now, these are the things I want you to think about. And these are the things I want you to talk about. This election is about more than

Bill Clinton and Al Gore. It's about more than the Democrats and the Republicans. This is an election about what kind of people we are and what we're going to do.

But I want you to be fundamentally optimistic. You just remember, this is a very great country. We are the oldest democracy in the world because most of the time when the chips are down, we do the right thing. Nearly 50 years ago, when I was born in Arkansas, the per capita income of my State was barely half the national average. I was raised by my grandparents until I was 4. My grandfather had a sixth-grade education. Because of America, I became President, not because of my goodness or my ability or because I worked hard. There are people like me all over this world because this country stood for something and had the right values and gave people like me a chance.

And I am telling you, if we do the right thing now, the best days of this country are ahead of us, the best is yet to come. But it depends upon you and people like you.

So thank you for your contribution. But now go do your duty as citizens. The whole future of this country is riding on it.

God bless you. Thank you.

Note: The President spoke at 9:02 p.m. at the Marriott Center. In his remarks, he referred to Sunny Brownstein, executive committee member, Colorado Presidential Gala; Mayor Wellington E. Webb of Denver, CO, and his wife, Wilma; Governor Roy Romer of Colorado and his wife, Bea; and Terence McAuliffe, national finance chair, and Laura Hartigan, national finance director, Clinton/Gore '96.

Remarks at the Exploratorium in San Francisco, California
September 21, 1995

Thank you very much. First of all, I'd like to thank Mr. Delacôte and all the people who hosted us here. To Mayor Jordan and your outstanding California commissioner of education, Delaine Eastin, and to all of the others who are gathered here today, thank you very much for being here with us. I want to say to all the students here that the Vice President and I are delighted to see you. Normally, we would not want to be responsible for taking you out of class, but today we think maybe we have a good reason. And we hope we have a chance to shake hands with a lot of you as soon as this brief ceremony is over. I want to say to all of the executives of the information companies that we just met with how very grateful I am to you, and I'll say a few words about them in a moment.

I came here to San Francisco today to issue a challenge to America to see to it that every classroom in our country, every classroom in our country, is connected to the information superhighway. To demonstrate that this is possible, we are all here today to announce a giant step toward that future.

By the end of this school year, every school in California, 12,000 of them, will have access to the Internet and its vast world of knowledge. By the end of this school year, fully 20 percent of California's classrooms, 2,500 kindergartens, elementary, middle, and high schools, from one end of this State to the other, will be connected for computers. If that can be done in California, we can do it in the rest of America.

But the key is to have the kind of partnership that we are celebrating here. The job of connecting California schools will be undertaken by a wide alliance of private sector companies, among them, Sun Microsystems, Apple, Xerox Park, Oracle, 3Com, Silicon Graphics, Applied Materials, TCI, Cisco Systems, and others. Our administration has brought these companies together, we have set goals, but they are doing the rest. Just as the connecting of our classrooms is a model for the 21st century, so is the way we are doing it here today, with Government as a catalyst, not a blank check.

So today, I challenge business and industry and local government throughout our country to make a commitment of time and resources so that by the year 2000, every classroom in America will be connected.

Tens of millions of parents all across our Nation have watched their children play every kind of video game from Mortal Kombat and Primal Rage to Killer Instinct and Super Streetfighter. But the really important new computer game in America is learning. And we are going to put it at the disposal of every child in this country by the end of the century.

Last month, I announced a broad initiative to stop our children from being addicted to tobacco because it was bad for them. Today I hope to encourage a good habit, a lifelong commitment to learning. I want to get the children of America hooked on education through computers.

Our country was built on a simple value that we have an obligation to pass better lives and better opportunities on to the next generation. And we see them all here. Education is the way we make this promise real. Today, at the dawn of a new century, in the midst of an information and communications revolution, education depends upon computers. If we make an opportunity for every student a fact in the world of modems and megabytes, we can go a long way toward making the American dream a reality for every student, not virtual reality, reality for every student.

The facts speak for themselves. Children with access to computers learn faster and learn better. Scores on standardized tests for children taught with computers, according to "Apple Classrooms of Tomorrow," a 10-year report that is coming out in a few days, caused scores to go up by 10 to 15 percent. Children mastered basic skills in 30 percent less time than would normally have been the case. Also, they stayed in school. Absenteeism dropped from over 8 percent to under 5 percent.

I cannot emphasize how important this is at a time when we want people to stay in school and get as much education as they possibly can. Technology enriches education; it teaches our children how to learn better, as the Vice President and I saw with the young people who walked in with us and their three different exhibitions of learning, and we thank them for that today.

We must make technological literacy a standard. Preparing our children for a lifetime of computer use is now just as essential as teaching them to read and write and do math. With this effort, we are also reinforcing the core convictions that have stood us so well for so long. Computers offer a world that lives up to our highest hopes of equal opportunity for all. And

look what we need equal opportunity for all for.

Computers give us a world where people are judged not by the color of their skin or their gender or their family's income but by their minds, how well they can express themselves on those screens. If we can teach our children these values, if they can learn to respect themselves and each other, then we can be certain we'll have stronger families, stronger communities, and a stronger America in the 21st century.

I could think of no better place for us to begin than here in California, the State that leads the world in technological innovation. Until now, this leadership too often has stopped at the schoolroom door, for California ranks 45th in the Nation in the ratio of students to computers. While suburban children often have access to computers in their homes, other children in rural areas and inner cities pass their school years without coming close to the information superhighway. The longer they're kept away, the less chance they have of building good lives in a global economy.

Well, thanks to the dedicated Americans gathered here today, all that is going to change. These companies who compete vigorously every day in the marketplace have come together in the classroom. We shared with them our vision, and they shared with us their ideas, their resources, and their know-how. Every company represented here today is making a different contribution, but they're all committed to the goal of connecting California because they know the future depends upon it.

Sun Microsystems is organizing a coalition of companies and volunteering for net day, an effort to install networks in at least 2,000 schools. And the number is growing with each new company joining the effort. In the morning, volunteers will arrive at each school. By noon, they will have wired the library, the labs, the classrooms. By nightfall, those schools will have the technology they deserve.

Smart Valley, a coalition of Silicon Valley companies, has contributed $15 million to putting technology in our schools. Smart Valley has agreed to develop 500 model technology schools over the next 2 years.

America Online has offered Internet services for a year. Even those phone companies that are always going after each other on TV have joined forces in this cause. AT&T will provide

Internet access and voice mail to all California schools. Sprint will help to connect the schools. MCI will provide software for entry into the Internet and help to connect the schools. And Pacific Bell, which has led the way in linking California schools, is accelerating its efforts this school year by hooking them up to high-speed phone lines.

I want to thank them all, and I'd like to ask the leaders of these companies here to stand, and I hope the children will give them a hand, because they've done a great thing for your future. Please stand up, all of you who met with me earlier today. Thank you so much. [*Applause*]

This is an enormous effort. It will take the same spirit and tenacity that built our railroads and highways. It will take leadership and dedication of groups like the advisory council I have appointed on the information superhighway. So let us begin. Let today mark the start of our mission to connect every school in America by the year 2000. If we can connect 20 percent of the schools in the largest State in the Nation in less than a year, we can surely connect the rest of the country by the end of the decade.

In the coming days, I will announce the winners of our technology learning challenge. And over the next several weeks, I will put forward a public-private partnership plan that lays out how we can move our entire nation toward the goal of technological literacy for every young person in America.

Here are its guiding principles: modern computers in every classroom, accessible to every student from kindergarten through 12th grade; networks that connect students to other students, schools to other schools, and both to the world outside; educational software that is worthy of our children and their best aspirations; and finally, teachers with the training and the assistance they need to make the most of these new technologies.

Make no mistake: You can count on us for leadership, but the goal we have set cannot be set and cannot be achieved by Government alone. It can only be met the way these companies are doing it, with communities, businesses, governments, teachers, parents, and students all joining together, a high-tech barn-raising.

What we are doing is the equivalent of going to a dusty adobe settlement in early 19th century California and giving every child a slate and a piece of chalk to write with. It's akin to walking into a rough-hewn classroom in the Sierras of the 1860's and wiring it for electricity for the first time. It's like going to the Central Valley in the 1930's to the canvas classrooms of the Dust Bowl refugees and giving every child a book. Chalk boards, electricity, accessible books, there was a time, believe it or not, when all these were rare. Now, every one is such a familiar part of our lives that we take them for granted.

If we stay on course, we'll soon reach a day when children and their parents and their teachers will walk into a classroom filled with computers and not even give it a second thought. Let's go to work. Our future depends upon it, and these children's lives will be better for it.

Thank you very much.

NOTE: The President spoke at 10:42 a.m. in the Rotunda. In his remarks, he referred to Goéry Delacôte, Exploratorium director, and Mayor Frank Jordan of San Francisco.

Remarks at a Clinton/Gore '96 Luncheon in San Francisco
September 21, 1995

Well, Mr. Vice President, you convinced me. [*Laughter*] I think I'll just play you a tune on Clarence's saxophone and leave. [*Laughter*]

I want to thank you all so much for being here, for the support that you have given to me and to Al Gore and to our family and our administration. I wish that Hillary could be here today, but we've been gone all week, and she had to stay in Washington to receive an award a couple of days ago from the Save the Children Foundation. So we're sort of out here on our own, but—[*applause*]. I thank Dick Bloom and Walter Shorenstein and Ernest Gallo and Sean Lowe and my friend Susie Tompkins, all of you, for your leadership on this very outstanding event and all the rest of you who have done so much to help this administration to continue to do the work that we are about. I thank Reverend Cecil Williams for being here to pray over us and get us off to a good start. And I thank Clarence Clemons who, whenever I played saxophone with him, I loved it, because he was big enough and loud enough and good enough to cover all my sins. [*Laughter*] I loved that. And I thank the Glide Memorial Ensemble from your gospel choir for being here. You were wonderful today. Thank you so much. They put me in the proper frame of mind for what I want to say to you. You know, my first exposure to Reverend Williams and Glide Memorial was on Mother's Day in 1992 when I was running for office. And I got to talk about my mother. And at the time, I couldn't have known it, but I just had one more Mother's Day with her. And I never will forget the way I felt in that magnificent church with all those people coming together. They were all so different. Some were very wealthy, and some were living on the street. They were of all different backgrounds and all different dispositions toward life, but they were united there. That's what America is when we're at our best, when we're getting together and working together.

It is no secret to anyone who lives in California and who's been through all the tumultuous ups and downs of the last few years that we are living in a time of profound change. And we have to decide how we're going to respond to that change. The challenge that I issue is more complicated because it requires all of us to do something. The other prevailing vision just tells you the Government's the problem, and if you get rid of it, everything will be all right.

I understand from long experience why that's more attractive. One of Clinton's laws of politics is that everybody's for change in general, but they're against in particular. [*Laughter*] And I have one famous story that comes out of my own political heritage in the South about Huey Long during the Depression when he was going around telling everyone in Louisiana they should share the wealth because 30 percent of the people were out of work and the rest of them were poor, and he could always get elected on his share-the-wealth platform in the Depression. And once he was out on a country crossroads, and he was giving his speech. And he identified a farmer in the crowd that he knew, who he thought was absolutely certain that he could make the point he wanted to make. And he said, "I see Farmer Jones out there." He said, "Now let me ask you something. If you had three Cadillacs, wouldn't you give us one of them to go around on all these country roads and gather up the children and take them to school during the week and take them to church on the weekends?" He said, "Of course I would." He said, "And if you had $3 million, wouldn't you give us a million dollars so that we could put a roof over every family's head in this county and feed every family?" He said, "Of course I would." He said, "And if you had three hogs—" And the farmer said, "Now, wait a minute, Governor, I've got three hogs." [*Laughter*] So every one is for change in general, but when you get particular, then it's another thing altogether.

And what I want to say to you is, we have no choice. I believe when the history of this era is written, people will say that the period from about—well, the—sometime around the mid-1980's until the first decade or so of the next century was the period of greatest economic and social change, the biggest changes in the way we live and work that America has experienced in 100 years, since roughly 1895 to 1916 when we moved from being an agricultural and rural country to a more urbanized and more industrial nation.

That's the depth of the change that is going on. We're now moving into, as all of you know in California, an age dominated by information and technology, even in agriculture and industry. We're moving out of a cold war environment, where the world was largely organized among nation-states and two big camps into a global economy, where the world is often disorganized, and where all the forces are toward economic unity and global trade but political and social disintegration. In its sharpest sense, you see it manifested in racial and ethnic and religious hatred, whether it's a war in the Balkans or the horrible things in Rwanda and Burundi or a bus blowing up in Israel or sarin gas breaking open in the subway in Japan or the awful bombing of the Federal building in Oklahoma City.

It is, in short, a world that is full of possibility, the most exciting period the world has ever known and full of challenge. And it is clear that we have to bring to this new world a flexibility, an openness, a willingness to embrace new ideas and new approaches. It is also clear that we have to have a clear idea about where we want to go. My vision for this country in the 21st century is of a high opportunity nation, where we grow a lot of entrepreneurs every year and we expand our middle class and shrink our under class, where we empower individuals to make the most of their own lives and families and communities to solve their own problems and where we define ourselves in terms of what we can do together, not how we can divide one another.

The Governor of Florida was with the Vice President and me a couple of days ago, and he said—in another fast-growing, multiethnic State—he said, "We have to decide whether we are going to be a community or a crowd. A crowd is a collection of people in the same place who swarm all over each other seeking their individual interests, and the fittest survive and the others don't do very well. A community is a collection of people that band together and think they'll all do better if they all do well. And so they have obligations to one another which they recognize."

That's my vision. To get there, we've got to a have a lot of new ideas, but we have to be faithful to our fundamental values, to supporting freedom and responsibility; to helping families raise their children; to helping all people make the most of their own lives; to holding people accountable for what they do that is destructive of our common purposes; to standing up for America here at home and for our best values and our better selves around the world; to finding common ground instead of cheap, short-run, partisan gain; and to doing what is important for the long run, even if it's unpopular in the short run.

I say that because there are a lot of perplexing problems that require us to do this. And I'll just give you two. If I had told any of you the day I was inaugurated that within 30 months we would have, working with the American people, created conditions which would produce 7½ million new jobs; 2½ million new homeowners; 2 million new small businesses with entrepreneurs growing in America; businesses at three-quarter of a million a year, a rate never before achieved; the largest number of new self-made millionaires in our history; a stock market at 4,700; that all of these things would occur, but the earnings of the guy in the middle would go down one percent, you'd have a hard time believing that, wouldn't you? But that's what's happened, because in the global economy, those in wealthy countries, not just the United States but in all wealthy countries, who are not plugged in to the growth and opportunity of the future will be punished, will be rendered more insecure. And within their family lives, their community lives, their aspirations for the future, their ability to impart the American dream to their children will be impaired.

So we have to figure out how to keep these good things going but how to bring the rest of America on board. That's why this computer initiative being undertaken by these major California companies was so important. I looked at those schoolchildren that we had gathered today, from all their different backgrounds, from all walks of life; I saw the Asian children and the Hispanic children and the white children. And then I ran up to a little girl, and she said, "Mr. President, I was born in Stevens, Arkansas, and I'm living here in California with my grandmother." Stevens is a little country town full of people who go to church every Sunday and sing songs like you just heard. All this is a very different country. We've got to get everybody on board.

I'll give you another example. The Vice President talked about our crime bill. America is, believe it or not, is actually making progress in the war against crime and in the war to reassert social responsibility. In virtually every major area in this country, the crime rate is down. The murder rate is down. The welfare rolls are down as the economy improves. The food stamp rolls are down. Almost everywhere this is so. Drug use among people between the ages of 18 and 34 is down. That's the good news. Against this background, it is shocking that the rate of violent crimes committed by juveniles between 12 and 17 years of age is up. And casual drug use among people between the ages of 12 and 17 is up. This is a perplexing thing. Too many of these children are out there raising themselves. Too many of them get out of school too early with nothing else to do. Too many of them have problems that are treated only with the kind of harshness that may be appropriate for some but won't save anybody from getting in trouble in the first place.

And nobody has all the answers. So we have to be open to new ideas, rooted in old values, because we want this to be a strong country, but we've got to get these kids on board. We can't lose a whole generation of Americans. We can't have people think that life is only about power and money.

1423

Did you see the story the other day that said two-thirds of kids between—who belong to gangs who are under 18 think it's okay to shoot somebody who disrespects them? And then about a week later you had a 16-year-old in New York kill a 12-year-old because he thought he'd been disrespected. It turned out the kid had a great sense of humor and was just—made fun of everybody. It cost him his life. What about counting to 10 before you do anything? What about, "Sticks and stones will break my bones." Or the family, you know, that was subject to the hail of bullets because they lost their way in Los Angeles the other day? It's not just violence—we have come to see children as a class of people as something to be marketed. What I said yesterday in Denver—maybe I'm just getting old-fashioned, but I just came out of my shoes when I saw those teenagers depicted the way they were in those Calvin Klein ads. I thought it was wrong. I thought it was wrong.

But the main point I want to make is, we've got to realize that we're making progress on these big problems, but we have these problems underneath. So we need to keep doing what we're doing, but we need to be humble about it and recognize that we've got to have new ideas rooted in old-fashioned values. That's what this budget debate is all about. It is not fundamentally about money. Fundamentally it's about whether we're going to be a community or a crowd and what our obligations to each other are.

And I just want to mention one or two things. I favor balancing the budget. We never had a permanent deficit in our budget that was structural until 1981. We quadrupled the debt of this country in 12 years. It's so bad that the budget would be in balance today, and we'd have more money to give California for defense conversion, but the interest rate we pay on the debt run up between 1981 and the day I became President has thrown us into a deficit this year. That's the only thing putting us in deficit. And if we don't do something about it, next year interest payments on the debt will be bigger than the defense budget.

So no one has a stake in this kind of permanent spending. But the question is, how are we going to do it? We know how important education is to our future. And we know that we have programs that give young kids a chance to get off to a better start in life, that make

for smaller classes and more computers and higher standards in our public schools; that give young people who don't go to 4-year schools the chance to get good training opportunities; that offer opportunities like AmeriCorps, to work and serve your community and earn money to go to college; that provide for more scholarships for poor children and provide for better loans at lower cost for other young people to go to school.

We know that if you raise the cost of a college education, you'll drive down the enrollment. Look at California: college enrollment down 10 percent in the last 2 years in the face of a bad economy. It should have been exploding in the face of a bad economy. So I say to you, it is a violation of our solemn obligation to give people the chance to make the most of their own lives, to have a budget in the name of balance that takes children off Head Start, raises the cost of going to college, abolishes AmeriCorps, and takes the American dream away from millions of Americans. It is wrong. It is a violation of our basic values.

It is not necessary to balance the budget. We have given a balanced budget plan that increases our investment in education. You heard the Vice President talking about the environment. Hillary and Chelsea and I spent a wonderful summer vacation in Grand Teton, in Yellowstone National Park. I want you to know one thing, that any family in America that can get in an automobile can go in that national park for 10 bucks a car. That's an incredible thing. It's a priceless wonder.

There are people who think we ought to close a bunch of the parks or we ought to have no restraint on whether you can have a diamond mine next door or who actually have the idea that it is oppressive for us to try to preserve clean air, clean water, and safe food; people who tried to stop us from implementing new regulations on food safety after all those people died from *E. coli*. And believe it or not, until we developed these new standards, when I became President, we were still inspecting meat the way dogs do. [*Laughter*] You laugh about it—we were looking at it, touching it, and smelling it. [*Laughter*] And we've finished with all that. We want to put in these new regulations. People are trying to stop us. It is funny, but you're really laughing to keep from crying. It's inconceivable that anybody would say, don't do that. Cryptosporidium killed all those people in

Milwaukee—do you remember that—polluting the water supply. We don't want it to happen to San Francisco. There were people who wanted to stop us from implementing them, who want to take away from the EPA the budget they need to enforce these things.

Now, we want to reduce Government regulation, but America needs clean air, clean water, safe food, and a devotion to our natural resources. That is a part of our moral obligation to our children and our future as well.

There are those who want us to take away our commitment to put 100,000 police on the street and just send a smaller check to local governments. We were in Jacksonville, Florida, the other day—a Republican county with an African-American Democratic sheriff. Why? Because out there where people live, crime and preventing it is a bipartisan issue. Out on the streets of America there's not much of a constituency for raising the crime rate. I'm having a hard time finding anybody for it. [*Laughter*] But back in Washington there are people who are perfectly prepared to do things that will lead to an increase in the crime rate in the name of a balanced budget. But it is not necessary.

If you look at the Medicare and the Medicaid issues, we have to slow the rate of growth in these entitlement programs. They're growing faster than the rate of inflation. We have to do something about that. Our budget does it. Their budget says, "In order to get a $250 billion tax cut and a 7-year balanced budget, we'll just take $450 billion out of the health care system over the next 7 years." Well, how did you arrive at that number? Was there a study done? "No. It's how much we have to take out to have the $250 billion and a balanced budget in 7 years." Well, what about a little smaller tax cut and take another year or two to balance the budget? "No, no, no. The most important thing is 7 years and $250 billion."

Well, what about our obligation to elderly people? Three-quarters of them are living on less than $25,000 a year. How much can they pay in Medicare premiums? "It doesn't matter; we've got to do this." Well, what about the fact that inner city hospitals here in San Francisco can't operate without Medicaid funding for poor children or poor elderly people? What are all these folks with HIV going to do if—[*inaudible*]—not for Medicaid, trying to keep them alive in some dignity so they can continue to

work and be productive members of society but have some access to Medicaid? And then when they really get sick, how are they going to get the care they need without it? "It doesn't matter, we've got to have 7 years and a $250 billion tax cut."

These are choices, folks. These are ethical choices. We can balance the budget in a credible way, in a short time. We can actually have a modest tax cut directed to childrearing and education and still fulfill our fundamental obligations to one another. But this is not fundamentally about money; it's about whether we're going to be a community or a crowd, whether we're going to have common ground or division.

I think I know where you stand. What I want to tell you is, I thank you for the contribution, but the contribution won't amount to much if we don't also have the contribution of your time, your effort, your passion, your willingness to engage your fellow citizens in saying that we have to have common ground, and we can have a balanced budget and we can have a good economy and we can have a good education system, we can have it all, but only if we proceed based on our rooted values that have taken America to this point in time. That's what I want you to do from now until November of 1996.

I want to close now with two brief points that I want you to think about. America has a lot of problems to face that require us to make difficult choices. And whether we make the right decision depends as much as anything else on our attitude and on whether we're willing to do the right thing for the long run. We have to find common ground. We need to reform the welfare system, but we need to do it because people on welfare will be better off if they can raise their children and get an education and be successful workers.

It's not a lot of the budget, but it's good for our values to do that. Therefore, when we reform welfare, we should do it in a way that lifts people up, not that divides people and tries to—[*inaudible*]—ethnic background. It's no longer necessary to make a conscious effort. I say to you, I'm against quotas. I'm against reverse discrimination. We've brought lawsuits against people for practicing reverse discrimination. But when Federal law enforcement officials who happen to be African-American get discriminated against in a restaurant that's part of a national chain, that is just one single example of the fact that we have not yet succeeded in creating an environment in this country where there is no more discrimination. So let's keep making the efforts and fix the program without doing away with it. That's what I think we ought to do. I feel the same way.

Immigration—do we need to make some changes in immigration? Of course, we do. We have spent more money in California trying to stop illegal immigration and return illegal immigrants than any previous administration. Congresswoman Jordan—former Congresswoman Jordan from Texas, a very distinguished American—has made some strong recommendations on what the volume of immigration of the United States should have on an annual basis so that we can have a stable economy. But let's not forget one thing: Except for the Native Americans, all the rest of us came from somewhere else. We are a nation of immigrants. And we should be proud to be a nation of immigrants. Our gateway to the 21st century resides in the fact that we are the most diverse, successful big country in the world, and we need to keep it that way and remain committed to it.

The last point is this: I'll bet you anything that I have done at least one thing and probably a half dozen things that everybody in this room has disagreed with in the last 2½ years. And that's because a lot of our decisions that come to me are hard ones and because we are always pushing the envelope of possible change. But what I want you to know is that at least every day I am trying to do what I think is right. And I know that a lot of times it will not be good in the short run politically. There's hardly anybody that thought we were in our right mind when I sent our forces to Haiti to restore President Aristide and to remove the military dictators. But I would remind you that those people, those dictators, came to our country and promised on our ground in front of our Statue of Liberty that they would go and that democracy would be restored, that every country but one in all of Central and South America is—in the Caribbean—is a democracy. We had to do that. The United States—if people can't look to us to make sure people keep their word to us and to freedom, we would be in terrible shape. And it was the right thing to do.

I had all these people tell me that Hillary should not go to China. On both sides, they'd say, "Gosh, if she goes, it'll be like saying everything that happens over there in human rights is all right," and others who said, "If she goes

and she says what she ought to say, it will ruin our developing relationship with China." But I knew that she would be able to say what was in the heart of every American about what we believe ought to be the condition of women and young girls, not in China but in the United States, in India, in every other place in the world. And she did a great job. It was the right thing to do.

I had lots of people tell me—and they turned out to be right in the short run—that if we did what we ought to do and we passed the Brady bill and we passed the assault weapons ban and I became the first sitting President ever to publicly clash with and prevail against an organized effort by the National Rifle Association, that it would be a political disaster, because the people who disagreed with me about that would be against everybody who supported what I believed in. And the people who agreed with me would find some other reason to be against those people.

And I can tell you today that one of the reasons that my party lost the House of Representatives, perhaps the main reason, is that people in close race, after close race, after close race in rural areas were stampeded and scared into believing we were trying to take away their right to hunt and to own weapons and to protect themselves. It wasn't true, but they prevailed.

So they said, don't do it. But I kept thinking to myself, you know, sooner or later somebody's got to stand up and tell the truth. There are tens of thousands of people who could not get weapons since the Brady bill became law because of their criminal backgrounds. And if we can get a few more Uzis out of a few more high schools and off of a few more streets and stop a few more innocent kids from being shot down standing on the street corners, it is worth the consequences. We've got to stand up for what will be right 10 and 20 and 30 years from now. That's what I want to say to you. I want all of you to believe that.

The Vice President and I sat in meeting after meeting when they said, "Don't do this teenage smoking thing. Oh, everybody will tell you it's a great idea, but the tobacco companies will gut you. They will terrify all those tobacco farmers that are good, fine, honest people. They will convince them that you're trying to bankrupt them. They will mobilize people against you, and everybody in America that agrees with you will find some other reason not to be for you. Don't do it. It's a terrible mistake." They would say, "There's got to be some reason no other President ever did this." Every other President always made a deal, made an agreement, did all this. But you know what? After 14 months of study, they came back and said two things. These people have known for 30 years that what they were doing was addictive and dangerous. They are marketing to children. They are trying to sell to children. And every day 3,000 children start smoking, and 1,000 of them will die early because of it. And it just seems to me that if we can give 1,000 more kids a day a chance at a full, good American way of life, it is worth whatever the near-term political consequences are.

That is how we all have to begin to think about our future. That's the way I want you to think about our future. And I want you to go out of here just remembering with all of our difficulties, with all the problems California's been through, there's a reason we're still around here after 220 years nearly. This is a very great country. And when we remember our basic values and when we work together and when we look to the future, we always do all right.

So I just want you to remember that. You stay with us, stay with what you know is right, and the best is yet to come.

Thank you, and God bless you all.

Note: The President spoke at 12:27 p.m. in the Grand Ballroom at the Fairmont Hotel. In his remarks, he referred to luncheon cochairs Richard Blum, Walter H. Shorenstein, Ernest Gallo, Chang Lo, and Susie Tompkins.

Interview With Larry King in Culver City, California
September 21, 1995

President's Trip

Mr. King. Thank you for joining us. This is a campaign trip or a Presidential trip?

The President. Well, a little of both.

Mr. King. Why so early?

The President. Because we have to get out now and raise our funds. And if I can do it in a regular, disciplined way, then I can maintain as much time as possible for my job even next year when the election begins.

Mr. King. Is it hard to run a country and run for office?

The President. It is if you have to do it full-time. And I just determined that the best thing to do would be to try to handle the fundraising in a regular way this year and try to get it out of the way so I could spend as much time as possible being President next year and defer the campaign as long as possible.

Mr. King. Oh, so next year the campaign is going to come late to you.

The President. Well, it depends what happens. But what I'd like to do is to work as much as I can. Even on this trip we've done several official things. This morning I was up in San Francisco with 19 executives of major information firms announcing that we were going to provide computer hookups for all the schools in California over the next couple of years and challenging the rest of the country to follow the lead. And over the next few weeks, I'll be trying to put together a national plan for this sort of thing. We know we can get computers in all of the schools, and if we can get the teachers trained, have good software, we're going to do very well, indeed.

Mr. King. Was Bill Gates there?

The President. He was not, although I know him quite well, and I expect that he will be very supportive of this.

Mr. King. Because he said recently on a show we did on television that he would be very supportive.

Mr. President. Yes, he—I know him quite well, and we've talked about this extensively. But he couldn't come today. We had lots and lots of other people there. There's a great feeling that California ought to lead the way because the State is now only 45th in students—computers per student—but they have the—they're the technological leader of the world. So I'm encouraged by it. It's a very exciting thing.

1996 Election

Mr. King. All right. This is the audience's show, but let's cover some bases right up front. When are you going to announce?

The President. Don't know.

Mr. King. This is just pro forma, right?

The President. It's a pro forma thing. Everyone knows I intend to run again. And again, I would like to put it off as long as possible. I——

Mr. King. Because?

The President. Because there is so much work that needs to be done. In the next 60 days, in the working out of this budget, we're going to define in some measure what our country is going to be like for the next several years. And I just want to continue to focus on the substance of the changes we ought to make and the values we ought to put up front in protecting families and individuals and trying to bring our country together and give people a chance to make the most of their own lives and try to write that into the budget. And I think the less politics, the less partisanship we have, the better off we're going to be.

Mr. King. And Al Gore will run again, too?

The President. He will unless he decides not to. I think—you know, he's plainly the most influential and effective Vice President in the history of the country, what he's done with technology, what he's done with the environment, what he has done with reinventing the Government. We have done more than any previous administration, Republican or Democratic, to shrink the size of Government, reduce regulation, and basically make Government more entrepreneurial. And he's led that effort. And of course, he's been the leading voice in what we've done in foreign policy as well. So I'm looking forward to running with him, and I like working with him.

Mr. King. A few areas. I don't even have to ask a question, I just say a name. Colin Powell—what do you make of it?

The President. Well, as you know, I've worked with him and I like him and I think he's got a very compelling life story and he's a very appealing man. And I think his book will do very well. I have no idea what he's going to do, and I can't—I don't really have any influence over it. So what I have to do is——

Mr. King. You have to think about it, though. I mean, the polls coming out that he's doing great and——

The President. Believe it or not—well, and you would expect that. I mean, he's a very impressive man, and he's gotten a lot of very favorable publicity, much of it very well deserved. And so that's just a part of it.

But I have no control over that. What I have to do is to do the job the people gave me. And I really believe, in the world we're living in, with so much change going on and people being bombarded from all sides with so much information, people like me who are in office should not worry so much about being popular. We ought to do what we think is right for the long run and then hope—believe the election can be our friend. Because only when the election starts do people really begin to focus on it.

Public's Mistrust of Government

Mr. King. Are you, though, concerned about this apparent feeling in the country—Powell said it the other night on my television show—a plague on both the Houses, the Democrats, the Republicans. Bill Bradley is a classic example—he leaves the Senate. What's going on? Both parties seem to be in disfavor.

The President. Well, I think they're in disfavor right now because the American people have seen them fighting in the Congress and they've seen few results since the last election and because in the previous election they didn't understand what results had actually occurred. But if you look at the facts—first, I think there's a good chance that we will get a budget agreement that will both balance the budget, which both parties want, but which will preserve our fundamental obligations to our children in terms of education and technology in the future——

Mr. King. And that will change the feelings?

The President. ——and to the elderly in terms of having—reducing the rate at which Medicare and Medicaid grow but still not really hurting a lot of the older people of the country. If we get a good balanced budget, if we can get a decent welfare reform bill, if the people see the system working, then I think they will not have such negative feelings about both parties.

But I also believe, in fairness, that the Democratic Party has done a lot of things that most Americans never thought they would. I mean, the Democrats took the lead alone in reducing the deficit from $290 billion to $160 billion a year. They passed a crime bill that increased the death penalty but also invested more in prevention, that had "three strikes and you're out" but also put 100,000 police on the street. The crime rate is going down in every State in the country. The murder rate is down. The only——

Mr. King. So why are we upset?

The President. Well, because we still have troubles and because it's an unsettling time. If you look at what's happened all over the world, you've got this global economy that's going from an information society to a technology and— I mean, it's going from an industrial society to a technology and informational economy——

Mr. King. Look at all this here tonight.

The President. Yes. And you—look at all this, yes. And you've got—people are going to be faxing us; they're going to be E-mailing us; they're going to be doing all this stuff on the Internet. We don't have the cold war anymore, with nation-states organized in roughly two different camps. We've got instead a global economy. And the good news is you've got economic integration. The bad news is there's all this pressure for unsettling people's lives, whether it's people being less secure in their jobs or working harder for less or being subject to smaller fanatic groups who practice destruction like the sarin gas attack in the Tokyo subway or the Oklahoma City bombing or a bus blowing up in Israel.

So it's a time of great ferment and upheaval where there are a lot of wonderful things going on and a lot of very troubling things going on. And the United States has—our job now, all of us in positions of authority and all of our citizens, is to embrace new ideas and change to try to create a new economy in which we can grow the middle class and shrink the under class, to try to create a social policy which rewards work and family and freedom and responsibility and to try to give us a different kind of Government that's more entrepreneurial and less bureaucratic but helps people solve their own problems.

Now, this has only happened—the last time this happened to this extent was 100 years ago. This is a 100–year change period we're going through. And it is not surprising in a period like this that people would be looking around at all their options because they think there are so many balls up in the air.

Mr. King. So, therefore, come independent candidates and disfavor and people leaving politics.

The President. Yes. And not only that, if you've got—look, if you go home at night and you've got 40 channels on television, and they say, which would you rather have, three parties or two, you'd say three. And if you ask five or four, they might say five.

But I think that if this system that we have, which has made us the oldest democracy in human history, the longest lasting one, if it produces a balanced budget with a commitment to our children and our future and being decent to the seniors on Medicare and Medicaid, if it produces welfare reform that promotes work and responsibility without hurting innocent children, if it shows that it can come to grips with the fundamental challenges of the time, then it will generate more support. If it doesn't solve the problems, then it won't. It's pretty simple.

1996 Election

Mr. King. Would you welcome an independent candidate? Is that good for the mix?

The President. I think it——

Mr. King. You ran against it last time.

The President. I did. And I think it all depends. I think it depends on who the candidate is, what the person says, what the issues are. But the main——

Mr. King. What Powell would be for?

The President. Yes.

Mr. King. Could we elect a black President? Are we ready?

The President. Oh, I think the American people—I would hope the American people would judge any candidate based on his or her merits, without regard to race or gender. That's what I hope, and that's the America I've worked for all my life. If you look at my appointments, if you look at the policies I've pursued, that's the America I've worked for.

But I think—again, I will say it takes almost all the concentration I can muster every day to do the job I was hired to do. And that's what I'm going to work on.

Mr. King. But you love it.

The President. I love it. I love working every day.

Mr. King. You told me once, "My bad days are good days."

The President. Yes, because of—it is an incredible gift, with all the difficulties, to be given the opportunity to meet these challenges. And as I said, I honestly believe, when the history of this era is written people will say this was the period of the biggest change in the way we work and live in 100 years. So who could not be grateful to do that for a day, a week, a month, 4 years? If I get 8 years, that's so much the better. I'm working hard at it.

Welfare Reform

Mr. King. We're going to turn it over to the public. Are you going to sign off on this welfare bill?

The President. It depends on what it looks like. The Senate bill—I still have a few problems with the Senate bill. But it basically is much, much better. They took a lot of the extreme, kind of right-wing ideological things out of it. They've put in a bonus for moving people to work. They require people to sign personal responsibility contracts. They've put in a lot more funds for child care so people can go to work and still be good parents. These are all ideas that I have been pressing a long time. So I like it.

It really would end welfare as we know it. And I think we can make it—if we can make it a little better in conference, I'll be happy to sign it. If they make it a lot worse, they could kill it. I think it wouldn't even get back to the Senate again.

Mr. King. Right now you're leaning toward yes?

The President. Well, right now I like a lot of—the changes in the Senate bill that were made in the last 2 weeks were very good. If that's the direction the Congress is going in, we're going to have a great welfare reform proposal. But it still could get off the track. I just hope they'll keep going in that direction.

Mr. King. This is Westwood One. You're listening to Larry King with President Bill Clinton.

[*At this point, the stations took a commercial break.*]

Mr. King. Our guest is President Bill Clinton. Granada Hills, California. Hello?

Q. Hello?

Mr. King. Yes. Go right ahead.

The Environment

[*A participant asked what the administration had done to help the environment.*]

Mr. King. Did you hear that clear?

The President. Yes. What have we done in the last 4 years to help the environment?

Mr. King. We don't hear a lot about Clinton and environment?

The President. We have, first of all, faithfully advanced the cause of the Clean Air Act and the Clean Water Act. Secondly, we have done a great deal to try to promote public health in dealing with problems like the cryptosporidium problem that—that was the thing that got into the water in Milwaukee that killed all the people. We're trying to deal with that.

Mr. King. Only you would know the actual name.

The President. We've also tried to improve public health through improving the food testing, like dealing with the problems with E. coli that caused the deaths from eating the meat.

Mr. King. Would you say you've kept your promises?

The President. Oh, absolutely. I have pushed through the California Desert Protection Act here, which was the biggest single land protection act and that kind of legislation in history. We worked very hard to solve the problems of the old-growth forests in the Pacific Northwest—which the Congress has kind of messed up now—to get that out of court to protect the old-growth forests and to try at the same time to permit responsible logging. We reached an accord between the environmentalists and the farmers here in this so-called Bay Delta accord, in the farming area of California. We have worked to try to reduce the global warming and hazardous emissions through working on the clean car project with Detroit. We've supported the development of electric cars and natural gas-burning cars and other things to promote clean air.

Those are just some of the many things we've done in the environment. And in addition to that, I'm obviously carrying on a vigorous fight now to prevent this Congress from using the budget process to undermine our ability to stick up for clean air, clean water, and the other basic environmental protections of the country.

Mr. King. Sacramento with President Clinton on Westwood One. Hello?

Q. Hello. Can you hear me?

Mr. King. Yes, sure.

Education Funding

[*A participant asked about focusing on a stronger education system to provide opportunity and prevent crime, instead of spending money on building prisons.*]

Mr. King. Are we too much one way?

The President. Well, I think it is a terrible mistake to neglect education funding in favor of building prisons. On the other hand, you still have to have strong criminal justice laws. The crime rate is going down in almost every State in the country——

Mr. King. Prison's the answer?

The President. The murder rate is going down. It's not the only answer, but some people need to be sent to prison. Now, when we passed the crime bill last year, in addition to providing for "three strikes and you're out" and more funds to help States build prisons, we also gave the States and the communities of our country a good deal of money to promote prevention through education, through community activities and recreation, to give our young people something to say yes to.

And in addition to that, our administration has worked very hard to give the States and the schools of this country and the young people of this country more educational opportunities, everything from getting kids off to a better start in school, to giving the school districts money for smaller classes, more computers, higher standards, to more scholarships and national service opportunities to pay for college education, to many, many more low-cost, easier repayment college loans.

Mr. King. So it doesn't have to be either/or?

The President. It's not either/or. We have to be tough on crime, but we have to be smart about prevention and we have to continue to invest in education. You know, we've got 7½ million new jobs in this country and an economic explosion by conventional measures, but half the people are still working harder for no raise. And the reason is education. We have got to increase the skill level. So I agree with the questioner.

You know, in California the cost of education has been increased so much and the funding decreased, that enrollment here has gone down in colleges by 10 percent at a time when it ought to be exploding. So I do want to reverse that, and I do think one of my fundamental

obligations as President is to help our young people make the most of their own lives by getting a good education. And we can't sacrifice that; that is the most important thing we can invest in for the future.

1996 Election

Mr. King. Based on that, are you surprised that Governor Wilson got into the Presidential primaries?

The President. No. I have no opinion about that. Let the Republicans pick their nominees. All I'm saying is, my obligation is to try to make sure that people like that caller can make the most of their own lives, and education is perhaps the critical element of that.

Mr. King. We have an E-mail question. By the way, do you expect it to be Bob Dole? Is that logical?

The President. I don't know. One of the things I learned is that you can't predict, just as nobody predicted that much that I would be nominated and elected.

Mr. King. Correct.

The President. It's very difficult to predict. I'm going to be President, work on being President, and let them make their own decision.

NAFTA

Mr. King. E-mail question. With Mexico in an economic and social tailspin, is NAFTA dead or jeopardized?

The President. No, it's not dead. And because I think Mexico is beginning to come back, I think it is not jeopardized. I still believe it was the right thing to do.

Mr. King. Wouldn't change it?

The President. Yes. And let me tell you why. NAFTA gives us a chance to have more access to Mexican markets and not to have a permanent trade deficit with Mexico just because their wages are lower than ours. In the first year of NAFTA's existence, we had a huge surplus with Mexico and generated many thousands of jobs.

The truth is that the Mexicans expanded too quickly, borrowed too much money, and got in trouble. But now, under President Zedillo, they're slowly working their way back into a stable situation.

Over the long run, NAFTA means more opportunities for Americans to sell products that bring higher wages to our workers, it means more stability in Mexico, it means less illegal immigration, it means better partnerships in Mexico and in Canada and then throughout Latin America for the long run.

We have to make these decisions in this period of change not just on what might be good next month but on what will be good for America 10 or 20 or 30 years from now, and I'm convinced that NAFTA and the GATT world trade agreement will be very good for America over the long run.

Bosnia

Mr. King. A report just in, Mr. President, from Reuters, that all the factions in Bosnia are going to meet in New York this week. What can you tell us?

The President. We just released that information, I think, from our plane. Ambassador Holbrooke, who is handling those negotiations for me, has been working very hard. I believe that a combination of factors, including the firm resolve of our NATO allies in the United Nations in stopping the siege of Sarajevo with the air campaign, some changes on the ground there in Bosnia, and the willingness of parties to work with Mr. Holbrooke and with our partners in Europe in Russia to get a negotiated settlement, give us some hope.

Now, I want to caution everybody, this is Bosnia, and it's tough.

Mr. King. Why New York?

The President. But I feel better than I have in a long time.

Mr. King. Better getting them on turf here?

The President. Yes. Well, they're coming to New York, as I understand it, in part for the United Nations.

Mr. King. And since they're here, why not?

The President. So it is convenient for them, and it is good for us. So we'll be working—we talked for a long time today. I talked with the Secretary of State and my National Security Adviser and Mr. Holbrooke; we had an extended talk and we agreed on what the agenda was going to be, and I feel good about the process. But I want to caution the American people, this is Bosnia, we've got a long way to go.

Mr. King. Are you hands-on in this?

The President. Yes, I've been very involved in it, and I feel that we're doing the right thing and we have a chance to put an end to the misery and to limit once and for all the possibility that this could spread into a wider war that can involve our people.

Mr. King. This is the Larry King special on Westwood One, if you've just joined us, with the President of the United States.

Spokane, Washington. Hello.

Balanced Budget

[A participant asked if the President could make across-the-board cuts in Government spending to balance the budget.]

Mr. King. Let's knock everything off.

The President. Well, let me first of all say that we have been doing a version of that. When we took the deficit from $290 billion down to $160 billion in the first three budgets that I was involved with, the first time since President Truman was office that we had a three-year-in-a-row reduction of the deficit, we eliminated hundreds of programs, we cut others, and we cut domestic discretionary spending and defense spending in the aggregate and then tried to make our priorities within them.

Now what we're trying to do is to agree on a timetable for going to zero, and instead of—we're cutting categories, if you will, as you suggest. But within those categories, I still believe we ought to preserve our commitment to education, to technology, to research and development, to the things that will generate the jobs and the opportunities of the future for Americans, because that's an important value. But we are doing, in general terms, what you suggest. The reason you can't take the politics out of it is because there is so much difference between the various Members of Congress and the administration on what should and shouldn't be funded. But I do believe that what we need is an automatic mechanism to say that if in any year we miss our deficit reduction targets, then there will be some sort of across-the-board cut.

Now, that's what we did when I was a Governor, and it worked very well. So I'd like to see us make our priority decisions now over the next 60 days, and then say if, in these years, these out-years we miss it and we have a bigger deficit than we thought, then there ought to be some sort of across-the-board shaving so that we can keep faith with the American people and take that process out of politics.

Mr. King. Someone by fax wants to know where you draw the line in sand? What would you definitely veto that's a Republican proposal?

The President. Well, I have issued a lot of those things. The veto threats, if you will, or veto notices, I do not want this balanced budget process to be a pretext for destroying our ability to protect clean air and clean water. I do not want the balanced budget process to lead to massive cuts in our efforts to give our young people a chance to make the most of their own lives through education investments.

And I don't want the balanced budget to be a pretext for really hurting the elderly, the disabled, and the poorest children in this country with excessive reductions in Medicare and Medicaid just to meet the 7-year target and mostly to meet this very large tax cut that benefits the upper income people like you and me who really haven't asked for it.

Now, I think we can have a tax cut targeted to the childrearing and to education and still balance the budget in a timely fashion. But we shouldn't just jerk the rug out from under the health care of the most vulnerable people in this country.

Line-Item Veto

Mr. King. Have you asked Mr. Dole and Mr. Gingrich about the conference committee on the line-item veto?

The President. Oh, repeatedly.

Mr. King. And what do they say? We have less than a minute because I've got to get an on-time break here.

The President. They basically said that—they said they were for the line-item veto, but once I became President and they had the Congress so they were in charge of the spending, they didn't want to give me the line-item veto.

Mr. King. So you think there's no doubt it's just deliberate because of Bill Clinton? If it were a Republican President, they'd have had it done?

The President. Well, I don't even know if they'd do that. They've got the Congress, and so now they like the spending. When they were in the minority, they liked the line-item veto. I have been consistent on this. I have always believed in the line-item veto. It imposes some discipline on the process. It's not a cure-all, but it gives you much more discipline.

Mr. King. This is Larry King. We have more to come. We're going to take a break, and then when we come back, more from President Clinton, more E-mail, more faxes overseas, in the United States, phone calls, et cetera, in this

kind of historic town meeting. This in Westwood One, and you're listening to Larry King with President Bill Clinton.

[*The stations took a commercial break.*]

American Justice System

Mr. King. I guess this is from America Online. This is a question from the United Kingdom: Due to the fiasco surrounding the O.J. Simpson trial, what's its effect on the American justice system? How do you see that trial—they're going into the jury next week?

The President. Well, I think it depends in part on things that still have to happen. But I would hope neither the American people nor our friends in the United Kingdom would judge the American justice system entirely on this trial, because the facts are so unusual.

First of all, the trial was televised, which I think contributed to the circus-like atmosphere and some of the developments.

Mr. King. You're opposed to televising?

The President. Well, I just think that you run a serious risk when you do it in a high-profile trial.

Secondly, you had a very excellent defense, and you've had a lot of—in terms of—and they're famous, they're well-known, and they're able. And then you had all these extraneous elements coming in that don't normally come in a murder trial.

So I would just say, we should be hesitant to recommend sweeping changes in the American justice system based on this trial, which is unlike any one in my experience.

Mr. King. As an Attorney General in—which you were in Arkansas——

The President. In Arkansas, yes.

Mr. King. Did you ever have a televised trial?

The President. Never. And I just think—on balance—I think all criminal trials can be heavily covered in the press and then reported on by television. But I think on balance, you run the risk of having more derailments and distractions if you have televised trials.

Mr. King. To Tucson, Arizona, for President Clinton. Hello.

Japan-U.S. Relations

[*A participant asked about the recent rape of a 12-year-old girl in Japan by U.S. military personnel and what effect that would have on Japan-U.S. relations.*]

Mr. King. Yes, we've got problems there, don't we?

The President. Well, the case obviously has been very traumatic, as you would imagine. And it's a much more rare occurrence in Japan, unfortunately, than it is here——

Mr. King. Yes.

The President. ——unfortunately for us.

But I would say to you that we will first of all make it clear that the United States deeply regrets the incident, that we do not condone any misconduct or any abuse of the Japanese people. We think that anybody who violates any laws should be treated accordingly.

But we have been a good partner with Japan. And even though we've had some differences over trade matters, for example, when we had to have a real conflict over the treatment of automobiles and the auto parts, the Japanese are a great democracy and a strong ally for us, and our forces have been there now for quite a long time in genuine partnership.

So if they think there's any kind of procedures we ought to take to improve things, we obviously are open to that. But I think as long as they know that we are not turning a blind eye to this, that we are outraged, that our heart goes out to them, they know that we have been a good partner and we respect them and we'll continue to be.

Mr. King. Is Vice President Mondale doing a good job of being up front with the Japanese?

The President. Yes, he's been a terrific Ambassador. I think it's fair to say that he has exceeded the expectations even of his biggest fans in both showing the Japanese that we are deeply committed to our friendship and partnership with them and that we respect them in every way but that there must be some changes in our trading relationship. He has been very tough and very strong and, at the same time, very supportive of them. He's struck just the right balance.

First Lady's Trip to China

Mr. King. Hillary's decision to go to Beijing—her own?

The President. Well, it was a decision that we made together. I strongly felt that she ought to go. Everybody said that it was bad politics—the people who said that if she went it would be condoning their human rights record and then if she went and said it was strong, that she would upset our developing relationship with the Chinese.

But I felt that she has invested so much of her life in the welfare of women and children in our country and then around the world, and I thought that she could speak for our American values and about conditions that exist, not only in China but in other countries, even here in the United States, that are bad for the future of women and little girls—that it would be a good thing.

And I think now everyone sees that it was a wonderful thing for our country and for the cause of freedom and human rights around the world.

Equal Access to Technology

Mr. King. From America Online: I'm sitting in an office in the middle of our farmyard in the middle of North Dakota. The information highway is open to us, but the long-distance charges are much too heavy. Can we expect equal access for rural America in the future?

The President. Great question. That is one of the things that we have worked very hard on. The Vice President and I strongly feel that we've got to have equal and affordable access, whether people are isolated in rural areas or whether they are low-income people in inner-cities or whether they're small business people or people in schools and hospitals and libraries.

And so one of the things that we're looking for, for example, in this telecommunications bill is a bill that will guarantee genuine competition to bring prices down and the quality and variety of services up. Rural America actually is in a position perhaps to benefit more than any other part of America by putting America into the information superhighway because you can bring all—everything to the smallest rural hamlet in North Dakota or in North Arkansas. But equal access is a big issue. It's going to be a big issue in the telecommunications bill, and it will continue to be a big issue for us.

And I do believe the answer to your question is, I think this will be like all technology. I think the more of it there is, and the more competition there is, the lower your prices will be.

Media Ownership Restrictions

Mr. King. In that regard, this legislation might remove all ownership restrictions for radio and television, meaning we could own anything in any amount. Do you favor it?

The President. No. Now there are restrictions now on how many—what percentage of the national television stations you can own—it's at 35 percent, I think—but the present bill has no restrictions in local markets. For example, in any——

Mr. King. You could own five stations.

The President. Well, no, you could own two television stations, the radio stations, and the town newspaper.

Mr. King. You're against that.

The President. I'm against that. You might say, well, look at Los Angeles, we have so many television stations, but most places have three television stations, a handful of radio stations, and one newspaper. And I just think that's too much. So I think the local concentration provisions ought to be changed before they send the bill to me.

Media Responsibility

Mr. King. You got into criticizing Calvin Klein. Any change of heart in that regard?

The President. No. I want to emphasize this: I have no judgment about whether whatever they did violated the law. That's not the question.

The point I was trying to make—Calvin Klein are not the only people who do this—but let me just say, here's the situation in America: The crime rate's coming down, and the murder rate's coming down. Drug use by people 18 to 34 is coming down. But violent crime among people between the ages of 12 and 17 is going up, casual drug use between—about people between 12 and 17 is going up.

And these young people, in their most vulnerable years, trying to come to grips with their physical developments, with their intellectual challenges, where the world may seem bewildering to them, I just don't think they ought to be used as commercial objects. I don't think you ought to put teenagers out there selling jeans where you show their underwear. And basically, you send a message to all these kids out there that are struggling to try to come to grips with the world that what's really important is how they look in jeans and whether they can show their underwear and whether they can basically be sex objects when they're teenagers. I just think it's wrong.

And it was an emotional, visceral reaction on my part. It has nothing to do with the law. I just think it's wrong. And I think the American people are going to have to reassert some things are important—more important than commerce, and the welfare of children is one of them.

Mr. King. And speaking of nothing to do with the law, was Senator Dole also right in his criticism of what some of the things Hollywood turns out? And I know you're supported here very well—tonight there's going to be a gala with a lot of those people there.

The President. Yes, but I think that the general comments he made were correct; the specific ones I don't have a judgment about. That is, the general thrust of saying that we need more sensitivity on the part of everybody in our culture—all the cultural influences in society, not just movies and not just records but all cultural influences in terms of the welfare of our children and their future, I think that is accurate.

Now, having said that, let me remind you that this was an issue that I raised before when I was Governor in the 1992 campaign. In '93, instead of attacking Hollywood, I came to Hollywood and challenged the people here—and in television, which I think is a bigger problem just because kids watch more of it—to join with me in trying to deal with this issue. And one of the things that came out of that meeting—and I want to compliment the networks on this—I think the major networks and I believe Fox was involved with this—commissioned UCLA to do an annual study of the violent content of television programs. And UCLA recently issued their first report. So that's something positive that the networks are doing. Now we'll have to see—will they act on those reports.

Mr. King. But again, you don't want laws.

The President. No, I'm not interested in censorship. What I'm interested in is asking all of us in American society to be accountable for what we do. You can't say the first amendment makes you unaccountable. The more freedom you have, the more responsibility you have to exercise, in any area of life.

And I think these things should become open for public debate, not because we want to gag people with laws, not because we want to be unrealistic but because our children, large numbers of our children are in deep trouble, and we all ought to be trying to rescue as many of them as we can and give them a good start in life.

Mr. King. This is Westwood One. You're listening to Larry King with President Bill Clinton.

[*The stations took a commercial break.*]

Q. Hello, Mr. President. My name is Brandon Kaplan, and I'm 6 years old. And I want to know how I can become President.

Mr. King. Okay. All right. Thanks for calling, kid.

The President. Brandon, I'd say you're off to a good start just the way you handled the question. I want to compliment you for calling in and——

Mr. King. By the way, it's appropriate because the President planned on being President when he was 6.

The President. That's not so.

Mr. King. [*Inaudible*]—directly to him.

The President. It's not so, but it's not too soon for you to think about it. I think you should—I would give you just a little simple advice. Number one, I think you should devote yourself to learning as much as you can in school. Study hard. Learn as much as you can in school. Develop your mind.

Number two, I think you should try to make friends with and understand all different kinds of people because in a democracy like America, many different kinds of people make up our country and get to vote.

And number three, when you're old enough, I think you should start to work for people you believe in in elections and learn how the election system works. So I would do those things.

If you like people and you understand them, if you learn a lot in school and you develop your mind, and then you understand how the political system works, you might grow up to be President.

Mr. King. Caller from Scotland, hello.

Native Americans

[*A participant asked what the U.S. Government was doing to redress the grievances of Native Americans.*]

Mr. King. Have we redressed that grievance?

The President. Well, it's interesting that you would ask that because I have—our administration has spent a great deal of time with the Native American tribes. And we now recognize in our country a government-to-government relationship with the American Indian tribes. We

are trying to do things that recognize their integrity, that recognize their right to exist, their right to make many autonomous decisions, and that give them more support in trying to become more independent and to overcome some of the economic and other problems they have.

As a matter of fact, I invited the heads of all the American Indian tribes to the White House, and I was the first President since James Monroe in the 1820's to do that. So we are working on having the right kind of relationship with the Native Americans, and I think we're making some good progress. And I hope we won't see that progress reversed in this Congress.

[*The stations took a commercial break.*]

Medicare

Mr. King. Before we take the next call, if we can capsulize it, what's happening today with Medicare? It seems to change daily.

The President. Well, essentially, here's what's happened. I presented a balanced budget that balanced the budget in 10 years and had a smaller but still sizable tax cut than the Republican congressional cut. Mine was basically targeted to middle income people to help them raise their kids and to deduct the cost of education after high school.

They presented a 7 year balanced budget with a $250 billion tax cut and then basically made an arbitrary decision that they had to cut Medicare and Medicaid. Together, they had to reduce that spending by $450 billion over the next 7 years.

With regard to Medicare, the problem with that is if you try to reduce it that much you either have to take so much out of the hospitals and doctors and other Medicare providers that you run the risk that they won't stay in the program or can't stay afloat, or you have to excessively increase premiums and copays and other costs for seniors. And keep in mind, three-quarters of our seniors live on less than $24,000 a year.

So what I am trying to do is to find some common ground with the Republicans to say we have to bail out the Medicare Trust Fund and lengthen its life. We have to slow the rate of medical inflation, but your cuts are simply too big and will cost too much hardship for the seniors of this country or to the health care system.

Mr. King. Are they going to change them?

The President. Well, we're trying to find a way to work through to an agreement. There are lots of possibilities, and you know, the details are probably too complicated to go into here now. But that's basically the difference between us. And I'm working hard to—because Medicare is a program that has integrity, it works, but it needs to be preserved for the future.

Mr. King. May I ask if you are confident that we're going to see a compromised Medicare bill?

The President. I believe the chances are 50/50 or slightly better that we will ultimately reach a good faith agreement which balances the budget, preserves the integrity of Medicare and Medicaid, increases our investment in our children's future, and protects our environment. I think that—because those are all American values we need to all advance.

President's Trip

[*A participant asked if the President's current trip to nine cities was a Presidential trip or a campaign trip.*]

Mr. King. In other words, what is this?

The President. Oh, well, it's not hidden. I mean, at night I've been doing——

Mr. King. Campaigning. Or raising money.

The President. Yes, I've been doing fundraisers, and I've made addresses. But even the speeches I've given at my fundraisers have been reasonably nonpolitical, and then I'm mostly trying to explain to the American people what I think we are going through right now and how I think we need to embrace new ideas based on old-fashioned American values and try to come together. I am really doing my best to see the American people go beyond partisanship to reach some common ground.

Mr. King. Does the party pay, then, for part of this trip?

The President. Well, my campaign pays for all—if I do anything political, my campaign pays 100 percent of it. The taxpayers can't pay for it. They don't pay for it.

Mr. King. So even if you work 5 hours and you do politics 6 hours, politics pays?

The President. That's correct. Unless I take a separate and distinct trip that is solely for the purpose of dealing with an issue before my job. Like the other day, for example, I flew to Colorado to do a fundraiser. My campaign paid for that. I left and went to another small town that was completely an educational event, and that was a public part of my job.

[*The stations took a commercial break.*]

President's Leadership Abilities

[*A participant asked what the President had learned about leadership since his election.*]

Mr. King. What have you learned? Good question.

The President. Well, I think the most significant thing I have learned is that the President—being President and being an effective President and a good leader for our country is about more than actually what you accomplish. It's about more than the bills you pass in Congress or the executive actions you take. It's also about the words that you say and how you say them.

And I have learned that, for example, the President has to be much more careful, much more clear, much more unambiguous than, for example, a Governor can in discussing an issue. And I am much more, I think, sensitive to the impact of my words and the way the decisions are made and the way they are communicated to the American people since Washington is so far from Boulder, Colorado, and all the other places that have called in today. And I think that giving the American people the understanding that we're making the decisions based on my convictions about American values, even though I know some of my decisions, whether it's to go into Haiti or to take on the NRA over the assault weapons ban or to take on the cigarette companies on teen smoking, may be wildly unpopular in the short run—I am trying to do things that are good for the long run.

And I think I have to communicate to the American people clearly what the basic values are that animate my decisions and why I'm doing this even though it may be unpopular because I think it will be good for the country over the long run. And that's a real lesson I had to learn, because when you're Governor, being Governor is more about whether you accomplish things and what you actually do in terms of the day-to-day work. Now, that's very important for a President, but very often it's almost impossible for people even to keep up with that until the election starts. So I've learned that. And if I were to win another term, I would try constantly, because I believe we're in a period of historic change, as I said earlier, to bring the American people together around shared values and a willingness to take bold steps and embrace new ideas even if they seem to be unpopular in the moment.

1996 Election

Mr. King. By the way, you will be participating in many debates in this campaign? We can count on it.

The President. Oh, yes, you know, I—you can. I believe the President should be accountable, and I think debates are a good way to do it. So I've always been willing to do that.

Proposed Special Education Cuts

[*A mother of two special-needs children voiced her concern over proposed cuts in special education.*]

The President. Basically I would be opposed to those changes. Our education budget preserves the commitment to special-needs children. My Domestic Policy Adviser, Carol Rasco, has a child who is almost—about grown now. But he had cerebral palsy. I've known him since he was 5. And I watched him come up through our public schools and develop and flower and get to the point where he could live in his own apartment. My college roommate for 4 years adopted a special-needs child. And I watched that child grow and flower. And I think the commitment of our Nation to let every child live up to the fullest of his or her own ability is something that we should not abandon. And we do not have to abandon it to balance the budget.

Tobacco Industry

Q. Hello. How are you?

Mr. King. Fine.

The President. Fine.

[*The participant asked about the influence of the tobacco industry on future legislation.*]

The President. Well, as you know, I believe the tobacco industry has made two great mistakes in the last several years. First of all, it is now clear that at least a couple of the big companies have been aware for years that tobacco was both addictive and harmful and that it was concealed. And secondly, it is clear that many of the tobacco companies definitely market to teenagers to get more customers because they lose customers every year even though it's illegal to sell cigarettes to teenagers, I think, in every State in the country.

So I would like to see a firm effort against teen smoking. I don't really care, as I made it clear, whether the FDA does it or whether the Congress does it by law. But if the Congress does it by law, I expect them to adopt all the restrictions in substance that we have recommended.

Now, many Congressmen are very loath to take on the tobacco companies because they are very wealthy, they have massive informational capacity to communicate to smokers, they have the ability to incite, inflame, and terrify the tobacco farmers who are really good, old-fashioned American hard-working people but who can be frightened by the tobacco companies. And so they do have a lot of influence, and frankly, all my political advisers told me that it was bad politics to take on the tobacco companies and there was a reason why no other living President had ever done it and that it was dangerous.

But we had evidence that for 30 years companies had known that tobacco was addictive and dangerous and that 3,000 kids start smoking a day and 1,000 kids will have their lives ended sooner because of it. So if we can save 1,000 kids a day, that's worth a lot of political damage to me. I think it's the right thing to do, and I hope they won't have so much influence in Congress that they will try to undermine this important effort.

Mr. King. Should it come under the FDA?

The President. It should come under the FDA unless Congress is willing to write these requirements into law. Now, the FDA itself, Dr. Kessler said he didn't care about regulating tobacco. If Congress would take the things we want to do and put it into law, the FDA would lose jurisdiction. They wouldn't be able to do it on an ongoing basis, but the benefit we would get is then the move against teen smoking would begin right away whereas tobacco companies can tie us up in court for a while otherwise.

So the FDA head, Dr. Kessler, has said that he will do it either way. But he would gladly give up jurisdiction to the Congress if, but only if, the Congress would take the same tough stand that we have recommended.

Agriculture

[*A participant asked how agreements such as NAFTA or GATT would affect American agriculture.*]

Mr. King. Well, we're all over the board today.

The President. I believe on balance that both NAFTA and GATT will be a major boon to American agriculture. I was just out in California meeting with a lot of farmers there. And virtually all of them talked about how much stronger agriculture was as a result of it.

With regard to NAFTA and Mexico, some of our livestock people have been concerned about how NAFTA would play and whether it would hurt them. With the GATT agreement, which is a worldwide trade agreement, there's no question that our farmers will be better off because other countries subsidize their farmers more than we subsidize ours. So if everybody has to reduce subsidies to an equal basis, American farmers will come out way ahead because we have the best, most competitive, most productive farmers in the world.

If we can get a decent farm bill out of the Congress, that is, one that continues to reduce the cost of the farm programs but doesn't take us out of global competition and doesn't really wreck the family farm, then I think the future of agriculture is bright. In fact, I think we may have seen a bottoming out of the number of farmers. We may see the same or even a larger number of farms in the years ahead because global population would probably outstrip the ability of other countries to produce food.

So farming should do very well in America for the next 20 or 30 years if we have a good farm bill and if these trade agreements are faithfully followed by all the countries.

Unabomber

[*A participant questioned the decision to publish the Unabomber's tract in newspapers.*]

Mr. King. What did you think of what the Post and Times did?

The President. Well, first of all——

Mr. King. I might add, the FBI praised them today.

The President. Yes. Just for the reason that the caller said, I thought it took a lot of real courage on the part of the Post and Times to do what they did because our country has basically taken a very hard line in not cooperating with terrorists of any kind, not being blackmailed and not being subject to blackmail.

The FBI recommended to the Attorney General, and she recommended to the Post and Times, after careful consideration, that they publish this for two reasons. One is they really felt, based on the best psychological profile they had of the Unabomber, that he would honor his commitment and stop killing people, stop trying to kill people. And secondly, they felt that the publication of the document, if it could be widely read, might actually help Federal authorities who have been looking for this person for nearly 20 years now, to identify a range of potential suspects.

And they thought that this was not like, you know, like asking for a million dollars or asking to swap hostages or anything like that. There were no people involved. So it was for that reason, with great reluctance, that the FBI recommended, that the Attorney General recommended, and that the Times and the Post did it.

Mr. King. And you agree with it?

The President. I do agree with it under these circumstances. It is a tough call. I sympathize with the comments of the gentleman that just called in. Our basic policy is strictly to not cooperate with terrorists of any kind. But under these circumstances, this narrow case, I think the Post and the Times did the right thing. And I appreciate the risks that they took with their journalistic integrity and with their principles to try to save lives and help us to finish this case.

Colin Powell

Mr. King. One other quick fax in a closing question. Do you plan to read Colin Powell's book? You're an avid reader.

The President. You know, I was kind of hoping he'd send me an autographed copy. I haven't gotten one yet, but I was kind of hoping he would.

Mr. King. He's autographed every other one in America. He might as well send one to you. By the way, would you—I know this happened once with Mr. Gingrich in New Hampshire. Would you sit down with Colin Powell and Ross Perot and others who are critical and semi-critical——

The President. Yes.

Mr. King. I know you like—discussions in the White House.

The President. Everything, as you—Mr. McLarty, my special Counselor, pointed out at Ross Perot's convention, we have done almost everything he said ought to be done in the '92 campaign. And all of the comments that General Powell has made so far with regard to the issues of the day, including our efforts to deal with assault weapons and the Brady bill, have been supportive of our position.

Mr. King. Do you think he's a Democrat at heart?

The President. Well, I think at heart he's kind of a new Democrat. I think he probably is trying—would like to see the country take generally the direction that I've tried to advocate. But I don't know that because we've never discussed anything about domestic policy other than what he said. I've talked to him a lot about foreign policy matters——

Mr. King. ——him to be Vice President? Or was that one of many?

The President. No, no, that's true. It was one of many, but we did. He was one of the people that I thought that should be considered based on what I knew about him. And there were many that we thought about, and I thought he should be.

Mr. King. Any closing comments on this kind of thing we did here today? Could do more of it?

The President. I'd really like to do more of it. I want to thank all of the people who called, all the people who sent their faxes, all the people that used America Online, and the E-mail and everything. I thought it was great.

Mr. King. It was great having you with us.

The President. Thank you.

NOTE: The interview began at 3:30 p.m. at Westwood One Radio Studio. In his remarks, the President referred to Bill Gates, chairman of the board, Microsoft Corp.

Remarks at a Clinton/Gore '96 Dinner in Los Angeles, California
September 21, 1995

Thank you very much. Thank you. Well, Mr. Vice President, you sure convinced me. [*Laughter*] One down; 110 million to go. [*Laughter*]

I want to thank all of you so much for being here. Thank you, Tom Hanks, for introducing Al Gore. Thank you for not introducing me. [*Laughter*] Somebody's talked to Al Gore about playing Tom Hanks in an autobiography. [*Laughter*] I want to thank young Ashley Ballard. She looked so beautiful up here, and she sang so well. I wish her well. I thank the chairs and the vice chairs and the executive committee and the host committee, everybody who is responsible for this, this very wonderful night. I thank you all for being here. A lot of you come to a lot of these things, I know, and they may get old to you, but you know it's important.

But I want to say something rather unconventional tonight about this dinner. We're doing our best to finance our campaign early and in a disciplined way so that I can spend the maximum possible time doing the job the American people elected me to do in 1992, being President. And it's very important. But the most important thing you can do is to take the little article and the summary of the record and leave here and make up your mind that between now and November of 1996, you're going to take every opportunity you can to talk to the people you come in contact with about what's really at stake in this election.

And I was trying to think if there was some simple and halfway hilarious characterization I could give you about what's really at stake here. I think it's fair to say that everybody has figured out this is a time of great change, and the people who would like to see someone else be elected President have an enormous and psychological advantage because they're telling you, "All you have to do to change this country is to destroy the Federal Government. It's all their fault. You know, it's just their fault. Nothing wrong with the rest of us, it's just them, those slugs in Washington." It's interesting, because nearly all of them have been in Washington a lot longer than I have. I still have a hard time finding my way in from Andrews Air Force Base when I—[*laughter*]. But you know, "It's just them. And they're taking all of your money, and they're squandering it on welfare and immigration and they're just throwing it away and just get rid of them. But you don't have to do anything."

I have a harder burden because I think we all have to do things. I think we all have to change if we're going to make this country what it ought to be, and that's a very big burden to carry.

And I was making this little speech to my senior Senator, Dale Bumpers, a couple of months ago, who is one of the funniest people I ever heard. And he said, "Now, don't you forget about that story I told you about years ago, before you go out and try to convince people we've all got to change." I said, "What's that?" He said, "You remember, the one about Huey Long in the Depression." Those of you who are old enough to remember this know that when Huey Long was the Governor of Louisiana and later Senator and a thorn in Franklin Roosevelt's side, his whole theory was share the wealth, that if we could just share the wealth, we wouldn't have 25 percent unemployed, we wouldn't have people poor as church mice, everything would be fine. But we'd have to share the wealth. And he was giving a speech one day in a country crossroads and trying to find someone to illustrate his point. And he saw a farmer in overalls out there and he recognized him, and he said, "For example," he said, "Farmer Jones, if you had three Cadillacs, wouldn't you give up one of them so we could go around here on these country roads and take all these kids to school every day, take them to church on Sunday?" He said, "Sure I would, Governor." He said, "And if you had $3 million, wouldn't you give up $1 million just so we could put a roof over every kid's head and feed them three good meals a day?" He said, "You bet I would." He said, "And if you had three hogs—" And he said, "Now, wait a minute, Governor, I've got three hogs." [*Laughter*]

So you get the point. The problem is that in this case the hard side of the argument is the right one. I mean, I believe, I believe much more than when I became President, that when the history of this era is written, people will look back on this period and they will say this was the most profound period of change in the way Americans live and work that we had experienced in 100 years. That not since the late 1800's, in the early 1900's, when we moved from being a rural agricultural society to being a more urbanized industrial society, when we moved from being a country in splendid isolation, the one that had to assume the burdens of world leadership in World War I, not since then has there been such a change in the way Americans live and work; as we move from our industrial age into a post-industrial, information-technology-based society of which many of you are the world's most glittering embodiment; as we move from a cold war period when the world is more or less organized around functioning nation-states that are divided into two opposing camps but all more or less capable of delivering basic services and sustenance to their people, into a global economy characterized by free markets and openness and rapid movement of money and management and people and technology, where there are all kinds of pressures to have global integration and a lot of pressures of economic disintegration on individual workers and families and communities throughout the world, of a world in which we think we're moving toward peace but we still see madness everywhere. In other words, there's a lot of good and a lot that's troubling.

And we need a vision for what we want America to look like, because all the good things and all the troubling things are occurring in this great diverse cauldron we call the United States, every day. And my vision is that we ought to build an America for the 21st century that's a high-opportunity place where hard-working entrepreneurs can live out their dreams, where we grow the middle class and shrink the under class, where we do what is necessary to help individuals make the most of their own lives and help families and communities to solve their own problems and where we come together across all these lines that divide us, these income and racial and regional and religious and other lines that divide us so that the 21st century can still be an American century, so that we can be the world's force for freedom and peace and human rights and prosperity. That's my vision.

And I think to get there we have to have a lot of new ideas, but I really believe they have to be rooted in old-fashioned American values, things that sound corny like freedom and responsibility and work and family and community, seeking the common good instead of the short-term wedge issue that divides us politically and being willing to do things that are unpopular in the moment because you know that when your children are grown and look back, they'll look like the right decisions. That's what I think we have to do.

And just let me give you a couple of illustrations why. The Vice President talked about the economy, and I'm very proud of our economic record. We've had a very serious strategy, the first time the United States has had one in a long time. We wanted to reduce the deficit while increasing investment in defense conversion to help California and other places, in new technologies, and in education and training. We wanted a vast increase in trade. We wanted to be for free but also for fair trade. And we thought we could do some good economically.

But if I had told you on the day I was inaugurated President that after 30 months the following things would happen, would you have believed it? That we would have 7½ million new jobs, 2½ million new homeowners, 2 million new small businesses, a record number of self-made millionaires, the stock market would be at 4,700, but the guy in the middle had an income that dropped. It has never happened before in the history of the Republic. More than half the people are working harder for the same or lower wages. Why? Because that's the way the global economy affects us today. And if we want a future where we grow the middle class and shrink the under class, we have to figure out how to deal with that.

Or look at our social problems. You heard the Vice President say it's true. In every State in the country, the crime rate is down, the murder rate is down, believe it or not, notwithstanding the rhetoric in Washington, because the economy is better, the welfare rolls are down, and the food stamp rolls are down.

People are actually trying to hang together more; the divorce rate is down. Drug use among people between the ages of 18 and 34 is down. Sounds great. But underneath it, just like on the economy, in spite of a falling crime rate, the rate of random violence and crime by people between the ages of 12 and 17 is up, and the rate of casual drug use by children between the ages of 12 and 17 is up. So we've got to figure out what to do about that. We've got a lot of heart-wrenching publicity, and everybody was moved by that terrible encounter in which the child lost his life here just a few days ago. But we've become inured to all the children that lose their lives every day in these violence-ridden places in America.

The other day we had a study come out of the Justice Department that said that two-thirds of the gang members in America felt justified in shooting someone just because they treated them with disrespect. And within a week, blaring headlines in the East of a 16-year-old boy who shot a 12-year-old, then ran over and stood over him and emptied his gun into him because he thought the 12-year-old treated him with disrespect. It turned out the 12-year-old was the neighborhood wit who made fun of everybody and lost his life for it.

Whatever happened to "Count to 10 before you say, much less do, something"? Whatever happened to "Sticks and stones can break my bones, but words can never hurt me"? I joked to somebody in the White House the other day that if I took that approach, everybody treated me with disrespect, there would be no ammunition left in America. [*Laughter*]

It's funny, but it's not. It isn't funny. You've got a whole generation of kids out there raising themselves, getting out of school an hour or two earlier than any of us ever got out of school, no place to go, nothing to do. We have to figure out what we're going to do to help them, too, because I believe we are a community. And I think we're going up or down together. So I'm proud of the fact that the crime rate is going down. But I'm really worried about these kids because when they all get grown, if enough of them do this and the next generation of 12 to 17-year-olds keep doing what they're doing, then the strategies we have for driving the crime rate down won't work anymore. It will go up again.

In foreign policy, the Vice President litanized all the things we'd done. I'm proud of the fact there are no Russian missiles pointed at our kids for the first time since the dawn of the nuclear age. I'm proud of what we were able to do in the Middle East and Northern Ireland and Southern Africa. I'm proud of the fact that in Bosnia we may be on the verge of a breakthrough because good people now in all those factions, the Muslims, the Croatians, and the Serbs, I think, have seen it is time to make a decent peace and quit killing each other. I'm proud of that.

But don't you forget: The real threat to the world today is that in an open world where you have to have free movement of people and technology, where the Internet is full of wonderful things that we celebrated today, we all are more vulnerable to the forces of organized evil. And there are people that are preying on hatred and paranoia, rooted in religious or ethnic or racial bigotry. And they can still do bad things. They can blow up buses full of kids in Israel. They can break open vials of sarin gas in subways in Tokyo. And yes, they can find out on the Internet how to make a simple bomb that will blow up a Federal building in Oklahoma City.

So until we have a way of dealing with that, we have to celebrate our progress, but we have to realize that there have to be some changes in the way we look at ourselves and our responsibilities to get to where we want to go. I believe with all my heart that the best days of the United States are ahead of us if, but only if, we face these changes and if we do it with new ideas rooted in old-fashioned values.

Now, the big news in Washington today is the fight about the budget. The budget is more about values than it is about money. Both parties now agree we ought to balance the budget. I say, high time. We never had a structural deficit in the United States of America until 1981. Never. We quadrupled the debt of the country in the 12 years before I showed up. It's so bad that the budget would be in balance today but for the interest we pay on the debt run up in the 12 years before I became President.

We've got to quit this. Next year interest on the debt will be bigger than the defense budget. If we weren't paying so much interest on the debt, we could invest more money in California to help you overcome the big defense downsizing and what has traumatized your economy so.

So we should balance the budget. The question is how? And are we interested in balancing the budget consistent with our values? I told you what my values are. Their argument is, the people who disagree with us, is that you don't have to believe in all that, you don't have to change anything, all you've got to do is get rid of the Government. Therefore, the differences.

We ought to balance the budget, but we don't have to cut education to balance the budget. You want to know what will happen if we stop giving little kids a chance to get off to a good start in school; if the Federal Government walks

away from its responsibility to help with smaller class sizes, more computers, and higher standards; if the National Government walks away from its responsibility to give kids the opportunity to serve in national service programs, the AmeriCorps program, to earn their way to college, or get more Pell grants if they're poor or have better access to lower cost college loans like we've done? Look at California. You raised the costs of higher education. You made it less accessible. And in the teeth of a bad economy, enrollment in higher education went down here when it should have gone up. We cannot let that happen to the United States. It is not necessary to balance the budget, and it would be wrong. It would be wrong.

There ought not to be a constituency in this country for ignorance and building a second-rate economy and building a two-tiered society. And that's exactly what walking away from our responsibilities in education is.

You look at this debate over the environment—under the guise of balancing the budget, gutting the ability of the EPA to enforce the clean air law, putting on the budget all these riders, these limitations on our ability to protect our natural resources. You know, Hillary and Chelsea and I went to the West, to Wyoming, and we went to the Grand Tetons and Yellowstone National Parks this summer. We got lucky; we got to do one or two things that most people couldn't do. We got to feed the wolves in Yellowstone because we happened to be there at feeding time. But basically, everything we did there, any American family could do. They could drive a car up there and fork over 10 bucks. And all across America we have this network of parks preserving our natural heritage.

Some of these people say that in order to balance the budget we need to close half the parks or that it's okay to put a big mine right next to Yellowstone, even if we don't know how we're going to protect the water quality. Or it's okay, now that we created a California Desert Protection Act, just not to fund it and hope it will go away and die.

Now, I know that sometimes we make mistakes with the Nation's environmental laws. I thought it was kind of crazy to see that guy indicted for killing a kangaroo right on his farm. But that stuff happened for a long time before we showed up. And under Al Gore's leadership, we've actually reduced the burden of crazy regulation. But I'm telling you something, the world is not free of environmental problems. The world is not free of public health problems. People died just a couple years ago in Milwaukee because their water supply was poison. Children died just a couple of years ago in the Pacific Northwest from poison meat from *E. coli,* partly because the Government still inspects meat, as I said yesterday, believe it or not, the way dogs do. That's how your Government inspects meat. They touch it, they look at it, and they smell it. But we wanted to put in new regulations using high-technology equipment to stop *E. coli,* and there were people that actually voted not once but twice in the House of Representatives under the guise of cutting Government spending to stop us from doing that.

So, yes, let's balance the budget, but don't tell me that we should sacrifice the clean air, clean water, and natural heritage of the United States. It is the rightful, rightful legacy of every American to do it. It's wrong.

Look at the crime bill. The Vice President talked about the crime bill. We did some important things in the crime bill because people in law enforcement told us to do it. They said, "Don't spend all your money on prisons; spend some money to keep these kids out of trouble. Spend some money to give kids something to say yes to, something to believe in. And put 100,000 police out there on the street so they can help prevent crime as well as catch criminals."

I started the week in Jacksonville, Florida, on Tuesday morning with an African-American Democrat who was elected sheriff in an overwhelmingly white Republican county. Then he got elected sheriff because people thought he'd be a good sheriff and because there was no partisan constituency for crime.

Out here in the country, I can't find anybody for raising the crime rate. It's only in Washington that people say, "Well, that's what the Democrats put in the crime bill; we've got to gut the prevention money, and we've got to kill the 100,000 cops. And we'll just give the cities and the counties and the States a little less money and we'll give it to them in a block grant, and we don't care how they spend it. Now, we know what lowers the crime rate, but we're going to stop doing it anyway."

Well, I'm sorry, we ought to balance the budget, but there is no constituency and no conscience in doing things that you know will

interrupt the fight to lower the crime rate. That's one of the great triumphs of the last 5 years, America proved we could lower the crime rate. Before, people didn't think we could do it. Let's stop trying to undo it, stick with what works, and balance the budget and still do our justice to the streets of Los Angeles and the other places in the United States. It's the right thing to do.

I could give you a lot of other examples, but let me just mention one. There's a lot of talk about Medicare and Medicaid. And you've heard all this, and the numbers are so confusing it probably makes your head hurt. Let me tell you what the basic facts are. Medicare is a program that provides health care to people over 65. Part A of Medicare is hospital care; it's funded by a payroll tax. Part B is all of the other things you get on Medicare, and it's funded by general tax money and what elderly people pay out of their own pocket. Medicaid is a program that takes care of old people on low incomes and disabled people who need nursing home care or get care in their homes, and it provides medical care for all these poor children and their parents. You know, it's not fashionable to stick up for the poor anymore, but those kids are going to grow up and be part of our country. Why do you think the Los Angeles health care system's in trouble? Because they've got a lot of poor kids to care for.

Now, we need to slow the growth of both those programs. They've been growing too fast, and they're crowding out our ability to invest in education and technology and the future. Everybody knows it. And we need to make sure that the so-called Medicare Trust Fund that guarantees hospital care for the elderly is secure. And everybody knows that. But that's not what's going on. The congressional majority has made a decision that in order to balance the budget in 7 years and get $250 billion in tax cuts, they have to take $450 billion out of the health care system over the next 7 years that we thought they were going to have to spend.

Now, we should take some money out. But I'm telling you, we cannot take that much money out without charging elderly people more than they can afford—and keep in mind, three-quarters of the people in this country over 65 live on less than $24,000 a year—we cannot do that without risking closing rural hospitals and urban hospitals, and we can't do it without hurting all those poor kids. We can't do it.

So I say, of course, let's slow the growth in medical inflation. But don't say, "The most important thing is my 7-year target, my economic assumption, my $250 billion tax cut. I do not care what happens to the health care system, this is how much I am going to jerk out." That is inconsistent with our values. This is not about money. This is about our values.

Yesterday in Denver I was with the Little Sisters of the Poor, an order of Roman Catholic nuns who spend their whole life serving in ways that most of us could never even dream of doing. And they run a home there for elderly people that you could eat breakfast off of any morning. You'd be proud to have any member of your family there. And they are giving their whole lives to do this. But with all of their sacrifice, they cannot do it unless the rest of us chip in a little money through Medicaid to keep those folks there. And I don't know about you, but I'm glad they do it. And if we can balance the budget without gutting them, we ought to. And we can and we will, if I have anything to say about it.

I just want to make two more points because California is on the forefront of both these issues. The first is that our meal ticket to the future is our diversity. If we can learn to live together and work together and respect each other, that is our meal ticket to the future. In a global economy, who is better positioned than the United States to take advantage of the blizzard of interconnections that will be the best of tomorrow? Nobody.

So I say to you, when we have issues that are troubling, we need to solve them in ways that bring us together, not use them as wedges used to drive us apart. I'll just give you three: Welfare reform. I led the fight to reform welfare. While the Congress has been fighting for 3 years, we've given 70 percent of the States permission to get rid of Federal rules to figure out how to move people from welfare to work. I did it not because it's costing you a lot of money. The welfare budget is a tiny part of the Federal budget. I did it because it's inconsistent with American values for people to be trapped in dependency when they want to be free, because most parents in this country have to work and people on welfare should be able to work, but they ought to be able to be good parents as well. So I want to change the welfare system, and I don't mind being very tough on requiring people to work. But you have to give

them education and training and you have to give them child care, and we ought to collect the child support enforcement that people owe them as well. That's what I believe.

So we should do this together. We shouldn't look for some way to put people down; we should look for ways to lift people up. You look at the affirmative action issue, this affirmative action issue. There are problems with affirmative action. We have to fix some. We've already fixed some. But let me tell you, I have hired hundreds of people in my life. I have worked with all kinds of people. I've been in all kinds of different circumstances. And I believe with all my heart we have not yet reached the point in our country when we are totally oblivious to our gender and racial differences. And as long as we are not, as long as we see troubling reminders of what may lurk in the hearts of people that they never say, I think it is appropriate not for Government to practice reverse discrimination, not for Government to have quotas, not for Government to guarantee anything to somebody who is unqualified to receive it but for the Government to say you should be conscious, you should be aware when you make decisions of the abilities and the potential of all the people in the community without regard to their race or gender. So I say fix affirmative action, but don't throw it away for a short-term political gain until we have solved this problem.

And I feel the same way, as all of you know, because of what I said 2 years ago about immigration. I knew we had immigration problems, and I had never dealt with them before 2½ years ago. So I asked former Congresswoman Barbara Jordan to set up a commission to deal with immigration in a forthright, humane, hardheaded way to just try to talk sense and not to use it for political benefits. And we have done more than any previous administration to try to close the borders and send illegal immigrants back. We have recommended a disciplined reduction in the annual quota of immigration until we get our own low-skill workers back in the work force and until we can manage our own economy better. But let's not forget something: Except for the Native Americans that are here tonight—and I thank them for being here—everybody else here came from somewhere else, and we should never, ever forget that.

The last thing I want to tell you is this: I'll bet you everybody here has disagreed with five or six things I've done in the last 2½ years. But one thing I have learned is that when things are really changing fast, you can absolutely not calculate what is the popular thing to do because what's popular today may look terrible 6 days from now. And what I try to do is figure out what this is going to look like when my daughter's my age. What's the 21st century going to be like for the United States? And so I do a lot of things that aren't popular. But when we do things like that, if you agree that we should keep leading, then you have to step into the breach as well and be heard.

All the political advice I got was, "Don't you be the first President in American history to take on the NRA over the Brady bill and assault weapons. Don't do it, because what will happen is they will gut you, and they will gut your Congressmen who stand with you. And all the people who agree with you will find some other reason to vote against them." And sure enough, last fall in '94, that's what happened.

I can tell you today that the Democrats would still be in the majority in the House of Representatives if they had not fought to ban assault weapons and for the Brady bill. I don't care what anybody else said. I've looked at those votes district by district, and I know what I'm talking about. That's why they lost. There were other reasons for the gain, the promise of the tax cut and all that; the Christian Coalition's great outpouring, they had a lot to do with it. But in the close races, the NRA took them down, the people that stood up for taking Uzis off the street and Uzis out of the schools, for making people check to see if they had a criminal or a mental health background. And there are thousands and thousands of people who now have not gotten guns because the Brady bill passed. There are people who are alive. There are children who are going to live because of the assault weapons ban. It was the right thing to do. And you ought to stand up for those people who did it. It was the right thing to do.

Same thing happened with Haiti. People said, "You've got to be out of your mind." Al Gore and I were 50 percent of all the people in Washington, DC, that thought it was a good idea to send our forces to Haiti. [*Laughter*] They said, "You'll never be able to explain this to the American people; everybody knows our national security is not at stake." You know what we said? Those military dictators came to the United States, to New York City, stood in the shadow of the Statue of Liberty, and promised to leave and let President Aristide come back.

If the United States can be lied to on its own soil in the shadow of the Statue of Liberty when we say we want every country in our hemisphere to be a democracy, how can we turn away the hoards of people who are risking their lives and dying in the seas from Haiti. How can we ever say we are the force for freedom and democracy? And so we did it. And we did it without firing a shot. And we were right. But it wasn't popular.

When Hillary was trying to decide about going to China, everybody said, "This is a really dumb idea. If you go, the people who are against their human rights practices will say you have legitimized them just by going. And then if you say what you need to do, the people that want to have stronger trade relationship will say you are wrecking our relationship." But you know what we decided? All over the world the kind of future we have depends in large measure on how we treat women and their little children, especially their little female children. Do you know—[*applause*]—just for an example, in all of Asia today, there are now 77 million more boys than there are girls, because little girl children are still being killed because they're not supposed to be worth anything?

I can give you a lot of other examples. And so we decided that she ought to go because she could stick up for the women and the children and especially the girl children of this world, and she could talk not only about China and not singling China out but about what's happening in other countries including our own country that isn't right. And now it looks like a great decision. But the reason it was is because it was the right thing to do, not because it was the political thing to do.

I could give you a lot of others, but I'll give you one more, because the Vice President had a lot to do with this. We were trying to decide whether to go forward with our campaign to try to stamp out, or at least dramatically discourage, illegal smoking by teenagers. And all the political advice was, "Wait til the next election is over. These tobacco companies never lose in court; they never lose anywhere. They got a double ton of money, and they will gut you, not because they will get on television and run ads saying we think kids ought to smoke but because they have mailing lists, they can write people, they can inflame people. There are all these wonderful, wonderful Americans who grow tobacco like their families have been growing it for 100 and 200 years. But they can terrify them, and they will give them all kinds of propaganda about how you're going to drive them into the dirt, and those people will become a political force against you. And all the Americans who agree with you, they'll find some other reason to be against you. That's why people don't ever take on organized interests. So don't you be—you've already been the first President to take on the NRA; for goodness sakes, don't take on the tobacco companies, everybody else gave that one a pass."

But we knew 2 things after 14 months of study. We knew, number one, that for 30 years some of these companies have known that tobacco was addictive and dangerous and that they were consciously marketing it to children. And the second thing we knew was that 3,000 kids a day begin to smoke, and 1,000 of them will end their lives early.

So finally, we decided, how in God's name can we walk away from this? A thousand kids a day living a better, fuller, longer life is worth any amount of political sacrifice. It is the right thing to do.

There's so many other things like this that I could tell you about, but you get the idea. This is a great country. I do not want you to be upset about what you think is going on in Washington; I want you to be determined to do what you think is best for America, consistent with our values.

This debate was inevitable, as inevitable as the sun coming up in the morning, because of the depth of the changes that are going on. Because we're changing the way we work, we're changing the way we live, we have to change the way we do government. This was inevitable.

Don't you forget—we've been around for nearly 220 years now because most of the time when the chips are down, the American people do the right thing. And we come out pretty good.

I was born nearly 50 years ago to a widowed mother in a State where the per capita income was barely half the national average. My granddaddy raised me til I was 4. He had a sixth grade education. And I got to be President, not because I was so smart or so good or because I worked like crazy—because there are hundreds of people like me in this country and hundreds of people all over the world. America made that possible. America said, no matter who you are, here's a chance at an education. No matter who you are, here's a chance at a job. No matter who you are, you can run for office. No matter who you are, you can go anywhere and stand up for what you believe in. This is a very great country, and every one of you should be happy and proud that you happen to be alive at this period of profound change. If we do our job, the best is yet to come.

Thank you, and God bless you all.

NOTE: The President spoke at 8:32 p.m. at the Century Plaza Hotel. In his remarks, he referred to actor Tom Hanks and Ashley Ballard, who sang the national anthem.

Message to the Congress Transmitting Transportation Department Reports
September 21, 1995

To the Congress of the United States:

I transmit herewith the 1994 calendar year reports as prepared by the Department of Transportation on activities under the Highway Safety Act, the National Traffic and Motor Vehicle Safety Act of 1966, and the Motor Vehicle

Information and Cost Savings Act of 1972, as amended.

WILLIAM J. CLINTON

The White House,
September 21, 1995.

Remarks on the Los Angeles County Fiscal Relief Plan and an Exchange With Reporters in Santa Monica, California
September 22, 1995

The President. Good morning. I am very pleased to announce today that a fiscal relief plan for Los Angeles County has been developed by a team of officials from the county, State of California, and the Federal Government. Overall, the package will provide $364 million in additional relief in resources to the county. It will allow the county to avoid closing any of its hospitals and to keep open a majority of the clinics it had planned to close.

The plan is structured around a 5-year Federal waiver that will allow the county to restructure its health care system in a rational and planned way and to move from its current reliance on hospital care to a system that emphasizes more preventive and primary care.

Reaching this unique agreement was possible because we had tremendous cooperation from both local and State officials. The development of this plan is an excellent example of intergovernmental cooperation at the local, State, and Federal levels. I want to thank the members of the county board of supervisors for their leadership during this difficult time, including the board chair, Gloria Molina, Yvonne Burke, Zev Yaroslavsky, Deane Dana, and Michael Antonovich. I also want to thank Mr. Margolin for the work that he did on this project. I know that they are committed to a meaningful restructuring of the current health care system, while continuing to ensure that the communities of Los Angeles County have access to critical health care services.

I also want to say that this agreement was reached after critical consultations with the Service Employees International Union. This agreement is an important breakthrough in continuing to provide critical care as well as saving thousands of health care jobs. As part of the implementation process, we're committed to working with the SEIU to help to protect the jobs and benefits of health care workers to ensure the provision of high-quality care. I also want to thank the State officials who've been extremely helpful in developing this solution. The State will be instrumental in working with the county to implement the plan.

I should mention that this plan underlines why we cannot afford the so-called Medicaid reforms that pulled billions of dollars out of critical health care facilities without any idea of what the consequences will be. Most of all, let me say that I am very pleased that the patients, the communities, and the workers and all of their families will not have to suffer the impacts of a crisis shutdown of county hospitals and clinics and that the county will continue to be able to maintain an appropriate safety net for those who depend upon these facilities for their health care.

Let me again thank everyone for their work on this and say that I am very pleased that we were able to be of assistance. I'm glad to be here with the county board of supervisors and with Mayor Riordan. And I'd like to now ask the chair, Gloria Molina, to come forward for whatever remarks she would like to make.

[At this point, members of the county board of supervisors made brief remarks.]

The President. If I might, just listening to the county supervisors talk, it occurred to me that, for the benefit of the people in this county and in this State who are interested in this problem, I ought to make two general points. First of all, this is an example of the kind of teamwork we need to solve the transitional problems, the many kinds of transitional problems that are plaguing the United States today as we move into a different kind of economy and a different kind of world.

They don't necessarily have a partisan tinge. They really require people to be creative, to be willing to embrace new ideas, to remember what the fundamental mission is, and to achieve that mission. And I want to applaud the people here who have spoken today for the way they work together across party lines. We need to do more of that in Washington right now in this budget process.

The second thing I want to emphasize to the people of this county—and this is true, by the way, to a greater or lesser extent in every State in this country and in very rural areas as well as more urbanized areas—you heard one of the commissioners say that one in three people in this county is uninsured. Well, one in three people in this county is not unemployed. Most uninsured people today are working people. And the reason the Medicaid program is so important is that it provides places like Los Angeles County with that extra amount of assistance, even though it's targeted to the poor, that helps them to keep their public health clinics and public hospitals open to deal with what is an increasingly difficult problem in America, which is working families without health insurance.

I tried to fix that last year, and my proposed solution didn't find favor. But if we're not going to have a comprehensive solution to it, then the only other alternative, if you believe as I do that you can't simply turn working families away when their children are sick or when the breadwinners are sick, the only alternative is to place greater emphasis on public health clinics and hospitals that can help with primary and preventive care as well as with people when they get very ill.

So this is a very important model, this restructuring that will take place over the next few years. And it won't be easy for them. But what they're trying to do is absolutely critical, given the fact that another million Americans every year who are in working families are without insurance. It would have been criminal to permit all of these clinics to close and all this crisis to develop, not just because of the very poorest people in this county but because of the working families on very limited incomes who don't have insurance.

And that's a national issue; it's not a Los Angeles County issue. And if it can be solved here with the restructuring, a lot of people all over America will be learning a lot from what you're doing, and the working families of our country will be better served by it.

Thank you very much.

Debt Limit Legislation

Q. Mr. President, what does that say about the spirit of cooperation and problem solving: Speaker Gingrich says that he won't bring a debt limit bill to the floor of the House unless you agree to the Republican budget tax cuts.

The President. Well, a lot of things have been said, you know. All I can say is that it's important for me to try to keep the rhetoric down and to keep calm. But I will say this: The United States has never failed to recognize its obligations to pay its debts. And the failure to raise the debt limit has nothing to do with holding the deficit down or balancing the budget. It is basically saying you're going to be a piker and welsh on your debts, and the United States has never done that. And it would be irresponsible to do that.

And let me emphasize that if the United States were to refuse to raise its debt limit, the real consequence to the Speaker and to the Republican majority in Congress would be to dramatically raise the risk that their own budget plan would fail because what would happen immediately is people would start to charge us more interest on our debt.

And most of the leaders in the Congress were around in the 12 years that we quadrupled the national debt. I wasn't there. But I can tell you today that our budget would be balanced but for the debts run up in the 12 years before I showed up in Washington. And if we don't— if we didn't raise the debt limit, the only practical impact would be, since we eventually would have to pay our debts, is that interest rates would go up, more and more of our budget would go to interest on the debt. It could raise our interest rates for a decade, and it could wreck their own budget plan.

So I just don't believe in the end that they will do that. There's going to be a lot of verbal back-and-forth between now and then, but it would be so irresponsible and it would undermine their own objectives, that I can't believe that it would happen.

The United States is a good citizen. We don't welsh on our debts, and we're not about to start doing it now.

Thank you.

NOTE: The President spoke at 9:20 a.m. at the Santa Monica Airport. In his remarks, the President referred to Burt Margolin, legislative strategist, Los Angeles County.

Remarks to the Community in Santa Ana, California
September 22, 1995

Thank you very much, Jason, for the introduction. I am delighted to be here with all the officers and members of the Boys and Girls Clubs; Mayor Pulido; to the president of the Police Officers Association, Don Blankenship. Ken Stevens, thank you for this wonderful gift on behalf of Taco Bell for the future of the United States of America. Aren't we proud of Taco Bell for doing this? Isn't it a great thing? I was glad to be standing there with—is it on now? Can you hear me? I was glad to be standing there receiving that check with Jason Reese and Karina Martinez and Shaquille O'Neal. And I thought, the young people make me feel so big, and he makes me feel so small. I can see the headlines tomorrow: "Shaq Visits Santa Ana; President Clinton Also Shows Up." [*Laughter*] I want to thank the police officers who are here, Chief Walters and Sergeant Follo, for what you said and all the students from the Santa Ana Unified School District high schools and the Pio Pico Elementary School and the Lowell Elementary School.

I am honored to be here, first and most importantly, to support this teen supreme alliance between the Boys and Girls Clubs and Taco Bell to fight youth violence and to give our young people a better start in life. And I really want to thank Shaquille O'Neal for getting on an airplane and coming all the way out here to be with us today and most importantly for wearing his magnificent talent and his great success in a humble and straightforward way that's a good role model for all the young people of this country and for the message he gave you today.

You know, when I was the Governor of Arkansas and Shaquille O'Neal was in college playing at LSU, our schools used to play all the time. And I woke up this morning thinking about a particular basketball game, and I thought, he's going to make me relive that game all over again. And right before we came out, I was in such a good humor. And he put his hand on my shoulder, and I looked at him; he said, "You remember the time we beat Arkansas' brains out and I scored 58 points?" [*Laughter*] And it was worth losing that game to see him giving the message to you today.

You listen to what Shaquille O'Neal said and you won't go wrong with your lives, and you'll have a good life. And that's really what we're all here about.

I want to say to all you young people, every day when I go to work as President I try to spend my time and make decisions thinking about your future. I try to think about what America will be like when you are out of high school, when you are grown, when you have children of your own here at the school where you are today. And I know that we need to do a lot of things in our country to give you a strong economy and the opportunity to make a good living. We desperately, all of us, owe you the opportunity to get a good education. And every young person in this country should be able to go to a good school and then should be able to go on to college, and money should not be an object. And I am working hard for that.

But one of the things that has burdened me the most—is it on again? There it is. One of the things that has burdened me the most is the knowledge that unless we can give our young people a safe and secure childhood free of crime and violence, a lot of people will never have the life they ought to have. And when I went to Washington 2½ years ago, I made a promise to myself that I would do everything I can to put more police on our streets, to get more guns and drugs off our streets, to give young people a chance to be in positive situations and out of gangs.

And what we are really here celebrating today is the kind of partnership that makes that possible, because the initiatives of the mayor and the Boys and Girls Clubs here, the initiatives of Taco Bell, the work of citizen leaders like Shaq, and the work of the police officers here all mean that you can have a safer and more secure future.

I did work hard to make sure these police officers behind me would be in this community and communities like it throughout the country. In the last year, under our crime bill, we have put out 25,000 more police officers in the United States of America to be on the streets protecting our children, preventing crime as well as catching criminals. These people are now working your neighborhoods, patrolling by foot or bicycle, and some are even on electric carts. In some of the small towns in the more rural Western parts of our country, they ride horses. But—is it on again? Is it on now? Now? Well, some of you can hear, and the others should pretend to hear. [*Laughter*] Now is it on? Half of you are saying yes; half are saying no. Now? [*Applause*]

These police officers are trying to do something that's very important. They're trying not only to catch criminals, they're trying to prevent crime by being with people in the neighborhoods, in the schools, on the streets, where they live. After all, our objective ultimately is to prevent crime, to keep bad things from happening to our children and their parents. And that's what they represent.

I also think it's important that we try to do some other things to make people safer. That's why last year we banned 19 deadly assault weapons from our streets. We don't need Uzis in our schools and on our streets, threatening our children. That's why we passed the "three strikes and you're out" law, because after people commit three serious violent crimes, they shouldn't be back on the streets to terrorize our children and their future. That's why we passed the Brady law which requires people to be checked for their criminal backgrounds before they get a handgun. And last year, last year alone, over 40,000 people who had committed serious crimes were prevented from purchasing handguns. And a lot of little children are alive as a result of that.

What I want to say to all of you today real simply is that we can't do this alone. And we can't do it solely with law enforcement. We have to have people who are working with our kids, making the speech that Shaq made to you today, telling young people they can have a good life, telling them they have to do right and avoid doing the wrong thing, telling them they ought to be in good organizations and out of gangs that want to hurt people, where people define how important they are by how many people they can hurt and how tough they can be.

You know, one of the most troubling things to me today—and I want to say this especially to the high school students who are here—the mayor said something that was absolutely true, that the crime rate is going down here. Four or 5 years ago, most Americans didn't believe

we could drive the crime rate down. The crime rate is down in every State. The crime rate is down in almost every city. But arbitrary crime by teenagers is still going up. And I think it's because there are too many young people who haven't been given the opportunity to be part of a positive environment, where they can have something to say yes to as well as something to say no to, where they know they're going to have a good future, where they're told that they matter, where they're important to everybody and they know that they matter and they can have a good life and they can live out their dreams. Nothing, nothing that we do can take the place of what you can do here in this community to reach out and touch these young people one by one by one, to tell them that they matter, to tell them that they are a gift of God and they can become anything they are willing to work hard enough to be. That is your job, and I'm proud that you're doing it.

Now meanwhile, those of us in Washington have a job, and that is to keep doing what we know works. One of the most troubling things to me about the debate in Washington today is that Congress is actually considering abolishing the program that put these police officers behind me, cutting back on the funding and sending a check to the cities and basically saying, "You do what you want with this money." The last time this was tried, some local governments used the money to buy airplanes, accountants, and tanks. What we want to do is to keep putting people like these fine men and women in uniform, who are behind me. We need to have more of these police officers. We don't want more young people being shot. We want more people being saved.

So I say to you, I say to you, today the American people are more threatened by what can happen on their own streets than by some country going to war with us. If the United States Congress were going to reduce the national defense of this country to the point where you felt insecure and dangerous, people would be outraged. Well, let me tell you, the gangs of this country, the armed criminals of this country, the people who are willing to shoot people on the street for no other reason than they happen to be there, they represent a threat to the security of America. And it is wrong, wrong, wrong to turn away from our obligation to protect our children with these police officers.

If all of you here will keep doing your job, if you will keep the light in the eyes of these children, if you will convince teenagers in their most difficult years that there is a country that cares about them and there is a good future for them out there, and if we do our job in Washington to keep giving communities the tools they need to bring the crime rate down, we can make the American dream live for all these young people into the next century. And 20 or 30 years from now, they can be here making their speeches, looking at another generation of young people, proud and secure in the fact that they had the chance to live out their dreams.

We have to do something about gangs and violence. We have to do something about our children being given up too young, too easily. And we know what to do. We have to do what the Girls and Boys Clubs do. We have to do what this city is doing. We have to do what

Taco Bell is doing. And we've got to keep the United States Government on the side of our children, their future, and safety in the streets with this police program. Help us do that, and we'll try to help you.

God bless you all, and thank you for having me here.

NOTE: The President spoke at 11:18 a.m. at the Boys & Girls Club of Santa Ana. In his remarks, he referred to Jason Reese, Boys & Girls Clubs of America 1995 national youth of the year; Mayor Miguel Pulido of Santa Ana; Kenneth T. Stevens, vice chairman, Taco Bell Foundation and member, national board of governors, Boys & Girls Clubs of America; Karina Martinez, Boys & Girls Club of Santa Ana 1995 local youth of the year; Paul Walters, chief, and John Follo, sergeant, Santa Ana Police Department; and basketball player Shaquille O'Neal.

Remarks at the O'Farrell Community School in San Diego, California
September 22, 1995

Thank you so much. Let's give Henry Walker another hand. Didn't he do a great job? [*Applause*] I sort of want him to keep on talking; I was having a good time. [*Laughter*]

Ladies and gentlemen, thank you for the warm welcome. Thank you, Congressman Filner. Thank you, Dr. Bertha Pendleton, for doing such a good job with this school district. Thank you, Dr. Bob Stein, the O'Farrell chief educational officer. I want to say a special word of thanks to a group of parents and teachers and students and others who help to make this school successful, who met with me for about a half an hour, before we came out here, to talk about what they were doing. I'd like to ask them to stand up and be recognized. Let's give them a hand. They gave me an education today. [*Applause*]

I want to say to all of you how grateful I am to this school and to all the other schools here present for believing in our children. I believe in zero tolerance, and I thank you for that. I'm trying to get every place in the country to adopt that policy. And most importantly, I believe in the high expectations that are given

to all children in this school, because all of your children can learn, and we should expect them to and help them to.

I want you to know why I came here today. You know, I like San Diego, and I came here to sign the Goals 2000 bill, and I like to be in a community that cares about education. But I wanted to come to this school today for a particular reason, and that is because O'Farrell is organized as a charter school. They call it a family. And as a school organized in this way, it's freed of a lot of the rules and regulations that keep some of our schools all across America from designing their own ways of educating children. They also are held accountable for results, and they do a good job.

I want the American people to see this because there are too many people in America that not only don't have high expectations of our students, they don't have high expectations of our schools anymore, and they don't understand how much good can be done in a good school when people are working together and they believe in their children and the promise of this future.

I have been promoting schools that are organized and operated like this school for more than 3 years now, and I asked the United States Congress to appropriate just a little money, as a part of the Goals 2000 program Congressman Filner referred to, to give schools all across America just a little start-up money if they wanted to become schools that were independent, that were energized, that were high-expectation schools like O'Farrell.

Today I'm pleased to say that the Department of Education has granted another $6 million to open schools just like this one in 11 States across our country, including more schools in the State of California.

America has to be serious about education. We have to be serious about education if we want to have a strong economy, if we want these young people to live up to the fullest of their God-given abilities. If we really believe that our obligation to our children is to give them the ability to make the most of their own lives in the world we are living in, that means education, education, education. We must face it, embrace it, and be glad about it.

I wouldn't be President of the United States today if it weren't for the educational opportunities I had. I was raised by my grandparents until I was 4, boys and girls, and my grandfather left school after the 6th grade. But because I had a chance to go to a good school, I had a chance to get scholarships and loans and jobs to go to college, I had a chance to become President. None of it would have happened if it hadn't been for teachers like your teachers, parents like your parents, community leaders like your community leaders. It means everything, and it is more important today than it even was when I was your age. We have to give the children of this country a chance to get a good education.

There are a lot of things that have to be done here school by school, that a President can't do much about: teaching our young people to believe in themselves, organizing a system for high expectations and zero tolerance of destructive conduct, pointing out that freedom and opportunity requires a lot of personal responsibility. But I'll tell you something, there are a lot of things that we in public office can do to help. And I am tired of people in public life pointing the fingers at others and saying, you should do better, and then running away from their own responsibilities to education.

That's not the example we should be setting for our children in this country.

Just yesterday in San Francisco, I announced a breakthrough that will enable, by the year 2000, every classroom in America to be connected for computers, if we do what people in California have promised to do—business leaders—which is to wire every school in California for the Internet and to do it soon. This is the kind of thing we have to do together.

But you heard Dr. Pendleton talk about the money that these schools get from the National Government to fight for better education for these children. Don't you let anyone convince you that this money cannot be well spent to improve education. And don't you let anyone convince you that we have to cut out this money to balance the Federal budget. It is not true.

I favor balancing the Federal budget, and I have given Congress a plan to do it. I hate the fact that we were up to our ears in debt when I took office. We had a deficit of $290 billion a year when I became President, and in 3 years we've cut it from $290 billion to $160 billion. I want to go all the way and balance the budget.

But why are we balancing the budget? Because we care about our children. We want to lift the burden of debt off of them. We want to have a stronger economy for them. We want America to work better. Those are our values. If those are our values, we cannot balance the budget by destroying our commitment to education. Otherwise, we won't help our children, and we won't strengthen our economy. So I say to you, my fellow Americans, we can balance the budget and increase our investment in education. And that is exactly what we ought to do.

We need to make sure our schools are safe and drug-free. We need to make sure when little children show up for school that they've been given a chance to get off to a good start. We need to make sure that schools that don't have the resources on their own can still have smaller classes and have technology and have the ability to have those higher expectations that were talked about here today. And your National Government has an obligation to help you do that. That is what I am fighting for in Washington today.

The right way to balance the budget is to balance the budget while keeping our commitments and our values to the future of our children intact. That's what I am fighting for. You heard Congressman Filner talk about it.

The alternative budget in Washington today, proposed by the congressional majority, would undermine dramatically our commitment to education. It would cut back on our ability to promote charter schools like this one. It would cut back on our ability to help with smaller classes and more computers. It would cut back on our ability to help assure safe and drug-free schools. It would cut back on our ability to make sure little kids from poor families show up ready to learn. It would cut back on the availability of scholarships to go to college and on the availability of low-cost college loans.

Now, California has seen what happens when you cut back on the availability of people to go to college. You have a decline in enrollment in your colleges because of the cost. I want to lower the cost and increase the enrollment of ordinary Americans in a college education.

I come here to San Diego to say to you that when things are really important in America, we ought to act like a family the way the O'Farrell family works.

Education is our meal ticket to the future. Let me tell you something, folks: There's not a country in the world in a better position for the next century, for the global economy, for the rapid movement of people and money and ideas and technology around the world. No one is better suited for that than the United States, because we are the greatest country, that has people from everywhere in our country and in our communities. Look around here today and you can see that. Look around here and you can see that.

But if we are going to fulfill our potential as a nation, these children have to fulfill their potential, every one of them. We have to believe in what they can become. We have to believe they can learn. We have to insist that they do learn. We have to help them to learn. And they can learn a very great deal. We have to believe that our schools can work. And yes, we've got to embrace all these new ideas, like charter schools, but we also have to invest in them.

Before I came out here, the students were given a chance to ask me questions, and one of the students who is sitting right back there stood up and said, "If we really care about education, how come we pay professional athletes who never get off the bench 10 times as much as the schoolteachers make?"

This is not about money. It is about our values. It's about what kind of people we are. If you believe that every person should be responsible, that every person should be a good citizen, but that every person should have the opportunity to make the most of his or her own life, then you are required to say we have obligations to each other. We owe something to each other. Yes, we can put a bunch of our money into entertainment and let those folks make a lot, but we have to invest some of our money where our values are, where our future lies, where everybody can come together.

This should not be a partisan political deal. America's existence as a great, free, democracy depends upon developing the ability of all the children who are here and the people they represent all over America. So I ask you, I ask you, without regard to your political party, your income, what you do for a living, your ethnic background, if you believe this, if you believe this, if you believe that one of these little kids could grow up to be President of the United States, with a good education, if you believe that all of these little children can assure that America will remain the strongest, greatest country in the world, if you believe it is not an accident that people here have gotten together and done something that is the envy of America in education, then I plead with you, send a message to the Congress that it shouldn't be a matter of partisan politics, we must balance the budget and invest in education to keep faith with the future of our children and the future of America.

Thank you, and God bless you all.

NOTE: The President spoke at 4:39 p.m. in the courtyard. In his remarks, he referred to Henry Walker, parent of an O'Farrell Community School student; Bertha Pendleton, superintendent, San Diego Unified School District; and Bob Stein, chief educational officer, O'Farrell Community School.

Exchange With Reporters Aboard Air Force One
September 22, 1995

Charter Schools

[The President's remarks are joined in progress.]

The President. ——education speech, but when I saw the venue today, I couldn't do it. There were kids; they were happy; I just couldn't do it. But this school, I have been—we got the DLC interested in this before I ever thought I'd be running for President in '92, the whole idea of charter schools, because one of the biggest problems with public education is there are too many people telling the teachers and the principals what to do—levels of authority—but not enough genuine accountability and not a sort of organized entrepreneurialism in the schools.

So these charter schools—like this guy calls himself the CEO of the school instead of the principal. And they come up with a theme, and they develop a culture and develop all the kind of community services as well as all the parents. They have an organized influence. It's a tough neighborhood. And those children that were talking to me were very articulate. They showed me their work, very high-quality work. And they really just hammer on these kids that they can all learn, doesn't matter what their background or their income is, they matter, they can learn.

They got rid of the—there's no principal, no vice principal, no counselors, no nothing. Everybody is organized in these small clusters that they call families, Family A or Family B.

Q. Oh, so that's what's the Family B——

The President. Yes. Yes, Family B is—that's the way they organize it. And they've got a certain number of teachers per students. They've got like a 1 to 20 ratio, because they don't have any sort of administrative-service infrastructure. I think it's a little more—it was 7 to 160, I think. And so every student has a teacher who is also a counselor, a friend, a mentor, as well as an educator. And they've reduced the dropout rate, and their performance levels on the basic scores are basically at or above the California and the national averages, even though their social-economic profile would tend to put them way below.

And it's very interesting to watch it. And I'm convinced it's because—these charter schools, in effect, it's a way of having school choice that's

as close as you can get to vouchers without going to vouchers and still keep the money you need in the public schools, because it's not like a magnet school where the people that go there may tend to be super—the more intelligent kids only or higher I.Q. kids, because—and that case, although it's a school of choice, you can opt not to go there or opt to go there. Most of them are neighborhood kids that you saw. They were basic—*[inaudible]*.

But the whole idea of the charter school is that you're part of the school district for funding purposes but you're an independent operating unit. And Bertha Davenport, the woman who is a school superintendent, a very impressive woman, and she succeeded Tom Payzant, who was also very successful, and Dick Riley brought him to the Department of Education to try to promote this. So a lot of superintendents don't like charter schools because they lose control of the schools, but her idea is—she said, "I'm not running these schools; I just created a climate, set expectations, make sure the trains run on time." So she's got nine of them.

And one of the things we did with the Goals 2000 program and with the rewrite of the Elementary and Secondary Education Act last year was to get the Congress to put out a little money just to fund school reforms, because if you switch from a regular school to one of these charter schools you need some extra money that aren't in the school districts' budgets, the money is—like to organize kind of planning sessions and figure out how you're going to redo the whole thing. So that's what I announced today. But it is an example of what we tried to do to invest more in education but to deregulate it, without lowering the standards—in fact, we're trying to deregulate it and raise the level of accountability.

So it's great. So these little independent operating—*[inaudible]*—and they will basically have contracts with their school districts with performance standards. And they'll either meet or exceed them, or they won't. And if they won't, then their charter can be jerked.

It's very exciting. There's no such thing as a cure-all, but you saw what happened. I mean, one of the things that I always was amazed by is that when schools had a monopoly on customers and a monopoly on money and districts were sort of independent of one another, there were not incentives to copy what works. And I think one of the most—the thing that I keep hammering home is, almost every problem in our country's education system has been solved pretty well by somebody, somewhere. But there's no—it's not centralized like the Japanese system, for example, where they can say, "This works in Kyoto; here's how it works. Everybody will institute this in 60 days; show up 10 days from now, and we'll have a training session about how to do it." We don't have that, but it's not entrepreneurially decentralized like a competitive environment.

For example, Sam Walton was the best entrepreneur I ever met. And way into his old age, until he got very sick, he was still getting on his one-horse airplane and flying to some town where he was opening a new store. And he'd go check out his store; then he'd go down to K-Mart and start wandering, and he'd say hello, and he'd introduce—he'd say, "Who are you?" He wouldn't tell them he was Sam Walton. You'd say, "I'm John Palmer," and he'd say, "Well, Mr. Palmer, how long have you been shopping at K-Mart? If you don't mind my asking, what are you in to buy? How do these people treat you? If you have a defective product can you get your money back?" He did that, and he did it in the large stores and he did it in small stores. In other words, he thought, no matter how big he got he had to at least equal his competition. And if they were doing something for his customers, it was not only bad business, it was unethical for him not to do for his customers what his competition was doing. And in different, less explicit, less organized ways, that's the way a market works in the best sense.

But I found that when—we had a little old school that was a semi-version of this, a great school in a little rural county in Arkansas. And we got them permission from the Federal Government to take all their Title I funds and some of this special-ed funds in the first grade and get rid of all the separate classes and put them all together. And we went down to 1 to 15 in this poor school district. There were three kids that had been held back. The next year they quadrupled their test scores. There was an 80 percent increase in the scores of the Chapter I kids the next year over the previous

year and a 67 percent increase in overall scores in the first grade. They even had first graders working in teams, learning together, doing collective work, which, by the way, we know how that really works. And I actually was paying people from other school districts, their expenses, to come look at what these people did.

And we found that there were school districts that were reluctant to copy it because it would be like admitting failure. And others who didn't copy it because it was too much trouble, everybody—[*inaudible*]—or they thought it was some fad that—[*inaudible*]. But the lesson is that things can get better, schools can perform at world-class standards, more kids in racially integrated—[*inaudible*]—economically   isolated places can do well.

Q. [Inaudible]

The President. It's like trying to turn a battleship around or it's basically trying to hold 400 ping-pong balls in your arms, because it's—but the point is when you get something that works, if you can get enough visibility to it, people can be looking at it and involved in it, and you basically—you empower the parents and the students and all these other people who come in here.

There was a very impressive man from the State social services there who talked about how he brought in—if all these kids had any problems, about all the services at the school. And he said, "All these pathologies are in our communities, but all the antibodies are, too," which I thought was a real—great one-liner.

So what I tried to do is to put the Federal Government in the business of adding funding where it's needed, holding up things that work, having high standards but not adding to the problem of over-regulation. Riley has reduced Federal regulations in education by about 40 percent since he's been there. And this is a program that has, at the State level, an enormous amount of support—[*inaudible*]—as you might imagine.

So parenthetically, it helps make the case for why we should cut the education funding in the balanced budget debate. But it also shows that there is a way to make schools work better, to have high expectations of kids, and to get some results. One of the things I find is that there's so much—people tend to give up now. They tend to think, "Oh, the schools can't be made to work well," or "The crime rate will never go down." But those things just aren't true.

So—and this was an extraordinary school, which is why I really wanted to go there. I thought we could really juice it up.

Mood of the Country

Q. Is it hard to explain to people how these sort of public-private or public-local partners— I mean, the technology initiative yesterday, the Goals 2000—I mean, they are a lot more complicated than most people understand.

The President. Yes.

Q. But in the face of everybody saying less Government, it's hard to explain this sort of thing.

The President. Well, what I'm trying to—like I said in my speeches this week, psychologically, they've got an easier argument. If a majority of people are anxiety-ridden and worried about the country, they can say, "We're moving into a new era, and the problem is the Government, and the Government is spending too much time on immigration, welfare, and affirmative action—too much of your money. Therefore, just get rid of it; less is better." It's a harder argument to say, "We're moving into a time of change; we're all going to have to change. We need to be faithful to our values. What works is having the right vision, working together, and working for the future." But if you can find some summary ways to say that, then the San Francisco announcement on the computers or the San Diego announcement on the charter schools, they become like ornaments on a Christmas tree. But the programs have to be secondary to people's understanding of what's happening and the vision and the values behind it, so that the programs become like ornaments on a Christmas tree.

That's why I keep saying this budget debate fundamentally is not about funding. It's about the choices we make about money.

Q. Mr. President, what was it that got you thinking about this sort of 100-year change that—I mean, were you just sort of reading since——

The President. Well, for years I felt like most people, I've been aware for a long—I began to talk about the wage stagnation and the relationship in the social disintegration and the wage stagnation at least 8 or 9 years ago, before I heard anybody else talking about it. I just studied—because I study data all the time. When

I was a Governor and I was trying to restructure the economy, I just studied a lot of things that were—looked like boring numbers but could be made—but had real-life stories around them.

But when I ran for President, I believed that if I had the right sort of economic policy, which was to grow jobs in the private sector and try to pursue strategies that will increase the number of high-wage jobs, facilitate defense conversion, and raise skill levels in the work force, we could grow jobs, grow entrepreneurs, and raise the incomes. I thought if we had a social policy that emphasized helping people to help themselves, helping people that need help but imposing responsibility and accountability, that we could reform welfare and do all these other things. And I thought if we had a Government that was strong but smaller and more entrepreneurial, that was more oriented toward results and less oriented toward regulation, we could build broad support for it.

And we did all that. We had a huge amount of success in the first 2 years. And the Congress—the Democrats actually moved a long way—however you want to say it—either to the center or into the future. But there was no perception of it on the part of the voters. Part of it the Republicans spent a lot more time and money on communication, as opposed to governance. But they hadn't been in the governing business for a long time, so they could do it. And part of it was that there was no way for people to feel it. They had these feelings about the way their lives were.

And after the election was over, I basically spent—I spent a lot of time trying to understand what was driving the mind-set of voters in terms of what was happening in their lives and try to tie what's going on here to what's going on in the rest of the world. And I finally realized that the depth of the changes—you know, it's one thing to say it's a post-cold-war era, the global economy, the information age, and another thing to try to come to grips with the fact that the depth of the changes in the way we live and work and relate to each other and the rest of the world are, in my judgment, greater than at any time in 100 years.

So I started looking for historical parallels. And it started with people saying, you know, this is going to be like Truman, all that kind of stuff—you know, what people say about '48. And I think the psychological dynamics are a lot like '48, where we had to come down off

World War II, we had to make all these economic adjustments, there was no common—[inaudible]—to weld us together. If there was, it was—[inaudible]—into exhaustion. The psychological dynamics were—[inaudible]—but the underlying reality was different, because, basically, even in the Great Depression, we knew we had a great industrial country; we just had to figure out how to make it work again, how to get out of this Depression.

But this is something different. The way we live and the way we work is really changing. And so I started going back into history, and I read—and I started trying to read things that would—triggered it. And finally, I realized, thinking about the beginning of the progressive era, basically, from Teddy Roosevelt to Woodrow Wilson, that the same kinds of things were being done. We changed the way we live; we changed the way we work; we changed the idea of what the role of Government was; we defined our relationships to each other in different ways. We never had to worry about child labor on the farm; nobody would have thought of—a farmer couldn't let his kid work 12 hours a day, 6 days a week on the farm, except when he was in school, you know. And we changed our relationship to the rest of the world.

I mean, when we got into World War I—it started with Teddy Roosevelt, even a little before Roosevelt, with the antitrust laws which said we were not going for socialism in the industrial age but we had to have competition to avoid the evils of a monopoly. Then we got into child labor. Then we got into the idea that we could destroy our natural heritage by abusing the environment—Teddy Roosevelt wanted to preserve the environment. And then Woodrow Wilson did a lot of other progressive things. We enacted the progressive income tax, to pay for things that we had to do together in an industrial society, that we couldn't do apart.

And then, lo and behold, after this whole tradition of isolationism—the biggest war we ever fought was the one we fought with each other—we wound up having to come into World War I basically to ensure the victory of the good guys and what we believed in. And if you go back—and it took about 20 years. So if you look at the way things are today, you see the same sort of thing, with a lot of good things and a lot of bad things and all these anomalies. The economy comes back, the wages stay flat. The crime rate goes down, our juvenile crime

goes bad. Peace in our time, with all these isolated acts of madness. And it's the same sort of deal. And so we have to work our way through it.

And as President, one of my big jobs is—and I neglected that the first 2 years, I think. The first 2 years, I knew exactly what I wanted to do, and I went about doing them. And I was obsessed with doing them. A lot of it required the Congress to go along. And I would have been better served, I think, and the country probably would have been better served if maybe we had done—even if we had done just slightly less, if people had understood sort of the big picture more. And the President, in a way, has to impart that big picture.

And there were times when I did it, like in that Memphis speech, for example. But if you go back and look at Lincoln's speeches, for example, he was always explaining the time people were living in and putting the big issues in terms of choices that had to be made, so that he basically never let the people off the hook.

Q. You mean like now we are engaged in the great Civil War, testing whether or not——

The President. Yes, yes, his second Inaugural—one side could make war rather than stay in the Union, and the other side would accept war rather than see the Union rend apart. And the war came. It was all about choices.

And one of the—the traditional rap on the Republican and Democrats' tradition is that the Democrats believe that Government could solve all the problems; the Republicans believe that Government was useless. And they were both too extreme, and the Americans were in the middle. But the real problem now is the Democrats have really moved a lot, and when we move this way the Republicans move this way.

But the real problem is, if we talk only in terms of programs and dollars, right, and they talk only in terms of the evils of Government and how the President is doing too much for them—[inaudible]—both sides are letting the people off the hook. That's what—you go back and read Lincoln. You know, the people were always—he would never let the people off the hook. We were making choices.

And Teddy Roosevelt and Woodrow Wilson, if you go back and read their speeches, there's a lot of that in there. And even when FDR was railing against the trust and all the enemies that he'd created, he still in the fireside chats was always reminding people that they had things to do.

So what I try to do—even the speeches I gave in my fundraisers, which were not your traditional campaign speeches, is I'm trying to find ways to explain as best as I understand it what is happening to our people and trying to get us to make choices that are consistent with the new realities and the basic values that I believe we all have to hold. And it's a very exciting thing. And I'm also trying to tell the Democrats that they need to just relax and say what they believe and not worry about this debate—a lot of people are, you know—there are Members in the Republican House that say things like Medicare's the worst thing that happened to the sixties, Janet Reno ought to be indicted, and all this stuff. It's driving some of our people crazy. But what I'm trying to tell them is—and I'm trying to tell the Republicans the same thing—this debate had to come because of the transition period. And in a period like this, new things become possible which are good, but then things become thinkable which caused people to shudder for the same reason, because all the conventional wisdom breaks down and then you have to create a new one.

Congress

Q. Why do you say the problem that Truman faced is the one you're facing? There were Republican Congresses both times, but that was a do-nothing Congress. This is sort of a do-too-much Congress in terms of activism. Do you draw—think the analogy—[*inaudible*]—do you see that as a different——

The President. But the difference is perception. The truth is the last Congress was not a do-nothing—you mean, Truman had a do-nothing Congress.

Q. Yes. But the current Congress is an activist Congress.

The President. Well, the House is an activist House. The Senate wants to be activist, but they're trying to find a more dynamic center that can be a bipartisan center. And the real interesting thing is whether the chemistry between the House, the Senate, and the President can lead to a creative kind of tension that will move us forward. That's the argument I keep making to the Speaker, or the personal plea I made to Bob Dole on welfare reform, which, frankly, to which he responded and we worked through a lot of that stuff. A lot of those ideas

that are in there, the giving States a bonus for putting people to work, requiring people to sign personal responsibility contracts, all those things are ideas we've been advocating for years. And I'm excited—I don't agree with everything in that Senate bill, but I'm excited about the direction it took, that it really is a new-ideas direction rooted in the idea of both work and family, which I think is—one of the central realities for you and for every other American is we have to create a country which you can succeed at work and at home. And if we get in a position where even the poorest among us have to choose, we're in deep trouble.

Welfare Reform

Q. Has Dole told you he thinks he can get most of that bill?

The President. No, he didn't say. But before he brought the bill up, we had a visit when he came to the White House one time, and I just told him that I would really go a long way to try to meet him in agreement and I thought that welfare reform had become a symbol for the country and I didn't want it to become a symbol of division because I didn't think we ought to kick poor people around and beat them up. But I did think it was bad to have a system of permanent dependency that was created for a different age. As Moynihan never tires of telling us, it was created for the West Virginia miner's widow, who had a fourth-grade education and kids at home and there wasn't anyplace in the work force for her anyway.

We live in a world now where work and family are merged much more clearly and which we cannot afford to have a whole class of our people in a state of permanent dependency. It draws upon their dignity; it's bad for their children. So welfare should be a temporary help to people in need.

So, anyway, that's a hopeful sign anyway. But we can do a lot of good for this country. We can balance the budget. We can strengthen the economy. We can maintain our commitment to education and technology, which means people will be able to make more of their own lives and they'll have a stronger economy. We have to slow the rate of growth in Medicare and Medicaid—I don't disagree with all the specific Medicare reforms that have been advanced. Some of them are common to what I recommended in '94, if you go back to my health care plan. What I think is wrong is to jerk an arbitrary amount of money out of a health care system without considering what the consequences are.

I was in Orange County after I left the—you all were down there with me, but after I did the public deal, I went in and did a roundtable with business executives in Orange County and some education leaders. And most of them were Republicans. But I started a dialog with them in '92. Some of them supported me and some of them didn't, but I've kept up the dialog because there are a lot of forward-thinking people around there. And one man spoke up in this room; he said, "You know, nobody has talked about the impact of the Medicaid program, all these cuts, on the great teaching hospitals," that basically this is typical of the Democrats—it's a problem they solved a few years ago in an indirect way and they never thought to explain to America that, basically, Medicaid, because so many of the great teaching hospitals are located in and around cities with large numbers of poor people and because those teaching hospitals need patients, Medicaid funds have actually supported medical education in America and indirectly supported institutions of—[*inaudible*]—resource.

So he was telling me—now, one of the things we estimate is that California will rebound from the defense downsizing by having a huge advance in medical and biological sciences over the next 20 years as we move into the age—[*inaudible*]. And he said, "If we just arbitrarily take all this money out of the Medicaid system without really thinking about what it's going to do to these great centers of learning and research, it's a bad deal." So that's an issue that nobody has even thought about in the actual debate.

But the point is, we can work this out. We do have to slow the rate of—is this going to become another Washington paralysis, like it was before I showed up? They fought about the crime bill for 6 years and fought about family aid for 7 years and fought about all this other—where each side can walk away and say, well, I tried, but the others were unreasonable. Or will we find a creative tension here which enables us to do—make real progress on all these—[*inaudible*]—so that we're throwing the country into the future but in a way that keeps us together and really preserves our obligations to our children, our parents, and our obligation to keep opportunity—[*inaudible*]?

It's going to be a very interesting 2 months.

Administration Accomplishments

Q. [Inaudible]

The President. Well, it did that. And also it came about because I realized that either—right before or right at the election there were a few sort of revisionist articles that came out in magazines saying, "People think nothing has been done, but this Congress has given Bill Clinton 80 percent of his programs in 2 years, very ambitious programs; it's only the third time since World War II this has happened, and why don't they link it? Maybe they don't feel it. The Democrats govern better than they talk. Health care was a $300 billion fight by those who were—so health care overshadowed everything else." There were all these reasons, but when you stripped it all away, I was doing all these things that 70 percent of the American people really agreed with when they heard about it, but it didn't connect in their lives and their minds. And a lot of them couldn't even receive it. A lot couldn't even receive it.

I'm going to tell you an interesting story. Mack McLarty—two stories. Mack McLarty spoke at the Perot convention for us, and basically—and I now think we took slightly the wrong tack there. But anyway—and there were some—a lot of them were Republican political people, but there were some real Perot people there, too. And so Mack talks to this—he's working the crowd after he talks. He basically said, we did 80 percent of what Ross Perot advocated in his book, and here's what he advocated and here's what we did and here's what we still have to do. So he talks his heart out, you know. And this woman comes up to him—he's working the crowd—and this woman says, "You're a nice young man, and you're a very attractive, nice young man. But I don't agree with anything you and your President stand for." So he says, "What is it that you don't agree with? Do you disagree with the fact that we took the deficit from $290 billion to $160 billion?" She said, "Did you really do that?" He'd just spoken about that. He said, "Yes, we really did that." He talked about it. She said, "Well, I do agree with that." He said, "Well, what do you do?" She said, "I'm a retired schoolteacher." He said, "Do you have children?" She said, "One; my son works for Dupont"—or some company. I think it was Dupont; I can't remember. And he said, "You don't agree with NAFTA, do you?" He said, "You know, 30 percent of that company's profits last year came from trade with Mexico." She said, "Is that right?"

It was interesting. But the point is she literally could not hear him when he was standing up there talking to her because her resistance is to her preconceptions about Democrats and me and Government and Washington. She couldn't absorb it.

And a lot of you have heard me talk about my Cabinet member whose sister called her one day and said, "I'm so excited because my tax bill went down $600"—or whatever it was. This woman was a working mother with two kids and a modest income. She said, "Yes, I know, that was a big part of the President's program." And she said, "No, it wasn't." She said, "What do you mean? I'm in the Cabinet; it was a big part of our program." She said, "All you do is defend him." She said, "He went around the table and made us all give up money to pay for that earned-income tax credit so people like you get a tax break." She said, "I watch the news every night; if anything that important had happened—that's the most important thing that's happened in years—I would know that if he had."

But you see, it was buried amidst all the bigger conflicts of the economic plan, just like the direct student loan program was, which is why they can never—[inaudible]. The point I want to make is what struck me is in a democracy it is not enough to do a lot of particular things that will make the general points you're trying to make. Things are changing so much that a lot of what is unsettling is not so much in reality as it also is in people's heads. And it's very important that—I mean, the most important thing in a democracy is how—is not who happens to be President at one given moment, it is how the people understand their time, their obligations, and their opportunities.

Which is why I don't like the argument going on between the two parties, even though in specifics I normally agree with—I don't think we ought to frame it just in terms of we're for this much money and this program, and they say the Government—[inaudible]. What we really have to do is say, this is the change, this is what's happening in your life, and the money is incidental to the value choices you're making and the vision you have about the future. Don't kid yourself; this is a decision we're all making. These are changes we're all going

through. You can't just blame somebody or drive a wedge through the country and expect us to get results. Neither will all your problems be solved if we win this money battle over this program.

And I just began to see that, and I realized that if you go back and read the really important things that Presidents said in history, very often what they tried to do is to explain to the American people that—[inaudible]—and how the American idea can be preserved and enhanced in that moment by taking a different course rooted in the basic things that have always been at the guts of this—[inaudible].

The Media

Q. [Inaudible]—modern Presidency people do—[inaudible]—because they see this on the TV——

Press Secretary Mike McCurry. Time out. This is good food for thought, but these guys need real food, too.

Q. Lincoln—if he suggested the same kind of scrutiny that you are—[inaudible].

The President. Well, I think in the information age, too much exposure and too much information and too much sort of quasi-information— I mean, you guys have to compete with near-news, too. It's like when we were kids, we'd drink near-beer. You've got all this information and a lot of competition among news sources, and then you're competing with the near-news. And there is a danger that too much stuff cramming in on people's lives is just as bad for them as too little in terms of the ability to understand, to comprehend.

Which is why, again I say, I underestimated in my first 2 years the importance of continually not just—even the town meetings, one of the problems is—like yesterday in the Larry King thing—I don't know if you listened to it—I thought it was good. I loved doing it, but I found myself about three questions in, I said, No, no, no, no, I'm doing too much of the details of the specific issue they're asking without trying to keep putting it in the larger context. Because we need to develop sort of a common understanding.

Now, people intuitively respond to that. When in Colin's book, he talks about the American family or if I talk about common ground or I say what it is that brings us together or Ross Perot says we shouldn't have politics or, you know, or when the leaders in the Congress make some outreach that they resonate to intuitively, but there's no sort of, "Well, what does that mean at this time?" which is what I'm trying to do.

I had so many people on this trip, even at these fundraisers, come up to me and say that they were really glad they were there because they had been themselves trying to understand what was going on and make sense of it, to kind of incorporate it into their lives.

Colin Powell and the Mood of the Country

Q. [*Inaudible*]—you have an autographed copy of General Powell's book tomorrow night when you see him?

The President. I certainly hope so. [*Laughter*]

Q. Are you looking forward to that? It will be the first time you will share the platform with——

Q. Is he going to be at the Congressional Black Caucus?

Q. Yes.

The President. Maybe I'll get my book. [*Laughter*]

Anyway, it's very—I'm also trying to get people to get out of their funk about it.

Q. Get out of their funk?

The President. Yes. Yes, because the truth is that we have proved that we can make this economy perform under these circumstances. But it used to be that a high-performance economy, a lot of entrepreneurs, a lot of new millionaires was inexorably—inevitably meant higher wages for everybody. It doesn't anymore. So we've got to go to the second problem. We've proved we can perform. We've proved we can make progress in social problems. I mean, it's—just last night on the news it said teen pregnancies down in America for the second year in a row. And you heard me—the divorce rate is down, food stamps, welfare, crime, murder. But the wrinkle on it is the teenager is still in trouble.

But we've proved—you know, 5 years ago most Americans basically thought the crime rate was going to go up forever. And you now know—so we can do things if we have the right understanding and we understand that we just have been given the gift or the burden of living through this time and we've just go to do our job.

I think it's really—it's quite exciting. But I believe, to go back to what you said, John, my own belief is that human beings, particularly the American people, are capable of enduring a lot of difficulty and a lot of tumult and upheaval if they understand it. What makes people insecure is when they feel like they're lost in the funhouse. They're in a room where something can hit them from any direction any time. They always feel living life is like walking across a running river on slippery rocks and you can lose your footing at any time.

If people kind of—if you understand what's happening to you, you can make the necessary—not just changes but necessary psychological adaptions. So you define security in a different way, and you can rear back and go on then. So that—I find it—and I really feel that this is important for me to do.

President Ronald Reagan

Q. [*Inaudible*]—in California what do you hear about President Reagan? I understand it was possible you might visit him, but he is in pretty bad shape. Have you heard any word on him lately?

The President. I called Mrs. Reagan some—a couple months ago, I guess. I haven't heard anything since then.

Mood of the Country

Q. On what we were talking about, do you feel after this trip that you found the words that can explain the time to people, or are you still searching for it?

The President. Yes, but I can't do it in 30 seconds.

Q. But when you talk about getting people out of their funk, there was this period where you were so—consistently reported—a long time ago now, but to be in one yourself. Are you long since out of it, and is this part of why?

The President. Oh, yes. Yes. But what bothered—I don't mind adversity. I have difficulty when I—I don't think I can do my job as President if I don't understand what's happening. And I really spent a lot of time trying to understand what was going on, and I really think what I said is true. I think that I and all of us had underestimated the dimensions of the changes and the challenges facing us. And so now I feel quite good about it.

Q. [*Inaudible*]—30 seconds in this day and age?

The President. I'll—eventually, I'll get it in 30 seconds. I'll be able to do it in 30 seconds, in a minute, 2 minutes, 5 minutes, and 30 minutes. It's what you've got to do. You need to—if you can go 30 minutes down, you know.

President's Schedule

Q. It's a long way to November in 1996——

Press Secretary McCurry. I get the last question. These guys—you've had so much energy this week, they all want to know are you going to try to keep this same pace all the way through to November of 1996.

The President. No. [*Laughter*]

Q. Can you tell us how to get by on 4 hours sleep a night? Are there things you learned in Oxford or——

The President. I never slept—I slept more than 4 hours every night we were gone. I never slept less than 5 hours. But except that night we were in Denver—I slept 6 hours, but it was 2 and 4.

Q. Not continuous.

The President. Two and four. So it was tough. When I have a difficult day like that, particularly if I can't exercise, I try to drink lots and lots and lots of water. I try to make an extra effort to concentrate on what other people are saying, to listen——

Q. [*Inaudible*]—don't fall asleep.

Q. Good advice to us.

The President. Well, so you don't fall asleep—not fall asleep, but just don't get blah, you know.

Q. Mr. President, when you run at 7 a.m. it means that we have to run at 5:30 a.m. [*Laughter*] Seriously. When you run at 7 a.m., I have to get up and run at 5:30 a.m. to catch the pool for you running.

The President. Why couldn't you make a deal with the pool that you could be the designated runner, then you could run at 7 a.m.

Q. Believe me, that would be the most popular innovation you could make.

Q. Hey, I'll take pool duty.

The President. I would love to have the pool run with me, any day.

Q. They should. I'm not sure Lew Merletti would love it, but I mean——

The President. Oh, no, it would be fine.

Q. Because that's what the public thinks. They think jogging with the President is running alongside of him. They don't think it's the 10th and 11th cars in a 12-car motorcade, passing beside him around the corner.

The President. The Secret Service would not care if anybody in the pool wanted to run with me.

Press Secretary McCurry. That's not the—the problem is, have you ever had Helen Thomas [United Press International] sit in your office at 7 a.m. in the morning? [*Laughter*] That's what I do every morning. Now, it's like a running press conference.

The President. No, I couldn't talk while I was running.

Q. We couldn't either, believe you me.

The President. I laid off for a couple of months. And one of the things I always have to do when I start running again, particularly the older I get and the harder it gets, is concentrate real hard on my breathing patterns. Because most people can run a lot more than they think; it's their breathing that gives out. They get into irregular breathing, and they start gasping instead of pushing out. So I can't—when I get in real good shape again I can talk when I'm running. But right now I can only concentrate on——

Q. Why did you lay off? Had you had a sprain or a strain or just——

The President. Well, this summer, the heat and allergies bothered me. So I just worked out. And then when I went to—by the time I got on vacation I was as tired as I've ever been in my life, I think. And I just didn't want to do it. I just wanted to lay around my family or fool around on the golf course or go climb mountains if you're going to do it. I just didn't want to do it.

Press Secretary McCurry. Let's let these guys have dinner.

Q. Thank you, sir.

Q. I was going to ask, can you come back again and say hello to——

The President. Thanks, guys.

NOTE: The exchange began at approximately 7:30 p.m. aboard Air Force One en route from San Diego, CA, to Washington, DC. In his remarks, the President referred to Bertha Pendleton, superintendent, San Diego Unified School District; the late Samuel M. Walton, founder, Wal-Mart Stores, Inc.; and Secret Service agent Lewis Merletti. The press release issued by the Office of the Press Secretary did not include the complete opening portion of the exchange. A tape was not available for verification of the content of this exchange.

Statement on the Aircraft Tragedy at Elmendorf Air Force Base in Alaska
September 22, 1995

Hillary and I were very saddened to learn of the death of the American and Canadian service members in the crash of a U.S. Air Force AWACS aircraft at Elmendorf Air Force Base in Alaska this morning. Their loss reminds us how much we owe those who serve our Nation's Armed Forces. Our hearts and prayers go out to the families, friends, and loved ones of those who were killed, both in the United States and in Canada.

The President's Radio Address
September 23, 1995

Good morning. I want to talk to you today about the prospects for peace in Bosnia. Over the past weeks, American leadership and the determination demonstrated by NATO and the United Nations have helped to bring Bosnia closer to peace than at any time since the war began there 4 years ago. Let me be clear: There are many tough obstacles still to overcome, but we are determined to press forward for a lasting peaceful settlement.

At the end of the cold war, Serbian nationalism forced the breakup of Yugoslavia. An ugly and dangerous war broke out in the heart of Europe, risking an even wider conflict in the Balkans which could have drawn the United States and many other countries in. Bosnia, a land in which Muslims, Serbs, and Croats had lived together peacefully for centuries, was literally torn apart.

As President, I have worked to do everything in our power to support the search for peace in Bosnia, to stop the conflict from spreading beyond its borders, and to ease the terrible suffering of the Bosnian people. We can't force peace on the parties; only they themselves can make it. That's why I have refused to let American ground troops become combatants in Bosnia. But we can press the parties to resolve their differences at the bargaining table and not on the battlefield. We will spare no effort to find a peaceful solution, and we will work through NATO to implement a settlement once the parties reach it.

Working closely with our partners from Europe and Russia, last year we proposed a peace plan that would preserve Bosnia as a state with Bosnia's Muslims and Croats holding 51 percent of the land and 49 percent going to the Bosnian Serbs. The Muslims and the Croats accepted our plan. But the Bosnian Serbs did not. Instead, they laid siege to Sarajevo and the other U.N.-declared safe areas, denying food, denying medicine, denying supplies to innocent civilians. They continued to make war. They refused to make peace.

This July, as the Serbs continue their assaults against the safe areas, America pressed NATO and the U.N. to take a tougher stand, and our allies agreed. When a Bosnian Serb shell slaughtered 38 people in Sarajevo just 3 weeks ago, we insisted that NATO and the U.N. make good on their commitment to protect Sarajevo and the other safe areas from further attacks. We demanded that the Serbs stop offensive actions against the safe areas, withdraw their heavy weapons from around Sarajevo, and allow road and air access to the city. When they refused, NATO began heavy and continuous air strikes against Bosnian Serb military targets.

These NATO air strikes, many, many of them flown by courageous American pilots and crews, convinced the Bosnian Serbs to comply with our demands. They stopped shelling Sarajevo. They moved their heavy weapons away from Sarajevo. They opened the roads and the airports to convoys carrying food and medicine and other supplies.

I salute our pilots and crews and their NATO colleagues. Because they did their job so well, today the people of Sarajevo can walk the streets of their city more free from fear than at any time in many months. And I want to make absolutely clear that if the Bosnian Serbs strike again at Sarajevo or the other safe areas, NATO's air strikes will resume.

Over the past weeks I also ordered our negotiators to step up their efforts to get the parties back to the peace negotiating table and to respond to shifting military circumstances in Bosnia where Croatian and Bosnian Government forces have made significant gains. The negotiators shuttled throughout the region, and they brought forth the Foreign Ministers of Bosnia, Croatia, and Serbia together in Geneva. Their hard work got the Serbs to agree to the principles of our peace plan. Thanks to the combination of military muscle and diplomatic determination, there is now a real chance for peace in Bosnia. We must seize it.

I have instructed our negotiating team to go to New York on Tuesday to meet with the Foreign Ministers of Bosnia, Croatia, and Serbia and our allies to push the peace process forward. Then I've asked them to return to the region to continue their intensive shuttle diplomacy and to keep the parties focused on an overall settlement. As I have said, there's no guarantee that we can reach a settlement. There are still deep, deep divisions among the parties. But there has been genuine progress.

What's happening today in Bosnia demonstrates once again the importance of American leadership around the world at the end of the cold war. Just think of the extraordinary achievements of the past year: democracy restored to Haiti, greater peace in the Middle East and in Northern Ireland, Russian nuclear weapons

no longer aimed at our people, the indefinite extension of a nuclear nonproliferation treaty, real progress toward a comprehensive nuclear test ban treaty, North Korea's agreement to end its nuclear weapons program. Each one of these is a product of American leadership. In the new and changing world we live in, America is the one country that can nearly always make a difference.

But if we want to continue to make a difference, if we want to continue to lead, we must have the resources that leadership requires. I intend to do everything in my power to make sure our military remains the best fighting force in the world and that our diplomats have the tools they need to help those who are taking risks for peace. We must not let our foreign policy and America's place in the world fall victim to partisan politics or petty fights. Every American, Democrats, Republicans, independents, all of us, should agree on the need for America to keep leading around the world.

That is the lesson of the progress we're seeing in Bosnia. That's the lesson of the foreign policy actions we've taken over the last year, actions that have made the world a safer place and every American more secure.

Thanks for listening.

NOTE. The address was recorded at 1:35 p.m. on September 22 at the Tustin Officers' Club in Tustin, CA, for broadcast at 10:06 a.m. on September 23.

Remarks at the Congressional Black Caucus Foundation Dinner
September 23, 1994

Thank you very much, Congressman Jefferson, for chairing this dinner and for being my longtime friend. He has such a nice name: William Jefferson. [*Laughter*] One day we were on a platform together in Louisiana, and we both kind of got to ventilating, and he said after I spoke, "It's a good thing you've got a last name or no one could tell us apart." [*Laughter*]

Congressman Payne, the CBC chair; Cardiss Collins, the foundation chair; to all the distinguished awardees, General Powell, Congressman Lewis, Muhammad Ali, Congressman Ford,

Renee Gaters, all very deserving; Ms. Gaters for your charity and your generosity over so many years; my longtime friend John Lewis for being a living reminder of what it means to live by what you say you believe; my friend Congressman Ford, who was working on welfare reform before the other crowd knew what it was. I thank you, sir.

Of course, one of your recipients has been on the front page of every magazine in this country, deluged with TV and radio requests, written a book, and has a name and face instantly recognized all around the world. I'm honored to share the spotlight tonight with Muhammad Ali and with General Colin Powell. [*Applause*] Thank you.

There are many things to be said about Colin Powell's lifetime of service to our country and service to three Presidents on matters on national security, but I know he is being honored tonight in large measure because just a year ago this week, he played an important part in our successful effort to end Haiti's long night of terror. Because of America's leadership, backing sanctions and diplomacy with force, because of the courage of President Aristide and the Haitian people and the support they received from so many of you in this room, today Haiti has its best chance in generations to build a strong democracy and to tackle the poverty that has been a scourge to those good people for too long.

In this great drama, General Powell answered my call to service. And along with President Carter and Senator Sam Nunn, he made sure the Haitian dictators understood the message of the United States that they had just one last chance to leave peacefully or suffer the consequences of being removed by military force. In no small measure because Colin Powell delivered that message so graphically, democracy was restored miraculously without the loss of a single American life or a single Haitian life.

Tonight is special for all of us because it's the 25th anniversary of the Congressional Black Caucus, now 40-strong. I think that we should pay special tribute to the founding members here tonight, and especially to the five who are still serving: Louis Stokes, Ron Dellums, Bill Clay, John Conyers, and Charlie Rangel. And let me say that after watching that film and after watching Charlie Rangel stand up for the rights of poor children and elderly Americans just the other day, I feel confident that they've still got a lot of juice, a lot of energy, a lot of good ideas, and a lot to give this country.

I don't know where our country would be today without the Congressional Black Caucus. I want to thank you, all of you, for standing up for the values we all hold dear, for freedom and for responsibility, for work and for family, for the idea that we are, as my friend the Governor of Florida said the other day, a community, not a crowd. A crowd is a collection of people occupying the same space, elbowing one another until the strongest and most powerful win without regard to what happens to the others. A community is a group of people who occupy the same space and believe they're going up or down together and they have responsibilities to one another. A community is a group of people led by people who do what's right for the long run, even if it defies the conventional wisdom and is unpopular in the short run. The Congressional Black Caucus has helped to keep America a community. Thank you, and God bless you all.

I have special reasons to be grateful to the Black Caucus. When I became President, we had a stagnant and suffering economy. The Congressional Black Caucus supported an economic policy that in 2½ years has produced 7½ million new jobs, 2½ million new homeowners, 2 million new small businesses, the largest number of new self-made millionaires in any time period in the history of the country, and an African-American unemployment rate back down in single digits for the first time since the Vietnam war. Thank you for doing that.

Three years ago, most Americans despaired that anything could ever be done about crime. Acting on old values and embracing new ideas, the Congressional Black Caucus played an active role in shaping a crime bill that had people and punishment and prevention. It put more police officers on our streets, punished people who should be, but gave our people something to say yes to, some opportunities to live positive, good, constructive lives, and to know they were important to someone else. And because of that, in every State in this country and in almost every major urban area, the crime rate is down, the murder rate is down, and people believe we can make a difference. And I thank you for that.

Because you supported the policies of this administration to advance peace and freedom and democracy, from the Middle East to Northern Ireland to Russia and the other places of the former Soviet Union, there are no missiles pointed at the people of the United States tonight for the first time since the dawn of the nuclear age. Peace is making progress in the Middle East and in Northern Ireland; democracy was restored to Haiti; we have supported South Africa, all because of people like you who made it possible. You have been a steadfast partner in standing up for America's best interests and America's best values.

I want to say a special word of thanks to you for the crucial role you have played in expanding freedom and opportunity in Africa. Today, two-thirds of the nations of Africa are moving toward democracy and market opportunities, with the help of American leadership and American assistance. Whether we supported historic elections in South Africa and Mozambique, provided dramatic humanitarian relief in Rwanda, assisted in the opening of stock markets in Botswana and Namibia, the United States has been committed to making a difference in Africa. Much remains to be done, fostering peace in Liberia and Angola, standing up for democracy in Nigeria, but with your help, America can remain a force for progress.

And in this debate on the budget, I implore you to remind the other Members of the Congress that we must remain a force for democracy and progress, not only in Africa but throughout the world. We cannot walk away from people who look to us for support and encouragement.

But this is still a difficult and unsettling time. In each area I mentioned, you could have said, "I heard what you said, Mr. President, but—" For example, if I had told you 30 months ago that this country could produce 7½ million jobs, 2½ million homeowners, 2 million entrepreneurs, a 4,700 stock market, the largest number of self-made millionaires in history, but the average wage of the person in the middle would go down, not up, it would have been hard to believe, but it happened.

We can say all we want that the crime rate is down, the murder rate is down, the number of people on welfare and food stamps are down, the teen pregnancy rate is down, the drug use rate among people between 18 and 34 is down. But the rate of violent crime, death, and casual drug use among our teenagers is still going up.

We can say all we want about all the peace and prosperity that is coming to the world and how democracy is sweeping the world, but in every country, forces of extremism have a stronger voice than they have had in years. And organized groups, committed to destruction, based on racial or ethnic or religious or political extremism, have enormous capacity to do that destruction. You see it in a school bus blowing up in the Middle East. You see it when a fanatic breaks open a little vial of sarin gas in a subway in Japan. You see it in a bomb blowing up the Federal building in Oklahoma City. And you see it in more subtle ways, yes, even in America.

Like when five children in an upper class suburb in this country write the hated word "nigger" in code word in their school album.

What is going on here? How do we account for all the good things and all the bad things that are happening at the same time? I've spent a lot of time thinking about this, and since last November, I've had a little more time to think about it. I believe with all my heart when the history of this era is written and people look back on it, they will say that this was the most profound period of change in the way the American people live and work and relate to the rest of the world in a hundred years.

One hundred years ago, most of our forebears lived out in the country or in little towns. Most of us farmed the land or made a living because other people were farming the land. Then we began to move to cities, and we became an industrial country. A hundred years ago, we were keeping to ourselves, but within 20 years we had to get into World War I so that the forces of freedom could win. And we began to assert national leadership.

Now, we're moving away from this industrial age to an age characterized by information and technology, where people will soon be able to do most of the work they do wherever they want to live—in a city or in an isolated place in the mountains somewhere. We are moving from a cold war in which nation-states look at each other across a great divide but still are able to provide most of people's needs, to a global economy where there's a lot of integration economically but a lot of pressures of disintegration on ordinary working people everywhere.

And what we have to do is to try to understand this time in which we live, embrace the new ideas that we need to embrace to preserve our vision of the future, which has to be rooted in the values for which you have always stood.

Don't you want a 21st century in which America is the leading opportunity society: growing entrepreneurs, growing the middle class, shrinking the under class; where everybody has a chance to live up to their God-given ability; where families and communities have a chance to solve their own problems; where the streets are safe and the schools are good and we have a clean environment and a strong health care system; and where we're still a force for peace and freedom in the world? I think that's what most of us want.

To get it, we need new ideas. We need a devotion to our old-fashioned values. We need to stop looking for ways to be divided and instead seeking common ground and higher ground. And we've got to be prepared to stand up for the future, even if it's not popular in the present. That's what this budget debate is all about. It's really not about money and programs; it's about what kind of people we're going to be. What are we going to look like in the 21st century? What are we going to look like? What are our obligations to each other? If we're a community and not a crowd, what kind of obligations do we have to our parents and to our children, to those who aren't as well off as we are, to those who through no fault of their own are not doing so well, to people all around the world who look to us for leadership? What are our obligations?

I agree with the leadership of the Republican majority in Congress that we ought to balance the budget. We never had a permanent structural deficit until about 12 years before I showed up. And to be fair to the caucus—again, this defies conventional wisdom—but the plain truth is that in the previous 12 years, in every year but one, the Congress appropriated less money than the executive branch asked for. But we wound up quadrupling the debt.

Next year, if we don't do something about it, interest payments on the debt will be bigger than the defense budget. But we have begun, you and I, to do something about it because this year the budget would be in balance but for the interest we're paying on those 12 years. The deficit was $290 billion when we started; it's down to $160 billion now. And that's not bad, a 40 percent cut in 3 years, for the first time since Harry Truman was President.

But why are we going to do this? Why should we balance the budget anyway? Because we believe it will take debt off our kids. Because we believe it will lower interest rates and free up money for the entrepreneurs who are here to borrow more money and put more people to work and make America stronger. Because we think it will fulfill our vision of the future. Therefore, when we do it, we have to do it in a way that supports that vision, otherwise there's no point in doing it in the first place. It is where we want to go that matters.

So I say to you, we ought to do this. But we ought to do it in a way that is consistent with our values, maintaining our investments in

the things that make us strong, keeping our commitments as a community. That's what we have to do.

The proposal I put forward balances the budget but increases our investment in education. We will never stop the decline in learning until we give lifetime educational opportunities to every person in this country no matter what their race, no matter what their income, no matter what their background. We will never do it.

We ought to secure the Medicare Trust Fund, but we can do that without breaking our contract with the elderly of this country. Three-quarters of them live on less than $24,000 a year. It's pretty hard to charge them several hundred dollars more a year for what they thought was already going to be paid for.

Now, let me just say that a lot of the things that I believed when I showed up here, I thought were matters of bipartisan consensus, are almost nonpartisan. When a country goes through a great period of change, it is important that people try to join hands on those things that are critical to its security and its character. That's what we did in the cold war. I think education is an important part of our security. I think growing the middle class and shrinking the under class is an important part of our security. I think reminding us, ourselves, that in the global economy of the 21st century our racial diversity is our great meal ticket to the future if we can all figure out how to get along and how to lift each other up. That's a part of our security. And we ought to treat it that way.

So I say, balance the budget, but don't deprive hundreds of thousands of young kids of a chance to get off to a good start in school. Don't deprive schools that happen to be poor of the chance to have smaller classes or computers in the classroom or high standards and high expectations or just the chance to be safe and drug-free. Don't raise the cost of going to college at a time when it's more important to go to college than ever before just because the people that used to make a lot of money out of the student loan program aren't making it anymore. Don't do that.

I want to emphasize this: My goal is to see every young person in this country get out of high school and get at least, at least, 2 years of further education. That's my goal. That ought to be your goal. That's what the economy tells us has to be everybody's goal.

And yet today, because of the rising cost of college, enrollment is already dropping for poor people and, therefore, disproportionately for minorities. And if you don't believe it's a problem, just look at California. They've been through such wrenching problems that the cost of education has gone up almost 20 percent and enrollment has dropped 10 percent. And when a State's in trouble, you need more people going, not fewer. This is a big deal, and we don't have to do it to balance the budget.

I believe, as all of you know, in reforming the welfare system but not as a way of dividing the American people but as a way of liberating people who are trapped in the system. Most people in this country work. Most parents work. So it's not unreasonable to say most people who have children who happen to be on welfare should move toward work.

But what we want in America is for every parent to be able to succeed at home and, if they must work, at work as well. We don't need to tear people down; we need to lift people up. Most people who are poor and on welfare would give anything in the world to be somewhere else doing something else. We ought to help them do it. And we ought to help them succeed as parents and workers.

We say—everybody says—if you took a poll in the Congress on Monday morning, "Everybody that does not believe in work, please stand up." Nobody would stand. "Everybody that believes we ought to encourage welfare over work, please stand up." Nobody would stand. But their budget proposal proposes to cut taxes for nearly everybody in America, including upper income people like me that don't ask for it and don't want it and sure don't need it. General Powell is about to move into that category—[laughter]—with his book.

They propose that, but you know what? They want to raise taxes on some Americans. The 14 million working families that we lowered taxes on in 1993, who are working full-time, have children in the homes, barely have enough to get by, the Congressional Black Caucus voted to lower their taxes. Now this congressional proposal is to raise their taxes by $40 billion. This is wrong. Ronald Reagan said that the earned-income credit for working families was the best antipoverty program in history because it rewarded work. We increased it so dramatically

that it was the biggest effort to lift the incomes of low-income working people and to equalize the middle class in America in 20 years. And now, while everybody else's taxes are being cut, those people's taxes are going to be raised by people who say they want to get people off welfare and into work. That is wrong. It violates our values. It's not about money; it's about families and rewarding work and standing up for what's right.

Medicare, Medicaid—for 3 years we said that health care costs were growing too fast, they had to be slowed down. The Congressional Black Caucus, with no help from members of the other party, added 3 years to the life of the Medicare Trust Fund when nobody was looking and some were denying it was there. Now, the Medicare trustees say we need to add more life to it, and it costs $90 billion to $100 billion to do it. I offered a balanced budget plan to do it, to save the Trust Fund, and add a decade of life.

Under the guise of saving the trust fund and balancing the budget, they propose to take 3 times that much out of Medicare and so much out of Medicaid that it will endanger the life of urban hospitals and rural hospitals, elderly people in nursing homes and getting care in their home, and the health care of all the poor children in the country who through no fault of their own are poor.

And so I say to you, let's save the Medicare Trust Fund. Let's slow the rate of growth in inflation in Medicare and Medicaid. But let's don't pretend that we can just jerk $450 billion out of health care system of America without hurting anybody and that we can do it without absolutely ignoring our obligations to our parents and our grandparents and to the children of this country. It is wrong. We should not do it. We can balance the budget without doing it. And we should listen to those who tell us that.

Let me just say one last thing about crime. Earlier this week I had the privilege of going to Jacksonville, Florida. Jacksonville, as a united city and county government—got some people clapping back there. It's a county that normally votes Republican and increasingly so. But they elected an African-American Democrat sheriff. Why? Because he promised to make his office the streets. Because he promised to put law enforcement officers on the streets in the neighborhood. Because he promised to make the safety of all the people in the county his first priority. And within 6 months the crime rate had gone down 9 percent, in only 6 months. And he was there with me expressing his thanks to you through me for the crime bill and the 100,000 police officers it put on the street.

The Attorney General was there with me. We had all the children from the community there. We were in a poor neighborhood. We walked the streets talking to these people who said nobody ever paid any attention to their safety before, and they were so glad to see that they could have law enforcement officers on the street.

So this sheriff stood up and said, "This is working. The crime rate's going down." The Congress should not abolish the national commitment to 100,000 police and say that they're going to meet it in some other way by cutting the money they're giving and writing a blank check to local governments or to the State. It'll never happen.

Now, out there in the country, fighting crime is a bipartisan issue. There is no constituency anywhere in America for raising the crime rate with the possible exception of Washington, DC, and this debate that's going on over the crime bill here. That also is not necessary to balance the budget, and it is wrong.

Let me just say one last thing to you about all this. Nobody knows how this is going to come out, so I've got a suggestion. We're in a 100-year period of change. You and I can no more calculate what will be popular next week or next month than a man in the Moon. In 1992, I wasn't smart enough to figure this out back then; I thought it had something to do with my ability. But in 1992, when I was nominated, on June 2, I was in third place in the polls. Six weeks later, I was in first place in the polls. Who could have predicted that? Nobody.

It is idle speculation. We have to now go back in these next 2 months and tell people with whom we disagree, Look, we want to find common ground. But we have to balance the budget in a way that is consistent with our vision. And we may have to do some things that are unpopular just because you think they're going to be right over the long run.

You know, two-thirds of the American people thought I was wrong in Haiti, but I'm glad I did it. And I think history will prove us right.

And a lot of you caucus members will have to say you lost some good colleagues out of the Congress because we voted for the Brady bill and we voted for the assault weapons ban. But you know, last year alone over 40,000 people with criminal records were unable to get handguns. And if we just take a few Uzis off the streets and out of the schools and we have a few fewer kids being shot dead standing by bus stops, having their lives robbed from them, it is worth the political price. They said, "Don't you do it," but it was worth it. We did the right thing. We did the right thing.

A few weeks ago we were trying to decide how to handle the studies of the FDA on teenage smoking. And every political adviser I had in and out of the White House said, "You can do this if you want to, but it's terrible politics, because the tobacco companies will get you. And they'll terrify all those good country tobacco farmers that are good, decent people. They work hard, but they can be scared to death. And then they'll wipe out—they'll vote against anybody in your party. And all the Americans that agree with you will find some other reason to vote against you, but they will stay against you. So don't you be the first person in office to take them on. You were already the first person in office to take the NRA on; don't do that."

But the research showed that for 30 years some of those folks were aware of the danger of tobacco. And the evidence showed that there is still targeted efforts to advertise to teenagers, even though it's illegal for children to smoke in every State in the country. And most important of all, the evidence showed that 3,000 young people a day start to smoke, and 1,000 of them will end their lives early. And if it saves a thousand lives a day for longer, fuller, better lives, then who cares what the consequences are? Twenty years from now in the 21st century, people will say they did what was right. And that is exactly what we ought to do on every single issue.

Finally, I thank Bill Jefferson for what he said about affirmative action. We reviewed every one of those programs. We looked at them all. I argued it nine ways from Sunday. It was obvious that the politics was one place and the merits were somewhere else. It's obvious that a lot of people in our country feel anxiety-ridden about the economy. And the easy answer is, "There's nothing wrong with you; you don't have to change in this time of change; we just need to get rid of the Government; and they're spending all their money on affirmative action, welfare," you know, whatever that list is.

That was the easy answer, but it's the wrong answer, not because all those programs are perfect, not because they don't need to be changed but because in the heart of America we still, we still, are not able to make all of our decisions without regard to race or gender. We ought to be able to. I pray to God someday we will. But you know it, and I know it; we still need to make a conscious effort to make sure that we get the most of every American's ability and we give every American a fair shot. That's what this is all about.

And I will say again, if it were not for our racial diversity, we wouldn't be as well positioned as we are for the 21st century. I know that it makes a difference in the administration that we have people like Ron Brown and Lee Brown and Jesse Brown and Hazel O'Leary. And I'll tell you something else, Mike Espy was the best Agriculture Secretary in 25 years. It makes a difference that we have people like Deval Patrick and Rodney Slater and Jim Joseph, who's going to be the Ambassador to South Africa. That makes a difference to how America works. Alexis Herman and Bob Nash and Maggie Williams and others make a difference in the White House. It makes a difference.

I was so attacked by the conventional wisdom for being committed to diversity. But after nearly 3 years, we're appointing Federal judges at a more rapid rate than the previous administration. We have appointed more African-Americans than the last three administrations combined. And according to the American Bar Association, they have the highest qualified ratings in the last 20 years. So I don't want to hear that you can't have excellence and equal opportunity at the same time. You can, we must, and we will.

Let me say that there is a lot of talk about personal responsibility. What we have to do is practice it. There's a lot of talk about valuing family and work and community. What we have to do is value them.

Let me close by talking about one particular American citizen that I think would be a pretty good role model for the President, the Speaker, the Senate majority leader, the Congressional Black Caucus, and everybody else that's going to be making decisions about America's future

in the next 60 days. I got permission from my wonderful wife tonight to have a date with another woman to the Congressional Black Caucus. Her name is Oseola McCarty.

At the young age of 87, she is a stellar example of what it means to live a life of dignity, service, values, and personal responsibility. Before today she had never been to Washington. She had never flown on an airplane, and when I invited her to do it, she said she'd like to come see me, but not if she had to get on an airplane. [*Laughter*] So Oseola has come all the way from Hattiesburg, Mississippi, by train.

You may have read about her in the last few weeks. A lot of people talk about the dignity of work, but from the time before she was a teenager, she worked all her life washing clothes for people. She started out charging $1.50 to $2 a bundle. She lived modestly and was able to accumulate savings over the years. In fact, while she earned what by any stretch of the imagination was a very meager income, she saved such an enormous percentage of what she earned, and she and her local banker invested it so well that she amassed a sizable sum. Last month, after a lifetime of work, this woman, who did that job for decades and decades and decades quietly and with dignity and with excellence, donated $150,000 to the University of Southern Mississippi for scholarships for African-American students.

When people ask her why in the world she did this, she said, "I just want the scholarship to go to some child who needs it, to whoever's not able to help their children. I'm too old to get an education, but they can." Well, the University has already given $1,000 scholarship in her name to an 18-year-old graduate of Hattiesburg High School named Stephanie Bullock. Someday Stephanie Bullock may be a lawyer, a doctor, perhaps a member of the Congressional Black Caucus, because of Oseola McCarty.

Our country needs more people like her, people who don't just talk about responsibility and community but who live those values. I'm proud that she's my guest tonight. Before we came over, I brought her into the Oval Office and awarded her the Presidential Citizens Medal for her extraordinary act of generosity. I'd like to ask her to come up here so you can all get a good look at her. [*Applause*]

I want to make you a promise, and I want to issue a challenge. My promise to you is that in the next few weeks when we make decisions that will shape the future of our great country into the 21st century, I'll try to keep her example in mind. And my challenge is that everyone else do the same. If we do, this great country is going to do just fine.

Thank you, and God bless you all.

NOTE: The President spoke at 9:24 p.m. in the Grand Ballroom at the Washington Convention Center. In his remarks, he referred to former boxing champion Muhammad Ali and civil rights attorney Renee Gaters.

Remarks on the Middle East Peace Process
September 24, 1995

The President. Good morning. Not long ago, Israel and the Palestinians announced that they have reached a full agreement on implementing the next phase of the Declaration of Principles. This is a big step on the road to a just and lasting peace in the Middle East. And on behalf of the American people, I want to congratulate the negotiators and their leaders who continue to work and persevere and to prevail over the enemies of peace, including some who are willing to use terror to try to derail the peace process.

At the request of the parties, I have gladly agreed to host a signing ceremony at the White House on September 28th. We will also be inviting other regional leaders and, obviously, other interested parties who have to be involved in this—entire venture a success. But this is a good day for peace in the Middle East and a good omen for good steps in the future.

Q. What do you think the impact will be on the hope for a comprehensive Middle East peace between Israel and all of its Arab neighbors?

The President. I don't think it can be anything but positive. But we've learned from experience to take these things one at a time and to hammer out step-by-step progress and not to read too much into it. But I feel quite good about this; this is a major step. And as you know from your own observations, they have worked very hard over some very contentious issues that were quite difficult and complex. And I've been encouraged by what I've heard this morning about the progress that's been made.

Thank you.

NOTE: The President spoke at 9:52 a.m. at Andrews Air Force Base, prior to his departure for Avoca, PA. A tape was not available for verification of the content of these remarks.

Remarks on Arrival in Avoca, Pennsylvania
September 24, 1995

Thank you very much. Good morning, and thank you for coming out. I want to say, first of all, how very much I appreciate the kindness that so many of you have shown to my wife and to the members of our family. And if we ever cause an interruption in ordinary flow of life here when the Rodham family comes back to its roots, I apologize for that. But you can't imagine how much they all love it.

We're going back to Lake Winola today for the first time since our daughter was not quite

2 years old. So she doesn't have much of a memory of the first time we took her up there. We were talking about that this morning, getting ready to come up here.

Let me also give you a little good news. I'm sorry we're a few minutes late this morning, but I got up early this morning at the White House and was on the phone for a couple of hours because this morning, or morning our time, not very long ago, the Israelis and the Palestinians have reached agreement on the next phase of their peace process. It's a big step forward toward ending the long, long state of siege in the Middle East. And on this day of worship, a thanksgiving for so many of us, I thought that would be a good way to get this Sunday off to the right kind of start.

I want to thank you also for the support that you have given to me and to our administration. We are doing everything we possibly can to try to lift up the values of work and family and freedom and responsibility and community in this country, to move the economy forward, to tackle the tough problems, and to bring the American people together.

And I am gratified that with all of our difficulties, we see the unemployment rate dropping, more jobs being created. The crime rate, believe it or not, now is going down in all 50 States. And we seem to be coming together again as a country and looking toward the future again.

And so I want to say that, for me at least, every day is an enormous opportunity as we go through this period of historic change for America's economy and in the whole world, to try to elevate the things that all of you live by day-in and day-out here, to try to restore economic opportunity where it was taken away in the 1980's, and to try to give people the opportunity to make the most of their own lives and families and communities the chance to solve their own problems and realize their own possibilities. It is a great honor, a great joy. And for every day you have given me to be your President, I thank you.

God bless you all.

NOTE: The President spoke at approximately 10:55 a.m. at Wilkes-Barre/Scranton International Airport.

Remarks in a Question-and-Answer Session at the Godfrey Sperling Luncheon
September 25, 1995

Godfrey Sperling. Well, Mr. President, what can I say, except it's wonderful to be over here. And as I've said before, in other times we've been at the White House, we'd love to have our breakfasts or lunches over here, maybe every week or two. Maybe Mike could work it out. [*Laughter*] But having said all that, we can get started. I hate to ask the President to sit down, but—[*laughter*]——

The President. Please, be seated, everyone.

Mr. Sperling. ——that's what we do. Our ground rules—you've been to our breakfast before and lunch, whatever we want to call this today, and you know the ground rules; everything's on the record. And you've seen this bunch of rascals before, at least a few of them. And they haven't changed; they're the same ones that you've seen in the past. So I'm giving you a little warning.

So you all know, I understand there will be transcripts of this later in the afternoon. And beyond that, I just have to say welcome to you and thank you so much for coming to my 80th birthday.

The President. I'm glad to have you here. I would like to say just to begin that the Vice President and I are delighted to have you and your family here. It's a special day. Someone told me that you had done 2,800 of these now. And——

Mr. Sperling. Almost.

The President. I was trying to think of the significance of them. One of them is that I noticed from the breakfasts that I've been to, they are notoriously high cholesterol. And so you are—you're very aging condition is a stunning rebuke to all of those who advocate healthy eating. [*Laughter*]

Mr. Sperling. I stay away from it.

The President. I don't know what the consequences of all that are, but it's a remarkable thing.

Let me also say, as you know, this is going to be a busy week around here. And you may have heard already, but in case you haven't, not too long ago, this morning, the Bosnian Government announced that they would participate in the resumption of the peace talks tomorrow in New York, which is very good news. And we do have the best chance we've had, I think, since the beginning of the conflict now to have a peace agreement come out of this. And of course, later in the week we'll have the signing here of the agreement between the Palestinians and the Israelis in the next phase of the peace agreement there.

So I'm very encouraged. I think both these things are examples of the imperative for United States leadership. And I think the world's better off because of what's happened in the last couple of years. And of course, there are a lot of things at issue there, which you might want to ask about. But I don't want to take up any more of your time.

Mood of the Country

Mr. Sperling. Well, since I own the football, I usually ask the first question. You know, I was feeling quite perky over the weekend, Mr. President, with my birthday coming up and everything. And then I read in the papers, you know, we all were in a deep blue funk. And I just have to ask you, how did we get into that funk, and how are you going to get us out of it?

The President. Well, first of all, before you draw that conclusion, I would urge you to read the entire pool report, on which the stories were——

Mr. Sperling. They weren't good translations I read in the——

The President. No, but I was basically very optimistic and upbeat about it. What I said was that the—there are a lot of contradictory things happening in American life now as a result of the fact that we're going through a period of profound change, and as you know from the stories, I believe the biggest change in the way we work, live, and relate to the rest of the world in 100 years, since we became an industrialized, more urbanized country, and since we got involved in World War I.

And I believe that in this time, there are a lot of things that seem contradictory and that are unsettling to people. And the American people have basically helped me to understand that, especially in the last year or so, just going out and listening to people talk about their own lives. I'll give you just, if I might, a couple of examples. If I had told you 30 months ago, when I became President, that we'd have 7½ million new jobs, 2½ million new homeowners, 2 million new businesses, a stock market at

4,700, the largest number of self-made millionaires in history, the entrepreneurial economy flourishing, and the median wage would go down, that would have been counter-intuitive.

But it has happened because of the complex forces in the global economy. Or if you look at the same thing happening in our society, we've got the crime rate down, the murder rate down, the welfare rolls down, the food stamp rolls down, the teenage pregnancy rate down 2 years in a row, even the divorce rate down, but violent crime among teenagers is up. Drug use among people between the ages of 18 and 34 down, but casual drug use among teenagers up. So there are these cross-cutting things. And it's perplexing to people, I think, and they feel it in their own lives.

And I think that the challenge for us all is to basically keep working for the future. You can't get—these periods of transitions come along every so often, and I feel very good about it. I feel very optimistic about the country. I think if you were betting on which country is likely to be in the strongest shape 20, 30 years from now in the 21st century, you'd have to bet on the United States because of the strength and diversity of our economy and our society. But we have some very, very important decisions to make, many of which will be made here in the next 60 days.

1996 Election

Mr. Sperling. Mr. President, with the Republicans always trying to trip you up, and sometimes successfully, why in the world do you want 4 more years in the White House? Why not go home, you know, and go fishing?

The President. Because I believe that my vision of this country is the one that's best for the country. I believe that our policies best embody the values of the American people who want to see our country preserve the American dream and our country's ability to lead the world and want to see families strengthened, want to see ordinary Americans have the chance to make the most of their own lives, and want to, in the words of Governor Chiles from Florida, want to see us be a community, not a crowd, a set of people who don't just occupy the same space of ground and elbow each other until the strongest win and the weakest fall, but a group of people who believe that we're all better off when we recognize obligations to one another and act on those obligations within our families and across generational and income and other lines.

So I feel very optimistic about the future of this country, but especially now, I think it's more important to run than it was 4 years ago. Four years ago I ran because I thought there was no action being taken to give us a new economic policy based on opportunity, a new social policy based on responsibility, and to try to bring this country together and change the way the Government works. Now I think the alternative vision out there is destructive of the future we want.

Mr. Sperling. Bob Thompson, I think, has a question. Then we'll move around the best we can. Carl.

The Presidency

Q. Mr. President, you've had 30 rather stormy months here. What are the lessons you've learned that you didn't know before about your office and its power and its authority?

The President. I think I had underestimated the importance of the President, even though I had read all the books and seen it all and experienced it in my lifetime. I think I had underestimated the importance of the Presidency as a bully pulpit and the importance of what the President says and is seen to be saying and doing as well as what the President does.

And I think that I underestimated—I had overemphasized in my first 2 years to some extent the importance of legislative battles as opposed to other things that the President ought to be doing. And I think now we have a better balance of both using the Presidency as a bully pulpit and the President's power of the Presidency to do things, actually accomplish things, and working on the process in Congress but not defining—permitting the Presidency to be defined only by relationships with the Congress.

But I must say, they've been a stormy 30 months. It's been a stormy time for the country, but if you look at what has been accomplished, I think the record has been good for America and will be good for our future. The economy is in better shape. We passed the toughest crime bill in American history, and it's plainly playing a role in driving the crime rate down throughout the country. When there was no action on welfare reform, we gave two-thirds of the States— I think more than two-thirds now—the right to pursue their own reforms. And we have lowered the cost and increased the availability of

a college education. We gave more kids a chance to get off to a good start in school. We've pushed school reforms that led to smaller classes, more computers, and higher standards. We've advanced the cause of the environment while growing the economy. And we've downsized the Government and made it more efficient, far more than our predecessors who talked about doing that but didn't. And if you look at the record in foreign policy, the world is a safer, more prosperous place today because of the initiatives we've taken, I mean, just in the last year, the efforts in the Middle East and Northern Ireland, in Haiti, the Japanese trade agreement, the North Korea nuclear initiative, the First Lady's trip to Beijing coming on the heels of the Cairo conference, and of course, the progress being made in Bosnia today. So it's a stormy time. But I think it's been a pretty productive time. And the American people, I think, are better off because of the things that we've done.

Mood of the Country

Q. Mr. President, I wanted to go back to the more philosophic view that you started out with and have been talking about recently, you've claimed that this is sort of a turning point, in 100-year cycles. Speaker Gingrich talks in those terms also. And when we—in fact, was in the breakfast a couple of weeks ago—he talked a bit more in terms of the country has had several, seven or eight, cycles of history and that we're in a period now—he really ly compares it to the early 1930's. A new majority is being built, and he portrays it as that he's on the cutting edge of the new majority and last year's election and that you're—I think he referred to once as perhaps the last defender of German socialism, but that you represent the old big Government style and that he's the new style. Now, why—maybe you're both right. Is that possible?

The President. No. [*Laughter*] I mean, it's possible that there are elements in both our analyses that are right. But you know, as we say at home, that's their party line, and they have enough access and enough unity and enough discipline to spout the party line that they may be able to convince people of it. But it's blatantly untrue—I mean, to say that I'm the last defender of German socialism.

It is true that I don't approve of their plans to deny more children access to a healthy start in school or putting more old people out of nursing homes or walk away from all the lessons we've learned in the last 20 years, whether it's preserving our environment or maintaining some human standards in the way we run these nursing homes. It's true that I don't think that we ought to—I don't think a good reform for the future is making it harder for young people to go to college, thereby ensuring a decline in the college enrollment rate and continued aggravation of the income differentials.

It's true that I don't believe that it's a great idea to raise taxes on working families making $15,000 a year to lower taxes on me, the people in my income group. That's true; I don't agree with that. But to talk about German socialism is ludicrous.

Let me just—we had two Republican Presidents before I showed up. Who reduced the size of the Government more? There are 163,000 fewer people working for the Federal Government today than there were the day I became President, I might add, without one vote from a Republican in Congress supporting me. The Democrats did it; all the Republicans voted against it.

Who reduced the number of regulations more—16,000 pages of regulations reduced by the Vice President's program? We supported school reforms, like charter schools, which allow private groups of individuals to get a charter from school districts to run schools. I visited one of them in San Diego the other day.

Who gave more authority to States to pursue reforms in welfare and education—I mean, in health care? I did, more than the two previous Presidents combined. Who reduced regulation more in the Small Business Administration, the Department of Education, the EPA, you name it? We did. So that may be their line, but it's not the right line.

The truth is that I still believe that we have certain obligations to each other—that is really the difference—and that the Federal Government's job, to some extent, is to try to make sure that we are stronger as a community and that we give people an opportunity to make the most of their own lives and that we give their families and their communities a chance to solve their own problems and that when we walk away from that, experience shows us we pay a very high price.

So I think that if their view prevails, it may be more like the twenties than the thirties.

Russian Nuclear Cooperation With Iran

Q. Mr. President—[*inaudible*]—on to serious matters on foreign policy. Two things that so far you have been unable to solve, I want to ask you about them. Number one, the Russians are apparently sending not one, but four nuclear reactors to Iran. And there's a move in the Senate—in fact, the Senate passed an amendment last week—cutting off American aid to Russia if those reactors actually go to Iran. And second, the Russians have violated the CFE, Conventional Forces in Europe Treaty, although it only takes effect I think in the next couple of weeks. I think both parties have been honored to keep it. And you have said on both these issues in the past, sir, you have said we will not allow reactors to go to Iran and we do not think the Russians have any legal right to break that treaty. What is your position on those two issues right now, sir?

The President. Well, first of all, on the treaty, we are working very hard with them and where the two sides, I believe, are getting somewhat closer together. And I think if you talk—even the Europeans believe that some accommodation can be reached, some agreement can be reached on the Conventional Forces in Europe Treaty that is fair to the Russian position and still fulfills the purposes of the treaty. So I'm hopeful that there will be an accord reached there, and until we fail to reach one, I don't think I should comment further.

On the Iranian nuclear reactor, you know what our position is. We think it's wrong. The Vice President—maybe he wants to say a word about it—has worked very hard through the Gore-Chernomyrdin commission to try to work through this. You know, their position is that this contract was made at a previous time and that they are basically giving them the same kind of reactor we proposed to help the North Koreans build. And so they disagree with our position. Our position is the North Koreans have certain nuclear capacity, and we're building it down, why should we give the Iranians anything?

And so we're continuing to work with them on it. And I hope that ultimately we will be able to work this out. I do believe that a lot of these threats, given the present state of play in Russia and where their Duma is and the way they talk, may be counterproductive. I mean, it may not further the objectives that the Congress seeks. Do you want to add anything to that?

The Vice President. Well, I think, you began by referencing a report on multiple reactors that I think was based on a news story that was garbled in the telling. And we can go into more detail later on that one. I just urge you not to give too much credence to that particular report.

But as the President said, the dialog is continuing, and they've agreed to——

Q. They're not sending—they're not sending the reactors——

The Vice President. You mentioned four reactors, that was—well, the one negotiation is the one that is still the subject of our dealings with them. It antedated our time in office, but they have agreed to continue a dialog on possibly canceling that sale. It is, as the President said, not a violation of any international law or treaty. Notwithstanding that fact, they understand the seriousness with which we do it. We're pressing it very hard. We do not accept that it is a good thing for them to do, and we hope to be able to convince them to back off it.

Wage Levels

Q. Mr. President, if during the first 3 years of your administration, the economy has basically been doing well but the median wage has been going down, then that suggests that whatever it was that you were doing for the economy, especially when the Democrats were fully in control of Congress and the Presidency, was not enough. Now, if you were re-elected, what would you do to help the average working person in the country? And what would you be able to do, especially if the Congress remained in Republican hands?

The President. Well, first of all, what I suggest is that, keep in mind, these trends of wage stagnation go—depending on whose numbers you look at—go back at least 15, and perhaps 20, years. So I think it's unrealistic to think that you can turn them around in 2 years. But I believe there are certain things that we need to do.

First of all, I think that if we can—the expansion of trade, which we have pushed, has generated about 2 million new jobs. On average, those have been higher wage-paying jobs. I think we need to do things that change the job mix. That is a slow but an important remedy. So that a high percentage of the total number of

jobs in America have a higher average income. In order to do that, we not only have to continue our trade policies, we must continue to invest in research and development and in new technologies.

Now that has been something that hasn't been noticed at all in this budget debate. But one of the quarrels I have with the congressional budget is that it takes our R&D budget down by roughly six-tenths of a percent of GDP. And a lot of Republican high-tech executives are very concerned about it. They believe it will lead to a loss of America's position in a lot of important industries over the next 5 years. So changing the job mix is an important part of it.

Continuing to get a higher and higher percentage of people in education is an important part of it. I have given the Congress one proposal, which I thought looked very much like a Republican program, which I expected them to embrace, the so-called "GI bill" for America's workers, in which we proposed to consolidate 70 Labor Department training programs and not block grant them to the States but give them in the form of vouchers to unemployed people and welfare people so that when people lose their jobs, they can immediately go back to a new training program.

Thirty years ago, 80 percent of the people who were laid off from work were called back to their old jobs. Today, 80 percent of the people who are laid off are not called back to their old jobs. And it's bad for employers and for employees—because employers pay unemployment—bad for employers and employees to let people traipse around looking for jobs when what they really need is to immediately be in a retraining program.

I think we should raise the minimum wage. It's going to go to a 40-year low if we don't. I think we should avoid gutting the earned-income tax credit for working families. I think that's one of the two or three worst things in the congressional budget. It will aggravate income inequality.

And I think, frankly, the proposals that we have endorsed that the Congress is working on from the Jordan commission will have some impact. If we lower the aggregate number of legal immigrants coming into the country, even by a modest amount, it will free up more jobs to people who now don't have any, and it will tighten the labor market some.

I talked to the Governor of Nebraska the other day, the State with our lowest unemployment rate, and I said, "Do you think when we're creating all these jobs, it's going to ever raise wages?" He said, "Yes." He said, "I just don't think the markets are quite tight enough in the country." He said, "In Nebraska, wages are up, and even at the places that used to not give benefits—fast food places—they're all giving health care benefits now and wages are up." So he said, "I think if you can get the unemployment rate down maybe another half a point, you can get that done."

So those are my ideas for raising the wages levels: change the job mix, improve the training, continue to expand trade, raise the minimum wage, and have a modest reduction in the number of legal immigrants. We'll still be a country of immigrants, but we should lower the total. We raised it, after all, dramatically, in 1990 to help deal with the cold war. We've done a lot of that, and I think we should come back down now.

Colin Powell

Q. Mr. President, how do you explain the Colin Powell phenomenon?

The President. That's your job, not mine. [*Laughter*]

Q. We need help. [*Laughter*]

The President. No, you do just fine. I'm the President. [*Laughter*]

President's Popularity

Q. Mr. President, you started off with a great laundry list of things that have happened in your administration so far, and yet, we had a Republican dominated Congress come into office last fall. And there's a lot of animosity toward you personally out there in the public. How do you account for that?

The President. That requires political analysis, too. Look, I took on a lot of tough issues, and I made a lot of people mad. You know, look at what they said about my economic program in 1993. They tried to convince every American I'd raise their income taxes when I haven't. They said it would bring on a recession.

You all ever ask them when they're having their press conferences how they won the Congress on a false premise? They said, you know, it was going to be the end of the world if— the end of the world if the Clinton economic program were passed, we'd have a terrible reces-

sion. Instead, we had the best economic performance we've had in two or three decades.

I made a lot of people—you know, the House—I still believe if you analyze those races, race by race by race, the House of Representatives is in Republican hands today because we took on the Brady bill and the assault weapons ban. And everybody knew they were unpopular. People said to me, "Don't do this. There's a reason no President has ever taken on the NRA. There is a reason for this. I don't care what the poll says, the people who are against this will vote against everybody who votes for it, and the people who are for it will find another reason to vote against it. They won't have any convictions. Only the antis will have convictions." But I'll tell you something, 40,000 people last year didn't get guns because of it, 40,000 people with criminal records.

And if we keep a few Uzis off the streets and out of the schools and we keep a few more innocent kids from being shot down at bus stops, it was worth it. You know, I had the same argument here on the tobacco thing. They said, "You've got to be crazy. There's a reason no sitting President has ever taken these people on. They'll scare all those good tobacco farmers to death. They'll vote out Democrats. They'll say you're trying to have the Government take over people's lives. Don't do this. This is a dumb thing to do. I don't care what the polls say. They'll all be against you, and the people that are for you will find another reason to vote against you."

Q. And——

The President. And—let me finish. You asked this question, I want to—and I believe—you know, we know 3,000 kids a day start smoking. We know that—at least we know some of those tobacco interests have known for 30 years it was destructive and addictive. We know 1,000 of those kids are going to die early. If you want to do things, you've got to make people mad. And if the people you make mad have access to television programs, radio programs, access to channels of communication, they will go wacky, and they will generate animosity.

Now, I will say this, my sense is that the level of personal animosity has gone down as people see who's really fighting for real family values and real interests of American families and real interests of small business and trying to give ordinary people a chance to make the most of their own lives. But you know, I did not take this job to try to maintain high levels of popularity.

You go back and look; I had a very specific agenda I was going to try to implement. And I was well aware that people would be against it. Look at this—look at this budget debate on the student loans. They even went through an accounting gimmick to try to convince people that the direct student loan program was more expensive than the guaranteed student loan program, when everybody in America knows it's not true. Why? Because they want to take money away from students and give it back to bankers.

Well, the people that lost their money weren't happy. The people that were going to benefit from the student loan program—there weren't enough of them to know that at election time. I think the main thing that we all have to do is to figure out what we believe and fight for it and be willing to work together with people who disagree with us, if we can find honest common ground. And we'll let the popularity take care of itself. I just tried to do what I said I would do when I ran.

Q. Just to follow up, do you wish, in retrospect, you might not have taken on a few of those, like gays in the military?

The President. Well, to be fair, I didn't take that on. That was an issue that was visited on the Presidency. I mean, I could have said, "We'll just let the courts go through that." But let's talk about that. That's become more of a slogan than a fact. The position I took, remember, was not that we should change the rules of conduct, which prohibited homosexual activity, but that we should not ask people or persecute people for their failure to lie about their sexual orientation. That position was endorsed by Barry Goldwater and by most of the combat veterans of the Vietnam war serving in the United States Congress.

Now, the military thought it went too far, so what did we do? We changed the position. We studied it for a few months. We changed it. We wound up with a position with which we fought two World Wars, Korea, and Vietnam. We did not bring an end to military order in our time. All we did was to change the position that was put in in President Reagan's tenure.

And look, the United States Government was covered up with lawsuits. We were losing lawsuits. I suppose the easy thing to do would say, "Oh, well, let the courts go forward." I was

trying to find a way to put an end to this so that the military could just put this issue behind it and go on being the world's best military. And you may disagree with the position I took or the position that we came out with, but the position we're in now is roughly how we won two World Wars and fought through Korea and Vietnam. It's hardly the end of civilization as we know it.

And the other position would not have been either.

Q. [*Inaudible*].

The President. Well, I didn't have any choice. The people who brought it up were the Republican Senators. They made it their number one legislative—go back and read the chronology of how all this came up. They stirred it and swung it and made sure it was the number one issue of the world. Do I wish I had never taken a position on it? You know, I often say what I think. My position on this was basically taken in the campaign when someone asked me about it. And by the way, don't forget one other thing. There was also evidence which was being put into all these court cases that the military knew that they had some gay service members who were permitted to serve in Desert Storm because they were needed and they were good service members, and then they were kicked out, which I thought was not a very good thing. All this happened before I showed up.

Civil Rights

Q. Mr. President, your home State in 1968 voted for George Wallace, the State that produced Orval Faubus, Little Rock Central High School. Even your severest critics—[*inaudible*]—acknowledge your own long and strong commitment to civil rights. Do you think—[*inaudible*]—see the country change, that America is ready to elect a black President?

The President. I would hope that the American people could evaluate any candidate without regard to their race or their gender. And I would hope that that would be the case. You know, that's the way I've lived my life. That's the way I've staffed my administration. That's the way I've done my work, and that's what I hope is the case in this country.

Debt Limit Legislation

Q. Mr. President, Speaker Gingrich has—[*inaudible*]—unilateral right to refuse to schedule a vote which would then suspend the raging debt limit. Does that create problems for you—both the procedure where the Speaker claims a unilateral veto and the threat to raise the debt limit?

The President. Well, I think it's wrong. I mean, I think it is wrong not to raise the debt limit. The United States in over 200 years has never defaulted on its debt. We have paid our debts. We have been an honorable citizen in that sense. And it is simply wrong.

I would also say it would ultimately be self-defeating. If what the Republicans in Congress want to do is to balance the budget, rather than to destroy the Federal Government, then I share their goal. And I have given them a balanced budget plan, and my door has been open from the beginning to work with them on that.

If we were to default on our debt, you have seen already in other countries, in events just in the last 12 months, how rapidly the financial markets react to such things. And what they would do is to say that the United States is no longer reliable. Then the cost of carrying our debt, the interest rates, would be raised, and that would make it harder to balance the budget. We'd spend more and more and more of taxpayers' money on interest payments on the debt and less and less on national defense or education or anything else. It's ultimately self-defeating, and it's wrong and it's irresponsible and it's not necessary.

We can reach an accord here on balancing the budget. But there is a process that we have to go through to do that. We are not going to have a unilaterally dictated budget; we are going to have a discussion about it. And as I said, more than any Democrat in many years, I've shown not only a willingness but a desire to make the Government smaller, less bureaucratic, more entrepreneurial, and to target investments while reducing unnecessary spending. We can make this work.

But blackmail is not they way to do it, and I'm not going to be blackmailed. And I'm not going to just sign a budget that I know will put people out of nursing homes or deprive people of the chance to go to college or children the chance to be in Head Start or compromise the environment. I'm not going to do that; I'm just not going to do that. We can get a balanced budget that the entire financial world thinks is a great thing. But it has to be done in an honor-

able way, and defaulting on our debts is not an honorable thing to do.

NAFTA

Q. Mr. President, just to follow up on your remarks here about the trade policy. The initial Commerce Department numbers indicate a modest dropoff—[*inaudible*]—NAFTA. That was expected. What wasn't expected is that what was a U.S. trade surplus with Mexico has become a trade deficit. Given the job loss and given the worsening trade numbers, has NAFTA turned out to be a worse deal than you expected? And politically, given the strength of economic nationalism in many parts of the country, do you have any fear that NAFTA is going to end up hurting you in a lot of key industrial States next year?

The President. Well, let's analyze it. Let me answer the question on the merit first. What happened in the short run was that NAFTA was a much better deal for us in the first year than we thought it would be. We had a much bigger trade surplus than we thought we'd have. We generated far more new jobs than we thought we would, and they were basically high-wage jobs. And because of the financial difficulties of Mexico, which were unanticipated, it turned out to be a worse deal in the second year than we thought it would be. And because we ran a trade deficit, which we did anticipate once the Mexican economy went down, we have a slight net job loss.

Does that mean NAFTA was a mistake? No, for two reasons. Number one, if the Mexican economy had gone through what it has just gone through without NAFTA and without the trading relationship with the United States, they would be in even worse shape. We would have a bigger illegal immigration problem. We would have a bigger period of instability down there. Democracy would be more at risk in Mexico. And we would be worse off than we are with NAFTA.

It is unfortunate that the Mexican economy—that they tried to expand it too fast and in some ways it were improvident and they didn't cut back in an election year. And then, from my point of view, there was an overcorrection by the financial markets. They punished them too much. But still, we are better off vis-a-vis Mexico than we would have been if NAFTA hadn't passed. If NAFTA hadn't passed we'd have a trade deficit with Mexico this year because they wouldn't be able to buy anything from us.

The second reason it was the right thing to do is, in a period like this where things are changing so rapidly, you cannot calculate from month to month or year to year. If you look at 10 years from now, 20 years from now, 25 years from now, it is plainly the right thing to do. A strong, stable, healthy, democratic Mexico with a sensible economy is plainly in our interest. It will stabilize our borders. It will help us economically. And it will promote our goal of a world trading system and a world moving toward democracy and peace. So I think it's the right to do.

On the politics of it, it was always a political risk for a Democrat to do what I did on NAFTA. But I believed in it. And it was one of the changes I thought the Democratic Party had to go for, not to give up fair trade, which is embodied in the Japanese trade agreement, but to go for free trade as well, to go for more open trade. It's just what I believe is the right thing to do, and I'll live with the political consequences.

Capital Gains Tax

Q. Mr. President, I'd like to ask you a question that I hear a lot of people around the country asking, and that is, would the cut in the capital gains tax that is enacted by both the Senate and the House in itself be reason enough for you to veto a bill that contains those provisions?

The President. I probably should be a little chagrined to admit this, but I am not absolutely sure what the precise provisions were of their tax. Let me say this: I believe my obligation is to try to reach a balanced budget. There will be a tax cut in this balanced budget. I want the tax cut, as much as possible, directed toward people who are out there working for a living, dealing with the economic uncertainties in the marketplace, trying to raise their children and educate themselves and their children. That's what I believe.

I also believe that we have provided quite a good environment for investors in this country. As I said, we have more self-made millionaires in the last 2 years than any comparable time period in American history, and the stock market is at 4,700. You know that I'm not philosophically opposed to all capital gains taxes because we had a capital gains tax in the '93 eco-

nomic plan that cut the tax rate 50 percent on people that invested in new or small businesses for 5 years. And I was prepared to go with the Bumpers bill, which would have taken it down to zero, if the investments went longer.

So, my answer to you, sir, is it depends on what form the capital gains tax is in in the final bill and how it works and will it really fulfill our objectives. What are our objectives? We want more jobs and higher incomes. If it's consistent with an overall package that gives more jobs and higher incomes, certainly I would consider that. I would be obliged to consider that. I cannot tell the Republican majority that they have to consider compromising with me and then we not considering trying to reach out to them. But the test should be, does it give you jobs and incomes? That's really what we need to do in this country.

Mood of the Country

Q. I just wanted to return to the original question—[*inaudible*]—asked about the funk that the Nation appears to be in. And I wonder if you could explain to us what your point is there and what it is a President can do about a nation that's in a funk? And are we going to see any more appearances of the Blues Brothers? [*Laughter*]

The President. If I thought it would help, I'd sure do it.

Last year, last November, plainly the country was in kind of an anxious mood, a negative mood, a frustrated mood about the Government. And I was saying that I thought that one of the reasons that it happened is that I had inadequately fulfilled—to go back to the first question that was asked back here—I had inadequately filled the first responsibility of the President, in terms of the bully pulpit, in terms of trying to say, here's the change we're going through. Here's how I think it's going to come out all right. Here's my vision for it. Let's do this based on our fundamental values of work and family and responsibility.

I think the country is sort of moving into a more positive frame of mind as we see more and more good economic news and as we see more and more evidence that some problems we thought couldn't be solved, you can actually make progress on them. I mean, 5 years ago, if you had asked people, do you think you could ever bring the crime rate down, they'd probably say no. Well, now the crime rate's going down in virtually every city and State in the country, largely because people have figured out that these community policing strategies, among other things, really work.

So what I'm saying is, what I think we have to do is to be optimistic about the future. But to do it, we have to understand that the news—we live in a good news/bad news time, like all tumultuous times. And we have to understand what we have to do to get more good news and what we have to do to attack the bad. And I think once you understand that, that increases your level of security and your level of optimism. And this country thrives on optimism. We have to maintain our optimism.

These problems we have are not insoluble. But we have to just keep that upbeat outlook. And I sense that more and more people are looking at the future in that way and balancing the scales in what I would consider to be an accurate way. And I think it's because the American people are pretty smart and they are sensing all these things in their own lives.

Medicare

Q. [*Inaudible*]—lead editorial accusing the House Democrats of demagoging the Medicare issue. Are you concerned that the tactics taken by the House Democrats are losing the battle of public opinion? And how would you characterize your view on Medicare vis-a-vis the House Democrats?

The President. Well, I think institutionally we have different responsibilities. And you can see that, I think, by the way the majority carried out their responsibilities when they were in the minority.

My job, I believe, is to present a balanced budget, and I have done it. My job is to present an alternative plan for Medicare and Medicaid which will be part of a balanced budget and which will also help the Medicare Trust Fund to lengthen its life. That is my job.

Historically, minority parties in the Congress have thought that their main job was to point out what they disagreed with with the majority's proposal. And that is, after all, what the people who are now in the majority did for the last 2 years before they became the majority, on every conceivable issue.

Now, so the idea that they should fashion an alternative is—there are cases in which they have—they did have an alternative welfare reform bill, for example. But I think in the end

they will be voting for an alternative. They think their job right now is to point out some facts which have been lost in this debate. For example, let's just take the Medicare issue. The congressional majority relies on the report of the trustees in Medicare coming out of the HHS process. They say Medicare is in trouble, and we have to help it. And we have, as you know, added 3 years to the life of the Trust Fund in the first 2 years of my administration.

But then they say—we agree with them on that, but they're not right about medical inflation, and they're not right about how much it costs to fix it. So what the Democrats are pointing out is that basically that the Republican proposal cuts Medicare 3 times as much as the trustees say is necessary to stabilize the Trust Fund and that at least half of the Medicare cuts are coming from beneficiaries, out of a pot that has nothing to do with the Trust Fund.

So that since a lot of these people live on $400, $500, $600 a month Social Security, these proposals, if you look at the Senate proposal, these proposals will in effect lower their income by 5 to 10 percent in the context of a budget which will raise the income of some of the wealthiest people in the country by cutting their taxes. Now, I think that's a very useful thing for them to be doing. As long as we know that in the end we've got to balance the budget and bail out the Trust Fund, it needs to be pointed out that the Medicare cuts are 3 times what is necessary to fix the Trust Fund. And it needs to be pointed out that the impact, therefore, is to lower the incomes of the elderly poor while we're going to raise other people's incomes.

Q. Why do you suppose that the Washington Post and other normally sympathetic newspapers and other institutions see that as demagoguery?

The President. Well, you'd have to ask them. But I think that part of it is, they see that, over the long run, this entitlements question is going to have to be dealt with. And so they figure that anybody that—they just want to see as many proposals as possible dealing with the entitlements question. I agree with that.

But keep in mind—let me just say—there are two issues here in Medicare that shouldn't be lost, and I don't want to overcomplicate this. The first question is, right now, from now until the end of the decade and into the first few years of the next century, let's stabilize the Medicare trust fund so that we get back up to where it normally has been over the last 30 years. You know, let's get—we ought to—excuse me—ought to always have a life of, you know, 10, 11 years, something like that to stabilize it.

The second issue is a very big issue, but it's totally unaddressed here, and that is what happens when the baby boom retires and how will that change things? There ought to be a long-term effort to address that. But that is not addressed by any of these proposals here, and so we shouldn't confuse them.

Colin Powell

Q. Mr. President, I realize this is probably our job, too, but I wonder if you would help us and tell us what you think is the defining difference between you and Colin Powell?

The President. Near as I can tell, he's—I will tell you this. I was grateful for his statement—and this is no criticism of him to say this, I want to emphasize that—I wish that more Americans who agreed on the assault weapons ban and the Brady bill had been out there last November. It might have made a difference. But that's not a criticism of him because he's coming out of a period of military service when he didn't feel that he should be a public spokesman.

I was grateful for what he said about abortion, that he didn't want to criminalize it, but that we should reduce it and emphasize adoption more because that's what I've worked very hard to do. And the First Lady's emphasized that, and we've done a lot to facilitate, for example, cross-racial adoptions and things of that kind.

I was grateful for what he said about affirmative action, because I believe in the kind of affirmative action practiced in the United States Army, and I don't believe it constitutes quotas or reverse discrimination or giving unqualified people things they shouldn't have.

So all I can say to you is that on those statements that he has made, I am profoundly appreciative. I think it's helped America to stay kind of in the sensible center and moving forward instead of being pulled too far in one direction or the other.

Speaker of the House Newt Gingrich

Q. Mr. President, I know you have many defining differences with Newt Gingrich, but what is your working relationship like with him? Do you find it productive? And secondly, do you think you'll be able to come to agreement on

most of these big issues this year, whether it's Medicare, welfare, the budget, tort reform, maybe even regulatory reform?

The President. Our personal relationship has basically been candid and cordial. And I've enjoyed our conversations, and they're basically—our private conversations are basically free of political posturing; they're candid, and they're straightforward. I'm sure that I do things that frustrate him, and sometimes he does things that frustrate me. I think this debt ceiling issue is wrong. And I think when he shook hands with me in New Hampshire on political reform and lobby reform and said we'd appoint a commission, we should have done it. I mean, that frustrates me. But we have, I think, a basically a decent working relationship on a personal level.

Do I think we'll reach an agreement on most of the issues? I do. I believe in America. I believe in the process. I believe that it's time for us to adopt a balanced budget. I think it's the right thing to do. But it is time to adopt a balanced budget consistent with growing the economy and growing the middle class and shrinking the under class and making this country stronger, which means we can't just turn away from things like education and technology and research. And it's time to do it consistent with our obligations to our children and our parents, which means we can't turn away from what we should be doing on the environment, for example.

So I think—but do I believe we will get an agreement? I do. This country's not around here after all this time because we let the trains run off the tracks. It's around here because people of good faith who have honest differences find principle compromises and common ground. And that's what I think will happen here; that's what I believe will happen. I think there's too much energy in the country saying, make this country work and move this country forward, for us to turn back.

Q. So you expect to have a series of signing ceremonies——

The President. I do. I think there will be some—there may be some vetoes first, but I think in the end, we'll reach accord. That's what I believe will happen.

Legalized Gambling

Q. Mr. President—[*inaudible*]—this morning on the spread of legalized gambling. More and more cities and States are relying on it as a source of income. And at the same time, there's been an increase in the social consequences of gambling, has prompted Senators Lugar and Simon to call for a Government commission on the subject. One scientist estimated that three dollars in social costs for every dollar that the States and cities take in. What's your position on legalized gambling? Are you for a national lottery, or——

The President. No.

Q. ——or are you somewhere down the line?

The President. I've always been against it, all my——

Q. What's your feeling about this?

The President. Well, first of all, let me just say, I mean, this is another one of my unpopular positions, I know, because it's very popular everywhere, because it looks like easy money. It's tax money that doesn't seem to be tax money. People give it up freely, instead of by paying—you know, filling out a form. But let me give you a little background.

When I grew up in Hot Springs, Arkansas, until I was a teenager, my hometown had the largest illegal gambling establishment in America. And it was basically permitted to operate with a wink and a nod from the State and local law enforcement officials. The only good thing about it being illegal was that it kept all the national syndicates out of it. It was sort of a homegrown deal that had existed for many, many years, going back to the twenties. But I'm quite familiar with this. And then there was a move to legalize it in the late sixties, which failed a vote.

And then when I was Governor, we had another vote on legalizing gambling in very limited ways and in just certain places. And I opposed it, and we defeated it again. And we did it because I believe that it disguised the social costs and because I believed it was not a good way to raise public funds. The lotteries are not so onerous; they're much more—they're more benign than other legalized gambling, I think. And States obviously have a right to do it.

But I wouldn't favor a national lottery because all we'd do is just saturate the market. We would weaken the States that are already doing it. We'd be taking money away from them and complicating it. And I don't favor any other kind of national legalized gambling efforts just because, based on my own personal experience and what I saw and what I know are the side effects, I just would not be in favor of it.

Q. Do you support the commission? The idea—[*inaudible*]—Federal commission?

The President. I would be glad to consider it. This is the first I've ever heard of it so I don't have an opinion.

Bosnia

Q. Mr. President, if NATO air strikes have helped advance the cause of peace in Bosnia, in hindsight should we have done this earlier?

The President. Well, as you know, the United States was willing to do it earlier. And I think we—let me—let's review the last 2½ years. We had a pretty peaceful 1994 because of the threat of NATO air power. We had a pretty peaceful 1994. The death rate went way down in Bosnia. But there was no progress made at the negotiating table. And then the Bosnian Serbs determined that they could take hostages and avoid the threat of air power. And they wound up doing it, and it worked. That is, we were unable to persuade our allies to take action through the air until after Srebrenica and Zepa fell. Then the London conference occurred. There was a renewed commitment, and I was convinced at the time that our allies really meant it. And that air action combined with the diplomatic initiative of Dick Holbrooke and the members of his team and the gains on the ground of the Croatian and the Bosnian armies, all those things together contributed to the circumstance which we have now.

So if there had been a stronger allied response earlier, would it have made a difference? I think it quite likely could have. But I—and, you know, we can revisit that. The main thing we need to say is that we have a chance now to make a decent and an honorable peace. The changes on the ground, the diplomatic mission, and the bombing campaign all contributed to it.

Two-Party System

Q. Mr. President, you've mentioned the frustration in the country. You think that one of the things you're going to be dealing with next year is a climate politically where people don't like either party, where basically it's sort of "a plague in both your houses." And how do you really—how do you deal with that? Isn't that one of the reasons for the increasing popularity of people like Colin Powell?

The President. Well, I think, first of all, if you look historically, that is not an atypical development in a transition period, because the debate becomes wider and people become more open to different things. Some of them are quite good and sensible; some of them are, in my judgment, too extreme. But we had, I think, four parties on the ballot in the 1948 Presidential election, just to mention one period of transition.

Both psychologically and substantively, things, you know, began to be more open. I think in this time period—I think the—you know, when people have 50 channels on their television station at night, if you say would you rather have 3 parties instead of 2, it's pretty obvious what the answer's going to be.

And the third thing I would say is—and this is a challenge that I think, frankly, those of you who are in the print media can perhaps help us to meet. The information age is a mixed blessing for serious public policy and politics, because the pressures on people who live in Washington to speak in terms that aggravate the differences and simplify the issues so that they can get their 10 or 15 seconds over to the American people at night are enormous. And sometimes it benefits one party, sometimes it benefits another, and they win a big election victory over it. But the aggregate impact of it is, if it doesn't quite resonate with what people think is the whole truth—all the facts—is to make people disillusioned with the process, even as they reward people who may be kind of shaving it in ways that are not good.

So, one of the things I'm looking forward to in the next election is to try to restore what I thought we had in 1992, that I thought was so good, you know, the town meetings, the debates and the different formats, the debates in which people were involved and could ask their questions. All those things, I felt, helped to restore people's faith in the system.

So I do believe—one thing I agree with Speaker Gingrich on, I think that over time, the American people have been well served by basically having two stable political parties.

But I would remind you that one reason that's worked is that both parties have had a rather broad tent. They have had philosophical convictions. There have been clear differences, but they have made room in their parties for people of different views so they could make principle compromises and keep moving the country forward.

I think that is what has worked best for America over the long run. The American people will be the final judge of what will work best in the future.

Campaign Finance Reform

Q. Mr. President, we've been talking, really since—[*inaudible*]—first question about the frustration, and you've answered somewhat philosophically. There's one thing that hasn't really changed since 1992 and that's the way we raise money to pay for this thing. You spent much of last week, some of it in semi-private forums, basically building your kitty so you could run next year, before the public money kicks in. Isn't there a better way? And isn't some of the frustration that we see in the country related to the cynicism that develops from the way we fund our politics?

The President. I believe it is, of course. And I think some of the things that were done in 1974, in an attempt to promote reform after Watergate, in a curious way, within a period of 20 years, may have made the process worse because it tended to mean that a higher percentage of fundraising, particularly for Members of Congress, was more concentrated around specific issues. So that I don't think that's what the people meant to do in '74, but I think it had the—you know, devolving things to PAC's and all that gives the appearance, if not the reality, that more and more of the fundraising is tied to specific decisions. And I don't think that's good.

And I did what I could to persuade the previous Congress, as you know, unsuccessfully, to pass campaign finance reform. And I thought that in this Congress, the only way we could do it is if we had some sort of commission, like the gentleman from New Hampshire suggested, kind of a base closing commission, which would in effect bring both the parties together. I still think that's a good idea.

I have done everything I know to do. I wrote the Speaker back; I accepted his offer. I even named two people that I would have participate in the commission. I cannot force Congress to do this. But I believe we would be better off. I think the Presidential elections—I think in the general election, I think the American people—there is one other problem here, though, to be fair, and that is, the American people themselves have very ambivalent feelings about public financing. They can—and the people that are against campaign finance reform can always say, "Can't you think of something better to do with your money than give it to a politician?"

So I think, to make the next steps—that's why I was hoping a commission would also spark a lot of public debate here. But I do believe that in the general election, like in 1992, when it was all publicly funded, everybody had a fair chance, and we devoted a lot of our time to these more open discussions and not just the sound bites, I think public confidence in the institution rose. And I think that when Congress is dealing with issues and, simultaneously, people see the fundraising going on, it sparks cynicism even if everybody is in there doing exactly what they believe, even if you read it in the best times.

So I still believe campaign finance reform is important. I can't think of any way to get there except a commission. And I still hope the Speaker will accept my offer again and act on it.

Mood of the Country

Q. Well, Mr. President, I've come here today thinking that the Nation is in somewhat of a funk. You've just about convinced me otherwise. [Laughter] And so, in view of the way Pat Caddell hung "malaise" around Jimmy Carter's neck back in '79, an editorialist may be having a lot of fun with "funk." I wondered if possibly that was a bad—not an accurate word, or would you maybe change it?

The President. It was no doubt a poor choice of words. And it was more of a characterization of how people felt a year ago, maybe, than they do now. But I do believe—to be fair, what I think is that times—we all are for change in general, but we tend to oppose it in particular. That is, there's a limit to how much change that almost any of us can endure in our own lives at one time. And what I really do believe has happened is as people go through these kinds of sweeping changes in the way they live and work and the way their nation relates to the rest of the world and apparently contradictory events occur, you know, we just have to—I think that there needs to be an extra effort to keep the American people positive about our future, upbeat about our prospects, and realistic

about what our opportunities as well as our problems are. And I think it will be difficult to convince people that I am advocating the politics of a national funk—[laughter]—because, you know, it's so inconsistent with my own outlook toward life and the way we try to do things around here. And so I'm hopeful.

I hope I didn't—I hope I served a valuable purpose with that rather long discourse. And again, I would urge you all to read it because I was trying to explain to the people who were on the plane and through them to all the rest of you, because I figured they'd write it up in the pool report, kind of how I have analyzed this period, but not because I'm down about the prospects of the future. I'm, to the contrary, quite optimistic.

Mr. Sperling. Mr. President, we are told we have to close this extraordinarily fine——

Q. One followup.

Mr. Sperling. I'd really like to—I'd like to close the session early. And what I want to talk about it is how grateful I am that you're sitting down with a bunch of us print journalists, because we see you again and again on television—[laughter]—and yeah, we're not that bad a lot. And I think it's worthwhile. [Laughter] I hope you come in again. And thank you so very much.

The President. Thank you. Now, wait, wait. We're not done yet.

Mr. Sperling. We're going to take care of Rollie?

The President. No, we're going to take care of you. [Laughter]

Mr. Sperling. Sorry, Rollie, I had to——

The President. Now—but we're going to do what Rollie wanted to do in the beginning. Come on. Are we ready?

[At this point, a cake was brought in, and the group sang "Happy Birthday" to Mr. Sperling.]

NOTE: The President spoke at 12:40 p.m. in the State Dining Room at the White House. In his remarks, the President referred to Gov. E. Benjamin Nelson of Nebraska and Assistant Secretary of State for European and Canadian Affairs Richard Holbrooke.

Statement on the Future of Federal Laboratories
September 25, 1995

On May 5, 1994, I directed the Department of Defense, the Department of Energy, and the National Aeronautics and Space Administration to review their major laboratories. These three laboratory systems account for approximately one-fifth of the Federal investment in research and development (R&D)—approximately $15 billion out of a total of about $70 billion. I sought a study that would assess the continuing value of these laboratories in serving vital public needs, and I wanted an evaluation of options for change within these labs for the purpose of cutting costs and improving R&D productivity.

Informed by that review, I am announcing today an initial set of directives which will affect these laboratories well into the future.

I have concluded that these laboratories provide essential services to the Nation in fundamental science, national security, environmental protection and cleanup, and industrial competitiveness. Many of these laboratories are equipped with research tools that are among the finest in the world. They employ personnel with extraordinary and, in many cases, irreplaceable talent. These labs have contributed greatly to our Nation in the past and hold the potential for contributions of tremendous importance in the future.

One example where the national laboratories can help change the course of history is with respect to nuclear weapons. On August 11, 1995, I announced my decision to seek a "zero" yield Comprehensive Test Ban Treaty (CTBT). I was able to make that decision based on assurances by the Secretary of Energy and the Directors of the Department of Energy's nuclear weapons labs that we can meet the challenge of maintaining our nuclear deterrent under a CTBT through a science-based stockpile stewardship program without nuclear testing.

To meet the challenge of ensuring confidence in the safety and reliability of our stockpile, I have concluded that the continued vitality of all three DOE nuclear weapons laboratories will be essential.

In accordance with this conclusion, I have directed the Department of Energy to maintain nuclear weapons responsibilities and capabilities adequate to support the science-based stockpile stewardship program required to ensure continued confidence in the safety and reliability of the nuclear weapons stockpile in the absence of nuclear testing. Stable funding for this effort based on bipartisan support will be necessary in order to meet this requirement.

Strong bipartisan support equally is necessary across a broad range of other science and technology programs being performed in Federal laboratories, academia, and the private sector. Since the beginning of my administration, we have placed a high priority on investments in science and technology. We believe that few areas of Federal spending will be more important to the well-being of future generations than R&D. We are deeply concerned about budget actions that could cripple our capacity to find new ways of solving the scientific and technological challenges of the 21st century.

Among our greatest strengths as our Nation moves into the next century will be our ability to innovate, to design new drugs, to find new ways to enhance our national security, to develop new tools for managing enormous amounts of information, to generate new ways of harnessing energy, to produce new materials and processes that result in new products and industries at lower cost and with less pollution, and to expand the frontiers of our knowledge of the universe. These laboratories have excelled in such innovations as these and will continue to yield great public dividends for our Federal investment.

At the same time, these labs must be run as efficiently as possible. I have directed the agencies to review and, as appropriate, to rescind internal management instructions and oversight that impede laboratory performance. I have directed the agencies to clarify and focus the mission assignments of their laboratories. I also have directed the agencies to achieve all possible budget savings through streamlining and management improvements before productive R&D programs are sacrificed. Many agencies and laboratories already are making important progress in each of these areas of management reform.

1487

It has been said that R&D investments are an expression of our confidence as a Nation in our future. Today we are reaping the benefits of those who wisely invested in Federal R&D in the past. While it would be easy to destroy premier Federal laboratories through severe budget cuts or senseless closures, that is not a path that this administration will follow. We will invest in our Federal laboratories while pursuing aggressive management reforms that ensure the maximum productive output for the taxpayers' investments.

Letter to Congressional Leaders and the Federal Communications Commission Chair on Radio Spectrum Reallocation
September 25, 1995

Dear Mr. Speaker: (Dear Mr. President:)
(Dear Mr. Chairman:)

Title VI of the Omnibus Budget Reconciliation Act of 1993 requires that the Secretary of Commerce identify 200 megahertz (MHz) of the radio spectrum assigned to Federal Government use for reallocation to the Federal Communications Commission for nonfederal use.

Under delegated authority, the National Telecommunications and Information Administration (NTIA) is responsible for managing the Federal Government's use of the radio spectrum. On March 22, 1995, Secretary of Commerce Ronald Brown submitted to you NTIA's Spectrum Reallocation Final Report that identified for reallocation in August 1995, the 2300–2310 and 2400–2402 MHz bands for exclusive nonfederal use and the 2417–2450 MHz band for mixed Federal and nonfederal use.

I am pleased to inform you that the Federal Government frequency assignments in the spectrum identified for reallocation for exclusive nonfederal use have been withdrawn by NTIA in compliance with section 114 of the Act. In addition, modifications were made to the National Table of Frequency Allocations for Government stations to reflect the reallocation of the spectrum.

Sincerely,

WILLIAM J. CLINTON

NOTE: Identical letters were sent to Newt Gingrich, Speaker of the House of Representatives, Albert Gore, Jr., President of the Senate, and Reed E. Hundt, Chair, Federal Communications Commission.

Remarks on the Federal Budget and an Exchange with Reporters
September 26, 1995

The President. First of all, let me say, as you can see here, I am meeting with the Democratic members of the House Ways and Means Committee. I am delighted to be here with them to discuss the budget decisions that have to be made in the next few weeks.

As you know, I strongly favor balancing the budget to lift the burden of debt off of our children and to strengthen our economy. But I think we have to do it in a way that is consistent with our values, giving people the chance to make the most of their own lives, strengthening our families, protecting our children, honoring our parents, growing the middle class, and shrinking the under class. Those are the values that we ought to be making these decisions on.

In my judgment, the congressional budget that the Republican majority has offered violates those values. And the American people need to be a part of this, and they need to ask some basic questions: Do we want to support that budget when it will deny 300,000 elderly people the right to be in nursing homes that they have today? Do we really want to eliminate all the quality standards for nursing homes?

What about—can anybody remember what it was like to go in those places when there were no quality standards? Do we really want to tax 17 million working families and put millions of them back into poverty even though they're working? Do we want to say to a woman whose husband has to go to a nursing home, "In order for your husband to qualify for any assistance you have to sell your car, your house; you have to spend all your life savings; you have to be totally impoverished"? And do we want to let corporations loot their pension funds and compromise the retirement of their workers' future? How can we forget—it just was a couple of years ago when we had all these pension funds going broke. Do we really want to go and make that mistake all over again? Now, this budget does all those things. Those are the choices.

I have offered the Congress a budget that balances the budget without destroying education, without undermining our commitment to the environment, and without violating our commitments to working families, the elderly, and poor children.

It seems to me that we have to ask these questions. We have to move beyond the level of rhetoric to the values that are embodied in the choices that are being made. And I want to see us make the right choices for America. We need to balance the budget, but we need to do it in a way that strengthens our families, strengthens opportunity, and honors our obligations. That's the only way to help this country, and I am determined to see that we work together to do that in the next few weeks.

Ross Perot

Q. Mr. President, what do you think about Ross Perot's decision to form a third party?

Congressman. Give us a break, will you? [*Laughter*]

Q. How about the President?

The President. I try to balance the budget, and I'm an ardent promoter of political reform, as you know. But he'll have to do whatever he wants to do, and the American people can make their judgment.

NOTE: The President spoke at 11:20 a.m. in the Cabinet Room at the White House, prior to a meeting with Members of Congress. A tape was not available for verification of the content of these remarks.

Teleconference Remarks to the United Mine Workers
September 26, 1995

Thank you. Thank you, President Trumka, for that great introduction, and thank all of you for that wonderful welcome you just gave me. I got to know your president, Rich Trumka, well in 1992, when we were campaigning together in Pennsylvania, and I learned that we have a lot in common. He's a kid from a small town, born just after the end of World War II. He still likes fifties rock and roll. He's the first person in his family to go to college and to law school. And when he first ran for president, nobody but his mother thought he had a chance. But he kept plugging away in that modest, low-key way of his, and look where he is today. I'm also glad to be where he is today, and with him. I also want to acknowledge another friend from 1992, who helped show me around West Virginia, your vice president, Cecil Roberts, and your great secretary-treasurer, Jerry Jones, of Illinois. I'm sorry I couldn't be with you in person, but I am there in spirit.

From your founding 105 years ago, the members of the United Mine Workers have always been the shock-troops of American labor. And I'm proud we're fighting today for the same things. If your brave founders could be with you today, they'd find another time of great change and great challenge for American workers. At the end of the 19th century, when your union got started, America was first entering the industrial age. Now we're the world's leading industrial power, and we're moving full-speed ahead into the global economy. Once again, we're challenged to make great decisions, decisions that will shape the lives of our children and our children's children.

The industrial age brought us great opportunities, to be sure, but it also brought us child labor, the sweatshops, the company towns and the company stores, and the working men and women in our factories who grew old before their time with injured bodies and broken spirits. That's why we built strong unions in our country and we built a caring Government to help Americans make the most of their own lives and to protect them from abuses from which they could not protect themselves. The unions build the middle class, and the middle class built America on the American dream.

Now we find ourselves at another moment of great change. Even as we still depend upon the industrial might of coal miners and other workers, all of you know we're moving into an age characterized by information and technology and this new global economy that links more of us together economically but also presents extraordinary new pressures on ordinary working people everywhere.

Our challenge is to recognize and embrace new ideas to preserve our vision for the future, a vision of high opportunity where the middle class is growing and the under class is shrinking, people have the opportunities to live up to their own God-given abilities, and families and communities have the ability to solve their own problems. We've got to hold on to that vision by holding on to the values which have always made this country great: freedom and responsibility, work and family, opportunity, and the idea that we are, as my friend Governor Chiles of Florida said the other day, we are a community, not a crowd.

Now, a crowd is a collection of people who occupy the same space, just elbowing one another until the strongest and most powerful win, without regard of what happens to the others. A community is a group of people who occupy the same space, who believe that they're going up or down together, and that they have responsibilities to one another. The United Mine Workers has helped to keep America a community, and I thank you for that.

You know, that's what this budget debate is really all about in Washington, whether the America of the 21st century will be a community, as we want it to be, or a crowd, as so many in the Republican majority in Congress want it to be. We need to stop looking for ways to be divided and start looking for ways to reach common ground and higher ground. We've got to be forward-thinking enough to stand up for the future, even if it's not popular

in the present. But we've got to be sensible enough to hold on to those core values which have made this country what it is.

The debate about the balanced budget is the biggest case in point. Let me be clear, I strongly favor balancing the budget to lift the burden of debt off our children and to strengthen our economy. But I think we have to do it in a way that is consistent with those basic values. We've got to give people a chance to make the most of their own lives. We've got to strengthen our families; we've got to protect our children; we must honor our parents. We have to do things that will grow the middle class and shrink the under class, not increase the insecurity of working families.

These are the values we ought to be making decisions on about the budget. In my judgment, the congressional budget that the Republican majority has offered violates those values. We, the American people, need to be a part of this. We need to ask them basic questions. When we look at their budget, do we really want to support a budget that will deny 300,000 elderly people the right to be in the nursing homes they have today? Do we really want to eliminate all those quality standards for nursing homes? Can't anybody remember what it was like to go in those places when there were no quality standards? Do we really want to tax 17 million working families, increasing taxes on them to the point that many of them will be put back into poverty, even though they're working, and take that money and give a tax break to upper income people who don't need it and most of whom haven't asked for it?

Do we really want to say to a woman whose husband has to go to a nursing home that "in order for your husband to qualify for any Government assistance, you have to sell your car, your house; you have to spend all your life savings; you have to be totally impoverished"? Do we really want to make it harder for poor young children to get off to a good start in school? Do we want to make it harder for our schools to have smaller classes and computers, even in the poor areas? Do we want to make it more costly for young people to get college loans?

Do we want to make fewer and fewer scholarships available so that more and more young people won't go to college and won't get good jobs with growing incomes? And do we want to let corporations loot their pension funds and compromise the retirement of their workers' future? How can we forget—it was just a couple of years ago—when we had all these pension funds going broke? Just last December, I signed a bill that we passed through the last Congress to save the pensions of 8½ million American workers and stabilize the pensions of 40 million more. Now, do we want to go along with the congressional budget plan to let corporations go and make that same mistake all over again and to loot their pension funds legally?

Now, this budget does all those things. Those are the choices. If you want their budget in 7 years, with their tax cut and their assumptions and their plan, those are the choices in that budget. But there is another way. I have offered Congress a plan that balances the budget without destroying education, without undermining our commitment to the environment, and without violating our commitments to working families, the elderly, and our children.

The budget debate forces us to answer a simple question: Do we want a Government that upholds our values as a community and stands on the side of working people, struggling to build better lives for themselves? I think the answer is yes. And that is exactly what I have been working to do.

Two and a half years ago, you sent me to Washington to generate jobs, increase income, shrink the under class, grow the middle class, give America a better, stronger future. Since I started my job, our economy has created more than 7 million new jobs, 2½ million new homeowners, 2 million new small businesses. Unemployment is down 20 percent. We're also cutting the deficit. You know, the deficit was $290 billion when we started. It's down to $160 billion now. That's a 40 percent cut, a cut for 3 years in a row, the best performance since Harry Truman was President.

But you know better than anyone that we have a lot more to do to make sure America keeps working for and not against working families. That's why I fought for the passage of the Family and Medical Leave Act. That's why we gave a tax cut to 14 million working families with incomes under $28,000. That's why I support an increase in the minimum wage. That's why I proposed a new "GI bill" for America's workers, to give people a check or a voucher when they're unemployed or underemployed, so they can take the money and take it to a local community college or any other training pro-

gram for up to 2 years to get the kind of training they decide they need.

When people lose their jobs in this country today, too often the rest of our people walk away from them. And that's wrong. Our administration is pro-family, pro-worker, and pro-union. Right after I took office, I got rid of my predecessor's antiworker, antiunion Executive orders that weakened unions from public service to private industry.

With an Executive order this spring, our administration said in no uncertain terms that we won't allow companies that do business with the Government to permanently replace striking workers. We want to make sure that if you're forced to exercise your right to strike, you won't be fired for it. Make no mistake about it, we believe collective bargaining is a right and firing striking workers is wrong.

I've often spoken about how America has to keep faith with the people who work hard and play by the rules. That means we must honor our obligations to those who risk their lives to go beneath the earth and mine our coal. Your workplace is unique. It can change in an instant from one of safety to one of danger. That's why we need to keep the Mine Safety and Health Administration and maintain it as a separate agency.

Under the outstanding leadership of Secretary Reich and Davitt McAteer, MSHA is enforcing the law, protecting workers, and saving lives. You know better than anyone that in the 25 years since Congress passed the Mine Safety Act, the deaths in the coal mines have decreased by 77 percent. Now there are those in Congress who want to destroy MSHA, to limit inspections in unsafe mines and leave miners out in the cold who dare to blow the whistle and stand up for safety.

Well, there are no coal mines in Washington, DC, and here, sometimes the voice of big money can shout down the voice of the people. That's why it is so important when United Mine Workers miners and Rich Trumka come to the Capital, as they did, to tell why saving MSHA is literally a matter of life and death. And that's why I will fight and fight against any bill to cut or gut MSHA.

Keeping faith with people who have worked hard all their lives also means protecting coal miner retirees' health care, as guaranteed in the Rockefeller act, also known as the coal act. The coal act is our country's solemn covenant with more than 100,000 retired miners and their families to protect their health benefits and their peace of mind. It is not a matter of partisanship. This act was signed into law by President Bush and is supported to this day by the major coal companies.

Yesterday, you heard the author of that act, Senator Jay Rockefeller, explain how it is threatened and how it must be maintained. Today, let me tell you, we're going to fight to preserve your health benefits as guaranteed in the coal act.

Let me close by saying that I understand what's at stake as we fight to protect the health and safety of coal miners. When I was a young lawyer in Arkansas, just out of law school, back in the early 1970's, I handled several black lung cases for retired coal miners who could breathe only with great difficulty after a lifetime in the mines.

Some of the folks from MSHA found a letter that was found on the body of a coal miner who died in a mine explosion in Tennessee. Although a barricade held out the bad air for over 7 hours, the trapped miners eventually succumbed to the suffocating gas. Here is what the miner, Jacob Vowell, wrote to his wife, Ellen:

"Ellen, darling, goodbye for us both. We're all praying for air to support us, but it's getting bad without any air.

"Ellen, I want you to live right and come to heaven. Raise the children as best you can. Oh, how I wish to be with you. It's 25 minutes after 2. There are a few of us alive yet. Oh, God, for one more breath. Ellen, remember me for as long as you live.

"Goodbye, darling."

That letter was written 93 years ago. Today, thanks to the United Mine Workers, a better America, and the grace of God, our miners are working in greater safety and living with greater dignity.

The future of our Nation depends upon rewarding the efforts of people like you with safety, prosperity, and dignity. You and your families and the millions and millions of working families like you, you are heart and soul of the American dream. We have to keep working together not just to preserve what's been won but to continue to fight for better jobs, better wages, and more justice.

The 21st century can be America's greatest time. Our children and our grandchildren can enjoy more freedom, more opportunity if we do what is right. But we can't let the people in Washington who are trying to do it, turn back the clock. We have to keep America moving forward, strong, proud, and united, in the words of your own banner. Let's stay that way and march into the 21st century victorious for the values of ordinary Americans.

God bless you, and thank you very much.

NOTE: The President spoke by satellite at 2:15 p.m. from Room 459 in the Old Executive Office Building to the United Mine Workers convention in Miami, FL.

Remarks at the Swearing-In of Mark Gearan as Director of the Peace Corps
September 26, 1995

Well, Mark, congratulations to you and your family, to all the Members of Congress who are here and other former Peace Corps volunteers and others.

I have always been impressed by many things about the Peace Corps, one of which is the contributions made by Peace Corps volunteers after they come home. Senator Dodd was a member of the Peace Corps. Congressman Farr was a member of the Peace Corps. Donna Shalala served in the Peace Corps. The Vice President's beloved sister, Nancy Gore Hunger, was one of the first two people to join the Peace Corps, working with Sarge Shriver, all those years ago.

And it is a remarkable tradition that emphasizes that our country is about more than power and wealth. It is also about the power of our values and the power of a helping hand and the ethic of service and the understanding that we have an obligation not only to our own people but to people around the world to help them make the most of their own lives, and that the best guarantee of peace and freedom and democracy is the ability of people freely to develop their God-given capacities to strengthen their families and see their communities succeed. That's really what the Peace Corps is all about.

It is the symbol of everything that got my generation into public service. And it has animated a whole generation of people. It is the inspiration for so much of the service that goes on today, whether it is in the AmeriCorps program that was started in our administration or—I just came from taping a public service announcement for Nickelodeon, the children's television network. One year ago this week, I asked the children in Nickelodeon to volunteer to do community service. And 5 million-plus of them did so by telephone. They called in and actually served. And so this year, we're trying to increase. These are grade-school children by and large.

So this whole ethic of service that has spread across our country in part is inspired by and defined by the work that was begun so many years ago by President Kennedy and by Sargent Shriver. I think it's really fitting that Mark Gearan should be here in this program inspired by President Kennedy. I mean, look around at this family and notice that Father Leo O'Donovan—operative word, O'Donovan—the

president of Georgetown, is here. Notice—I was wondering how Mark got so much bipartisan support. Look at the chairman of the committee, Chairman Callahan—[*Laughter*]—and Peter King—King, in this case, is a very Irish name. [*Laughter*] As a matter of fact, Mark said, "Mr. President, I love the Peace Corps just the way it is. I only have one serious change I want to make. I think we should send 6,500 of the 7,000 volunteers to Ireland." [*Laughter*]

Congressman Moran, we're glad you're here. And Congresswoman Pelosi, we're certainly glad you're here to show that we're not trying to ethnically purify the Peace Corps here. [*Laughter*]

The Peace Corps is really the reflection of our better selves, isn't it? And one of the reasons we're all so happy to see Mark Gearan become the Director of it is that, on most days, he is the reflection of our better selves. We wish him well. We love him, we respect him, and we know that he will do great honor to this very important position for the United States and for all the good-hearted people of the entire world.

Thank you very much.

NOTE: The President spoke at approximately 3:20 p.m. in the Indian Treaty Room of the Old Executive Office Building.

Remarks on the Peace Process in Bosnia and an Exchange With Reporters
September 26, 1995

The President. Good afternoon. I have just spoken with Secretary Christopher and the rest of our negotiating team in New York, and I am pleased to announce another positive step on the path to peace in Bosnia. The Foreign Ministers of Bosnia, Serbia, and Croatia have endorsed a set of further agreed basic principles for an overall settlement to the war, building on the agreement they reached in Geneva on September 8th.

These principles spell out in greater detail the constitutional structures of the state of Bosnia, including the establishment of a national Presidency, a Parliament, and a constitutional court. They commit the parties to hold free

and democratic elections under international supervision. And they further provide that a central government will be responsible for conducting Bosnia's foreign policy as well as other key functions that are still being discussed.

The American people must realize that there are many difficult obstacles still to overcome along the path to peace. There is no guarantee of success. But today's agreement moves us closer to the ultimate goal of a genuine peace, and it makes clear that Bosnia will remain a single internationally recognized state. America will strongly oppose the partition of Bosnia, and America will continue working for peace.

We hope the progress we are making finally reflects the will of the parties to end this terrible war. We know it's a result of the international community's resolve and a determined diplomacy on the part of our negotiating team and our European and Russian partners.

I have instructed our team to return to the Balkans on Thursday to press forward in the search for peace. If and when the parties reach a settlement, America should help to secure it. The path to a lasting peace in Bosnia remains long and difficult, but we are making progress, and we are determined to succeed.

As you know now, our team in New York will have a press conference, and they will be able to answer your more detailed questions about the specifics of the agreement.

Thank you.

Q. What about your response to Senator Dole, Mr. President?

Q. What else has to be decided?

Q. What about that letter that Senator Dole sent you yesterday?

The President. Well, I intend to write him a response and to make it available. But remember, I have said since February of 1993, since February of 1993, constantly, for more than 2½ years now, that the United States should participate in implementing a peace agreement. We should not have ground troops on the ground, under the present U.N. mandate. We should not have ground troops on the ground in combat.

But the United States is the leader of NATO. No peace agreement could be fairly implemented without the involvement of NATO, and we cannot walk away from our responsibility to try to end this terrible conflict, not only for the people of Bosnia but for what it means for ultimate peace throughout the Balkans and the ultimate security of the United States and the ultimate avoiding of war and involvement by the United States. And that has been my position for 2½ years.

We have had several congressional consultations about it, and of course, as developments proceed here, if there is a peace and we have a good implementation agreement that I believe the United States should be a part of, I will, of course, extensively further consult with Congress.

But this has been my public position, well-known, and members of the press corps have asked me about it now for more than 2½ years. And it will continue to be my position, and I will continue to consult with Congress.

Thank you.

NOTE: The President spoke at 3:50 p.m. in the Briefing Room at the White House.

Remarks to the Saxophone Club
September 26, 1995

Well, if I had any sense, I would quit while I'm ahead. [*Laughter*] I believe Terry's about to get the hang of this. [*Laughter*]

I want to thank Terry McAuliffe for the magnificent job that he has done, along with Laura Hartigan and all of our staff. I want to thank Sean, who thought up the idea of the Saxophone Club in his office about 3 years ago. And it, I think you could say, has sort of caught on, thanks to you. And I appreciate that. I thank you. I thank Matt and all the people who have worked hard to make the Saxophone Club a success.

This, in some ways, is my favorite part of the campaign, the Saxophone Club, because a lot of you have come here and have contributed, and it hasn't been easy for you. But those of you who have joined the Saxophone Club who are basically in Sean's generation—some a little younger, maybe some a little older—you're the people that I ran for President for. I wanted so badly to see our country go into the next century still the strongest country in the world, the strongest force for peace and freedom and democracy, the American dream alive and well here at home, and with people coming together instead of being split apart. That's why I ran, and that's why I'm running for reelection.

I think every day of what I want this country to look like 10, 20, 30 years from now when your children are coming up and growing up and looking forward to their futures. I want this to be a country with great opportunity for entrepreneurs; a country where we can, through hard work, grow the middle class and shrink the under class; a country with good schools and a clean environment and safe streets; a country that is characterized by fairness, not meanness, and by unity, not division.

We're having this great debate in Washington now which is more extreme in the options being discussed than has been the case in previous times. And part of it is because we're going through a period of change, and whenever we go through a period of change, extreme debates tend to arise and old alliances tend to get unsettled.

But the fundamental questions are clear: How are we going to get into the 21st century, rewarding the values that made America great with the new ideas that are always required in a time of change? How are we going to reward both freedom and responsibility? How are we going to lift up both work and family? How are we going to empower individuals to make the most of their own lives and families and communities to solve their own problems? How are we going to honor our obligations across the generations to our parents and our children, across our racial and ethnic lines, across our income lines?

Fundamentally, we have to decide, as my friend Lawton Chiles, the Governor of Florida, said the other day, whether we're going to be a community or a crowd. You think about it. That's what the fairness and meanness debate is all about. It's also about whether you believe that you will do better in the 21st century if you live in a community or a crowd.

You obviously have decided you want to live in a community, even though most of you could do pretty well in a crowd. A crowd is a group of people occupying the same space who basically have no rules and they can just elbow each other until the strongest prevail and the weak are left behind. A community is a group of people occupying the same space who believe that their success and meaning and richness in life depends upon other people's success as well, that we go up or down together and therefore we have certain obligations to one another and to our land and to our future.

I want this country to be a community, not a crowd. I want it to be a country where huge opportunity exists for individuals but where we do it with fairness and not meanness. That's basically what this debate is all about now.

When I look to the future, I see an economic policy that has worked. My friends in the other party, they all said if my economic plan passed it would be the end of the world, we'd have the awfullest recession you ever saw. I keep waiting for all those fellows who want to be President in the Republican primary to be just quoted back what they said about our economic plan in '93. [*Laughter*] Where are they? Sooner or later we should stop rewarding people for being wrong, wrong, wrong every time.

But in spite of everything Terry said, in spite of the fact that we had over 7 million new jobs and 2½ million new homeowners and 2 million new small businesses and the largest number of self-made millionaires than any time period in history that's comparable and a 4,700 stock market, the median wage dropped. So if we're going to be a community, not a crowd, we have to find a way to give everybody a shot at the American dream, which means that we should invest more money in education and research and development and new technologies, not less. We should give everybody a chance to go forward.

If we really believe in responsibility along with opportunity and along with freedom, then we have to believe in safe streets and a clean environment; we have to believe in child support enforcement; we have to believe in genuine welfare reform which rewards work and parenting, instead of punishing children. If we really believe in that.

I am proud of the fact that, since our crime bill passed—the same crowd, you know, they said, "If the President's crime bill passes, he claims there will be 100,000 police in 6 years, but they'll never get to 20,000." Well, in the first year we're over 25,000 and rising. And I keep hoping somebody will ask them about what they said. Maybe I'll get a chance to one day. But I'm proud of that. I'm proud of the fact that we have stiffened child support enforcement. I'm proud of the fact that we have cracked down on fraud in the Medicare and Medicaid and food stamp programs. I am proud of the fact that we have done the things we've done. We've had the first conviction this week under the Violence Against Women Act. We've begun to convict people under the "three strikes and you're out" bill. I'm proud of that.

And I am proud of the fact that we seem to be coming back to our senses in many ways as a society. In every State just about, the crime rate's down, the murder rate's down, the welfare rolls are down, the food stamp rolls are down. The teen pregnancy rate is down in America 2 years in a row now. Even the divorce rate is down. We seem to be coming back together.

But it's just like on the economic side. The drug use rate is down for people over 18, but among young children, between 12 and 17, the rate of random violence and random drug use is up again. So we have to keep doing what works, but we have to also have an agenda for those young people, which means we shouldn't abandon a crime bill that is working with both prevention and preventive policing. It means we shouldn't cut out things like summer jobs and other programs designed to give these kids something to say yes to, instead of just something to say no to. It means we shouldn't walk away from our commitment to safe and drug-free schools and giving these children access to role models that give them a chance to make something positive of their lives. Because a lot of them are just out there kind of raising themselves, and they've been kind of cut loose. And we can't walk away from them.

If you look at what we have tried to do in the way we run our Government—our adversaries, they always talked about big Government and how they wanted to do something about it. But there are 163,000 fewer people working for the National Government today than there were the day I took office. We have downsized the Government. We took 16,000 pages of regulation away. We reduced SBA regulations, for example, by 50 percent and the budget by 40 percent and doubled the loan volume including an 85-percent increase in loans to women and a 75-percent increase in loans to minorities, without making one single loan below our normal standards. We did those things.

So I'm all for that. But there's still work to be done. We still have to say there are some things as a community we do through our Nation that we don't want to just leave alone. In the world, I'm proud of the foreign policy accomplishments that Terry mentioned. I'm glad for what happened here in Bosnia today with the new agreement. And I am glad that on Thursday we will have a second signing between Israel and the Palestinians, moving forward on peace in the Middle East.

But we are still vulnerable in our country to the forces of organized destruction, from terrorism and religious and ethnic and racial hatred and fanaticism. So there's more to do. We've got an antiterrorism bill to pass. I was told that bill would pass by Memorial Day, and I am still waiting for it. We still have things to do to make the world a better place.

I want a comprehensive nuclear test ban. I want the chemical weapons treaty to pass. I want the START II treaty to pass. I want us to have ultimate real peace in Bosnia and in Northern Ireland. I want the world to be moving in the right direction so that you will have less chaos and madness to deal with. And I want the United Nations and NATO to work. That means the United States has to lead.

All those things are issues. But they're all rooted in whether we want to be a community or a crowd, whether we want to reward responsibility as well as freedom, whether we want to reward opportunity for individuals and strength for families and communities. And that's really what this debate about the budget is. It's really not much about money, it's about what kind of people we're going to be.

We have proved—I have given the Congress a budget that the Chairman of the Federal Reserve says is credible, based on economic estimates that have been more accurate than those of Congress in the previous 2 years. It is a good, solid budget. But this is not about balancing the budget. Both parties agreed now we should balance the budget, and we should. The Democrats should never be in the position of being for a permanent deficit. We never had one until the 12 years before I showed up here.

But let balanced budgeting be a goal in and of itself, done consistent with our values. Don't use the balanced budget as an excuse to destroy programs that you don't like that will make us more uneven, less healthy, undermine our environment, and weaken our community. Let's do it in the right way.

When I learned, for example, that among the proposals in this budget is a gimmick to make the cost of college loans more expensive to students and to take away options that students have to repay those loans so that bankers and other middlemen can get more money back— that's not about cutting the budget; that's about our values. If we want to grow the economy by cutting the budget, why would we undermine economic growth by taking college out of the reach of more and more Americans? It doesn't make sense. It's not consistent with our values.

Why would we make it harder for little poor children to get off to a good start in school or for districts that don't have so much money to have smaller classes and more computers and higher standards? Those children may not be your children, but they'll be a big part of your future, because when those of you who are young or my age, they will be who you'll be looking at to care for you, to strengthen your country, to drive us forward. We have to be thinking about 20 years, 30 years down the road. This is not a smart thing to do. And it violates our values as well as our interests.

If you look at the environment, my idea of balancing the budget does not include gutting the EPA so they can't enforce the Clean Air Act. This administration—not the previous Republican administration, this administration—has gone to big industries and said, "Look, if you can meet the standards of the Clean Air Act and you're willing to be tested for it, you can throw the rule book away. We're tired of over-regulating America. We just want a clean environment, and we'll look for ways to get it." Our administration has gone in partnership to Detroit and other automotive interests and said, we will work with you to develop a clean car, but we have to triple the auto mileage that we're going to get out of our automobiles. And we have to do it soon, otherwise the greenhouse gas emissions from all this automobile driving around the world is going to choke the future.

We have to do it. But we did it in a partnership. I could give you example after example after example. But to jump in the tank and claim that the environment doesn't matter anymore? You see, just last week, we had a new scientific report that said now there is virtually unanimity among all the established scientists in the world that the globe is heating up, that the hole in the ozone layer is bigger than we thought, that if we could—we could see the temperature of the Earth grow up to 8 degrees in the next hundred years. If you do that, you'll have the polar ice caps breaking up; you'll have the water level rising; you'll have temperature extremes going wacky. And the world will be a very different world for your great-grand-children.

We cannot let that happen. We don't have to let that happen. We owe it to our country to preserve our heritage. And we sure don't

need a commission on closing the national parks, which is another part of their budget. It's wrong.

I grew up in one of those little national parks they say they want to close. And I can tell you we had a lot of elderly people coming down and retiring in our hometown from the Middle West, living in little rooming houses, barely had enough money to live on. They came there because of the national park, because of what it offered, because they could for no money be in 5 minutes from downtown in peaceful, beautiful surroundings. And they can have access to the sulfur springs and all the other things that were there. And that story is replicated all over America.

When our family went to Yellowstone and Grand Teton this summer, and we drove through there for 10 bucks—for 10 bucks, our family could go through there and visit the national park, just like any other family. For $25 you can get a year pass, and your car can get into any national park in America. [*Laughter*] Now, listen, we're laughing, but there are a lot of Americans who haven't had a pay raise in 15 years; they can still have the dignity and the rest and the exhilaration of seeing the most beautiful places on God's Earth at an affordable price because your country has the national parks.

My idea of balancing the budget does not include a Medicare program where, as they told us in both Houses in the last week, "We want to double the deductibles, double the premiums, not give anybody Medicare until they're 67, and, oh, by the way, in Medicaid we're going to abolish all the national standards for nursing homes"—signed into law by Ronald Reagan, hardly a liberal Democrat—[*laughter*]—"we're going to get rid of all them, and we're going to adopt a rule that says before an elderly person can get any help, if they're married, the State has the right to make their spouse sell the car, the house, and clean out the savings account and live in abject poverty."

That is not the America I want you to live in in the 21st century. It is wrong. I don't want you to live in that America. I don't want you to be living in Maryland making a living and have your parents in Indiana or some other place out there in the country and worried to death because there are no national quality standards for nursing homes if your parents have to be there. I don't want you to have to work that way. That's not right, and it's not necessary. I don't want that.

And I'll tell you something else: Look at what happened to working families this week in this budget. They proposed to cut my taxes but to just erode the working family tax credit that we put in, so that they're going to raise taxes on families with incomes of less than $25,000 a year to lower mine. No thank you. That's not right. That's not pro-work. It's not pro-family. It's not good for America. It is not right. It is not right. How can you do that?

I'm telling you, there are a huge number of American families out there where there's one or two parents, where people are working full-time, where they have children in the home and they're living on $11,000, $12,000, $13,000, $15,000, $16,000 a year. It is all they can do to educate their children and put clothes on their back and make sure they get to the doctor if they're sick. It is all they can do.

And in 1993, when we passed our economic plan, we lowered taxes on 14 million of those families—with 50 million Americans in them—because we wanted always to encourage work over welfare and because we wanted to have an elemental principle in our country: If you're a parent and you're trying to be a good parent and you're willing to work 40 hours a week, you should not be in poverty. That is right, and we should say this.

And let me tell you something else that you may not know about their budget. They voted this week to say that a company keeping a retirement plan can deposit money into workers' retirement funds and then take it out and spend it for whatever they want, for whatever they want. As long as they leave a minor and inadequate cushion there, you can put money into your workers' retirement and then take it out and spend it on whatever you want.

Is there no memory? Just last December, just last December, I signed a bill to strengthen our national pension benefit guaranty system. It saved the pensions of 8½ million Americans. It secured the pensions of 40 million other Americans. Have we no memory? We just saw people losing their whole retirement. Now they propose to let people loot their workers' pension plans for whatever reason, take it out of the pension and give it in dividends, take it out of the pension and give it to managers in extra pay, for a third home or something.

Let me say this: I want people to do well in this country. I am proud of the fact that under our administration we've had record numbers of new businesses and record numbers of self-made millionaires. And I want every one of you who wants to be a millionaire or a successful entrepreneur to do it. But we don't have to hurt the rest of America. This is a middle class country with middle class values, committed to families and children and their parents and doing right by everybody. We don't have to hurt people to do that. We don't have to.

So I say to you, it is about values. And it's also about leadership, and leadership includes making policies like this based on principle, not mere politics—based on principle, not mere politics—and being willing to do certain things that are unpopular. You heard Terry reel off a few of them. The conventional wisdom was that we shouldn't take on the NRA over the Brady bill and the assault weapons ban. You all clapped and cheered, but the Democrats lost the House because of it; don't you ever forget it. There were a lot of people who laid down their careers so that last year, 40,000 people with criminal records would not be able to get handguns. And they did because there were actually people out there who were willing to frighten good, God-fearing Americans who owned guns and engage in sporting contests and actually convinced them that that threatened their weapons. It didn't, and they knew it, but they did it anyway. And yes, they won a short-term political battle, but there are more people alive today because of that. There are more people alive today because we're going to take those assault weapons out of the schools and off the streets. And nobody's going to lose the right to have a hunting weapon or a sporting weapon.

And everybody says that this tobacco thing is going to be chapter two of the same thing. They'll terrify all those good, God-fearing tobacco farmers into thinking that we're going to put them in the street. They'll try to convince people that Big Brother, the Government's going to take over these decisions. And maybe it's bad politics, but let me tell you something, folks. You know what the 14-month study by the FDA showed? It showed that, number one, there were some people in the industry who had known for decades about the dangers of tobacco and how addictive it was; number two, that there was advertising still having a heavy attraction for children. And since they lose a certain number of customers every year, they've got to get a few more. [*Laughter*] And number three—you're laughing, but it's true. Number three showed that of the 3,000 young people a day who begin to smoke, 1,000 will have their lives shortened. Now, if we can give 1,000 kids a day, for the next however many months I've got to be President—you know, whether it's 64 or some less—1,000 people a day—it's worth the political consequences. For the long run, it is the right thing to do.

But there are lots of other examples where I have to do what I think is right. I knew the Haiti thing was unpopular, but it was right. And we're in better shape in Latin America and the world, and democracy's in better shape because we restored democracy to Haiti, and because of the way we did it without having to kill a bunch of them or our people as well. It was the right thing to do, even if it wasn't popular in the moment.

I can see it now building up. In Bosnia, people say, "Well, we like the fact that now our allies decided to go along with our strategy, and we did the strong and right thing in Bosnia and now we have a chance to make peace. But if we make peace, because we're the world's leader and because we're the leader of NATO, we'll have the same obligation here we had when Egypt and Israel made peace in the late seventies. We have to help enforce that."

We never lost a person in the Sinai as a result of the Middle East peace. And if we have a good peace agreement here, in all probability none of our soldiers will be put in harm's way. But there will be people who try to stir folks up and say it's a bad thing to do. But if you want your country to be a leader for peace and freedom, we cannot say, "We're the leader; here's what you should do; now, you go do it." We've got to—we have to show up for work in the morning. We have to.

I could give you lots of other examples. I knew, when I gave my affirmative action speech, I know what the politics of that is. But I'm nearly 50 years old. I have lived through the worst of racial segregation in this country. I was raised by a working grandmother and a working mother, and I have seen women's opportunities expand and discrimination continue. I know in my own mind that we are not yet able to fully make decisions, all of us, totally

disregarding the gender and race of the people with whom we deal. Now, that doesn't mean that we don't have to fix affirmative action, there weren't a bunch of things wrong with it that we need to clean up and deal with. And I'm trying to do that.

The popular thing is just say get rid of it. But it's not the right thing. The right thing is for us to band together and to grow together. Our ethnic diversity and the fact that we are willing to give all of our people, regardless of their gender, a chance to live up to the fullest of their God-given abilities, is our meal ticket in the global society of the 21st century, if we can live together instead of using cheap politics to drive each other apart. It is our meal ticket.

So I say to you, when people ask you why you're involved in this campaign and why you're fighting for my reelection, say, "I'm not fighting for the President; I'm fighting for myself and my children and my future and my country. That's what I'm interested in." When people ask you why they should support this campaign, you can tell them what Terry did about our record. And I hope you will become familiar with it. And I hope you will be able to say that.

But the real thing is, what are we going to do tomorrow to make it better? We've got to have a strong economy. We've got to have strong families. We've got to have good individual opportunity. We have to have a Government that is leaner and makes more sense. We have to be leaders in the world.

But most important, if we want the 21st century to look right, we've got to stand up for responsibility as well as freedom, for family and for work, and for the elemental proposition that the reason we're around here after more than 200 years is that at all critical junctures we have deepened our understanding and our willingness to act on what it means to be a community instead of a crowd.

Thank you, and God bless you all.

NOTE: The President spoke at 10:05 p.m. at the Omni Shoreham Hotel. In his remarks, he referred to Terry McAuliffe, national finance chairman, and Laura Hartigan, national finance director, Clinton/Gore '96; and Sean Foley, chairman, and Matt Gobush, director, Saxophone Club.

Remarks to Oklahoma City "Thank You America" Participants
September 27, 1995

Thank you, Governor Keating. I want to thank so many people who are here who made me immensely proud to be an American and to have the opportunity to serve during this sad but amazing episode in our Nation's history.

First, I thank Governor Keating for his outstanding leadership. It's a little-known fact, but about 30 years ago in this city, Frank Keating and I were college classmates. And life took us in different directions and to different parties and different pursuits. But when I watched him during this crisis, I saw the same person I had admired 30 years ago and had felt good about, about his strength and his eloquence and his conviction. And the people of Oklahoma were very fortunate to have him as their Governor during this period. I thank Mrs. Keating for the work she did, especially on that memorial service which will live in the minds and hearts of every one of us who participated in it, and I imagine every American who saw it, for as long as we live. I thank Mayor Norick and Mrs. Norick. I saw the mayor earlier, and the first time I talked to him and then when I came down to see him, I thought, of all the things you ever imagined could happen to you when you run for mayor, this is the one thing you never signed on for. But I think that he and his representatives here from the police and fire department and the people from the Oklahoma National Guard and the Oklahoma Emergency Management Agency who are represented here did a very, very fine job.

I think you saw once again, when my old friend James Lee Witt was up here talking about it—he lives this job more than anybody who has ever headed the Federal Emergency Management Agency. And I think he has done great credit to that agency, and he's made America feel secure in times of trouble, whatever the trouble is. And I thank him for that.

I want to say to Mr. Stinnett and the people from Fairfax County, Mr. Mathias and the people from Virginia Beach, Lieutenant Carr and the people from Montgomery County, and all the brave men and women who answered the call, I thank you very much. Let me also thank the Governor and the mayor for bringing our new Miss America here. I thought she did magnificently well in the contest the other night. Congratulations to you. We're glad to see you here.

It is a tribute to the leadership and to the strength of Oklahomans that in the midst of their own continuing recovery, they took the trouble and time to come here and tour this country to thank those of you who assisted them in their hour of need. As I said at the time, and I want to say again, one of the lessons of the Oklahoma City tragedy is that, although they lost a very great deal, they did not lose America. They have not forgotten that. And I really appreciated what the Governor said when he said that if any of us ever needed them, they would be there.

I was in Florida the other day, walking the streets of Jacksonville in a high-crime area with a man who had just been elected sheriff. And we had a lot of children there who were living there in this neighborhood. And in the last 6 months, they've been able to drive the crime rate down dramatically. And the Governor of Florida said, "You know, one of the continuing struggles in America is for us to decide whether we're going to be a community or a crowd." He said, "A crowd of people occupy the same piece of land, but they don't really relate to each other very well. They just kind of shove each other back and forth, and some win and some are left behind. A community occupies the same piece of land, and they recognize that they really are obligated to one another and that everybody's life is better when they recognize those obligations and act on them."

Oklahoma City turned the entire United States into a community. In fact, it turned us all into a family. We somehow found our better selves in the horror of what had happened to people with whom we identified. The feelings of the rescuers, I think, is best summed up in a note I got from the Fairfax County team. And they wrote:

"We'll never forget our time in Oklahoma City. We still are healing and searching for the reason why someone could do something this evil to people that are so good. Now, whenever we find ourselves angry over something, we think about the people of Oklahoma and our anger abates. Whenever we're asked about what we did there, the answer always includes meeting the most wonderful people in the country. We'd like to thank the people of Oklahoma City for reminding us of what being an American really means."

No one could have said it better than the team. Thank you very much.

One of the best things we can do to continue this healing process is to all carry on as best we can with the work that was left undone there, to reach out to the children, especially those who lost a parent or whose parents were severely disabled by the bombing.

America believes in extending a helping hand to people who are in trouble through no fault of their own. And a lot of things have been announced to help those children and those families. We have established a scholarship fund here, and various Federal agencies are working on making sure that the children of people who were killed who worked for the agencies will all be able to go on to college and have their educational needs met. And so we decided to establish a Presidential scholarship fund to assist the children of the victims.

One of the nicest things that's happened to me in the last 3 years is that this year on my birthday, the present my staff gave to me was that each of them contributed to the scholarship fund for the children of Oklahoma City. Since there will be many different circumstances for these young people, we thought it best to set up an advisory board to direct the proceeds of the scholarship fund. And my long-time friend former Governor George Nigh has agreed to chair it. Former Governor and Senator Henry Bellmon has agreed to serve on the board. We will be assisted by the Governor's office and the mayor's office. And James Lee Witt has also agreed to serve on the board.

So this fund will be administered at absolutely no cost, and therefore, 100 percent of all the contributions given by Federal employees and others here in Washington and throughout the country to help the children will go to educate those children. And I think that is very, very important.

Gandhi once said that if we are ever to reach real peace in this world, we shall have to begin with the children. For those of you who are being honored here today who brought your children, let me thank you for that. I hope they will always remember and always be very proud of what you did for their Nation in the hour of need of the people of Oklahoma City.

Let me now say that I hope and pray that this will never happen again in our country. We are doing everything we can to prevent it from happening again. But we learned something about ourselves when it did happen that we should never forget. And I just hope that we can follow the lesson of the note in the Fairfax County team's statement. When we feel ourselves getting angry or drifting away from our fellow citizens or being less than we ought to be, we ought to remember how all of us were in the aftermath of Oklahoma City and how that magnificent spirit made everyone a little more human, a little more alive, and a lot more proud to just have the opportunity to help our fellow human beings and our fellow Americans who needed it. If we can remember that, then that lasting tragedy will always have changed America for the better.

Thank you very much.

NOTE: The President spoke at 5:40 p.m. at the National Guard Memorial. In his remarks, he referred to Governor Frank Keating of Oklahoma, and his wife, Cathy; Mayor Ronald Norick of Oklahoma City, OK, and his wife, Carolyn; Edward L. Stinnett, member, FEMA Urban Search and Rescue Virginia Task Force 1 (Fairfax County); Melven R. Mathias, member, FEMA Urban Search and Rescue Virginia Task Force 2 (Virginia Beach); Thomas Carr, leader, FEMA Urban Search and Rescue Maryland Task Force 1 (Montgomery County); and Shawntel Smith, Miss America 1995.

Remarks to the Congressional Hispanic Caucus Institute
September 27, 1995

Thank you all. Please be seated. It is wonderful to be here, wonderful to be back. I thank Congressman and Mrs. Pastor for coming out here with me, and I thank Ed for that fine introduction. To your mistress of ceremonies, Giselle Fernandez; members of the Congressional Hispanic Caucus; the Institute Board; your executive director, Rita Elizondo; and Secretary Cisneros and Mary Alice; Secretary Peña and Ellen; Secretary Riley and Tunky; Attorney General Reno; and all your honored guests: I thank you for inviting me to come again this year.

For 18 years you have held this event, and it's become a part of our Nation's important Hispanic Heritage Month. I have been here for 3 years running, and during these 3 years my daughter has been studying Spanish. So I hope you'll keep inviting me back; it's getting a little better each year. How's this? *Y me gusta hablar Español.* Is that okay? [*Applause*]

I was thinking tonight coming over here— it's not in my prepared remarks, but I was thinking of two connected events that shape what I wish to say to you tonight. The first was the honor I had to be a part of the premiere here a few months ago of that wonderful movie "Mi Familia." And the second was the experience I had just today to be with the Governor of the State of Oklahoma and Mrs. Keating, and the Mayor of Oklahoma City and Mrs. Norick, and a group from Oklahoma as they came here on their national tour, thanking all the volunteer workers who went to Oklahoma City in the aftermath of the horrible bombing of the Federal building. And what I thought and said there was that in that moment we all became a family, the whole country.

In Florida last week, Governor Lawton Chiles said that the central question of our time was whether we were going to be a community or a crowd. The Hispanic community in America has always been a community, always tried to live by family values, not just talk about them. Now, a crowd is a group that occupies the same piece of land but really has no particular connection to one another. And so they elbow and shove and go to and fro until the strongest win and others are left behind. A community is a group of people who occupy the same piece of land and recognize their obligations to one another, people who believe they're going up or down together, people who believe they should help protect children and do honor to the elderly and help people make the most of their own lives, people who believe in freedom and responsibility, people who believe that we have an obligation to find common ground and sometimes to do the right thing because it's right, even if it's unpopular in the short run.

And in this period of change, as we move out of an industrial to an information society, out of the cold war into the global economy, that is what we need more than ever before, the values of your family and your community and your work.

The work of the Hispanic Caucus has never been more important than it is today, because you have stood for the values that are the very heart of the Latino culture and the very best of America. Some seek to divide us by spreading fear and laying blame. But the Hispanic Caucus has always sought to unite us all in America. I have counted on your support, literally from everything from A to Z, from affirmative action to zero tolerance gun policies in our schools.

The Hispanic Caucus has been my partner in 3 years of hard-won progress. When I became President, we had a stagnant and suffering economy. When I proposed a remedy to drive down this terrible deficit and increase investment in our people and in our economy and in our future, the naysayers who turned away said it would wreck the economy. But with the help of the Hispanic Caucus we passed an economic policy, and after 3 years, they were wrong and we were right.

We have 7.3 million new jobs, 2½ million new homeowners. Secretary Cisneros has a plan that will take home ownership above two-thirds of the American people by the year 2000 for the first time in American history. We have the largest number of new small businesses incorporated in any 2½-year period in American history, about 2 million. We have the largest number of new self-made millionaires in any 2½-year period in American history, and we have the lowest combined rate of unemployment and inflation in nearly three decades.

The Hispanic Caucus helped this administration to tackle the problem of crime. When I showed up here, for 6 years Washington rhetoric had paralyzed the crime bill while everybody made speeches about it. We broke through that rhetoric and the partisan discord and passed a crime bill at a time when most Americans believed that nothing, nothing, could really be done about the crime problem. Our crime bill put more police officers on our street. It did punish serious criminals more, but it also gave our young people something to say yes to. And in every State in the country now, in virtually every urban area, the crime rate is down, the murder rate is down.

I was in Jacksonville, Florida, last week, and I saw that for the first time, people really believed that crime could go down in their neighborhoods, as they saw these police officers that we have put on the street. Again, we did it in the face of intense partisan opposition, but you were right, and I thank you. And America is a safer place tonight because of the leadership of the Hispanic Caucus.

Last year at the Summit of the Americas, we saw what a vital role Hispanic-Americans can play as we expand trade with all of Latin America, through NAFTA and the free trade area we agreed on by the year 2005. When Mexico got in trouble, so many of you stood by my side in what had the least popular support of anything I think I've done since I've been President.

But think what would have happened if we had not gone to Mexico's aid. Look what was happening in Mexico. Look what was happening in Argentina. Look what was happening in Brazil. Look what would have happened in terms of illegal immigration, in terms of political discord, in terms of economic dislocation. Maybe those of you who stood with me were part of only 15 percent approval of the policy at the time, but when the President of Mexico gets here in the next week or in the next couple of weeks for his state visit, we will see a Mexico coming back in the right direction, moving toward constructive partnership with the United States, with a future that we can be hopeful about, instead of one we can rue, because of you and your leadership. And I thank you for that.

I also thank you for your support for our policies designed to improve the security and prosperity and advance the values of the American people around the world. It is no longer possible in this global society to talk about domestic and foreign policy; they're all blurred. And I thank you for your support in policies that have led us to the point where I can say that for the first time since the dawn of the nuclear age there are now no foreign missiles pointed at the people of the United States of America.

I thank you for our efforts to make peace in Haiti and Northern Ireland and for the celebration we will have tomorrow on the next step on the road to peace in the Middle East. I thank you for the work we have done to bring a genuine peace in Bosnia. And one of your members, of course, I must thank specifically, because through his combination of energy and imagination, heart and diplomacy, he has helped time and time again to make the world a safer place, Congressman Bill Richardson. Thank you.

On Friday, I will have the honor of acknowledging the work of another great American when I present the family of Willie Velasquez with the Presidential Medal of Freedom, the highest civilian honor in the land. I wish he could be here tonight to see how much he has helped citizenship to bloom among Hispanic-Americans throughout this country.

I also want to say a special word of thanks to the Hispanic-Americans who have helped to enrich the work of our administration. Beginning with Henry Cisneros and Federico Peña and the Latinos who have been appointed to the Federal District and Circuit Court of Appeals, those who occupy senior levels in Government in both categories, considerably more than any previous administration. You have proved, as I said in my speech on affirmative action, that excellence and diversity can go hand in hand; they must go hand in hand. And if they do, that is our ticket to a very, very bright future.

I thank those from my administration who are here tonight, including Gil Casellas, Norma Cantu, Maria Echaveste, Nelson Diaz, George Muñoz, Aida Alvarez, Fernando Torres-Gil, Katherine Archuleta, Jack Otero; the people from the White House who have been wonderful to be part of my family, Janet Murguia, Suzanna Valdez, Carolyn Curiel, Ray Martinez, Alfred Ramirez, Liz Montoya, and Grace Garcia, my advance person who got me in here tonight.

I couldn't get around without her anymore. I thank her. I also want to thank someone who recently left the White House, Isabelle Rodriguez Tapia, who was the Deputy Assistant to the President and Director of Advance for both the First Lady and for me. All of these people and so many others are a part of what America is in its Government. And this is terribly important.

As we look at this balanced budget, I ask you to think about the people, the values, the vision you have for the future. It's really about values. Should we balance the budget? Of course, we should. Of course, we should. We never had a permanent deficit, never, until the 12 years before I come to Washington. We never had one before. And lest anyone blame any one party or the other, I would remind you that in 11 of those 12 years, the Congress appropriated less money, not more, than the President asked for. This was not a partisan thing, but Presidents have a responsibility to lead. And thanks to the efforts of many of you here, we reduced our Government deficit from $290 billion to $160 billion, a 40 percent reduction in 3 years, the first time since President Truman that had been done.

So, should we balance the budget? Of course, we should. Otherwise we will spend more and more of your money on paying interest on the debt, and we'll have less to spend on the things that make us strong and good and give us a better future. Otherwise we will take too much money at interest rates that are too high away from the business community in America that needs to borrow that money to generate jobs in the private sector, which is where we're trying to grow our future.

But the question is, how should we do this, and don't we have to do it in a way that is consistent with our most fundamental values, with work and family, with responsibility, with our obligations to the elderly and to our children, with our obligations to help those who cannot help themselves through no fault of their own, and perhaps to stop helping those who can help themselves just as well without it? What are we going to do? How are we going to do this?

Let me just offer a few observations. I don't think it is consistent with our values to balance the budget by reducing the number of college scholarships and more affordable college loans or by depriving hundreds of thousands of little children who happen to be poor the chance to get off to a good start in school or by depriving schools of the chance to have smaller classes and computers in the classroom and meet the higher standards that we're holding out for them, just because the districts happen to be poor.

Why are we trying to balance the budget to strengthen America's future? We cannot strengthen America's future in a global economy, where what we earn depends on what we can learn, by weakening our commitment to education at the moment we should be strengthening that commitment to education. And let me say this as an aside: neither should we use the balanced budget as an excuse just to go after things that we do not like and cannot find a more open way to deal with.

And I want to just say a word in that context about bilingual education. Of course, English is the language of the United States. Of course, it is. That is not the issue. The issue is whether children who come here, while they are learning English, should also be able to learn other things. The issue is whether American citizens who work hard and pay taxes and are older and haven't mastered English yet should be able to vote like other citizens. The issue, in short, is not whether English is our language; it is. The issue is whether or not we're going to value the culture, the traditions of everybody and also recognize that we have a solemn obligation every day in every way to let these children live up to the fullest of their God-given capacities. That's what this is about.

Look at the balanced budget on the tax issue. Can we afford to reduce taxes and balance the budget? I believe we can. But we should do it consistent with our values. We should not cut taxes more than we can afford to do and provide our other obligations and meet them. And we should focus tax relief on the most important and most stressed things in our society, the need that middle class families have to get help with raising their children and to get help with financing the cost of education after high school. That's what we ought to do.

And the last thing we ought to do is what is now proposed, unbelievably, by the congressional majority. They want to raise the family tax credit by $40 billion. One of the most important things we did in 1993 with our economic proposal was to give over 14 million working families who lived on modest incomes a reduction in their income taxes to send out two very important messages: Number one, this country should never favor welfare over work. And number two, if someone is working 40 hours a week and they have children in their home, they should not live in poverty because of a tax system. We must not reverse that. How in the world—how in the world anyone could justify cutting the taxes of someone in my income group and raising the taxes on working mothers with children who have an income of $11,500 a year is beyond me. It is wrong, and we must stop it. We must not permit it to be done.

And let me say this: There's a lot of budget balancing to be done in the name of welfare reform. This administration has given 35 States the right to get out from under various Federal rules and regulations, to do more to move people from welfare to work. But what is our objective with welfare reform? It is to see people who are poor who may have made some mistakes in their lives have the chance to live good, strong, pro-work, pro-family lives. Our objective is to look at the reality of America where most parents work and most parents have to work and to say what we want is for everybody who can work to work, but we also want people to succeed as parents, for that is still our most important job.

And we must do both those things with welfare reform. Therefore, I say to you, it's all right to be very tough in child support enforcement. The Congress has adopted my provisions because there aren't any that are tougher. It is all right to be strong in saying you must, if you can, be in school or be in a training program or take a job when it is offered. And it is good that the Congress seems to be willing now to give some funds for child support so that you don't have to neglect your children if you go to work and you're poor. But it is wrong to use this as an excuse to punish people just because they're poor or they made a mistake or they happen to be children who, through no fault of their own, are in the family they're in.

Democratic, Republican Governors, the Catholic Church, they've all helped us to try to take some of these extreme provisions out of the welfare reform debate. And I say we have to keep them out. And let's remember, what we want is for people to be able to work and raise their children with dignity in this country. That is the purpose of welfare reform.

Finally, let me just give you one last example. There's a lot of talk about Medicare and Medicaid. We have to slow the rate of inflation in those programs. If we don't, they will soon be taking virtually all the discretionary money of the Government. We won't have money to invest in education or Secretary Peña's infrastructure programs that can put people back to work and rebuild communities. So we do have to do that.

It is true that the Medicare Trust Fund needs help. But the trustees that are so often cited by the congressional majority say that it costs $90 billion to fix the Medicare Trust Fund for more than a decade. That money comes from slowing the reimbursement rates to medical providers. Their proposal to double the premiums, double the deductibles, stop giving Medicare to anybody under 67 years old, to raise 3 times as much as it takes to bail out the Trust Fund has nothing to do with saving Medicare; it has everything to do with funding their budget priorities.

My priorities say, we owe it to the elderly not to do that to them. Most of them have very limited incomes. The average senior lady in the country, a woman over 65 living alone, is living on less than $9,000 a year average. In many States, 75 percent of those folks are living on less than $7,500 a year. They cannot afford to have their premiums and deductibles doubled. It is wrong. It is not necessary. And we should not do it.

And finally, let me say just a word about the Medicaid program. It's not popular to stand up for poor children anymore, but the Medicaid program, two-thirds of that money in Medicaid goes to the elderly and the disabled Americans of this country. It pays for their nursing home care, for in-home care to avoid the costs of going to nursing homes, and for hospital care. About a third of the money goes to the poor children of America to pay for their medical bills. And a lot of that money goes to hospitals in big cities and isolated rural areas.

And if you take a third of that money away over the next 7 years, 3 times as much as I have recommended in my balanced budget plan, there is no way you will not do grievous harm to the elderly, the disabled, and the poorest, most vulnerable children in America. And to all those who say, "Well, I'd rather have mine now; I don't care about them," just remember, those children will be, will be, the adults of the future. And we—those in my age group—will be depending on those kids to take care of us when we are retired. We are a family. We better act like a family. We cannot afford to do these things that violate our family values.

Lastly, let me say how very proud I am that the Hispanic Caucus mirrors these values every day in their work. And let me encourage all of you who may be discouraged by what I have just said—and I left a lot of things out. They also have proposed, for example, that if an elderly couple has one of—the husband or the wife needs to go into the nursing home, they've proposed letting States require the one that's not in a nursing home to have to sell their house, their car, and clean out their bank accounts before the one who's in the nursing home can get any kind of help. I don't think that's right, either.

My idea of the America of the 21st century is a high-opportunity country where everybody has a chance to live up to the fullest of their ability. I do not want my child to get ahead by driving elderly people into poverty. That is not my idea of family values. That is not the right thing to do.

Now, I want to ask all of you, without regard to your political party or where you live or what your income is, in these next few weeks to urge the Congress to live by the values of Hispanic America, to decide by the values of Hispanic America, to lift up work and family, to work for more freedom and responsibility, to remember our obligations to our children and to our parents, and to remember the future belongs to the United States if we can just remember that we're a community, not a crowd.

Look at America and imagine what the world's going to be like in 20 or 25 years, the global economy, people moving around, technology, ideas, information moving around. There is no country in this world as well-suited to seize the 21st century as the United States, if we will just remember how we got to where we are: by being a community, not a crowd.

Thank you, and God bless you all.

NOTE: The President spoke at 7:50 p.m. at the Washington Hilton Hotel. In his remarks, he referred to Giselle Fernandez, NBC News correspondent, and the late Willie Velasquez, founder, Southwest Voter Registration Education Project.

Exchange With Reporters Prior to Discussions With Chairman Yasser Arafat of the Palestine Liberation Organization
September 28, 1995

Middle East Peace Process

Q. Mr. Chairman, do you think this will lead to a Palestinian state, this signing today?

Chairman Arafat. The most important thing, it will lead to a permanent and just solution and peace in the Middle East.

Q. But will it lead to a Palestinian state? You want a Palestinian state; you want a capital in Jerusalem. Is this a step in that direction?

Chairman Arafat. And we have expressed our—from the first day, we were talking with the Israelis, even during the Sadat period, when he was making his invitation with Mr. Begin.

Q. Mr. Chairman, are you worried about another outbreak of terrorism in the wake of this agreement, as there have been in the past? Are you worried about another outbreak of terrorism?

Chairman Arafat. Look, there are many enemies against this, the peace process, and for this, we call it "the peace of the braves." And we are in need of all our efforts and this extensive help to overcome all of these obstacles, including the terror and the oppositions on the two sides.

Q. Have you solved all the problems with the Israelis, particularly the date for a military pullout from——

Chairman Arafat. Yes, the last one has been informed to us from Mr. Dennis on the phone. And there is—there was a contact with Abu Alaa when we were in the meeting with His Excellency, Prime Minister Major, which were the most important points which had been changed——

Q. But all the issues have been solved?

Chairman Arafat. Yes.

Q. Including the—[*inaudible*]

Chairman Arafat. There is now—there is now a committee to finalize the whole situation.

Q. Mr. President, what is the U.S. policy on a Palestinian state? What is the U.S. policy, currently? What is the U.S. policy?

Q. President Clinton, could you maybe tell us how you defined the U.S. role in today's events and what transpired here?

The President. Well, we've continued to work to try to help the parties make peace and to help them reach their own agreements. And that is what they have done in good faith and with very difficult negotiations. And now that they have taken this other important step, as they take successive steps, we will try to make sure each step succeeds, that we build on it and we keep working until we have a just and comprehensive peace in the Middle East.

And I am very proud of the work that the Secretary of State has done, that Dennis Ross has done, and that the others involved in our team have done. But the credit here, the ultimate credit, belongs to the parties, to the Palestinians and the Israelis, who have been working through this in a very difficult way. We have said that our job was to support the peace process and to help make sure it succeeds once an agreement is reached. This is another important agreement. We'll do our best to make sure it succeeds.

[*At this point, one group of reporters left the room, and another group entered.*]

Q. Mr. President, do you think after this signing ceremony that you will be going to the Middle East and visit these peripheries, the Palestinian periphery, the Israeli periphery, the Egyptian periphery, and the Jordanian periphery as well as Syria and Lebanon?

The President. I don't know the answer to that, but I know we will do everything we can to make sure these signing ceremonies are successful. We have worked very hard, the United States has, with your leaders, with the Israelis, with others, to try to help make peace in the Middle East and to try to help make sure each step along the way is successful. And we will keep working until we finish the job.

[*At this point, a question was asked in Arabic, and a translation was not provided.*]

Chairman Arafat. According to the agreement, they will be released, all—[*inaudible*]—on three schedules. The first one, directly after the signing of this agreement here, under his extensive supervision and after that, before the election. And the third one, later on.

[*A question was asked in Arabic, and a translation was not provided.*]

Chairman Arafat. The most important thing is we work together for the new history in the Middle East on the platform of comprehensive, lasting peaceful solution in the whole—[*inaudible*]—not only with the Egyptians, not only with the Palestinians, not only with the Jordanians. And also we hope that it will continue to be with the Syrians and with the Lebanese, too.

NOTE: The exchange began at 8:45 a.m. in the Oval Office at the White House. During the exchange, the following persons were referred to: Dennis Ross, Special Middle East Coordinator; Abu Alaa (Ahmed Qurei), chief Palestinian negotiator; and Prime Minister John Major of the United Kingdom. A tape was not available for verification of the content of this exchange.

Exchange With Reporters Prior to Discussions With Prime Minister Yitzhak Rabin of Israel
September 28, 1995

Middle East Peace Process

Q. Mr. Prime Minister, do you think this agreement today will be a step toward a Palestinian state?

Prime Minister Rabin. I'll answer questions later. We came to visit with the President. After the signing he will be able to ask questions. I prefer not to answer—not to respond to them at this stage.

Q. Maybe the President will be less shy. Mr. President, U.S. policy has been against Palestinian statehood. But you appear to be moving in that direction. Has U.S. policy shifted?

The President. We're not moving anywhere. We're moving with the parties to help make a peace. The parties are making the peace. Every agreement along the way is an agreement between the parties. We are supporting the peace process, and that's all we're doing, and that's all we will continue to do.

Q. [*Inaudible*]—need their own state, Mr. President?

Prime Minister Rabin. Allow me not to answer you on specifics. I would like to thank the President for the way that he encouraged, assisted, and helped the peace process in the last almost 3 years. I believe that the approach that was taken by the President, the way that he just said so, is to encourage the parties to the conflict to be the parties for peace. The responsibility, the main responsibility of the peacemaking process lies with the parties to the conflict. We appreciate and are thankful to the President for his assistance and encouragement to reach agreements, the kind that we have reached—started 2 years ago almost in signing the DOP, then the Washington Declaration with Jordan, then the peace treaty with Jordan, hopefully today, the second phase of the implementation of the DOP after the Cairo agreement to the whole West Bank. And I believe what has happened in the last over 2 years is a remarkable progress with tranquility, stability, and peace in the region.

Q. Mr. Rabin, progress on the Syrian front hasn't been very swift. Do you have any thoughts about whether this will provide impetus for agreement on another front?

Prime Minister Rabin. Be patient.

[*At this point, one group of reporters left the room, and another group entered.*]

Q. Mr. President, is there a chance to see President Asad sitting in this room next to you and the Prime Minister?

The President. Well, we would like to see a peace, a comprehensive peace in the Middle East, but that's up to the parties involved. We'll keep working, and we'll just keep working at it.

Q. Mr. President, how do you see the chances of implementation, this current Oslo B agreement between Israel and the Palestinians? Do you perceive that this—that there are fair chances that it will be implemented correctly, positively?

The President. Yes, I believe that if the parties make a good-faith effort, I will do what I can to see that it's properly implemented and to get the necessary support from around the world.

You know, a lot of people have been cheering this process on, and those who cheer need to support it. And the United States will do what we can to support it. And I will encourage a bipartisan support within the United States and around the world. I think the parties will do their part. And those of us who support peace should do ours.

Q. Do you mean political or economically?

Q. Mr. President, do you think Israel should release all the Palestinian prisoners when the agreement is signed?

The President. Excuse me?

Q. Do you think Israel should release all the Palestinian prisoners now when the agreement is signed?

The President. I think that the United States will take the position we have always taken. The parties are working these matters out, and the parties will continue to do it, and we will support the peace process.

NOTE: The exchange began at 9:28 a.m. in the Oval Office at the White House. A reporter referred to President Hafiz al-Asad of Syria. A tape was not available for verification of the content of this exchange.

Exchange With Reporters Prior to Discussions With Middle East Leaders
September 28, 1995

Middle East Peace Process

Q. Mr. President, what message should the world get from seeing this group assembled here together today?

President Clinton. Well, first of all, this is truly an historic meeting. The people here represented have never sat together before. And we have the Foreign Ministers of virtually the entire Arab League here. There's never been, even when we were here last—September 2 years ago, we didn't have this kind of representation.

And the message to the world is that the peoples of the Middle East are coming together. They're moving toward peace. They're determined to reach an honorable, a just, and a lasting peace.

Q. When do you expect President Asad to join you here, Mr. President? When do you expect President Asad of Syria to be here with you?

President Clinton. We don't want to give expectations. All I can tell you is that the message that should come out of this meeting is the peoples of the Middle East are moving toward peace.

Q. President Mubarak, what do you think of this accord? And do you think it is the biggest step in the right direction?

President Hosni Mubarak. I think it's a very good accord. And I can say that it's a very historic one. It's a very good indication about the peace which all of us hope can be maintained and cover all the Middle East.

Q. Are the toughest decisions yet to come?

President Clinton. There are always tough decisions on the road to peace. But look at what's happened. Look at what His Majesty King Hussein and—look at this agreement today. We're moving in the right direction. That's all anyone

could ask. And the United States is very, very pleased about it.

[*At this point, one group of reporters left the room, and another group entered.*]

Q. Mr. President, to what limit can the United States guarantee the honest implementation for that agreement?

President Clinton. I don't know that the United States is in a position of guaranteeing it, but we have worked with these parties, and we have confidence that there will be an honest effort made to implement the agreement.

And I think the fact that President Mubarak would come here—he has been a very positive force in these negotiations—His Majesty King Hussein would come here for this should be evidence that all of us have a high level of confidence that we will be able to work together to help this agreement be implemented.

And that will be my message to the others who are coming here from around the world today. Every nation says that it is a friend of peace in the Middle East. Now we must all help this peace to succeed in every way that we possibly can. And the leaders of your region by coming here today have, I think, given great energy and inspiration to that and will increase the chances that this historic meeting will lead to the proper implementation of the agreement and to rewarding the courage of the Israelis and the Palestinians who have made it.

NOTE: The exchange began at 10:50 a.m. in the Oval Office at the White House prior to discussions with King Hussein I of Jordan, President Hosni Mubarak of Egypt, Chairman Yasser Arafat of the Palestine Liberation Organization, and Prime Minister Yitzhak Rabin of Israel. A tape was not available for verification of the content of this exchange.

Remarks at the Signing Ceremony for the Israeli-Palestinian West Bank Accord
September 28, 1995

The President. Prime Minister Rabin; Chairman Arafat; Your Majesty King Hussein; President Mubarak; Foreign Minister Peres; Mr. Abu Mazin; Prime Ministers Gonzalez, Filali, Bin Shakir; Foreign Minister Kozyrev, our cosponsor of the Middle East peace negotiations; distinguished Foreign Ministers and members of the Diplomatic Corps; and honored guests:

I welcome you to the White House for this milestone on the path to reconciliation. Today we make a great stride toward the fulfillment of a vision toward the day when two peoples divided by generations, by conflict, are bound now by peace. Finally, the time is approaching when there will be safety in Israel's house, when the Palestinian people will write their own destiny, when the clash of arms will be banished from God's Holy Land.

Two years ago, on another brilliant September day here at the White House, two men reached across one of history's widest chasms with a simple handshake. That moment is etched forever in our memory. With the eyes of the world upon you, Mr. Prime Minister, you declared your wish to live side by side with the Palestinian people in dignity, in empathy, as human beings, as free men. And you, Mr. Chairman, vowed to wage what you called the most difficult battle of our lives, the battle for peace.

In the days of labor that have followed, you have both shown profound courage in bringing us to this moment, and you have kept your word.

The enemies of peace have fought the tide of history with terror and violence. We grieve for their victims, and we renew our vow to redeem the sacrifice of those victims. We will defeat those who will resort to terror. And we revere the determination of these leaders who chose peace, who rejected the old habits of hatred and revenge. Because they broke so bravely with the past, the bridges have multiplied, bridges of communication, of commerce, of understanding. Today, the landscape changes and the chasm narrows.

The agreement that now will be signed means that Israel's mothers and fathers need no longer worry that their sons will face the dangers of patrolling Nablus or confronting the hostile streets of Ramallah. And it means that Palestinians will be able to decide for themselves what their schools teach, how their houses should be built, and who they choose to govern.

You, the children of Abraham, have made a peace worthy of your great forebear. Abraham, patriarch of both Arabs and Jews, sacrificed power for peace when he said to his nephew, Lot, "Let there be no strife between thee and me. If thou will take the left hand, then I will go to the right." Patience and persistence, courage and sacrifice: These are the virtues, then as now, that set peacemakers apart.

Mr. Prime Minister and Mr. Chairman, you are showing that it is not by weapons but by will and by word that dreams best become reality. Your achievement shines as an inspiration to others all around this world who seek to overcome their own conflicts and to secure for themselves the blessings of peace.

Chapter by chapter, Jews and Arabs are writing a new history for their ancient lands. Camp David; the Declaration of Principles, signed here 2 years ago; the peace of the Arava last year between Jordan and Israel: With each of these, the truth of this book has become clear to the world. As courageous leaders stepped beyond the bounds of convention, they build for their peoples a new world of hope and peace.

Now, as this new chapter begins, it is fitting that we are joined by so many from the camp of peace. Egypt's President Mubarak has carried forth the commitment to peace that began with Anwar el-Sadat and the miracle at Camp David. Before there was a glimpse of a breakthrough, President Mubarak stood for reconciliation. And he added his strength, his personal strength, time and time again in the days of the negotiations.

Almost a year ago, on the border that had known only barbed wire and armed patrols, King Hussein and Prime Minister Rabin brought their nations together in peace. Already that border has been transformed, as have the lives of Israelis and Jordanians, after 46 years as enemies. King Hussein stands a rock on which peace can be built. In only a few weeks, he will host the economic summit in Amman that will bring together Israelis and Arabs from throughout the region, business and government leaders from throughout the world, to map the promise of tomorrow.

Today we are also joined by the largest group of Arab Foreign Ministers ever assembled to support the growth of peace. Prime Minister Filali of Morocco has traveled here to represent King Hassan, who has done so much to advance progress in the region. With us as well are representatives of nations that have provided vital support for peace, including the countries of the European Union, Japan, Canada, and of course, Norway, whose assistance 2 years ago opened the way to this moment.

All those who doubt the spirit of peace should remember this day and this extraordinary array of leaders who have joined together to bring a new era of hope to the Middle East. The United States is proud to stand with all of them.

Much remains to be done. But we will continue to walk each step of the way with those who work and risk for peace. We will press forward with our efforts until the circle of peace is closed, a circle which must include Syria and Lebanon if peace is to be complete. We will not rest until Muslims and Jews can turn their backs to pray without any fear, until all the region's children can grow up untouched by conflict, until the shadow of violence is lifted from the land of light and gold.

Thank you very much.

[At this point, the Israeli-Palestinian West Bank Accord was signed. Following the signing, King Hussein of Jordan, President Hosni Mubarak of Egypt, Chairman Yasser Arafat of the PLO, and Prime Minister Yitzhak Rabin of Israel made remarks.]

The President. As we adjourn, let me once again thank all of our guests from across the world who have come here to be a part of this and to wish all the parties well. Let me thank those who spoke today for their contributions to the peace process.

Let me say a special word of thanks to the Members of Congress who have come here from both parties, including both Jewish-Americans and Arab-Americans represented in our United States Congress, for their support of the United States effort.

And let me close with this simple thought. As the cold war has given way to a global village in which the enemies of peace are many and dispersed all across the world, the United States is honored and obligated to be a force for peace, from Northern Ireland to Southern Africa, from Bosnia to Haiti, to reducing the nuclear threat and the threat of biological and chemical weapons to fighting against terrorism and organized crime.

But this is special, for it is in this place that those of us who believe that the world was created by, is looked over by, and ultimately will be accountable to one great God. All of us came from there, whether we find that wisdom in the Torah or the Koran or the Christian Holy Bible. If we could all learn in that place to find the secret of peace, then perhaps the dream of peace on Earth can truly be realized.

Thank you, and God bless you all.

NOTE: The President spoke at 12:23 p.m. in the East Room at the White House. In his remarks, he referred to Foreign Minister Shimon Peres of Israel; Mahmud Abbas (Abu Mazin), head of the PLO committee on negotiations; Prime Minister Felipe Gonzalez of Spain, representing the European Union; Prime Minister Abdellatif Filali of Morocco; Prime Minister Zayd Bin Shakir of Jordan; and Foreign Minister Andrey Kozyrev of Russia.

Remarks at a Reception for Heads of State
September 28, 1995

Thank you very much. On behalf of the First Lady and myself, the Vice President and Mrs. Gore, and Secretary Christopher, we are delighted to welcome all of our visitors from around the world and especially from the Middle East, the Prime Ministers, the Foreign Ministers, especially Mrs. Rabin and Mrs. Arafat, Mrs. Mubarak, and Her Majesty Queen Noor.

We are delighted to be here again with these four great leaders who have just spoken. I was looking at His Majesty King Hussein when he said he was almost 60, thinking that he has been on the throne for more than 40 years. What I thought to myself was, for myself, I don't object to term limits, but I'm awfully glad he was not subject to them—[*laughter*]—because the Middle East is a different place because of the way King Hussein has lived his life for peace all these decades.

I thank President Mubarak for the power of his example, the constant strength of his determination. Not so very long ago, my family and I were, as with many Americans, praying for his safety. We are glad to see him strong, leading the world working toward peace.

I agree with Prime Minister Rabin that Chairman Arafat makes a good speech and a passionate one. What an interesting turn of events his life has taken, and how fortunate we all are that he decided to take his risks for peace.

Mr. Prime Minister, you give a pretty good speech yourself. I think you give such a good speech because it is obvious to everyone that every word you utter comes from your heart and your mind together, and we thank you.

And to all my fellow Americans and all of you here present, we've heard a lot of wonderful words today. I would like to close with three brief points that I believe should be emphasized. First, I want to recognize the negotiators, Foreign Minister Peres, Mr. Abu Mazin, Mr. Uri Savir, and Mr. Abu Alaa and their teams. They did this, and we should applaud them. We should applaud them. [*Applause*]

I watched today in the Cabinet Room while the Prime Minister and Chairman Arafat literally signed, initialed, the annex to this agreement, which included 26 different maps, comprising literally thousands and thousands of decisions that these two sides made. After long and arduous argument, they found common ground. It was an astonishing achievement, the care, the detail, the concern that they manifested and the effort it took to reach agreement was truly extraordinary. And I do not want that to escape anyone's attention.

The second thing I want to say is that this agreement embodies, for those of us who are Americans, the things that we believe in the most, for this agreement required the acceptance of responsibility, along with the assertion of freedom and independence. This agreement required people to think about the interests of their children and the sacrifices of their parents.

This agreement required a real effort to reach principled compromise, common ground, and higher ground. And make no mistake about it, this agreement required these decisionmakers to do things that may be unpopular in the short run, because they know that 10, 20, 30 years from now, it is the only course for the future of the people that they love.

And that brings me to the second point: What are our obligations, the rest of us? We can clap for them. But they have to go back to work tomorrow. When the glamour is gone and the applause has died out, they will be back at the hard work. There are two things we can do for them. The first thing we have to do is to stand with them against terrorism. It is the enemy of peace everywhere.

Now we in America know what it is like to see parents grieving over the bodies of their children and children grieving over the bodies of their parents because people believe that terrorism is simply politics by other means. We have had our hearts ripped out, and now we know better. So we must stand with them against terrorism.

The second thing we have to do is to work with them to achieve the benefits of peace, for the peace has to bring people the opportunity to work with dignity, to educate their children, to clean up their environment, to invest in their future. Hundreds and hundreds of Arab-Americans and Jewish-Americans have the capacity to work with these people in partnership to transform the future of the Middle East. And I say again, let us do our part.

Finally, let me say to all the Members of Congress here present and those who were there this afternoon, I thank you for your presence and your support of this process.

We know that in this era where we have gone from the bipolar world of the cold war to a global village with all kinds of new and different threats to our security, only the United States can stand consistently throughout the world for the cause of freedom and democracy and opportunity. We know that, and we must continue to do that, not simply for the people of the Middle East but for ourselves as well. For when we work for peace in Northern Ireland, in Southern Africa, in Haiti, in Bosnia, when we work to dismantle the threat of nuclear war and fight terrorism, we help ourselves and our children's future.

But I will say again what I said today: If we can make peace in the Middle East, if we can help the people who live there to make their own peace, it will have a special meaning for ourselves and for the world in the 21st century for the simple reason that the world's three great religions who believe that one God created us, watches over us, and ultimately will hold us to account for what we do—we all study through the Koran, through the Torah, through the Holy Bible those lessons—surely if those people can resolve all their differences, we can bring peace to all the world.

Thank you, and God bless you all.

NOTE: The President spoke at approximately 8:15 p.m. at the Corcoran Gallery. In his remarks, he referred to President Hosni Mubarak of Egypt and his wife, Suzanne; Prime Minister Yitzhak Rabin of Israel and his wife, Leah; PLO Chairman Yasser Arafat and his wife, Suha; Queen Noor, wife of King Hussein; Foreign Minister Shimon Peres of Israel; and Director General Uri Savir, Israeli Ministry of Foreign Affairs.

Remarks on Presenting the Presidential Medal of Freedom
September 29, 1995

Good morning, and welcome to all of you, especially to the honorees, their family members, their friends, the distinguished Members of Congress.

The Presidential Medal of Freedom is the highest honor given to civilians in the United States. It has a special history, established 50 years ago by President Truman to honor noble service in time of war. In 1963, President Kennedy expanded its purpose, making it an honor for distinguished civilian service in peacetime. The 12 Americans we honor today embody the best qualities in our national character. All have committed themselves, both publicly and privately, to expanding the circle of freedom and the opportunities the responsible exercise of freedom brings, at home and around the world.

In this time of change, where people's living patterns and working patterns are undergoing such dramatic transformation, it is necessary and fashionable to focus on new ideas and new visions of the future. We are here today to celebrate people who have always been for change and who have changed America for the better but who have done it based on the enduring values that make this country great: the belief that we have to give all of our citizens the chance to live up to the fullest of their God-given capacities; the conviction that we have to do everything we can to strengthen our families and our communities; the certainty that when the chips are down, we have to do what is good and right, even if it is unpopular in the short run; the understanding that we have the obligation to honor those who came before us by passing better lives and brighter opportunities on to those who come after.

This medal commemorates the remarkable service and indelible spirit of individual Americans. But it also serves as a beacon to all Americans and especially to our children. For our children, especially now when so many of their lives have been darkened by violence and irresponsible or absent role models, the robbers of innocence, of poverty and drug abuse and gang life, the excesses of our modern commercial media culture and other forces that are undermining the fabric of good lives, all of these things require more and more people to live by the values and measure up to the example of the winners of the Presidential Medal of Freedom. They represent in so many ways the true face of American heroism today.

Let me begin now by introducing each of them in turn.

As a young mother 27 years ago, Peggy Charren took a good look at her children's frequent companion, television, and she did not like what she saw. But unlike others who simply bemoan the problem, she actually did something about it. She took a stand against entrenched and powerful institutions in Government and in business, and she made them listen. She started Action for Children's Television. As a result, she uplifted the quality of what comes into our homes and inspired a whole generation of citizen activists. In 1990, the campaign that began in front of Peggy Charren's television set reached Capitol Hill when Congress passed the Children's Television Act. And for the first time, the television industry was challenged to fulfill its responsibility to educate our children, not just to entertain them. Peggy Charren, mother and now grandmother, leader and reformer in the best American tradition, has put all of our children first, and we thank her for it.

Now, I'm going to change the order here a minute, just a little, and go to Joan Ganz Cooney. While Peggy Charren forced television to change its ways from the outside, Joan Ganz Cooney did the same thing from the inside. In 1968, she launched the Children's Television Workshop, and a whole new landscape of joyful education opened up before our children's eyes. Out of this effort came "Sesame Street," "The Electric Company," "3-2-1 Contact," and other programs that enlighten not only our youngsters but older people as well. With a host of lovable characters like the Cookie Monster and Big Bird, who became as familiar to me at one point in our family life as the people I grew up with— [*laughter*]—these shows have helped teach a generation of children to count and to read and to think. They also teach us more about how we should live together. We all know that Grover and Kermit reinforce rather than undermine the values we work so hard to teach our children, showing kids every day what it means to share, to respect differences, and to recognize that it's not easy being green. [*Laughter*]

Joan Ganz Cooney has proven in living color that the powerful medium of television can be a tool to build reason, not reaction, for growth, not stifling, to help build young lives up rather than tear them down. We all know that TV is here to stay. Most of us, frankly, love it even when we curse it. But we also know that there are clear damaging effects to excessive exposure to destructive patterns of television. As the Vice President and Mrs. Gore have pointed out on so many occasions and as their recent family conference on media and the family demonstrated, the numbing effects of violence or the numbing inability to concentrate that comes from overexposure to mindless, repetitive programming are things that we have to fight against.

Peggy Charren sounded the alarm; Joan Ganz Cooney developed an alternative. And even today as we grapple with this challenge—how to get the best and repress the worst—we know that we would be nowhere near where we are were it not for these two remarkable American heroes. We thank them. Thank you so much.

William T. Coleman, Jr.'s first public act to advance equal opportunity came early in his life. He tried out for his high school swim team, and in response, the school disbanded the team. [*Laughter*] For four decades in the courtroom, the boardroom, the halls of power, Bill Coleman has put his brilliant legal intellect in service to our country. He was the first African-American accepted on the Harvard Law Review, the first to serve as a clerk on the United States Supreme Court, the first to serve in the President's Cabinet—the second to serve in the President's Cabinet, and the first to reach the pinnacle of the corporate bar. As Secretary of Transportation to President Ford, he helped to open the doors of opportunity to thousands of black entrepreneurs. As a corporate director, he broke the color barrier in the Nation's executive suites. Today, as chairman of the board of the NAACP Legal Defense and Education Fund, he continues the fight.

I have known Bill Coleman for a long time. I had the honor and pleasure of being his son's roommate for a year in law school. I think it is fair to say that the first time we saw each other, he never dreamed that I would be here and he would be there. [*Laughter*] But I can honestly say, if you are looking for an example of constancy, consistency, disciplined devotion to the things that make this country a great place, you have no further to look than William Coleman, Jr. Thank you.

Fifty years ago, John Hope Franklin was on a train in North Carolina, jammed into a compartment reserved for baggage and for African-Americans. When he asked the conductor if he and his fellow passengers could move to a near-empty car occupied by just five white men, he was told it couldn't be done, for the men, the conductor said, were German prisoners of war. John Hope Franklin and those with him were prisoners of something else, American racism.

John Hope Franklin has both lived and chronicled the history of race in America. He is the author of many books, including the classic "From Slavery to Freedom: A History of African-Americans." He provided Thurgood Marshall with critical historical research for the landmark case of *Brown* v. *Board of Education*. He has taught throughout America and around the world, and he has influenced countless, countless students of the American scene with his profound scholarship.

"I look history straight in the eye and call it like it is," John Hope Franklin has said. This has meant telling the untold stories of northern racism and of slaves successfully striking for better conditions under the sinful confines of slavery. It has meant blazing a trail through the academy, but never confusing his role as an advocate with his role as a scholar. It has meant holding to the conviction that integration is a national necessity if we are to truly live by the values enshrined in the Constitution.

John Hope Franklin, the son of the South, has always been a moral compass for America, always pointing us in the direction of truth. I think I can speak for Hillary and for the Vice President and Mrs. Gore in saying that one of the most memorable moments of our campaign in 1992 was having John Hope Franklin take a ride with us on our campaign bus. And he sat in the front. [*Laughter*]

In 1944, at the age of 16, Leon Higginbotham arrived at his Midwestern college only to be pushed back by the icy hand of racism. There, he and 12 other African-American students were housed in an unheated attic. Fed up with sub-zero nights, Leon Higginbotham went to the university president to protest. "Higginbotham," the president said, "the law doesn't require us to let colored students in the dorm, and you either accept things as they are or leave the university." So Leon Higginbotham set out to change the law. He went to Yale law school, and after he was rejected by every major Philadelphia law firm because of his race, he turned to public service, working as a community lawyer and a State and Federal official.

When Leon Higginbotham was named to the Federal bench at the age of 36 by President Kennedy, he was the youngest Federal judge to be appointed in three decades. He served with distinction and eventually became judge of the Third Circuit Court of Appeals. He also found the time to write and speak with idealism and rigor on the great dilemmas of race and justice.

His retirement has been spent, remarkably, helping to draft the constitution for a democratic South Africa and teaching a fresh generation of students at Harvard. We honor Judge Higginbotham, whose life as much as his scholarship has set an example of commitment, en-

largement, and service to new minds at home and now, thank God, to a newly free South Africa an ocean away.

Thank you, Leon Higginbotham.

Judge Frank Johnson could not be here today and so had to send the young gentleman to my left to receive his award for him. He was advised by his doctor not to travel. I admire that doctor. I imagine that he is the first person who ever got Frank Johnson to do something he did not want to do. [*Laughter*]

For his steadfastness, his constitutional vision, his courage to uphold the value of equal opportunity, even at the expense of his own personal safety, for these things, we honor Frank Johnson with the Presidential Medal of Freedom.

During 40 years on the bench, Judge Johnson made it his mission to see to it that justice was done within the framework of law. In the face of unremitting social and political pressure to uphold the traditions of oppression and neglect in his native South, never once did he yield. His landmark decisions in the areas of desegregation, voting rights, and civil liberties transformed our understanding of the Constitution. He fought for the right of Rosa Parks to sit where she wanted on the bus and battled for the right of Martin Luther King and others to march from Selma to Montgomery.

Armed with a gavel and the Constitution, Frank Johnson changed the face of the South. He challenged America to move closer to the ideals upon which it is founded and forever will be an inspiration to all who admire courage and value freedom. We wish you were here with us today, but his spirit is in this place, and we thank him.

For a good long while now, Dr. C. Everett Koop, as Surgeon General of the United States and afterward as America's most well-known private doctor, has told the Nation the truth as he sees it, whether we want to hear it or not. In so doing, he has saved countless lives and left an enduring legacy of the doctor as a healer in the broadest and deepest sense of the word.

Dr. Koop's life has been defined by doing the right thing. He chose children's medicine for the simple reason that his colleagues were ignoring it. He refused to let political considerations leave Americans vulnerable to the epidemics of AIDS and teen pregnancy. He fought for sex education, knowing that if he were to be true to the value of protecting our children, we could not let them live in perilous ignorance. He told America that tobacco is addictive, that it kills, and that we have to get cigarettes out of our children's hands.

He helped us to come to grips with the painful shortcomings in America's health care delivery system and what it means for children that over 40 million of our people have no health insurance. And we value his support for the action now being taken to try to protect children's lives from the epidemic of smoking, which embraces 3,000 of them a day and will shorten 1,000 of their lives every day.

Dr. Koop's record is a priceless reminder that disease is immune to ideology and that viruses do not play politics. Over the course of his career, I have seen him attacked from both the left and the right for his strong convictions. But all of us who have watched him, not only in public but as Hillary and I have had the chance to do in private, know that in the very best sense, he stands for life in America and for the potential of all of our children. And for that, the United States should be eternally grateful to C. Everett Koop.

Twenty-five years ago this year, Americans came together for the very first Earth Day. They came together to make it clear that dirty air, poison water, spoiled land were simply unacceptable. They came together to say that preserving our natural heritage for our children is a national value. And they came together, more than anything else, because of one American, Gaylord Nelson. His career as Wisconsin's Governor, United States Senator, and now as counselor of the Wilderness Society has been marked by integrity, civility, and vision. His legacy is inscribed in legislation, including the National Environmental Education Act and the 1964 Wilderness Act,

As the father of Earth Day, he is the grandfather of all that grew out of that event: the Environmental Protection Act, the Clean Air Act, the Clean Water Act, the Safe Drinking Water Act. He also set a standard for people in public service to care about the environment and to try to do something about it. And I think that the Vice President would want me to say that young people like Al Gore, back in 1970, realized, because of Gaylord Nelson, that if they got into public service, they could do something to preserve our environment for future generations.

In the 1970's, when a river was so polluted it actually caught on fire, Gaylord Nelson spoke up. He insisted that Americans deserved the safety that comes from knowing the world we live in will not make us sick. He warned that our leaders should never let partisan politics divert us from responsibility to our shared environment. He inspired us to remember that the stewardship of our natural resources is the stewardship of the American dream. He is the worthy heir of the tradition of Theodore Roosevelt, and the Vice President's work and that of all other environmentalists today is the worthy heir of Gaylord Nelson.

Today as much as at any time in modern American history, we need to remember what we share on this precious planet and in this beloved country. And I hope that Gaylord Nelson's shining example will illuminate all the debates in this city for years to come.

Walter Reuther was an American visionary so far ahead of his times that although he died a quarter of a century ago, our Nation has yet to catch up to his dreams. A tool and die maker by trade, Walter Reuther built a great union that lifted industrial workers into the middle class. But he always understood that the UAW stood for something greater and nobler than a few more dollars in the paycheck. So he fought for causes on the edge of America's horizon, from racial justice to small cars that would conserve fuel and compete successfully both here and abroad.

He wanted America to create an economy strong and supple enough to convert from peacetime production to defense work and back again without costing workers and their families their livelihoods. As the journalist Murray Kempton said later, "Walter Reuther was one man who could reminisce about the future." The union he led and the future he built stand as a memorial to what is bravest and best in the American spirit. Would that we had more people like him today. We are honored that his daughters are here and that his award will be received by his young grandson.

Walter Reuther.

Our homes, our cities, our neighborhoods, our communities, all these represent who we are. With the helping hand of James Rouse, many of these places have come to reflect our best values. In the 1960's, James Rouse saw a problem. Poorly planned suburban neighborhoods did more than take away from the landscape, they had a corrosive effect on our sense of community. So he did something about it; he con-

Photographic Portfolio

Overleaf: In North Miami Beach,
FL, September 19.
Left: At the Parliament in London,
United Kingdom, November 29.
Above: Congratulating consecutive
game recordbreaker Cal Ripken, Jr.,
at Oriole Park at Camden Yards,
Baltimore, MD, September 6.
Right: Visiting U.S. troops at
Baumholder Army Base, Germany,
December 2.

Left: Speaking at Fort Armistead Park in Baltimore, MD, August 8.

Below: Participating in a demonstration of educational technology at the Exploratorium in San Francisco, CA, September 21.

Right: Meeting with Secretary of State Warren M. Christopher, National Security Adviser Anthony Lake, Secretary of Defense William J. Perry, and Gen. John M. Shalikashvili, Chairman of the Joint Chiefs of Staff, in Mr. Lake's office, July 17.

Below right: Enjoying Christmas carolers in the Residence, December 6.

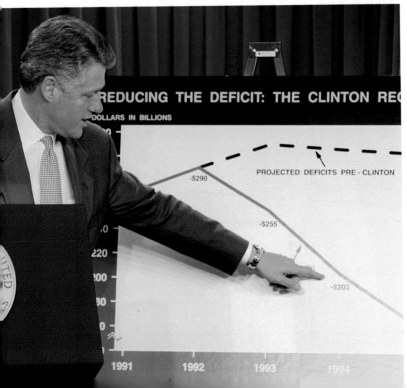

Above: Meeting with the law enforcement community in Jacksonville, FL, September 19.
Left: Holding a news conference in the Briefing Room, October 25.
Right: Speaking at the National Archives and Records Administration, July 19.
Overleaf: Enjoying an early birthday celebration on the South Lawn August 10.

UNITED STATES OF AMERICA
AND THE
BILL OF RIGHTS
SEAL OF THE PRESIDENT OF THE UNITED STATES

ceived and built Columbia, Maryland. By updating the colonial village for modern times, he gave a generation of architects and designers a blueprint for reviving community all across our Nation.

A decade later, James Rouse turned to another monumental task, healing the torn-out heart of America's cities. He met the challenge head-on. With Boston's Faneuil Hall, Baltimore Harbor Place, and other developments, he put the town square squarely back into America's urban life. He proved that we could reclaim and recreate our urban frontiers. Adviser to Presidents, foe of economic and racial segregation, champion of high-quality, affordable housing, James Rouse's life has been defined by faith in the American spirit. He has made our cities and our neighborhoods as beautiful as the lives that pass through them.

He has shown us that we can build communities worthy of the character and optimism of our people. I know that he has had a special impact on our Secretary of Housing and Urban Development, Henry Cisneros. And I can tell you that he has had a very special impact on my life. Every time I see James Rouse I think if every American developer had done what James Rouse has done with his life, we would have lower crime rates, fewer gangs, less drugs; our children would have a better future; our cities would be delightful places to live; we would not walk in fear, we would walk in pride down the streets of our cities, just as we still can in the small towns in America. James Rouse has changed this country. And if more will follow his lead, we can do the entire job we need to do in our cities.

Mr. James Rouse.

His name was William C. Velasquez, but everyone knew him as Willie. Willie was and is now a name synonymous with democracy in America. Through the organization he founded, the Southwest Voter Registration Education Project, he nearly doubled Hispanic voter registration and dramatically increased the number of Latino elected officials in this Nation. His appeal to the Hispanic community was simple, passionate, and direct: *"Su voto es su voz,"* your vote is your voice.

The movement he began here at home went on to support democracy abroad in El Salvador, Nicaragua, and Mexico, and in South Africa. From the farm fields of California, where he organized workers with Cesar Chavez, to the halls of Harvard, where he taught politics, Willie Velasquez was driven by an unwavering belief that every American should have a role in our democracy and a share in the opportunities of our great Nation.

Willie Velasquez died too young. He was just 44 when he passed away in 1988. But in his vibrant life, he restored faith in our ideals and in ourselves. And no person in modern America who has run for public office wherever Hispanic Americans live has failed to feel the hand of Willie Velasquez. He made this a greater country and we're honored that his wife is here with us today.

It is not surprising that Lew Wasserman has devoted his life to helping others to see. For it was his vision that led him from the streets of Cleveland to the top of Hollywood and his perspective that inspired him to give so much back to a nation that had given so much to him. Lew Wasserman helped to build MCA from a small booking agency into a vast multimedia company. His feat awakened the world to the infinite promise of the American entertainment industry.

It also showed a new generation of American business leaders that a company's success can be measured by the depth of its values as well as by the size of its revenues. In honor of MCA's founder, the eye doctor Jules Stein, Lew Wasserman has made an astonishing contribution to treat and to cure blindness. He has devoted himself to strengthening the American community through his role as citizen adviser to almost a half century of Presidents of both parties and with his support for countless humanitarian efforts.

Never for a moment has he forgotten his roots, the value of hard work, or the importance of giving people in far, far less fortunate conditions a chance to make something of their lives. The story of Lew Wasserman is the story of the American dream, not—not—just for what he has achieved but far more important for what he has given back. I have met a lot of philanthropists and successful people in my life. I don't know that I ever met anybody that more consistently every day looked for another opportunity to do something for somebody else, to give somebody else the chance to enjoy the success that he had in life.

I thank you, Lew Wasserman.

Let me close, before we hear from the official citation and present the medals, by saying that

I think that all the people who are here, were they to speak, would tell you that they did not come here alone. They were guided by parents and teachers, by neighbors and mentors. Many were inspired by other great Americans who themselves at some time in the past received this very medal.

The miracle of American life is that this cycle can be repeated over and over again with each succeeding generation and that with each succeeding generation, we make freedom a little more real and full to all Americans. I ask all of you to think about that. You couldn't help feeling, when you heard these stories, that this is a very great country. And we do not have to give in to our lesser selves. We do not have to be divided. We do not have to achieve less than we can. If we will follow their examples, we will make sure that in the next century, this country will be all it was meant to be for all of our children.

I'd like to now ask the military aide to read the citations as I present the Medals of Freedom.

NOTE: The President spoke at 9:45 a.m. in the East Room at the White House.

Exchange With Reporters Prior to Discussions With President Hosni Mubarak of Egypt
September 29, 1995

President Clinton. I thought it was great. I thought your talk was great, what you said. There were some unusual things said yesterday, even more so in some ways than the last time when they were here. What you said and—we've got a transcript we haven't made up our mind about—[*laughter*].

Good morning, everyone.

Vice President Gore. Your picture is all over the United States today in the morning newspapers.

President Clinton. Yes. I thought it was interesting. The picture that most of them showed was the one in the New York Times today. Most—[*inaudible*]—showed us, the five of us, you know—have you seen it? [*Inaudible*]—every time. That's the picture that was mostly in the country.

President Mubarak. Yes.

President Clinton. That was great.

Good morning.

Jerusalem

Q. Mr. President, what do you think is going to happen to Jerusalem when there is a final settlement?

President Clinton. Are you addressing me or President Mubarak? [*Laughter*]

Q. First Mubarak, then you.

President Clinton. That's good. [*Laughter*]

Q. Or vice-versa. I think you heard Chairman Arafat say something about a joint cornerstone.

President Mubarak. I think, as Chairman Arafat mentioned yesterday, there should be access of the holy places for all the religions in Eastern Jerusalem. And we know beforehand that Jerusalem will be very difficult to be divided. So any kind of arrangement for Jerusalem, east and west, without dividing it, I think, may have a problem.

Q. Well, that would be the Israeli position, wouldn't it?

President Mubarak. Look, it's—we should listen to all of the statements coming here and there, but this will be decided during the negotiations. All of us are going to act in that direction, with the help of President Clinton and the administration.

Q. Mr. President, do you want to elaborate on that?

President Clinton. You know what our position is, that the less we say about this at this moment, the better, because the parties have agreed themselves to make this a part of the final status talks. And what we want to do is to create the maximum chance that they will actually reach a good-faith agreement, because if they actually reach a good-faith agreement, then the chances are much greater that it will then be accepted by all the people in the area.

I think everyone expects that because of the importance of Jerusalem to Muslims, to Jews, and to Christians, that all of us believers from all over the world will be able to show up there and have access to our holy sites. But I think that it's very important that we not prejudge exactly what the structure be. We should let the negotiators work. They have done a marvelous job. I mean, look at yesterday, Prime Minister Rabin and Chairman Arafat initialed 26 maps in here. There were thousands and thousands and thousands of excruciatingly detailed decisions made by those negotiators. That is good evidence that they can actually work through these things. And I believe in the end, they will reach whatever they believe is a fair and livable accommodation on Jerusalem, and I want to see them have a chance to do it.

Foreign Policy

Q. Do you think, Mr. President, that your foreign policy, foreign policy in general is beginning to fall into place as you see some of the problems that you've had over the past 2½ years get resolved?

President Clinton. Well, I thought we had a pretty good year last year as well. I think what's happening is that these two events of this week show that the announcement in the Middle East in 1993 was not a fluke, not an aberration, that there really is a process unfolding in the Middle East and that we have a chance to go all the way. And of course, President Mubarak and I will be talking about that today. Until we finish these agreements between the Palestinians and the Israelis and until we have an agreement between Syria and Lebanon and Israel, we won't be able to go all the way, but I think there is a sense of that.

And in Bosnia, I think there is at least a sense that what has been our thorniest and most difficult problem, we may be able to work through. Now, we're a long way from getting there, but we are making progress. And I'm hopeful and—these things will make the American people more secure and more prosperous. And they'll live in a world that they feel better about. And I'm happy for our people, but I'm particularly pleased for the people in the affected areas.

Bosnia

Q. Are you bringing to the leaders today a specific price tag for Bosnia when a peace settle-

ment is reached? What is it you will be asking them?

President Clinton. No, because we have no way of knowing that. We have to see whether there is a peace agreement reached and what the map looks like and what the conditions are and what we're asked to do as a world community. So we have no way of knowing that right now.

Q. But you're still committed to sending U.S. troops to implement the peace?

President Clinton. I believe the United States should be a part of implementing the peace process. I have said that for almost 3 years. I don't see how, as the leader of NATO and basically the leader of the West, we can walk away from that. And I think the American people, once I explain it to them, will be supportive. And I believe the Congress will.

Q. How many?

President Clinton. I'll have more to say about that in the congressional meeting. You can ask more Bosnia questions in there because we're going to talk about that.

Continuing Resolution

Q. Are you going to sign a CR today?

President Clinton. I'll talk about that at the congressional meeting as well.

Q. Got to have something later.

President Clinton. Never satisfied. [*Laughter*] Thank you all.

Q. Nothing ventured. [*Laughter*]

[*At this point, one group of reporters left the room, and another group entered.*]

Middle East Peace Process

Q. Mr. President Mubarak, can we ask what main issues will be discussed with President Clinton?

President Mubarak. We have various issues to be discussed—implementation of the peace process; we'll speak on Bosnia; we'll speak of cooperation in the area; about the economic summit in Jordan. We have so many issues to discuss.

Q. President Clinton, actually, I have two questions. I wanted to ask you about what you plan to do in the next stage on bilateral ties with Egypt in order to boost investment, American investment in Egypt. And also, the other question is, we've been talking to many Palestinians about good intentions on the part of the Israelis in order to implement the peace process, and good intentions are the key for the implementation of the peace process——

President Clinton. Well, let me answer—I'll try to answer both of them. First of all, our bilateral relations are important with Egypt, but one of the things that is shaping our bilateral relations is the leadership that Egypt is showing in the region and throughout the Arab world as a force for peace and the strong stand taken against terrorism, which we want to cooperate with and support. I believe that that is very important not only for the strong tourism industry in Egypt but for getting investment and growth into the country and over the long run.

Secondly, I think Egypt's role as a regional leader will help us to strengthen our bilateral relationship. For example, if we can locate the Middle Eastern development bank there, that's not just to develop things for the Palestinians, that's for the whole region. What we want to do is to bring in a huge influx of capital into the Middle East to bring the benefits of peace to all the people who have fought for it. And since Egypt was the first nation to make peace and since President Mubarak has been a leading, consistent, unwavering force for the peace process, I think Egypt would benefit dramatically from that. So we will work on that.

Now secondly, with regard to the intentions of the Israelis, I believe that the Prime Minister and his government are completely committed to this. And I saw yesterday these maps that were signed in here that are the annexes to the words of the agreement. They signed—Chairman Arafat and Prime Minister Rabin signed 26 maps that had literally thousands and thousands of decisions on them. So they know

exactly what they're getting into. They have made very, very detailed commitments to one another.

And just as I believe that Chairman Arafat is going to do his best to try to diminish terror, I believe that the Prime Minister will do everything he can to fulfill both the letter and the spirit of the agreement. And that is one of the things that the United States has been able to do with the leadership of the Secretary of State and Mr. Ross. And our whole team is to try to work with the parties to make sure that their relationship ripens.

And I will say this: I would urge you to go back and carefully review the text of the statements made not only yesterday at the ceremony but last night at the reception by both Prime Minister Rabin and Chairman Arafat. They said some remarkable things, some things that they certainly didn't say here 2 years ago, which, to me, showed that they are kind of opening up to one another and that the level of trust is growing.

Now, we all know that none of us have total control over people who are, in theory, within our dominion. Here in the United States we have crimes committed every day that the President cannot stop. But I think they are proceeding in good faith, and I think that the people in the Middle East will have a high level of confidence in the way the Israelis proceed now.

NOTE: The exchange began at 11:20 a.m. in the Oval Office at the White House. A tape was not available for verification of the content of this exchange.

Exchange With Reporters on the 1996 Election
September 29, 1995

Q. Mr. President, I don't know if you've heard that Governor Pete Wilson is going to drop out of the Presidential race this afternoon.

The President. No. Are you sure? [*Laughter*] Well, I—that's a very personal decision. It's a difficult road, and I respect the judgment that he would make, or anybody would make under these circumstances, since I've been through it. I hope we will continue to be able to work

together on some of our common problems. I said in Los Angeles when I was there a couple of days ago that the Governor's office worked very closely with us when we were trying to solve the problems of the medical center for Los Angeles County, and there's a lot of important work to do and he still has a very important job.

Q. Does this help your prospects in California?

The President. I don't know.

NOTE: The exchange began at 11:45 a.m. in the Oval Office at the White House prior to discussions with King Hussein of Jordan. In his remarks, the President referred to Governor Pete Wilson of California. A tape was not available for verification of the content of this exchange.

Exchange With Reporters Prior to a Meeting With Congressional Leaders
September 29, 1995

The President. Is everyone in? Ladies and gentlemen, we are about to begin a meeting between the congressional leadership and the administration to discuss our progress in Bosnia and where we're going from here. But before we do, let me begin by saying a thank you to the leadership of Congress for their successful effort to avoid any kind of interruption in our Government operations as we work toward a balanced budget over the next several weeks.

This is the kind of cooperation that makes it possible for our country not only to work but to be great. And I hope that we will have more of it. It is also the kind of cooperation, frankly, that was really being celebrated yesterday when we marked another important milestone on the road to peace in the Middle East.

American leadership has worked for peace in the Middle East through Democratic and Republican administrations for a very long time now, step by step, with discipline and determination over years. And yesterday, we celebrated the product of that kind of effort.

Let me also say that I believe we must continue to work together in Bosnia, and I very much appreciate the expressions of support that have come from leaders in both parties for the efforts that we have been making in recent weeks.

We are now closer to a settlement because of the initiatives we've taken than at any time in the last 4 years because of the combined impacts of the NATO air strikes, the United States diplomatic initiative, and the changes that have occurred on the ground. If and when there is a peace agreement, as I have said since early 1993, I believe America must be a part of helping to implement that agreement, because NATO will have to do it in order for it to work, and we are the leaders of NATO.

I have consistently opposed the involvement of our troops in any combat and in this United Nations mission, but this is a very different thing, and I believe it's very, very important that we play a part of it.

I just received an update from our team and the work they're doing, and I can tell you that we are now seeing some serious discussion of the possibility of a cease-fire, which I hope can be successfully concluded as a prelude to getting into the other details of the agreement.

But I'm looking forward to this meeting. I thank Senator Dole, the Speaker, for being here, and Senator Daschle, Congressman Bonior, and all of the others who are here. And we're looking forward to the meeting.

And I thank you for the continuing resolution. If, as expected, it passes today, I expect to sign it as soon as it hits my desk. And as I said, that's a good omen for our efforts to successfully conclude an effort to balance the budget.

1996 Election

Q. Can I ask Senator Dole to comment on Pete Wilson's decision to drop out of the Presidential race? Is this going to help your prospects of challenging the President next November?

Q. That's a fast jump from Bosnia.

Senator Bob Dole. No, I haven't had a chance to talk to the President about it, so—*[laughter]*.

Q. Does this mean there's no room in the Republican Party for moderate Republicans?

Senator Strom Thurmond. This is not a political meeting.

Senator Dole. Yes—I don't like to answer questions at the President's meeting. I'll be happy to do it later.

Bosnia

Q. Excuse me. Can you tell us more about this possible cease-fire?

The President. No. I mean—and I literally can't tell you more about it. I can tell you that it's being seriously discussed and the parties are talking about how they feel about it and what the obstacles to it are at the present moment. And that's all I can tell you at the present time.

Q. Do you think it's—[inaudible].

The President. No, I didn't say that. I don't know that. I don't know that it's not. I don't know. The answer to that is, I don't know.

Q. Will it happen today or——

The President. I don't know. I think that's highly unlikely.

Thank you.

NOTE: The President spoke at 1:20 p.m. in the Truman Conference Center of the New Executive Office Building.

Statement on Congressional Support for Administration Efforts To Reduce Juvenile Tobacco Use
September 29, 1995

All Americans agree that we must protect the lives and future health of our children. The bipartisan "Commitment to Our Children"—in support of this administration's efforts to reduce children's smoking or use of smokeless tobacco products—shows just how deep that sentiment runs through our country. The Representatives and Senators who stood up today for our children deserve the Nation's thanks. These Democrats and Republicans showed that this is not about partisan politics; it is about doing the right thing for our children and families. Public health leaders, children and family advocates, and elected State and local officials from across the Nation have also pledged to support our efforts.

Each day, 3,000 young people become regular smokers. Nearly 1,000 of them will die early from smoking-related diseases. We must reduce children's access to tobacco products and limit the advertising and promotions that tell our children it is cool or glamorous to smoke but do not tell them about the disease and death that also come with smoking. The stakes are too high not to act.

Message to the Congress on the South Africa-United States Agreement on the Peaceful Use of Nuclear Energy
September 29, 1995

To the Congress of the United States:

I am pleased to transmit to the Congress, pursuant to sections 123 b. and 123 d. of the Atomic Energy Act of 1954, as amended (42 U.S.C. 2153(b), (d)), the text of a proposed Agreement for Cooperation Between the United States of America and the Republic of South Africa Concerning Peaceful uses of Nuclear Energy, with accompanying annex and agreed minute. I am also pleased to transmit my written approval, authorization, and determination concerning the agreement, and the memorandum of the Director of the United States Arms Control and Disarmament Agency with the Nuclear Proliferation Assessment Statement concerning the agreement. The joint memorandum submitted to me by the Acting Secretary of State and the Secretary of Energy, which includes a summary of the provisions of the agreement and various other attachments, including agency views, is also enclosed.

The proposed agreement with the Republic of South Africa has been negotiated in accordance with the Atomic Energy Act of 1954, as amended by the Nuclear Non-Proliferation Act of 1978 (NNPA) and as otherwise amended. In my judgment, the proposed agreement meets all statutory requirements and will advance the non-proliferation and other foreign policy interests of the United States. It provides a comprehensive framework for peaceful nuclear cooperation between the United States and South Africa under appropriate conditions and controls reflecting a strong common commitment to nuclear non-proliferation goals.

The proposed new agreement will replace an existing U.S.-South Africa agreement for peaceful nuclear cooperation that entered into force on August 22, 1957, and by its terms would expire on August 22, 2007. The United States suspended cooperation with South Africa under the 1957 agreement in the 1970's because of evidence that South Africa was embarked on a nuclear weapons program. Moreover, following passage of the NNPA in 1978, South Africa did not satisfy a provision of section 128 of the Atomic Energy Act (added by the NNPA) that requires full-scope IAEA safeguards in non-nuclear weapon states such as South Africa as a condition for continued significant U.S. nuclear exports.

In July 1991 South Africa, in a momentous policy reversal, acceded to the Treaty on the Non-Proliferation of Nuclear Weapons (NPT) and promptly entered into a full-scope safeguards agreement with the IAEA as required by the Treaty. South Africa has been fully cooperative with the IAEA in carrying out its safeguards responsibilities.

Further, in March 1993 South Africa took the dramatic and candid step of revealing the existence of its past nuclear weapons program and reported that it had dismantled all of its six nuclear devices prior to its accession to the NPT. It also invited the IAEA to inspect its formerly nuclear weapons-related facilities to demonstrate the openness of its nuclear program and its genuine commitment to non-proliferation.

South Africa has also taken a number of additional important non-proliferation steps. In July 1993 it put into effect a law banning all weapons of mass destruction. In April 1995 it became a member of the Nuclear Suppliers Group (NSG), formally committing itself to abide by the NSG's stringent guidelines for nuclear exports. At the 1995 NPT Review and Extension Conference it played a decisive role in the achievement of indefinite NPT extension—a top U.S. foreign policy and national security goal.

These steps are strong and compelling evidence that South Africa is now firmly committed to stopping the spread of weapons of mass destruction and to conducting its nuclear program for peaceful purposes only.

In view of South Africa's fundamental reorientation of its nuclear program, the United States proposes to enter into a new agreement for peaceful nuclear cooperation with South Africa. Although cooperation could have been resumed under the 1957 agreement, both we and South Africa believe that it is preferable to have a new agreement completely satisfying, as the proposed new agreement does, the current legal and policy criteria of both sides, and that reflects, among other things:

—Additional international non-proliferation commitments entered into by the parties since 1974, when the old agreement was last amended, including, for South Africa, its adherence to the Treaty on the Non-Proliferation of Nuclear Weapons;

—Reciprocity in the application of the terms and conditions of cooperation between the parties; and

—An updating of terms and conditions to take account of intervening changes in the respective domestic legal and regulatory frameworks of the parties in the area of peaceful nuclear cooperation.

For the United States, the proposed new agreement also represents an additional instance of compliance with section 404(a) of the NNPA, which calls for an effort to renegotiate existing agreements for cooperation to include the more stringent requirements established by the NNPA.

The proposed new agreement with South Africa permits the transfer of technology, material, equipment (including reactors), and components for nuclear research and nuclear power production. It provides for U.S. consent rights to retransfers, enrichment, and reprocessing as required by U.S. law. It does not permit transfers of any sensitive nuclear technology, restricted data, or sensitive nuclear facilities or major critical components thereof. In the event of termination, key conditions and controls continue with respect to material and equipment subject to the agreement.

From the United States perspective the proposed new agreement improves on the 1957 agreement by the addition of a number of important provisions. These include the provisions for full-scope safeguard; perpetuity of safeguards; a ban on "peaceful" nuclear explosives; a right to require the return of exported nuclear items in certain circumstances; a guarantee of adequate physical security; and a consent right to enrichment of nuclear material subject to the agreement.

I have considered the views and recommendations of the interested agencies in reviewing the proposed agreement and have determined that its performance will promote, and will not constitute an unreasonable risk to, the common defense and security. Accordingly, I have approved the agreement and authorized its execution and urge that the Congress give it favorable consideration.

Because this agreement meets all applicable requirements of the Atomic Energy Act, as amended, for agreements for peaceful nuclear cooperation, I am transmitting it to the Congress without exempting it from any requirement contained in section 123 a. of that Act. This transmission shall constitute a submittal for purposes of both sections 123 b. and 123 d. of the Atomic Energy Act. The Administration is prepared to begin immediately the consultations with the Senate Foreign Relations and House International Relations Committees as provided in section 123 b. Upon completion of the 30-day continuous session period provided for in section 123 b., the 60-day continuous session period provided for in section 123 d. shall commence.

WILLIAM J. CLINTON

The White House,
September 29, 1995.

Message to the Congress Transmitting a Report on the Lapse of the Export Administration Act of 1979
September 29, 1995

To the Congress of the United States:

As required by section 204 of the International Emergency Economic Powers Act (50 U.S.C. 1703(c)) and section 401(c) of the National Emergencies Act (50 U.S.C. 1641(c)), I transmit herewith a 6-month periodic report on the national emergency declared by Executive Order No. 12924 of August 19, 1994, to deal with the threat to the national security, foreign policy, and economy of the United States caused by the lapse of the Export Administration Act of 1979.

WILLIAM J. CLINTON

The White House,
September 29, 1995.

The President's Radio Address
September 30, 1995

Good morning. I want to talk to you about the budget debate now unfolding in Washington and about how the wrong decisions can threaten the independence and the dignity of elderly Americans.

I strongly believe we must balance the budget to lift the burden of debt off our children and to strengthen our economy. But we must balance the budget in a way that is consistent with our values and our vision for America's future, giving our people the chance to make the most of their own lives, strengthening our families, protecting our children, honoring our parents, growing the middle class and shrinking the under class, preserving America as the world's strongest nation. Those are the values that must anchor our budget decisions.

For our parents and grandparents who sacrificed so much, no value is more important than independence. All Americans deserve to live out their lives in dignity, and nobody wants to be a burden to their children. So we should do everything in our power to offer elderly Americans the chance to live with respect and with independence, and the Government shouldn't make it worse.

But the Republicans in Congress have proposed a budget that will undermine the dignity and independence of our senior citizens. Here's how: Medicaid's the way our country helps families pay for nursing homes, home care, or other long-term care for elderly or disabled persons. Some people would have you think that Medicaid just helps poor children. Well, it does do that, and that is very important. Almost one in four American children are poor enough to need help from Medicaid.

But the truth is, two-thirds of Medicare—Medicaid—goes to help to pay for nursing homes and other care for senior citizens and the disabled. Nearly 7 of every 10 nursing home residents gets some help from Medicaid. And no wonder, for nursing homes cost an average of $38,000 a year, and not many of our families can afford that.

Now this Republican budget would break this promise to our families. It ends the national commitment that any senior citizen, regardless of how much money they have or don't have, will have access to quality doctors and good facilities.

This budget actually provides for $180 billion in cuts. Now, we do need to slow the rate of medical inflation in the Medicaid program. But these cuts are way, way too much. They are far, far more than the health care system can handle. Over the next few years, this plan and its cuts would deny nursing home care to 300,000 seniors who are eligible for it today. And it will also cut off home care services to 300,000 more. That's bad enough. But listen to what's buried in the fine print; it's even worse.

Under the plan put forward by the House of Representatives, because they know there's not enough money in it to maintain the health care system, any State government can force people whose husbands or wives have to go into nursing homes to give up their car, their furniture, even their home before their spouse can qualify for any medical support. Everything they've worked for their whole lives, gone.

Think about it. Who wants a Medicaid police with vast power to seize your assets and put you out of your home and make sure you have nothing left to pass on to your children? I don't think it should be a precondition that if a husband has to go into a nursing home, his wife has to go into the poorhouse.

Once, this kind of abuse was the norm. In the mid-1980's, one elderly couple in Texas was forced to live in nursing homes 700 miles apart. Another woman in New York had to actually sue her husband for support while he lay helpless in a nursing home. The Government had tried to force her onto food stamps, but she refused. The Government was literally out of control. Then, a bipartisan law signed by President Reagan protected spouses.

The Republican budget plan will also devastate the quality of medical care for seniors who need it. Little more than a decade ago, if you went to a nursing home, what could you see? Some patients tied to their beds, others in a drug-induced stupor, undertrained nurses, and fumbling technicians. All told, back then 40 percent of nursing home residents were either overrestrained or overmedicated.

Reforms signed by President Reagan changed all that. But now, the Republican plan would eliminate all national standards for nursing home care. It would turn back the clock to the days when children worried about whether their parents in nursing homes had to actually be afraid of danger and degradation.

Congress should strip these outrageous provisions from the budget bill. They're inconsistent with our core values. They're not what America is all about, and they are certainly not necessary to balance the budget. Congress is trying to cut Medicaid too much, and Congress is also trying to cut Medicare too much. It is not necessary to balance the budget or to save the Medicare Trust Fund.

Now, the truth is that we do need—we do need to slow the rate of inflation in Medicare and to extend the life of the Medicaid Trust Fund. But the congressional cuts of over $270 billion are less than half—and less than half of those cuts are going to the Trust Fund.

Late yesterday, the House Republicans finally told us what these big numbers mean. Their massive Medicare cuts, by far the biggest in history, now are clear in terms of their impact on individual senior citizens.

Remember now: More than half their cuts don't go to secure Medicare; they're using the money for other purposes. How are they going to raise the money? They want to double premiums, double deductibles, lower quality, give less choice, and have no Medicare at all for Americans under 67.

I have proposed a balanced budget plan that reflects our fundamental values. It eliminates the deficit without destroying education or undermining our environment or violating our commitments to working families, poor children, or seniors. It gives the American people a tax cut targeted to education and childrearing, and it secures Medicare and its Trust Fund, and it restrains inflation on Medicaid without imposing new costs on seniors, threatening their independence, or destroying their dignity.

Let's be clear, of course—of course, we need to balance the budget. But we need to do it in a way that strengthens our families, enhances opportunity for Americans, and honors our obligations to our parents.

I am determined to see that people of good faith work together to find common ground in meeting this challenge.

Thanks for listening.

NOTE: The address was recorded at 6 p.m. on September 29 in Room 453 of the Old Executive Office Building for broadcast at 10:06 a.m. on September 30.

Remarks in Observance of National Domestic Violence Awareness Month
October 2, 1995

Thank you very much, Sergeant Wynn, for your remarks and for dedicating your life to this important work. Thank you, Bonnie Campbell, for doing a great job as head of the Violence Against Women Program in the Justice Department. Thank you, Attorney General Reno, for believing in this and for driving it. Thank you, Secretary Shalala, for reminding us this is a human tragedy.

Thank you, Jerry Rossi. You stood up here and you tried to convince us that you were really worried about the bottom line, and everybody who saw you knew that what you were really worried about was all those people out there, right and wrong. And every American who can see you would be proud of you and would wish that every person in business in this country would have those values and that kind of passion. Thank you so much.

And thank you, Tana Sherman, for being brave enough to tell us your story. Before we came over here, Tana and the five people who are on the back row with Bonnie Campbell all told me their stories. One of them had to have her back broken before she actually asked for help. Another waited until her oldest child was assaulted with a meat cleaver.

This is not just a woman's problem. I was glad to hear that. This is a children's problem, and it's a man's problem. And we're not doing anybody any favors, least of all the abusers, by ignoring it any longer. And I thank all these

brave women for the power of their example. And there are others in this audience who have been severely abused in domestic situations; I thank them all for having the courage to be here and for the fight they are fighting.

I'd also like to thank the Congress for the support that they gave this program a year ago and to say a special word of appreciation to the United States Senate for restoring funding for the Violence Against Women Program just last week. Thank you, Senator Leahy; thank you, Congresswoman Morella; thank you, Congresswoman Zoe Lofgren. And I have to thank my good friend Senator Joe Biden, in his absence, for all of their work on behalf of this program.

Last week we had a great week in Washington. We celebrated progress in peace in the Middle East. We celebrated the beginnings of peaceful agreements in Bosnia. I spend a whole lot of my time trying to make or keep peace, Northern Ireland, Southern Africa, Haiti, trying to get rid of the nuclear weapons that have threatened to disturb our peace profoundly and permanently. But we don't need just peace with other countries, we need peace on our streets, in our schools, and perhaps most of all, in our homes. All of us should want a peaceful world, but we know a peaceful world has to start with each of us, in our homes and at work and in our lives.

This problem has been swept under the rug for quite a long while now. It's really always existed at some level or another. It is time to recognize that domestic violence can quickly and easily become criminal violent activity that affects us all, regardless of our race, our income, or our age, regardless of where we live or what we do.

You've heard about how it increases health costs and absenteeism and reduces the productivity of businesses. You know the most important thing is that it undermines the most important things in life; it undermines the most important institution in the world.

Most of us have been privileged to know, in greater or lesser degree, the joys of family life. And everyone who has ever been part of any family knows there's no such thing as a perfect family and they all have their problems. But there's a whole lot of difference between a family with joys and problems and a family dominated by violence and abuse.

If there is anything I could say to you today that would leave a lasting impression, I would hope it would be to echo what the fine man who introduced me said, and that is that we don't have to put up with this. We do not have to put up with this. We can do something about it. It can be changed. It can be better.

And everybody, not just the battered women but their children who suffer psychological wounds that can only be imagined and can never be fully predicted, and the abusers themselves, will be better off if we determine that we are going to put a quick, firm, rapid, unambiguous stop to every single case we find out about, as soon as we find out about it. That is what we should all leave here determined to do.

I wish the First Lady could be here today, but Hillary has to—she's going to New York, and she couldn't be here. But when we lived in Little Rock, we spent a lot of time at the shelter for battered and abused women and children. It was run by some saintly people we knew and respected. We enjoyed, if you can use that word, the time we spent there. We learned a lot. And it sort of stiffened my resolve to see this as a problem of society, not just an unfortunate thing that happens to some families on occasion, including mine.

And when we were debating the crime bill a year ago, I was so moved by the commitment that the Attorney General had and that many in the Congress had to make a bipartisan departure from national policy and say that we were actually going to single this out, that we were

going to pass a crime bill that was comprehensive and meaningful, that carried the real potential of lowering the crime rate, changing the conditions in which crime would occur. And it really was a brilliant piece of legislation. It had the assault weapons ban. It had stronger penalties for serious offenders.

You see now people are beginning to be put away for good under the "three strikes and you're out" law, and the two cases that I've seen, I'd say the law has been properly implemented. It had money for prevention, for community strategies. It had money for 100,000 police officers. We see all over the country now community policing lowering the crime rate. You do not have to put up with this; we can make this better. We can bring the crime rate down, and we can certainly reduce the rate of domestic violence.

But the Violence Against Women Act is really a peculiar part of the genius of the crime bill because of its commitment to raise to national prominence an issue that had never, ever been there before and because it combines tough sanctions against abusers with assistance to police and to prosecutors and to shelters. And I don't know—several of the people who talked with me before I came out here were emphasizing how important it is to educate and train not only the police officers but also the prosecutors and the judges. All the police can do is to bring the case to the criminal justice system. Prosecutors and the courts have to do the rest.

To make sure this act had a good chance to work, we created the Office of Violence Against Women in the Justice Department, and we named Bonnie Campbell, the former attorney general of Iowa, to head it. And we hope that we can say now that as a matter of national policy, with the support of people all across America in uniform, in women's groups, in support groups, the days of men using physical violence to control the lives of their wives, their girlfriends, and their children are over. And it is not a women's issue; it's an American issue, it's a values issue, and it is now an issue around the world.

A lot of kind things have been said about the speech that Hillary made at the women's conference in Beijing, speaking out against abuses against women and little girls in other parts of the world. But I would remind you, she also spoke out against the problem of family violence. And the Beijing conference made that an international goal for improving the condition of women the world over. And since we had so much to do with that, we ought to say, "We've got a lot of work to do right here in the United States, and we want to lead the way to guarantee women and their children a safe life and a chance at a good, constructive family."

Again, let me say, I'm grateful to all the corporations who have worked on this. Jerry Rossi made an eloquent statement. There are many others; the GAP, Liz Claiborne, Aetna, Polaroid are among the great companies in this country who have made a difference in the way their employees are treated and the way they think about themselves and their options and their possibilities. I thank them for that.

I want to thank the Congress again—I mean the Senate, for restoring the funding. I want to say again, we will not be able to do this right unless there are police officers like Sergeant Wynn who will give themselves to this work. And I often say this in Washington—very often a national movement like this starts with someone like him, who had to live with the reality of domestic abuse. But we can't bring it all the way home with only police officers who grew up in families where there was abuse. We now have to have a systematic commitment to sensitize people who, thank God, did not have to live through it to be a part of this movement, to sensitize prosecutors, to sensitize judges, to sensitize all of us in decisionmaking capacities, whether or not we had domestic abuse in our homes.

And let me finally say that as a kickoff to the National Domestic Violence Awareness Month, I signed today an Executive memorandum to ensure that our Federal Government continues to be a leader in this national effort. I've asked the heads of all the executive departments to conduct employee awareness campaigns modeled after the one that the Attorney General has put in place at the Department of Justice, to provide information and the re-

sources to deal with domestic violence. After all, we know there must be Federal employees at work, even as we speak, who themselves are the victims of domestic violence and who are sitting there at their desks staring blankly at a piece of paper while we here proclaim victory in this fight, and they haven't even taken the first step. So we want to set a good example.

Let me lastly say that, to all the women here and all across America who are abused or who have been abused, you are not invisible. The people who have stood with you today can now say that you are being heard, you are being seen, you are being understood.

The following quote is from one of Hillary's favorite books, and I asked if I could use it today. It's called "In the Spirit," by Susan Taylor, the editor of Essence magazine, and it talks about your courage, your strength, and your hope. She writes, quote, "While we cannot change the past, with the wisdom of spirit, we can change what it means to us and to our future. With understanding and compassion, we can break a cycle of despair, rise above our sorrows, and find a new emotional home from which to create a brighter tomorrow. Each breath we take offers us a chance to create a better life."

Now, I hope because of all these efforts, we will all, with each breath we take, resolve that a part of that better life will be less and less and less domestic violence and abuse, until we have taken it out of the spirit and the soul and the life of the United States of America.

Thank you, and God bless you all.

NOTE: The President spoke at 2:06 p.m. in the East Room at the White House. In his remarks, he referred to Sgt. Mark Wynn, detective, Nashville-Davidson, TN, police department; Jerry Rossi, president, Marshalls, Inc.; and Tana Sherman, survivor of domestic violence. The proclamation on National Domestic Violence Awareness Month and the related memorandum is listed in Appendix D at the end of this volume.

Statement on House of Representatives Inaction on Political Reform
October 2, 1995

The American people have made it clear that they want political reform. It is plain that lobbyists have too much influence in the Halls of power and that reforms are needed to change the way we finance campaigns. I believe that a bipartisan consensus exists to enact reform. By an overwhelming margin, the Senate passed legislation that would require lobbyists to fully disclose their activities and that ended the practice of lobbyists giving lawmakers expensive gifts, meals, and travel.

However, this past weekend, in an abrupt reversal of a previous commitment, the House Republican leadership announced that it would refuse to schedule a vote on lobby reform this year. This may please Washington's professional lobbyists, but it will only deepen the American people's cynicism about the way Government works. There can be no excuse for delay.

This is the starkest indication yet that the new congressional majority simply is not serious about political reform. But it is not the first such indication. It is now nearly 4 months since Speaker Gingrich and I agreed to create a bipartisan commission on political reform. I have sought in good faith to move forward on this proposal. I asked two distinguished Americans, John Gardner and Doris Kearns Goodwin, to reach out to the congressional leadership to make this commission a reality. Mr. Gardner made repeated attempts to contact the Speaker, but the Speaker did not even show him the courtesy of a direct reply. In light of this extraordinary unresponsiveness, Mr. Gardner has indicated that he does not believe the commission has any chance of success.

We must move forward with rapid action on reform that is bipartisan and real. Congress should quickly enact lobby reform, gift reform, and campaign finance reform legislation. In the meantime, I am not waiting. In my first days in office, I barred senior officials from lobbying their agencies for 5 years after leaving office and from ever lobbying for foreign governments. We repealed the tax loophole that let lobbyists deduct their expenses. We have fought for tough lobby reform and campaign reform legislation. And now, my administration is moving forward with an Executive order that will require lobbyists who contact the executive branch to fully disclose their activities.

Message on the Observance of Yom Kippur
October 2, 1995

Warm greetings to all who are observing the holy day of Yom Kippur.

Jews around the world mark this solemn Day of Atonement with stringent fasting for the body and careful examination of the soul. Yom Kippur is a deeply personal holiday, inviting worshippers to confess transgressions and to make reparation for sins, striving in this way to reaffirm their bonds with God and to repair and renew human relationships.

Yom Kippur teaches us all that peace and reconciliation can come only through committed human effort and humility before God. The conclusion of the Israeli-Palestinian Interim Agreement, signed at the White House September 28, is a shining example of such resolve. Two peoples, divided for generations by conflict, have now taken another courageous step toward peace. In this season of renewal, there is more reason than ever before to hope that one day soon there will be safety in Israel's house and that the clash of arms will be banished from God's Holy Land. Let us treasure this lesson in our hearts and work to bring healing and harmony to our nation and our world.

Best wishes for a meaningful and rewarding holiday.

BILL CLINTON

Remarks on Accepting the Report of the Advisory Committee on Human Radiation Experiments
October 3, 1995

Let me begin with a simple thank you to everyone who participated in this extraordinary project and to everyone who supported them.

I am especially glad to see here today Senator Glenn, who's been so active in working on the medical ethics issue; Congressman Markey, who's worked on this issue for a very long time; Congressman Frost, Secretary Shalala; Deputy Secretary of Veterans Affairs Hershel Gober; and of course, the Attorney General who basically tries to get us all to do the right thing all the time. [*Laughter*]

I want to thank Secretary O'Leary for her extraordinary devotion to this cause. And you heard in her remarks basically the way that she views this. It's a part of her ongoing commitment to finish the end of the cold war. And perhaps no Energy Secretary has ever done as much as she has to be an advocate, whether it is for continued reforms within the Energy Department or her outspoken endorsement of the strongest possible commitment on the part of the United States to a Comprehensive Test Ban Treaty, which I believe we will achieve next year in no small measure thanks to the support of the Secretary of Energy.

And of course, I want to thank Dr. Ruth Faden for her extraordinary commitment of about a year and a half of her life to this unusual but important task. And all of you who served on the Committee—I remember the first time we put this Committee together. I looked—I said, that's a pretty distinguished outfit. I wish I could give them five or six jobs to do. [*Laughter*] I'll expect you back next Monday and then we'll—[*laughter*]. I do thank you so much for the work you have done.

Let me tell you that, just as this is an important part of the efforts that Secretary O'Leary outlined, I saw this Committee as an indispensable part of our effort to restore the confidence of the American people in the integrity of their Government. All of these political reform issues to me are integrated. When I became the President, I realized we had great new economic challenges, we had profound social problems, that a lot of these things had to be done by an energized American citizenry, but that our

National Government had a role to play in moving our country through this period of transition. And in order to do it, we needed to increase the capacity of the Government to do it through political reform, but we also needed, as much as anything else, to increase the confidence of the American people that, at the very least, they could trust the United States Government to tell the truth and to do the right things.

So you have to understand that, for me, one reason this is so important is that I see it as part of our ongoing effort to give this Government back to the American people: Senator Glenn's long effort to get Congress to apply to itself the same laws it imposes on the private sector; the restrictions that I imposed on members of my administration in high positions for lobbying for foreign governments; and when the lobby bill failed in the Congress, I just imposed it by Executive order on members of the executive branch. All these efforts at political reform, it seems to me, are important.

But none of these efforts can succeed unless people believe that they can rely on their Government to tell them the truth and to do the right thing. We have declassified thousands of Government documents, files from the Second World War, the cold war, President Kennedy's assassination. These actions are not only consistent with our national security, they are essential to advance our values.

So to me, that's what this is all about. And to all those who represent the families who have been involved in these incidents, let me say to you, I hope you feel that your Government has kept its commitment to the American people to tell the truth and to do the right thing.

We discovered soon after I entered office that with the specter of an atomic war looming like Armageddon far nearer than it does today, the United States Government actually did carry out on our citizens experiments involving radiation. That's when I ordered the creation of this Committee. Dr. Faden and the others did a superb job. They enlisted many of our Nation's most significant and important medical and scientific ethicists. They had to determine first whether experiments conducted or sponsored by our

Government between 1944 and 1974 met the ethical and scientific standards of that time and of our time. And then they had to see to it that our research today lives up to nothing less than our highest values and our most deeply held beliefs.

From the beginning, it was obvious to me that this energetic Committee was prepared to do its part. We declassified thousands of pages of documents. We gave Committee members the keys to the Government's doors, file cabinets, and safes. For the last year and a half, the only thing that stood between them and the truth were all the late nights and hard work they had to put in.

This report I received today is a monumental document—[*laughter*]—in more ways than one. But it is a very, very important piece of America's history, and it will shape America's future in ways that will make us a more honorable, more successful, and more ethical country.

What this Committee learned I would like to review today with a little more detail than Dr. Faden said, because I think it must be engraved on our national memory. Thousands of Government-sponsored experiments did take place at hospitals, universities, and military bases around our Nation. The goal was to understand the effects of radiation exposure on the human body. While most of the tests were ethical by any standards, some were unethical, not only by today's standards but by the standards of the time in which they were conducted. They failed both the test of our national values and the test of humanity.

In one experience, scientists—experiment—scientists injected plutonium into 18 patients without their knowledge. In another, doctors exposed indigent cancer patients to excessive doses of radiation, a treatment from which it is virtually impossible that they could ever benefit.

The report also demonstrates that these and other experiments were carried out on precisely those citizens who count most on the Government for its help, the destitute and the gravely ill. But the dispossessed were not alone. Members of the military—precisely those on whom we and our Government count most—they were also test subjects.

Informed consent means your doctor tells you the risk of the treatment you are about to undergo. In too many cases, informed consent was withheld. Americans were kept in the dark about the effects of what was being done to them.

The deception extended beyond the test subjects themselves to encompass their families and the American people as a whole, for these experiments were kept secret. And they were shrouded not for a compelling reason of national security but for the simple fear of embarrassment, and that was wrong.

Those who led the Government when these decisions were made are no longer here to take responsibility for what they did. They are not here to apologize to the survivors, the family members, or the communities whose lives were darkened by the shadow of the atom and these choices. So today, on behalf of another generation of American leaders and another generation of American citizens, the United States of America offers a sincere apology to those of our citizens who were subjected to these experiments, to their families, and to their communities.

When the Government does wrong, we have a moral responsibility to admit it. The duty we owe to one another to tell the truth and to protect our fellow citizens from excesses like these is one we can never walk away from. Our Government failed in that duty, and it offers an apology to the survivors and their families and to all the American people who must—who must be able to rely upon the United States to keep its word, to tell the truth, and to do the right thing.

We know there are moments when words alone are not enough. That's why I am instructing my Cabinet to use and build on these recommendations, to devise promptly a system of relief, including compensation, that meets the standards of justice and conscience.

When called for, we will work with Congress to serve the best needs of those who were harmed. Make no mistake, as the Committee report says, there are circumstances where compensation is appropriate as a matter of ethics and principle. I am committed to seeing to it that the United States of America lives up to its responsibility.

Our greatness is measured not only in how we so frequently do right but also how we act when we know we've done the wrong thing, how we confront our mistakes, make our apologies, and take action.

That's why this morning, I signed an Executive order instructing every arm and agency of our Government that conducts, supports, or regulates research involving human beings to review immediately their procedures in light of the recommendations of this report and the best knowledge and standards available today and to report back to me by Christmas. I have also created a Bioethics Advisory Commission to supervise the process, to watch over all such research, and to see to it that never again do we stray from the basic values of protecting our people and being straight with them.

The report I received today will not be left on a shelf to gather dust. Every one of its pages offers a lesson, and every lesson will be learned from these good people who put a year and a half of their lives into the effort to set America straight.

Medical and scientific progress depends upon learning about people's responses to new medicines, to new cutting-edge treatments. Without this kind of research, our children would still be dying from polio and other killers. Without responsible radiation research, we wouldn't be making the progress we are in the war on cancer. We have to continue to research, but there is a right way and a wrong way to do it. There are local citizens' review boards; there are regulations that establish proper informed consent and ensure that experiments are conducted ethically. But in overseeing this necessary research, we must never relax our vigilance.

The breathtaking advances in science and technology demand that we always keep our ethical watchlight burning. No matter how rapid the pace of change, it can never outrun our core convictions that have stood us so well as a nation for more than 200 years now, through many different scientific revolutions.

I believe we will meet the test of our times, that as science and technology evolve, our ethical conscience will grow, not shrink. Informed consent, community right-to-know, our entire battery of essential human protections, all these grew up in response to the health and humanitarian crises of this 20th century. They are proof that we are equal to our challenges.

Science is not ever simply objective. It emerges from the crucible of historical circumstances and personal experience. Times of crisis and fear can call forth bad science, even science we know in retrospect to be unethical.

Let us remember the difficult years chronicled in this report and think about how good people could have done things that we know were wrong.

Let these pages serve as an eternal reminder to hold humility and moral accountability in higher esteem than we do the latest development in technology. Let us remember, too, that cynicism about Government has roots in historical circumstances. Because of stonewallings and evasions in the past, times when a family member or a neighbor suffered an injustice and had nowhere to turn and couldn't even get the facts, some Americans lost faith in the promise of our democracy. Government was very powerful but very far away and not trusted to be ethical.

So today, by making ourselves accountable for the sins of the past, I hope more than anything else, we are laying the foundation stone for a new era. Good people—like these Members of Congress who have labored on this issue for a long time and have devoted their careers to trying to do the right thing and having people justifiably feel confidence in the work of their Representatives—they will continue to work to see that we implement these recommendations.

And under our watch, we will no longer hide the truth from our citizens. We will act as if all that we do will see the light of day. Nothing that happens in Washington will ever be more important in anyone's life affected by these experiments, perhaps, than these reports we issue today. But all of us as Americans will be better off because of the larger lesson we learned in this exercise and because of our continuing effort to demonstrate to our people that we can be faithful to their values.

Thank you very much.

NOTE: The President spoke at 11:07 a.m. in Room 450 of the Old Executive Office Building. In his remarks, he referred to Ruth R. Faden, Chair, Advisory Committee on Human Radiation Experiments. The Executive order on protection of human research subjects and creation of the National Bioethics Advisory Commission is listed in Appendix D at the end of this volume.

Statement on Signing the Military Construction Appropriations Act, FY 1996
October 3, 1995

Today I have signed into law H.R. 1817, the "Military Construction Appropriations Act, FY 1996," which provides funding for military construction and family housing programs of the Department of Defense.

I am pleased that the Act provides my full request for the vast majority of military construction projects, the military family housing program, other quality of life facilities for our military personnel and their families, and the Defense Department base closure and realignment program. Especially noteworthy, the bill funds my request for the Defense Department Family Housing Improvement Fund, which will give the Department a new vehicle for acquiring and improving military housing and supporting facilities more quickly and at lower cost than with conventional funding and acquisition methods.

Although I am disappointed that the Act provides more funding than requested, most of the unrequested appropriations are for legitimate defense requirements. Funding was provided in FY 1996 rather than in future years.

I am concerned, however, that Congress has chosen to spend $70 million on unneeded projects. The Defense Department has not identified these projects as priorities, and they will not help improve the quality of life for our service members. These projects are clear examples of why the President needs line-item veto authority. The taxpayers deserve protection from this kind of wasteful spending, and if I had the line-item veto, I would use it to strike this $70 million. Unfortunately, Congress still has not completed action on legislation to provide the President with line-item veto authority. The American people have waited long enough. I strongly urge the Congress to complete action on line-item veto legislation now so I can eliminate wasteful spending this year.

The American people sent us here to change the way Washington does business. Passing the line-item veto would be a good place for this Congress to start.

WILLIAM J. CLINTON

The White House,
October 3, 1995.

NOTE: H.R. 1817, approved October 3, was assigned Public Law No. 104–32.

Message to the House of Representatives Returning Without Approval the Legislative Branch Appropriations Bill, FY 1996
October 3, 1995

To the House of Representatives:

I am returning today without my approval H.R. 1854, the "Legislative Branch Appropriations Bill, FY 1996."

H.R. 1854 is, in fact, a disciplined bill, one that I would sign under different circumstances. But, at this point, Congress has completed action on only two of the 13 FY 1996 appropriations bills: this one and H.R. 1817, the Military Construction appropriations bill. Thus, the vast majority of Federal activities lack final FY 1996 funding and are operating under a short-term continuing resolution.

I appreciate the willingness of Congress to work with my Administration to produce an acceptable short-term continuing resolution before completing action on the regular, full-year appropriations bills for FY 1996. I believe, however, that it would be inappropriate to provide full-year regular funding for Congress and its offices while funding for most other activities of Government remains incomplete, unresolved, and uncertain.

As I said two months ago, I don't think Congress should take care of its own business before it takes care of the people's business. I stated that if the congressional leadership were to follow through on its plan to send me its own funding bill before finishing work on the rest of the budget, I would veto it. I am now following through on that commitment.

I urge the Congress to move forward promptly on completing the FY 1996 appropriations bills in a form that I can accept.

WILLIAM J. CLINTON

The White House,
October 3, 1995.

Remarks Welcoming Pope John Paul II in Newark, New Jersey
October 4, 1995

Archbishop McCarrick, Archbishop Cacciavillan, Cardinal Keeler, Father Theroux, the members of the Cabinet, the Members of the Congress, Governor Whitman, Mayor James, honored guests: Your Holiness, it is a great pleasure and an honor to welcome you back to the United States.

You seemed to bring us the rain, but we need the rain, and we thank you for that. Your return has been greatly anticipated by the American people, and as you have gathered from the welcome of the children and the not-so-young, all Americans are very, very happy to see you.

This is our third opportunity to visit. I look forward to our discussion, and I am grateful that your voice—for peace and hope and for the values that support every family and the family of humanity.

On this, your fourth visit to our Nation, you will see an America striving to build on our ideals of peace and charity, justice and tolerance. When you visit the United Nations and you speak to the General Assembly, you will be retracing the steps of Pope Paul VI in his visit to the United States which began 30 years ago this day. He became the first Pontiff to visit our beloved country when he spoke to the United Nations in the name of peace.

The Catholic faithful here in America have always taken an active role in making our country better. The Catholic Church helps the poor, the children, the elderly, the afflicted, and our families. You will see their handiwork here in the city of Newark and throughout your visit. The Church has given life to the idea that in the human community we all have obligations to one another. This idea is rooted in Church institutions, including thousands of charitable ac-

tivities, the Catholic Charities, the Campaign for Human Development, the network of Catholic hospitals, and other agencies that help all Americans, and of course, it is rooted in the 9,000 Catholic elementary and high schools, and more than 200 Catholic colleges here in the United States. And they too, thankfully, serve all Americans.

As distinct as Catholicism is, it shares something with many other faiths in our Nation, the unshakable values that are at the core of our society that hold us together as a country. We Americans are a people of faith, expressed in many ways. With the most diverse population on Earth, our Nation counts more religions than any other, more than 1,500, and more places of worship than any other. Indeed, even as we gather here now, many of our fellow citizens are in their synagogues fasting and observing the holiest day of the Jewish calendar, Yom Kippur, the day of atonement.

Our great American poet, Walt Whitman, who I know is a favorite of yours, once wrote about America, "The real and permanent grandeur of these States must be their religion. Otherwise, there is no real and permanent grandeur." That is the America that awaits you and your visit, Your Holiness. Our faith matters to us as individuals and as families. Our faith supports our families, strengthens them, and keeps them together.

Your Holiness, you have written and spoken so eloquently of family rights, and women and men everywhere welcomed your recent open letter on the dignity and rights of women. The First Lady and I thank you, especially, for the words of support from the Holy See regarding her speech on the rights of families, women, and their children, at the recent conference on women in Beijing, China. Your words supported the statement she made on behalf of all Americans, that if women are healthy and educated, free from violence, if they have a chance to work and earn as full and equal partners, their families will flourish. And when families flourish, communities and nations will flourish.

We know that if we value our families, as we must, public policy must also support them. It must see to it that children live free of poverty with the opportunity of a good and decent education. If we value our families, we must let them know the dignity of work with decent wages. If we value our families, we must care for them across the generations from the oldest to the youngest.

Your Holiness, it is most fitting that you have arrived to be with us today on the feast day of St. Francis of Assisi, the champion of the poor, the defender of the defenseless. His prayer, carried to this day in the pockets, the purses, the billfolds of many American Catholics, and revered by many who are not Catholics, is a simple clarion to unity. It begins: "Lord, make me an instrument of your peace. Where there is hatred, let me so love." Today, these words hold special meaning for us, for with God's help, we recently celebrated the advance of peace in the Middle East, and we are trying, earnestly, with your support, to knock on the door of peace in Bosnia.

We see peace advancing in Northern Ireland, in Haiti, in Southern Africa. All this has been

an answer to many, many prayers around the world, but many of them were led by you, Holy Father, and for that, you have the gratitude of all the American people.

On the threshold of a new millennium, more than ever, we need your message of faith and family, community and peace. That is what we must work toward for millions of reasons, as many reasons as there are children on this Earth.

It has been said that you can see the future by looking into the eyes of a child. Well, we are joined here today by 2,000 children from the Archdiocese of Newark and surrounding parishes. Your Holiness, looking out at them now and into their eyes, we can see that the future is very bright indeed. For them and for all Americans, we thank you, Holy Father, for coming back to the United States, and we welcome you.

NOTE: The President spoke at 3:35 p.m. at Newark International Airport. In his remarks, he referred to Archbishop Theodore McCarrick, Archbishop of Newark; Archbishop Agostino Cacciavillan, Apostolic Pronuncio to the United States; William Cardinal Keeler, president, National Conference of Bishops; Father Paul Theroux, national coordinator for the Papal visit; Gov. Christine T. Whitman of New Jersey; and Mayor Sharpe James of Newark.

Statement on Hurricane Opal
October 4, 1995

As Hurricane Opal hits the coast of the Southern United States, our hearts and prayers go out to all whose lives have been disrupted by the devastation. The people of Florida and Alabama have shown great courage and strength in dealing with the damage that has already been done, and I know they will continue to show courage as the hours progress.

I want the States affected by this terrible storm to know that the rest of America is with them. One of the basic values of America is the responsibility to stand with each other in times of need. I will do all I can to ensure

you the Federal support you need for successful recovery efforts. Tonight I have signed emergency declarations to supplement State and local recovery efforts in both Florida and Alabama. James Lee Witt, the Director of the Federal Emergency Management Agency, will be on the ground coordinating efforts in the South to save lives and protect the health, safety, and property of those affected by Hurricane Opal.

The action I am taking tonight will now enable us to immediately send rescue teams into the affected areas. Please be assured that the Federal Emergency Management Agency will mobilize all necessary resources to help these States recover from the damage. And be assured that the prayers of our entire Nation are with you.

Remarks Announcing the Bosnia-Herzegovina Cease-Fire Agreement and an Exchange With Reporters
October 5, 1995

The President. Good morning. Today we take another solid step on the hard but hopeful road to peace in Bosnia. I'm pleased to announce that the parties in Bosnia have agreed to a cease-fire to terminate all hostile military activities throughout the territory of Bosnia-Herzegovina to become effective on October 10th, if certain conditions are met.

At the same time, the Governments of Bosnia, Croatia, and Serbia have agreed to proximity peace talks in the United States, beginning about October 25th, aimed at bringing them closer to a peace agreement. Those negotiations will take place with the assistance of our able negotiating team, led by Assistant Secretary Holbrooke, together with our Contact Group partners.

The talks will continue, then, at an international peace conference in Paris that can help to achieve an enduring end to the struggle. This is an important moment in the painful history in Bosnia, for today the parties have agreed to put down their arms and roll up their sleeves and work for peace.

We need to be clear-eyed about this. What matters is what the parties do, not simply what they say. There remain deep divisions to overcome. We are now on the right road, but we have by no means reached our destination, which is a serious and lasting peace in Bosnia. This cease-fire, however, greatly increases our chances to end the war and to achieve a peace. The United States, together with our European and our Russian partners, intends to use all of our influence and every ounce of our energy to seize this historic opportunity for peace.

Q. Do you think it's fair to make this statement, and do you wish you had done it sooner? If you had moved more aggressively——

The President. All I know is that we're on the verge of a cease-fire. We're going to do our best to get the cease-fire. We have 5 days of hard work to do on that.

Q. Will NATO police this cease-fire? How will this be enforced?

The President. We're going to brief you on all the details of the cease-fire. We intend to go forward with the cease-fire, then go forward with the talks here in Washington. We hope we can start the talks in Washington by October 25th, and we feel very strongly that that will increase the chances of peace.

NOTE: The President spoke at 11 a.m. in the Briefing Room at the White House.

Remarks on Presenting the Arts and Humanities Awards
October 5, 1995

The President. Thank you very much. It's an eerie feeling being introduced by your wife. [*Laughter*] You never know what's going to be said. [*Laughter*] You're steeling yourself for the discipline not to show any adverse reaction. [*Laughter*] We're having a good time today, Hillary and I are. We love this day; we look forward to it. And we thank all of you for coming. We thank especially Senator Pell and Senator Simpson. Thank you for coming. We're glad to see you.

We thank the members of the administration who are here. I see Secretary Riley and Deputy Secretary Kunin of Education; and Roger Johnson, the Director of the General Services Administration. There may be others here. I thank all of you for being here. I want to say a special word of thanks for the service of Jane Alexander and Sheldon Hackney for the great job that they have done. I thank my good friend John Brademas, the Chairman of the President's Committee on the Arts and Humanities, and Diane Frankel, the Director of the Institute for Museum Services. And I thank all the members of the Arts and the Humanities Councils who are here for their willingness to serve.

It's a great honor for me to be able to present today the National Medal of Arts and the Charles Frankel Prize in the Humanities to a distinguished group of Americans who have lived their lives as builders, bringing people enlightenment, bringing people enjoyment, advancing the cause of human knowledge and human understanding and the joy in life. Before I do that, I think I ought to say, we've had a couple of pieces of good news this morning at the White House, which at least are not inconsistent with what so many of these people have given their lives to.

The President of Mexico called me this morning and told me that, after all the difficulties his country had faced in recent months, that he was making an early repayment of $700 million of the money they borrowed from the United States to keep their economy going. And I think that's a good thing.

You know, when you loan money, you never know whether it's a good thing or not until it's too late to do anything about it. [*Laughter*] Some of you have been in that position. But they're our friends; they're our allies; they're our partners for the future. They're fighting for their democracy, and they're fighting for the quality of their country's economy. They hit a rough spot in the road, and they borrowed less money than we authorized them to, and they're paying it back more quickly. And we're going to have a brighter future as a result of it and a safer, more secure future and a better partnership. And that's a good thing.

And perhaps even more importantly, I learned early this morning that in 5 days from now, if we can just get a couple of things done, the parties in Bosnia have agreed to a complete cease-fire of all military hostilities. They have furthermore agreed to come for what are called "proximity peace talks"—I'll tell you about that in a minute; that's a Government language word—to the United States to actually talk about hammering out a final peace agreement

in late October. So this is a good day for the cause of peace and prosperity in the world and in the United States.

Proximity peace talks means that they'll all come to the same country, to the same town, to the same place, but they'll let us talk to them, and they won't talk to each other until— [*laughter*]—but that's better than it's been. [*Laughter*] And sooner or later, we'll all find out we have more in common than we do dividing us. And that's the lesson that we hope the American people keep in mind us we go through the next months and years as well.

I think it's fair to say that no President has ever enjoyed these award ceremonies more than I have because every year I get a chance to recognize the lifetime achievements of people who have been heroes to me in various ways, men and women who, unbeknownst to them, have been my teachers, my role models, my inspiration, because, as President, I am no different than any other American who enjoys literature or music or art and architecture. And I have benefited, as so many of you have, from the work of the people we recognize today.

These awards call attention to the lives of 17 individuals and one organization who have worked to enrich the lives of millions and millions of Americans, millions of people around the world, and have made this country a stronger, better, richer place. They are genuine examples of the American ideal, and their work as a whole is a national treasure.

The arts and humanities have energized the American dream in so many ways. The soul of our country has literally been shaped by the vision of our artists and the creativity of those whom we honor here today. And many others in the past have helped America to become and to remain the freest, most democratic nation in the world. Through the arts and humanities, we assert both our oneness and our diversity. And in celebrating this ideal, we move forward together.

Human creativity is clearly the most powerful force on Earth. And these awardees have exercised that power to the fullest. They have woven for us a wonderful mosaic of music and dance, art and literature to comfort and inspire a troubled world.

The importance of this work is more important now, perhaps, than ever before as our country and our world go through a period of unprecedented change, changes that are both bringing us together and ripping up the bonds that have united us in the past. In a nation as diverse as ours, our arts and our humanities are bridges to help us reach out to one another and understand one another better. Projects like the NEH's national conversation are truly helping us to accomplish this.

In the face of those who would divide us, we must remain steadfast in supporting the arts and humanities as a way of coming together while we celebrate our diversity. Our support for them is not the preservation of some extravagant cultural elite, it is the preservation of our cultural tradition for all Americans and especially for those who, unlike me and so many of us, are not part of anybody's elite, and they need their country to make sure they have access to the great heritage of America as well.

For the last 30 years, the National Endowment for the Arts and the National Endowment for the Humanities have made the arts and humanities accessible to millions of our fellow citizens from schoolchildren to people in our inner cities to citizens in our most isolated rural communities, many of whom would never have experienced these gifts had they not been offered so freely by our Nation's artists and scholars and by their Nation's Government.

For a very small contribution, both the NEA and the NEH have made vital contributions to the life of this Nation. Each of the awardees we recognize here today has been a pioneer. Sometimes they've made us laugh. Sometimes they've helped us cry. Sometimes they've challenged us to see the error of our ways. Sometimes they've helped us to celebrate the strength of our goodness. But always they have lifted us to higher ground.

I am honored to confer upon this wonderful group of Americans the National Medal of the Arts and the Charles Frankel Prize. First, the Medal of the Arts winners.

Licia Albanese: the beginning of her career came as something of a surprise. When the lead soprano in a Milan production of "Madame Butterfly" fell ill during the performance, this young singer was called upon to finish the opera. Her performance that evening brought the house down. And a career that spanned more than 30 years was launched.

She went on to leading roles in operas all around the world, always creating characters memorable not only for the arias they sang but for their intense vitality. She had the rare ability to combine her great talent as a singer with equal talent as an actress. It was once said that Licia Albanese had the two qualities which all great artists have, simplicity and sincerity. Most recently, she and her late husband founded the Puccini Foundation, and she has worked tirelessly for the benefit of opera and its survival as an art form.

Please welcome our first honoree, Licia Albanese.

[*At this point, the President and Hillary Clinton presented the medal and congratulated Ms. Albanese.*]

Gwendolyn Brooks began writing poetry when she was only 11. And at the age of 13, her first poem was published. More than 75 others followed, while she was still a teenager. For four decades, Gwendolyn Brooks has drawn on the black experience to create poetry that speaks to all of us in a frank and familiar way. She served as the poetry consultant to the Library of Congress, and today is the poet laureate of Illinois. In 1949, she was awarded the Pulitzer Prize for poetry. She has kept alive the culture of her roots through the cultivation of her words.

Gwendolyn Brooks.

[*The President and Hillary Clinton presented the medal and congratulated Ms. Brooks.*]

Each painter, performer, or thinker here today has in one way or another served to create a legacy in the halls of American art. Their contributions shall be forever remembered in their fields and beyond. But their work might never have seen the light of day were it not for generous, committed, and visionary citizens like two of those whom we honor, Iris and Bernie Cantor.

They have helped literally countless young artists to succeed. They've introduced countless young people to the joys of art. The grants and gifts bestowed by the Cantor family have built and filled the galleries and museums across our Nation. From the Rodin sculptures given to New York's Metropolitan Museum of Art to the grants for exhibitions at institutions such as our own Arkansas Art Center at home to the sculpture exhibit here at the White House, the Cantors' love for art has known no bounds. They've done much to keep the arts alive in America, and we owe them our thanks. Bernie could not be with us here today. But Hillary and I are delighted that our good friend Iris Cantor is here to accept the award on behalf of both of them.

Iris and Bernie Cantor.

[*The President and Hillary Clinton presented the medal and congratulated Mrs. Cantor.*]

It's a special honor for me today to honor another husband and wife team that has shown that a commitment to the issues facing the world around us can be just as important a part of their lives and our lives as a commitment to the art one creates. Ossie Davis and Ruby Dee met in 1946, performing in a Broadway version of "Jeb Turner". I want to say that again. They met in 1946, while performing in a Broadway version of "Jeb Turner"—[*laughter*]—a play in which she was violating the child labor laws at the time. [*Laughter*] They were married a year later. And they have performed individually and together now for almost 50 years.

While the stage and screen have kept them busy with such projects as "A Raisin in the Sun," "The Jackie Robinson Story," and "Do The Right Thing," they have continued to fight for others' struggle for equality. Ossie Davis and Ruby Dee have helped groups such as the NAACP, the Urban League, the AIDS projects, like Housing Works. In 1986 they produced a PBS tribute entitled "Martin Luther King: The Dream and the Drum." Their vision and their talent shine as brightly today as they did on that first day when they met on Broadway so long ago, and our country is very much a better place because of their life and their work.

[*The President and Hillary Clinton presented the medal and congratulated Mr. Davis and Ms. Dee.*]

Having written no fewer than 100 pieces of music by the time he graduated from high school, David Diamond was well on his way to becoming one of America's most accomplished and disciplined composers very early in his youth. His dedication and commitment throughout his distinguished career has made him a master at the craft of creating music.

He's a proud adherent to the classical tradition and has made outstanding contributions to the field for more than 60 years now. An inspiration both to those within his field as well as those who simply enjoy the music he creates, David Diamond truly exemplifies the spirit of American creativity.

Mr. Diamond.

[*The President and Hillary Clinton presented the medal and congratulated Mr. Diamond.*]

Born in Germany, James Ingo Freed came to the United States as a 9-year-old refugee in 1939. After earning his architectural degree in 1953, he joined the offices of I.M. Pei and Partners. Widely published and respected within the world of architecture, he has been the recipient of many major awards, and most recently, he has been justifiably celebrated for his creation of the magnificent, for most of us, overwhelming United States Holocaust Memorial Museum, an extraordinary structure that houses many painful memories but ultimately inspires its visitors to strive for a better future. We're honoring him today for that monumental achievement but also for his lifelong dedication to his craft which continues in this city at this moment as the Federal Triangle building comes up and moves toward completion. Let's give him a warm welcome.

James Ingo Freed.

[*The President and Hillary Clinton presented the medal and congratulated Mr. Freed.*]

Our next awardee obviously needs no introduction. He was cited by the Guiness Book of Records as the most honored entertainer in the world. [*Laughter*] Maybe we ought not to do this. [*Laughter*] Bob Hope has more than 1,000 awards and citations for his humanitarian and professional success. He's been honored more than—I think, five times by the Motion Picture Academy, including receiving an honorary Oscar and the Jean Hersholt Humanitarian Award. But I know something that some of you probably don't know. He would far rather go down in history as a great golfer. [*Laughter*] This morning when I saw him, Bob said, "Well, how's your golf game?" I said, "It's pretty good, but it's too rainy today. We can't play." He said, "That's too bad, I'll miss taking your money." [*Laughter*] Unfortunately, that's not as funny as you think it is. [*Laughter*] Known the world over for his wonderful wit and sense of humor, Bob Hope has brought laughter and pleasure and a happier outlook on life to generations of American citizens and especially to our troops in uniform all around the world.

He began entertaining American service men and women even before World War II, and he's done it in every conflict since. In 1971,

Bob Hope took his commitment to the people of America one step further by applying for a visa to Laos to help negotiate the release of our prisoners there. When he wasn't performing across oceans, Bob Hope was making films and making people laugh here in America. I can honestly say that those films are still making all the members of my family laugh every time they're shown on the television here.

But even with his busy career, Bob Hope never lost sight of the truly important things in life, helping people in need. He's helped raise more than $1 billion for hospitals, for the disabled, the Boy Scouts, and numerous other health and human service causes. His annual golf tournament every year, which he still plays in, directs, and manages, is an example of a man whose commitment to doing this kind of work truly is a lifetime endeavor.

He is perhaps the finest example of a successful American entertainer whose greatest performance is in what he does off stage every day. I am so delighted that Bob Hope and his wonderful wife, Dolores, are both here today. And I'd like to ask Bob now to come up and receive his award.

Mr. Bob Hope.

[The President and Hillary Clinton presented the medal and congratulated Mr. Hope.]

Mr. Hope. I just want to say a couple of words. I appreciate this, Mr. President. [*Laughter*] But last year during our golf tournament, I called the President, and I said, "Do you think you could get out here and play with us during our tournament?" And he said, "I don't know." And I got a hold of Mr. Bush, George Bush, and I got a hold of President Ford. And the four of us played, and we raised $1,400,000 for the hospital out there. And I just wanted to thank him right now in person. That's it; that's it. [*Laughter*]

The President. American art is not limited to portraits or landscapes or still lifes. The broad range of subjects reflects the diversity of American experience. Roy Lichtenstein is one of the pioneers who challenged convention and opened our eyes to new styles of expression. In the early sixties, he was one of just a small group to experiment with popular icons as subject material. I hope that doesn't make a comeback. [*Laughter*]

His works are well known and have appeared in numerous exhibitions all around this country.

In addition, Roy was one of several artists commissioned to work on the New York State Pavilion for the 1964 World Fair. I hope that the pioneering spirit exemplified by Roy Lichtenstein will always, always live in the artists of America. It's been a real honor for Hillary and for me to get to know Roy and his wife and his work. And we're very grateful for it and glad to honor him here today.

Roy Lichtenstein.

[The President and Hillary Clinton presented the medal and congratulated Mr. Lichtenstein.]

For nearly four decades, Arthur Mitchell has been a pivotal figure in American dance. The protege of the great George Balanchine, he was the first African-American dancer to become a principal artist in the New York City Ballet. After leaving the company in 1966, he went on to a career on Broadway and as an artistic director. But always, always, there was the call of his home, Harlem.

Following the death of Martin Luther King, Jr., in 1968, the next year Arthur Mitchell realized a dream by returning to Harlem as the founder of the Dance Theater of Harlem. It is now recognized as one of the world's premier dance troupes. His dedication to young people and to dance are truly legendary. We are honored by his presence here today and by the lifetime of creativity, achievement he has demonstrated and, most of all, that he found a way to go back to his roots and lift people up with their God-given talents.

Mr. Arthur Mitchell.

[The President and Hillary Clinton presented the medal and congratulated Mr. Mitchell.]

Speaking of roots, this next awardee is one from mine. Bill Monroe is heralded as the father of bluegrass music, a title that is a fitting tribute to his truly innovative and inventive style. Bluegrass is known for its free improvisation, and in its way, it embodies the essence of the American spirit. Bill's own roots stem from rural Kentucky. When he was just 10 years old, he began to play the guitar and the mandolin. Along with his two older brothers, Charlie and Birch, he made music on the front porch of their family home. Later, Bill Monroe and his Blue Grass Boys established themselves as more than just a string band by blending different vocal harmonies with instrumental solos. And over the years, the band continued to gain recognition for its novel combination of instruments.

Bill Monroe was inducted into the Country Music Hall of Fame in 1970 and joined the International Bluegrass Music Association's Hall of Honor in 1991. For people who follow and love that music, Bill Monroe is truly an American legend. He's added so much through his lifetime career to the rich heritage of this great Nation's music.

Mr. Bill Monroe.

[The President and Hillary Clinton presented the medal and congratulated Mr. Monroe.]

He said, "I'm younger than Bob Hope, but I'd still like to say a thing or two." *[Laughter]*

Mr. Monroe. Bob Hope is a great man. I'm glad that he's here. But what I wanted to tell you folks, I have played for the last four Presidents of the United States, President Carter, President Reagan, President Bush, President Clinton here. And they all tell me that the music I originated belongs to America. And I'm really proud of that. It's a great honor. Thank you.

The President. Thank you. God bless you.

Now, it is a great honor for me to present the award we give every year to an arts organization. As the largest and most comprehensive arts and education program in the entire Nation, Urban Gateways has been cited as a model by the National Endowment for the Arts. In 1994 alone, Urban Gateways reached over 1 million people in over 11,000 programs established in Chicago area schools. Armed with the belief that exposure to the arts is crucial to personal development, the program helps bridge the gap between Chicago's vast cultural wealth and the huge number of children from disadvantaged communities. At a time when so many of our children are being lost to the horrors of drugs and violence, Urban Gateways has assumed responsibility for our young people's youth. The organization gives them guidance and an important outlet for their creative energies.

Here today to accept the award is Urban Gateways' executive director, Sandra Furey. She has led Urban Gateways to the frontlines in the campaign to keep the arts alive in the minds of our children and, in so doing, to keep our children alive and well and strong for the future of this great Nation. Let's give her a big hand. *[Applause]*

[The President and Hillary Clinton presented the medal and congratulated Ms. Furey.]

And now it is my honor to introduce the winners of the 1995 Charles Frankel Prize. The first winner, Bill Ferris, leads the sort of life I'd like to lead if I had another one to live. I mean, he lives in the Deep South. He writes funny, wonderful books. And he's still trying to find out if Elvis is alive. He's probably done more than anyone else to bring national recognition and understanding to the field of Southern studies. As many of you know, he seriously was one of the organizers of the recent, highly successful Elvis conference at the University of Mississippi at Oxford. Since 1979, he has directed the Center for the Study of Southern Culture at Ole Miss, where he's built Southern studies curriculum into the most extensive in the Nation. He was a consultant to the movie "The Color Purple," and for nearly a decade until 1994, as the blues doctor, he hosted "Highway 61," a weekly blues music program that airs on Mississippi public radio. His scholarship covers the fields of folklore, American literature, music, and photography.

I want to thank him for bringing the culture and music of my homeland to all Americans. A remarkable person.

Mr. Bill Ferris.

[The President and Hillary Clinton presented the prize and congratulated Mr. Ferris.]

Too often, television overlooks the lives and poignant stories of ordinary Americans who may not show up on the evening news, but whose extraordinary lives keep our country going. Charles Kuralt recognized this problem nearly 30 years ago. In 1967, he asked his boss to let him wander around the country for 3 months, and the critically acclaimed show "On the Road" was born. Through his travels, Charles Kuralt brought hundreds of courageous Americans into the living rooms of our country. And in so doing, he helped raise issues of social concern, such as funding for education, the problems of poverty, the plight of small businesses. But understanding the needs of others comes naturally to Charles Kuralt. His father, Wallace, was a North Carolina social worker who worked all his life on programs that provided day care, substance abuse counseling, and planned parenthood services. That spirit is alive and well in his son today.

The numerous awards and 13 Emmys Charles Kuralt holds are but a small reward for what he has given to all the rest of us. It's unfortunate that he was unable to attend today. We send him our wishes for a very speedy recovery from surgery that he had earlier this week, and we're glad that here to receive his award is his daughter, Lisa Kuralt White.

[The President and Hillary Clinton presented the prize and congratulated Ms. White.]

David Macaulay has written several books detailing the insides of complicated machines. He can even explain "the way things work." *[Laughter]* We could use him around here in the next couple of weeks. *[Laughter]* He has devoted his professional life to the investigation of architecture and mechanics. His books have helped children and adults alike to understand the world's rich history of construction and architecture. Using detailed illustrations, his books help to unfold the mysteries of both man and machine. David Macaulay's works serve as a bridge between humankind's earliest attempts at building and the most modern techniques of today. His painstaking efforts have made knowledge and investigation more accessible to the rest of us who could never have understood them on our own but whose lives were richer and more enlightened and whose citizenship more informed as a result of his work.

Mr. David Macaulay.

[The President and Hillary Clinton presented the prize and congratulated Mr. Macaulay.]

All of us know that history well-written and well-learned can be a great teacher. It can demonstrate what we are capable of at our best and what we may do wrong at our worst. In his remarkable body of work, David McCullough has shown us the true character of many of our country's most heroic figures and many of its most important events and eras.

From his wonderfully successful and enlightening biography on President Truman to his look at the building of the Brooklyn Bridge to his work as the voice of the highly regarded PBS series "The American Experience," David McCullough has given us a window into the lives of outstanding Americans and important events. His work emphasizes the value of history and our place in it. Along with his research, he spends many hours working for the preservation of historic sites, of public libraries, and of other institutions across America which enable us to preserve and learn about our roots. We should never forget what David McCullough has asked us to remember. And we should never forget his incredible contribution in helping us to preserve that memory.

Mr. David McCullough.

[The President and Hillary Clinton presented the prize and congratulated Mr. McCullough.]

Bernice Johnson Reagon is perhaps best known as the guiding spirit and resonant alto voice of Sweet Honey in the Rock, the famous *a cappella* quintet she founded in 1973. Singing an eclectic blend of gospel, jazz, folk, and rhythm and blues, the group has carried its message of world peace, women's rights, and racial harmony on tour throughout our Nation and throughout the world. If that were all she had done, Professor Reagon would be worthy of this award. But her creative energy is truly unlimited.

For nearly 35 years, she's helped to preserve, celebrate, and illuminate the rich heritage of African-American music as a civil rights activist, as a singer-composer, an author, an historian, a museum curator. Since 1993, she's been distinguished professor of history at American University here in Washington. Her latest contribution to public understanding of African-American music is the 26-part radio documentary "Wade in the Water: African-American Sacred Music Traditions," which aired beginning in 1994 on National Public Radio stations nationwide. She is a messenger of peace, and I am deeply honored that she is with us today.

"Sweet Honey in the Rock," for those of you who haven't heard it, is a truly inspiring experience, but the work of her life is even more inspiring.

[The President and Hillary Clinton presented the prize and congratulated Ms. Reagon.]

Let me thank again all the honorees and congratulate them. Thank all of you for coming. Let me thank all the distinguished saxophonists who came here to be with us today for their work. *[Applause]* Thank you all for your contributions and your devotion to the American way of life.

God bless you all. Thank you.

NOTE: The President spoke at 1:15 p.m. on the South Lawn at the White House. In his remarks,

the President referred to President Ernesto
Zedillo of Mexico.

Statement on the Financial Recovery in Mexico
October 5, 1995

This morning I received a call from Mexican
President Ernesto Zedillo. I am pleased to announce that he informed me that Mexico is
ready to repay $700 million of the U.S. financial
assistance we provided earlier this year to address Mexico's financial crisis. This news is another important step on the road to financial
recovery for Mexico, and I am very pleased that
this repayment comes sooner than expected. I
congratulated President Zedillo on his resolve
to implement the tough measures needed to
restore economic stability and growth.

Last winter, an imminent financial collapse
of Mexico threatened the economic and national
security of the United States. At my direction,
the United States took action to form an international coalition to provide Mexico sufficient
funds to refinance its debts. It is critically important that Mexico remain a stable neighbor,
continuing to grow as a market for our exports
and to cooperate with us on a broad range of
issues of mutual concern.

Today's decision sends a positive signal to the
financial markets that the tough financial measures Mexico has undertaken are succeeding and
the American taxpayer is being repaid ahead
of schedule.

I look forward to meeting with President
Zedillo next week when he visits Washington
on his first state visit and discussing the broad
range of issues affecting our two countries.

Remarks at the Arts and Humanities Awards Dinner
October 5, 1995

The President. Ladies and gentlemen, I want
to welcome all of you here and say again to
our honorees today how very much Hillary and
I enjoyed having all of you here and having
the great honor of presenting your awards to
you.

Helen Hayes once said that, "We rely upon
the poets, the philosophers, and the playwrights
to articulate what most of us can only feel in
joy and in sorrow. They illuminate the thoughts
for which we only grope. They give us the
strength and bond we cannot find in ourselves,
the wisdom of acceptance, the will and resilience to move on."

Those words have special meaning today as
America and, indeed, our entire world work to
find their way into a new era, an era in which
people are dramatically changing the way they
work and live and relate to one another.

We must dare, as artists and poets do, to
break free of the past to create a better future
rooted in the values that never change. That
is a great lesson our artists, our thinkers, our
scholars, our supporters and advocates of the
arts and humanities teach us. We thank you
for your lives, your dedication. We honor all
of you.

In every period of change and upheaval, there
is always great new opportunity and there is
always a struggle between those who are best
positioned to receive that opportunity and those
who work but aren't so well-positioned. I want
to thank tonight, especially, the National Endowment of the Arts and the National Endowment of the Humanities because, in a world
where some fear we're moving to a winner-
take-all society, you work so that all people can
win in their access to the arts and humanities.
And that is a goal worth pursuing and worth
achieving.

I thank you all for your work, and again,
I say on behalf of the First Lady and the Vice

President and Mrs. Gore, we're honored to have our honorees here in the White House tonight and deeply grateful for your many contributions to America.

I'd like to propose a toast to the winners of the awards today.

[At this point, the musical entertainment continued, and then the President resumed speaking.]

The President. Thank you so very much. You were both wonderful. You know, one of our awardees is over there in the cowboy hat there, Mr. Monroe, sort of the founder of bluegrass music. And I could tell by looking at him that I am authorized on his behalf to offer you a place in his next bluegrass band. [Laughter]

We need somebody here who can play "Blue Moon of Kentucky" in A—is there a volunteer? [Laughter] Great. Bill, make sure he does it right.

[Bill Monroe sang "Blue Moon of Kentucky," and then dinner participants sang "God Bless America."]

The President. Can I ask you all to give Mr. Zuckerman and our wonderful pianist a big hand? Weren't they terrific? Thank you. You were wonderful. [Applause] Let's give them a wonderful hand. They were terrific. Please come back. Come on up. Now, there is only one way we can end this magnificent evening. Come on up. You were wonderful. Thank you for being here. Thank you, Tuesday, for being here.

I think we should end—I think Bob Hope should sing "Thanks for the Memories." It's the only way you can end.

[Bob Hope sang "Thanks for the Memories."]

The President. We want you all to join us out there for dancing and more music, and maybe you can get the rest of them to sing, if we're lucky. [Laughter] Come on. Let's go out—everybody. Thanks, again, to everyone and especially to our wonderful musicians.

Thank you, and good night.

NOTE: The President spoke at 8:31 p.m. in the State Dining Room at the White House.

Remarks at a Freedom House Breakfast
October 6, 1995

Thank you very much. I'm honored to be introduced by someone who writes so powerfully about the past and is working so effectively to shape the future. The Secretary of State and I have tried to encourage both those activities by keeping Win Lord busy at the State Department.

I'm honored to be here with all of you and to be here at Freedom House. For more than 50 years, Freedom House has been a voice for tolerance for human dignity. People all over the world are better off because of your work. And I'm very grateful that Freedom House has rallied this diverse and dynamic group. It's not every day that the Carnegie Endowment, the Progressive Policy Institute, the Heritage Foundation, and the American Foreign Policy Council share the same masthead. I feel that I should try out a whole list of issues and try to get check-off here—[laughter]—before the meeting goes any further.

It does prove that there is a strong, dynamic center in our country that supports America's continued leadership in the world. We have all worked for that. And I want to publicly thank the Secretary of State and Tony Lake, the others in our foreign policy team, my Counselor, Mr. McLarty, up here who's been especially active on our behalf in Latin America. And I want to thank all of you who have supported that continued endeavor.

You know, in 1991 I sought the Presidency because I believed it was essential to restore the American dream for all Americans and to reassert America's leadership in the post-cold-war world. As we move from the industrial to the information age, from the cold war world to the global village, we have an extraordinary opportunity to advance our values at home and around the world. But we face some stiff challenges in doing so as well.

We know that at home we have the responsibility to create opportunity for all of our citizens to make the most of their own lives, to strengthen their families and their communities. We know that abroad we have the responsibility to advance freedom and democracy, to advance prosperity and the preservation of our planet. We know that the forces of integration and economic progress also contain the seeds of disruption and of greater inequality. We know that families, communities, and nations are vulnerable to the organized forces of disintegration and the winner-take-all mentality in politics and economics. We know all this, and therefore, we have an even heavier responsibility to advance our values and our interests.

Freedom House, in my view, deserves extraordinary praise for your sense of timing of this meeting. I wonder if Adrian Karatnycky and his colleagues knew that in the days prior to this discussion the United States would have the opportunity to demonstrate so vividly once again the proposition this conference seeks to advance, that American leadership and bipartisan support for that leadership is absolutely essential as a source of our strength at home and our success abroad. We must stand for democracy and freedom. We must stand for opportunity and responsibility in a world where the dividing line between domestic and foreign policy is increasingly blurred.

Our personal, family, and national security is affected by our policy on terrorism at home and abroad. Our personal, family, and national prosperity is affected by our policy on market economics at home and abroad. Our personal, family, and national future is affected by our policies on the environment at home and abroad. The common good at home is simply not separate from our efforts to advance the common good around the world. They must be one and the same if we are to be truly secure in the world of the 21st century.

We see the benefits of American leadership in the progress now being made in Bosnia. In recent weeks, our military muscle through NATO, our determined diplomacy throughout the region, have brought the parties closer to a settlement than at any time since this terrible war began 4 years ago. Yesterday, we helped to produce an agreement on a Bosnia-wide cease-fire. Now, the parties will come to the United States to pursue their peace talks mediated by our negotiating team and our European and Russian counterparts.

We have a long way to go, and there's no guarantee of success. But we will use every ounce of our influence to help the parties make a peace that preserves Bosnia as a single democratic state and protects the rights of all citizens, regardless of their ethnic group.

If and when peace comes, the international community's responsibility will not end. After all the bloodshed, the hatred, the loss of the last years, peace will surely be fragile. The international community must help to secure it. The only organization that can meet that responsibility strongly and effectively is NATO. And as NATO's leader, the United States must do its part and send in troops to join those of our allies under NATO command with clear rules of engagement. If we fail, the consequences for Bosnia and for the future of NATO would be severe. We must not fail.

The United States will not be sending our forces into combat in Bosnia. We will not send them into a peace that cannot be maintained, but we must use our power to secure that peace. I have pledged to consult with Congress before authorizing our participation in such an action. These consultations have already begun.

I believe Congress understands the importance of this moment and of American leadership. I'm glad to see Chairman Livingston here at the head table today. As I have said consistently for 2 years, we want and welcome congressional support. But in Bosnia as elsewhere, if the United States does not lead, the job will not be done.

We also saw the benefits of America's leadership last week at the White House where leaders from all over the Middle East gathered to support the agreement between Israel and the Palestinian Authority. For nearly a half-century now, Democratic and Republican administrations have worked to facilitate the cause of peace in the Middle East. The credit here belongs to the peacemakers. But we should all be proud that at critical moments along the way, our efforts helped to make the difference between failure and success.

It was almost exactly a year ago that the United States led the international effort to remove Haiti's military regime and give the people of Haiti a real chance at democracy. We've succeeded because we've backed diplomacy with sanctions and ultimately with force. We've succeeded because we understood that standing up for democracy in our own hemisphere was right for the Haitian people and right for America.

American efforts in Bosnia, the Middle East, and Haiti and elsewhere have required investments of time and energy and resources. They've required persistent diplomacy and the measured use of the world's strongest military. They have required both determination and flexibility in our efforts to work as leaders and to work with other nations. And sometimes they've called on us to make decisions that were, of necessity, unpopular in the short run, knowing that the payoff would not come in days or weeks but in months or years. Sometimes they have been difficult for many Americans to understand because they have to be made, as many decisions did right after World War II, without the benefit of some overarching framework, the kind of framework the bipolar cold war world provided for so many years.

To use the popular analogy of the present day, there seems to be no mainframe explanation for the PC world in which we're living. We have to drop the abstractions and dogma and pursue, based on trial and error and persistent experimentation, a policy that advances our values of freedom and democracy, peace, and security.

We must continue to bear the responsibility of the world's leadership. That is what you came here to do, and that's what I want to discuss today. It is more than a happy coincidence that the birth of bipartisan support for America's leadership in the world coincides with the founding of this organization by Eleanor Roosevelt and Wendell Willkie in 1941 when for the first time Americans, both Democrats and Republicans, liberals and conservatives and moderates, understood our special obligation to lead in the world.

The results of that responsible leadership were truly stunning: victory in the war and the construction of a post-cold-war world. Not with abstract dogma but again, over a 5-year period, basing experience on new realities, through trial and error with a relentless pursuit of our own values, we created NATO, the Marshall plan, Bretton Woods, the institutions that kept the peace in Europe, avoided nuclear conflict, helped to spread democracy, brought us unparalleled prosperity, and ultimately ensured the triumph of freedom in the cold war.

In that struggle, Freedom House and organizations like it reminded Americans that our leadership is essential and that to advance our interests, that leadership must remain rooted in our values, must continue to advance democracy and freedom to promote peace and security, to enhance prosperity and preserve our planet.

When it comes to the pursuit of these goals, it is important that we never forget that our values and our interests are one in the same. Promoting democracies that participate in this new global marketplace is the right thing to do. For all their imperfections, they advance what all people want and often fight and die for: human dignity, security, and prosperity. We know these democracies are less likely to go to war, less likely to traffic in terrorism, more likely to stand against the forces of hatred and intolerance and organized destruction.

Throughout what we now call the American century, Republicans and Democrats disagreed on specific policies, often heatedly from time to time, but we have always agreed on the need for American leadership in the cause of democracy, freedom, security, and prosperity. Now that consensus is truly in danger, and interestingly enough, it is in danger in both parties. Voices from the left and the right are calling on us to step back from, instead of stepping up to, the challenges of the present day. They threaten to reverse the bipartisan support for our leadership that has been essential to our strength for 50 years. Some really believe that after the cold war the United States can play a secondary role in the world, just as some thought we could after World War II, and some made sure we did after World War I.

But if you look at the results from Bosnia to Haiti, from the Middle East to Northern Ireland, it proves once again that American leadership is indispensable and that without it our values, our interests, and peace itself would be at risk.

It has now become a truism to blame the current isolationism on the end of the cold war because there is no longer a mainframe threat in this PC world. But when I took office, I made it clear that we had a lot of work to do to get our own house in order.

I agree that America has challenges at home that have to be addressed. We have to revive our economy and create opportunity for all of our citizens. We have to put responsibility back into our social programs and strengthen our families and our communities. We have to reform our own Government to make it leaner and more effective. But we cannot do any of these things in isolation from the world which we have done so much to make and which we must continue to lead.

Look at what is going on. Many of the new democracies in this world, they're working so hard. I see their leaders all the time. They believe in the cause of freedom, and they are laboring out there in these countries against almost unbelievable obstacles. But their progress is fragile. And we must never forget that. We have to see them as growing, growing things that have to be nurtured in a process that could still be reversed.

And we also have to recognize that we confront a host of threats that have assumed new and quite dangerous dimensions, the proliferation of weapons of mass destruction. In the technology age, that can mean simply breaking open a vial of sarin gas in a Tokyo subway. It can mean hooking into the Internet and learning how to build a bomb that will blow up a Federal building in the heart of America. These forces, just as surely as fascism and communism, would spread darkness over light, disintegration over integration, chaos over community. And these forces still demand the leadership of the United States.

Let me say again, the once bright line between domestic and foreign policy is blurring. If I could do anything to change the speech patterns of those of us in public life, I would almost like to stop hearing people talk about foreign policy and domestic policy and instead start discussing economic policy, security policy, environmental policy, you name it.

When you think about the world and the way that you live in it, you readily see that the foreign-domestic distinction begins to evaporate in so many profound ways. And if we could learn to speak differently about it, the very act of speaking and thinking in the way we live, I believe, would make isolationism seem absolutely impossible as an alternative to public policy.

When the President of Mexico comes here in a few days and we talk about drug problems, are we talking about domestic problems or foreign problems? If we talk about immigration, are we discussing a domestic issue or a foreign issue? If we talk about NAFTA and trade, is it their foreign politics or our domestic economics? We have to understand this in a totally different way. And we must learn to speak about it in different ways.

The isolationists are simply wrong. The environment we face may be new and different, but to meet it with the challenges and opportunities it presents and to advance our enduring values, we have to be more engaged in the world, not less engaged in the world. That's why we have done everything we could in our administration to lead the fight to reduce the nuclear threat, to spread democracy in human rights, to support peace, to open markets, to enlarge and defend the community of nations around the world, to share our aspirations and our values, not in abstract but in ways that are quite practical and immediately of benefit to the American people.

Consider just a few examples. Every American today is safer because we're stepping back from the nuclear precipice. Russian missiles are no longer pointed at our citizens, and there are no longer American missiles pointed at their citizens. Thanks to agreements reached by President Reagan, President Bush, and our administration, both our countries are cutting back their nuclear arsenal.

Over the past 3 years, we've been able to persuade Ukraine, Kazakhstan, and Belarus to give up nuclear weapons left on their land when the Soviet Union collapsed. We've convinced North Korea to freeze its nuclear program. We've secured the indefinite extension of the Nuclear Non-proliferation Treaty. We're working hard to make sure nuclear materials don't wind up in the hands of terrorists or international criminals. And I hope and pray that next year we'll succeed in getting a comprehensive nuclear test ban treaty.

Americans are safer because of the tough counterterrorism campaign we have been waging, including closer cooperation with foreign governments, sanctions against states that sponsor terrorism, and increasing the funding, the manpower, the training for our own law enforcement. These have helped us to get results, big, visible results, like the conviction just this week of those who conspired to wage a campaign of terror in New York, and things that aren't so visible but are very important, the planned terrorist attacks that have been thwarted in the United States and on American citizens, the arrests that have been secured in other countries through our cooperation.

We have an obligation to work more and more and more on this. And if there is any area in the world where there is no difference between domestic and foreign policy, surely it is in our common obligation to work together to combat terrorism.

That is why, even before Oklahoma City, I had sent legislation to the Hill asking for additional resources and help to deal with the threat of terrorism. And after Oklahoma City, I modified and strengthened that legislation. The Senate passed the bill quickly, but I am very disappointed that the bill is now stalled in the House. We need this legislation.

I believe Federal law enforcement authorities must be held accountable. I believe we must be open about whatever has happened in the past. But that has nothing to do with our obligation to make sure that the American people have the tools that they need to combat the threat of terrorism. So, once again, I say I hope the antiterrorism legislation will pass. We need it. The threat is growing, not receding.

When we gave democracy another chance in Haiti, a lot of people said this has nothing to do with the United States. Well, it did. It did. It mattered that, when somebody came to our country and gave their word that they would leave and bring back democracy, that we enforce that commitment. And in a more immediate sense, in the month before our intervention, 16,000 Haitians fled tyranny for sanctuary in Florida and elsewhere in our region, but 3 months after the intervention, the refugee flow was practically zero.

When Mexico ran into a cash flow crisis, we put together an emergency support package to help put our neighbor back on the course of stability and economic progress. And to their credit, the Republican leaders of the Congress supported that effort. But it was impossible to pass a bill through the Congress endorsing it because of all the surveys which showed that the American people were opposed to the Mexican bailout by about 80–15, as I remember the poll on the day that I took executive action to do it. This is another case, however, when what may be unpopular in the short run is plainly in the interest of the United States in the long run.

When your neighbors are in trouble and they're trying to do the right thing, you normally try to help them, because it's good for the neighborhood. Look what's happened since the United States stepped in to try to be a good neighbor to Mexico. Economic growth has returned, even though in a fragile state, more quickly than it was anticipated; exports have returned to levels that exceed what they were pre-NAFTA; and just yesterday, President Zedillo called me to say that Mexico will repay $700 million of its debt to the United States well ahead of schedule.

Consider what would have happened if we would have taken the isolationist position. What would have happened to their economy? What would have happened to the international financial market's reaction to that in Argentina, in Brazil, throughout Latin America and other fragile, emerging democracies? What would have happened to our relationships and our cooperation on a host of issues between us? It was the right thing to do. Was it a domestic issue or a foreign issue? You tell me. All I know is we have a better neighborly relationship and the future is brighter for the American people and for the people of Mexico because we are pursuing a strategy of engagement, not isolation.

You can see that in what's happening in Europe, where we're trying to bring the nations of Europe closer together, working for democracy and economic reform in the Soviet Union and Central Europe and modernizing NATO, strengthening the Partnership For Peace. And again I will say, these things also further our interests.

I was told just last week that by all the trade initiatives which have been taken, from NAFTA and GATT to over 80 separate individual trade agreements that Ambassador Kantor has conducted, 15 of them with Japan alone, the expanded volume of exports for the United States has created more than 2 million jobs in the last 2½ years, paying well above the national average. With the Summit of the Americas, with the APEC process that we have agreed on, there are more to come.

The Commerce Department and the State Department have worked together more and have worked harder than ever before to try to help Americans take advantage of these new opportunities. They are a part and parcel of our foreign policy and our domestic policy.

And let me say one other thing. We have tried to make it a constant refrain that while we seek to engage all countries on terms of goodwill, we must continue to stand up for the values that we believe make life worth living.

We must continue to stand up for the proposition that all people, without regard to their nationality, their race, their ethnic group, their religion, or their gender, should have a chance to make the most of their own lives, to taste both freedom and opportunity.

The most powerful statement of that by anyone in our administration recently was a statement made by the First Lady at the women's conference in Beijing, where she condemned abuses of women and their little children, and especially their little girl children, throughout the world, not sparing the problems of domestic violence and street crime here in the United States.

These are the kinds of things that America must continue to do. From Belfast to Jerusalem, American leadership has helped Catholics and Protestants, Jews and Arabs to walk the streets of their cities with less fear of bombs and violence. From Prague to Port-au-Prince, we're working to consolidate the benefits of democracy and market economics. From Kuwait to Sarajevo, the brave men and women of our Armed Forces are working to stand down aggression and stand up for freedom.

In our own hemisphere, only one country, Cuba, continues to resist the trend toward democracy. Today we are announcing new steps to encourage its peaceful transition to a free and open society. We will tighten the enforcement of our embargo to keep the pressure for reform on, but we will promote democracy and the free flow of ideas more actively. I have authorized our news media to open bureaus in Cuba. We will allow more people to travel to and from Cuba for educational, religious, and human rights purposes. We will now permit American nongovernmental organizations to engage in a fuller range of activities in Cuba. And today, it gives me great pleasure to announce that our first grant to fund NGO work in Cuba will be awarded to Freedom House to promote peaceful change and protect human rights.

Just mentioning this range of activities and the possibilities for positive American leadership demonstrates once again how vital it is to our security and to our prosperity, demonstrates once again that advancing our values and promoting our self-interests are one in the same.

I suppose, given the purpose of this conference and the unique sponsorship of it, that everybody here shares that belief and that, in a way, I'm just preaching to the choir. But this isolationist backlash, which is present in both parties, is very real. And if you look at it from the point of view of people who feel threatened by the changes in the world, it is even completely understandable. So it is important that we not simply condemn it. It is even more important that we explain the way the world is working. And as the world works its way through this period of transition toward a new order of things in which we can garner all of the benefits of change and technology and opportunity and still reinforce the importance of giving everybody a chance, giving all families the chances to be strong, solidifying communities, as we work our way through this period, it is more and more important that we not simply condemn the isolationists but that we seek to explain how the world works and why we must be engaged and lead.

Condemnation is not enough. Characterization is not enough. We must work through these issues. The American people are good people. They have common sense. They care when people are being murdered around the world. They understand that a war somewhere else could one day involve our sons and daughters. They know that we cannot simply pretend .that the rest of the world is not there. But many of them have their own difficulties. We must work and work and work on the basic values and interests and arguments until we beat back the forces of isolation, with both intense passion and reason.

You can do that. That is what you must help us to do. Every one of you, each in your own way, with your own centers of influence, you can do that, with assertion and with argument.

Let me just give you one specific example: I am determined to do everything I can to preserve our international affairs budget. It represents, after all, less than 2 percent of our overall budget. Foreign aid is unpopular in the abstract because Americans believe we spend a lot more of their money on foreign aid than we do. But when you ask the American people how much we should spend, they will tell you 3 percent, 4 percent, 5 percent, more than we in fact spend.

No agency in this era when we're trying to balance the budget can be exempt from conscious cost-cutting. Vice President Gore and I have worked very hard to give the American people the smallest Government, in terms of Federal employees, we've had since President

Kennedy was in office, to eliminate hundreds of programs. But we must have the tools of diplomacy.

American leadership is more than words and the military budget. Although the military budget is important, we must have a diplomacy budget. Some in Congress literally want to gut foreign assistance, to hack the State Department's budget, to slash the Arms Control and Disarmament Agency, the USIA, AID. They would shirk our responsibilities to the United Nations. I want to go give this speech to the United Nations. Wouldn't you like it if I did? Wouldn't you like it if I did? [*Applause*] I appreciate the applause, but you tell me what I'm supposed to say. I will go give this speech, and they will say, "Thank you very much, Mr. President, where's your $1 billion?" [*Laughter*] Why is the United States the biggest piker in the U.N.?

Now, let me say, does the United Nations need to be reformed? Has a lot of our money and everybody else's money been wasted? Does there need to be greater oversight? Of course there does. Is that an argument for taking a dive on the United Nations? No.

We need your support for this. We must do this. It is the right thing to do. It is the responsible thing to do. Those who really would have us walk away from the U.N., not to mention the international financial institutions, they would really threaten our ability to lead.

As you know, in instances from Bosnia to Haiti, working out how we can lead and still maintain our alliances and cooperate through the United Nations and through NATO is sometimes frustrating and almost always difficult. But it is very important. We don't want to run off into the future all by ourselves, and that means we have to work responsibly through these international organizations and we have to pay our fair share. Every dollar we spend on foreign assistance comes back to us many times over.

By reducing the threat of nuclear war in the Newly Independent States, we've been able to cut our own spending on strategic weapons. By supporting democratic reforms and the transition to free markets in the Soviet Union and in Central Europe, we promote stability and prosperity in an area that will in the future become a vast market for the United States. By assisting developing nations who are fighting against overpopulation, AIDS, drug smuggling, environmental degradation, the whole range of problems they face, we're making sure the prob-

lems they face today don't become our problems tomorrow. The money we devote to development or peacekeeping or disaster relief, it helps to avert future crises whose cost will be far greater. And it is the right thing to do. It is the right thing to do.

I am very worried that all these budgets are at risk—some of them in an almost deliberate attempt to cut the United States off from partnership. I'll just give you one other example so I can go home and tell the Vice President I did it. [*Laughter*]

We have a little bit of money devoted to a comprehensive, worldwide effort to deal with the threat of global warming. It is simply a matter of science and evidence. Just in the last several days, there have been a whole new rush of scientific evidence that 1995 is the warmest year on our entire planet in 20,000 years, that the hole in the ozone layer is bigger than we had imagined it to be, and that global warming is a real threat. We spend a pittance on it. That is one of the items targeted for elimination. This is not budget-cutting; this is ideology. This is another example of what the teenagers say about "denial" being more than a river in Egypt. [*Laughter*] This is wrong. It is not necessary to balance the budget, and it is necessary to reverse it to stand up for America's values and America's interests.

Let me just cite one more example. Radio Free Europe and Radio Liberty were key weapons in the war of ideas waged against communism. Many of you stood up for it and fought for them. To meet the challenges of the new era, they have been dramatically downsized and moved from Munich to Prague. But some want to squeeze their already vastly reduced budget on the eve of major Russian elections, at the very time the Russian reformers most need objective information and the free exchange of ideas. They would do the same for the Voice of America, which serves on the frontlines of democracy all around the world from Burma to the Balkans.

Reckless budget cutters would shut down our Embassies first and consider the consequences later. Last year alone, our Embassies responded to nearly 2 million requests for assistance from Americans overseas. They helped American companies win billions of dollars in contracts. And every international business leader will tell you that the State Department and its Embassies are working harder to advance our economic interests than at any time in the history of the global economy.

If we didn't have diplomats in Asia and Latin America to help stem the flow of drugs to our shores, imagine how much harder that task would be. In Northern Ireland and the Middle East, if we didn't have people representing us, it would be a lot harder to move the peace process forward. In Burundi or Rwanda, if we didn't have brave people there, like Ambassador Bob Krueger, it would be even harder to avoid human tragedy. We don't need half-strength and part-time diplomacy in a world of fast-moving opportunities and 24-hour-a-day crises.

The last point I want to make is this. There are people who say, "Oh, Mr. President, I am for a strong America. I just don't understand why you fool with the U.N. What we need is for America to stand up alone. We'll decide what the right thing to do is and do it. Let the rest of the world like it or lump it. That's what it means to be the world's only superpower." That also is a disguised form of isolationism.

Unilateralism in the world that we live in is not a viable option. When our vital interests are at stake, of course, we might have to act alone. But we need the wisdom to work with the United Nations and to pay our bills. We need the flexibility to build coalitions that spread the risk and responsibility and the cost of leadership, as President Bush did in Desert Storm and we did in Haiti.

If the past 50 years have taught us anything, it is that the United States has a unique responsibility and a unique ability to be a force for peace and progress around the world, while building coalitions of people that can work together in genuine partnership.

But we can only succeed if we continue to lead. Our purpose has to be the same in this new era as it has ever been. Whatever our political persuasions, I believe we all share the same goals. I think we want a future where people all over the world know the benefits of democracy; in which our own people can live their lives free from fear; in which our sons and daughters won't be called to fight in wars that could have been prevented; in which people no longer flee tyranny in their own countries to come to our shores; in which markets are open to our products and services, where they give our own people good, high-wage jobs; a country in which we know an unparalleled amount of peace and prosperity because we have fulfilled a traditional American mandate of the 20th century well into the 21st, because we, we, have led the world toward democracy and freedom, toward peace and prosperity.

If we want the kind of future I described, we have to assume the burden of leadership. There is simply not another alternative. So I ask you, bring your passion to this task, bring your argument to this task, and bring the sense of urgency that has animated this country in its times of greatest challenge for the last 50 years to this task.

The future, I believe, will be even brighter for the American people than the last 50 years if, if, we can preserve our leadership in pursuit of our values.

Thank you, and God bless you all.

NOTE: The President spoke at 9:37 a.m. at the Hyatt Regency Hotel. In his remarks, he referred to Adrian Karatnycky, president, Freedom House, and Representative Robert Livingston.

Statement on Reform of Computer Export Controls
October 6, 1995

Today I am pleased to announce a major reform of our computer export controls that will adjust to the global spread of technology while preserving our vital national security interests.

Effective export controls are a critical part of national security, especially a strong nonproliferation policy. Our control regulations must focus principally on exports that have significant national security applications and which are not so widely available in open commerce that controls are ineffective.

When I came into office, virtually all computers more powerful than a basic desktop required an export license from the Government, even though many of these machines could be purchased in electronics stores from Hong Kong to Frankfurt as well as in cities across America. Both the U.S. Government and American exporters spent millions of dollars and thousands of hours implementing and complying with a tangled web of export control regulations.

Two years ago, to bring our export control system into line with new developments in computer technology and the changing nature of the threats to our national security, I relieved billions of dollars worth of exports from outdated and unnecessary controls and instructed my administration thoroughly and periodically to review the controls on computer exports. The purpose of this review was to determine how changes in computer technology and its military applications should affect our export control regulations.

Now, in the wake of a careful reevaluation by the Department of Defense, I have instructed my administration to update our controls to ensure that computers that could have a significant military impact on U.S. and allied security interests remain carefully controlled, while controls that are unnecessary or ineffective are eliminated.

Specifically, I have decided to eliminate controls on the export of all computers to countries in North America, most of Europe, and parts of Asia. For a number of other countries, including many in Latin America and Central and Eastern Europe, we will ease but not eliminate computer export controls. For the former Soviet Union, China, and a number of other countries, we will focus our controls on computers intended for military end uses or users, while easing them on the export of computers to civilian

customers. Finally, we will continue to deny computer technology to terrorist countries around the world.

This decision will relieve U.S. computer manufacturers of unnecessary and ineffective regulations which often have tied their hands while foreign competitors won major contracts or built their own systems. It will help preserve the strength of the U.S. computer industry, which also is key to our national security. It is good for U.S. workers and U.S. business.

This decision will benefit our national security in a number of other ways. Trying to regulate the export of computers that are increasingly available in markets abroad is a recipe for an ineffective nonproliferation policy. It imposes serious regulatory burdens without improving our national security and diverts resources from the pursuit of other important nonproliferation objectives.

Today's action will strengthen our nonproliferation policy by targeting our export control resources on those areas where they can make a difference. It will complement our work in the New Forum, the multilateral regime we are forming to control arms and sensitive dual-use technologies, where we will work with our partners to encourage development of multilateral transparency and controls on computers consistent with our national controls. It will reinforce other steps we have taken in this administration to achieve concrete goals—such as the indefinite extension of the Nuclear Non-Proliferation Treaty, denuclearization of Ukraine, stopping the North Korean nuclear weapons program, and a negotiation of a comprehensive test ban—in our efforts to combat proliferation.

Memorandum on Absence of Federal Employees in the Aftermath of Hurricane Opal
October 6, 1995

Memorandum for the Heads of Executive Departments and Agencies

Subject: Excused Absence for Employees Affected by Hurricane Opal and Its Aftermath

I am deeply concerned about the devastating losses caused by Hurricane Opal and the impact

on the well-being and livelihood of our fellow Americans who have been affected by this disaster. Elements of the Federal Government have been mobilized to respond to this disaster.

As part of this effort, I request the heads of executive departments and agencies who have Federal civilian employees in the areas designated as disaster areas because of the effects of Hurricane Opal and its aftermath to use their discretion to excuse from duty, without charge to leave or loss of pay, any such employee who is faced with a personal emergency because of this storm and who can be spared from his or her usual responsibilities. This policy should also be applied to any employee who is needed for emergency law enforcement, relief, or clean-up efforts authorized by Federal, State, or local officials having jurisdiction.

WILLIAM J. CLINTON

NOTE: This memorandum was released by the Office of the Press Secretary on October 7.

The President's Radio Address
October 7, 1995

Good morning. As you know, we're working in Washington to try to balance the budget. But we're working on two very different approaches. I want to balance the budget because if it's done right, it will help us to restore the American dream and to keep America the strongest nation in the world. It will help to improve our economy, create jobs, raise incomes, and take debt off our children.

That's why we've worked so hard in our administration to bring the deficit down from $290 billion a year when I took office to $160 billion this year, to expand our exports, and to increase investment in education. That's helped to give us 7½ million new jobs, a record number of new small businesses. And just last week, the Census Bureau announced that the poverty rate has dropped in America for the first time in 5 years, as more families are sticking together and doing better.

Still, we all know that many working families are finding it harder than ever to live the American dream. And that's why we have to do even more to ensure opportunity for all working people, to grow the middle class and to shrink our under class. Above all, as we balance the Federal budget, we must make sure we don't make it harder for people to educate their children, care for their parents, strengthen their families. That would defeat the very purpose of balancing the budget.

Yet that's exactly what the budget proposals of the Republican majority in Congress would do. At a time when we're growing the middle class, they would make it harder for poor people to work their way into the middle class. They'd even kick a lot of American families out of the middle class and hurt families, for many of their so-called cuts are in fact hidden direct and indirect tax increases.

The congressional leadership says they want to cut taxes. Well, I do, too. I think we should have a tax cut targeted at working families to help them with childrearing and to permit families to deduct the cost of college education. But we can do that without the back-door tax increases on millions of American families the Republican leaders claim to be cutting taxes on.

You see, buried deep within their plan is a vast collection of tax increases and other costs on working people, $148 billion worth of direct and indirect hidden taxes that hit working families in America hard. Some will claim these tax hikes aren't really taxes. They'll search the dictionary to find every possible way to avoid using that "T" word. Well, in Washington they may not call it a tax increase, but when the Government makes a working family pay more, it sure feels like a tax to them.

Here are the facts. You can decide for yourself. We want parents to care for their children. But under the Republican plan, single mothers struggling to preserve their families will have to pay $4 billion in fees for the Government's help in collecting child support they're legally due. That's a tax hike on responsible mothers and their children which will lower their already modest incomes.

The elderly, who have a right to expect that we will do our duty to them so they can live their lives in dignity, will be asked to pay thousands of dollars more per couple in extra premiums, extra copayments, extra deductibles for Medicare over the next 7 years. People who are old and sick and poor, regardless of how hard they've worked in their lives, will have to pay $10 billion more for their Medicare because the Republican budget proposes to repeal the extra help now given to the elderly poor with their Medicare bills. Experts say up to a million seniors could be driven out of Medicare.

And the Republican Congress proposes to do away with the law that now prevents States from forcing seniors whose spouses have to go into nursing homes to sell their cars, their homes, even empty their bank accounts before their husbands and wives can get the Government help for the care they need.

Young people and their families who are seeking to secure America's promise of opportunity could wind up paying thousands of dollars more in additional fees and interest to get student loans. That's a tax hike on middle class families and students that we can't afford for our future.

Most unbelievably of all, 17 million working families who seek to share in the American dream will have to pay $42 billion more in income taxes through reductions in the earned-income tax credit for working families. In 1993, I worked hard to expand this working family tax credit so that we in America could say that anybody who works full-time with children in their homes will not be in poverty. Now what the Congress wants to do is to roll back that working families' tax credit in a way that will impose a tax increase averaging $500 a family on families least able to pay it. This is a tax hike that literally will push many working families back into poverty.

All told, there are about $148 billion of these hidden taxes and fees. They represent a cynical assault on America's values by targeting working families, the elderly, poor people who work hard at their jobs, mothers seeking child support, young people struggling their way through college. These are the very people we should be helping. I want to reward responsibility, not punish it; to increase opportunity, not shrink it; to strengthen our families, not weaken them. That's why my budget plan includes none of these new taxes.

The taxes imposed by the Republican budget are deceptive and unfair. I urge Congress to defeat them. We don't need to raise taxes on working people and lower their incomes to balance the budget. We have enough income inequality in America as it is.

I've proposed a balanced budget that reflects our fundamental values, that eliminates the deficit without undermining education or weakening our environment or violating our commitments to working families, seniors, and poor children. It secures Medicare and the Trust Fund without imposing big new costs on seniors, threatening their independence, or destroying their dignity. And it gives a tax cut targeted to education and childrearing, the very things that working families need. And they're helping the very working families who are hit with the tax increases under the Republican budget.

I'm deeply committed to balancing the Federal budget. But we have to do it in a way that is consistent with our values and our vision for our future, to give our people the chance to make the most of their own lives, to strengthen our families and protect our children and honor our parents, to grow the middle class and shrink the under class, and to preserve our Nation as the world's strongest. Let's all keep those values fixed firmly in our sight in the weeks ahead as we work toward a balanced budget that advances the American dream.

Thanks for listening.

NOTE: The address was recorded at 8:49 a.m. in the Old Whaling Church, Edgartown, MA, for broadcast at 10:06 a.m.

Statement on Senator Sam Nunn's Decision Not To Seek Reelection
October 9, 1995

For the last 23 years, Senator Nunn has served our country with tireless devotion and steady leadership. He has earned the respect and appreciation of all Americans for his leadership in national security, defense, and foreign policy. He has urged us to deal with the long-term challenges of our economy and to move beyond established political rhetoric to new policies that reward responsibility and work and to strengthen families and communities.

I am grateful for his wise counsel and personal friendship and look forward to his continued leadership in setting the new Democratic agenda and America's agenda in 1996 and beyond. I wish him and his fine family well.

Remarks Announcing the Technology Learning Challenge Grants
October 10, 1995

Thank you, Mr. Vice President, for your outstanding work on this issue. And thank you, Secretary Riley and Secretary Brown, for your work as well.

I want to say a few more things about the people behind me and those in front of me, but if I might, in the beginning, I think it would be appropriate for me to make a few comments about what has happened to the Amtrak train in Arizona.

We believe it was a case of sabotage. And I am profoundly outraged by it. I want to make it clear that we will do everything we can with the Federal Government to catch whoever is responsible. I am determined that we will make sure that in the United States we will have the tools, the means we need to keep the American people safe. We will get to the bottom of this. We will punish those who are responsible. We will not tolerate acts of cowardice like this in the United States, regardless of the motive. And when I know more about it, I'll be glad to comment more about it.

I have just finished a meeting, along with the Vice President and other members of our administration, with leaders who are here behind me, leaders of many of the American companies on the cutting edge of the information age. They are helping to lead our Nation into the world of the 21st century as the strongest economic power in the world.

Two and a half weeks ago in California, I met with some other business leaders, and I called on the representatives of business, government, teachers, schools, parents, students to become involved in a high-tech venture with a guaranteed return. I asked for a national public-private partnership to connect every classroom in America to the information superhighway by the year 2000.

This today, this meeting, is the next step. Today these business and education leaders have joined with me to launch a partnership that will ensure that every child in America is technologically literate for the dawn of the 21st century and that every child in America has the resources, the means, by which to become technologically literate by the dawn of the 21st century.

The idea that every child deserves the opportunity to build a bright future has been at the heart of America's education system and America's entire value system. Education is the way we keep the promise of the American dream to all of our children without regard to their circumstances.

Today that means computers, knowing how to make the most of them, having teachers who can work with students to make the most of them, and having the right software to make the computers make sense. Technological literacy must become the standard in our country. Preparing children for a lifetime of computer use is just as essential today as teaching them the basics of reading, writing, and arithmetic.

This isn't just computers for computers' sake. We're going to work together to help our schools use technology to revolutionize American education so that all children will be able to learn better and teachers will be able to be more effective.

In the next few months, the leaders here behind me will be working with us to produce a plan based on the four pillars I outlined in California: modern computers in every classroom, accessible to every student from kindergarten through the 12th grade; connections from every classroom to the incredible educational resources flowing throughout the world; teachers in every classroom who are trained to make the most of new technology to educate every student—and I want to emphasize, one of the most important aspects of the technological revolution is the opportunities being opened to children so many Americans had given up on and schools that too many Americans had given up on—and finally, a rich array of educational software and information resources.

Today I'm announcing three steps forward that show we are turning these principles into reality. First, we're awarding Technology Learning Challenge Grants to 19 communities. In each community there's a partnership of educators, businesses, libraries, museums, and community groups that have come together to retool their schools for the 21st century. They are matching these grants. They are committing hardware and software, hard work, and know-how. For example, in Dover, Delaware, Bell Atlantic, Lightspan Partnership, and the State education department are linking homes and schools through family TV sets to improve reading and arithmetic in the early grades. This is how these partnerships will work.

Let me say that it costs a very modest amount of money. This is one of the discussions we have to have in the weeks ahead as we continue our progress toward a balanced budget. We can balance the budget without cutting back on our commitment to our educational future. For a very small amount of national money, we are leveraging much larger amounts of local resources. And I would say again, this is the kind of thing that the Nation ought to be doing now in the area of education and the sort of thing I will be trying to preserve as we negotiate the shoals of the budget discussions.

The second thing I want to announce is a private sector effort making a difference in one State is now going nationwide. We must rely on the expertise of millions of Americans working in the high-tech professions. The Technology Corps brings private sector volunteers into our schools so that they can bring technology into our classrooms. It's already working in Massachusetts where it was started by Gary Beach, who is here with us today, to connect Massachusetts schools. And now we want to do this around the country.

Finally, we're launching the American Technology Honor Society to harness the high-tech skills of exceptional students so they can help to expand their own school's use of technology. We have to remember that people born in the information age are more comfortable with it than people like me, who weren't. [*Laughter*]

The American Technology Honor Society will be rooted in the National Honor Society, and it will be run by the National Association of Secondary School Principals. Communities, businesses, and governments; parents, teachers, and students—this could be the largest merger in history, with no questions from the Justice Department. [*Laughter*] Certainly it will be the most important partnership for the future in the United States today, working together to put a computer in every classroom and a computer whiz at every desk.

Every child in America deserves the chance to get the high-tech know-how to unlock the promises of the 21st century—every child in America. And thanks to the statesmanship and vision of the people who are here with me today and many like them all around America, we are going to forge a partnership to do just that.

Thank you very much.

NOTE: The President spoke at 9:28 a.m. in the Roosevelt Room at the White House.

Remarks Welcoming President Ernesto Zedillo of Mexico
October 10, 1995

President and Mrs. Zedillo, members of the Mexican delegation, distinguished guests. On behalf of the American people, it is my honor to welcome you to the United States as our neighbors, our partners, and our friends.

I know I speak for all Americans when I send my condolences to the victims of yesterday's terrible earthquake in western Mexico and to their families. Our thoughts and prayers are with all the people of your nation as the relief effort gets underway.

Mr. President, the bonds between our nations have never been stronger or more important. Over the last decade, and with renewed vitality since you took office, Mexico has embarked upon a course of political and economic transformation. Openness and participation are the watchwords of the future as the people of your great nation take control of shaping their destiny.

Mexico's triumph in this epic endeavor will be America's triumph as well. A prosperous Mexico will be an even greater partner in trade, and this means more high-paying jobs for citizens in both our nations. A strong, democratic Mexico will be an even more effective partner in the struggle against drugs and crime and pollution.

President Zedillo, the American people are proud to support your efforts. We know we share a stake in your success. That is why, when Mexico fell into financial crisis, the United States answered with action, not only for the sake of the Mexican people but also for the sake of thousands of Americans whose jobs depend upon Mexico's well-being.

We saw the threat of economic dislocation all along our 2,000-mile border, and we recognized that trouble next door would spread to other markets all around the world. The United States, with bipartisan backing, assembled a package of international support to help lift the Mexican economy back on track. And you, President Zedillo, rose to your daunting challenge with courage and determination. You implemented hard measures to stabilize the economy, while holding to the road of reform. You knew that the costs of your action were high but the costs of inaction were far greater. You recognized your truly historic responsibilities, and you met them.

We overcame tough challenges by making tough decisions and by standing together and standing firm for the long-term best interests of both our nations. Mexico's early repayment of $700 million serves proof that our actions were proper and that they will be rewarded. The Mexican economy has turned the corner, and the markets have taken notice.

The North American Free Trade Agreement helped to speed the recovery of international confidence. Even during the financial crisis, Mexico kept its NAFTA commitments, lowering its tariffs on American products. Today, despite the economic downturn, our exports to Mexico exceed their pre-NAFTA levels. And as Mexico's economy regains its strength, not only will your people benefit but so, too, will tens of thousands of Americans whose well-being also advances when Mexico prospers.

Mr. President, the United States applauds your grace under pressure, your vision for your people, and your unflinching resolve. You have coupled far-reaching economic reform with unprecedented progress for democracy, throwing open the doors of political participation and welcoming every Mexican inside.

We salute the Mexican people for their extraordinary perseverance. They have borne tremendous hardship to build a stronger, more prosperous nation. We support your goal of an open, dynamic, and democratic Mexico, an inspiration for the region and the entire world.

President and Mrs. Zedillo, we're glad to have you with us again. Welcome to the White House. Welcome back to the United States.

NOTE: The President spoke at 10:19 a.m. on the South Lawn at the White House. In his remarks, he referred to President's Zedillo's wife, Anilda Patricia Zedillo.

Remarks Prior to Discussions With President Ernesto Zedillo of Mexico and an Exchange With Reporters
October 10, 1995

Mexican Financial Recovery

President Clinton. Let me say again how very pleased I am to have President Zedillo here and to congratulate him on his strong, determined leadership during this period of economic difficulty for Mexico. Inflation is down, the peso is stable, the stock market is stabilized, and interest rates have been cut in half. I think Mexico has clearly turned the corner, thanks to his leadership.

I also would point out that he has continued to implement the NAFTA agreement and to lower tariffs on American products during this difficult time, and he deserves a lot of credit for that. As a result of that, our exports to Mexico are now above where they were before

NAFTA was passed, even though Mexico is going through this difficult time.

So I have nothing but the highest compliments for the way Mexico has handled this difficult period, and I think it's due to the leadership of the President and his team who are here. And I am delighted to have this chance to visit with him.

President Zedillo. I also want to congratulate you for the international leadership that you have shown regarding the Mexican situation. I think that your decisive, effective action avoided a major crisis in the international financial system and a much higher cost for many other countries, perhaps including your own country. You have proven to have a vision, courage, perseverance. And the Mexican people recognize you for that.

President Clinton. Thank you very much.

Antiterrorism Legislation

Q. Mr. President, earlier you mentioned the derailment of the train. And after you spoke to us, your Press Secretary talked about the unhappiness within the administration about Congress' failure to pass the terrorism bill. I wondered if you could give us your thoughts on that and whether you think there's any legitimacy in what some Members are saying, that is, the FBI behavior at Waco and Government behavior at Ruby Ridge have made people a little bit leery about passing that kind of legislation.

President Clinton. First of all, what we asked for in the antiterrorism bill would not make more likely any kind of actual or alleged abuse of police authority. It would just give us the ability to deal with terrorism.

Secondly, I have been very eager to be accountable and to see this administration accountable and to see Government generally accountable for the mistakes that are made in the past, whether it was on—whether someone believes we did something wrong at Waco— we've had an independent review of that—or on the Ruby Ridge thing, which happened before I became President, or what we've done with the announcement we made on the radiation experiments, which happened a long time before I became President.

So I think the answer is, give us the tools we need to fight the problems of today and tomorrow with antiterrorism, but hold us strictly,

strictly accountable. That's the answer. That's the balanced, fair answer. We can achieve both.

There are some things—if the House, for example, wanted to make some modifications in the habeas corpus provisions, some other things to try to guard against abuse or protect people, they could do that. We could work that out. But to do nothing is a mistake. That's the point I want to make. It's a mistake to do nothing.

Q. Is Congress playing games here, do you think?

President Clinton. I don't want to characterize their motives. I just think they should act. They said that we'd have a bill by, I think, Memorial Day, and that was months ago. So we should not do nothing. We should act. If they want to work on how we should change the bill, I'd be happy to discuss that. But we need the bill.

[*At this point, one group of reporters left the room, and another group entered.*]

Mexican Financial Recovery

President Clinton. I would like to again welcome President Zedillo to the United States, along with his very able governmental representatives here, and to say again how much the United States appreciates the difficulty that Mexico and the Mexican people have been through in the last several months and how much we respect the leadership that the President has shown.

It is clear to us, looking from the outside, that the worst is past, that the economy is turning around. And it is clear that the United States did the right thing in trying to provide some financial support to Mexico in that difficult period. I think the future looks good.

I know there are difficult times ahead, but I have been very impressed by the strong and steady leadership of the President. And I hope that we can continue to work together until prosperity is fully restored to Mexico and we can have the kind of partnership for the 21st century that I believe will benefit both the people of Mexico and the people of the United States.

NOTE: The President spoke at 11:09 a.m. in the Oval Office at the White House. Following President Clinton's remarks, President Zedillo made brief remarks in Spanish, but a translation was not provided. A tape was not available for verification of the content of these remarks.

The President's News Conference With President Ernesto Zedillo of Mexico
October 10, 1995

President Clinton. Let me say again how delighted I am to welcome President Zedillo to the White House and take this opportunity to say again, on behalf of the American people, how terribly sorry we are for the terrible earthquake in Mexico yesterday. Our thoughts and prayers are with the victims and with their families.

My meeting with President Zedillo marks an extraordinary moment for relations between the United States and Mexico. Never has our partnership had so much potential. Never has it yielded such clear results.

Each of us is uplifted by the strength of the other's economy, as we create good, high-paying jobs that benefit both our peoples. Each of us is made stronger by the support of the other in our common efforts to fight drugs, crime, and pollution. Each of us is enriched by the wealth of the other's heritage. We celebrate Hispanic Heritage Month this month, and we should honor the Mexican-American community that has contributed and continues to contribute so very much to the life of the United States.

President Zedillo and I are joined in a common endeavor to advance the security and prosperity of both our nations. The events of the last year have demonstrated how crucial it is that we work together.

When the peso collapsed just 10 months ago, America's deepest interests were affected. The crisis threatened 700,000 Americans whose jobs depend on exports to Mexico. It raised the specter of severe dislocation along our 2,000-mile border and in emerging markets throughout Latin America and, indeed, throughout the entire world. By making tough decisions together, we steered through those days of uncertainty and averted far graver consequences. The United States put together an international package of support to stabilize Mexico's economy. And President Zedillo showed tremendous vision and courage implementing tough measures that laid the basis for recovery.

To be sure, the road ahead will be difficult. But the Mexican people, with President Zedillo's leadership, are determined to hold onto reform, courageously accepting today's hardship for the sake of a better tomorrow. Already we see the results. When the financial crisis struck in 1982, it took 7 long years before Mexico could return to international capital markets. Under President Zedillo's skillful guidance, it took just 7 months this time. Interest rates have fallen by half, monthly inflation is down, and the stock market is back up to pre-crisis levels. Last Thursday, President Zedillo informed me that Mexico would repay $700 million of our financial support ahead of schedule.

The North American Free Trade Agreement bolstered that recovery of confidence. Despite Mexico's economic downturn, American exports to Mexico still exceed their levels before NAFTA. And I want to emphasize that. The last time the Mexican economy was in crisis in 1982, there was a steep increase in tariffs, and Mexican exports were cut in half. It did not happen this time because of NAFTA. Therefore, if the NAFTA agreement had not been in place, the recent difficulties would have been far, far worse from the United States point of view. Our overall exports to NAFTA partners have grown by 25 percent since the agreement took effect, supporting about 340,000 good American jobs.

Mexico is already one of our most important partners in the global fight against drugs, and we are determined to do more. Helping Mexico to fight crime before it crosses the border is an investment in America's security. We will do all we can to strengthen Mexico's ability to detect and to deter drug traffickers by providing 12 helicopters, helping Mexico obtain radars, intensifying our training to help fight money laundering. President Zedillo's major reform of Mexican law enforcement will make our cooperation even more effective.

The United States is a nation of immigrants and a nation of laws. We must control our borders even as we work to protect the dignity and rights of individuals. Working with Mexico, we have made important strides to prevent illegal immigration and to promote public safety.

By the end of 1996, the United States aims to increase our Southwest Border Patrol personnel by 60 percent above its 1993 levels. The

Mexican Government has taken concrete steps to fight border crime, prevent alien smuggling, and close illegal gateways to our country. I welcome President Zedillo's agreement to begin a pilot repatriation program in the San Diego region. Under this program, Mexicans who repeatedly cross our border illegally will be voluntarily returned to their hometowns instead of to the border area.

President Zedillo and I also discussed the environment. Thanks to the efforts set in motion by NAFTA, our nations are working more closely than ever to solve pollution problems, protect public health, and deal with our long-term common environmental interests. Together we are helping border communities find ways to improve sanitation and to ensure clean drinking water.

The vitality of these relations between the United States and Mexico reflects and reinforces the new spirit of cooperation that indeed is sweeping our entire hemisphere. As we witnessed at the Summit of the Americas in Miami last December, our interests and our values increasingly coincide.

Again, let me say how very much I appreciate the leadership and strength that President Zedillo has shown. We know that the core of our long-term future with our partnership in the Americas lies in a strong relationship and a strong working partnership between the United States and Mexico.

Mr. President, welcome back.

President Zedillo. Thank you, Mr. President, ladies and gentlemen. I would like to thank President Clinton for his kind words. In the conversations that we have held, we carried out a very complete analysis of the basic issues, the main issues, on our bilateral agenda.

We have spoken of the relationship of the two economies. Especially we have spoken of the results offered by NAFTA and of its enormous potential. NAFTA is a reality, and it is yielding impressive results. Even in this difficult year, Mexico now purchases nearly 4 times more goods and services from the United States than it did 10 years ago. And the United States is exporting to Mexico more than in the years prior to NAFTA. Trade between the two countries is in excess of $100 billion a year.

We discussed some of the aspects of our bilateral relations, and we were pleased to find solutions in some of the cases. We also hope that very soon we will find a modification or amendment to the legislation which imposed the tuna embargo. This has been the result of acknowledging the great effort that Mexico has carried out in this field.

We trust that the trade between the two nations will increase again as of 1996 when Mexico's economy will begin to recover significantly. The recovery in economic growth will prove that the economic program put in practice by Mexico and the decisions reached have been the appropriate decisions.

The vigorous economic growth and the creation of more and better jobs will be the best response to the migration of Mexicans to the United States. We agree that our respective legislation must be respected, as well as the dignity and the rights of individuals must be respected. We have reached agreements for the orderly repatriation of undocumented Mexicans to different entry ports.

Drug trafficking is our common enemy. It is the most threatening of all enemies because it brings corruption, corruption in health, in social living, and in institutions. We agree to fight firmly the war against drug trafficking in both nations and to severely punish money laundering. We have also agreed to intensify the efforts against drug use.

Mexico is doing its share in this regard. Just a few days ago, as part of a new, stronger policy, we put in practice a national drug control program. The three basic avenues comprise an important social campaign against drug use. It is an unprecedented effort also to eradicate crops and to combat the trafficking of prohibited or forbidden drug substances and against money laundering. In our conversations we reaffirmed our mutual commitment to cooperate with the sovereignty of each nation in an unprecedented struggle against drug trafficking.

We have spoken about our border, and we agreed to work to make it clean and safe and to make it an opportunity for productive activities and well-being. This is the intention of the *Frontera Veinte-Uno* program or the Border 21 program between our nations.

At important times, at decisionmaking times, President Clinton has shown Mexico friendship and respect. He has shown vision, commitment, perseverance, and leadership. Because of all this, Mr. President, as Mexicans, we acknowledge your friendship, your commitment, and your respect to Mexico.

In brief, ladies and gentlemen, in sum, this has been an opportunity which has allowed us to carry out a very constructive and detailed analysis of our bilateral agenda. And at the same time, it has allowed us to assert a new understanding that will ensure what is most important, that is, our will to hold a permanent dialog with mutual knowledge and friendship between our peoples.

Thank you very much.

President Clinton. Thank you.

Helen [Helen Thomas, United Press International].

Divisive Domestic Issues

Q. Mr. President, how concerned are you over the two social problems, one, the vengeful violence against law enforcement officers as manifested by Oklahoma City and the apparent sabotage of Amtrak, and of course, the racial divide as exposed by the Simpson trial? And what are you going to do about it?

President Clinton. Well, first, let me say I'm very concerned about it. I'm concerned about anything that makes the American people less secure or that divides them along racial or other lines. And it should be clear what we are trying to do about it.

What we are trying to do on the law enforcement side, obviously, is to improve our capacity to enforce the law, which is why we have asked for the antiterrorism legislation from the Congress and why we have done the things that we have done in this administration which have averted several terrorist incidents against Americans and which have succeeded in bringing suspected criminals back to the United States and which have secured convictions. So we are working very hard there to bring down the crime rate and make the American people safer.

With regard to the racial divisions, without commenting, again, on the trial itself, I think what has struck all Americans in the aftermath of the trial is the apparent differences of perception of the same set of facts based on the race of American citizens. And I have always believed that the best way to deal with that is to try to get us to identify common objectives and work toward them together and agree that we have achieved them together.

That's why I've worked so hard, often in the face of intense criticism, to assure that we had both diversity and excellence in our administration, to promote affirmative action but to get

rid of its abuses, and to do other things that would give all Americans a common stake in a common future.

But I have been thinking about this a lot over the last several days. And you know, the whole issue of reconciling races in America has been a passion of my life, even before I was an elected official. The fact that we are still polarized in some ways is a source of great concern to me, not only as President but as an American, as a father, as someone who desperately wants his country to do very well for a long time.

I have spoken about this elsewhere, but I may have some more to say about it in the next few days. I'm really going to think through this and talk to some people and try to absorb the impact of what I have been learning here. Because I must say that even I—I thought I knew a lot about how people of different races viewed things in America, but I have been surprised by the depth of the divergence in so many areas. And I do think we need to work on it, because we don't have a stake in drifting apart. We need to see—we can have differences of opinion, but at least we ought to be able to look at facts and reach some common judgment more frequently than apparently we're able to today.

Mr. President, do you want to——

Drug Abuse and Trafficking

Q. Yes, President Zedillo, at different times, on different occasions, you and other Latin American Presidents have spoken of the need for large countries—large drug consuming countries to take on the role of coresponsibility or shared responsibility with the countries where there is drug trafficking. I'd like to know if you discussed this with President Clinton and what he answered to you.

President Zedillo. This vision regarding the drug trafficking problem is a concern that is shared by the two nations. This was expressed in the agreements in Miami at the summit meeting convened by President Clinton, in the Declaration of Principles and in the Program of Action. It was very clear that we must tackle the drug trafficking problem from a global perspective, in the supply, in the trafficking, and also in the demand for drugs or drug consumption.

That is why this year the two Governments together have intensified our cooperation. It has always been in full respect of the sovereignty of the other nation, and we have acknowledged the importance of increasing our efforts to combat consumption in an integral fashion.

President Clinton. I'd like to answer that.

I think it is a legitimate thing for countries—other countries to ask the United States to do more to reduce its demand for drugs. We have roughly 5 percent of the world's population; we consume roughly half of the world's illegal drugs. So I think that's a legitimate thing.

When we passed the crime bill last year through our Congress, there was a real commitment there to increase our investment in community-based prevention programs and in drug treatment programs and in punishment programs. And I would like to point out that in the United States now we are first or second in the world in the percentage of our people that we have in prison, and half of them are there because of violating our drug laws. The crime rate is down in the United States in almost every major category. And drug use among adults is down in the United States, although casual drug use among teenagers seems to be creeping up a little. And we're intensely involved in discussions about how to drive that down.

So I accept that responsibility. And we have to do more. We also have to do more to interdict drugs coming into our country. And we've tried to do more of that on our own and have made some major progress there. So we want to do our part in what will be a genuine partnership against the scourge of drugs and the organizations that sell them and, therefore, threaten the vitality of democracy in our neighbors.

Yes, Terry [Terence Hunt, Associated Press].

Budget Negotiations

Q. Mr. President, in a speech last night, Speaker Gingrich challenged your administration to begin serious negotiations on the budget. He said—or else you'd face the loss of some Government functions that you like. And he specifically mentioned that Labor Secretary Reich might be out of a job. What would it take to begin the serious negotiations that he's talking about? What will trigger these? And what will it take to break this impasse?

President Clinton. Well, first of all, they—let me say, I don't want to get into a word war here. My door has been open to negotiations all along. I have made it clear what I would do, which is to support a balanced budg-

et; that I would support and think it's important that we increase the life of the Medicare Trust Fund; and I would support a tax cut, properly targeted and affordable, for the American people. Those are the things that the Speaker says that he wants out of the budget. I will support those things.

But I disagree with the magnitude and the pace of the cuts in the medical programs, Medicare and Medicaid. I disagree with the dramatic walking away of our responsibilities in education and in the areas of technology and research that are key to our economic future. I disagree with the significant erosion in our commitment to the environment and public health in the budget.

And the options for achieving agreement are, I think, many and fairly clear. But this legislative process has to unfold. After all, we have some of the—it's not clear to me what is going on in the Congress. You know, last year, we passed all the appropriation bills before October 1st, and in 1993 when we passed our multiyear budget, the reconciliation bill, it passed in August. And so I worked with the Congress on a regular schedule that I understood.

I have—you know, if we're going to have an honest conversation about this which—and by the way, we've had many conversations about it—I think that we have to say we have to find common ground here.

But I want to balance the budget so we can grow the economy and strengthen the American people. They've offered the American people a budget which says, "If you pass our budget with our tax cut, we will give you slower economic growth than you've had for 25 years." That's the message of their budget. I find that astonishing that they have no confidence in their own budget.

We adopted very conservative economic projections and said we thought we would grow at least as fast as we had for the last 25 years with the very difficult years in the seventies and eighties. In fact, I think we'll grow more if we do it in the right way.

So there are a lot of ways that we can meet and talk together. But we don't need to get into a fight about it; we need to work through it. And my door is open, and we'll work through it, and I think we'll get it.

Mexico-U.S. Relations

Q. President Clinton, you took on the personal risk of this financial package, the largest financial package existing. I'd like to know why in policies it appears as if you never do anything for anyone. President Zedillo, is there something that people can come and ask you for accountability on later on?

President Clinton. I'm not sure I understand the question.

Q. Would you like me to repeat the question?

President Clinton. Yes, please do.

Q. What are you expecting in exchange for the credit package that you offered Mexico? What are you expecting? [*Laughter*]

President Clinton. I see. All I want is for Mexico to stay on the path to democracy and prosperity through open markets. I seek no special favors for the United States, no special concessions. We share this great border together. Americans of Mexican heritage are one of our largest groups of Americans. Mexico is one of our largest trading partners in both directions. And our future is bound up together.

What I want is for Mexico to be strong and healthy and free and successful. That means an America with a good partner, with a bright future, with a growing economy, with stable borders, with the ability to fight the scourge of drugs and organized crime and raise the resources necessary to fight environmental pollution. And it means that there will be two countries, along with our friends in Canada, that can lead this hemispheric-wide partnership for the Americas into the 21st century. That's what I want out of this.

And the flip side of it is that if Mexico's economy had been permitted to deteriorate further because of the speculation which was existing in the financial markets at that time, then one of modern history's great examples of democracy and economic reform would have been lost because of a short-term problem. It would have been a tragedy for the American people— I mean for the Mexican people—and for the American people. And we would have paid a much dearer price because then you would have had problems in Argentina, in Brazil, in other developing countries all over the world.

So I did it because I wanted to stop bad things from happening. I did it because I have a vision of what our partnership will be in the future. But I seek no special advantage for the

United States and certainly no influence over the internal affairs of Mexico.

President Zedillo. There is nothing in what we have done this year to face the adverse situation that Mexico's economy is facing—there is nothing that we will regret in the future. Thus, all of the decisions that we have reached to tackle the crisis have been indispensable decisions, so that very soon the Mexican economy will be clearly on the path to recovery, to economic growth and the path to creating jobs.

The agreements that we have reached with the Government of the United States of America, headed by President Clinton, have been agreements that have been in full respect of our national sovereignty. We have received a very understanding and supportive attitude from the Government of the United States. And we understand that this is in benefit of Mexico. But as President Clinton has already emphasized, these decisions and these agreements were reached in the interest of international coexistence, of the international financial system as well, to safeguard its stability, and also in the interest of the U.S. economy.

Q. The Mexicans are very worried that Mexico will become an issue in the political campaign and Mexico-bashing has no political—[*inaudible*]. Have you given President Zedillo any assurances that every time that happens you will condemn that?

And I would like a quick question for Mr. Zedillo in Spanish. Mr. President, how would you respond to the allegations that your campaign has received the money from the Cali cartel?

President Clinton. First of all, I think I have established, beyond any question, my position on that issue. My view is that Mexico is our partner and that we have to work together. When we have honest differences, they should be honestly discussed. But to imagine a future for the United States that is successful into the 21st century without a successful partnership with Mexico is difficult indeed.

So my answer is the way to avoid Mexicobashing, first of all, is to deal with the facts. For example, the facts on NAFTA are that, sure, after Mexico had an economic downturn, our exports suffered. But they suffered so much less than they did just a little over a decade ago when there was no NAFTA. So we're better off.

First, we must deal with facts, not emotions. Secondly, we have to be good partners in working on the real problems that give rise to emotional and anxiety-ridden responses. We have to work on the drug problem together. We have to work on immigration and the border problems together. We have to work on these things together in an open, honest way so that people on both sides of the border can see what we're doing and that we are laboring away to make the situations better. That is the answer.

Cali Cartel

President Zedillo. That information is absolutely false, of unknown origin. It is information that appeared in a Colombian magazine, quoting supposed DEA sources. Yesterday the DEA issued a communique saying that they did not authorize that information. And as we said the first day that this information was published, we will begin legal actions against the Colombian magazine that published this information.

The data having to do with the financing of all political federal campaigns in Mexico were delivered and analyzed by the electoral authori-

ties. So we could say that that investigation has been done and completed.

Cuba

Q. President Clinton, President Zedillo, apparently there are subjects in the foreign policy where you each maintain your own position. Today in your meeting, did you speak of Cuba? It appears that the United States has changed its position regarding Cuba. Was that subject discussed in your conversations, and will it have any effect on the bilateral relations?

President Zedillo. The response, Mr. President, is very simple. We did not discuss that.

Thank you very much.

President Clinton. But it will not have any effect on our bilateral relations. [*Laughter*]

Thank you very much.

NOTE: The President's 102d news conference began at 12:45 p.m. in Room 450 of the Old Executive Office Building. President Zedillo spoke in Spanish, and his remarks were translated by an interpreter.

Message to the Congress Transmitting the Germany-United States Social Security Agreement
October 10, 1995

To the Congress of the United States:

Pursuant to section 233(e)(1) of the Social Security Act (the "Act"), as amended by the Social Security Amendments of 1977 (Public Law 95–216; 42 U.S.C. 433(e)(1)), I transmit herewith the Second Supplementary Agreement Amending the Agreement Between the United States of America and the Federal Republic of Germany on Social Security (the Second Supplementary Agreement), which consists of two separate instruments: a principal agreement and an administrative arrangement. The Second Supplementary Agreement, signed at Bonn on March 6, 1995, is intended to modify certain provisions of the original United States-Germany Social Security Agreement, signed January 7, 1976, which was amended once before by the Supplementary Agreement of October 2, 1986.

The United States-Germany Social Security Agreement is similar in objective to the social

security agreements with Austria, Belgium, Canada, Finland, France, Greece, Ireland, Italy, Luxembourg, the Netherlands, Norway, Portugal, Spain, Sweden, Switzerland, and the United Kingdom. Such bilateral agreements provide for limited coordination between the United States and foreign social security systems to eliminate dual social security coverage and taxation, and to help prevent the loss of benefit protection that can occur when workers divide their careers between two countries.

The present Second Supplementary Agreement, which would further amend the 1976 Agreement to update and clarify several of its provisions, is necessitated by changes that have occurred in U.S. and German law in recent years. Among other things, it would extend to U.S. residents the advantages of recent German Social Security legislation that allows certain ethnic German Jews from Eastern Europe to receive German benefits based on their Social Security coverage in their former homelands.

The United States-Germany Social Security Agreement, as amended, would continue to contain all provisions mandated by section 233 and other provisions that I deem appropriate to carry out the provisions of section 233, pursuant to section 233(c)(4) of the Act.

I also transmit for the information of the Congress a report prepared by the Social Security Administration explaining the key points of the Second Supplementary Agreement, along with a paragraph-by-paragraph explanation of the effect of the amendments on the principal agreement and the related administrative arrangement. Annexed to this report is the report required by section 233(e)(1) of the Act on the effect of the agreement on income and expenditures of the U.S. Social Security program and the number of individuals affected by the agreement. The Department of State and the Social Security Administration have recommended the Second Supplementary Agreement and related documents to me.

I commend the United States-Germany Second Supplementary Social Security Agreement and related documents.

WILLIAM J. CLINTON

The White House,
October 10, 1995.

Message to the Senate Transmitting the Bolivia-United States Extradition Treaty
October 10, 1995

To the Senate of the United States:

With a view to receiving the advice and consent of the Senate to ratification, I transmit herewith the Extradition Treaty Between the Government of the United States of America and the Government of the Republic of Bolivia, signed at La Paz on June 27, 1995.

I transmit also, for the information of the Senate, the report of the Department of State with respect to the Treaty, and copies of diplomatic notes dated June 27, 1995, which were exchanged at the time of signing of the Treaty. Those notes set forth the expectations of the two Governments regarding the types of assistance each Government would provide to the other in extradition proceedings, pursuant to Article XVI of the Treaty.

The Treaty establishes the conditions and procedures for extradition between the United States and Bolivia. It also provides a legal basis for temporarily surrendering prisoners to stand trial for crimes against the laws of the Requesting State.

The Treaty represents an important step in combatting narcotics trafficking and terrorism, by providing for the mandatory extradition of nationals of the Requested State in a broad range of serious criminal offenses.

The provisions in this Treaty are substantively similar to those of other extradition treaties recently concluded by the United States.

This Treaty will make a significant contribution to international cooperation in law enforcement. I recommend that the Senate give early and favorable consideration to the Treaty and give its advice and consent to ratification.

WILLIAM J. CLINTON

The White House,
October 10, 1995.

Remarks at a State Dinner for President Ernesto Zedillo of Mexico
October 10, 1995

Ladies and gentlemen, I want to begin by again welcoming President and Mrs. Zedillo and the members of the Mexican delegation. To all of our distinguished guests, Hillary and I are pleased to welcome you back to the White House.

I have known President Zedillo less than a year now, but I feel as if I have known him for a very long time because of the remarkable similarities in our lives, some of which will surprise you, perhaps some of which will amuse you.

Both of us were lucky enough to come from families where everyone worked hard. His mother was a nurse, and so was mine. We both had the chance to do graduate work in England and both continued our studies at Yale on scholarships. We both married up. [Laughter] Like her husband, Mrs. Zedillo is a trained economist, and a quite good one. And I thought I would be a pretty good lawyer until I met Hillary. [Laughter] Most important of all, and most unbelievably to me, we both went to Acapulco on our honeymoons. [Laughter] And we both went on our honeymoons not only with our wives but with our in-laws. [Laughter] Now, what that says about our judgment, character, and vision, I leave for you to determine. [Laughter] But Mr. President, we clearly have a lot in common.

We are also privileged to lead two great nations whose histories and destinies are intertwined. Our strides are longer and our burdens are lighter because we advance together in partnership.

President Zedillo, you took office at a time of great challenge for your country. You held up a vision of Mexico for the future, a Mexico united in democracy and in prosperity. You also knew that Mexico would have to change to succeed, and you called on the Mexican people to join in your campaign for progress.

Only 3 short weeks later, financial crisis struck, and pessimists predicted collapse. But while those people were wringing their hands, Mr. President, you and I were ringing each other on the telephone. I knew that you were determined to lead Mexico forward, and we both knew that we were in the fight for the future together. The United States rallied the international community to Mexico's cause, and you, Mr. President, made the courageous and difficult choices that opened the door to recovery without closing the door to reform.

Because of your faith in the people of Mexico, because of your love for your homeland, because of your willingness to lead by example, putting long-term good ahead of short-term gain, Mexico's economy is back on track, and its democracy is stronger than ever. And Mr. President, the United States is proud to be your partner.

In your inaugural address, you offered the following challenge: Let it be said of us that we have dared have high aspirations and we knew how to make our dreams come true.

With respect to your achievements, let us raise a glass to your dreams and honor the President and the people of Mexico, the ties that bind us and the friendship between us, and our common vision and destiny in the future.

Viva Mexico.

NOTE: The President spoke at 8:25 p.m. in the State Dining Room at the White House.

Remarks to the International Monetary Fund and the World Bank
October 11, 1995

Mr. Chairman, Mr. Secretaries, Mr. Camdessus, President Wolfensohn, to the governors of the International Monetary Fund and the World Bank Group, honored guests: On behalf of the United States, it's an honor to welcome you to Washington for your 50th annual meeting. And I am especially pleased to have the opportunity to speak to this group at a moment when you can see the fruits of your labors.

Ordinarily, accomplishments of great institutions like these come slowly. Yet, today the visit of President Zedillo of Mexico reminds us that in only 9 months, with the help of the international community, Mexico has pulled back from the brink of financial disaster. After one of the most severe financial emergencies in the postwar era, Mexico again is on the road to stability and growth. The Mexican stock exchange has recovered. Inflation is stable. Interest rates are down. International markets have been reassured. And most impressively, in only

7 months, Mexico was able to return to private capital markets.

As you have heard, President Zedillo has announced that Mexico will begin repaying its short-term debt with a $700 million installment this month, well ahead of schedule.

Mexico's success is a tribute first to President Zedillo's leadership, his courage, and his government's steadfast commitment to carry through tough economic reforms, though they have required great sacrifices from the Mexican people. They have borne these sacrifices, the austerity, the increased unemployment in the short run, with the hope that they will pay off in long-term growth and the better lives that ordinary Mexican citizens deserve.

That of course is the hope of people throughout the world, the hope we must address, the hope to which we must give reality as we move into the next century.

The international financial institutions, the IMF, the World Bank, the Inter-American Development Bank, all your swift and decisive support for the stabilization package played a vital role in bringing this hopeful moment to pass. I particularly want to thank Mr. Camdessus for his leadership.

The United States also acted decisively. We acted decisively for Mexico and for America, for helping Mexico helped to protect one of our biggest export markets and 700,000 jobs that depend upon our trade with Mexico. It helped to prevent an economic collapse that could have caused serious dislocation along our 2,000-mile border and had a grave impact on our common efforts to limit immigration to legal immigration. But more importantly, it was the right thing to do, because the United States and Mexico are neighbors.

The truth is, in the global economy of the 21st century, we are all neighbors. Helping Mexico not only prevented a national crisis, it prevented this national crisis from turning into a multinational catastrophe by arresting the spread of uncertainty throughout the world's emerging markets. At that time, which many of you will remember well, every sign on exchanges in South America, in Asia, in Europe, registered a looming disaster for the developing countries. Those emerging markets support more than 3 million American jobs. They're essential to our economy and to the well-being of our people, but they're more important for our common commitment to a more peaceful, more democratic, more free world.

In many of the nations embracing free enterprise for the first time, the very ideas that underpin market economies were thrown into doubt, into severe doubt, by the Mexican crisis. Open markets, privatization, deregulation: these things came under a cloud of suspicion. The decision of the countries in the developing world, Central and Eastern Europe, the Newly Independent States of the former Soviet Union, and other nations, to embrace these ideas has been one of the great achievements of this century. No American leader could allow one setback in one nation to undermine this tremendous wave of history.

But I ask you to remember also that the Mexican crisis put into high relief tensions that are less evident in many, many emerging economies throughout the world in the new realities of the 21st century. It therefore provides for us a powerful reminder of why we must continue to lead in the face of these extraordinary new challenges and these new opportunities.

History will look back on us and judge how well we responded to this time of intense economic transformation. It is the most intensive period of economic change since the industrial revolution. The revolutions in communications and technology, the development of nonstop global markets, the vast currency flows that are now the tides of international business, all these have brought enormous advantages for those who can embrace and succeed in the new global economy.

But these forces have also made all our societies more vulnerable to disturbances that once may have seemed distant but which now directly affect the jobs and livelihoods in every nation in the world, from the richest to the poorest. The unbridled forces of the global market make it more difficult for every nation to sustain the social contract, to sustain individual opportunity for all citizens, to keep families strong, to keep communities thriving, to keep hope alive.

The truth is, in this new world there are powerful forces of integration and powerful forces of disintegration. And as we approach the 21st century, we must adapt our thoughts and our actions to this new reality. No nation can turn its back, and we will all have to work together if we want the promise of the 21st century to outweigh its peril in every nation in the globe.

The trend toward globalization, after all, has far surpassed anything the great figures of Bretton Woods could have imagined. Interdependence among nations has grown so deep that literally it is now meaningless to speak of a sharp dividing line between foreign and domestic policy. In the United States, when we think of economic policy, we can't divide that which is domestic from that which is global. When we think of security policy, we know that our efforts to combat terrorism, whether it's in the World Trade Center incident or in Oklahoma City, have very much in common with our efforts to help our friends around the world to deal with a bus blowing up in the Middle East or a vial of sarin gas being broken open in a Japanese subway or in so many other instances that all of you can well relate to.

We simply must adjust the world's financial architecture to these new conditions. We must forge a system strong enough, yet flexible enough, to make the most of the historic opportunities and the historic obligations before us.

Billions of people, after all, in Asia, in Latin America, in Africa, in Europe, who are turning to democracy and free markets need to see that there can be tangible benefits from their decision and a better life after breaking the shackles of the past.

Today, a child born in Bangkok or Buenos Aires or Johannesburg enjoys the possibility of a vastly better life than his or her forebears could ever have imagined. But to redeem that promise, we must work to exalt the forces of integration and to overcome the forces of disintegration that globalization brings. We must see that a future crisis like Mexico's does not rob children of the better lives before those lives ever get started.

Fifty-one years ago, at another moment of historic change, President Roosevelt urged our Congress to approve the Bretton Woods agreements. He drew a dark picture of—or a clear picture of stark contrast. The choice, he said then, was, and I quote, "between a world caught again in a maelstrom of panic and economic warfare or a world that will move toward unity and widely shared prosperity. This point in history," he said, "is full of promise and of danger." Today, as we stand on the verge of a new century and confront a radically new international economy, I say to you that we are at a point of history full of promise and of danger.

To master the challenge before us, we must focus our efforts on expanding trade, improving investment and capital flows, and promoting sustainable development here. And we must do it in the context of our devotion to human freedom and democracy.

In the last 2½ years, our administration, working together with many of you in this room, has taken tremendous strides toward opening world markets and promoting global growth. First, we tried to become a better international citizen by putting our own economic house in order. When I became President, our Government deficit was $290 billion a year, claiming capital from around the world that needed to be properly put to other uses and keeping interest rates unnecessarily high. In 3 years, that deficit has been reduced to $160 billion a year, and we are working in good faith to bring our budget into balance across the party lines here in America.

Second, we promoted a higher rate of growth, led by investment and free of inflation, with the result that we now have the best combined rates of unemployment and inflation in the United States in 25 years.

Third, we worked with like-minded people throughout the world to advance the cause of global trade. We have worked to increase our exports, to create high-wage jobs, to improve our own standards of living and those of other nations, and to sustain growth. We brought the Uruguay round into force. We made NAFTA a reality. Our trade Ambassador, Mr. Kantor, has negotiated over 80 other separate bilateral trade agreements to expand trade. We are forging agreements with the Asia-Pacific region and with the Americas that mean that early in the next century trade will flow freely over most of the Earth.

The best way to grow our economies is to expand trade. Our experience shows that. In the last 3 years, there has been a stunning explosion in American exports, up 4 percent in 1993, 10 percent in 1994, 16 percent in 1995. At the same time, global trade has increased over 12 percent over the last 3 years, and the United States, as we have sold more, has been in a position to buy even more from other countries all around the world.

This is not an abstract concept. This makes a difference in the real lives of people throughout the entire globe. Opening markets has helped to create almost 2 million American jobs here in our own economy. But as barriers fall elsewhere, our ability to trade, our ability to purchase others' exports, our ability to invest in others' countries have created many, many more jobs in other nations around the world.

We have to do more, of course. We have to maintain our efforts to resolve trade disputes and to fight protectionism. I am pleased to say that with the establishment of the World Trade Organization, we have made real progress toward removing barriers and preventing conflicts.

Ironically, just when the advantages of expanded trade have become so dramatic, we are again hearing the voices of retreat here in our own country. There are those who say that America should simply erect a wall and live within its own borders economically and, when it comes to foreign policy, we should just go it alone. But my fellow citizens of our shared planet, economic interdependence is a fact of life. The goal must be to have it benefit all people, consistent with our shared vision for a world of freedom and peace and security and prosperity, consistent with shared values of responsibility and opportunity for all people, of stronger families and stronger communities, of nations with sustainable levels of economic growth that preserve our common environment.

That is what is happening all over the world today. I could just give you one example that coincides with President Zedillo's visit. We have a company called U.S. Filter in Palm Desert, California, with only 50 workers. But they have jobs because the Mexican city of Cuernavaca is buying a water treatment system from their company. We are fostering growth, trade, jobs, and sustainable development. We must do more of that, and turning away from one another is not the way to achieve that objective.

Mexico understands this. When the trouble hit earlier this year, because of NAFTA Mexico did not turn back and close its markets as it did during its 1980's crisis. Back then it took Mexico almost a decade to recover. But because Mexico has stayed on course, it is on the way to recovery now. There will be no lost decade for Mexico because of its own policies and because of the work done in the international community to assist it to recover. This can now be a decade of opportunity springing from short-term sacrifice.

Mexico's troubles and the other recent events have shown that reforms in the international financial system have to continue. We don't have

this all worked out as it needs to be. We should spread the benefits of financial integration around the world so that more and more borrowers have access to capital markets. We have to devise better ways to prevent financial crises and to cope with the crises that inevitably occur. People will turn away from free markets if they feel helpless, if they feel that they are simply pawns in a global game of winner-take-all, rather than partners in a global endeavor that seeks to make it possible for all to win.

Since the peso crisis, we have moved from crisis management to institutional reform. At the G–7 summit in Halifax, we put forward far-reaching proposals to help the international financial institutions meet these new needs. They aim to increase disclosure of nations' financial information and identify possible crises early, before they rock the world economy. And they include steps to mobilize the international community quickly when future crises occur. Next time there's a problem like Mexico's, the system will be better prepared. I'm pleased that over the last few days the broader membership of the IMF has endorsed these proposals, made them more concrete, brought them closer to implementation. I thank you for that, and I congratulate you for it.

Fulfilling the hopes of this moment demands that we also renew our efforts to help those who still suffer the curse of poverty. Development that improves standards of living, strengthens democracy, conserves resources, and restrains population growth; development that lifts people up and builds societies of citizens and consumers, not victims and dependents, these, these objectives benefit all nations, rich and poor.

To succeed, we must change the approaches of the past to meet the demands of the future. The international financial institutions, the multilateral development banks must continue to sharpen their focus on giving all people the chance to make the most of their own lives. That means investing in education, in health care, in other programs that attack the roots of poverty. It means responding to the problems that were highlighted in such stark and clear relief at the Beijing conference on women. It means encouraging private sector development. It means that our development programs must support democracy, accountability, and the rule of law. It means we must have a common global commitment to environmental protection and sustainable development.

Developing nations must shoulder their own responsibilities, sticking to sound economic policies, liberalizing trade practices, creating financial markets that work, and above all, being the primary investor in the human capacity of their citizens. Achieving these goals will require the banks to continue reforming their own operations and striving for greater efficiency.

Jim Wolfensohn is devoting all of his famous energy to that task. I thank him for it and for carrying forward the work of his fine predecessor, Lew Preston. I applaud Jim's progress and look forward to further accomplishments in the months and years ahead from the World Bank.

Before closing, I'd like to say just a few words about the United States commitment to helping the poorest nations of the world help themselves through our partnership in the International Development Association. It is simple: The IDA is essential. Its loans provide a crucial tool for nations that seek to escape from poverty to sustain growth. It serves our fundamental values, as well as our economic interests, by lowering trade and investment barriers, supporting private sector growth, opening the markets of tomorrow, and giving people a chance to succeed.

A lot of people don't remember this, but the IDA was the brainchild of President Eisenhower. He believed deeply that when, as he put it, "people despair that their labor will ever decently shelter their families or protect them against disease, peace and freedom will be in danger, and the seeds of conflict will be sown."

For decades, Democrats and Republicans shared President Eisenhower's sentiments, and they supported IDA. Unfortunately, that is no longer always the case. Many in the Congress have forgotten that IDA recipients of yesterday, countries like South Korea, Indonesia, Turkey, China, Chile, are today among America's most important trading partners, are among America's most important strategic partners working for global security. Those who are reminded of this perhaps will be tempted to change their position. But I want to say clearly that those who are determined to make reckless cuts in the funding of the United States for IDA should look at the facts. They should remember the vision of a great Republican President, Dwight Eisenhower.

Today's despair breeds tomorrow's conflicts. Resolving the funding for dealing with today's despair will save the world and the United States a lot of money and perhaps even precious lives in the future. Restoring funding for IDA is one of our administration's top priorities because it is the right thing to do. Of course, it serves our interests, but it is the right thing do to.

And let me assure you, if you believe as I do that balancing our Federal budget will permit higher levels of growth in the United States and throughout the world, then this is a good investment. And it is not necessary—not necessary—for the United States to walk away from its commitment to balance the national budget. Don't let anybody tell you that it is.

When these two institutions opened for business, the IMF and the World Bank, there were 38 nations standing behind them. Even then, John Maynard Keynes likened the affair to the Tower of Babel. Well, today, there are 179 nations represented here. But even though we are larger in number and some of us are larger and more wealthy than others, this increase in numbers does not mean that any one of us, including the United States, can afford to detach itself from the business at hand and hope that others will take up the slack. More than ever, we must all participate in the reform of the international economic system, and we must all do our part.

In a world that grows rapidly closer, every one of us is called upon to help harness the forces of integration for the benefit of our people and to make the forces work for all our communities and for the community of nations that is increasingly bound together. Only then can we fulfill the potential of the advances in technology and trade and knowledge. Only in that way will we defeat the forces of disintegration, extreme nationalism and ethnic strife, isolation, and protectionism.

I believe that the 21st century will be the period of greatest possibility in all human history. I hope it will be a period of unparalleled growth, achievement, prosperity, and human fulfillment. It certainly has the potential to be.

What these institutions do in the next 20 years will have a large say in what the 21st century looks like for all the people of the world. What we do individually, as nations and as leaders, will have a large say in what that world looks like.

The institutions that we honor today and that you participate in deserve and require our support. They also deserve and require our best efforts to make constructive changes to meet the new opportunities and the new challenges we face.

We must, we must, lay the foundation for prosperity, security, and freedom that will benefit all the people of the world well into the next century. These next few years are a critical point, an historic turning point. And if we do our job, the history of the next century will be less bloody than the history of the 20th century and even more filled with prosperity and freedom and common human decency.

Thank you very much.

NOTE: The President spoke at 11:15 a.m. in the Grand Ballroom at the Sheraton Washington Hotel. In his remarks, he referred to Paul Dossou, chairman, 1995 IMF/World Bank annual meeting; Timothy Thahane, Vice President and Secretary, World Bank; Leo Van Houtven, Secretary and Counsellor, IMF; James D. Wolfensohn, President, World Bank; and Michel Camdessus, Managing Director and Chairman of the Executive Board, IMF.

Remarks at a Luncheon Honoring President Ernesto Zedillo of Mexico
October 11, 1995

Thank you. Thank you so much, Mr. Vice President, for the introduction and for your leadership in these important endeavors. President Zedillo, Secretary General Gaviria, World Bank President Wolfensohn, the IMF's Managing Director Camdessus, President Iglesias, members of the United States and American Cabinets, Ambassador Babbitt, and the other OAS Ambassadors; to the very important members of our business communities in the United States and throughout Latin America; to all of our distinguished guests:

Just 9 months ago, I had the honor of hosting all the democratically elected leaders in our hemisphere at the Summit of the Americas in Miami. Together we laid out a bold and broad vision for the future of the region we all share. We imagined a community of nations committed to freedom and prosperity. And we set out a plan of action to realize that vision, to create a free trade area throughout our hemisphere, to strengthen the remarkable trend toward democracy, to improve the quality of life for all our people.

What all of us in Miami recognized is that increasingly our values and our interests coincide. Our futures are joined. As each of us prospers, all of us benefit.

For 45 years, the Organization for American States has worked tirelessly to strengthen the ties that bind us together. Now, its members have challenged us to implement many of the summit's initiatives, especially in the area of democracy and human rights. And in turn, we have asked the OAS to help turn our goal of a free trade area of the Americas into a concrete reality.

Under Secretary General Gaviria's dynamic guidance, I am confident the OAS will meet the responsibilities of its mandate and help to build a new era of democratic progress throughout the Americas.

Nowhere is the potential for progress clearer than in our relationship with Mexico. The stronger our trade, the greater the well-being of all of our people. The deeper our cooperation, the better we will be able to fight together our common problems like drugs and crime and pollution. The more effective our partnership, the stronger an example we will be able to set for all the nations of our hemisphere.

That's why when the peso collapsed, the United States stepped forward. The international support package we assembled, with the IMF, the World Bank, the Inter-American Development Bank, helped Mexico to get back on the path of stability and growth. It also protected hundreds of thousands of American jobs, and it prevented the crisis from spreading throughout our region and, indeed, to other emerging markets throughout the world. To put it mildly, the action the United States took was not popular here at home at the time it was taken. But it was the right thing to do.

In the months since the crisis, Mexico has demonstrated more strongly than ever that it is not only our neighbor, it is a very good neighbor. The Mexican people, led by President Zedillo, have courageously stayed on the road to reform.

Mr. President, the tough steps you took required courage and the ability to convince the Mexican people of the need for short-term pain in return for long-term gain. But now your resolve is paying off. Mexico has turned the corner toward recovery. And all of your partners in our region applaud your leadership and your success and the basic character and vision of the people of Mexico who have supported your direction.

During his visit to Washington, President Zedillo and I discussed how we can move our partnership forward, not only to benefit our two nations but the entire hemisphere. By spreading the success of NAFTA, leading the fight against crime and corruption and drugs, clearing our air and cleaning our water, modernizing our educational systems for the 21st century, we hope to inspire the efforts of our neighbors throughout the Americas.

All of us in the Americas have an extraordinary opportunity, if we work together. We can build a future where our borders serve as bridges; where open societies and open markets flourish; where ordinary citizens, their families, and their communities see the benefits of a free-market economy without being swept away by its excesses; where our horizons know no limits and we prove the promise of our common commitment to democracy and human dignity.

If we achieve that vision, it will be thanks in no small measure to the steady hand and the clear-sightedness of my friend and partner who is here, the distinguished President of Mexico, President Zedillo.

Thank you, Mr. President. Thank you, ladies and gentlemen.

NOTE: The President spoke at 12:13 p.m. in the Hall of the Americas at the Organization of American States. In his remarks, he referred to Cesar Gaviria, Secretary General, Organization of American States, and Enrique V. Iglesias, President, Inter-American Development Bank.

Message to the Congress Transmitting a Report on Hazardous Materials Transportation
October 11, 1995

To the Congress of the United States:

In accordance with Public Law 103–272, as amended (49 U.S.C. 5121(e)), I transmit herewith the Biennial Report on Hazardous Materials Transportation for Calendar Years 1992–1993 of the Department of Transportation.

WILLIAM J. CLINTON

The White House,
October 11, 1995.

Teleconference Remarks With Rural Hospital Administrators and an Exchange With Reporters
October 12, 1995

The President. First of all, let me thank you very much for participating in this conference call to discuss the importance of continuing to invest in health care in rural America.

As you all know, we are involved here in a serious attempt to balance the budget. I want to balance the budget. I have offered the Congress a proposal to do it. I think it will help to lift the burden of debt off our children, it will help to strengthen our economy if we do it in a way that is consistent with our values and our interests.

And one of the most important values we have is the obligation we have to strengthen our families and preserve the health care of our children and our parents. And the balanced budget I presented to the Congress does call for slowing the rate of growth in the Medicare and Medicaid programs, and it does secure the Medicare Trust Fund. But it strengthens rather than guts our Medicare program, and it recognizes that Medicaid is the principal source of funding not only for health care for poor children but for a lot of our seniors and for an enormous number of our hospitals in rural areas and in urban areas.

And I believe that the Medicare/Medicaid budget that the Republicans in Congress are pushing violates both our basic values and our interests and it is not necessary, not necessary, to balance the budget. The level of Medicare cuts are more than twice what I propose. The level of Medicaid cuts are 3 times what I propose. And I believe it will force American families to choose between educating their children and making sure their families have the health care that they need.

And as all of you know—and I want to hear from you in a moment—these cuts will be especially devastating to rural communities and to rural families because Medicare and Medicaid are the backbone of the health care system in so many rural areas. Hospitals in rural areas already are struggling to make ends meet and are closing at far more rapid rates than hospitals in urban areas and tend to depend a lot more on Medicare and Medicaid than urban hospitals do.

Therefore, if this budget passes that the Congress has proposed, it can mean, I think, devastating consequences for rural health care. And of course, we want to hear what it will mean for your local hospitals. And if more of them close, they won't be there for families in emergencies or for families with a child that needs to be immunized or for people who need longer term care.

And let me say, having been a Governor for 12 years in a rural State and having presided over a lot of hospital closings in the 1980's and having spent hours and hours and hours inside rural hospitals in all different kinds of communities, I think I have a good feel for this. But

I wanted to hear from you because I want America to know what the real consequences are.

This budget debate should not be a matter of abstract ideologies. We know we have to slow the rate of medical inflation. We know we have to deal with entitlements. We know we have to balance the budget. But we have to do it in a way that is prudent, humane, and decent and that is consistent with our values. So that's my objective, that's what I'm fighting for, and I need your help.

Now, before I close, I'd like to say one more word about the Republican Medicare plan because it affects hospitals directly. Two days ago, we saw further evidence that the Congress is prepared to walk away from the impact of this plan on people. In the dark of night, the Republican leadership cut a deal with the AMA that put—once again—put their interests ahead of the interests of the patients.

It may help the Republicans to pass their plan, but the rest of America needs to know who's going to pay for the payoff to the AMA to get them to support it. Older Americans who rely on Medicare are going to pay for it. Rural hospitals are going to pay for it. They took $3 billion more in cuts and they shifted them to patients, which means they shifted them also to rural hospitals. They give less protection for laboratory results in doctor's offices. And worst of all, it's another hidden tax on elderly people who rely on Medicare.

Under their plan, seniors can be forced into managed care networks which then can impose new fees on top of new premium increases. Under the Medicare program we have today, as all of you know, doctors can charge the Medicare-approved fee and no more. The new Republican plan would give doctors the power to charge any amount of additional out-of-pocket costs they want to older Americans every time they go to the doctor, whether or not they can afford the plan. And if you look at that and you add to that the fact that they cut out the Medicaid payments to low-income elderly people to help them pay their copays under the Medicare program, one group has estimated that as many as a million seniors may actually drop out of the Medicare system. And of course, that's going to make it even more difficult for rural hospitals.

So I'm very disappointed that the AMA supported this plan. It may look better to doctors in the short run, but it's going to be a lot tougher on their patients and a lot tougher on the hospitals in which they practice, especially the rural hospitals. They will be dealing with this.

And I'd like to ask Secretary Shalala to say a few words and talk about this from her perspective. And then I'd just like to hear from all of you, and we'll have a little conversation about it.

[At this point, Secretary of Health and Human Services Donna Shalala stated that the Republican health care proposals would have a negative impact on rural health care affordability, security, and quality.]

The President. The only other point I'd like to make, and then I'll call on you, is that when I served as Governor of my State, I worked from the late seventies through the early nineties to try to provide all kinds of incentives for doctors to go out and practice in rural areas, to try to keep the quality of health care up in rural areas. And a lot of States have done that. And I know a lot of rural hospitals have done things like have really sophisticated interconnections with urban hospitals and with teaching hospitals. And a big portion of these efforts are going to be undermined by this budget.

And again I will say, this should not be a matter of ideology. We should just practically look at the consequences. We do not have to slow this train down so fast we cause the train to run off the tracks. The health care system of America is too important.

But I'd like to hear from you now to talk about what you think you will be personally experiencing. Let's start with Don Sipes, who's the CEO of St. Luke's Northland Hospital, a hospital with 92 beds and 150 employees in Smithville, Missouri, which is a community of 2,500.

Mr. Sipes.

[Mr. Sipes described the potentially devastating impact of the proposed Medicare cuts on rural Missouri hospitals as health care providers and employers, noting that many of them were already struggling financially.]

The President. I'd like to just emphasize two things here that kind of came out of your remarks. Number one, the 1980's were tough on rural hospitals. Rural hospitals—about 17 percent of our rural hospitals closed in the decade

of the eighties, and only about 2 percent of our nonrural hospitals did. And we knew that some of that consolidation had to occur. But the important thing for the people of the United States to understand is that rural hospitals have undergone significant changes in management and the way they allocate their resources, and they have achieved enormous efficiencies, and their ability to do more is constrained by the remarkable progress that was made in the eighties and the enormous changes that were made.

The second point I'd like to make is that no one has an answer to what happens to these folks if you close. I mean, who's going to be—how are these people going to be taken care of?

What is the percentage of your Medicare—what percentage of your revenue comes from Medicare and Medicaid?

Mr. Sipes. At the Smithville campus, 71 percent.

Secretary Shalala. And you're going to lose at least $1 million under the Senate plan, I think. I think that's our calculation.

The President. A year.

[Secretary Shalala noted that other businesses in the community would be adversely affected by the closing of a major rural health care employer.]

The President. That's right. The other point I want to make is that in this debate you will frequently hear the congressional leaders say, "Look, we're not giving anybody less money; we're giving everybody more money." And that is true. But the real issue is, is the more money sufficient to deal with more patients and the cost of inflation?

The real answer here is to bring medical costs per patient, per treatment closer to the general rate of inflation. And we're working on that. This year, premium costs for insurance were at or below the rate of inflation for the first time in a decade. But these numbers, the budget numbers, will not permit many of our health care providers to deal with increased case loads plus inflation.

So even though it may look like more money 7 years from now than we're spending today, the real question is, in real dollar terms will it be more? And the answer is, for many, many of you, no. And I think that's really important because just to say we're giving more money obscures the question of whether you'll really be able to deal with your patient loads, with the cost of health care, and with inflation.

I'd like to call on Mr. Cannington now. H.D. Cannington is the administrator of the Jay Hospital, which has 55 beds and 110 employees in Jay, Florida.

Mr. Cannington.

[*Mr. Cannington explained that the cuts would probably force his hospital to close, disrupting the entire health care system in that rural area.*]

The President. That's another thing I'd like to emphasize that's special about rural America. You just described the kind of services you provide. A lot of people say, "Well, if we cut the budget this much and these hospitals close, it's no big deal; we'll just convert them into clinics, to primary care clinics. Then if they need a serious hospital, they can go to the nearest city somewhere." The problem is that a lot of these rural hospitals, most of the ones I know in my State, do just exactly what you said. They're running—they are the public health outreach. They are the home health outreach. They are doing these things that those who say, "If we close the hospital, they'd be replaced by other people." There's just no reason to believe that.

And we all know, anybody that's ever worked or lived in a rural area knows that one of the biggest problems in getting doctors to go to rural areas and stay there is having access to a decent hospital. And they just won't stay if all they have is their own clinics. We just see it over and over and over again in America.

So I really appreciate your saying that very important point.

[*Mr. Cannington stated the importance of a hospital's proximity to its patients' homes.*]

The President. What percentage of your revenues come from Medicare and Medicaid?

Mr. Cannington. About 69 percent of our revenue and about 71 percent of our patients are Medicare and Medicaid.

The President. Thanks.

Mr. Kelly, John Kelly, is the administrator of the Soldier and Sailors Memorial Hospital, which has 217 beds and 500 people on the staff in Penn Yan, New York, which has a population of 5,500.

Mr. Kelly.

Mr. Kelly. Yes, Mr. President. Some of our people up here wanted to wish you a happy anniversary, sir.

The President. Thank you. I had a wonderful day. It was a great day.

[*Mr. Kelly described the services provided by his hospital as a result of changes in the previous decade and expressed concern about the systematic failure to address rural health care issues.*]

The President. First of all, let me emphasize something you said that Mr. Cannington also said, that typical rural hospitals, an awful lot of them now, are far more than traditional hospitals. They are long-term care centers; they offer psychiatric care; they perform home health functions; they perform public health clinic functions.

When I started working on all these problems over a decade ago, our big struggle was to try to convince all these hospitals in rural areas in our home State, if they wanted to survive they had to diversify, they had to use their beds in the most efficient way, they had to provide all these services; that rural areas couldn't afford to have separate institutions for all these different things.

That has now been done. We now have in so many rural communities in our country what we call hospitals, but they're basically comprehensive care centers. And they are now in a position to do what needs to be done. What we believe is that we have to lower the rate of medical inflation and that now you have the infrastructure and the organization to do that. But if you cut too much too fast, we're going to wind up wrecking the system that we built through a lot painstaking effort and often trial and error throughout the 1980's.

I don't think most Americans—they wouldn't have any way to know—but I don't think they understand the dramatic, breathtaking changes that rural hospitals went through in the 1980's and how many rural hospitals are now the kind of flexible, entrepreneurial, comprehensive health care systems that we all could only imagine just a decade ago. So I really appreciate what you said, because we need to—the American people need to know that we're not dealing with some big, fat, bloated, outdated bureaucracy that's been living off the fat of the land for the last 20 years. That's not what happened in rural America. But you are going to get a disproportionate hit out of this.

I'd like to talk to Margo Arnold now—or hear from her. She is the CEO of the West Side District Hospital in Taft, California, which has a population of 5,900 and has 84 beds and 160 employees.

Ms. Arnold.

[*Ms. Arnold stated that her hospital and others would face cuts at both Federal and State levels and expressed concern that the onslaught would continue.*]

The President. What percentage of your revenues come from Medicare and Medicaid?

[*Ms. Arnold stated that approximately 69 percent of revenues came from Medicare and Medicaid and reiterated her concern for the future of the facility and its clients.*]

The President. Thank you very much.

Peter Hofstetter is the CEO at Northwestern Medical Center, with 70 beds and 400 employees, in Saint Alban's, Vermont. Peter, would you like to comment?

[*Mr. Hofstetter expressed concern about the impact of the cuts on his hospital's efforts to maintain a high-quality staff and institute community health programs. Secretary Shalala then questioned Republican proposals that rural hospitals shift costs to their clients.*]

The President. Yes. I think of all the people we're talking to, Mr. Hofstetter's Medicare-Medicaid reliance is the smallest. And yours is what? What percentage of revenue—

Mr. Hofstetter. Sixty percent.

The President. And that's the smallest of anybody we're talking to, 60 percent.

It's important to emphasize that rural populations tend to be older and that their average incomes tend to be lower. It's also important to emphasize that what is rural in Washington, DC, may not be rural in Vermont. I mean, it's extraordinary to have 48 doctors in a town of 7,300. But the reason is there's so many other many, many smaller towns in Vermont that you're probably serving near there. And of course, we don't have anybody on this telephone call today who's from one of the High Plains States or Intermountain States, a place like South Dakota or North Dakota or rural Colorado or some of those places where you're not talking about 30 miles, you're talking about 100 miles or 150 miles or 200 miles to the nearest town of any size. We're talking about breathtaking distances in some of our rural States which are very sparsely populated.

So I think it's an astonishing thing that you were able to go from 17 to 48 doctors and to solve those—to do what you're doing in the 1980's. I wish I had known you 10 years ago when I had a different job. That's an amazing achievement.

Secretary Shalala. How critical are you to the economy of the area that you're in, with that large of a facility?

Mr. Hofstetter. Saint Alban's?

Secretary Shalala. Yes.

Mr. Hofstetter. Oh, we're about the second- or third-largest employer in the county. We've got a couple of large manufacturers and some other industries. But we're consistently in the top two, three, four. And we put about, oh, $8 million and change, with payroll and stuff, back into the economy.

The President. How many of those doctors are on the hospital payroll?

Mr. Hofstetter. Well, just one primary care doctor and then pathologists, that kind of thing. But most of the physicians that came here in the eighties and early nineties, it was a quality of life thing, and they set up a traditional solo practice situation. And I have to tell you, honestly, they're all—not all of them but a number of them are starting to question that whole aspect of life as well, being sort of the lone cowboy out there practicing medicine.

The President. And of course, a lot of them, in addition to their hospital practice, a lot of their patients who don't come into the hospital are probably Medicaid and Medicare patients as well.

Mr. Hofstetter. Oh, sure. We still have a lot of docs that do home visits. It's textbook primary care.

Secretary Shalala. Not much quality of life if you don't have good health care, though.

Mr. Hofstetter. No.

The President. Let's go on to Todd Linden, who is the president and CEO of the Grinnell Regional Medical Center in Grinnell, Iowa. He has 81 beds and 350 employees in a community with a population of 8,900.

Mr. Linden, would you like to talk?

Mr. Linden. Good morning, Mr. President.

The President. Good morning.

[*Mr. Linden described his facility's task of dealing with one of the Nation's highest Medicare populations coupled with one of the lowest reimbursement rates, noting that the problem would increase as the baby boom generation became more of a senior boom.*]

The President. I wish you hadn't said that. [*Laughter*]

[*Mr. Linden then expressed his concern that Medicare reforms be achieved in the most responsible manner possible, avoiding regional inequities.*]

The President. I want to thank you for what you said. Let me—you made a point that I want to reemphasize that everybody who talked today did. No one questions the fact that we have to slow the rate of medical inflation. That is not an issue here. The issue is—and no one knows, frankly, how much more progress we might make with telemedicine, with HMO's. And all of us recognize that you need to have more options, like for providers to directly sponsor managed care plans. And I certainly agree with you, we need to constantly review the equity of the reimbursement system.

There is—however, one thing has been—there has been a consensus on one thing in this entire debate, which is that the number selected by the majority in Congress for their medical cuts in Medicare and Medicaid had nothing to do with a study of what the system would bear and what it could accommodate over the next 7 years. It was a number picked out of the air arbitrarily to fit a certain set of economic assumptions which are questionable, a 7-year balanced budget and a tax cut of $250 billion. So they said, "Well, that leads us to these cuts, and so we're going to make them, even though we have no idea what the impact on the system will be."

The people I talk to all across America—I was with senior citizens in Florida the other day—everybody in America is willing to make an effort to do what it takes to bring medical inflation down. Everybody knows that we can't continue to have medical inflation go up at 3 times the rate of inflation. But enormous efforts have been made by health care providers, especially in rural areas, in the last several years. And there is a consensus among providers with whom I talk that no one knows how and no one believes that this volume of cuts can be

just taken out of the system in the next 7 years without severe adverse impact.

And so I think it's important again to say this is not about ideology and this is certainly not about irresponsibility. The health care providers, the seniors in this country, everybody is trying to respond to this situation in a responsible way, but nobody, nobody, believes that this arbitrary very high number can be reached, based on all the evidence and experience we have today. That is the important thing.

We have to do this in a way that is consistent with what we believe the facts and evidence are. We have to be honest and we have to be concerned about our primary mission, which is to provide decent health care. We don't want to make it worse.

There's one other point I want to make about Iowa that relates to a lot of other States. I have been a big proponent of managed care as an option for seniors. And I'm glad that the Congress—the congressional majority now supports that. But I think we have to go into this with our eyes wide open. If we sell this as an end-all and be-all, what's going to happen is a lot of these networks, if there's not some real discipline here in how we do it, will cream the healthiest seniors. And the oldest seniors that have the highest health care costs will be left not in managed care networks and will be back either dependent on the Government—which either means they won't get health care, or we'll wind up spending a lot more than we think we will on the system because of that. And because Iowa has the highest percentage of Americans over 80, I think that's worth focusing on.

It depends on who sets up these networks and how they serve them, whether everybody really gets served. This thing could get out of hand, and a lot of older people could get—and less healthy seniors could get left in the dust by this managed care movement if we don't do it in a decent and humane way.

[*Mr. Linden concurred on the complexity of the issue and stressed the primary importance of preserving health over curing disease. Secretary Shalala then noted that the Trust Fund would be adequately secured by $90 billion in cuts rather than the $270 billion Republican proposal.*]

The President. Let me say to all of you how much I appreciate the time you've given this, and even more, how much I appreciate the work you've done with your lives. As I said, because of the job I had before I became President, because I lived in a rural State, I know how hard it's been for you in the last 10 years, and I know what dramatic advances have been made in the face of these difficulties and challenges.

And we can do more, we can do better, and we will. But it is important that when we have this budget finalized that we don't have an arbitrary number, that we make an honest effort to discipline this system in a way that will save the Medicare Trust Fund, slow the rate of medical inflation, but do it in a way that will enable us to enhance the quality of medical care and the quality of life for seniors, for children, and for poor people, particularly those that are in more isolated areas and the rural areas.

I'm going to do my best to take care of those concerns here and to defend them. And we will do our very, very best to achieve in the end a balanced budget that is decent and fair and based on our values when it comes to health care, and that's based on the evidence that you've given us. And I can't thank you enough.

But if I could just say one thing in closing, I would implore you to personally contact the Members of the Congress in your area without regard to their party and say that you have done your part in the eighties, you are willing to do your part in the nineties, you understand why we want to balance the budget, but we have to do it in a prudent, disciplined way that does not wreck the health care system. We have worked so hard to reconstruct a comprehensive health care network in rural America, and there's still great difficulties in maintaining it. And to take it out now would be a tragedy. And it would be wrong, and it is not necessary to balance the budget.

So I thank you from the bottom of my heart. And I just want to urge you to share your experiences and your knowledge with the Members of Congress, because many of them are having to vote on these issues without the experience base that you have—or that I have, frankly, or that any of us who have actually been through this and lived through it. So I would just close with that.

There are a lot of good people up here trying to do the right thing, and we've got to just stick to our values, stick to the evidence, and do what is doable.

And so—but, please, please, continue to reach out to the Congress in these next few weeks so that we can make the right kind of decisions for our country.

Mr. Kelly. Mr. President?

The President. Yes.

Mr. Kelly. This is John Kelly up in Penn Yan. Could you just tell us what do you think the next step would be from your perspective in this process?

The President. Well, I keep trying to engage the Congress in this. They're going to have to decide when and how they want to work with us to try to come to some agreement. But meanwhile, I think the next step is, that will either happen or they'll pass a budget that I find unacceptable and I will manifest that with a veto and then we'll talk about it then.

And I don't know how this is going to unfold. But I do know this, that the more information, the more information you can get for the Members of Congress, based on what is real and what is going on in their districts and what their constituents are living with, the better chance we have to do the right thing on this budget.

It is not clear to me yet exactly how the congressional leaders will determine they're going to proceed. But however it's going to proceed, in the end, I'm going to do my part in this process. And my responsibility is to basically advance the values and the interests of the American people and stand up for the people who I believe have been left behind in the process. That is what I'm going to do; that's my responsibility.

But the mechanics of it are not yet clear because we're in somewhat of an unprecedented situation now. We're already past the time when the budgets are normally done. So I can't tell you that. But I can tell you this: It is never too late for you to contact them and explain your experiences and say, "Look, this is just not doable; these numbers are arbitrary and they're not achievable. We're willing to help, we're willing to contribute, but we can't do that." And I urge you to do it.

Thank you very much.

Q. Thank you, Mr. President.

The President. Goodbye.

[*At this point, the teleconference ended, and the President took questions from reporters.*]

Federal Budget

Q. Mr. President, a short time ago, Speaker Gingrich said of you—and I quote—"If he plans to run for reelection, I think it's a very big step for him to say, 'I'm going to veto the balanced budget, tax cuts, welfare reform, and save Medicare.' I'm not at all certain by the time we're done in early November that he is not going to sign these things." Could you react to that?

The President. Well, those words sound good, but what stands behind them? What kind of balanced budget plan? What kind of tax cuts?

My job is to protect the families of this country, the children of this country, and the future of this country, the elderly. The President's job is to stand up for the fundamental values of the country. Those are nothing more than slogans. There are ways—if what the Speaker wants to achieve is a balanced budget with a tax cut that secures the Medicare Trust Fund, well, I'm for that. I'm for that. And I will work with him to help him to achieve that. But underneath that very appealing slogan there are $148 billion in taxes and fee increases on the elderly and on working people with very low incomes.

This budget would take people out of the middle class and put them back into poverty. This budget would jerk up the ladder that poor people are now using to work their own way into the middle class. This budget would say, "We're going to cut taxes on the President if he has capital gains income, but we're going to raise taxes on working people with children living on 15,000 bucks a year." This budget would say, "If you're a senior citizen now on Medicare and you're living on 300 bucks a month, we're no longer going to make your copay from the Medicaid program, we're going to raise your cost of living, even if you're living on $300 or $400 a month." This budget would say, "If you're going to college, we're going to charge you more for your college loan and make it more expensive and make it more difficult for you to get. And we're going to give more money that we used to allocate to students and their loans to middlemen like banks and others in the middle of the process." I don't believe that's consistent with American values. I just— and it is not necessary.

And so, these goals sound very good, but how you achieve them is very important. And they

have, apparently, very little confidence—much less confidence than I have—that a balanced budget would lead to a growth in the economy. I mean, they say they want to grow the economy, but they have given us a budget that says, "If you adopt our budget just like we've given it to you, we're going to have a big tax cut including—that goes to some people that don't want it and don't need it, and we're going to have huge cuts in Medicare and Medicaid, and we're going to balance the budget, and it's going to give America the slowest economic growth it's had in 25 years." That's the message of their budget.

You know, I'd be proud of it if I were them. Now, what I did to show fiscal prudence was to give them a budget which says that I am assuming only that we will grow as fast as we have for the last 25 years, when we've had some very, very bad years. I believe we're going to grow faster than that, but I wanted to be prudent. But they say, "No, adopt our budget. Do all these really tough things to the middle class, to the elderly, to the children, and we will slow the economy down. That's your reward, America, for adopting our budget." I think that's a very curious message.

So, you know, I don't want to get into a shouting match on this, but would I sign a budget like this because they would maybe hide some of the severe consequences in the election year just to get reelected? The answer is, no. I won't do that. Because whether I get reelected or not, I hope to live to be an old man, I hope to live to see my grandchildren grow up in the America of the 21st century, and I want it to be a country with opportunity for everybody, with strong families and strong communities leading the world, that's a place where the things that we all believe in are alive and well. And I would gladly, gladly terminate my tenure here if the price of continuing it was just shelving everything I believe in about this country.

So we need to take this debate out of the politics of it and take it out of the ideology, and let's talk about the facts. You heard these people. They're running these rural hospitals. They've all slowed their cost of inflation down. They're all willing to do more. None of them believe they can make the numbers in the congressional budget. Let's get out of politics and ideology and personal gain and all this rhetoric, and let's talk about what the impact is going to be as a factual matter on the American people and how we can sign a credible budget that will grow the economy. Grow the economy, create jobs, raise incomes. We're going to be able to balance the budget quite easily, and we don't have to do all this.

Q. What do you think about the AMA, Mr. President? What do you think about the AMA?

Q. Mr. President, how do you suggest that the White House works with Republicans and vice versa? The two sides aren't even talking at this point.

The President. I have a conversation with the Speaker every week about a lot of things. And we try to find ways that we can work together. But they have tensions within their own caucus, as you know. They have ideological tensions in the House and they have in the Senate—they have ideological tensions and political tensions that I can't reach or influence at this moment, because they're sort of encased in the way the Republican Party is today.

A genuine discussion and negotiation about what we can do involving the leaders of the Republican Party—there are a lot of Democrats who want to vote for a balanced budget, a ton of them. You know, it's been largely ignored here, but the Democrats in the Congress took the lead in reducing the deficit. They took it without any support from the Republican Party. They took the deficit from $290 billion down to $160 billion. So there are a whole bunch of Democrats that are literally yearning to vote for a bipartisan budget that reflects the best of the budget I put forward and the best of the budget they put forward and is better than both of them. We're not talking about a compromise that just splits the difference, we're talking about something that is better for America.

So we can have these conversations before, during, and after they cast whatever votes they're going to take, but we have to get beyond this sort of line-in-the-sand rhetoric where—my door's been open since I gave my budget. That's why I gave them a balanced budget.

Q. Will it take a budget summit, Mr. President?

Q. Why don't you invite them over for a budget summit here? You're getting the Bosnians——

Q. Will it take a budget summit?

The President. I don't know. I don't know.

Q. —for peace talks. Why don't you have peace talks with the Republicans?

The President. Well, you know, like I said, I try to talk to as many of them as I can, all the time. I think, to be fair to them in terms of the timetable, to be fair to them, they have to—they're in a better position than we were 2 years ago, because 2 years ago, the week I got here, I was informed by the Republican leaders that there would be no votes for my budget. Whatever I did, there would be no votes. And so what we had to do was to work through our budget and figure out how to cut the deficit by $500 billion with Democrats only, which made it—which meant, compared to what I wished, there was a little more tax on upper income people and a little less cuts than I wanted. But we passed it. And it had a terrific impact. It drove down interest rates. It drove up the economy. It got us where we are today, with 7½ million jobs and 2½ million new homeowners and 2 million new small businesses.

What they have to do—the timing on this will be, I think, determined as much by—will have to be determined by where they are within their own caucus. But they know something that we didn't know 2 years ago. They know that we want to balance the budget, too—not just the President but a large number of Democrats in Congress in both Houses are willing to work with them. But they can't say working with us is, "We're going to pass what we want, we're going to put it on your desk, and you will sign it or veto it." That's not my idea of working together.

If their real objectives are a balanced budget, tax cuts that are reasonable, extending the life of the Medicare Trust Fund, we can achieve those objectives. But we cannot do it if the objective—or the real objective is to raise taxes on the lowest income working families of the country, to raise the cost of living to the poorest elderly people of America, do significant damage to the health care system, and to undermine the education investments of America and the environmental responsibilities of America, just because there's an ideological desire to wreck the Federal Government. And they have to work through that.

But at some point, we'll all get together and work this out. I believe in the system and I wouldn't—and I don't think you all should overreact to this. I believe we're going to work this out. But meanwhile, I'm going to do my best to take care of the American people.

Q. Thank you, Mr. President.

President's Wedding Anniversary

Q. What did you get for your anniversary? [*Laughter*]

The President. I got a number of things, but one of the most interesting things I got was from my wife. It was two old pictures of us together 20 years ago blown up.

Q. Show us. [*Laughter*]

The President. My daughter had unfavorable comments on men's styles in the 1970's. [*Laughter*]

NOTE: The President spoke at 11:45 a.m. from the Roosevelt Room at the White House.

Remarks at a Swearing-In Ceremony for AmeriCorps Volunteers
October 12, 1995

If she hasn't made the case, there's nothing for me to say. [*Laughter*]

Thank you, Michelle Johnson Harvey, for that remarkable statement. And thank you and all of your colleagues here for your dedication to your country, to your community and your participation in AmeriCorps. Thank you, Don Doran, for the work that you have permitted AmeriCorps to do with you and your school in Atlanta.

And I thank Senator Harris Wofford for his willingness to take up this service at this important time in the history of our country and the history of AmeriCorps. We just swore him in—the Vice President swore him in over in the Oval Office with Mrs. Wofford and his entire family and his extended family of friends. And he pointed out that at least I had told him what I expected him to do. He said that once before he was sworn in in the Oval Office, and President Kennedy swore him in and then told him what his job was going to be. [*Laughter*] So I feel that after 30 years we're at least making some progress in the Government's obligation to fully disclose to its—[*laughter*]—public servants what they are expected to do.

I want to thank Jim Joseph, the Chairman of the Board, who is about to become our distinguished Ambassador to South Africa, and all the other supporters of the AmeriCorps program and the other volunteer efforts that are here.

And I want to say, of course, a special word of thanks to my friend of 25 years, Eli Segal, for the remarkable job he did in creating AmeriCorps and getting it off to a good start. Thank you for a brilliant job.

I want to thank the supporters of AmeriCorps in the Congress, including those who are here, Senator Jeffords from Vermont, Congressman Sawyer from Ohio, Congresswoman Karen McCarthy from Kansas City. She got one of her constituents up here, and I saw her bursting with pride. Congressman Green from Texas and Congressman Tim Roemer from Indiana. We're glad to see all of you. And we thank you for your support.

A year ago, in one of my proudest moments as President, I challenged 20,000 citizens to join us in a new American adventure, rooted in our most fundamental values of personal responsibility, educational opportunities, service to others, and commitment to community. I asked those 20,000 Americans to put their values into action through AmeriCorps, because service is a spark to rekindle the spirit of democracy in an age of uncertainty. Well, the times may be uncertain because they're changing so rapidly, but I am certain that the flame of democracy is burning brighter all across America today because of people like Michelle Johnson Harvey and her friends who helped to close those crack houses and give those children safe streets to walk, and because of the thousands and thousands of other AmeriCorps volunteers and the many thousands more whom they recruited to work to build houses, to immunize children, to educate, to help to solve all the community problems that are being faced at the grassroots level.

You know, it is true that this idea was consciously born as a nonbureaucratic, grassroots, community-based, totally nonpartisan idea. I became enamored of the idea of community service because I saw what it could do as a Governor and because I was working with a group in the late eighties and early nineties, the Democratic Leadership Council, and we devised a proposal. And Senator Nunn, who just a couple of days ago announced his retirement from the Congress, and some others, when President Bush was in office, proposed a pilot project. And President Bush was good enough to sign the bill that passed, and we did begin this.

And then when I ran for President, I saw all over America these community groups like the City Year group in Boston, which is now spreading across the country like wildfire. I saw them everywhere, these young people full of energy and ideas, across racial lines, across income lines, people who had never shared any common experiences before coming together and literally creating a new future for people one-on-one and for communities and solving problems that we could never begin to solve here in Washington, DC. And I was determined that if I ever had the chance to do it as President, I would try to create a national commitment to community service all across the country that would give our young people a chance to give something back to their communities and to advance their education at the same time. That is what we are doing.

At a time when, once again, we are asking ourselves whether we are too divided in our perceptions of reality and our attitudes toward all the things that are going on in America to be a real community, the members of AmeriCorps put the lie to all of that. They show us once again that if you can just get good people together, no matter how different their backgrounds are, and you give them a chance to share common values and to work on a common problem or to seize a common opportunity, and you give them a chance to do it together, day-in and day-out, they will change everybody's preconceived notions of what is possible in America. They will prove, once and for all, again in this age, that the American idea is a universal idea, that the notion of personal responsibility, the notion of opportunity for everybody, the notion that we're all better and stronger when we work together than when we are divided, that those things are universal, that they are rooted in a fundamental truth about human nature and that there is no power like it anywhere. That's what these young people in AmeriCorps prove day-in and day-out.

I'm so grateful for all of the things they've done. They've fought forest fires in Idaho. They've helped people after floods in Houston. They've built homes in Miami. They've, as you heard, helped to raise reading scores dramatically in Kentucky, a model I hope will be copied in schools all across America. They've helped to prevent lead poisoning in Portland. They've helped troubled youths to care for people in nursing homes in Boston. They certainly came to the rescue after Oklahoma City, some of them in truly remarkable ways. They simply put themselves on the line to prove that things are still possible in America.

No one could ever meet these young people and listen to their stories and continue to be cynical about the prospect of Americans working together. I met a young woman named Velaida "Cricket" Shepard when we had our economic conference in Portland, Oregon, last June. And she was trying to talk about AmeriCorps, and she began to cry. She almost couldn't get through her statement. Michelle didn't have that problem. [Laughter] I thought she was going to declare for President right here in the middle of her speech. [Laughter] But this young woman talked about getting up at 6 o'clock every morning so she could make sure a young girl she was mentoring got to school on time; so she could make sure that no family problem this child had—nothing would keep that child from school; so she could make sure that no amount of disappointment in her own life, no amount of personal injury that child had suffered, emotional injury, would keep her from becoming what she ought to be.

That young girl, who was troubled, was marked for failure, has now become a role model in her school. And at the same time, Cricket Shepard has gone on to other challenges to help other young people do the same, and AmeriCorps is helping her to get an education at Portland State University.

This is the kind of thing that we ought to be doing, folks. No one knows here in Washington what the really most important problem is in Kansas City, but the people in Kansas City know. No one wakes up every morning in Washington thinking about whether, in a given community, they need most to close crack houses or build Habitat for Humanity homes or keep beaches clean or tutor students. But the people in those communities know.

I have been overwhelmed by the broad and deep support for AmeriCorps from people from all walks of life. We know that it is not only consistent with our values and a good thing to do, it also happens to be cost-efficient and it works. We know that from independent economists, from evaluators, even the GAO says that it more than pays its way and actually costs less than we had originally estimated it would.

So I say to you today that as we debate this great national question of how to balance the budget, we can balance the budget without turning our backs on these young people. We can balance the budget without forgetting the fundamental lesson, which is that if you can create a national movement with no bureaucracy that explodes human energy at the grassroots level, you can put the lie to all this business about how we are bound to be divided by race, by region, by income, by walk of life, just by letting them live and do what they know to do. And that is what we ought to do.

AmeriCorps should be continued for far more than the some 25,000 young people that will be involved in it this year, far more than the 2,000 communities in all 50 States that will be benefited, far more than the many, many tens of thousands of other volunteers, that they will make it possible to work because they will organize them. It should be continued if, for no other reason, that it proves that the American idea is alive and well and can meet the challenges of the 21st century, to restore our values, to strengthen us at the grassroots level. It can

be a shining symbol that there is no need for cynicism, no need for defeatism, and no need for tolerance of division in the United States of America. That's why we should continue AmeriCorps.

So I would like to begin this next year of AmeriCorps by asking all of the members who are here and all of those who are with us via satellite in Kansas City to join me in taking the AmeriCorps pledge.

Please stand and repeat after me, if you're not all standing. Stand up—it'll be good for all of us to do it. [*Laughter*] This would be a good pledge for the citizens of the United States:

I will get things done for America, to make our people safer, smarter, and healthier. I will bring Americans together to strengthen our communities. Faced with apathy, I will take action. Faced with conflict, I will seek common ground. Faced with adversity, I will persevere. I will carry this commitment with me this year and beyond. I am an AmeriCorps member. And I am going to get things done.

[*The AmeriCorps volunteers repeated each line of the pledge after the President.*]

Thank you, and God bless you all.

NOTE: The President spoke at 2:40 p.m. in the East Room at the White House. In his remarks, he referred to Michelle Johnson Harvey, AmeriCorps member, and Don Doran, principal, Benteen Elementary School.

Statement on Signing the Small Business Lending Enhancement Act of 1995
October 12, 1995

I am pleased to sign into law today S. 895, the "Small Business Lending Enhancement Act of 1995." This Act would, among other things, establish new guarantee levels for guaranteed loan programs of the Small Business Administration (SBA).

S. 895, which the Congress passed at my Administration's urging, contains important elements of the Vice President's National Performance Review proposals and SBA's reinvention proposal. The Act is also consistent with rec-

ommendations from this spring's White House Conference on Small Business.

S. 895 reduces the Government's cost of small business financing, thereby enabling even more customers to be served. With the program reforms contained in this Act, SBA will be able to extend up to $33 million in additional loan guarantees per day with no additional cost to the taxpayer.

I am pleased to sign this measure into law because it reflects my Administration's commitment to customer service and to "doing more with less."

WILLIAM J. CLINTON

The White House,

October 12, 1995.

NOTE: S. 895, approved October 12, was assigned Public Law No. 104–36.

Remarks at a Celebration of the Anniversary of the Restoration of Democracy in Haiti
October 12, 1995

Thank you very much, Mr. Secretary General. This marks the second time in 2 days I have been here. I promise I won't come back tomorrow and interrupt your lives. [*Laughter*] Madam Foreign Minister, to the distinguished Prime Minister of St. Kitts and others who are here who were part of that remarkable coalition that restored democracy to Haiti a year ago. Let me say I was looking out at this crowd tonight, and when my friend of 25 years, Taylor Branch, told me that this event was going to come to pass, I redid my schedule just so I could come by here and thank so many of you for what you did. I want to thank my longtime friend Bill Gray for agreeing to be pressed back into public service for the work that he did.

I want to thank all the people in the United States who cared about Haiti, who wrote me letters and called me on the phone and came to see me about it and talked to me about what was at stake. Randall Robinson even went on a diet for Haiti. [*Laughter*] Jonathan Demme wrote me letters that were even more eloquent than the films that he makes. [*Laughter*] And many others did as well. I thank you all for your concern.

I want to thank our partners in the hemisphere. When the United States decided that if necessary we would use force to remove the military regime and to restore President Aristide and democracy, I was so determined that no one would think we were trying to revive any hemispheric imperialism. I have worked very hard to establish a new sense of partnership, a new sense of common bond, a new sense of common mission with all the nations of the Caribbean, of Central and South America.

The First Lady would like to be here tonight. She is in Nicaragua as we speak, on her way to a four-nation tour of Latin America. We care deeply about how other people who share our neighborhoods feel about the United States and that they understand that we believe we have a common destiny.

And so I don't think this operation ever would have worked as it should have worked had it not been for all the other countries who were willing to participate with us. Even though we had a United Nations mandate, what really made it go was all of our neighbors participating, sending their soldiers, sending their police monitors, participating, standing up for it. It made an enormous difference.

I want to say a special word of thanks to all the people within our administration who supported my action. And needless to say, it was hotly debated. And all the political polls said it was a dumb thing to do. And I said, well, I do a lot of things that the polls—[*laughter*]. But it seemed to be the right thing to do. Two of them are here, the Deputy Secretary of State, Strobe Talbott, and Sandy Berger. And people that aren't here, Tony Lake and the Vice President, were all very strongly in support of the action that our administration took. And I appreciate that very much.

And finally let me say to General Fisher and to everyone who was involved first in the multinational force and then in the United Nations force, I am very proud and grateful for the performance of the United States military in Haiti. They made all Americans proud. And they made this whole thing possible, and we thank you, too, sir.

One of the best things that's happened to me in the last year is a few months after the restoration of President Aristide, one of the military officers who was involved in the operation—and I don't want to embarrass him, so I won't say his name—but I was having a rather interesting conversation with him, and he looked at me, and he said, "You know, Mr. President, when you did this, I just didn't know. But you know, that was a good thing we did. It was the right thing to do." And I was—coming from a person of few words and high performance, I treasured that.

I thank Brian Atwood and the work that AID is doing in Haiti. And all of you should relish this celebration for all of the work that all of you did and the contributions you made, all of the groups and the individuals. Tonight I hope you will think about what we all have to do to make sure that this extraordinary endeavor succeeds.

The United States has worked hard in the last year to help to establish an electoral process which is proceeding. We have worked hard to try to establish a system of law and order which is making progress. But in the end, the Foreign Minister and all of the people in her government and President Aristide have to be able to prove that freedom and democracy can bring the benefits that we know it can bring.

And Haiti was plundered for a very long time. It has been environmentally ravaged. When I went back to Haiti for the first time since my wife and I went there in December of 1975, I was literally shocked to see the deterioration of the environment, the topsoil running thin, and all of the things that had happened.

We all have a lot of work to do there. And in the end, we have to make it possible for the people of Haiti who are willing to work and learn and grow to compose a life, to stabilize their families, to live out their dreams. And we have a lot more work to do there.

So I ask you to celebrate this extraordinary evening by reaffirming your determination to help the people who live there keep their democracy alive and bring its benefits to ordinary citizens, to infuse new investment, to create new jobs, to develop a sustainable economic program while restoring the environment, to do all those things that they might have done for themselves had they had a longer period of time free of oppression.

I must say that when I went to Haiti, I was very moved by what I saw, by the spirit of the people and the openness to the possibilities of the future. But we all know that the future is not free of difficulties.

So if you are still today as firmly convinced as you were a year ago that this is the right thing to do, if you feel as deeply proud today as you did a year ago, then you have to make your convictions good by making sure that we do not fail in this common endeavor, that democracy ultimately triumphs, that freedom is ultimately the victor, and that there is some prosperity for those good people who have suffered too long, borne too much, and now have to have our continued partnership to build the kind of future that all of us want for ourselves, our families, and our children. I know we can do it but we must get about it, and we must stay with it until the job is done.

Thank you, good luck, and God bless you all.

NOTE: The President spoke at 7:10 p.m. at the Organization of American States. In his remarks, he referred to Secretary General Cesar Gavirio of the Organization of American States; Foreign Minister Claudette Werleigh of Haiti; Prime Minister Kennedy Simmonds of St. Kitts and Nevis; author Taylor Branch; Special Adviser on Haiti William H. Gray III; Randall Robinson, executive director, TransAfrica Forum; movie director Jonathan Demme; President Jean-Bertrand Aristide of Haiti; and Maj. Gen. George A. Fisher, USA, Commander, 25th Infantry Division.

Remarks to the Business Council in Williamsburg, Virginia
October 13, 1995

Thank you very much. The last time I was with the Woolards we were in Jackson Hole, Wyoming, in the Grand Tetons. And this outfit would have been highly inappropriate there. I felt more at home, but I saw Ed tonight and I kind of—I'm jealous of the beautiful shirt. I want to know where you got it. [*Laughter*] I'm so glad to see all of you. I know some of our administration members have been here—Secretary Rubin, who feels right at home.

I still can't believe Bob Rubin is a Democrat. [*Laughter*] He told me not very long ago we were going to have to change the currency to avoid counterfeiting. And I said, "Well, all right." And he said, "But I want to start with $100 bills." [*Laughter*] So that's where we started. I have reviewed a little bit about who spoke here today and what they said, and, Ed, if Hugh Sidey really said that, he must have been awful tough on the people who are running against me. [*Laughter*]

I want to talk to you tonight about, obviously, about the major controversy presently raging in Washington about the balanced budget. But I want to try to set the stage for what this really means and what's really going on. And I'd like to begin with what I think is the most important thing, which is what kind of country we live in and what kind of country we wish to live in and what kind of country we wish to leave for our children and our grandchildren. That, after all, is the most important thing of all.

When I sought this job in 1992, I did it because I wanted to restore the American dream for all of our people and because I wanted this country to go into the next century still as the world's leader for freedom and peace and prosperity and democracy. Because I really believe that we're all better off in a country where people have opportunity but exercise responsibility, where we strengthen work but we also strengthen our families, and where we recognize that the real power in America should be at the community level where people work together and where they deal with each other directly, instead of through the filters that exist between me and Washington and you where you live.

This is a remarkable period of success for America's economy. All of you are doing a remarkable job. We've had a great 2½ years. And I believe there are better times ahead if we make the right decisions. It's a time of profound change. We're moving from the industrial to the information and technology age. We've moved out of the cold war into a global marketplace. We have problems, to be sure, but they're nowhere near as great as the opportunities we have.

When I sought the Presidency, I said that I wanted to do three things: I wanted to restore pro-growth economics. I wanted to put mainstream values back at the heart of our social policy. And I wanted to give America a modern Government that was more entrepreneurial and smaller and gave more authority to the State and local governments, to the private sector, and operated more as a partner with others to build a better America.

I said then, and I believe I have been true to this, that I wanted to see new ideas injected into our political life, everything from welfare reform to national service to empowerment zones for our inner cities to the reinventing Government program that the Vice President has done such a good job with. I said I would make a good-faith effort to move beyond the partisan labels that had divided people so much in the past. And believe it or not, I have done my best to do that. It's a lot harder in Washington than it is in the State capitals and the cities of the country, but it can be done and it will be done again, I believe, in the next few weeks.

I also believed then and I believe more strongly now that in a time of change, it's important that the President make decisions based on their long-term impact as opposed to their short-term benefits or burdens.

Now, if you look at the last 2½ years, you must all be very proud. Our country has produced 7½ million jobs, 2½ million new homeowners, about 2 million new small business owners, the largest number of new small businesses in such a time period in the history of the United States, a record number of new self-made millionaires. Trade has increased in the last 3 years from 4 percent in '93, 10 percent in '94, and it's going up 16 percent this year— our exports. The deficit has come from $290 billion a year down to $160 billion a year.

Of course, there are still problems. In any period of profound change, there tends to be a big disruption and a significant problem of income inequality. We have that in America. We need to get more energy and growth back into middle class families' incomes. We have still some isolated areas in our country that have not felt the benefits of this recovery. And I believe that the budget proposal now in Congress would undermine our economic growth in the future unless it's modified significantly, and I'll say more about that in a moment.

I think the policies of this administration have made a contribution to that economic record by reducing the deficit; by expanding trade through NAFTA and GATT and taking all those outdated cold war controls off of our high technology exports; by concluding over 80 trade agreements through the efforts of Ambassador

Kantor, including 15 with Japan alone; by investing in technology, research and development, and defense conversion; and by working with so many of you to manifest the real commitment to the education of all Americans, more money but also higher standards, higher expectations, and more accountability in education.

If you look at the question of our social problems and whether we've been successful in putting middle class values into our approach, you can all be somewhat hopeful there. The crime rate is down in almost every place in America. The murder rate is down. The welfare rolls are down. The food stamp rolls are down. The poverty rate is down. The teen pregnancy rate has gone down for 2 years in a row. Americans are reasserting their beliefs in old-fashioned personal, family, and community responsibility. And it is beginning to work.

Yes, we have some problems. We still need to pass a national welfare reform plan, I believe. We still need to avoid the tendency that's now alive in Congress to believe that all you need to do on the crime problem is to put people in jail and we don't need anything to do with prevention and giving our young people something to say yes to. But basically we are moving in the right direction to reassert and reinsert into American life mainstream values.

And I believe the initiatives of our administration have played a role in that: The crime bill, which is putting 100,000 more police on the street, keeping repeat offenders off the street; passing the Brady bill; passing the assault weapons ban; doing things that enable our local communities to help prevent crimes. I think it's making a difference.

I believe the work we've done in what the New York Times called "a quiet revolution" in welfare—our administration has given 35 States over 40 separate approvals to get around Federal rules and regulations to move people from welfare to work. When the Congress wouldn't pass the bill, we just decided to reform welfare State by State, community by community. We have offered all 50 States within any 30-day period a complete relief from any number of Federal rules and regulations if they will present a comprehensive plan to move people from welfare to work without hurting their children.

I think when we almost doubled the family tax credit that President Reagan said was the best antipoverty program the country had ever come up with, so that we can now say that anybody who works 40 hours a week and has children in the home will not live in poverty, that was a major step toward rewarding work and family and helping us to reform welfare and get people out of welfare into the work rolls.

I think the national service program is an important advance. We celebrated its first year yesterday with a young woman from Kansas City who's working her way through college from an inner-city neighborhood in Kansas City with a project of young volunteers who have closed 44 crack houses in Kansas City in the last year. And this is the kind of thing being done by these young people all over America, whether they're building houses with Habitat for Humanity, tutoring kids in rural Kentucky where they have increased the grade level in reading by threefold in one year, or helping to fight the crime problem.

All these things manifest our values. And something I know that means a lot to all of you, we have tried to give the American people a more modern Government. The size of the Federal Government tonight when I left Washington was 163,000 smaller than it was the day I became President. It's the smallest Federal Government since John Kennedy was President. We will reduce it by another 110,000 in the next 2 years, no matter what the Congress does with this budget. This Government as a percentage of the civilian nonfarm payroll is the smallest Government the United States has had in Washington since 1933.

Now, those are facts. We've reduced 16,000 pages of regulations, cut the regulations of the Small Business Administration by 50 percent, the regulations of the Education Department by 40 percent. Next year, the paperwork time that businesses spend fooling with the Environmental Protection Agency will be down by 25 percent.

More important than all that to me, I think our Government's working better. The Small Business Administration has cut its budget by 40 percent and doubled its loan output. The Export-Import Bank is helping small businesses that never knew what it was before to sell their products all around the world. The Commerce Department and the State Department have done more good for American businesses overseas than any Commerce Department and State Department in modern history. And every one of you who has worked with them knows that

that is the absolute truth. We are moving forward to give you a Government that works.

The automobile industry has been working with us in partnership to produce a clean car. It is a big deal. Nineteen ninety-five was the hottest year for the planet Earth since the present temperature system was devised. China is growing rapidly. If everybody in China winds up with a car and you don't want the atmosphere of this Earth to burn up, we had better find an efficient way of moving people around. And this is the sort of thing that we're trying to do.

Now, let me tell you this; this will probably surprise you more than anything. Every year, Business Week—hardly an arm of the Democratic Party or of my administration—recognizes outstanding businesses for performance in various categories. This year in the category of service to consumers by telephone, the winner was not L.L. Bean or Federal Express but the Social Security Administration of your Federal Government. So I think that we have made a contribution to modernizing the Federal Government. It's smaller. It's less bureaucratic. It is more entrepreneurial. It still has dumb things in the rules, and it does dumb things that drive me crazy that I find out about after it's over. But it is better than it was before by a very, very long shot.

The most important thing is, we're trying to help move decisions back where people make them. The mayor of Chicago is here. Chicago received one of our empowerment zones, a new idea helping to attract private investment into inner cities to grow the economy and give people a stake in America's future. Chicago received more funds for police not because we know how to prevent crime, but they do, if they have the means to do it, and funds for prevention to support programs like the ones in Chicago that have lowered the crime rate, even though they make fodder for congressional speeches like midnight basketball. Better a kid on a basketball court than on a corner selling drugs or mugging somebody and winding up in jail. We didn't make the decisions; they make the decisions at the local level.

We finally passed a bill to stop mandating costs on State and local governments that we don't help them pay for. These are the kinds of things that are going on. We are moving in the right direction, your country is, and you ought to be proud of it.

And America has been gratified to be a part of making peace in the Middle East, progress in Northern Ireland, the cease-fire in Bosnia, making sure that for the first time since the dawn of the nuclear age there aren't any missiles pointed at Americans or their children tonight. North Korea is moving away from its nuclear program, and, by the grace of God, we might get a comprehensive test ban treaty on all nuclear testing next year. We seem to be headed in that direction.

Now, what does the future hold? First, we do have to balance the budget. It's the right thing to do to take the burden of debt off our children and free up capital for private sector investment. I'm really proud of the fact that way over 90 percent of the new jobs created in this recovery were created not by Government but in the private sector. That is exactly what we wanted to happen. So as we reduce the size of Government, the private sector is growing more. We have to do it, but we have to do it consistent with our values and with our interests.

The second thing we have to do is to expand trade. We have our friends here from the Americas. Mack McLarty, who's here with me, worked so hard last December on the Summit of the Americas. And we have worked to follow up on that. We believe that our partners in this hemisphere are a very, very important part of our future. We believe we have to build on NAFTA until we have partnerships with all these democratic governments, to reward their moves to democracy, to freedom, to market economics with a genuine and respectful partnership with the United States.

In that connection, I say I was very well pleased with the remarkable visit I just had with the President of Mexico and the fact that they have already paid back $700 million of the loan they received through our international financial package ahead of schedule, being faithful to their commitment to modernize Mexico politically and economically.

We have to continue to invest in technology and make it our friend, not our foe. People cannot afford to be afraid of the technological revolution that is sweeping the world. We just have to make sure that everybody can have access to it. And we have to give people the tools they need to succeed.

In that connection, let me say I am very grateful for the support that we've gotten from the business community for every education initiative of our administration, from expanding Head Start to the Goals 2000 program, which focuses on national standards and grassroots reforms, to the expansion of student loans.

And just a couple of days ago—I know the Secretary of Labor said this earlier, but I want to emphasize this because it achieved almost no public notice, largely because there were only two votes against this bill in the Senate, and when there's no controversy, it is often deemed not important. But with no controversy, a couple of days ago, the United States Senate adopted what I thought was one of the most important new ideas that I advocated in the State of the Union message: the "GI bill" for America's workers, consolidating 70 separate, marginally impacting Federal training programs into a big fund and saying to unemployed people, we will just send you a voucher, we will send you a voucher if you lose your job and you can immediately take it to the nearest community college and begin to start your life again.

Now, that's very important. A lot of you pay a lot of unemployment tax. The unemployment system today is not relevant to the times in which we live. When the unemployment system in America was developed, 85 percent of the people were called back to the jobs they were laid off from. Today, 85 percent of the people who are laid off are never called back to those jobs. If we want people to feel secure about the future, to have a stake in the future, we have to increase their sense of empowerment about it. That's what this "GI bill" for America's workers will do. It's a very important idea, and we ought to stick with it and support it and properly fund it.

Now, let me say something in all candor. To have—if we're going to continue to move forward in a time of change, you have to expect the leadership of the country to do what you have to do in a time of change, and that's to make decisions that are unpopular in the short run because they're right over the long run. Now, I have found as an elected official that everybody is for that in general, but they're against it in particular. And let me just give you some examples of the kind of things I've faced. I bet I've done five things that have made everybody in this room mad in the last 2½ years, at least five. But I want to give you a few.

When I became President I knew, based on my conversations with Mr. Greenspan, with people in the private markets, with others, that if we could reduce the deficit at least $500 billion in 5 years, we'd get a big drop in interest rates and a big boom in this economy. I knew that. And I knew, conversely, if we failed to do it that we would continue to lengthen the sluggish economy which I confronted when I took office. So I made up my mind, come hell or high water, we were going to reduce the deficit $500 billion. In the first week I showed up in Washington, the leaders of the minority in Congress, who are now the majority leader and the Speaker of the House, told me that I would not get one vote for my budget no matter what I did, not a single, solitary vote. The policy was going to be "just say no."

As a consequence, I had to raise your taxes more and cut spending less than I wanted to, which made a lot of you furious. All I know is, we got a huge drop in the interest rates and a big boom in the economy, and most everybody who paid more made more than they paid. And it was the right thing for the United States. It was wrong for them to refuse to cooperate with me, but they were richly rewarded for it later on. But our country is better off because we passed a deficit reduction plan which, over a 7-year period, is about as big as the one we're debating in the Congress today. And that's what got this country going again. And we did it without cutting education or investment in technology or the environment or our future.

I'll give you another example that affects the mayor here. When we were debating the Brady bill to require people to wait 5 days before they got a handgun, and the assault weapons ban, all my political advisers said, "Don't do this; this is crazy." And I said, "Why do you think it's crazy?" And they said, "Because everybody that's against this will vote against everybody who's for it, but all the people that are for it, they'll find some other reason to oppose you."

That's why things don't get done in your country, because organized interests and their intense opposition always overcome the generalized feeling of good will, which is not manifest in the same intensity of support. But you know what? Last year 40,000 people with criminal records did not get handguns because of the Brady law. And it was the right thing to do.

And I am tired of picking up the newspaper and seeing kids that are honor students in school getting shot down standing at bus stops by nuts with assault weapons. And by election time next time, every hunter in my State will know that nobody lost their hunting rifle and it was all a big canard, there was nothing to it. But people are alive today because those decisions were made.

The teenage smoking initiative—the same thing. Same folks came and said, "Oh, don't do this. By the time the tobacco companies get through working on you, they'll convince every tobacco farmer in North Carolina and Tennessee that you're going to drive them in the poorhouse; they all vote against everybody with a "D" behind their name; they will bury you. And everybody in America that agrees with you will find some other reason not to support you. This is dumb politics." Well, it might be. But we studied that issue for 14 months. We found out two companies knew for 30 years what they were doing and kept on doing it and didn't own up to it. We found out that there were still deliberate attempts to advertise to young people. And most important, we found out that 3,000 kids a day start smoking and 1,000 of them are going to die sooner because of it. I don't know what you think a thousand kids a day are worth, but to me, that's the kind of America I want to live in, where another thousand kids a day have longer, better, fuller lives because somebody doesn't sucker-punch them into doing something they shouldn't do while they are still children. So it may be unpopular, but I think it was the right thing to do.

The same thing—something where most of you agree with me, I think—the affirmative action issue. Everybody said, "Oh, you don't need to—you need to be against this; we need to stop this." But there is still racial discrimination in America, folks. When five Federal law enforcement officials can't even get served in Denny's, there's a problem there. And I could give you a lot of other examples.

I don't favor unfair preferences or quotas or reverse discrimination. Our administration has actually joined lawsuits against reverse discrimination in States. But everybody has to be considered in this country. The great meal ticket we've got for the future is that this is the most diverse, big, rich country in the world. Los Angeles County has 150 different racial and ethnic groups in one county. In the global village, it is a manna from heaven. But we have to learn to live together and work together with common values and a common chance to succeed. So we said, let's mend affirmative action, but let's don't end it. And I hope and believe it made it possible for the people who lead large companies in our country to follow the same policies.

I could give you lots of other examples, but you get the idea. When you're going through a period of change like this, you can't even predict what's going to be popular.

Last night we celebrated one year of the restoration of democracy in Haiti. Well, when we threw the dictators out of Haiti, hardly anybody was for it. But it was the right thing to do. You can't let dictators come to the United States and stand in the shadow of the Statue of Liberty and promise they're going to leave and then go home and keep killing people in the street and never even blink an eye. The United States couldn't do that.

When we helped our friends and neighbors in Mexico, most of you probably supported that. But the day I made the decision, there was a poll in the paper that said by 81 to 15 the American people were opposed to that. Half the people in the country who were for it were in the room at the time I decided to do it. [*Laughter*] But it was the right thing to do, because they're our neighbors, because they want to do the right thing, because they have the capacity to grow and become our strong partners and generate opportunities for you and incomes and jobs for America, because our real future here, no matter what happens to the movement toward free trade, is with our friends here in our backyard, in our neighborhood.

So I would ask all of you as people who have to make difficult decisions to expect people who lead your governmental institutions to do the same thing and to be perfectly willing to be held accountable for the consequences of them.

And that brings me to the budget issue. Let me say what this is not about, this squabble in Washington. It is not—I say again—it is not about balancing the budget. There are two plans to balance the budget, both of which have been blessed as perfectly credible by every neutral observer.

Our plan would, now we know, would balance the budget in 9 years and continue to increase investment in education, research and development, technology, and the environment. It would invest enough in things like the Commerce Department, the State Department, and our aid programs to maintain our world leadership, which is very important. You see what happens when we have a chance to exercise it. It would lengthen the life of the Medicare Trust Fund just as much as the Republican budget. It would slow the rate of medical inflation but not as much as their budget. Why? Because nobody I know in the health care field believes that we can take $450 billion out of Medicare and Medicaid over the next 7 years, based on what we now know, without causing serious problems to the medical schools of the country, to the children's hospitals of the country, to the ability of the elderly poor to get into nursing homes or their middle class children to have them there and afford to educate their children, and devastating problems to our ability to care for the over 20 percent of America's children who are so poor they qualify for medical assistance under the Medicaid program.

We do have to slow the rate of medical inflation. I've been working at this for 2 years. We do have to bail out the Medicare Trust Fund. But we have to recognize that we have to listen to the people who do this for a living and have some sense of the practical implications of how much we can cut. My budget has a tax cut, but it's smaller than the congressional one. The congressional budget balances the budget in 7 years. It cuts education, research and development, technology, investment in the environment. It drastically cuts back on our ability to exercise world leadership through the Commerce Department, the State Department, and the aid programs. The tax cut they offer is bigger, and there's a big tax increase on the lower income working poor—a big one.

I think one of our values ought to be to grow the middle class and shrink the under class. I think it's not a very good idea, on the edge of the 21st century, to grow the under class and shrink the middle class. That is not my idea of what kind of country I want my child and her children to grow up in.

So, can we resolve this? You bet we can. Here's the practical thing; this is what I want to ask you to do. There are four or five big issues where there's a lot of money involved. One is, we differ on how much we estimate we'll grow. I picked a conservative figure, 2½ percent, because that's what the economy has

grown for the last 25 years. They said, "Oh, no, we're not going to grow that fast." Well, why are we balancing the budget and giving a capital gains tax cut and doing all this stuff if we think we're going to get lower growth than we've had for the last 25 years?

I don't want to argue it either way, but I mean, I think my growth estimate is not a rosy scenario, it is lower than what a lot of you pay for. The blue chip forecast is for a higher economic growth and, therefore, more revenues than I estimate.

Then we are arguing about the rate of medical inflation. Then there's the question of whether we should reassign or redesign and recalculate the amount of inflation in the Consumer Price Index, which determines how much we increase Social Security and retirement. And we're talking about the size of the tax cut.

We can work this out, folks. The only thing I won't do—I will not do this—I will not let balancing the budget serve as a cover for destroying the social compact, for cutting back on education, wrecking the environment, or undermining our obligations to help protect our children and treat our elderly people decently, because it is not necessary to balance the budget.

Now, I don't want you to take my side or theirs on any of these big questions. Here's what I'm asking you to do. What I want is to get together with the Congress and get a budget out that is an honorable compromise that is better than theirs and better than mine. That's the best kind of get-together, where everybody puts their ideas together and you come out with something that's better than what anybody had. I'm not the source of all wisdom. But I know this: There's not a single one of you looking at the 21st century and the position of your company that would knowingly cut back on research and development or investment in technology or education and training. You wouldn't do it, not if you didn't have to, and we don't have to.

So all I'm asking you to do is to say, "Just get together; come up with something. If you do it in good faith, it will be better than the President's budget, and it will be better than the Congress' budget. Because when people get together, that's what they do."

I am prepared to make some decisions that I think are right over the long run, and I believe they are. There is no earthly reason why we shouldn't do this. America needs and deserves a balanced budget. America needs and deserves a balanced budget consistent with our values that will give us the kind of world that we would be proud to have our children and our grandchildren and their children grow up in.

This country is doing well, and it's going to do better. And a lot of it is because of what you are doing. And a lot of it is because of what mayors are doing all over the country. And a lot of it is because of what plain old American citizens are doing. We are moving in the right direction. And there is no country on Earth better positioned to do well in the 21st century than the United States of America. And ironically, all we have to do to get there, I believe, is to be faithful to our basic values and what we know is right.

That's a commitment I make to you. And I'm asking you tonight to do what you can, because you have more influence with most of those folks than I do, to make sure that we get together and do this, do it right, do it for America, and do it for the future.

Thank you very much.

NOTE: The President spoke at 7:34 p.m. at the Williamsburg Inn. In his remarks, he referred to Edgar Woolard, chairman and CEO, E.I. Dupont de Nemours & Co., Inc., and author and journalist Hugh Sidey.

The President's Radio Address
October 14, 1995

Good morning. In recent weeks, all of us have had reason to focus on two of the biggest problems facing our country: the problem of continuing racial divisions and the problem of violence in our homes, violence against women and children.

Today, I want to talk to you about that violence in our homes. It is prevalent, unforgivable, and sometimes deadly. In the latest statistics from the Justice Department, we find that close to a third of all women murdered in this country were killed by their husbands, former husbands, or boyfriends.

For too long, domestic violence has been swept under the rug, treated as a private family matter that was nobody's business but those involved. Fortunately, that's changing. In recent years, a huge public outcry against domestic violence has been rising all across the Nation. In our churches, schools, and throughout communities, we've begun to bring this problem out in the open and deal with it. Now everyone knows it is cowardly, destructive of families, immoral, and criminal to abuse the women in our families.

Just last week at the White House, I met with a group of women who are survivors of domestic abuse. One woman told me of being battered and terrorized for more than 20 years, all the while blaming herself for the brutality she endured. It wasn't until her husband attacked her son that she got up the courage to leave the marriage and to seek help.

It's important to remember that when children witness or are victimized by violence in the home, they often later grow up to abuse their own families. So it can become a vicious cycle, as many abusers were once those abused themselves.

The good news is we can do something about this. The same day I met with the women survivors, I also met a remarkable Nashville police sergeant named Mark Wynn, a young man who himself grew up in a home where his father abused his mother and the children. But that experience motivated him to become a police officer and to dedicate his life to preventing domestic violence. For the past 10 years, he's been educating police nationwide about the seriousness of this problem and what to do about it. And he spearheaded the creation of a special domestic violence unit in the Nashville Police Department that has helped to reduce domestic murders by 70 percent in the last 6 months alone.

One year ago, we made a major commitment in Washington to ensuring the securities of our families with the bipartisan passage of my anticrime bill. That law banned assault weapons from our streets and our schools, imposed tougher penalties for repeat offenders, including the "three strikes and you're out" law. It provided resources for community-based prevention programs to give our children something to say yes to. And it put 100,000 more police officers behind our efforts at effective community policing. That's an increase of about 20 percent in the number of police who are protecting our citizens. In just a year, 25,000 of these new officers are already out there working to help make your life safer. And I've put aside $20 million to train our police to effectively deal with the problems of domestic violence.

The crime bill also included the landmark Violence Against Women Act. For the first time in our history, the Federal Government is now a full partner in the effort to stop domestic violence. The Violence Against Women Act combines tough new sanctions against abusers with assistance to police, to prosecutors, and to shelters in the fight against domestic violence.

Just last week, we awarded grants to organizations in 16 different States to assist in their efforts to stop the violence and support the victims. And soon we'll establish an 800 number where women facing abuse can get assistance, counseling, and shelter.

Yet at the very moment our Nation has been focused on the abuse against women by their husbands—or former husbands or boyfriends— the House of Representatives has voted to cut $50 million from our efforts to protect battered women and their children, to preserve families, and to punish these crimes. I'm happy that the Senate agreed with me to fully fund the Violence Against Women Act, and I certainly hope the House will reconsider its decision.

Violence against women within our families will not go away unless we all take responsibility for ending it. So let me close today by speaking directly to the men of America, not just as President or a father or a husband but also as a son who has seen domestic violence firsthand.

We all know how much we owe to the sacrifices of the women who are our mothers, our wives, our sisters, our daughters. I was fortunate enough to be raised by a loving mother who taught me right from wrong and made me believe I could accomplish anything I was willing to work hard for. Hillary and I were blessed to celebrate our 20th wedding anniversary just this week. And of course, our daughter Chelsea is the great joy of our lives.

I know that all of us support stronger law enforcement efforts to deal with violence against all of the mothers, all of the wives, all of the daughters in America. But the real solution to this problem starts with us, with our personal responsibility and a simple pledge that we will never, never lift a hand against a woman for as long as we live and that we will teach our children that violence is never the answer. Then we can do all we can to end violence in our homes, in our neighborhoods, and in everyone else's homes and neighborhoods throughout our beloved country.

Thank you for listening.

NOTE: The address was recorded at 1:48 p.m. on October 13 in the Roosevelt Room at the White House for broadcast at 10:06 a.m. on October 14.

Remarks at the Dedication of the Thomas J. Dodd Archives and Research Center in Storrs, Connecticut
October 15, 1995

Thank you very much, President Hartley. Governor Rowland; Senator Lieberman, Members of Congress, and distinguished United States Senators and former Senators who have come today; Chairman Rome; members of the Diplomatic Corps; to all of you who have done anything to make this great day come to pass; to my friend and former colleague Governor O'Neill; and most of all, to Senator Dodd, Am-

bassador Dodd, and the Dodd family: I am delighted to be here.

I have so many thoughts now. I can't help mentioning one. Since President Hartley mentioned the day we had your magnificent women's basketball team there, we also had the UCLA men's team there. You may not remember who UCLA defeated for the national championship—[*laughter*]—but I do remember that UConn defeated the University of Tennessee.

And that made my life with Al Gore much more bearable. [*Laughter*] So I was doubly pleased when UConn won the national championship.

I also did not know until it was stated here at the outset of this ceremony that no sitting President had the privilege of coming to the University of Connecticut before, but they don't know what they missed. I'm glad to be the first, and I know I won't be the last.

I also want to pay a special public tribute to the Dodd family for their work on this enterprise and for their devotion to each other and the memory of Senator Thomas Dodd. If, as so many of us believe, this country rests in the end upon its devotion to freedom and liberty and democracy and upon the strength of its families, you could hardly find a better example than the Dodd family, not only for their devotion to liberty and democracy but also for their devotion to family and to the memory of Senator Tom Dodd. It has deeply moved all of us, and we thank you for your example.

Tom Dodd spent his life serving America. He demonstrated an extraordinary commitment to the rule of law, beginning with his early days as an FBI agent, then Federal attorney. He was equally passionate in his opposition to tyranny in all its forms. He fought the tyranny of racism, prosecuting civil rights cases in the South in the 1930's, long before it was popular anywhere in the United States, and helping to shepherd the landmark Civil Rights Act of 1964 into law. He fought the tyranny of communism throughout his years in elected office. And while he bowed to none in his devotion to freedom, he also stood bravely against those who wrapped themselves in the flag and turned anticommunism into demagoguery.

Tom Dodd was in so many ways a man ahead of his time. He was passionate about civil rights three decades before the civil rights movement changed the face of our Nation. In the Senate, he pioneered programs to fight delinquency and to give the young people of our country a chance at a good education and a good job. And that is a task, my fellow Americans, we have not yet finished doing. He saw the dangers of guns and drugs on our streets, and he acted to do something about that. Had we done it in his time, we would not have so much work to do in this time.

Tom Dodd's passion for justice and his hatred of oppression came together, as all of you know, most powerfully when he served as America's executive trial counsel at the Nuremberg War Crimes Tribunal. It was the pivotal event of his life. He helped to bring justice to bear against those responsible for the Holocaust, for the acts that redefined our understanding of man's capacity for evil. Through that pathbreaking work, he and his fellow jurists pushed one step forward the historic effort to bring the crimes of war under the sanction of law.

Senator Dodd left many good works and reminders of his achievement. Some bear his name, the children who have followed in his steps and served the public, who carried forward his ardent support for an American foreign policy that stands for democracy and freedom, who maintain his commitment to social justice, to strong communities and strong families. They have also upheld their father's tradition of loyalty. And as one of the chief beneficiaries of that lesson, let me say that I am grateful for it and again grateful for its expression in this remarkable project which will help the people of Connecticut and the United States to understand their history.

I am delighted that this center will bear the Dodd name because it is fitting that a library, a place that keeps and honors books and records, will honor Tom Dodd's service, his passion for justice, and his hatred of tyranny. Where books are preserved, studied, and revered, human beings will also be treated with respect and dignity and liberty will be strengthened.

Dedicating this research center today, we remember that when the Nazis came to power, one of the very first things they did was burn books they deemed subversive. The road to tyranny, we must never forget, begins with the destruction of the truth.

In the darkest days of the war, President Roosevelt, with those awful bonfires fresh in his memory, reflected upon how the free pursuit of knowledge protects our liberty, and he put it well when he called books "the weapons for man's freedom." I am glad that Tom Dodd will be remembered here, in this place, in this building, with this center, in the State he loved, with the very best arsenal for the freedom he fought to defend his entire life.

Thank you very much.

NOTE: The President spoke at 1:40 p.m. at the University of Connecticut. In his remarks, he referred to Harry Hartley, president, and Lewis

Rome, chairman, University of Connecticut; and Gov. John G. Rowland and former Gov. William A. O'Neill of Connecticut.

Remarks at the University of Connecticut in Storrs
October 15, 1995

Thank you very much, first, Senator Dodd, for your dedication and your service, your friendship, and your wonderful, wonderful introduction. It's worth three more strokes the next time we play golf. [*Laughter*] Chairman Rome, President Hartley, Governor Rowland, Senator Lieberman, members of the congressional delegation, and especially your Congressman, Representative Gejdenson, thank you for your fine remarks here today. To the State officials who are here and the Senators and former Members of the United States Senate; to my friend Governor O'Neill and all others who have served this great State; the faculty, students, and friends of the University of Connecticut; and to the remarkable American treasure, Morton Gould, who composed that awesome piece of music we heard just before we started the program.

Ladies and gentlemen, I am delighted to be here. As an old musician, I'd like to begin by congratulating the wind ensemble. They were quite wonderful in every way, I thought. As a near fanatic basketball fan, I am glad to be in a place where it can truly be said there is no other place in America where both men and women play basketball so well under the same roof. And at the risk of offending the Dodd family and all the other Irish who are here, I want to say that your new football coach, with his remarkable record, learned at his father's knee, not at Notre Dame but when he spent 9 years in my home State as a football coach. [*Laughter*] But congratulations on that great start for the University of Connecticut football team. That is a remarkable thing.

When Governor Rowland made his fine remarks and talked about the Special Olympians turning their cameras around and turning their camera sighting into the telescope, I thought it was a remarkable story. And I was wondering if he could identify them and arrange to send them to Washington for a few weeks—[*laugh-*

ter]—so that we might clear vision down there as we make these decisions.

Let me also say just one other thing by way of introduction. The State of Connecticut is really fortunate to have two such remarkable United States Senators, and I am very fortunate to have known both of them a long, long time before I became the President and a long, long time before either one of them thought that was even a remote possibility for the United States. [*Laughter*]

I was a student at Yale Law School and a sometime volunteer when Joe Lieberman first ran for the State senate back in 1970. He still barely looks old enough to be a State senator. [*Laughter*] And I thank him for the remarkable blend of new ideas and common sense and old-fashioned values he brings to the Senate.

And in many, many ways I have enjoyed a long and rich personal friendship with Chris Dodd. I can't add anything to what Senator Lieberman said, but I will say this: At a time when every person in public life talks about family values, it is quite one thing to talk and another thing to do. And I have been very moved by the family values of the Dodd family and what they have done together that has brought this magnificent day to pass. And I honor them all and especially my friend Senator Chris Dodd.

I have been asked today to inaugurate the first Dodd center symposium on the topic of "50 Years After Nuremberg." I am honored to do that. I was born just after World War II, and I grew up as a part of a generation of young students who were literally fascinated by every aspect of the Nuremberg trials and what their ramifications were and were not for every unfolding event in the world that was disturbing to human conscience.

I wish that Tom Dodd could be here today to see this center take life, not only because of what his family and friends and this State have done but because now, for all time, we will be able to study this great question as we strive to overcome human evil and human failing to be better.

Senator Dodd, as we know, was a man of extraordinary breadth and depth, who was passionate about civil rights three decades before the civil rights movement changed the face of our Nation; who fought to provide the young people of America with an education and a decent job, a fight that is never-ending; who understood then the menace of violence and guns and drugs on the streets of our cities. And if only others had joined him firmly then, think what we might have avoided today.

But most important, we look today at his experience at Nuremberg as a prosecutor, an experience that compelled him for the rest of his life to stand up for freedom and human dignity all around the world. He made a great deal of difference. And now, because his spirit lives on in the Dodd center, he will be able to make a difference forever.

A few moments ago, in the powerful documentary we watched on Nuremberg, our chief prosecutor, Mr. Justice Jackson's words spoke to us across three decades: "The wrongs which we seek to condemn and punish have been so calculated, so malignant, and so devastating, that civilization cannot tolerate their being ignored because it cannot survive their being repeated."

At Nuremberg, the international community declared that those responsible for crimes against humanity will be held accountable without the usual defenses afforded to people in times of war. The very existence of the Tribunal was a triumph for justice and for humanity and for the proposition that there must be limits even in wartime. Flush with victory, outraged by the evil of the Nazi death camps, the Allies easily could have simply lashed out in revenge. But the terrible struggle of World War II was a struggle for the very soul of humankind. To deny its oppressors the rights they had stripped from their victims would have been to win the war but to lose the larger struggle. The Allies understood that the only answer to inhumanity is justice. And as Senator Dodd said, three of the defendants were actually acquitted, even in that tumultuous, passionate environment.

In the years since Nuremberg, the hope that convicting those guilty of making aggressive war would deter future wars and prevent future crimes against humanity, including genocide,

frankly, has gone unfulfilled too often. From 1945 until the present day, wars between and within nations, including practices which were found to be illegal at Nuremberg, have cost more than 20 million lives. The wrongs Justice Jackson hoped Nuremberg would end have not been repeated on the scale of Nazi Germany, in the way that they did it, but they have been repeated and repeated on a scale that still staggers the imagination.

Still, Nuremberg was a crucial first step. It rendered a clear verdict on atrocities. It placed human rights on a higher ground. It set a timeless precedent by stripping away convenient excuses for abominable conduct. Now it falls to our generation to make good on its promise, to put into practice the principle that those who violate universal human rights must be called to account for those actions.

This mission demands the abiding commitment of all people. And like many of the other challenges of our time, it requires the power of our Nation's example and the strength of our leadership, first, because America was founded on the proposition that all God's children have the right to life, liberty, and the pursuit of happiness. These are values that define us as a nation, but they are not unique to our experience. All over the world, from Russia to South Africa, from Poland to Cambodia, people have been willing to fight and to die for them.

Second, we have to do it because, while fascism and communism are dead or discredited, the forces of hatred and intolerance live on as they will for as long as human beings are permitted to exist on this planet Earth. Today, it is ethnic violence, religious strife, terrorism. These threats confront our generation in a way that still would spread darkness over light, disintegration over integration, chaos over community. Our purpose is to fight them, to defeat them, to support and sustain the powerful worldwide aspirations of democracy, dignity, and freedom.

And finally, we must do it because, in the aftermath of the cold war, we are the world's only superpower. We have to do it because while we seek to do everything we possibly can in the world in cooperation with other nations, they find it difficult to proceed in cooperation if we are not there as a partner and very often as a leader.

With our purpose and with our position comes the responsibility to help shine the light of justice on those who would deny to others their most basic human rights. We have an obligation to carry forward the lessons of Nuremberg. That is why we strongly support the United Nations War Crimes Tribunals for the former Yugoslavia and for Rwanda.

The goals of these tribunals are straightforward: to punish those responsible for genocide, war crimes, and crimes against humanity; to deter future such crimes; and to help nations that were torn apart by violence begin the process of healing and reconciliation.

The tribunal for the former Yugoslavia has made excellent progress. It has collected volumes of evidence of atrocities, including the establishment of death camps, mass executions, and systematic campaigns of rape and terror. This evidence is the basis for the indictments the tribunal already has issued against 43 separate individuals. And this week, 10 witnesses gave dramatic, compelling testimony against one of the indictees in a public proceeding. These indictments are not negotiable. Those accused of war crimes, crimes against humanity, and genocide must be brought to justice. They must be tried and, if found guilty, they must be held accountable. Some people are concerned that pursuing peace in Bosnia and prosecuting war criminals are incompatible goals. But I believe they are wrong. There must be peace for justice to prevail, but there must be justice when peace prevails.

In recent weeks, the combination of American leadership, NATO's resolve, the international community's diplomatic determination: these elements have brought us closer to a settlement in Bosnia than at any time since the war began there 4 years ago.

So let me repeat again what I have said consistently for over 2 years: If and when the parties do make peace, the United States, through NATO, must help to secure it. Only NATO can strongly and effectively implement a settlement. And the United States, as NATO's leader, must do its part and join our troops to those of our allies in such an operation. If you were moved by the film we saw and you believe that it carries lessons for the present day and you accept the fact that not only our values but our position as the world's only superpower impose upon us an obligation to carry through, then the conclusion is inevitable: We must help to secure a peace if a peace can be reached in Bosnia. We will not send our troops into com-

bat. We will not ask them to keep a peace that cannot be maintained. But we must use our power to secure a peace and to implement the agreement.

We have an opportunity and a responsibility to help resolve this, the most difficult security challenge in the heart of Europe since World War II. When His Holiness the Pope was here just a few days ago, we spent a little over a half an hour alone, and we talked of many things. But in the end, he said, "Mr. President, I am not a young man. I have a long memory. This century began with a war in Sarajevo. We must not let this century end with a war in Sarajevo."

Even if a peace agreement is reached, and I hope that we can do that, no peace will endure for long without justice. For only justice can break finally the cycle of violence and retribution that fuels war and crimes against humanity. Only justice can lift the burden of collective guilt. It weighs upon a society where unspeakable acts of destruction have occurred. Only justice can assign responsibility to the guilty and allow everyone else to get on with the hard work of rebuilding and reconciliation. So as the United States leads the international effort to forge a lasting peace in Bosnia, the War Crimes Tribunal must carry on its work to find justice.

The United States is contributing more than $16 million in funds and services to that tribunal and to the one regarding Rwanda. We have 20 prosecutors, investigators, and other personnel on the staffs. And at the United Nations, we have led the effort to secure adequate funding for these tribunals. And we continue to press others to make voluntary contributions. We do this because we believe doing it is part of acting on the lessons that Senator Dodd and others taught us at Nuremberg.

By successfully prosecuting war criminals in the former Yugoslavia and Rwanda, we can send a strong signal to those who would use the cover of war to commit terrible atrocities that they cannot escape the consequences of such actions. And a signal will come across even more loudly and clearly if nations all around the world who value freedom and tolerance establish a permanent international court to prosecute, with the support of the United Nations Security Council, serious violations of humanitarian law. This, it seems to me, would be the ultimate tribute to the people who did such important work at Nuremberg, a permanent international court to prosecute such violations. And we are working today at the United Nations to see whether it can be done.

But my fellow Americans and my fellow citizens of the world, let me also say that our commitment to punish these crimes against humanity must be matched by our commitment to prevent them in the first place. As we work to support these tribunals, let's not forget what our ultimate goal is. Our ultimate goal must be to render them completely obsolete because such things no longer occur.

Accountability is a powerful deterrent, but it isn't enough. It doesn't get to the root cause of such atrocities. Only a profound change in the nature of societies can begin to reach the heart of the matter. And I believe the basis of that profound change is democracy.

Democracy is the best guarantor of human rights—not a perfect one, to be sure; you can see that in the history of the United States— but it is still the system that demands respect for the individual, and it requires responsibility from the individual to thrive. Democracy cannot eliminate all violations of human rights or outlaw human frailty, nor does promoting democracy relieve us of the obligation to press others who do not operate democracies to respect human rights. But more than any other system of government we know, democracy protects those rights, defends the victims of their abuse, punishes the perpetrators, and prevents a downward spiral of revenge.

So promoting democracy does more than advance our ideals. It reinforces our interests. Where the rule of law prevails, where governments are held accountable, where ideas and information flow freely, economic development and political stability are more likely to take hold and human rights are more likely to thrive. History teaches us that democracies are less likely to go to war, less likely to traffic in terrorism and more likely to stand against the forces of hatred and destruction, more likely to become good partners in diplomacy and trade. So promoting democracy and defending human rights is good for the world and good for America.

These aims have always had a powerful advocate in Senator Chris Dodd, who has defended the vulnerable and championed democracy, especially here in our own hemisphere, as has his brother, Tom, first as a distinguished academic at our common alma mater, Georgetown, and then as America's Ambassador to Uruguay.

As a Peace Corps volunteer in the Dominican Republic, Senator Dodd helped some of our poorest neighbors to build homes for their families. Twenty-five years later, when a brutal dictatorship overthrew the legitimate government of Haiti, murdering, mutilating, and raping thousands and causing tens of thousands more to flee in fear, Chris Dodd was the conscience of the Senate on Haiti. He urged America and the world to take action.

On this very day one year ago, an American-led multinational force returned the duly elected President of Haiti, Jean-Bertrand Aristide, to his country. The anniversary we celebrate today was the culmination of a 3-year effort by the United States and the international community to remove the dictators and restore democracy. Because we backed diplomacy with the force of our military, the dictators finally did step down. And Haiti's democrats stepped back into their rightful place.

Our actions ended a reign of terror that did violence not only to innocent Haitians but to the values and the principles of the civilized world. We renewed hope in Haiti's future where once there was only despair. We upheld the reliability of our own commitments and the commitments that others make to us. We sent a powerful message to the would-be despots in the region: Democracy in the Americas cannot be overthrown with impunity.

We have seen extraordinary progress in this year. The democratic government has been restored. Human rights are its purpose, not its disgrace. Violence has subsided, though not ended altogether. Peaceful elections have occurred. Reform is underway. A new civilian police force has already more than 1,000 officers on the street. A growing private sector is beginning to generate jobs and opportunity. After so much blood and terror, the people of Haiti have resumed their long journey to security and prosperity with dignity.

There is a lot of work to do. Haiti is still the poorest nation in our hemisphere, and that is a breeding ground for the things we all come here to condemn today. Its democratic institutions are fragile, and all those years of vicious oppression have left scars and some still thirsting for revenge.

For reform to take root and to endure, trust must be fully established not only between the Government and the people but among the people of Haiti themselves. President Aristide understands that when he says, no to violence, yes to justice; no to vengeance, yes to reconciliation.

This is very important. Assigning individual responsibilities for crimes of the past is also important there. Haiti now has a national commission for truth and justice, launching investigations of past human rights abuses. And with our support, Haiti is improving the effectiveness, accessibility, and accountability of its own justice system, again, to prevent future violations as well as to punish those which occur.

The people of Haiti know it's up to them to safeguard their freedom. But we know, as President Kennedy said, that democracy is never a final achievement. And just as the American people, after 200 years, are continually struggling to perfect our own democracy, we must and we will stand with the people of Haiti as they struggle to build their own. Indeed, the Vice President is just today in Haiti celebrating the one-year anniversary.

And let me say one final thing about this. I thank Senator Dodd and Ambassador Dodd for their concern with freedom, democracy, and getting rid of the horrible human rights abuses that have occurred in the past throughout the Americas. The First Lady is in South America today—or she would be here with me—partly because of the path that has been blazed by the Dodd family in this generation to stand up for democracy, so that every single country of the Americas, save one, now has a democratically elected leader. And human rights abuses and the kinds of crimes that Senator Thomas Dodd stood up against at Nuremberg are dramatically, dramatically reduced because of that process and this family's leadership.

In closing, let me say that, for all of the work we might do through tribunals to bring the guilty to account, it is our daily commitment to the ideals of human dignity, democracy, and peace that has been and will continue to be the source of our strength in the world and our capacity to work with others to prevent such terrible things from occurring in the first place.

We will continue to defend the values we believe make life worth living. We will continue to defend the proposition that all people, without regard to their nationality, their race, their ethnic group, their religion, their gender, should have the chance to live free, should have the chance to make the most of their God-given potential. For too long, all across the globe,

women and their children, in particular, were denied these human rights. Those were the rights for which the First Lady spoke so forcefully in China at the women's conference and for which the United States will work hard in the years ahead.

Ladies and gentlemen, we are living in a moment of great hope and possibility. The capacity of the United States to lead has been energized by our ability to succeed economically in the global economy and by the efforts we are making to come to grips with our own problems here at home. But I leave you with this thought that was referred to by the Governor in his fine remarks and that the president of this University has emphasized in his comments today.

It is important that we be able to act upon our values. And what enables us to do it is our success as a nation, our strength as a people, the fact that people can see that if you live as we say we should live, that people can work together across racial and ethnic and other divides to create one from many, as our motto says, and to do well.

Therefore, we should in the weeks ahead in Washington find a way to come together across our political divide to balance the budget after the deficit has taken such a toll on our economy over the last dozen years. But I ask you to remember this: We must do it in a way that is consistent with our values and with our ability to live by and implement and support those values here at home and all around the world.

Therefore, if our goal is to preserve our ideals and our dreams and our leadership and to extend them to all Americans, when we balance the budget we must not turn our backs on our obligation to give all Americans a chance to get an education, including a college education; to honor our fathers and our mothers in terms of how we treat their legitimate needs which they have earned the right to have addressed, including their health care needs; and not to forget the poor children, even though it is unfashionable to talk about poverty in this world today. They will be the adults of this country someday.

We are strong because we honor each other across the generations. We are strong when we reach across the racial and ethnic divides. We are strong when we continue to invest in education and the technology which opens all the mysterious doors of the future. We are strong when we preserve the environment that God gave us here at home and around our increasingly interconnected planet. We are strong when we continue to determine to lead the world.

These are the things which make it possible for us to meet here in Connecticut today and advocate the responsibility of the United States to lead in the protection of human rights around the world and the prevention of future horrendous circumstances such as those that Senator Dodd had to address at Nuremberg.

So I ask you to remember those lessons as well. If we have an obligation to stand up for what is right, to advance what is right, to lift up human potential, we must be able to fulfill that obligation.

If there is one last lesson of this day, I believe it should be that prosperity for the United States is not the most important thing and not an end in itself. We should seek it only, only, as a means to enhance the human spirit, to enhance human dignity, to enhance the ability of every person in our country and those whom we have the means to help around the world to become the people God meant for them to be. If we can remember that, then we can be faithful to the generation that won World War II, to the outstanding leaders which established the important precedents at Nuremberg, and to the mission and the spirit of the Dodd center.

Thank you, and God bless you all.

NOTE: The President spoke at 4:18 p.m. at Gampel Pavilion.

Remarks at the University of Texas at Austin
October 16, 1995

Thank you. You know, when I was a boy growing up in Arkansas, I thought it highly— [*applause*]—I thought it highly unlikely that I would ever become President of the United States. Perhaps the only thing even more unlikely was that I should ever have the opportunity to be cheered at the University of Texas. I must say I am very grateful for both of them. [*Laughter*]

President Berdahl, Chancellor Cunningham, Dean Olson; to the Texas Longhorn Band, thank you for playing "Hail to the Chief." You were magnificent. To my longtime friend of nearly 25 years now, Bernard Rapoport, thank you for your statement and your inspiration and your life of generous giving to this great university and so many other good causes. All the distinguished guests in the audience—I hesitate to start, but I thank my friend and your fellow Texan, Henry Cisneros, for coming down here with me and for his magnificent work as Secretary of HUD. I thank your Congressman, Lloyd Doggett, and his wife, Libby, for flying down with me. And I'm glad to see my dear friend Congressman Jake Pickle here; I miss you. Your attorney general, Dan Morales; the land commissioner, Garry Mauro, I thank all of them for being here. Thank you, Luci Johnson, for being here, and please give my regards to your wonderful mother. I have not seen her here—there she is. And I have to recognize and thank your former Congresswoman and now distinguished professor, Barbara Jordan, for the magnificent job you did on the immigration issue. Thank you so much. [*Applause*] Thank you. Thank you.

My wife told me about coming here so much, I wanted to come and see for myself. I also know, as all of you do, that there is no such thing as saying no to Liz Carpenter. [*Laughter*] I drug it out as long as I could just to hear a few more jokes. [*Laughter*]

My fellow Americans, I want to begin by telling you that I am hopeful about America. When I looked at Nikole Bell up here introducing me and I shook hands with these other young students—I looked into their eyes; I saw the AmeriCorps button on that gentleman's shirt— I was reminded—as I talk about this thorny subject of race today—I was reminded of what Winston Churchill said about the United States when President Roosevelt was trying to pass the Lend-Lease Act so that we could help Britain in their war against Nazi Germany before we, ourselves, were involved. And for a good while the issue was hanging fire, and it was unclear whether the Congress would permit us to help Britain, who at that time was the only bulwark against tyranny in Europe. And Winston Churchill said, "I have great confidence in the judgment and the common sense of the American people and their leaders. They invariably do the right thing after they have examined every other alternative." [*Laughter*] So I say to you, let me begin by saying that I can see in the eyes of these students and in the spirit of this moment, we will do the right thing.

In recent weeks, every one of us has been made aware of a simple truth: White Americans and black Americans often see the same world in drastically different ways, ways that go beyond and beneath the Simpson trial and its aftermath, which brought these perceptions so starkly into the open.

The rift we see before us that is tearing at the heart of America exists in spite of the remarkable progress black Americans have made in the last generation, since Martin Luther King swept America up in his dream and President Johnson spoke so powerfully for the dignity of man and the destiny of democracy in demanding that Congress guarantee full voting rights to blacks. The rift between blacks and whites exists still in a very special way in America, in spite of the fact that we have become much more racially and ethnically diverse and that Hispanic-Americans, themselves no strangers to discrimination, are now almost 10 percent of our national population.

The reasons for this divide are many. Some are rooted in the awful history and stubborn persistence of racism. Some are rooted in the different ways we experience the threats of modern life to personal security, family values, and strong communities. Some are rooted in the fact that we still haven't learned to talk frankly, to listen carefully, and to work together across racial lines.

Almost 30 years ago, Dr. Martin Luther King took his last march with sanitation workers in Memphis. They marched for dignity, equality, and economic justice. Many carried placards that read simply, "I am a man." The throngs of men marching in Washington today, almost all of them, are doing so for the same stated reason. But there is a profound difference between this march today and those of 30 years ago. Thirty years ago, the marchers were demanding the dignity and opportunity they were due because in the face of terrible discrimination, they had worked hard, raised their children, paid their taxes, obeyed the laws, and fought our wars.

Well, today's march is also about pride and dignity and respect. But after a generation of deepening social problems that disproportionately impact black Americans, it is also about black men taking renewed responsibility for themselves, their families, and their communities. It's about saying no to crime and drugs and violence. It's about standing up for atonement and reconciliation. It's about insisting that others do the same and offering to help them. It's about the frank admission that unless black men shoulder their load, no one else can help them or their brothers, their sisters, and their children escape the hard, bleak lives that too many of them still face.

Of course, some of those in the march do have a history that is far from its message of atonement and reconciliation. One million men are right to be standing up for personal responsibility. But one million men do not make right one man's message of malice and division. No good house was ever built on a bad foundation. Nothing good ever came of hate. So let us pray today that all who march and all who speak will stand for atonement, for reconciliation, for responsibility. Let us pray that those who have spoken for hatred and division in the past will turn away from that past and give voice to the true message of those ordinary Americans who march. If that happens, the men and the women who are there with them will be marching into better lives for themselves and their families. And they could be marching into a better future for America.

Today we face a choice. One way leads to further separation and bitterness and more lost futures. The other way, the path of courage and wisdom, leads to unity, to reconciliation, to a rich opportunity for all Americans to make the most of the lives God gave them. This moment in which the racial divide is so clearly out in the open need not be a setback for us. It presents us with a great opportunity, and we dare not let it pass us by.

In the past, when we've had the courage to face the truth about our failure to live up to our own best ideals, we've grown stronger, moved forward, and restored proud American optimism. At such turning points, America moved to preserve the Union and abolish slavery, to embrace women's suffrage, to guarantee basic legal rights to America without regard to race, under the leadership of President Johnson. At each of these moments, we looked in the national mirror and were brave enough to say, this is not who we are; we're better than that.

Abraham Lincoln reminded us that a house divided against itself cannot stand. When divisions have threatened to bring our house down, somehow we have always moved together to shore it up. My fellow Americans, our house is the greatest democracy in all human history. And with all its racial and ethnic diversity, it has beaten the odds of human history. But we know that divisions remain, and we still have work to do.

The two worlds we see now each contain both truth and distortion. Both black and white Americans must face this, for honesty is the only gateway to the many acts of reconciliation that will unite our worlds at last into one America.

White America must understand and acknowledge the roots of black pain. It began with unequal treatment, first in law and later in fact. African-Americans indeed have lived too long with a justice system that in too many cases has been and continues to be less than just. The record of abuses extends from lynchings and trumped up charges to false arrests and police brutality. The tragedies of Emmett Till and Rodney King are bloody markers on the very same road. Still today, too many of our police officers play by the rules of the bad old days. It is beyond wrong when law-abiding black parents have to tell their law-abiding children to fear the police whose salaries are paid by their own taxes.

And blacks are right to think something is terribly wrong when African-American men are many times more likely to be victims of homicide than any other group in this country, when there are more African-American men in our corrections system than in our colleges, when almost one in three African-American men in their twenties are either in jail, on parole, or otherwise under the supervision of the criminal justice system, nearly one in three. And that is a disproportionate percentage in comparison to the percentage of blacks who use drugs in our society. Now, I would like every white person here and in America to take a moment to think how he or she would feel if one in three white men were in similar circumstances.

And there is still unacceptable economic disparity between blacks and whites. It is so fashionable to talk today about African-Americans as if they have been some sort of protected class. Many whites think blacks are getting more than their fair share in terms of jobs and promotions. That is not true. That is not true.

The truth is that African-Americans still make on average about 60 percent of what white people do, that more than half of African-American children live in poverty. And at the very time our young Americans need access to college more than ever before, black college enrollment is dropping in America.

On the other hand, blacks must understand and acknowledge the roots of white fear in America. There is a legitimate fear of the violence that is too prevalent in our urban areas. And often, by experience or at least what people see on the news at night, violence for those white people too often has a black face.

It isn't racist for a parent to pull his or her child close when walking through a high-crime neighborhood or to wish to stay away from neighborhoods where innocent children can be shot in school or standing at bus stops by thugs driving by with assault weapons or toting handguns like Old West desperadoes. It isn't racist for parents to recoil in disgust when they read about a national survey of gang members saying that two-thirds of them feel justified in shooting someone simply for showing them disrespect. It isn't racist for whites to say they don't understand why people put up with gangs on the corner or in the projects or with drugs being sold in the schools or in the open. It's not racist for whites to assert that the culture of welfare dependency, out-of-wedlock pregnancy, and absent fatherhood cannot be broken by social programs unless there is first more personal responsibility.

The great potential for this march today, beyond the black community, is that whites will come to see a larger truth: that blacks share their fears and embrace their convictions, openly assert that without changes in the black community and within individuals, real change for our society will not come.

This march could remind white people that most black people share their old-fashioned American values, for most black Americans still do work hard, care for their families, pay their taxes, and obey the law, often under circumstances which are far more difficult than those their white counterparts face. Imagine how you would feel if you were a young parent in your twenties with a young child living in a housing project, working somewhere for $5 an hour with no health insurance, passing every day people on the street selling drugs, making 100 times what you make. Those people are the real heroes of America today, and we should recognize that.

And white people too often forget that they are not immune to the problems black Americans face, crime, drugs, domestic abuse, and teen pregnancy. They are too prevalent among whites as well, and some of those problems are growing faster in our white population than in our minority population.

So we all have a stake in solving these common problems together. It is therefore wrong for white Americans to do what they have done too often, simply to move further away from the problems and support policies that will only make them worse.

Finally, both sides seem to fear deep down inside that they'll never quite be able to see each other as more than enemy faces, all of whom carry at least a sliver of bigotry in their hearts. Differences of opinion rooted in different experiences are healthy, indeed essential, for democracies. But differences so great and so rooted in race threaten to divide the house Mr. Lincoln gave his life to save. As Dr. King said, "We must learn to live together as brothers, or we will perish as fools."

Recognizing one another's real grievances is only the first step. We must all take responsibility for ourselves, our conduct, and our attitudes. America, we must clean our house of racism.

To our white citizens, I say, I know most of you every day do your very best by your own lights to live a life free of discrimination. Nevertheless, too many destructive ideas are gaining currency in our midst. The taped voice of one policeman should fill you with outrage. And so I say, we must clean the house of white America of racism. Americans who are in the white majority should be proud to stand up and be heard denouncing the sort of racist rhetoric we heard on that tape, so loudly and clearly denouncing it that our black fellow citizens can hear us. White racism may be black people's burden, but it's white people's problem. We must clean our house.

To our black citizens, I honor the presence of hundreds of thousands of men in Washington today committed to atonement and to personal responsibility and the commitment of millions of other men and women who are African-Americans to this cause. I call upon you to build

on this effort, to share equally in the promise of America. But to do that, your house, too, must be cleaned of racism. There are too many today, white and black, on the left and the right, on the street corners and the radio waves, who seek to sow division for their own purposes. To them I say, no more. We must be one.

Long before we were so diverse, our Nation's motto was *E Pluribus Unum*, out of many, we are one. We must be one, as neighbors, as fellow citizens, not separate camps but family, white, black, Latino, all of us, no matter how different, who share basic American values and are willing to live by them.

When a child is gunned down on a street in the Bronx, no matter what our race, he is our American child. When a woman dies from a beating, no matter what our race or hers, she is our American sister. And every time drugs course through the vein of another child, it clouds the future of all our American children. Whether we like it or not, we are one nation, one family, indivisible. And for us, divorce or separation are not options.

Here in 1995, on the edge of the 21st century, we dare not tolerate the existence of two Americas. Under my watch, I will do everything I can to see that as soon as possible there is only one, one America under the rule of law, one social contract committed not to winner-take-all but to giving all Americans a chance to win together, one America.

Well, how do we get there? First, today I ask every Governor, every mayor, every business leader, every church leader, every civic leader, every union steward, every student leader, most important, every citizen, in every workplace and learning place and meeting place all across America to take personal responsibility for reaching out to people of different races, for taking time to sit down and talk through this issue, to have the courage to speak honestly and frankly, and then to have the discipline to listen quietly with an open mind and an open heart, as others do the same.

This may seem like a simple request, but for tens of millions of Americans, this has never been a reality. They have never spoken, and they have never listened, not really, not really. I am convinced, based on a rich lifetime of friendships and common endeavors with people of different races, that the American people will find out they have a lot more in common than they think they do.

The second thing we have to do is to defend and enhance real opportunity. I'm not talking about opportunity for black Americans or opportunity for white Americans; I'm talking about opportunity for all Americans. Sooner or later, all our speaking, all our listening, all our caring has to lead to constructive action together for our words and our intentions to have meaning. We can do this first by truly rewarding work and family in Government policies, in employment policies, in community practices.

We also have to realize that there are some areas of our country, whether in urban areas or poor rural areas like south Texas or eastern Arkansas, where these problems are going to be more prevalent just because there is no opportunity. There is only so much temptation some people can stand when they turn up against a brick wall day after day after day. And if we can spread the benefits of education and free enterprise to those who have been denied them too long and who are isolated in enclaves in this country, then we have a moral obligation to do it. It will be good for our country.

Third and perhaps most important of all, we have to give every child in this country, and every adult who still needs it, the opportunity to get a good education. President Johnson understood that, and now that I am privileged to have this job and to look back across the whole sweep of American history, I can appreciate how truly historic his commitment to the simple idea that every child in this country ought to have an opportunity to get a good, safe, decent, fulfilling education was. It was revolutionary then, and it is revolutionary today.

Today that matters more than ever. I'm trying to do my part. I am fighting hard against efforts to roll back family security, aid to distressed communities, and support for education. I want it to be easier for poor children to get off to a good start in school, not harder. I want it to be easier for everybody to go to college and stay there, not harder. I want to mend affirmative action, but I do not think America is at a place today where we can end it. The evidence of the last several weeks shows that.

But let us remember, the people marching in Washington today are right about one fundamental thing: At its base, this issue of race is not about government or political leaders, it is about what is in the heart and minds and life of the American people. There will be no progress in the absence of real responsibility on the part of all Americans. Nowhere is that responsibility more important than in our efforts to promote public safety and preserve the rule of law.

Law and order is the first responsibility of government. Our citizens must respect the law and those who enforce it. Police have a life-and-death responsibility never, never to abuse the power granted them by the people. We know, by the way, what works in fighting crime also happens to improve relationships between the races. What works in fighting crime is community policing. We have seen it working all across America. The crime rate is down, the murder rate is down where people relate to each other across the lines of police and community in an open, honest, respectful, supportive way. We can lower crime and raise the state of race relations in America if we will remember this simple truth.

But if this is going to work, police departments have to be fair and engaged with, not estranged from, their communities. I am committed to making this kind of community policing a reality all across our country. But you must be committed to making it a reality in your communities. We have to root out the remnants of racism in our police departments. We've got to get it out of our entire criminal justice system. But just as the police have a sacred duty to protect the community fairly, all of our citizens have a sacred responsibility to respect the police, to teach our young people to respect them, and then to support them and work with them so that they can succeed in making us safer.

Let's not forget, most police officers of whatever race are honest people who love the law and put their lives on the lines so that the citizens they're protecting can lead decent, secure lives and so that their children can grow up to do the same.

Finally, I want to say, on the day of this march, a moment about a crucial area of responsibility, the responsibility of fatherhood. The single biggest social problem in our society may be the growing absence of fathers from their children's homes, because it contributes to so many other social problems. One child in four grows up in a fatherless home. Without a father to help guide, without a father to care, without a father to teach boys to be men and to teach girls to expect respect from men, it's harder.

There are a lot of mothers out there doing a magnificent job alone, a magnificent job alone, but it is harder. It is harder. This, of course, is not a black problem or a Latino problem or a white problem, it is an American problem. But it aggravates the conditions of the racial divide.

I know from my own life it is harder, because my own father died before I was born, and my stepfather's battle with alcohol kept him from being the father he might have been. But for all fathers, parenting is not easy, and every parent makes mistakes. I know that, too, from my own experience. The point is that we need people to be there for their children day after day. Building a family is the hardest job a man can do, but it's also the most important.

For those who are neglecting their children, I say it is not too late; your children still need you. To those who only send money in the form of child support, I say keep sending the checks; your kids count on them, and we'll catch you and enforce the law if you stop. But the message of this march today—one message is that your money is no replacement for your guiding, your caring, your loving the children you brought into this world.

We can only build strong families when men and women respect each other, when they have partnerships, when men are as involved in the homeplace as women have become involved in the workplace. It means, among other things, that we must keep working until we end domestic violence against women and children. I hope those men in Washington today pledge among other things to never, never raise their hand in violence against a woman.

So today, my fellow Americans, I honor the black men marching in Washington to demonstrate their commitment to themselves, their families, and their communities. I honor the millions of men and women in America, the vast majority of every color, who without fanfare or recognition do what it takes to be good fathers and good mothers, good workers and good citizens. They all deserve the thanks of America.

But when we leave here today, what are you going to do? What are you going to do? Let all of us who want to stand up against racism do our part to roll back the divide. Begin by seeking out people in the workplace, the classroom, the community, the neighborhood across town, the places of worship to actually sit down and have those honest conversations I talked about, conversations where we speak openly and listen and understand how others view this world of ours.

Make no mistake about it, we can bridge this great divide. This is, after all, a very great country. And we have become great by what we have overcome. We have the world's strongest economy, and it's on the move. But we've really lasted because we have understood that our success could never be measured solely by the size of our gross national product.

I believe the march in Washington today spawned such an outpouring because it is a reflection of something deeper and stronger that is running throughout our American community. I believe that in millions and millions of different ways, our entire country is reasserting our commitment to the bedrock values that made our country great and that make life worth living.

The great divides of the past called for and were addressed by legal and legislative changes. They were addressed by leaders like Lyndon Johnson, who passed the Civil Rights Act and the Voting Rights Act. And to be sure, this great divide requires a public response by democratically elected leaders. But today, we are really dealing, and we know it, with problems that grow in large measure out of the way all of us look at the world with our minds and the way we feel about the world with our hearts.

And therefore, while leaders and legislation may be important, this is work that has to be done by every single one of you. And this is the ultimate test of our democracy, for today the house divided exists largely in the minds and hearts of the American people. And it must be united there, in the minds and hearts of our people.

Yes, there are some who would poison our progress by selling short the great character of our people and our enormous capacity to change and grow. But they will not win the day; we will win the day. With your help, with your help, that day will come a lot sooner. I will do my part, but you, my fellow citizens, must do yours.

Thank you, and God bless you.

NOTE: The President spoke at 9:34 a.m. at the Frank Erwin Center, as part of the Liz Sutherland Carpenter Distinguished Lectureship in the Humanities and Sciences. In his remarks, he referred to Robert Berdahl, president, William

Cunningham, chancellor, Sheldon Ekland-Olson, dean, college of liberal arts, Bernard Rapoport, chairman, board of regents, and Nikole Bell, student, University of Texas at Austin. A portion of these remarks could not be verified because the tape was incomplete.

Remarks at a Luncheon in Dallas, Texas
October 16, 1995

Thank you very much. Lloyd Bentsen already said this, but I want to reemphasize that in my opinion, when the history of our administration has been written, even those who disagreed with a lot of things I did will say that, unquestionably, Al Gore was the most important and influential Vice President in the history of the United States of America. No other person has been given so much responsibility, and no other person has fulfilled it so well, whether it was in the reinventing Government movement or in setting environmental and technology policy or dealing with our attempts to work more closely with the Russians across a wide range of issues—and I tell you now there are no Russian missiles pointed at the people of the United States for the first time since the dawn of the nuclear age because of the things that we've been doing—or working with Secretary Cisneros on our community empowerment strategy. Right across the board he has made a terrific difference, and besides that, he gives great introductions. [*Laughter*]

I want to thank Frank and Debbie for doing such a wonderful job, along with all of you on the steering committee. Thank you very, very much.

I thank Secretary Bentsen for being here, for his remarks and for his remarkable service to our country. This country has had very, very few Treasury Secretaries in its long and distinguished history that have had anything like the impact that Lloyd Bentsen had on the economic policy of the United States, as you can see from what others have said about the statistics, to very, very good effect. And a lot of the things we had to do were not easy at the time. I'll say a little more about that in a moment. But I want to say thank you, and I miss you.

I look around this room and I see some people in this room, like my dear friend B. Rapoport who spoke with me at the University of Texas this morning, and Jess Hay and Audrey

and Betty Jo, people I've known more than 20 years and others that I just met since I have been running for or become President. Perhaps there are a few people here I have never met before. I'm going to try to correct that before I leave this office—all over the country. But I want to thank all of you for coming here, and I hope you're coming here in common cause.

This is a remarkable day for our country. In Washington, DC, there may be as many as one million black men actually marching even as we speak here today. And they are doing it, I believe, for the same reasons and based on the same values that the people of Dallas elected Ron Kirk the mayor. They are saying that we have to do two things in this country: We have to see people who are in difficult circumstances reassert their own discipline and dedication to personal responsibility for themselves, their families, and their communities; and then we have to bridge this foolish racial divide that continues to plague us, even 30 years after President Johnson saw through the passage of the Voting Rights Act and the Civil Rights Act, because we tend to see the world so differently through our different experiences and lenses. And that's what I went to the University of Texas to talk about today. I don't want to reiterate what I said there, except to say that I think there is fault on both sides and merit on both sides.

I think that the better part of wisdom now is to do two things, first of all, to really have every citizen seek out someone of a different racial or ethnic group and engage in the kind of conversations people think they have but don't really, in which people can be frank and brutally honest about what they honestly feel but in which they have the discipline to listen and open their ears and their minds and their hearts and hear others. I find so often in Washington, DC, perhaps especially in Washington, DC, people say a lot, but they don't listen very well. And I've taken to calling the Speaker of the House once a week and just trying to listen, whether I need to or not—[laughter]—just because I think that it's important for us to listen to one another, for people of different views to actually hear and be able to say what someone on the other side of an issue really believes.

The second thing I think we have to do is to follow people like your mayor or our wonderful Secretary of Housing and Urban Development who actually bring people together to get things done.

I'm deeply indebted to Texas for so many reasons, for Lloyd Bentsen and Henry Cisneros and, of course, for Bill White, who until recently was the Deputy Secretary of Energy. And my lifetime friend Mr. McLarty has a car dealership in Texarkana. I don't know if that counts or not, but I think it does. [Laughter] We're still trying to sell Ross Perot down there. [Laughter]

We've tried to work hard with the people of Texas, and one thing that I've been really proud of is the support that we've been able to maintain through both Congresses—one in Democratic hands, one in Republican hands—for the space program, something that I strongly support and believe in, and the Vice President does as well. And I thank the Members of the Congress who are here for representing Texas so well and for helping us to move this country forward.

I'd like to—there's hardly anything left for me to say because everybody who's spoken before did so well. And maybe I ought to sit down while I'm ahead. But what I'd like to do today is just to make a few points that I hope you can make to others in the days and weeks and months ahead, because I think the election in 1996 and the budget debate we are having now in 1995 will shape the kind of people we're going to be well into the 21st century.

Let me begin by saying that I am very upbeat about where we are and where we're going, not only because the economic news—although it's good; we do have the lowest combined rates of unemployment and inflation we've had in 25 years, and I'm proud of the work that everyone did on that. Of course, there's still things to be done. We're going through a period of profound change from an industrial to a technology-based, information-based economy, from the cold war to a global village. And whenever these kind of big changes happen and the shakeout

is occurring, there are a lot of people who kind of fall behind, and we have to catch them up.

We have to not only create jobs, we have to figure out how to raise incomes. That's why we are trying, even in this Congress, to pass the "GI bill" for America's workers that would permit people who lose their jobs to get a voucher from the Federal Government to take to the nearest community college to immediately begin job training. That's why we want the tax cut to emphasize giving families a deduction for the cost of education after high school, so people can continue to strengthen their ability to earn good incomes.

But basically, this economy is going in the right direction. And the most important thing is that we permit those of you in the private sector to succeed by following good, sound policies on the deficit, on trade, on investment in education, on research and development, on technology, on helping the communities that have been left behind to attract investment and to put people to work.

The Vice President talked about our successes on the social front. There is a real reawakening today. What you see in this march in Washington is really not confined, by any means, to black men, or black men and black women. What is going on today in Washington is a manifestation of a sweeping feeling in the country that the time has come for everyone to assume a higher measure of personal responsibility, to try to come to grips with the incredible dimensions of the social problems that we have allowed to foster and fester in this country over the last generation.

And I believe our policies have played a role. I believe our welfare reform policies, I believe our crime bill, I believe a lot of the things we have done have played a role. But the American people are leading the way to bring the crime rate down. The welfare rolls are down. The food stamp rolls are down. The poverty rate is down. The teen pregnancy rate is down in America.

Now, they're all still too high, every one of them. But the point is that we are at least gaining on it for a change. And what we need to do is to keep gaining on it. There will be problems in this old world as long as people like you and me inhabit the planet because we're not perfect. But the issue is, are we gaining on it, are we getting closer every day to living by the values we believe in, to lifting up the potential of every person, to giving everybody the chance to be the kind of person that they ought to be? The answer is, we are. And what we ought to do is to continue that.

We still have some troubling problems. For example—can you explain this—drug use is down among young adults, but casual drug use is up among juveniles. The crime rate is down among young adults, but random crime is up among juveniles. Why? We're gaining on it, but there's still too many kids out there raising themselves. And we have to keep working on that.

We know now that we can make progress. For years, I heard people talk about social problems in almost hopeless terms. Now we know we can do something about this. And now there is no excuse for our not doing it. But we can do this.

There is a lot of talk—I don't want to be too political today, but we all know every time I come to Texas a hundred of my friends say, "You know, if you just spend more time down here, we could carry this State." Then I leave, and all the Republicans say, "Oh, you know, he's just another one of those Democratic liberals." And I hate to say it, but every one of them that wants to replace me, except one or two, has spent a whole lot more time in Washington, DC, in the last 20 years than I have. [*Laughter*]

But next time you hear that, ask them, of the last three administrations which one reduced the deficit more, which was the only one to produce a balanced budget, which one reduced the size of the Government, the number of regulations more, which one gave more authority to State and local governments and the private sector and reduced it from the Government, which one passed the toughest crime bill? The answer to all of that, obviously, is our administration.

I say that not to be political myself but to say that the political attacks on this administration may be helpful at election time, but they actually cause a lot of voters to do something that's not in their own interests. And sometimes the conventional wisdom just kind of gets a leg up and people just keep on repeating it. So I want you to go out and help refute the conventional wisdom, not because I think anything I've done in the past justifies reelection—I think people should be reelected based on what's going to happen in the future—but because it

is evidence of the values this administration has and the record of performance we will make if we continue into the future.

And you should confront people. You should talk to people. Just in the way I want us to bridge the racial divide, we have to bridge the political divide. The thing I think that surprised me most when I got to Washington was how intensely partisan the place was and how people got away with doing that. Because mostly in a State capital around the country or in a city hall, you'd just collapse; people would just get rid of you if you were so intensely partisan you never worked with anybody else. You'd never do anything else.

And it's one of the reasons we had to make some tough decisions. I'll just give you one. Lloyd Bentsen will vouch for me on this. When I went to Washington, I knew from talking to Alan Greenspan and a lot of economic experts that if we could get the deficit down at least $500 billion over 5 years, we'd have a big drop in interest rates and a big boom in the economy—we knew that—and that the $500 billion, as Secretary Bentsen said to me over and over and over again, was sort of a psychological barrier. If we could just get by it, boy, we could get this economy going again. So we decided that come hell or high water, that's exactly what we were going to do.

And after I'd been in Washington about a week, I was informed by the then minority leaders of the Senate and House, now the Senate majority leader and the Speaker, it didn't matter what I did, I would not get one single, solitary Republican vote for deficit reduction for my budget. And one of them was candid enough to say, "It's great because this is a free thing for us. If it works, we'll deny that it worked and claim it's a tax increase. If it doesn't, we can blame you. You won't get any votes from us, not one." And they were as good as their word. They didn't have a single one for it. [*Laughter*]

Now what did that mean? Since—and you ask your Members of the House here. What it meant was, since we had to pass the budget with only Democrats and we had to reduce the deficit $500 billion, we had to raise taxes on a lot of you more than we wanted to, and we had to cut spending less. In the end, Lloyd Bentsen said, "We have to do this because all the people that pay more in taxes will make even more in income if we get this economy going again." And so we did it. He didn't want to do it. I didn't want to do it. We wound up with a budget that was not ideal but was still right for America in an intensely partisan atmosphere.

I had never been in anything like that before, and I still think it's not good for America. I think there's enough differences between Republicans and Democrats to run 500 elections, much less just this one coming up in 1996. So there ought to be some argument for just getting up tomorrow and trying to work something out so the country's interest will be served and still let people make their decisions. That is what I am committed to doing. But I am not, I am not going to do anything as President that I believe will make the America of the 21st century, that the children that are here in this luncheon today will grow up and live in, less than it ought to be. That's what this whole budget debate is about.

Don't let anyone tell you this is a debate about balancing the budget. Every outside credible source says both these budget plans are good plans to balance the budget. Every one. Every one. Our plan gets a balanced budget in 9 years; theirs does in 7. Our plan has a smaller tax cut more targeted toward education and childrearing. Our plan uses conservative economic forecasts that are consistent with our historic performance, even though we're going to grow more, I think, if we do this right.

But their plan, I believe, violates our most basic values. I believe this is really a contrast between those who really think that winner-take-all is all right, let the market decide everything, and those of us who believe that America is a place where everybody ought to have a chance to win. It's a contrast between a plan that is committed to growing the middle class and shrinking the under class and a plan that would certainly shrink the middle class and grow the under class. That's not the 21st century I want to live in. It's a contrast between a plan that would continue to honor our obligations to our parents and to our children, especially the poorest children among us, and one that would say that's somebody else's problem. That is the difference.

Everybody knows we have to slow the rate of growth in medical care. But their plan would impose great new burdens on some of the poorest elderly people in this country. They would say to all of these people out there living on

$300 or $400 a month that you have to pay more for your Medicare and Medicaid, even if you can't afford to pay it. They would say to medical centers and urban hospitals that we're going to cut way back on your Medicaid payments, and we hope you don't have to close, but if you do, it's too bad.

We have to slow the rate of medical inflation, but we have to do it in a disciplined way so that we understand the consequences to the University of Texas Medical Center, to the urban hospitals throughout Texas, to the rural hospitals that provide the only health care people have out in the country, and to elderly people, many of whom barely have enough to live on, not to mention the fact that 1 in 5 children today—more than 1 in 5, 22 percent, are eligible for help from the National Government to deal with their health care needs. And they're our children, too, not just the kids that can afford to be at a luncheon like this because their parents have done well. But they're our children, too, and they're our future, too. And we owe them something.

So, yes, I propose to slow the rate of medical inflation, but I don't want us to go plumb off the side of a mountain before we know where we're going. It is not prudent, and it is not consistent with our values.

I don't support one incredible provision of that budget of theirs which would actually raise taxes on families making about $20,000 a year with two kids by cutting back on the working families tax credit, a credit signed into law under President Ford, a credit expanded under President Bush, a credit President Reagan said was the best antipoverty program ever devised because all it does is to cut taxes and give tax credits to working people who don't have enough money, even though they work full-time, to get above the poverty line because they've got kids at home.

And Lloyd Bentsen and I designed a program that, over a period of years, would enable the United States of America to say, if you will work 40 hours a week and you have children in your house, you will not be taxed into poverty by your Government; your Government will lift you out of poverty. We want people to work, not be on welfare. And we want people to be successful when they're doing their best to work and raise their children. Why in the world we would do that is beyond me.

I don't think it's smart to cut back on our environmental investments. The Vice President could have told you, but he's too modest to say this. He told me, the first time I ever met him, that all this scientific dispute about whether the globe was warming up was bogus, that it really was, and we were going to be in trouble. Just a couple of weeks ago, we see a whole new raft of scientific evidence and almost unanimity of opinion now that global warming is real, that there is a hole in the ozone layer that is going to affect the whole future of the planet, including the future of the United States. I don't believe eliminating the modest amount of money we invest in studying global warming and what our response ought to be to it is a very good way to balance the budget.

And at a time—we just came to the University of Texas, which every Texan is proud of—I don't think on the edge of the 21st century there's a single business person in this audience who would knowingly cut a corporate budget for education and training, research and development, or technology. The idea that we would consider on the edge of the 20th century cutting back our investment in helping poor kids get off to a good start in school or providing scholarships and loans to people going to college is a mystery to me, since we don't have to do any of that to balance the budget. And you don't have to take my word for it, ask Lloyd Bentsen. We do not have to do any of that to balance the budget.

So don't be fooled. This fight over the balanced budget—when you see your Representatives go back to Washington, it is not about balancing the budget. We can balance the budget, cut taxes, protect Medicare without destroying the social contract and forgetting about our obligations to one another. That is what this is about.

So I ask you to leave here doing two things: One, go out and talk to people who are different from you, just like I asked the people at the University of Texas today, tell them what you heard here and listen to what they think; two, tell the people of Texas we can balance the budget without stepping on our values and trampling on our future and walking away from our obligations to one another.

And that is what we are determined to do. I go back to Washington with that determination because I believe that we're going in the right direction economically, we're going in the right direction socially, we are better positioned for the next century than any country on the face of the Earth, if we will simply face up to our responsibilities and deal with them with common sense and good values instead of turning them into some sort of ideological fight that will tear the American people apart. I want to bring us together and move us forward.

Thank you very much.

NOTE: The President spoke at 1:20 p.m. in the Plaza Ballroom at Le Meridien Hotel. In his remarks, he referred to Debbie and Frank Branson, luncheon cochairs; Bernard Rapoport, chairman, board of regents, University of Texas, and his wife, Audrey; and Democratic fundraiser Jess Hay and his wife, Betty Jo.

Remarks at the Concert For Hope in Hollywood, California
October 16, 1995

Thank you very much. Thank you, Joe Califano, for your singular determination to keep this issue before the American people. There is not another citizen in the entire United States of America who has done as much as Joe Califano to help us all to come to grips with the implications of substance abuse. And every American is in his debt.

I also want to thank the other honorees for the work they have done, the late Frank Wells and Tony Bennett and our friend Betty Ford. I want to thank the Center on Addiction and Substance Abuse at Columbia for helping us all to learn more about this, and all the performers tonight for making this a very special evening for the United States.

This mission of ours cuts across politics, geography, income, and race. It must unite all of our people in a common purpose. Tonight in 3,500 cities and towns all across our beloved country, community antidrug coalitions are gathered in auditoriums and town halls to watch this broadcast. These people have played a large role in our antidrug efforts, many of them part of an important campaign led by Lee Brown, our Director of National Drug Control Policy, who accompanied me here tonight. With their help, he is getting an urgent and very straightforward message to our teenagers: Stay drug-free; you have the power. With marijuana use on the rise among our teens, that's a message every one of us must now help to spread every day.

Tonight the antidrug coalitions all across our country who are sharing this evening with us are honoring some of their own and some of our Nation's finest. I applaud these honorees as well, the parents, the police officers, the prosecutors, the clergy, the social service workers, the doctors, the recovering drug addicts and alcoholics, and all of their families, for they are the true foot soldiers and the real heroes in this, our common national crusade. To them I say, we know your battle is not easy, but you are not alone, and you must keep fighting for all of us and especially for our children.

Like millions of Americans, I know firsthand how a family suffers from both drug and alcohol abuse. The consequences of this kind of abuse are many. But since December 1st is World AIDS Day, we should take special note that 25 percent of AIDS cases are the result of drug abuse. Many other cases can be blamed on the risks our young people take under the influence of drugs or alcohol.

The battle against substance abuse must be waged a person at a time, a family at a time, a school at a time, community by community. But it must be backed by all of our efforts, including the President. We are doing what we can at the national level, with punishment, with working to keep drugs out of the country, with helping our community-based efforts to promote safe and drug-free schools and prevention and treatment programs that are so important. And I will keep fighting to keep these things funded.

But I also hope all of you will help me in this battle against teen smoking. We know that every day 3,000 of our young people begin to smoke and that 1,000 of them will have their lives end prematurely because of it. Children who reach the age of 20 almost never start smoking if they haven't started by then.

These are our common goals and our common endeavors. We wish for all of our children a drug-free America. It's up to each of us to take the kind of responsibility that your honorees, and the honorees in all those town halls and auditoriums all across America, have assumed. If we can do our part, we can give this country a drug-free America in the 21st century.

Thank you, and God bless you all.

NOTE: The President spoke at 9:40 p.m. in the Pantages Theater. In his remarks, he referred to Joseph A. Califano, Jr., director, Center on Addiction and Substance Abuse, Columbia University; Frank G. Wells, former chief operating officer, Walt Disney Productions; entertainer Tony Bennett; and former First Lady Betty Ford.

Remarks Prior to a Meeting With the Initial Base Adjustment Strategy Committee in San Antonio, Texas
October 17, 1995

Well, I'd like to begin by making an opening statement and to say how very pleased I am to have a chance to come here to San Antonio and to Kelly Air Force Base to follow up on the meeting that I had with the fine committee in Washington 2 months ago.

I know that officials from the Defense Department, John White and Rudy de Leon, were here in August, and they're back here with me here today. And we have done a lot of work with this community. I have been very, very impressed with their Kelly 21 project, the vision of it, the energy of it. I hope that you have seen the commitment of the administration to try to maintain employment at appropriate levels, to try to have a reasonable period of transition, and to try to make sure that in the end you are as successful as you possibly can be.

We believe that if we do this right, we can generate even more employment in this area as we go through this transition period.

I want to say a special word of thanks to your former mayor, Secretary Cisneros, who has worked with me very closely on this and advised me. General Viccellio, I want to say I know that this community is very encouraged by the fact that you're going to be overseeing this process. And I want to say a word of appreciation, too, to Congressman Henry B. Gonzalez, who can't be here today—he's in Washington—and of course, to Congressman Frank Tejeda, our prayers go out to him. I had a quick conversation with him just a few days ago.

The most important thing, I think, to announce today for the San Antonio community is that we have reached an agreement on joint use of the base which will, obviously, permit you to do precisely what you proposed to do. We are committed to implementing that agreement on joint use in good faith. And as I said, my goal is to do this in such a way that the strengths of this community and the strengths of this great resource will generate even more employment and more stability for you at the end of this 5-year process—really an 8-year process—than you had when we began it and than you would have had given the fact that we have to lower our presence all across the country in the aftermath of the cold war. Mr. Mayor, that's my commitment, and I think we're going to deliver on it.

Thank you very much.

NOTE: The President spoke at 1 p.m. in the Pilots Lounge in the Base Operations Building. In his remarks, he referred to Deputy Secretary of Defense John White; Under Secretary of the Air Force Rudy de Leon; Gen. Henry Viccellio, Jr., USAF, Commander, Air Force Materiel Command; and Mayor William E. Thornton of San Antonio. A tape was not available for verification of the content of these remarks.

Remarks to the Community at Kelly Air Force Base in San Antonio
October 17, 1995

Thank you. Let's give Frances another hand. Wasn't she great? I thought she did a great job. Mayor Thornton, thank you for your remarks and for your remarkable and energetic leadership during this important time for San Antonio. General Viccellio, thank you for your assumption of this new, important task. General Curtis, thank you for your strong leadership here; to the other dignitaries here present, including the Deputy Secretary of Defense, John White, who has worked so hard on this project at my instruction, but also with his own heart in it; to the members of the Initial Base Adjustment Strategy Committee, or IBASC, as you call it, Jose Villareal, Juan Solis, and Tullos Wells; to your county judge, Cynthia Taylor Krier; and to the workers here at Team Kelly.

And I'd like to say a special word of acknowledgement to one of the people who came down here with me today, your former mayor and the finest Secretary of Housing and Urban Development this country ever had, Henry Cisneros.

I want to thank the Sky Country and the Band of the West from Lackland for the music they provided before I came here. I want to thank Frances Garza-Alvarado for her introduction and for the example she's set of professionalism and dedication, a model for the people, both men and women, that she helps to train for the jobs of tomorrow. When she talked about how she felt when she came here 30 years ago, I knew that I was right to fight for the families and the people of Kelly and the future of this base and this community, because Frances represents what America is all about.

Before I get into my remarks, I'd also like to acknowledge two friends of Kelly Air Force Base who could not be with us today for different reasons: my friend of many, many years, over 20 years now, Congressman Henry B. Gonzalez, who is working in Washington, and his colleague, Congressman Frank Tejeda.

Frank is in a different sort of fight now, and I want to say a word about him. Many of you know him as more than a Congressman. He's your neighbor; he's your friend. He comes home to his old neighborhood every weekend without fail. He's a decorated Vietnam veteran and a proud son of Texas. He has always been one of *la gente*. If an issue matters to working people, you can bet that Frank Tejeda is there working on it, fighting for them. He's a fighter; he's a winner. I had a wonderful talk with him just a few days ago, and we're all praying that he wins the fight he's involved in now. God bless you, Congressman, and good luck.

San Antonio has made special contributions to the security of this country, not only with Kelly but also with the Randolph Air Training Command, with Brooke Air Force Base, with Lackland Air Force Base, with Fort Sam Houston, and the Brooke Army Medical Center.

There are a lot of Presidents who have had special ties to San Antonio because of its commitment to our Nation's military. Most of you probably know that President Roosevelt trained the Rough Riders here. One of the gifts that I was pleased to receive since I became President is an original printing of Teddy Roosevelt's account of how he organized and trained the Rough Riders in San Antonio. President Eisenhower served as a young lieutenant at Fort Sam Houston and met his wife, Mamie, here. President Johnson married Lady Bird in San Antonio, and later was pronounced dead at the Brooke Army Medical Center.

This is an important part of America, and San Antonio's contribution and Kelly's contribution to the security of this country must never be forgotten. Our Nation owes a profound debt of gratitude to all the workers at Kelly for giving our country something that cannot be measured and certainly cannot be purchased, patriotism, service, and heart.

Recently I was so moved, just before I came out here, to hear two things about all of you that I want to repeat for the benefit of all the people of Texas and the people of the United States who will know about this event today. After it was announced that the BRAC commission's decision was to close Kelly and phase out its operations, your commander told me—General Curtis—that he was walking through the crowd just a few days ago, through the workplace here, and that two of the workers here stopped and said they wanted to ask him something about the new realignment plan we had put in place for Privatization in Place. They didn't ask him about their jobs. They didn't ask him about their retirement. They asked him in-

stead whether he thought that the readiness of the United States of America could be maintained with this new plan. That is the kind of patriotism the United States of America should know about, in this place, among you people. And I am grateful to you.

The other thing I was told about today was that after the announcement was made, when you would normally expect a big decline in morale, that the productivity of operations here went up, not down. If everybody in America had that kind of character, we wouldn't have half the problems we have in this country. And I thank you for that.

You have been a model of what I believe our country has to do, a model of what I talked about yesterday in my speech on race relations at the University of Texas in Austin, a model of what those people who marched in Washington yesterday were calling on all of us to represent. You have shown personal responsibility and responsibility for your families, your communities, and your country. You have proved that you could work together across racial and ethnic lines. And now we're going to prove that we can harness the changes going on in the world today to make America and San Antonio and the families of Kelly stronger and better.

My mission as your President at this moment in our history is to harness the changes that are going on for the better. As we move from an industrial to an information and technology age, as we move from the cold war, in which you played such a pivotal role, to a global village with different kinds of threats to democracy and freedom, I want to see that we keep the American dream alive for all of our people and that we keep America as the strongest country in the world. Those are our two objectives as we move to the 21st century.

We know that we have to create a modern economy that will grow jobs and enable people to grow good families. We know we have to create a modern Government that is smaller and more flexible. We know we have to maintain America's leadership in the world. And most important of all, we know we have to make all these changes consistent with our basic values as people with responsibility and opportunity, with the idea that people have to be able to succeed at work and in their family lives, with the idea that we are all one community and we have certain obligations to our parents, to our children, to the needy among us so that we can go forward together.

One of the most important things to recognize today in that framework of values is that the people who won the cold war cannot be left out in the cold. We are going through a period of change; everyone knows that. Well, that's fine if you're winning from it, but it's pretty scary if you're not sure what the future holds. By your work, you have honored your commitment to America. And I came here today to tell you I want you to have hope for the future because we intend to honor our commitment to you.

On July 1st, you were dealt a serious blow when the independent base closing commission said that we ought to shut Kelly down. At my insistence and my refusal to go along with that specific recommendation, the Air Force developed the Privatization in Place plan that will keep thousands of jobs here at this depot. I am here to say that, of course, Kelly will change; that was inevitable because the world has changed. But we are not leaving you out in the cold. We will work with you in partnership to protect jobs, to protect workers, to help the families and communities here, and to make sure you are still contributing to America's mission in the 21st century.

Kelly has been far more than an important military base. It's also been an avenue of opportunity for so many people who could not have found it in other jobs. So many families were lifted into the middle class because of Kelly. And each generation of people in San Antonio and the communities around here have built upon that opportunity.

Henry Cisneros tells me that he grew up on the west side of the city under the flight pattern of Kelly's aircraft. He grew up hearing the prop B–36's, the C–124's, and later the powerful F–16's. He said his entire block worked at Kelly. It's no wonder, from that block of military employed families came the first Cabinet Secretary in the United States Government from San Antonio, and with him came some of the best people in our administration. I want to just name one who is here today, Frank Wing, who after 38 years in the Air Force here at Kelly came to serve under Henry Cisneros in Washington. Thank you, sir, for your lifetime of devoted service.

This base has been a cornerstone for the Hispanic middle class, indeed, for much of middle class San Antonio. The larger area has played

a role in our Nation's security for a very long time, as I have already said. I told the Air Force and the Department of Defense when this BRAC decision was announced to take all the time the law allows to reduce the economic impact on the community and to create the strongest possible economic base at Kelly and to work with the local leaders to plan a future that would give you a chance to have even more prosperity.

That means we're not shutting this base down, we're transforming it. We're maintaining jobs here because it is good for San Antonio, but it's also good for the Air Force. With our plan to move jobs here to the private sector, we'll be helping national security and helping the people of San Antonio.

We call this plan Privatization in Place. It means that for 5 more years, Kelly will keep the jobs that would be here if closure had not been recommended, and even 8 years from now, more than two-thirds of Kelly's jobs will still be here, working for the Department of Defense. But at the same time, we'll create even more jobs. We've seen this work already in other places. For example, at the Sacramento Army Depot in California, private investment there has actually produced thousands of more jobs than the base had at the time it was closed. If you look at this incredible resource here, we can do that and more.

Our plan for Kelly does more than just provide breathing room; it gives you the time we all need for a transition to the future for Kelly and for San Antonio. This base still has an important role in the future of San Antonio, an important role in the security of our Nation. With the 5 extra years we have won for Kelly, the city will have time to diversify its economic base. And we'll have a new opportunity to build another kind of base for jobs, grounded firmly in the private sector and in the strengths of San Antonio, the people, the culture, the ideal location to become a leading center of trade for the 21st century.

More than almost any other place, you are ready for the future. Your workers are among the best trained anywhere. You have the best specialized equipment and the facilities for the future, part of our national investment and part of something private industry really needs. So the incentive for private investment is here, as you found out last weekend when you had hundreds of businesses coming here to look over the potential for the future.

And then of course, there is San Antonio, the ninth-largest city in our Nation, a city that is very large but still is a community, not a crowd. People like Mayor Thornton and Frank Tejeda and my good friend Jose Villareal and all of the others who have worked on this committee, they have worked hard to prove that you could bring all parts of this community together with a clear-eyed vision for the future. In the name of Kelly and its workers, the people of San Antonio have done something very important. They have given all people here the opportunity to build a better and stronger life.

I know that this plan can work. Deputy Secretary White and Under Secretary of the Air Force Rudy de Leon are working closely with the community here. And because there is no better person to help direct a transition than a former vice commander at Kelly, we do have the best in General Butch Viccellio, and I thank him for his dedication to this effort.

At the same time—yes, you could clap for him; I think you ought to. [*Applause*] I know generals don't run for office, but they love to hear the applause. [*Laughter*] They love to hear the applause.

At the same time, your local IBASC commission has been working hard to coordinate the reuse effort here, to develop the strategy and the vision to propel Kelly and San Antonio into the next century. We aren't wasting a second. From day one, we've been pursuing creative initiatives, providing planning funds to help in the effort. We've allocated more than half a billion dollars for construction, personnel, and support help to Kelly and its workers. Just this past weekend, as I said, the open house that was sponsored by the city and the base drew hundreds of contractors and others from the private sector. They saw the potential for success here.

Today I am proud to announce that we have reached an agreement between the community and the Air Force and the Federal Aviation Administration to allow the joint use of the Kelly runway between the Air Force and private sector.

That puts San Antonio in a prime position to handle the growth of trade from all over our hemisphere, all the way down to the tip of Tierra del Fuego. If diversity is America's strength, and it is, San Antonio will have the muscle when it comes to trade with Latin America.

More action is on the way. Let me say that this is a time of hope for San Antonio. You're one of the youngest cities in the country. You have the position, the resources, the proven character and ability to take advantage of the future. You are organized, skilled, and now sitting on some of the best real estate and biggest opportunities in the entire United States.

I know the BRAC decision last summer was a disappointment. And if you saw me in my rare, unguarded moments, you knew that I was disappointed, too. But I believe that San Antonio will come out a winner with a healthier, more diversified economic base and better jobs, a community moving confidently into the next century as a center of trade and a vital player in our national security. And let me emphasize again, for the benefit of the two workers who asked the general that the other day, this plan is designed to strengthen our national security, not to weaken it.

No American should forget that. If our mission as a people is to go into the 21st century with the American dream alive for all people and to keep America the strongest country in the world, then we have to have a good economic plan, a modern Government, mainstream values driving everything we do. And that means we have to maintain America's leadership in the world. It is not an option for us to walk away from our role and our responsibilities. And you will be helping us do that well into the next century.

Let me close by saying something that you must already know. Your local leaders here have a vision and a plan. I believed all along that we could not walk away from San Antonio or from Kelly or from the people here. And we have a national plan that will permit you the time you need to take advantage of the changes going on in the world and to maintain an important role in our national security. But the real strength of these plans will come from you, from your character, your work, and your own vision, and your willingness to believe in yourselves and the future.

If you look at how we in the United States are positioned now and imagine what the world will look like 10 or 20 or 30 years from now when all the children in this audience have their children at meetings like this, I tell you, there is no nation in the world in a better position to do well in the global village of the 21st century, if we will seize our opportunities. And to do that, we have to believe in ourselves, stay true to our mainstream values, and make the changes we know that will harness the future for a better America.

That's what you can do. I will be there with you. I know that you can do it. If you believe you can do it, there is no stopping you.

Thank you, and God bless you.

NOTE: The President spoke at 2:06 p.m. In his remarks, he referred to Maj. Gen. Lewis E. Curtis III, USAF, Commander, San Antonio Air Logistics Center.

Remarks at a Dinner in Houston, Texas
October 17, 1995

Well, Secretary Bentsen, that was such a wonderful introduction, I almost forgive you for leaving. [*Laughter*] The operative word is "almost." I thank Lloyd and B.A. for their friendship and the gifts they've given our country. And I tell you that when the history of the last 50 years of the 20th century is written in the United States, the work that Lloyd Bentsen did to not only help to get hold of this terrible out-of-control deficit but to do it in a way that would permit us to invest in our people and our future and to connect the United States to the rest of the world through NAFTA, through the GATT world trade agreement, and in so many other ways will mark him as one of the greatest Secretaries of the Treasury in the history of the United States of America.

I want to thank two other Texans who are here who made immeasurable contributions to our administration: the Secretary of Housing and Urban Development, Henry Cisneros. If you ask anybody who has followed the work of that Department in the few decades that it has existed, they will tell you that without question he is the best Secretary of Housing and Urban Development ever to serve in that position. And we're very proud of him. And my good friend Bill White, who just came home to Houston after being Deputy Secretary of Energy, thank you, sir. I will say again that between Bill White and Hazel O'Leary and Ron Brown, the Secretary of Commerce, they did more to further the energy interest of the United States and to create jobs in the United States by getting investment abroad than any previous administration has ever done. Thank you, sir, for what you did in that, and I appreciate that very much.

My heart is full of gratitude tonight and so many wonderful things have been said that if I had any sense I'd just sit down. [*Laughter*] I'm afraid if I talk on now I'll disqualify myself for reelection. But I'm going to talk anyway. [*Laughter*]

I want to thank the statewide chairs of these galas we've had. I have had 2 wonderful days in Texas. I thank Arthur Schecter, who made a wonderful statement earlier, and Joyce; Lee and Sandra Godfrey and Stan McClellan; Lou Congillan; Sheldon and Sunny Smith; and George Bristol and Frank and Debbie Branson, who did such a wonderful job for us in Dallas yesterday. Thank you very much. Thank you, all of you.

My good friend of nearly 25 years, who is only a year younger than me and looks 15 years younger than me—I resent it bitterly, but I still love Garry Mauro. Thank you, my friend, and Judith, his wife.

I'm really glad to see Ann Richards and Mark White here. I used to be a Governor, you know, back when I had a real life. And we served together, and we enjoyed it immensely.

I appreciate Attorney General Morales and former Attorney General Mattox being here. I told somebody the other day—he said, "What's the best job you ever had?" And I said, "I was attorney general; that was the best job I ever had." And they said, "Why?" And I said, "Well, I didn't have to hire or fire or appoint or disappoint, raise taxes or cut spending. And every time I did something unpopular, I blamed it on the Constitution." [*Laughter*] So, remember that.

I want to say a special word of thanks to Congresswoman Sheila Jackson Lee and Congressman Jim Chapman for their work for our country and for your State in the Congress. And let me say a great word of thanks, too, to Bob Bullock for what he said and for the private things that he has said to me in the last 2 days. It's been a great inspiration to me. And I was sitting there thinking that I could play that talk he was giving in several States, and it would help us. I wish I could patent it and send it around like that Ozark water you talked about. [*Laughter*]

And finally, let me say a special word of thanks, too, to Mayor Bob Lanier and his wife, Elise. We came in and we got out of the car—I spend a lot of time with a lot of mayors and I have many, many very close friends who are mayors, but I'm not sure there is any mayor in America who has the particular combination of compassion and intellect and old-fashioned practical insight. It's really quite ingenious, you know, to not just talk about problems but to actually do something about them. And in so many ways, Bob Lanier has done that. And I guess that's why he got 91 percent last time. He has promised that if you beat it this time, that he will give me a few that he has to spare in '96. [*Laughter*] So I hope that you will do that.

I want to thank Reverend Caldwell for praying over us tonight and for his mission and his ministry and for bringing his wonderful wife, who is a native of my State. His mother-in-law was a supporter and a woman I got to know, a remarkable woman. I'm delighted to see you here, sir. Thank you both for coming.

I'd like to thank Terry McAuliffe and Laura Hartigan and Meredith Jones, our Texas finance director, for the work they did and all those who helped them for this fine night. I thank you.

I also want to say a word on behalf of two people who are not here tonight. The Vice President had meant to come with me when we were going to do this last night, but I—thanks to the sponsors here in Houston, we were able to defer this until this evening so that I could go out to California last night and participate in a national benefit for the Center on Alcohol and Substance Abuse Prevention, something that is very important to me because I've dealt with both those issues in my family and because our administration is committed to

making progress on that. And I thank you for your indulgence, but that kept the Vice President from coming.

I just want to say that even my severest detractors, when our administration's history is written, will say that Al Gore was the most influential Vice President in 219 years of the American Republic. And I thank him for his work on the environment, on reinventing Government, on technology, on helping us with Russia. But most of all, I thank him just for being there.

When we work together, I wonder what all of those other Presidents did and why they didn't do more with this incredibly flexible office. The only thing the Vice President really has to do is to sort of show up in the Senate when there is a tie vote and hang around waiting for something to happen to me. [*Laughter*] Every day I think about that, I do a few more sit-ups and—[*laughter*]—you know, do what I can to avoid that. So you know, you've got a fellow with a high IQ and a reasonable amount of energy, it seems like a shame just to let him hang around. [*Laughter*] And I really think he's done a magnificent job. I'm so proud of him, and we have a genuine partnership.

I'd also like to say that I know that the First Lady would like to be here with us tonight, but as some of you doubtless know, she has been on a very, very successful trip to Latin America. She went to Nicaragua, to Chile, to Brazil, and to Paraguay. And since the people of Texas understand better than any other people in the United States how important our partnership with Latin America is, I hope you will excuse her absence.

I've been trying to think of what I ought to talk about tonight. You saw a movie about the accomplishments of the administration, and then Secretary Bentsen was kind enough to get up and talk about it, and others did. What I'd like to do is to give you some arguments for the next year. I've heard all this talk about how the Democratic Party is dead because we don't have any new ideas or we're too liberal or we're slaves to Government. And I have concluded that since they keep winning elections with those arguments, we're better at doing and they're better at talking. So I want to give you some talking tonight, if I could.

I have learned a few things about the limits of liberalism. I heard a story the other day—my senior Senator, Dale Bumpers, called me and told me a story I want to share with you about the limits of liberalism, involving Huey Long, the famous populist Governor and Senator of Kentucky. One day, you know, when we were in the middle of the Depression and we had—I mean, Louisiana. [*Laughter*] I've got a Kentucky story I wanted to tell, but I decided, upon reflection, I shouldn't tell it. So my conscience is clicking in on me.

Anyway, when—do you remember Huey Long? Those of you who are old enough to remember when he was Governor and then later Senator, he campaigned around the State and then around the country on this "share the wealth" platform. He came up north to Arkansas, actually, and helped a woman named Hattie Caraway get elected to the Senate. The first woman in American history ever elected to the Senate in her own right was Hattie Caraway from Arkansas. And the only time anybody ever came into our State as an outsider and helped anybody win an election was Huey Long. He was a great politician. And unemployment was 25 percent in America, and the per capita income of Arkansas, Louisiana, and Mississippi was only about half the national average. So you could say whatever you want to about sharing the wealth, and you had a pretty willing audience.

And he was out on a country crossroads one day, talking about how we ought to share the wealth. And there were all these farmers standing around. He saw this old boy in overalls, and he said, "Farmer Jones," he said, "let me ask you something." He said, "Now, if you had three Cadillacs, wouldn't you give us one so we could go around here on these country roads and pick up these kids and take them to school during the week and take them to church on Sunday?" He said, "Of course, I would." He said, "If you had $3 million, wouldn't you give us a million dollars so we could put a roof over every family's head and give them a good meal at night and breakfast in the morning?" He said, "You bet I would." He said, "If you had three hogs—" And he said, "Now, wait a minute, Governor, I've got three hogs." [*Laughter*] So the Democrats, to be fair, have learned a few things about the limits of liberalism. [*Laughter*]

Here's what I think is going on. This is a time of extraordinary change but very great promise for this country. We're moving from an industrial age to an information and a technology age. We're moving out of the cold-war era into a global village, where we're all closer together than ever before and where there are vast new opportunities for cooperation existing alongside the new security threats of terrorism, biological and chemical warfare, organized crime, and global drug trafficking. What we have to do is to harness all this change to make America a better place.

I ran for President with a clear mission in my own mind to try to take good care of this country to achieve two objectives in the 21st century. One was to make sure that the American dream was alive and well for all people without regard to their race, their income, or their region. And the second was to make sure that America continued to be the strongest country in the world, so that someone could lead the world after the cold war toward greater freedom and greater democracy and greater security and greater prosperity. That's what I wanted to do.

I said at the time that I thought we would have to move beyond the old political debate that parties had been having for many years toward what I called a new democratic philosophy. And I'd just like to go over what those elements were that I told you I would try to bring to the Presidency.

I said I thought our economic policy ought to be based on growth, not dividing the pie but growing the economy more; that we ought to do whatever it took to maintain our world leadership but that we couldn't be involved in everybody's problem everywhere; that we needed a new form of Government that would be smaller and less bureaucratic, would be more entrepreneurial, would give more responsibility to State and local governments and to the private sector, would embrace all kinds of new ideas, but would still fulfill our fundamental obligations that can only be done by the National Government; and that all of this ought to be done based on a reassertion of old-fashioned, mainstream values that I think got lost over the last 10 or 20 years, that we needed both responsibility and opportunity in our country, that people had to be able to succeed both at work and in their family lives, that we had to have both growth and fairness in our country, and that in the end we had to decide, as Mayor Lanier said, to be a community. We had to decide that we had certain obligations to one another. That's what people in a community feel.

If we have no obligations to one another, then we're not a community, we're just a crowd. We occupy the same piece of land, but we're just going to elbow each other until whoever is strongest winds up at the front of the line. And we never will turn over our shoulder to see what happened to the others. Being a community means you have obligations to our parents, to our children, to those who need help through no fault of their own. It also means that we revel in and cherish and build up our diversity, we don't use it as a cheap political trick to divide the American people. That's what it means.

Now, what I want to say to you tonight is that I believe I've been faithful to that and I believe this country is moving in the right direction, thanks mostly to the American people. But I believe that our administration has made its contributions.

You heard what was said about the economy, about the growth of the economy. The misery index that the other party used to talk about so much, the combined rates of unemployment and inflation, you never hear them mention it anymore because it's at the lowest level it's been in 25 years.

And beyond the new jobs, I'm really proud of the fact that we've had the largest number of new small businesses incorporated in the last 2½ years of any comparable period in American history, that we've got, thanks in no small measure to the remarkable partnership Henry Cisneros has established with the housing industry in America, we have 2½ million new homeowners, a record number for such a short time. And if he keeps going, we're going to have two-thirds of the American people in their own homes by the end of the decade, something that has never been done before.

Most of the credit goes to the American people, but the fact that we drove down the deficit while increasing our investment in technology, in research, in the education of our people, and that we expanded trade dramatically—up 4 percent in '93, 10 percent in '94, 16 percent in '95—those things have made a contribution to that economic picture because we broke the mold.

We brought down the deficit and invested in our people. We went for free trade with NAFTA and GATT in 80 agreements with other countries, including 15 with Japan. But we also went for fair trade that looked after labor standards and the environment and that finally, finally, got an agreement with Japan that we can enforce on automobile related issues. These are important things that will make a difference over the long run. And I think they're worthy of support.

You heard what Mr. Schecter said about the role the United States has played in world peace; I won't belabor that. I will tell you that this is also a safer country than it was 2½ years ago. There are no Russian missiles pointed at anyone in America for the first time since the dawn of the nuclear age. We are moving toward a comprehensive nuclear test ban treaty next year. We have extended indefinitely the agreement of over 170 nations not to be proliferators of nuclear weapons. We are making progress in working with other countries in fighting terrorism, in fighting the spread of biological and chemical weapons, in trying to make the American people safer. I am proud of that. And we have to continue to do it.

This Bosnia issue has been difficult, but we must lead here. And if we can get a peace agreement, as the leader of NATO we have to help implement it. Otherwise, we will have a terrible problem in the middle of Europe that can engulf us in the future.

Do we have problems? Yes, of course, we do. We still have too much income inequality. You always have that when you change from one economic arrangement to another and everything gets shaken up. The people that are best positioned to do well do very well. Those that aren't positioned to do well get hurt worse. And we have to do something about that. And I've put forward a program to do that, to offer more educational opportunities, to raise the minimum wage, to give middle income families a tax deduction for the cost of a college education so that more people can get that education.

We have to deal with that, but let's see it in the context of what's happening. This country is generating jobs and growth and opportunity. There will always be problems as long as the world exists. We need to focus on the problems but keep doing what is working in America.

If you look at the issue of Government— Lloyd Bentsen said the Government's 165,000 smaller than it was when I took office; let me tell you what that means. Next year, the Federal

Government will be the smallest it's been since Kennedy was President. But more importantly, as a percentage of the work force, the Federal Government today is the smallest it's been since 1933. I hardly think that qualifies us to be the party of big Government.

We've done more to give authority to States to get out from under Federal rules on welfare and health care experiments than the last two administrations combined did in 12 years. We have done more to get rid of thousands and thousands of pages of regulations. We are trying to make this Government work. Does it still do dumb things? Of course. Do we make mistakes? You bet we do. Is the answer to abolish the Federal Government? No. No. The answer is to have it be smaller but make it so it can still protect people.

This is a fundamental decision that's at issue in this election season, that's at issue in this budget fight. Do you really believe that the market will solve all problems and we'd be better off without any Government? Are you willing to tolerate the occasional mistake of a Government that is transforming itself radically in order to know that somebody is there looking out for the public interest and our obligations to one another as a community.

Do we need to do more? Of course, we do. I still want the line-item veto, lobby reform, campaign finance reform. There's lots of things we can do. But the point is, we're going in the right direction. The answer is to reform the National Government, not to dismantle it. That is the answer. That's what will work for America. That is the right approach.

If you look at whether we've furthered our values or not, let me tell you that I want to give you some statistics that will support what you saw yesterday in that march. Forget about all the speeches and all the politics about it and everything; just remember the faces of the people that were at that march yesterday. Listen to what they said. That march was about them and their desire to reassert responsibility for themselves, their families, their communities. Their understanding that until everybody in America is willing to do their part, then the Government can't fix the problems, no one else can—that is a beautiful and awesome thing, and no one should denigrate it and no one should underestimate it.

What I tried to do at the University of Texas yesterday was to give a clear voice to what I believe was in the hearts and minds of most of the people who showed up there yesterday. But I believe it's in the hearts and minds of most Americans. And I think it is a great tragedy that people who basically share the same values and, frankly, have a lot of the same problems, often cannot reach across the divide at one another.

But what I want to tell you is, this country, even more than what you saw at the march yesterday, across racial and gender and age and regional lines, there is a reawakening in this country, a sort of a coming back to common sense and shared values and a determination to go into the future with greater strength and character and devotion to the things that make life worth living.

And I'll just give you a few examples of that. In the last 2½ years, the crime rate is down, the murder rate is down, the welfare rolls are down, the food stamp rolls are down, the poverty rate is down, the teen pregnancy rate is down. A lot of people don't know that. Now, no Government program did that. That's the folks that live in this country getting themselves together and sort of—you know, we're a great big, complicated country, and we change slowly, but that's an awesome thing when you think about that.

Now, I think our policies helped. I think we helped when we cut taxes on 15 million working families who were making modest incomes, so that we'd be able to say, if you work 40 hours a week and you've got kids in your house, you won't be in poverty anymore. I think that was a good thing to do. I think that was an honorable thing to do.

I think the family and medical leave law helped. I don't think people ought to lose their jobs if their parents get sick or their baby's born and they need to be there.

I think the 35 States who we gave permission to experiment with welfare reform—I think that helped. I'll give you an example. One thing that they're doing in Texas that I agree with is they have asked for permission to get out from under Federal rules so that they can say, if you want a welfare check and you've got a child, you have to prove your child has been immunized against serious diseases. We have one of the lowest immunization rates in the country. I think it's a great idea. It's a great idea.

And I hope—I think the crime bill helped. I appreciate what Mayor Lanier said. I was very moved by what I saw that he was trying to do in Houston when I ran for President. And that crime bill, by putting 100,000 police on the street and community policing, is helping America to lower the crime rate. But also by emphasizing the prevention and giving these kids something to say yes to, that's also helping to lower the crime rate. And I want to say more about that in a minute.

I just want you to remember this little moment from yesterday's speech in Texas—at the University of Texas, I mean. I tried to say that a lot of what has to be done to bridge the racial divide requires first the assumption of personal responsibility by all Americans without regard to race. Second, the ability to talk honestly and listen carefully to one another—we don't do enough of that. We still haven't even scratched the surface of that. But thirdly, there are responsibilities of things we have to do. One of the big fights I'm in now with Congress is whether we ought to just get rid of all this money for prevention. Now, they say they like this, giving the States and localities the right to spend the money; that's what we did. We said, here's the prevention money. I don't know what works in Houston and whether it would work in Hartford, Connecticut. I know one thing, you get enough kids in these programs playing soccer after school or learning to play golf or doing whatever else these kids are doing, you get all of them in there, and your crime rate is going to go down. You're going to save a lot of kids' lives. You won't have to spend all that money building jails and putting them in prison. You can spend less money and educate them and have them do well. I believe that.

I have always believed we should be very tough on crime. I have always believed that in some crimes you just have to give up and be unforgiving. But I am often reminded of one of my favorite lines of poetry that was written in the context of the turmoil in Ireland but applies to the children growing up alone on these mean streets today. William Butler Yeats once said, "Too long a sacrifice can make a stone of the heart." And we shouldn't forget that.

Our biggest problem today is, in spite of all those good numbers I told you, in spite of the fact—one thing I didn't say is that drug usage among young adults is down—in spite of all that, the violent crime rate among juveniles in most cities is up. Casual drug use, especially marijuana, among young teenagers—not young adults, among teenagers—is up. Why? Because there's too many of those kids out there raising themselves. And nobody's looking after them and making sure they have something to do, something to say yes to. The mayor told me that the juvenile crime rate is not going up in Houston because those kids are being engaged.

So I say to you, we're moving in the right direction. The answer is to do more of this, to do more things consistent with our basic values, not to do less, not to do less.

This is a great country. We are getting our act together culturally and socially. And our economy is going great. What we have to do is to figure out how to spread the benefits of the economy to people who don't have it and how to deal with the social and cultural problems that need some help from the outside, that can't be totally solved by individuals and families on their own. This is what I want you to think about. That means that a great deal of the rhetoric in Washington today is irrelevant to what we have to do, to the future, and that's what bothers me about it.

Now, you want to deal with yesterday's rhetoric—and the Republicans say, "Well, Clinton's liberal; the Democrats are liberal; they love big Government"—you got a few questions you can ask them. You say, "Well, if that's true, of the last three Presidents, who cut the deficit more? Who was the only one to present a balanced budget? Who reduced regulation more? Who gave more authority to State and local governments to get out from under the Federal Government more of the last three Presidents? Who cut the size of Government more? Who cut taxes more for small businesses?" Believe it or not, we did in 1993, thanks to Lloyd Bentsen. Those are all facts. Who had the most pro-family welfare and child support and tax policies? We did.

But that is not the argument we need to make. I want you to say that; maybe that will open some people's ears and eyes. But that's not what this is about. This is not about politics. This is about the people of the United States, about our future, about how we're going to get into the 21st century, remember, with the American dream alive for everybody, with America the strongest country in the world. That is the mission. The mission is what happens to the people, not what happens to the politicians, not what happens to the political parties, what happens to the people of the United States of America.

And I ask you to consider just two things as I move out of this and leave you here and go back to work. First is, in a time of change the President has to do what is right for the long run, which means inevitably he will do things that will be unpopular in the short run. Now, that is absolutely true. I'd bet everything I've got in the bank, which isn't all that much—[*laughter*]—that I've done four or five things that made everybody in this room mad in the last 2½ years. And sometimes I've been wrong. But I show up every day. [*Laughter*] But the point I want to make here, what I want to say is, you have to understand that when things are changing so quickly and the moment is there, you cannot even imagine what will be popular in a month or a year in a time of change like this. You have to think about what it would look like in 10 or 20 years.

When Lloyd Bentsen and I—he didn't tell you the whole story—I'll tell you the whole story about that budget—probably people in this room still mad at me at that budget because you think I raised your taxes too much. It might surprise you to know that I think I raised them too much, too. But you know why we did it? Because we had been in Washington—you ask—we had been in Washington one week when the then-minority leaders of the House and Senate, now the Senate majority leader and the Speaker of the House, informed us that we would not get not one single, solitary vote from the other party for our budget, no matter what we did, and were very candid. They said, "We want to be in a position to blame you if the economy continues to go down. And if it goes up, we want to be in a position to attack you for raising taxes, whether you raise taxes on people or not. You're going to raise taxes on some, and that's the attack we want, so we're not going to vote for it, not a one of us."

Well, needless to say, we had information, as you heard Secretary Bentsen say, that if we could get the deficit down $500 billion in 5 years, we could lower interest rates and boom the economy. And so we decided, even with only Democrats voting for it, we would have to make whatever decisions would be necessary to do that, even though it meant a little more tax and a little less spending cut than we want-

ed. And we reasoned—and I remember him telling me this, he said, "I'm going to pay more, but most people will make a whole lot more money if we get this economy going than they'll pay in extra taxes." And that's exactly what happened. It was the right thing for America for the long run, even though it was difficult politics in the short run. It was the right thing to do.

You know and I know they cut us a new one in Texas over the assault weapons ban and the Brady bill. [*Laughter*] But let me tell you something. Since we adopted the Brady bill, last year, 1994, there were 40,000 felons who did not get handguns and didn't have a chance to shoot innocent Americans because of it.

I know when we had to decide whether we should move the administration through the FDA to try to crack down on teenage smoking and restrain advertising directed at teenagers, all the political advice was, "Don't do that. Don't do that, because if you do that, everybody that's against you will vote against you, and everybody that's for you can find some other reason to vote against you."

That's why things often don't get done, by the way, in national politics. [*Laughter*] Because organized, intense, minority interests will all vote against you and will terrify whoever they can terrify if you do such and such a thing. And then everybody that agrees with you will find some other reason to be against you. So it paralyzes the political system.

But we studied this problem for 14 months. Three thousand kids a day start smoking; 1,000 of them are going to die earlier because of it. How much political hit is 1,000 lives a day worth? I think it's worth a whole lot. It's the right thing to do. Twenty years from now, there will be a lot more kids alive because of the initiatives of the administration. It is the right thing to do.

Most of you liked it when I helped Mexico, but the day I did it, there's a poll in—the Washington Post came out, the poll was 81–15 against what I did. I thought it just another day at the office. [*Laughter*] But the American people could not possibly see ahead 10, 20 years to what would happen to the United States if the economy of Mexico failed and the financial markets in Argentina and Brazil collapsed. And our whole strategy for growing the American economy in the 21st century in a world economy, but starting in our backyard with Mexico and the rest of Latin America and then moving to

Asia, Europe, and other places would be wrecked. And our ability to cooperate in fighting drugs and in dealing with illegal immigration and all these things would have been undermined.

So I said to myself, "Yes, it's unpopular, but this is a good country. People are fairminded. Maybe it will work out in the next year or two. But whether it does or not, 20 years from now, it will look like a very good decision." That is the way we all have to begin to think. And when we do, then we can begin to dismiss out of hand these trivial wedge issues that are designed to divide us and drive a stake in our hearts.

I applaud the mayor for not abandoning affirmative action. It's not time yet. It's not time yet. It's not time yet. We had so many different programs in Washington, there were things wrong with them. We're trying to fix them. And any time you do anything, if you do it long enough, somebody will make a mistake, and then someone else can go find it, and they can blow it up in a 30-second ad and make it look like, you know, you can't find your way home at night. [*Laughter*] But it is not time yet. If we haven't learned anything from the last few weeks, we should have learned that. We have still got work to do to make sure everybody has a chance to participate on fair and equal terms in the bounty of America.

So these are the things we have to do, and that's what I want you to see. Now, having said that, I want you to see this fight over the budget in these terms.

Let me tell you as you leave here, this is not about balancing the budget. For the first time since Lyndon Johnson was President, the President and the leaders of Congress are committed to balancing the budget. That is a very good thing. I applaud the Republican leadership for that. This is not about slowing the rate of medical inflation and securing the Medicare Trust Fund for the first time in a good while. We're both committed to that. The issue is, how are we going to do it, and are we going to do it in a way that is consistent with our values and with common sense and bringing us together?

Now, my budget is a good, credible, conservative budget. It gets rid of hundreds of programs. But it does not, it does not, in this age, gut education or research or technology. I want everybody to get on that information super-

highway and ride straight into the 21st century, and it is nuts for us to cut education if we're going to do that. It is wrong. And it doesn't hurt families. I can't imagine my getting a deduction for Chelsea's college costs, which is what would happen under their bill, and turn around and raising taxes on families making $20,000 a year trying to support three children. But that's exactly what they'd do. That's wrong. That is wrong. It doesn't make sense, and it's wrong.

And on the health care issue, you may think there's a lot of demagoguery in it, but let me tell you—we have got to slow the rate of medical inflation, but that is happening. Health insurance premiums went up less than inflation this year for the first time in 10 years. We can fix this. But we do not want to cut Medicare so much.

Listen to this. This is their proposal: Cut Medicare so much that we stop paying the copay requirements for really poor elderly people. You've got a bunch of old folks out there living on $300 a month. And the way this budget, their budget, is written now, they get hit the hardest. We stopped—because right now, we pay their copays and their deductibles because they don't have enough money to live on. And it's estimated a million elderly people could drop out of the Medicare system if the budget passed. We don't have to do that. We don't have to do that.

And we don't have to go back to the time where we say to an elderly couple, if they're lucky enough to both live and be happy, and they're way up in their seventies or eighties, and they're still together, but they don't have much money, and one of them needs to go into a nursing home, we don't have to go back to the time when you could tell the person that's not going into the nursing home, "You've got to sell your house. You've got to sell your car. You've got to clean out your bank account, or your spouse can't get any help." Do you really want to give those people that choice? I don't. We don't have to. It's in their budget, but we don't need it to balance the budget. And I'm going to fight it. It's not right. It's not right.

Do you really want to take thousands of kids out of the chance to be in the Head Start program or cut the number of college scholarships for poor kids at the time when we need more children going to college? What do you think it's going to do to the racial dialog in this country when you need more and more and more education? Look around here. If we'd had this dinner 20 years ago and charged us to get in, would there have been any black people here? Would there have been any Hispanic people here? No. How do you think they got here? They have good educations. What are we going to do—does that make any sense? No.

I could go on and on and on. This is—they want to get rid of the Commerce Department. Who do you think is opening all these doors for all these Texas energy companies in these countries that many people just learned existed a couple of years ago? [*Laughter*] The Commerce Department, the Energy Department, the United States of America, working in partnership with our business interests to create jobs here in America by building bridges of commerce around the world. Why should we do that? We don't have to, and it doesn't make any sense.

Let me tell you something about the Medicaid program. This is the last one I'll mention. This is big for Houston, the Medicaid program. Most people think that that's that program for health care for poor people on welfare. Well, that's sort of true. About 30 percent of the Medicaid program goes to pay for health care mostly for children of welfare families; 70 percent of it goes to help older people who don't have a lot of money in their nursing homes or home health care or to help the disabled population in America.

And when that happens, it means that their middle class children, if you're talking about nursing homes, or their middle class brothers and sisters and parents, if you're talking about the disabled, are therefore able to save the money they have and educate their children and maintain a middle class lifestyle. And it holds us together. I don't know a single, solitary health care provider in the United States of America who believes we can maintain the quality of health care we've got now for all those people if we put these Medicaid cuts in.

Not only that, the Medicaid program helps cities like Houston big time. Why? Because the Medicaid program gives extra money to university teaching hospitals, gives extra money to children's hospitals, gives extra money to inner-city hospitals, gives extra money to rural hospitals in all those little towns in Texas that are 90 miles from nowhere and wouldn't be able to give health care if they didn't have country hospitals out there. What's going to happen to that? Is that what you want? I'm not for that. We don't have to do that.

And then there are all those little curlicues in the budget. You know how they're giving everything to the States, right? The States are the source of all wisdom now—[*laughter*]—all wisdom. They're never going to make a mistake. We're giving everything to the States except a few things. For example, they've decided that Texas, even though Texas just passed a tort reform law, you don't have enough sense to do your own laws. So they want to take away your right to decide what your malpractice laws are and what all your other laws are. They want to just take that away. All of a sudden, you can do everything but decide what your legal system is.

And last week—you know what they did last week? This is an amazing thing. One of their committees, last week they said, "We're going to give the Medicaid program back to the States in a block grant. Now, we're going to cut their money by 30 percent, but we're sure they'll do fine because they're so much more efficient than we are, they can get lower costs." And the next vote—I mean within the same hour they voted to stop States from being able to bargain with drug companies to get cheaper prescription drugs. [*Laughter*]

This is not about balancing the budget. This is about whether you believe America should be a winner-take-all society or a society where everybody has a chance to win. That's what this is about. It's about whether you believe that the market can solve every problem in the world or that all human systems are imperfect and democracies are instituted to find fair ways to treat people fairly so we can go forward together.

I'm telling you, folks, this country is in better shape than it was 2 years ago. Part of it is because we have had a good economic policy. We've had good social policies. We've done the right things by the Government. We stood up for America around the world. But a big part of it is, the American people are changing the way they live and think, and they are moving into the future. And you deserve better than what is in that budget. And I'm going to do my best to see that you get it. It is the right thing for America. And I want you to help me.

And I want you to fight for it because it's right for you.

Thank you, and God bless you all.

NOTE: The President spoke at 8:15 p.m. in the Westin Galleria Hotel. In his remarks, he referred to former Secretary of the Treasury Lloyd Bentsen and his wife, B.A.; former Texas Governors Ann Richards and Mark White; Texas Attorney General Dan Morales and former Texas Attorney General Jim Mattox; Lt. Gov. Bob Bullock; Texas Land Commissioner Garry Mauro; and Terence McAuliffe, national finance chair, and Laura Hartigan, national finance director, Clinton/Gore '96.

Remarks on Presenting the National Medals of Science and Technology
October 18, 1995

Thank you very much, Mr. Vice President, Senator Glenn, Senator DeWine, distinguished members of our administration involved in science and technology and research and development, to our honorees, their friends, and other distinguished visitors to the White House today. I was looking at the Vice President, listening to him eloquently lay the case out and thinking to myself how fortunate we are to have a Vice President who knows so much and cares so much about these issues and wishing that you could all do something for him, those of you who are being honored today. You see, since Sunday, he has been in Haiti, Texas, and Tennessee, and I have been in Connecticut, Texas, California, Texas, and back here. And what we need is some nonbiologically damaging way to stay awake and on the job today. If any of you could come up with an idea before you leave today with your medals, we would be immensely grateful to you. [*Laughter*]

Today it is a great honor for both the Vice President and me to honor outstanding Americans whose contributions to science and technology have enriched not only the United States but the entire world. Through persistence and focused intellectual energy, they have stretched our horizons, expanded the frontiers of knowledge, peeled away the secrets of nature, cured disease, created new industries such as that of optical storage. Through technologies like virtual reality, they will let doctors treat soldiers on the battlefield and let children on our prairies learn from teachers in our cities.

They have even affected the lives of people of this country in more direct ways. They have invented the adhesive used for Post-Its. All of them have performed research that will pay off richly for the United States in the 21st century. In whatever their field or specialty, their spark of genius has lighted the landscape of human knowledge and pushed back the shrouds of ignorance.

We are proud of all of you and what you have done. Your achievements give us confidence that the United States will continue to lead in science and technology for many years to come.

In a year when seven of nine Nobel laureates for science and mathematics were Americans, we can feel assured that our scientific leadership is unchallenged. We can also feel proud that every one of these Nobel Prize winners has been supported in their research efforts by the United States Government.

In honoring these pioneers, we must ask and answer a fundamental question: At the edge of the 21st century, how will we ensure that America remains the strongest nation in the world? How can we pass on to every child the American dream of opportunity?

The world is changing rapidly from the industrial to the information technology age, from the cold war to the global village. We live at a time of remarkable promise, when dazzling new technologies are poised to transform how we work, how we learn, how we get information, indeed, how we organize our patterns of living. Consider that at the turn of the century, nearly half of American people were living on farms. At the midpoint of the century, 4 of 10 of us worked in industries. At the end of this century, most of us will be knowledge workers. That remaking of the economic landscape will only accelerate in the years to come, as we morph from the machine age to the information age.

Al told me to say that. Did I do okay? [*Laughter*] You promised you wouldn't laugh if I'd say it, and then there you are. It's part of my training in virtual reality, which is becoming the norm around here. [*Laughter*]

Our ability to offer people opportunity clearly depends upon our ability to spread the fruits of our knowledge. In other words, our leadership depends upon our commitment to science, to technology, to research, to learning. We have always revered science and its implicit promise of progress. We are in a way a whole nation of inventors and explorers and tinkerers. We believe in technology, and we are determined to pursue technology in all of its manifestations. These things seem to me to be deeply embedded in our national character and our national history. We also recognize that these benefits are far from abstract, for throughout our history, from the steam engine to the telegraph, from the assembly line to the microchip, our prosperity has surged forward on wave after wave after wave of technological change. Since World War II, innovation has been responsible for clearly as much as half of our national economic growth.

The private businesses represented here today will always be the most important investors in research and development. But throughout our history, we have recognized that Government, working in partnership with the private sector, does have a critical role to play.

The defense and space programs help make America the world's leader in aircraft, aerospace, and electronics. Because our troops are equipped with the world's most sophisticated weapons, our Nation is secure. The work of the National Institutes of Health led to new drugs and therapies that have made America a leader in biotechnology. And a unique partnership between Government, business, and university researchers spawned the Internet, a pathway for knowledge and creativity, the likes of which our parents could only have imagined, and some of us who are parents today can just barely imagine. [*Laughter*] Sales of products through on-line services will soar from $200 million this year to $4.8 billion in 1998.

Today, global competition and rapid change have made technology clearly more central to our future than ever before. And because it is so often difficult for individual firms to reap the benefits of discovery and innovation, the public sector must continue to play a role.

Since I became President, I have continued this commitment to invest in science and technology. Our comprehensive economic strategy began by reducing the deficit by a trillion dollars over 7 years, which lowered the cost of capital and freed up funds for investment. But we strengthened our investments in basic science research. And we put in place pragmatic industry-led efforts such as the Commerce Department's advanced technology program, manufacturing extension programs, and our work to enhance market-led solutions to our Nation's environmental challenges.

Throughout our history, at least throughout modern history when we've been clearly aware of these scientific matters, this future and this kind of policy has been broadly supported by members of both parties. It has been a part of our national common ground, a part of our sense of who we are, what our security requires, and what will bring us the best future. Today that commitment is at risk in the great debate over balancing the Federal budget.

I have proposed a balanced budget plan that sustains our investment in scientific endeavors, in technology, in research and development. The plan now being considered by the Congress will cut vital research and development by a third and any number of other related endeavors by that much or more. We could have a balanced budget to show for it tomorrow, but a decade or a generation from now our Nation will be much the poorer for doing that.

At a time of real and crushing budget pressures, the Congress deserves credit for its commitment to balance the budget and to slow the rate of growth of medical inflation. But it is tempting to cut other things without considering what the consequences are, including investments in science and technology, which may not have the biggest lobby here in Washington.

The future, it is often said, has no constituency. But the truth is, we must all be the constituency of the future. If we want a future in which the world's libraries are at every child's fingertips, in which gene therapy enables us to cure diseases like cystic fibrosis, in which a car can travel across the country on one tankful of gas with virtually no pollution, then we must strengthen, not weaken, our investments in science, technology, and research. We must sustain our universities, a critical national resource and still the envy of the entire world. We must allow ourselves always to see the world through fresh eyes. We must never allow those who fear change to subvert progress. And we must resist these drastic cuts, for constant churning innovation is the key to economic growth and national strength in the 21st century.

If we're going to make real the promise of the American dream to all Americans, which would plainly do a lot to help us deal with the kind of racial difficulties that we began so bravely as a nation to come to grips with this last week, we have to go further in this area.

Those of us in this room who care about science and technology, all of us have a duty to ensure that every child has the chance to take part in the new information age. Technological literacy must become the standard in our country. Computers can enrich the education of any child but only if the child has access to a computer, good software, and a competent, good teacher who can help that child learn how to use it. Preparing children for a lifetime of computer use is just as essential today as teaching basic skills was a few years ago.

Over the past month I have been gratified that so many leaders of the high-tech industry have joined with us to launch a national effort to connect every classroom by the year 2000, a plan that rests upon four pillars: modern computers in every classroom accessible to all students; connections from every classroom to the incredible educational resources flowing throughout the world; teachers in every classroom who are trained to make the most of the technology; and a rich array of educational software and information resources.

Already, significant progress is being made. In California, a voluntary private effort will provide Internet access to every elementary and secondary school by the end of the decade and will wire one out of every five classrooms by the end of this year. That is an astonishing achievement led by private sector companies in California.

These goals are important to our future. And this balanced budget debate has to be seen in that context. It is a very good thing to balance the budget if we do it in a way that is consistent with our values and our clear long-term goals of strengthening our economy, growing our middle class, shrinking our under class, keeping America the world's greatest home for entrepreneurs. If it's consistent with our values and our economic interests, that's what we ought to do. We can't do that if we destroy the public responsibility in these critical areas.

I, however, have to tell you I am basically optimistic, maybe because I am genetically programmed that way. [*Laughter*] We are going through sort of a tortured version of a scientific method now. It reminds me—I say tortured because, unlike the scientific method, it ignores the experiments of the past. [*Laughter*] But still, it's sort of like that.

And I'm reminded of what Winston Churchill said about the United States when we were trying to decide in the Congress whether to support the Lend-Lease Act and help Britain when Britain was alone in World War II. And there was a great question about whether President Roosevelt could pass the Lend-Lease Act through Congress because many thought it was a backdoor way of getting the United States into the war. And Mr. Churchill said, "I have great confidence in the judgment and the common sense of the American people and their leaders. They invariably do the right thing, after they have considered every other alternative." [*Laughter*]

So I urge you to inject some rigor into this scientific experimentation. I thank you for your achievements and your contributions. I do believe that the 21st century can be a golden age for all Americans and that we can help to lead the world to a new era of freedom and peace and prosperity, if we make the right decisions in this critical time of change.

Your very achievements, the example of your life work have increased the odds that we will do exactly that. And on behalf of all Americans, I thank you and congratulate you.

Thank you very much.

NOTE: The President spoke at 2:54 p.m. in the East Room at the White House.

The President's News Conference
October 19, 1995

The President. Good morning. The Congress is about to take some votes that I believe will move this country in the wrong direction. Before they do it, I want to urge them to think again. There's a right way to balance this budget and a wrong way. I strongly believe the Republicans in Congress are taking the wrong way.

On Medicare, the House is voting on a $270 billion cut in Medicare that will eviscerate the health care system for our older Americans. It goes far beyond what is necessary to secure the Medicare Trust Fund. Our plan to secure the Medicare Trust Fund secures it for just as long as the Republican plan at less than half the cost and with far less burden on our seniors.

The House plan, by contrast, actually weakens existing law on waste, fraud, and abuse in the Medicare program, which is a serious problem. And therefore, it will undermine our efforts to save funds through cracking down on waste, fraud, and abuse, as the Attorney General has outlined. On the other hand, it increases costs on older Americans dramatically. That is the wrong way.

So my message to the Republicans is simple: I hope you will think again. I will not let you destroy Medicare, and I will veto this bill. I have to do that to protect the people of the United States and to protect the integrity of this program.

On taxes, just last night we learned from the Republicans' own Joint Committee on Taxation that more than half of the American people who live in the group earning under $30,000 will pay more taxes if the Republican economic plan passes. Why? Because they have a $43 billion tax hike targeted at working families. Now this doesn't count the cost to working families of the increases in college loans, the child support collection fees, the Medicare increases, the Medicaid increases, all told, over $140 billion of taxes, fees, and other increases on the most vulnerable people in our country and on working families.

So again, I would say, think again. I won't let you raise taxes on working families $48 billion. That is not the right way to balance the budget. It isn't fair, and it won't happen. These bills undermine our values, our values of supporting both work and family, our values of being responsible and creating opportunity. They are not necessary to balance the budget.

Meanwhile, Congress is lagging behind on its other business. For the budget this year—the fiscal year, as all of you know, ended 3 weeks ago, and they have still sent me only 3 of the 13 appropriations bills. Last year, all 13 were here and signed into law by the beginning of the fiscal year.

It's been 6 months since the Oklahoma City bombing killed 169 of our fellow Americans and 6 months since congressional leaders promised that they would pass the anti-terrorism legislation by Memorial Day. They still haven't passed the bill. They haven't even scheduled it for a final vote. I might add also, one of the important items in their contract which I did support, the line-item veto, has still not been passed by the Congress and sent to me. And perhaps most troubling of all, because they refuse to extend the debt limit, they are threatening to plunge our country into default for the first time in the entire history of the Republic. This would, of course, mean higher interest rates, which would increase the deficit we both want to reduce, and it would also lead to higher home mortgage costs for millions of homeowners whose mortgages are tied to Federal interest rates. I was told this morning by the Council of Economic Advisers probably somewhere between 7 and 10 million homeowners have mortgages that are tied to Federal interest rates.

So again, my message to Congress on this issue is simple: We must not play political games with the good faith and credit of the United States. Pass the debt limit, and I will sign it.

It's time for Congress to turn back from passing extreme measures that never will become law and instead to work with me for the American people to balance this budget in a way that advances our values and supports our interests. That is what we ought to do. We can still do that; it is what I still believe we will do.

1993 Budget

Now, I can only imagine what the first question is. [*Laughter*] Wait a minute, let me just say one thing. Before you ask this question, I want to say something about my speech—well, the two speeches I gave in which I made reference to the economic plan of 1993. If anything I said was interpreted by anybody to imply that I am not proud of that program, proud of the people who voted for it, or that I don't believe it was the right thing to do, then I shouldn't have said that, because I am very proud of it. I think it was absolutely the right thing to do. I am proud of the people in Congress who voted for it. And the results speak for themselves. After all, that program actually did reduce the deficit by $1 trillion over 7 years. That program drove down interest rates. That program created an economic climate in which the American people were able to produce 7½ million new jobs, 2½ million new homeowners, a record number of new businesses, and put this country moving in the right direction.

So if I said anything which can be read in any other way, then I should not have said that. And I certainly did not mean to do that, and I accept responsibility for it, because I am very, very proud of what I did. And I have tried to make that clear in every talk I have made this year, and I reaffirm it to you here today— all of the parts of the program. We did the right thing for America, and I'm proud of it today, and I'm proud of the people who voted for it.

Q. Mr. President, did you mean to say what you said, that you regret having raised taxes as much as you did?

The President. What I said was—what I meant to say is, I think nobody enjoys raising taxes. I think our system works better when Democrats and Republicans work together to reach consensus, and I think it would work better now if we did. That's what I meant to say.

But I do not believe that when we had the decision to make and we had the vote to cast, I take full responsibility, proudly, for what we did. It was the right thing to do. I believe all the people who have heard me talk about it knew what I meant to say, and I'm proud of the Congress for voting for it. And if we hadn't done it, we'd really be in a fix today. And I might say, the Republicans who criticize us obviously think we did the right thing since they're not trying to undo much of it at all.

Q. But did you raise taxes too much?

Medicare Legislation

Q. Mr. President, you said that you'd veto the Republican Medicare bill for $270 billion worth of cuts. Your own Medicare bill is $124 billion in cuts. Where do you see a compromise between the two? How far are you willing to go?

The President. Well, first of all, I think we have to draw a—I am willing to do what they want to do, which is to extend the life of the Medicare Trust Fund to 2006. That's what we both do. Now beyond that, I don't believe we ought to be raising costs on the elderly poor through the Medicare program and the far worse things that are in the Medicaid program. You know, the Medicaid program supplies the copays and the deductible for very poor elderly people, and they propose to stop doing that.

It's estimated we could lose a million seniors out of the Medicare program, and I just don't think we need to do that. We can balance the budget with the cuts that I have proposed, and that's what I think we ought to do. I believe that they are more than adequate to balance the budget and to secure the Medicare Trust Fund without really burning our seniors.

Helen [Helen Thomas, United Press International].

Bosnia

Q. Mr. President, slight change of subject. Would you send peacekeeping troops to Bosnia if we do not get congressional approval? And you have never stated that you would only keep them for one year. Your people have and the Cabinet has, but is that a flat commitment?

The President. Let me answer the question carefully. The reason I have never said that is that I wanted to define our mission and have the mission be defined in the way that we did in Haiti. We defined our mission in Haiti, and we said, okay, this is when we think we will complete our mission, and we did it. And then we said the United Nations would complete its mission with the next Presidential election, which occurs early next year.

In Bosnia, I wanted to make sure that we had a clear notion of what our mission was. Yesterday, General Joulwan, who is our NATO Commander, came in with the national security team, and we had a very extended session about the plans that are now being developed, which, of course, cannot be finalized until we get a peace agreement, because the nature of the map and the nature of the agreement among the parties will determine in part the nature of the commitments that the United Nations and that NATO will have to make.

But our commanders believe we can complete our mission in a year. That's what they believe. Before I make that pledge to the American people, I want to know what the peace agreement is finally, and I want to have a very high level of confidence that I can make that commitment and keep it. But it looks like we're talking about a commitment in the nature—in the range of a year.

Q. Wait a minute. Would you go ahead then and send the troops, even if Congress does not approve?

The President. I am not going to lay down any of my constitutional prerogatives here today. I have said before and I will say again, I would welcome and I hope I get an expression of congressional support. I think it's important for the United States to be united in doing this. I believe that we had a very good meeting with the Speaker and Senator Dole and a large number of Congressmen, as you know, a couple of weeks ago. I expect that our people will be asked and will have to answer difficult questions; that's the job of the Congress. But I believe in the end, the Congress will support this operation.

1993 Budget

Q. Mr. President, may we take it—just a final followup on this—may we take it from what you said here today that what you meant to say on taxes was that while you raised them more than you would have liked to, that it was perhaps a mistake to say you raised them too much?

The President. If I said anything which implies that I think that we didn't do what we should have done, given the choices we faced at the time, I shouldn't have said that.

My mother once said I should never give a talk after 7 o'clock at night, especially if I'm tired. And she sure turned out to be right, is all I can say. [*Laughter*]

Bosnia

Q. Mr. President, back on the subject of the deployment in Bosnia, many experts feel that by the very nature of a deployment, American troops would become targets for various groups who want to disrupt the situation. How do you prevent that? And having committed troops to Europe twice in this century because they got into a mess they couldn't resolve, why does the United States have to continue to come to Europe's rescue?

The President. Because now what we're trying to do is to avoid just what drug us into Europe. If you remember, I said we would not go into a situation in which we'd be in combat in Bosnia on one side of the conflict, nor would we be engaged with the United Nations mission because of the rules of engagement there, but that if we can make a peace, since NATO would have to be involved in implementing the peace agreement and assuring its success and we are the leaders of NATO, we would have to go into it. The reason we need to do this is to—precisely to avoid the kind of convulsive conflict with massive consequences that drug us into Europe twice before and got huge numbers of Americans killed in the defense of freedom and decency. I strongly believe we can do that.

Now one of the things we are concerned about, obviously, is that if a peace is made, even in good faith, there may be people who don't like the peace. And we don't want—not only the United States but any of the NATO soldiers or any of our allies not in NATO who will be taking part in this, and we expect a significant number of non-NATO members to contribute—we don't want anybody to be targets, and we've given quite a bit of thought to that. And as this plan proceeds, we'll see what happens.

Let me just emphasize—first of all, first things first. The leaders of the three countries have agreed to come here to the United States to meet in Ohio at the end of this month. We are very pleased by that, and that is the next big step. The most important thing, the thing that will reduce danger to everybody, is if these leaders will agree to an honorable peace and then do everything they can in good faith to keep it.

I must tell you, I'm somewhat encouraged by the fact that the cease-fire seems to be taking hold. The incidents seem to be dropping throughout Bosnia. There seems to be an atmosphere of mutual commitment taking hold there, and we obviously hope that can be sustained.

Budget Negotiations

Q. Mr. President, yesterday you said you were perhaps genetically optimistic by nature that there would in the end be a deal when all is said and done. But Speaker Gingrich keeps saying he's willing to cooperate, but he's not willing to compromise on his bottom line in the tax cut, the Medicare cuts, and all these other issues. Why are you optimistic that there still will be a deal?

The President. Because this is America and people usually do the right thing, and because we've been around here for a long, long time. Now, I know that at least in reading between the lines, it appears that the extreme conservative wing in the House continues to move the Speaker back and affect what happens in the Senate and make the possibility of honorable compromise more remote. But I believe in the end, that's the right thing for the country.

My goal, I will say again, and what I try to capture from time to time, sometimes not too well, as we see, is that if you have two people who both make a good-faith effort at reaching a common stated goal, the balanced budget in this case, and they have different approaches, if they get together in genuine honesty and openness—I think there's a way for me to meet their stated objectives, which is a balanced budget in 7 years with a family tax cut, and I think they want a capital gains tax cut and extending the Medicare Trust Fund until 2006, and for them to meet our stated goals, which is to maintain our commitments to our investments in education and our obligations to the elderly through the Medicare program and to the elderly and our children, the disabled people in America through the Medicaid program, and our obligations to the environment and to technology and to the things that will make our economy grow—we can both meet our objectives. And if we do it in good faith, we might wind up with a budget that is better than either one of us proposed. That's what I hope will happen, and I'm going to leave the door open for that. But meanwhile, my job is to protect the American people if something happens that I think is very wrong. And I think the Medicare budget is wrong for America.

Presidential Commission on Race

Q. Mr. President, the University of Texas speech included several challenges on race to blacks and whites alike. How do you plan to further the conversation? Are there any next steps? What are your thoughts about a Presidential commission on race?

The President. Well, as you know, I received a letter signed by a number of House Members asking for that. And I have that and a number of other ideas under consideration. After I spoke at the University of Texas, and after so many came here to Washington in that march in what I thought was such a profoundly moving spirit, an open spirit and is clearly a manifestation of a desire to assume more responsibilities for themselves, for their families, their communities, and to reach out to the white community and their fellow Americans and to try to figure out how we can work together, I think that there is a big responsibility on me and on others to carry forward with that. And as you know, in the last few days I've been quite active with previously scheduled events. But we are turning our attention now very carefully to what should be done to follow up. I think we owe the country a followup, and I'm going to do my best to do it right.

I'll take one more question. Mara [Mara Liasson, National Public Radio].

Budget Negotiations

Q. Mr. President, just to follow up. This, I believe, is the first time you've said that you think you can reach a balanced budget in 7 years. How would the Republicans' plans need to alter so that you could reach that goal and still meet your——

The President. Well, I think we could reach it in 7 years; I think we could reach it in 8 years; I think we could reach it in 9 years. Our budget has moved forward from 10 to 9 years just because of the improvements in the economy and our deficit reduction package since we started. So we're between 7 and 9 now.

So I think it's obvious—what would have to happen is that we would have to find a formula in which we would monitor the reduction of the deficit as we go toward balance because under either of these programs, no one can predict with any exactitude—I mean, no American corporation has a 7-year budget. They may have a 7-year plan or a 10-year plan or a 5-year plan, but they don't have budgets in that sense, because you can't project what all will happen.

So we have to have sort of checks along the way to make sure we're on our downward target.

And then we'd have to find a way to take care of these concerns that I have repeatedly expressed. I do not want us to make education less available. I don't want us to have retrenchment on technology and research. I do not want us to burden, unnecessarily, people who barely have enough money to get by on, who depend on Medicare and Medicaid. I don't want to damage the university hospitals, the children's hospitals, and the urban and rural hospital network of this country with what I think the Medicare budget will do. I don't want to damage the environment. And I do not want to tolerate a $48-billion tax increase on working families with incomes under $30,000. That's wrong.

Thank you very much.

NOTE: The President's 103d news conference began at 11:29 a.m. in the Briefing Room at the White House.

Message to the Congress Transmitting Budget Deferrals
October 19, 1995

To the Congress of the United States:

In accordance with the Congressional Budget and Impoundment Control Act of 1974, I herewith report three deferrals of budgetary resources, totaling $122.8 million.

These deferrals affect the International Security Assistance program, and the Departments of Health and Human Services and State.

WILLIAM J. CLINTON

The White House,
October 19, 1995.

Letter to Senator Edward M. Kennedy on Proposed Employment Non-Discrimination Legislation
October 19, 1995

Dear Ted:

I am writing in regard to the Employment Non-Discrimination Act, which you and Senator Jeffords have reintroduced in the current session of Congress.

As you know, discrimination in employment on the basis of sexual orientation is currently legal in 41 states. Men and women in those states may be fired from their jobs solely because of their sexual orientation, even when it has no bearing on their job performance. Those who face this kind of job discrimination have no legal recourse, in either our state or federal courts. This is wrong.

Individuals should not be denied a job on the basis of something that has no relationship to their ability to perform their work. Sadly, as the Labor and Human Resources Committee documented last year, this kind of job discrimination is not rare. Cases of job discrimination on the basis of sexual orientation are seen in every area of our country.

The Employment Non-Discrimination Act, however, is careful to apply some exemptions in certain areas. I understand that your bill provides an exemption for small businesses, the Armed Forces, and religious organizations, including schools and other educational institutions that are substantially controlled or supported by religious organizations. This provision, which I believe is essential, respects the deeply held religious beliefs of many Americans.

Moreover, your bill specifically prohibits preferential treatment on the basis of sexual orientation, including quotas. It also does not require employers to provide special benefits.

The bill, therefore, appears to answer all the legitimate objections previously raised against it, while ensuring that Americans, regardless of their sexual orientation, can find and keep their jobs based on their ability and the quality of their work. The Employment Non-Discrimination Act is designed to protect the rights of all Americans to participate in the job market without fear of unfair discrimination. I support it.

Sincerely,

BILL CLINTON

Remarks at the Opening Session of the Midwest Economic Conference in Columbus, Ohio
October 20, 1995

Thank you very much, Mr. Vice President, Mr. Mayor. President Gee, you were kind enough to point out that when Ohio State was playing Notre Dame, I was meeting with His Holiness, the Pope. I hope that at election time the people of Ohio will remember that I single-handedly prevented papal intervention in that game. [*Laughter*] And when they say, "What did Bill Clinton ever do for Ohio?" you'll have an answer. [*Laughter*] These are—lightning is about to come through that window right now. [*Laughter*] Forgive me, God.

These are very good days for Ohio, not only because the Buckeyes are winning on the football field and Cleveland has become the comeback team of the ages, winning 100 games in a shortened season and is now in the World Series but because the economy of Ohio has come back. You can drive through this city, you see its vibrancy, its aliveness, its beauty, and the strength that the university and the other parts of the community here give to what is going on. It's very exuberant. And you see this throughout the Middle West.

I want to make a few comments today, if I might, about how what we're doing here relates to what is going on back in Washington. But let me, first, just follow up on some things the Vice President said.

Economic policy is very important to this administration. And when I became President, I determined to do everything I could to put economic policy beyond partisan politics, to forge a partnership between our Government and the private sector, to try to support cooperative efforts between business and labor, and to try to share ideas and work together with people at the State and local level, in other words, to try to move America together toward realizing its maximum economic potential in creating jobs, in raising incomes, in fulfilling the dreams of the American people.

And I believe that the results of the last 2½ years point to the proposition that every administration from here on out in the foreseeable future should seek to put economic policy beyond partisan politics and the traditional wrangling that goes on in Washington, because that is a very important part of our national security and what it means to be an American.

Everyone knows now that we're in a period of profound change, moving from the cold war to the global village, from the industrial era to the information and technology era, when even in a State like Ohio, you know, even our industries are becoming more information- and technology-driven. The Midwest is emerging from years of economic trouble with a hopeful future built around a very, very diversified economy.

At the turn of the century, half of the people in this country worked or lived on farms. At the midpoint of the century, 4 out of 10 Americans worked in factories. By the end of the century, just 5 years from now, half of all Americans will be knowledge workers. We have to find ways to harness this change to make the American dream available to all of our people, to keep our country the strongest nation in the world, and to help people strengthen their families and their communities. That is the great challenge now: How are we going to harness the change so it benefits everyone?

We are engaged in a great debate now over balancing the Federal budget. The real issue is not whether to balance the Federal budget. We now have broad agreement on that after several years of exploding the deficit. The real question is how we should do it. I believe we should try to do it as much as possible based on common sense and the way it would be done if the decision were being made in a town meeting in Ohio instead of through the glare of national publicity and partisan filters in Washington, DC.

We ought to do it in a way that guarantees maximum opportunity for every American, that preserves and strengthens our families, that recognizes that if you live in a country that is a community, it means you have obligations to other people and not just yourself. We ought to recognize what those obligations are, to our parents and to our children, to those who through no fault of their own need our help. We ought to be building our great middle class and shrinking the under class, not the other way around. And I will say again: We must keep our Nation the strongest nation in the world.

So all the decisions that we make about this budget ought to mirror those goals. And everything we talk about today about the Midwest economy or what we found about the economy of the Pacific Northwest or the economy of the South when we had the other regional conferences, all the things we do should be consistent with helping Americans in every region fulfill their aspirations. That's what I think we ought to be doing.

You heard the Vice President say that the American economy is on the move. In the last 2½ years, we've not only seen 7½ million new jobs but a record number of new small businesses within that time period, 2½ million new homeowners, the smallest misery index—the combined rate of unemployment and inflation—in 25 years, a huge expansion in trade. We have seen our exports go from increasing 4 percent to 10 percent to 16 percent in the last 3 years. And the result of all that has been a very good movement for the American economy. It has been fueled in no small measure by the fact that the deficit has been reduced from $290 billion a year to $160 billion while increasing our investment in education, in technology, in research, and in partnerships to help promote the economic strength of the United States. So I feel very good about that.

I have to say that, in the aftermath of the great march in Washington earlier this week, there is also kind of a renewal of common sense and shared values in dealing with social problems in the United States. We have—a lot of people don't know this, but generally throughout the country, the crime rate is down, the welfare rolls are down, the food stamp rolls are down,

the poverty rate is down, the teen pregnancy rate is down. Now, these problems are still very profound in our country, but the American people are reasserting responsibility for themselves, their families, their communities. They're moving this country in the right direction.

And I believe that the work we have tried to do with the crime bill—and I want to thank your mayor and all the mayors for working with us on that in such a bipartisan fashion—to put more police officers on the street, to have more prevention programs, to deal with the problems of our young people and try to keep them from flowering into lives of crime; the work we've done on helping States reform welfare and health care on a State-by-State basis; the work we did to try to help families that are working for modest incomes by lowering their taxes and passing the family leave law—I think these things have supported this great movement by the American people to try to bring our country back together and move our country forward.

And that is the sort of thing that we ought to be trying to accelerate in this budget debate. And we certainly shouldn't be doing anything to get in the way of what you're doing out here and what the American people are trying to do in their own lives and their own communities. That is the kind of balanced budget I want.

I have proposed a balanced budget that balances the budget in 9 years, secures the Medicare Trust Fund, continues to invest more in education and research and technology because I think that's important to our future, and cuts out hundreds of other programs without unduly crippling either the Medicare or the Medicaid program and hurting the people who depend on them and without the kind of tax increases on working people that are in the congressional majority plan.

Yesterday I know you all saw that the House of Representatives voted for the Medicare plan that reduces projected expenditures and Medicare by $270 billion over the next 7 years. And I think that's too much because it will hurt working people too much, hurt the seniors too much and their children, who will have to pay more to help their parents and will have less to educate their children. I think that is a mistake. And you should know that the plan I proposed, which has less than half that many cuts, has exactly the same strengthening effect on the

Medicare Trust Fund. So we're going to argue about that. But I think it's a mistake.

This city and many others have huge, huge, interests and investments in the health care system of this country. University medical hospitals, children's hospitals, medical research facilities, urban hospitals dealing with large numbers of poor people, rural hospitals, all of those folks are going to be hurt quite significantly if we just jerk $450 billion out of the health care system over the next 7 years with no sense of exactly how these budget targets will be met.

And of course, a lot of our most fragile elderly people, under this plan, will be hurt the worst. A lot of older people living on $300 or $400 a month will pay among the largest increases because of the way the plan is structured. I believe that that is inconsistent with our values. And since it is not necessary to balance the budget, I think it's a mistake to do it.

I think it's a mistake to single out education and the environment for deep and devastating cuts. We shouldn't be reducing key programs and environmental protections. As I said, we have already eliminated, under the Vice President's leadership in the reinventing Government plan, we've eliminated hundreds of Government programs, hundreds. We've cut hundreds more. We have reduced the size of Government. There are 163,000 fewer people working for your Government today than there were the day I became President. Next year the Federal Government will be the smallest it's been since John Kennedy was President and—listen to this—as a percentage of the civilian work force, the smallest it's been since 1933. There is no more big Government.

The issue is not maintaining some big bloated Government. We have reduced the size of this Government more rapidly than ever before. We've eliminated 16,000 pages of regulations. We've got some more to do on that, and I'm sure we'll hear from some of you about that today. And I'm more than happy to help with that. But we shouldn't undermine the fundamental ability of the United States to educate our young people, to invest in education and technology, to maintain these health care programs at an appropriate level, to protect our common environment. These are commonsense commitments that are important to achieving a good future. And I just believe it's a mistake.

I also think it is a terrible mistake to raise taxes on working families with incomes under $30,000. I mean, after all, these people are the ones that we want to reward; we want to say, "Don't go on welfare. Work." What we did was the reverse. We dramatically increased the family tax credit, the earned-income tax credit, so that I would be able to say to you by next year, any American with a child in the home working 40 hours a week will not be in poverty. There will never be an economic incentive to be on welfare instead of work because we will not tax people into poverty; we will use the tax system to lift them out of poverty. That is a good, commonsense national goal.

So I say to you, that is what I'm fighting for. I don't want a big partisan fight in Washington, but I am going to stand up for the values that I think would be embedded in this budget decision if it were being made in this room by the people who live in this community. That's my simple test. If the budget decisions were being made by people in this room who live in this community, who reflect a broad cross-section of the people who work here, the people who go to Ohio State as students, the people who teach here, the people who work in the hospitals, the people who work in city hall, the people who do all these things, I believe they would come up with a budget far more like mine than the one that is working its way through Congress. If the crowd was divided equally between Republicans and Democrats, if there were more Republicans than Democrats in the crowd, that's what I believe would happen. And so, I'm going to do my best to do that.

Now, there are some who say that if I stand up for these commonsense values, that they'll just shut the Government down and, for the first time in the history of the Republic, refuse to honor our national debt. Well, I just showed up there 2½ years ago, so I didn't have as much as some of them did to do with running up the debt in the first place. [*Laughter*] But it does seem to me that if we're going to be good neighbors and good citizens, we ought to pay our bills. And I can't imagine that the United States would not pay its debt.

Let me say, again, this just sounds like a rhetorical debate, but this could have practical consequences in the Midwest. If we don't pay our bills, our interest rates on our own debt will go up. If it goes up a tenth of a percent, it adds $40 billion to the deficit over 10 years. What does that mean? No balanced budget, even with this plan, just by letting—or even with their plan, it means no balanced budget if you let the debt limit expire.

I also want you to know that there are $400 billion worth of mortgages held by between 7 and 10 million American homeowners that are tied to Federal interest rates. So if we don't pay our debt on time, if we let this debt limit expire, you have friends and neighbors with home mortgages tied to the Federal interest rates whose monthly mortgage payment could go up. This is not a good idea, either.

We do not need to overly politicize this debate. We need to settle down and pass a budget that will bring our budget into balance, based on commonsense values. That is my commitment.

So I will say to you again, I cannot in good conscience sign a budget that cuts thousands of young, poor children out of getting in the Head Start program, or that makes it harder for young people to go to Ohio State because we raise the interest rates on their loan or charge them fees, or that makes it harder for single mothers out there really working hard to raise their kids because we're going to charge them a bigger fee for collecting the child support they're legally due, or that says to a senior citizen who is living on $300 a month, we're not going to help you with your copays and deductible anymore, even if you drop out of the Medicare system. I can't do that.

I signed on to protect the fundamental interests of the American people, and it has nothing to do with partisan politics. I'm just not going to do it; it's not right.

But there are other economic issues. We gave out the scientific medals—the Vice President and I did—gave out the annual medals for science and technology this week. Do you know that nine of the Nobel Prize winners this year— nine of the Nobel Prize winners in science and technology, of those nine, seven were Americans. Seven were Americans, seven. And all seven benefited in their work from research grants from the United States Government.

Now, this is a small part of our budget. I cannot in good conscience watch us cut 30 percent of our research and development and basic science budget when I know it is critical to our economic future and I know the Japanese just voted to double theirs. They just voted to double theirs. We shouldn't cut ours by 30 per-

cent. That's not right. It defies common sense. It's not necessary.

Secretary Brown—is he on this panel? Secretary Brown got back from China at 11:30 last night. The Commerce Department is a central reason for why exports have increased 4 percent, 10 percent, and 16 percent in the last 3 years. Ohio needs that. That's a good thing for you. The Middle West needs that. Michigan, a State a long way from Mexico, is like the fourth or fifth biggest exporter to Mexico. We've got a lot of people from Michigan here today. It would be a mistake for us to shut down the operations of the Commerce Department and to undermine the work they're doing in technology, especially to help people who lost their defense contracts but are looking for ways to put all these technological benefits to work in the post-cold-war world. It is not necessary to balance the budget, and it would be wrong.

It would be a mistake to cut back on education and training when so many people are having to change jobs more rapidly. We are going to have to redefine security. The most important initiative we've got up there in the Congress today, arguably, is the one that Secretary Reich and I and Secretary Riley have pushed so hard to collapse a lot of these education and training programs and create a large pool so that anybody who loses a job or anybody on welfare can just get a voucher, instead of having to figure out how to get in the Government program, and take it to the nearest community college and immediately begin to get in a program that will give them a skill that will lead to a good job.

This is a practical thing. This has nothing to do with partisan politics. Half the community college board members in America are Republicans. This is not a partisan deal. This is the difference between the way Washington looks at the world and the way the world works on the ground where you live.

So I say to you, my fellow Americans, look what's happened in the Midwest. Look at the renaissance that's occurred here, the resurgence of manufacturing, the infusion of high technology, the strength of agriculture still in this region, something that's often overlooked—this is a huge agricultural region for our country— and the way this region is doing compared to the rest of the country and compared to the rest of the world.

All I want to do is to pass a balanced budget that will strengthen our economy, that will continue the good things that all of you are doing, and that doesn't get in the way of our fundamental values but permits them to continue to advance. That is my commitment. And I don't want to see, after all the progress of the last few years, I don't want to see us get in the way of what we have to do.

And let me just mention, there are three or four things I think we have to do. I think we have to accelerate our ability to innovate. I think we have to accelerate our ability to give people a lifetime of educational opportunity, starting with young children and going through adults who need retraining throughout their lives. I think if we're going to have a tax cut, it ought to be focused on childrearing and education, helping people to finance their education and training. That ought to be the emphasis; there can be other things in it, but we ought to help that. And we ought to pass this "GI bill" for America's workers. I think we ought to do some more for small businesses and for the areas that have been left behind, either in inner cities or rural areas. We began that in the last 2 years, but we ought to do more.

In the last 2 years, we also helped to bail out a lot of the pension systems in the country that were in trouble. Last December, we passed a bill that saved 8½ million pensioners their pensions. We now have a bill working through Congress that would make it much easier for small businesses to take out retirement plans for themselves and their employees. That would be a huge deal. Most of the new jobs are being created by small businesses now. It's much more difficult for small business to provide for health care and retirement and things like that than it is for bigger business or for Government. So I'm hoping that this is one bill we'll have strong bipartisan support on to help.

The last point I want to make is this. I went to the University of Texas earlier this week and gave a speech about race in America. The racial and ethnic diversity of this country is one of the two or three most important assets we have in the global economy. If we can prove we can have a democracy that is a multiracial, multiethnic democracy, where people work together, get along and are honest with each other, we are going to do very, very well in the 21st century. We are going to do very, very well.

That's the last point I want to make to you. We have got to—whether on this issue or any other, we have to learn as Americans to be honest with each other, both in what we say and in how well we listen. We've got to bridge these gaps. Most of the problems we have in this country today, most of the challenges we have are not ideological, they are practical. There is no reason in the wide world to let the country be split in two over most of the real challenges we face. They are practical problems, and they are human problems.

And since I believe most people are good people and most people share the same values, if we learn to speak more clearly and more honestly, if we learn to listen more openly and we learn to sort of leave our ideological blinders at the door, I believe that the next 50 years, even though the United States will not have the same percentage of wealth in the world we had in the last 50 years, in the next 50 years we can have a better life for Americans and in profound ways we can have a more positive influence on the world, because we can prove that all the things other people say they believe in and say they want, we actually are living and doing. That is my goal. And today I want us to focus on what we're doing here in the Middle West and what more we can do to help you to achieve those goals more quickly.

Thank you, and thank you for coming.

NOTE: The President spoke at approximately 10:10 a.m. in the Fawcett Center Dining Room at Ohio State University. In his remarks, he referred to Mayor Gregory Lashutka of Columbus and E. Gordon Gee, president, Ohio State University.

Remarks to the Community in Columbus
October 20, 1995

Thank you, Holly. Thank you, Dr. Gee. Thank you, Richard. And thank you, Mr. Vice President. Ladies and gentlemen, when we came here in 1992, I knew that if I could be elected President that Al Gore would be the most influential and positive Vice President in American history, and he has been exactly that. And I am very proud of him.

I am delighted to be back at Ohio State, delighted to be here when you're on the verge of such an incredible, successful football season, when Cleveland is on the verge of starting the World Series. And I know you're proud of that.

I have so many people in our administration from Ohio: the United States Treasurer, Mary Ellen Withrow; the Federal Railroad Administrator, Jolene Molitoris; most important, my personal photographer, Sharon Farmer, over here, was the vice president of the OSU student body when she was a student. I'm glad to be here with her.

I will be very brief. You've waited a long time, and it's cold, but I want to make a few points to you. I believe that my first responsibility is to guarantee you the best possible future. I want the 21st century to be a time when every American has the chance to live up to the fullest of his or her God-given abilities. I want America to be the strongest force for freedom and peace and decency and prosperity in the entire world. I want your life to be exciting and wonderful and hopeful. And in order to do that, we have to have a strong economy. We have to have a Government that works, that is smaller and less bureaucratic but still fulfills our basic values: giving people the chance to make to most of their own lives, strengthening families, building up communities, helping people, the elderly, the poor children, those who, through no fault of their own, need some help to get along in life. This is part of having a good society.

This country is in much better shape than it was 2½ years ago. We are coming back. We have 7½ million more jobs, millions of more small businesses, the so-called misery index—the combination of unemployment and inflation—is at its lowest point in 25 years. We are moving in the right direction. And we see the American people coming back together and reasserting a sense of responsibility for themselves and their families and their communities, responsibility in a personal way. The welfare rolls are down; the food stamp rolls are down; the poverty rate is down; the crime rate is down; the teen pregnancy rate is down. And community service through things like AmeriCorps, the national service program, is up. This country is moving in the right direction.

We are facing a challenge today in Washington that is a very important one. We do need to balance the budget. When I became President, I was worried that the debt of this country was going to hang over your future like a dark cloud and make your future less than it ought to be. And in 3 years, we took the deficit from $290 billion a year down to $160 billion, the biggest drop in American history.

I want to balance the Federal budget. That is not the question. The question is, how shall we do it? What is the honorable way? What do we need to do? If you want the kind of future that I believe you do, we have to invest as well as cut. We have to guarantee that we have enough to educate all of our people to the fullest of their abilities. We have to guarantee that we have enough to protect our environment. We have to guarantee that we have enough to protect the Medicare and Medicaid of our seniors and our poorest children and the disabled. We have to guarantee that.

And we have to guarantee that we can maintain America's leadership in the world. In just a few days, Ohio will become the center of the world's attention for quite another reason, when the heads of Bosnia and Croatia and Serbia come to Wright-Patterson Air Force Base to try to make peace in Bosnia.

And I have to tell you that—I have to say one sad thing today. A very distinguished graduate of Ohio State University, Joe Kruzel, was one of the three Americans who was killed in Bosnia recently, working for that elusive peace. But he served his country well. You can be proud of him. And when they come here to Ohio and the world looks at Ohio, it will be happening because America has been able to lead the world toward peace, from the Middle

East to Northern Ireland to Haiti to Bosnia. This is important. It matters. It's a big part of your future.

What I want to say to you is this: So many of these things that I am trying to do should not have much to do with partisan politics. It is a part of our basic value structure that we believe people should be able to strengthen their families and make the most of their own lives and protect their parents and their children and protect our environment and make sure it's going to be around for our grandchildren and our grandchildren's grandchildren. That ought to be what America is all about. It shouldn't be a partisan issue.

I have tried very much to work with this Congress, and I will continue to try to do that. But I will not tolerate raising the costs of student loans and student scholarships and cutting out opportunities.

I do not believe America would be stronger if we denied tens of thousands of young children the chance to be in the Head Start program. I do not believe America will be stronger if we deny poor school districts the chance to have small classes and computers in their schools. I do not believe America will be stronger if we wreck the ability of the National Government to provide for clean air and clean water and safe drinking water and pure food. I do not believe that.

I do not believe America will be stronger if we say to the elderly in this country who have worked their entire lives, "We don't really care anymore what happens to you and your health care. It's all right with us if some State tells you that if you or your husband or your wife have to go into a nursing home, before they can get any help from the Government, you've got to clean out your bank account; you've got to sell your car; you've got to sell your home." That's not the kind of America I want to live in, and I do not believe we will be stronger if we do that.

And I know we won't be stronger if we are not given the ability to stand up for basic decency and peace and freedom and prosperity around the world, if we are not given the ability to help to lead the way toward peace in Bosnia and Northern Ireland and the Middle East and Haiti and these other places.

This is what America is all about. And what I want to tell you is, if you look at the future, there is no nation in the world as well-positioned

as the United States for the 21st century. All we have to do is to remember our basic values. And all I ask you to do today is to do the following: Number one, ask yourself, what do I have at stake in this debate for a balanced budget? I need the budget balanced, because I don't want a big debt on my future and my children's future. But it has to be done in the right way so that we can protect education and health care and the environment and the leadership of the United States in the world, because that's a big part of what I want.

And I want to leave you with this last thought as you look at your future. On Monday, nearly a million people gathered in Washington, DC, in a remarkable, remarkable march. And they had a simple message: We want to take responsibility for ourselves, for our families, and for our communities. But we want the rest of America to join hands with us in making this great country what it ought to be.

So I ask you to do one last thing. Look around this crowd today. We are a multiracial, multiethnic country. In a global village where people relate to each other across national lines, nothing, nothing, could give us a greater asset for the 21st century than our racial and ethnic diversity. It is a godsend. It is a godsend.

But all the surveys show, of public opinion, when people are called personally and asked in the privacy of their home, that there are still great differences in the way we view the world based on our racial or ethnic background. And even on our college campuses today, there are too many people whose lives are too segregated.

And so I want to repeat to you what I said at the University of Texas to the students there earlier this week. Make sure, make sure, that you have taken the time to really know and care about and understand somebody who is of a different race. Make sure you have told them the truth about how you feel. Make sure you have listened carefully to how they feel. And make sure you have done what you could in your way personally to bring your community together.

I am telling you, there are a lot of days when I wish I were your age, looking to the future that I think you'll have. It can be a great and beautiful thing. But we have got to go there together. And we have got to go there consistent with the values that made this country great. We can harness all this technology. We can harness all these changes to your benefit, to make your life the most exciting life any generation of Americans ever had. But you have to help us. You've got to stand up for what you believe. You've got to insist that we do it right. I will veto, if I have to, any attempt to mortgage your future. I will not let it happen. But you have to help me claim your future. That's something only you can do. I want you to do it.

I'm honored to be here with you today. I wish you well tomorrow and for the rest of your lives.

God bless you, and thank you very much.

NOTE: The President spoke at 3:07 p.m. at the Oval Mall at Ohio State University. In his remarks, he referred to Holly Smith, student trustee, Ohio State University Board of Trustees, and actor and comedian Richard Lewis, OSU alumnus.

Remarks at the Jefferson-Jackson Day Dinner in Des Moines, Iowa
October 20, 1995

The President. I like to see a Democratic crowd just a little rowdy. I like to see a meeting in Iowa where we don't have to bus people in to raise a crowd.

I want to thank your State chair, Mike Peterson, for inviting me here, and give my regards to your attorney general, Tom Miller; to Treasurer Mike Fitzgerald; to your secretary of agriculture, Dale Cochran; the senate president, Leonard Boswell; the majority leader, Wally Horn; your house minority leader, Dave Schraeder; and to all the other Iowans who are here. And I want to say a special word of thanks to the Iowans who have been a part of our administration: Ruth Harkin, the President of the Overseas Private Investment Corporation; Bonnie Campbell, who does a wonderful job running our Violence Against Women Office; Joel Hern at HUD; Rich Running and Dave O'Brien at Labor; John Miller at FEMA. All these Iowans are doing a great job to serve the United States in the National Government, and I thank them very much.

You know, 4 years ago I was here in the middle of the beginning of the Presidential process. I made a courtesy call because I knew I wouldn't do very well in the Iowa caucuses. [*Laughter*] I hope that it works out differently this time. I had the great honor of coming here to speak to your legislature, and then to come back to Ames for the rural conference. And I was very glad to do that.

I didn't exactly enjoy it, but I was deeply moved by what I saw when I came here during the floods. And I think there is something quite remarkable about this State. And you're going to have a very important role in the direction of the country for many, many years to come. I came here because I wanted to see the Democratic Party alive and well and I wanted to speak to what I believe we have to stand for, clearly, unambiguously, and proudly, and how I believe we can reach out to others to broaden our ranks and deepen our resolve.

I think we have to think first and foremost about the young people here. I'm glad to see all these students who are here. I just spoke to somewhere between 900 and 1,000 of them in the basement. As an old musician, let me tell you that even though I wasn't in the room, I very much enjoyed the Carroll High School Jazz Band; they did a great job. I thank them for that.

I want to say a special word of thanks and admiration to Senator Harkin for his friendship, his leadership, and for what he said tonight. What he said was wise and good and true. I want you to keep him in the Senate; we need him. We need him. America needs him.

You know, Tom Harkin was for balancing the budget when the other guys were still running up the debt. He was for doing it in a way that honors our values and our interests. He worked with me to reduce the deficit but to increase our investment in education, in technology, in research, especially in medical research. He fought for the proposition that we do have certain obligations to one another in this country. That's what the Americans with Disabilities Act is really all about, bringing out the best in everyone so that we'll all be stronger.

He has always been a leader in our fight against crime. And the Vice President and the Attorney General will be coming into Iowa for a violence prevention conference on Monday morning. And I honor him for having led the fight to remind us that we not only have to be strong in dealing with crime, we have to be aggressive in preventing crime. That's one of the many lessons that the majority in Congress seems to have forgotten that Tom Harkin has not.

The last thing I wanted to say about the other guys in my introduction is that I was proud to see Senator Harkin invite independents and Republicans to our cause. If you think about the sharp differences in values being expressed in Washington today, we would be historically accurate to call this the Jefferson-Jackson-Abraham Lincoln-Theodore Roosevelt dinner. They were all on our side, compared to what is going on today in Washington, DC.

My fellow Americans, I come to you tonight with a simple and straightforward message. You know we live in a very great country, on the edge of a new era, a new century, a new millennium, a time of great change. We are moving from an industrial age into an information and technology-driven age where even agriculture and industry will be driven by information and technology. We are moving from the cold war to a global village where all of us will be more closely in contact, more closely bound up. We'll have common possibilities and common vulnerabilities, as we see every day with terrorism around the world and here at home.

This is a time of enormous potential, and your country is on the move. There is no nation in the world remotely as well-positioned to enable its people to fulfill their dreams and to lead the world toward peace and freedom and prosperity as the United States. But we must be true to our values, and we must have a clear vision of that future.

I ran for President in 1992 for the same reason Tom Harkin did. We thought our country was going in the wrong direction, without a clear sense of vision. I said that if I were honored by the American people with the Presidency, I would try to do the following things: I would try to restore the American dream for all our people and make sure we went into the next century as the most powerful country in the world, the greatest force for peace and freedom and prosperity by having an economic policy that produced jobs and growth, that expanded the middle class and shrinks the under class; by giving us a modern Government that is smaller, less bureaucratic, more entrepreneurial, but can still fulfill our fundamental responsibilities to one another; by making sure that America was still the leading nation in the world in a positive sense; and most important of all, by being true to old-fashioned American values in this very new age, of responsibility and opportunity for all, of valuing work, yes, but understanding that families count, too, and we have to help them to stay strong and be together, and of a sense of community which means that we are stronger when we work together.

We're going forward or backward together, and that means we have obligations to one another. It isn't popular in Washington to talk about that today, but it is true. We have obligations to our parents when they need us and to our poor children when, through no fault of their own, they need a hand up in life. We have obligations to those who are disabled or who otherwise need a helping hand who are willing to do their part. We have obligations to take off our own blinders and the chains on our own spirit, which is why I was so proud to see all those people in Washington saying in that march, "I intend to take greater responsibility for myself, for my family, and for my community, but I want to reach out to you to ask you to work with me to make America a better place."

And my message to you is very plain and simple: This country is in better shape than it was 2½ years ago because we have worked hard to do what we said we would do. We still have real and significant challenges that require us to keep going in the right direction, toward a better and brighter future. And we're in the midst of a struggle in Washington that is not about balancing the budget and is far more important than economics, that goes to the very heart of who we are as a people, what we believe and what we are willing to stand for and what kind of America we want our children and our grandchildren to live in in the 21st century. That is what is going on.

You know, in 1993, when we passed our economic program in the most intense partisan environment in modern American political history, the other side said, "Oh, the sky will fall." There were Chicken Littles everywhere. "The world will come to an end if you pass this program.

A recession is just around the corner." Well, 2½ years later we have 7½ million more jobs, 2½ million more homeowners, a record number of new small businesses, the lowest combined rate of inflation and unemployment in 25 years. They were wrong, and we were right.

Do we have more to do? Of course we do. In any time of great change like this, inequality is a danger because some people aren't very well suited to the world toward which we're leaving—toward which we're moving. And we've got to do more in the area of education and training. We've got to do more for rural areas and urban areas that have been left behind. We have got to do more to spread opportunity. But the answer is to build on the successes of the last 2½ years, not to turn around and do the wrong thing.

In the area of Government, I heard the other side complain about Government year-in and year-out and how terrible it was. Well, we didn't do that. We did something about it. I put the Vice President in charge of a reinventing Government task force. Two and a half years later— we didn't just rail against the Federal Government—2½ years later there are 163,000 fewer people working for the National Government. Next year it will be the smallest Federal Government since President Kennedy was President. And as a percentage of the Federal work force, we'll be the smallest Federal Government since 1933. The big Government myth is just that; it's a myth. And we brought it down, the Democrats brought it down. We did it.

There are 16,000 fewer pages of Federal regulations. Hundreds of programs have been eliminated. But the most important thing is performance has been increased. Take the Small Business Administration—a 40 percent cut in the budget, but they doubled the loan volume, more loans to women, more loans to minorities, no reduction in loans to men and, most important, no watering down of the standards for eligibility, just a commitment to old-fashioned American entrepreneurialism. That's the kind of Government we're trying to give you.

For the first time, we realized if we're in a global economy fighting for opportunities, we need to give small businesses a chance to sell their products and services around the world. We need to get everybody involved in having a chance to create jobs in America by relating to the rest of the world. And so, Ruth Harkin and her organization and the Export-Import Bank and the Commerce Department and the State Department, for the first time ever, are all working together to help create jobs. And 2 million, 2 million, of our 7½ million new jobs came because of the expansion of the ability to sell American products overseas in the last 2½ years. And we should thank those people for the work they did on it.

I am proud of the work the Federal Emergency Management Agency did in Iowa and in the other States of the Midwest when they had the 500-year flood. That used to be the most criticized agency in Government. I did a novel thing. I appointed a qualified person to head it, not a politician. And people are proud of it, and Iowans remember it.

And I'll tell you something that will surprise you. Every year, Business Week—Business Week magazine, not an arm of our party— [laughter]—gives awards for outstanding performance in various areas of business. One of the awards they give is for the best consumer service and customer service over the telephone—Federal Express, L.L. Bean, you name it. You know who won this year? The Social Security Administration of the United States Government.

I want you to go out on the street and tell people these things. We made big Government a thing of the past. Are there still stupid regulations? Of course there are, but at least we have a system for trying to do something about it. We are trying to make this Government more entrepreneurial. But that's a lot different than turning our backs on the American people. We are not about to do that.

And I know we live in a time when people are more preoccupied with their own problems. But we cannot run away from the world either. And America is safer tonight because we didn't give up our leadership, because we are in a situation where we're destroying nuclear missiles more rapidly. And for the first time since the dawn of the nuclear age, there is not a single, solitary nuclear missile pointed at an American child tonight, not one, not one, not a single one.

We got over 170 countries to agree to indefinitely extend their commitment not to proliferate nuclear weapons. And next year, God willing, we will have a comprehensive test ban on all nuclear testing.

The United States is stronger when these things happen, when we work against terrorism, when we work against drug trafficking, when we help to make peace from Northern Ireland to Haiti to Bosnia to the Middle East. We are stronger in a more peaceful world where we are living by our values and the power of our example.

But most important of all, this country is coming together around its values again. In almost every State, believe it or not, the crime rate is down, the murder rate is down, the welfare rolls are down, the food stamp rolls are down. The teen pregnancy rate has dropped for 2 years in a row, and the poverty rate is down. America is coming back together and moving forward together. And I believe—I believe the commitments that we have had to family-friendly policies, to community-oriented solutions to our problems have made a difference.

I think it matters that we passed the Family and Medical Leave Act so people don't lose their jobs when their children are sick. I think it matters that we're collecting record amounts of child support. I think it matters that we gave working families in 1993 a tax cut so that we could say, "If you work 40 hours a week and you have children in your house, you should not and you will not be in poverty. We want to reward work and parenting." I believe that matters. I think it's important.

And yes, I think it matters that we decided we had to give all of our young people a chance to live up to the fullest of their God-given abilities, whether it was helping more poor little kids go into a Head Start program or helping States that have difficulties that most Iowa school districts don't have, to have smaller classes and computers in the classrooms or making sure all the young people in this country could go to college by giving them more affordable college loans. It was the right thing to do.

And let me say this. What I have tried to do in this time is to always think about how this is going to impact the future, the future of these children, the future of these young people up here. You know, there are so many controversial decisions a President has to make in a time like this. There is no way—I'll bet you I've done four or five things that made everybody in this room mad. [*Laughter*] And I doubtless have made some mistakes. But I do show up every day—[*laughter*]—and I do work every day, and I do think about your future every day. And that means every day—every day!

Audience members. Four more years! Four more years! Four more years!

The President. Thank you. I'll just give you some examples. I knew that when we passed the Brady bill and the ban on assault weapons that the NRA would be able to terrify a lot of good, God-fearing, hard-working American gun owners into thinking we were trying to take their guns away. And I knew it would hurt a lot of people who stood up for what was right. And don't kid yourself, it's one of the big reasons the Democrats lost the House.

But you know, last year 40,000 criminals who would have been able to get guns didn't because of the Brady bill, 40,000. And not a single American hunter or sportsman has lost a gun, not a single one. And there will not be one. But there are some mean streets and some schools where some thug can't show up with an Uzi and gun down a bunch of innocent kids. And that's worth a little political heat, I think. It's the right thing to do.

When the Food and Drug Administration came to me and they said, "Oh, Mr. President, we have completed our 14-year study of children smoking"—14-month study—"and we know, know, based on the records, that the big tobacco companies know this is hazardous to the health of young people, that they continue to advertise to young people, that 3,000 young people a day start smoking, and 1,000 of them will die sooner because of it," the conventional political advice was, "For goodness sakes, you have made enough people mad, Mr. President, don't fool with this because they will take all those good, hard-working, God-fearing tobacco farmers and convince them that you want to put them in the poorhouse, that you're trying to have the Government take over everybody's private decisions, and everybody who's against you on that will be against you, and the people that are for you will find some other reason to be against you."

That was the conventional politics. But folks, 1,000 kids a day taking up a habit that will end their lives early, what is that worth? That's worth a lot of political heat. Think about 10, 20, 30 years from now. I want those kids to be alive in a great America of the 21st century, and I think it was the right thing to do.

When the First Lady went to Beijing to stand up for the rights of women and children everywhere—[*applause*]—thank you—the conventional wisdom was, notwithstanding your ovation, that that was a bad idea. People said, "Well now, look, if she goes, just the act of her going will legitimize human rights practices we don't agree with." People on the other side said, "Oh, oh, if she goes and says what's true, it might offend the Chinese and we'll mess up our trade relations and will it cost a few jobs."

But let me tell you something, folks. We're going to live in a world with all of these other countries. In South Asia alone, there are 77 million more—listen to this—77 million more young boys than young girls. Why? These little girls are being killed. They're not valued as people. Boys are still thought of as more important economically and therefore as human beings than girls. We can't live in a world at peace and harmony, consistent with our values, until we live in a world where women everywhere, including women here, subject to domestic violence and abuse on the street, can live in dignity and freedom and equality. We cannot do that.

And I just want to say one more thing. When I went to the University of Texas Monday morning, some people said, "This is a very dangerous thing for you to embrace the people that are showing up in Washington and stand up for racial reconciliation. You don't know what's going to happen there." But I know one thing. I didn't know what was going to happen there—I thought I did—I knew that march was about the people that were showing up, not about the leaders. I knew it was about what was in people's heart on that day, not what some people had said in political speeches. I knew that the same thread that's running through America that's driving down the teen pregnancy rate and the crime rate and all of these other things was running through the spirit of those people there. And it seems to me that as President I have a responsibility to speak to that. You look around this room, you've got a fair amount of diversity. You look up in that crowd of young people, you'll see a lot more. Generationally, there will be more and more and more.

In a global village, old-fashioned American values, the power of American free enterprise and technology, the power of America's example, combined with the fact that we are so diverse across racial and ethnic groups, is our meal ticket to the future. It is not only morally the right thing to do, it is a gold mine for us if we will turn away from those who would divide us. That's why I said to the American people last week, every American needs to make a per-

sonal commitment that they're going to establish some sort of a personal relationship with someone of a different racial or ethnic group. And if you work with a lot of people from different groups, ask yourself if you've ever really had an honest conversation, have you ever really told anybody what you thought?

The most stunning thing to most Americans in the aftermath of the Simpson trial was all that public research saying that people from different races saw the same set of facts in a completely different light. But most of us share the same values. That's what the march proved. People showed up saying, "We do have to take more responsibility for ourselves, our families, and our communities, and we are going to do it. And we want to reach out to you." So we have to do that. All of you do. We have to set an example. We have to be honest with one another. We have to listen to one another. And we have got to find a way to come together. Because, I'm telling you, if you solve this diversity problem, America, there is no stopping this country in the 21st century; it is ours to lead and to enjoy and to profit from.

So that is the background. This country is on a roll. We're moving in the right direction. We have problems. We'll always have problems. We know what to do. We need to have a good economic policy, a Government that works and doesn't get in our way too much but protects our fundamental interests. We need to make sure we maintain our leadership in the world. And we need to have a set of policies as a people consistent with our values.

Now, that is really what is going on in Washington. That's what we're debating up there today. We are not debating the balanced budget. That is not the issue. I have presented a balanced budget that Mr. Greenspan, who was appointed by my predecessors and is a Republican, and many others—and all the market analysts say it is a perfectly credible balanced budget. I have given them a balanced budget. This is not about balancing the budget. What is at stake here is what kind of people we are going to be in the 21st century, what kind of future are we going to have. And I just want to ask you a few questions.

You heard Senator Harkin talk about the Medicare cuts and how they want to save money, but they've actually made it harder for us to prosecute waste, fraud, and abuse in Medicare. We have set records in our administration for collections of waste, fraud, and abuse, and we haven't scratched the surface. And now they want to stop us. They don't think that's important.

Well, my idea of the future of America is not a Medicare program where it's easier to commit waste, fraud, and abuse, but harder for a senior citizen to live from month to month because their Medicare premiums have been doubled when they can't afford to pay for it. That's not my idea of the future I think we ought to have in America.

The Medicaid program has not gotten as much coverage, but my idea of the future of America is not living in a country where we cut Medicaid so much we're closing more rural hospitals, we're closing inner city hospitals, we're putting unbearable burdens on our teaching hospitals and our children's hospitals, we're making it harder for poor little kids to get care.

And I'll tell you something else that's in this bill. They want to take away the money that we presently give under the Medicaid program to help the poor elderly pay their copays and their deductibles, people living on $300 and $400 a month, so the people under this plan that are going to get hit the hardest are not the wealthiest seniors but the poorest seniors. And a study has been put out that said as many as 1 million seniors might drop out of the Medicare system.

I don't know about you, folks, but I don't want somebody to give me a tax cut and put a million old people out of the Medicare system. That's not the America that I want to live in. I don't think it is right, and I do not support it.

Let me tell you—I want to reiterate—I do support the goal of balancing the budget. I agree with them we have to save the Medicare Trust Fund. To do it, we have to slow the rate of growth in medical inflation in Medicare and Medicaid. We don't have to take 450 billion bucks out of the health care system to do it.

Do you know what else is in one of those plans? They want to repeal the prohibition against spousal impoverishment. Now, that's a Government phrase. Let me tell you what that means. That means if a married couple are lucky enough to be 78 or 80 years old, they've been together 50 years, and they've saved their money and been frugal, one of them gets real sick and has to go to a nursing home—which is heartbreaking enough as it is—they want to go

back to the dark old days when the State can tell the spouse that doesn't have to go to the nursing home, "We'll give you help, but only after you sell your car, your house, and clean out your bank account. Now, then, we'll take your spouse in the nursing home. I don't know what you're going to do. That's not our problem." I don't know about you, folks, that is not the America that I want to live in the 21st century. I don't believe in that. I don't believe in that.

Look at those young—how many college students do we have up there? How many of you get student aid? The only thing that has grown faster than the cost of health care in the last 15 years is the cost of higher education. And yet we know we need more and more and more young people to be able to go to college and be able to finish college.

I pledged if elected President I would provide a more efficient, more cost-effective student loan program that would get the money out quicker, that would lower the cost to students, and that would provide for easier repayment terms. I also promised to crack down on people that didn't repay their loans. We have cut the loan default rate in half by cracking down. But you know what else we've done? We're getting those young people their money quicker at lower cost with better repayment terms, so that young people who get out of college and don't get jobs making a lot of money can pay the loan off as a percentage of their income. And there will never, never, never, never be an incentive not to borrow the money to go to college because you're afraid you can't pay it back. Now, that's what we did. And it's a good, good thing to do.

Their budget limits or totally destroys, depending on which House you look at, this direct loan program. It goes back to the old way where we just shove money to the private sector, total Government guarantees, no performance standards, no costs, nothing, raises the cost to the taxpayers and cuts out good loans to them and, for good measure, eliminates somewhere between 150,000 and 380,000 college scholarships, depending on whether the Senate or the House version passes.

I don't know about you, but the 21st century I want to live in does not include kicking middle class kids out of college, taking scholarships away from poor kids, and doing things that will not help us to build the great American dream for all Americans. I don't want that kind of 21st century. That is not my idea of how we ought to be living.

I don't believe we ought to go into the 21st century gutting our budgets to protect clean air, clean water, pure food, to preserve our natural heritage, and letting the lobbyists for the biggest polluters in the country write the clean water laws. That's not my idea of the 21st century that I want.

I don't believe we should walk away from our crime bill, which is lowering the crime rate, and stop people from putting these police on the street and stop communities from having prevention programs to give our children something to say yes to. I don't believe we should refuse to raise the minimum wage. That's their position. Next year it will get to a 40-year low in purchasing power if we do that. I don't believe that's right, either.

I don't believe, notwithstanding what one of your Senators believes, that we should abolish AmeriCorps. It would be a terrible mistake to get rid of the national service program. The national service program involves young people and working with other people to solve community problems. It has no bureaucracy. It ought to be a Republican's dream. But because it involves the National Government bringing people together to do something positive and good and decent to move people forward, they say, no, no, no.

That's not my idea of the 21st century. My idea of the 21st century has all young people serving their communities, working together, building this country from the grassroots up, earning their way to college and moving forward.

There is a provision in this budget that would allow companies who have been in deep trouble to withdraw money from their pension funds, even if it puts the retirement of their workers in trouble. Now, last December, I signed a piece of legislation that saved 8½ million Americans' pensions and stabilized 40 million more Americans' pensions. Do you really want me to sign a budget that would permit pension funds to be looted and have people's pensions and retirements put at risk?

Audience members. No-o-o!

The President. I don't think that's what we ought to be doing in the 21st century.

And here's the last thing. This is the last on my top 10 list. There are $148 billion of new taxes, fees, and costs imposed on middle class America and poor America in this budget, including a $42 billion tax increase on working people with the most modest incomes in our country.

The Wall Street Journal—again, this is not me, hardly an arm of the Democratic Party—the Wall Street Journal yesterday reported—the Wall Street Journal reported that if this budget passes with all of its tax cuts in it, the group of people making less than $30,000 a year, 51 percent of the American people, will have greater tax hikes than they have tax cuts. Can you believe it? Why? Ronald Reagan said that the working family tax credit was the best antipoverty program the country had ever devised. All we did was double it so people could say, "If I work 40 hours a week and I've got children in my house, I will not be taxed into poverty. The tax system will lift me out of poverty. My country values my work and values my being a good parent."

I do not want to live in a country that throws people out of the middle class and puts them back in the under class, and I don't think you do, either. I don't think you do, either. I don't think any of you want to live in that kind of America.

So, look—I'm nearly done. You don't even have to sit down. [*Laughter*] I just want you to think about this. This country is on a roll. We're coming back. It's in better shape than it was 2½ years ago. The American people deserve the lion's share of the credit. But our economic policies and our social policies and our anticrime bill and our welfare reform, those things have all played a role. We are moving in the right direction.

And the choice now is whether we're going to be a society in which everybody has a chance to win or become a winner-take-all country, a society where we're growing the middle class and shrinking the under class or one in which we're kicking people out of the middle class and swelling the under class, a society in which special interest and short-term greed override the long-term concern for the welfare of all Americans.

This is a very, very great country. We are a great country. And you look at these children tonight. And when you walk out of here, I want you to keep their faces in your mind, and I want you to promise yourself that you will realize that this could be a Jefferson-Jackson-Abraham Lincoln-Theodore Roosevelt dinner. This is about American values, American interests, America's future. And I want you to promise yourself that when you walk out of this room tonight, for the next year you are going to engage your fellow Americans in talking about these fundamental values and the fundamental vision we have for our future. The 21st century is ours if we will simply be true to our values and follow our vision and think about these children and what kind of America we want for them.

Thank you, and God bless you all.

NOTE: The President spoke at 9:15 p.m. in the Veterans Memorial Auditorium.

The President's Radio Address
October 21, 1995

Good morning. I want to talk to you today about American renewal. Not economic renewal, though our economy is certainly on the move. Not the renewal of peace, though the United States is leading hopeful efforts toward peace from the Middle East to Northern Ireland to Bosnia. Not even the renewal of the American spirit, though there is a tide of optimism rising over our country as we harness technology and other changes to increase opportunities for all our people and strengthen our families and communities. No, the American renewal I want to talk to you about today is the renewal of our national pastime, the renewal of baseball.

A year ago, for the first time in 90 years, we found ourselves without a World Series, and boy, did we miss it. We missed those nail-biting extra-inning nights. We missed a game that for so many of us is so much more than a game. Well, tonight, with the start of the World Series, baseball is back. And we couldn't be happier.

Baseball is a part of our common heritage. Its simple virtues—teamwork, playing by the rules, dedication, and optimism—demonstrate basic American values. We can look out at the green grass of the outfield or feel the worn leather of an old glove or watch a Latino shortstop scoop the ball to a black second baseman, who then throws it to a white first baseman in a perfect double play, and say, yes, this sure is America. This is who we are.

At its best, baseball is more than just a field of dreams. Every season brings our children and many adults face to face with heroes to look up to and goals to work toward. This year was no different. Greg Maddux's 1.63 ERA; Albert Belle's 50 home runs and 50 doubles; and of course, most important, Cal Ripken's 2,131st consecutive game: All these inspire countless young people to play the game and those of us who are older to make the most of the talents God has given us, no matter what kind of work we do.

While baseball provides role models, it also helps us recognize these American values in everyday life. Just before Cal Ripken broke Lou Gehrig's record, I saw a story about other dedicated workers, featuring a bus driver who hadn't missed a day's work in 18 years. This man said he didn't see anything unusual about himself; after all, his father had told him we're all supposed to work hard and show up every day. But had it not been for Cal Ripken, we would never have had the opportunity to meet this wonderful man or to appreciate the hard work that he and millions and millions of other Americans do every day just by showing up for work like Cal Ripken did.

Baseball does something more. It helps to hold us together; it helps us to come together. I've been fortunate enough to see a lot of our great country. Just about everywhere I've ever been I've come across a baseball diamond. No matter where you go in America, sooner or later there will be a patch of green, a path of dirt, and a homeplate.

When I was growing up in Arkansas, baseball connected me to the rest of America. My team was the St. Louis Cardinals, the closest team to my home State. They were the ones we got on the radio. And I spent a lot of hot summer nights listening to the heroics of Stan Musial come over my transistor, like thousands of other young kids all over America.

Baseball also teaches us tolerance. It teaches us to play as hard as we can and still be friends when the game's over, to respect our differences, and to be able to lose with dignity as well as win with joy—but real tolerance for differences. I mean, after all, my wife was raised in Chicago as a Cubs fan, and she married me even though I'd grown up rooting for the Cardinals. And everybody in the Midwest knows that when Cubs fans and Cardinal fans can sit down together, that's real tolerance.

If you watch one of the 178,000 Little League teams in this country, you also will see real community in America. Two and a half million of our children get together to play this sport, boys and girls. And that's not counting everyone who supports the teams and shows up for the games and practices and bake sales. Communities large and small grow up around baseball: kids playing a pick-up game until it's too dark to see, folks getting together for softball after work, families walking together to see a home game at their local ball park.

This has been a wonderful baseball season. When it's over and the owners and players sit down to resolve their labor dispute, I hope they'll remember the spirit of the season, the spirit we all feel right now, and use it to come together to build a lasting agreement. America doesn't need to lose baseball in a squabble. America needs to keep baseball.

During World War II, there was a debate about whether baseball should continue while so many of our young Americans were fighting for freedom around the world. President Roosevelt knew we should play ball. He wrote, "It would be best for the country to keep baseball going. Everybody will work longer hours and harder than ever before, and that means they ought to have a chance for taking their minds off their work even more than before."

Well, we still need baseball. We know we have many important challenges facing us as a nation as we prepare for the 21st century. We know that we're having important debates in Washington and real differences. But tonight, I just hope Americans will be able to take their minds off all that and their own work for a moment. I hope they'll be able to wonder instead at the arc of a home run, a catch at the wall, the snap of the ball in the back of a mitt. Soon these sights and sounds will become a new part of our shared national memory of baseball.

Tonight fans of the Cleveland Indians and the Atlanta Braves will watch with special interest. But all of us Americans have reason to smile, for baseball is back.

Thanks for listening, and play ball.

NOTE: The address was recorded at 10:20 a.m. on October 20 in the Veterans Memorial Auditorium in Des Moines, IA, for broadcast at 10:06 a.m. on October 21.

Remarks at the Dedication of the National Czech and Slovak Museum in Cedar Rapids, Iowa
October 21, 1995

Thank you very much. President Havel, President Kovac, Governor Branstad, Senator Harkin, Congressman Leach, Mayor Serbousek, Mr. Schaeffer, Mr. Hruska, Ambassador Albright. Ladies and gentlemen, if we have not demonstrated anything else about the Czech and the Slovak heritage of Iowa, we have certainly shown to these two Presidents that you are a hearty people. I thank the Czech Plus Band for playing today. I thought they did a marvelous job, and we thank them.

I am proud to stand here with these two Presidents, each a pioneer and a patriot, each leading his nation through an epic trans-

formation, each representing the promise of Europe's future, and their presence today reflects our growing partnership as well as the deep roots of their people in the soil of Iowa.

I will never forget visiting Prague in January of 1994, the first time I had been there in 24 years, and walking across the magnificent Charles Bridge with President Havel. I remembered then all the young people I had met there a quarter century before and how desperately then they had longed for the freedom they now enjoy. In his devotion to democracy and through his courage and sacrifice, Vaclav Havel helped to make the dreams of those young people a reality, and the world is in his debt.

President Kovac stands with us as a leader of a newly independent nation with a proud heritage and a hopeful future. Mr. President, we know your job has been and continues to be difficult. And the United States supports your personal strong commitment to openness and reform as Slovakia takes its place within the family of democratic nations. And we thank you for your leadership.

Here in America's heartland, the heart of Europe beats loud and clear. Czech immigrants first came to Cedar Rapids in the middle of the 19th century. Soon, a little Bohemia had blossomed in the city where Czech culture flourished in journalism, music, and drama.

Today that proud heritage is as vibrant as ever. One in five residents of Cedar Rapids is of Czech descent, including your mayor. There are eight major Czech-American organizations in this city, and through the Czech school, American children learn the language and traditions of their ancestors an ocean away. Just a few steps from here, the shops of Czech Village are filled with authentic crafts and home cooking. I think it's fitting that in this celebration of American diversity, we have a city which produces both Quaker Oats and kolaches. [*Laughter*]

In Iowa and beyond, Americans of Czech and Slovak descent have added richness and texture to our American quilt. The values they, like so many other immigrants, brought from their homelands—love of family, devotion to community, taking responsibility, and working hard—these values flourished in America and helped America to flourish.

In the mid-19th century, thousands of Czech settlers farmed America's new frontiers, an experience immortalized in Willa Cather's novel "My Antonia." Slovak immigrants brought their skill and strength to the urban Northeast and the Midwest, where they helped to build heavy industry and oil and steel and coal.

The children and grandchildren of these early pioneers, as well as more recent arrivals, have been generous with their gifts to America: Filmmakers like Milos Forman have challenged our imagination; students of the humanities have been enlightened by Jaroslav Pelikan; and stargazers stand in awe of Captain Eugene Cernan, the last human being to leave his footprints on the Moon. From city hall to Capitol Hill, indi-

viduals like Congressman Peter Visclosky of Indiana, former Congressman Charles Vanick of Ohio, and former Senator Roman Hruska of Nebraska have served our country with distinction. Our dynamic Ambassador to the United Nations, Madeleine Albright, who is here with me today, was born in Prague. And as I have told President Havel several times, the Czech Republic is the only nation in the world that has two Ambassadors at the United Nations. [*Laughter*]

The National Czech and Slovak Museum and Library we are privileged to dedicate here today is a wonderful tribute to two cultures and two peoples and to the contributions Czech and Slovak immigrants and their descendants have made and continue to make to our great Nation. In keeping with tradition, a dozen eggs have been added to the mortar of the cornerstone, guaranteeing that the museum will serve the public as long and proudly as the Charles Bridge in Prague. To all who have played a part in creating this great place, congratulations on your marvelous achievement.

My fellow Americans, I ask you to take just one more minute to reflect on what our history and this moment mean for us today and in our tomorrows. We celebrate a special corner of our rich and varied mosaic of race and ethnicity and culture and tradition that is America. We are many different peoples who all cherish faith and family, work and community and country. We strive to live lives that are free and honest and responsible. We know we have to build our foundation, even in all of our differences, on unity, not division; on peace, not hatred; and on a common vision for a better tomorrow. We know that our motto, *E Pluribus Unum*, is more than a motto, it's a national commitment.

As we deal with all the remarkable changes that are moving us from the cold war to the global village, from the industrial to the information and technology age, we have to remember that we cannot keep the American dream alive here at home unless we continue to make common cause with people like President Havel and President Kovac, unless we continue to stand for freedom and democracy and peace around the world.

The United States has made a real contribution to the march of freedom, democracy, and peace, in accelerating the dismantling of our nuclear weapons so that now, for the first time since the dawn of the nuclear age, there's not a single nuclear missile pointed at a single American citizen.

We are working with people all around the world to combat the dangers of terrorism and the proliferation of weapons of destruction. We have tried to be a force for peace and freedom from the Middle East to Northern Ireland to Haiti and, most recently, in Bosnia, where we are hoping and praying that the peace talks will succeed and that the cease-fire will turn into a genuine peace agreement. All of that, of course, especially affects the efforts of these two Presidents to secure their own people and their future.

The Czech Republic, Slovakia, other nations in Central Europe, they are working hard to build the democracy and foster the prosperity that we sometimes take for granted. They've made an awful lot of progress in the face of real challenges, and we have to continue to stand by them by opening the door to new NATO members, by supporting their integration into the other institutions of Europe, by improving access to our own markets and enabling them to move from aid to trade. The Czech and the Slovak people who came to the United States helped us to build our country. It's time for us to return the favor.

More and more Americans are investing in becoming economic partners. There was $300 million worth of economic transactions with the Czech Republic and about $100 million with Slovakia last year, with much more in the pipeline. And I have to say, a lot of that was due to the extraordinary personal efforts of one distinguished citizen of Iowa, the head of the Overseas Private Investment Corporation, Ruth Harkin, who is here with us today. And I thank her for her efforts.

Making these countries economically strong and helping them to be free and to stay free is the best way to ensure that American soldiers never again have to shed their blood on Europe's soil. It's also good business for us, as you well know. Cedar Rapids is the largest exporting city per capita in the entire United States. Foreign trade creates jobs here.

But we have to do this because it's also the right thing to do. For 45 years we challenged the people of these nations to cast off the yoke of communism. They have done it, and we dare not abandon them now. We have an obligation to work together so that all our people can enjoy the rewards of freedom and prosperity in the 21st century.

I believe the citizens of Cedar Rapids understand that. Those of you of Central European descent have to know it and feel it in your bones. But all of us as Americans should feel it in our hearts, for we believe the American dream is not for Americans only. It is for every hard-working man and woman who seeks to build a brighter future, every boy or girl who studies hard and wants to learn and live up to their dreams, every community trying to clean its streets of crime and pollution and build a better future for all the people who live there, every nation committed to peace and progress. That dream belongs to every citizen of the world who shares our values and will work to support them.

President Havel, President Kovac, my fellow Americans, as we celebrate the opening of this marvelous museum, a monument to those who had faith in the American dream and who struggled to make it come true for themselves and their children, let us resolve to work together for hope and opportunity for all who are reaching for their dreams.

Thank you, and God bless you all.

NOTE: The President spoke at approximately 11:30 a.m. In his remarks, he referred to President Vaclav Havel of the Czech Republic; President Michal Kovac of the Slovak Republic; Governor Terry E. Branstad of Iowa; Mayor Larry Serbousek of Cedar Rapids, IA; and Robert Schaeffer, president, and Roman Hruska, chairman of the board, National Czech and Slovak Museum.

Remarks at the National Italian-American Foundation Dinner
October 21, 1995

Thank you, ladies and gentlemen. Thank you, Frank Guarini, for that wonderful introduction. Chairman Frank Stella, Vice Chairman Art Gajarsa, Senator Domenici—always does a good job at these dinners. I must say I was delighted this was not one of those annual roasts, because otherwise I would have been the object of his wonderful humor. [*Laughter*] I am delighted to be here with you and with all the Members of Congress tonight. To the Most Reverend Cacciavillan, the Ambassador from the Holy See; the Italian Ambassador, Ambassador Biancheri; to the Foreign Minister of Italy, Foreign Minister Agnelli, I'm delighted to see you here tonight. And I want to say a special word of thanks on behalf of the United States to our Ambassador to Italy, Reginald Bartholomew, for what a fine job he has done. To all the board members and friends of the foundation, some of whom—hundreds, indeed, of whom have come here tonight from Italy, I am deeply honored to be with you tonight for the fourth time in a row on the occasion of your 20th dinner. And I would like to say one thing to the Italians here present, beginning with the Foreign Minister.

Last year I came to this dinner direct from a trip to the Middle East and a signing of the peace treaty between Israel and Jordan. In the last year, in many ways the world has moved closer to peace in Northern Ireland and Haiti, another signal event on the road to peace in the Middle East. And by the grace of God, we will continue the road to peace, beginning on October 31st, when the leaders of all the countries involved in the conflict in Bosnia meet in the United States in Ohio. If we are able to make a peace and enforce it, I want all my fellow Americans to know that it would not have been possible but for the strong and firm leadership and involvement of Italy. And I am very grateful for what they have done to bring about peace in Bosnia.

I know a lot of your honorees. Last Monday, I was in Los Angeles with Tony Bennett, who was the headliner for a wonderful concert put together as a benefit for the Center for Alcohol and Substance Abuse at Columbia University. Just a couple of days ago, Joe Montana and

his lovely wife and their four wonderful children and some of their friends came to the White House. And as their children were examining— I think that's the appropriate word, examining— everything in the Oval Office, I thought to myself, now, there are real family values. And since we're—I have to say, since this event is held in Washington, DC, and given all that's going on here in Washington, I think it's quite appropriate that you're honoring on the same night Joe Montana and John Travolta, because what's going on here reminds me of a cross between a pro football game and "Pulp Fiction" half the time. [*Laughter*]

Earlier this month, I was with Cardinal Bevilacqua when I had the great honor to welcome His Holiness Pope John Paul II to Newark, New Jersey. It was our third meeting since I've been President. I don't want to commit heresy here, and I'm not a Roman Catholic, but there are some important parallels between the Holy Father's career and mine. [*Laughter*] He came from Poland to the Vatican; I came from Arkansas to the White House. [*Laughter*] We were both outsiders who got jobs that usually go to insiders. [*Laughter*] And sometime in 1993 or early '94 or so, I saw the obvious, that he seemed to be doing better than I was. [*Laughter*] And I searched for the reasons why, and I realized it was because he had named an Italian chief of staff. By blind coincidence, about 30 minutes after that light dawned in my brain, Leon Panetta walked in for a meeting, and that's how he got the job. [*Laughter*]

I want to thank all the Italian-Americans who are active in this administration: the Ambassador; Mr. Panetta; Laura D'Andrea Tyson; Pat Griffin, the head of our Congressional Liaison; the Director of the FBI, Louis Freeh; Bob Balancato, the executive director of our conference on aging. And one person I want to mention especially tonight who doesn't get mentioned enough, Marilyn DiGiacobbe, who did such a wonderful job of coordinating for us during the Pope's visit and tonight and so many other times.

These people have done a lot to help our administration move our country forward and do the things that Frank Guarini was kind enough to mention. I want to thank this organization for the support that you have given us in our common efforts to move this country forward.

I love to come to this dinner for a lot of reasons. There are always a lot of laughs. There are always a lot of distinguished people here. I always learn a lot. But most importantly, I think it's important that the President acknowledge that Italian-Americans have given us a model, all of us, for valuing our families, caring for our communities, celebrating our unique cultures while respecting those of others. Italian-Americans have given a great deal to our Nation. And they've shown us the importance of preserving and creating opportunity for generations to come.

It's these values that I believe should guide all Americans without regard to party or position. I honestly believe the best days of this country lie before us. I believe there is no country in the world better positioned for the 21st century than we are. As we move from the cold war to the global—[*applause*]. Thank you. I'm glad you believe that. But we have to realize we're going through a period of more profound change in the way we work and live and relate to the rest of the world than perhaps in any time in a hundred years. And we have to be visionary about the future while holding fast to the values that got us where we are and make life worth living.

We are moving our economy forward. We've tried to address our most serious problems at home. We're trying to change the Government in a way that befits the 21st century. You might be interested to know that your Federal Government now has 163,000 fewer people working for it than it did the day I was inaugurated. I didn't know it until Laura Tyson told me last week, but she went back and checked. As a percentage of the civilian work force, the Federal Government is the smallest it has been since 1933. So the era of big Government is a big myth in that sense. We, too, have to become more productive. We, too, know we have to do more with less. But we also have to, together, continue to honor our basic values and pursue our common interests. We have to give our kids a better future. We have to give Americans a chance to make the most of their own lives and hold their families together.

We have to recognize that, as the Governor of Florida said the other day, we are, in fact, a community, not a crowd. He said a crowd is a group of people that occupy the same piece of land but have no obligations to each other, so they just elbow one another until the strongest get ahead and the others fall behind. A community is a group of people that recognize that they will go forward or fall back together, that they have obligations to one another, and that they become better and fuller and richer by fulfilling those obligations.

You might be interested to know, and you might find it difficult to believe, but there is moving in America, in this big country that moves ever so slowly, a new spirit of community and family and personal responsibility. In almost every State the crime rate is down. In our Nation the welfare rolls are down, the food stamp rolls are down, the poverty rate is down, and the teen pregnancy rate is down now for 2 years in a row. Our country is beginning to move together and move forward.

What I want to say to you tonight is that I believe these decisions we are now making in Washington about the budget are not really about the budget. They must be about our basic values and what we imagine America should look like in the 21st century. And because we are changing so rapidly—frankly, no one can predict anyway what will be popular a month or 6 months or a year from now—we all have to try to imagine what we want America to look like 10 or 20 or 30 years from now.

My friend Cardinal Bernardin once said, "Families give life, and giving life means more than procreation. It means education and nurturing children to the full status as sons and daughters of God and citizens of their country and their world." The United Nations calls the family the smallest democracy at the heart of society. Where will new generations learn about democracy's rights and responsibilities if not at home? That is the question that we have to answer: What will the home of America be? What will our communities be? What will our families be? And I urge you, whether you're a Republican or a Democrat, whether you live here or all the way across the country, whatever you do for a living, as we debate these great issues, imagine what you want America to look like for your children and your grandchildren. It's changing so fast you can't predict how it's going to look in a month or 6 months, in a year.

That is the context in which I hope this debate over the budget will play itself out. We all want a strong economy. We all want a strong America. To do it we have to have strong individuals, strong families, and strong communities.

I believe that the budget debate is not about balancing the budget. Everybody's for that. I couldn't believe what had happened to the debt when I came here. And we've taken the deficit from $290 billion a year down to $160 billion in just 3 years. I am proud of that. I think it's important and it matters. And every one of you, no matter what your party or political philosophy, should want us to finish that job. We should not leave this crushing burden of debt on our children. We should not take money away that is needed in our private sector to create jobs and invest and grow America and make us stronger. Everybody should be for it, but how we do it is a function of what we imagine our common responsibilities to be.

I believe we have to do it in a way that permits us to invest in education and invest in technology and invest in research, so that we can grow the economy and grow strong individuals. I believe we have to do it in a way that permits us to preserve the fundamental health care system that enables us to honor our responsibilities to our parents, to the disabled, to poor children. I believe we have to do it in a way that enables us to protect our natural environment and to recognize that there is a certain elemental sense of fairness that Americans always have, a certain compass that always guides us, and if we will hew to that and do what is common-sensical and consistent with our basic values, we will be fine.

I have done my best and will continue to do my best to move beyond traditional partisan politics at this very untraditional time, to work with the United States Congress to achieve a balanced budget in which all Americans can win. But I have to say, and I want you to know, I do not believe any major American company on the verge of the 21st century would cut its investment in education or research or technology, and I don't think we should either. I do not believe any family would willingly say that its poorest elderly members should be forced to pay for health care they cannot afford or its most vulnerable children should be put at risk of losing that health care. And I don't think we should either. I do not believe we should hamper our common responsibilities to

protect the environment of the United States or to work with other nations to secure the environment of the planet. I do not believe anybody would knowingly do that, and I don't think we should either.

I hope very much that we will see a coming together in this process. Everybody knows that the President under our Constitution has a veto and has to be prepared to use it. Everybody knows what the rules are in Congress. They're going to do what they're going to do, and if I have to use my veto pen, well, I'll do that. But in the end, what we need to do is to come together to build a stronger America, good for our children, good for our families, good for our communities.

You know, the lesson—I will just say this, and I want you to reflect on it—the ultimate lesson of what I saw in the faces of the thousands and thousands and thousands of African-American men who came here last week to march was people in a total spirit of reconciliation and personal atonement saying, "Yes, I do intend to take more responsibility for myself, for my family, and for my community. But I would like it very much if I do that"—[applause]—but the other message was, "I would like it very much if I do that, if you would reach out and join hands with me and help us solve our common problems and move our country forward together."

That's why I said at the University of Texas something that I think Italian-Americans, especially who came here at a time when immigrants from Italy and Ireland were discriminated against, can identify with this. We still have too many people in America passing each other like ships in the night. I saw the other day an old book I had by Will Rogers. He said, for example, he said, "The Congress is someplace where somebody gets up and talks real loud, no one listens, and then everybody says they disagree." [*Laughter*] Well, that's not just in Congress, and it's not just there. That happens in America, and it happens among people of different racial and ethnic groups.

And so I leave you with this challenge. I think we need, each of us as Americans, not only to value our own ethnic solidarity and our shared values but to share them with other people. We need to find somebody who is different from us and tell them what we really think for a change, even if it hurts. And then we need to have the discipline to listen to what they say. And we need to work slowly to bridge these gaps in the way we view reality that have become so present and prevalent in our country.

I am telling you if you look at the facts, this country is better positioned for the 21st century than any country on Earth. Why? Because we're the most ethnically diverse, with the most flexible economy, with all these resources that God has given us and that our forebears have developed. We are well-positioned. We have to learn how to use—to make our diversity as an asset instead of letting it tear us apart. We have to relish in our diversity.

You're happy to be Italian here, but you're also proud to be Americans. We want everybody in America to feel that way, and we want everybody to feel that way about other groups as well. And we know if we do that we'll be all right.

So I say to you, I want you to think about this. Every time a decision is called upon to be made in this Nation's Capital or in your community, ask yourself what's it going to look

like in 20 years? What kind of America do I want my grandchildren to grow up in? Will we give people the right and the ability to make the most of their own lives? Will we help families become stronger? Will we be more of a community and less of a crowd? If the answer is yes, that's what we ought to do. And if we do it, you will be very proud of the America you leave to your children and your grandchildren, worthy of your Italian-American heritage.

Thank you, and God bless you all.

NOTE: The President spoke at 9:30 p.m. at the Washington Hilton Hotel. In his remarks, he referred to Frank Guarini, president, Frank Stella, chairman, and Arthur Gajarsa, vice chairman, National Italian-American Foundation; singer Tony Bennett; former NFL football player Joe Montana; actor John Travolta; Gov. Lawton Chiles of Florida; Anthony Cardinal Bevilacqua, Archbishop of Philadelphia; and Joseph Cardinal Bernardin, Archbishop of Chicago.

Remarks to the United Nations General Assembly in New York City
October 22, 1995

Mr. President, Mr. Secretary-General, Excellencies, distinguished guests. This week the United Nations is 50 years old. The dreams of its founders have not been fully realized, but its promise endures. The value of the United Nations can be seen the world over in the nourished bodies of once-starving children; in the full lives of those immunized against disease; in the eyes of students eager to learn; in the environment sustained, the refugees saved, the peace kept; and most recently, in standing up for the human rights and human possibilities of women and their children at the Beijing conference.

The United Nations is the product of faith and knowledge: Faith that different peoples can work together for tolerance, decency, and peace; knowledge that this faith will be forever tested by the forces of intolerance, depravity, and aggression. Now we must summon that faith and act on that knowledge to meet the challenges of a new era.

In the United States, some people ask, "Why should we bother with the U.N.? America is strong; we can go it alone." Well, we will act, if we have to, alone. But my fellow Americans should not forget that our values and our interests are also served by working with the U.N.

The U.N. helps the peacemakers, the care providers, the defenders of freedom and human rights, the architects of economic prosperity, and the protectors of our planet to spread the risk, share the burden, and increase the impact of our common efforts.

Last year I pledged that the United States would continue to contribute substantially to the U.N.'s finances. Historically, the United States has been, and today it remains, the largest contributor to the United Nations. But I am determined that we must fully meet our obligations, and I am working with our Congress on a plan to do so.

All who contribute to the U.N.'s work and care about its future must also be committed to reform, to ending bureaucratic inefficiencies and outdated priorities. The U.N. must be able to show that the money it receives supports saving and enriching people's lives, not unneeded overhead. Reform requires breaking up bureaucratic fiefdoms, eliminating obsolete agencies, and doing more with less. The U.N. must reform to remain relevant and to play a still stronger role in the march of freedom, peace, and prosperity.

We see it around the world in the Middle East and Northern Ireland, people turning from a violent past to a future of peace. In South Africa and Haiti, long nights and fears have given way to new days of freedom. Throughout this hemisphere, every nation except one has chosen democracy, and the goal of an integrated, peaceful, and democratic Europe is now within our reach for the first time. In the Balkans, the international community's determination and NATO's resolve have made prospects for peace brighter than they have been for 4 long years.

Let me salute the U.N.'s efforts on behalf of the people of Bosnia. The nations that took part in UNPROFOR kept the toll of this terrible war in lives lost, wounds left unhealed, children left unfed from being far graver still.

Next week, the parties to the war in Bosnia will meet in Dayton, Ohio, under the auspices of the United States and our Contact Group partners, Russia, the United Kingdom, France, and Germany, to intensify the search for peace. Many fundamental differences remain. But I urge the parties to seize this chance for a settlement. If they achieve peace, the United States will be there with our friends and allies to help secure it.

All over the world, people yearn to live in peace. And that dream is becoming a reality. But our time is not free of peril. As the cold war gives way to the global village, too many people remain vulnerable to poverty, disease, and underdevelopment. And all of us are exposed to ethnic and religious hatred, the reckless aggression of rogue states, terrorism, organized crime, drug trafficking, the proliferation of weapons of mass destruction.

The emergence of the information and technology age has brought us all closer together and given us extraordinary opportunities to build a better future. But in our global village, progress can spread quickly, but trouble can, too. Trouble on the far end of town soon becomes a plague on everyone's house. We can't

free our own neighborhoods from drug-related crime without the help of countries where the drugs are produced. We can't track down terrorists without assistance from other governments. We can't prosper or preserve our environment unless sustainable development is a reality for all nations. And our vigilance alone can't keep nuclear weapons stored half a world away from falling into the wrong hands.

Nowhere is cooperation more vital than in fighting the increasingly interconnected groups that traffic in terror, organized crime, drug smuggling, and the spread of weapons of mass destruction. No one is immune: not the people of Japan, where terrorists unleash nerve gas in the subway and poison thousands; not the people of Latin America or Southeast Asia, where drug traffickers wielding imported weapons have murdered judges, journalists, police officers, and innocent passers-by; not the people of Israel and France where hatemongers have blown up buses and trains full of children with suitcase bombs made from smuggled explosives; not the people of the former Soviet Union and Central Europe, where organized criminals seek to weaken new democracies and prey on decent, hard-working men and women; and not the people of the United States, where homegrown terrorists blew up a Federal building in the heart of America and foreign terrorists tried to topple the World Trade Center and plotted to destroy the very hall we gather in today.

These forces jeopardize the global trend toward peace and freedom, undermine fragile new democracies, sap the strength from developing countries, threaten our efforts to build a safer, more prosperous world.

So today I call upon all nations to join us in the fight against them. Our common efforts can produce results. To reduce the threat of weapons of mass destruction, we are working with Russia to reduce our nuclear arsenals by two-thirds. We supported Ukraine, Kazakhstan, and Belarus in removing nuclear weapons from their soil. We worked with the states of the former Soviet Union to safeguard nuclear materials and convert them to peaceful use. North Korea has agreed to freeze its nuclear program under international monitoring. Many of the nations in this room succeeded in getting the indefinite extension of the Non-Proliferation Treaty.

To stem the flow of narcotics and stop the spread of organized crime, we are cooperating with many nations, sharing information, providing military support, initiating anticorruption efforts. And results are coming. With Colombian authorities, we have cracked down on the cartels that control the world's cocaine market. Two years ago, they lived as billionaires beyond the law; now many are living as prisoners behind bars.

To take on terrorists, we maintain strong sanctions against states that sponsor terrorism and defy the rule of law, such as Iran, Iraq, Libya, and Sudan. We ask them today again to turn from that path. Meanwhile, we increase our own law enforcement efforts and our cooperation with other nations.

Nothing we do will make us invulnerable, but we all can become less vulnerable if we work together. That is why today I am announcing new initiatives to fight international organized crime, drug trafficking, terrorism, and the spread of weapons of mass destruction, initiatives we can take on our own and others we hope we will take together in the form of an international declaration to promote the safety of the world's citizens.

First, the steps we will take: Yesterday, I directed our Government to identify and put on notice nations that tolerate money laundering. Criminal enterprises are moving vast sums of ill-gotten gains through the international financial system with absolute impunity. We must not allow them to wash the blood off profits from the sale of drugs from terror or organized crimes. Nations should bring their banks and financial systems into conformity with the international anti-money-laundering standards. We will work to help them to do so. And if they refuse, we will consider appropriate sanctions. Next, I directed our Government to identify the front companies and to freeze the assets of the largest drug ring in the world, the Cali cartel, to cut off its economic lifelines and to stop our own people from dealing unknowingly with its companies. Finally, I have instructed the Justice Department to prepare legislation to provide our other agencies with the tools they need to respond to organized criminal activity.

But because we must win this battle together, I now invite every country to join in negotiating and endorsing a declaration on international crime and citizen safety, a declaration which would first include a no-sanctuary pledge, so that we could say together to organized criminals, terrorists, drug traffickers, and smugglers,

"You have nowhere to run and nowhere to hide."

Second, a counterterrorism pact, so that we would together urge more states to ratify existing antiterrorism treaties and work with us to shut down the gray markets that outfit terrorists and criminals with firearms and false documents.

Third, an antinarcotics offensive. The international drug trade poisons people, breeds violence, tears at the moral fabric of our society. We must intensify action against the cartels and the destruction of drug crops. And we, in consumer nations like the United States, must decrease demand for drugs.

Fourth, an effective police force partnership. International criminal organizations target nations whose law enforcement agencies lack the experience and capacity to stop them. To help police in the new democracies of Central Europe, Hungary and the United States established an international law enforcement academy in Budapest. Now we should consider a network of centers all around the world to share the latest crime-fighting techniques and technology.

Fifth, we need an illegal arms and deadly materials control effort that we all participate in. A package the size of a child's lunch bag held the poison gas used to terrorize Tokyo. A lump of plutonium no bigger than a soda can is enough to make an atomic bomb. Building on efforts already underway with the states of the former Soviet Union and with our G–7 partners, we will seek to better account for, store, and safeguard materials with massive destructive power. We should strengthen the Biological Weapons Convention, pass the comprehensive test ban treaty next year, and ultimately eliminate the deadly scourge of landmines. We must press other countries and our own Congress to ratify the Chemical Weapons Convention and to intensify our efforts to combat the global illegal arms network that fuels terrorism, equips drug cartels, and prolongs deadly conflicts. This is a full and challenging agenda, but we must complete it, and we must do it together.

Fifty years ago, as the conference that gave birth to the United Nations got underway in San Francisco, a young American war hero recorded his impressions of that event for a newspaper. "The average GI in the street doesn't seem to have a very clear-cut conception of what this meeting's about," wrote the young John F. Kennedy. But one bemedaled Marine sergeant gave the general reaction when he said, "I don't know much about what's going on, but if they just fix it so we don't have to fight anymore, they can count me in."

Well, the United Nations has not ended war, but it has made it less likely and helped many nations to turn from war to peace. The United Nations has not stopped human suffering, but it has healed the wounds and lengthened the lives of millions of human beings. The United Nations has not banished repression or poverty from the Earth, but it has advanced the cause of freedom and prosperity on every continent. The United Nations has not been all that we wished it would be, but it has been a force for good and a bulwark against evil.

So at the dawn of a new century so full of promise, yet plagued by peril, we still need the United Nations. And so, for another 50 years and beyond, you can count the United States in.

Thank you very much.

NOTE: The President spoke at 10:30 a.m. in the General Assembly Hall at United Nations Headquarters. In his remarks, he referred to United Nations General Assembly President Diogo Freitas do Amaral and United Nations Secretary-General Boutros Boutros-Ghali.

Remarks Prior to Discussions With President Nelson Mandela of South Africa and an Exchange With Reporters in New York City
October 22, 1995

President Clinton. Hello. Is everyone in?

President Mandela. They're the only people who can order the President of a superpower around. [*Laughter*]

President Clinton. Let me just begin by saying that it's a great honor for me to have a chance to meet with my friend President Mandela again. He is a symbol of the best of what has occurred in the world in the last 50 years, since the United Nations has been in existence. And we honor the progress South Africa has made and is making. We value our partnership and look forward to doing more together.

I want to thank again the President for making it possible to establish the Gore-Mbeki commission so that we'll have a very high-level way of working together systematically over the long run. And we are very excited about it, and I'm looking forward to our meeting.

President Mandela. [*Inaudible*]—is in power in South Africa, it is the duty of the new government to solve the problems facing the country and not to be pointing the finger—fingers—at what happened before we came into power. But for the purpose of appreciating what the United States of America has done to facilitate the transformation that has taken place in our country and the trend of democracy, we must start from the point that we faced one of the brutal systems of racial oppression in our country. And the fact that in our anti-apartheid fight we had the support of a country like the United States of America strengthened the democratic forces in our country and enabled us to win. It is in that spirit that I always look forward to meeting the President of the United States of America. And it is in that spirit that I'm going to have discussions with him.

Thank you.

[*At this point, one group of reporters left the room, and another group entered.*]

President Clinton. Let me begin by saying it is a great honor for me to welcome my friend President Mandela back to the United States. He is a hero to so many people in our country because of his long fight for freedom and democracy and justice in South Africa. And on this 50th anniversary of the United Nations, I think we can fairly say that the example that he and his country have set really embodies the best of what the United Nations is trying to do throughout the world.

Vice President Gore and Mr. Mbeki have established a remarkable commission where we're going to have a high-level, ongoing, significant partnership with South Africa. And I believe that this relationship is in good shape. And I look forward to making it better.

And I'm delighted to welcome you here, Mr. President. Would you like to say anything before we let them ask a question or two?

President Mandela. Thank you. We have had very good relations with the United States of America. I must point out that the first head of state to congratulate me when I came out of prison was the President of the United States of America at the time. And he invited me to this country.

Our relations have deepened considerably since President Clinton took over power. He has helped us to ensure that democracy in our country is deeply entrenched. And it is always in that spirit that we think of him. And it is in that spirit that I'm here today to have these discussions with the President.

I look forward to reaching agreement on a wide variety of issues. This has been my experience before in having discussions with him. And I have no reason to doubt whatsoever that from this short meeting that we're going to have, we'll come out stronger and more close to one another as never before.

Thank you.

United Nations Funding

Q. Mr. President, what makes you think the Republican Congress will be in any mood to give you the money to make up the back payments the U.S. owes the U.N.?

President Mandela. Can you just repeat that?

President Clinton. Excuse me.

President Mandela. He was talking to you. I'm so sorry. Very sorry. I am very sorry.

President Clinton. I wish you would answer that question. [*Laughter*]

Q. Do you think they might—the money until—

President Clinton. Well, the Secretary of State and Ambassador Albright are working on that in the Congress now. There are some supporters of the United Nations in the Congress and the Republican Party. And again I say—you know, we're having this argument on another subject— I just believe America ought to be a good citizen. I think we ought to pay our bills.

Now, we have made it clear that our contribution should be more commensurate with our share of the world's wealth, and it will be. We have made it clear that there have to be reforms in the United Nations, and we're working hard

on that. But I don't think the United States wants to be known as the biggest deadbeat in the U.N. That's not the kind of reputation I think we should cultivate. And we are still the largest contributor to the United Nations, but we ought to pay our obligations. I was raised to believe we should pay our obligations. I was raised to believe the United States set a standard for the world in honoring its obligations. And I do not believe that we should depart from that now. I worked hard to get our arrears paid back in a disciplined, regular way, and the Secretary of State and Ambassador Albright will be working with Congress to see if we can do that.

Cuba

Q. Mr. President, if President Mandela was able to speak to the apartheid government when he came out of prison, why is it the United States can't talk to Cuba's Fidel Castro?

President Clinton. He was speaking to his own country and his own country trying to change his own country.

We have a Cuban Democracy Act which sets the framework of our relationship. And we have a mechanism within which we have dealt with the Cubans on matters of common concern for some years now. And that mechanism has operated since I've been President. And the Cuban Democracy Act provides for a measured improvement of our relationships in direct response to measured steps by the Cubans moving toward greater freedom and openness and democracy. And we have taken some steps in the last few days, as you know, to try to open contacts and to try to facilitate travel by Cuban-Americans to go see their families. So we're moving in a direction that we can continue to move in if Cuba continues to move in that direction.

I think the Cuban Democracy Act and its framework sets a good way of seeing this relationship mature when there are changes in Cuba that warrant it.

NOTE: The President spoke at 12:20 p.m. at the United States Mission to the United Nations. In his remarks, he referred to Executive Deputy President Thabo Mbeki of South Africa. A tape was not available for verification of the content of these remarks.

Remarks at a United Nations Luncheon in New York City
October 22, 1995

Mr. Secretary-General, first, on behalf of all of us here present, let me thank you for your hospitality. But far more important, I thank you for your leadership, your energy, your resolve, and the vision of the United Nations and the world for the next 50 years that you have just painted for us. To be sure, the United Nations will face greater demands, but the potential for doing greater good is there as well. And we believe that your leadership has played a very important role in bringing us to this point.

This morning, I was able to speak about many of the specific activities of the United Nations and some that I hope we will undertake in the future. At this luncheon, I would just like to thank you for something that has been done by the United Nations in the last couple of years that I believe has been also very important, and that is the effort that you have made through the international conferences sponsored by the U.N. to change the way we think and to deepen our understanding. From Rio to Vienna to Copenhagen to Cairo to Beijing, you have brought the peoples of the world together to help us to learn about one another and to change the way we think about the present and the way we imagine the future. And that, in the end, may be the most important legacy of the last few years.

Finally, let me say to you, Mr. Secretary-General, and to all of you here present, it has been a profound honor for the United States to host the U.N. for these last 50 years. We know that from time to time, because of the differences between our nations, during the cold war and in other ways, it has not always been easy for other countries to have the United States as the host. But we have always tried to provide here at the U.N., notwithstanding the differences among countries from time to time, a haven where all the members can come, have their say, and be weighed in the court of public opinion.

I would say to you that we here in the United States still treasure the opportunity that was given to us 50 years ago to be the host of the United Nations. We have benefited from it in ways that even our own citizens are often unaware. And we hope that the next 50 years will be an even richer, more profoundly successful endeavor by all of us because of what we have learned by working together in this last half century.

I'd like to conclude by offering a toast to the Secretary-General and to the United Nations.

NOTE: The President spoke at approximately 1:39 p.m. in the North Lounge at the United Nations Headquarters.

Message to the Congress on Sanctions Against Narcotics Traffickers Centered in Colombia
October 21, 1995

To the Congress of the United States:

Pursuant to section 240(b) of the International Emergency Economic Powers Act, 50 U.S.C. 1703(b) and section 301 of the National Emergencies Act, 50 U.S.C. 1631, I hereby report that I have exercised my statutory authority to declare a national emergency in response to the unusual and extraordinary threat posed to the national security, foreign policy, and economy of the United States by the actions of significant foreign narcotics traffickers centered in Colombia and to issue an Executive order that:

blocks all property and interests in property in the United States or within the possession or control of United States persons of significant foreign narcotics traffickers centered in Colombia designated in the Executive order or other persons designated pursuant thereto; and prohibits any transaction or dealing by United States persons or within the United States in property of the persons designated in the Executive order or other persons designated pursuant thereto.

In the Executive order (copy attached) I have designated four significant foreign narcotics traffickers who are principals in the so-called Cali cartel in Colombia. I have also authorized the Secretary of the Treasury, in consultation with the Attorney General and the Secretary of State, to designate additional foreign persons who play a significant role in international narcotics trafficking centered in Colombia or who materially support such trafficking, and other persons determined to be owned or controlled by or to act for or on behalf of designated persons, whose property or transactions or dealings in property in the United States or with United States persons shall be subject to the prohibitions contained in the order.

I have authorized these measures in response to the relentless threat posed by significant foreign narcotics traffickers centered in Colombia to the national security, foreign policy, and economy of the United States.

Narcotics production has grown substantially in recent years. Potential cocaine production—a majority of which is bound for the United States—is approximately 850 metric tons per year. Narcotics traffickers centered in Colombia have exercised control over more than 80 percent of the cocaine entering the United States.

Narcotics trafficking centered in Colombia undermines dramatically the health and well-being of United States citizens as well as the domestic economy. Such trafficking also harms trade and commercial relations between our countries. The penetration of legitimate sectors of the Colombian economy by the so-called Cali cartel has frequently permitted it to corrupt various institutions of Colombian government and society and to disrupt Colombian commerce and economic development.

The economic impact and corrupting financial influence of such narcotics trafficking is not limited to Colombia but affects commerce and finance in the United States and beyond. United States law enforcement authorities estimate that the traffickers are responsible for the repatriation of $4.7 to $7 billion in illicit drug profits from the United States to Colombia annually, some of which is invested in ostensibly legitimate businesses. Financial resources of that magnitude, which have been illicitly generated and injected into the legitimate channels of international commerce, threaten the integrity of the domestic and international financial systems on which the economies of many nations now rely.

For all of these reasons, I have determined that the actions of significant narcotics traffickers centered in Colombia, and the unparalleled violence, corruption, and harm that they cause in the United States and abroad, constitute an unusual and extraordinary threat to the national security, foreign policy, and economy of the United States. I have, accordingly, declared a national emergency in response to this threat.

The measures I am taking are designed to deny these traffickers the benefit of any assets subject to the jurisdiction of the United States and to prevent United States persons from engaging in any commercial dealings with them, their front companies, and their agents. These measures demonstrate firmly and decisively the commitment of the United States to end the scourge that such traffickers have wrought upon society in the United States and beyond. The magnitude and dimension of the current problem warrant utilizing all available tools to wrest the destructive hold that these traffickers have on society and governments.

WILLIAM J. CLINTON

The White House,
October 21, 1995.

NOTE: This message was released by the Office of the Press Secretary on October 23. The Executive order is listed in Appendix D at the end of this volume.

The President's News Conference With President Boris Yeltsin of Russia in Hyde Park, New York
October 23, 1995

President Clinton. We don't have prepared statements, but we will each make a very brief statement, and then we'll take a couple of questions.

This was our eighth visit as heads of state. It was a good and productive one which emphasized the stability and the strength of the partnership between the United States and Russia.

We spent the vast majority of our time discussing Bosnia, and we reached complete agreement about how we would work together for peace there. We reached agreement on the importance of the involvement of Russia and the other Contact Group partners in the peace process. On the question of what our roles would be in the implementation of a peace agreement, we made some progress, and we agreed that our representatives, Secretary Perry and Minister Grachev, would continue to work on this in the coming days, literally in just a matter of days.

We discussed a number of other issues. I think I should mention three very briefly. First, we agreed that we would both push hard for the ratification of START II. Second, we agreed that we would continue our close cooperation on nuclear security, and we have a statement that we have already agreed on prepared by our experts which will be released today. And finally, we agreed—and this is very, very important—that we would work together to succeed in getting a zero-yield comprehensive test ban treaty next year. This is a major, major step, and it dramatically increases the chances of our success for a sweeping comprehensive test ban treaty in 1996. And I want to thank President Yeltsin for that.

Mr. President.

President Yeltsin. Dear ladies and gentlemen, dear journalists: I want to say, first of all, that when I came here to the United States for this visit at the invitation of the President of the United States, Bill Clinton, I did not at that time have the degree of optimism with which I now am departing.

And this is all due to you because, coming from my statement yesterday in the United Nations, and if you looked at the press reports, one could see that what you were writing was that today's meeting with President Bill Clinton was going to be a disaster. [*Laughter*] Well, now for the first time, I can tell you that you're a disaster. [*Laughter*]

President Clinton. Be sure you get the right attribution there. [*Laughter*]

President Yeltsin. This proves that our partnership is not calculated for one year or for 5 years but for years and years to come—tens of years, for a century; that we're friends, and that it's only together, together we're going to be trying to solve not only our joint bilateral issues but issues affecting the whole world.

How many journalists' brains are used to constantly try to figure out what kinds of different versions and options the two Presidents are going to try to come up with regarding Bosnia? I can't say that your brains turned out to be useless—[*laughter*]—of course, you also helped us, and we are grateful. And so you did help us because when Bill and I sat down to look at the different options, we used even some of your seemingly most unbelievable options. [*Laughter*]

Bill said also that we agreed on nuclear disarmament. We agreed on a whole host of issues, not just those that affect our two countries but that affect all the countries of the world. Bill neglected to say we also came to terms on the flank limits that have been placed. And I want to say a big, big thank you to Bill for supporting us so strongly on this score.

I want to say a big, big thank you, Bill, for inviting me here to this most magnificent site. If all of you look around you, look behind you—the most incredible scenery—you will find this a most lovely place to host such a meeting. I want to thank Bill from the bottom of my heart, to bow my head before all of the people, the people who work here, who support this wonderful museum, the staff who made this visit so wonderful, all of you who support not only the museum but also the persona, the personality of President Roosevelt, the one who was a personality not only for the United States but for all the peoples of the world for all time.

I do want to bow my head and thank all of you for this wonderful occasion.

So with this, I want to stop with my introductory remarks. We'll have just a couple of questions. And as soon as we start we're going to finish, so very short. First question to the President of the United States.

Bosnia

Q. Mr. President, could you tell us what progress——

Q. Could you tell us——

Q. Could you tell us, Mr. President—President Yeltsin, are Russians now willing to work under the command and control of NATO in a peacekeeping mission in Bosnia? And then a followup for President Clinton.

President Clinton. I understand that, but let me just say first, we agreed that it was important for Russia to participate in the implementation of the agreement. We discussed some specifics on which we were in accord and some on which we agreed that we had to let our defense experts work. And we decided that we would say nothing here which would make their work any harder than it already is.

Russia-U.S. Relations

Q. Mr. Clinton, as the Russian press, we'd like to ask you the following question. You were saying that not only has it not caved in, our partnership has not caved in but it has become stronger and better. Does that indicate that Russia and the United States will be for the future generations the guarantor of peace, that there will be no wars?

President Yeltsin. With the faith of two big Presidents like us, our faith is getting stronger. And with this faith, it means that we have decided that there shall be no disagreement between our two countries, that our partnership will in fact be strengthened, and having this faith means that we will move into the future toward peace, either with no war or a minimum of war.

Bosnia

Q. Could we get the answer to President Yeltsin's original question, and that is whether or not he could ever accept the idea of Russian forces being under a NATO command? And for those of us in this country who've followed this dispute, it is difficult to understand how you could have made progress given how different your positions have been in the past, and especially after what you said at the United Nations yesterday.

President Yeltsin. We agreed today that Russian armed forces will participate in these operations. But how they go about doing it is the affair of the military; it is not a question for us two Presidents. We have done our task.

Russia-U.S. Relations

Q. How would you characterize, President Yeltsin, the way the talks went today, as a whole, in general?

President Yeltsin. When I came here I thought we were going to have very, very tough meetings. I was not looking forward to the very difficult, complicated discussions. I had a lot of apprehensions. However, on my way here, I flew into Paris, had detailed talks with Jacques Chirac. On the phone I had discussions with Helmut Kohl. I met also very actively with other leaders. President Bill Clinton was very active in meeting with world leaders.

And in spite of the forecasts that said that this would be a breakdown, that this would not be a success, this turns out to be today the friendliest meeting, the best meeting, the most understandable meeting, not only for each other but for all the people of the world.

And we discussed individual positions; then we arrived at common positions. And I must say that this kind of meeting is not an official summit, it is a working meeting. But this most successful working meeting is worthy of meetings that would last hundreds of days, and these big issues, global issues that affect the lives of all the peoples on this planet.

President Clinton. I'll take one more question, but I'd like to say something about your question as well. If I could speak directly to the Russian people, I would say that the United States and Russia have established an important partnership. It's a partnership of mutual respect based on a shared commitment to democracy, a shared commitment to working for the prosperity of the Russian people, and ultimately a partnership which helps us both economically and, perhaps most important, working together to make the 21st century a time of greater peace and greater freedom and greater prosperity for all the people of the world.

That is the larger truth in which all these issues should be seen. That is why we have made such remarkable progress in dealing with the nuclear issues. There is no relationship between two human beings, much less two countries, with their own unique histories, their own unique aspirations, their own unique fears and understandings, that does not have occasional differences of opinion. That would happen in any friendship, in any marriage, in any business; certainly it will happen between two countries. But if we keep the larger truth in mind, we will be able to work together and sustain this partnership. And it is very important for our people and for the people of the world that we do so.

Interpreter. Thank you very much.

President Clinton. They cut it, sorry.

President Yeltsin. Thank you.

President Clinton. Well, I promised him one more. Go ahead. Boris—President Yeltsin insisted that an American have the last question, so go ahead.

Bosnia

Q. Mr. President, members of your administration said coming into this meeting that a Bosnia peacekeeping operation in which Russian forces were not under NATO command and control or there was some type of dual key arrangement wouldn't work. Is that still the U.S. position?

President Clinton. Our position is that we're going to have an operation that works. We want Russia to be involved in it. We made some progress today consistent with both of our objectives, with neither side giving up the things that were most important to it. We made some progress today on that. And we recognized that some of the things that needed to be decided neither of us could in good conscience decide without giving our military leaders the chance to work through that. So we agreed that this week, this week, our military leaders would keep working.

That is all I can tell you; the more we say about it, the worse it will be. We are moving toward peace. The first and most important thing is, make peace in Bosnia. That has not been done yet. If that happens—and we hope it will, and we've agreed on that completely, how we will approach it—then we have the responsibility to work together to make the peace work. And we will do that.

President Yeltsin. I want to add, you are underestimating the Presidents of two such great powers. Maybe something didn't quite reach you. Maybe you can't quite figure out how we can solve it, but it came to us; it reached us.

NOTE: The President's 104th news conference began at 3:44 p.m. on the front steps of the Franklin D. Roosevelt home. In his remarks, he referred to Russian Minister of Defense Pavel Grachev. President Yeltsin spoke in Russian, and his remarks were translated by an interpreter.

Joint Statement With President Yeltsin on Nuclear Materials Security
October 23, 1995

Presidents Clinton and Yeltsin noted the importance they attach to ensuring the security of nuclear weapons and nuclear materials, maintaining effective control over them, and combating illegal trafficking in nuclear materials. They underscored their strong support for the efforts underway in the Russian Federation and the United States to achieve these objectives, including the rapidly growing range of cooperative activities being pursued jointly by US and Russian experts. The Presidents noted with satisfaction that bilateral and multilateral cooperation in these areas has grown rapidly over the past year and includes joint activities on law enforcement, customs, intelligence liaison and on-the-ground cooperation to improve nuclear materials security at ten sites, protecting tons of nuclear material. The Presidents also welcomed cooperative efforts to improve the security of nuclear weapons in transport or storage in connection with their dismantlement.

The two Presidents welcomed the joint report on steps that have been accomplished and additional steps that should be taken to ensure the security of nuclear materials, prepared by the Gore-Chernomyrdin Commission in implementation of the May 10 summit declaration on nonproliferation. This report outlines current and planned U.S.-Russian programs of bilateral cooperation that will result in broad improvements in nuclear materials security, including several important sites with weapons-usable nuclear material, increased security for nuclear weapons in connection with their dismantlement, and construction of a safe and secure long-term storage facility for fissile material from dismantled weapons. The Presidents endorsed speedy implementation of these plans and directed that they be expanded and accelerated to the greatest extent possible.

NOTE: An original was not available for verification of the content of this statement.

Remarks to the AFL–CIO Convention in New York City
October 23, 1995

The President. Thank you very much for the wonderful welcome. Thank you, Tom, for the great introduction. I wish I'd been here to hear it. [*Laughter*] But I appreciate it.

You know, I've taken so many controversial positions in the last 3 years, I thought I'd come here and tell you what you ought to do in this election. [*Laughter*] You should elect—listen to this—you ought to elect an Irish-American from the Bronx who comes out of the Service Employees Union. [*Laughter*] I just want you to know that whatever you do, I intend to be there with you every step of the way. And I know how important this is. [*Applause*] Thank you.

Let me say before I get into my remarks, I have just come, as I think all of you know, from Hyde Park and a meeting with President Yeltsin of Russia. We made a lot of progress today in agreeing to work toward peace in Bosnia, something that concerns every citizen of the world whose conscience has been shocked by all the children and other innocent people who have been killed there.

We also agreed on working together, very importantly, to control the spread of nuclear materials, something that is a very serious problem in the aftermath of the cold war, to minimize the prospect that terrorists will ever be able to get small amounts of nuclear material and make bombs out of them.

And finally, President Yeltsin agreed with me that we should go for the strongest possible comprehensive nuclear test ban treaty next year. And that means we will probably get it, and the world will be much safer as a result of it.

I know that you have—all of you—and I came here more than anything else just to thank you, because I know that you have waged a strong and passionate grassroots campaign for a year now to oppose the cuts in worker safety and job training, in education and health care, being considered in the Congress. The White House mailroom is jammed with postcards from union retirees. [*Applause*] Thank you. This may be the high-tech age, but you have got the Capitol Hill switchboards groaning with calls from your members. And I say, send more. And I know that those ads you're running have gotten some Members of Congress suffering with heartburn. And we just need to pour it on a little more. I thank you for that.

I come here today with a simple message: This is a very great country. You helped to make it that way. We're on the edge of a new century. We're living in a time of great change. No one can perceive clearly all the implications of that change.

We know that we've moved from an industrial age to an information and technology age, which, as all of you know in your own experience, even industry and agriculture is infused today with more technology. We know we have moved from the bipolar world of the cold war to a global village in which we have dreamed of new possibilities but also a lot of new vulnerabilities because of the changes that are going on.

And we know we've got to somehow harness this change to benefit ordinary people in our country and throughout the world. We have to do it consistent with the basic values that made America great and that make life worth living, values that your movement embodies: a commitment to opportunity for every American; to the dignity of work; to the commitment that the family should be strengthened and children should be nurtured and parents should be honored; a recognition that we have to go forward or backward together and therefore it is crazy for us to be divided by race, by region, by income, in any way that in any way saps our strength; and the determination to keep this country the strongest nation on Earth. Those are the things which have animated the labor movement in the later half of the 20th century. And those are the values that will take us into the 21st century.

Three years ago, you helped the American people to send me to Washington to uphold these values and to turn our economy around. I had a commitment to make the American dream real for all Americans in the 21st century and to make sure that our country would remain the strongest country in the world. I had a simple strategy to harness change to benefit all of us. I thought we needed to be faithful to the mainstream values I just mentioned. I thought we needed a middle class economic strategy to grow the middle class and shrink the under class. I thought we needed a modern Government that would be less bureaucratic, more entrepreneurial, but still strong enough to take care of the business that the people need done.

The lion's share of the credit belongs to you and the rest of the American people, but we're moving in the right direction. And I know that our policies had something to do with it. We've got 7½ million new jobs in this country, after the slowest job growth in the country since the Great Depression, in the 4 years before I took office. We've got 2½ million more homeowners, 2 million new small business people, the lowest combined rate of inflation and unemployment in 25 years. Our country is safer and stronger. For the first time since the dawn of the nuclear age, there's not a single solitary nuclear missile pointed at the people of the United States of America. And I'm proud of that. And by the grace of God, from Northern Ireland to Haiti to the Middle East, now to Bosnia, the United States is a strong partner in pushing for peace.

Maybe most important of all, this country seems to be slowly coming together around its values again. It's hard to turn a great country around, but when we get going in a certain direction, we can make a real difference. In almost every State, in this great city where you're meeting, the crime rate is down; the murder rate is down; the welfare rolls are down; the food stamp rolls are down. Believe it or not, the poverty rate is down, and the teen

pregnancy rate has dropped for 2 years in a row. America is coming back and moving together.

And we proved you could do it together. Instead of just condemning the Government the way my predecessors did, we made a partnership with the Federal employees, and in a balanced and fair and disciplined way, we tried to downsize the Government so that this big Government attack is a myth today. But we left our Government strong enough for the employees that are there to do their jobs. And we just didn't throw anybody on the street; we gave them good buyout provisions. We tried to protect their retirement. We treated them and their families with decency and the honor and the respect they were entitled to after the years they had served the United States of America. And that's the way this ought to be done everywhere.

Let me tell you what the Federal employees are doing, just a few things. I could talk all day about it. But Federal employees working in the Commerce Department, in the Export-Import Bank, in other areas, have helped to create good jobs, many of them union jobs, in America by increasing our exports 4 percent, 10 percent, and 16 percent this year, in the last 3 years. A lot of that was done because of aggressive actions by people who work for the United States Government.

The Federal Emergency Management Agency—we've had as many natural disasters to deal with in the last 3 years as any time I can remember. And it is probably the most popular arm of the Federal Government because the Federal employees have been there in a timely, aggressive, effective fashion when they were needed, whether it was for floods in the Middle West or fires and earthquakes in the West or anything else. And I am proud of that.

And let me tell you something I'm especially proud of. Business Week magazine, which is hardly an arm of the Federal Government or the Democratic Party, every year gives awards to businesses that perform at the highest level of efficiency in a number of categories. And one of their categories is for customer service over the telephone. So the businesses that compete, for example, are Southwest Airlines or L.L. Bean or, you know, anybody that you call on the telephone. You know who won this year? The Social Security Administration of the Federal Government won that award.

These Federal employees operate a Medicare program that has a 2 percent administrative cost, lower than any private insurance program in the United States of America, something you rarely hear about in the debate going on in Congress today. They have implemented a crime bill that's putting 100,000 police on the streets of America, and they're doing it on time and under budget. They have implemented the motor voter law, the family leave law, both those things that you helped to get.

They have been able to be much tougher in capturing large quantities of drugs before they come into this country. Without going into a bunch of immigrant bashing, they have been able to in a disciplined way strengthen our ability to reduce the problems of illegal immigration in the United States. And they have fought discrimination, something that was out of fashion for the Federal Government to do until this administration came in. And I thank them for it.

And guess what? We've been able to prove you can grow the economy and be decent to working people, something that the people who were there before and the people who are in the Congress today in dominant positions apparently don't believe. If you look at what's happened—and I'm sure Tom mentioned a lot of this—but when we repealed my predecessors' antiunion Executive orders that denied American workers their rights from private industry to public service, it didn't hurt the economy. The economy got better, not worse. When we said in no uncertain terms that you ought to have a fair, decent, effective NLRB, and we did our best to provide that, the economy got better, not worse. It didn't undermine the American economy.

When we refused to go along with repealing Davis-Bacon and the service contract law, the economy didn't collapse; it helped to create more high-wage jobs, not fewer. And when we began to crack down on sweatshops where unscrupulous employers make illegal immigrants work in prisonlike conditions, depriving them of the minimum wage, overtime pay, a safe workplace, and the right to organize, it will make us stronger, not weaker.

And when we have refused to go along with the attempts of some people to weaken our ability to provide a safe workplace, it has not weakened the economy; it has helped to make the American economy stronger. It is time we accepted a fundamental lesson: Treating working people in a decent, fair, humane, enlightened way gives you a stronger American economy, not a weaker one.

Audience members. Four more years! Four more years! Four more years!

The President. Thank you.

Now, we do have some real challenges before us. You and I know that this recovery's benefits have not been spread evenly to all Americans. We know that we've been in a time of increasing inequality. By the way, this is what usually happens when you move from one economic model to another. When we move from the agricultural age to the industrial age, the labor movement grew up because there were so many people who were being exploited, not benefiting from the benefits of the new industrial age. So whenever you change in a huge way the way people work and live and relate to each other and the rest of the world, some will be well-positioned and do well; others will not be.

That's why people need to come together, because you know in the end you cannot sustain progress unless everybody can benefit. That's one of the big reasons we had the Great Depression, because people did not understand that everybody had to have a stake in the future in order for free enterprise to flourish.

And so we have that happening today, where people who are well-positioned tend to do well; others work harder for less and become more insecure. There are some fundamental things we have to do about it. First and most elementally, it is high time we raise the minimum wage. It is wrong—[*applause*]. Thank you. If we do not do that, next year the minimum wage will reach a 40-year low in purchasing power. That is not my idea of the 21st century America I want our children and grandchildren to live in. I want us to go up together.

It also will be good business. People will have more money to consume, and people who are presently out of the work force will be attracted to get back into it. There is no evidence, no evidence, and I have read all the studies—at least I've read fair summaries of all the studies. I don't want to—[*laughter*]—there is no evidence that the minimum wage, a modest increase in the minimum wage, will cause unemployment. There is every evidence that it will strengthen America and bring us together.

The second thing I think we need to do is to make some changes that recognize that there is a fundamental difference in the nature of unemployment today and unemployment 30 years ago. The unemployment compensation system, the whole setup was designed for people who were laid off when there was a slowdown and then picked right back up by their employers when the economy picked up again. It was designed to give people a way to just get by until they got called back.

As recently as 30 years ago, 80 percent— 85 percent of the people who were laid off and collected unemployment were called back to the same job from which they were laid off. Today, over 80 percent of the people who are laid off are not called back to the same job from which they are laid off. All of you know that. Therefore, I have proposed having the Labor Department, working with the Education Department, create a "GI bill" for America's workers, which consolidates all of our training programs, puts more money into it, and gives every person who loses a job a right to get a voucher to take to the program that you want, whether it's a union apprenticeship program, a union training program, the local community college. Whatever is best needed for the people that are unemployed, they ought to have it. And I think we ought to do it immediately.

The second thing that we ought to do—if we're going to have a tax cut we ought to target it to working families and what they need the most, which is help raising their children, paying for their child care, and getting an education. So I think we ought to have a tax deduction for the cost of all education after high school. Now, that would help working people a lot. That would help.

The third thing I will say is—and I know we have sometimes disagreed on this—I believe that we win when we expand trade. So it's not enough to have more free trade, which I favor, we also have to have more fair trade. That's what the Japanese auto agreement was about. And thank you, Owen Bieber, for supporting us and for finally giving us a chance to crack some of those markets that have been denied American workers for too long. And we're going to keep doing things like that all the way down.

Against that background, this is how I think you ought to see this balanced budget fight. What has worked for us the last 2½ years? Mainstream values, work and family and responsibility and community and treating people with dignity, all people, without regard to their race or their region or income; believing that you have to lift working people up if you want other people to do well: That has worked for us. What's worked for us? Middle class economics, help the small business people, help the entrepreneurs, also help to grow the middle class working people and shrink the under class: That's what works. That's what is at stake in this budget battle.

This is not—I want to say this, and I want you to go home and tell everybody you know this—this is not a battle about balancing the budget. That has nothing to do with what is going on in Washington today. I gave the Congress a balanced budget. You'd be better off if we could balance the budget. When we quadrupled the debt in 12 years before I showed up, what happened? We had to spend more and more money on interest on the debt. We had less and less money to invest in worker training, in new technology, and the kinds of things that will grow the economy, raise incomes, educate our children.

It would be a good thing to do. But we have to do that, like everything else, consistent with our values and our objectives. That is what is at stake. It is, what kind of America are we going to live in?

I've given the Congress a balanced budget. It cuts all kinds of spending. It eliminates hundreds of programs. But it increases our investment in education, in technology, in research. It protects instead of hurts the old, the poor, the disabled, the little children on Medicare and Medicaid. It supports investment in worker safety and in a clean environment and in the kinds of national treasures that we share together. That is the kind of balanced budget we need.

And that is what I want to talk to you about. I am not about to do something that I think will prevent us from doing what I ran for President to do: giving every American a shot at the American dream and making sure this is the strongest, finest country in the world in the 21st century. I am not going to do that. And you shouldn't put up with it. You shouldn't put up with it.

Now, here's what I mean. I'm going to give you the 10 greatest hits or so of this present budget. This is not the Letterman show, and so it won't all be funny. You may have to laugh a couple of times to keep from crying, but here's what this is really about. Here's what the real contract is.

We all say we believe in honoring our parents for what they have done for us. And Medicare is a way of honoring our parents. We have to slow the rate of growth of medical inflation. We have to secure the Medicare Trust Fund. I presented a budget which will do that.

We have to recognize that health care is changing. I have no problem with giving seniors the option to join managed care plans if they can get lower costs or better services. I think we should do that. I'm sympathetic with doctors and hospitals and their need to have some changes in the law so they can work together to compete with insurance companies to provide managed care. I'm not against that. But I'll tell you what I am against. I'm against this budget that was passed that, believe it or not, makes it easier to commit waste, fraud, and abuse. When the Federal Government says up to 10 percent of the money may be wasted, they passed a budget to make it easier to commit waste, fraud, and abuse but harder for the poorest, the oldest, and the sickest seniors to make sure their health care needs are met. That is wrong. I don't like it. I won't support it. And if it passes, I will veto it. It is wrong.

I want to talk to you about the Medicaid program. There's a lot of AFSCME workers here who work in health care institutions that depend upon Medicaid. New York City has a whole health care network that depends not just on Medicare but Medicaid. Most people think Medicaid is the welfare health program. Let me tell you—70 percent of the Medicaid money goes to the elderly and the disabled for nursing home care, for in-home care, for physician care. Thirty percent of the Medicaid money does go to poor people, not all of them on welfare, some of them even working for very poor wages. And most of that money goes to take care of the little children. Over one in five children in the United States of America is eligible for Medicaid help for health care. And all those kids, they may not be in your family, but they're your kids. And 20 years from now, they're either going to be in jail or in school or in the workplace. And they're going to be a big part of our future. And I don't know about you, but when I retire, I want them out there working, making lots of money, taking care of me. And I want to take care of their health right now.

So my idea of the 21st century is not a Medicaid program that takes away the money that helps the poorest seniors to pay their part of the Medicare program. That's right; they get rid of it, $10 billion. We help the poorest old folks pay their copays. We help them pay the fees they owe under Medicare because they don't have any money. There's a lot of old folks out there. There's folks still living on $300 a month. This budget takes it all away. And there's been a study which estimates that it may take at least a million elderly people out of the Medicare program.

I was in Texas the other night at a fundraiser, and a doctor came up to me. A doctor came up to me, and he said, "You keep fighting on this." He said, "I've been a doctor a long time. I remember when I did not have any older patients, before Medicare, before Medicaid, when I had no older patients, because older people were too proud to come to the doctor if they couldn't pay their bills. So a lot of them just stayed home and got sick and died." It is wrong. I will not put up with it. It is not right. And you shouldn't put up with it either. It is not right. It is not right.

I want to tell you one more thing about this Medicaid plan. It says, "Oh, we're going to block-grant this to the States. We're going to get these terrible Federal rules and regulations out of the States' hair." I was a Governor for 12 years. I used to sing that song. [Laughter] I believe in that.

Our administration—don't you let anybody tell you this is about States' rights—our administration has given more waivers, more freedom to get out from under Federal rules to State governments to experiment with moving people from welfare to work or serving more people, getting health insurance to more people, than the last two administrations combined. More in 2½ years than they did in 12 years. This is not about giving the States flexibility.

But let me tell you the kind of things they want to let the States do and what they don't want to let the States do, and it will tell you what's really behind this. They've adopted their Medicaid programs. And among other things, they say that the State ought to get Medicaid block-granted and they ought to have the right to get rid of the so-called spousal impoverishment rule. That's Government language. You know what that means? That means if an elderly couple lived to be 78 years old and they've been married 50 years and they're living on their Social Security and one of them gets so sick that he or she needs to go in the nursing home, they want to give back to the State governments the right to tell the one that doesn't go to the nursing home, "You want your wife or your husband to get any help? You've got to sell your car, sell your house, clean out your bank account, give it to us, and then we'll give you a little help. We don't know how you're going to live." I don't like that. That is not my idea of the 21st century I want to live in.

But you know what? In the next breath, do you know what they did? They took away from the States—they say, "We're going to give you lots of flexibility and a little less money. And we want you to run it however you want to, but, oh, oh, there's one thing you've been doing we're not going to let you do anymore. Right now you can bargain with the drug companies to get the lowest possible price for drugs for elderly people and little kids. And we're not going to let you do that anymore, because the drug companies don't want us to. So I'm sorry, you will have to do more with less money, but here's something you can't do." I don't know about you, but I don't get driving up the price of drugs and driving old folks into the poorhouse. I don't think that's right. That's not the America I want to live in. And I'm going to do everything I can to stop it. And I want you to help me.

Now, I want to talk to you about education. Everybody's for education. You ask anybody in the Congress, are you for education? They say, absolutely. But you've always got to ask the next question; the first question is never enough. I'll tell you—you know, the best story I know about that—you know, there's a—this minister was sort of a—not a very effective minister, and people would go to sleep in his sermons. And he was overcome, and he prayed day-in and day-out for inspiration so he could finally give a barn-burning sermon and everybody would stand up. And their hearts would be purified, and their spiritual zeal would be great.

So he worked so hard on this. And he showed up, and he gave the sermon of his life. And people were stomping and clapping and even in this staid church were shouting amen. And he got to the final line of his sermon; he said, "I want everybody that wants to go to heaven to stand up." And the whole congregation stood up, except one woman that hadn't missed church in 45 years. And he was crestfallen. He said, "Sister Jones, don't you want to go to heaven when you die?" And she leapt up, she said,

"I'm sorry, I thought you were trying to get up a load to go right now." [*Laughter*]

So you always got to ask the next question. Everybody's for education. Our budget balances the budget and increases our investment in education by \$40 billion—by \$40 billion over 7 years—by making choices and setting priorities. Why? Because if 22 percent of the kids in this country are poor enough to be on Medicaid, they need a little extra help through Head Start to get off to a good start in school, because a lot of schools are too poor to have the class sizes they need or the computers we want them to have; because a lot of kids are in danger going to and from school, and we need to give schools more help to remain safe and drug-free; because we want to make it possible for everybody to go to college.

When I ran for President, I came here and I made a specific commitment. I said if you will vote for me and get me elected, I'll do everything I can to cut the cost of college loans, to improve the repayment on college loans, and then to be tougher on people who default. We cut the default rate in half, but we also cut the cost of college loans. We made repayment easier. And to boot, we added more scholarships.

And enrollment is going up, but nowhere near what we need. I want every middle class family in this country and every poor family in this country to be able to send their kids to college. And I don't want anybody ever from now on to have to walk away from a college education because of the cost. That's my idea of the 21st century.

So when the Congress presents a budget that says, "No, it's all right if several thousand more kids—20, 30, whatever it is—more kids don't get to go to Head Start and we have to remove them; it's all right if we don't help as many schools with safe and drug-free programs as we were; it's all right if a whole lot of schools now can't use that money for their poor kids for the smaller classes and the computers; it's okay if because the people that lost money on the direct loan program, the special interests, want their money back, so we're just going to kill this program that the Government's running that's got lower cost college loans and better repayment terms. We're going to get rid of that, and to boot, we'll get rid of somewhere between 150,000 and 380,000 scholarships." I don't know about you folks, that is not the kind of America

I want for the 21st century. And I'm going to do everything I can to stop it. It is wrong. And it's bad for our economy. It doesn't make sense.

And we're getting a little closer to home now. You say to people, are you for family values? Why, of course we are. Who could be against it? Most of those who were there last time—they're in the majority now—when we asked them to stand up for family values by adopting the family and medical leave law, they said no. And we said yes. And there are families that are stronger today because of the family and medical leave law because they don't lose their jobs when there's a kid sick or a parent dying or one of them gets sick. It's a better country. It's a stronger country. And it's a stronger economy because of that.

So what do we mean? Well, family values to me means safe streets, a clean environment, economic opportunity, fair taxes, secure pensions; let's just start there. Well, at least one House of Congress wants to eliminate our program to put 100,000 police on the street and to give communities—the only block grant they don't like is the one we passed to give communities the power to do what they can to prevent crime, to give our children something to say yes to instead of something to say no to, the one all the mayors love, all the Governors love, everybody thinks is great—they don't like that. Well, making us less safe is not my idea of family values.

Then they want to put 315 of our national parks and other national facilities up for sale, including Franklin Roosevelt's home where I was today. I know you find some of this unbelievable, but it's true. That's on the list. They have proposed to do all kinds of things to make it harder to preserve clean air, clean water, safe food. That's not my idea of family values. In economic opportunity, there's not a company in America that if they could avoid it in 1995 would cut research, technology, or training. But this budget cuts research, technology, and training. That's not my idea of how to build strong families. And worst of all, there's $148 billion of hidden taxes and fees on working families while they propose to give people in my income group a tax cut. And that's not my idea of the kind of 21st century I want to live in.

Now, I want you to listen to this. The Wall Street Journal—hardly an arm of the Democratic Party—[*laughter*]—reported the other day that if this budget passes with all of the taxes in it and all the tax cuts in it, with all the tax cuts in it the group of Americans as a group who make less than $30,000 a year, which is 51 percent of the American people, will have greater tax hikes than tax cuts. I get a tax cut, and we're going to soak people like that?

You know, in 1993, one of the best things about our economic program was that we doubled the family tax credit, the earned-income tax credit, which had bipartisan support, signed into law by Gerald Ford, supported by Ronald Reagan, increased by George Bush, and we doubled it. Why? Because I wanted to be able to say to the American people, "Look, you've got to choose work and family over welfare and dependence. And anybody who'll work 40 hours a week with children in the house—I don't care how low their pay is—we will not tax them into poverty. We will use the tax system to lift them out of poverty." That is the principle. That is the principle. And it's the right thing to do.

I mean, I thought the game plan was we were supposed to be growing the middle class and shrinking the under class. They want to cut this by more than I increased it. They want to kick people out of the middle class and then pull the ladder up so poor people can't work their way into it. You want to get more people on welfare? Raise taxes on people with two kids making $11,000, $12,000 a year, and they will say, no thank you. This does not make sense. It violates our values. It violates our interest. It is bad for the economy. It is wrong for America. And if I can stop it with a veto pen or with my voice or whatever it takes, I am going to do everything I can to stop it. And I want you to help me, too.

Audience members. Veto! Veto! Veto!

The President. This is the last issue I want you to focus on. These are great hits. I want you to remember this. I want you to go home, I want you to talk to friends in the workplace, and I want you to talk to friends who aren't in your union. I want you to talk to people at church, at the bowling alley, at the ball park, wherever two or more are gathered. I want you to talk to people. I want people to know about this. This is their country, just like it's your country. This is not about me or the Republicans in Congress. It's about the future of the American family, the future of the American workplace, the future of the United States. And so I want you to listen to this. This is the greatest last hit.

During the 1980's, when—you know, that "everything goes" decade where everything was going to trickle down to ordinary people—thousands and thousands of corporations transferred some $20 billion out of their employees' pension funds for buyouts and other purposes. An awful lot of workers lost their life savings. Last December, one of the proudest things I was able to do in the last Congress, even after the November election, the Congress passed a bill that saved 8½ million American pensions and stabilized 40 million others that were in danger of being in trouble. I don't know what the retirement income of 48½ million Americans is worth to the strength, the stability of America; to our pro-family, pro-work values; to our economic future, but I think it's worth an awful lot.

Now, as if we haven't learned anything from the eighties and didn't have to do that, this Republican budget would allow companies to withdraw money from their workers' pension funds to use it for whatever reason they want.

Audience members. No-o-o!

The President. For whatever reason they want, corporate buyouts, bonuses, any reason.

Now, folks, we just had to fix this last year. You know, I don't remember as well as I used to; my circuits are kind of jammed. But I can at least remember what I did last year. [*Laughter*] That is not my idea of what I want America to look like in the 21st century, taking good middle class people that worked hard all their lives, paid into their pension, showed up at work, did everything they were supposed to, and, "Oh, I'm sorry, your pension is gone." One of two things is going to happen. Either the Government will have to bail it out again, in which case the deficit reduction won't take place. Or we'll throw them into the street, and we'll one more time shrink the middle class and grow the under class. Say no to that. Say no to looting the pension funds. Say no. It's wrong. It's wrong.

And look, the thing that bothers me about this is that this budget would snatch defeat from

the jaws of victory This country is in better shape than it was 2½ years ago. We're moving in the right direction. What we need to do is build on what we've done, not tear it down. We need to build on middle class economics. We need to build on an economy that has the largest number of new small businesses in history. We need to build on the best time for education in the last 30 years, in the last Congress. We need to build on medical reforms that are slowing the rate of medical inflation without stripping elderly people of the security and dignity of knowing that their health care is there. We do not need to tear it down. We need to prove we can make the environment and the economy go together, not walk away from our common responsibilities.

Folks, this is about more, even more, than all the things that we are concerned about that directly affect any of us individually. This is about what kind of country we're going to be. This is about what kind of people we're going to be. It's about whether we're going to live by the values we all say we believe in. It's about whether the American dream is going to be alive in the 21st century. And what we really have to do is to do what that sign says. If we'll just stand up for America's working families, if we'll just do what we know is right, if we'll use every tool at our command—I will use the tools at my command, but I want you to go home, and I want you to talk to people in the streets and say we're moving this country. This country is going into the 21st century. Don't let these people take us back. If it takes a veto, you'll have it. But I need you in the streets standing up for America's future.

God bless you, and thank you.

NOTE: The President spoke at 5:35 p.m. in the Imperial Ballroom at the Sheraton New York Hotel and Towers. In his remarks, he referred to Tom Donahue, president, AFL–CIO, and Owen Bieber, former president, United Auto Workers.

Letter to Congressional Leaders Reporting on Iraq's Compliance With United Nations Security Council Resolutions
October 23, 1995

Dear Mr. Speaker: (Dear Mr. President:)

Consistent with the Authorization for Use of Military Force Against Iraq Resolution (Public Law 102–1), and as part of my effort to keep the Congress fully informed, I am reporting on the status of efforts to obtain Iraq's compliance with the resolutions adopted by the U.N. Security Council.

Events in Iraq unfolded dramatically in the weeks following my August 3, 1995, letter to you on Iraq in a way that makes absolutely clear our firm policy has been the correct one. In the first half of August, Iraqi leaders, in both public statements and private remarks to U.N. officials, threatened retaliation if the Security Council failed to lift sanctions by August 31, 1995. The retaliation was not specified, but the Iraqi remarks echoed those made before previous Iraqi acts of belligerence. Ambassador Albright and her colleagues from the United Kingdom and France called upon the Iraqi U.N. Ambassador, made clear that such threats were unacceptable, and urged that Iraq implement all relevant Security Council resolutions.

On August 9, 1995, two of Saddam Hussein's sons-in-law left Iraq and were granted refuge in Amman. One of these men, Hussein Kamil, directed Iraq's weapons of mass destruction (WMD) programs while holding various high level government positions during the 1980s and 1990s. Evidently fearful of what the defectors might reveal, Saddam Hussein hurriedly invited U.N. weapons inspectors to Baghdad to examine previously undisclosed information on his weapons programs. Saddam Hussein offered the extraordinary explanation that Hussein Kamil had hid all this information from inspectors and Saddam Hussein himself.

While the international community had long understood that Saddam Hussein had pursued a vigorous and extensive weapons program, the revelations were still staggering. Ambassador Ekeus, head of the U.N. Special Commission on Iraq, reported to the Council that, among other things, Iraq had placed biological agents such as anthrax and botulin into bombs and missiles and deployed these weapons of terror to military bases and airfields in December

1990; lied about the extent of its biological weapons program as recently as a few months ago; launched a crash program after the invasion of Kuwait to produce nuclear weapons within a year; and continued its weapons research and procurement activities, including work on uranium enrichment, after the Security Council cease-fire resolutions, possibly until quite recently.

The August 1995 revelations virtually erased what little credibility Saddam Hussein may have had left. It seems clear that, were it not for the defections, Iraq never would have revealed this information. Saddam clearly planned to hide this weapons information until he could use it to facilitate the reconstitution of his WMD programs. Saddam Hussein's intentions are hardly peaceful. There is every reason to believe that they are as aggressive and expansionist as they were in 1990. It is more important than ever that the Security Council demand Iraqi compliance with all relevant Council resolutions prior to any change to the sanctions regime.

The August 1995 WMD program revelations have overshadowed the fact that Iraq has done nothing to comply with its other obligations. Iraq continues to drag its feet on its obligations to account for hundreds of Kuwaitis and third country nationals missing since the invasion. Iraq has not returned the millions of dollars worth of Kuwaiti property looted during the occupation. The Iraqi Republican Guards still use a large quantity of stolen Kuwaiti military equipment. Iraq continues to provide safe haven for terrorist groups. Given this Iraqi track record of disrespect for its international obligations, the Security Council maintained the sanctions regime without change at the September 8, 1995, review.

Saddam Hussein's unwillingness to comply with the norms of international behavior extends to his regime's continuing threat to Iraqi citizens throughout the country. We and our allies continue to enforce the no-fly zones over northern and southern Iraq as part of our efforts to deter Iraq's use of aircraft against its population. As reported by Max van der Stoel, the Special Rapporteur of the U.N. Commission on Human

Rights, Iraq's repression of its southern Shi'a population continues, with policies aimed at destroying the Marsh Arabs' way of life and important environmental resources. Along with international and local relief organizations, we continue to provide humanitarian assistance to the people of northern Iraq. We have facilitated talks between the two major Kurdish groups in an effort to help them resolve their differences and increase stability in northern Iraq.

The human rights situation throughout Iraq remains unchanged. Saddam Hussein shows no signs of complying with U.N. Security Council Resolution 688, which demands that Iraq cease the repression of its own people. Iraq announced an "amnesty" in July for all opponents of the regime, but the announcement was seen by most Iraqis and by international human rights observers as an ill-conceived ploy. The regime's recently announced plans to amend the Iraqi constitution are viewed by Iraqi exiles as a transparent effort to bless an extension of Saddam Hussein's presidency.

Last October, the U.N. Security Council adopted Resolution 949, which demanded that Iraq not utilize its forces to threaten its neighbors or U.N. operations, and that it not redeploy or enhance its military capacity in southern Iraq. However, Saddam Hussein has continued to conduct military activities that we believe are intended to threaten Kuwait. The defections of Saddam Hussein's family members, coupled with indications of heightened Iraqi military readiness, increased our concerns that Iraqi leadership might lash out as it did last October when we responded during Operation Vigilant Warrior. In this time of uncertainty, we felt it prudent to improve the deterrence and warfighting capability of U.S. forces within the U.S. Central Command area of responsibility. Accordingly, the deployment of a mechanized task force was accelerated to participate in a scheduled exercise in Kuwait and a ground theater air control system was deployed to improve our command and control capability within the region. Additionally, 13 prepositioning ships were moved into the Gulf to increase our deterrence posture.

We continue to receive good support from the Gulf States in our sanctions enforcement efforts. The Multinational Interception Force (MIF) conducting the maritime enforcement of U.N. economic sanctions against Iraq continues to serve magnificently. Since October 1994, the MIF has diverted to various Gulf ports 14 sanc-

tions-violating vessels, which were carrying cargoes of oil or dates having an estimated cumulative value of over $10 million. The multinational composition of the MIF has been significantly strengthened. Ships from Belgium, New Zealand, Italy, Canada, and the United Kingdom have been committed to participate in MIF operations for the remainder of 1995.

The expeditious acceptance of two recently diverted sanctions-violating vessels by Saudi Arabia and Kuwait has greatly contributed to the deterrent effect of MIF sanctions enforcement operations and has also freed enforcement vessels escorting the diverted vessels to return to patrol operations. Panama and St. Vincent and the Grenadines have deflagged three sanctions-violating vessels while Honduras has enacted stricter sanctions enforcement measures and has continued deflagging proceedings against vessels involved in violating Iraqi sanctions.

Security Council Resolution 687 affirmed that Iraq is liable under international law for compensating the victims of its unlawful invasion and occupation of Kuwait. Although the U.N. Compensation Commission (UNCC) has approved some 355,000 individual awards against Iraq worth about $1.39 billion, it has been able to pay only the first small awards for serious personal injury or death (aggregating $2.7 million). The remainder of the awards cannot be paid because the U.N. Compensation Fund lacks sufficient funding. The awards are supposed to be financed by a deduction from the proceeds of future Iraqi oil sales, once such sales are permitted to resume. However, Iraq's refusal to meet the Security Council's terms for a resumption of oil sales has left the UNCC without adequate financial resources to pay the awards. Iraq's intransigence means that the victims of its aggression remain uncompensated for their losses 4 years after the end of the Gulf War.

To conclude, Iraq remains a serious threat to regional peace and stability. I remain determined that Iraq comply fully with all its obligations under the U.N. Security Council Resolutions. My Administration will continue to oppose any relaxation of sanctions until Iraq demonstrates peaceful intentions through its overall compliance with the relevant resolutions.

I appreciate the support of the Congress for our efforts, and shall continue to keep the Congress informed about this important issue.

Sincerely,

WILLIAM J. CLINTON

NOTE: Identical letters were sent to Newt Gingrich, Speaker of the House of Representatives, and Strom Thurmond, President pro tempore of the Senate.

Exchange With Reporters in New York City Prior to Discussions With Balkan Leaders
October 24, 1995

Balkan Peace Process

President Clinton. Let me begin by saying that I am delighted to have this opportunity to meet with President Izetbegovic and President Tudjman. We are very much looking forward to having the chance to discuss the prospects of peace.

As all of you know, the United States is committed to peace in Bosnia, but an honorable peace, which preserves a unified state that respects the rights of all of its citizens. And we are very much looking forward to the proximity talks, which will begin in a few days in Ohio. And of course, if a peace agreement can be reached, we expect NATO and the United States to help to implement it. And we'll be discussing that today.

Q. Mr. President, are you troubled by Senator Dole's effort to bar President Milosevic from attending those talks?

President Clinton. I believe the proximity talks will be held, and I think they should be. And I don't think anyone in the United States should do anything to undermine the prospects of bringing this horrible war to a close. And I would remind anyone who thinks otherwise to remember the wisdom of Prime Minister Rabin, who told us in 1993 that you cannot make peace with your friends.

Q. How do you rate those prospects, Mr. President? Do you think this is the last best chance for peace in Bosnia?

President Clinton. It's clearly the best chance in the last 4 years. And I think I would rate the prospects as good, thanks in no small measure to the wide range of efforts made by these two Presidents, to the diplomatic mission that Mr. Holbrooke has headed so ably, and to the resolve of NATO and the United Nations in dealing with the violations of human rights in previous agreements. So I think the moment is here if we can seize it to make a successful peace agreement.

Q. Do you think Dole's proposal, as you say, would undermine the proximity peace talks?

President Clinton. I think the proximity talks are necessary to make a peace. And I believe they——

Q. [*Inaudible*]—will undermine that?

President Clinton. I've already answered that. I don't think we should do anything which undermines the prospects of having these talks go forward. And they require people who have been on all sides of the conflict to get together to make peace. That is the responsible position, and it is the one the United States should follow and I believe will follow.

Q. Just what results do you expect out of the talks in Ohio? What is the best possible scenario?

President Clinton. That they will agree to make a peace.

Q. Can there be a solution here in Ohio, do you think, or is this just one more step?

President Clinton. Well, that's up to them. The United States will be there to be supportive. Our Contact Group partners all—Germany, United Kingdom, France, and Russia will be there. We will all be working hard. We'll do our best to get it done.

Thank you.

American Media

Q. Do you think we're a disaster, sir?

President Clinton. That's why I laughed yesterday. I wanted to make sure you got the attribution right. You have to admit it was kind of funny, though. [*Laughter*]

Q. It was.

Q. It was a moment. [*Laughter*]

President Clinton. We all need those moments.

[*At this point, one group of reporters left the room, and another group entered.*]

Balkan Peace Process

Q. President Clinton, what mechanisms are you going to use in Dayton, Ohio, to convince the Serbian side that the reintegration of Eastern Slovenia is the only solution?

President Clinton. Well, first of all, the United States is hosting these talks along with our Contact Group partners—the Germans, the British, the French, and the Russians—to give the leaders the opportunity to come here to make their own peace. And we will do whatever we can to be useful in that regard. But my position is that we have to seize this moment. This is by far the best chance we have had because

of the circumstances on the ground and because of the resolve of the international community, because of the diplomatic mission. And we have to seize this moment and resolve these issues. And I believe it can be done diplomatically if all the leaders proceed in good faith. And I have no reason to believe they won't.

NOTE: The President spoke at 12:30 p.m. in the Waldorf Astoria Hotel prior to meeting with President Alija Izetbegovic of Bosnia-Herzegovina and President Franjo Tudjman of Croatia. In his remarks, he referred to President Slobodan Milosevic of Serbia and Prime Minister Yitzhak Rabin of Israel. A tape was not available for verification of the content of this exchange.

Exchange With Reporters in New York City Prior to Discussions With President Jiang Zemin of China
October 24, 1995

China-U.S. Relations

Q. President Jiang, are you still hoping for a promise from President Clinton that the Taiwan President will not be allowed to visit America again?

President Jiang. We will discuss this issue. We will—[*inaudible*]—discuss this issue.

[*At this point, one group of reporters left the room, and another group entered.*]

Q. Mr. President, will human rights be an issue in your talks today with President Jiang?

President Clinton. We'll talk about a lot of things, but we're just meeting. We haven't even had a chance to say anything yet, but we'll give you a report later.

Q. Mr. President, with symbolism being so important with these kind of meetings, why would you allow the Chinese to dictate the

meeting place so they could avoid confronting a Tiananmen Square display?

President Clinton. The important thing is that we're going to have this meeting. It's very important. And we'll have it. It'll be a good exchange. And then afterwards we will report about it.

Q. Well, what is the purpose of this meeting, Mr. President? Is it a face-saving gesture on both sides?

President Clinton. No. These are two great countries that have a real interest in maintaining a constructive dialog with each other and, wherever possible, a partnership.

NOTE: The exchange began at 3:05 p.m. at the Lincoln Center. A tape was not available for verification of the content of this exchange.

The President's News Conference
October 25, 1995

Budget Legislation

The President. Good afternoon. Three years ago, I ran for President promising to put the American economy back on track and to cut the Federal deficit in half. In 1993, without a single Republican vote, the Democratic Congress adopted our deficit reduction plan. It was a plan that shrunk the deficit while investing in our people, their education, and the technological future of America.

We took firm steps toward a balanced budget, but we did it in a way that honors our values of responsibility and opportunity, work and family, a strong American community, and a strong America around the world. We did deficit reduction consistent with our values, and it was very good economic policy.

Today, America is on the move. The economy is growing. The American people have produced 7½ million new jobs, 2½ million new homeowners, over 2 million new small businesses, and the lowest combined rates of unemployment and inflation in 25 years. And I am pleased to announce today that the deficit in fiscal year '95 is $164 billion, cut almost in half in just 3 years. The deficit was projected to be $302 billion, as you can see here, before our plan was adopted. It was $290 billion in 1992. We began immediately to bring it down. It came down to $255 billion, to $203 billion, now to $164 billion in 3 years.

This is the first time since Harry Truman was President that the deficit has actually dropped 3 years in a row. The plan has worked better than we projected that it would. And as the chart shows, the deficit reduction is for real.

Now it is time to finish this job, to take that red line down to zero. We must balance the budget to take the burden of debt off of our children and to free up more funds for investing in our future. But we have to do it in the way we did it in 1993, that is in a way that is consistent with our values and consistent with a strategy that will actually grow the American economy. I have proposed a plan that cuts wasteful Government spending and reflects our values. It is the right way to balance the budget.

By contrast, the Republican Congress is taking the wrong way. Last week it passed the biggest Medicare cuts in our history. They're about to pass about $148 billion in taxes and fees on working families and elderly people and low-income Americans. And their budget slashes education and technology. It undercuts the environment. In other words, it balances the budget but it still mortgages our future. That's the wrong way to go, and I don't intend to let it happen. If the Republicans plunge ahead and pass this budget, I will veto it and demand a budget that is balanced in a way that reflects our values and promotes our economy.

Before I close, I'd like to be very clear on my determination that no one should toy with the full faith and credit of the United States. Republican congressional leaders have said they won't pass a debt ceiling bill unless I accept their misguided budget priorities.

For more than two centuries, through wars and depression, our Nation has always paid its bills and honored its obligations. For all their loose talk, the congressional leaders know that if they were to allow us to go into default, this would have a severe impact on our economy, on financial markets, and on the interest rates paid by Government, thereby increasing the deficit; paid by business, therefore slowing economic growth; and paid by millions of homeowners, thereby increasing their mortgage rates. That is not a responsible thing to do for the United States, and it is certainly not responsible budget strategy. It is economic blackmail, pure and simple.

The Republicans are saying, "Either you accept what we're doing to Medicare, what we're doing to health care, what we're doing to educational opportunities, what we're doing to the environment, what we're doing to raise taxes on working families with incomes of $25,000 a year or less and children in their homes, or we'll just stop America from honoring its obligations for the first time in history."

I am not going to let anybody hold Medicare or education or the environment or the future of this country hostage. If they send me a budget that says simply, "You take our cuts, or we'll let the country go into default," I will veto it.

Threats to our future are not an acceptable basis for good-faith efforts to resolve our differences.

The most important thing about this, folks, is that America is moving in the right direction. The deficit is coming down. The jobs are going up. The crime rate is down. The welfare rolls are down. The food stamp rolls are down. Defaults in child support are down. The poverty rate is down. The teen pregnancy rate is down. Small businesses are up. Business failures are down. We are moving in the right direction. We know what strategy works. The strategy that works is to reduce the deficit and invest in people, invest in technology, and grow the economy. Why would we abandon a proven strategy that works and that will take us all the way to a balanced budget to adopt an extreme budget that absolutely shreds our values and will weaken our economy?

We should pass the right kind of balanced budget and finish this job. But if people want to know what kind of balanced budget is right, look at the record, look at what works. We ought to do what's right for America.

This country is on a roll economically. There is no nation in the world better positioned than the United States for the 21st century. And all we have to do is to honor our values, learn how to live with all of our diversity, and have sound, sensible policies. That's what I'm fighting for. And this number today shows that we're on the right side of this battle.

Q. What are your options, and what do you think is going to happen if you do veto? Then where do we go?

The President. Well, we'll do what we've always done in cases like this. I will veto, and then they'll either pass legislation that's acceptable or they won't. But that is their choice.

You know, before they ever adopted a budget resolution, as soon as they proposed a balanced budget I proposed one. I proposed one without frills, one that eliminated hundreds of programs, one that continues to shrink the Federal Government, one that continues to invest in our future, and one with the kind of sensible economic assumptions that have characterized my first budgets. And so far, the response was, "Well, we'd be glad to talk to you, but we're not going to change anything." So the ball is basically in their court. They have to enact the laws.

Yes, Rita [Rita Braver, CBS News].

Q. Mr. President, what have you done to reach out to the Republicans and try to talk with them? Have you made any personal calls?

The President. Absolutely.

Q. Have you been rebuffed? Can you tell us what's been going on?

The President. I don't think that going into the details of what's going on would be helpful. But I have—I talk—every time I meet with or see Republican Members of Congress, every time I talk to Republican business leaders, every time I talk to anybody that I think can have any influence in this process, I make privately and in greater detail and with more specifics the argument I have just made to you. So I have not shut the door; I have kept the door open. And every time there has been any kind of public discussion of this, the leaders of the Congress have said, "Well, we'd be glad to talk, but we're not going to change anything."

Q. Mr. President, you went from a 10-year balanced budget plan down to 9 years based on improved economic conditions. Based on this, with this decline, can you see it going down every further? Is there any narrowing?

The President. Well, the question is—let me just say, I don't want to get into all the complex, technical details. But one of the things that has caused all this difference between us is their assumption that if their budget is passed, we will have lower growth and lower business profits than we have averaged for the last 25 years.

Now, that's amazing to me. They're saying to America, on the one hand, "Support our plan. We have to slash Medicare and slash medical care for poor children so we can have a big tax cut and so we can balance the budget. But if we do it, it will give you lower economic growth for the next 7 years than we've averaged for the last 25." To me, that is an amazing admission by them. I don't know why they're doing that. But that requires them to make hundreds of billions of dollars in cuts in education, in technology, in the environment, and aid to poor children and needy elderly people that would otherwise not be there.

So that is a big part of the difference between us. They say, "Well, if you adopt this incredibly complicated Medicare plan that we only allowed one day of public hearings on—we have lots of time for hearings on other subjects, but only one day for this profoundly important issue—well, it will control medical costs." And then they turn around and estimate a rate of inflation a half a percent higher than mine. That's over $100 billion dollars of difference between us.

So I think it's interesting. There's a lot of extreme ideology going on here that is driving them under the guise of balancing the budget to make cuts that will undermine the ability of our Nation to honor its commitment, to give all children a chance at an opportunity in life, to honor its commitment to our parents and to our environment, to many other things. And I think that's something that we ought to look at.

We have proven what works. Cut and invest works. Reduce the deficit but invest in our future works. That's what works.

Q. Mr. President, politically, though—politically, doesn't this chart allow you now, after you cast your veto, to come back and compromise to something closer to the Republican 7-year model if you're both heading toward ground zero?

The President. That depends entirely on what is in the budget. It depends entirely on what is in the budget.

You know, my idea of what America should look like in the 21st century does not include denying tens of thousands of children the chance to be in a Head Start program or raising the cost of college loans or cutting the number of scholarships by hundreds of thousands or putting the biggest burden for Medicare changes on the seniors in our country who are the poorest, the eldest, and the sickest. My idea is not raising taxes on working families to give people in my income group a tax break. I just don't understand that. So it depends on what is there.

Yes, sir, in the back.

Canada-U.S. Relations

Q. Mr. President, are you concerned about the possible breakup of Canada and the impact that could have on the North American economy and Canada-U.S. trade relations?

The President. Let me give you a careful answer. When I was in Canada last year, I said that I thought Canada had served as a model to the United States and to the entire world about how people of different cultures could live together in harmony, respecting their differences, but working together. This vote is a Canadian internal issue for the Canadian people to decide. And I would not presume to interfere with that. I can tell you that a strong and united Canada has been a wonderful partner for the United States and an incredibly important and constructive citizen throughout the entire world.

Just since I have been President, I have seen how it works, how our partnership works, how the leadership of Canada in so many ways throughout the world works, and what it means to the rest of the world to think that there's a country like Canada where things basically work. Everybody's got problems, but it looks like a country that's doing the right things, moving in the right direction, has the kind of values that we'd all be proud of. And they've been a strong and powerful ally of ours. And I have to tell you that I hope we'll be able to continue that. I have to say that I hope that will continue. That's been good for the United States.

Now the Canadian people, the people of Quebec will have to cast their votes as their lights guide them. But Canada has been a great model for the rest of the world and has been a great partner for the United States, and I hope that can continue.

Political Strategist Dick Morris

Q. Mr. President, in the last few days you've probably read several articles about Dick Morris. Would you care to tell us about your relationship with Dick Morris, given all of these stories that have surfaced?

The President. Well, the only thing I can tell you is that he worked in my first campaign for Governor, and I think he's an able man; he's a creative man. And when you have a long time relationship with somebody, you know when to listen and then you do what you think is right. And that's the kind of relationship I have. I listen to him, he's been helpful to me, and I do what I think is right.

Budget Legislation

Q. Mr. President, the chart you point out here today indicates that things have turned out a lot better than you thought they would, even a year ago. Why then would you propose now to go all the way to zero and balance the budget, which is something you did not propose to do a year ago when things looked a lot worse?

The President. Because now I believe we can do the job. Keep in mind—look here, we're going from $290 billion to $164 billion. That's why I proposed to do it over a 9-year period.

I believe that economic growth—to go back to the question that, I think, Brian [Brian Williams, NBC News] asked earlier, someone asked this earlier—I think it's quite conceivable that if my budget were adopted just as I propose it, that economic growth could take the deficit down even more quickly. But I didn't estimate, that is—my budget is premised on the economy growing at about the same rate it has for the last 25 years, with the profits of our business enterprises at about the same level. If the same thing happens in the next 3 to 5 years as happened in the last 3, we would have quicker growth and a quicker resolution of this.

But that's why I think we should not be pessimistic about the future. The more we can get this deficit down, the lower interest rates will be for people in the private sector; that means they'll borrow more money, they'll build more houses, they'll have more home mortgages, they'll invest in more plant and equipment, and the economy will grow quicker; also the lower our interest payments on our own debt will be, which means we'll have more funds to invest in education, health care, and the environment.

So I now believe—I just didn't want to over-promise, Brit [Brit Hume, ABC News]. I didn't want to say that I knew we could do something we couldn't. I know we can take this down to balance, and we can do it in a disciplined way. But I have ordered—excuse me—offered a balanced plan that says, let's keep doing what works, and let's don't over-promise. And let's don't pretend that we can do things we can't do, like tell you right now we can jerk $450 billion out of the health care system with no adverse consequences.

Q. You don't mean to be saying—take it to balance now because it would be easier, do you?

The President. No. I believe—what we know, though, is that we can—when I ran for President, I didn't think I should make more than a 4-year pledge. [*Laughter*] And what I said was that I thought we could get the deficit to half what it was when I took office as a percentage of our income. That's been done, and it's nearly, in real dollar numbers, half of what it was. Now, we've had a lot of success with our reinventing Government program. I know a lot more about how the Federal Government and the budget works than I did the day I showed up here. I believe we can take it into balance. But we've got to do it in a way that permits us to invest in education, invest in technology, and do right by people that have a right to rely on things like Medicare and Medicaid.

Q. Mr. President, you know that eventually you'll have to work out this budget dispute with Congress, assuming that they can't override your veto. Instead of going through the veto scenario and tiptoeing right up to default, why don't you just invite the Republican leaders over here and work it out ahead of all of that?

The President. Well, let me say again, when I proposed this budget, before they even voted for their budget resolution, I had my hand outstretched. My hand has been outstretched ever since, in all kinds of public and private ways. Frankly, let me say, that I believe the same is the case of the vast majority of the Democrats in the Congress. I believe we'd like to have a huge bipartisan vote for the right sort of balanced budget.

But at every turn, what have I been told? "We'll be glad to talk to you, but we're not changing anything. If you don't change our deficit, we just won't pay the debts of the United States. We'll abandon a 200-year history of honoring our obligations to pay our debts."

So that really is not a question that should properly be directed to me. The Congress has to finish its business, and they will make a decision. They know exactly where I stand. They know what my principles are. And now the American people know that the philosophy that I have, the ideas that I have, the values that are in my budget also turn out to be very good for the economy and good for reducing the deficit.

Thank you very much.

NOTE: The President's 105th news conference began at 4:15 p.m. in the Briefing Room at the White House.

Statement on the AFL-CIO Election
October 25, 1995

There were plenty of winners in today's AFL-CIO election. The working men and women of the labor movement benefit the most. If every American got to choose in every election between candidates such as these, this country would be a better place.

I offer my hearty congratulations to John Sweeney, who has led one of the most progressive, growing, and innovative unions in America. He has been a force for inclusion and activism and has already left a deep and positive imprint on the labor movement.

The outgoing president, Tom Donahue, has been a source of strength and leadership in the labor movement for decades. Working men and women are fortunate for his many years of service, his integrity, and his dedication.

The theme of AFL-CIO convention was "Stand Up for America's Working Families." My administration stands with John and the other newly elected officers as we work together in the months and years ahead on issues important to America's working families.

Remarks at a United Jewish Appeal Reception
October 25, 1995

Thank you very much, Stan Chesley. Thank you for your friendship and for your leadership. Mr. Secretary, thank you for what you have done, along with Dennis Ross and so many others here to hasten the day of peace in the Middle East. Senator Lautenberg, distinguished foreign guests, my fellow Americans, and most of all, to Prime Minister and Mrs. Rabin and all the friends who are here from Israel, we're delighted to have you back.

It is a great honor for me to receive this award, an honor amplified by its association with the United Jewish Appeal and with all of you who contribute so much to the UJA and its mission. But it's a special honor to receive it from the Prime Minister.

As the journey toward Middle East peace advances, the courageous leadership and vision of the Prime Minister will become more clear to all the world, and they will serve not only the people of Israel but all people in our generation and those who will inherit the Earth.

This is a time of remarkable progress for peace. You heard the Secretary talk about what we hope and pray will happen when the parties to the war in Bosnia meet in the next few days. We have seen a remarkable transformation in South Africa. In Northern Ireland they have laid down their arms, and we are working and hoping and praying for peace there. But nowhere

has the progress been more dramatic and nowhere has it moved more people than in the Middle East.

We have tried to be a full and reliable partner. I am proud of the agreements that we have worked hard to bring about. I am proud of the handshakes that sealed them, handshakes I never thought I would live to see. I'm not sure he did either. [*Laughter*] I am proud of our efforts to secure the economic underpinnings of the peace.

We will continue to stand with the peacemakers. But let's be clear on one thing here: The real credit belongs to them. Could we have made peace in the Middle East had Israel not had a Prime Minister like the one who stands before us? He and the members of his government, but most of all, the Prime Minister, a man willing to risk his own political fortunes, a man who for decades had risked his own life to secure the life and the future of Israel. Could we have made it had it not been for King Hussein and had Chairman Arafat not determined that he would take a different course, if President Mubarak had not been supportive? Could we have made it if people who have already reached their mature years had not looked into the eyes of the young people of the Middle East, like the Israeli and Arab children who participated in the Seeds of Peace program?

Can we make it stick without the Jewish and Arab-American business leaders who have pledged their personal efforts to bring the rewards of peace to all the people of the Middle East, without others in the region who are now supporting it?

These are the people to whom the credit goes. It is the responsibility of the United States, at this moment in history, to do what we, and only we can do to try to be a force for freedom, for prosperity, and for peace.

Each of us still has work to do, as I'm sure you all know. It takes many backs to bear the burden of peace and the awful burden of change, many hearts to conquer hatred with humanity, many hands to build a sturdy house within which all can live on honorable terms. No one can sit on the sidelines. This work is not done.

The United States will remain a force for peace. We will continue to support those who take risks for peace, and yes, we will continue to do everything we can to minimize those risks. We will continue also and we will intensify our efforts to fight the forces of terror who would turn back the march of history. And we will continue to defend human rights and human dignity for all the people on this planet.

The road ahead will not be easy, and it will not be even. But we must remain steadfast, remembering with Isaiah that those who do the Lord's work will have their strength renewed. I believe they will mount up with wings as eagles; they will run and not grow weary; they will walk and not faint.

The United Jewish Appeal and all the committed donors who gather tonight give life to Isaiah's admonition. And in the United States and Israel and throughout the world, you renew our strength. In more than 50 countries you bring hope and relief to the needy. I thank you for everything you do, for the hot meals for the homebound, the wheelchairs for the disabled, the shelter for the refugees, the comfort to the victims of Alzheimer's and AIDS, protecting the weakest among us, the newborn, the aged, the frail. To those who have lost their jobs, their homes, their way, or their strength,

you have been their strength and a second chance.

I think it's fair to say that all of us who believe that we are loved and cared for by one God, no matter how imperfect we are, know that our God is a God of second chances. That is what the movement for peace in the Middle East is all about.

I thank you for reminding all of us of that and of our obligations to each other in one community. I thank you for what you've done to strengthen families and improve education, to honor traditions and celebrate culture, to embody the values that make this country a great nation.

I thank you for this award. But let me say, more important than anything else, I look forward to our continued partnership as we struggle on behalf of peace and dignity and humanity. I leave here honored and doubly burdened by the instruction of the prophet Isaiah, "Cease to do evil; learn to do well. Prepare ye the way of the Lord." With God's will, that is exactly what we will do together.

Thank you.

I could tell you an interesting little aside here. When we were about to come out tonight, the Prime Minister insisted that I stand on his right, even though he's in the United States. In the American State Department, I am his host. Protocol dictates that he stand on my right. I told him that. [*Laughter*] He said, "Tonight we reverse the order." [*Laughter*] Then I looked at all of you, and I looked back at him, and I said, "Well, it's appropriate; after all, they may be more your crowd than mine." [*Laughter*]

Thank you very much.

NOTE: The President spoke at 7:30 p.m. in the Benjamin Franklin Room at the State Department. In his remarks, he referred to Stanley M. Chesley, cochairman, International Leadership Reunion; Secretary of State Warren Christopher; Dennis B. Ross, Special Middle East Coordinator; Prime Minister Yitzhak Rabin of Israel and his wife, Leah; King Hussein of Jordan; Chairman Yasser Arafat of the Palestinian Authority; and President Hosni Mubarak of Egypt.

Remarks at the Harry S. Truman Library Institute Legacy of Leadership Dinner
October 25, 1995

Thank you very much, Clifton, for that very fine introduction, and I hope that what you said is true about both of us. President Ford, President Carter, thank you for your service to our Nation and for what you said and for the work you have done to continue America's mission since you have left office; the work you have done in supporting our common efforts in expanding trade; and for that very unusual trip President Carter took to Haiti not very long ago, which has now given them one year of freedom and democracy. Thank you, sir, for that.

Vice President Gore; General and Mrs. Dawson; my good friend Lindy Boggs; Mr. and Mrs. Hackman; Senator and Mrs. Nunn; Governor and Mrs. Carlin; Mr. Symington; David and Rosalee McCullough; Congresswoman McCarthy; the other Members of Congress who are here. I always love to be at events honoring Harry Truman because I come from a family that was for him when he was alive. [*Laughter*]

I loved hearing the story about the—that President Ford told about the tour President Truman gave of the White House. You know, President Truman oversaw the last great renovation of the White House, although many fine things have been done within the house by subsequent Presidents and their wives. And he gave us the Truman Balcony, and fated almost as much heat for that as he did some of the more famous things he did. Every first family since then has thanked their lucky stars for Harry Truman's persistence in hanging on to the Truman Balcony.

It was my great honor, along with the First Lady, who had the privilege of hosting many of you at the White House today, to have Mr. Daniel's parents come to dinner. Margaret Truman Daniel was uncommonly kind to my wife and to my daughter during the course of the '92 campaign and on occasion thereafter. And we wanted to have them for dinner. And as we were having dinner in the Family Dining Room upstairs, which used to be the room in which Margaret Truman had her piano and did her practicing—it was her room—and President and Mrs. Kennedy converted it into the Family

Dining Room, and for the first time in 160 years, the First Family no longer had to go downstairs to dinner at night. And I thought this was quite a great thing, you know, and so I thought we should have dinner in this room with the beautiful Revolutionary wallpaper that Mrs. Kennedy put up.

And we got sort of into the dinner. We were having a wonderful conversation; I was marveling at how much Margaret Truman reminded me of her father. And so, as the conversation warmed, I said, "Tell me, Margaret, how do you like this Family Dining Room?" And she got a very stern look in her face, and she said, "Well, Mr. President, I like you." But she said, "You know, I just don't think people should eat on the same floor they sleep." [*Laughter*] And I thought to myself, the Trumans are still speaking their mind. [*Laughter*] And thank God for that.

I have been asked to talk about the meaning of Harry Truman's legacy for today and tomorrow. And because of the meetings that I have just had at the United Nations and the work that we are doing 50 years after its beginning, I thought it might be worth my sharing with you a few thoughts about Harry Truman's legacy and what it means for today and tomorrow.

Every American President, including my two distinguished predecessors who spoke here tonight, has followed in Harry Truman's footsteps in carrying forward America's leadership in the world. This tradition of sustained American leadership and involvement has been so successful and has been so consistently maintained by Democratic and Republican Presidents alike that some of us forget what a bold departure it was.

Just before I came here tonight I was with Prime Minister Rabin at another meeting talking about peace in the Middle East. Harry Truman was the first world leader to recognize the State of Israel. And his commitment to giving us the capacity to lead and work for peace started a single silver thread that runs right through the terrific accomplishments of President Carter and all of the things which have been done since. But we forget what a bold departure it was. The Truman doctrine, the Marshall plan, the

NATO alliance, each was a step unlike anything before.

Indeed, NATO, which President Truman rightly considered one of his finest achievements, was our very first peacetime alliance ever. We never had a military alliance in peacetime before NATO. This decisive change grew out of the belief that was shared by General Marshall, Senator Vandenberg, and Dean Acheson and so many others that we could never again remain apart from the world. We had, after all, isolated ourselves after the First World War, and because of that, we had to fight another. Harry Truman was determined that would not happen again. And he had to face, almost immediately, the chilling prospect of the cold war and to make all of the decisions which set in motion the policies which enabled, ultimately, freedom to prevail in that war.

He had to do it with a nation that was weary from war and weary from engagement, where people were longing to just focus on the little everyday things of life that mean the most to most of us. But because he did it, we just celebrated 50 years of the United Nations. No more world war, no nuclear device ever dropped again, and we see the movement for peace and freedom and democracy all over the world.

What are we going to do to build on his achievement? What do we have to do to secure a peace for the next century? Freedom's new gains, I believe, make it possible for us to help to build a Europe that is democratic, that is peaceful, and that, for the first time since nation-states appeared on that continent, is undivided.

We can build a Europe committed to freedom, democracy, and prosperity, genuinely secure throughout the continent and allied with other like-minded people throughout the world for the first time ever. And I am committed to doing what we can to build that kind of Europe based on three principles: First, to support democracy in Europe's newly free nations; second, to work to increase economic vitality in Europe with America and other partners through open markets and expanded trade and to help the former Communist countries complete their transition to market economies, a move that will strengthen democracy there and help to block the advance of ultranationalism and ethnic hatred; and finally, we're building the transatlantic community of tomorrow by

deepening, not withdrawing, from our security cooperation.

Today, with the overarching threat of communism gone, the faces of hatred and intolerance are still there with different faces: ethnic and religious conflicts, organized crime and drug dealing, state-sponsored terrorism, the spread of weapons of mass destruction. America cannot insulate itself from these threats any more than they could insulate themselves after World War II. Indeed, we have less option to do so because the world is becoming a global village.

By joining with our allies and embracing others who share our values, we can't insulate ourselves from these threats, but we can sure create a better defense. NATO's success gives us proof of what we can do when we work together. NATO binds the Western democracies in a common purpose with shared values. And I strongly believe that NATO does not depend upon an ever-present enemy to maintain its unity or its usefulness.

The alliance strengthens all of its members from within and defends them from threats without. If you just compare the stability, the economic strength, the harmony in Western Europe today with the conditions that existed just a few decades ago in President Truman's time, you can see that. The alliance has brought former foes together, strengthened democracy, and along with the Marshall plan, it sheltered fragile economies and got them going again. It gave countries confidence to look past their ancient hatreds. It gave them the safety to sow the prosperity they enjoy today.

By establishing NATO, of course, America also did something even more important from our point of view. We established the security that we require to flourish and to grow. Now we have to build upon President Truman's accomplishments. He said when he announced the Truman doctrine, "The world is not static. The status quo is not sacred. We have to adapt NATO, and I believe we should open NATO's doors to new members." The end of the cold war cannot mean the end of NATO, and it cannot mean a NATO frozen in the past, because there is no other cornerstone for an integrated, secure, and stable Europe for the future.

NATO's success has involved promoting security interests, advancing values, supporting democracy and economic opportunity. We have literally created a community of shared values and shared interests as well as an alliance for the common defense. Now the new democracies of Central and Eastern Europe and the former Soviet Union want to be a part of enlarging the circle of common purpose and, in so doing, increasing our own security.

That's why we established the Partnership For Peace. In less than 2 years, we've brought 26 nations into a program to create confidence and friendship, former enemies now joining in field exercises throughout the year, building bonds together instead of battle plans against one another. This has been good for us and good for Europe.

Now those nations in the region that maintain their democracies and continue to promote economic reform and behave responsibly should be able to become members of NATO. That will give them the confidence to consolidate their freedom and to build their economies and to make us more secure.

NATO's completed a study of how it should bring on new members. We intend to move carefully and deliberately and openly and share the conclusions of that study with all of those who have joined us in the Partnership For Peace. But we have to move to the next phase in a steady, careful way, to consider who the new members should be and when they would be invited to join the alliance. Throughout this, I will engage with the Congress and the American people and seek the kind of bipartisan partnership that made Harry Truman's important work possible.

Let me emphasize one important point: Bringing new members into this alliance will enhance, not undermine, the security of everyone in Europe, including Russia, Ukraine, the other former Soviet republics. We've assured Russia that NATO is as it has always been, a defensive alliance. Extending the zone of security and democracy in Europe can help to prevent new conflicts that have been building up, in many cases, for centuries. For Russia and all of her neighbors, this is a better path than the alternative.

I also want you to know, as you saw from the laughing photograph with President Yeltsin, we are still building a positive relationship with Russia. Those of you familiar with the history of that great country know that its heroic effort to become a confident and stable democracy is one of the most significant developments of our time.

One of our former colleagues, President Nixon, who is no longer with us, wrote me a letter about Russia a month to the day before he died, which I still have and reread from time to time, emphasizing the extraordinary historic significance of Russia's courageous reach for democracy and liberty.

Russia, too, has a contribution to make in the new Europe, and we have offered them a strong alliance with NATO and working through the Partnership For Peace. Let me just tell you, that partnership is going to deepen. Tomorrow, United States and Russian armed forces will begin a peacekeeping exercise together at Fort Riley, Kansas, under the auspices of the Partnership For Peace. We want our relationships with them to be daily, comprehensive, routine. We want to go every step of the way to build confidence and security and a democratic Russia. But we don't think NATO's opening to the East and our relationship with Russia are mutually exclusive choices.

I want to emphasize one other thing. NATO is at work for us right now, as we speak, demonstrating in Bosnia how vital it is to securing the peace in Europe. The efforts of our negotiators, the military changes on the ground, and NATO's air strikes have brought these parties to the negotiating table and to an agreement on the basic principles of a settlement and a nationwide cease-fire.

Next week, in an historic meeting, the Presidents of Bosnia, Croatia, and Serbia will travel here to Dayton, Ohio, to resolve the remaining issues. The political settlement that is taking shape will preserve Bosnia as a single state and provide for a fair territorial compromise. It will commit the parties to hold free elections, establish democratic institutions, and respect human rights.

There are many people who have played a role in bringing this process this far. I want to thank one of them tonight for his extraordinary efforts, President Carter. Thank you so much for what you have done.

I want to say to all of you, there is no guarantee of peace, but it is possible in large measure because of NATO. And let me ask you one final thing. If the peace is negotiated, NATO must be prepared to help implement the agreement. There will be no peace without an international military presence in Bosnia, a presence that must be credible. NATO is indispensable to this to give the parties the reassurance they need to make peace.

The question I have is this: If Harry Truman were President, would he expect the United States as the leader of NATO to be a part of the force in Bosnia? I think you know what the answer is. The answer is, yes. And so must we.

My fellow Americans, make no mistake about this: If we're not there, many of our partners will reconsider their commitments; if we're not there, America will sacrifice its leadership in NATO; if we're not there, we will be making a sad mistake. I am determined that we will be part of this NATO mission.

I am working with Congress, engaging in an important dialog. I met not very long ago with a bipartisan group of leaders, and I want to say a special word of thanks to Senator Nunn for his remarkable contribution to that meeting and for his remarkable contributions to our country, which we will all miss when he is gone.

My fellow Americans, if you want 4 years of bloody conflict to end, you have to support the United States being involved with NATO in enforcing the peace agreement. We have not sent troops into battle. We have not taken sides. We have not been a part of the UNPROFOR mission on the ground. But we must do this if you want your country and NATO to be effective in our time as it was in President Truman's vision and in his time.

Let me also say again, if we don't do this, the consequences for our country could be grave, indeed. This is the most serious conflict on the continent of Europe since World War II. NATO must help to end it. If we fail to secure this peace, how can we achieve an integrated, peaceful, and united Europe? If we fail to secure this peace, our success around the world and much of our success at home, which has come from American leadership, will be weakened. If we fail to secure this peace, the conflict in the former Yugoslavia could spread to other nations and involve our sons and daughters in a conflict in Europe.

Let me say in closing that just a few days ago, we were fortunate to have a visit in the United States from His Holiness John Paul II. And I spent about a half an hour with him alone, and he started with the most unusual conversation I've ever had with him or, in some ways, with any other world leader. He said, "I want to talk about the world, and I want to know what you think." I said, "The world?" He said, "Yes, the whole deal." I said, "Well, where shall I start?" He said, "Start in Bosnia." So we talked about Bosnia. Then we went around the world. At the end he said, "You know, I am not a young man. I have lived through most of this century. The 20th century began with a war in Sarajevo. Mr. President, you must not let the 20th century end with a war in Sarajevo."

I ask you to think of this, my fellow Americans, that first war in Sarajevo, that was Harry Truman's war. That's the war that he joined up in even though he was old enough and his eyesight was bad enough for him to get out of it. That's the war he showed people the kind of leadership capacity he had. And our failures after that war led Franklin Roosevelt into another war, led Harry Truman to end that war with a set of difficult painful decisions, including dropping the atomic bomb, and led him to determine that it would never happen again. That's why he did all the things we celebrate tonight.

If he were here he would say, "If you want to really honor me, prepare for the future as I did."

Thank you, and God bless you all.

NOTE: The President spoke at 9:35 p.m. in the Main Hall at the National Building Museum. In his remarks, he referred to Clifton Truman Daniel, President Truman's grandson; Maj. Gen. Donald S. Dawson, USAF (Ret.), president, Harry S. Truman Library Institute for National and International Affairs, and his wife, Jenny; Lindy Boggs, dinner chair; Larry Hackman, Director, Harry S. Truman Library, and his wife, Sandi; Senator Sam Nunn and his wife, Colleen; Archivist of the United States John W. Carlin and his wife, Diana; master of ceremonies James Symington; and author and historian David McCullough and his wife, Rosalee.

Statement on the Gun-Free Schools Act
October 26, 1995

A year ago I launched a national effort to get guns out of America's schools. Today, almost one year after I signed the Gun-Free Schools Act, I'm very pleased to announce that our message of zero tolerance has been made a reality around the country. The Gun-Free Schools Act is working and working well.

Guns have no place in our schools, and this directive ensures that any student in America who brings a gun to school will be expelled for at least a year. Our message is clear: We will not tolerate threats to the safety of America's students and teachers. Period. Parents have a right to expect that their children will be safe when they go to school in the morning.

We still need more good parents and strong communities if we are to win the fight against crime in America. But through efforts like this one, my administration is committed to doing its part to protect our children and ensure that they can learn in safety, free from fear and violence.

Exchange With Reporters Following the Departure of President Soeharto of Indonesia
October 27, 1995

Gross Domestic Product Report

Q. [*Inaudible*]—growth figures?

The President. Well, the growth figures clearly show that the economy of the United States is moving, that we're on the right track. Today we have this very high growth figure. Just a few days ago we got the good news that the deficit has dropped dramatically now for 3 years in a row. We need to build on this. We do not need to reverse our economic course. That's the message I have for the Congress on the deficit reduction. We should balance the budget. We should continue to reduce the size of the Federal Government. But we need to do it in a prudent way that continues to invest in our people, in our education, our technology, for the health care of our seniors and the future of our children and our environment.

We are moving in the right direction. This is the right direction. Why would we reverse course? We now have virtually 3 years of complete economic data showing that this policy that we have followed with great discipline and determination is good for the American people. So I hope we can stay right with it.

Budget Legislation

Q. Mr. President, some liberal Democrats are afraid that as part of the end game, after the veto and after the real negotiations begin, they may be left alone out there, that you'll make a deal in the center somewhere with some moderate Republicans that would be enough to see a compromise go through.

The President. Well, first of all, my goal would be to have a budget that would be—get a huge bipartisan vote. And my principles have been clear. If there are those even in my own party who do not favor a balanced budget at all, then there will come a time when we'll be on different sides of the fence on that.

But I would ask you to remember, look how much the liberal Democrats have done to move to a dynamic center in the last 3 years: They voted for deficit reduction; they voted for a very tough crime bill; they voted for an education reform bill that had high standards and let us let all kinds of States and school districts get out from under Federal regulations. They are moving. And I think most of the traditional liberal Democrats are trying to create a dynamic future. I believe they will vote for a balanced budget if it's the right kind of one.

You know, the Republicans' leaders say they have certain principles. And they are—what are those principles? Balance the budget, secure the Medicare Trust Fund—excuse me—balance the budget, secure the Medicare Trust Fund, have a tax cut, and have more authority being given to the States and the local governments. I have said I would embrace all those principles. I do believe a tax cut should be targeted toward childrearing and education and toward the broad middle class of America.

But I have certain principles. What are my principles? Don't reduce Medicare and Medicaid more rapidly, more radically than the system can contain and that will be fair to our seniors and to others that depend upon the program. Don't cut investment in education, technology, and research when education, technology, and research will determine our economic growth. Don't destroy the environment or our ability to regulate and maintain the public health. Those things, it seems to me, are pretty clear principles.

Now, I have already said, you know, the principles they say are important to them, they're important to me. I want to balance the budget. I'm determined to secure the Medicare Trust Fund. I want a reasonable tax cut targeted to the middle class, childrearing, and education. But I have these other principles on health care, on education, on the environment, on technology. And one other thing, I cannot in good conscience support a budget that actually raises taxes on people with incomes under $30,000 a year more than they're cut. That is wrong. It is wrong to raise taxes on working people with children at that income level.

So if we can—I've already said these are my principles. And I believe these principles, if furthered and if there are some other adjustments made in the budget—if we don't do too much to harm rural America and the farming sector and a few other things—I think you could get a huge, huge bipartisan vote for a balanced budget. But we are a long way from there right now.

Fort Bragg, NC, Tragedy and GDP Report

Q. [*Inaudible*]—this new figure what does it say that could possibly—[*inaudible*]—interest rates? And second of all, do you know anything about the shooting at Fort Bragg?

The President. Let me answer the second question first. I received very early this morning a briefing. I know something about it, but I don't believe that I know enough, more than has been in the press, that I should comment at this moment. Obviously, I'm very concerned about it, but I don't think I should comment.

Now, the growth figure—I don't believe the growth figure should raise interest rates because

inflation is so low. Keep in mind, the inflation rate is hovering around 2 percent. So that's the extraordinary thing about this. The combined rates of unemployment and inflation are at a 25-year low. The danger in the economy is not inflation now. The problem in the economy, the challenge of the economy is it's a time of rapid change, so there are a lot of people who aren't getting raises, even though there's growth, and there are a lot people who are still worried about losing their jobs, even though there's growth.

Those are the challenges we have to face. That's why I want the education tax deduction. That's why I want to increase investment in education, not cut it. That's why I want to raise the minimum wage. That's why I want the "GI bill" for America's workers to pass, so when people lose their jobs, they can immediately start new training programs.

We should be focusing on the challenges this economy poses, not undermining its strengths. That's why this budget battle ultimately is important. It's our values and what works for the economy. Both are at issue here. We can get this done, but we've got to do what's right, and we've got to do what's right for the economy.

Q. Mr. President, some of that growth was due to Government purchases. Do you think this growth pace can be maintained in the face of all the budget cutting that's going on?

The President. Well, they say their budget will give us a slower growth for the next 7 years than we've averaged in the last 25. I find that hard to believe, but that's what they say. They say their budget will give us lower business profits for the next 7 years than we've averaged. I find that hard to believe, but that's what they say. They say their budget will give us higher inflation in health care costs even though they claim they're going to lower health care inflation.

There are a lot of things about their budget I don't agree with. But if we cut Government expenditures, obviously, a lot of Government expenditures are with private contractors. If we— for example, if we build a new airplane, most of the people who build the airplane are— they're private sector employees. If we build a building, the people who build the building are private sector employees. But if we do this in a disciplined way, and we keep our investments up and focus on shrinking Government consumption—that is, lowering the programs that are of marginal benefit or getting rid of them, and slowly downsizing the Government, although we've been in a rapid downsize period—and we keep investing in America, then the activity in the private sector with growth will more than overcome the shrinking of the public sector. But we have to do it in a disciplined way.

That's another thing that bothers me about this health care business. I have been talking about the need to reduce health care inflation since the day I became President. I've been talking about the need to give more options for managed care since the day I became President and since long before I became President. But you cannot just say, "Well, we're going to take $450 billion out of it, even though we don't know what's going to happen." It is too much. It is too extreme. It is not necessary.

So the thing for us to do is to ultimately—what my goal is, to ultimately come out with a budget which satisfies their stated principles, which I have embraced, but which honors my stated principles, which they have yet to embrace. The stated principles that I've put out are more important for standing up for what's right for America, number one, and more important for growing our economy, number two, than what's in their budget.

And so we're going to keep working on this, but I am not going to bend on my principles. I cannot, and it's not good for America. This program—now we have 3 years of evidence. It's not only morally right, it is working for the country, and we need to keep going in this direction.

Thank you.

NOTE: The exchange began at 11 a.m. at the West Wing Portico at the White House. A tape was not available for verification of the content of this exchange.

Remarks in a Telephone Conversation With Democratic Congressional Leaders
October 27, 1995

Senator Thomas A. Daschle. Hello, Mr. President.

Representative Richard A. Gephardt. Hello, Mr. President.

The President. How are you?

Senator Daschle. Not good.

The President. Tell me what's going on.

Senator Daschle. Well, we're still working on our reconciliation bill. Democrats are offering a series of amendments that deal directly with each of the concerns that we have. But I must say it doesn't appear that there is any prospect of improving this bill. This bill is just as mean and as extreme as it was when it was introduced. It ends Medicare, it rewards the rich, and ravages the rest. And so I must tell you, I am very disappointed to report that every Democrat here in the Senate tonight at some point will be voting against this piece of legislation.

The President. Tell them not to worry about it; I'm going to veto it anyway.

Senator Daschle. Well, I applaud you for that because I must tell you it is a terrible piece of legislation. It's the wrong plan for the wrong reason, done the wrong way to help the wrong people. And I——

The President. Otherwise you don't feel strongly about it. [*Laughter*] You know, this is one of those moments in our history when I'm grateful for the wisdom of the Founding Fathers. I mean, the Congress gets to propose, but the President has to sign or veto. And the Constitution gave me that authority, and one of the reasons for the veto is to prevent excess. And this is—we are willing to work with them in good faith to balance this budget. We believe in that. You saw what—and America saw earlier this week—what the Democrats did to bring the deficit from 290 billion down to 255, then to 205, then to 164, when we were all working together. And that approach has been rejected. So I will have no alternative but to veto it. It's excessive, and it's wrong for all the reasons you said.

I just want to urge you to keep offering your amendments, standing up, make it clear what you believe in, and tell everybody to just stay positive and just stand up there, stand for what we believe in.

Senator Daschle. Mr. President, I've consulted with virtually every member of our caucus, and they have all indicated that if you veto it, we will have the votes and then some to sustain that veto.

The President. Dick?

Representative Gephardt. Mr. President, we have the very same situation in the House. We had a very united Democratic Party. As you know, yesterday, we had 203 votes against their plan. We even picked up 10 Republicans who voted against the plan.

The President. Brave souls.

Representative Gephardt. So the phalanx is beginning to splinter a little bit. But they will stand behind you and sustain this veto. And I must tell you that I really believe the American people will be behind you as well.

I was at Cambridge Hospital this morning with Joe Kennedy, and Hillary had been there I think about a year ago. This is a hospital, as you know, that has about 60 percent Medicare and Medicaid. It's a public hospital. And they really believe that if cuts of this magnitude go through, they'll have to close the hospital. And I met with the doctors and nurses and the staff there and told them that I believed you would veto this legislation if it got through and that we would stand behind that veto. And they applauded and applauded and applauded because it means whether or not there's going to be health care in that community and communities all over the country.

So we're behind you, and we're going to stay there. And we appreciate what you're doing.

Senator Daschle. Mr. President, I would say not only are we willing to support you in your position on vetoing this legislation, but I think it's also fair to say that every Democrat is prepared to go to work the day after you veto that bill to work in a constructive way to find alternatives and to work with Republicans to find some positive conclusion to this whole affair. It's important we learn to govern, that we work with Republicans in doing that. But obviously, they have concluded, as we have, that this veto is the only way that we're going to get it done. And so we look forward to working with you.

The President. Well, we want to work with them, but we've got to stick with our principles,

you know. They talk about their principles of balancing the budget and securing Medicare and having some kind of tax cut. And, you know, I accept that. I think we ought to balance the budget, secure Medicare, and I'm not opposed to a tax cut if it's properly targeted and emphasizes childrearing and education for middle class people.

But I believe that the more important principles are the ones that have been rejected by them that we had to stand up for. I mean, here we are on the verge of the 21st century; no major American company would cut education and training and cut technology and cut research, but they do. We can't tolerate that.

Nobody would—with any sense of fairness— would raise taxes on working families with children with incomes of $27,000 a year or less. That will discourage people moving from welfare to work. But that's what they do. Nobody who understands what the world is going to be like 10 years from now would have the kind of cuts and crippling provisions related to the environment that they do.

And of course we've been treated to a real education on Medicare and Medicaid which is the most grievous thing of all. I mean, we have obligations to our parents, to the poor children of this country, to the disabled people, and also to the hospitals and to the doctors and the others that are participating in these programs. It's just not right.

And so we have our principles to stand for, and we'll stand for them. And I'm glad you're going to stand with me. And eventually America will be better for this. If we stand up for America and for the future and for the things we believe in, it's going to be all right.

But as I said in this phone conversation, I'm probably more grateful today for the wisdom of the Founding Fathers than I have ever been in my life. They knew what they were doing, and we're going to use the Constitution they gave us to stand up for what's right.

Senator Daschle. Well, thank you, Mr. President. We appreciate your leadership and look forward to working with you.

The President. Thank you. Thank you, Dick.

Representative Gephardt. Thank you, Mr. President. There's a lot of people that are glad you're there and glad you've got the veto pen today, believe me.

The President. Well, just be of good cheer. Just go out there and debate these things and tell them what we believe in, and it will all work out. We'll make it work out for America.

Representative Gephardt. Great.

Senator Daschle. Thank you.

The President. Thanks.

NOTE: The President spoke at 4:23 p.m. from the Oval Office in the White House.

Statement on Signing the Agriculture, Rural Development, Food and Drug Administration, and Related Agencies Appropriations Act, 1996
October 27, 1995

I have signed into law H.R. 1976, the "Agriculture, Rural Development, Food and Drug Administration, and Related Agencies Appropriations Act, 1996."

I urge the Congress to complete action on the remaining regular FY 1996 appropriations bills and to send them to me in acceptable form. Last year, the Congress sent to me—and I signed—all 13 appropriations bills by September 30. Regrettably, this is only the second bill that I have been able to sign for this fiscal year.

This Act provides $13.4 billion in discretionary budget authority for programs of the Department of Agriculture and the Food and Drug Administration, including the Special Supplemental Feeding Program for Women, Infants, and Children (WIC); food safety programs; and various programs to protect and support rural communities.

The Act also provides a total of $41.2 billion for the Food Stamp program, the Child Nutrition program, the Commodity Credit Corporation, and other mandatory programs.

In signing this bill, I have made it possible for USDA to promptly send full-year payments of nearly $1.8 billion for the Conservation Reserve Program. This program compensates farmers for protecting environmentally sensitive cropland.

I am pleased that H.R. 1976 provides the resources necessary to keep the Special Supplemental Nutrition Program for Women, Infants, and Children on the Administration's path to full funding. An estimated 7.5 million women and children will be served, 400,000 more than in FY 1995. This program provides important nutrition benefits and health-related services.

I am also pleased that the Congress continued funding at my requested level for the Child Nutrition program and other important nutrition programs for needy Americans, including the Commodity Supplemental Food Program, Soup Kitchens, and the Nutrition Program for the Elderly.

Funds included in the bill for the Agricultural Conservation Program will provide Federal cost-share financing to farmers for needed soil and water conservation practices and structures, including water quality improvements.

The bill also includes funds I requested for farm operating and farm ownership loans, which help new farmers get started in agriculture, as well as those farmers who do not quality for private-sector financing.

In addition, H.R. 1976 omits many of the troublesome provisions contained in earlier versions of the bill that would have compromised the ability of Federal nutrition programs to assist low-income Americans. However, I am concerned about the provisions to reduce food stamp spending in an appropriations bill. This action may lead to proposals for additional food stamp cuts in the reconciliation process. This program, which assists almost 27 million low-income children, elderly, and working family members, continues to be the cornerstone of the Federal nutrition safety net.

The Act permits full funding for the Export Enhancement Program, as I requested. This program assists exports of American agricultural products, which reached an all-time high in FY 1995 of $53 billion—a trend we would like to continue.

While funding provided by H.R. 1976 is an improvement over funding levels in earlier versions of the bill, I am still disappointed by its reductions from my request for rural development. By contrast the Act includes $58 million in unrequested funds for earmarked university research facilities. I believe rural Americans would have been better served had these funds instead been channeled into rural development programs. Doing so could have, for example, helped 7,000 rural families realize the American dream of owning their own home through USDA's single-family loan program.

Section 726 raises constitutional concerns and I have therefore asked the Department of Justice to advise me as to the validity and enforceability of that section.

Despite these concerns the overall bill is acceptable because of the very positive provisions I have already mentioned and because of the benefits its programs provide to farm families and rural communities.

Again, I urge the Congress to meet its responsibilities by sending me the remaining regular FY 1996 appropriations bills in acceptable form.

WILLIAM J. CLINTON

The White House,
October 27, 1995.

NOTE: H.R. 1976, approved October 27, was assigned Public Law No. 104–37.

The President's Radio Address
October 28, 1995

Good morning. I want to talk to you today about what's at stake for the American people in the great budget debate now taking place in Washington. But first, I've got some good news to report.

Our country is on the move. Our economy is the strongest in the world, and it's growing. Yesterday, the official report on the economy for the last 3 months showed continued strong economic growth with very low inflation. And this week we also learned that we've cut the budget deficit nearly in half since I became President. It has dropped for 3 years in a row for the first time since President Truman was in office. The American people should be proud of their accomplishment.

Now it's time to finish the job and balance the budget, so that we don't pass a mountain of debt on to our children and we free up more funds to be invested in our economy. But we need to do it in a way that reflects our core values: opportunity for all Americans to make the most of their own lives; responsibility—we all must do our part, no more something for nothing; and third, recognizing our community, our common obligations to preserve and strengthen our families, to do our duty to our parents, to fulfill our obligation to give our children the best future possible with good schools and good health care and safe streets and a clean environment; and finally, a determination to keep our Nation the strongest in the world.

I have proposed a balanced budget that secures Medicare into the future, that increases our investment in education and technology, that protects the environment, that keeps our country the strongest in the world. Because working people do deserve a tax break, it includes a tax cut targeted at education and childrearing. My balanced budget reflects our national values.

It's also in our national interest. We now have 3 years of evidence that our economic strategy works. Reduce the deficit, sell more American products around the world, invest in education and technology—it gives you more jobs, more new businesses, more homeowners, a stronger future for all Americans. But this week the Republican Congress voted to enact an extreme budget that violates our values and I believe is bad for our long-term interest.

All Americans believe in honoring our parents and keeping our pledge that they'll live out their last years in dignity. But the Republican budget cuts $450 billion out of the health care system, doubles premiums for senior citizens. And the House budget actually repeals the rule called spousal impoverishment. What this means is they would let a State say to an elderly couple that if the husband or the wife has to go into a nursing home, the other has to sell the house, the car, and clean out the bank account before there can be any help from the Government. They say, "We'll then help you, and how you get along afterward is your own problem."

The Republicans say they support Medicare. They say they just want to reform it. But just this week we learned that the Senate majority leader is bragging that he opposed Medicare from the beginning, and the Speaker of the House admitted that his goal is to have Medicare, quote, "wither on the vine." When they say those things, it's clear that the Republicans come not to praise Medicare but to bury it.

All Americans believe we have a fundamental duty to provide opportunity for our young people and to protect the world that God gave us. But the Republican budget singles out education and the environment for deep and devastating cuts.

And it's a basic American value to honor hard work. But the congressional Republicans impose billions of dollars in new taxes and fees directly on working people. On average, families who earn less than $30,000 a year get a tax hike, not a tax cut, under their plan. Let me put it another way. They want to increase taxes on working families with children living on $20,000 a year or less and give people in my income group a tax cut. That is wrong. A country where Medicare withers on the vine, where our children are denied educational opportunity, where pollution worsens, where working people get a tax increase, that's not the kind of America I want for the 21st century. I want a nation that promotes opportunity and demands responsibility; that preserves families, increases work; that recognizes the duty we owe to each other; and that still is the strongest country in the world.

The more the American people see of this budget the less they like it. That's why the Republicans in Congress have resorted to extraordinary blackmail tactics to try to ram their program through. They have said they won't pass a bill letting the Government pay its bills unless I accept their extreme and misguided budget priorities.

Well, for more than two centuries, through war and depression, the United States has always paid its bills, always honored its obligations. For all their loose talk, the congressional leaders know that a default would have a severe impact on our country. By making it more expensive for the Government to raise money, it would expand the deficit, unsettle financial markets, and increase interest rates. Higher interest rates mean higher mortgage rates for homeowners, especially the 10 million of them whose mortgages are tied to Federal interest rates. Higher interest rates means higher credit card rates for

consumers and bigger borrowing costs for businesses.

Now, I'm not about to give in to that kind of blackmail. So Congress should simply stop playing political games with the full faith and credit of the United States of America. They should send me the debt limit bill to sign, as every Congress has done when necessary throughout American history.

Just yesterday the Secretary of the Treasury once again asked Congress to remove the debt limit from the budget bill or, at the very least, to extend it through mid-January. That way we can resolve this budget impasse without hurting our economy. Even this offer was brushed aside.

I will not let anyone hold health care, education, or the environment hostage. If they send me a budget bill that says simply, "Take our cuts or we'll let the country go into default," I will still veto it. And hear this: Before or after a veto, I am not prepared to discuss the destruction of Medicare and Medicaid, the gutting of our commitment to education, the ravaging of our environment, or raising taxes on working people.

So I say to the Republican leaders: Back off your cuts in these vital areas. Until you do, there's nothing for us to talk about. You say your principles are a balanced budget, a tax cut, extending the life of the Medicare Trust Fund. I want all those things. They're my principles, too. But there are other important principles, the ones that I have outlined. They are morally right for America, and they're good for our economy.

This is a time of genuine promise for our country. We're on the move. Our economy is the envy of the world. No nation on Earth is better positioned for the new century than America because of the diversity of our economy and our citizens, because of our commitment to excellence, because of our technological advantages. The 21st century will be ours if we make the right choices and do the right thing for the American people.

Thanks for listening.

NOTE: The address was recorded at 5:25 p.m. on October 27 in the Roosevelt Room at the White House for broadcast at 10:06 a.m. on October 28.

Statement on the Court Decision on Timber Sales
October 28, 1995

I am deeply disappointed in the court's decision to force the Forest Service and the Bureau of Land Management to release these sales of healthy ancient timber.

My administration's agreement with the Congress on this issue was significantly different from the interpretation upheld this week by the courts. We agreed that the administration would not have to violate our standards and guidelines for our forest plan and for forest management in general, but only speed up sales that met those standards. We do not believe that this extreme expansion of ancient timber sales was authorized by the 1995 rescission act. My administration will actively pursue a legislative remedy to correct this extreme result.

At this time, however, there is no choice but to comply with the court's decision. The decision forces the release of timber that may lead to grave environmental injury to chinook salmon and other wildlife and damage our rivers and streams. This could jeopardize the livelihoods of thousands of people who depend on the Pacific Northwest's vibrant commercial and sport fisheries.

I have directed the Secretaries of Agriculture and the Interior to work with the companies awarded contracts to seek changes to mitigate any harm to salmon and other species and water quality.

In signing the rescission legislation and in subsequent directives to my Cabinet, I pledged to uphold existing environmental laws and standards. I will continue to fight for those laws and standards.

Letter to Senator Ernest F. Hollings on Telecommunications Reform Legislation
October 26, 1995

Dear Fritz:

I enjoyed our telephone conversation today regarding the upcoming conference on the telecommunications reform bill and would like to follow-up on your request regarding the specific issues of concern to me in the proposed legislation.

As I said in our discussion, I am committed to promoting competition in every aspect of the telecommunications and information industries. I believe that the legislation should protect and promote diversity of ownership and opinions in the mass media, should protect consumers from unjustified rate increases for cable and telephone services, and, in particular, should include a test specifically designed to ensure that the Bell companies entering into long distance markets will not impede competition.

Earlier this year, my Administration provided comments on S. 652 and H.R. 1555 as passed. I remain concerned that neither bill provides a meaningful role for the Department of Justice in safeguarding competition before local telephone companies enter new markets. I continue to be concerned that the bills allow too much concentration within the mass media and in individual markets, which could reduce the diversity of news and information available to the public. I also believe that the provisions allowing mergers of cable and telephone companies are overly broad. In addition, I oppose deregulating cable programming services and equipment rates before cable operators face real competition. I remain committed, as well, to the other concerns contained in those earlier statements on the two bills.

I applaud the Senate and the House for including provisions requiring all new televisions to contain technology that will allow parents to block out programs with violent or objectionable content. I strongly support retention in the final bill of the Snowe-Rockefeller provision that will ensure that schools, libraries and hospitals have access to advanced telecommunications services.

I look forward to working with you and your colleagues during the conference to produce legislation that effectively addresses these concerns.

Sincerely,

BILL CLINTON

NOTE: Senator Ernest F. Hollings was the ranking member of the Communications Subcommittee of the Senate Commerce, Science, and Transportation Committee. This letter was released by the Office of the Press Secretary on October 30.

Remarks to the White House Conference on Travel and Tourism
October 30, 1995

Thank you. Please sit down. This is not an endurance contest. [*Laughter*] I am delighted to be here, delighted that this day has finally come. I want to thank Greg Farmer for the fine job that he has done, and the others who are here: the FAA Administrator, David Hinson; the Deputy Transportation Secretary, Mort Downey; Bill Norman, the president of the Travel Industry Association of America. I want to say a special word of thanks to Loranne Ausley Ellis, who was the executive director of this conference. I don't know if she's had any sleep for the last week or two, waiting for you all to appear. And a thanks to my good friend Congressman Oberstar.

I was telling Greg Farmer when Jim was up here speaking that Jim Oberstar, once he gets the bit in his teeth, he never lets go. If Jim had been a dog, half the people in Washington would have rabies. [*Laughter*] He is the most determined person I ever saw. And it might not be so bad, depending on which half it was. [*Laughter*]

Jim Oberstar came to me with this idea, and I could look in his eyes and tell it was going to happen. I might tell you also, on a totally different subject, for a very long time he was one of only literally a handful of Members of the Congress who supported me in what I ultimately had to do in Haiti. Because he speaks Creole—he'd lived in Haiti—he knew it was the right thing to do. He knew it was the right thing for our country, for the cause of freedom. And when we celebrated one year of democratic freedom in Haiti just a couple weeks ago, I thought to myself, if it hadn't been for Jim Oberstar and just a couple of more, this might not have happened. So he, in a real way, is the father of this conference, and I thank him for it very much.

I do want to thank the Members of Congress and the citizens of both political parties who worked so hard to make this day possible. I want to thank those of you who took time away to attend this conference. I know there are a lot of people here today, as there were at the White House Conference on Small Business, who don't work for big companies, who don't have generous leave policies and travel allowances, and who really had to make a personal effort and a personal sacrifice to come. And I thank you for coming because I know what an important part of the tourism industry you are.

I want to thank the State employees who are here who work with tourism and the local employees and elected officials who are here. I want to thank the students from the Academy of Travel and Tourism programs who wrote essays that won prizes about encouraging people to visit the United States.

I am very proud that this is the first White House Conference on Travel and Tourism. And I know all of you agree that it's about time.

This industry has been near and dear to my heart since I was a little boy. I grew up in a resort town that also embraced a national park. As an adult I've had the good fortune to travel a fair amount, although as President I must say one of the more frustrating aspects of the job is I go to a lot of interesting places and never get to be a tourist.

As Governor, I enthusiastically attended our Governor's conference on tourism every year. And I want you to know that this is very important to me personally and that this time is a very important time for you to be gathering here.

This industry holds much promise for the future of America. It has a lot to teach us as Americans, as we stand on the dawn of a new era, moving from an industrial age to one that will be dominated by technology and information and our ability to relate to one another and to move quickly in terms of ideas and technology and people across the globe. We've moved at a breathtaking pace from the divided world of the cold war to a global village. If the 21st century is going to be an American century, we have to master this transition as surely as we mastered the shift from the agricultural to the industrial economy. And we will.

To meet the test of the time, we have to dedicate ourselves to promoting and strengthening those aspects of American society which will clearly work best in the global economy. And we know that trade and tourism and travel, all these things are tailor-made for what we do well and what the 21st century will value.

That's why I have dedicated myself to helping this industry grow. A healthy travel and tourism industry is good for the economy, and it also gives Americans a larger service. If you think back to the first time as a child you left home to go somewhere new, recall the first time you met someone who was visiting you from a far-off place, I know that you came away from the experience with a greater knowledge of other people and other communities, a stronger sense of the common humanity that unites us all. And I would guess that you returned with an increased appreciation for something just as important, your own home, your own community, your own roots.

Travel leads to understanding. It increases the chances of peace, and therefore, it increases the chances of a better life for all. When you just travel this land you learn the miracle of America. Our people are as diverse and wonderful as our landscape. Going to another State can almost be like going to another country, and if you come from another State to Washington, it's almost like space travel. [*Laughter*]

Travel is also democratic, with a small "d." It used to be a luxury reserved for the aristocracy. But in the history of American travel and tourism you can see that the marvelously optimistic quality of our people made this something that everybody ought to do. We look at something set aside for the very few at the top and we say, "Hold on, everybody ought to have the opportunity to work hard and then enjoy that." Most Americans may not travel first class, but for a long time now our families have been able to load up the car and head for a fall-

colored national park or a warm beach or a clean motel on the side of a road leading to a place they have never been before.

Of course, the travel and tourism industries are also essential to providing opportunity for all Americans in the 21st century. You are our largest business service export. As Greg said, in 1993 you generated a $22 billion trade surplus for the United States. You're the second largest employer in the Nation, providing jobs for over 6 million Americans. And of course, you employ millions more through the industries that thrive when you do well. As the circle of freedom expands around the globe, the tourism industry will keep growing all around the world. And as you grow, here at home the hardworking Americans whose jobs are changing along with our economy will have a chance to find a home with you.

Many Americans have general worries about all service-sector jobs. Somehow they think they're not as steady and don't have as good of prospects for the future. But I know that we're all working to prove otherwise. Service industry wages are among the fastest rising wages in our economy. And I support your efforts to reward hard work and to give people incomes that they can build solid lives on and raise children with. For all these reasons, I have committed myself to giving your industry the opportunity to flourish that it deserves. It is part of a strategy that I have embraced to restore the American economy and to ensure the American dream and America's leadership into the 21st century.

The first thing I want to tell you is that your country is clearly on a roll. We have a resurgence of economic growth. We have a dramatic reform in the size and scope and way of operating of our Government. And most important of all, we have a reassertion of basic American values in every community in this country.

In the last 2½ years since I have been privileged to be your President, Americans have produced 7½ million new jobs; 2½ million new homeowners, bringing home ownership to a 15-year high; over 2 million new small businesses, the most rapid growth of small businesses in American history, with the lowest combined rates of unemployment and inflation in 25 years. The Government's role in this economic resurgence was to reduce the deficit while increasing our investment in education, in training, in technology, in research, and in partnerships with the private sector to promote American products and services all around the world.

Our trade with other countries has increased by 4 percent in '93, 10 percent in '94, and 15 percent in '95. As a percentage of our national income, the deficit is less than half of what it was when I became President. For the first time since Harry Truman, the deficit has actually been driven down for 3 years in a row. As a percentage of income, the United States of America now has the lowest Government deficit of any industrial country in the world except Norway. Every other country has a higher deficit as a percentage of their income than we do. I'm proud of that, and you should be proud of it, too.

We are now debating here in Washington how to balance the budget. But the good news is the leaders of both parties want to finish the job. I believe we have to do it in a way that is consistent with our values, that keeps our economy going, and that maintains our leadership in the world.

More important even than the economy to me is the encouraging signs that Americans are getting back together around the values that make life worth living. In almost every State and significant community in America the crime rate is down, the murder rate is down, the welfare rolls are down, the food stamp rolls are down, the poverty rate is down, the teen pregnancy rate is down, and child support collections have increased 40 percent in the last 3 years. Our country is moving in the right direction and coming back together. That is a terribly important development.

Specifically with regard to the tourism and travel industry, we have taken a series of very specific steps designed to help you succeed at what you do. First of all, we have a disciplined, coordinated leadership effort and a commitment to promoting travel and tourism, beginning with the Secretaries of State, Commerce, and Transportation; our Trade Representative, Ambassador Kantor; the Overseas Private Investment Corporation, led by Ruth Harkin; and the Export-Import Bank, led by Ken Brody. Secondly, we have worked very hard to open markets and to support U.S. exports including travel and tourism around the world. We have concluded more than 80 separate trade agreements in less than 3 years. Tourism is an export, and we have fought for it just as we have fought for other industry.

The U.S. Trade and Tourism Association is leading a public-private partnership to double the number of Japanese visitors to the United States by the year 2000. The reason is clear: Of the 7½ million new jobs that have come into the United States since I have been President, 2 million, 2 million came from the expansion of the sale of American products and services overseas. International visitors spent $78 billion here last year.

The second thing we've worked to do is to sign open-skies agreements with more countries to facilitate air travel here. Earlier this year I signed an open-skies agreement with Canada, deregulating the world's largest aviation market: more flights, lower fares. Last month we concluded an open-skies pact with nine European countries. We've expanded air service around the world to Great Britain, Brazil, Ukraine, the Philippines.

We've worked hard to give you a healthy airlines industry. They were in deep trouble when I came into office. Every airline in America but one was losing money. Three were in bankruptcy. From 1988 to 1992, the industry lost $12 billion, more money lost in 4 years than it had made in its entire history. I appointed a special commission headed by the former Governor of Virginia, Gerry Baliles, to revive the industry. Secretary Peña has now carried out the vast majority of its recommendations. Today the airlines are healthy, the fares are down, the passengers are up, and they are turning a profit. We are moving in the right direction.

We've also worried about industry safety, to try to make America a safe harbor and to try to guarantee the safety of Americans around the world. We see today ironic and mostly encouraging developments, peace in the Middle East coming along, more peace and less violence in Northern Ireland, tomorrow peace talks opening about Bosnia here in the United States, something we are proud to host. We also know that there are new threats to our security that go across all national boundaries, that the organized forces of destruction and terror know no nationalism.

We saw terrorism at home blow up the Federal building in Oklahoma City and foreign terrorists try to take the World Trade Center down, plan to bomb the United Nations. We see abroad when a religious fanatic sect can take a small vial of sarin gas into a subway in Japan and break it open and kill scores of people and injure hundreds of others. And we know we have to work together, together with other countries, to reduce the menace of terrorism and violence and drug trafficking and organized crime in this world. That was the subject of the speech I gave to the United Nations last week on the occasion of its 50th anniversary.

But I also want you to know that we are doing everything we can to help your local officials and your community bring the homegrown crime rate down in America. The crime bill that was passed in 1994 was an astonishing piece of legislation. It provided for putting a hundred thousand more police officers on our street in community policing settings so that we could reduce the incidence of violent crime. It provided for prevention programs, not designed and run by the Federal Government but run by local communities to give our young people something to say yes to, constructive endeavors, avoiding a life of crime. It provided for tougher punishment. And we now have the first convictions coming in under the "three strikes and you're out" law, where we take career criminals and just put them away. It provided for all these things, plus the Brady bill, which kept 40,000 criminals from getting handguns last year—40,000. Next time somebody tells you that didn't work, tell them to think again.

Now, that's one big reason the crime rate is down. We're on time—we're actually slightly ahead of schedule in putting these police officers out there on the street. And we are trying to give you a safe America that everyone is happy to travel in and to be a part of, in every State in our community, in cities and rural areas alike. That is a very important priority with me. And we've got to keep this crime rate coming down, down, down.

The other thing we're trying to do is rooted in a lesson I learned as a Governor when I realized that every time we opened a new State park or refurbished an old one, or did something to one of our State's landmarks, we helped the private sector tourism in the area. We have done everything we could to promote and enhance our national parks and our national landmarks and our national monuments, as well as to maintain the ability of the United States to have clean air, clean water, safe drinking water, and a generally very healthy and high-standard environment. I am therefore opposed to changes which would undermine our ability to provide a clean environment or would require us to sell off any of our national parks or national assets.

I congratulated Congressman Oberstar on the victory won and headed by Congressman Richardson of New Mexico, in the Congress just last week to get rid of this hit list of over 300 American treasures that some in the Congress wanted to sell off, including the home of President Roosevelt, where I met with President Yeltsin last week. I hope that idea is dying a very timely death. We need to enhance our public investments.

So we are committed to doing things that will help the tourism industry, that will promote travel, that will enhance your efforts. Let me say, we are also doing it with a much smaller Government. There are 163,000 fewer people working for the Federal Government today than there were the day I became President. Next year, the Federal Government will be the smallest it's been since John Kennedy was President, under the budget we passed in 1993. And as a percentage of the civilian work force, it will be the smallest it's been since 1933. The era of big Government is done. The era of smart Government is here. It is the right thing to do.

We have 16,000 fewer pages of Government regulations. My favorite, because I'm from Arkansas, was when I showed up I realized there was a whole page of Government regulations on what grits were. [*Laughter*] And I could have just given the name of 400 people they could teach something to, and they could say this is grits or it's not. [*Laughter*] So we're getting rid of a lot of that. We got rid of 16,000 pages—you think I'm kidding, it really was there—[*laughter*]—16,000 pages of regulations have been eliminated. We have proposed to eliminate hundreds of programs.

But we also want to make the Government work better. A lot of you are small business people. Maybe you've had some help from the Small Business Administration. In the last 3 years, we have cut the budget of the SBA by 40 percent, but we have doubled the loan volume. We have emphasized making loans to women business people and to minorities without in any way reducing the loans that white males were getting or without watering down the standards for making the loan one bit. The SBA is simply working in a more entrepreneurial, more effective way to try to help more small business people get started in the United States in every part of the United States no matter who they are or where they come from. That is the kind of Government that the taxpayers of this country are entitled to. And it will help the travel and tourism industry if we can accelerate the growth of small business in America.

Another thing we are trying to do in this Congress—and I think we have a good chance to get a bipartisan agreement on this—that affects an awful lot of small business people, and I would imagine a lot of you in this audience, is to make it easier for small business people to take out retirement plans for themselves and their employees. The present rules and regulations are a nightmare. They are too cumbersome; they are too expensive. The legal fees alone keep thousands of small business people from doing anything in this important area.

So if you're interested in this and this will affect you personally, I would urge you to contact your Member of Congress and get a status report on this. As far as I know, there is no partisan difference here. We just know that small business is creating most of the new jobs in this economy; that retirement programs, health care programs are often too burdensome, too inaccessible for small business people; and this legislation can make it much, much, much easier for people in small business to take out retirement plans for themselves and to help their employees. And I would urge you to help me get this done. I think we have a broad coalition for it. It just needs to be made a priority so that no matter how busy we are, we take care of this. I am committed to it, and I hope you will be as well.

Finally, let me say that we are trying to do two more things to make the Government work better and cost less that directly affect the travel and tourism industry. The Vice President is going to speak to you tomorrow, and he will talk about the work we've done in reinventing Government with the Customs Service and the Immigration and Naturalization Service which has changed the way we greet our own citizens and visitors as they enter the United States. If you're coming or going legally, we want to get the Government out of the way and get you on your way. And that will make a big difference if we do it right.

Now, finally, I want to mention this second point. We have worked very hard to enact reforms at the Federal Aviation Administration. Having a Federal Aviation Administration that

works, that has the confidence of all Americans, that operates the airports efficiently and safely, that has a lot to do with how well those of you in travel and tourism do, unless you get all your customers off the road. And it is a very important thing for the United States, for our economy, for the convenience and for the safety of our people.

The FAA controls the bottom-line efficiency of the airline industry. Yet, believe it or not, its air traffic control system in many places still depends upon stone age technology that's often older than the flight controllers using it. [Laughter] I know that's hard to believe. At a time when our private sector is building the most advanced airplanes in the world, the FAA is still buying vacuum tubes like this—the Vice President gave me this just before I came over—to run the computers and the radar systems that ought to be run by chips. We actually have to buy these vacuum tubes for some of the old computers and radar systems from other countries because they're not even produced here anymore.

Now, this is unacceptable. Americans have a right to believe that the FAA will be run with the highest technology in the world and that they will get where they're going on time at a reasonable cost and at maximum safety. I never want a parent to think twice when a child asks if the flying is safe.

Now, we've been very blessed by very safe and careful airlines, and our control and regulatory system has worked very well over time. But we also know that there's no point in pretending something's all right when it's not. It is not all right that the FAA does not have the highest technology, safest, most efficient equipment in the world. That is not all right. We have to change that.

That's why more than 2 years ago I made FAA reform a top priority and asked the Vice President to include it at the top of his list in the National Performance Review. In early 1994, almost 2 years ago, we sent Congress a plan to overhaul the Agency. Building on suggestions from the airline commission that helped us to turn the airline industry around, we called for a procurement system that gets the FAA new technology while it's still on the cutting edge, a new personnel system that puts controllers where they're needed and rewards them for good work, and a radically new financing system that ensures stability, demands accountability, and provides incentives for efficiency.

We've done everything we could to fix the FAA on our own. Secretary Peña and Administrator Hinson brought in a new management team and put in plans to modernize the system. We have speeded up the replacement of failing computers at some of our busiest air traffic centers, so there will be fewer of these and more of the chips. And we have stepped up training for controllers and technicians.

But unfortunately, we cannot do everything we need to do alone. We have to have some legislative help. And I am very pleased that Congress has put together finally a transportation appropriations bill that embraces the personnel and the procurement reforms we asked for 2 years ago. I am very gratified that members of both parties came together to create this important legislation, and I'd like to give a special word of thanks to Senator Mark Hatfield of Oregon. When this bill hits my desk—[*applause*]— we've got the Oregon group back there. When this bill hits my desk, I intend to sign it. And we will get FAA back on a glide path to the 21st century.

But there's more to do. We still have to overhaul the financing of FAA. Today's budget process simply does not guarantee the agency the long-range funding it needs to operate safely and efficiently. Again let me thank Congressman Oberstar and Senators McCain, Ford, and Hollings for their work on this. I want Congress to redouble their efforts. We have got to fix this problem once and for all.

Now, let me say that these are my ideas for what the National Government can do to support you in what you're trying to do. I'm sure that you have some ideas about that, too. I never met a group of people that I thought had more consistently higher levels of energy and more consistent openness to new ideas than the people I work with throughout my career who are in tourism and travel.

One big point of a White House Conference on Travel and Tourism is for us to listen to you, not for you to listen to us. I came here to make a report to you because you're entitled to that and it will help you to know where we are and how we're thinking. But when you leave, I want you to report back to me and tell me what more you think we can do to help you to succeed.

I will say again: Next year the whole world will be looking at the United States when the Olympics open in Atlanta. They may let the Braves carry the torch in now. [*Laughter*] But the world will be looking at us. It will give us a new opportunity, an even greater opportunity, as billions of people all over the world look at the United States, to enhance the chances that more and more and more of them will want to come here to see what America's like up close, to share in all the things that too many of our fellow countrymen sometimes take for granted.

We want to be ready for that. We want to keep this country on a roll. We want to keep coming back to our values, and we want to keep pushing our economy forward. And we want to keep being a leading force in the world for peace and freedom and prosperity.

In order to do that, we have to have a healthy travel and tourism industry. And by next year when the eyes of the world are on America in a clear and focused and open-hearted way, I want to know that you and I together have done everything we can to make sure that one of the things those eyes take away from the sight of the Olympics is a deep, yearning desire to come to America and to be with us in friendship and partnership as we pave the way for greater opportunity for these young people in the 21st century.

Thank you, and God bless you all.

NOTE: The President spoke at 10:35 a.m. in the Grand Ballroom at the Sheraton Washington Hotel. In his remarks, he referred to President Boris Yeltsin of Russia.

Statement on Signing Legislation Rejecting U.S. Sentencing Commission Recommendations
October 30, 1995

Today I reject United States Sentencing Commission proposals that would equalize penalties for crack and powder cocaine distribution by dramatically reducing the penalties for crack. The Sentencing Commission would also reduce the penalties for money laundering by combining the guidelines on money laundering with those on transactions in unlawfully acquired property. I am opposed to both of these changes.

Since I took office, my Administration has fought to stop drug abuse and to stamp out the crime and violence that are its constant companions. We are battling drug traffickers at every level of their networks—from the very top to the very bottom.

The Cali Cartel, which pumped drugs into America with seeming impunity, is now on the run. We have intensified our efforts to work with drug producing countries to stop drugs from coming into the United States and to capture major drug traffickers. We told criminals convicted time and again for serious violent crimes or drug trafficking that from now on, it's three strikes and you're out. And we established the death penalty for drug kingpins, because they should reap what they sow.

We are putting 100,000 police officers on America's streets. We banned assault weapons because America doesn't want drug dealers to be better armed than police officers. We are helping schools to rid themselves of guns, and we are also helping schools to prevent teenage drug use by teaching children about the dangers of drugs and gangs. And we support schools who test student athletes for drugs.

All of this is beginning to work. For the first time in a very long time, crime has decreased around the country. But we cannot stop now.

We have to send a constant message to our children that drugs are illegal, drugs are dangerous, drugs may cost you your life—and the penalties for dealing drugs are severe. I am not going to let anyone who peddles drugs get the idea that the cost of doing business is going down.

Trafficking in crack, and the violence it fosters, has a devastating impact on communities across America, especially inner-city communities. Tough penalties for crack trafficking are required because of the effect on individuals and families, related gang activity, turf battles, and other violence.

Current law does require a substantial disparity between sentences for crack as compared to equal amounts of powder cocaine. Some adjustment is warranted, and the bill I am signing today, S. 1254, directs the Sentencing Commission to undertake additional review of these issues and to report back with new recommendations.

Furthermore, the sentencing structure should reflect the fact that all crack starts as powder. When large-scale cocaine traffickers sell powder with the knowledge that it will be converted into crack, they should be punished as severely as those who distribute the crack itself. I have asked the Attorney General to immediately develop enforcement strategies to bring about this result. As I said before, we *are* going after drug traffickers at every level of their networks.

WILLIAM J. CLINTON

The White House,
October 30, 1995.

NOTE: S. 1254, approved October 30, was assigned Public Law No. 104–38.

Remarks on the Balkan Peace Process and an Exchange With Reporters
October 31, 1995

The President. Good morning. I have just met with Secretary Christopher and our Bosnia negotiating team, led by Ambassador Holbrooke. As you know, they are preparing to leave for Dayton, Ohio, in just a few moments. There, the Presidents of Bosnia, Croatia, and Serbia will start direct negotiations which we hope will lead to a peaceful, lasting settlement in Bosnia.

I want to repeat today what I told President Tudjman and President Izetbegovic when we met in New York last week. We have come to a defining moment in Bosnia. This is the best chance we've had for peace since the war began. It may be the last chance we have for a very long time. Only the parties to this terrible conflict can end it. The world now looks to them to turn the horror of war to the promise of peace. The United States and our partners, Russia, Germany, France, and the United Kingdom, must do everything in our power to support them. That is what I have just instructed Secretary Christopher and our team to do in the days ahead in Dayton. We will succeed only if America continues to lead.

Already our military strength through NATO and our diplomatic determination have advanced the possibility of peace in Bosnia. We can't stop now. The responsibilities of leadership are real, but the benefits are greater. We see them all around the world, a reduced nuclear threat, democracy in Haiti, peace breaking out in the Middle East and in Northern Ireland. In Bosnia, as elsewhere, when the United States leads we can make progress. And if we don't, progress will be much more problematic.

Making peace in Bosnia is important to America. Making peace will end the terrible toll of this war, the innocent lives lost, the futures destroyed. For 4 years, the people of Bosnia have suffered the worst atrocities in Europe since World War II: mass executions, ethnic cleansing, concentration camps, rape and terror, starvation and disease. We continue to learn more and more even in the present days about the slaughters in Srebrenica.

The only way to stop these horrors is to make peace. Making peace will prevent the war from spreading. So far, we have been able to contain this conflict to the former Yugoslavia. But the Balkans lie at the heart of Europe, next door to several of our key NATO allies and to some of the new, fragile European democracies. If the war there reignites, it could spread and spark a much larger conflict, the kind of conflict that has drawn Americans into two European wars in this century. We have to end the war in Bosnia and do it now.

Making peace will advance our goal of a peaceful, democratic, and undivided Europe, a Europe at peace with extraordinary benefits to our long-term security and prosperity, a Europe at peace with partners to meet the challenges of the new century, challenges that affect us here at home like terrorism and drug trafficking, organized crime, and the spread of weapons of mass destruction. A peaceful, democratic, undivided Europe will be that kind of partner.

In Dayton, our diplomats face a tremendous challenge. There is no guarantee they will succeed. America can help the parties negotiate a settlement, but we cannot impose a peace. In recent weeks, thanks to our mediation efforts, the parties to the war have made real progress. The parties have put into effect a Bosnia-wide cease-fire. They have agreed to the basic principles of a settlement. Bosnia will remain a single state comprised of two entities but, I repeat, a single state. There must be free elections and democratic institutions of government at the national and regional levels.

Now, beyond this, many difficult issues remain to be resolved. These include the internal boundary between the Bosnia-Croat Federation and the Serb Republic, the status of Sarajevo, the practical steps that need to be taken to separate hostile forces, and the procedures for free elections. That's just a few of the difficult issues this team will have to confront beginning today.

I urge the parties to negotiate seriously for the good of their own people. So much is riding on the success in Dayton, and the whole world is watching. If the parties do reach a settlement, NATO must help to secure it, and the United States, as NATO's leader, must participate in such an effort.

Again I say, there is no substitute for American leadership. After so many years of violence and bloodshed, a credible international military presence in Bosnia is needed to give the parties confidence to live up to their own agreements and to give them time to begin the long, hard work of rebuilding and living together again. NATO is the one organization with the track record and the strength to implement a settlement.

And as I've said many times, the United States, the source of NATO's military strength, must participate. If we don't participate in the Implementation Force, our NATO partners, understandably, would reconsider their own commitments. We would undermine American leadership of the alliance. We would weaken the alliance itself. And the hard-won peace in Bosnia could be lost.

American troops would not be deployed—I say this again—would not be deployed unless and until the parties reach a peace agreement. We must first have a peace agreement. And that is what I would urge the American people and the Members of Congress to focus on over the next few days. They would, if going into Bosnia, operate under NATO command, with clear rules of engagement and a clearly defined mission. They would not be asked to keep a peace that cannot be kept. But they would make sure we do our part in helping peace to hold.

As the peace process moves forward I will continue to consult closely with Congress. If a peace agreement is reached I will request an expression of support in Congress for committing United States troops to a NATO implementation force. Our foreign policy works best when we work together. I want the widest possible support for peace.

But now it would be premature to request an expression of support because we can't decide many of the details of implementation until an agreement is clearly shaped and defined. Let me stress again, we aren't there yet; there are still difficult obstacles ahead. The focus on Dayton must be on securing the peace. Without peace there will be nothing for us to secure.

Earlier this month in New Jersey, I had the privilege of spending time with His Holiness Pope Paul—Pope John Paul II. At the end of our meeting, the Pope said something to me I would like to repeat. He said, "You know, I am not a young man. I have lived through most of this century. This century began with a war in Sarajevo. Mr. President, you must not let it end with a war in Sarajevo."

All of us must do our part to hear the Pope's plea. Our conscience as a nation devoted to freedom and tolerance demands it. Our conscience as a nation that wants to end this mindless slaughter demands it. Our enduring interest in the security and stability of Europe demand it. This is our challenge. And I'm determined to do everything I can to see that America meets that challenge.

Thank you.

Q. Mr. President, what is the effect of the House resolution on these talks? And do you feel hemmed in by them?

The President. No. No, I wouldn't expect it to have any effect on the talks. I think we have to get the peace agreement first. I expect to consult intensively with the leaders of Congress, beginning—I believe tomorrow the congressional leadership is coming in, and I expect to talk to them about Bosnia in detail and then to keep working with the congressional leadership and with Members of Congress who are interested in this right along, all the way through the process. And I expect them to say that they want to ask questions and to have them answered before they would agree to the policy that I will embark on.

Q. Mr. President, looking back at the advice that General Colin Powell gave you on Bosnia when he was Chairman of the Joint Chiefs of Staff, was that bad advice, his reluctance to use air power to force the parties into negotiations?

The President. Let me tell you, today we're starting a peace process. And we have done things that have brought us to this point. I believe we have done the right things. But I think the American people should be focused on peace and on the process and the work before us.

Debt Limit Legislation

Q. Mr. President, are you going to make peace with the Republicans tomorrow and strike some sort of debt extension agreement?

The President. Well, I look forward to having the opportunity to discuss that with them. I know Senator Dole and Leon Panetta have had a brief conversation about it. I know that a lot of others are contacting the Congress about it. So we'll have a chance to talk about that tomorrow as well.

Q. Are you willing to accept a short-term, through November 29th, as has been suggested, extension?

The President. I think any responsible extension is a move forward. I think the main thing is we want to send a message to the world and to our own financial markets and to our own people that America honors its commitments, that we are not going to see the first example in the history of the Republic where we don't pay our bills.

Thank you very much.

Q. Mr. President, have you been briefed on the Aldrich Ames damage assessment?

Canadian Referendum

Q. Are you happy about Canada?
The President. Yes.

NOTE: The President spoke at 11:35 a.m. in the Roosevelt Room at the White House. In his remarks, he referred to President Franjo Tudjman of Croatia and President Alija Izetbegovic of Bosnia-Herzegovina.

Message to the Congress on Continuation of the National Emergency With Respect to Iran
October 31, 1995

To the Congress of the United States:

Section 202(d) of the National Emergencies Act (50 U.S.C. 1622(d)) provides for the automatic termination of a national emergency unless, prior to the anniversary date of its declaration, the President publishes in the *Federal Register* and transmits to the Congress a notice stating that the emergency is to continue in effect beyond the anniversary date. In accordance with this provision, I have sent the enclosed notice, stating that the Iran emergency is to continue in effect beyond November 14, 1995, to the *Federal Register* for publication. Similar notices have been sent annually to the Congress and the *Federal Register* since November 12, 1980. The most recent notice appeared in the *Federal Register* on November 1, 1994.

The crisis between the United States and Iran that began in 1979 has not been fully resolved. The international tribunal established to adjudicate claims of the United States and U.S. nationals against Iran and of the Iranian government and Iranian nationals against the United States continues to function, and normalization of commercial and diplomatic relations between the United States and Iran has not been achieved. Indeed, on March 15 of this year, I declared a separate national emergency with respect to Iran pursuant to the International Emergency Economic Powers Act and imposed separate sanctions. By Executive Order 12959, these sanctions were significantly augmented. In these circumstances, I have determined that it is necessary to maintain in force the broad authorities that are in place by virtue of the November 14, 1979, declaration of emergency, including the authority to block certain property of the Government of Iran, and which are needed in the process of implementing the January 1981 agreements with Iran.

WILLIAM J. CLINTON

The White House,
October 31, 1995.

NOTE: The notice is listed in Appendix D at the end of this volume.

Statement on Signing Biotechnology Process Patent Legislation
November 1, 1995

I am pleased to sign into law S. 1111, a bill to provide enhanced protection of biotechnology process patents. This bill will update current patent law to provide the protection American biotechnology companies need to continue developing new products. American consumers will benefit from improvements in the diagnosis, cure, or treatment of disease and from the production of healthier, more abundant foods.

Process patents are especially important in biotechnology, since part of the genius of that field is to produce commercial quantities of breakthrough products through new and inventive processes. If the innovative process used to make a biotechnology product is not protected by patent, American biotechnology will remain vulnerable to foreign imitation. This bill will provide necessary new protection for processes, spurring innovation and keeping American jobs in America.

In less than two decades, the biotechnology industry has created more than 100,000 high-wage American jobs and it now generates annual sales of over $7 billion. Originating in the United States, biotechnology has already produced life-saving drugs that dissolve blood clots in heart attack victims and treat anemia in patients suffering from chronic kidney failure. It has helped produce disease-resistant plants, more nutritious foods, effective waste treatment systems, and methods to clean and protect the environment. American companies working to commercialize breakthrough products should not be required to face unfair competition from overseas.

This bill addresses the need for current patent laws to keep pace with the rapid growth in biotechnology. It was passed with the strong support of this Administration and broad bipartisan support in the Congress. I am pleased to sign S. 1111 into law to ensure the continued development of important products for American consumers and continued U.S. job growth in this field.

WILLIAM J. CLINTON

The White House,
November 1, 1995.

NOTE: S. 1111, approved November 1, was assigned Public Law No. 104–41.

Remarks to the Community Anti-Drug Coalitions of America Forum
November 2, 1995

Thank you, Jim, my good friend Jim Burke. Thank you for devoting your life to this cause. Thank you, Alvah Chapman, CADCA's founding chair, who first talked to me about this some years ago now. Thank you, Lee Brown, for your distinguished work for all Americans and all American children. Thank you, Marni Vliet. I thank all the families who are here today who have sustained losses. And I want to say a special word of thanks to Lori Plank for having the courage to be here, just 2 weeks after she lost her husband, along with her husband's parents and her beautiful child. I thank them for coming and for devoting themselves to the proposition that the best way they can honor Ed Plank is to do whatever can be done to stop this madness from killing more Americans.

Let me say to all of you that this issue is especially close to me. Most of you, because of what you do, probably know I grew up in an alcoholic home, and I have a brother I love very much who could have been killed by the cocaine habit he had. This is madness, pure and simple. And we all have to do whatever we can to get it out of our lives.

We have to deal with the question of law enforcement and punishment. We have to deal with education and treatment and prevention. We have to deal with all those things that can

be done by the President and all those things that can be done by legislators at the national, State, and local level. But in the end, this problem will be changed when America changes, when we assume responsibility for ourselves, our families, and our communities. And therefore, what you are doing—what you are doing—and what other Americans are doing in attempting to assert that sort of responsibility over their own lives for their families and for their communities is the most important thing that can be done in America today. And it is up to the rest of us to support you as well as we possibly can.

Of course, parents have a special role to play because we all know that the best crime prevention, the best antidrug program in this country always has been a good family with strong parents. We know that it is the Government's job to uphold the law, to promote order, but parents must teach right from wrong, and we must all support that. And where the parents are not there or cannot do it, then the community must step in and do their best, which is what so many of you are trying to do.

I want to say again that I thank Lee Brown for the work he has done to get the urgent message out to our young people that they are wrong if they think that drug use is not dangerous as well as illegal and that they have the power to do something about it. That message has to be repeated over and over and over again. It is one of the cruel ironies of this battle that drug use has stabilized or is actually declining among young adults, but casual drug use, especially marijuana, continues to go up among teenagers. We have to get that message out there. We owe it to the generation of young people, some of whom are in this audience today.

I also want to say that we know that here in Washington, there are things that we can and must do to try to deal with the problems of the drug supply as well as the law enforcement problems in our country. And we have developed a strategy to tackle this problem from top to bottom. We began by taking on the notorious Cali cartel, the biggest drug cartel in the world. For years, the Cali cartel pumped drugs into the American economy and into the veins of the American people with impunity. But after years of operating largely untouched by Colombian law enforcement, I am proud to say that seven of the eight top drug traffickers in the Cali cocaine cartel were arrested by Colombian authorities with our support and cooperation in 1995.

Investigative activity by United States enforcement agencies provided much of the evidence against the Cali kingpins. We are also using our military and our law enforcement activities beyond our borders in other ways. We are working more closely together among ourselves and with other countries. We are beginning to have a real impact.

But we know that cutting off the supply is only half the equation. As long as the demand remains great in America, people will figure out how to provide some supply. We have to take more steps here in this country to reduce demand. We have to take more steps to punish people who are making a killing by killing other people. And we have to take more steps to empower people like you to do the education, the treatment, and the prevention work that will turn this generation of young people away from this madness.

A year ago with the enactment of the crime bill, we attempted to give the American people the tools they need to do what has to be done here at home. We put more police on the street, and we did more to get guns and drugs and children off the street.

The 100,000 police commitment of the Federal Government is running ahead of schedule and under budget. The crime rate is down in almost every State in America, in no small measure because people are out there in uniform, walking the streets in the communities, doing what they can to help prevent crime. More and more law enforcement officers are in our schools through programs like the D.A.R.E. program, trying to help educate children and prevent the drug problem from taking hold.

"Three strikes and you're out" is now the law of the land, and more and more career criminals are being tried under it and convicted under it. We are taking steps against the terrible problems of violence against women. And the crime bill, together with the education bills that were passed in our budget, have increased our commitment to drug treatment as well as to education and other prevention strategies, which is also important.

Throughout, there has been an emphasis on community empowerment. If you think about what your National Government does directly—well, we do the national defense directly. We do some law enforcement directly. We do some things directly through the mail, the Social Security checks, the Medicare checks. But a lot of what we do—in the form of education, in the form of protecting the environment, in the form of promoting law enforcement and safe streets, in the form of growing the economy—a lot of what we do, we do in partnership with individuals at the community level. And we have tried to focus on that very sharply. So we've tried to bring down the size of the Federal bureaucracy but to increase the commitment of the Federal Government at the grassroots level so you could do what needs to be done.

You know, this is beginning to work. We know that for the first time in a long time, as I said, the crime rate is down. There is a greater responsibility ethic in the country. There's a stronger sense of family in the country. There's a stronger sense of community in the country.

In addition to the crime rate being down, you might be interested to know that over the last 3 years, the welfare rolls are down, the food stamp rolls are down, the teen pregnancy rate has come down 2 years in a row, and the poverty rate is down. Child support payments are up 40 percent, and the college loan delinquency rate is down by 50 percent. There is a real sense that this country is coming back together around core values, and that's very important.

Having said that, we know that crime, welfare, poverty, violence, and drug abuse are still far too high. We know that random juvenile violence and casual juvenile drug use are both going up, even as the overall statistics seem to be getting better. There's still too many of our children out there raising themselves. There are too many kids out there who aren't a part of something wholesome and positive and bigger than themselves; the people are not taking responsibility for their future and trying to help them take responsibility for themselves. And there is still way too much violence in this country, as the tragic example of the Plank family shows.

So let me say—and Jim made a reference to it, but it is in this context that I want you all to see and make your own judgments about the budget battle now raging in Washington. We do have to continue to bring this deficit down, and we do need to balance our budget. I'm proud of the fact that it's gone from a $290 billion a year budget to $164 billion a year budget in just 3 years. And I'm—you might be interested to know that as a percentage of our income, the United States now has the lowest budget deficit of any industrial country in the world, except for Norway, in the entire world today.

Now, that doesn't mean that we don't need to do more. We built up such a huge debt in the 1980's and early nineties. We need to do more. But it means we have to do it in a way that's consistent with our values. Why do we need to eliminate the deficit? Because we want to grow the economy and raise incomes and give our children a brighter future. But we have to do it in a way that looks to our values, give people a chance to make the most of their own lives, to strengthen families, to reward work and family, and to help communities solve their problems. That is the purpose of this.

That's why I have said repeatedly I think it is a mistake to balance the budget if we cut education or if we harm the health care system or undermine the environment or weaken law enforcement or raise taxes on working families. I don't think those should be options. If you look at the work at which you are involved, you are doing this work, but it makes a difference if the Nation is contributing to law en-

forcement. It makes a difference if the Nation is contributing to drug education. It makes a real difference if the Nation is contributing to the treatment programs. All these things matter.

We simply cannot balance the budget in a way that puts our children at risk or that weakens our resolve to fight the drug problem. And we do not have to do that. We cannot walk away from the fight against drugs and violence. We have to walk right into it. If the Plank family, bearing the burden of their grief only 2 weeks old, have the courage to come here and stand up for making America a better place to live, a drug-free place to live, a violence-free place to live, if these other families that have sustained their terrible losses have the courage to come here, surely the rest of us can have the courage and vision and wisdom to say, we can deal with our budget problems in Washington without walking away from our values and our responsibilities.

Let me say that one of the things that concerns me most as President is to see the economy coming back and all these indicators that society is getting healthier, and then to see underneath it that juvenile violence is still going up and that casual juvenile drug use is still going up. If we don't turn that around, then all of these directions could be brought to a screeching halt as more and more of these juveniles become adults.

And I told the Attorney General that in terms of law enforcement we need to focus on the problem of juvenile violence more than ever before to see what can be done there. We can't tolerate the killing of an innocent child by gang members simply because her parents drove down the wrong street. We can't tolerate the killing of innocent children in schools or what happened in Maryland not very long ago, an honor student standing at a bus stop just happened to be in the way, in the crossfire of two gangs that took a notion to shoot at each other. We can't tolerate the shooting of one youth by another simply because the killer felt that he was shown disrespect and therefore had a right to shoot another child. That is not the America I grew up in. That is not the America that won World War II or the cold war or that stood for freedom and opportunity for the whole world. And that is not the America we can afford to leave to our children.

We also have to deal with this whole problem of casual drug use. You heard Jim Burke talk about it; you heard Lee Brown talk about it. There's a lot of evidence that young people simply have—starting in about 1991, began to believe that some kinds of casual drug use simply weren't dangerous and didn't have to be countenanced very seriously. That is not true. It is not true because as a pure medical matter, marijuana is more toxic than ever before, because people who do it are now mixing it with other things, like huffing all these dangerous fumes, because very often they get into other drugs. We have got to do something about it.

Most of our children are busy building good lives. Most of our kids are more than happy to show up for activities like this. They're not involved in violent activities. They're doing well in their schools. They, I would say, should be applauded. I think that we forget sometimes— [*applause*]—what we need to ask these young people to do is what these young people are doing here. If the kids are doing well—and the vast majority are—if the kids are emphasizing the importance of staying in school and staying drug-free—as the vast majority are—we need to ask more of them to do what these young people are, to be an example to their peers, because many of them can have far more influence over young people their age than the rest of us old fogies can. [*Laughter*] And we need to applaud them and give them encouragement.

The other thing I want to say, just to reemphasize what Jim Copple said and what Jim Burke said, we need every community in America to be a part of this alliance. Every community in America should have a group that's a part of this alliance, because we know that we can make a difference. It is simply not true that you cannot whip this problem. And a lot of you are living evidence of that.

The citizens of Pierce County, Washington, for example, who have the safe streets campaign to combat illegal drug and gang activity and violence that accompanies these problems, they know their efforts are making a difference. They have closed down over 600 drug dealing locations in 12 communities and reduced calls to 911 by 23,000. Not just an urban problem, Hamilton, Missouri, citizens are banding together, using such innovations as a youth peer court in conflict mediation beginning in the 4th grade to educate and empower young people.

There's a lot of things you folks are doing that are working. And as I look out at this whole array of energetic, wide-eyed, upbeat, positive

people, I think to myself: The real problem we have in America is that we have not learned yet to figure out how to take a solution that works in one community and put it into every community which is not doing anything. So I want to say to you, I want you to keep up the good work, but we have to find a way to say to every community in America, "If something is working somewhere else, you're really doing your children and your future a disservice if you haven't done it in your community." Every community in America should be a part of this alliance.

In an attempt to facilitate greater progress in dealing with the problems of juvenile violence and juvenile drug use, I will convene a White House Leadership Conference on Adolescent Drug Use and Violence in January. We want to bring together people like you to highlight successes in local communities, and we want to help you build a true, national coalition to combat drugs and violence. You'll be hearing more about that in the coming weeks.

One of the things we want to highlight is the positive role the media can play in the fight against drugs. Every day, as many of us have said, the children of this country are bombarded with messages that tell them it's cool, sexy, attractive to drink and smoke and do drugs. But conversely, let's not forget, that the media can also play a very positive role in influencing the attitudes of our young people about the harmfulness and the unacceptability of using drugs. The Partnership for a Drug-Free America, which Jim Burke has led so ably, has proven that over and over again. The media has donated over $2 billion in support of partnership antidrug messages on television and radio, in print and outdoor billboards. Lee Brown has been able to enlist the support of a number of sports and television celebrities in new TV and radio public service campaign spots aimed at our Nation's youth, telling them they do have the power to stay drug-free.

So these messages are working to change attitudes. They can make a difference. So what I want to say is, just like I want every community in the country to have an organization that's a member of CADCA, and I want you to go out to all them and get it done, just as I want the vast majority of our young people who are doing the right thing with their lives to do what these young people are doing and reach out to other kids and help them. We ask the media across this Nation, when it comes to the fight against drugs, turn up the volume.

I also ask you not to forget that the media is not a national thing entirely. Lee Brown and Bill Clinton and Jim Burke and Jim Copple and all the rest, we can go to the networks and to the large media centers and say, "Will you help us do this?" But the media in America is a many-faceted thing. And there are things that can be done in your community by people who are more than willing to help if you ask them to do it.

Oftentimes, too many of our young people spend too much time relating to the media as opposed to other people. They don't have enough time for a lot of things that time ought to be spent on, and too much time sitting in front of the television. We need to ask for help to turn up the volume. I have been profoundly impressed by the number of positive things that our media has done to help us in this battle. We need to come up with systematic plans in every community to do more.

So that's it. I feel pretty good about the future of this country, and you should, too. This is a very great country. We go through difficult periods from time to time. We will always have some bad people, as any society does. There will always be a measure of tragedy, as is the lot of human nature, as the Scripture teaches us. But America is coming back together. America is moving forward economically. But America dare not forget that our children are the future of this country. And if we want America to be the strongest, greatest nation in the world in the 21st century, we have got, we have got to stamp out this madness.

And you have to do your part; I have to do mine. In the end, we know that what you do to get people to take control of their own lives, their families' lives, and their community lives will tell the tale.

I think we are moving in the right direction. We know we've just got too many kids out there that are still raising themselves, and we have to help that. But if we do it, if we do it, we can make the service and the sacrifice of people like Trooper Plank a shining memory in the life of our country. We owe it to them. Let's deliver.

Thank you, and God bless you.

NOTE: The President spoke at 10:55 a.m. at the J.W. Marriott Hotel. In his remarks, he referred to Lori Plank, widow of Maryland State Trooper Edward A. Plank, Jr., who was killed in the line of duty by an alleged drug runner; and James E. Copple, president, and Marni Vliet, board chair, Community Anti-Drug Coalitions of America.

Statement on Congressional Action on Proposed Environmental Legislation
November 2, 1995

Today's vote on the 17 special interest environmental riders is a step in the right direction, but we still have a long way to go if we are to stop Congress' assault on public health and the environment.

Even with the elimination of the riders, the Republican budget still dismantles vital protections that keep our Nation healthy, safe, and secure. It still cuts funding for enforcement of environmental laws in half. America cannot protect the environment if we gut enforcement of antipollution laws.

As important as today's vote was, Congress' responsibility does not end here. Now, congressional Republicans must take the next steps and change their bill to fully protect public health and the environment. As we balance the budget in the interest of our children, we must not leave them a world that is more polluted and less livable.

Remarks to the National Jewish Democratic Council
November 2, 1995

Thank you very much, first of all, ladies and gentlemen, for that wonderful, wonderful welcome. Thank you, Jeff, for your introduction and for this beautiful Tzedakah box. Did I say it right—Tzedakah? [*Applause*] I'm very glad that you explained its significance, otherwise I was afraid that others would interpret it as something I might as well carry around, since whenever I see you, we seem to be—[*laughter*]. I was very moved by the story, and I'm very grateful. And that will have a happy place in the White House tonight.

Thank you, Monte Friedkin, for your work here; and David Steiner, Nancy Jacobson, Liz Schrayer, all the others who worked on this tonight; Senator Dodd and Senator Daschle and Congressman Gephardt, Congressman Frost, Congressman Bentsen; and to your wonderful honorees behind me.

You know, when Jeff said something about, look at this lineup, eight Jewish Senators, I thought he was going to say eight Jewish Senators and an Arkansas redneck. I didn't know what—[*laughter*]. I thought he was going to say, pick the person who's spoiling this lineup. [*Laughter*]

Let me say to all of you, I'm grateful to be here. I'm grateful to be here among friends. I'm honored to be here with these eight Senators whom you are honoring tonight. They richly deserve it. I know I don't have to tell you this, but if it weren't for them, for their steadfastness, for their belief in the values we all share, for their vision for the future, my work as President today in the midst of the battles that are going on in Washington would be not only difficult but indeed impossible.

I have never appreciated the wisdom of the Founding Fathers more than I have since this Republican budget has been working its way through Congress. They were really smart, those people who gave the President the veto. [*Laughter*] They understood the American system. They understood that there would be times in the history of our Republic, if we were going to last a very long time, when elections would produce unintended consequences and extreme conduct. And the President was given the veto because only the President has the responsibility

to look after all the people of this country and to look into the future, to imagine that future, and to keep the country on the right path. But none of that would be possible without these whom you honor tonight and their allies in the Congress. They reflect the very best contributions of Jewish-Americans to our way of life, as do the Jewish-American members of my Cabinet, Mickey Kantor and Secretary Reich and Secretary Glickman and Secretary Rubin and many others in our administration.

I am delighted, again, I want to say, that you're giving them the Hubert Humphrey Humanitarian Award, and I'm delighted that Attorney General Humphrey from Minnesota is here with you tonight to present it. And I thank him for his friendship and contribution.

I want to make a very brief argument to you tonight that I hope you will share with others throughout this country. When I sought the Presidency, I had a vision for what I wanted America to look like in the 21st century. I wanted our country to be a place with opportunity for everybody; a place where children had good schools and safe streets; where we had a clean environment; where we were all investing and growing together; where we made a virtue, not a problem, of our diversity, and we were coming together, not being driven apart; a country where we were still strong enough and good enough to lead the world to peace and freedom and democracy.

And I believe the only way to achieve that vision is to be open to new ideas consistent with the values that have made our country great and that make life worth living, both responsibility and opportunity; understanding the need of people not only for work but also for strong families; understanding that we are a community and we have responsibilities to each other, and that if we're going to make the most of our lives, we have to live by those responsibilities; understanding that standing up for America sometimes means doing what's unpopular in the short run because it's the right thing to do in the long run. These Members that you honor tonight and I have pursued for nearly 3 years now a very disciplined strategy to achieve that vision based on those values: pro-growth economics; a modern Government that is smaller and less bureaucratic but still strong enough to advance the public interest; and a genuine attempt to write these mainstream values into the public policy of America.

And I leave it for you to make a judgment. But if you look at where we are now compared to where we were 3 years ago, we have 7½ million more jobs. Home ownership is at a 15-year high. There have been more new businesses started in America in the last 3 years than in any comparable period in American history. Our sales to other countries of our products and services is up one-third in only 3 years. The deficit has gone from $290 billion a year to $164 billion a year. As a percentage of our income, the United States of America has the smallest Government deficit of any industrial country in the world except Norway. That is the record that these people have made in the last 3 years, and I think it is a very good record.

Others may condemn big Government; these Democrats changed it. Your National Government has 163,000 fewer people than it did the day I was inaugurated. Next year, we'll have the smallest Federal Government since John Kennedy was President. As a percentage of our work force, it will be the smallest Federal Government since 1933—1933. Sixteen thousand pages of Federal regulation gone out of a total of 86,000.

But we have not given up on the responsibility of the Government to work with the private sector to try to sell America's products abroad, to try to create jobs here at home, to try to protect the environment and public health, to try to empower all Americans to do what they need to do to make the most of their own lives.

We have given you a modern Government. The era of big Government is over, but the era of good Government and strong Government cannot be over, because the public interest still must be advanced by the American people working together through their elected representatives. That is what these people have given you. And they are entitled to the gratitude and support of the United States of America.

Most important of all to me, this country is getting its act together. We're coming back together as a people. In the last 3 years, compared with 3 years ago, the crime rate is down, the welfare rolls are down, the food stamp rolls are down, the poverty rate is down, the teen preg-nancy rate is down, the infant mortality rate is at an all-time low, child support collections are up 40 percent, and the delinquency rate of young people on student loans has been cut in half. That is what has happened in the United States in the last 3 years. And a lot of the policies that we adopted that they supported have contributed to that. This country is on a roll. We're moving in the right direction.

Do we have problems? Of course we do. Of course we'll all have problems as long as we're here on this Earth. The books of our faith tell us that. It is not given to people to be without problems. What are the problems of this time? Too many middle class people work harder without a pay raise and with increasing insecurity and no access to health care. Too many areas have not been affected by the economic recovery, and we have to find a way to get investment in enterprise into those areas; mostly they're in inner cities and isolated rural areas. And thirdly, even though all the social indicators look better, the truth is, a lot of our young teenagers are still in deep trouble. There are many places where the crime rate's going down but juvenile crime is going up. There are many places where drug use is going down but casual drug use by teenagers is going up. There are too many of our children still out there on the street raising themselves, frankly. And these are problems. But the answer to the problem is to do what we're doing and do more of it, to build on what we are doing, not to turn around and go in the other direction.

This country is a force for peace and freedom around the world. We have stood up for America's values and America's interests. We've been able to advance the cause of peace in the Middle East, in Northern Ireland, and God willing, our people are working as hard as they can now in Ohio for the cause of peace in Bosnia, to put an end to the horrible slaughter in that troubled land.

We have lessened the nuclear threat. We have fought terrorism and international drug running and organized crime. We are doing what can be done to stand up for this country's values. And yes, we were honored to be able to advance the cause of peace in the Middle East, but we're not done yet, and we have to keep working until the whole job is done. That's the only way that the people of Israel will ever be fully secure and the only way we will have ever finished our task there, when all the people are at peace with each other and pledge to one another's mutual existence, security, and freedom. And I pledge to you, I will keep working until the job is over.

You must see this fight that we're in over the budget in the context of the brief remarks I have just made, in the context of what your values are and what your vision is for the 21st century. Let me tell you what this is not about: This is not about balancing the budget. And it is not about securing the Medicare program. That is not what this is about. This is about what kind of country we're going to be, what kind of people we are, and whether we're going to balance the budget in a way that is consistent with our mainstream values and consistent with our pro-growth economic policy. That's really what this is about.

And you know, I have had to resist this whether it's popular or not. It seems that the public is coming back our way now. But the truth is that it is impossible to know from one year to the next what will be popular in a time of great change. The fundamental reality is we are changing dramatically the way we live and work and relate to the rest of the world. In a time like this, you can't read the polls; you have to fall back on your values and be open to new ideas.

I've done a lot of things that made a lot of people angry, but I think I was right. The people that are in the majority now, when we passed our economic program, they said it would bring the country down. They were wrong. It lifted the country up. When we passed that economic program, we provided for lower cost college loans so young people like this could go to school at lower cost and pay their loans back on better terms. And they all opposed it because the organized interest groups were against it. But they were wrong, and we were right. It was the right thing for the long term of America.

When these people were in the majority in Congress and we became the first National Government ever to take on the organized interest groups to pass the Brady bill and the assault weapons ban, they were all against it. But we were right, and they were wrong. And the American people are better off now.

When we passed the crime bill that Jeff mentioned that put 100,000 police on the street—and by the way, we're ahead of schedule and under budget. And you talk to any major police

officer in this country in any city, and they will tell you that these police officers walking the street are not only catching criminals quicker, they are preventing crime. And after all, that is our objective.

And when we gave the cities some money in block grants that they now are in love with, we were attacked for giving cities the money and letting them decide how best to tell our children that they don't have to turn to a life of crime; they don't have to turn to a life of drugs; they can solve their problems in ways other than violence. They were excoriated, these people were, because we gave that authority to cities to give our little children something to say yes to instead of something to say no to. But they were wrong, and we were right. And the crime rate is going down, and we are saving lives today because of the work these people are doing.

The reason the budget fight is important is because it violates our values and it will undermine our future—what they are trying to do. I don't know about you, but my idea of America in the 21st century is not wrecking the Medicare program and being tougher on the oldest, the poorest, and the sickest senior citizens in this country. That's not my idea.

My idea of the 21st century is not devastating the Medicaid program so that 4 million poor children will be denied medical care, hospitals will close in rural and urban areas, teaching hospitals and children's hospitals will stop doing the work they are now doing. That's not my idea of the 21st century. And we are better than that. We do not have to do that to balance the budget, and it is wrong to do it to advance some ideological theory.

My idea of the America of the 21st century is not crippling the ability of the National Government to promote clean water and clean air, to protect the integrity of the American food supply, and to undermine the whole movement that we have made, all the progress we have made, to try to prove we could, in partnership, have economic growth and environmental protection. I believe if we give away the economy for short-term greed, we will all live to regret it. And these young children deserve better. We ought to give them a better 21st century than that.

My idea of the 21st century does not include raising taxes on working families that make less than $27,000 a year in the most mean-spirited part of all of their budget to give people in my income group and yours a tax cut. If they can figure out how to do it, fine—not by raising taxes on people with incomes of less than $27,000. This Congress cut them, and we ought not to raise them.

There is no group in America devoted to the family more than Jewish-Americans. When we took office and we started our work, I had heard people condemn welfare forever and ever and ever. I had actually spent a lot of time in my life talking to people on welfare, and I knew that most of them hated it and were dying to get off. And one of the things that we have to do is to make work pay. So this Congress, that these people were in the majority in, that you honor tonight, voted to double the working family's tax credit so that we could make a simple statement: If you work 40 hours a week and you have children back at the house, we want you to succeed as a parent as well as as a worker. So we won't let the tax system put you into poverty even if you just make a little bit of money; we will use the tax system to lift you out of poverty. There will never be an excuse to choose welfare over work. And if you choose work, you can also be successful as a parent. That's what the working-family tax credit did. It was signed into law by Gerald Ford, lauded by Ronald Reagan as the best anti-poverty program in American history, expanded by George Bush. But because we doubled it, they are determined to cut it by more than we increased it. That is not my idea of the kind of America I want to live in in the 21st century. It is wrong. It is wrong. [*Applause*] Thank you.

I want you to think about this last point. A lot of you run companies that are doing very well and are positioned to do better in the 21st century. Is there a single, sensible American company on the edge of the global village of the 21st century that would cut its investment in research, in technology, in education, and in training? Of course not. Their budget cuts our investment in research, in technology, in education, and training. That is wrong.

Why would we make college education more expensive when we want more people to go? Why would we take 140,000 kids—or 45,000 kids—out of Head Start programs when we know young, poor kids need a chance to get off to a good start in school? Why would we do that? Why would we take college scholarships away from 150,000 young people when we need more people to go to college? Why would we cut the research budget of the United States when Japan, in the midst of a terrible recession, just voted to double their research budget? Why would we do these things?

It is my job to be true to our common values, to stand up for our economic interests, and to look down the road toward the future for the young people of this country. That is what this struggle is all about. This country is on a roll. The economy is going in the right direction. The Government has a lot of work to do, but it is changing in the right direction. And most important of all, the American people are getting their act together. There is a remarkable resurgence of personal responsibility for self, for family, and for community. It would be a travesty if we at this moment, when we have things going in the right direction, when all of the problems we have require us to keep going and do more in that direction, if we took a terrible veer off into the dark waters of some extremist theory that drug this country into more division, in more problems, in more heartache, and that compromised the future of these young people. There is no country in the world better positioned than the United States for the 21st century.

And so what I say to you tonight, these folks you're honoring and the person you helped to make President, we're going to do our best to give you that future. You rear back, relax, enjoy it, and help us fight for it.

Thank you, and God bless you.

NOTE: The President spoke at 7:59 p.m. at the National Museum of Women in the Arts. In his remarks, he referred to Jeffrey Hirschberg, chair, David Steiner, vice chair, and Nancy Jacobson, young leadership chair, Hubert H. Humphrey Award Committee; Monte Friedkin, national chairman, and Elizabeth Schrayer, acting executive director, National Jewish Democratic Council; and Hubert H. Humphrey III, Minnesota attorney general.

Remarks to Participants in Project XL
November 3, 1995

The President. Thank you very much, Scott, for your introduction and also for your very impressive remarks and your even more impressive work. Thank you, Mr. Vice President, for the work you have done on this project; and Administrator Carol Browner; the Chair of the Council of Environmental Quality, Katie McGinty; to Fred Hansen, the EPA Deputy Administrator who is in charge of Project XL, thank you. And thank you, Andy Lietz. I thought you were going to start trying to sell your product up here. [*Laughter*] I must say I was even more impressed when you talked about how you invited us to visit in New Hampshire, New York, and California. I thought, there's a man with a strategically placed company. [*Laughter*]

I want to thank every one of you for being here and for helping us to move a little closer to our vision of the 21st century.

Let me say that I sought the Presidency because I had a vision of what I wanted our country to look like in the 21st century. I wanted the American dream to be alive for all of our people, and I wanted our Nation to be the strongest force in the world for peace and freedom and prosperity. And we have a simple, straightforward, but quite comprehensive strategy for achieving that. We believe in pro-growth economics that rewards entrepreneurs and expands the middle class and shrinks the under class. We believe in commonsense Government that is smaller, less bureaucratic, more flexible, focusing on partnerships with the private sector and empowering communities and citizens. And we believe in rooting all this in old-fashioned, mainstream values, rewarding opportunity but insisting on responsibility, valuing work but recognizing that helping families to be strong and stay together is even more important, and what the Vice President referred to—we believe in community and common ground, not division in the United States.

The project we announce today reflects all those strategies. That's what Project XL is all about. It will advance our economic agenda. It is an example of commonsense Government. And it is rooted in our deepest American values. It will help us us to make the American dream available to all Americans in the 21st century,

and it will certainly help America to be the world's strongest nation in the 21st century.

In March I announced the creation of this project, which gives our companies the freedom to meet tough pollution standards in ways that make sense to them, instead of following a Government rule book. Today we are announcing the first eight pilot projects for this cutting-edge initiative: Anheuser-Busch, AT&T, Hadco, Intel, Merck, the Minnesota Pollution Control Agency, 3M, and the South Coast Air Quality Management District. All of them have put together projects which will help us to blaze the way to a new era of environmental protection. Two of them are represented in the Congress by my friend Senator Robb and Congressman Vento. I thank them for coming today and for their support of this from an economic and an environmental perspective.

I want to thank all of the companies here and the other organizations for their dedication. And I want you to know that we are here to honor your pledge to reduce pollution creatively, effectively, and in partnership with your neighbors.

I want to especially commend the Department of Defense, which is committed to undertaking a similar effort at military installations throughout our country. And this is very important because of all the base closings. And a lot of you are very familiar with our efforts to accelerate our ability to turn these closed bases back to communities and turn them into community assets. It's a huge issue. And the environmental difficulties and challenges have slowed that effort, and I thank all the representatives from the Defense Department here for their commitment to this endeavor because it will have a major impact on both the environment and our ability to spark economic opportunity in communities throughout the Nation.

To industry, Project XL shows that protecting the health and safety of our citizens doesn't have to come at the expense of a bottom line. And to those in the environmental community, XL shows that strengthening the economy doesn't have to come at the expense of the air we breathe, the food we eat, the water we drink. I hope to our citizens that this will stand as an example of what we can do when we work together and when we look out for one another, when we recognize that our obligations to one another, when properly fulfilled, actually help us to improve our own lot in life.

I guess there was a time not so long ago that if I said there was a Government program named XL, everybody would have thought it stood for extra large and was well-named. [*Laughter*] I want to say again, that not withstanding my own size, this does stand for excellence and leadership. [*Laughter*] We want to back our words up by action, and we intend to do so.

Much of our effort in developing commonsense Government has been devoted simply to reducing the sheer size of Government. Our Government was organized for a much more sort of top-down, bureaucratic industrial age than the one in which we are living.

Thanks to the Vice President, our reinventing Government task force, and the support we have received in the past from the Congress, there are now 163,000 fewer people working for the Federal Government than there were the day I was sworn in as President. With next year's already planned downsizing, the Government next year will be the smallest it's been since Mr. Kennedy was President. And as a percentage of the Federal—the civilian work force of the United States, next year the Federal Government will be the smallest it has been since 1933. That is an astonishing change in a short period of time.

And I want to say, I think we've done it in the right way. Like I say, that if you want to read about it, the Vice President's got a little book out here. [*Laughter*] He made me write a foreword to it. [*Laughter*]

The Vice President. It's available in New York, California—[*laughter*].

The President. Philip Howard, the author of the wonderful book "The Death of Common Sense," also wrote an introduction. And the Vice President gets no money out of the book. That's part of reinventing Government—[*laughter*]—work harder, be poorer. [*Laughter*] But this book reflects what it is we're trying to do. The reason I bring it up is that most Americans don't know that the Government is 163,000 smaller, don't know how much smaller it is. But there are maybe some bad reasons for that, but I think there are two good reasons I'd like to mention.

One reason is that the Federal employees were treated properly in the downsizing. They weren't just put on the street. There were generous early retirement packages approved by the Congress. There were generous separation packages. They were treated with the dignity and respect to which they were entitled. So we didn't just have a slash-and-burn policy. The other reason is that the Federal employees who stayed were able to dramatically increase their productivity so that people didn't notice it in diminished services.

And so I think what I'd like to do is to say I'm very proud of the fact that we have downsized the Government more rapidly and to a greater extent than at, as far as I know, any time in history. But the real credit goes to the Federal employees who have continued to do the work of America with good humor and increased creativity. And I'm very proud of that. And so the first thing we did was to try to shrink the Government.

The second thing we're doing is getting rid of 16,000 of the 86,000 pages of Government regulations. I think the most successful talk I've given since I've been President was at the White House Conference on Small Business where all I did was simply read them the Federal regulation on grits. [*Laughter*] Some of you not from the South don't even know what grits are, probably. [*Laughter*] But all of us who do found it amazing that there had to be a Federal regulation to define it and that it was two pages long. [*Laughter*] And there wasn't a dry eye in the place when I got done reading it. [*Laughter*] Most of them were laughing and crying; some of them were actually crying to think their Government had done such a thing. [*Laughter*] So every department has got a quota, a target, and we are in the process of getting rid of, just purely getting rid of 16,000 of the 86,000 pages of Federal regulations.

But that is only part of the vision because commonsense Government recognizes that there is still a public interest in America that has to be advanced, that can only be advanced when the elected representatives of the American people use the power given to them under the Constitution of the United States to deal with the problems of the moment in a public way, and to do it in the way that is the most efficient, the most effective for the moment. That is what we are celebrating today.

The environmental regulations that we are reforming today were designed for a time when the environmental problems were different, when there were in some places dark clouds of pollution literally blocking the sun, a time when the bald eagle was on the edge of extinction, a time when we had a river in America that actually caught fire. And for people who think it's been a bad thing, this environmental effort, I'll ask you to remember that all happened in the lifetime of everybody in this room.

These laws and regulations have served us well. Though we've got a lot more work to do, we've made a lot of progress as a people. Our environment is the envy of the world compared to other industrial countries. But what worked yesterday is not adequate for today, and we now know it certainly won't work tomorrow. And going through Washington is plainly not the only road to ensuring a cleaner or a safer world. That's why we have challenged our businesses and our communities to work together to achieve better results where they live and work at lower cost.

At the core of this whole approach are the values I mentioned earlier. We are saying the Government should enhance opportunity but should insist on responsibility. The people who are in Project XL are saying we want the opportunity to do this in a better, more sensible, less bureaucratic, more hassle-free way. But we recognize that before opportunity comes responsibility. And our commitment is to maintain high standards.

To understand what we're trying to do, the Vice President used a see-saw analogy, which I thought was pretty good, by the way. I may steal it from him tomorrow. [*Laughter*] Think of a high-jump competition. In this case, the Government would set the bar in the high-jump competition and set it high, as high as it takes to ensure that our people have the essential security of knowing that the world that we live in will be vibrant, healthy, and clean. But we wouldn't tell the Government how to jump over the bar. If you've ever watched a high-jump competition, people jump in different ways. The way it works today is the Government gives you a rule book, and if you can't jump over in the prescribed way you just never get over the bar. What we want to say is, "Here is the bar. If you can figure out how to jump over it any old way—the old way, the new way, a different way, forward or backward—all you have to do

is jump over the bar. Then you make the grade."

Project XL is built on the simple premise that in many cases companies know their business a whole lot better than the Government does; that they understand how best to reduce their own pollution; that we will all benefit if private enterprise brings its energy, its innovation, its creativity to the task of reducing pollution; and that cost-effective ways that are found to clear certain specific goals by certain companies and certain industries will certainly be adopted by others, and it will help us to create whole new sectors of economic opportunity by promoting a whole new round of entrepreneurialism in environmental cleanup. We also recognize that if companies have the freedom to devise their own strategies, they will have the obligation to work with and consult with their neighbors.

This project marks the end of one-size-fits-all Government regulations. We know what works for one community and one company simply doesn't necessarily work for others. This is real reform. It eases the burden of regulation. It helps to achieve superior environmental performance. It gives each company the chance to find its own way while always, always reaffirming the responsibilities that all companies have to their communities.

You know, I look at Project XL and I have a hard time understanding those who are still fighting yesterday's regulatory battles today, those who still think we're only faced with two choices: no regulation at all or more regulation. Under the banner of regulatory reform, some of these would weaken or even abolish previous environmental safeguards. The Republican majority in Congress would deny citizens the right to know what's in the air they breathe and the water they drink. They'd rob our agencies of the ability to enforce environmental laws at all. They'd slow the cleanup of toxic waste in our communities.

I tell you today that I do not intend to let this happen. As you know, I have been very clear about the 17 special interest provisions the congressional majority put in its EPA budget. These riders would seriously jeopardize the enforcement of our vital environmental laws. And I was very, very pleased yesterday to see what I hope is only the beginning of a trend that will sweep this Congress when a bipartisan majority in the House stood up for our basic values, for commonsense Government, and voted against these 17 riders. I hope there will be more of this in the future.

Project XL is proof that we can find a better way. We don't have to—it's also about common ground. Why should we have a fight about this when we all will be better served if we work together to protect our environment and to promote our economic interests? There is clearly a wrong way and a right way to change the regulatory environment of America and to get rid of outdated regulations. The wrong way is to toss away our essential health and environmental concerns just because we don't have the patience to sit down and fix them.

The right way is to roll up our sleeves, make regulations work, demand responsibility, but give opportunity. It may take a little longer. It may be a little harder, but it is the right way to meet the challenges of the next century. And I want to say again—the most important thing I want to say is I honor these eight projects and the people who are committed to doing it in this way. I honor the commitment the Defense Department has made to do this in its sites.

If we can prove that this works, we can literally change the way Americans look with fear either on environmental threats or on the Government or on some new economic enterprise. We can literally give the future back to the American people at the grassroots level and have the Government doing what it ought to do: be in the business of defining the public interest, making it clear, making sure it's advanced, but not prescribing every little jot-and-tittle detail about how people pursue it in every business,

in every community, in every enterprise all across the land. That is our goal.

Project XL is designed to put the focus back where it should be, on progress, not process, on families and businesses, not government. We have a model here that I think will be good not only for protecting the environment, not only as an example of effective regulatory reform—I think it's a blueprint for the future. I think it's a way we can deal with a whole range of our other economic and social problems.

A lot is riding on those of you who have agreed to participate in this project. I think we can really change the way people look at our common problems if we can prove, as I believe you will, that this works.

I am deeply indebted to the Vice President and to Carol Browner and to Katie McGinty, to all those in our administration who have done this. But as I said, we really respect more than anything the companies and the people from the Department of Defense that are prepared to engage in this great endeavor. We have to make this work. This is the only way to take our country into the 21st century with a growing economy, being steadfast to our values, with a commonsense Government that keeps the American dream alive for all. Let's prove the cynics wrong.

Thank you very much.

NOTE: The President spoke at 10:28 a.m. in Room 450 of the Old Executive Office Building. In his remarks, he referred to Scott Bernstein, president, Center for Neighborhood Technology, and Andy Lietz, chief executive officer, Hadco Company.

Remarks at the Dedication of the Pan American Flight 103 Memorial Cairn in Arlington, Virginia
November 3, 1995

Sir Hector, Jane Schultz, George Williams, Reverend Keegans, Reverend Miller, Reverend Neal, Rabbi Goldberg; to Members of Congress and the administration, the diplomatic corps; to our honored friends from Scotland; most of all, to the members of the family of Pan Am 103. Thank you, Sir Hector, for your good words. And thank you and the Lockerbie Trust for this

beautiful cairn which I accept on behalf of the people of the United States.

This simple monument speaks with a powerful voice. Each of its 270 Lockerbie stones tells of the loss beyond measure, a child or a parent, a brother or a sister stolen away through an act of unspeakable barbarism. Almost 7 years have now passed since that bomb cut short the lives of all 250 passengers of Pan Am 103 and the 11 villagers below. I know that I can speak for all the American people when I say that we have not forgotten and the families of the victims are still not alone in your sorrow.

Since Pan Am 103, there have been other attacks of terrorism on our own soil, the bombing of the World Trade Center, the tragedy in Oklahoma City. After each, our Nation has drawn closer, and some of the families here of the victims at Lockerbie have helped in that process. I thank all of you who reached out to those who were grieving most recently in Oklahoma City.

Despite the passage of time, nothing has dimmed our recollection of that day when death commanded the heavens. Nothing has diminished our outrage at that evil deed. Today the people of the United States understand terrorism better. We know it can strike anyone, anywhere. We know that each act of terrorism is a terrible assault on every person in the world who prizes freedom, on the values we share, on our Nation and every nation that respects human rights.

Today, America is more determined than ever to stand against terrorism, to fight it, to bring terrorists to answer for their crimes. We continue to tighten those sanctions on states that sponsor terrorism, and we ask other nations to help us in that endeavor.

We are strengthening our ability to act at home and around the world. Recently, we have been successful in apprehending terrorists abroad and in preventing planned terrorist attacks here in the United States. We are redoubling our efforts against those who target our liberties and our lives. And just a few days ago in the United Nations, I asked the nations of the world to join me in common cause against terrorism.

In the case of Pan Am 103, we continue to press for the extradition of the two Libyan suspects. We want to maintain and tighten the enforcement of our sanctions, and we want to increase the pressure on Libya. This cairn reminds us that we must never, never relax our efforts until the criminals are brought to justice.

I thank those who have spoken before for their reference to this hallowed ground. It is fitting that this memorial to the citizens of 21 nations has been erected here in the sacred place of our Nation, surrounded by so many who fell fighting for our freedom. It is fitting, too, that this cairn was chosen as the embodiment of our common concern, not only because of the strong bonds that have grown up between the people of Scotland and America out of this tragedy but because this cairn was built stone by stone.

From the time of the Bible, men and women have piled stones to mark a covenant between them as the patriarch Jacob did with Laban. So let us take this cairn as the sign of our bond with the victims of Pan Am 103 to remember the life they brought into so many lives, to work to bring justice down on those who committed the murders, to keep our own people safe, and to rid the world of terrorism and never to forget until this job is done.

We must all labor for the day, my fellow Americans and citizens of the world, when, in the words of the Psalm, "we shall not be afraid for the terror by night, nor for the arrow that flieth by day, nor for the pestilence that walketh in darkness, nor for the destruction that wasteth at noonday."

The days are now shortening, and December 21st approaches once again. I hope, to those of you who are members of the families, that the honor done your loved ones here today brings you some solace. And I pray that when this anniversary day comes again you will have a measure of peace. Your country men and women are with you in spirit and in determination.

God bless you. God bless Scotland. And God bless the United States of America.

NOTE: The President spoke at 2:37 p.m. at Arlington National Cemetery. In his remarks, he referred to Sir Hector Monro, who presented the memorial cairn; Jane Schultz, chief organizer of the memorial; George H. Williams, president, Victims of Pan Am Flight 103; Rev. Patrick Keegans, Rev. John Miller, and Rev. Alan Neal, who gave the blessing; and Rabbi Jacob Goldberg, who gave the benediction.

Statement on Signing the Fisheries Act of 1995
November 3, 1995

Today I have signed into law H.R. 716, the "Fisheries Act of 1995." This comprehensive legislation demonstrates the extent to which the United States is involved, and must remain involved, in international initiatives with global impact. It implements international agreements designed to protect important fish stocks both in high seas areas of the world's oceans and off our coasts. Many of these measures implement agreements that required major negotiating efforts over a number of years.

This Act implements and would allow the United States to become a party to the United Nations Food and Agriculture Organization Agreement to Promote Compliance with International Conservation and Management Measures by Fishing Vessels on the High Seas. Our negotiators were the principal drafters of the agreement, designed to end the practice of "reflagging" fishing vessels to evade international conservation rules. The provisions of H.R. 716 that implement this Agreement also provide a basis for the United States to ratify the Convention on Conservation and Management of Pollock Resources in the Central Bering Sea. This will preserve jobs for American fishermen in Alaska and the Pacific Northwest, while protecting fish stocks from over-harvesting. The Act also implements a fisheries convention in the Northwest Atlantic and allows the Administration to seek fishing quota shares for our fishermen in that region.

The Act reauthorizes the Atlantic Tunas Convention Act, enhancing U.S. efforts to ensure that all of the countries fishing for tuna in the Atlantic follow internationally agreed upon conservation measures, and providing enforcement authority, which can be particularly effective when its use is based on international consensus. In addition, H.R. 716 strengthens the U.S. role in maintaining the global moratorium on large-scale high seas driftnet fishing, implements an agreement to conserve salmon originating from the Yukon River in Canada, and contains other provisions to promote sound fisheries management.

Several provisions in the Act, specifically sections 603–605 and 302(b), could be taken to direct how the Nation's foreign affairs should be conducted. The Constitution, however, vests the President with special authority to conduct the Nation's foreign affairs. My constitutional authority over foreign affairs necessarily entails discretion over these matters. Accordingly, I shall construe these provisions to be advisory, and I hereby direct all executive branch officials to do likewise.

A provision in section 802 of the Act allows the Secretary of Commerce to issue certain fishing permits if the application has been recommended by a regional fishery management council. Because regional fishery management councils are entities within the Federal Government and comprise officials who are not appointed pursuant to the Appointments Clause of the Constitution, they may not exercise significant governmental authority. To avoid this constitutional problem, I hereby direct the Secretary to treat this provision as advisory.

I am pleased to approve this comprehensive legislation, which will conserve fishery resources and allow for their continued harvesting at sustainable levels.

WILLIAM J. CLINTON

The White House,
November 3, 1995.

NOTE: H.R. 716, approved November 3, was assigned Public Law No. 104–43. This statement was released by the Office of the Press Secretary on November 4.

The President's Radio Address
November 4, 1995

Good morning. What I have to say today is clear and simple: Under the cover of balancing the budget, the Republican Congress is going after the essential environmental protections that have guaranteed the health and safety of all Americans for a long time now, and I am determined to stop them.

I'm for balancing the budget; it's part of my vision to keep the American dream alive for all Americans in the 21st century. It's a core part of our strategy to promote economic growth, commonsense Government, and the mainstream values of responsibility, opportunity, work, family, and community.

But protecting our environment is a fundamental community value for all Americans, and it can't be sacrificed to balance the budget. Because we cherish our children, we want to be sure the water they drink and the food they eat won't make them sick. Because we honor our parents, we want the air they breathe to be clean so they can live long and healthy lives and not be housebound by smog. Because we believe that what God created we must not destroy, each of us has a sacred obligation to pass on a clean planet to future generations. For nearly three decades, all Americans have agreed we must do what we have to to protect our environment. And America is cleaner and healthier because of it.

Since our environmental laws were put in place, toxic emissions by factories have been cut in half. Lead levels in children's blood have dropped 70 percent. Lake Erie, for example, once declared dead, is now teeming with fish. But all this progress is now at risk. In the last few months, a small army of lobbyists for polluters has descended on Capitol Hill, mounting a full-scale assault on our environmental and public health protections. And this Congress has actually allowed these lobbyists to sit down and rewrite important environmental laws to weaken our safeguards. And now they're trying to use the budget bill to further weaken these protections. It's an incredible fact that this Republican budget actually singles out the environment and its protections for extra cuts.

This budget will mean dirtier water, more smog, more illness, and a diminished quality of life. Here's how. It's plain that there are two ways to legalize pollution: You can change the laws or just stop enforcing them by firing the enforcers. The pollution lobby knows it could never repeal half our environmental protections, so the Republican budget cuts the resources for environmental enforcement in half. Quite simply, it just pulls the cop from the environmental beat. The budget also would cut off money now going to communities to invest to keep their drinking water clean. And the cuts mean that toxic waste cleanups across America would slow to a crawl.

The Republican leadership even tried to slip 17 special interest provisions into the spending bill, loopholes that would end enforcement of the Clean Air and the Clean Water Acts, let more dangerous arsenic into our drinking water, allow raw sewage on our beaches. I'm happy to report that earlier this week, a bipartisan majority of the House, on the third try, rejected the efforts of the Republican leadership. But this fight isn't over.

There's another important issue here, too. There's nothing more American than the idea that citizens have the right to know what's happening to them. But this budget tries to roll back the law that gives people the right to know what toxic chemicals are being released into their neighborhoods. So I've acted, issuing a pollution prevention Executive order to limit the damage of their efforts to deprive citizens of the right to know. But this fight isn't over yet, either.

This budget also treats our Nation's great and precious store of public lands as a platform for destruction. The Republican budget, for example, would give oil companies the right to drill in the last unspoiled Arctic wilderness in Alaska. And it allows a giveaway of mining rights to companies at a fraction of their worth. Just recently, a law on the books since 1872 that I am trying hard to change forced the Government to sell minerals worth $1 billion to a private company for $275. That is taxpayer robbery, and it's going to keep right on happening under the Republican budget.

Just think of it: The Republican budget proposes to raise taxes on working families with incomes of less than $27,000, to increase the cost of college loans and cut the number of college scholarships, but they're determined to keep giving away $1 billion worth of minerals on Government land for $275.

Well, I've got bad news for the lobbyists and their allies. We don't need more pollution to balance the budget. We don't need dirtier water to close the deficit. If Congress sends me a budget that guts environmental protection, that protects polluters, not the public, I will veto it. As President, it is my duty to protect our environment, and on my watch, America will not be for sale.

On the other hand, we do have to be vigilant to make sure environmental protection doesn't become a tangle of redtape and bureaucracy, so we're stripping away thousands of pages of unnecessary rules and regulations and changing the way we protect the environment. Instead of a long list of do's and don'ts, we're telling responsible businesses, if you can meet the tough pollution goals, you figure out how to do it as cheaply and efficiently as you can. That's

the way to cut regulation without hurting public health.

After all, America's families don't care much about the rules and regulations. They look at the results, at a son who comes home from a playground with a rash from playing near an industrial site or a daughter with asthma, simply because she breathed the air.

My fellow Americans, let's never forget: The decisions we make today will live on long after we're gone. I don't think we Americans have lost our sense of the past or our dedication to the future. We're balancing the budget in a way that will be good for future generations. That means that in balancing the budget, we have to preserve the planet—clean air, clean water, safe food, a decent environment—for those future generations, too.

Thanks for listening.

NOTE: The address was recorded at 12:57 p.m. on November 3 in the Roosevelt Room at the White House for broadcast at 10:06 a.m. on November 4.

Statement on the Shooting of Prime Minister Yitzhak Rabin of Israel
November 4, 1995

I am outraged at the news of this attempt on the life of Yitzhak Rabin, a great leader for peace and a good friend. I join all Americans in prayers for his recovery.

Remarks on the Death of Prime Minister Yitzhak Rabin of Israel
November 4, 1995

The world has lost one of its greatest men, a warrior for his nation's freedom and now a martyr for his nation's peace.

To Leah Rabin and her children, Hillary and I send our love and our prayers. To the people of Israel, I want you to know that the hearts and prayers of all Americans are with you. Just as America has stood by you in moments of crisis and triumph, so now we all stand by you in this moment of grieving and loss.

For half a century, Yitzhak Rabin risked his life to defend his country. Today, he gave his life to bring it a lasting peace. His last act, his last words were in defense of that peace he did so much to create. Peace must be and peace will be Prime Minister Rabin's lasting legacy.

Tonight, the land for which he gave his life is in mourning. But I want the world to remember what Prime Minister Rabin said here at the White House barely one month ago, and I quote: "We should not let the land flowing with milk and honey become a land flowing with blood and tears. Don't let it happen."

Now it falls to us, all those in Israel, throughout the Middle East, and around the world who yearn for and love peace to make sure it doesn't happen.

Yitzhak Rabin was my partner and my friend. I admired him, and I loved him very much. Because words cannot express my true feelings, let me just say, *shalom, chaver,* goodbye, friend.

NOTE: The President spoke at 5:48 p.m. in the Rose Garden at the White House. In his remarks, he referred to Prime Minister Rabin's widow, Leah.

Statement of Condolence on the Death of Prime Minister Yitzhak Rabin of Israel
November 5, 1995

Prime Minister Rabin gave his life to Israel, first as a soldier for its freedom, then finally as a martyr for its lasting peace.

For his example, his friendship to the United States, and his warm friendship to me, I am eternally grateful.

WILLIAM J. CLINTON

NOTE: The President inscribed this statement in a condolence book at the Israeli Embassy. An original was not available for verification of the content of this statement.

Exchange With Reporters Aboard Air Force One
November 5, 1995

Middle East Peace Process

Q. This is quite a President gathering, Mr. President, your thoughts as the flight of this——

President Clinton. We're all going to pay our respects to Prime Minister Rabin. We all knew him. And we're going to express our support for Israel and for the peace process.

Q. President Carter said the other day when he was being interviewed that he thought, given the circumstances, there logically enough would be a pause, not a pause in peacemaking but a reflective pause, and then, of course, the process should gather again. How quickly do you think the Israelis can pull themselves together?

President Clinton. I don't have any idea. We don't know yet. We are going to have meetings when we're there. We're going to visit and then maybe we'll have some more—some better thoughts for you then.

Q. Mr. President, collectively when you look at the manifest of this trip, what message does it send to the Israelis, Middle East, and the entire world for that matter?

President Clinton. Well, I think it should send, first of all, the message that the United States still stands as a genuine friend and a partner to the people of Israel, Republicans and Democrats alike. We have decades of dedication to the cause of peace here, from the work President Carter did with the Camp David accords to the work President Bush did in starting this process that has been consummated in the last couple of years, the Secretaries of State that are here, the leaders of both parties in the Congress. The United States is standing with Israel and standing for the cause of peace. And we're standing strong and deep.

Q. President Bush, what goes through your mind, sir, as you consider all the familiar faces on this trip and the message that it may be sending to the rest of the world?

President Bush. Well, of course, I'm very grateful to President Clinton for personally inviting me. Barbara and I felt close to Prime Minister Rabin, as do the others here, very close to him. I remember when he visited us in our home up in Maine and all of that.

And so I would simply leave the policy to President Clinton but simply say I'm sure it will be a very emotional event, and I hope that it conveys that the Republicans, Democrats, whatever, are together in the support of Israel and clearly in support of the peace process. And that's all I think we can expect from this.

Q. The Syrian track seems awfully tough, even before this. Various approaches have been tried; President Carter actually mediated 16 tough days. You've talked to us on it. Do you have some new tactic? I don't know how many ways there are to go about it, but have you thought of some way to break this stalemate that might work?

President Clinton. I think I should defer all substantive conversations about this until after the funeral and after the meetings. Then I will—on the way back perhaps I'll have something more to say about it. But I think it would be inappropriate—this is a time of national mourning for the people of Israel and a time when all of us who knew Prime Minister Rabin feel a great sense of loss and an enormous sense of respect, even awe, for what he did and for the sacrifice he paid. I'd like for us to take the time to properly honor that, and then on the way back perhaps something will emerge from our meetings which will be useful for me to comment on.

Q. Will you be seeing Mr. Netanyahu, or can you give us an idea of who you will see?

Press Secretary Mike McCurry. We'll do that for all of you here.

President Clinton. Mike has that.

Q. President Carter, we haven't heard from you. What are your thoughts about the message that should be sent by this delegation that includes people who were in your administration—yourself of course?

President Carter. Well, I've known Prime Minister Rabin for 24 years and admired him personally and as a great leader. I'm honored to be invited by President Clinton to participate. I think it was a very wise thing on the part of the President to put together this tremendously impressive delegation because in this time of sorrow and grief and uncertainty, I think it is very important to every Israeli to know the United States stands beside us with full support.

I wasn't insinuating that the peace process should be delayed, but the comment I made was that the Israelis would have to make this decision, and for a few days at least we shouldn't be pushing them on an exact schedule for the peace process.

But I think it's important, too, for the Israelis to not only know that we are supportive of Israel but also supportive of the peace process. And our coming, I think, is closely related to that.

So I hope that President Clinton's ideas for this mission, burdened as we are with sadness and the personal loss, will be productive for Israel and for the peace process.

Q. People have said that one of the causes of this is the polarization that has occurred in Israel because of the peace process and the very vigorous opposition to it. Is there any lesson for us in the United States with what happened yesterday?

President Clinton. Well, of course we've dealt with some polarization of our own. And I think the lesson is that in a free and vital society, you want the widest range of freedom of speech. But words can have consequences; people can be driven to extremes. And our society only works when—any democracy only works when freedom is handled responsibly. And I think that's the lesson here.

The Israelis have been through all these wars, all this tension for all these decades and never had a political assassination before. And I hope, I hope, it will never happen again. I admire their flourishing democracy; I like the big and raucous arguments they have. But they should do it respecting one another's innate patriotism and dignity and fundamental right to participate. We've got to keep this thing within proper bounds.

But you know, that's something we all have to work on; all democracies have to work on that. Israel doesn't—that's not just a comment about Israel. I'm sure they'll have the time to reflect on all of that. And they are a very great people, a very great democracy, and I'm sure they'll work it out.

NOTE: The exchange began at 6:05 p.m. aboard Air Force One en route to Tel Aviv, Israel. Former Presidents George Bush and Jimmy Carter were members of the U.S. delegation attending Prime Minister Rabin's funeral. A reporter referred to Likud Party leader Binyamin Netanyahu.

Remarks at the Funeral of Prime Minister Yitzhak Rabin in Jerusalem, Israel
November 6, 1995

Leah, to the Rabin children and grandchildren and other family members, President Weizman, Acting Prime Minister Peres, members of the Israeli Government and the Knesset, distinguished leaders from the Middle East and around the world, especially His Majesty King Hussein for those remarkable and wonderful comments and President Mubarak for taking this historic trip here, and to all the people of Israel.

The American people mourn with you in the loss of your leader. And I mourn with you, for he was my partner and friend. Every moment we shared was a joy because he was a good man and an inspiration because he was also a great man.

Leah, I know that too many times in the life of this country you were called upon to comfort and console the mothers and the fathers, the husbands and the wives, the sons and the daughters who lost their loved ones to violence and vengeance. You gave them strength. Now, we here, and millions of people all around the world, in all humility and honor, offer you our strength. May God comfort you among all the mourners of Zion and Jerusalem.

Yitzhak Rabin lived the history of Israel. Through every trial and triumph, the struggle for independence, the wars for survival, the pursuit of peace—in all he served on the frontlines. This son of David and of Solomon took up arms to defend Israel's freedom and laid down his life to secure Israel's future.

He was a man completely without pretense, as all of his friends knew. I read that in 1949, after the War of Independence, David Ben-Gurion sent him to represent Israel at the armistice talks at Rhodes, and he had never before worn a necktie and did not know how to tie the knot. So the problem was solved by a friend who tied it for him before he left and showed him how to preserve the knot simply by loosening the tie and pulling it over his head. Well, the last time we were together, not 2 weeks ago, he showed up for a black-tie event on time but without the black tie. And so he borrowed a tie, and I was privileged to straighten it for him. It is a moment I will cherish as long as I live.

To him, ceremonies and words were less important than actions and deeds. Six weeks ago, the King and President Mubarak will remember, we were at the White House for signing the Israel-Palestinian agreement. And a lot of people spoke. I spoke; the King spoke; Chairman Arafat spoke; President Mubarak spoke; our foreign ministers all spoke. And finally Prime Minister Rabin got up to speak, and he said, "First, the good news: I am the last speaker." But he also understood the power of words and symbolism. "Take a look at the stage," he said in Washington. "The King of Jordan, the President of Egypt, Chairman Arafat, and us, the Prime Minister and Foreign Minister of Israel, on one platform. Please take a good, hard look. The sight you see before you was impossible, was unthinkable just 3 years ago. Only poets dreamt of it. And to our great pain, soldier and civilian went to their deaths to make this moment possible." Those were his words.

Today, my fellow citizens of the world, I ask all of you to take a good, hard look at this picture. Look at the leaders from all over the Middle East and around the world who have journeyed here today for Yitzhak Rabin and for peace. Though we no longer hear his deep and booming voice, it is he who has brought us together again here in word and deed for peace.

Now it falls to all of us who love peace and all of us who loved him to carry on the struggle to which he gave life and for which he gave his life. He cleared the path, and his spirit continues to light the way. His spirit lives on in the growing peace between Israel and her neighbors. It lives in the eyes of the children, the Jewish and the Arab children who are leaving behind a past of fear for a future of hope. It lives on in the promise of true security.

So let me say to the people of Israel, even in your hour of darkness, his spirit lives on, and so you must not lose your spirit. Look at what you have accomplished: making a once barren desert bloom, building a thriving democracy in a hostile terrain, winning battles and wars and now winning the peace, which is the only enduring victory. Your Prime Minister was a martyr for peace, but he was a victim of hate.

Surely we must learn from his martyrdom that if people cannot let go of the hatred of their enemies, they risk sowing the seeds of hatred among themselves. I ask you, the people of Israel, on behalf of my Nation that knows its own long litany of loss, from Abraham Lincoln to President Kennedy to Martin Luther King, do not let that happen to you.

In the Knesset, in your homes, in your places of worship, stay the righteous course. As Moses said to the children of Israel when he knew he would not cross over into the Promised Land, "Be strong and of good courage, fear not for God will go with you. He will not fail you. He will not forsake you." President Weizman, Acting Prime Minister Peres, to all the people of Israel, as you stay the course of peace, I make this pledge: Neither will America forsake you.

Legend has it that in every generation of Jews from time immemorial, a just leader emerged to protect his people and show them the way to safety. Prime Minister Rabin was such a leader. He knew as he declared to the world on the White House lawn 2 years ago that the time had come, in his words, "to begin a new reckoning in the relations between people, between parents tired of war, between children who will not know war." Here in Jerusalem, I believe with perfect faiths that he was leading his people to that promised land.

This week, Jews all around the world are studying the Torah portion in which God tests the faith of Abraham, patriarch of the Jews and the Arabs. He commands Abraham to sacrifice Yitzhak. "Take your son, the one you love, Yitzhak." As we all know, as Abraham in loyalty to God was about to kill his son, God spared Yitzhak. Now, God tests our faith even more terribly, for he has taken our Yitzhak.

But Israel's covenant with God, for freedom, for tolerance, for security, for peace, that covenant must hold. That covenant was Prime Minister Rabin's life's work. Now we must make it his lasting legacy. His spirit must live on in us.

The Kaddish, the Jewish prayer for mourning, never speaks of death but often speaks of peace. In its closing words, may our hearts find a measure of comfort and our souls the eternal touch of hope: *Oseh shalom bimromov hu ya'aseh shalom aleinu ve'al kol Yisrael, ve'imru amen.* And *shalom, chaver.*

NOTE: The President spoke at 2:24 p.m. at Har Herzl Cemetery. In his remarks, he referred to President Ezer Weizman and Acting Prime Minister Shimon Peres of Israel; King Hussein I of Jordan; President Hosni Mubarak of Egypt; and Chairman Yasser Arafat of the Palestinian Authority

Remarks Following a Meeting With President Ezer Weizman of Israel in Jerusalem
November 6, 1995

First, let me just say how pleased I am to have had the opportunity to come here for a second time to visit with President Weizman on this very, very sad day for Israel and for the United States. I want to emphasize today the support of the American people for the people of Israel. It is evidenced by our delegation here. We have three American Presidents, three American Secretaries of State, almost 40 Members of our Congress, including the leadership of both parties in both Houses of our Congress, and a very distinguished group of American religious and business leaders, all coming here to express our support and our solidarity, our grief

over the death of Prime Minister Rabin and our support for the process of peace.

But for me, this is not a day to discuss the future or policies beyond what I have already said. I think you can see, by the kind of delegation that came from the United States, how strongly we feel about our support for Israel and how strongly we feel about our support for peace.

Thank you.

NOTE: The President spoke at approximately 5:20 p.m. outside President Weizman's residence. A tape was not available for verification of the content of these remarks.

Message to the Congress on the Proliferation of Weapons of Mass Destruction
November 8, 1995

To the Congress of the United States:

On November 14, 1994, in light of the dangers of the proliferation of nuclear, biological, and chemical weapons ("weapons of mass destruction") and of the means of delivering such weapons, I issued Executive Order No. 12938, and declared a national emergency under the International Emergency Economic Powers Act (50 U.S.C. 1701 *et seq.*). Under section 202(d) of the National Emergencies Act (50 U.S.C. 1622(d)), the national emergency terminates on the anniversary date of its declaration, unless I publish in the *Federal Register* and transmit to the Congress a notice of its continuation.

The proliferation of weapons of mass destruction continues to pose an unusual and extraordinary threat to the national security, foreign policy, and economy of the United States. Therefore, I am hereby advising the Congress that the national emergency declared on November 14, 1994, must continue in effect beyond November 14, 1995. Accordingly, I have extended the national emergency declared in Executive Order No. 12938 and have sent the attached notice of extension to the *Federal Register* for publication.

As I described in the report transmitting Executive Order No. 12938, the Executive order consolidated the functions of and revoked Executive Order No. 12735 of November 16, 1990, which declared a national emergency with respect to the proliferation of chemical and biological weapons, and Executive Order No. 12930 of September 29, 1994, which declared a national emergency with respect to nuclear, biological, and chemical weapons, and their means of delivery.

The following report is made pursuant to section 204 of the International Emergency Economic Powers Act (50 U.S.C. 1703) and section 401(c) of the National Emergencies Act (50 U.S.C. 1641(c)), regarding activities taken and money spent pursuant to the emergency declaration. Additional information on nuclear, missile, and/or chemical and biological weapons (CBW) nonproliferation efforts is contained in the annual Report on the Proliferation of Missiles and Essential Components of Nuclear, Biological and Chemical Weapons, provided to the Congress pursuant to section 1097 of the National Defense Authorization Act for Fiscal Years 1992 and 1993 (Public Law 102–190), also known as the "Nonproliferation Report," and the annual report provided to the Congress pursuant to section 308 of the Chemical and Biological Weapons Control and Warfare Elimination Act of 1991 (Public Law 102–182).

The three export control regulations issued under the Enhanced Proliferation Control Initiative (EPCI) are fully in force and continue to be used to control the export of items with potential use in chemical or biological weapons or unmanned delivery systems for weapons of mass destruction.

In the 12 months since I issued Executive Order No. 12938, 26 additional countries ratified the Convention on the Prohibition of the Development, Production, Stockpiling and Use of Chemical Weapons and on Their Destruction (CWC) for a total of 42 of the 159 signatories; the CWC must be ratified by 65 signatories to enter into force. I must report my disappointment that the United States is not yet among those who have ratified. The CWC is a critical element of U.S. nonproliferation policy and an urgent next step in our effort to end the development, production, stockpiling, transfer, and use of chemical weapons. As we have seen this year in Japan, chemical weapons can threaten our security and that of our allies, whether as a instrument of war or of terrorism. The CWC will make every American safer, and we need it now.

The international community is watching. It is vitally important that the United States continue to lead the fight against weapons of mass destruction by being among the first 65 countries to ratify the CWC. The Senate recognized the importance of this agreement by adopting a bipartisan amendment on September 5, 1995, expressing the sense of the Senate that the United States should promptly ratify the CWC. I urge the Senate to give its advice and consent as soon as possible.

In parallel with seeking Senate ratification of the CWC, the United States is working hard in the CWC Preparatory Commission (PrepCom) in The Hague to draft administrative and implementing procedures for the CWC and to create a strong organization for verifying compliance once the CWC enters into force.

The United States also is working vigorously to end the threat of biological weapons (BW). We are an active participant in the Convention on the Prohibition of the Development and Stockpiling of Bacteriological (Biological) and Toxin Weapons and Their Destruction (BWC) Ad Hoc Group, which was commissioned September 1994 by the BWC Special Conference to draft a legally binding instrument to strengthen the effectiveness and improve the implementation of the Convention. The Group convened its first meeting in January 1995 and agreed upon a program of work for this year. The first substantive meeting took place in July, making important progress in outlining the key issues. The next meeting is scheduled for November 27 to December 8, 1995. The U.S. objective is to have a draft protocol for consideration and adoption at the Fourth BWC Review Conference in December 1996.

The United States continues to be active in the work of the 29-member Australia Group (AG) CBW nonproliferation regime, and attended the October 16–19 AG consultations. The Group agreed to a United States proposal to ensure the AG export controls and information-sharing adequately address the threat of CBW terrorism, a threat that became all too apparent in the Tokyo subway nerve gas incident. This U.S. initiative was the AG's first policy-level action on CBW terrorism. Participants also agreed to several amendments to strengthen the AG's harmonized export controls on materials and equipment relevant to biological weapons, taking into account new developments since the last review of the biological weapons lists and, in particular, new insights into Iraq's BW activities.

The Group also reaffirmed the members' collective belief that full adherence to the CWC and the BCW will be the only way to achieve a permanent global ban on CBW, and that all states adhering to these Conventions have an obligation to ensure that their national activities support these goals.

Australia Group participants are taking steps to ensure that all relevant national measures promote the object and purposes of the BWC and CWC, and will be fully consistent with the CWC upon its entry into force. The AG considers that national export licensing policies on chemical weapons-related items fulfill the obligation established under Article I of the CWC that States Parties never assist, in any way, the acquisition of chemical weapons. Moreover, inasmuch as these measures are focused solely on preventing activities banned under the CWC, they are consistent with the undertaking in Article XI of the CWC to facilitate the fullest possible exchange of chemical materials and related information for purposes not prohibited by the CWC.

The AG agreed to continue its active program of briefings for non-AG countries, and to promote regional consultations on export controls and nonproliferation to further awareness and understanding of national policies in these areas.

The United States Government determined that two foreign companies—Mainway Limited and GE Plan—had engaged in chemical weapons proliferation activities that required the imposition of sanctions against them, effective May 18, 1995. Additional information on this determination is contained in a classified report to the Congress, provided pursuant to the Chemical and Biological Weapons Control and Warfare Elimination Act of 1991.

The United States carefully controlled exports which could contribute to unmanned delivery systems for weapons of mass destruction, exercising restraint in considering all such proposed transfers consistent with the Guidelines of the Missile Technology Control Regime (MTCR). The MTCR Partners continued to share information about proliferation problems with each other and with other possible supplier, consumer, and transshipment states. Partners also emphasized the need for implementing effective export control systems.

The United States worked unilaterally and in coordination with its MTCR partners in multilateral efforts to combat missile proliferation by nonmembers and to encourage nonmembers to export responsibly and to adhere to the MTCR Guidelines. Three new Partners were admitted to the MTCR with U.S. support: Russia, South Africa, and Brazil.

In May 1995, the United States participated in an MTCR team visit to Kiev to discuss missile nonproliferation and MTCR membership criteria. Under Secretary of State Davis met with Ukraine's Deputy Foreign Minister Hryshchenko in May, July, and October to discuss nonproliferation issues and MTCR membership. As a result of the July meeting, a United States delegation traveled to Kiev in October to conduct nonproliferation talks with representatives of Ukraine, brief them on the upcoming MTCR Plenary, and discuss U.S. criteria for MTCR membership. From August 29-September 1, the U.S. participated in an informal seminar with 18 other MTCR Partners in Montreux, Switzerland, to explore future approaches to strengthening missile nonproliferation.

The MTCR held its Tenth Plenary Meeting in Bonn October 10–12. The Partners reaffirmed their commitment to controlling exports to prevent proliferation of delivery systems for weapons of mass destruction. They also reiterated their readiness for international cooperation in peaceful space activities consistent with MTCR policies. The Bonn Plenary made minor amendments to the MTCR Equipment and Technology Annex in the light of technical developments. Partners also agreed to U.S. initiatives to deal more effectively with missile-related aspects of regional tensions, coordinate in impeding shipments of missile proliferation concern, and deal with the proliferation risks posed by transshipment. Finally, MTCR Partners will increase their efforts to develop a dialogue with countries outside the Regime to encourage voluntary adherence to the MTCR Guidelines and heightened awareness of missile proliferation risks.

The United States has continued to pursue my Administration's nuclear nonproliferation goals with success. Parties to the Treaty on the Non-Proliferation of Nuclear Weapons (NPT) agreed last May at the NPT Review and Extension Conference to extend the NPT indefinitely and without conditions. Since the conference, more nations have acceded to the Treaty. There now are 180 parties, making the NPT nearly universal.

The Nuclear Suppliers Group (NSG) continues its efforts to improve member states' export policies and controls. Nuclear Suppliers Group members have agreed to apply technology controls to all items on the nuclear trigger list and to adopt the principle that the intent of the NSG Guidelines should not be undermined by the export of parts of trigger list and dual-use items without appropriate controls. In 1995, the NSG agreed to over 30 changes to update and clarify the list of controlled items in the Nuclear-Related Dual-Use Annex. The NSG also pursued efforts to enhance information sharing among members by establishment of a permanent Joint Information Exchange group and by moving toward adoption of a United States Department of Energy-supplied computerized automated information exchange system, which is currently being tested by most of the members.

The increasing number of countries capable of exporting nuclear commodities and technology is a major challenge for the NSG. The ultimate goal of the NSG is to obtain the agreement of all suppliers, including nations not members of the regime, to control nuclear exports in accordance with the NSG guidelines. Members continued contacts with Belarus, Brazil, China, Kazakhstan, Lithuania, the Republic of Korea (ROK), and Ukraine regarding NSG activities. Ambassador Patokallio of Finland, the current NSG Chair, led a five-member NSG outreach visit to Brazil in early November 1995 as part of this effort.

As a result of such contacts, the ROK has been accepted as a member of the NSG. Ukraine is expected to apply for membership in the near future. The United States maintains bilateral contacts with emerging suppliers, including the New Independent States of the former Soviet Union, to encourage early adherence to NSG guidelines.

Pursuant to section 401(c) of the National Emergencies Act (50 U.S.C. 1641(c)), I report that there were no expenses directly attributable to the exercise of authorities conferred by the declaration of the national emergency in Executive Order No. 12938 during the period from May 14, 1995, through November 14, 1995.

WILLIAM J. CLINTON

The White House,

November 8, 1995.

NOTE: This message was released by the Office of the Press Secretary on November 9. The notice is listed in Appendix D at the end of this volume.

Letter to Congressional Leaders Transmitting the Report on International Exchange and Training Activities
November 9, 1995

Dear Mr. Speaker: (Dear Mr. Chairman:)

As required by section 229(a) of the Foreign Relations Authorization Act, Fiscal Years 1994 and 1995 (Public Law 103–236), I am submitting the enclosed Fiscal Year 1994 report, *International Exchange and Training Activities of the U.S. Government,* prepared by the United States Information Agency (USIA) in coordination with the Vice President's National Performance Review.

United States Government educational, cultural, scientific, and professional exchange and training programs enhance communication and understanding between the United States and other societies. They are among our more effective tools to achieve long and intermediate range objectives of U.S. foreign policy.

The enclosed report summarizes the work of 38 departments and agencies engaged in international exchange and training totaling more than 123,000 exchange participants. The report includes foreign area summaries as well as individual country data profiles. In Fiscal Year 1994,

these programs were funded at $2.2 billion, including $1.6 billion in Federal support and $600 million in private sector and foreign government contributions.

It is important that international exchanges and training programs be administered in a manner that not only ensures clarity of objectives, but also has a system of measurements to review its outcomes and its cost effectiveness. My report to you on the extent to which such activities are duplicative requires additional time for analysis by the Vice President's National Performance Review.

My Administration will continue to work with the Congress to realize our shared goals of improving efficiency and reducing costs.

Sincerely,

WILLIAM J. CLINTON

NOTE: Identical letters were sent to Newt Gingrich, Speaker of the House of Representatives, and Jesse Helms, chairman, Senate Committee on Foreign Relations.

Message to the Congress Transmitting the Report of the Federal Labor Relations Authority
November 9, 1995

To the Congress of the United States:

In accordance with section 701 of the Civil Service Reform Act of 1978 (Public Law 95–454; 5 U.S.C. 7104(e)), I have the pleasure of transmitting to you the Sixteenth Annual Report of the Federal Labor Relations Authority for Fiscal Year 1994.

The report includes information on the cases heard and decisions rendered by the Federal

Labor Relations Authority, the General Counsel of the Authority, and the Federal Service Impasses Panel.

WILLIAM J. CLINTON

The White House,

November 9, 1995.

Message to the Congress Transmitting the Report of the Commodity Credit Corporation
November 9, 1995

To the Congress of the United States:

In accordance with the provisions of section 13, Public Law 806, 80th Congress (15 U.S.C. 714k), I transmit herewith the report of the Commodity Credit Corporation for fiscal year 1993.

WILLIAM J. CLINTON

The White House,

November 9, 1995.

NOTE: This message was released by the Office of the Press Secretary on November 10.

Message to the Congress Transmitting the Report of the National Corporation for Housing Partnerships
November 9, 1995

To the Congress of the United States:

I transmit herewith the annual report of the National Corporation for Housing Partnerships and the National Housing Partnership for fiscal years 1993 and 1994, as required by section 3938(a)(1) of title 42 of the United States Code.

WILLIAM J. CLINTON

The White House,

November 9, 1995.

NOTE: This message was released by the Office of the Press Secretary on November 10.

Letter to Congressional Leaders Transmitting a Report on Cyprus
November 9, 1995

Dear Mr. Speaker: (Dear Mr. Chairman:)

In accordance with Public Law 95–384 (22 U.S.C. 2373(c)), I submit to you this report on progress toward a negotiated settlement of the Cyprus question. The previous report covered progress through July 31, 1995. The current report covers the period August 1, 1995, through September 30, 1995.

I can assure you of my continuing interest in helping find a solution to this long-standing issue, but I also believe that peace can result only through the will and determination of the parties themselves. I remain concerned about the current lack of progress. My Administration is working to ensure that preparations for Spe-cial Emissary Beattie's renewed effort later this year will be successful.

We continue to believe strongly that the European Union (EU) accession process for Cyprus can have a positive impact on efforts to achieve a negotiated settlement. In that context, there are substantive questions arising from prospective EU membership. Accordingly, the EU must maintain frequent contacts with both Cypriot communities to address these key questions. This subject is a constant theme in our discussions with EU representatives.

Sincerely,

WILLIAM J. CLINTON

NOTE: Identical letters were sent to Newt Gingrich, Speaker of the House of Representatives, and Jesse Helms, chairman, Senate Committee on Foreign Relations. This letter was released by the Office of the Press Secretary on November 10.

Remarks on the Budget Debate
November 10, 1995

Good afternoon. The budget debate we are now engaged in is a serious and critical moment for this country. The debate is about whether we will balance this budget in a way that is consistent with our fundamental values: our responsibility to our parents and to our children; our determination to provide opportunity for all Americans to make the most of their own lives through good jobs and education and technology; our obligation to protect the environment and to maintain America's ability to be the world's strongest force for peace and freedom, for democracy and prosperity.

In a larger sense, I believe this budget debate is about two very different futures for America: about whether we will continue to go forward under our motto, E Pluribus Unum, out of many, one; whether we will continue to unite and grow; or whether we will become a more divided, winner-take-all society.

I recognize that the Republican Congress has a very different view. The American people deserve a serious debate over these two approaches to balancing the budget. But we cannot have that serious debate under the threat of a Government default or shutdown. And we cannot cut Medicare, education, and the environment as a condition of keeping the Government open.

The bills Congress voted on last night are not ordinary measures designed simply to keep the Government open while we continue the debate over how to balance the budget. Instead, last night Republicans in Congress voted to raise Medicare premiums; they voted to cut education and to cut it deeply; and they voted to overturn three decades of bipartisan environmental safeguards.

Beyond that, these measures would make a Government default almost inevitable, for the first time in our history, because they take away from the Secretary of the Treasury the tools now available to avoid default under extraordinary circumstances. This is deeply irresponsible. It has never happened before, and it should not happen now.

Republicans in Congress have a responsibility to keep the Government running without cutting Medicare and increasing premiums, without cutting education and undercutting the environment. I want to work with Congress to resolve these differences and to keep the Government running in the interest of the American people. After all, we have shown we can work together on this. Just last September we agreed on an appropriate measure to keep the Government running while we finish the job of balancing the budget. We should simply do now what was done in September so that the Government and the budget debate can go on. And I believe Congress should stay in this weekend and finish this work.

Thank you.

NOTE: The President spoke at 1:05 p.m. in the Briefing Room at the White House.

The President's Radio Address
November 11, 1995

Good morning. At midnight this Monday night, unless Congress passes legislation to keep the Government running, the Federal Government will be required by law to begin shutting down. For months, the congressional Republicans have made a consistent threat: If I don't sign legislation cutting Medicare, education and the environment, they'll plunge the Government into default and force it to close its doors.

I don't want to shut down basic Government services for the American people, but I can't allow that to be used to force us to accept extreme budget measures that would violate our basic values as a nation and undermine the long-term welfare of the American people.

A very great deal is at stake in this debate. This budget debate is not about whether we will balance the budget. Both parties support that. It's about whether we will balance our budget in a way that is consistent with our fundamental values: our responsibility to our parents and to our children; our determination to provide opportunity for all Americans to make the most of their own lives through good jobs and education and technology; our obligation to protect the environment and to keep America the world's strongest force for peace and free-dom, democracy and prosperity.

This budget debate is about two very different futures for America: about whether we'll continue to go forward under our motto, *E Pluribus Unum*, out of many, one; whether we will continue to unite and grow together; or whether we will become a more divided winner-take-all society.

Today as I speak with you, the congressional Republicans are on the verge of carrying out their threat. I want to explain how we have come to this juncture and why it is so important that we stand firm against measures that would endanger our future. The congressional Republicans propose to balance the budget in 7 years, but they would get there with deep cuts in Medicare, education, protection for the environment, and by raising taxes on working people. Five full months ago, I proposed an alternative plan to balance the budget in 10 years while protecting Medicare and Medicaid, increasing our investment in education and technology, protecting the environment, without raising taxes on working families. Since then, the Republican Congress has dismissed my proposal at every turn and has not met the deadlines established by law for setting this year's budget.

The new Federal fiscal year started back on October 1st. Now it's November 11th, Veterans Day, and still they haven't sent me a budget, even though the Republicans control both Houses of Congress. This is very unusual. In

my first 2 years, we passed budgets to reduce the deficit in a timely fashion.

Also this year, the Republicans have not come close to resolving their own internal differences in their overall budget plan between measures passed in the House and the Senate. Back in 1993, we passed our deficit reduction plan 3 months earlier than this, in August. That plan has now given us 3 years of deficit reduction in a row for the first time since Mr. Truman was President. And the United States now has the lowest deficit as a percentage of our income of any industrial nation in the world except one. Let me say that again, we now have the lowest deficit as a percentage of our income of any industrial nation in the world except one.

Now, there have been times in our history when our budget process has run late before. I want to acknowledge that. But when that happens, the differing sides, regardless of party, usually agree to find a fair and unbiased way to keep the Government going and to enable the United States to pay its bills, while the broader debate about budget priorities goes on.

That is what I worked out with Congress in September. They passed and I signed a simple, straightforward bill to keep the Government running and to prevent America from going into default. That was the serious and responsible thing to do, and I applauded them for doing it at the time. Last week, I met with the Republican congressional leadership to try to find a way, again, to keep our Government open and to keep it from falling into default. As I told them then, we should balance the budget. But we cannot do it under a threat of Government shutdown and default.

Instead of following the path of reconciliation, however, they have, once again, gone their own way. This week, they voted on an unprecedented measure. On Thursday night, as a part of their bill to keep the Government going, both Houses voted a 25 percent increase in Medicare premiums for every single senior citizen on Medicare. That is an extraordinary act. No Congress in our history has ever demanded an increase in Medicare premiums as a condition of keeping the Government open. That is wrong, and I will not accept it.

And on this Veterans Day, they have a strange way of honoring all of those men and women who have sacrificed for our country. Eight million of the senior citizens and disabled Americans whose Medicare premiums would be raised by Congress are veterans, and they, too, deserve better.

The Republicans in Congress are also demanding deep cuts in education and the environment and a profound weakening of environmental laws as a condition of keeping the Government open and our bills paid. And they have added conditions to the debt limit legislation that amount to a shortcut to default on the full faith and credit of the United States.

Think of it this way, my fellow Americans. Imagine the Republican Congress as a banker and the United States as a family that has to go to the bank for a short-term loan for a family emergency. The banker says to the family, "I'll give you the loan, but only if you'll throw the grandparents and the kids out of the house first."

Well, speaking on behalf of the family, I say, no thanks. I believe we can find a good-faith way to keep the Government open and make good on its obligations. So I've asked my Chief of Staff, Leon Panetta, to meet with the Republican and the Democratic leaders of Congress this afternoon. I've instructed him to present them with the straightforward ideas to keep the Government open, just like we did in September

and just as Congress has done dozens of times before. But I will not allow them to impose new, immediate cuts in Medicare, education, and the environment as a condition of keeping the Government open.

I believe we can resolve these differences without hurting the American people or our future. All around us we see evidence that America is on the move. Our economy is the envy of the world. The unemployment and inflation rates together are at a 25-year low, new businesses and exports of American products at an all-time high.

As I said, our deficit already is the smallest of any major economy in the world but one. Our Government as a percentage of the work force is the smallest it's been since 1933. We're making a serious assault on our social problems, like crime. Now our challenge is to balance our budget in a way that is consistent with our fundamental values and to do it without threats and without partisan rancor. We can do that, so let's get it done.

Thank you for listening.

NOTE: The President spoke at 10:06 a.m. from the Oval Office at the White House.

Remarks at a Veterans Day Ceremony in Arlington, Virginia
November 11, 1995

Thank you, Secretary Brown, for your introduction and for your remarkable service on behalf of the veterans of the United States. General Foley, Commander Liwack, distinguished leaders of all our veterans organizations, Secretary Brown, Secretary Perry, General Shalikashvili, Attorney General Reno, Senator Simpson; especially to my friend Congressman Montgomery. I want to join the remarks that were earlier made and thank you, sir, for your lifetime of service to the United States and for your unparalleled service to the veterans of the United States. We will all miss you, and we thank you. To our men and women in uniform and their families here today and most of all, of course, to all of our veterans and their families and the Gold Star mothers and wives, their survivors who are here today; my fellow Americans.

On this day that marked the end of World War I, we close the 50-year commemoration of the end of World War II. Together on this day we offer a prayer for peace and a tribute to those who defend it. All across this land a symphony of 50 bells will soar. Together on this day we say thank you to those who stepped forward to safeguard our security and our ideals. Today, this day, our grateful Nation is united to honor America's veterans.

This year we have paid special homage to the World War II generation. From the windswept beaches of Normandy to the craggy rocks of Corregidor, meeting the Americans who fought in that struggle has been one of the great privileges I have had as your President. Later today we will honor all of them in dedicating the site of the World War II memorial, ensuring that we will never, never forget those who suffered and sacrificed so that future generations of Americans might be free.

They followed in the footsteps of others who came before them, from those who battled for our independence to those who braved the trenches in "the war to end all wars." And clearly they inspired successive generations of heroes, men and women who fought in Korea, Vietnam, and the Persian Gulf; who steadily won the cold war; who served with such skill and compassion in Haiti; who saved so many lives in more than one place in Africa; who halted the Bosnia Serb attacks against innocent civilians; and the men and women who, even as we gather here, safeguard the frontiers of freedom with their courage, their commitment, and their confidence.

Our Nation has obligations to all those who wear our uniform, ensuring that our military remains the strongest in the world, leaving no stone unturned in the search for the fullest possible accounting for Americans who never came home, supporting our citizen soldiers, the Guard and the Reserves, whom we call on increasingly to serve overseas, and ensuring that when our men and women in uniform leave the service we do not leave them. From education to employment, from buying a home to getting quality medical care, our veterans deserve and must have their Nation's unfaltering support, for our peace, our freedom, our prosperity is surely the legacy of their service.

Much of this responsibility still falls upon our Federal Government. We must uphold the commitment established first by President Franklin Roosevelt to give veterans preference for Federal jobs, and we are. Even as we shrink the work force of the National Government to its lowest level since President Kennedy served here, the percentage of permanent jobs in the Government going to our veterans has grown over the last 3 years.

We must rally the resources for veterans benefits, and we are. Even as we cut Government spending—and my fellow Americans, our annual deficit as a percentage of our income is now lower than that of any other industrial country in the entire world except for Norway—even as we do that, I have sought more than a $1 billion increase in health funding for the VA so that we can provide better care for even more veterans.

And even as we enjoy a 15-year high in home-ownership among Americans, we must not forget that there are too many homeless Americans,

and an extraordinary percentage of them are veterans. Later today, a group of distinguished American entertainers will attempt to make America laugh to raise funds and increase awareness of the problems of the homeless. And they do it on this Veterans Day to remind us that it is a national disgrace that people who are willing to lay down their lives for this country do not have a roof over which they will lay down their heads tonight. And we must continue to fight that.

We are committed to active communication with our veterans. We have to do more to bring the men in on the decisions that affect their lives. We will continue to pursue answers and provide relief for Gulf war veterans with unexplained illnesses. Just 3 days ago, we launched a major study to help address the concerns of Persian Gulf veterans about their health and that of their spouses and their children. And we are working hard to meet the special concerns of women veterans, the needs of disabled veterans, and the precious debt we owe to veterans' families.

But Government cannot and should not do this job alone. Supporting our veterans is not the Government's job; it's America's job. Over the last 3 years, I have visited our troops all around the world. I have stood in the desert of Kuwait with our vigilant warriors who stopped Iraqi aggression this time before it could start. I have met our fliers in Ramstein, Germany, who delivered supplies and hope to Bosnia in the largest humanitarian airlift of all time. I have visited the men and women of Operation Uphold Democracy who ended the terror and turned on the lights for the freedom-loving people in Haiti. I have been to Korea, where the steady presence of our Americans in uniform has been indispensable to our successful efforts to end the nuclear threat and maintain the peace there.

Wherever I go, I see firsthand the dedication, the skill, the ingenuity of our men and women in uniform. I see the legacy of World War I, World War II, Korea, Vietnam, the cold war, Desert Storm, all of our other encounters, in these young people who get better and better and better at what they do.

Every year, more than 275,000 of these talented Americans finish their military service and return to civilian life. The strength they bring to our Armed Forces can and indeed must fortify our Nation's civilian economy and fiber of civic life. So on this Veterans Day, let me urge every employer in America in the public and the private sector to tap the invaluable resource of America's veterans, to recognize their loyalty and their commitment—after all, they volunteered, sometimes for jobs of great danger and risk—to recognize their skill, their creativity, their dedication. There are so many ways in which we can now say, nobody does it better. America's veterans are leaders and winners, and they can help America to compete and win. But they must be given the opportunity to serve and to work.

As we reflect on the challenges that these veterans have met so successfully in the recent and in the distant past, my fellow Americans, let us today rededicate ourselves to meet the new challenges we face today. Because of the work of our veterans, our Nation remains the world's strongest force for peace and freedom, for democracy and prosperity. And the world is moving in our direction.

We can be very thankful that on this Veterans Day, for the first time since the dawn of the nuclear era, there are no Russian missiles pointed at the children of the United States. We can be thankful for that.

But as the painful events of recent days have reminded us, the forces of darkness and division have not been destroyed. Threats like the proliferation of weapons of mass destruction; violence rooted in ethnic, religious, and racial hatred; organized crime and drug trafficking; and especially terrorism call upon us to respond. Just as our veterans faced down the threats of a previous era, so now we must confront these challenges of this time. Just as Congress and the President join in bipartisan spirit over the last 50 years to protect our Nation's security, so we must join today.

I am proud of the work our military is doing in the fight to keep illegal drugs out of America and the fight to break the terrible drug cartels of the world. I am proud of the work our law enforcement people have done here at home and abroad to combat terrorism, from bringing terrorists to justice from all across the world to actually stopping terrorists plots in the United States before they succeed.

But as we saw in the World Trade Center and at Oklahoma City and as we saw so recently in the tragic, tragic murder of Israel's great leader and military hero, Prime Minister Rabin, there is more to be done. Giving our officials the tools they need to defeat terrorism is now a part of our national security mission, just as maintaining a strong national defense is. This matter must be beyond party. All of us must rise to the challenge to meet it.

As we close this commemoration of World War II, let me thank again General Kicklighter and all those who helped to make it possible and let me urge all of us to summon the spirit that joined that generation that stood together and cared for one another. The ideas they fought for are now ours to sustain. The dreams they defended are now ours to guarantee. In war they crossed racial and religious, sectional and social divisions to become one force for freedom.

Now, in a world where lives are literally being torn apart all over the globe by those very divisions, let us again lead by the power of example. Let us remember their example. Let us live our motto, *E Pluribus Unum*, from many, one. Let us grow strong together, not be divided and weakened. Let us find that common ground for which so many have fought and died.

On this hillside of honor and respects, let us once again humbly thank our veterans for answering the call to duty for what they did in times of crisis and war and what they did to preserve the peace. Let us remain ever grateful for all they have done. And for what we owe them, let us never be forgetful. We must and we will meet our obligations and secure our future if we remember all of that. My fellow Americans, that is our mission, and we must fulfill it.

Thank you, God bless you, and God bless America.

NOTE: The President spoke at 11:44 a.m. at the Tomb of the Unknowns at Arlington National Cemetery. In his remarks, he referred to Maj. Gen. Robert Foley, USA, commanding general, Military District of Washington; Joseph Liwack, commander, Polish Legion of American Veterans; and General C.M. Kicklighter, chairman, 50th Anniversary of World War II Commemorative Committee.

Teleconference Remarks With World War II Veterans
November 11, 1995

The President. Hello. Grace?

Ms. Ellen Grace Forgey. Yes, this is Grace Forgey.

The President. Carl Crabtree? Are you there?

Ms. Forgey. This is Grace Forgey. Hello?

Carl Crabtree. Yes, sir.

The President. Yes, I hear you, Grace.

Ms. Forgey. Oh, Mr. President?

The President. Yes. And is William Frizzell there?

William Frizzell. Yes.

The President. And John Byrnes?

John Byrnes. Yes, Mr. President. John Byrnes of New York City.

The President. Well, you're all on the line, and you sound like you're next door.

Ms. Forgey. That's the wonderful telephone company. There's one thing that we're——

Mr. Frizzell. We're on the line, and you can get us.

The President. That's great. Well, I'm just calling to wish all of you a happy Veterans Day and to say to you and veterans like you in the hospitals all across our country that we're thinking about you, we're pulling for you, and we're very excited about these phones in your room now, thanks to the PT Phone Home project.

Ms. Forgey. Yes, it's wonderful.

The President. And I'm here with Frank Dosio, who came up with the idea, and also with the leaders of the groups that implemented it, the Communications Workers of America, the International Brotherhood of Electrical Workers, Bell Atlantic, and NYNEX Corporation and the Telephone Pioneers of America. They have done a wonderful job, and they have saved our Government literally millions and millions of dollars because of the volunteer work and the contributions they have made to make this opportunity available to all of you.

Ms. Forgey. And I want to say that it's made life——

Mr. Frizzell. Well, I put in 4 years—something.

Ms. Forgey. It's made life at the veterans hospital the last word, you know, in contact with the outside. It's wonderful. The hospital is wonderful.

The President. Well, I'm very glad, and I know you're grateful to all of these folks that

are here. That's why I wanted to tell you they were here.

Ms. Forgey. I certainly am.

Mr. Byrnes. It's a blessing, Mr. President, it really is.

Ms. Forgey. Yes. You should be very proud of your employees.

The President. You know, within an hour I'm going to leave the White House here and go dedicate the memorial to the veterans who fought in World War II 50 years ago.

Ms. Forgey. That's me.

The President. That will join the similar tributes to the Korean war and the Vietnam war veterans that we have on The Mall in Washington. I know that three of you, I believe, were in World War II. Grace, you were a nurse. Isn't that right?

Ms. Forgey. That's right, yes.

The President. And I think you have a son in the—and a grandson in the Army now.

Ms. Forgey. My grandson's in the Army, yes.

The President. Where is he?

Ms. Forgey. Fort Riley, Texas. Where is it?

The President. Kansas.

Ms. Forgey. That's right. I don't know one State from the other. It's wonderful to talk to you. How nice of you to do this.

The President. Thank you.

Ms. Forgey. It makes you feel like you belong to the right country.

The President. Mr. Frizzell? You're from Chillicothe, Ohio?

Mr. Frizzell. No, I'm from Columbus, Ohio.

The President. Oh, you're at Chillicothe?

Mr. Frizzell. I'm at Chillicothe.

The President. Yes. I visited that community once, and I went running around the city park. It was three degrees.

Mr. Frizzell. Yes.

The President. They thought I needed a mental examination for doing it, but it was a great morning. [*Laughter*]

Mr. Frizzell. I walked over to the 9 building, and ended up in the 31 building, and I'll never tell you how in the hell I did that.

The President. You were at Pearl Harbor, weren't you?

Mr. Frizzell. Yes.

Ms. Forgey. My husband was at Pearl Harbor.

Mr. Frizzell. Camp Cameron—about a mile and a half from Pearl Harbor.

The President. Well, good for you. Mr. Byrnes?

Mr. Byrnes. Yes, sir.

The President. You were in the Navy in World War II, isn't that right?

Mr. Byrnes. U.S.S. *Alaska*, CV–1. The best battleship the United States Navy ever had.

The President. Otherwise, you don't have strong feelings about it. [*Laughter*]

Mr. Byrnes. No, I—a little more than strong, sir.

The President. And you were at Iwo Jima, weren't you?

Mr. Byrnes. Iwo Jima, Okinawa, Japan, all through the Pacific.

The President. Well, we thank you for what you did.

Mr. Byrnes. Thank you, Mr. President.

The President. Mr. Crabtree?

Mr. Crabtree. Yes, sir.

The President. You were in—I'm told that you were in the military police.

Mr. Crabtree. Yes, sir.

The President. I wonder if that means you still have the power to arrest the rest of us if we don't behave. [*Laughter*] You were on duty in Japan?

Mr. Crabtree. Yes, sir.

The President. After the war, right?

Mr. Crabtree. Yes, sir.

The President. I'm grateful to all of you, and I hope the VA has taken good care of you.

Ms. Forgey. It has.

The President. I wish you the best of health. We're doing everything we can to try to preserve the quality of health care in the veterans' network, and it's for people like you. We know on this Veterans Day that we owe our freedom to people like you who have served our country, and I just wanted to say how grateful I am to you for your service and how grateful I am to all of these people who are here with me for providing this PT Phone Home project. We're expanding it just as rapidly as we can, and I look forward to the day when every veteran like you in every hospital in this country has access to it.

Ms. Forgey. It's wonderful. They did a wonderful job.

The President. I hope you'll all have a good day. Grace and Carl and William and John, you have a wonderful day and know that we're all thinking about you.

Mr. Byrnes. Thank you, Mr. President.

Ms. Forgey. Thank you, Mr. President.

The President. God bless you.

Mr. Frizzell. God bless you, and you have a wonderful day, too.

The President. We'll do it.

Ms. Forgey. Take care of yourself.

Mr. Byrnes. Have a good Thanksgiving and a good Christmas.

The President. Thank you. Bye-bye.

NOTE: The President spoke at 1:05 p.m. from the Oval Office at the White House. In his remarks he referred to Frank Dosio, coordinator, PT Phone Home.

Remarks in a Telephone Conversation With Gaetano Maggio
November 11, 1995

The President. Hello.

Mr. Maggio. Hello, Mr. President.

The President. Mr. Maggio?

Mr. Maggio. Yes, sir.

The President. Happy birthday.

Mr. Maggio. Thank you, sir.

The President. I heard you're in Tampa with a big group of family members and friends.

Mr. Maggio. Right. That's my home in Tampa. Been in Tampa—my home since 1903.

The President. That's great. And this is your actual birthday, on this Veterans Day, is that right?

Mr. Maggio. Actual birthday, November the 11th at 11 o'clock at night.

The President. That's amazing. And you were among the first group of people from Tampa to volunteer for World War I, weren't you?

Mr. Maggio. Yes, sir. I sure did.

The President. Well, I really appreciate you.

Mr. Maggio. Thank you.

The President. I appreciate you and—do you have all your children there?

Mr. Maggio. All here.

The President. And a lot of grandchildren there?

Mr. Maggio. I got grandchildren and a great-grandchild here. It's the fifth generation.

The President. That's great.

Mr. Maggio. They come from Fort Lauderdale just to celebrate my birthday.

The President. I bet you're proud of that.

Mr. Maggio. I sure am.

The President. You've been very fortunate, haven't you?

Mr. Maggio. I've been very fortunate with my family. Got a beautiful family. And all—all of the boys that were servicemen—ex-servicemen—all have been servicemen.

The President. I know you're proud of them.

Mr. Maggio. And I'm proud of them. The whole six of them.

The President. Well, I just wanted to wish you a happy birthday, and I wanted to tell you that I'm proud of you, and I'm very grateful that our country has had someone like you——

Mr. Maggio. Thank you.

The President. ——living here throughout the 20th century, seeing all the changes you've seen, and making the sacrifices you've made so that we could stay a free country and——

Mr. Maggio. I've seen plenty.

The President. You have seen a lot, haven't you.

Mr. Maggio. Yes, good and bad.

The President. Yes. But we can still bring immigrants to our shores and give them a shot at a better life because of people like you. And I really thank you for it.

Mr. Maggio. Thank you.

The President. And you have a wonderful day.

Mr. Maggio. Have a beautiful day, too. Thank you.

The President. Tell your family I said hello.

Mr. Maggio. Mr. President says hello to the family.

The Maggio Family. Hello, Mr. President.

The President. [*Laughter*] They sound great! Thank you, sir, and God bless you.

Mr. Maggio. Thank you, sir.

The President. Bye-bye.

NOTE: The President spoke at 1:21 p.m. from the Oval Office at the White House.

Remarks at the Dedication of the World War II Memorial Site
November 11, 1995

Thank you, Dr. Encinias, for that introduction and for your truly remarkable service to our Nation. General Woerner, Governor Carey, Chairman Wheeler, Congresswoman Kaptur, I thank you all for what you have done to bring us to this day. I want to thank Mr. Durbin for his idea and for the triumph of his idea today and the triumph of the idea that an American citizen can have a good idea and take it to the proper authorities and actually get something done. To all the Members of Congress, and especially to Congressman Montgomery on his retirement, for all of his service to our veterans; to Mrs. Boyajian, thank you for your wonderful remarks today; General Shalikashvili, Secretary Perry, Secretary Brown, my fellow Americans.

I would like to begin by asking on the occasion of this last observance of the 50th anniversary of World War II that all of us express our appreciation to those who served on the World War II Commemorative Commission, and especially to its leader, General Kicklighter, for a magnificent job. Thank you all, and thank you, General.

On this Veterans Day, we gather in special memory of World War II, and we dedicate this site to ensure that we will never forget. That war claimed 55 million lives, soldiers and civilians, children, the millions murdered in the death camps. It engulfed more of the Earth than any war before it or any war since. It was, as Governor Carey said, the coming of age not only for many Americans but for America, the moment that we understood that we could save the world for freedom and only we could save the world for freedom, and so we had to do it.

Today, we honor those who did just that, the fighting men and women who wore our uniform all around the world and the millions of civilians on our Nation's homefront who did the remarkable things embodied by Mrs. Boyajian. For all they did for our troops and for all they did without, all the sacrificing at home to help the cause abroad, we thank them, too.

My fellow Americans, the World War II generation emerged from the darkness of global war to strengthen our economy, to enlighten our society, and to lead our world to greater heights. More than 16 million women worked in our factories and cared for our soldiers. After the war, they began to play a larger role in our economy and, over time, a remarkable role in our military.

Many thousands of African-Americans served their country with courage and distinction as Tuskegee Airmen and Triple Nickel paratroopers and Sherman tank drivers and Navy Seabees. After the war, we began slowly to act on a truth too long denied, that if people of different races could serve as brothers abroad, surely, surely, they could live as neighbors at home.

I cannot let this moment pass without expressing my gratitude to all those of other ethnic and racial groups, who themselves knew discrimination, who also served in World War II, and the especially brave and heroic Japanese-Americans who served in World War II, many of them with their own relatives in internment camps.

All these people took a fuller and larger and more meaningful role in American life after the war, and we were stronger for it. And instead of turning its back on the world the way the previous generation did after World War I, the World War II generation stood with its allies and reached out to its former adversaries to cement the partnerships and create the institutions that secured a half-century of unparalleled prosperity in the West, no return of world war and victory in the cold war. We owe that generation a very great deal. And this monument will tell us we must never forget that either.

This memorial whose site we dedicate today will be a permanent reminder of just how much we Americans can do when we work together, instead of fighting among ourselves. It will honor those who served and those who made the ultimate sacrifice. It will pay tribute to the millions of civilians who supported the war effort in spirit and action. It will stand as a monument to the values that joined us in common cause, that are worth defending and that make our life worth living. All these things we must never forget.

Here in the company of President Lincoln and President Jefferson, the White House in which every President but George Washington has lived, and the monument to George Washington just behind you, with the stately Capitol dome beyond, the World War II Memorial will join the ranks of our greatest landmarks because it was one of the greatest and most important periods in our history.

We will seal this plaque soon with the earth of 16 World War II cemeteries, and so, in our small way, infuse this place with the spirit and the souls of those who died for freedom.

I want to thank all of those who have worked so hard to raise the funds for this project, including my good friend Jess Haye from Dallas. I want to thank Secretary Perry and the Department of Defense for making an initial contribution. And to all of you in the future who will give to make sure that this project is done and done right, I thank you.

America must never forget the debt we owe the World War II generation. It is a small downpayment on that debt to build this monument as magnificently as we can.

From this day forward, this place belongs to the World War II generation and to their families. Let us honor their achievements by upholding always the ideals they defended and by guarding always the dreams they fought and died for, for our children and our children's children.

Thank you very much.

NOTE: The President spoke at 2:40 p.m. on The Mall. In his remarks, he referred to Miguel Encinias, World War II veteran and prisoner of war; Gen. Fred Woerner, USA (Ret.), chairman, and Hugh L. Carey, vice chairman, American Battle Monuments Commission; Peter Wheeler, chairman, World War II Memorial Advisory Board; Roger Durbin, World War II veteran and activist for the memorial; and Helen Boyajian, Home Front Representative. A portion of these remarks could not be verified because the tape was incomplete.

Statement on the Report on Juvenile Crime
November 11, 1995

These statistics are a chilling reminder to all of us—parents, teachers, police officers, and elected leaders—that juvenile violence remains the number one crime problem in America.

I am proud of the landmark legislation we have passed to fight the scourge of youth violence, such as the juvenile handgun ban and zero-tolerance for guns in schools. But if we are to win this fight against crime and violence, more parents must begin to teach their children right from wrong.

And to anyone who would undo the steps I have taken to fight crime and violence in America's streets and on her schoolyards, I say, look at the facts. Now is not the time to weaken our laws.

NOTE: This statement was embargoed for release by the Office of the Press Secretary until 5:01 p.m. on November 12.

Statement on the Balkan Peace Process
November 12, 1995

Today's agreement between the Government of Croatia and the leaders of the local Serbian community on the region of Eastern Slavonia is a major step toward the achievement of an overall peace settlement in the Balkans. This agreement provides for the peaceful reintegration of the region under Croatian sovereignty, following a period of transitional administration by the United Nations.

I congratulate the parties for the wisdom they have shown in entering into this agreement and avoiding renewed conflict. I also congratulate Secretary of State Warren Christopher, who played a direct role in assisting the parties to arrive at this agreement, along with Ambassador Richard Holbrooke and the U.S. and U.N. mediators, Ambassador Peter Galbraith and Thorvald Stoltenberg.

Remarks on Vetoing Temporary Public Debt Limit Increase Legislation and an Exchange With Reporters
November 13, 1995

The President. Good morning. Today I am vetoing H.R. 2586, which the congressional leadership sent to me last night. It would allow the United States to pay its debts for another month but only at a price too high for the American people to pay. Here are the reasons why.

First, the bill actually increases the likelihood of a default on America's obligations for the first time in our history by taking away from the Secretary of the Treasury the tools he now has to avoid default under extraordinary circumstances.

Second, the bill obligates the Government—Congress and the President—to pass the Republican congressional budget plan with its huge cuts in Medicare and Medicaid, education and technology, the environment, and its tax increases on working families.

Third, the bill implements the Republican congressional proposal to reverse a 30-year bipartisan commitment to environmental protection and public health. It would increase pollution and decrease the purity and safety of our air, water, and food.

This legislation is part of an overall back-door effort by the congressional Republicans to impose their priorities on our Nation. Here is what is really going on.

Last spring, Speaker Gingrich said he and his new Republican congressional majority would force me, the congressional Democrats, and the American people to accept their budget and their contract by bringing about a crisis in the fall, by shutting down the Government and pushing America into default, unless I accepted their extreme proposals. In this way, the congressional Republicans sought to get around the United States Constitution which gives the President the power to veto measures not in the public interest.

They are now implementing the strategy Speaker Gingrich told us about last spring. And because I refuse to go along with it, they say I am refusing with them to solve these short-term problems.

When the time came for the Republicans to announce their balanced budget plan, I said I supported a balanced budget. I said I agreed with balancing the budget, but I did not agree with the way they proposed to do it. So I offered an alternative plan, and I offered then to work with them. I offered it repeatedly, beginning 5 months ago. They dismissed my offer and said at every turn that I would simply have to accept their budget conditions. That is what this legislation says again today.

When the time came for them to pass their own budget, however, they did not do their work. It is now 6 full weeks into the new budget year, and they have passed only 3 of the required 13 budget bills. Furthermore, they have not yet resolved the differences between the Republican House and Senate versions of the balanced budget. Instead, they propose to attach elements of a budget plan and their contract to essential bills to raise the debt ceiling so that America can meet its obligations and to keep the Government running until they do finish their budget work and a proper budget is passed. Their goal is to force me to sign legislation which I know to be harmful to our Nation and to its future or to veto the legislation, also with harmful consequences.

This is a critical moment of decision for our country. But the issue is not whether we will balance the budget and not whether I will work with them to solve this short-term problem. I do want to balance the budget. Remember that in 1993 when I took office, we had a huge deficit that was growing larger. Congress passed

my economic plan, and since then we have reduced our deficit 3 years in a row for the first time in nearly 50 years. Today, only one industrialized nation has a lower deficit than the United States. We've also reduced the size of the Federal Government dramatically, so that today, as a percentage of the civilian work force, our Federal Government is the smallest it has been since 1933. The American economy has done well since 1993, since this budget plan was passed, as everyone knows.

The balanced budget plan that I have proposed would finish the job. It would eliminate the deficit in a way that strengthens our economy and, most important, reinforces our most important values: our responsibility to our parents and to our children; to provide opportunity to all Americans to make the most of their own lives through education and technology; to strengthen our families; to preserve our environment; to keep America the world's strongest force for freedom and democracy, for peace and prosperity.

So that is the issue here. I believe we must pass a budget that is consistent with our values and our interests. I have said for months that I will not sign a budget that violates these values and undermines our economic interests. This bill I veto today is a big downpayment on that Republican congressional budget. It is not good for America.

Our country has to choose between two very different options, two very different visions and paths to the 21st century. Throughout our history, our Nation has been able to reach important decisions on matters like this about national priorities through proper channels of deliberation and debate as set out in our Constitution. This year, the Republican Congress has failed to pass most of its spending bills, has not yet passed its overall budget plan, but instead has sought to impose some of its most objectionable proposals on the American people by attaching them to bills to raise the debt limit and to keep the Government running.

Now, the appropriate step for Congress to take would be to authorize America to meet its obligations and to pass temporary legislation to keep the Government running while this overall budget battle is taking place. This has been the course of action taken at other moments in history when Congress failed to meet its budget deadlines. That is exactly what we did just last September when the Congress did pass and I signed legislation to keep the Government running.

Our agreement in September was fair. It was unbiased. It kept the Government going, able to pay its bills and meet its obligations. That agreement was an honorable compromise. In recent days, Congress has chosen the path of confrontation. It is not in the national interest, but it is exactly what they said they would do last April.

They have attached these controversial, long-range proposals to emergency legislation, not only to meet our financial obligations but just to keep the Government running. In the bill to keep the Government running, they voted to raise Medicare premiums by 25 percent for every single senior citizen who uses Medicare, $264 a year for the typical couple, beginning the first of January. They voted to roll back three decades of environmental laws. Now they voted to put the United States on the path to default.

This is an unacceptable choice. Congress has said it will pass emergency legislation to keep the Government going and paying its bills only if we increase Medicare, cut education, cut the environment, take other unacceptable steps.

I know the American people want us to balance the budget with common sense and without bitterness, to drop the extreme proposals and get to work. Congress should take the sensible step of passing the legislation necessary to keep the Government going and to have America meet its financial obligations. Therefore, today, I am transmitting legislation to Congress that would enable the Government to pay its bills without forcing the acceptance of extreme cuts in Medicare, education, and the environment. This legislation would enable us to have a fair debate on our country's direction without rancor or threats. Congress should pass it without delay. This is not the time or the place for them to backdoor their budget proposals. It is not the right thing to do. I cannot, and I will not accept it.

Government Shutdown

Q. What happens now? Is the Government going to shut down? Will we default on our bills?

The President. That's up to the Congress. That is entirely up to them. I am certainly willing to work with the bipartisan leadership of the Congress to resolve this problem, but it

is important that the American people have a forthright debate over this budget in the ordinary constitutional way. That is important. It is critically important that the President not permit this budget to be passed in a backdoor way, because we have to keep the Government running, because we have to meet our financial obligations.

This budget is a dramatic, even a radical, departure from the deliberate, disciplined, and I might add, highly successful plan that this administration has pursued over the last 2 years. It is also an dramatic and unacceptable departure from the appropriate way of doing business in this Government. America does not react well to this kind of pressure.

Budget Negotiations

Q. Mr. President, Speaker Gingrich yesterday appeared to offer what may be an olive branch when he said that everything was on the table if you would just agree to sit down and talk and agree in principle to a balanced budget in 7 years. Is that possible? Could you do that? And why not?

The President. I cannot agree in principle—we had a discussion in here the other day, I did with the Speaker and Senator Dole, I would remind you, about the budget and other things. We can have any discussion we want on the budget. But I will not agree as a matter of principle to any discussion in which they say, we want to raise Medicare premiums by 25 percent in a bill designed to keep the Government running or that we want to do it in a bill designed to enable America to meet its financial obligations.

I have asked them to do only one thing. I have asked them to say forthrightly that they're willing to meet with me and the bipartisan congressional leadership in an atmosphere in which they can pass whatever bills they want to pass in the budget process, but they will not attempt to raise Medicare premiums just as the price of letting the Government run for 2 more weeks or another month. I don't think that is right. I don't think the American people think that is right.

There is a procedure for passing budgets and for passing the budget plan. That is a procedure they have chosen not to follow. I don't know how many years, how many decades it's been since the Congress got 6 years into a new budget plan, having voted on only 3 of the 13 budget bills for the year. They have still not even met and resolved the differences between the House and Senate balanced budget plans.

There is a procedure for dealing with this. Now they have to resolve those differences. And it is time to get on the timetable. But avoiding that, they seek to tack on to measures necessary to simply go through the ordinary business of the Government their budget, including a dramatic increase in Medicare premiums. All I have asked them to do is to say that they will not seek to increase Medicare premiums on this interim legislation to keep the Government running and that we will have this bipartisan meeting of the congressional leadership. And we will talk about everything if they do that. That is all I have asked them to do.

But America has never liked—ordinary Americans don't like pressure tactics. And I would be wrong to permit these kind of pressure tactics to dramatically change the course of American life. I cannot do it, and I will not do it.

Terrorist Attack in Riyadh, Saudi Arabia

Q. Mr. President, what do you know about Riyadh?

The President. At this moment, I know very little more than you do. I know that Americans were killed in an explosion. We have expressed our condolences and deep regret to the families of those who were killed, and we have already begun the process of determining what happened and who, if anyone, was responsible if it was not an accident. And we will devote an enormous effort to that.

NOTE: The President spoke at 8:26 a.m. in the Oval Office at the White House.

Message to the House of Representatives Returning Without Approval Temporary Public Debt Limit Increase Legislation
November 13, 1995

To the House of Representatives:

I am returning herewith without my approval H.R. 2586, a bill that would provide a temporary increase in the public debt limit while adding extraneous measures that have no place on legislation of this kind.

This bill would make it almost inevitable that the Government would default for the first time in our history. This is deeply irresponsible. A default has never happened before, and it should not happen now.

I have repeatedly urged the Congress to pass promptly legislation raising the debt limit for a reasonable period of time to protect the Nation's creditworthiness and avoid default. Republicans in the Congress have acknowledged the need to raise the debt limit; the budget resolution calls for raising it to $5.5 trillion, and House and Senate voted to raise it to that level in passing their reconciliation bills.

This bill, however, would threaten the Nation with default after December 12—the day on which the debt limit increase in the bill would expire—for two reasons:

First, under this bill, on December 13 the debt limit would fall to $4.8 trillion, an amount $100 billion below the current level of $4.9 trillion. The next day, more than $44 billion in Government securities mature, and the Federal Government would be unable to borrow the funds to redeem them. The owners of those securities would not be paid on time.

Second, the bill would severely limit the cash management options that the Treasury may be able to use to avert a default. Specifically, it would limit the Secretary's flexibility to manage the investments of certain Government funds— flexibility that the Congress first gave to President Reagan. Finally, while the bill purports to protect benefit recipients, it would make it very likely that after December 12, the Federal Government would be unable to make full or timely payments for a wide variety of Government obligations, including interest on the public debt, Medicare, Medicaid, military pay, certain veterans' benefits, and payments to Government contractors.

As I have said clearly and repeatedly, the Congress should keep the debt limit separate from the debate over how to balance the budget. The debt limit has nothing to do with reducing the deficit; it has to do with meeting the obligations that the Government has already incurred.

Nevertheless, Republicans in the Congress have resorted to extraordinary tactics to try to force their extreme budget and priorities into law. In essence, they have said they will not pass legislation to let the Government pay its bills unless I accept their extreme, misguided priorities.

This is an unacceptable choice, and I must veto this legislation.

The Administration also strongly opposes the addition of extraneous provisions on this bill. Items like habeas corpus and regulatory reform are matters that should be considered and debated separately. Extraneous issues of this kind have no place in this bill.

The Congress should pass a clean bill that I can sign. With that in mind, I am sending the Congress a measure to raise the permanent debt limit to $5.5 trillion as the Congress called for in the budget resolution, without any extraneous provisions.

WILLIAM J. CLINTON

The White House
November 13, 1995.

Message to the Congress Transmitting Proposed Temporary Public Debt Limit Increase Legislation
November 13, 1995

To the Congress of the United States:

In disapproving H.R. 2586, a bill that would have, among other things, provided for a temporary increase in the public debt, I stated my desire to approve promptly a simple increase in the debt limit. Accordingly, I am forwarding the enclosed legislation that would provide for such an increase.

I urge the Congress to act on this legislation promptly and to return it to me for signing.

WILLIAM J. CLINTON

The White House,
November 13, 1995.

Remarks to the Democratic Leadership Council
November 13, 1995

Thank you very much, Senator Lieberman, for your work, your example, and your wonderful introduction. You know, I knew 25 years ago when I worked for that guy that I'd have a big payoff some day. [*Laughter*] Thank you, Al From, for your long and devoted work for the DLC, to you and all the other staff members, to the other leaders of the DLC who are here, my good friends Senator Robb and Governor Romer. I see Congressman McCurdy and others in the crowd who have worked so hard for this organization for so many years.

A week ago today I was in Israel, representing America at the funeral of Prime Minister Rabin. As I reflected on the terrible events that took his life, it was clear to me, again, how in the world of the global village, the post-cold-war world, the information technology age, we are both coming together and coming apart. Precisely because Prime Minister Rabin tried to unite his portion of the world in peace, an assassin took his life.

Last night I went to Ford's Theatre for its annual benefit performance. And as I looked at the balcony where President Lincoln lost his life to an assassin, because he was determined to preserve the Union and end slavery, I was struck by the fact that the entire history of our great land has been dominated by three great ideas: love of liberty, belief in progress, and the struggle to find common ground.

We have worked throughout this entire life of our country to make our motto, *E Pluribus Unum*, from many, one, more than a slogan; instead, a driving force of unity and of strength. We have now to face the fact that we cannot achieve the first two objectives, liberty and freedom or progress and prosperity, unless we can achieve the third, common ground.

We established in our country a Constitution and a rule of laws, limitations of powers, separation of powers, authority at the State and local level. All these things were designed to give us a way to resolve or differences in a lawful, reconciling manner so that we could preserve our liberty and always make progress. It's worked pretty well for us for well over 200 years now.

If you look at the world and the problems it faces and you look at home and the problems we face, it is clear that the responsibility of the United States today is to lead the world away from division, to show the world that the center can hold, that a free and diverse people, through democratic means, can form a lasting union. This is the challenge of our time and our responsibility as Americans.

That is, in a larger sense, why you and I joined the Democratic Leadership Council. We knew that to keep America strong, the old ways of governing would have to be abandoned. We wanted a Government committed to standing up for the values and interests of ordinary Americans, a Government that offers more opportunity with less bureaucracy, that insists on responsibility from all its citizens, that strengthens our sense of community, the idea that we are all in this together and that everyone counts.

I ran for President in 1992 to restore the American dream for all our people, to bring the American people together, and to assure that America would remain the world's strongest force for peace and freedom, democracy and prosperity, into the 21st century. I have pressed that vision with a simple strategy rooted in economic growth, commonsense Government, and mainstream values. And my fellow Americans, this country is in better shape than it was 3 years ago.

Of course, we still have formidable challenges. But America is on the move. We passed our economic plan, and when we did, our critics said it would bring on a deep recession. But they were wrong. Today the economy is growing. The American people have produced 7½

million new jobs, a 15-year high in home ownership, an all-time high in new business formation, and the lowest combined rates of inflation and unemployment in 25 years. It is a good thing for the country.

A child born today has a better chance of going to college and getting a good job. It's a little easier for people to be good parents and good workers. The infant mortality rate is at an all-time low. Every day there are more opportunities for more Americans to tap into the technological marvels of the information economy and to build a prosperous future.

Commonsense Government is moving forward, thanks in no small measure to the DLC members who have come to work at the White House. According to the Office of Management and Budget this morning, there are now 200,000 fewer people working for the United States Government than on the day I became President. And I might say, almost no Americans have noticed that for two very good reasons. One is, as an employer the United States treated the Federal employees with dignity and respect, with genuinely good severance packages and early retirement packages. And I am proud of that. We didn't just throw those people into the street. The second is that the Federal employees who stayed behind working for you are doing more with less, and they deserve our respect and appreciation. If no one noticed that 200,000 are gone, it's because those who are left are doing their jobs better. And I'm proud of that.

It is not only true that we are now moving quickly to the smallest Federal Government we have had since President Kennedy was here, but listen to this: Today, Federal employees are a smaller percentage of the civilian work force than at any time since 1933, before the New Deal. That is an astonishing statistic. Does it mean that Government still never does anything it shouldn't or that there's never a regulation that doesn't make sense? No, it doesn't, but it means that the Democrats have taken the lead in reducing the deficit and reducing the burden of unnecessary Government, while keeping a Government strong enough to advance our values and our interests. That is our mission, and we are achieving it, and you should be proud of it.

This country is stronger and safer. For the first time since the dawn of the nuclear age, there is not a single nuclear missile pointed at an American child. And from Northern Ireland to Haiti to the Middle East, the United States is leading the world to peace.

Now, we are working for peace in Bosnia, to stop the slaughter of innocents, to prevent the war from spreading, to bring real peace to Europe. Our military might, through NATO, stopped the Bosnian-Serb attacks on the safe areas. Our mediators helped the parties to reach a cease-fire and agree on principles of a settlement and now to come to Dayton, Ohio, to forge a lasting peace. If this peace is achieved, my fellow Americans, our responsibility does not end, for NATO must help to secure it, and as NATO's leader, the United States must participate.

The war of ethnic and religious hatred in Bosnia strikes at the heart of our ideal. It's the sort of thing that led to hatred in the hearts of people in the Middle East and cost Prime Minister Rabin his life. It's the sort of thing that cost Abraham Lincoln his life. We have to, we have to, stand against this.

It's convenient now to forget, but there was a time when Bosnia, too, found unity in its diversity, when Sarajevo was one of the most beautiful and peaceful multiethnic cities in all of Europe. It can happen again if we stand up for our principles and stand up for our interests, if we are willing to be leaders for peace.

That responsibility extends to the other threats in the world today that are related to racial and ethnic and religious divisions, especially to terrorism. Just this morning, the terrorist attacks against American citizens in Saudi Arabia provided a brutal reminder that our people are not immune, not immune here at home as we learned at the World Trade Center and Oklahoma City and not immune abroad.

Our thoughts and prayers are with the victims and their loved ones at this time of their loss. We owe it to them and to all of our citizens to increase our efforts to deter terrorism, to make sure that those responsible for this hideous act are brought to justice, to intensify and pressure the isolation of countries that support terrorism. And we must spare no effort to make sure our own law enforcement officials have what they need to protect our citizens. That's why, even before Oklahoma City, I sent legislation to Capitol Hill asking for additional resources to deal with the threat of terrorism. The Senate passed the bill quickly, but the bill has stalled for months and months in the House.

I ask again for the House of Representatives to pass the antiterrorism legislation.

Just as we try to advance our principles abroad, we know we have, first and more importantly, to stand by them at home. Our Nation is coming together around traditional values even as we move forward economically and try to bring more common sense to our Government. All across America though they are still too high, the American people should know that the crime rate is down, the welfare rolls and food stamp rolls are down, teen pregnancy has dropped for 2 years in a row, and for the first time in more than a decade, the poverty rate is down.

We still have a lot to do; you know that better than anyone. And I encourage the development of the new ideas that you are pushing, how you are going beyond what we are advocating now in the "GI bill" of rights and tax benefits for childrearing and education. I encourage this project.

There are still too many people who are in trouble. There are too many young people without parents or others to teach them right from wrong who are turning to drugs and to violence. There are too many places in our country that still have both too little opportunity and too little responsibility. But we are coming together.

And I'm proud of what we did in the administration with welfare reform efforts to support 35 States, with the crime bill that Senator Lieberman mentioned, with a 40 percent increase in child support collections, and a cut in the student loan default rate by 50 percent since this administration took office. I am proud of that.

My fellow Americans, we have to see this debate about the budget in the context of the remarks I have just made. This is a very great country. No one is so well-positioned for the 21st century as the United States, as long as we stick to our strategy of economic growth, commonsense Government, and mainstream values. There is no country so well-positioned.

But we now have to make a fundamental choice. In 1992, most voters believed the choice was between an active approach to our problems and a more passive one. Today in the budget debate you see two very different active approaches to America's challenges. We face a choice that will be a test of our values, a test of our vision, a choice that goes to the very heart of our identity as a nation and to the very core of the future we will chart.

What is the vision of the congressional Republicans as manifest in their budget? Their budget would render our Government incapable of supporting our values and advancing our common interests. It is bereft of the simple understanding that we rise or fall together. They would support policies that would make us far more a divided, winner-take-all society, a community with fewer connections and less common purpose, in which we say to all Americans without regard to opportunity or obligation, fend for yourselves.

Ours is a vastly different vision. We know Government cannot do everything. We know there is not a program for every problem. We know we should not ask Government to do for people what they ought to be doing for themselves. We know more must be done at the State and local level and in partnership with private citizens. But we know our Government has fundamental responsibilities to lead, to act, to move forward.

We know that the Government of the 21st century must be a constant challenge to our people to seize opportunities and assume responsibilities. We know that, above all, we must give people the tools, the skills, the opportunities they need to make the most of their own lives, not through a one-size-fits-all, old-style bureaucracy but by liberating the creative energies of millions and millions of Americans in their homes, their businesses, their schools, and their communities. This must be the vision that animates our Nation. We don't want a winner-take-all society. We want a society in which all have a chance to win together.

I think it is very important that you understand that this great debate in Washington is not, is not, about balancing the budget. It is about balancing our values as a people. The American people want and deserve a balanced budget. Since I took the oath of office, we have cut the Federal deficit in half. And listen to this: When I became President, we had the highest deficit we've had ever. And the prospect was for it getting larger. Today, today, the United States of America has the smallest deficit of any industrialized country in the world except Norway. Every other country has a deficit that is a larger percentage of its income than we do. You should be proud of that, my fellow Democrats, and I am, too.

Five months ago, I proposed a balanced budget that eliminates the deficit, cuts hundreds of wasteful and outdated programs, but preserves Medicare and Medicaid, invests in education, technology, and research, protects the environment, and defends and strengthens working families. And it maintains the ability of the United States to lead the world toward peace and freedom and democracy and prosperity. My budget reflects those values and fulfills our interests. The Republican congressional budget simply does not.

I believe we have a duty to care for our parents so that they can live their lives in dignity. That duty includes securing Medicare, slowing the rate of growth of inflation, protecting our senior citizens and giving them every opportunity to maximize the options that are out there.

But the Republican budget rests on massive cuts, 3 times bigger than any previous ones in our history, designed apparently to let the system wither away. We believe our children should have the opportunity to make the most of their own lives. We think schools should be run by teachers and principals, not by bureaucrats in the central office or in Washington, DC. But the Republican budget slashes college scholarships and college loans, funds to cut class size and provide computers, and rewards schools which agree to be held accountable for meeting the highest standards, in direct contradiction to the work that Democrats and Republicans have done to establish national education goals, high standards, and more accountability, the things that Governor Romer has led this country in for 5 or 6 years. The last Congress was supporting that direction; this budget would undermine it.

We believe we have a duty to preserve God's Earth for future generations. We are committed to reform so that environmental protection doesn't trap business in a tangle of redtape. And indeed, we are now reducing by 25 percent the time businesses have to spend in filling out compliance forms with the EPA. But we must not, we must not, abandon our commitment to clean air, clean water, safe drinking water, safe food. These things are at the core of the quality of life we owe to ourselves and, most important, to our future.

And we believe, as Senator Lieberman says, that we should not tax working people into poverty. The working family tax cut is something the DLC supported for years. But I want to make it clear that we were building on an idea supported by Republicans at least as much as Democrats.

President Ford signed the earned-income tax credit into law. President Reagan said it was the best antipoverty program ever designed because it rewarded work. It was increased under President Bush. The DLC idea was simple. We would simply double it so we could say to everybody in America, "If you are willing to work 40 hours a week and you have children in the home, you will not be in poverty. Therefore, there is no incentive to be on welfare. Move to work. Your tax system will not put you in poverty; it will lift you out of it." That is what we did, and it was the right thing to do.

Now, the Republican budget would cut the tax credit by even more than we raised it, raising taxes on 17 million working families, rising to an average of $574 a year for families with two or more children. If you've got a breadwinner out there trying to feed two children on $12,000 a year or $13,000 a year, $574 is a lot of money. And it is wrong, and I will fight it.

I support a balanced budget, but I oppose the Republican budget plan. I had looked forward to working with this Congress to achieve a balanced budget consistent with our values and consistent with our obligation to keep this economy growing. This week, instead of following a path of reconciliation, they have gone their own way and brought the Government to the brink of two serious problems.

They're following a strategy announced by the Speaker last April. In an unprecedented move, they have passed one bill and sent it to me and apparently are about to send another that say that we will keep the Government going and we will raise the debt limit so America can meet its financial obligations, if and only if, we can in this interim legislation increase Medicare premiums on all senior citizens by 25 percent, have deep cuts in education and the environment, and repeal 30 years of bipartisan Republican and Democratic commitments to protect the environment and the public health in ways that will increase pollution and decrease support for clean air, clean water, and safe food. This is irresponsible, and it is wrong.

For example, if Congress forces the Government to default on its obligations and interest costs rise, they will rise for Government, thereby undermining the ability of the Republicans to meet their balanced budget targets. One-tenth of one percent interest rate increase adds $42 billion to the deficit over a 10-year period. But interest rates would also rise for businesses and for the 10 million American homeowners whose variable mortgage rates are tied to Federal interests rates and for consumers.

Here we are trying to drive interest rates down so we can keep the economic recovery going. That is what we should be doing, not putting a ball and chain on every American who is trying to soar in the global economy.

The Republican Congress has said to me with brutal simplicity, "You will sign our cuts in Medicare, education, the environment, or we will shut the Government down. You will agree to support our budget and all of its major elements. You will agree to support what we have called regulatory reform, repealing 30 years of bipartisan commitment to a clean environment and a safe food supply or we will push the Government into default."

Well, America doesn't respond very well to those kind of pressure tactics. It's no way to find common ground. So this morning, just before I came here, I vetoed their bill on the debt ceiling. [*Applause*] Thank you very much. I did not relish doing this. My job as President is to take care of the American people. And I have done my best to take good care of this country. We are safer. We are more secure. We are more prosperous. We have a Government that helps more and costs less in the last 3 years. That is what I am for America.

But in the end, what we stand for, the values we embrace, and the things we fight for will shape the future that we will all live with. I will do everything I can to minimize disruption in these next several days. There are limits to what we can do until Congress does its job and allows us to resolve our budget differences in a forthright manner.

But I was elected President to restore the American dream for all of our people, to keep our Nation the strongest in the world and to bring our people together. I cannot and will not under pressure sign a budget that will rob the American dream for millions of Americans, divide our people instead of uniting them, and undermine our ability to remain the strongest Nation in the world and the greatest force for those things we believe in.

You have to understand what is going on here. The strategy that was adopted and announced last April was to precipitate this crisis in the hope of forcing me to accept the budget and the other priorities in their contract. They have not done the normal work of budgeting.

Here we are, 6 weeks into the new budget year, 6 weeks into the new budget year, and this Congress has only passed 3 of the 13 required budget bills. The Senate and the House have each passed balanced budget plans, which I find objectionable but which are different from one another, and they have not met, resolved their differences, and sent it to me.

The Founding Fathers set up a system to deal with this. The Congress passes bills. The President signs or vetoes them. Then the Congress can either override the veto or work with the President to find a bill that either the President will sign or they can get two-thirds of the Congress to support so they can override the veto. That is the wisdom of the Founding Fathers. This strategy is nothing more or less than an attempt to evade that system.

As long as they insist on plunging ahead with a budget that violates our values in a process that is characterized more by pressure than constitutional practice, I will fight it. I am fighting it today. I will fight it tomorrow. I will fight it next week and next month. I will fight it until we get a budget that is fair to all Americans. [*Applause*] Thank you.

And let me say to you that I am honored to have been given the opportunity to wage this contest, to stand up for the values and the interests of ordinary Americans. And I ask you to think about this, as I close, in two ways. This struggle is about things that the Founding Fathers knew we would always have to face, so it is as old as our history. It is also about our challenge as Americans and as leaders in the world moving to the 21st century.

Our Founding Fathers had this dream that people of different religious backgrounds and beliefs could build a strong nation together. They knew it was flawed. Thomas Jefferson knew it was flawed on slavery. But they set up a system where we could just keep working on it, year-in and year-out, decade-in a decade-out, as we work through the problems and became better and fashioned a life that was a

purer and purer and purer example of the values which they enshrined.

We are now called upon to be faithful to the vision of our Founders, the vision that Andrew Jackson had that true and lasting prosperity rests on equal opportunity for all and special privileges for none; the wisdom of Abraham Lincoln that a house divided against itself cannot stand; the wisdom of Theodore Roosevelt that the heritage of America is in no small measure the heritage of the natural resources and bounty that God gifted us with here in our own land.

This is also the challenge of the modern times. The forces of integration which offer so much hope are pitted against the forces of disintegration: the people who killed Americans in Iraq; the fanatic who killed that brave and good Prime Minister in Israel, our partner for peace; the people who everywhere would sow discord over harmony.

At the end of this month, I hope I will be going to Great Britain and to Ireland to do what I can to continue to further the peace process there. How many people have died in Ireland in the 20th century because of hatred and division—religious hatred and division? In his great poem, "The Second Coming," about the Irish civil war, William Butler Yeats said this: Things fall apart. The center cannot hold. Mere anarchy is loosed upon the world. The blood-dimmed tide is loosed, and everywhere the ceremony of innocence is drowned. The best lack all conviction, while the worst are full of passionate intensity.

My fellow Americans, we have worked too hard for too long to bring our country to this point. If we have our convictions and we stand for them firmly, reasonably, responsibly, if we hold out our hands in cooperation but always stand up for what we know is right, this country's future will be even brighter than its brilliant past. It is our responsibility to make that happen.

Thank you, and God bless you all.

NOTE: The President spoke at 10:50 a.m. at the Washington Convention Center. In his remarks, he referred to Senator Joseph Lieberman, chairman, and Al From, president, Democratic Leadership Council.

Teleconference Remarks to the New England Regional Health Care Conference
November 13, 1995

The President. I want to thank you for joining me on the conference call to talk about the proposed Medicare and Medicaid cuts in the congressional budget. And I want to apologize for not coming to Lawrence Memorial today, but I know you understand why I couldn't come.

Let me just begin by emphasizing again, the answer is not—excuse me, the question here in Washington we're debating is not whether we will balance the budget but how. I've been working for 3 years to eliminate this deficit, and we've gone from having one of the largest deficits in the world to the point now where our budget deficit today is the smallest of any industrialized nation in the world as a percentage of our income, except for Norway. Every other country has a higher deficit.

So I want to finish the job. But it seems to me clear that if you look at how the American economy is doing and if you look at how we're beginning to come to grips with some of our most serious social problems under the system we're now operating under, it would be a great mistake to have a dramatic departure that would eliminate the deficit by undermining our values and our interests, including our obligations to our parents and our children in the area of health care.

So I want to balance the budget. I want to strengthen the Medicare Trust Fund. But I don't want to destroy Medicare or Medicaid. And that's what I want to emphasize today. I believe that the proposed congressional budget, with $440 billion in reductions in Medicare and Medicaid over the next 7 years, would have quite harmful consequences. Eight million Americans could lose their Medicaid coverage. People on Medicare will be forced to pay more, whether they can afford it or not. And the people who choose to stay in the Medicare program may have a program that doesn't meet their fundamental needs.

And of course, I'm very worried about what's going to happen to hospitals and nursing homes, teaching hospitals, children's hospitals. These are the concerns that I have. And what I wanted to do today in person with you we'll now have to do over the telephone, but I want to just

give all of you the chance to just specifically talk about, from your personal experience, what do you think is likely to happen here? And we'll start with our host, Charles Johnson. And let me again apologize for not being there with you. But I appreciate you taking this call, and I'd like for you to go first and comment.

Charles Johnson. Well, thank you very much, Mr. President. I appreciate that. And needless to say, we were very disappointed that you weren't coming, but we certainly understand.

The President. Give me a raincheck.

[*At this point, Mr. Johnson, president, Lawrence Memorial Hospital of Medford, thanked the President for his leadership on health care issues and explained how proposed Medicare and Medicaid cuts would affect the hospital and its patients.*]

The President. Well, thank you, sir. I just wanted to emphasize a couple of things, since you said what you did, that the medical community, the health care community in America has recognized that we can't go on for another 10 years with the costs of Medicare and Medicaid going up as much as they have in the previous 10 years.

On the other hand, as you know better than anyone, there are changes now occurring every day which are bringing the inflation rate down. Last year, for the first time in a decade, private insurance premiums went up less than the rate of inflation. And if together we can continue to manage these changes in a responsible way, then the inflation in health care costs will come down, but they will come down as people in the health care sector of our economy learn to cope and to find other options for dealing with these problems so that we won't say, "Well, we're going to cut an arbitrary amount of money, and we don't care about the consequences."

That's what our plan is focused on. It's focused on giving people more choices, more options, including giving hospitals and doctors the options to do some more participation in managed care options. But I also think we have to leave these seniors with a good, vital, vibrant

Medicare program that operates in the way the present one does. After all, it has lower administrative costs than any private insurance plan, and the inflation per Medicare recipient has not gone up more than the general rate of inflation in health care.

So I think we need to give you the chance to keep dealing with and implementing the changes that we've got. We need to give you some more options. But I think you've made it clear that just to pick an arbitrary number like this without any knowledge that it can be reached is a hazardous undertaking.

Mr. Hall?

Philo Hall. Yes, Mr. President.

The President. Perhaps you'd like to comment. I know that you live in a State like my home State that has an awful lot of people in small towns and rural areas. And I can tell you from 15 years of experience, I know what a hard time real hospitals had just staying open in the eighties and meeting all of the needs of their people, and I know what kinds of changes you must have already undertaken. But perhaps you could talk a little about the impact of Medicare and Medicaid on your hospital.

[*Mr. Hall, president, Central Vermont Medical Center, Berlin, VT, explained that Medicare and Medicaid paid about 75 percent of the hospital's costs and the proposed cuts would force the hospital to make drastic changes, including increased cost-shifting, to avoid closing.*]

The President. Thank you very much. You've made a very important point that I want to emphasize because I think it's been lost in this debate a little bit over the understandable concentration of what's in the Federal budget, and that is that if we move too far too fast and we put a lot of these hospitals at risk, one of two things is going to happen. Since there are plainly limits to how much more money can be taken out of the Medicare and Medicaid population, either the hospitals won't have the money they need to stay open and they'll close, which will cause a lot of disruption and a cost to our society far greater than any benefit to these cuts, or you will have to cost-shift onto people with private insurance, which will aggravate a problem that already exists where a lot of private employers and their employees are paying more than they should today.

And if that happens, in the end that's a defeating strategy, too, because as I'm sure you know, we have a million Americans a year in working families who are losing their health insurance because their employers can't afford to maintain it. Now that we have inflation coming down in private health insurance premiums and we've got—we're trying to steer more and more of the smaller employees into big buying pools so they can buy competitive insurance at competitive rates, it would be a terrible mistake to do something that we know will accelerate the number of Americans losing their health insurance.

This is the only advanced country in the world where more people are losing their health insurance every year and there are a smaller percentage of people who are non-seniors—that is, who don't have Medicare—smaller percentage of people with health insurance today than there were 10 years ago. And I really appreciate your saying that because that's an important thing, that we've lost too much. This is not just something that will affect the senior population or the poor. It will affect the middle class who have health insurance for the very reason you said. And I appreciate that.

I'd like to go on now to Barbara Corey, who is a senior activist with the Quabbin Community Coalition in Petersham, Massachusetts. And Barbara, you're on the line——

Barbara Corey. Yes, I am, Mr. President.

The President. ——and I wish you would talk to us about what you think the impact of these cuts will be on the people you represent.

[*Ms. Corey said that most Medicare and Medicaid recipients were hard-working people in need of a helping hand and that tax breaks for the wealthy and cuts in these services would be detrimental to hospitals and patients.*]

The President. Thank you very much. I'd like to just sort of emphasize one of the things you said there, and that is that I don't think many Americans yet, unless they have parents who relied on Medicare and Medicaid, have really grasped the fact that there are an enormous percentage of these seniors out here who have a decent life——

Ms. Corey. That's right.

The President. ——on a low income, only because of Social Security and Medicare——

Ms. Corey. That's right.

The President. ——and that we have to make sure that as we lower the rate of increase in Medicare that we're doing it in a fair way. And

$400 a month is not a lot to live on, but there are—there are not just a few, there are millions and millions of seniors out there living on that.

Ms. Corey. That's right. That's right. Good people. And real people.

The President. And their children.

Ms. Corey. Absolutely. And you're right when you talk about the fact that it's all the generations. It's the elderly population's children that are going to be devastated by this as well. It's a tough time.

The President. It is a tough time. But the other thing I'd like to emphasize on this is that we don't have to do this. That's another thing I'd like to say.

Ms. Corey. That's right.

The President. We are succeeding in slowing the rate of medical inflation.

Ms. Corey. Exactly.

The President. Creative people, not the Government, but all these creative people out here working together, in the hospitals, in the nursing homes, are finding ways to lower costs. We can do this. But if we go too far too fast, we're going to hurt not just the elderly, but we're going to hurt their children and their children's children. You think about all the middle class children of these folks in the nursing homes, just for example, or the—[*inaudible*]—premiums double. All the money they then have to give to their parents is money they won't be able to invest in their children's education.

So this is not just an elderly issue. This is an issue for all Americans, and it's not just a poor person's issue, it's a middle class issue.

Ms. Corey. Exactly, exactly. And I'm grateful to you for the concerns that you're showing.

The President. Thank you so much.

I'd like to ask Alan Solomont, whom I've known for some years now and who does a very good job in running a significant number of nursing homes, to talk a little bit about the impact of these cuts on his employees and perhaps on the quality of service that the patients get.

What do you think is going to happen with the Medicaid cuts? We've heard a lot about Medicare and not so much about Medicaid, perhaps because the program's not as familiar to the American people, so maybe you could talk a little about that, Alan.

[*Mr. Solomont, president, ADS Group, Andover, MA, explained that proposed cuts would ad-versely affect middle class families who depended on Medicaid to help them take care of their elderly parents, as well as causing the quality of care in nursing homes to decline and many employees to lose their jobs.*]

The President. Thank you very much. And I want to thank you and your employees, through you, for the quality of care you are providing. You know, I'm old enough to remember now—and I've been involved in public life for about 20 years now—I remember what nursing homes were like when there was no Medicaid investment and no standards. And we've seen a combination of appropriate standards and better investment over the last 20 years and a dramatic increase in the professionalization of the care in nursing homes. And that's something, I think—I'd just like to ask all of our country men and women who are old enough to remember this, to remember what it was like before this sort of thing happened.

And we now have—we're a fortunate nation. We're getting older. We're living longer. We can look forward to longer lives. But the fastest growing group of Americans are people over 80. And there is no quick or easy way to avoid the fact that we need to be providing adequate, appropriate levels of care. And as you well know, a lot of people in nursing homes have done all kinds of things to be more efficient, forming partnerships with hospitals, having boarding homes, doing more—sometimes doing more home health care. But in the end, there are people who need to be in the homes, and they need to be properly cared for.

I also appreciate what you said about the people you're hiring. The Republican Congress and I, we both say we want to move more people from welfare to work. If you look at the realistic options for moving people from welfare to work, among those are in the caring profession, particularly moving into nursing homes or, on the other end of the age spectrum, into child care, into helping our young children.

When I was Governor, I sponsored a whole program to try to create more child care training slots and put child care centers in our training schools so that—our technical schools—so that welfare mothers could begin to get jobs there, and then the nursing homes were hiring them when they got out of the training program.

These are the kinds of things that we have to do. So if we expect to have welfare reform, we have to have jobs for these people when they get out. And we need these jobs in the caring professions. And we will need more of them, not fewer of them, as time goes on.

There again, I would say, that's why you don't want to cut too much too fast before you know what the consequences will be, because we do not know—these budget numbers were basically plucked out of thin air once they decided that they were going to have a 7 year balanced budget with unrealistic economic assumptions and a $250 billion tax cut. We ought to put health first and say, how are we going to lower the rate of inflation? That's what I tried to do in the budget that I presented.

So I thank you for what you said, because I think it's important that people focus on these employees as well as on the fact that, you know, this budget will not repeal demographic trends in the United States.

Mr. Solomont. That's right.

The President. People over 80 continue to be the fastest growing group of our population.

Mr. Solomont. Absolutely.

The President. Mr. McDowell?

[*Donald McDowell, president, Maine Medical Center, Portland, ME, explained that cuts in Medicare and Medicaid would jeopardize community access to health care. He then stated that the health care industry must be given the freedom to restructure the health care system and that the State of Maine must receive financial assistance to attract medical students who would later practice in the State.*]

The President. Thank you. I'd just like to make two comments, one hopeful and one sort of on the lines we're talking about here. The hopeful comment is that I do believe this is one area where we can reach agreement with the Congress. I have long advocated changes in the present law which would permit doctors and hospitals to have the flexibility they need to establish their managed care networks and to provide the most cost-effective direct way to provide these kinds of services to patients. So I think that in the end, we might be able to get some very good legislation on that, and I am encouraged by that. I do think that we'll have broad agreement on that.

But again, I go back to the point you made about doctors staying where they're trained. It's not just that. You know, in my rural State, when I worked for years and years to get doctors

out all across the State and we had all kinds of regional educational programs and outreach programs and rural training programs, we also found that doctors simply would not stay where they did not have adequate support.

So if there is no hospital, if they don't have that clinical support, if they don't have the things that make it possible for them to know they can succeed in family practice, you may wind up with a serious doctor shortage no matter where you train them. And so, that's another argument for making sure that before we just kind of jump off a cliff here, we know exactly what we're doing and that we're going to have the necessary physician network out there in rural America.

Mr. McDowell. I think those that say that we have too many doctors in America need to visit Aroostook County, Maine.

The President. You've got it. No rural resident of the United States believes that we have too many family practitioners in this country and out there serving people, and I appreciate you saying that.

Mr. MacLeod?

[*Leslie MacLeod, president, Huggins Hospital, Wolfeboro, NH, explained that proposed Medicare and Medicaid cuts would have a great impact on New Hampshire hospitals and the surrounding communities. He then stated that senior citizens who had worked hard to build the Nation should not bear the major burden of cutting costs.*]

The President. Thank you for making that point. You know, I just have two observations about what you just said. First of all, I have been impressed by the extent to which seniors all over the country are willing to do their part to try to help this country slow the rate of medical inflation and make sure that we have money to invest in education and technology and the future of the country. But they just don't want to be asked to jump off a cliff, to go into a forest with no path to the other side. And that's what I think we're all concerned about.

When I went to Florida a few weeks ago, I was so impressed by the willingness of the seniors there to try to, based on their own personal experience, to suggest ways that we might reduce costs. But no one, no serious student of this subject believes that cuts of this magnitude can be absorbed without serious adverse consequences, both to the seniors and the health care system. And I think that's—you have articulately said why that's not fair.

The other point I want to emphasize, because there will be people all across America who will read about this, is that these comments are coming in part from people who come from the three northeasternmost States in our country, Maine, Vermont, and New Hampshire, where Yankee frugality is still alive and well, where people don't want a big Federal Government, where they want the budget balanced, where they expect us to stop wasting money. But it's important that we recognize that Yankee frugality is something that is consistent with living by basic values.

And I want to say again, we've reduced the size of this Federal Government by 200,000 people since I've been President. And as a percentage of the civilian work force, your Federal Government is now the smallest it's been since 1933, as a percentage of the work force. We are bringing down the Government. But we're doing it in a disciplined way that has—frankly, almost no one in America has noticed that we've downsized it this much because we've done it in a way that enabled us to maintain services with higher productivity and to treat the Federal employees who left our Federal service with dignity and honor.

That's the way we ought to approach the health care issue. We ought to be able to slow the rate of inflation in ways that people won't notice because we will do it at a pace and in a way that will continue to enhance the quality of health care and meet the challenges that we face. And I think that's what you're all telling me. You think you could do it if people don't throw an arbitrary number at you that no serious student of health care believes can be absorbed.

There's one serious issue we really haven't talked about yet, and I want Dr. Rabkin to wrap up this conversation by dealing with that, the whole issue of medical education and how these programs have worked to further that.

[*Mitchell Rabkin, M.D., president, Beth Israel Hospital, Boston, MA, stated that many Boston academic medical centers which had already reduced operating expenses and employment were concerned that future cuts would affect education, training, and research.*]

The President. Thank you very much. Let me say that I believe that this is the one aspect of this debate that most Americans don't know about, that the Medicare and Medicaid programs over time have been used by the Congress to funnel some extra money to our teaching hospitals, our children's hospitals in the form of the disproportionate share payments, among others, to support medical education and to make sure that the patients are there for the young doctors to treat. And I think that it would be fair to say that not more than 5 or 10 percent of the people in the United States would be aware of that; there's no reason they should be.

But when Congress decided to support medical education in this way, it served as a vital lifeline to keep our medical schools going and doing well and also meeting an important community need. And again, just to cut at this level in this way will really be a blow to the medical schools.

As you well know, we've tightened up on those payments in the last several years anyway. We've tried to practice certain economies. But to put what is clearly the world's finest system of medical education at risk I think would be a grave error. And that's another reason that I don't want to see cuts of this magnitude, because every, every American, even Americans who may never spend a dollar of the Government's money through the Medicare program and certainly may never be eligible for Medicaid, every American has a clear interest in having the best trained doctors in the world. And Medicare and Medicaid have contributed to that and need to be able to continue to contribute to that in an appropriate way. And I thank you.

Dr. Rabkin. Well, thank you, Mr. President.

The President. I thank all of you. I've enjoyed this conversation very much. I wish it had happened face-to-face. And I thank you for your concern and your interest. Just keep speaking up, keep going forward, and we'll keep working here to make sure that we do the right thing.

NOTE: The President spoke at 12:50 p.m. from the Oval Office at the White House to the conference at Lawrence Memorial Hospital of Medford, MA.

Statement on the Terrorist Attack in Riyadh, Saudi Arabia
November 13, 1995

This morning's attack in Riyadh against an American facility is an outrage. Our condolences and prayers go out to the victims and their families. We appreciate the speed and professionalism with which Saudi authorities have responded to this emergency and will work closely with them in identifying those responsible for this cowardly act and bringing them to justice.

Statement on Signing the Energy and Water Development Appropriations Act, 1996
November 13, 1995

Today I have signed into law H.R. 1905, the "Energy and Water Development Appropriations Act, 1996."

I urge the Congress to complete action on the remaining regular FY 1996 appropriations bills and to send them to me in an acceptable form. Last year, the Congress had sent—and I had signed—all 13 appropriations bills by September 30th. Regrettably, this is only the third bill that I have been able to sign for this fiscal year.

The Act provides $19.3 billion in budgetary resources for programs of the Department of Energy, portions of the Departments of Interior and Defense, the Army Corps of Engineers, and several smaller agencies. While the bill does not fully fund my budget requests in a number of programs, the bill provides important funding for many major programs in these agencies.

The bill supports the Administration's proposal to reinvent the Department of Energy to improve the way it serves the American people. The bill provides $6.1 billion for a critical environmental mission to continue working cooperatively with States and all other interested stakeholders to clean up the Department's former weapons production facilities. The bill also fully funds my request for the Department of Energy's Stockpile Stewardship and Management program, assuring the safety and reliability of the nuclear weapons stockpile without nuclear testing. In addition, the bill provides full funding for one of my key science initiatives to enhance the operation and availability of the Department of Energy's science facilities, giving more researchers access to these facilities to conduct more basic and applied research. This is a modest investment that will leverage a significant return from the scientific community.

The enrolled bill provides $4.0 billion for water resources programs at the Corps of Engineers and the Bureau of Reclamation—98 percent of the amount I requested. At the same time, the Congress added 14 unrequested Corps of Engineers new start construction projects that will require over $1.1 billion in total Federal funds to complete, potentially causing delays in ongoing projects. I look forward to maintaining a dialogue with the Congress to formulate a mutually acceptable reinvention strategy for the Corps of Engineers.

I am particularly pleased that the Congress satisfactorily resolved sensitive language issues that the Administration was concerned about, including some cases in which language contained in earlier versions of the bill would have overridden environmental laws.

Again, I urge the Congress to meet its responsibilities by sending me the remaining regular FY 1996 appropriations bills in acceptable form.

WILLIAM J. CLINTON

The White House,
November 13, 1995.

NOTE: H.R. 1905, approved November 13, was assigned Public Law No. 104–46.

Message to the House of Representatives Returning Without Approval Continuing Resolution Legislation
November 13, 1995

To the House of Representatives:

I am returning herewith without my approval H.J. 115, the Second Continuing Resolution for fiscal year 1996.

This legislation would raise Medicare premiums on senior citizens, and deeply cut education and environmental protection, as the cost for keeping the government running. Those are conditions that are not necessary to meet my goal of balancing the budget.

If I signed my name to this bill now, millions of elderly couples all across this country would be forced to sign away $264 more in Medicare premiums next year, premium hikes that are not necessary to balance the budget. If America must close down access to quality education, a clean environment and affordable health care for our seniors, in order to keep the government open, then that price is too high.

We don't need these cuts to balance the budget. And we do not need big cuts in education and the environment to balance the budget. I have proposed a balanced budget without these cuts.

I will continue to fight for my principles: a balanced budget that does not undermine Medicare, education or the environment, and that does not raise taxes on working families. I will not take steps that I believe will weaken our nation, harm our people and limit our future as the cost of temporarily keeping the government open.

I continue to be hopeful that we can find common ground on balancing the budget. With this veto, it is now up to the Congress to take the reasonable and responsible course. They can still avoid a government shutdown.

Congress still has the opportunity to pass clean continuing resolution and debt ceiling bills. These straightforward measures would allow the United States government to keep functioning and meet its obligations, without attempting to force the acceptance of Republican budget priorities.

Indeed, when Congress did not pass the 13 appropriations bills to fund the government for fiscal year 1996 by September 30, we agreed on a fair continuing resolution that kept the Government operating and established a level playing field while Congress completed its work.

Now, more than six weeks later, Congress still has sent me only three bills that I have been able to sign. Indeed, I am pleased to be signing the Energy and Water bill today. This bill is the result of a cooperative effort between my Administration and the Congress. It shows that when we work together, we can produce good legislation.

We can have a fair and open debate about the best way to balance the budget. America can balance the budget without extreme cuts in Medicare, Medicaid, education or the environment—and that is what we must do.

WILLIAM J. CLINTON

The White House,
November 13, 1995.

Remarks on the Federal Government Shutdown
November 14, 1995

Good afternoon. Today, as of noon, almost half of the Federal Government employees are idle. The Government is partially shutting down because Congress has failed to pass the straightforward legislation necessary to keep the Government running without imposing sharp hikes in Medicare premiums and deep cuts in education and the environment.

It is particularly unfortunate that the Republican Congress has brought us to this juncture because, after all, we share a central goal, balancing the Federal budget. We must lift the burden of debt that threatens the future of our children and grandchildren. And we must free up money so that the private sector can invest, create jobs, and our economy can continue its healthy growth.

Since I took office, we have cut the Federal deficit nearly in half. It is important that the people of the United States know that the United States now has proportionately the lowest Government budget deficit of any large industrial nation. We have eliminated 200,000 positions from the Federal bureaucracy since I took office. Our Federal Government is now the smallest percentage of the civilian work force it has been since 1933, before the New Deal. We have made enormous progress, and now we must finish the job.

Let me be clear: We must balance the budget. I proposed to Congress a balanced budget, but Congress refused to enact it. Congress has even refused to give me the line-item veto to help me achieve further deficit reduction. But we must balance this budget without resorting to their priorities, without their unwise cuts in Medicare and Medicaid, in education and the environment.

Five months ago I proposed my balanced budget plan. It balances the budget in the right way. It cuts hundreds of wasteful and outdated programs. But it upholds our fundamental values to provide opportunity, to respect our obligations to our parents and our children, to strengthen families, and to strengthen America because it preserves Medicare and Medicaid, it invests in education and technology, it protects the environment, and it gives the tax cuts to working families for childrearing and for education.

Unfortunately, Republican leaders in Washington have put ideology ahead of common sense and shared values in their pursuit of a budget plan. We can balance the budget without doing what they seek to do. We can balance the budget without the deep cuts in education, without the deep cuts in the environment, without letting Medicare wither on the vine, without imposing tax increases on the hardest pressed working families in America.

I am fighting for a balanced budget that is good for America and consistent with our values. If they'll give me the tools, I'll balance the budget.

I vetoed the spending bill sent to me by Congress last night because America can never accept under pressure what it would not accept

in free and open debate. I strongly believe their budget plan is bad for America. I believe it will undermine opportunity, make it harder for families to do the work that they have to do, weaken our obligations to our parents and our children, and make our country more divided. So I will continue to fight for the right kind of balanced budget.

Remember, the Republicans are following a very explicit strategy announced last April by Speaker Gingrich to use the threat of a Government shutdown to force America to accept their cuts in Medicare and Medicaid, to accept their cuts in education and technology and the environment. Yesterday they sent me legislation that said we will only keep the Government going and we will only let it pay its debts if, and only if, we accept their cuts in Medicare, their cuts in education, their cuts in the environment, and their repeal of 25 years of bipartisan commitments to protect the environment and public health.

On behalf of the American people, I said no. If America has to close down access to education, to a clean environment, to affordable health care to keep our Government open, then the price is too high.

My message to Congress is simple: You say you want to balance the budget, so let's say yes to balancing the budget. But let us together say no to these deep and unwise cuts in education, technology, the environment, Medicare, and Medicaid. Let's say no to raising taxes on the hardest pressed working families in America. These things are not necessary to balance the budget. Yes to balancing the budget; no to the cuts.

I know the loss of Government service will cause disruption in the lives of millions of Americans. We will do our very best to minimize this hardship. But there is, after all, a simple solution to the problem. All Congress has to do is to pass a straightforward bill to let Government perform its duties and pay its debts. Then we can get back to work and resolve our differences over the budget in an open, honest, and straightforward manner.

Before I conclude, I'd like to say a word to the hundreds of thousands of Federal employees who will be affected by this partial shutdown. I know, as your fellow citizens know, that the people who are affected by this shutdown are public servants. They're the people who process our Social Security applications, help our veterans apply for benefits, care for the national parks that are our natural heritage. They conduct the medical research that saves people's lives. They are important to America, and they deserve to be treated with dignity and respect. I will do everything I can to see that they receive back pay and that their families do not suffer because of this.

But it is my solemn responsibility to stand against a budget plan that is bad for America and to stand up for a balanced budget that is good for America. And that is exactly what I intend to do.

Thank you very much.

NOTE: The President spoke at 2:38 p.m. in the Briefing Room at the White House.

Statement on Action To Prevent Default on the Public Debt
November 15, 1995

The Republican Congress has failed to take responsible action to prevent default for the first time in our history and to ensure that the Government can meet its obligations, including paying next month's Social Security benefits. To prevent against default and all of its subsequent harmful consequences, my Secretary of Treasury has been forced today to take extraordinary but necessary actions. I won't allow the Republican Congress to force us into default or put Social Security beneficiaries at risk. If the Republican Congress won't take action to prevent default and protect Social Security recipients, I will.

The President's News Conference
November 16, 1995

The President. Good afternoon. Today the Congress is considering a bill I find objectionable because once again it requires acceptance of the congressional Republican budget as a condition of reopening the Government.

Let me repeat: Holding the Government, the Federal employees, and the millions of Americans who depend upon them hostage to the congressional Republican budget is not the way to do this work. And it won't work, because I will still veto any bill that requires crippling cuts in Medicare, weakens the environment, reduces educational opportunity, or raises taxes on working families.

I have proposed a plan to balance the budget without undermining Medicare and Medicaid, education, the environment, or working families' incomes. If I were to sign their 7-year plan, in effect, I would be approving these cuts. I won't do that because I believe it would be bad for America.

We must balance the budget in a way that doesn't weaken our economy or violate our val-

ues, including providing the opportunity for Americans to make the most of their own lives, helping families to grow stronger and to stay together, strengthening our communities and our country.

Congress should act responsibly and pass a straightforward legislation to open the Government and enable it to meet its financial obligations. They should do it right now. That's what Congresses in the past have done, and that's what this Congress did last September.

The American people should not be held hostage anymore to the Republican budget priorities. So today I am sending Congress straightforward legislation that would reopen the Government without delay and without enacting into law the Republican budget.

We have to get to work on this in a serious way. I will work, I will work, with Congress in good faith to balance the budget. But I want to do it in a way that is good for America. It is not the fault of the Federal employees or the millions of Americans who depend upon them that Congress did not pass a budget for this fiscal year by October 1st, as required by its own laws. And it's time for the Republicans in Congress to stop punishing them for that.

This is a new experience for our country. Congress has never before shut the Government down for an extended period of time. I'm determined to do what I can to reduce the damage to our people. I'm especially concerned that every day 28,000 people apply for Social Security benefits, 10,000 people seek to enroll in Medicare, 7,500 veterans make claims for benefits they are owed.

I asked the Social Security Administration and the Department of Veterans Affairs to examine their operations and see if there are necessary services that can lawfully be provided to the public. As a result of this request, this coming Monday the Social Security Administration and the VA will recall to work additional staff to process applications and claims. If the Government shutdown continues to prevent action to accept applications for Medicare, Social Security, and veterans benefits made by seniors and veterans, this backlog would be so great that service to these citizens would not return to normal for months to come. Our elderly and veterans deserve better, and I believe we are permitted to do better under the law.

Finally, let me say again, let us reopen the budget—the Government. Let's reopen the Government, and then get down to the business of balancing the budget in the right way.

Air Force One

Q. Mr. President, the Speaker has complained about the treatment that he and the other Republican leaders received aboard Air Force One on the flight to and from Israel. Is there any reason that he was treated as shabbily as he says he was? And is that reason for him to put forward a tougher CR than would have normally been the case?

The President. Let me, first of all, say, when, on short notice, the Speaker and Senator Dole, Senator Daschle and Leader Gephardt, two former Presidents, two former Secretaries of State, and 40 Members of Congress of both parties—when all of them agreed to go to Israel to Prime Minister Rabin's funeral, I was very grateful. It was a good thing for Israel, for the Middle East peace process, and for the United States. And I was deeply appreciative of that,

and I told them that on the plane flight going to and from Israel repeatedly.

Now as to your question about whether that is a reason, I don't know. But it seems to be in the atmosphere these days in Washington that we are connecting things together that don't properly belong together. I can tell you this: If it would get the Government open, I'd be glad to tell him I'm sorry. But I was clear in expressing my gratitude to everyone for going. It was an arduous trip. It was hard on them. They did it on short notice, and I was very grateful. And I still think it was a very important thing that they did.

Balanced Budget

Q. Mr. President, all of the numbers that you're arguing about from the OMB and the CBO in the out-years are just educated guesswork anyway, aren't they, and if so, would you agree to balancing the budget in 7 years if some neutral arbitrator, someone with stature like the Fed Chairman, were able to mediate some agreed-on set of numbers?

The President. First of all, I'm not going to make any agreements to do anything that would require me to agree to reductions in Medicare, Medicaid, funds to meet national standards in our schools, or to provide Head Start for our children or scholarships and college loans to people who need them and make the most of their own lives or to undermine the environment. It is clearly not necessary.

I would remind you that when I presented my 10-year balanced budget plan to Congress, which our own people say can now be achieved in 9 years, Chairman Greenspan said it was a perfectly credible budget. And I would also remind you, as Senator Conrad pointed out today with his charts, that if you look at what we did in 1993, we have outstripped what the Congressional Budget Office said we would achieve in our 5-year deficit reduction plan by well over $100 billion.

So the methodology they are using is one no one accepts. And this is not one of those split-the-difference things. I split the difference between all the economic forecasts. I gave a very moderate and disciplined recommendation to the Congress based on the experts. I did not cook the books. Our growth figure for this budget is what the country has grown for the last 25 years. I cannot believe that the Congress seriously believes that if we balance the budget in the right way our economy would grow more slowly in the next 7 years than it has in the last 25 years. Why then would you estimate that? Because that enables you to cut more. I do believe that there is a controlling element with an ideological bias toward cutting education and the environment and making as many cuts as possible in Medicaid and Medicare. But I think that's wrong.

And so I can tell you, I have proved something that they have not yet proved. I have proved that we know how to balance the budget and grow the economy. It was our administration and the Democrats in the Congress that voted for the last deficit reduction plan that has given us the lowest deficit of any large economy in the world, the strongest economy in the world, and a growing economy. We have proved we know how to do it. I am not going to engage in any negotiations now that would possibly compromise the principles that I know are good for America.

Q. Mr. President, Speaker Gingrich has contended now that 7 years is the most effective time period to get a balanced budget. He says he bases that on intuition. What's your current time target? You mentioned several different time targets over the weeks and months, and what do you base that estimate on?

The President. Well, first of all, if you go back to all my comments, with the exception of a comment I made in 1992 on the Larry King show, which we clarified within, I think, 2 days, what I have said is how long it takes to balance the budget obviously depends upon the assumptions you use and the other elements of the budget, how big will the tax cut be, for example. But I can tell you that we believe and we have said that we can implement the plan that I have put forward in 9 years.

What I did—the difference in the way we put our balanced budget together and the way they did is quite stark. That is we both had to have some estimate of how fast they thought the economy would grow and what we thought inflation and health programs would be. But they make it plain that they started with 7 years and started with their $245 billion tax cut and then decided at a totally arbitrary way how much they had to take out of Medicare and Medicaid and these other programs.

That's not what we did. We said, "We have to balance the budget in a reasonable period of time. Here's how much we think the econ-

omy will grow. Now, how much can we cut? How much can we slow the rate of medical inflation in these programs? What can we cut? How can we continue to cut these hundreds and hundreds of programs like we've been cutting for 3 years and still have the investments left we need in educational opportunity, in the environment, in technology and research, and in the health care programs?" That's how we did it.

So we think we balanced the budget consistent with our values and our economic interests instead of the other way around. And therefore—and when I entered into these negotiations that's the way I'll discuss it. There is no magic timeline. You know, if we had 3 percent growth, the budget would be balanced more quickly than any of us calculate.

So this is a—to go back to the earlier question, it's important that the American people understand that this is a multiyear balanced budget plan. The budget is done on a yearly basis.This is a balanced budget plan. And the only thing I want to do is to have a plan that balances the budget consistent with our values and our interests. And I don't think you can discuss one item in isolation with the others. It's not—you can't talk about 7 years in isolation from everything else, or—so we put together our budget from the ground up in the right way. That's the way I'd like for these negotiations to proceed.

House Democrats

Q. Mr. President, are you concerned that you lost 48 House Democrats on the vote last night? They voted with Republicans, putting Republicans within sort of spitting distance of being able to override your veto.

The President. No. I would have been concerned if they made enough for a veto override. But to be fair to those House Democrats, they did—their budget is much closer to mine than the Republican budget, except they don't permit any kind of tax cut at all for working families, for education and childrearing. And as you know, I would like to provide one.

But if you go back and look at what the House Democrats did, they have much lower Medicaid, Medicare, education, and environmental restrictions cuts than the Republican budget, and they do it by having no tax cut at all and a reduction in the CPI. So what they thought was that they ought to say, "We can do it within these frameworks, and we did it before so we want to own up to the fact that we did it before."

But they have no intention, those House Democrats, except for maybe just a handful of them, of supporting the Republican budget. The argument I was making is that their vote would be misinterpreted as an endorsement of the Republican budget framework, which it manifestly was not. So I'm satisfied with the vote and how it came out.

Budget Negotiations

Q. So how do we get out of this mess? Where do we go from here?

The President. Well, I will keep working to find a way to open the Government and permit the budget negotiation to continue. But the American people just need to know, the Federal employees need to know that I believe I would be remiss in agreeing, in effect, to the Republican budget plan as a condition of reopening the Government.

I have demonstrated I want to balance the budget. I have demonstrated I am committed to deficit reduction. We endured a withering array of criticism from the House Republicans from which they benefited in '93 and '94 when they claimed we were going to bring on a recession. And we proved we could reduce the deficit and grow the economy. So I will deal with them in good faith. But I cannot agree to, on the front end, to their budget framework when I know what it really means is big cuts in Medicare, Medicaid, educational opportunity, and the environment. I can't do that.

Now, we will keep working with them in every way we know how, but I'm not going to be pushed into that position because—someone has to stand up here for what's right for America instead of for this exercise of political power.

Q. [*Inaudible*]—there's no room for any compromise on your part, that there's no flexibility? I mean, usually in negotiations——

The President. No, there's—I didn't say that. I didn't say that. There are many elements in this budget which are variable. What I did say was, and what I will say again, is that I don't propose to negotiate away 60 to 70 percent of the budget simply to get a continuing resolution to reopen the Government. And that's what all this is about, an attempt to get the President

to negotiate away a majority of what could be the basis for compromise.

If I ask you to compromise with me, and then you say, "I will compromise with you, but only if you give me 60 percent of what I want on the front end." Then we sit down, and we say, "Okay, let's split the difference." That's a good compromise. You split the difference between 40 percent. You wind up with 80 percent. I wind up with 20. That's what this resolution is all about. And no one should be confused by it.

And if we did it, it would be bad for America. I will not do something I know is bad for our country. That is my responsibility, to try to make sure that all the interests of the country are furthered.

White House Travel Office Verdict

Q. Do you have anything to say, sir, about the acquittal of Billy Dale?

The President. I do. First of all, I think it's clear that there were some problems in the way the Travel Office was run, but there were also clearly some serious problems in the way it was handled by the White House. And all of you will remember we issued quite a self-critical report on how it was handled. And in light of that, I'm very sorry about what Mr. Dale had to go through, and I wish him well. And I hope that now he'll be able to get on with his life and put this behind him.

Q. Will you offer him a job?

Japan-U.S. Relations

Q. What about relations with Japan in the aftermath of your forcing yourself to cancel the visit to the APEC conference and the state visit to Tokyo?

The President. Well, I want to reschedule the trip and take it as soon as I can, because the Japanese-United States relationship is very important. We've had a big increase in our exports to Japan. We've negotiated 15 trade agreements with them, and in each one of these trade agreement areas we've had an even bigger increase in our exports. We're making progress in our economic relationship.

They are going through some tough times. If they weren't having some tough times—some of the things that we went through, frankly, back in the eighties—with their financial system, we'd even be doing better because they'd be doing better. We've had some issues to deal with in our security relationship, but it's still fundamentally strong. And I have the greatest respect for the nation and for its people, and I think all of us know that a strong U.S.-Japan relationship is critical for the world as we move into the 21st century.

So I called Prime Minister Murayama; we had a very good talk. I have already talked to two of the other APEC leaders, President Kim of South Korea, and President Soeharto of Indonesia. I expect at least to talk to the President of China, perhaps some others before the meeting. The Vice President is going to the meeting, and then we'll have a bilateral meeting with Prime Minister Murayama. So we're determined to keep this relationship on track.

I assured him that my absence from Japan has nothing to do with our relationship or my importance—the importance to which that I attach to it. So I think we'll be fine. But we need to—when you say you're going to go visit your neighbor and you have to cancel the visit, you have to reschedule and show up. And I intend to do it.

Thank you.

NOTE: The President's 106th news conference began at 3 p.m. in the Oval Office at the White House. In his remarks, he referred to Prime Minister Tomiichi Murayama of Japan; President Kim Yong-sam of South Korea; and President Jiang Zemin of China.

Statement on Signing the Department of Transportation and Related Agencies Appropriations Act, 1996
November 16, 1995

Last night I signed into law H.R. 2002, the "Department of Transportation and Related Agencies Appropriations Act, 1996."

I urge the Congress to complete action on the remaining regular FY 1996 appropriations bills and to send them to me in acceptable form. Last year, the Congress had sent me—and I had signed—all 13 appropriations bills by September 30. Regrettably, this is only the fourth bill that I have been able to sign for this fiscal year. The Congress has failed to send to me the bills that fund over 88 percent of the discretionary programs of our Government.

The Act provides $36.9 billion in new budgetary resources for programs of the Department of Transportation and several smaller agencies. The bill is consistent with my request in most key areas.

I am particularly pleased that the Congress heeded my calls to increase funding for the Federal Aviation Administration's (FAA's) safety programs over what the Congress had originally proposed. The FAA manages the world's largest and safest aviation system. Nevertheless, Secretary Pena and FAA Administrator Hinson are working to make it safer, both for today and the future. The bill's FAA personnel and procurement reforms, which the Vice President's National Performance Review first proposed,

will contribute greatly to that effort. I encourage the Congress to move quickly on the rest of my comprehensive FAA reform package.

The FAA personnel and procurement reforms contained in the Act will contribute greatly to our safety effort. They permit the FAA to improve its hiring, training, compensation, and relocation practices to better meet its unique personnel needs. They also allow for streamlined contracting practices that will speed up the deployment of new technologies into the field. Both new systems will be developed with the participation of the aviation community, including FAA employees and their representatives. They will build upon, not diminish or redefine, FAA's current beneficial management-labor relationship. While we embrace the FAA personnel and procurement reforms in the Act, we will work with the Congress to ensure that personnel reforms enacted pursuant to any FAA reform legislation must be designed and implemented in consultation with FAA unions, consistent with their continuing role as the representatives of these key members of the Federal workforce.

I am also pleased that the Act provides the fast-track reorganization authority for the Department of Transportation, as I requested, because it will improve service while cutting costs to taxpayers. Secretary Pena and I look forward to working with the Congress as we reform and streamline the Department.

The Act provides funding for most of the Department's high-priority programs. I commend the Congress for not including new earmarked highway demonstration projects; States can better use these funds in determining their transportation infrastructure priorities.

I am disappointed that the Congress did not authorize the restructuring of transportation infrastructure programs, as I proposed, but I look forward to maintaining a dialogue with the Congress about how to best meet States' and local-ities' needs for flexibility to address their future, high-priority transportation needs.

Again, I urge the Congress to meet its responsibilities by sending me the remaining regular FY 1996 appropriations bills in acceptable form.

WILLIAM J. CLINTON

The White House,
November 16, 1995.

NOTE: H.R. 2002, approved November 15, was assigned Public Law No. 104–50.

Message to the Congress Transmitting Proposed Legislation To Compensate Furloughed Federal Government Employees
November 16, 1995

To the Congress of the United States:

In declaring my intention to disapprove House Joint Resolution 122, the further continuing resolution for fiscal year 1996, I stated my desire to approve promptly a clean extension of the continuing resolution that expired on November 13. Accordingly, I am forwarding the enclosed legislation that would provide for such an extension. This legislation also provides that all Federal employees furloughed during the Government shutdown through no fault of their own will be compensated at their ordinary rate for the period of the furlough.

I urge the Congress to act on this legislation promptly and to return it to me for signing.

WILLIAM J. CLINTON

The White House,
November 16, 1995.

NOTE: This message was released by the Office of the Press Secretary on November 17.

Interview With NHK Television of Japan
November 17, 1995

President's Trip to Japan

Q. Thank you very much, Mr. President, for joining us. The Japanese people are greatly disappointed that you have suddenly canceled your visit to Japan. Was it really inevitable?

The President. Yes, it was inevitable. And let me begin by saying that I am greatly disappointed, more disappointed perhaps than I can even convey to you and through you to the Japanese people, to cancel this trip. My first overseas trip as President was to Japan. One of the first actions I took as President was to try to elevate the Asian Pacific Economic Council to a leaders meeting so that we could all work more closely together throughout Asia. And I have had many, many meetings and telephone calls with not only Prime Minister Murayama but his predecessors. When I ran for President, I said the Japanese-American relationship was of supreme importance to the United States. And so I am very, very disappointed.

But I would ask the Japanese people to understand what is happening here. We are having a debate here which will have great implications for the United States for decades to come. And our Government is closed down for the first time in history for this length of time. This is unprecedented. So that if I were to leave the United States now, the American people, and particularly the employees of the Federal Government, would not understand how the President could leave the country while the Government was shut down and when the Congress might be passing bills to me that I would either have to veto, disapprove, or to sign.

I will go to Japan as soon as I possibly can. I look forward to rescheduling this trip. And I can only ask the Japanese people to understand that this has nothing to do with Japan and America's relationship and everything to do with the pressing emergency that I must now deal with.

Q. Mr. President, we all know that you will always come back, even to Japan.

The President. Thank you.

Q. But we would like to know exactly when you will be able to go there. January or——

The President. Well, I don't know. We have begun to look over the calendar. And I have talked this morning with the Vice President. I called him on the airplane. He's on his way—he's almost in Japan. And I talked with Ambassador Kantor this morning, who is in Japan now, again reaffirming my desire to come as quickly as possible.

As I'm sure you know, we're about to begin our Thanksgiving and Christmas season here, a major holiday time—the major holiday time in the United States. And then next year we begin the Congress in early January and all the Presidential primaries. But I will come as soon as I can. This is very, very important to me. And I want—I have conveyed my deep regrets to Prime Minister Murayama, and I appreciate his understanding.

But I—again, I want to say I hope the Japanese people will understand this is no expression of disrespect by me either to the Government or the people of Japan. As a matter of fact, my wife and I had looked very much forward to being with the Emperor and Empress again in the Imperial Palace because we had such a wonderful time with them when they visited us and stayed here. So I'm anxious to have that experience, and I'm looking forward to it.

Q. Any guesstimates as to when—like spring?

The President. I can't say. We're in the middle of this difficulty now, and we have to resolve—see our way through it. And I'm looking at the calendar. I will set the date just as soon as I can. I will come as quickly as I can. But I want to make sure we have a good visit and

we have enough time to do it right. I think it's important when I do come that we have the time to do it right.

Q. But you're going to get busier and busier next year.

The President. Not necessarily. There will be certain down times in our schedule next year. And it doesn't matter, I will put some of my business aside to come to Japan. I would happily put some of my business aside. If it hadn't been for this unprecedented emergency, I would have put this aside.

Okinawa and the Japan-U.S. Security Relationship

Q. Well, your cancellation is especially significant since the Okinawa incident by the three marines, and emotions are running high. And people are starting to question the most—the linchpin of the U.S. security—linchpin of the U.S.-Japan relations, which is the security threat. How would you define the treaty after the cold war, the importance of the treaty?

The President. If I might, I'd like to first say something about the incident at Okinawa. On behalf of the American people, we want the Japanese people to know that we share their outrage and their pain. And I want to express my personal regret and outrage to the family, to the young woman, to all the people of Okinawa. This was—it's a terrible thing. And every father in the world of a young daughter, including the President of the United States, was struck by the incident. The United States, obviously, has cooperated and supported the turning over of the people who were charged. We have tried to improve our procedures for cooperating in these criminal matters, and we will continue to do that. So I feel very strongly about this.

Now, however, I think that, notwithstanding this terrible incident and the end of the cold war, we shouldn't minimize the importance of continuing this partnership. We've had 50 years of relative security in Asia because of the partnership that the United States and Japan have had for security. We still have an unresolved situation on the Korean Peninsula. North Korea has more than a million people under arms. We have an agreement, thanks to the cooperation of Japan and the United States, with China and Russia and others to dismantle North Korea's nuclear program. But it isn't finished yet. And there are many uncertainties in the future.

We also know we're going to have to deal with problems of proliferation of weapons of destruction, of terrorism, of organized crime. Both Japan and the United States have been victimized by terrorism recently. So there are still very compelling reasons for us to maintain our security partnership. We are reviewing that. We want to clarify that in the form of a declaration.

As you know, we have established a high-level committee to review the specifics of our relationship with Japan and particularly the problems in Okinawa. We want to show the people of Okinawa that we can continue to respond to the specific objections. But the need for a security partnership, I think, is still very, very strong. And I hope it will remain one of the real pillars of our relationship.

Q. I think very few people suspect about the need of the continued security partnership between Japan and the United States. But many people think that since the treaty was written 35 years ago based on the conditions prevailing in the Far Fast then, maybe this is a time to review the entire system and check it and modify it if there is a need.

The President. Well, I think—I would say there are two things that I think we should do. First of all, we should make clear to the people of Japan and the United States and all the people in Asia who are affected by this what we believe the security, the common shared security interest and the common values we share are as we look toward the 21st century. Then I also believe that this group of people we have put together to work with your people on the specifics of the relationship within Japan and on Okinawa, that we should finish that and do that over the next year and look at whether there are further things we could do in our operating procedures to accommodate the people of Okinawa, look if there is something we can do in the size and the distribution of our forces on Okinawa, look at the size of the land we occupy and how we occupy it, and then consider whether maybe even we could transfer some of our forces elsewhere in Japan.

You know, there are all these things we need to look at in a very disciplined way. And I think that we will do that. But I don't believe we should, without great discipline and care, just revise a relationship that has plainly contributed to economic growth and political security and stability not only for Japan but for the rest of Asia as well.

Q. What do you think about the Governor of Okinawa, Mr. Ota? You used to be the Governor of Arkansas. I think he is presenting a good case that Okinawa people are having unfair burden by excessive concentration of U.S. bases.

The President. Well, I believe that his concerns have to be carefully considered. You know, we have—for example, in the last few years, we've tried to change our training schedules, reducing the firing of live ammunition, for example, trying to be concerned about the impact of noise on the people of Okinawa. I think that we have to consider his concerns very carefully. And as I said, I think we have to look at what our options are. I think the United States should be openminded about that. I think that we will discuss with the Government of Japan what other options we might have within Japan for pursing this relationship.

But his job as the Governor of Okinawa, like my job when I was a Governor, is to represent the real concerns of the people there who have a right to want to carry on their daily lives, to make the most of their own lives, and to take care of their families. And we should be careful to listen to them and see whether or not we can resolve this. And I believe we can do better.

Q. One more point I want to ask you, Mr. President, is the so-called free-ride argument in the United States. The asymmetry where the United States protects Japan but Japan cannot fight for the United States constitutionally is the course of nation we chose 50 years ago under the guidance of the United States. And Japanese are, to be frank, quite proud of their peace constitution. Is the United Stated growing—becoming dissatisfied with such Japanese course?

The President. I don't think so, for two reasons. First of all, the Japanese people have been willing to bear an appropriate level of cost for the location of our troops in Japan. And we cannot complain about that—and have improved that cost ratio over the last couple of years. And the United States needs to recognize that. Secondly, Japan has become increasingly willing to assume other kinds of global responsibilities. You have been very forthright and strong in Cambodia. You have even committed to help in the reconstruction of Bosnia, a long way from home, and many, many other examples I could cite. So my view is that this is still a fair partnership for security matters. And barring some dramatic change of circumstances, we should try to modify the partnership to meet the demands of this time, not have a dramatic departure from it.

Q. In that sense, Mr. President, do you think Japanese peaceful constitution is still viable for peace?

The President. Well, I believe it is because I believe that one of the things we ought to be trying to do is to get the rest of the world to move toward less armaments. You know, Japan is working with the United States, for example, and we hope we'll be able to persuade the rest of the world to join us in a comprehensive test ban treaty, nuclear test ban treaty, next year. We hope that we'll be able to do more together in the world to reduce the danger of chemical and biological weapons. We worked very hard just a few months ago, Japan and the United States, to get almost 180 countries to join the Nuclear Non-Proliferation Treaty. So our objective in the world should be to reduce the volume, the danger of arms, to reduce the millions of landmines that are in the ground in places that your people in Cambodia have been subject to, for example, not to try to have a massive arms buildup everywhere.

Q. Going back to Okinawa, you sympathized with the burden of the Okinawan people having bases concentrated there. Would you bring a specific package, a concrete proposal, in reducing the bases, the U.S. bases there?

The President. That depends on what the alternatives are. And that's why I think it—for me, I should leave it to our negotiators. I have gotten—I have put a high-level team in place— Mr. Lord, Mr. Nye, and others will be working on this. And I think that they need to see what the options are. I do not know enough to know what the alternative options are to make a specific proposal. All I can say is that I have followed very, very carefully here the specific concerns of the people of Okinawa. And I know what it's like for people to feel that they are being oppressed by those over whom they have no influence. And I don't want that to be the feeling of the people of Okinawa. I want this to be a partnership of which they can be proud as well. And therefore, we're going to work very hard to—in total good faith—to try to resolve this.

Q. Are you in agreement with Secretary Perry when he says that the number of 47,000 U.S.

troops in Japan as a whole will not be reduced? Bases in Okinawa could be withdrawn, but they would have to go somewhere else in Japan— is that your stance?

The President. Well, my feeling is that that is the general consensus not only of the United States but of other nations as well, that we would be sending the wrong signal at this time if we had a substantial reduction in our overall commitment, either in Japan or Korea, that this is the time for stability, for working toward reducing the possibility of any kind of war, any kind of exchange of missiles, any kind of military problem, whatever. And that is what we're trying to do. We believe that there's a consensus among our allies to try to maintain a sense of stability. And we don't want to do anything that could send the wrong signal there.

Asia-U.S. Security Agreement

Q. Do you have a vision as to the post security—post-cold-war security vision in Asia? So far it has mainly been characterized by bilateral relationship with Japan and the U.S., South Korea and the United States. Do you have a vision or a plan that would stabilize that part of the area?

The President. Well, of course, I hope that we will have more and more cooperation with other countries which could lead us, eventually, to regional agreements like the regional trade relationship we're attempting to develop through APEC.

For example, we have had military-to-military contacts with China which we are now resuming. And while we still have some concerns, and we hope the Chinese will issue a white paper on defense and be very forthright about it, the truth is that the Chinese have put most of their emphasis into growing their economy, not growing their military. So we hope that we can see further progress there. There are many issues to be resolved there, as you know, and we saw some of them in the recent flareup of tensions with Taiwan and the testing in that area. But my hope would be that by early in the next century we would see other countries coming forward to work with Japan and work with South Korea so that we can broaden the responsibilities that we all share there.

Q. So you can envision maybe a military exercise together with four or five different countries?

The President. It could well happen. That's what we've tried to do in Europe. In Europe, if I could just draw a parallel, as long as nation-states have existed on the continent of Europe, there's always some sort of political or military division. We are now trying to work with the Europeans to try to create a united Europe for the first time in history through something called the Partnership For Peace, among other things. But the Partnership For Peace is a NATO security partnership.

We've done military training with Russia. We just had, in Kansas, a Russian-United States military training exercise. We have had military exercises in Poland. We have all these countries working together to reinforce each others security, instead of planning to fight with each other. That's what I hope will happen throughout the world.

Japan-U.S. Security Relationship

Q. So I gather you have recognized that U.S.-Japan security treaty has become more important?

The President. Yes. I think it would be a great mistake to think it is less important. If you look at the economic power of Japan and the United States, at the fact that we are both great democracies, at the fact that our—I believe—I know this is not the prevailing opinion, perhaps, but I believe our relationship has grown much stronger in the last few years, just since I've been President because we are now more open about our differences and more steadfast in holding on to our strengths and the things we share. That is the way great democracies have to behave. And I think until we live in a very different world than we now live in, we should maintain our security relationship as well as our economic partnership and our political commitment to democracy and freedom. The things go together, and it's not time to change that.

Japan-U.S. Trade

Q. If I may turn the topic a little bit more to economics. The small, tragic incident in Okinawa flared up into such a major diplomatic incident. Perhaps it is because for the past 2½ years while you have been in office, Japan and United States has been engaged in very severe trade negotiations that maybe—concentration on the economy has brought adverse feelings among us.

The President. Well, you see, I believe that—let's take it back to where we were when I became President. The United States had just experienced the slowest job growth rate we'd had in 4 years, in the last 4 years—since we had a Great Depression—for 60 years. The feelings of resentment in the United States were building up over the enormous trade surplus Japan had in our dealings. And the feeling was that nothing ever happens.

So what I did was to launch a broad-based outreach to Japan to reaffirm the security relationship, to reaffirm our political partnership, to say that ultimately we needed a regional and a global approach to trade. So we had this world leaders meeting at APEC, and Japan and the United States helped to resolve the GATT world trade agreement so we'd have a global trading system. And we had an aggressive approach to our individual bilateral trade differences.

But look what's happened. Because of good-faith efforts in Japan and the United States, we have conducted and completed an unprecedented 20 trade agreements. The Japanese trade surplus with the United States has gone down for 5 months in a row. We have had a big increase in our exports in the 20 areas where we have agreements and overall. And the Japanese, at a time of economic difficulty for Japan, have gotten a wider choice of goods at lower cost. So I believe we are working toward a much stronger and more balanced partnership.

Again, I would say, I would hope the people—there is no American who ever would defend or be insensitive to what happened in Okinawa. We felt the same way about that the Japanese people did. And again, I would say that's why I so much wanted to come now, to say these things directly to the people of Japan. But these trade difficulties should be seen in the context of our long-term partnership. And we are working through difficulties in the way that mature democracies must. So I see it as a plus, not a negative, over time. No one likes to read about conflict or hear about it on the evening news, but conflict is also a part of life—that mature and disciplined people resolve their conflicts in a way that is consistent with their values and the long-term interests of their people. And I believe that's what we're doing.

Q. I think you are right in saying that there have been many economic progresses, but there does seem times the level of inflammatory rhetoric has unfortunately gone up, partly because we lost a common enemy, partly because of our protracted trade imbalance. People are seeing that the "special relationship," quote and unquote, does no longer exist between the two countries. In that case, we have to lower our mutual expectations. What are your comments?

The President. I think that's very wrong, at least in the United States. It's my experience—you know, we have a few politicians here who still engage in inflammatory rhetoric against Japan—but not just Japan. If they—anybody here who engages in inflammatory rhetoric against Japan is probably engaging in inflammatory rhetoric against a lot of other places, too——

Q. That's right.

The President. ——always trying to blame America's problem on someone else. What I tried to do was to preserve and strengthen this special relationship by setting up a system through Ambassador Kantor, who is in Japan today, to handle the trade problems in a very disciplined way in the context of our overall partnership with Japan. It is a very special relationship.

We are still the world's two most powerful economies. We are still committed to democracy. We have this unusual, wonderful security partnership that has helped to keep war out of the lives of the people of Asia for the last 50 years. These are major, major important things. And we cannot abandon our special relationship until there are others who have as much commitment to the future of the world as we do and who have the same ability we do to secure peace and prosperity. No one else can do that in the way America and Japan have. So to me, the relationship is more important than ever. And I hope it would not be abandoned just because the cold war is over. We still have our affirmative responsibilities.

Q. Well, we are very must gratified to hear your comments. But still, some people think that the major cause of imbalance is a rather microscopic savings investment imbalance, whereas too much political emphasis has been given to individual trade issues.

The President. My own view is that they're both to blame. And if you look at what I have done since I've been President—we had one of the highest deficits of all the large economies in the world when I became President—trade deficits—and a very low savings rate. We have

now taken our deficit down to the point where—this year at least—it's the lowest of all the G–7 countries.

And we're committed to balancing the budget. Our debate here is over how to balance the budget, not whether. We are looking at ways to increase the savings rate. We are trying to increase our own productivity. And we know that we will never, ever have an overall balance of trade in the world until we have done something about our Government deficit, done something about our savings and investment rate.

But we also know that it's important that, insofar as possible, all countries move toward open, transparent trading systems and treat each other fairly. So to me, both things must be done. And I have never tried to ask Japan or any other nation to do anything as an excuse for not having America do what we must do as well.

Q. So would you like to concentrate next phase on structure issues like debt regulation with Japanese counterparts?

The President. Well, I think as Japan goes through its deregulation program, prices will drop in Japan and the quality of life for average Japanese families will go way up. It will also lead to the purchase of more American products, and that will create more good, high-wage jobs for Americans. But you ought to pursue these policies primarily because it's good for the Japanese people. Incidentally, it will help our people. But great nations must obviously look after the interests of their own people first.

At this point, your economy is so advanced and so powerful, you even have Japanese companies now, if you will, out-sourcing some of your manufacturing in other Asian countries that are still developing.

The reason for opening your economy and deregulating now is not to make me happy—although it will create a lot more American jobs and I want you to do it for that reason—but because it's also good for the Japanese people. The Japanese people have worked so hard for so many years and now, with these changes, you can bring the benefits of their hard work to them in the form of a better quality of life. That's why I think it should be done.

Q. Another bad news that came from the United States to Japan recently was the fact that one of the Japanese commercial banks, Daiwa Bank, was ordered to stop their operations in the United States. Your view on that decision?

The President. Well, because it's under active investigation here, under our system, I can't really comment on it, except to say that I regret it very much. But it should not be taken as a signal that we do not welcome Japanese investment in our financial institutions or the establishment of Japanese financial operations here. You have a lot of other extremely successful operations in America—the Mura Securities I just think of as one I could mention off the top of my head.

So we have to enforce our laws in the way we are required to. And I can't comment on that specific case, but please do not believe we do not want your country to have the opportunity to send its people here to compete, because we do.

Japanese Economy

Q. But in general, Japan has been suffering—the Japanese Bank has been suffering with huge amounts of bad debt. Are you concerned about the Japanese economy, where it's going and what effect it might have in the global economy?

The President. Obviously, we're concerned about the financial system problems that are reported here. But keep in mind, we went through a terrible situation here 10 years ago, where because of a lot of imprudent things that were done in many—10, 15 years ago, we had a collapse of our savings and loan sector. It cost a lot of money to fix it, but fundamentally, the American people were working hard and becoming more productive. And we got through it.

And I think that you'll—I'm not familiar enough to know the details and what the options are, but this is something the Japanese people will have to address. But don't forget, fundamentally, you have this enormously powerful economy. You have a great technology base. You have an enormously competitive citizenry. The underlying health and power of the Japanese economy is great. So you'll just have to figure out what has to be done, and I'm sure the people will do it. And it won't permanently weaken the country.

All these problems—I find that whether we have them or you have them or some other country has them, people will always have problems as long as we live on this planet. And the important thing is to address them quickly

and in a disciplined way and so that the underlying strengths of the people involved can rise to the top.

Japanese Investment

Q. May I tell you on a negative case, Japanese companies have had bad investment here in the States like yours in Whitewater—I might be wrong——

The President. If you invest money, you might lose it; that's the way the market system goes. [*Laughter.*]

Q. And the result is that more Japanese companies are investing more into Asia. What would you like to think about that?

The President. Well, I think, partly that's quite understandable because in those rapidly growing countries which are near to you, if you put more investment in, it is logical to assume that they will become better markets for your products. And a lot of those countries are close at hand, and they have rapidly growing economies.

In our country, some of the Japanese investments—which were, just like a lot of Americans, somewhat speculative in nature in certain areas—when the markets turned down, a lot of money was lost. On the other hand, I think there will always be a healthy level of Japanese investment in America because of the importance of the American market. And the long-term, stable Japanese investments that are tied to production and to productivity are doing very well in this country, and I expect they will continue to do well.

And I might say, the American people have benefited from that. We have learned a lot in our own efforts to improve the productivity of our people, especially in manufacturing, from the investments of Japanese companies in the United States and from watching how your companies operate and the relationships between management and labor and the power given to the workers in the productive sector to grow the economy. So I think it will be quite good in the future.

U.S. Economy

Q. Well, let me complement the question by asking you something more positive. As you say, the productivity in this country is going up. The basis of manufacturing industry has become robust. Consumer confidence is back. But what we are seeing is your phenomenal growth in export performance. Is the United States transforming itself from import-oriented country to an export-oriented country?

The President. Oh, I think what we want is a more balanced economy. That's what I work for. And you're right, it's working. We have the stock market at an all-time high in this country, the creation of small businesses at a record pace. And we have the lowest combined rates of unemployment and inflation we've had in 25 years, because we're following a balanced approach: bring down the deficit, investment in technology and education, push for more exports, do it in a balanced way.

Our exports have increased in only 3 years by something like 35 percent to the world and even more in Asia. So there, again, I would say the special relationship is important. Over half of America's exports go to Asia. Over 3 million American jobs are tied directly to the health and welfare of the Asian economies. And again, that makes our partnership with Japan, from my point of view, even more important.

But if I could bring it back at home, that's one reason, unfortunately, I have to stay here now, because what we have done is to follow a balanced approach: bring the deficit down, work to balance the budget, but keep investing in people and technology and keep the power to promote America's business interest and the workers' interest around the world.

And so, if you look at the fight we're having here, I want the Japanese people to know we're not fighting about whether we should balance our budget and be more responsible so we don't take so much money out of the world's economy. We agree we must balance our budget. But I think—what we have here is—how to balance the budget is a debate between two different visions of the future for our own society. I want a society where we grow in strength together, and I believe the alternative proposal would have us growing apart.

For example, I don't think we have to balance the budget by raising the medical costs of our poorest senior citizens. I don't think we have to balance the budget by depriving our younger people of the opportunity to be in Head Start programs. I think it's a mistake to say we have to balance the budget by reducing the number of college scholarships or raising the cost of university loans or by cutting aid to disabled children and their families. These are matters really important to debate here. I know we don't

have to do that to balance the budget, and I think that would be bad for our economy.

I believe the strength of the Japanese economy rests more than anything else in the disciplined pursuit, over a long period of time, of a responsible investment policy, a responsible production policy, a responsible export policy, and the investment into people—education, technology, and having all the people do well. That's what we have to do in the United States. That's the debate we're having here. That's why, in a way, the people of Japan are better off if I stay here now, because a strong Japan needs a strong America to be a good partner. We have to grow together.

Asia-Pacific Economic Cooperation

Q. Since you mentioned the importance of Asia for the United States, I'd like to ask a question in relation to APEC. You convened a summit meeting 2 years ago in Seattle, and this year you're not present. Perhaps your leadership and credibility in Asia might diminish.

The President. It might. And I had to think of that. But when the President of the United States takes the oath of office of the President, he must first promise to deal with the responsibilities that the Constitution of our country imposes. If I were to leave now, I would be running away from decisions that I have to make here imposed on me by the oath that I swore to uphold.

I have already called not only Prime Minister Murayama but President Kim of South Korea, President Soeharto of Indonesia. I'm trying to reach President Jiang Zemin now. I'm going to talk to as many of the APEC leaders personally as I can to apologize for not being there and to say the Vice President's going to be there, because we—this APEC leaders partnership is very important to our country and very important to your country, because what we want is a growing Asia in the context of a global trade system and the agreement. And I want to say one thing before we run out of time. Prime Minister Murayama and his government have done an excellent job in leading APEC this year. And the agreement that will be announced there to deal with comprehensive trade issues, to do it in a flexible way, to have regular reviews of how we're doing and moving toward an integrated economy, it's a very, very important agreement. And it proves that we need APEC.

And I hope that my one-time absence will not be interpreted by my colleagues and friends, the leaders of the other nations, as a loss of interest, because this is a big APEC meeting, thanks largely to the leadership of your government.

President's Vision for the 21st Century

Q. Mr. President, we have two great native Arkansans; one is the President, the other one is General Douglas MacArthur. Both of them gave us great influence. What would you like to do to the Japanese?

The President. What I would like to do as President with regard to Japan? I would like to be known in the future as the President who created a partnership with Japan that took the world beyond the cold war into the global village of the 21st century, that together we led the world to be a more peaceful and a more prosperous place where more people enjoyed freedom and could make the most of their own lives and that this is something we did together, that because of our wealth and because of our vision and because of our values, that together we were the driving forces in making the global village of the 21st century the kind of place we would all be proud for our children to grow up in.

Q. The year 2000 will presumably be the last year in your reelected office. And your dreams about the 21st century—short of the United States becoming world's policeman, how are you going to bring about the safer world?

The President. Well, my dream for the 21st century is that people, nations will define their greatness not in terms of their military power but in terms of the quality of life their people enjoy, their ability to preserve our common natural environment and our ability to give every person the right to make the most of his or her own life. That's how we'll define our greatness.

My vision includes the ability of nation-states to open up their systems enough to have a global trading system but to still be strong enough to stamp out the organized forces of destruction, to stamp out those who would use terrorism and organized crime and drug trafficking to kill innocent people. That really is going to be our great challenge, to take advantage of all these forces that are pulling the world together—essentially, economics and culture pulling the world together—and to stamp out these forces

that are threatening to tear us apart, the forces of racial and religious and ethnic hatred—what we're trying to deal with now in Bosnia, hoping to bring peace there—and the forces of terrorism, organized crime, and drug trafficking. Those things are the great security challenges of the 21st century, along with the proliferation of weapons. Those people that want to proliferate weapons—we've got to do something about it. When Japan went into Cambodia to try to help make the peace—there is something like 10 million landmines there. We have to do something about that.

But if we can deal with our differences, our cultural, racial, ethnic, religious differences, and deal with the organized criminal and the terrorists, then I think the 21st century will be the greatest time in all of human history.

1996 Election

Q. But, Mr. President, he meant you'll be reelected next year.

The President. I hope he's right. *[Laughter.]* I let it pass, but I hope he's right.

The main thing is that in a time of change, you can't predict the future. And you can't predict what will be popular next month, much less next year. The important thing is for us to say, "Here's what we believe in; here's the future we're trying to achieve and the work to achieve it." And the elections will take care of themselves.

Japan–U.S. Relations

Q. Finally, we are running out of time so I'd like to ask you if there's anything else that you left out to tell the Japanese public?

The President. I just want to say that I have been coming to Japan for many years, first as a Governor, then as President. I have enjoyed and been moved by every trip I have ever made there. Again, I personally regret that I cannot come now. But I'm doing the right thing for our country and for our relationships with Japan by staying here in this unprecedented moment. I will come as soon as I can.

But the important thing is that the Japanese people must know that our partnership with Japan is secure and must grow stronger. We owe it to ourselves; we owe it to the rest of the world. It is the right thing to do, and I will do everything in my power to see that we achieve it.

Q. Mr. President, we'd like to thank you very much for joining us.

The President. Thank you very much. Glad to see you.

Q. Thank you.

The President. Thank you.

NOTE: The interview began at 12:30 p.m. in the Roosevelt Room at the White House.

Statement on the Conventional Forces in Europe Treaty
November 17, 1995

Today marks a milestone in our common effort to build a transatlantic community where cooperation, not confrontation, is the key to security. The parties to the CFE Treaty have achieved a goal that was thought unattainable less than a decade ago: They have destroyed more than 50,000 pieces of military equipment to establish a stable balance of conventional forces in Europe at levels dramatically lower than existed only a few years ago. CFE's implementation—including the conduct of thousands of onsite inspections and the exchange of detailed information on military forces, in addition to the destruction of thousands of pieces of armor, artillery, combat aircraft, and attack helicopters—is tangible evidence that the era of cold war confrontation is behind us.

We owe this remarkable achievement to the determination of the 30 governments represented in the CFE Joint Consultative Group. As envisaged when the CFE Treaty was signed in 1990, this group has been the key to finding cooperative solutions to countless implementa-

tion problems, large and small. You have made the treaty work.

CFE has been a flexible instrument in promoting our common security. This has been demonstrated by our ability together in the joint statement approved today to agree on the broad outline of a solution to the issue of the flanks, which preserves the integrity of the treaty and does not diminish the security of any state. I urge all parties to this landmark treaty to work intensively to complete the task of resolving this issue as soon as possible.

There are other implementation concerns as well, relating to equipment destruction and other issues. The United States expects all parties to CFE to meet their treaty obligations. This must be done if we are to achieve the full promise of this treaty. Working through these remaining problems will be a key task for the Joint Consultative Group in the days to come. Given the record of the past, I know that our work will succeed.

Statement on House of Representatives Action on Budget Reconciliation Legislation
November 17, 1995

Today the Republicans in the House of Representatives voted to enact the biggest Medicare and Medicaid cuts in history, unprecedented cuts in education and the environment, and steep tax increases on working families. I will veto this bill. I am determined to balance the budget, but I will not go along with a plan

that cuts care for disabled children, reduces educational opportunity by cutting college scholarships, denies preschool to thousands of poor children, slashes enforcement of environmental laws, and doubles Medicare premiums for the elderly. We should balance the budget in a way that reflects our values.

The President's Radio Address
November 18, 1995

Good morning. Last night I went the extra mile to bring Republicans and Democrats together to open the Government up and get down to the hard work of balancing the budget. I sent my Chief of Staff, Leon Panetta, to Capitol Hill to forge a common ground. I had hoped the Republicans and Democrats of good faith would be able to work together to reopen Government and to continue our larger debate over national budget priorities.

But this morning it looks like this chance to reopen the Government may be slipping away. I hope that's not true, and I call on reasonable Republicans to join with Democrats in Congress to pass a bill to reopen the Government and open the way to real, serious talks on how to balance the budget.

I know that for many people across our country, all this conflict and drama looks just like people in Washington are playing politics again. What every American has to realize is that this is way beyond politics. There are very, very profound, fundamental issues involved. What's at stake is nothing less than two different visions of our country and two different futures for our people.

I believe we must balance the budget. I'm determined to eliminate the Federal deficit to avoid passing a legacy of debt on to our children. I am proud that in my first 3 years in office, our administration has cut the deficit in half and that now we already have the smallest deficit of any major economy in the world. It's time to finish the job and pass a balanced budget plan.

So what's at issue is not whether to balance the budget, but how. And we and the Republican Congress are offering two very different visions for our country and two different futures. You need to know the whole reason the Government is shut down is that the Republican Congress, following a plan announced last spring by Speaker Gingrich, has shut the Government down unless I accept the framework of their budget.

Well, last night the House of Representatives passed their budget. This is what they say we have to accept as the price of reopening the Government. First, on Medicare, just a few weeks ago the Speaker of the House said their goal was to let Medicare, and I quote, "wither on the vine." Now we know that's exactly what will happen. We know the Medicare program that has worked for everyone and guaranteed a dignified retirement for senior citizens, that program's days are numbered, even though it's efficient and effective. Under the Republican plan there will be two Medicares in America: one for the healthy, one for the sick; one for the rich, and one for the poor, with everyone in the middle getting squeezed with fewer choices, higher costs, and less quality. Most sadly, the oldest, the poorest, and the sickest senior citizens will get hit too hard.

The Republican budget would also deny 360,000 deserving students the scholarships they need to go to college and make the most of their lives. And it would make college loans harder to get for millions more Americans at the very time when more people need to go on to college and when the costs are going up.

Unbelievably, this budget would deny Head Start preschool programs to 180,000 young children at a time when we know that on our mean streets, too many of our young people are raising themselves. This budget of theirs would make it much harder for our Government to guarantee the safety of the water we drink, the air we breathe, the food we put on the table. Unbelievably, too, their budget would actually raise taxes on 15 million of our hardest pressed working families. Oh, and by the way, it also cuts the School Lunch Program. And it would even prevent thousands of disabled children from being able to live with their parents by cutting off assistance for home care.

In recent days, I've heard from Americans all across our country about the real impact this will have on the lives of our people. One of my friends called to tell me about a woman he knows with a disabled child. This woman rides an hour a day to work on subsidized transportation. And she works for barely above the minimum wage. She comes home to care for her child. Under their budget she loses three ways: Her transportation to work is going to be more costly because we're cutting aid to transportation in cities under their budget; her ability to help her disabled child will be less because the disabled child will lose Federal assistance; and unbelievably, at her low income with her child at home, she gets a tax increase under their plan so that people in my income group can get a tax cut. It doesn't make sense.

Another friend of mine, the chairman of the board of a technical college, wrote to say how important it is that we help our young people get scholarships to go on to college today. My friend remembers that in the 1960's he got help from Government to pay for his college education. And because all of us took a risk in lending him the money for college, today he pays a lot more in taxes every year than the total he borrowed. He asked a very simple question: If we can't invest in our people, how can we ensure the future of our country?

My fellow Americans, none of these extreme cuts, not one of them, are necessary to balance the budget. This extreme budget reflects not economic necessity but a philosophy that would strip the ability of our National Government to be an instrument of meeting our national goals. It would make us a more divided, winner-take-all society, a community with fewer connections and less common purpose. Its economic assumptions operate on the premise that our country will not grow very much if their plan is passed, that our best days are behind us.

I have proposed a balanced budget rooted in our fundamental values, providing opportunity but expecting responsibility from people, honoring our obligations to our parents and our children, helping our families to be stronger and to stay together, and making sure our country is the strongest force for peace and freedom, democracy, and prosperity in the world.

My budget cuts hundreds of wasteful programs. We have already reduced the size of the Federal Government by 200,000. It's the smallest it's been in 30 years and, as a percentage of the civilian work force, the smallest it's been since 1933. But my budget also invests in our people and our future. It secures Medicare and Medicaid into the future. It invests in education. It ensures the protection of the environment. It gives working families a tax cut targeted at education and childrearing. Now, that's the right way to balance the budget.

I'll say again, I want to balance the budget. But any budget that cuts funding for disabled children and school lunches, for Head Start for our youngest children, for college scholarships and loans, that doubles Medicare premiums and undermines the entire Medicaid program that provides for nursing home care and home health care for the elderly, the disabled, and health care for poor children—this budget's dead on arrival when it comes to the White House. And if the price of any deal are cuts like these, my message is, no deal.

The effort to make the American people swallow a budget that will hurt our country is over. Let's get back to work, together, to balance the budget without unbalancing our values.

To the Republicans in Congress, I say, listen to the American people. Let's all say yes to a balanced budget and no to extremism in cuts in health care, education, and the environment. If we do that, America will be strong and true to its values and its vision as we enter the 21st century. Now let's get the job done.

Thanks for listening.

NOTE: The President spoke at 10:06 a.m. from the Oval Office at the White House.

Statement on Action To Reopen the Federal Government
November 19, 1995

Today I took concrete steps to put the Government back to work for the American people.

I have signed the Treasury-Postal and Legislative Branch appropriations bills. In addition, the Department of Defense is recalling to work the people who staff Armed Forces Recruiting Centers. And the Department of Housing and Urban Development is recalling employees who process public housing funds.

Last Friday, I took steps that resulted in furloughed employees being recalled to work to process Social Security and Medicare claims and accept applications for veterans benefits. Earlier in the week, I signed the funding bill for the

Department of Transportation. All told, these actions bring back to work over 200,000 of the 800,000 Federal employees who were furloughed last week.

These bipartisan bills mark real progress in our efforts to fully reopen the Government so it can serve the American people. I am determined that we should fully reopen the Government. Then we can openly and fairly decide the best way to balance the Federal budget while protecting Medicare, Medicaid, education, and the environment.

Statement on the Decline in the National Crime Rate
November 19, 1995

The continued decline in our national crime rate shows that the efforts by citizens and their police are making a difference. My 1994 crime bill's putting 100,000 cops on the street, taking assault weapons off the street, and cracking down on violent drug crimes. Today, all Americans must double their efforts to eliminate the scourge of juvenile violence from our communities. This will only be accomplished by more parents teaching their children right from wrong.

Remarks Announcing an Agreement To Reopen the Federal Government and an Exchange With Reporters
November 19, 1995

The President. Good evening. As you know, an agreement has been reached to reopen our Government beginning tomorrow. The bill I have agreed to sign will allow our Government to once again begin to serve the American people while broader discussions about how best to balance the budget take place.

I have made clear from the beginning my principles in this budget debate. We must balance the budget, but we must do it in a way that is good for our economy and that maintains our values. That means we have to do it without devastating cuts in Medicare and Medicaid, in education and the environment. And we have to do it without raising taxes on working families.

This agreement reflects my principles. And for the first time, the Republican leaders in Congress have acknowledged the importance of those principles. As I have said throughout this debate, I could only agree to move forward if that occurred.

Tonight represents the first sign of their willingness to move forward without forcing unacceptable cuts in health care, education, and the environment on the American people. The Republican budget which was passed just yesterday clearly does not come close to meeting that test, as I have said repeatedly. Therefore, I will veto that budget.

As you know, I have expressed strong doubts that the budget can be balanced in 7 years if we use the current Republican congressional budget assumptions. But I am nevertheless committed to working in the coming weeks to see if we can reach common ground on balancing the budget. The key is that nothing will be agreed to unless all elements are agreed to. I simply cannot sign a budget that devastates Medicare to the elderly or Medicaid to senior citizens and disabled people and poor children, that robs educational opportunity or educational standards from our children in the future, or that hurts our environment. And I can't support a tax increase on working families.

Well, tomorrow the Government will go back to work. And now the debate will begin in earnest on how to balance the budget in a way that is consistent with the interests and the values of the American people.

I appreciate the work that was done by both Democrats and Republicans tonight. I applaud the leadership. I applaud the leaders of the budget committee. I applaud all of them for the work that they did. This is the way our Government ought to work. We ought to be able to find common ground, and we ought to be able to do it and permit the day-to-day work of the United States and the American people to go forward.

So from my point of view this is a very good thing, and a good and somewhat unexpected development on this Sunday evening.

Budget Compromise

Q. Are there any winners or losers in this, Mr. President——

The President. Yes.

Q. ——in the sense that you—you may be interpreted as a loser to the extent on the binding 7 years?

The President. But nothing is binding unless everything is binding. And if you read the whole agreement, both paragraphs and the way it's written, essentially we agree to do something that I said we ought to agree to a long time ago. We ought to both say, we'll try to balance the budget. There's no magic to the timetable,

but if we can do it, you know, as quickly— we ought to do it as quickly as we can, consistent with economic growth and the values of the American people that hold us together.

So I would say that the real winners tonight are the American people. The American people have won in two ways: Number one, the Government will go back to work tomorrow, and the good Federal employees are real winners, too. And the real winners tonight are the American people because now we can have an open, honest, straightforward discussion about how best to balance the budget. So the victors tonight are the people that sent us all up here and that pay our salaries.

Q. Mr. President, how optimistic are you you can reach a compromise by December 15th?

The President. I don't know. All I know is that I can go to work. But you know what my— you know what my standards are, and you know what I'll do if we meet them and what I'll do if we won't. So we'll just go to work tomorrow and see if we can do it.

NOTE: This President spoke at 7:33 p.m. in the Briefing Room at the White House.

Statement on Signing the Treasury, Postal Service, and General Government Appropriations Act, 1996
November 20, 1995

Last night I signed into law H.R. 2020, the "Treasury, Postal Service, and General Government Appropriations Act, 1996."

The Act provides a total of $11.3 billion in discretionary budget authority for various programs in the Department of the Treasury, the U.S. Postal Service, the General Services Administration, the Office of Personnel Management, the Executive Office of the President, and several smaller agencies. With this legislation enacted into law, over 140,000 furloughed employees were able to go back to work.

I am pleased that a provision contained in an earlier version of the bill, which would have limited the political advocacy rights of non-profit organizations that receive Federal funding, was removed from the bill. This unacceptable provision would have presented a broad attack on

the exercise of fundamental rights protected by the First Amendment.

Regrettably, the Congress has not funded the Internal Revenue Service at a sufficient level to ensure the kind of service that the taxpayers deserve. I am disappointed that the Congress eliminated the FY 1995 funding of $405 million for the compliance initiative as it creates serious risks to the levels of tax compliance. At the very least, this action is expected to result in the loss of additional revenue over the next five years. Major compliance cuts send the wrong signal and reward tax cheats. The Internal Revenue Service's FY 1996 funding level is not consistent with the efforts of the Administration and the Congress to balance the Federal budget.

Again, I urge the Congress to meet its responsibilities by sending me the remaining regular FY 1996 appropriations bills in acceptable form.

WILLIAM J. CLINTON

The White House,
November 20, 1995.

NOTE: H.R. 2020, approved November 19, was assigned Public Law No. 104–52.

Statement on Signing the Legislative Branch Appropriations Act, 1996
November 20, 1995

Last night I signed into law H.R. 2492, the "Legislative Branch Appropriations Act, 1996."

The Act provides fiscal year 1996 appropriations for the Congress, the Congressional Budget Office, the Architect of the Capitol, the General Accounting Office, the Government Printing Office, and the Library of Congress.

On October 3, 1995, I vetoed the first Legislative Branch Appropriations bill, indicating at the time that the bill was acceptable but that the Congress should not take care of its own business before it takes care of the people's business. At the time the Legislative Branch bill was sent to the White House, the Congress had passed only one other of the 13 appropriations bills. The Congress has now completed action on six bills that I have been able to sign.

While much work remains to be done and the Congress remains behind schedule, I signed this bill recognizing that the Congress has indeed made some progress since October 3.

I urge the Congress to meet its responsibilities by sending me the remaining FY 1996 appropriations bills in an acceptable form.

WILLIAM J. CLINTON

The White House,
November 20, 1995.

NOTE: H.R. 2492, approved November 19, was assigned Public Law No. 104–53.

Remarks Announcing the Bosnia-Herzegovina Peace Agreement and an Exchange With Reporters
November 21, 1995

Good morning. About an hour ago I spoke with Secretary Christopher in Dayton, Ohio. He informed me that the Presidents of Bosnia, Croatia, and Serbia have reached a peace agreement to end the war in Bosnia, to end the worst conflict in Europe since World War II.

After nearly 4 years of 250,000 people killed, 2 million refugees, atrocities that have appalled people all over the world, the people of Bosnia finally have a chance to turn from the horror of war to the promise of peace.

The Presidents of Bosnia, Croatia, and Serbia have made a historic and heroic choice. They have heeded the will of their people. Whatever their ethnic group, the overwhelming majority of Bosnia citizens and the citizens of Croatia and Serbia want the same thing. They want to stop the slaughter; they want to put an end to the violence and war; they want to give their children and their grandchildren a chance to lead a normal life. Today, thank God, the voices of those people have been heard.

I want to congratulate America's negotiating team, led by Secretary Christopher and Ambassador Holbrooke, for their extraordinary service. Their determination, along with that of our European and Russian partners, along with NATO's resolve, brought the parties to the negotiating table. Then their single-minded pursuit of peace in Dayton made today's agreement a possibility and eventually a reality.

The people of Bosnia, the American people, indeed people throughout the world, should be very thankful for this event today. The peace plan agreed to would preserve Bosnia as a single state, within its present borders and with international recognition. The state will be made up of two parts, the Bosnian Croat Federation and the Bosnian Serb Republic, with a fair distribution of land between the two. The capital city of Sarajevo will remain united.

There will be an effective central government, including a national parliament, a presidency, and a constitutional court, with responsibility for foreign policy, foreign trade, monetary policy, citizenship, immigration, and other important functions. The presidency and the parliament will be chosen through free democratic elections, held under international supervision. Refugees will be allowed to return to their homes. People will be able to move freely throughout Bosnia. And the human rights of every Bosnian citizen will be monitored by an independent commission and an internationally trained civilian police. Those individuals charged with war crimes will be excluded from political life.

Now that the parties to the war have made a serious commitment to peace, we must help them to make it work. All the parties have asked for a strong international force to supervise the separation of forces and to give them confidence that each side will live up to their agreements. Only NATO can do that job. And the United States as NATO's leader must play an essential role in this mission. Without us, the hard-won peace would be lost, the war would resume, the slaughter of innocents would begin again, and the conflict that already has claimed so many people could spread like poison throughout the entire region.

We are at a decisive moment. The parties have chosen peace. America must choose peace as well. Now that a detailed settlement has been reached, NATO will rapidly complete its planning for the implementation force known as IFOR. The plan soon will be submitted to me for review and for approval. As of now, we expect that about one-third of IFOR's force will be American. The rest will come from our NATO partners and from other nations throughout the world.

At the same time, once the agreement is signed, the international community will initiate a parallel program to provide humanitarian relief, to begin the job of rebuilding, to help the thousands of refugees return to their homes, to monitor free elections, in short, to help the Bosnian people create the conditions of lasting peace.

The NATO military mission will be clear and limited. Our troops will take their orders only from the American general who commands NATO. They will have authority to meet any threat to their safety or any violation of the peace agreement with immediate and decisive force. And there will be a reasonable timetable for their withdrawal.

I am satisfied that the NATO implementation plan is clear, limited, and achievable and that the risks to our troops are minimized. I will promptly consult with Congress when I receive this plan, and if I am fully satisfied with it when I see it in its final form, I will ask Congress to support American participation.

The central fact for us as Americans is this: Our leadership made this peace agreement possible and helped to bring an end to the senseless slaughter of so many innocent people that our fellow citizens had to watch night after night after night for 4 long years on their television screens. Now American leadership, together with our allies, is needed to make this peace real and enduring. Our values, our interests, and our leadership all over the world are at stake.

I ask all Americans in this Thanksgiving week to take some time to say a simple prayer of thanksgiving that this peace has been reached, that our Nation was able to play an important role in stopping the suffering and the slaughter.

May God bless the peace and the United States.

Q. Mr. President, Congress seems deeply skeptical of sending American troops to Bosnia right now. How are you going to turn that around, and how soon would American forces have to go into Bosnia?

The President. Well, first of all, I believe it's important for the Congress to have a chance to review this peace agreement and to receive the assurances from the leaders of Bosnia, Croatia, and Serbia that they intend to do everything in their power to make sure the agreement is implemented in good faith and with peaceful intent and absolutely minimal violence. I think that will be an imperative part of this endeavor.

I will work with the leaders of Congress to establish a schedule for implementing that. I have placed calls to the Speaker, the majority leader of the Senate, and the minority leaders of the Senate and the House shortly before I came out here. I was only able to reach the

Speaker. The others were in transit, but I will speak to them all today. And I will work with them to establish a schedule for consultation with Congress that will begin as soon as I approve the final NATO plan.

I have had extensive briefings on this plan. And as I said, I am satisfied that based on what we knew at the time I was briefed, we had a clear, limited, achievable mission that minimized the risks to not only the uniformed forces of the United States but others who would participate as well. When I see the final plan, if I remain of that opinion, I will immediately consult with Congress and we will have an agreed-upon schedule for consultations, which I think will begin immediately in terms of the detail of the peace agreement itself. And that is the responsibility that I have to bear, and I intend to assume it.

Now, we have assured Congress that there will be no complete deployment until they have a chance to be heard on this issue. The only things that will be done in the preliminary period, assuming that things go forward as we anticipate today and you hear what I think you will hear shortly from the three Presidents, is that there will be some preliminary planning done in the Bosnia area, which is absolutely essential and which we have already fully disclosed to the Congress. But beyond that, the Congress will have a period of weeks before the final formal signing ceremony, which would trigger the involvement of NATO's forces. So that's what I expect will happen.

Let me say that I know you will have other questions about the details of this peace agree-

ment, how it was reached, the number of eleventh hours that came and passed. And even last night at midnight, when I had my last conversation with Secretary Christopher, we were not sure whether there would be peace this morning. When I got up and we began to work on this, we were not sure there would be peace. As often happens in a process like this, as I think happened in the Middle East, something stirred among the leaders themselves and they decided that they should not let this moment pass for the benefit of their people.

So I believe we'll be able to answer all the other questions in the days ahead, and the people in Dayton will be able to answer more of your questions when they have their press conference. The main thing is, I ask all Americans to remember what we have seen and heard and read about for the last 4 years and remember what the implications were not only for our consciences but for the prospect that that conflict could spread.

The fact that these leaders have voted to bring an end to this and to give the people of Bosnia a peaceful Christmas and a peaceful future is something for which we should be very, very thankful.

Thank you very much.

NOTE: The President spoke at 11:40 a.m. in the Rose Garden at the White House. In his remarks, he referred to President Alija Izetbegovic of Bosnia-Herzegovina, President Franjo Tudjman of Croatia, and President Slobodan Milosevic of Serbia.

Remarks at the Blair Homeless Shelter
November 22, 1995

I'd like to just say one word, if I might. I want to say that Hillary and I came here to be with you at Thanksgiving and to celebrate Thanksgiving with our country because we wanted to thank the people who run this wonderful service here for their commitment, for their service.

I also want to say a word of thanks to my friend Henry Cisneros, the Secretary of Housing and Urban Development, because he put to-

gether a homeless initiative for the District of Columbia that helps this project and many others, because after I became President, I said I was just tired of seeing people on the street. I want us to do something to give people some hope, to give people a place to be.

And on this Thanksgiving Day, Mr. Mayor, I say again, we are honored to be citizens of the District of Columbia. We are honored to have the chance to be with you and to work with people in DC to try to deal with the problems here. We know we have a lot of challenges in dealing with homelessness, not the least of which is that the fastest growing group of homeless people are women and their children. And we've got to stay after this.

I'd like to say one other thing, too, on this Thanksgiving. Yesterday I made an announcement that an agreement for peace has been made in Bosnia. A lot of people today are asking questions about how it will all be implemented. I'd just like to ask you to think of one human

fact. In that little country so much smaller than ours, in that little bitty country, there are one million homeless families because of that war. So I hope on this Thanksgiving we can help more of our own people to find homes and we can help them to go home.

Thank you, and God bless you all.

NOTE: The President spoke at 1:49 p.m. In his remarks, he referred to Mayor Marion Barry of the District of Columbia. A tape was not available for verification of the content of these remarks.

Remarks at the Thanksgiving Turkey Presentation Ceremony
November 22, 1995

The President. Ladies and gentlemen, welcome to the Rose Garden, and Happy Thanksgiving. I want to acknowledge, especially, Kenneth Rutledge, the chairman of the National Turkey Federation, his wife, Brenda, his son, John; Stuart Proctor—Kenneth is the chairman; Stuart Proctor is the president of the Turkey Federation, his wife, Sherry. I also want to recognize the presence here of Congressman Cal Dooley. And I want to on this cold day warmly welcome the young people and the volunteers who are here from the Boys Club, the Girls Club of America, the Big Brothers and Big Sisters program, and the members of the AmeriCorps program from Baltimore. [*Applause*] Thank you. I also want to say that's the most multicolored, best looking turkey we've had here since I've been President.

You know, we're here today to have a little fun and to begin the official Thanksgiving in our country that we give every year at this time for the blessings that God has given us, for the personal gifts he's given us, the gifts of our families and communities and to our great country.

Thanksgiving is a uniquely American holiday, as all of you know. It goes back to our foundings. But I think it's important to note that the first official proclamation of Thanksgiving, issued by a United States President, was issued by Abraham Lincoln during the Civil War, when our people were overwhelmingly preoccupied with their problems and indeed with whether our country would even continue

to exist. Nevertheless, Mr. Lincoln reminded us that we had things to be thankful for.

On this Thanksgiving here in America, we've got a lot to be thankful for. The combined rates of unemployment and inflation in our country are at their lowest in 27 years. Home ownership and new business formation and the stock market now are at an all-time high, all three of them. Maybe even more important, the crime rate, the welfare rates, the poverty rates, they're all down this year, and we're grateful for that. I'm grateful that the United States has been a force for peace, from the Middle East to Northern Ireland and to Haiti and now of course, we hope, in Bosnia.

But we should never forget that there are still people in our country that need our concern and our caring. The young people who are here today are interested in making the most of their own lives and serving those in their community. And that's an important part of Thanksgiving as well. We have obligations to our parents and to our children, to people who are disabled or otherwise, through no fault of their own, need a helping hand.

And just before I came here, I was with Secretary Cisneros and the First Lady at a homeless shelter here in Washington, DC, where we were feeding people. And I'm sad to say I saw a fresh and personal example of the fact that the fastest growing group of homeless people in our country are young women and their young children.

So on this Thanksgiving we should be thankful for our blessings, and we should redouble our resolve to do everything we can to make America a place of honor and decency and community, where we can all give thanks.

I'd like to say one other thing, too. I'm very proud of the United States negotiators who did so much to help to bring about the peace agreement in Bosnia yesterday. There will be many questions in the days ahead about all the things that have to be answered before we can go forward with this project. And I expect to be addressing the Nation about it shortly.

But let me just remind you of one thing on this Thanksgiving eve. Among other things, in that tiny country, so much smaller than the United States, there are one million homeless people. So I say, on this Thanksgiving, I hope God will bless the peace and bring those folks home again as well.

Let me now turn to the moment at hand, which I look forward to every day—every year, I mean. This is a—[*laughter*]—I wouldn't mind having it every day, actually. In 1947, President Truman began this great tradition of accepting a Thanksgiving turkey and then granting it a Presidential pardon.

[*At this point, the turkey gobbled.*]

The President. You can see one person thoroughly agrees with my decision here. [*Laughter*] This year, I guess we can say, since the Government is back to work, I can at least grant to one living thing in America, a permanent furlough. [*Laughter*]

Approximately 45 million turkeys will be consumed tomorrow all across our country but not this one. As in previous years, it will be donated to Kidwell Farms, a petting zoo in Fairfax, Virginia. I am glad to be able to give this turkey a pardon. And as I said, if you look at his very patriotic red, white, and blue face and feathers, it seems like the American thing to do on Thanksgiving.

I believe this turkey was born in the State of California and raised there. And we're delighted to have the turkey and the turkey's owner come all the way from California. And to all the farmers who raise turkeys in North Carolina, Minnesota, California, my home State of Arkansas, and throughout the country, let me say we appreciate what you do for our agricultural sector and for the nutrition of the United States.

But I'm very glad that one of your products is going to be exempt from the cruel fate that will make so many of us happy tomorrow. And by this action, I hereby pardon this turkey. There are so many turkeys in Washington, I should pardon at least one a year, I think. [*Laughter*]

Thank you very much.

NOTE: The President spoke at 2:04 p.m. in the Rose Garden at the White House.

The President's Radio Address
November 25, 1995

Good morning. All across our Nation this weekend, American families are coming together to give thanks for the good things in our lives. Hillary and I wish all of you a happy and healthy Thanksgiving weekend. As we rejoice in our blessings in the company of our loved ones, let's also give thanks for America's blessings and for all we have achieved as a nation.

This week, after a tough debate on the Federal budget, we made important strides toward what I hope will be common ground. Our Government is open again, and the Republican leaders in Congress have agreed to work with me to find a process so that we can establish our Nation's priorities together.

I hope we can balance the budget in a way that is true to our fundamental values: expecting responsibility from all our citizens but also providing opportunity so that we become a society in which everybody has a chance to win, not a winner-take-all society; honoring our obligations to our senior citizens through Medicare and Medicaid while also making investments for the next generation in education, environment, research, and technology; helping our families to be stronger and stay together; and ensuring that America remains the strongest force in the world for peace and freedom, democracy and prosperity.

All around the world we are seeing the results of America's willingness to work and to lead for peace. We see it in the Middle East, where even in the wake of the tragic loss of Prime Minister Rabin, Arabs and Israelis continue to turn the page on past conflict. We see it in Northern Ireland, where bombs and bullets have given way to hope for the future—where I will visit next week. And in this week of Thanksgiving, we have seen the results of America's leadership for peace in Bosnia.

After 4 years of terrible conflict, we have helped the people of Bosnia turn from the horror of war to the promise of peace. America's negotiating team, backed by NATO's resolve and airpower, brokered a cease-fire. We got the parties to agree on the principles of the settlement and brought them to the peace table in Dayton, Ohio. And now, the skill and dedication of our negotiators, working with our European and Russian partners, has enabled them to reach a comprehensive peace agreement.

Peace in Bosnia is important to America, to both our values and our interests. The Bosnian people have suffered unspeakable atrocities: mass executions, ethnic cleansing, campaigns of rape and terror. Two hundred and fifty thousand people have died; 2 million have been driven from their homes, with over a million of them still homeless. The violence done to those innocent civilians does violence to the principles on which America stands. The only way to end the killing for good is to secure a commitment to peace. Now our conscience demands that we act.

Securing the peace will also prevent the war in Bosnia from reigniting and then from spreading, sparking an even wider and more dangerous conflict right in the heart of Europe in the Balkan regions where there is still a lot of tension and potential for conflict in areas near Bosnia. In 1914, a gunshot in Bosnia's capital, Sarajevo, launched the first of two World Wars that drew America in to make great sacrifices for freedom. We must not let this century close with gunfire ringing in Sarajevo.

The peace agreement preserves Bosnia as a single state within its present borders and with international recognition. It settles the territorial disputes over which the war began. Refugees can return to their homes. People will be able to move freely throughout the country. The parties have accepted strong safeguards for human rights. They've pledged to cooperate fully with the international war crimes tribunal so that those responsible for crimes against humanity can be brought to justice.

Now that all the parties, including the Bosnian Serbs, have made a serious commitment to peace, America must help them to make it work. All the parties have asked for a strong international force to give them the confidence and the breathing room they need to implement the peace agreement and to begin the hard task of rebuilding.

NATO, the alliance of democracies that has preserved our security since the end of World War II, is clearly that force. And America, as NATO's leader, clearly must participate. Without our support the hard-won peace would be lost, the terrible slaughter would resume, the conflict that already has claimed so many lives could spread like a cancer throughout the region.

. In the days ahead I will review the NATO implementation plan and continue to consult closely with Congress. As of now, we expect that about a third of the NATO force will be American, approximately 20,000 troops. Two-thirds will be from our NATO allies in other supportive countries.

Our men and women will take their orders from the American general who commands NATO forces. They will have the authority to meet any threat to their safety or any violation of the peace agreement with immediate and decisive force. They will not be deployed until I am satisfied that the NATO mission is clear, limited, and achievable and until Congress has a chance to be heard.

I will discuss the peace agreement and the NATO mission in more detail when I speak to the Nation on Monday. I will also be visiting with American troops in Germany next week to talk directly with them about the important mission their Nation is asking them to carry out.

But on this Thanksgiving weekend, I ask my fellow Americans to think about who we are as a people, what we are as a nation. All around the world others look to us not just because of our economic and military might, because of what we stand for and what we're willing to stand against.

In Bosnia, our Nation has led the way from horror to hope, hope for no more Srebrenicas, no more shelling of children's playgrounds, no more desperate winters, no more shattered lives. Now we have a responsibility to see this achievement for peace through. Our values, our interests, and our leadership are at stake.

So let us give thanks for America's role in bringing Bosnia's nightmare to an end, and let us share the blessing of our Nation's strength to secure a lasting peace.

May God bless the United States on this Thanksgiving weekend.

NOTE: The address was recorded at 9:30 a.m. on November 24 at Camp David, MD, for broadcast at 10:06 a.m. on November 25.

Statement on Signing the Veterans' Compensation Cost-of-Living Adjustment Act of 1995
November 22, 1995

Today I have signed into law H.R. 2394, the "Veterans' Compensation Cost-of-Living Adjustment Act of 1995."

In signing H.R. 2394, I am pleased to extend a most deserved benefit to our Nation's service-disabled veterans and the surviving spouses and children of those who made the supreme sacrifice in defense of our freedom. In acting to maintain the value of these payments, we keep faith with those who have given so much in service to us all.

The Act provides a 2.6 percent increase in compensation and dependency and indemnity compensation benefits, effective December 1, 1995. This is the same percentage increase that

Social Security beneficiaries and veterans' pension recipients will be receiving in January.

On Veterans Day, we paused to salute all men and women in uniform. Today, it is altogether fitting that we give tangible expression to our enduring commitment to honor our obligations to them.

WILLIAM J. CLINTON

The White House,
November 22, 1995.

NOTE: H.R. 2394, approved November 22, was assigned Public Law No. 104–57. This statement was released by the Office of the Press Secretary on November 27.

Remarks Announcing the Child Survival Initiative for Bosnia-Herzegovina and an Exchange With Reporters
November 27, 1995

The President. Ladies and gentlemen, I am honored to be here today, especially with Congressman Tony Hall, a longstanding champion of children in our own country and throughout the world and the leading fighter in the Congress and perhaps in the entire United States in combating hunger. After visiting Bosnia this fall, Representative Hall worked with UNICEF to design the important child survival initiative that we announce today. I thank UNICEF Director Carol Bellamy, not only for her work at UNICEF but for her previous service in our administration as the Director of the Peace

Corps; and the USAID Administrator, Brian Atwood, who has been a tireless advocate of America's role in promoting sustainable development, in providing developmental assistance, and protecting the welfare of children throughout the world.

I want to especially welcome here two Bosnian families, the Kapetanovic family and the Mundzahasic family, who fled the fighting in their homeland and have been resettled as refugees here in the United States. Welcome to both of you.

These families know firsthand the terrible costs of war, the breakdown of basic human services, the lack of medical care, the forced closure of schools. They know how desperately the people of Bosnia need support and assistance from the international community right now.

Since the conflict in Bosnia began nearly 4 years ago, our Nation has played a major role in providing emergency assistance, including support for children, clean water and sanitation, food, shelter, and health care. But even with these efforts, the war in Bosnia has seriously harmed the most innocent and most vulnerable members of that society, its children.

Immunization rates have declined dramatically, putting tens of thousands of children at risk of potentially deadly whooping cough, measles, and diphtheria. The situation has been aggravated by the onset of harsh winters and overcrowded living conditions. Half of Bosnia's prewar population was driven from their homes during the conflict, and even today, more than one million of them remain homeless.

In addition, the basic education systems in the region are in deep crisis. It is estimated that 40 percent of the primary schools in Croatia and 55 percent of those in Bosnia have been either damaged or destroyed.

Now that a lasting peace is at hand, we have to bring the Bosnian people the benefits of that peace, starting with the children. And that is exactly what USAID and UNICEF are doing. Together, they will lead a new, multinational initiative to immunize the children of Bosnia, Croatia, and the Federal Republic of Yugoslavia who have not had access to decent health care during this war. Efforts should begin before Christmas. Most of the approximately 150,000 needy children in the region should be immunized within just 6 months.

This initiative will also provide support for basic education systems. Remember the comment of Zlata Filpovic, the Sarajevan girl who shared her experience of the war through her remarkable diary, "For me," she said, "the school is a symbol of normal life. When they take away my school, I said this really means something. They took my childhood; they took my school." With this program we can at least begin to give those children back their childhoods which were stolen.

USAID and UNICEF are finalizing plans for this $15 million initiative. The United States will devote $2 million to back the effort now, and our goal is to contribute $5 million. We'll also do our part to mobilize other donors. We hope our friends and our allies will join us in supporting this important program for the children of the former Yugoslavia.

We have just celebrated one of our most treasured holidays, Thanksgiving. All across our country, Americans came together to give thanks for the blessings in their lives and the lives of their families. This Thanksgiving, our Nation helped to give the people of Bosnia a blessing as well: the first real hope of peace in nearly 4 years. I want to say a special thanks again to the citizens of Dayton, Ohio, who welcomed the Balkan leaders to Dayton and who demonstrated on our behalf our vast and diverse Nation all committed to living together in peace.

Now we have a responsibility to see this achievement through. That is who we are as a people. That is what we stand for as a nation. The people of Bosnia, the children of Bosnia, have suffered unspeakable atrocities. We must not, and we will not, turn our backs on peace. And I am very proud to begin this very important day of discussion with the American people with this important announcement.

And again, I want to say a special word of thanks to Congressman Tony Hall for coming to me with this idea and helping me to develop it and push it through to the point where we could announce it today.

Thank you all, and thank you, Congressman.

President's Address to the Nation

Q. Mr. President, how hard a sell do you face tonight with your speech?

The President. I think the American people will respond. I believe that they're entitled to an explanation, that our values and our interests are very much at stake in the decision we make. And they're also entitled to an explanation about what exactly I propose to have our troops do there as part of the NATO mission. And I will do that this evening.

But I believe they will respond. This is an extraordinary opportunity and we have a very compelling responsibility, and I expect the American people to support it.

Thank you.

NOTE: The President spoke at 1:44 p.m. in the Roosevelt Room at the White House.

Address to the Nation on Implementation of the Peace Agreement in Bosnia-Herzegovina
November 27, 1995

Good evening. Last week, the warring factions in Bosnia reached a peace agreement as a result of our efforts in Dayton, Ohio, and the support of our European and Russian partners. Tonight I want to speak with you about implementing the Bosnian peace agreement and why our values and interests as Americans require that we participate.

Let me say at the outset, America's role will not be about fighting a war. It will be about helping the people of Bosnia to secure their own peace agreement. Our mission will be limited, focused, and under the command of an American general. In fulfilling this mission, we will have the chance to help stop the killing of innocent civilians, especially children, and at the same time, to bring stability to Central Europe, a region of the world that is vital to our national interests. It is the right thing to do.

From our birth, America has always been more than just a place. America has embodied an idea that has become the ideal for billions of people throughout the world. Our Founders said it best: America is about life, liberty, and the pursuit of happiness. In this century especially, America has done more than simply stand for these ideals. We have acted on them and sacrificed for them. Our people fought two World Wars so that freedom could triumph over tyranny. After World War I, we pulled back from the world, leaving a vacuum that was filled by the forces of hatred. After World War II, we continued to lead the world. We made the commitments that kept the peace, that helped to spread democracy, that created unparalleled prosperity, and that brought victory in the cold war.

Today, because of our dedication, America's ideals—liberty, democracy, and peace—are more and more the aspirations of people everywhere in the world. It is the power of our ideas, even more than our size, our wealth, and our military might, that makes America a uniquely trusted nation.

With the cold war over, some people now question the need for our continued active leadership in the world. They believe that, much like after World War I, America can now step back from the responsibilities of leadership. They argue that to be secure we need only to keep our own borders safe and that the time has come now to leave to others the hard work of leadership beyond our borders. I strongly disagree.

As the cold war gives way to the global village, our leadership is needed more than ever because problems that start beyond our borders can quickly become problems within them. We're all vulnerable to the organized forces of intolerance and destruction; terrorism; ethnic, religious, and regional rivalries; the spread of organized crime and weapons of mass destruction and drug trafficking. Just as surely as fascism and communism, these forces also threaten freedom and democracy, peace and prosperity. And they, too, demand American leadership.

But nowhere has the argument for our leadership been more clearly justified than in the struggle to stop or prevent war and civil violence. From Iraq to Haiti, from South Africa to Korea, from the Middle East to Northern Ireland, we have stood up for peace and freedom because it's in our interest to do so and because it is the right thing to do.

Now, that doesn't mean we can solve every problem. My duty as President is to match the demands for American leadership to our strategic interest and to our ability to make a difference. America cannot and must not be the world's policeman. We cannot stop all war for all time, but we can stop some wars. We cannot save all women and all children, but we can save many of them. We can't do everything, but we must do what we can.

There are times and places where our leadership can mean the difference between peace and war, and where we can defend our fundamental values as a people and serve our most basic, strategic interests. My fellow Americans, in this new era there are still times when America and America alone can and should make the difference for peace.

The terrible war in Bosnia is such a case. Nowhere today is the need for American leadership more stark or more immediate than in Bosnia. For nearly 4 years a terrible war has torn Bosnia apart. Horrors we prayed had been banished from Europe forever have been seared into our minds again: skeletal prisoners caged behind barbed-wire fences; women and girls raped as a tool of war; defenseless men and boys shot down into mass graves, evoking visions of World War II concentration camps; and endless lines of refugees marching toward a future of despair.

When I took office, some were urging immediate intervention in the conflict. I decided that American ground troops should not fight a war in Bosnia because the United States could not force peace on Bosnia's warring ethnic groups, the Serbs, Croats, and Muslims. Instead, America has worked with our European allies in searching for peace, stopping the war from spreading, and easing the suffering of the Bosnian people.

We imposed tough economic sanctions on Serbia. We used our airpower to conduct the longest humanitarian airlift in history and to enforce a no-fly zone that took the war out of the skies. We helped to make peace between two of the three warring parties, the Muslims and the Croats. But as the months of war turned into years, it became clear that Europe alone could not end the conflict.

This summer, Bosnian Serb shelling once again turned Bosnia's playgrounds and marketplaces into killing fields. In response, the United States led NATO's heavy and continuous air strikes, many of them flown by skilled and brave American pilots. Those air strikes, together with the renewed determination of our European partners and the Bosnian and Croat gains on the battlefield, convinced the Serbs, finally, to start thinking about making peace.

At the same time, the United States initiated an intensive diplomatic effort that forged a Bosnia-wide cease-fire and got the parties to agree to the basic principles of peace. Three dedicated American diplomats, Bob Frasure, Joe Kruzel, and Nelson Drew, lost their lives in that effort. Tonight we remember their sacrifice and that of their families. And we will never forget their exceptional service to our Nation.

Finally, just 3 weeks ago, the Muslims, Croats, and Serbs came to Dayton, Ohio, in America's heartland, to negotiate a settlement. There, exhausted by war, they made a commitment to peace. They agreed to put down their guns, to preserve Bosnia as a single state, to investigate and prosecute war criminals, to protect the human rights of all citizens, to try to build a peaceful, democratic future. And they asked for America's help as they implement this peace agreement.

America has a responsibility to answer that request, to help to turn this moment of hope into an enduring reality. To do that, troops from our country and around the world would go into Bosnia to give them the confidence and support they need to implement their peace plan. I refuse to send American troops to fight a war in Bosnia, but I believe we must help to secure the Bosnian peace.

I want you to know tonight what is at stake, exactly what our troops will be asked to accomplish, and why we must carry out our responsibility to help implement the peace agreement. Implementing the agreement in Bosnia can end the terrible suffering of the people, the warfare, the mass executions, the ethnic cleansing, the campaigns of rape and terror. Let us never forget a quarter of a million men, women, and children have been shelled, shot, and tortured to death. Two million people, half of the population, were forced from their homes and into a miserable life as refugees. And these faceless numbers hide millions of real personal tragedies, for each of the war's victims was a mother or daughter, a father or son, a brother or sister.

Now the war is over. American leadership created the chance to build a peace and stop the suffering. Securing peace in Bosnia will also help to build a free and stable Europe. Bosnia lies at the very heart of Europe, next-door to many of its fragile new democracies and some of our closest allies. Generations of Americans have understood that Europe's freedom and Europe's stability is vital to our own national security. That's why we fought two wars in Europe. That's why we launched the Marshall plan to restore Europe. That's why we created NATO and waged the cold war. And that's why we must help the nations of Europe to end their worst nightmare since World War II, now.

The only force capable of getting this job done is NATO, the powerful military alliance of democracies that has guaranteed our security for half a century now. And as NATO's leader and the primary broker of the peace agreement, the United States must be an essential part of the mission. If we're not there, NATO will not be there; the peace will collapse; the war will reignite; the slaughter of innocents will begin again. A conflict that already has claimed so many victims could spread like poison throughout the region, eat away at Europe's stability, and erode our partnership with our European allies.

And America's commitment to leadership will be questioned if we refuse to participate in implementing a peace agreement we brokered right here in the United States, especially since the Presidents of Bosnia, Croatia, and Serbia all asked us to participate and all pledged their best efforts to the security of our troops.

When America's partnerships are weak and our leadership is in doubt, it undermines our ability to secure our interests and to convince others to work with us. If we do maintain our partnerships and our leadership, we need not act alone. As we saw in the Gulf war and in Haiti, many other nations who share our goals will also share our burdens. But when America does not lead, the consequences can be very grave, not only for others but eventually for us as well.

As I speak to you, NATO is completing its planning for IFOR, an international force for peace in Bosnia of about 60,000 troops. Already more than 25 other nations, including our major NATO allies, have pledged to take part. They will contribute about two-thirds of the total implementation force, some 40,000 troops. The United States would contribute the rest, about 20,000 soldiers.

Later this week, the final NATO plan will be submitted to me for review and approval. Let me make clear what I expect it to include and what it must include for me to give final approval to the participation of our Armed Forces.

First, the mission will be precisely defined with clear, realistic goals that can be achieved in a definite period of time. Our troops will make sure that each side withdraws its forces behind the frontlines and keeps them there. They will maintain the cease-fire to prevent the war from accidentally starting again. These efforts, in turn, will help to create a secure environment so that the people of Bosnia can return to their homes, vote in free elections, and begin to rebuild their lives. Our Joint Chiefs of Staff have concluded that this mission should and will take about one year.

Second, the risks to our troops will be minimized. American troops will take their orders from the American general who commands NATO. They will be heavily armed and thor-

oughly trained. By making an overwhelming show of force, they will lessen the need to use force. But unlike the U.N. forces, they will have the authority to respond immediately and the training and the equipment to respond with overwhelming force to any threat to their own safety or any violations of the military provisions of the peace agreement.

If the NATO plan meets with my approval, I will immediately send it to Congress and request its support. I will also authorize the participation of a small number of American troops in a NATO advance mission that will lay the groundwork for IFOR, starting sometime next week. They will establish headquarters and set up the sophisticated communication systems that must be in place before NATO can send in its troops, tanks, and trucks to Bosnia.

The Implementation Force itself would begin deploying in Bosnia in the days following the formal signature of the peace agreement in mid-December. The international community will help to implement arms control provisions of the agreement so that future hostilities are less likely and armaments are limited, while the world community, the United States and others, will also make sure that the Bosnian Federation has the means to defend itself once IFOR withdraws. IFOR will not be a part of this effort.

Civilian agencies from around the world will begin a separate program of humanitarian relief and reconstruction, principally paid for by our European allies and other interested countries. This effort is also absolutely essential to making the peace endure. It will bring the people of Bosnia the food, shelter, clothing, and medicine so many have been denied for so long. It will help them to rebuild, to rebuild their roads and schools, their power plants and hospitals, their factories and shops. It will reunite children with their parents and families with their homes. It will allow the Bosnians freely to choose their own leaders. It will give all the people of Bosnia a much greater stake in peace than war, so that peace takes on a life and a logic of its own.

In Bosnia we can and will succeed because our mission is clear and limited and our troops are strong and very well-prepared. But my fellow Americans, no deployment of American troops is risk-free, and this one may well involve casualties. There may be accidents in the field or incidents with people who have not given up their hatred. I will take every measure possible to minimize these risks, but we must be prepared for that possibility.

As President, my most difficult duty is to put the men and women who volunteer to serve our Nation in harm's way when our interests and values demand it. I assume full responsibility for any harm that may come to them. But anyone contemplating any action that would endanger our troops should know this: America protects its own. Anyone, anyone, who takes on our troops will suffer the consequences. We will fight fire with fire and then some.

After so much bloodshed and loss, after so many outrageous acts of inhuman brutality, it will take an extraordinary effort of will for the people of Bosnia to pull themselves from their past and start building a future of peace. But with our leadership and the commitment of our allies, the people of Bosnia can have the chance to decide their future in peace. They have a chance to remind the world that just a few short years ago the mosques and churches of Sarajevo were a shining symbol of multiethnic tolerance, that Bosnia once found unity in its diversity. Indeed, the cemetery in the center of the city was just a few short years ago a magnificent stadium which hosted the Olympics, our universal symbol of peace and harmony. Bosnia can be that kind of place again. We must not turn our backs on Bosnia now.

And so I ask all Americans and I ask every Member of Congress, Democrat and Republican alike, to make the choice for peace. In the choice between peace and war, America must choose peace.

My fellow Americans, I ask you to think just for a moment about this century that is drawing to close and the new one that will soon begin. Because previous generations of Americans stood up for freedom and because we continue to do so, the American people are more secure and more prosperous. And all around the world, more people than ever before live in freedom. More people than ever before are treated with dignity. More people than ever before can hope to build a better life. That is what America's leadership is all about.

We know that these are the blessings of freedom. And America has always been freedom's greatest champion. If we continue to do everything we can to share these blessings with people around the world, if we continue to be leaders for peace, then the next century can be the greatest time our Nation has ever known.

A few weeks ago, I was privileged to spend some time with His Holiness Pope John Paul II, when he came to America. At the very end of our meeting, the Pope looked at me and said, "I have lived through most of this century. I remember that it began with a war in Sarajevo. Mr. President, you must not let it end with a war in Sarajevo."

In Bosnia, this terrible war has challenged our interests and troubled our souls. Thankfully, we can do something about it. I say again, our mission will be clear, limited, and achievable. The people of Bosnia, our NATO allies, and people all around the world are now looking to America for leadership. So let us lead. That is our responsibility as Americans.

Good night, and God bless America.

NOTE: The President spoke at 8 p.m. from the Oval Office at the White House.

Remarks Prior to a Meeting With Congressional Leaders and an Exchange With Reporters
November 28, 1995

Bosnia

The President. Well, thank you very much for coming today. I just wanted to say, again, I appreciate the interest here in the Congress, the remarkable turnout. I'm looking forward to this meeting.

As I said last night, the United States faces an historic choice between peace and war. I believe we will choose peace. I'm looking forward to having the chance to answer these questions. I know there are many questions, and good questions, that have to be answered to the Members of Congress and on behalf of the American people coming through the Members of Congress. This is the first of many, many more meetings we will have in the aftermath of the talk I gave to the American people last night. And I'm looking forward to beginning it.

Thank you.

Q. What has been the response of the Republican leadership so far, Mr. President?

The President. As you know, we had a meeting before this meeting with the Republican and Democratic leadership of the Congress to discuss scheduling of hearings, debate, and vote. And we had a very constructive meeting. I think I should let them speak for themselves, but I was very pleased by the meeting.

Q. What will you do to overcome public skepticism, Mr. President?

The President. Just more of what we're doing. We'll keep answering questions and reasserting what is at stake here in terms of the values, the interests of the American people, and the leadership of our country and our partnerships with our allies.

Thank you.

NOTE: The President spoke at 4:03 p.m. in the State Dining Room at the White House. A portion of these remarks could not be verified because the tape was incomplete.

Statement on Signing the National Highway System Designation Act of 1995
November 28, 1995

Today I have signed into law S. 440, the "National Highway System Designation Act of 1995." This Act advances my Administration's continued commitment to strategic investment in our Nation's infrastructure. It releases immediately more than $5 billion in funding for highway and other transportation projects. It also implements my proposal for a "Zero Tolerance" policy toward drinking and driving by those under age 21.

I am disturbed, however, by the repeal of certain key safety measures and will work to mitigate the impact of their repeal.

This Act is the culmination of several years' work by all levels of government to identify highways of national significance—routes that will support our Nation's needs for efficient, safe, and reliable transportation. The designation of the National Highway System makes clear that transportation infrastructure should be viewed as a single system, with each mode complementing the others. Manufacturers and shippers rely on several modes of transportation to deliver their products to consumers in the most efficient manner possible. The National Highway System unites these different modes by providing access to major ports, airports, rail stations, and public transit facilities. The National Highway System also provides 53 critical connections to Canada and Mexico so that goods can move across our Nation's borders efficiently.

In 1992, I saw the way in which our Nation's highways reach all Americans. Vice President Gore and I traveled much of this great land in buses, and we met the American people where they live and where they work. Whether at a truck stop in Carlisle, Pennsylvania, or at dusk on U.S. Highway 51 in Sandoval, Illinois, we saw and heard what access and mobility mean to opportunity and economic well-being. It was during our first bus trip, from New York City to St. Louis, Missouri, that I made a commitment to rebuild America. And I'm proud to say, this National Highway System bill builds on all the work we have done in the last 3 years to do just that.

But the National Highway System is also something more. It is a prime example of the strategic investment of Federal resources. The National Highway System comprises only 4 percent of our Nation's highways, but these roads carry almost half of our highway traffic and most of our Nation's truck and tourist traffic. The improvements made to these roads will not only support our Nation's economic, national defense, and mobility needs, but directly and significantly improve the safety of these key national roadways. The funds released by this legislation and used to upgrade noninterstate highways will provide significant safety benefits.

This Act also includes an essential and commonsense highway safety measure. Last June,

I called on the Congress to make "Zero Tolerance" the law of the land and require States to adopt a Zero Tolerance standard for drivers under the age of 21. It is already against the law for young people to consume alcohol. This national standard will reinforce these laws by making it effectively illegal for young people who have been drinking to drive an automobile.

Many States have already enacted Zero Tolerance laws. These laws work—alcohol-related crashes involving teenage drivers are down as much as 20 percent in those States. When all States have these laws, hundreds more lives will be saved and thousands of injuries will be prevented. I commend the Congress for heeding my call and making Zero Tolerance the standard nationwide for drivers under the age of 21.

S. 440 establishes innovative ways to attract new forms of investment in transportation and gives States greater flexibility and more options to utilize limited Federal transportation funds effectively. It also eliminates unnecessary Federal requirements such as those concerning highway building materials and program management. This will enable Federal transportation officials to focus their efforts on the most useful and cost-effective ways of achieving important safety aims and increase States' discretion to implement their highway programs in ways best suited to their own circumstances.

In approving S. 440, however, I must note that some of my most serious concerns with this legislation have not been remedied. I am deeply disturbed by the repeal of both the national maximum speed limit law and the law encouraging States to enact motorcycle helmet use laws. I am also disturbed that this Act could potentially exempt large numbers of small- to medium-sized trucks and their drivers from critical safety regulations governing driver qualifications and truck maintenance.

Without question, these laws have saved lives. The States, now given greater authority over issues of highway safety, must exercise this authority responsibly. I am, therefore, strongly committed to the requirement in this Act for Federal and State officials to work together to assess the costs and benefits of any change in speed limits. I have instructed the Secretary of Transportation to develop an action plan to promote safety consistent with my Administration's continuing commitment to highway safety. My Administration will redouble our efforts to protect those who travel on our Nation's highways.

Although I am disappointed by the Congress' actions on these important safety measures, I believe that this legislation will benefit the Nation by designating and funding the National Highway System, strengthening the backbone of our transportation system, providing jobs and economic opportunities, funding vital transportation projects in every State, and making Zero Tolerance the law of the land.

WILLIAM J. CLINTON

The White House,
November 28, 1995.

NOTE: S. 440, approved November 28, was assigned Public Law No. 104–59.

Message to the Congress Reporting on the National Emergency With Respect to Iran
November 28, 1995

To the Congress of the United States:

I hereby report to the Congress on developments since the last Presidential report of May 18, 1995, concerning the national emergency with respect to Iran that was declared in Executive Order No. 12170 of November 14, 1979. This report is submitted pursuant to section 204(c) of the International Emergency Economic Powers Act, 50 U.S.C. 1703(c) and section 505(c) of the International Security and Development Cooperation Act of 1985, 22 U.S.C. 2349aa–9(c). This report covers events through September 29, 1995. My last report, dated May 18, 1995, covered events through April 18, 1995.

1. On March 15 of this year by Executive Order No. 12957, I declared a separate national emergency pursuant to the International Emergency Economic Powers Act and imposed separate sanctions. Executive Order No. 12959, issued May 6, 1995, then significantly augmented

those new sanctions. As a result, as I reported on September 18, 1995, in conjunction with the declaration of a separate emergency and the imposition of new sanctions, the Iranian Transactions Regulations, 31 CFR Part 560, have been comprehensively amended.

There have been no amendments to the Iranian Assets Control Regulations, 31 CFR Part 535, since the last report. However, the amendments to the Iranian Transactions Regulations that implement the new separate national emergency are of some relevance to the Iran-United States Claims Tribunal (the "Tribunal") and related activities. For example, sections 560.510, 560.513, and 560.525 contain general licenses with respect to, and provide for specific licensing of, certain transactions related to arbitral activities.

2. The Tribunal, established at The Hague pursuant to the Algiers Accords, continues to make progress in arbitrating the claims before it. Since my last report, the Tribunal has rendered four awards, bringing the total number to 566. As of September 29, 1995, the value of awards to successful American claimants from the Security Account held by the NV Settlement Bank stood at $2,368,274,541.67.

Iran has not replenished the Security Account established by the Accords to ensure payment of awards to successful U.S. claimants since October 8, 1992. The Account has remained continuously below the $500 million balance required by the Algiers Accords since November 5, 1992. As of September 29, 1995, the total amount in the Security Account was $188,105,627.95, and the total amount in the Interest Account was $32,066,870.62.

Therefore, the United States continues to pursue Case A/28, filed in September 1993, to require Iran to meet its obligations under the Accords to replenish the Security Account. Iran filed its Statement of Defense in that case on August 31, 1995. The United States is preparing a Reply for filing on December 4, 1995.

3. The Department of State continues to present other United States Government claims against Iran, in coordination with concerned government agencies, and to respond to claims brought against the United States by Iran, in coordination with concerned government agencies.

In September 1995, the Departments of Justice and State represented the United States in the first Tribunal hearing on a government-

to-government claim in 5 years. The Full Tribunal heard arguments in Cases A/15(IV) and A/24. Case A/15(IV) is an interpretive dispute in which Iran claims that the United States has violated the Algiers Accords by its alleged failure to terminate all litigation against Iran in U.S. courts. Case A/24 involves a similar interpretive dispute in which, specifically, Iran claims that the obligation of the United States under the Accords to terminate litigation prohibits a lawsuit against Iran by the McKesson Corporation from proceeding in U.S. District Court for the District of Columbia. The McKesson Corporation reactivated that litigation against Iran in the United States following the Tribunal's negative ruling on Foremost McKesson Incorporated's claim before the Tribunal.

Also in September 1995, Iran filed briefs in two cases, to which the United States is now preparing responses. In Case A/11, Iran filed its Hearing Memorial and Evidence. In that case, Iran has sued the United States for $10 billion, alleging that the United States failed to fulfill its obligations under the Accords to assist Iran in recovering the assets of the former Shah of Iran. Iran alleges that the United States improperly failed to (1) freeze the U.S. assets of the Shah's estate and certain U.S. assets of close relatives of the Shah; (2) report to Iran all known information about such assets; and (3) otherwise assist Iran in such litigation.

In Case A/15(II:A), 3 years after the Tribunal's partial award in the case, Iran filed briefs and evidence relating to 10 of Iran's claims against the United States Government for non-military property allegedly held by private companies in the United States. Although Iran's submission was made in response to a Tribunal order directing Iran to file its brief and evidence "concerning all remaining issues to be decided by this Case," Iran's filing failed to address many claims in the case.

In August 1995, the United States filed the second of two parts of its consolidated submission on the merits in Case B/61, addressing issues of liability and compensation. As reported in my May 1995 Report, Case B/61 involves a claim by Iran for compensation with respect to primarily military equipment that Iran alleges it did not receive. The equipment was purchased pursuant to commercial contracts with more than 50 private American companies. Iran alleges that it suffered direct losses and consequential damages in excess of $2 billion in total because of the United States Government's refusal to allow the export of the equipment after January 19, 1981, in alleged contravention of the Algiers Accords.

4. Since my last report, the Tribunal has issued two important awards in favor of U.S. nationals considered dual U.S.-Iranian nationals by the Tribunal. On July 7, 1995, the Tribunal issued Award No. 565, awarding a claimant $1.1 million plus interest for Iran's expropriation of the claimant's shares in the Iranian architectural firm of Abdolaziz Farmafarmaian & Associates. On July 14, 1995, the Tribunal issued Award No. 566, awarding two claimants $129,869 each, plus interest, as compensation for Iran's taking of real property inherited by the claimants from their father. Award No. 566 is significant in that it is the Tribunal's first decision awarding dual national claimants compensation for Iran's expropriation of real property in Iran.

5. The situation reviewed above continues to implicate important diplomatic, financial, and legal interests of the United States and its nationals and presents an unusual challenge to the national security and foreign policy of the United States. The Iranian Assets Control Regulations issued pursuant to Executive Order No. 12170 continue to play an important role in structuring our relationship with Iran and in enabling the United States to implement properly the Algiers Accords. I shall continue to exercise the powers at my disposal to deal with these problems and will continue to report periodically to the Congress on significant developments.

WILLIAM J. CLINTON

The White House,
November 28, 1995.

Message to the Congress Transmitting the Railroad Retirement Board Report
November 28, 1995

To the Congress of the United States:
I transmit herewith the Annual Report of the Railroad Retirement Board for Fiscal Year 1994, pursuant to the provisions of section 7(b)(6) of the Railroad Retirement Act and section 12(1) of the Railroad Unemployment Insurance Act.

WILLIAM J. CLINTON

The White House,
November 28, 1995.

Remarks on the Northern Ireland Peace Process
November 28, 1995

I have just come from a meeting with the congressional leadership, where we discussed the importance of continuing America's leadership in the search for peace in Bosnia. I emphasized to them this afternoon, as I did to the American people last evening, that our mission will be clear, limited, and achievable and that the risks to our troops will be minimized. Bosnia is a case where our leadership can make the difference between peace and war. And America must choose peace.

Now I am departing for Europe, where British Prime Minister Major and Irish Prime Minister Bruton have just announced the launching of a promising new twin-track initiative to advance the peace process in Northern Ireland. I want to salute both these leaders for their vision, their courage, and for their leadership for peace.

The twin-track initiative will establish an international body to address the issue of arms decommissioning, while at the same time organizing preliminary political talks in which all parties, all parties, will be invited to participate. I am pleased that former Senator George Mitchell will chair the international body. The goal is to bring all the parties together for political talks on the future of Northern Ireland. This is an opportunity to begin a dialog in which all views are presented and all are heard.

In just a few days, I will become the first American President ever to visit Northern Ireland. Last year's cease-fire and the process of negotiations has sparked a remarkable transformation in that land. For the first time in 25 years, children can walk to school without fear. Bomb-shattered shopfronts have both been replaced by new businesses. People can visit their relatives and friends without the burdens of checkpoints or barricades. Crossing the border between north and south is as simple as going over a speed bump.

The twin-track initiative builds on those achievements. It brings the people of Northern Ireland one step closer to the day when the only barriers their children will face are the limits of their dreams.

Today's announcement also brings hope and strength to all those who struggle for peace around the world. It demonstrates that the will for peace is more powerful than bombs and bullets. And it reminds us once again that, with courage and resolve, bitter legacies of conflict can be overcome.

The United States is proud to support the peacemakers in Northern Ireland, in the Middle East, in Bosnia, and throughout the world. Those who stand up for peace will have the United States standing with them.

Thank you very much.

NOTE: The President spoke at 7:26 p.m. on the South Lawn at the White House, prior to his departure for the United Kingdom. In his remarks, he referred to Prime Minister John Major of the United Kingdom and Prime Minister John Bruton of Ireland.

The President's News Conference With Prime Minister John Major of the United Kingdom in London, England
November 29, 1995

Prime Minister Major. Can I, firstly, welcome the President here to London. I'm delighted he's been able to come in what is, I know, for him an extremely busy time. And he and Mrs. Clinton are extremely welcome guests here.

The President's come to London fresh from explaining to Congress and the American people his plans for a very large United States contribution to the peace implementation force in Bosnia. Bosnia is, and has been for some years, a shared responsibility. British troops have been there now for something over 3 years, in numbers ranging up to 8,000 at a time. And both of our countries have made huge contributions to the international aid effort.

What I think we now need to do is to carry the remarkable Dayton agreements through to a successful conclusion. Dayton was a very hard-won and hugely important breakthrough by the United States and her Contact Group partners. And for the first time in the many discussions over the years that the President and I have had on Bosnia, we can look this morning at a realistic prospect of a real and lasting peace in Bosnia.

But it is still a fragile prospect, and we need to make sure that it doesn't in some fashion just slip away from us. And that is why we both agree that it's vital to deploy a genuinely effective implementation force to Bosnia as soon as the peace agreements come into effect. I very much welcome the President's intention to contribute a large force to that particular cause.

I can certainly confirm that we shall do the same. We intend to make a large contribution; around 13,000 troops will be the size of the British contribution to that force. They will find themselves working in the future, as so many times in the past, with their American colleagues in a common endeavor. And I believe it's an endeavor of immense importance to the future of Bosnia and for many places beyond it. And I look forward to the peace implementation conference in London in a couple of weeks' time, which will work on the very important civil aspects of that peace agreement.

The President and I this morning have also had the opportunity of talking about Northern Ireland and about the twin-track initiative that I launched yesterday with the Irish Prime Minister. I am delighted that the President will tomorrow become the first serving United States President to visit Northern Ireland. I have no doubt that that will give a huge encouragement to the people in Northern Ireland who have been working for peace. And I'm sure that it will boost the very valuable help that George Mitchell will be giving us in his work, for he has generously agreed to undertake the work as chairman of the new body to look at the question of decommissioning.

George Mitchell, of course, is no stranger to the situation in Northern Ireland and over the years has given us very great help in promoting investment in Northern Ireland's economy. So I think the chairmanship of the international body is in very good hands. And I'm very grateful to Senator Mitchell for undertaking it and for the President for permitting that.

I had the opportunity with the President this morning of discussing the present situation in Northern Ireland. What I hope people will see with his visit there in a day or so is the changed life in Northern Ireland. For far too long, the world has been very familiar with the negative side of Northern Ireland. I think the President's visit will enable him and his colleagues to see how very dramatically life has changed there over the past 15 months. And we look forward to carrying that further.

We had the opportunity of discussing a number of other matters, but I think in the limited time available, I won't touch upon those at the moment, but I will invite the President to say a few words.

The President. Thank you very much, Prime Minister. This is my sixth trip to Europe as President and the latest of the many, many sessions I have had with Prime Minister Major. Europe and the United States have unbreakable ties, but the United Kingdom and the United States enjoy a unique and enduring relationship.

Because of our values and the work we have done together over the last 50 years, the things we stand for are more and more becoming widely accepted all around the world. Today we discussed our ongoing efforts to reinforce our partnership; to reduce the threat of weapons of mass destruction; to combat terrorism, international crime, and drug trafficking; and to advance the global march of peace. And of course, we mostly discussed Northern Ireland and Bosnia.

Let me begin by just congratulating the Prime Minister on the important initiative that he and Prime Minister Bruton announced yesterday to advance the process of peace in Northern Ireland. The twin-track initiative will establish an international body to address arms decommissioning and at the same time will initiate preliminary political talks in which all parties will be invited to participate. This is an opportunity for them to begin a dialog in which all views are represented and all voices are heard.

I cannot say enough to the British people how much I appreciate and admire the Prime Minister in taking this kind of risk for peace. This was not an easy action for him to take, not an easy action for Prime Minister Bruton to take. Very often, people who take risks for peace are not appreciated for doing so. But we in the United States appreciate this work and hope very much that it will prove fruitful. Tomorrow I will visit a Northern Ireland that is closer to true peace than at any time in a generation. And the risks that have been taken to date by the Prime Minister and by the Irish Prime Minister and his predecessor are a big reason why.

The United Kingdom has also taken extraordinary risks for peace in Bosnia. The United States deeply appreciates all this country has done to end the suffering in Bosnia, your brave soldiers who risked their lives as part of UNPROFOR, your countless humanitarian relief efforts to aid the people of that wartorn land, your diplomatic and military strength as members of the Contact Group and NATO.

Now the people of Bosnia have made a commitment to peace, and we have to do our part to help it succeed. That means participating in NATO's Implementation Force, not to fight a war in Bosnia but to help secure a peace. It means implementing the arms controls provisions of that agreement while ensuring that the Bosnian Federation has the means to defend itself once NATO withdraws. And it means supporting the reconstruction in Bosnia so that all the people there can share in the benefits of peace. If we can secure the peace in Bosnia—and I am convinced that we can and will—

that will bring us a step closer to the goal of a free, peaceful, and undivided Europe.

The Prime Minister and I discussed developments in Russia, including the upcoming parliamentary elections, and agreed that fuller integration of Russia and Europe remains a key goal that both of us share. We also reaffirmed our joint determination to open NATO to new membership in a gradual and open way.

I also welcome the priority the United Kingdom has given to strengthening the Atlantic community. This weekend at the summit meeting between the United States and the European Union in Madrid, I hope we can agree on a vigorous Atlantic agenda that we can both work to implement.

Let me just close by saying that we live in a time of remarkable opportunity for peace and prosperity, for open markets and open societies, for human dignity and human decency. Together the United States and the United Kingdom have helped to shape this hopeful moment in our history. We have some more work to do. We just talked about two of our biggest challenges. But I am confident that our people are up to those challenges and that that work will be done.

Thank you.

Prime Minister Major. Now, the President has a speech to deliver in Parliament not very long ahead, but we can take just a few questions.

Yes, the lady in the red scarf.

Bosnia

Q. President Clinton, could you let us know if one of the things you discussed was arming and training the Bosnian military and how that will work as part of this peace process?

The President. Yes, we discussed that, but in our roles as a part of the NATO mission, neither the NATO forces of the United States or the United Kingdom will be involved in that. There is an agreement among the parties that they will work for 6 months to achieve an arms control agreement; that they will do everything they can to agree on a fair way to reduce the number of arms in Bosnia; that if they fail to reach agreement there will be a 25 percent reduction by all the parties in the region, preserving roughly the ratio of arms that exists now between Serbia, Croatia, and Bosnia but at a smaller level, and that within Bosnia proper, the Bosnian Federation will have a roughly 2-to-1 ratio of arms and that that will have to be

supplied in terms of equipment and training by third parties, which we are confident will occur.

Northern Ireland Peace Process

Q. Mr. President, do you accept the British Government's position that there must be some giving up of arms by the paramilitaries and especially by Sinn Fein IRA, before all-party talks can begin?

The President. I accept the British Government's position announced yesterday in the twin tracks. That is, I believe the agreement represented—or reflected in what Prime Minister Bruton and Prime Minister Major announced yesterday has set forth a framework within which these differences of opinion can be resolved. And I hope the framework will be accepted by all the parties.

My answer to you, sir, is that the United States, whether it's in the Middle East or Bosnia or in Northern Ireland, has tried to support a reasonable peace process, not to dictate the terms or make the decisions. The twin-track process is a reasonable peace process. And it is not for us to get into the details of the judgment that the countries and the parties will have to make.

Prime Minister Major. Yes, Helen [Helen Thomas, United Press International].

Q. What broke the camel's back on this? You were arguing for so long on this one issue. Was there one thing that turned the tide, one catalyst?

Prime Minister Major. Well, there were a whole range of points we've been discussing over the last few days. It wasn't just the decommissioning issue. There were a range of other issues as well. And I think time wore away the difference—time and patience on both sides.

I think the number of meetings that there have been over the last few weeks, the numbers of discussions I've had with John Bruton—I've absolutely no doubt both our telephone bills will be astronomical, but we think it's worthwhile. It was simply that we saw that a deal needed to be reached if we were to regain the momentum and carry this process forward.

We can't deliver peace, John Bruton and I. We can't do that. What we can do is facilitate peace. And what we are putting in place is a process that will help to carry that capacity for peace forward. Now, that can be achieved if the politicians in the north are able to reach themselves an agreement that this conflict is over. And what we were seeking was a mechanism of carrying this forward so that that work would continue.

But I emphasize the point, peace isn't in my gift or in John Bruton's gift. It is in the gift of all the people who at present have caused the conflict. We must bring them together. Constant examining of the detailed problems found a way through.

Q. Did the President's trip have anything to do with it?

Prime Minister Major. I think the fact that the President's trip—the President was coming concentrated the mind.

Q. Now that you have agreement, are you prepared to accompany the President to Belfast on any part of his trip? And like the President, are you prepared to meet all the party leaders in Northern Ireland now?

Prime Minister Major. Well, I've met most of the party leaders in Northern Ireland. In due course I will meet them all. I won't be meeting them all quite yet. And I think the President is being accompanied by the Secretary of State to Northern Ireland. I will be answering questions in Parliament.

Q. Mr. President, is your message to the IRA that they should start surrendering their weapons and explosives now, immediately?

The President. My message to the IRA is that the twin-tracks process has provided a mechanism for all of the parties honorably now to bring their concerns to the table and to be heard and that, in the end, peace means peace, and we're all going to have to support that.

But the message I should give in public is the same message I would give in private: I think the framework set out by Prime Minister Major and Prime Minister Bruton is the best opportunity I have seen to resolve all of these issues, and I think it should be embraced and I hope it will be.

Prime Minister Major. Have we time for one more? Yes, gentleman there.

Q. Mr. Prime Minister, do you think Mr. President—the President has been too accommodating to Mr. Adams, or do you think it's now—his efforts have been worthwhile?

Prime Minister Major. I don't think it's a question of being accommodating at all. American support in this process has always been immensely helpful, and the President has always taken a very great interest in that process. There is a communal interest in achieving a satisfactory settlement in Northern Ireland. It's very much in the interest of everybody in Northern Ireland, very close to my heart and something very close to the President's heart as well. And I welcome the tremendous support he's been, both publicly and privately. I think that has been very helpful, and I'm very pleased to have the opportunity of thanking him for it in public. Thank you very much, indeed.

The President. Thank you.

NOTE: The President's 106th news conference began at 11:20 a.m. at 10 Downing Street. A reporter referred to Gerry Adams, leader of Sinn Fein.

Remarks to the Parliament of the United Kingdom in London
November 29, 1995

My Lord Chancellor, Madam Speaker, Lord Privy Seal, the Lord President of the Council, Mr. Prime Minister, my Lords, and Members of the House of Commons. To the Lord Chancellor, the longer I hear you talk the more I wish we had an institution like this in American Government. I look out and see so many of your distinguished leaders in the House of Lords, and I think it might not be a bad place to be after a long and troublesome political career. [*Laughter*] My wife and I are honored

to be here today, and I thank you for inviting me to address you.

I have been here to Westminster many times before. As a student, I visited often, and over the last 20 years I have often returned. Always I have felt the power of this place, where the voices of free people who love liberty, believe in reason, and struggle for truth have for centuries kept your great nation a beacon of hope for all the world and a very special model for your former colonies which became the United States of America.

Here, where the voices of Pitt and Burke, Disraeli and Gladstone rang out; here, where the rights of English men and women were secured and enlarged; here, where the British people's determination to stand against the tyrannies of this century were shouted to the entire world: Here is a monument to liberty to which every free person owes honor and gratitude.

As one whose ancestors came from these isles, I cherish this opportunity. Since I entered public life I have often thought of the words of Prime Minister Churchill when he spoke to our Congress in 1941. He said that if his father had been American and his mother British, instead of the other way around, he might have gotten there on his own. [*Laughter*] Well, for a long time I thought that if my forebears had not left this country, perhaps I might have gotten here on my own, at least to the House of Commons.

But I have to tell you, now our American television carries your "question time." And I have seen Prime Minister Major and Mr. Blair and the other members slicing each other up face-to-face—[*laughter*]—with such great wit and skill, against the din of cheers and jeers. I am now convinced my forebears did me a great favor by coming to America. [*Laughter*]

Today the United States and the United Kingdom glory in an extraordinary relationship that unites us in a way never before seen in the ties between two such great nations. It is perhaps all the more remarkable because of our history, first, the war we waged for our independence, and then barely three decades later, another war we waged in which your able forces laid siege to our Capitol. Indeed, the White House still bears the burn marks of that earlier stage in our relationship. And now, whenever we have even the most minor disagreement, I walk out on the Truman Balcony and I look at those burn marks, just to remind myself that I dare not let this relationship get out of hand again. [*Laughter*]

In this century we overcame the legacy of our differences. We discovered our common heritage again, and even more important, we rediscovered our shared values. This November, we are reminded of how exactly the bonds that now join us grew, of the three great trials our nations have faced together in this century.

A few weeks ago we marked the anniversary of that day in 1918 when the guns fell silent in World War I, a war we fought side by side

to defend democracy against militarism and reaction. On this Veterans Day for us and Remembrance Day for you, we both paid special tribute to the British and American generation that, 50 years ago now, in the skies over the Channel, on the craggy hills of Italy, in the jungles of Burma, in the flights over the Hump, did not fail or falter. In the greatest struggle for freedom in all of history, they saved the world.

Our nations emerged from that war with the resolve to prevent another like it. We bound ourselves together with other democracies in the West and with Japan, and we stood firm throughout the long twilight struggle of the cold war, from the Berlin Airlift of 1948 to the fall of the Berlin Wall on another November day just 6 years ago.

In the years since, we have also stood together, fighting together for victory in the Persian Gulf, standing together against terrorism, working together to remove the nuclear cloud from our children's bright future, and together preparing the way for peace in Bosnia, where your peacekeepers have performed heroically and saved the lives of so many innocent people. I thank the British nation for its strength and its sacrifice through all these struggles. And I am proud to stand here on behalf of the American people to salute you.

Ladies and gentlemen, in this century, democracy has not merely endured, it has prevailed. Now it falls to us to advance the cause that so many fought and sacrificed and died for. In this new era, we must rise not in a call to arms but in a call to peace.

The great American philosopher John Dewey once said, "The only way to abolish war is to make peace heroic." Well, we know we will never abolish war or all the forces that cause it because we cannot abolish human nature or the certainty of human error. But we can make peace heroic. And in so doing, we can create a future even more true to our ideals than all our glorious past. To do so, we must maintain the resolve in peace we shared in war when everything was at stake.

In this new world our lives are not so very much at risk, but much of what makes life worth living is still very much at stake. We have fought our wars. Now let us wage our peace.

This time is full of possibility. The chasm of ideology has disappeared. Around the world, the ideals we defended and advanced are now shared by more people than ever before. In Europe and many other nations, long-suffering peoples at last control their our destinies. And as the cold war gives way to the global village, economic freedom is spreading alongside political freedom, bringing with it renewed hope for a better life, rooted in the honorable and healthy competition of effort and ideas.

America is determined to maintain our alliance for freedom and peace with you and determined to seek the partnership of all like-minded nations to confront the threats still before us. We know the way. Together we have seen how we succeed when we work together.

When President Roosevelt and Prime Minister Churchill first met on the deck of the HMS *Prince of Wales* in 1941 at one of the loneliest moments in your nation's history, they joined in prayer, and the Prime Minister was filled with hope. Afterwards, he said, "The same language, the same hymns, more or less the same ideals. Something big may be happening, something very big."

Well, once again, he was right. Something really big happened. On the basis of those ideals, Churchill and Roosevelt and all of their successors built an enduring alliance and a genuine friendship between our nations. Other times in other places are littered with the vows of friendship sworn during battle and then abandoned in peacetime. This one stands alone, unbroken, above all the rest, a model for the ties that should bind all democracies.

To honor that alliance and the Prime Minister who worked so mightily to create it, I am pleased to announce here, in the home of British freedom, that the United States will name one of the newest and most powerful of its surface ships, a guided missile destroyer, the United States Ship *Winston Churchill*. When that ship slips down the ways in the final year of this century, its name will ride the seas as a reminder for the coming century of an indomitable man who shaped our age, who stood always for freedom, who showed anew the glorious strength of the human spirit. I thank the members of the Churchill family who are here today with us, Lady Soames, Nicholas Soames, Winston Churchill, and I thank the British people for their friendship and their strength over these many years.

After so much success together we know that our relationship with the United Kingdom must be at the heart of our striving in this new era.

Because of the history we have lived, because of the power and prosperity we enjoy, because of the accepted truth that you and we have no dark motives in our dealings with other nations, we still bear a burden of special responsibility.

In these few years since the cold war we have met that burden by making gains for peace and security that ordinary people feel every day. We have stepped back from the nuclear precipice with the indefinite extension of the Nuclear Non-proliferation Treaty, and we hope next year a comprehensive test ban treaty.

For the first time in a generation, parents in Los Angeles and Manchester and, yes, in Moscow, can now turn out the lights at night knowing there are no nuclear weapons pointed at their children. Our nations are working together to lay the foundation for lasting prosperity. We are bringing down economic barriers between nations with the historic GATT agreement and other actions that are creating millions of good jobs for our own people and for people throughout the world. The United States and the United Kingdom are supporting men and women who embrace freedom and democracy the world over with good results, from South Africa to Central Europe, from Haiti to the Middle East.

In the United States, we feel a special gratitude for your efforts in Northern Ireland. With every passing month, more people walk the streets and live their lives safely, people who otherwise would have been added to the toll of the Troubles.

Tomorrow I will have the privilege of being the first American President to visit Northern Ireland, a Northern Ireland where the guns are quiet and the children play without fear. I applaud the efforts of Prime Minister Major and Irish Prime Minister Bruton who announced yesterday their new twin-track initiative to advance the peace process, an initiative that provides an opportunity to begin a dialog in which all views are represented and all views can be heard. This is a bold step forward for peace. I applaud the Prime Minister for taking this risk for peace. It is always a hard choice, the choice for peace, for success is far from guaranteed. And even if you fail, there will be those who resent you for trying. But it is the right thing to do. And in the end, the right will win.

Despite all of the progress we have made in all these areas and despite the problems clearly still out there, there are those who say at this moment of hope we can afford to relax now behind our secure borders. Now is the time, they say, to let others worry about the world's troubles. These are the siren songs of myth. They once lured the United States into isolationism after World War I. They counseled appeasement to Britain on the very brink of World War II. We have gone down that road before. We must never go down that road again. We will never go down that road again.

Though the cold war is over, the forces of destruction challenge us still. Today they are armed with a full array of threats, not just the single weapon of frontal war. We see them at work in the spread of weapons of mass destruction, from nuclear smuggling in Europe to a vial of sarin gas being broken open in the Tokyo subway to the bombing of the World Trade Center in New York. We see it in the growth of ethnic hatred, extreme nationalism, and religious fanaticism, which most recently took the life of one of the greatest champions of peace in the entire world, the Prime Minister of Israel. We see it in the terrorism that just in recent months has murdered innocent people from Islamabad to Paris, from Riyadh to Oklahoma City. And we see it in the international organized crime and drug trade that poisons our children and our communities.

In their variety these forces of disintegration are waging guerrilla wars against humanity. Like communism and fascism, they spread darkness over light, barbarism over civilization. And like communism and fascism, they will be defeated only because free nations join against them in common cause.

We will prevail again if, and only if, our people support the mission. We are, after all, democracies. And they are the ultimate bosses of our fate. I believe the people will support this. I believe free people, given the information, will make the decisions that will make it possible for their leaders to stand against the new threat to security and freedom, to peace and prosperity.

I believe they will see that this hopeful moment cannot be lost without grave consequences to the future. We must go out to meet the challenges before they come to threaten us. Today, for the United States and for Great Britain, that means we must make the difference between peace and war in Bosnia.

For nearly 4 years, a terrible war has torn Bosnia apart, bringing horrors we prayed had vanished from the face of Europe forever: the mass killings, the endless columns of refugees, the campaigns of deliberate rape, the skeletal persons imprisoned in concentration camps. These crimes did violence to the conscience of Britons and Americans. Now we have a chance to make sure they don't return. And we must seize it.

We must help peace to take hold in Bosnia because so long as that fire rages at the heart of the European Continent, so long as the emerging democracies and our allies are threatened by fighting in Bosnia, there will be no stable, undivided, free Europe; there will be no realization of our greatest hopes for Europe; but most important of all, innocent people will continue to suffer and die.

America fought two World Wars and stood with you in the cold war because of our vital stake in a Europe that is stable, strong, and free. With the end of the cold war, all of Europe has a chance to be stable, strong, and free for the very first time since nation-states appeared on the European Continent.

Now the warring parties in Bosnia have committed themselves to peace, and they have asked us to help them make it hold, not by fighting a war but by implementing their own peace agreement. Our nations have a responsibility to answer the request of those people to secure their peace. Without our leadership and without the presence of NATO, there will be no peace in Bosnia.

I thank the United Kingdom that has already sacrificed so much for its swift agreement to play a central role in the peace implementation. With this act, Britain holds true to its history and to its values. And I pledge to you that America will live up to its history and its ideals as well.

We know that if we do not participate in Bosnia our leadership will be questioned and our partnerships will be weakened, partnerships we must have if we are to help each other in the fight against the common threats we face. We can help the people of Bosnia as they seek a way back from savagery to civility. And we can build a peaceful, undivided Europe.

Today I reaffirm to you that the United States, as it did during the defense of democracy during the cold war, will help lead in building this Europe by working for a broader and more lasting peace and by supporting a Europe bound together in a woven fabric of vital democracies, market economies, and security cooperation.

Our cooperation with you through NATO, the sword and shield of democracy, can help the nations that once lay behind the Iron Curtain to become a part of the new Europe. In the cold war the alliance kept our Nation secure and bound the Western democracies together in common cause. It brought former adversaries together and gave them the confidence to look past ancient enmities. Now NATO will grow and expand the circle of common purpose, first through its Partnership For Peace, which is already having a remarkable impact on the member countries, and then, as we agree, with the admissions of new democratic members. It will threaten no one. But it will give its new allies the confidence they need to consolidate their freedoms, build their economies, strengthen peace, and become your partners for tomorrow.

Members of the House of Commons and Noble Lords, long before there was a United States, one of your most powerful champions of liberty and one of the greatest poets of our shared language wrote "Peace hath her victories, no less renowned than war." In our time, at last, we can prove the truth of John Milton's words.

As this month of remembrance passes and the holidays approach, I leave you with the words Winston Churchill spoke to America during America's darkest holiday season of the century. As he lit the White House Christmas Tree in 1941, he said, "Let the children have their night of fun and laughter. Let us share to the full in their unstinted pleasure before we turn again to the stern tasks in the year that lies before us. But now, by our sacrifice and bearing, these same children shall not be robbed of their inheritance or denied their right to live in a free and decent world."

My friends, we have stood together in the darkest moments of our century. Let us now resolve to stand together for the bright and shining prospect of the next century. It can be the age of possibility and the age of peace. Our forebears won the war. Let us now win the peace.

May God bless the United Kingdom, the United States, and our solemn alliance.

Thank you very much.

NOTE: The President spoke at 12:38 p.m. in the Royal Gallery of Westminster Palace. In his remarks, he referred to Lord MacKay of Clashfern, Lord Chancellor; Speaker of the House of Commons Betty Boothroyd; Viscount Cranborne, Lord Privy Seal and Leader of the House of Lords; and Anthony Newton, Lord President of the Council and Leader of the House of Commons.

Remarks Prior to Discussions With British Labour Party Leader Tony Blair and an Exchange With Reporters in London
November 29, 1995

The President. Good afternoon. Let me say, first of all, I'm delighted to have this opportunity to meet with the British Labour leader, Tony Blair. I have followed his career with great interest, and I am anxious to have this time to visit with him about his views on conditions here and matters affecting both of our countries, especially the Bosnian question. And I don't know whether he was looking forward to coming here or not because he's just come from that "question time" that I referred to in my speech to the Parliament today.

Northern Ireland Peace Process

Q. Are you interested in his views on Ireland?
The President. Of course I am.
Q. What are they?
The President. Well, that's for him to say. I haven't had a chance to talk to him.

Mr. Blair. First of all, let me say, I'm absolutely delighted to meet the President and to express my admiration, not merely for his magnificent speech this morning that I think will have a great impact here and abroad but also for the work that he's done in bringing peace to Bosnia and the Middle East, to Ireland and to other parts of the world.

And our views on Ireland—in fact, today in the House of Commons, you wouldn't have seen any of the cut-and-thrust at all. It was one of these rare moments of agreement between myself and John Major. We've supported the government in that push for peace in Northern Ireland. We will continue to do so.

Q. Mr. President, what kind of advice are you giving Mr. Blair, and I'm wondering if Mr. Blair can explain what lessons you've learned from President Clinton?

The President. I have no advice to give him. And let me say, one of the things that I'm going to do privately—I might as well do it publicly—is to thank him for the position that he and his party have taken on this, the question of the initiatives of the British Government in Northern Ireland.

A country is always stronger when, in its foreign policy and its difficult decisions, it moves forward together so that the country can be strong, can be united, and the people essentially can both claim the credit and shoulder the responsibility. And I think this is a very exceptional act of statesmanship on his part, and I very much appreciate it.

Q. Which you'd like to see on the part of the Republicans?

Q. What's your message tomorrow going to be, sir?

The President. Well, we've already answered too many questions, I can tell now. [*Laughter*]

NOTE: The President spoke at 4:10 p.m. at the U.S. Ambassador's residence. A tape was not available for verification of the content of these remarks.

Statement on Congressional Action on Lobby Reform Legislation
November 29, 1995

I am delighted that Congress has passed lobby reform legislation. This bill will help change the way Washington does business. For too long, Washington's influence industry has operated out of the sunlight of public scrutiny. This new law will require professional lobbyists, for the first time, to fully disclose who they are working for and what legislation they are trying to pass or kill. Lobby reform will be good for American democracy and will help restore the trust of the people in their Government.

This is precisely the sort of change that the American people have demanded and that I championed during my campaign for the Presidency and as President. I am particularly pleased that a strong bipartisan coalition in both the House and Senate stood firm for reform. I want to especially thank Senator Carl Levin, who championed this legislation for many years, and the other Members for their leadership, including Senator Bill Cohen and Representatives Barney Frank, John Bryant, and Charles Canady.

Since I took office, I have challenged Congress to enact four significant political reform measures: legislation applying laws to Congress, a ban on gifts to lawmakers, lobby disclosure, and campaign finance reform. The Congress has now acted on the first three of these reform priorities. It is time to finish the job.

Message to the Congress Transmitting the EURATOM–United States Nuclear Energy Cooperation Agreement
November 29, 1995

To the Congress of the United States:

I am pleased to transmit to the Congress, pursuant to sections 123 b. and 123 d. of the Atomic Energy Act of 1954, as amended (42 U.S.C. 2153(b), (d)), the text of a proposed Agreement for Cooperation in the Peaceful Uses of Nuclear Energy Between the United States of America and the European Atomic Energy

Community (EURATOM) with accompanying agreed minute, annexes, and other attachments. (The confidential list of EURATOM storage facilities covered by the Agreement is being transmitted directly to the Senate Foreign Relations Committee and the House International Relations Committee.) I am also pleased to transmit my written approval, authorization and determination concerning the agreement, and the memorandum of the Director of the United States Arms Control and Disarmament Agency with the Nuclear Proliferation Assessment Statement concerning the agreement. The joint memorandum submitted to me by the Secretary of State and the Secretary of Energy, which includes a summary of the provisions of the agreement and other attachments, including the views of the Nuclear Regulatory Commission, is also enclosed.

The proposed new agreement with EURATOM has been negotiated in accordance with the Atomic Energy Act of 1954, as amended by the Nuclear Non-Proliferation Act of 1978 (NNPA) and as otherwise amended. It replaces two existing agreements for peaceful nuclear cooperation with EURATOM, including the 1960 agreement that has served as our primary legal framework for cooperation in recent years and that will expire by its terms on December 31 of this year. The proposed new agreement will provide an updated, comprehensive framework for peaceful nuclear cooperation between the United States and EURATOM, will facilitate such cooperation, and will establish strengthened nonproliferation conditions and controls including all those required by the NNPA. The new agreement provides for the transfer of non-nuclear material, nuclear material, and equipment for both nuclear research and nuclear power purposes. It does not provide for transfers under the agreement of any sensitive nuclear technology (SNT).

The proposed agreement has an initial term of 30 years, and will continue in force indefinitely thereafter in increments of 5 years each until terminated in accordance with its provisions. In the event of termination, key nonproliferation conditions and controls, including guarantees of safeguards, peaceful use and adequate physical protection, and the U.S. right to approve retransfers to third parties, will remain effective with respect to transferred non-nuclear material, nuclear material, and equipment, as well as nuclear material produced through their use. Procedures are also established for determining the survival of additional controls.

The member states of EURATOM and the European Union itself have impeccable nuclear nonproliferation credentials. All EURATOM member states are party to the Treaty on the Non-Proliferation of Nuclear Weapons (NPT). EURATOM and all its nonnuclear weapon state member states have an agreement with the International Atomic Energy Agency (IAEA) for the application of full-scope IAEA safeguards within the respective territories of the nonnuclear weapon states. The two EURATOM nuclear weapon states, France and the United Kingdom, like the United States, have voluntary safeguards agreements with the IAEA. In addition, EURATOM itself applies its own stringent safeguards at all peaceful facilities within the territories of all member states. The United States and EURATOM are of one mind in their unswerving commitment to achieving global nuclear nonproliferation goals. I call the attention of the Congress to the joint U.S.-EURATOM "Declaration on Non-Proliferation Policy" appended to the text of the agreement I am transmitting herewith.

The proposed new agreement provides for very stringent controls over certain fuel cycle activities, including enrichment, reprocessing, and alteration in form or content and storage of plutonium and other sensitive nuclear materials. The United States and EURATOM have accepted these controls on a reciprocal basis, not as a sign of either Party's distrust of the other, and not for the purpose of interfering with each other's fuel cycle choices, which are for each Party to determine for itself, but rather as a reflection of their common conviction that the provisions in question represent an important norm for peaceful nuclear commerce.

In view of the strong commitment of EURATOM and its member states to the international nonproliferation regime, the comprehensive nonproliferation commitments they have made, the advanced technological character of the EURATOM civil nuclear program, the long history of extensive transatlantic cooperation in the peaceful uses of nuclear energy without any risk of proliferation, and the fact that all member states are close allies or close friends of the United States, the proposed new agreement provides to EURATOM (and on a reciprocal basis, to the United States) advance, long-term approval for specified enrichment, retransfers, reprocessing, alteration in form or content, and storage of specified nuclear material, and for retransfers of nonnuclear material and equipment. The approval for reprocessing and alteration in form or content may be suspended if either activity ceases to meet the criteria set out in U.S. law, including criteria relating to safeguards and physical protection.

In providing advance, long-term approval for certain nuclear fuel cycle activities, the proposed agreement has features similar to those in several other agreements for cooperation that the United States has entered into subsequent to enactment of the NNPA. These include bilateral U.S. agreements with Japan, Finland, Norway and Sweden. (The U.S. agreements with Finland and Sweden will be automatically terminated upon entry into force of the new U.S.-EURATOM agreement, as Finland and Sweden joined the European Union on January 1, 1995.) Among the documents I am transmitting herewith to the Congress is an analysis by the Secretary of Energy of the advance, long-term approvals contained in the proposed U.S. agreement with EURATOM. The analysis concludes that the approvals meet all requirements of the Atomic Energy Act.

I believe that the proposed agreement for cooperation with EURATOM will make an important contribution to achieving our nonproliferation, trade and other significant foreign policy goals.

In particular, I am convinced that this agreement will strengthen the international nuclear nonproliferation regime, support of which is a fundamental objective of U.S. national security and foreign policy, by setting a high standard for rigorous nonproliferation conditions and controls.

It will substantially upgrade U.S. controls over nuclear items subject to the current U.S.-EURATOM agreement as well as over future cooperation.

I believe that the new agreement will also demonstrate the U.S. intention to be a reliable nuclear trading partner, and thus help ensure the continuation and, I hope, growth of U.S. civil nuclear exports to EURATOM member states.

I have considered the views and recommendations of the interested agencies in reviewing the proposed agreement and have determined that its performance will promote, and will not constitute an unreasonable risk to, the common defense and security. Accordingly, I have approved the agreement and authorized its execution and urge that the Congress give it favorable consideration.

Because this agreement meets all applicable requirements of the Atomic Energy Act of 1954, as amended, for agreements for peaceful nuclear cooperation, I am transmitting it to the Congress without exempting it from any requirement contained in section 123 a. of that Act. This transmission shall constitute a submittal for purposes of both sections 123 b. and 123 d. of the Atomic Energy Act. The Administration is prepared to begin immediately the consultations with the Senate Foreign Relations and House International Relations Committees as provided in section 123 b. Upon completion of the 30-day continuous session period provided for in section 123 b., the 60-day continuous session period provided for in section 123 d. shall commence.

WILLIAM J. CLINTON

The White House,
November 29, 1995.

Remarks at a Dinner Hosted by Prime Minister John Major of the United Kingdom in London
November 29, 1995

Prime Minister and Mrs. Major, ladies and gentlemen, let me begin by saying how very grateful Hillary and I are to be here personally and representing the people of the United States. This has been a fine opportunity for me to meet with the Prime Minister and representatives of Her Majesty's Government to talk about our common interests, our shared values, our future agenda. It's also been a great opportunity for me personally to come back to this wonderful city which I love so much and where I have such warm memories.

Prime Minister, I want to thank you especially for welcoming here at your table my stepfather, for a personal reason. My late mother would love to be here tonight, and I miss her tonight especially because I tried in vain for 25 years to convince her that not every meal in London was steak and kidney pie or fish and chips. [*Laughter*]

I want to say to all of you that I meant every word of the speech I gave in Parliament today. We have a relationship that is enduring and very special. If I might paraphrase one of my very favorite British citizens, 007, our relationship can never be stirred nor shaken. [*Laughter*] It will always be there; it will always be strong.

And now we have a special responsibility. We have all the unique opportunities that are apparent to us to make peace and to make progress. But it will not happen unless we work at it, and it will not happen if we try to work at it alone. It will only happen if we work at it together.

In Northern Ireland—I thank the Prime Minister for what he said—but the real thanks go to Prime Minister Major and to Prime Minister Bruton and his predecessor who were willing to take risks for peace. The United States supports those who take risks for peace. The risks may be political. We know they are severe. There's always a high risk of failure, as I said in Parliament today, and even if you fail, the people who wish you hadn't tried will hold it against you. Sometimes the risks are far, far greater, as the Prime Minister and I saw not so long ago when we buried our friend Prime Minister Rabin. But the work of peace is always important. Today, it is imperative because we can achieve it in so many places where just a short while ago it was impossible.

The philosophy of the United States is simple and consistent. It runs in a seamless way from Northern Ireland to Bosnia to the Middle East. We will support those who take risks for peace. We will not attempt to tell people what peace they should make but only to urge on them the need to make peace at the soonest possible date in a fair and honorable and decent way.

I look forward to my trip to Northern Ireland, and I look forward to doing whatever we can,

consistent with our policy and the willingness of the parties to move on the path to peace.

I'd like to also thank the Prime Minister and again the British people for the sacrifices they have made in Bosnia over the course of that long and painful war, for the risks to your soldiers, for the extraordinary humanitarian aid, for all the nameless people who are alive today because of what Great Britain has done in that terrible and difficult conflict.

And I want to thank you anew for the very strong statement you made today in terms of the depth of commitment that you are prepared to make to implement this peace agreement. Together with our French and other allies, through NATO and with other nations who work in partnership with us, I believe we have a better than even chance to help bring peace to Bosnia because the parties made their peace at Dayton. And the parties, if they will keep their minds straight and their hearts pure, can make the peace live in the lives of the people of Sarajevo and throughout the nation. These are the kinds of things we have to do.

I believe that the best days for democracy and freedom are before us but only if we face our challenges and only if we face them together.

I brought only one note tonight I wanted to read because I don't want to mix the words up. In one of history's stranger coincidental meetings, Mark Twain appeared in New York City on a cold night in the year 1900 to introduce a lecture by a young adventurer and writer by the name of Winston Churchill. So much for your—I'm trying to remember—Rudyard Kipling said, "Never the twain shall meet." He was wrong. [*Laughter*] In the introduction, this is what Mark Twain said about the British and the Americans: "We have always been kin, kin in blood, kin in religion, kin in representative government, kin in ideals, kin in just and lofty purposes." Mark Twain was not being humorous on that night. He was right then; he is right tonight.

I ask you to join me in a toast to Prime Minister and Mrs. Major and to the people of the wonderful nation of Great Britain.

NOTE: The President spoke at approximately 8:05 p.m. at 10 Downing Street. In his remarks, he referred to the Prime Minister's wife, Norma.

Remarks to Mackie International Employees in Belfast, Northern Ireland
November 30, 1995

This is one of those occasions where I really feel that all that needs to be said has already been said. I thank Catherine and David for introducing me, for all the schoolchildren of Northern Ireland who are here today, and for all whom they represent. A big part of peace is children growing up safely, learning together, and growing together. I thank Patrick Dougan and Ronnie Lewis for their remarks, for their work here, for all the members of the Mackie's team who are with us today in welcoming us to this factory. I was hoping we could have an event like this in Northern Ireland at a place where people work and reach out to the rest of the world in a positive way, because a big part of peace is working together for family and community and for the welfare of the common enterprise.

It is good to be among the people of Northern Ireland who have given so much to America and the world and good to be here with such a large delegation of my fellow Americans, including of course my wife. And I see the Secretary of Commerce here and the Ambassador to Great Britain and a number of others. But we have quite a large delegation from both parties in the United States Congress, so we've sort of got a truce of our own going on here today. [*Laughter*] And I'd like to ask the Members of Congress who have come all the way from Washington, DC, to stand up and be recognized. Would you all stand? [*Applause*]

Many of you perhaps know that one in four of America's Presidents trace their roots to Ireland's shores, beginning with Andrew Jackson, the son of immigrants from Carrickfergus, to John Fitzgerald Kennedy, whose forebears came from County Wexford. I know I am only the latest in this time-honored tradition, but I'm proud to be the first sitting American President to make it back to Belfast.

At this holiday season all around the world, the promise of peace is in the air. The barriers of the cold war are giving way to a global village where communication and cooperation are the order of the day. From South Africa to the Middle East and now to troubled Bosnia, conflicts long thought impossible to solve are moving along the road to resolution. Once-bitter foes are clasping hands and changing history, and long-suffering people are moving closer to normal lives.

Here in Northern Ireland, you are making a miracle, a miracle symbolized by those two children who held hands and told us what this whole thing is all about. In the land of the harp and the fiddle, the fife and the lambeg drum, two proud traditions are coming together in the harmonies of peace. The cease-fire and the negotiations have sparked a powerful transformation.

Mackie's plant is a symbol of Northern Ireland's rebirth. It has long been a symbol of world-class engineering. The textile machines you make permit people to weave disparate threads into remarkable fabrics. That is now what you must do here with the people of Northern Ireland.

Here we lie along the peace line, the wall of steel and stone separating Protestant from Catholic. But today, under the leadership of Pat Dougan, you are bridging the divide, overcoming a legacy of discrimination where fair employment and integration are the watchwords of the future. On this shop floor, men and women of both traditions are working together to achieve common goals.

Peace, once a distant dream, is now making a real difference in everyday life in this land. Soldiers have left the streets of Belfast; many have gone home. People can go to the pub or the store without the burden of the search or the threat of a bomb. As barriers disappear along the border, families and communities divided for decades are becoming whole once more.

This year in Armagh on St. Patrick's Day, Protestant and Catholic children led the parade together for the first time since the Troubles began. A bystander's words marked the wonder of the occasion when he said, "Even the normal is beginning to seem normal."

The economic rewards of peace are evident as well. Unemployment has fallen here to its lowest level in 14 years, while retail sales and investment are surging. Far from the gleaming city center to the new shop fronts of Belfast, to the Enterprise Center in East Belfast, business is thriving, and opportunities are expanding. With every extra day that the guns are still, business confidence grows stronger, and the promise of prosperity grows as well.

As the shroud of terror melts away, Northern Ireland's beauty has been revealed again to all the world: the castles and coasts, the Giant's Causeway, the lush green hills, the high white cliffs, a magical backdrop to your greatest asset which I saw all along the way from the airport here today, the warmth and good feeling of your people. Visitors are now coming in record numbers. Indeed, today the air route between Belfast and London is the second busiest in all of Europe.

I want to honor those whose courage and vision have brought us to this point. Prime Minister Major, Prime Minister Bruton, and before him, Prime Minister Reynolds, laid the background and the basis for this era of reconciliation. From the Downing Street declaration to the joint framework document, they altered the course of history. Now, just in the last few days, by launching the twin-track initiative, they have opened a promising new gateway to a just and lasting peace. Foreign Minister Spring, Sir Patrick Mayhew, David Trimble, and John Hume all have labored to realize the promise of peace. And Gerry Adams, along with Loyalist leaders such as David Ervine and Gary McMichael, helped to silence the guns on the streets and to bring about the first peace in a generation.

But most of all, America salutes all the people of Northern Ireland who have shown the world in concrete ways that here the will for peace is now stronger than the weapons of war. With mixed sporting events encouraging competition on the playing field, not the battlefield, with women's support groups, literacy programs, job training centers that serve both communities, these and countless other initiatives bolster the foundations of peace as well.

Last year's cease-fire of the Irish Republican Army, joined by the combined Loyalist Military Command, marked a turning point in the history of Northern Ireland. Now is the time to sustain that momentum and lock in the gains of peace. Neither community wants to go back to the violence of the past. The children told us that today. Both parties must do their part to move this process forward now.

Let me begin by saying that the search for common ground demands the courage of an open mind. This twin-track initiative gives the parties a chance to begin preliminary talks in ways in which all views will be represented and all voices will be heard. It also establishes an international body to address the issue of arms decommissioning. I hope the parties will seize this opportunity. Engaging in honest dialog is not an act of surrender, it is an act of strength and common sense. Moving from cease-fire to peace requires dialog. For 25 years now, the history of Northern Ireland has been written in the blood of its children and their parents. The cease-fire turned the page on that history. It must not be allowed to turn back.

There must also be progress away from the negotiating table. Violence has lessened, but it has not disappeared. The leaders of the four main churches recently condemned the so-called punishment beatings and called for an end to such attacks. I add my voice to theirs.

As the church leaders said, this is a time when the utmost efforts on all sides are needed to build a peaceful and confident community in the future. But true peace requires more than a treaty, even more than the absence of violence. Those who have suffered most in the fighting must share fairly in the fruits of renewal. The frustration that gave rise to violence must give way to faith in the future.

The United States will help to secure the tangible benefits of peace. Ours is the first American administration ever to support in the Congress the International Fund for Ireland, which has become an engine for economic development and for reconciliation. We will continue to encourage trade and investment and to help end the cycle of unemployment.

We are proud to support Northern Ireland. You have given America a very great deal. Irish Protestant and Irish Catholic together have added to America's strength. From our battle for independence down to the present day, the Irish have not only fought in our wars, they have built our Nation, and we owe you a very great debt.

Let me say that of all the gifts we can offer in return, perhaps the most enduring and the most precious is the example of what is possible when people find unity and strength in their diversity. We know from our own experience even today how hard that is to do. After all, we fought a great Civil War over the issue of race and slavery in which hundreds of thousands of our people were killed.

Today, in one of our counties alone, in Los Angeles, there are over 150 different ethnic and racial groups represented. We know we can become stronger if we bridge our differences. But we learned in our own Civil War that that has to begin with a change of the heart.

I grew up in the American South, in one of the States that tried to break from the American Union. My forebears on my father's side were soldiers in the Confederate Army. I was reading the other day a book about our first Governor after the Civil War who fought for the Union Army and who lost members of his own family. They lived the experience so many of you have lived. When this Governor took office and looked out over a sea of his fellow citizens who fought on the other side, he said these words: "We have all done wrong. No one can say his heart is altogether clean and his hands altogether pure. Thus, as we wish to be forgiven, let us forgive those who have sinned against us and ours." That was the beginning of America's reconciliation, and it must be the beginning of Northern Ireland's reconciliation.

It is so much easier to believe that our differences matter more than what we have in common. It is easier, but it is wrong. We all cherish family and faith, work and community. We all strive to live lives that are free and honest and responsible. We all want our children to grow up in a world where their talents are matched by their opportunities. And I believe those values are just as strong in County Londonderry as they are in Londonderry, New Hampshire; in Belfast, Northern Ireland, as in Belfast, Maine.

I am proud to be of Ulster Scots stock. I am proud to be also of Irish stock. I share these roots with millions and millions of Americans, now over 40 million Americans. And we rejoice at things being various, as Louis MacNeice once wrote. It is one of the things that makes America special.

Because our greatness flows from the wealth of our diversity as well as the strength of the ideals we share in common, we feel bound to support others around the world who seek to bridge their own divides. This is an important part of our country's mission on the eve of the 21st century, because we know that the chain of peace that protects us grows stronger with every new link that is forged.

For the first time in half a century now, we can put our children to bed at night knowing that the nuclear weapons of the former Soviet Union are no longer pointed at those children. In South Africa, the long night of apartheid has given way to a new freedom for all peoples. In the Middle East, Arabs and Israelis are stepping beyond war to peace in an area where many believed peace would never come. In Haiti, a brutal dictatorship has given way to a fragile new democracy. In Europe, the dream of a stable, undivided, free continent seems finally within reach as the people of Bosnia have the first real hope for peace since the terrible fighting began there nearly 4 years ago.

The United States looks forward to working with our allies here in Europe and others to help the people in Bosnia, the Muslims, the Croats, the Serbs, to move beyond their divisions and their destructions to make the peace agreement they have made a reality in the lives of their people.

Those who work for peace have got to support one another. We know that when leaders stand up for peace, they place their fortunes on the line and sometimes their very lives on the line, as we learned so recently in the tragic murder of the brave Prime Minister of Israel. For just as peace has its pioneers, peace will always have its rivals. Even when children stand up and say what these children said today, there will always be people who, deep down inside, will never be able to give up the past.

Over the last 3 years, I have had the privilege of meeting with and closely listening to both Nationalists and Unionists from Northern Ireland. And I believe that the greatest struggle you face now is not between opposing ideas or opposing interests. The greatest struggle you face is between those who deep down inside are inclined to be peacemakers and those who deep down inside cannot yet embrace the cause of peace, between those who are in the ship of peace and those who are trying to sink it. Old habits die hard.

There will always be those who define the worth of their lives not by who they are but by who they aren't, not by what they're for but by what they are against. They will never escape the dead-end street of violence. But you, the vast majority, Protestant and Catholic alike, must not allow the ship of peace to sink on the rocks of old habits and hard grudges. You must stand firm against terror. You must say to those who still would use violence for political objectives, "You are the past. Your day is over.

Violence has no place at the table of democracy and no role in the future of this land." By the same token, you must also be willing to say to those who renounce violence and who do take their own risks for peace that they are entitled to be full participants in the democratic process. Those who do show the courage to break with the past are entitled to their stake in the future.

As leaders for peace become invested in the process, as leaders make compromises and risk the backlash, people begin more and more— I have seen this all over the world—they begin more and more to develop a common interest in each other's success, in standing together rather than standing apart. They realize that the sooner they get to true peace, with all the rewards it brings, the sooner it will be easier to discredit and destroy the forces of destruction.

We will stand with those who take risks for peace in Northern Ireland and around the world. I pledge that we will do all we can, through the International Fund for Ireland and in many other ways, to ease your load. If you walk down this path continually, you will not walk alone. We are entering an era of possibility unparalleled in all of human history. If you enter that era determined to build a new age of peace, the United States of America will proudly stand with you.

But at the end of the day, as with all free people, your future is for you to decide. Your destiny is for you to determine. Only you can decide between division and unity, between hard lives and high hopes. Only you can create a lasting peace. It takes courage to let go of familiar divisions. It takes faith to walk down a new road. But when we see the bright gaze of these children, we know the risk is worth the reward.

I have been so touched by the thousands of letters I have received from schoolchildren here, telling me what peace means to them. One young girl from Ballymena wrote, and I quote,

"It is not easy to forgive and forget, especially for those who have lost a family member or a close friend. However, if people could look to the future with hope instead of the past with fear, we can only be moving in the right direction." I couldn't have said it nearly as well.

I believe you can summon the strength to keep moving forward. After all, you have come so far already. You have braved so many dangers. You have endured so many sacrifices. Surely, there can be no turning back. But peace must be waged with a warrior's resolve, bravely, proudly, and relentlessly, secure in the knowledge of the single greatest difference between war and peace: In peace, everybody can win.

I was overcome today, when I landed in my plane and I drove with Hillary up the highway to come here, by the phenomenal beauty of the place and the spirit and the good will of the people. Northern Ireland has a chance not only to begin anew but to be a real inspiration to the rest of the world, a model of progress through tolerance.

Let us join our efforts together as never before to make that dream a reality. Let us join our prayers in this season of peace for a future of peace in this good land.

Thank you very much.

NOTE: The President spoke at 11 a.m. on the factory floor. In his remarks, he referred to Catherine Hamill and David Sterritt, students who introduced the President; Patrick Dougan, president, and Ronnie Lewis, senior shop steward, Mackie International; Richard Spring, T.D., Foreign Minister of Ireland; Sir Patrick Mayhew, M.P., Secretary of State for Northern Ireland, United Kingdom; David Trimble, M.P., leader, Ulster Unionist Party; John Hume, M.P., leader, Social Democratic and Labour Party; Gerry Adams, leader, Sinn Fein; David Ervine, leader, Progressive Unionist Party; and Gary McMichael, leader, Ulster Democratic Party.

Remarks to Business Leaders in Belfast
November 30, 1995

The President. Well, first of all, I want to thank all of you, all the panelists and Mr. Thompson and your M.P. for the fine things that have been said. And I thank you for quoting the King James Version of the Bible. I read all the more modern ones, and sometimes they're easier to understand, but they're not nearly as eloquent. So King James is still my favorite, too.

I would like to make just three points very briefly. First, in the presence of the Members of Congress who are here, I want to thank them for funding the International Fund for Ireland. In the United States, it was really a congressional initiative. For many years, the President—until I became President, no President ever even made a recommendation to spend the money because it was thought to be unusual. But I can tell you, now, even though this connection was never made before, we fund programs through the Agency for International Development around the world in countries much poorer than Northern Ireland which are essentially trying to do the same things.

We know now that if you really want to grow jobs in places where there's not a lot of capital, you have to set up a mechanism for getting capital into entrepreneurial people who may be in one- or two- or three- or four- or five-person businesses. And if you do it right, you can create an enormous, enormous number of successful businesses and, in so doing, create the demand for the products and services that will be produced.

So I think what you are doing here is really an extraordinary thing. And I want to thank the Members of Congress who have consistently supported the International Fund for Ireland who are here and to say that I hope, frankly, that you will become, as we move forward down the road to peace—and Senator Mitchell and the others who worked so hard on the investment conference over on our side of the ocean—and you enjoy more success, I hope you will become a model for a lot of other countries as well who are struggling to build a system of free enterprise and give their energetic people the kinds of opportunities that you have found.

We see it even in our own country—some places that others had given up on, thought, you know, where there would never be any economic opportunity there again—the most successful thing that has been done even in our own country is starting things like the International Fund for Ireland. But it works better here, what you are doing through these community groups, than almost any other place that I'm aware of in the world.

And you said it yourself, sir. I think you said you have in this consortium 200 companies with 900 employees; that's an average number of employees somewhere between 4 and 5. But it you look at the cost—what did you say—13½ million pounds—I think I can still do exchange rates, even though I've been—Presidents are disabled from all practical things, you know. [*Laughter*] They don't get to buy food or drive cars or exchange money, but that's pretty low cost per job creation. And so I think that's very, very important. And I applaud all of you for what you're doing.

The second point I want to make is that the cease-fire, I'm convinced, made possible a lot of this growth. And some of you have said that. And you talked about how it's also changing the whole image of Northern Ireland. One of the things that I hope will come out of my trip here today is that people who have never been here will see the country in a different light. You know, we owe that to the media. But people all over the world will be seeing this trip tonight, and they will see your whole country in a different light, they will see people like you. They will see you on television; they will say, "Those are the kind of people I wouldn't mind being involved with". And I think that will help. But it's a real argument for continuing the peace.

And the third thing I would say is that—you might want to ask Senator Mitchell to comment on this—is the conference we had, the Washington conference last May. I think it's important to do more things like that, not just in the United States but elsewhere, so that people are aware, in a tangible way, of the grassroots, not only the grassroots commitment to peace but the extraordinary array of competence, the abilities, the ideas, that are coming out of here. Because I think—and I think as you do that, you'll become more integrated into the global economy in a positive way and it will be more difficult for anyone to turn the clock back on you.

George, would you like——

[*At this point, George Mitchell, Special Adviser to the President and Secretary of State on Economic Initiatives for Ireland, made brief remarks.*]

The President. Let me just say, I want to leave on a little bit lighter note. When I read my notes about what all of you do, and I was preparing for this and I knew I was bringing all the—the Ambassador for the United States to Great Britain and the British Ambassador to America and all these other people and especially all the politicians back there, and I saw that Lynn McGregor is the owner of a company called Altered Images, and I thought to myself, she could become an overnight millionaire in Washington, DC, just by putting up an office.

[*Laughter*] We all need to alter our image a little there.

Thank you very much. Congratulations to all of you. Thank you.

NOTE: The President spoke at 12:54 p.m. at the East Belfast Enterprise Park. In his remarks, he referred to Peter Thompson, board chairman, East Belfast Enterprise Park.

Remarks to the Community in Londonderry, Northern Ireland
November 30, 1995

Thank you. Thank you very much. Mr. Mayor, Mrs. Kerr, Mr. and Mrs. Hume, Sir Patrick and Lady Mayhew. And to this remarkable crowd, let me say that there have been many Presidents of the United States who had their roots in this soil. I can see today how lucky I am to be the first President of the United States to come back to this city to say thank you very much.

Hillary and I are proud to be here in the home of Ireland's most tireless champion for civil rights and its most eloquent voice of nonviolence, John Hume. I know that at least twice already I have had the honor of hosting John and Pat in Washington. And the last time I saw him I said, "You can't come back to Washington one more time until you let me come to Derry." And here I am.

I am delighted to be joined here today by a large number of Americans, including a distinguished delegation of Members of our United States Congress who have supported peace and reconciliation here and who have supported economic development through the International Fund for Ireland.

I'm also joined today by members of the O'Neill family. Among the last great chieftains of Ireland were the O'Neills of Ulster. But in America, we still have chieftains who are the O'Neills of Boston. They came all the way over here to inaugurate the Tip O'Neill Chair in Peace Studies here at the University of Ulster. This chair will honor the great Irish-American and late Speaker of the House of Representatives by furthering his dream of peace in Northern Ireland. And I am honored to be here with his family members today.

All of you know that this city is a very different place from what a visitor like me would have seen just a year and a half ago, before the cease-fire. Crossing the border now is as easy as crossing a speed bump. The soldiers are off the streets. The city walls are open to civilians. There are no more shakedowns as you walk into a store. Daily life has become more ordinary. But this will never be an ordinary city.

I came here because you are making a home for peace to flourish and endure—a local climate responsible this week for the announcement of new business operations that offer significant new opportunities to you as well as new hope. Let me applaud also the success of the Inner City Trust and Paddy Dogherty who have put people to work rebuilding bombed-out buildings, building new ones, and building up confidence and civic pride.

America's connections to this place go back a long, long time. One of our greatest cities, Philadelphia, was mapped out three centuries ago by a man who was inspired by the layout of the streets behind these walls. His name was William Penn. He was raised a Protestant in Ireland in a military family. He became a warrior, and he fought in Ulster. But he turned away from warfare, traded in his armor, converted to the Quaker faith, and became a champion of peace. Imprisoned for his religious views, William Penn wrote one of the greatest defenses of religious tolerance in history. Released from prison, he went to America in the 1680's, a divisive decade here, and founded Pennsylvania, a colony unique in the new world because it was based on the principle of religious tolerance.

Philadelphia quickly became the main port of entry for immigrants from the north of Ireland who made the Protestant and Catholic traditions valuable parts of our treasured traditions in America. Today when he travels to the States, John Hume is fond of reminding us about the phrase that Americans established in Philadelphia as the motto of our Nation, *E Pluribus Unum*, out of many, one, the belief that back then Quakers and Catholics, Anglicans and Presbyterians could practice their religion, celebrate their culture, honor their traditions, and live as neighbors in peace. In the United States today in just one county, Los Angeles, there are representatives of over 150 different racial, ethnic, and religious groups. We are struggling to live out William Penn's vision, and we pray that you will be able to live out that vision as well.

Over the last 3 years since I have had the privilege to be the President of the United States I have had occasion to meet with Nationalists and to meet with Unionists and to listen to their sides of the story. I have come to the conclusion that here, as in so many other places in the world, from the Middle East to Bosnia, the divisions that are most important here are not the divisions between opposing views or opposing interests. Those divisions can be reconciled. The deep divisions, the most important ones, are those between the peacemakers and the enemies of peace: those who, deep, deep down inside, want peace more than anything and those who, deep down inside, can't bring themselves to reach out for peace; those who are in the ship of peace and those who would sink it; those who bravely meet on the bridge of reconciliation and those who would blow it up.

My friends, everyone in life at some point has to decide what kind of person he or she is going to be. Are you going to be someone who defines yourself in terms of what you are against or what you are for? Will you be someone who defines yourself in terms of who you aren't or who you are? The time has come for the peacemakers to triumph in Northern Ireland, and the United States will support them as they do.

The world-renowned playwright from this city, Brian Friel, wrote a play called "Philadelphia, Here I Come." In it a character who is about to immigrate from Ireland thinks back on his past life and says to himself, "It's all over." But his alter ego reminds him of his future

and replies, "And it's about to begin." It's all over, and it's about to begin. If only change were that easy.

To leave one way of life behind in search of another takes a strong amount of faith and courage. But the world has seen here over the last 15 months that people from Londonderry County to County Down, from Antrim to Armagh, have made the transition from a time of ever-present fear to a time of fragile peace. The United States applauds the efforts of Prime Minister Major and Prime Minister Bruton who have launched the new twin-track initiative and have opened a process that gives the parties a chance to begin a dialog in which all views are represented and all can be heard.

Not far from this spot stands a new Statue of Reconciliation, two figures, 10 feet tall, each reaching out a hand toward the other but neither quite making it across the divide. It is a beautiful and powerful symbol of where many people stand today in this great land. Let it now point people to the handshake of reconciliation. Life cannot be lived with the stillness of statues. Life must go on. The hands must come closer together or drift further apart.

Your great Nobel Prize winning poet, Seamus Heaney, wrote the following words that some of you must know already but that for me capture this moment. He said:

History says, *Don't hope*
On this side of the grave,
But then, once in a lifetime
The longed-for tidal wave
Of justice can rise up,
And hope and history rhyme.

So hope for a great sea change
On the far side of revenge.
Believe that a further shore
Is reachable from here.
Believe in miracles
And cures and healing wells.

Well, my friends, I believe. I believe we live in a time of hope and history rhyming. Standing here in front of the Guildhall, looking out over these historic walls, I see a peaceful city, a safe city, a hopeful city, full of young people that should have a peaceful and prosperous future here where their roots and families are. That is what I see today with you.

And so I ask you to build on the opportunity you have before you, to believe that the future can be better than the past, to work together because you have so much more to gain by working together than by drifting apart. Have the patience to work for a just and lasting peace. Reach for it. The United States will reach with you. The further shore of that peace is within your reach.

Thank you, and God bless you all.

NOTE: The President spoke at 3:20 p.m. in the Guildhall Square. In his remarks, he referred to Lord Mayor John Kerr and his wife, Corita; John Hume's wife, Patricia; and Sir Patrick Mayhew's wife, Jean.

Remarks on the Inauguration of the Thomas P. O'Neill Chair for the Study of Peace in Londonderry
November 30, 1995

Mayor and Mrs. Kerr, Sir Patrick and Mrs. Mayhew, Mr. and Mrs. Hume; to the community and religious leaders who are here and to my fellow Americans who are here, Congressman Walsh and the congressional delegation; Senator Dodd, Senator Mack, and others. Let me thank you all for the wonderful reception you have given to Hillary and to me today and, through us, to the people of the United States. And let me thank Tom O'Neill for his incredibly generous remarks. I am honored to be here with him and with his family and with Loretta Brennan Glucksman and the other members of the American Ireland Fund to help inaugurate this Tip O'Neill Chair in Peace Studies. And thank you, Vice Chancellor Smith, for the degree. You know, I wonder how far it is from a degree to a professorship? [*Laughter*] See, I have this job without a lot of tenure, and I'm looking for one with more tenure.

Tip O'Neill was a model for many people he never knew. The model of public service, he proved that a person could be a national leader without losing the common touch, without ever forgetting that all these high-flown speeches we give and all these complex issues we talk about in the end have a real, tangible impact on the lives of ordinary people and that in any free land, in the end all that really counts are the lives of ordinary people.

He said he was a man of the House, but he was far more. He was fundamentally a man of the people, a bricklayer's son who became the most powerful person in Congress and our Nation's most prominent, most loyal champion of ordinary working families.

He loved politics because he loved people but also because he knew it could make a difference in people's lives. And you have proved here that political decisions by brave people can make a difference in people's lives. Along with Senators Kennedy and Moynihan and former Governor Hugh Carey of New York, he was among the first Irish-American politicians to oppose violence in Northern Ireland. And though we miss him sorely, he will long be remembered in the United States and now in Ireland with this O'Neill chair. It is a fitting tribute to his life and legacy, for he knew that peace had to be nurtured by a deeper understanding among people and greater opportunity for all.

Tip O'Neill was old enough to remember a time when Irish Catholics were actually discriminated against in the United States, and he had the last laugh when they wound up running the place. [*Laughter*] I was just thinking that in my conscious political lifetime we've had three Irish Speakers of the House of Representatives, John McCormick and Tip O'Neill of Boston and Tom Foley of Washington State, and goodness knows how many more we're destined to have.

I am very proud to be here to inaugurate this chair in peace studies. I have been privileged to come here at an important time in your history. I have been privileged to be President at an important time in your history and to do what I could on behalf of the United States to help the peace process go forward.

But the work of peace is really the work of a lifetime. First, you have to put the violence behind you. You have done that. Then, you have to make an agreement that recognizes the differences and the commonalities among you. And this twin-tracks process I believe is a way at least to begin that process where everyone can be heard. Then, you have to change the spirit of the people until it is as normal as getting up in the morning and having breakfast to feel a real affinity for the people who share this land with you without regard to their religion or their politics. This chair of peace studies can help you to do that. It can be symbol of the lifetime work of building a peaceful spirit and heart in every citizen of this land.

Our administration has been a strong supporter of the International Fund for Ireland. We will continue to do so because of projects like this one and because of the work still to be done. We were eager to sponsor the conference we had last May, aided by the diligent efforts of our friend, former Senator and Senate majority leader George Mitchell who now embarks for you on another historic mission of peace. I hope very much that Senator Mitchell will succeed. I think the voices I have heard on this trip indicate to me that you want him to succeed and that you want to succeed.

A lot of incredibly moving things have happened to us today, but I think to me, the most moving were the two children who stood and introduced me this morning in the Mackie plant in Belfast. They represented all those other children, including children here from Derry who have written me about what peace means to them over the last few weeks.

One young boy said—the young boy who introduced me said that he studied with and played with people who were both Protestant and Catholic, and he'd almost gotten to the point where he couldn't tell the difference. [*Laughter*] A beautiful young girl who introduced me—that beautiful child—started off by saying what her Daddy did for a living, and then she said she lost her first Daddy in the Troubles. And she thought about it every day. It was the worst day of her life, and she couldn't stand another loss. The upside and the downside, and those children joined hands to introduce me. I felt almost as if my speech were superfluous. But I know one thing: Tip O'Neill was smiling down on the whole thing today.

The other night I had a chance to go with Hillary to the Ford Theatre in Washington, DC, a wonderful, historic place—it's been there since before our Civil War—and where President Lin-

coln was assassinated. And I told the people there who come once a year to raise money for it so we can keep it going that we always thought of it as a sad and tragic place, but it was really a place where he came to laugh and escape the cares of our great Civil War. And there, I was thinking that America has always been about three great things, our country: love of liberty, belief in progress, and the struggle for unity.

And the last is in so many ways by far the most difficult. It is a continuing challenge for us to deal with the differences among us, to honestly respect our differences, to stand up where we feel differently about certain things and still to find that core of common humanity across all the sea of differences which permit us to preserve liberty, to make progress possible, and to live up to the deepest truths of our shared human nature.

In the end, that is what this chair is all about. And believe me, we need it everywhere. We need it in the streets of our toughest cities in the United States, where we are attempting to teach our children that when they have conflicts, they shouldn't go home and pick up a gun or a knife and hurt each other, they should figure out a way to work through to mutual respect. We need it in the Middle East, where the Prime Minister of Israel just gave his life to a religious fanatic of his own faith because he dared to make peace and give the children of his country a better future. We need it in Bosnia, where the leaders have agreed to make peace, but where the people must now purge their heart of the hatred borne of 4 years of merciless slaughter. We need this everywhere.

So, my friends, I pray not only for your success in making a peace, but I pray that through this chair and through your example, you will become a model for the rest of the world because the world will always need models for peace.

Thank you, and God bless you all.

NOTE: The President spoke at 4:48 p.m. in the Major Hall of Guildhall at the University of Ulster. In his remarks, he referred to Trevor Smith, vice chancellor, University of Ulster.

Statement on Approval of the Department of Defense Appropriations Act, 1996
November 30, 1995

I have decided this evening to approve the Department of Defense appropriations bill. This legislation is vital to fund our national defense, so that the United States remains the strongest force for peace in the world.

This bill provides for a strong national defense, supports our commitments to the quality of life of our forces and their families, maintains high military readiness, and funds investment programs necessary to modernize the equipment used by our combat forces. Continuing American global leadership is ensured by the support the bill provides for our forces.

I made this decision because my Administration has reached agreement with Congressional leaders to provide funding, out of the funds contained in this bill, for the troop deployment and other efforts to secure peace in Bosnia. The pressing demands of peace and of our military service men and women compel my approval of this measure.

I have expressed my strong concerns that this legislation contains excessive spending for projects that are not currently needed for our defense. I will forward to Congress rescission legislation that would eliminate funding for those projects, and I urge Congress to act on it. We should spend no more than we need to at a time when we are determined to balance the budget.

I am also concerned that section 8117 of the Act contains certain reporting requirements that could materially interfere with or impede this country's ability to provide necessary support to another nation or international organization in connection with peacekeeping or humanitarian assistance activities otherwise authorized by law.

I will interpret this provision consistent with my constitutional authority to conduct the foreign relations of the United States and my responsibilities as Commander in Chief.

In addition, I remain very concerned about provisions of the Act that restrict service women and female dependents of military personnel from obtaining privately funded abortions in military facilities overseas, except in cases in which the mother's life is endangered or the pregnancy is the result of rape or incest. In many countries, these U.S. facilities provide the only accessible, safe source for these medical services.

My Administration is continuing discussions with the Congress on the remaining spending bills, in order to protect necessary priorities in education, the environment and law enforcement. Over the past several days we have made progress in good faith discussions with the leadership of the House and Senate Appropriations Committees to close the gap between us on these issues. The decision I am making tonight is consistent with our understanding that these discussions will continue with the goal of reaching a satisfactory conclusion as rapidly as possible. We should promptly complete this task, so there is no unnecessary shutdown of the government.

WILLIAM J. CLINTON

The White House,
November 30, 1995.

NOTE: H.R. 2126 became law without the President's signature on December 1, and it was assigned Public Law No. 104–61.

Remarks on Lighting the City Christmas Tree in Belfast
November 30, 1995

Thank you very much. To the Lord Mayor and Lady Mayoress, let me begin by saying to all of you, Hillary and I thank you from the bottom of our hearts for making us feel so very, very welcome in Belfast and Northern Ireland. We thank you, Lord Mayor, for your cooperation and your help in making this trip so successful, and we trust that, for all of you, we haven't inconvenienced you too much. But this has been a wonderful way for us to begin the Christmas holidays.

Let me also say I understood just what an honor it was to be able to turn on this Christmas tree when I realized the competition. [*Laughter*] Now, to become President of the United States you have to undertake some considerable competition. But I have never confronted challengers with the name recognition, the understanding of the media, and the ability in the martial arts of the Mighty Morphin Power Rangers.

To all of you whose support enabled me to join you tonight and turn the Christmas tree on, I give you my heartfelt thanks. I know here in Belfast you've been lighting the Christmas tree for more than 20 years. But this year must be especially joyous to you, for you are entering your second Christmas of peace.

As I look down these beautiful streets, I think how wonderful it will be for people to do their holiday shopping without worry of searches or bombs, to visit loved ones on the other side of the border without the burden of checkpoints or roadblocks, to enjoy these magnificent Christmas lights without any fear of violence. Peace has brought real change to your lives.

Across the ocean, the American people are rejoicing with you. We are joined to you by strong ties of community and commerce and culture. Over the years, men and women of both traditions have flourished in our country and helped America to flourish.

And today, of course, we are forging new and special bonds. Belfast's sister city in the United States, Nashville, Tennessee, was proud to send this Christmas tree to friends across the Atlantic. I want to thank the most prominent present resident of Nashville, Tennessee, Vice President Al Gore, the Mayor, Phil Bredesen, and the United States Air Force for getting this big tree all the way across the Atlantic to be here with you tonight.

In this 50th anniversary year of the end of World War II, many Americans still remember the warmth the people of Northern Ireland showed them when the Army was stationed here under General Eisenhower. The people of Belfast named General Eisenhower an honorary burgess of the city. He viewed that honor, and I quote, "as a token of our common purpose to work together for a better world." That mission endures today. We remain Americans, and

as people of Northern Ireland, partners for security, partners for prosperity, and most important, partners for peace.

Two years ago, at this very spot, tens of thousands of you took part in a day for peace, as a response to some of the worst violence Northern Ireland had known in recent years. The two morning papers, representing both traditions, sponsored a telephone poll for peace that generated almost 160,000 calls. In the United States, for my fellow Americans who are here, that would be the equivalent to 25 million calls.

The response left no doubt that all across Northern Ireland the desire for peace was becoming a demand. I am honored to announce today that those same two newspapers, the Newsletter and the Irish News, have established the President's Prize, an annual award to those at the grassroots level who have contributed most to peace and reconciliation. The honorees will travel to the United States to exchange experiences on the issues we share, including community relations and conflict resolution. We have a lot to learn from one another. The President's Prize will underscore that Northern Ireland's two traditions have a common interest in peace.

As you know, and as the First Lady said, I have received thousands of letters from schoolchildren all over your remarkable land telling me what peace means to them. They poured in from villages and cities, from Catholic and Protestant communities, from mixed schools, primary schools, from schools for children with special needs. All the letters in their own way were truly wonderful for their honesty, their simple wisdom, and their passion. Many of the children showed tremendous pride in their homeland, in its beauty, and in its true nature. I congratulate the winners. They were wonderful, and I loved hearing their letters.

But let me tell you about another couple I received. Eleven-year-old Keith from Carrickfergus wrote, "Please tell everyone in America that we're not always fighting here and that it's only a small number of people who make the trouble." Like many of the children, Keith did not identify himself as Protestant or Catholic and did not distinguish between the sources of the violence.

So many children told me of loved ones they have lost, of lives disrupted and opportunities forsaken and families forced to move. Yet they showed remarkable courage and strength and a commitment to overcome the past. As 14-year-old Sharon of County Armagh wrote, "Both sides have been hurt. Both sides must forgive."

Despite the extraordinary hardships so many of these children have faced, their letters were full of hope and love and humor. To all of you who took the time to write me, you've brightened my holiday season with your words of faith and courage, and I thank you. To all of you who asked me to do what I could do to help peace take root, I pledge you America's support. We will stand with you as you take risks for peace.

And to all of you who have not lost your sense of humor, I say thank you. I got a letter from 13-year-old Ryan from Belfast. Now, Ryan, if you're out in the crowd tonight, here's the answer to your question. No, as far as I know, an alien spacecraft did not crash in Roswell, New Mexico, in 1947. [*Laughter*] And Ryan, if the United States Air Force did recover alien bodies, they didn't tell me about it, either, and I want to know.

Ladies and gentlemen, this day that Hillary and I have had here in Belfast and in Derry and Londonderry County will long be with us as one of the most remarkable days of our lives. I leave you with these thoughts. May the Christmas spirit of peace and good will flourish and grow in you. May you remember the words of the Lord Mayor, "This is Christmas. We celebrate the world in a new way because of the birth of Emmanuel: God with us." And when God was with us, he said no words more important than these, "Blessed are the peacemakers, for they shall inherit the Earth."

Merry Christmas, and God bless you all.

NOTE: The President spoke at approximately 7:45 p.m. outside Belfast City Hall. In his remarks, he referred to Lord Mayor Eric Smyth of Belfast and his wife, Frances Smyth.

Remarks at a Reception Hosted by Sir Patrick Mayhew in Belfast
November 30, 1995

The President. Thank you.

Audience member. Four more years!

The President. The plane for America leaves tomorrow morning. I want you to be on it. [*Laughter*] We'll take you back.

Thank you, Sir Patrick and Lady Mayhew. And thank you, Sir Patrick, for your tireless efforts for peace in Northern Ireland.

I want to thank the Vice Chancellor, Sir Gordon Beveridge, and everyone here at Queen's University for allowing us to meet at this wonderful place in the year of its sesquicentennial celebration. I am delighted to be here. And I'm also delighted that it was given to me the honor to make a little announcement involving Queen's. Under the auspices of the Fulbright program, named after the late Senator from my home State, J. William Fulbright, who gave me my first job in public life, we are establishing a distinguished Fulbright lecturer program here at Queen's University to bring distinguished Americans to share their experiences and their ideas with their academic colleagues here and to reach out to the community throughout Northern Ireland.

Let me say that Hillary and I are delighted to be here with a very large contingent of Americans from all walks of life and from both political parties. I am delighted to be the first American President ever to visit Northern Ireland while serving as President. And I think all of you here know that I would, given the choice, never miss a chance to go to an exciting place and make new friends. But the real reason I'm here is because of the hard work and the tough choices that many of you in this room have made to advance the cause of peace and reconciliation in this land. And I thank you for that.

I will take away from this visit a lot of enduring memories, a lot of lasting impressions of peace. When we were at the Mackie plant this morning, it really struck me as a symbol of Northern Ireland's rebirth since the cease-fire. On the shop floor, men and women who come to the plant by separated gates still, work together side by side with common goals for their families and their communities.

I went to the Enterprise Park in East Belfast, and I met with tenants and managers who were making the most of their ideas, their potential, assisted, among other things, by the International Fund for Ireland.

I went to Londonderry where we had an extraordinary crowd, and I saw the splendor of that beautiful old city wall and also the remarkable Statue of Reconciliation there, which is also a sharp reminder. If you've seen it, you know there are two tall figures with their hands outstretched, but they're not quite touching yet. And of course, tonight at the Christmas tree lighting, for Hillary and for me it was an especially poignant moment not only because it reaffirmed the ties between our two lands with the President's Prize and the Christmas tree from your sister city of Nashville and because of those remarkable letters that those children wrote but also because of what I saw and felt in that vast throng of people.

And when I was shaking hands in the crowd there when there were no microphones on and no cameras shining, person after person after person that I shook hands with said, "We're glad you're here. We're trying to do this. Please stay with us; we haven't finished yet. The peace is not certain yet. We have to do this." Person after person. Person after person said, "Surely we'll never go back to the way it used to be." Just people in the crowd with their passion and energy and intensity.

I will remember this day for as long as I live, with great gratitude. And let me say what I have said all day: I am proud that the United States stands with the peacemakers here. We respect each tradition equally. We believe peace can be built here on the basis of mutual consent and, in fact, only on that basis. We continue to stand with those who take risks. And we want to see that there are clear, concrete benefits to peace through trade and investments and new jobs and new futures. We will do everything we can to work with all of you to sustain the momentum that Northern Ireland has at this point.

Let me finally say that I have taken a strict and unyielding position about the role of the United States as a force for peace throughout the world. Whether in the Middle East or in Bosnia or here, it is that we cannot, and we could not even if we wanted to, impose a peace on anyone. People must make their own peace from their heads and from their hearts. All we can do is to do the very best we can to create the best conditions in which people can make peace, to give the greatest encouragement to the process of peace, and to offer the hope of every reward we can possibly help to provide.

That is our role. That will remain our role. The details, the direction, and the question of whether you will go forward, that, my friends, is all up to you. But if you do, we will be proud to walk with you.

Thank you, and Merry Christmas.

NOTE: The President spoke at 9:27 p.m. in Whitla Hall at Queen's University.

Exchange With Reporters Prior to Discussions With President Mary Robinson of Ireland in Dublin
December 1, 1995

President's Visit

Q. Mr. President, how did you like the reception when you came in?

The President. I liked it very well. I was delighted to see the people in the streets and delighted to be with President Robinson again.

Q. What's on the agenda for the discussions this morning?

The President. More of the same. [*Laughter*]

Bosnia

Q. How do you like Senator Dole's support of Bosnia?

The President. I'm very gratified by it. I appreciate it very much.

NOTE: The exchange began at 11:07 a.m. at Áras an Uachtaráin, President Robinson's residence. A tape was not available for verification of the content of this exchange.

Exchange With Reporters Prior to Discussions With Prime Minister John Bruton of Ireland in Dublin
December 1, 1995

President's Visit

Q. Welcome to Ireland.

The President. Thank you. I'm delighted to be here.

Q. Did you enjoy your trips to Belfast and Derry yesterday?

The President. Very, very much.

Northern Ireland Peace Process

Q. How significant do you think it's going to be for the peace process, your visit to Belfast yesterday? Both of you, would you answer briefly?

The President. Well, I hope it will be very significant, but I think, frankly, it will have more meaning because of what the Taoiseach and Prime Minister Major did in launching the twin-track proposal. They gave me something to talk about, to try to advance the peace process, as well as to hold out the hope that the United States would obviously support both communities in Northern Ireland if they would work toward peace.

It was a magnificent day, and it proved to me once again that people sometimes are far ahead of those of us in political life in their yearnings for the right things.

Q. Taoiseach, what do you think of yesterday?

Prime Minister Bruton. I think that the fact that the President came to Belfast and to Derry gave to the people of Northern Ireland who made the peace themselves that sense of international encouragement and support that is so important. They now see what they have won by making peace. So the recognition that came to those people from the most powerful, most significant politician in the world—if he came in their midst, that showed in the most tangible way possible an appreciation of the dividend of peace. And it was a great tribute for the President to pay.

And I would have to say I think also that the President has played a key role in bringing peace about, and he is now playing an equally important role in entrenching the peace and bringing reconciliation closer.

Q. Mr. President, do you believe that your visit and indeed all-party talks can begin by the February deadline? Would you be very anxious that those talks would begin?

The President. Well, of course, I hope that the process will succeed. I support it strongly. The Taoiseach and the Prime Minister took some risks, both of them did, to try to keep the peace process going. It is plainly in the interest of the citizens of Northern Ireland and of all those who wish them well here in Ireland and, frankly, throughout Great Britain and throughout the world. It's a very important thing. So of course I hope it will work, and I'm going to do everything I can to be supportive.

[At this point, one group of reporters left the room, and another group entered.]

Bosnia

Q. Will you be talking about Bosnia today, Mr. President?

The President. I expect we will, yes.

Q. What are some of the issues that you want to discuss about Bosnia?

The President. Well, I just want to basically give the Prime Minister an update on where we are now. And of course, I'm going, when I leave here, to see our troops in Germany who are preparing and then, on Sunday, to the European Union. And soon I expect Ireland will be in the leadership of the European Union at a time when we will be, obviously, just in the throes of implementing what we're supposed to do in Bosnia. So we have a lot to talk about.

Q. Are you optimistic about what you saw on Capitol Hill yesterday and what you know of how it went with your advisers testifying?

The President. Yes, I—first of all, I thank Senator Dole and Senator McCain for their willingness to support that resolution, which we certainly agree with. And I'm very—I'm gratified by their response. And I also am pleased that we're having all these hearings on Capitol Hill and that the witnesses are going up; they're giving the best answers they can about what we've done. And I'm looking forward to getting my briefing tomorrow from General Joulwan to see what the NATO planners finally do with the military plan that I authorized General Shalikashvili to support.

So I think right now we're moving toward implementation of the peace agreement. I feel good about it.

Q. [Inaudible]—to generate support in the House as well as the Senate?

The President. Well, I take it one step at a time. I think we're making progress. I think we're in better shape as days go by, and I think that the decision by Senator Dole and Senator McCain will help immeasurably, I think, to build the kind of bipartisan support that we need to make this an American effort.

I can tell you this: As I have been in London and Ireland, I can see that, in addition to the overwhelming preoccupation we've all had with our efforts in Northern Ireland, the ability of the United States to play a leading role in partnership with Europe in dealing with the world's problems in the years ahead is certainly heavily dependent upon our doing our part here in Bosnia, especially after we hosted and did so much to broker the peace.

Northern Ireland Peace Process

Q. When you talked to the leaders last night in Belfast, were you encouraged? Was there anything that you told them to hold back their old grudges or—do you have hopes for the future?

The President. Let me just say, yes, I was encouraged because I think that Mr. Bruton and Mr. Major came up with a brilliant formulation which enables them to continue to have dialog with one another without giving up their position—it seems to me that is the genius of that—and then asking Senator Mitchell, along with two other very distinguished people, to be on this arms decommissioning work, so that it can succeed in parallel. I think it was great foreign relations.

Obviously, none of the people with whom I spoke yesterday changed their positions in their brief meetings with me. The point I tried to make to them was that the two Prime Ministers had given them an honorable way to continue to engage in peace talks without giving up any of their previous positions; and if they looked in the streets of Belfast and Derry, they could see that the young people of their country, without regard to whether they were Protestant or Catholic, desperately wanted this to be resolved. They want to live together, they want to live

on equal and honorable terms, and they want to live in peace. Those were the only points that I could make, and I made them as forcefully as I could.

Q. If you would permit me, Mr. President, the decommissioning issue is going to be a very hard nut to crack, isn't it?

The President. Sure. But that's why they——

Q. How do you do it?

The President. Well, that's why they set it up the way they did. I think it's not just a rational issue, it's an emotional issue. And that's why, I will say again, what the United States—the role of the United States is not to tell anybody how to solve a specific problem, including the decommissioning problem. We've tried to support those who are taking risks for peace.

The two Prime Ministers have set up a process at considerable risk to themselves which permit all the parties to be heard and permit this very difficult decommissioning issue to be dealt with. And everyone can now proceed forward without giving up any of their own positions at the moment. That is what I thought was so important. We were stalled for too long.

And as I said in Derry, if you look at that statue—those two Statues of Reconciliation there; they're reaching out, and they're not quite touching. But people are not statues. When you get close like this, you don't stay in that position. You either shake hands, or you drift apart. They've given this process a chance to move to a handshake, and that's all we can hope for. Now we just have to redouble our efforts and keep our attitudes proper and remember the message of the people in the streets, which is that they want this done. They're not interested in all the last details. They want it worked out so they can live on equal and honorable terms and live in peace. And I think that's what the rest of us have to try to give them.

Prime Minister Bruton. I just want to say the key word is that this is a process, a process in which people can move closer together, a process in which people can give as well as take.

NOTE: The exchange began at 12:29 p.m. at the Government Buildings. In his remarks, the President referred to Prime Minister John Major of the United Kingdom and Gen. George A. Joulwan, USA, Supreme Allied Commander, Europe. A tape was not available for verification of the content of this exchange.

The President's News Conference With Prime Minister John Bruton of Ireland in Dublin
December 1, 1995

Prime Minister Bruton. Ladies and gentlemen, Mr. President: I'd like to welcome you warmly to Ireland, to thank you for all that you have done to help bring peace to our country, to thank you for all that you are continuing to do to bring the people that live on this island closer together and to improve the relations that exist between this island and its neighbors.

I'm delighted that it was possible for the British Prime Minister, John Major, to whom I pay tribute here, and myself to agree on a framework for moving forward towards a settlement of the differences that have existed on this island for 300 years now. And the fact that we were able to do that on the eve of your visit is no accident. Because we both realized, both John Major and I, that the sort of support that you have been able to give, yesterday and today, to the people of this island searching for peace, searching for reconciliation, searching to heal the wounds that have been there for so long, and looking positively to the future, we both appreciate it that your support gives them encouragement, gives us encouragement, and is something for which we from the bottom of our hearts sincerely thank you, Mr. President.

The President. Thank you very much. I'd like to begin by thanking the Prime Minister for his warm welcome, and more importantly, I want to say a special word of thanks to all of the people of Ireland and the people of Northern Ireland who have shown such extraordinary warmth and generosity to Hillary and me and now our American delegation. This has been an extraordinary experience for us, and I will never forget it.

I thank the Prime Minister for what he said, but the truth is that the credit for this latest progress belongs to the Taoiseach and to Prime Minister Major. They announced this twin-track initiative to advance the peace process of Northern Ireland shortly before I arrived here. It gives the parties a chance to engage in an honest dialog where all their views are represented and everybody's voice can be heard. And I certainly hope that it will be successful.

Let me also say, as you know, it establishes a means to address the issue of decommission-

ing, and I am gratified that my good friend Senator George Mitchell is going to lead the international body to deal with that issue. He is seizing this opportunity already. He has begun to organize the effort with other members, and I expect him to be at work shortly.

Let me again say, I know that I speak for all Americans who want peace and ultimate reconciliation on this island when I say that the Taoiseach has shown great courage in the pursuit of peace, and we intend to do whatever we can to help him, Prime Minister Major, Mr. Spring, and all others who are working for peace to succeed.

The United States is honored to stand with those who take risks for peace, and we are doing it all across the world, in the Middle East, in Bosnia, and here. It is a difficult road to travel. It is always easier to stay in the known way and to play on the known fears. But the right thing to do is to do what is being done here, and I applaud it and I want to do everything I can to support it.

Let me also say that we had the opportunity to discuss the situation in Bosnia, and I described as best I could the terms of the peace agreement and what we intend to do in the United States with our allies to implement it in a military way and what nonmilitary tasks have to be undertaken. I am very hopeful that after the peace agreement is signed in Paris in just a couple of weeks, we will see a dramatic change in that war-torn land.

Let me say that the kind of thing that the international community is going to have to do in Bosnia is consistent with what Ireland has done every day for nearly 40 years now. Irish peacekeepers have helped people to live in peace from Cyprus to Somalia, to feed the hungry, to do so much that most people in the world don't even know that the people of Ireland have done. And again, I want to say on behalf of the American people, I am very, very grateful for that.

So we had a good meeting, we've got a wonderful relationship, the Sun is shining, and I hope it's a good omen for peace in Northern Ireland.

Thank you.

Northern Ireland Peace Process

Q. The impasse has been broken at the moment, but the roadblock is still there. Senator Mitchell's committee is going to start its work. If at the end of the day the deadlock is still there, is your Government, your administration prepared to act as persuaders to get to all-party talks without preconditions?

The President. Well, first of all, let me say I think we ought to give these folks a chance to succeed. We shouldn't be talking about, "If at the end of the day..." The Prime Minister of Great Britain and the Taoiseach have announced, I think, a brilliant formulation which permits people to go forward in dealing with all of these issues without giving up any of the things they say they believe in and have to have.

I think we ought to give this process a chance to succeed. If it fails, then we'll reconnoiter and see what to do next. But I think the lesson of the last 15 months is that the people like peace, they like the absence of violence, and they want to go forward, not backward. They want to deal with the issues that are still before them. So I'm inclined to believe it will succeed. If it doesn't, then you can ask me that question.

Q. What has your visit done, in concrete terms, to change the way the United States will engage with the peace process? How has it affected where you go from here?

The President. I don't know that the visit has done anything to change, in concrete terms, the way we are engaged, except I believe that since we have quite a large number of Members of Congress here and quite a large number of business people here and quite a large contingent of people in the news media here, all seeing what is going on in Northern Ireland, I think it will deepen the support of the American people for our constructive involvement, and it might well intensify the pace at which people in the private sector are willing to make investments and try to bring the economic benefits of peace to the people there. But we are committed, we have been committed, and we're going to stay committed. And we'll be there until the work is finished.

Prime Minister Bruton. Now an American journalist.

Balkan Peace Process

Q. Mr. President, back home Republicans in Congress are expressing concern about snipers and bombs and ethnic hatreds that American forces are going to face in Bosnia. When you go to Germany tomorrow, what will you tell the American troops about the dangers they face, and have you heard any estimates about the casualties that they might suffer?

The President. Well, first of all, the American troops that have trained to go to Bosnia know every bit as much about the dangers they might face as I do. What I will tell them is that it is not a risk-free mission. Indeed, being in the military is not risk-free. We lose a significant number of our finest young people every year just in the training exercises because of the inherent danger of moving around and doing the things that they do in the air, on the land, and at sea.

I will tell them that we have done everything we can to minimize the risks, we have guaranteed for them very robust rules of engagement so that if anyone attempts to interfere with their mission or to take action against them, they can respond with decisive, indeed, with overwhelming force and that their peace and their security, their safety is uppermost in my mind and in the mind of their general officers who have done all the planning for this mission but that this is a mission very much in America's interest where we can make a huge difference and stop the worst slaughter in Europe since World War II, and that I'm very proud of them for doing it.

Q. Mr. President, are you escalating the U.S. involvement in Bosnia even before we go there? Suddenly, 20,000 troops have become 25,000 and the cost has gone from 1.5 billion to 3 billion.

The President. No. Well, first of all, I don't think it's going to be at 3 billion but we—the numbers keep getting bandied around here. Some people who count the money in Europe would be double-counting it. Some of this money is going to be spent anyway. I don't think we should count as a cost of the operation in Bosnia, for example, the salary of someone who's going to get paid their salary whether they're there or not.

The 25,000, let me say—well, I have always said we would have 20,000 people in the theater. We have been asked how many people are necessary to support them. We'll have another roughly 5,000 people outside of Bosnia in support of those who are in Bosnia, but they will not be in the Bosnian theater. There may be some extra costs associated with them that are sizable enough, and they ought to be included in the bill that we tell Congress we expect to pay here.

But if you look at it, again I will say, this is an appropriate level of contribution. This is no more than a third—may wind up being considerably less than a third of the total contribution, depending on how many other nations participate. You heard the British Prime Minister say 2 days ago that he expected that Great Britain, a country with a population of roughly—well, less than a fourth of ours, is going to send 13,000 troops to the theater. So the Europeans are going to take the major load, and we should support them.

Northern Ireland Peace Process

Q. It seems that this historic trip by President Clinton to Ireland has facilitated an agreement between yourself and John Major. Is that not ominous for the future of the peace process if it takes President Clinton's arrival to produce that level of movement forward? When we get to the really serious negotiations, won't it be more difficult?

Prime Minister Bruton. I think the ingredients for the agreement have been there for quite some time. But I think it is the case that we both recognized that the President's visit to Britain and Ireland was an opportunity for both of us to launch in the best possible circumstances an initiative which we were probably going to have to agree anyway very shortly. But we were able to do it on the eve of President Clinton's visit in such a fashion as to ensure that his presence here has given it the fairest possible wind.

Balkan Peace Process

Q. Mr. Prime Minister, why is it necessary for the United States for the third time in this century to send troops to Europe? Why aren't the Europeans capable, in your opinion, of resolving these kinds of problems in Bosnia by themselves?

Prime Minister Bruton. I think it's important to recognize that if you have genocide of the kind that was occurring in Bosnia, that's not just a European problem; that's a problem for the world at large. It's a problem for the common civilization which we all share. It's a common problem for all of us who have democratic values, democratic values which stem in Europe chiefly from the inspiration of the American War of Independence and the United States Declaration of Independence. Those values are universal, and therefore there is a universal responsibility, in my view, for all of us to do whatever we can in proportion to our means to facilitate the making of peace.

It is very important also to stress that the role that the United States, the European Union, and others have played in Bosnia is one of facilitating peacemaking. The peace is not being made by the United States, no more than it is being made by the European Union. The peace in Bosnia is being made by the people of Bosnia themselves. And that is the same situation in this country. We provide a framework. They must do the deal.

The President. And I just want to mention one other thing, too. I want you to think about these points: Number one, at the end of World War II, we established NATO, recognizing that we would try to stay together dealing with common security concerns. Admittedly, at the time, we thought those concerns might play themselves out in Central Europe in the contest between what was then the Soviet Union and the Western bloc, the NATO bloc. But we understood that we had shared concerns that would manifest themselves first on the Continent of Europe but could become much more immediate for us.

Now, the NATO powers have voted among themselves to work with others through the United Nations and on our own in brokering this peace agreement and trying to implement it. This is consistent with what we have done since World War II.

The second thing I'd like to ask every American is how you would have felt—I would like to ask every American how would you have felt when President Bush sent out the call for help in Desert Storm, which was a war, not a peacekeeping measure, if they said, "You handle that. You have more money, more soldiers, more interests there. You're concerned about the oil. You waste more oil than the rest of us do. You guys handle that"? Or think about all the countries that helped us in Haiti who didn't say, "I'm sorry. That's not our problem; that's your problem. You have the refugees in the

United States. We don't have them. They're on your shore. They're your problem. We can't be bothered with that." But instead, we have had dozens of countries rally to the United States to work with us in common cause when their values were violated by things that were of more immediate concern to us. That's what they did in Desert Storm. That's what they did in Haiti.

And I will say, every day, every day for almost 40 years, there has been a citizen of Ireland in some distant country working for peacekeeping in places where the United States did not go. And they did not ask, "What is the imme-diate interest of the people of Ireland in doing that?"

So I think the United States has been very well-served by countries that have been willing to stand up with us, to stand up for good things and right things that also affect our interest. And I believe we should do this now.

Prime Minister Bruton. Thank you. We must respect the timetable. I'm sorry. Thank you very much, indeed. Thank you.

NOTE: The President's 108th news conference began at 1:20 p.m. on the steps of the Government Buildings.

Remarks to the Community in Dublin
December 1, 1995

Thank you very much. First, let me say to all of you Dubliners and to all Ireland, Hillary and I have loved our trip to your wonderful country. To the Taoiseach and Mrs. Bruton; Lord Mayor Loftus and Lady Mayoress; City Manager Frank Feely; to all the aldermen who conferred this great honor on me. To the Americans in the audience, welcome to all of you. Are there any Irish in the audience? [*Laughter*] I want to say also how pleased I am to be here with a number of Irish-American Members of the United States Congress and the Irish-American Director of the Peace Corps, Mark Gearan; the Irish-American Secretary of Education, Richard Riley; and the Secretary of Commerce, Ron Brown, who wishes today he were Irish-American. Thank you all for being here.

I was on this College Green once before. Yes, in 1968, when I was almost as young as some of the young students over there. Lord Mayor, I never dreamed I would be back here on this College Green in this capacity, but I am delighted to be here. And I thank you.

I am told that in earlier times the honor I have just received, being awarded the Freedom of the City, meant you no longer had to pay tolls to the Vikings. I'm going to try that on the Internal Revenue Service when I get home. I hope it will work. [*Laughter*] Whether it does or not, I am proud to say that I am now a free man of Dublin.

To look out into this wonderful sea of Irish faces on this beautiful Irish day I feel like a real "Dub" today—is that what I'm supposed to say? [*Applause*] Not only that, I know we have a handy football team. [*Laughter*]

Let me say that, as a lot of you know, because of events developing in Bosnia and the prospect of peace there, I had to cut short my trip. But there are a few signs out there I want to respond to. I will return to Ballybunion for my golf game. [*Laughter*]

I am also pleased to announce that President Robinson has accepted my invitation to come to the United States next June to continue our friendship.

There's another special Irish-American I want to mention today and that is our distinguished Ambassador to Ireland, Jean Kennedy Smith, who came here with her brother President Kennedy 32 years ago and who has worked very hard also for the cause of peace in Northern Ireland.

Years ago, Americans learned about Dublin from the stories of James Joyce and Sean O'Casey. Today, America and the world still learn about Dublin and Ireland through the words of Sebastian Barry, Paula Meehan, Roddy Doyle; through the films of Jim Sheridan, Neil Jordan; through the voices of Mary Black and Delores Keane; and yes, through the Cranberries and U2. I hear all about how the world's global culture is becoming more American, but

I believe that if you want to grasp the global culture, you need to come to Ireland.

All of you know that I have family ties here. My mother was a Cassidy, and how I wish she were alive to be here with me today. She would have loved the small towns and she would have loved Dublin. Most of all, she would have loved the fact that in Ireland, you have nearly 300 racing days a year. [*Laughter*] She loved the horses. I understand that there are some Cassidys out in the audience today. And if they are, I want to say in my best Arkansas accent, *céad mile failte—beatha saol agus slainte.*

One hundred and fifty years ago, the crops of this gorgeous island turned black in the ground and one-fourth of your people either starved from the hunger or were lost to emigration. That famine was the greatest tragedy in Irish history. But out of that horrible curse came the most bittersweet of blessings, the arrival in my country of millions of new Americans who built the United States and climbed to the top of its best works. For every person here in Ireland today, 12 more in the United States have proud roots in Irish soil.

Perhaps the memory of the famine explains in part the extraordinary generosity of the Irish people, not just to needy neighbors in the local parish but to strangers all around the globe. You do not forget those who still go hungry in the world today, who yearn simply to put food on the table and clothes on their backs. In places as far away as the Holy Land, Asia, and Africa, the Irish are helping people to build a future of hope.

Your sons and daughters in the Gardai and the defense forces take part in some of the most demanding missions of good will, keeping the peace, helping people in war-torn lands turn from conflict to cooperation. Whenever the troubled places of the Earth call out for help, from Haiti to Lebanon, the Irish are always among the very first to answer the call.

Your commitment to peace helps conquer foes that threaten us all. And on behalf of the people of the United States, I say to the people of Ireland: We thank you for that from the bottom of our hearts.

Ireland is helping beat back the forces of hatred and destruction all around the world, the spread of weapons of mass destruction, terrorism, ethnic hatreds, religious fanaticism, the international drug trade. Ireland is helping to beat back these forces that wage war against all humanity. You are an inspiration to people around the world. You have made peace heroic. Nowhere are the people of Ireland more important in the cause of peace today than right here at home.

Tuesday night, before I left the United States to come here, I received the happy word that the Taoiseach and Prime Minister Major had opened a gateway to a just and lasting peace, a peace that will lift the lives of your neighbors in Northern Ireland and their neighbors in the towns and counties that share the northern border. That was the greatest welcome anyone could have asked for. I applaud the Taoiseach for his courage, but I know that the courage and the heart of the Irish people made it possible. And I thank you for what you did.

Waging peace is risky. It takes courage and strength that is a hard road. It is easier, as I said yesterday, to stay with the old grudges and the old habits. But the right thing to do is to reach for a new future of peace, not because peace is a document on paper or even a handshake among leaders but because it changes people's lives in fundamental and good ways.

Yesterday in Northern Ireland I saw that for myself. I saw it on the floor of the Mackie plant in Belfast, with Catholics and Protestants working side by side to build a better future for their families. I heard it in the voices of the two extraordinary children you may have seen on your television, one a Catholic girl, the other a Protestant boy, who introduced me to the people of Belfast with their hands joined, telling the world of their hopes for the future, a future without bullets or bombs, in which the only barriers they face are the limits to their dreams.

As I look out on this sea of people today, I tell you that the thing that moved me most in that extraordinary day in Northern Ireland yesterday was that the young people, Catholic and Protestant alike, made it clear to me, not only with their words but by the expressions on their faces, that they want peace and decency among all people.

I know well that the immigration from your country to the shores of mine helped to make America great. But I want more than anything for the young people of Ireland, wherever they live on this island, to be able to grow up and live out their dreams close to their roots in peace and honor and freedom and equality.

I could not say it better than your Nobel Prize winning poet, Seamus Heaney, has said: We are living in a moment when hope and history rhyme. In Dublin, if there is peace in Northern Ireland, it is your victory, too. And I ask all of you to think about the next steps we must take.

Stand with the Taoiseach as he takes risks for peace. Realize how difficult it is for them, having been in their patterns of opposition for so long to the north of you. And realize that those of you who have more emotional and physical space must reach out and help them to take those next hard steps. It is worth doing.

And to you, this vast, wonderful throng of people here, and all of the people of Ireland, I say: America will be with you as you walk the road of peace. We know from our own experience that making peace among people of different cultures is the work of a lifetime. It is a constant challenge to find strength amid diversity, to learn to respect differences instead of run from them. Every one of us must fight the struggle within our own spirit. We have to decide whether we will define our lives primarily based on who we are or who we are not, based on what we are for or what we are against. There are always things to be against in life, and we have to stand against the bad things we should stand against.

But the most important thing is that we have more in common with people who appear on the surface to be different from us than most of us know. And we have more to gain by reaching out in the spirit of brotherhood and sisterhood to those people than we can possibly know. That is the challenge the young people of this generation face.

When President Kennedy came here a generation ago and spoke in this city he said that he sincerely believed, and I quote, "that your future is as promising as your past is proud, that your destiny lies not as a peaceful island in a sea of troubles but as a maker and shaper of world peace."

A generation later, Ireland has claimed that destiny. Yours is a more peaceful land in a world that is ever more peaceful in significant measure because of the efforts of the citizens of Ireland. For touching the hearts and minds of peace-loving people in every corner of the world, for the risk you must now continue to take for peace, for inspiring the nations of the world by your example, and for giving so much to make America great, America says, thank you.

Thank you, Ireland, and God bless you all.

NOTE: The President spoke at 2:10 p.m. outside the Bank of Ireland at College Green. In his remarks, he referred to Prime Minister John Bruton and his wife, Fionnuala; and Lord Mayor Sean D. Loftus of Dublin and his wife, Patricia.

Remarks to the Parliament of Ireland in Dublin
December 1, 1995

Mr. Speaker Comhaile, you appear to be someone who can be trusted with the budget. [*Laughter*] Such are the vagaries of faith which confront us all. [*Laughter*]

To the Taoiseach, the Tánaiste, members of the Dáil and the Seanad, head of the Senate. I'm honored to be joined here, as all of you know, by my wife, members of our Cabinet, and Members of the United States Congress of both parties, the congressional delegation chaired by Congressman Walsh; they are up there. They got an enormous laugh out of the comments of the Comhaile. [*Laughter*] For different reasons they were laughing. [*Laughter*]

I thank you for the honor of inviting me here, and I am especially pleased to be here at this moment in your history, before the elected representatives of a strong, confident, democratic Ireland, a nation today playing a greater role in world affairs than ever before.

We live in a time of immense hope and immense possibility, a time captured, I believe, in the wonderful lines of your poet Seamus Heaney when he talked of the "longed-for tidal wave of justice can rise up and hope and history rhyme." That is the time in which we live. It's the world's good fortune that Ireland has become a force for fulfilling that hope and redeeming the possibilities of mankind, a force for good far beyond your numbers. And we are all the better for it.

Today I have traveled from the north, where I have seen the difference Ireland's leadership has made for peace there. At the lighting of Belfast's Christmas tree for tens of thousands of people there, in the faces of two communities divided by bitter history, we saw the radiance of optimism born, especially among the young of both communities. In the voices of the Shankill and the Falls, there was a harmony of new hope which we saw. I saw that the people want peace, and they will have it.

George Bernard Shaw, with his wonderful Irish love of irony, said, "Peace is not only better than war but infinitely more arduous." Well today I thank Prime Minister Bruton and former Prime Minister Reynolds and Deputy Prime Minister Spring and Britain's Prime Minister Major and others, but especially these, for their unfailing dedication to the arduous task of peace.

From the Downing Street declaration to the historic cease-fire that began 15 months ago to Tuesday's announcement of the twin-track initiative which will open a dialog in which all voices can be heard and all viewpoints can be represented, they have taken great risks without hesitation. They've chosen a harder road than the comfortable path of pleasant, present pieties. But what they have done is right. And the children and grandchildren of this generation of Irish will reap the rewards.

Today I renew America's pledge. Your road is our road. We want to walk it together. We will continue our support, political, financial, and moral, to those who take risks for peace. I am proud that our administration was the first to support in the executive budget sent to the Congress the International Fund for Ireland, because we believe that those on both sides of the border who have been denied so much for so long should see that their risks are rewarded with the tangible benefits of peace. In another context a long time ago, Mr. Yeats reminded us that too long a sacrifice can make a stone of the heart. We must not let the hearts of the young people who yearn for peace turn to stone.

I want to thank you here, not only for the support you have given your leaders in working for peace in Northern Ireland but for the extraordinary work you have done to wage peace over war all around the world. Almost 1,500 years ago, Ireland stood as a lone beacon of civilization to a continent shrouded in darkness. It has been said, probably without overstatement, that the Irish, in that dark period, saved civilization. Certainly you saved the records of our civilization, our shared ideas, our shared ideals, our priceless recordings of them.

Now, in our time, when so many nations seek to overcome conflict and barbarism, the light still shines out of Ireland. Since 1958, almost 40 years now, there has never been a single, solitary day that Irish troops did not stand watch for peace on a distant shore. In Lebanon, in Cyprus, in Somalia, in so many other places, more than 41,000 Irish military and police personnel have served over the years as peacekeepers, an immense contribution for a nation whose armed forces today number fewer than 13,000.

I know that during your Presidency of the European Union next year, Ireland will help to lead the effort to build security for a stable, strong, and free Europe. For all you have done and for your steadfast devotion to peace, I salute the people of Ireland.

Our Nation also has a vital stake in a Europe that is stable, strong, and free, something which is now in reach for the first time since nation-states appeared on the Continent of Europe so many centuries ago. But we know such a Europe can never be built as long as conflict tears at the heart of the Continent in Bosnia. The fire there threatens the emerging democracies of the region and our allies nearby. And it also breaks our heart and violates our conscience.

That is why, now that the parties have committed themselves to peace, we in the United States are determined to help them find the way back from savagery to civility, to end the atrocities and heal the wounds of that terrible war. That is why we are preparing our forces to participate there, not in fighting a war but in securing a peace rooted in the agreement they have freely made.

Standing here, thinking about the devastation in Bosnia, the long columns of hopeless refugees streaming from their homes, it is impossible not to recall the ravages that were visited on your wonderful country 150 years ago, not by war, of course, but by natural disaster when the crops rotted black in the ground. Today, still, the Great Famine is seared in the memory of the Irish nation and all caring peoples. The memory of a million dead, nearly 2 million more forced into exile, these memories will remain forever vivid to all of us whose heritage is rooted here.

But as an American, I must say, as I did just a few moments ago in Dublin downtown, that in that tragedy came the supreme gift of the Irish to the United States. The men, women, and children who braved the coffin ships when Galway and Mayo emptied, when Kerry and Cork took flight, brought a life and a spirit that has enormously enriched the life of our country.

The regimental banner brought by President Kennedy that hangs in this house reminds us of the nearly 200,000 Irishmen who took up arms in our Civil War. Many of them barely were off the ships when they joined the Union forces. They fought and died at Fredericksburg and Chancellorsville and Gettysburg. Theirs was only the first of countless contributions to our Nation from those who fled the famine. But that contribution enabled us to remain a nation and to be here with you today in partnership for peace for your nation and for the peoples who live on this island.

The Irish have been building America ever since, our cities, our industry, our culture, our public life. I am proud that the delegation that has accompanied me here today includes the latest generation of Irish-American leaders in the United States, men and women who remain devoted to increasing our strength and safeguarding our liberty.

In the last century, it was often said that the Irish who fled the great hunger were searching for *casleain na n-or,* castles of gold. I cannot say that they found those castles of gold in the United States, but I can tell you this: They built a lot of castles of gold for the United States in the prosperity and freedom of our Nation. We are grateful for what they did and for the deep ties to Ireland that they gave us in their sons and daughters.

Now we seek to repay that in some small way, by being a partner with you for peace. We seek somehow to communicate to every single person who lives here that we want for all of your children the right to grow up in an Ireland where this entire island gives every man and woman the right to live up to the fullest of their God-given abilities and gives people the right to live in equality and freedom and dignity.

That is the tide of history. We must make sure that the tide runs strong here, for no people deserve the brightest future more than the Irish.

God bless you, and thank you.

NOTE: The President spoke at 5:30 p.m. in the Dail Chamber at Leinster House. In his remarks, he referred to Chairman of the House of Deputies Sean Tracey.

Remarks at a Dinner Hosted by Prime Minister John Bruton of Ireland in Dublin
December 1, 1995

To the Taoiseach and Mrs. Bruton and to all of our hosts: Hillary and I are honored to be here tonight with all of you and to be here in the company of some of America's greatest Irish-Americans, including Senator George Mitchell, who has taken on such a great and difficult task; a bipartisan congressional delegation headed by Congressman Walsh; many members of the Ambassador's family, including Kathleen Kennedy Townsend, lieutenant governor of Maryland; the mayors of Chicago and Los Angeles; Secretary Riley, the Secretary of Education; Mark Gearan, Director of the Peace Corps. And as I said, we have the Secretary of Commerce, Ron Brown, tonight, who wishes more than ever before in his life that he were Irish. [*Laughter*] I think he is, down deep inside. I thank you also for—I see the mayor of Pittsburgh here. I know I've left out some others—my wonderful stepfather, Dick Kelley, who thought it was all right when I got elected President, but when I brought him home to Ireland he knew I had finally arrived. [*Laughter*]

You know, the Taoiseach has been not only a good friend to me in our work for peace but a good friend to the United States. Indeed, he and Fionnuala actually came to Washington, DC, to celebrate their honeymoon. I think it's fair to say that his honeymoon there lasted longer than mine did. [*Laughter*]

I managed to get even with at least one Member of Congress—or former Member of Congress—when I convinced Senator Mitchell to give in to the entreaties of the Taoiseach and the Prime Minister to head this arms decommissioning group. Now, there's any easy job for you. [*Laughter.*] You know, in Ireland I understand there's a—our American country music is very popular. Garth Brooks said the other day he sold more records in Ireland than any other place in the world outside America. So I told Senator Mitchell today that—he was telling me what a wonderful day we had yesterday in Derry and Belfast and what a wonderful day we had today in Dublin, and I said, "Yes, now you get to go to work." I said, "This reminds me of that great country song 'I Got the Gold Mine and You Got the Shaft.'" [*Laughter*] But if anybody can bring out more gold, George Mitchell can.

I want to thank the Taoiseach for the courage he showed in working with the Prime Minister of Great Britain, from the day he took office, taking up from his predecessor, Albert Reynolds, right through this remarkable breakthrough that he and Prime Minister Major made on the twin tracks that he helped to forge just 2 days ago. This is an astonishing development really because it is the first formulation anyone has come up with that permits all views to be heard, all voices to speak, all issues to be dealt with, without requiring people to give up the positions they have taken at the moment. We are very much in your debt.

This has been an experience like none I have ever had before. Yesterday John Hume, who's joined us, took me home to Derry with him. And I thought to myself, all my life "Danny Boy" has been my favorite song; I never thought I'd get to go there to hear it. But thanks to John, I did.

And then we were, before, in Belfast. And all of you I'm sure were so moved by those two children who introduced me, reading excerpts from the letters. You know, I've got thousands and thousands of letters from Irish children telling me what peace means to them. One thing I am convinced of as I leave here: that there is a global hunger among young people for their parents to put down the madness of war in favor of their childhood.

I received this letter from a teenager right here in Dublin. I thought I would read it to you, to make the point better than I could. This is just an excerpt: "With your help, the chance is given to reason and to reasonable people, so that the peace in my country becomes reality. What is lost is impossible to bring back. Children who were killed are gone forever. No one can bring them back, but for all those who survive these sufferings, there is future."

The young person from Dublin who wrote me that was Zlata Filpovic, the young teenager from Bosnia who is now living here, who wrote her wonderful diary that captured the imagination of people all over the world.

I am honored that at this moment in the history of the world the United States has had the great good fortune to stand for the future of children in Ireland, in Bosnia, in the Middle East, in Haiti, and on the toughest streets of our own land. And I thank you here in Ireland for taking your stand for those children's future as well.

Let me say in closing that in this 150th anniversary of the Great Famine, I would like everyone in the world to pay tribute to Ireland for coming out of the famine with perhaps a greater sense of compassion for the fate of people the world over than any other nation. I said today in my speech to the Parliament that there had not been a single, solitary day, not one day, since 1958 when someone representing the Government of Ireland was not somewhere in the world trying to aid the cause of peace. I think there is no other nation on Earth that can make that claim.

And as I leave you, I feel so full of hope for the situation here in Ireland and so much gratitude for you, for what you have given to us. And I leave you with these words, which I found as I was walking out the door from the Ambassador's residence. The Ambassador made it possible for Hillary and me to spend a few moments this evening with Seamus Heaney and his wife, since I have been running around the country quoting him for 2 days. [*Laughter*] I might say, without his permission. [*Laughter*] And he gave Hillary an inscribed copy of his book "The Cure at Troy." And as I skimmed through it, I found these words, with which I leave you:

Now it's high water mark
And floodtide in the heart

And time to go...
What's left to say?

Suspect too much sweet talk
But never close your mind.
It was a fortunate wind
That blew me here. I leave
Half-ready to believe
That a crippled trust might walk
And the half-true rhyme is love.

Thank you, and God bless you.

I thought I had done something for a moment
to offend the Taoiseach—he was forcing me on
water instead of wine. [*Laughter*]

Let me now, on behalf of every American
here present, bathed in the generosity and the
hospitality of Ireland, offer this toast to the
Taoiseach and Mrs. Bruton and to the wonderful
people of this great Republic.

NOTE: The President spoke at approximately 8:40
p.m. at Dublin Castle. In his remarks, he referred
to U.S. Ambassador to Ireland Jean Kennedy
Smith and Mayors Richard M. Daley of Chicago,
IL, Richard Riordan of Los Angeles, CA, and Tom
Murphy of Pittsburgh, PA.

Remarks to Troops in Baumholder, Germany
December 2, 1995

General Joulwan, General Nash, General
Crouch, Secretary West. A special word of
greeting to America's good friend Chancellor
Kohl, who has been a wonderful partner to our
country, with great thanks to Germany for their
partnership with this fine unit.

I am immensely proud to be here today with
the men and women of the 1st Armored Division. You truly are America's Iron Soldiers. Previous generations of Iron Soldiers have answered
our Nation's call with legendary skill and bravery. Each time before, it was a call to war.
From North Africa to Italy, they helped freedom
triumph over tyranny in World War II. Then
for 20 years, their powerful presence here stood
down the Soviet threat and helped to bring victory in the cold war. And just 4 years ago,
when Saddam Hussein attacked Kuwait, the 1st
Armored Division's awesome power turned back
Iraq and protected the security of the Persian
Gulf. I know many of you were there. But I
would like to remind you that in just 89 hours
of combat, you destroyed 440 enemy tanks, 485
armored personnel carriers, 190 pieces of artillery, and 137 air defense guns. You should be
very proud of that remarkable record.

Now America summons you to service again,
this time not with a call to war but a call to
peace. The leaders of Bosnia, Croatia, and Serbia have agreed to end 4 long years of war
and atrocities. They have asked for our help
to implement their peace agreement. It is in
our Nation's interest and consistent with our

values to see that this peace succeeds and endures. And we are counting on you, the men
and women of Task Force Eagle, to get that
job done.

For 3 years I refused to send our American
forces into Bosnia where they could have been
pulled into war. But I do want you to go there
on a mission of peace. After speaking to your
commanders and looking at all of you and listening to you, there is not a doubt in my mind
this task force is ready to roll. Your mission:
to help people exhausted from war make good
on the peace they have chosen, the peace they
have asked you to help them uphold.

Just 2 weeks ago in Dayton, Ohio, the warring
parties in Bosnia agreed to put down their arms,
to pull back their armies and their heavy weapons, to hold free elections, to start rebuilding
their homes, their towns, and their lives. But
they need help to do that, and they have asked
America and our NATO allies and other willing
countries to provide it.

They need that help because, after nearly 4
years of terrible brutality, trust is in short supply
in Bosnia, and they all trust you to do the job
right. Each side wants NATO to help them live
up to the commitments they've made, to make
sure each army withdraws behind the separation
line and stays there, to maintain the cease-fire
so that the war does not start again, and give
all the parties the confidence they need to keep
their word and also to give them the trust that
the other side will keep its word as well.

I pledged to the American people that I would not send you to Bosnia unless I was absolutely sure that the goals we set for you are clear, realistic, and achievable in about a year. This mission meets those essential standards. I also vowed that you would not go to Bosnia until I was sure that we had done everything we could to minimize the risks to your safety.

You know better than anyone that every deployment has risks. There could be accidents. In a formerly hostile environment, there could be incidents with people who have still not given up their hatred. As President, I take full responsibility for your well-being. But I also take pride in the knowledge that we are making this mission as safe as it can be.

You will take your orders from General Joulwan, who commands NATO. There will be no confusing chain of command. You are superbly prepared. You will be heavily armed. The reputation that you—[*applause*]—I didn't want anyone to think there was a division of the house on that point. [*Laughter*]

Perhaps even more important, you will be heavily armed with the reputation that proceeds you. That and the technology and training that protect you will make those who might wish to attack think twice. But you will also have very clear rules of engagement that spell out the most important rule of all in big, bold letters: If you are threatened with attack, you may respond immediately and with decisive force. Everyone should know that when America comes to help make the peace, America will still look after its own.

Your presence will help to create the climate of security Bosnia needs. It will allow the international community to begin a massive program of humanitarian relief and reconstruction. It will bring the people of Bosnia the food, the medicine, the shelter, the clothing they have been denied for too long. It will help them rebuild their roads and their towns, open their schools and their hospitals, their factories and their shops. It will reunite families torn apart by war and return refugees to their homes. It will help people recover the quiet blessings of normal life.

This morning, after 2 days of working for peace in Northern Ireland, I met at the airport in Dublin with Zlata Filpovic, the young Bosnian girl whose now famous diary of her wartime experience in Sarajevo has moved so many millions of people around the world. She's my

daughter's age, just 15, but she has seen things that no one 3 or 4 times her age should ever have to witness. I thanked her for a powerful letter of support for our efforts for peace in Bosnia that she wrote me just a few days ago. And then I told her I was on my way to visit with all of you. This is what she said: "Mr. President, when you're in Germany, please thank the American soldiers for me. I want to go home." She also asked me to thank you and all the American people for, in her words, "opening the door of the future for her and for all the children of Bosnia."

Without you, the door will close, the peace will collapse, the war will return, the atrocities will begin again. The conflict then could spread throughout the region, weaken our partnership with Europe, and undermine our leadership in other areas critical to our security. I know that you will not let that happen.

As you prepare for your mission, I ask you to remember what we have all seen in Bosnia for the last 4 years: ethnic cleansing, mass executions, the rape of women and young girls as a tool of war, young men forced to dig their own graves and then shot down in the ground like animals, endless lines of desperate refugees, starving people in concentration camps. Images of these terrible wrongs have flooded our living rooms all over the world for almost 4 years. Now the violence has ended. We must not let it return.

For decades, our people in America have recognized the importance of a stable, strong, and free Europe to our own security. That's why we fought two World Wars. That's why after World War II we made commitments that kept Europe free and at peace and created unparalleled prosperity for us and for the Europeans as well. And that's why you are still here, even after the cold war.

Europe can be our strongest partners in fighting the things that will threaten the security of your children: the terrorism, the organized crime, the drug trafficking, the spread of weapons of mass destruction. But it can only be a strong partner if we get rid of the war that rages in the heart of Europe in Bosnia. We have to work with the Europeans on this if we're going to work on all those other problems that will be the security problems of the future.

When people ask—as they sometimes do back home because they're so concerned about you— "Well, why can't the Europeans do this without us?" just remember that when you went to Desert Storm, we asked for help from a lot of nations who could have taken a pass, but they stood up with us. And when we led in Haiti, we were supported by a lot of other nations who had no direct interest in Haiti, but they answered our call and they stood up with us. Now in Bosnia, we are needed. You are needed.

Men and women of Task Force Eagle, I know the burden of our country's leadership now weighs most heavily on you and your families. Each and every one of you who have volunteered to serve this country makes hard sacrifices. We send you a long way from home for a long time. We take you away from your children and your loved ones. These are the burdens that you assume for America, to stand up for our values, to serve our interests, to keep our country strong in this time of challenge and change.

In Bosnia, your mission is clear. You are strong, you are well-prepared, and the stakes demand American leadership that you will provide. You don't have to take it just from me. I have gotten it myself from the words of your own children. A seventh-grade English teacher at Baumholder High School, Patricia Dengel, asked her students to write letters to their parents who are preparing to go to Bosnia. I've seen a few of those letters, and I was moved.

I was moved by the fears they expressed but even more by the pride and confidence they showed in you.

Justin Zimmerman's father, Captain Ronald Zimmerman, is a company commander with the 40th Engineering Battalion. This is what Justin wrote: "Dad, I know you'll be fine in Bosnia because of all the training you've had. I'll miss you and count the days until we see you again." And Rachel Bybee, whose father, Major Leon Bybee, is a doctor with the Medical Corps, tells him, "I'm proud of your job, which is to help others. It must make you feel great to know you save lives."

Your children know you are heroes for peace, and soon so will the children of Bosnia. Your country and I salute you. We wish you Godspeed in the days and months ahead. You are about to do something very important for your Nation, very important for the world, very important for the future that you want your own children to have.

God bless you all, and God bless America.

NOTE: The President spoke at 12:35 p.m. in the Smith Barracks at the Baumholder Army Base. In his remarks, he referred to Maj. Gen. William L. Nash, Commanding General, 1st Armored Division; Gen. William W. Crouch, Commanding General, U.S. Army Europe; and Secretary of the Army Togo D. West, Jr.

Remarks Following Discussions With Chancellor Helmut Kohl of Germany and an Exchange With Reporters in Baumholder
December 2, 1995

The President. Good afternoon. I have just finished a very good set of briefings from our military commanders about the plans to deploy in Bosnia to enforce the peace agreement. And I have received a report from General Joulwan about the meeting of the North Atlantic Council which has, in essence, approved the military plan for implementing the peace agreement, which I signed off on just a few days ago in the Oval Office.

So I feel very good about what I have seen, about the morale of our troops. As you saw, I shook hands with several hundred of them, and I then had lunch with a significant number

of them. I think their morale is high. They are well aware that they have been very well-trained. They are very supportive of the rules of engagement which give them the tools they need to do their job.

But I would say more than anything else, the men and women with whom I spoke today are committed to the humanitarian mission of saving the lives of the children and innocent civilians. And they understand that they are going there not in war but in peace, to facilitate a peace agreement, and that this is very different from having been involved in a conflict.

And so we're working hard, and I feel good about where we are.

I also had a wonderful extended visit with Chancellor Kohl on the way down here, and he shared a lot of his thoughts with me. And of course, Germany has been a great partner in this and in some ways has borne perhaps the heaviest financial burden of the Bosnian war because of the many hundreds of thousands of refugees which have been taken in and sustained by the German people.

So I would like to ask Chancellor Kohl to make whatever comments he would like to make, and then we'll have questions.

Chancellor Kohl. Mr. President, I would like to bid you once again a very warm welcome here to our country. This has been a very impressive day that we shared here today. And I must say that I'm gratified that I'm yet again able to say this here in Baumholder, to say once again what, for us here in Germany, the Alliance has meant these past four decades.

The Alliance for us meant peace and freedom for our country. It meant that we were given the opportunity, together with our American friends, to overcome the division of our country and to win unity for Germany. And I don't think there's any other place where one is in a better position to say something like that than here. Because, Bill, I'm confident that when this message is being sent here from Baumholder to the United States, then hundreds of thousands, even millions of Americans will remember the days when they themselves as soldiers or relatives spent time here in Baumholder. And I would like to state clearly that we have not forgotten what our American friends have done for us.

And it was a very impressive day for me, too, because it brought home to me the determination of the President of the United States and of the people of the United States to make, through their mission, possible that peace finally comes to Bosnia and that the agreement is being implemented.

And I would like to say to the mothers and fathers who send their sons and their daughters out with this mission out to Bosnia, that they send out their sons and their daughters in order to assure peace and to safeguard peace. And that is the best possible mission for any army in the world.

And I would like to use this opportunity here, Bill, to thank you, to thank the President of the United States for the determination to act that they have shown here. You are in a proud American tradition in so doing, a proud tradition that has always said that the United States should not look away but that they should show leadership and become active.

Obviously, I would never dare to interfere in American domestic politics. But I would like to know as many Americans as possible that we hope for the broadest possible support of the people of the United States of America for the President and the Army in this important endeavor.

We, ourselves, have made a decisive step in the right direction; 4,000 German soldiers will go, will be sent to the region. And I would like to wish all of the troops going into the region—American troops, British troops, French troops, German troops, from whatever nation they may be sent—I would like to wish them Godspeed and a safe return back to their families.

And I must say that I came away very much impressed from the luncheon, where I had the opportunity to talk to family members as well, impressed by the calm and the steadfastness of the wives and the relatives—the wives obviously being afraid, which is very understandable under the circumstances, but showing a quiet resolve to support their husbands and seeing how important this mission is.

Thank you.

Bosnia

Q. How many Americans will be spending Christmas in Bosnia?

The President. You'll have to ask General Joulwan that. I don't know that. We will—obviously, under the peace agreement, deployments have to begin shortly after the signing of the agreement. But it will take some considerable amount of time for a full buildup. So I would think there would be probably fewer than half of the total force could be there by Christmas, maybe even less than that. That's a question you should ask General Joulwan. Right now it's strictly a matter of military planning.

Q. Mr. President, have you approved the execute order for the deployment of U.S. troops? And also, you have said many times that it's expected that it would be one year for the U.S. troops. Does that also pertain to other NATO troops? How long would they be there?

The President. The timeframe is for the military mission, not specifically for the American troops. It is the military mission. Because of the specific functions delegated to the military, as opposed to the civilians—keep in mind, what the military is supposed to do is maintain the cease-fire, separate the forces, create the zone of separation, supervise the transfer of property and the redeployment of forces, and then maintain a secure environment so there can be free movement throughout the country, so the refugees can go home and the reconstruction can begin and the elections can be held. It is believed by all of our planners and agreed to by the people who signed the peace treaty that that should be done in about a year. And it's completely different from the civilian practices.

The answer to your first question is, no, I have not, but I will as soon as it's presented to me. I have given a prior general approval to our military planners, as I announced to the Congress, to send a small force in to do the planning work in anticipation of the signing of the treaty and no adverse developments between now and the treaty signing on the 14th in Paris. But that is all I intend to do before Congress has a chance to speak its mind. I believe that I have no alternative. So I have not done it now, yet, but I will as soon as presented with the decision.

Any German press have a question? No——

Q. Mr. President, as Commander in Chief, how difficult is it for you to look into the faces of these young men and women who are about to go into a dangerous situation to carry out your orders?

The President. Well, I wanted to come here to look into their faces and into the faces of their wives, their husbands, and their children because I think they are about to do a very noble and important thing for our country and for the world. And I wanted to come here and directly say to them, "Here is why I want you to go, and here is what you will be doing and what you will not be doing. We have done everything we could to minimize the risks, but there still are some, and here is what we expect to do about that."

I wanted to give them those straight answers. I wanted to look at them—you know, I spent quite a long time there today and I talked to several hundred of them briefly today, and I frankly was very moved by the responses they gave. I think they understand it's not a risk-free mission, but I believe they understand its importance and the fundamentally honorable nature of it.

Once again, the United States has no hidden or dark motives here. We simply want to restore peace and democracy and a decent life to those people.

Thank you.

Q. Mr. President, Chancellor Kohl expressed the hope that you would have the American people behind you. Do you think you do have the American people's support for it?

The President. I think that the support is building in the United States, and I think that the support for the troops and their mission will be universal. It always has been, and I believe it will be now.

NOTE: The President spoke at 3:40 p.m. in the Rheinlander Building at the Baumholder Army Base. A tape was not available for verification of the content of these remarks.

The President's Radio Address
December 2, 1995

Good morning. Today I am speaking to you from Germany, and I am with the men and women of the United States Army's 1st Armored Division. For the last 4 days, I have been on a journey of peace that has taken me from Britain to Ireland to Germany. I have shaken the hands, heard the voices, and seen the faces of those all over Europe who long for peace, peace in Northern Ireland and peace in Bosnia.

I will never forget the two young children in Belfast, one Catholic, who lost her father, and one Protestant. These children joined their hands and told the world of their dreams for a future of peace and their gratitude that America is working for peace.

I'll never forget the tens of thousands of people in Derry and in Dublin whose surging cheers and sea of American flags symbolized the friendship between our people and their appreciation that America is a force for a fair peace in Northern Ireland.

People in England and Germany and even people in Ireland also said they wanted peace and an end to the tragedy in Bosnia. Wherever I went and whomever I talked to, from ordinary citizens to Prime Ministers and parliamentarians, the message to me was the same: American leadership for peace matters. American leadership is welcome in Europe. American leadership is necessary in Europe, whether to achieve peace in Northern Ireland or join in implementing the peace in Bosnia.

Europe's freedom and strength and stability are essential to our own freedom, strength, and stability. That's why twice in this century American troops have fought in wars on European soil. That's why we stayed there during the cold war until victory was won. And that's why our soldiers are still stationed in Europe today.

Today I am visiting many of the brave young Americans who are preparing to leave for Bosnia. I spoke today to the 1st Armored Division, our country's Iron Soldiers. They are the frontline fighters of our country; they have been from World War II right through the Persian Gulf war. But this time, they're not being sent to war, they're being sent to guarantee peace. They have the noblest mission of all: to stop incredible human suffering and lift people's lives.

Over the last 4 years, a quarter of a million Bosnians have been killed. More than half of Bosnia's people have been driven from their homes; a million of them are still refugees. We have seen parents divided from their children, children deprived of their dreams, people caged like animals in concentration camps, women and young girls subject to systematic rape. We have seen unbelievable horrors. But now we have a chance to end this misery for good, and we have a responsibility to act.

This will be a difficult mission in a hard corner of the world. But let's remember, it is a peace that the people of Bosnia want. It is a peace that they have demanded. The leaders of Bosnia, Croatia, and Serbia understand that. That's why they reached a peace agreement in Dayton last month. And that's why they asked for America's help. They have made a serious commitment to peace, but they can't do it alone. There have been so many things happen in that poor, war-torn country that trust is a rare commodity, and they need our help to help reestablish the conditions under which people can live in decency and peace.

The three leaders of all three countries have emphasized in letters to me, and I quote, "that the NATO-led implementation force is essential to the success of the peace settlement." And they have pledged, and again I quote, "to take all possible measures to ensure the safety and security of all American and other forces and civilian personnel participating in the implementation force."

As of now, we expect that America will make up roughly a third of that implementation force, known as IFOR. More than 25 other nations, including our NATO allies, have also pledged to take part in this mission of peace. Because our Nation is willing to lead, our strength will be multiplied and our burdens will be shared.

Earlier today I met with General Joulwan, the American Commander of NATO, under whom our troops will serve. He and General Nash, who will command our Task Force Eagle in Bosnia, gave me a thorough briefing on NATO's plan. The force will be strong, with strong rules of engagement. Our young men and women will have the tools they need to do the job.

We do not expect significant opposition to IFOR, but in Bosnia, as in other places of the world, there will always be people who cannot move beyond their hatreds, who would still rather destroy than rebuild. If IFOR's safety is threatened by them in any way, I am confident that the strength, the speed, and the decisiveness of its response will cause other potential attackers to think again.

I'm satisfied that our military commanders have done all they can to minimize the risks to our troops while maximizing their ability to carry out a clearly defined mission with a clear endpoint. And here in Germany I have seen firsthand that our troops are the best trained, best equipped, best prepared fighting force in the world. They are skilled; they are strong; they are determined to succeed. They are also an extraordinary group of Americans. They are intelligent, they are good people, they are intensely patriotic, and they are proud of the mission they have been asked to carry out.

As soon as I return, I will be consulting closely with Congress on the details of the NATO plan. I welcome the statement of those leaders who said they will work with me in the national interest. And I hope and expect that after careful debate, others will join in supporting the plan and our troops.

The mission is clear and so are the stakes, for the Bosnian people, for the security of Europe, and for America's leadership around the world.

This morning in Dublin, I met with Zlata Filpovic, the young Bosnian girl who became famous the world over when she published her diary of life in war-torn Sarajevo. This morning she asked me to thank our American soldiers for giving her and other children the chance to live in peace in their homeland. In a letter she gave me, she spoke in the name of children. She said, "Thank you for helping civilization not to die over there, because ordinary people and children truly don't deserve it. Thank you for opening the door of future to our children."

My fellow Americans, we should be proud we have opened that door for the children of Bosnia, for the people of Bosnia. They have chosen the road of peace. Their road is our road, and we must stand with them. We must be leaders for peace.

Thanks for listening.

NOTE: The President spoke at 4:06 p.m. from the Rose Room at the Rheinlander Club, U.S. Army Base/Smith Barracks, Baumholder, Germany.

Interview With Joe Garvey of the Armed Forces Network in Baumholder
December 2, 1995

Mr. Garvey. The first question, Mr. President. You have spent the entire day talking to soldiers, shaking soldiers' hands. You've been briefed by the Task Force Eagle commanders. You've talked to spouses. What is the one thing that you'll walk away with here today?

The President. An immense feeling of gratitude that our country has people who are this well-trained, this highly motivated, this patriotic, and this good working for us. You know, these people have volunteered to serve their country, to go anywhere and do anything that their country needs. And they are an exceptional group of people, and their families are exceptional people.

Now, because of the training they've had in Germany, they believe that the training probably will be harder than the mission, and of course, we all hope it will be. So I think every American should feel an immense sense of pride and gratitude that people like the men and women of the 1st Armored Division are out there serving our country.

Mr. Garvey. Changing gears just a little bit, has having a U.S. forward-deployed force in Europe been an advantage for the planning and potential and ultimate execution of this Bosnia mission?

The President. Absolutely. It's been a huge advantage. For one thing, we are here, obviously part of the unified NATO Command, but we can do our planning not just through General Joulwan and the NATO Command Headquarters but right down through the Americans that are expected to do it and have it here in close proximity. It's made a big difference, and the training has made a huge difference.

We've been able, as you know, to recreate the conditions that our people will face in Bosnia here in Germany. We're fairly close by; we can get the same sort of topography, the same kind of weather conditions, and I think that that has made a huge difference.

I'm not sure we have ever sent a group of our men and women in uniform into a situation where they were better prepared in advance in almost on-site training. Neither of those things would have been nearly as good had we not had a forward deployment in Germany.

Mr. Garvey. I know you're a busy man. I have nothing else to ask you, Mr. President, unless you have something yourself you would like to add.

The President. Well, the only other thing I would like to add is that I think it's important for the American people to understand that with our volunteer Army now, it's more and more of a family place. It's more and more a place full of exceptional people with good values and deep ties, either to their spouses and children who are with them while they're in the service or to their parents back home.

And so when we make a decision, when I make a decision, like the decision to deploy our troops to carry out the peace mission in Bosnia, it's a family decision, it affects families, and I am very mindful of that. And one of the things that I really appreciate is the extent to which caring for the families, thinking about their needs, making sure that they're treated in the proper way is a big part of the mission now. And I think that's something that we have gotten better at and something I hope we will continue to get better at, because if we're going to have a volunteer Army, we want the very best people in it and we want people to be able to succeed in uniform but also in their family roles. And that is very, very important to me—especially at Christmastime I guess I'm thinking a lot about it, but all year long we have to be better and better and better at that, because this is a family commitment as well as an American commitment.

Mr. Garvey. Thank you. I appreciate your time.

The President. Thank you.

NOTE: The interview began at 4:40 p.m. at the Rheinlander Club.

Statement on the Death of General Maxwell R. Thurman
December 2, 1995

We mourn the passing yesterday of Gen. Maxwell R. Thurman, USA, Ret., whose dedicated and exceptional service is cherished by everyone who knew of his extraordinary courage, enduring vision, and selfless service. During a distinguished career which culminated in his service as commander in chief of the U.S. Southern Command, General Thurman achieved prominence as a disciplined thinker, organizer, and leader. His foresight and leadership in a succession of key recruiting, personnel, military doctrinal development, and training assignments during the 1970's and eighties helped shape the post-Vietnam Army and transform it into the high-quality, ready-to-fight force of today.

To General Thurman's family and friends and to the Army community, I extend my heartfelt condolences. We will remember him as one of America's finest soldiers and most capable military leaders.

The President's News Conference With European Union Leaders in Madrid, Spain
December 3, 1995

Prime Minister Gonzalez. Thank you very much. It is our pleasure to welcome to Madrid President Clinton as well as the President of the Commission. And as you have seen, we have just finished signing the new transatlantic agenda, along with an action plan. Thanks to this document and this summit between the European Union and the United States, we hope to be taking a new step forward, a quantitative leap forward, and to undertake new common action. This is enshrined in the documents we have just signed.

For the Spanish Presidency, I would like to state that this was one of our priorities. We had a meeting in Cannes in June, and we decided to prepare an agenda for the next years until the end of the century. Since then we have been working very hard, and the United States high-level group as well as the Commission and Spain have worked very efficiently. And as you will see clearly from these documents, we have a clear-cut vocation to work together from the political point of view in promoting democracy and human rights as well as from a commercial point of view, an economic point of view, and strengthening the bonds on both sides of the Atlantic as well as our struggle against terrorism and drug trafficking and organized violence.

We have common goals, and this morning we also spoke about converging actions such as the peace plan that was signed in Dayton with regard to Bosnia. I would like to point out that, keeping in mind our responsibility as the President of the European Union and the presence of Spanish troops and Spanish nongovernmental organizations in Bosnia, but I would like to point out how significant it is that the United States, that President Clinton has decided to send a large contingent of troops. And I think that this is of utmost importance for international solidarity. And this peace plan that will be signed on the 14th of December will become a lasting peace that will outlive the fight between the two communities of Bosnia and the former Yugoslavia.

So I would like to publicly thank President Clinton, his effort and the appeal he has launched to the American people to participate wholeheartedly in the peace plan. And I would also like to say that this new transatlantic plan is open to other countries on both sides of the Atlantic, such as Canada, Norway, and Iceland. And I would like to make this as broad an agenda as possible.

And now I would like to give the floor to Mr. Santer. And Mr. Clinton will be having the closing remarks.

Mr. Santer.

President Santer. Presidents, ladies and gentlemen, I would just like to add some comments on what President Gonzalez has said. In my inaugural speech to the European Parliament on January 17th this year, I emphasized the importance of transatlantic links. I stressed that the EU's commitment should be reaffirmed, and I concluded that I was personally in favor of a transatlantic treaty. So today, I believe, is an historic moment for transatlantic relations, and that I think for three reasons.

Firstly, because it shows that Europe and America now have the means and the will to provide the joint leadership that the world so urgently needs. We will not lead by threatening or excluding our partners, we will lead by example. And take Bosnia. You, President Clinton, have shown such an example in Dayton, Ohio. Europeans and Americans are taking the coura-

geous decision to send troops to enforce a peace in Bosnia. This shows that Europe and America can act together to promote peace, stability, democracy, and freedom. Moreover, we have already committed $2 billion to help the victims, and we are ready to give more in order to rebuild that shattered country. I am confident that our partners will help us share the burden.

Secondly, this is an historic moment for the people of Europe and America. This is not just an agenda for politicians and civil servants. We are determined to fight side by side in order to tackle those issues that most affect the lives of ordinary people. And together, we will see that the drug traffickers and criminals have nowhere to hide within our borders. Together, we will fight poverty and disease, and we will bring our citizens themselves closer together, students, academics, professionals, artists, and others. We want to ensure that our common cultural heritage remains the glue that binds our two continents together.

And finally, today we are making Europe and America more open for business, more open to each other, and more open to the world. If it's made in Europe, it must be good enough for America and vice-versa. That's what the new transatlantic marketplace is all about.

Thank you.

President Clinton. Thank you very much. Let me begin by thanking Prime Minister Gonzalez for hosting this meeting and for the very energetic leadership that he has provided to the European Community and to the partnership between the European Community and the United States. I want to thank President Santer for his consistent, firm direction to the Community, and both of them for working with me over the last 6 months to launch this new partnership between the United States and the Community.

As the cold war gives way to the global village, we have new opportunities and new security threats. We know what those security threats are. We see them every day, the ethnic and religious hatred, the reckless aggression of rogue states, the terrorism, the drug trafficking, the weapons of mass destruction that are increasingly threatening us all.

We know that poverty and job insecurity and barriers to open trade limit the reach of prosperity for all. We know that too many people remain vulnerable to disease and underdevelopment around the world. We know now that these threats respect no borders and that they demand the kind of concerted action that we adopt today with our agenda and action plan.

Until now, the relationship between the United States and the European Union has largely been one of consultation. Today we are moving beyond talk to action. These joint initiatives in our agenda will directly benefit citizens on both sides of the Atlantic.

I'd like to highlight just a few of the areas in which we have agreed to work more closely together; some have been mentioned already. First, we will together lead a global effort to organize the postwar reconstruction of Bosnia. After 4 years of war, the Bosnian leaders have agreed to peace. But now the Bosnian people need the support of the international community to revitalize their economy, to rebuild their lives, in short, to realize the promise of peace.

I have just come from visiting our troops in Germany who are training and who will soon travel to Bosnia. They are well-prepared, well-equipped, well-trained for this mission of peace. I am very proud of them. And I want to say a word of thanks to the Prime Minister and to the people of Spain for their contributions, for the people from Spain who have already done so much in Bosnia and those who will join us in securing this peace mission.

Next, we will create a transatlantic marketplace in which we continue progressively to reduce the barriers to trade, commerce, and investment. The worldwide GATT agreement was a very important step forward. But our advanced economies can do better, can grow faster. We aim to create more good new jobs on both sides of the Atlantic and to reinforce the world trading system that benefits every nation.

Third, we will continue and increase our support for the Middle East peace process.

Fourth, we will join in a new initiative to combat international criminals, terrorists, and drug traffickers. As President Santer says, they should have no place to hide.

Fifth, we will strengthen our environmental cooperation in important and specific ways. We will work to reduce lead exposure, a major threat to the health of all our children; to provide countries with sophisticated environmental technologies that are developing their own economies; and to better coordinate our disaster and our development assistance to the neediest people around the globe.

All these actions will further strengthen the transatlantic community, united around democ-racy, free markets, and respect for human rights. Our destiny in America is still linked to Europe. This action agenda makes it clear that we will remain as firmly engaged with Europe in the post-cold-war era as we have for the last 50 years. It also makes clear that our partnership is evolving, that we recognize new challenges but that we have to meet them together.

Finally, let me say that we in the United States are very pleased to welcome the nomination of the Spanish Foreign Minister, Mr. Solana, to be the next Secretary General of NATO. He is one of Europe's outstanding leaders. We believe he will be a firm hand and a strong voice for NATO. And we offer you our congratulations, sir.

Prime Minister Gonzalez. Thank you. And now we will have questions. Please tell us who you are asking the question of.

Bosnia and NATO Forces

Q. Good morning. A question to Prime Minister Gonzalez as to whether President Clinton has asked for a greater Spanish contribution in Bosnia of a military nature in NATO, more than the 1,200 people who are there—if you've spoken about this in the general framework.

And also a question for you, Mr. Clinton. In view of the changes in Europe since the fall of the Berlin Wall, do you think that it is fitting for Spain to become part of the central military command structure in NATO?

Prime Minister Gonzalez. With regard to the first question, which was directed to me, we have not yet established the contribution of each country. Right now, we have in Spain 1,200 people, plus the naval contingent and logistic support, which is about 2,400 people. So at present, we are going to keep up this effort, but of course, we would be willing to speak to all our allies to make sure that this is enough or if we need more.

Mr. President, sir.

President Clinton. If I might say that the most important thing is that we have enough troops and the right troops to perform the defined military mission. And we estimate that we need about 60,000. The United States has committed about 20,000; the British, about 13,000; the French, I think between 9,000 and 10,000. We have over two dozen other countries who want to contribute. Spain has made a very, very valuable contribution already, including the NATO contribution with the Spanish pilots which should not be overlooked. And so from my point of view, I think we'll be able to work together and achieve the kind of force we need.

With regard to the NATO question, I don't think that's a question for me to answer. That is a question that we will have to work through with NATO. I can only tell you this, that our American pilots and our American military personnel have been immensely impressed with the work they did through NATO in Bosnia, with the flying that we both did together and in coordination. And I can only say that I am very grateful for that.

Q. Two questions, Mr. President. Have you given the order for the 700 American troops in the NATO force to go into Bosnia? And also, the Bosnian Serb military leader, Ratko Mladic, is demanding changes in the peace agreement, and there are also some other questions being raised by the French military——

Q. [Inaudible]—start over.

President Clinton. I can repeat the questions.

Q. ——military commander in Sarajevo as well as by the Bosnian Government. Is this treaty in trouble? Is it going to have to be changed?

President Clinton. Let me answer the first question first. I have authorized the Secretary of Defense to order the deployment of the preliminary troops, the people who have to do the preparatory work, to Bosnia, as I said I would as soon as I was convinced that the military plan was appropriate. And so I have done that, and those people will be going into the area over the next couple of days. As I've emphasized to the American people and the Congress, that's a few hundred of our forces necessary to set up communications networks and things of that kind.

The answer to your second question is no, I don't think the treaty is in trouble, and no, I don't think it should be renegotiated. President Milosevic made strong commitments which he will have to fulfill to secure the support of the Bosnian Serb leaders for this agreement. And I would remind you that, of course, the Bosnian Serbs aren't happy with everything in the agreement; neither are the Croats; neither are the Muslims and the others in the Bosnian Government. That's what—when you make a peace agreement, not everybody is happy with it. So only those who were at the table have fully reconciled themselves, perhaps, to that, although a lot of the Bosnian Serb political leadership have endorsed this treaty.

So we expect, we fully expect that President Milosevic will take the appropriate steps to ensure that this treaty will be honored as it is written and that we will not have undue interference with implementing it. And we feel very strongly on that point.

European Union-U.S. Relationship

Q. Briefly, for President Clinton, with regard to the Dayton peace agreement, has this also changed the relationship between the United States and the European allies? It seems that there were several differences of opinion, politically and militarily, but also from a trade point of view. And I would like to know if in this document, which talks about a possibility of avoiding a trade war—and we have here Mr. Kantor and Mr. Brittan, who spent nights and nights trying to avoid this type of war—so I would like to know if in this new transatlantic agenda you have something against this.

And then a question for the Spanish Prime Minister. Does the fact that Spain will have the general secretariat here, does it mean that we will be in the central military command structure?

President Clinton. Let me say, first of all, this document commits both the European Union and the United States to take further steps to open our markets to each other. Mr. Brittan and Mr. Kantor worked very hard to hammer out the differences between Europe and the United States so that we could get the world GATT agreement, which is the biggest trade agreement in history and a very good step forward.

But we believe, given the development of our economies, that we can and should do more in our relationships with each other. They have committed themselves to do that, and there are already some action items on the agenda. So I feel that you will see less tension and more cooperation.

And in terms of the Dayton peace treaty, I think that that reflects—the positive European response there reflects a very high level of cooperation between the United States and Europe in foreign policy and security matters.

President Santer. I would only add that there is no—that in the transatlantic treaty or declaration we signed, there are some items to deal with—also with what we are calling now the new transatlantic marketplace. We can reduce our tariff barriers inside between the United States and the European Union.

We have also to stress our multilateral agreement between the world trade organizations. I think there are many things to do. We make a very good job in the Uruguay round. We can say that now more than $500 billion are flowing through goods and so on through the results of the Uruguay round. So we are not struggling together, but we are cooperating together, and there's a big change.

We are coming now from a consultation procedure to a joint action procedure and that—new spirit is underlying this new transatlantic declaration.

NATO Secretary General

Prime Minister Gonzalez. Very briefly, I would like to start by saying that I would like to publicly acknowledge the confidence deposited in Javier Solana, the Spanish Foreign Minister, in electing him as the Secretary General of NATO, in view of the tremendous challenges we have with regard to Bosnia in the short term and the broadening and the enlargement of the European Union to the Eastern and Central European countries in the long term.

Now, this is not a change for the Spaniards. It's merely progress of the alliance. We are going to be a loyal ally in everything we do and in everything that happens in the alliance. So we have to take things on board as they are, and I have full confidence in Javier Solana that he will undertake to carry out his responsibilities in the best possible manner. And I thank everyone again for voting him.

Bosnia and the Budget

Q. Mr. President, you've spent now almost a week on this side of the Atlantic, and you're about to get back to Washington. How, if at all, has this experience in Europe affected your thinking in regards to selling—Bosnia once to get back to a skeptical Congress and—American public, especially—and also the spill-over, if any, on how you will deal with the December 15th looming deadline with the budget? Is there any relationship between Bosnia and the budget?

The President. Let me answer the first question, and then I'll attempt to answer the second one. [*Laughter*] I know I can answer the first one.

I have seen again, from the address I made to the Parliament in London, to the people in the streets in Belfast and Derry, to the teeming throng in the streets of Dublin, to the Irish Parliament, and then on to a meeting with Chancellor Kohl as we met with the American troops and then coming here and having my meeting with Prime Minister Gonzalez and President Santer today, the importance of American leadership and American partnership in Europe.

You know, we fought two World Wars here. Most of our people came from here. We stayed here for 50 years after World War II, first to deal with the cold war, and then after the cold war was over we left our troops and many of our airbases here in Europe. And what we are seeing in Bosnia is an affront to the conscience of human beings everywhere, right in the heart of Europe. All the things that we need to do, all the things we talked about today—the need to build stronger economic ties, the need to confront the other security problems we have—none of that is going to happen as it should unless we deal with this problem in Bosnia, to try to stop the murders and the rapes and the butchery that has occurred. And I feel more strongly about that.

If you look—also, I think the American people should know that we have a unique responsibility at this moment in history. After the cold war, the United States was left with a certain superpower status and a certain economic standing that that imposes on us great responsibilities, along with the opportunities we have.

You know, when those people turned out in the streets in Ireland—all those young people, Protestant and Catholic alike—demanding the right to be heard on behalf of peace and their future, responding to an American President, it was because of everything America has stood for over 200 years, not just the initiatives of our administration and the things I have personally done to promote peace there but everything we represent. And I would hope that because we have the chance to do good things and because we have the chance to do it in a way that minimizes our risks and relies on our strengths, that the American people and the Congress would respond.

Now, on the budget. I do not expect Congress to link Bosnia and the budget, if that is the implication of your question. I do not believe they would do that. I think they understand that these are—both issues are too important.

The lesson I draw as an American from this trip in terms of the budget negotiations is that if we're going to be strong abroad, we have to be strong at home. And the policy we are following is working. The economy is better than it was 3 years ago. We're making progress on our social problems. We should not take a radical detour from the disciplined direction we have gone to grow the economy, to expand the middle class, to shrink the under class. And we should do nothing that would send the signal to the world that we are less successful economically, that we are promoting inequality, that we are being less humane and less caring and less sensitive as a country to our own people within our borders. That is what I know.

We have to continue—the power of the United States goes far beyond military might. What you saw in Ireland, for example, had not a wit to do with military might; it was all about values. And we should do nothing at home within our own borders that undermines our ability to project those values to the rest of the world.

Prime Minister Gonzalez. Thank you. I have promised firmly to keep on schedule, and we've reached the end. Thank you.

NOTE: The President's 109th news conference began at 11:50 a.m. at the Moncloa Palace. The President met with Prime Minister Felipe Gonzalez of Spain, President of the European Council, and Jacques Santer, President of the European Commission. Prime Minister Gonzalez spoke in Spanish, and his remarks were translated by an interpreter. In his remarks, the President referred to President Slobodan Milosevic of Serbia and Sir Leon Brittan, Vice President of the European Commission.

Remarks at the Kennedy Center Honors Reception
December 3, 1995

I am delighted to see you here. I am delighted to see you here on this, what is really the first day of our Christmas season. It is true that Hillary saw these decorations a couple of hours ago, but I went up and crashed. You saw them all before I did. [*Laughter*]

This is a happy time at the White House, and this is an appropriate way to begin. As all of you know, we've just come home from Europe, from a trip to London, Belfast, Dublin, to see our forces in Germany, and to Madrid.

I was especially moved again, as I think every person who goes to Ireland is, by the incredible power of the art of Ireland. The Irish playwright John Millington Synge wrote of artists that they know the stars, the flowers, and the birds and converse with the mountains, moors, and ferns. Today we honor five such artists, and I am delighted to see so many more in the audience tonight joining us.

I think all of us know that our Nation and our world are in a period of profound change, perhaps the most sweeping period of change in the way we work and live and relate to one another in a hundred years. We know that there is an enormous amount of possibility in this period and still a great deal to trouble the soul.

At such a time we have to do everything we can to imagine the right kind of future and to remember what is best and constant about human nature throughout all ages. And so at this time we need our artists in a special way, in a profound way. And so, especially at this Christmas season, I welcome all of you to the White House.

Joseph Jacques d'Amboise was a natural athlete and a tough street kid in New York City. He discovered his true gift one day when he took his sister to ballet class and discovered the new sport of dance. Ever since that day, he has taken ballet into the neighborhoods and consciousness of America in a way that no other performer has. He has made ballet strong as well as beautiful through his performances in "Carousel," "Seven Brides for Seven Brothers," and "Stars and Stripes," a distinctively American ballet created especially for him. He danced until he was 50, which may be young in some careers, but not in ballet; I'm not so sure it's young in others as well. [*Laughter*] Today we thank you for sharing your talents by teaching dance to a whole new generation of performers. We thank you for your work as a performer and choreographer and for giving new dimension to the world of ballet.

Marilyn Horne made her professional debut at the age of 4 when she sang at a fundraiser for President Roosevelt. That's Franklin Roosevelt—[*laughter*]—and it was very late in his term of service. [*Laughter*] Showing good judgment in art and politics, she still had a glitch or two in the road. Her career didn't exactly take off in a straight line. In fact, she was rejected from her grade school glee club because her voice was too powerful. By age 17, however, she was back on track giving a solo recital in the Hollywood Bowl and dubbing the music for the title role in the film "Carmen Jones." She went on to form a legendary partnership with Joan Sutherland, to record remarkable Christmas carols and, most of all, to light up the opera houses of the world with a spirit as magnificent as her songs. And today as she continues to perform, she is passing on her sheer love of music and her generous spirit.

In addition, Marilyn, to thanking you on behalf of the American people, let me thank you again for your several years of friendship to me and to Hillary and for gracing our Inauguration with your beautiful voice.

Thank you.

Riley B. King was known during his days on Memphis's Beale Street as "the blues boy." Eventually he became known to all America simply as B.B. King. For generations of Americans the music and the man are synonymous. Like nearly everyone else my age, I grew up listening to "Three O'Clock Blues." B.B. King was a troubadour on the American road. He spent decades touring, perfecting, and inventing. The sounds he created became the soul of a new music, with Jerry Garcia, Eric Clapton, and the Rolling Stones all modeling their music after his. He has traveled the world to represent our country and set hands clapping from London to Lagos. He still averages—listen to this—275 performances a year. Music is his life, and yes, the blues is B.B. King.

When Sidney Poitier left Cat Island in the Bahamas for Miami at the age of 15, he was stunned at the signs of segregation, signs that read "colored" and "white." More than any other person, he would remove those signs from the world of film. He broke these barriers by sheer force of his powerful presence on screen. From the start, he was a leading man, and his performances have become landmarks in America's consciousness of itself. When he filmed "Cry, the Beloved Country," he had to enter South Africa as an indentured servant to the director. But we are all grateful to him and in his service for the way he has graced the screen with films like "To Sir, With Love," "Guess Who's Coming to Dinner," "A Raisin in the Sun," and many, many others. He has captivated us with his performances and reminded us that excellence comes in all colors. Thank you for entertaining and educating America with dignity, strength, and grace, Sidney Poitier.

Marvin Neil Simon's humor distills the essence of his life and our lives, sometimes whether we like it or not. [*Laughter*] He has written the lines behind the laughs of Phil Silvers, Victor Borge, Buddy Hackett, and Jackie Gleason. He collaborated with Sid Caesar on what many people hailed as the best show ever on television. He has written a string of magnificent hit plays unprecedented in the history of the American theater. Audiences found them so funny that at first, that few people noticed the gentle, deep, and sometimes sharp truths behind the comedy. Felix and Oscar became American archetypes. We saw what it was to grow up in "Brighton Beach Memoirs" and to grow older in "The Sunshine Boys." We saw flaws and foibles and faults, but always, through them all, the indomitability of the human spirit. Neil Simon takes his work seriously, but he challenges us and himself never to take ourselves too seriously. Thank you for the wit and the wisdom.

Today we meet at the summit of five lives of artistic grace and greatness. Jacques d'Amboise, Marilyn Horne, B.B. King, Sidney Poitier and Neil Simon, we are pleased to honor all of you for your work. But more importantly, we honor you for your spirit and your heart.

Thank you, and congratulations.

NOTE: The President spoke at 6:03 p.m. in the East Room at the White House.

Remarks on Signing the Human Rights Proclamation
December 5, 1995

Thank you very much. Thank you for being here. And most important of all, thank you for your commitment to the people of Bosnia, for your care and your courage.

Many of you in this room have worked throughout the war to stop the human rights abuses that horrified the world and to ease the suffering of the people of Bosnia. Now the Balkan leaders have ended the war and have made a commitment to peace, so that now I can say to you, we need your help more than ever to make sure the peace takes hold and endures.

I have just had a remarkable meeting in the Oval Office with a group of Bosnians who just came in and took their seats. They were forced to flee their country, and they have resettled in ours: the Capin family, the Ibisevic family, and Dr. Oljaca. They are all here with me. They bear witness to loved ones lost, homes destroyed, careers shattered, families separated. They can tell us what it's like to leave the land they love, where they were born and went to school, where they married and raised families, where they should have been able to enjoy the basic human right to build a good future in peace.

These people and so many more like them are the human faces of the war in Bosnia. They are the story behind the unbelievable numbers of a quarter of a million dead, 2 million people displaced, more than half the population of pre-war Bosnia.

Many of you have actually witnessed and documented the war's atrocities firsthand, the executions, the ethnic cleansing, the rape of young women and girls as a tool of war, the endless lines of despairing refugees. We cannot bring back the war's victims. So many of them were little children. We cannot erase its horrors. But because the parties have said they will turn from war to peace, we can now prevent further suffering; we can now shine the light of justice in Bosnia; we can now help its people build a future of hope.

All of us have a role to play. This weekend, as you all know, I visited our troops in Germany, those who will soon set off for Bosnia not to make war but to wage peace. Each side in Bosnia has asked NATO to help secure their peace agreement, to make sure the armies withdraw behind the separation lines and stay there, to maintain the cease-fire so that the war does not start again, to give all the parties the mutual confidence they need so that all will keep their word. Creating a climate of security is the necessary first step toward rebuilding and reconciliation. That is NATO's mission, and it must be America's mission.

I have to say that the families who just visited with me said repeatedly that they felt that the presence of Americans in Bosnia, the American troops, was absolutely critical to giving the people of Bosnia the confidence they need to believe that they can once again live in peace together as they did before the war.

I am absolutely convinced that our goals are clear, they are limited, and they are achievable in about a year's time. I'm also satisfied that we have taken every possible precaution to minimize the risks to our troops. They will take their orders from the American general who commands NATO; there will be no confusing chain of command. Our troops are very well-trained, and they will be heavily armed. They will have very clear rules of engagement that will allow them to respond immediately and decisively to any threat to their security.

The climate of security NATO creates in Bosnia will allow a separate, broad international release effort for relief and reconstruction to begin. That's where many of you come in. I cannot overstate the importance of that effort. For peace to endure, the people of Bosnia must receive the tangible benefits of peace. They must have the food, the medicine, the shelter, the clothing so many have been denied for so long. Roads must be repaired, the schools and hospitals rebuilt, the factories and shops refurbished and reopened. Families must be reunited and refugees returned home. Elections must be held so that those devoted to reconciliation can lead their people to a future together. And those guilty of war crimes must be punished, because no peace will long endure without justice.

Over the next year the civilian relief and reconstruction effort will help to realize the promise of peace and give it a life of its own. It can so change the face of Bosnia that by the time the NATO mission is ready to leave, the people of Bosnia will have a much, much greater stake in peace than in war. That must be all of our goals.

Once the people of Bosnia lived in peace. Many people have forgotten that, but it wasn't so very long ago. It can happen again. It must happen again. And every one of us must do what we can to make sure that the stakes of peace and the faces of children are uppermost in the minds of the people of Bosnia when the NATO mission is completed.

Sunday is International Human Rights Day, the anniversary of the adoption by the United Nations of the universal declaration of human rights in 1948. For nearly 4 years the war in Bosnia did terrible violence to the principles of that declaration. It destroyed hundreds of thousands of lives. It ruined countless futures.

But on this Human Rights Day, we have something to celebrate. The war in Bosnia is over. The peace, however, is just beginning. Together, if we work hard to help it take hold, to help it endure, on the next Human Rights Day, the faces of Bosnia will not be the victims of war but the beneficiaries of peace.

I am now very pleased to sign this proclamation designating December 10th, 1995 as Human Rights Day, and December 10th through 16th as Human Rights Week. Let us make sure that for the next year, it will be a human rights year in Bosnia.

Thank you very much.

[At this point the President signed the proclamation.]

You look at these children, and they make you smile. They should not have to come here to look as good as they look and to be as happy as they are. I'm glad they're here. I'm honored to have such fine people strengthening the fabric of America. They are very welcome here. But the people like them who want to live at home and raise their children to look just like this ought to have the same rights. That's what this piece of paper is all about.

Thank you very much.

NOTE: The President spoke at 11:42 a.m. in Room 450 of the Old Executive Office Building. The proclamation is listed in Appendix D at the end of this volume.

Message to the Congress on Administration of Export Controls
December 5, 1995

To the Congress of the United States:

In order to take additional steps with respect to the national emergency described and declared in Executive Order No. 12924 of August 19, 1994, and continued on August 15, 1995, necessitated by the expiration of the Export Administration Act on August 20, 1994, I hereby report to the Congress that pursuant to section 204(b) of the International Emergency Economic Powers Act, 50 U.S.C. 1703(b) ("the Act"), I have today exercised the authority granted by the Act to issue an Executive order (a copy of which is attached) to revise the existing procedures for processing export license applications submitted to the Department of Commerce.

The Executive order establishes two basic principles for processing export license applications submitted to the Department of Commerce under the Act and the Regulations, or

under any renewal of, or successor to, the Export Administration Act and the Regulations. First, all such license applications must be resolved or referred to me for resolution no later than 90 calendar days after they are submitted to the Department of Commerce. Second, the Departments of State, Defense, and Energy, and the Arms Control and Disarmament Agency will have the authority to review any such license application. In addition, the Executive order sets forth specific procedures including intermediate time frames, for review and resolution of such license applications.

The Executive order is designed to make the licensing process more efficient and transparent for exporters while ensuring that our national security, foreign policy, and nonproliferation interests remain fully protected.

WILLIAM J. CLINTON

The White House,

December 5, 1995.

NOTE: This message was released by the Office of the Press Secretary on December 6. The Executive order is listed in Appendix D at the end of this volume.

Remarks to the Committee for American Leadership in Bosnia and an Exchange With Reporters
December 6, 1995

The President. I want to welcome this distinguished group of Americans to the White House. Each of you has worked very hard throughout your career to preserve and to project America's leadership around the world. Today you have joined across partisan lines to make a strong case for America's leadership in Bosnia, and I thank you for that.

I welcome the support that you and others, including Presidents Bush and Ford, have shown for our troops and our efforts to secure a peace in Bosnia. All of you represent a spirit that has helped to keep our country strong. Regardless of party or political differences, you've stood up for America's leadership on behalf of our interests and our values.

Many of you have been working for peace in Bosnia since that terrible war began. Now that the Balkan leaders have made a commitment to peace, you know that we must help that peace take hold. You understand the importance of our action and the costs of our failure to act, something, I might add, that has been under-discussed in the public arena in the last few weeks. Our conscience demands that we seize this chance to end the suffering, but our national security interests are deeply engaged as well.

Europe's security is still inextricably tied to America's. We need a strong Europe as a strong partner on the problems from terrorism to the spread of weapons of mass destruction. Europe's stability is threatened as long as this war burns at its center. We have to stand with the Europeans on Bosnia if we're going to stand with them and if we expect them to stand with us, on the whole range of other issues we clearly are going to face together in the years ahead.

Our engagement in Bosnia is also essential for the continued viability of NATO. All the parties, all the parties there, asked for NATO's help in securing this peace. If we're going to be NATO's leader, we have to be part of this mission. If we turn our backs on Bosnia now, our allies will do the same. The peace will fail; the conflict could spread; the slaughter will certainly resume. NATO would be shaken at its core. Its ability to shape a stable, undivided Europe would be thrown into doubt, and our leadership in Europe and around the world would pay a terrible, terrible price.

For 50 years, the bipartisan consensus for our leadership in the world has been a source of America's progress and strength. At the dawn of the post-cold-war era, that consensus is being questioned. But I believe that vision and unity are still called for.

During my recent trip to Europe, everywhere I went and every person with whom I talked, from people on the street to Prime Ministers, said the very same thing: American leadership matters; American leadership is welcome; American leadership is necessary. But leadership is not a spectator sport. In Bosnia, our leadership can make a difference between peace and war. It demands our participation.

I have to tell you that I knew how the European leaders felt, and I thought I knew how the people in the street felt. But the personal expression of support for America's willingness to help broker this peace agreement in Dayton and then to help participate in the peace mission in Bosnia was more intense, more persistent, and more urgent than I had imagined, from the Prime Minister of Great Britain to the Prime Minister of Germany to the Prime Minister of Spain to the Prime Minister of Ireland, everyone else I talked to. This is a very, very, very important thing in terms of our relationships with Europe and what we expect in terms of a partnership with Europe in the years ahead.

Let me say to those of you who come here from both parties, I understand that bipartisanship in foreign policy has never meant agreement on every detail of every policy. And while we may differ from time to time on the specifics of our policies, we still must agree and we have never fundamentally disagreed on our purpose: to defend our interests, to preserve peace, to protect human rights, to promote prosperity around the world.

That does not mean that we can solve every problem. We cannot be the world's policeman. But when our leadership can make a difference between war and peace and when our interests are engaged, we have a duty to act. We have seen the dividends of that from the Persian Gulf to the Middle East, from North Korea to Northern Ireland to Haiti. American leadership can also produce those dividends and more in Bosnia, because we can make a difference there.

I'm convinced that this mission is clear; it's achievable. Our troops will have strong rules of engagement. They will operate under an American general. They will be fully trained and heavily armed. Our commanders have done all they can to minimize the risks and to maximize their ability to carry out a clearly defined mission with a clear end point. There will be no mission creep.

The peace agreement has given these parties a real opportunity to have a peaceful future.

But they can't do it alone, and they're looking to us to help.

America is seen by all of them as an honest broker and a fair player. Each of you has played a role in creating that image, and I want to thank you for that as much as anything else. The thing that has constantly impressed me as I have dealt with people all around the world is that people believe we are a nation with no bad motives for them or their future.

That is what has made this moment possible in Bosnia; that is what has also imposed upon us our responsibilities at this moment. For all that you have done to bring that about and for your support today, I thank you very, very much.

Thank you.

Q. Do you think you can bring the House along with you, Mr. President?

The President. Well, one thing at a time. I think we're better off today than we were yesterday. We're working on it day-by-day. I'm encouraged. I had a good visit with the Speaker about it yesterday, and I talked with several Members who were here last night at the annual congressional ball. And we're working at it.

Thank you.

NOTE: The President spoke at 10 a.m. in the Cabinet Room at the White House.

Remarks to the White House Conference on HIV and AIDS
December 6, 1995

The President. First of all, thank you, Sean, and thank you, Eileen. Thank you, Patsy Fleming and Secretary Shalala, Secretary Cisneros. Thank you, Dr. Scott Hitt, and all the members of the President's advisory council. I think most of them were actually sitting in the overflow room so the rest of you can be here. But I thank them—[*Laughter*]. We heard them. Let's give them a hand; maybe they can hear us. [*Applause*] Thank you. I thank Dr. Varmus, Dr. Kessler, all the others here who are involved in the dramatic effort that they are making in the fight against AIDS. Most of all, I thank all of you for coming and for giving us a chance

to have this first-ever White House Conference on HIV and AIDS.

So much has been said by the speakers who have spoken before, and so much is still to be said by the panelists and perhaps by some of you in the audience, but I'm going to do what I can to shorten my remarks because I want to spend most of my time listening to you and focusing on where we go from here. But there are a few things that I would like to say.

First of all, this is a disease, and we have never before had a disease we could not conquer. We can conquer this. I believe that—in my lifetime, we've eliminated smallpox from the planet and polio from our hemisphere. We can do better, and we can do better until we prevail.

The threat of AIDS, just the very threat of it, has changed the lives of millions of people. And you heard from the talk about prevention, about which I want to say more in moment, it needs to change the lives of millions of more Americans. It has taken too many friends and loved ones from every one of us in this room. For millions of people it has shaken their very faith in the future.

But it's also inspired a remarkable community spirit. One of the people on this program today, Demetri Moshoyannis, who is right behind me, grew up in a typical American—I think he's still there—[Laughter]—grew up in typical American suburb in a typical American community. He attended college, became politically active. With a quick mind and an active spirit, he was clearly a rising star. After graduating, he joined the Corporation for National Service to help us start AmeriCorps.

While he was working for AmeriCorps, he found out he was HIV-positive at the ripe old age of 23. He took the news as a challenge, to use his communications skills, his organizational skills, and his leadership skills to educate and support his peers and help them escape the threat. He represents the combination of heartbreak and hope that makes this epidemic so unique. I am grateful to him, grateful to Sean, grateful to Eileen, grateful to every one of you who also represents that remarkable combination. We have to be worthy of your continuing courage.

Twelve days ago, the Centers for Disease Control reported that our Nation reached another sad milestone in the AIDS epidemic: A half million Americans have now been diagnosed with AIDS, and more than 300,000 have died. On this very day, and on every day from this day forward until we do something to change it, 120 more Americans will lose their lives, another 160 people will be diagnosed with the disease, nearly 140 will become infected with HIV.

That's why this meeting is important. It gives us an opportunity to say to America what the facts are, to rally our troops, to search our minds and hearts, to leave here with more weapons than we came to make progress in this battle.

Our common goal must ultimately be a cure, a cure for all those who are living with HIV and a vaccine to protect all the rest of us from the virus. A cure and a vaccine, that must be our first and top priority.

When I ran for President, I said that I would do everything I could to pull together the necessary resources and to organize them and to exercise real direction toward this goal. At a time of dramatic spending cuts, as Secretary Shalala said, we have nonetheless increased overall AIDS funding by about 40 percent. If my budget passes—and on this item, it actually might pass this year—we'll have a 26 percent increase in research. For the first time since the beginning of the epidemic, there is now one person in charge of the Nation's entire NIH AIDS research program, Dr. William Paul. And though more budget cuts are coming, we have got to protect the research budget and the Office of AIDS Research. I will oppose any effort to undermine the research effort or the Office of AIDS Research.

I want all our fellow Americans to know that this investment in science has paid tremendous dividends. Today people with AIDS live twice as long as they did just 10 years ago, especially those who seek early treatment. AIDS-related conditions that used to mean a quick and often very painful death for people living with HIV can now be treated and even prevented.

Since this administration began, I also want to compliment Dr. Kessler and the FDA. In record time they are now approving new classes of AIDS drugs that will help to restore the damaged immune systems of people with HIV. Indeed, there was a study released last week which says that the United States is now approving drugs faster than any European nation. And a drug company executive was recently quoted as saying that we are now 2 years ahead of Europe in the approval of AIDS drugs. Thank you; bring on more. This is a good direction.

Again, we have a lot to look forward to. Combination drug therapies are showing great promise as a means for controlling the virus in the human body. And just last year, we found that the use of drug therapy could actually block HIV transmission from mother to child. Our scientists tell me it's within our grasp to virtually eliminate pediatric AIDS by the end of the decade by offering all pregnant women HIV counseling and testing and guaranteeing that they have access to the treatment they need to protect their unborn children. We can give a generation of Americans the freedom of being born without HIV. We can do it, and we will.

I think all of us know we have to do more. And you may have ideas for us. In the end—I want to emphasize this over and over again, whenever we have these conferences, it's important for the President to speak, but it's also important for the President and the administration to hear. And you don't learn much when you're talking. So I want to urge you all here during this meeting today and afterward in following up, we are combing the country and the world for the best ideas about what to do next.

To move the search for a cure forward and to accelerate the pace, I have asked the Vice President to convene a meeting of scientists and leaders of the pharmaceutical industry to identify all the ways in which we might accelerate the development of vaccines, therapeutics, and microbicides that can protect people from HIV and the infections it causes. There are no guarantees in science, of course, but the collective will of government and industry can overcome huge obstacles as we have seen just in the last few years.

Second, let me say I am very pleased that the decision that was made at the NIH to put Dr. Paul in charge of coordinating the AIDS research of the NIH, for the first to have it all reconciled, coordinated, and directed, has worked out very well. But we need to extend this effort Government-wide. That's why I have asked Patsy Fleming to coordinate an inter-departmental working group that will be chaired by Dr. Paul to develop a coordinated plan for HIV and AIDS research all across every single Department of our Government, including developing a coordinated research budget. And I want a report in the next 90 days. That is the next important step to move forward.

We can't afford any unnecessary delays or missed opportunities. And I'm convinced that these two steps will help us to avoid those.

In addition to the work in research, we have to continue to do what we can to assure that those who are living with HIV and AIDS get the support and the care they need. And I want to talk about this in some detail.

For people with AIDS, the current debate over how to balance the Federal budget is far more than a question of political rhetoric. It is a matter of survival, primarily because of Medicaid. Even if we are successful, and I believe we will be, in reauthorizing the Ryan White CARE Act, at higher levels of funding—

and as you heard the Secretary say, we've increased funding by, I believe, 108 percent in the last 3 years—that is less than 20 percent of the total money spent to care for people with HIV and AIDS.

Medicaid is the lifeline of support. It provides health care for nearly half of the 190,000 Americans living with AIDS, including 90 percent of the children. It provides access to doctors, to hospitals, to drugs, to home care, the things that allow people to live their lives more fully. It pays for the drugs that keep HIV under control for longer and longer periods of time. And it pays for drugs that prevent the infections that often end the lives of those with AIDS. Medicaid pays for the care that allows families to stay together.

Yet today, Medicaid, a program that parenthetically also is eligible to cover one in five American children—that's how many—22 percent of our children are living in such difficult circumstances that they are eligible for Medicaid. And one of the things about the congressional budget that I objected to so strongly is that it slashes spending on Medicaid by over $160 billion and turns it into a block grant, thus eliminating a 30-year national commitment we have made to the poor, especially to poor children, which I might say has given us the lowest infant mortality rate in our history. It is the one thing we have done that has helped us to drive down infant mortality among poor people who otherwise never see doctors. It has given elderly people, millions of them, a dignified life in nursing home or getting home care. And it has helped people with disabilities, not just people with HIV and AIDS but millions and millions of families on limited incomes with children born with cerebral palsy, children born with spina bifida, families that could never afford to buy a decent wheelchair for their children, much less send them to camp in the summertime or have them in an appropriate living setting. And it is the lifeline for people with HIV and AIDS.

I say again, the Ryan White health care act is important. I'm proud of the fact that we have doubled the funding. I am fighting for more funding this year. I am proud of the fact that it enjoys some bipartisan support in the Congress. I am proud of the fact that when there was an attempt in the Senate to eviscerate it and turn it into a political football, the Senate almost unanimously turned it back. But be not deceived; we could double it. And if this Medicaid budget goes through, it is a stake in the heart of our efforts to guarantee dignity to the people with AIDS in this country. [*Applause*] Thank you.

I want to say one other thing. I want to thank the Secretary of Housing and Urban Development for the work that he has done to increase opportunities in housing for people living with AIDS. We have taken some tremendous hits in the HUD budget, some of them we have inflicted in an attempt to get the deficit down. And there will doubtless be further reductions which will require reorganization on an unprecedented scale at the Department. But Henry Cisneros and I were together on the day before Thanksgiving at a shelter serving food, and he told me again the one thing that we must not do is to undermine the ability of the Department of Housing and Urban Development to try to provide dignified, adequate, compassionate housing opportunities for people living with AIDS.

So I say to you, when we talk about balancing the budget, I'd like to remind you that our administration has cut the deficit nearly in half in ways that were honorable and fair and enabled us to increase our investment in things that mattered, not just the war against AIDS but education, technology, medical research, the environment, to bring the deficit down and lift the society up. And that's the way we ought to approach this.

I want to say more about this in a minute, but this budget debate, because it requires tough choices, will inevitably require us to define what kind of people we really are. When times are easy and you can just dole out money to everybody that shows up at the door, it's pretty hard to tell what your values are. When times are tough and you have to say yes some places and no others, it becomes far, far clearer.

So I ask you to help us in the fight against the Medicaid cuts, to help us to preserve Secretary Cisneros's ability to support housing opportunities.

I got the message. I heard what you said about prevention. I would point out that in the last 2 years we have asked for increases in our prevention budget. But I am very worried about what's happening there because of what has already been said.

We have to set a goal. And I hope you will suggest one coming out of this conference. We have to reduce the number of new infections each and every year until there are no more new infections. And we all have to do that.

We know that for this to work it has to be targeted and it has to be sustained, as the gay community demonstrated in the 1980's. We know now we have to pay particular attention to young people and those who abuse drugs. There is a lot of evidence that huge numbers of our young teenagers continue to be completely heedless of the risks of their behavior.

I was pleased to see the public service announcements that Secretary Shalala released to educate young people and to urge them to take responsibility to protect themselves. I would say we ought to go further, and you need to help us. We have to educate these kids, but we also have to tell them they cannot be heedless of the consequences of their behavior.

It is not enough to know; they must act. It is in the nature—it is one of the joys of childhood that children think they will live forever. It is one of the curses of childhood in some of our meanest neighborhoods that children think they won't live to be much beyond 25 anyway. In a perverse way, both of those attitudes are contributing to the problems, because one group of our children thinks that they are at no risk because nothing can ever happen to them; they're bulletproof. Another group believed that no matter what they do, they don't have much of a future anyway. And they are bound together in a death spiral when it comes to this. This is crazy. We have got to find some way to tell them: You must stop this.

We are doing what we can to make those toughest neighborhoods safer. Believe it or not, amidst all the talk here in Washington, you could hardly know it, but out there in America in almost every community, the crime rate is down, the welfare rolls are down, the food stamp rolls are down, the poverty rolls have dropped for the first time in over a decade. Why? Because if you invest in people and their future and jobs are created and people go to work and hope begins to be infused in people's lives, all the problems we talk about here in Washington give way to opportunities in the lives of people.

But we see with this problem, whether there is an atmosphere of opportunity or an atmosphere of hopelessness, too many teenagers are ignoring the responsibility they have to protect themselves. We have to find better ways and maybe more help from different people, to get inside their minds, to shake their spirits, to make them know we care about them and we want them to have a future. But we cannot do the one thing that only they can do, which is to control their own decisions. And we have to do more. And if you've got any better ideas for me, believe me, I am all ears.

I want to say, too, just a little word about the importance of trying to tie our prevention efforts with HIV and AIDS to our prevention efforts with drugs and substance abuse, because that's the second big problem area of populations. In 1993 and again in the crime bill in 1994, we increased our Federal investment with drug treatment. And I'm working to try to convince Congress to do even more. We know that the right kind of treatment programs work. We know that the right kind of prevention programs work. And we know that we can marry the two.

I've asked the CDC to convene a meeting of State and local people involved in both public health and drug prevention to develop an action plan that integrates HIV prevention and substance abuse prevention. And I hope that we can do that and do it now, because I think it will make a significant difference.

I have to tell you that I am very worried that what we see with the HIV rates among juveniles is now being mirrored in drug use. Last year's statistics showed unbelievably that drug use among people 18 to 34 was going down but casual drug use among people 12 to 17 was going up. I think it is clearly because there are too many kids out there raising themselves, thinking nobody cares about them, and not thinking there's much of a future. So we have to deal with these two things together.

And while we search for a cure, work to improve treatment, strive to prevent new cases and to protect the hard-won gains of the past, I'd also like to say just a word about the basic human rights of people living with HIV and AIDS.

AIDS-related discrimination unfortunately remains a problem that offends America's conscious. The Americans with Disabilities Act now offers more than 40 million Americans living with physical or mental disabilities, including those living with HIV and AIDS, protection against discrimination. And the Justice Department, the Department of Health and Human Services, the Equal Employment Opportunity Commission, they have been vigorously enforc-

ing the ADA. We're about to launch a new effort to ensure that health care facilities provide equal access to people with HIV and AIDS.

We simply cannot let our fears outweigh our common sense or our compassion. And as Sean said, we can't let our bigotry—to use his word, we can't let our homophobia blind us to our obligations. I say that for two reasons. One is that the fastest growing group of people with the HIV virus are not gay men. This is not a disease that fits into the homophobic world view. But the second reason is that regardless of sexual orientation or race or income or even whether a person has sadly fallen victim to drug abuse—as someone who has lived in a family with an alcoholic and with a drug abuser—every person—I say this with clear knowledge, experience, and conviction—every person with HIV or AIDS is somebody's son or daughter, somebody's brother or sister, somebody's parent, somebody's grandparent.

And when we forget this, when we forget that all the people who deal with this are our fellow Americans and that most of them share our values and our hopes and our dreams and deserve dignity and decency in the treatment we give them, we forget a very great thing that makes this a special country. And we forget it at our own peril.

In one way or another nearly every person in America at one time in his or her life has been subject to some sort of scorn. Woodrow Wilson once said that you could break a person with scornful words just as surely as with sticks and beat him. And I think that's an important thing, too, to remember.

The American people need to know that everybody in this country and, indeed, throughout the world, is now vulnerable to this disease. We need to identify what our responsibilities are in this country and our responsibilities to developing countries are to deal with the problem, to search for a cure, to search for a vaccine, to deal with the treatment issues. But I'm not sure it doesn't begin with dealing with our own hearts and minds on this. That's where you have to come in.

Frederick Douglass said, during the great struggle against slavery, that it was not light that is needed but fire; not the gentle shower but thunder; the feeling of the Nation must be quickened, the conscience of the Nation must be roused. That's what you came here to do.

Don't forget this: Most Americans are good people. The great burden we have as Americans is that when we have to deal with something new, too often we can't deal with it from imagination and empathy, we have to actually experience it first. I do not want to wait until every single family has somebody die before we have a good policy.

So I ask you—I understand anger and frustration, but I will never understand it until someday and something happens to me, and I know the sand is running out of my hourglass. So I can't totally understand it. But I ask all of you to remember this: This is fundamentally a good country. Alexis de Tocqueville said in the 1830's that this was a great country because we are a good country. And if we ever stop being a good country, we would no longer be a great country.

So I ask you to use this moment to give America a chance to be great about this issue, give our people a chance to feel this the way you feel it, to see it the way you see it, to know it the way you know it.

When I was getting ready for the conference yesterday, I called Bob Hattoy, sitting back there in the room. I said, "What do you think I ought to say tomorrow? What do you think is going to happen?" We were talking, and he said, "I think you ought to think about all the people who waged this battle with us in 1992 who aren't around anymore." And so we just went through them name by name. And then right before I came over here I looked at the picture of little Ricky Ray that I keep on my desk at the White House in the Oval Office, and I remembered his family and the members that are still struggling with it.

Give the country a chance to be great about this. Shake them up. Shake me up. Push us all hard. But do it in a way that remembers this is fundamentally a good country. Every now—when we stray, we get off the track a little bit, but we're still around for more than 200 years because most of the time, when the chips are down, we do the right thing. And I am convinced that people like you can get this country, starting here in Washington, to do the right thing.

Thank you, and God bless you all.

[*At this point, Dr. Renslow Sherer, director of the AIDS clinic at Cook County Hospital in* Chicago, IL, *discussed methods for improving primary care for HIV patients.*]

The President. Thank you.

I want to ask one brief question, if I might. One of the difficulties that we have in dealing responsibly with this issue involves the dilemma that you just laid out when you said we ought to have voluntary testing, not mandatory testing. And the issue is most clearly represented with the whole question of pregnant women now given the advances that have been shown. I've studied the CDC guidelines; I think they're—they make sense to me. I think the rest of us who don't know the facts ought to follow people that we hire to make these judgments. You know, if there's—it makes a lot of sense to me.

But you just said that there were 34,000 people that needed your services, and only 10,000 were getting them and we had to find a way to get more people to get voluntarily tested. So how do we close the gap between 10 and 34? What can we do? What can you do? What can the rest of us do? That's what's driving this whole mandatory testing thing. It's not the notion that people are out there hiding, trying to avoid getting tested; it's that there's this huge gap and that society is being burdened by it and so are these people. So how do we close that gap?

Dr. Sherer. I know other speakers today will address this, but let me start. Mandatory testing not only will not address this problem, it will further drive people away and be a disincentive to their coming into care.

The President. So how do you do it?

[*At this point, representatives reported on the various HIV/AIDS issues that were discussed by the nine working groups that comprised the conference.*]

The President. I would like to say just one thing before I go.

First of all, I have learned a lot. I even learned some things about some bills in Congress I thought I already knew all about. [*Laughter*] And I would like to encourage you to make sure that through our AIDS office or through the advisory council and Scott Hitt that we have an actual record of every question asked and every issue raised. I think it's very, very important that we do a systematic followup on every issue raised, every question asked.

Q. Mr. President, why didn't you do a systematic followup on the two previous Presidential commissions on AIDS? You promised in your campaign to adopt the recommendations. Why has it taken another year for you to—[*inaudible*].

The President. Didn't you listen to what we said before about what we've done the last 2 years? Most of the——

Q. I heard you talk about—[*inaudible*]——

The President. Do you want me to answer, or do you want to keep talking?

Q. ——I did not hear you talk about specific actions that will save lives today. And there's a list of 50 that have been followed by a range of New York organizations that have been submitted to officials in your administration. And it has taken 2 years, and now——

The President. First of all, that's not accurate. We implemented a lot of those recommendations, as you know. So I think that's a little unseemly for you to say. We had a set of recommendations we got when we got here, most of which have been implemented.

I am very sorry—I am very sorry—now, wait a minute. I listened to you; now you listen to me. I listened to you. Look, I am very sorry that there is not a cure. I am very sorry that there is not a vaccine. I regret that not everything I have asked for has been approved by the Congress. In the context of what has happened in this country in the last 3 years, I believe we have gone a long way toward doing what we said we would do. But I will never be satisfied, and you won't, and you shouldn't be, until we have solved the problem. That is what this meeting is about, and that's what I am trying to do. And I think all of us should do what we can to be constructive.

Q. [*Inaudible*]

The President. Well, that's a matter of dispute. You have your version of the facts and I have mine, and I'll leave it to others to make a judgment.

Q. [*Inaudible*]

The President. Let me just say, I believe this has been a good meeting. I think most people are glad they came, and I think most people believe they're better off than they were 4 years ago.

NOTE: The President spoke at 1:10 p.m. in the Cash Room at the Treasury Department. In his remarks, he referred to Sean Sasser, member, board of directors, AIDS Policy Center for Children, Youth & Families; Eileen Matzman, board member, Mothers' Voices; and Dr. Scott Hitt, Chair, and Bob Hattoy, member, Presidential Advisory Council on HIV/AIDS.

Remarks on Vetoing Budget Reconciliation Legislation
December 6, 1995

The President: Throughout our history, American Presidents have used the power of the veto to protect our values as a country. In that spirit today, I am acting to protect the values that bind us together in our national community.

My goals as President have been to preserve the American dream for all of our people, to bring the American people together, and to keep America the world's strongest force for peace and freedom and prosperity. In pursuit of that strategy, I have sought to grow the economy, to shrink the Government but leave it strong enough to do the job, and most important, to elevate mainstream values that all Americans share: opportunity and responsibility, work and family, and bringing our community together so that we can be stronger.

I have consistently said that if Congress sends me a budget that violates our values, I'll veto it. Three decades ago, this pen you see here was used to honor our values when President Johnson used it to sign Medicare into law. Today, I am vetoing the biggest Medicare and Medicaid cuts in history, deep cuts in education, a rollback in environmental protection, and a tax increase on working families. I am using this pen to preserve our commitment to our parents, to protect opportunity for our children, to defend the public health and our natural resources and natural beauty, and to stop a tax increase that actually undercuts the value of work.

We must balance the budget, but we must do it in a way that honors the commitments that we all have and that keeps our people together.

Therefore, today, I am vetoing this Republican budget because it would break those commitments and would lead us toward weakness and division when we must move toward strength and unity.

[*At this point, the President signed the veto message.*]

Can you bring me some more ink, boys? Here, Todd, I knew you had some. It's a small well. Leave it here and see if I need it.

Q. Mr. President, what happens next?

The President. I'm about to say. As I have said repeatedly, America must balance its budget. It's wrong to pass a legacy of debt onto our children. Our long-term growth depends on it. But we must do it in a way that is good for economic growth and for our values.

The budget I have vetoed in a very real sense, in very concrete ways, undermines our values and would restrict the future of families like the ones that are here with me today. American families want to make the most of their own lives and to pass opportunity onto their children. They deserve our respect and our support. Above all, we shouldn't make it harder for them to fulfill their dreams.

When it comes to health care, we owe a duty to our parents. We have to secure Medicare, and I've spelled out how to do that. But the budget I just vetoed would turn Medicare into a second-class system. The Medicare system has served all senior citizens well for 30 years; it would be over.

This budget would end Medicaid's guarantee that no senior citizen and no American in need would be denied medical care, including poor children and children with disabilities. It would deny care for hundreds of thousands of pregnant women and disabled children. It would repeal standards that ensure quality for nursing homes.

Education means opportunity, and opportunity is the key to the American dream. But this budget cuts education by $30 billion, even in this high technology age when education is more important than ever before. It would essentially end the direct student loan program. It would deny college scholarships to 360,000 deserving students. It would deny preschool opportunities to 180,000 children in the Head Start program.

We must protect the Earth that God gave us and guarantee our children safe food and clean water. This budget would give oil companies the right to drill in the last unspoiled arctic wilderness in Alaska. And it is loaded with special-interest provisions that squander our natural resources. Already, short-term budget cuts have forced us to pull back enforcement of clean air, clean water, even inspections of toxic waste sites in our neighborhoods.

People who work hard and save for retirement ought to be able to retire with dignity. We worked hard last year to secure the pension benefits of 40 million Americans with landmark reform legislation. This bill would give companies the green light to raid pension funds and put those retirements at risk again.

Americans know we have to reform the broken welfare system. But cutting child care that helps mothers move from welfare to work, cutting help for abused and disabled children, cutting school lunch, that's not welfare reform. Real welfare reform should be tough on work and tough on responsibility but not tough on children or tough on parents who are responsible and who want to work. We shouldn't lose this historic chance to end welfare as we know it by using the words welfare reform as just another cover to violate our values.

No one who works hard should be taxed into poverty. In 1993, we nearly doubled the earned-income tax credits so that we could say, "If you work 40 hours a week, you've got children in the home, you won't be taxed into poverty. The tax system will help lift you out of poverty." But this budget raises taxes on our hardest pressed working people, even as it gives unnecessarily large income tax relief and other tax relief to those who need it least. Nearly 8 million working families would pay more in new taxes than they would receive from any tax cut in this bill.

Beyond our principles, let me just say this budget is bad for the economy. No business on the edge of the 21st century would cut its investment in education and training, in research. No business would do that. No business would cut back on technology on the edge of the 21st century. The Japanese are in a recession, and they recently doubled their research budget. We are voting in this budget, if I were to allow it to become law, to cut our research budget by a year when we're in a period of economic growth, while another country, looking to the future in a recession, is doubling theirs. So this not only violates our values, it is bad, bad economics.

Now, with this veto, the extreme Republican effort to balance the budget through wrongheaded cuts and misplaced priorities is over. Now it's up to all of us to go back to work together to show we can balance the budget and be true to our values and our economic interests.

Tomorrow, I will present to the congressional leadership a plan that does balance the budget in 7 years, but it also protects health care, education, and the environment, and it does not raise taxes on working families. It is up to the Republicans now to show that they, too, want to protect these principles, as they pledged to do.

Let me say again, our country is on the move; our economy is growing. Many of our most difficult social problems are beginning to yield to the effort and commonsense values of the American people. We have proved again that we are a model for the entire world of peace and reconciliation. With all of our difficult problems, we are moving in the right direction. Now is not the time to derail this movement.

I have vetoed the budget. Now, the question is, will we get together and balance the budget in a way that is consistent with our values? It's time to finish the job of balancing the budget and do it in the right way.

Thank you.

Q. Mr. President,—[*inaudible*]—Medicare and Medicaid, how are you going to—where are you going to find——

The President. Tune in tomorrow.

NOTE: The President spoke at 3:36 p.m. in the Oval Office at the White House. In his remarks, he referred to White House Staff Secretary Todd Stern.

Message to the House of Representatives Returning Without Approval Budget Reconciliation Legislation
December 6, 1995

To the House of Representatives:

I am returning herewith without my approval H.R. 2491, the budget reconciliation bill adopted by the Republican majority, which seeks to make extreme cuts and other unacceptable changes in Medicare and Medicaid, and to raise taxes on millions of working Americans.

As I have repeatedly stressed, I want to find common ground with the Congress on a balanced budget plan that will best serve the American people. But, I have profound differences with the extreme approach that the Republican majority has adopted. It would hurt average Americans and help special interests.

My balanced budget plan reflects the values that Americans share—work and family, opportunity and responsibility. It would protect Medicare and retain Medicaid's guarantee of coverage; invest in education and training and other priorities; protect public health and the environment; and provide for a targeted tax cut to help middle-income Americans raise their children, save for the future, and pay for postsecondary education. To reach balance, my plan would eliminate wasteful spending, streamline programs, and end unneeded subsidies; take the first, serious steps toward health care reform; and reform welfare to reward work.

By contrast, H.R. 2491 would cut deeply into Medicare, Medicaid, student loans, and nutrition programs; hurt the environment; raise taxes on millions of working men and women and their families by slashing the Earned Income Tax Credit (EITC); and provide a huge tax cut whose benefits would flow disproportionately to those who are already the most well-off.

Moreover, this bill creates new fiscal pressures. Revenue losses from the tax cuts grow rapidly after 2002, with costs exploding for provisions that primarily benefit upper-income taxpayers. Taken together, the revenue losses for the 3 years after 2002 for the individual retirement account (IRA), capital gains, and estate tax provisions exceed the losses for the preceding 6 years.

Title VIII would cut Medicare by $270 billion over 7 years—by far the largest cut in Medicare's 30-year history. While we need to slow the rate of growth in Medicare spending, I believe Medicare must keep pace with anticipated increases in the costs of medical services and the growing number of elderly Americans. This bill would fall woefully short and would hurt beneficiaries, over half of whom are women. In addition, the bill introduces untested, and highly questionable, Medicare "choices" that could increase risks and costs for the most vulnerable beneficiaries.

Title VII would cut Federal Medicaid payments to States by $163 billion over 7 years and convert the program into a block grant, eliminating guaranteed coverage to millions of Americans and putting States at risk during economic downturns. States would face untenable choices: cutting benefits, dropping coverage for millions of beneficiaries, or reducing provider payments to a level that would undermine quality service to children, people with disabilities, the elderly, pregnant women, and others who depend on Medicaid. I am also concerned that the bill has inadequate quality and income protections for nursing home residents, the developmentally disabled, and their families, and that it would eliminate a program that guarantees immunizations to many children.

Title IV would virtually eliminate the Direct Student Loan Program, reversing its significant progress and ending the participation of over 1,300 schools and hundreds of thousands of students. These actions would hurt middle- and low-income families, make student loan programs less efficient, perpetuate unnecessary red tape, and deny students and schools the free-market choice of guaranteed or direct loans.

Title V would open the Arctic National Wildlife Refuge (ANWR) to oil and gas drilling, threatening a unique, pristine ecosystem, in hopes of generating $1.3 billion in Federal revenues—a revenue estimate based on wishful thinking and outdated analysis. I want to protect this biologically rich wilderness permanently. I am also concerned that the Congress has chosen to use the reconciliation bill as a catch-all for various objectionable natural resource and environmental policies. One would retain the notorious patenting provision whereby the government transfers billions of dollars of publicly owned minerals at little or no charge to private interests; another would transfer Federal land for a low-level radioactive waste site in California without public safeguards.

While making such devastating cuts in Medicare, Medicaid, and other vital programs, this bill would provide huge tax cuts for those who are already the most well-off. Over 47 percent of the tax benefits would go to families with incomes over $100,000—the top 12 percent. The bill would provide unwarranted benefits to corporations and new tax breaks for special interests. At the same time, it would raise taxes, on average, for the poorest one-fifth of all families.

The bill would make capital gains cuts retroactive to January 1, 1995, providing a windfall of $13 billion in about the first 9 months of 1995 alone to taxpayers who already have sold their assets. While my Administration supports limited reform of the alternative minimum tax (AMT), this bill's cuts in the corporate AMT would not adequately ensure that profitable corporations pay at least some Federal tax. The bill also would encourage businesses to avoid taxes by stockpiling foreign earnings in tax havens. And the bill does not include my proposal to close a loophole that allows wealthy Americans to avoid taxes on the gains they accrue by giving up their U.S. citizenship. Instead, it substitutes a provision that would prove ineffective.

While cutting taxes for the well-off, this bill would cut the EITC for almost 13 million working families. It would repeal part of the scheduled 1996 increase for taxpayers with two or more children, and end the credit for workers who do not live with qualifying children. Even after accounting for other tax cuts in this bill, about eight million families would face a net tax increase.

The bill would threaten the retirement benefits of workers and increase the exposure of the Pension Benefit Guaranty Corporation by making it easy for companies to withdraw tax-favored pension assets for nonpension purposes. It also would raise Federal employee retirement contributions, unduly burdening Federal workers. Moreover, the bill would eliminate the low-income housing tax credit and the community development corporation tax credit, which address critical housing needs and help rebuild communities. Finally, the bill would repeal the tax credit that encourages economic activity in Puerto Rico. We must not ignore the real needs of our citizens in Puerto Rico, and any legislation must contain effective mechanisms to promote job creation in the islands.

Title XII includes many welfare provisions. I strongly support real welfare reform that strengthens families and encourages work and responsibility. But the provisions in this bill, when added to the EITC cuts, would cut low-income programs too deeply. For welfare reform to succeed, savings should result from moving people from welfare to work, not from cutting people off and shifting costs to the States. The cost of excessive program cuts in human terms—to working families, single mothers with small children, abused and neglected children, low-income legal immigrants, and disabled children—would be grave. In addition, this bill threatens the national nutritional safety net by making unwarranted changes in child nutrition programs and the national food stamp program. The agriculture provisions would eliminate the safety net that farm programs provide for U.S. agriculture. Title I would provide windfall pay-ments to producers when prices are high, but not protect family farm income when prices are low. In addition, it would slash spending for agricultural export assistance and reduce the environmental benefits of the Conservation Reserve Program.

For all of these reasons, and for others detailed in the attachment, this bill is unacceptable.

Nevertheless, while I have major differences with the Congress, I want to work with Members to find a common path to balance the budget in a way that will honor our commitment to senior citizens, help working families, provide a better life for our children, and improve the standard of living of all Americans.

WILLIAM J. CLINTON

The White House,
December 6, 1995.

Remarks on Lighting the National Christmas Tree
December 6, 1995

Thank you so much. To John Betchkal, the Pageant of Peace Chairman; Reverend John Tavlarides; to the Sherando High School Choir, congratulations, you guys were great tonight; to Brendan and Bridget Walsh; the Washington Ballet; to Denyce Graves and Jack Jones and Kathie Lee Gifford and the Navy Band; and of course, to Santa Claus. I would come here every year just to see Santa Claus.

We gather to begin our Nation's celebration of the Christmas season with the lighting of this magnificent tree, a symbol, as evergreens have always been, of the infinite capacity of nature and people to renew themselves. We give gifts, and we count our blessings.

My fellow Americans, I have just returned from a very moving trip to Europe, to England and to Northern Ireland and the Republic of Ireland, to Germany to see our troops, and to Spain. And I can tell you that among the things that I feel most grateful for at this Christmas time is the way people around the world look at our America. They see a nation graced by peace and prosperity, a land of freedom and fairness. And even though it imposes extra bur-dens on us, they trust us to work with them to share the blessings of peace.

This is my second Christmas tree lighting of the season, for just a few days ago I was in Belfast with the people of Northern Ireland, Protestant and Catholic alike, searching, yearning, longing for peace, celebrating their second Christmas of peace. I'm proud that I was introduced there by two children, a little Catholic girl named Catherine Hamill and a young Protestant boy named David Sterritt, who joined hands and told the world of their hopes for the future, a future in which the only barriers they face are the limits of their dreams. That is the future we should want for our children and for all the children of the world.

I'm very pleased that Catherine Hamill, who touched the whole world with the story of her suffering and her family's losses in Northern Ireland, and her family are here with us tonight to celebrate this lighting of the Christmas tree. And I'd like to ask her to stand up right down here and ask all of you to give her a fine hand. She has come all the way from Northern Ireland. [*Applause*]

Remember at this Christmas time we celebrate the birth of a homeless child, whose only shelter was the straw of a manger but who grew to become the Prince of Peace. The Prince of Peace said, "Blessed are the peacemakers." Let us bless the peacemakers at this Christmas time from the Middle East to Northern Ireland to our own troops in Bosnia. Let us pray especially for our peacemakers, those who will go to Bosnia and those who are soon to come home from Haiti.

And let us resolve, my fellow Americans, to be peacemakers. For just as so many nations around the world and so many children around the world cry for peace, so do we need peace here at home in our toughest neighborhoods, where there are children, so many children who deserve to have their childhood and their future free and peaceful.

And let us remember from the example of the Prince of Peace how even the humblest of us can do, through acts of goodness and reconciliation, extraordinary things. And as we light this wonderful Christmas tree, let us all remember that together a million small lights add up to make a great blaze of glory, not for ourselves but for our families, our Nation and the world, and for the future of our children.

Merry Christmas, and blessed are the peacemakers.

NOTE: The President spoke at 5:45 p.m. on the Ellipse during the annual Christmas Pageant of Peace. In his remarks, he referred to Rev. John Tavlarides, who recited the Christmas prayer; Brendan and Bridget Walsh, Camp Fire Boys and Girls, Pittsburgh, PA; entertainers Denyce Graves, Jack Jones, and Kathie Lee Gifford; and television weatherman Willard Scott.

Letter to Congressional Leaders on the Deployment of United States Military Forces for Implementation of the Balkan Peace Process
December 6, 1995

Dear Mr. Speaker: (*Mr. President:*)

I last reported to the Congress on September 1, 1995, concerning the use of U.S. aircraft in support of United Nations and North Atlantic Treaty Organization (NATO) efforts in the former Yugoslavia. In that report I noted our diplomatic efforts to assist the parties to reach a negotiated settlement to the conflict. I am gratified to report that those efforts have borne fruit.

On November 21, 1995, the Presidents of the Republic of Bosnia and Herzegovina, the Republic of Croatia, and, on behalf of the Federal Republic of Yugoslavia, the President of the Republic of Serbia initialed a peace agreement to end the conflict in the former Yugoslavia. The agreement has 11 annexes including, among others, Military Aspects, Regional Stabilization, Elections, Human Rights, Refugees and Displaced Persons, and Civilian Implementation. These annexes were also signed or initialed by the state parties, and where appropriate, by officials from the Republika Srpska and the Federation of Bosnia and Herzegovina. This is the first

step in a process that will lead to formal signing of the agreement on December 14 in Paris.

As a result of this important first step, consistent with our consultations with the Congress, and pursuant to the North Atlantic Council (NAC) decision of December 1, 1995, I have ordered the deployment of approximately 1,500 U.S., military personnel to Bosnia and Herzegovina and Croatia as part of a NATO "enabling force" to lay the groundwork for the prompt and safe deployment of the NATO-led Implementation Force (IFOR). United States personnel participating in the enabling force will be under NATO operational control and rules of engagement. To date, I have also authorized the deployment of approximately 3,000 additional U.S. military personnel to Hungary, Italy, and Croatia in order to establish forward U.S. support infrastructure for the enabling force and the IFOR. These personnel will deploy in the very near future and will remain under U.S. command and control and rules of engagement.

As I have indicated before, now that I have approved the NATO operation plan for implementation, I will be requesting an expression of support from the Congress.

The enabling force will join previously deployed NATO communications personnel in Croatia as well as various national forces currently part of the United Nations Protection Force; these other national forces will come under NATO operational control when the IFOR main force is deployed. The enabling force consists of headquarters and administrative staff, communications units, movement control teams, logistics units, special forces units and civil affairs personnel under NATO operational control. The enabling force will have combat capability for force protection. These forces will be fully authorized and equipped to defend themselves, and will be backed by U.S. and NATO forces in the theater of operations, including U.S. air assets supporting Deny Flight and an amphibious reaction force in the Adriatic that are ready and able to counter any threat to their safety. In addition, British and other elements of the U.N. Protection Force/Rapid Reaction Force (UNPROFOR/RRF) in Bosnia will be available to protect U.S. forces. It is envisioned that the IFOR main body will begin to deploy following the signature of the peace agreement in Paris and the issuance of final NATO and U.S. orders. The enabling force will thereafter remain as part of the IFOR.

The U.S. forces participating in the enabling force being deployed to Bosnia and Herzegovina and Croatia are drawn largely from U.S. forces stationed in Germany. Among the nations providing forces to the enabling force are the United Kingdom, France, Germany, and Canada. In total, approximately 2,600 troops will be deployed as part of the enabling force.

I authorized these deployments in conjunction with our NATO allies following NAC decisions to permit implementation of the peace agreement following its formal signing. I have directed the participation of U.S. forces in these operations pursuant to my constitutional authority to conduct the foreign relations of the United States and as Commander in Chief and Chief Executive.

I am providing this report as part of my efforts to keep the Congress fully informed about developments in the former Yugoslavia, consistent with the War Powers Resolution.

Sincerely,

WILLIAM J. CLINTON

NOTE: Identical letters were sent to Newt Gingrich, Speaker of the House of Representatives, and Strom Thurmond, President pro tempore of the Senate. This letter was released by the Office of the Press Secretary on December 7.

Remarks Prior to a Meeting With Congressional Leaders and an Exchange With Reporters
December 7, 1995

Bosnia and the Budget

The President. I'd like to just say a couple of opening words. First, I want to welcome the bipartisan delegation of House Members who are here and thank them for coming as we continue to discuss the question of our mission in Bosnia and search for unity on that.

I also want to say that I took a step today which I hope will help us to find unity on the budget. I presented a budget that is a 7-year balanced budget that protects Medicare, Medicaid, education, and the environment, doesn't raise taxes on working families, and meets the conditions that were set out in the resolution to which we all agreed. And I hope it will be taken as a gesture in good faith that will start us on the road to real negotiations over this budget and that will bring about a constructive resolution for the American people.

So I'm very hopeful about that, and I'm looking forward to having the opportunity to have a discussion about Bosnia with the Members who are here present. And some of them I think have recently returned from a trip of their own to Bosnia, so I think we'll have a lot to discuss. And I thank you for being here. And I thank you for being here.

Q. Mr. President, Chairman Kasich said late today your budget came up there 400 in the hole. And he said by submitting this document you have breached the contract you signed with them a few days ago.

The President. Well, I disagree with that. You know, if you look at—we thought there would be new budget estimates coming out of the Congressional Budget Office by now, but they haven't been. That's fine, and I haven't attacked them for not doing it, even though they said they would. And I don't think that's very constructive.

Our budget—let me point out two things. All this is is a—the balanced budget plan is a plan over 7 years. No one can know what will happen between now and then, but we do know what's happened for the last 3 years. For the last 3 years, both the Congressional Budget Office and the Office of Management and Budget have un-derestimated the deficit reduction as a result of the 1993 economic plan, although we have been closer to accurate than the CBO.

We know that our plan was submitted based on basically splitting the difference of all the experts in America who predict what the economy will do. And therefore, it is mainstream, and it's good, and it's a good place to start discussions. And I think that's the attitude they ought to take. And if they have a—I've made a proposal; now I'd like to see what theirs is. Thank you.

NOTE: The President spoke at 6:05 p.m. in the Indian Treaty Room at the Old Executive Office Building.

Letter to Congressional Leaders on Proposed Legislation To Protect Retirement Plan Savings
December 7, 1995

Dear _____:

Since the beginning of this Administration, we have worked together to protect the retirement savings of hard-working Americans. Last year, Congress passed legislation proposed by the Administration that secured the retirement promises made to over 40 million workers in traditional pension plans.

Now we must all act to ensure that the savings of the 22 million American workers who put their hard-earned money into 401(k) plans are safe. We need to make certain the government has the tools to assure American workers they can put their savings—and their trust—into a system that will be there when they need it most.

I urge you to swiftly approve legislation we sent to Congress in July that would give both private auditors and the government new strength and more effective tools with which to enforce the law and prevent abuse of employee retirement savings by unscrupulous employers.

My Administration has consistently urged Americans to save for their retirement—a message echoed by financial planners, consumer groups and virtually everyone who has considered this issue. But Americans need to know their savings are safe if they are to follow this sound advice.

While the vast majority of employers fully respect and protect their employees' savings, some employers are abusing that trust. Last week, the Department of Labor, which protects private pensions, urged consumers to watch for warning signs to protect their 401(k) investments. The Department of Labor's Pension and Welfare Benefits Administration has begun a nationwide enforcement initiative that has already uncovered the misuse of millions of dollars of contributions by workers. Over $3.5 million has already been returned to workers; 310 investigations remain open, and more cases are coming.

On July 6, Secretary of Labor Reich transmitted to Congress the "ERISA Enforcement Improvement Act." Our legislation would help in early identification of potential abuses, strengthen pension plan auditing and subject abusers to new penalties. Since July, we have worked with members of Congress and the financial community to develop a bipartisan consensus to protect our workers.

I am sure you agree with the 22 million Americans who place their faith and trust in 401(k) plans that this is an issue of protection, not partisanship.

I strongly urge you to give this important legislation your immediate attention, and urge that it be enacted before the end of the year. America's workers shouldn't be asked to wait a day longer.

Sincerely,

BILL CLINTON

NOTE: Identical letters were sent to Senators Robert Dole, Thomas Daschle, Paul Simon, Edward M. Kennedy, Nancy Kassebaum, and Representatives Newt Gingrich, Dick Gephardt, Patsy T. Mink, Harris W. Fawell, William F. Goodling, William Clay, and Matthew G. Martinez.

Remarks on the Budget and an Exchange With Reporters
December 8, 1995

The President. Good morning. I am delighted to be here with a number of Governors from around our country to talk about the budget debate now in Washington. All these Governors who are here present and all those who are not have to balance the budget, but they're accountable for doing so in a way that increases opportunity for their people and holds the people together, maintains the bonds of community. That's what we're trying to do here.

Yesterday I gave the Congress a budget that balances in 7 years without devastating cuts in Medicare and Medicaid, education and the environment and that does not raise taxes on working families.

There are many differences between the budget that I vetoed, which Congress passed, and the one that I've presented. But perhaps the starkest one of all is the different treatment of Medicaid. The Republican budget would be a disaster for States and for the people who depend upon Medicaid. It would ask the States to do more and more and more for the elderly, for the disabled, for poor children and pregnant women and give them less help to do it. It would force them to make unconscionable and unnecessary choices between senior citizens and disabled people, between people with AIDS and nursing home residents.

The plan would end the guarantee of quality medical care that now exists for 26 million Americans, a guarantee that has been on the books for three decades now. The Republicans are insisting that we repeal the guarantee that no poor child, pregnant mother, poor senior citizen, or disabled person will be denied quality medical care. That would eliminate the guarantee of nursing home care for as many as 300,000 people. All told, if current patterns of coverage prevail, some 8 million people could be denied health care coverage under Medicaid, nearly half of them children. No one would want to do this in any State, but many States would have no choice under the budget now pending.

So I just want to be clear about this. I very much want to work with the Republican Congress to get a balanced budget. But I will not, I will not, permit the repeal of guaranteed medical coverage for senior citizens, for disabled people, for poor children and pregnant women. That would violate our values. It is not necessary, and therefore, if it continues to be a part of the budget, if necessary, I would veto it again.

We cannot, we must not, do this. This would do more harm to more people and do more to undermine the stability of State governments and the life of the States in our country than any other provision of this budget, in all probability, and we just cannot do it. So I want to make that clear.

On the other hand, let me say again, I am reaching out the hand of cooperation to Congress. I did yesterday. I do so again today. But there are some things that we cannot and should not change and back away from. That resolution that was passed that permitted the Government to go forward said that we would protect Medicare, Medicaid, education, and the environment. That's what it said. I've done my part. I've offered a 7-year budget. We cannot destroy Medicaid.

Federal Reserve Board Chairman

Q. Mr. President, are you going to reappoint Alan Greenspan, as the New York Times says?

The President. Did they say that? [*Laughter*] To be honest with you, that's very premature.

I haven't even given much thought to it, one way or the other. We've had a few other things on the griddle here.

Balkan Peace Process

Q. Speaking of that, Mr. President, do you think you'll have a resolution of support on Bosnia before the treaty signing in Paris next week?

The President. Will we have one? Well, I hope so. I don't know. I'm working on it, but I hope so.

Q. What do you think about half of the House Members signing a letter opposing the deployment?

The President. I hope that both Houses will vote to do it. It's the responsible thing to do. And those who paid any attention to the trip that I made to Europe last week know that all of the people in Europe are looking to see whether the United States will continue our 50-year partnership with Europe for security, will continue our leadership in NATO, and will do our part. They have only asked us to do a part. They, after all, are doing two-thirds of the work on the ground in Bosnia. They have asked us as the leader of NATO and the Alliance to send about a third of the troops. And in every nation I visited, people came up to me and said that

America had been able to make peace in Bosnia, and they were desperately hoping we would participate so that we could prevent any kind of a resumption of the slaughter there, prevent the conflict from spreading, and prove that Europe and the United States are still partners for security in the post-cold-war era. I feel far more strongly about it even than I did before I went last week.

It's clear to me that our Nation's ability to work with these European countries on every other security issue—reducing the nuclear threat, fighting terrorism, you name it—depends upon our partnership here. That is the issue of the day for them and for millions and millions and millions of them. And I think we have to do our part, and I'm going to do what I can to persuade the Congress of that.

Q. Is there any possibility, sir, that the Paris signing next week will slide because of what's going on there?

The President. I know of no plans to delay it. I believe it's going to go forward on time.

NOTE: The President spoke at 9:38 a.m. in the Cabinet Room at the White House prior to a meeting with Democratic Governors. A tape was not available for verification of the content of these remarks.

Remarks Prior to Discussions With President Jose dos Santos of Angola and an Exchange With Reporters
December 8, 1995

Angolan Peace Process

President Clinton. Hello. I'd like to say that I'm very pleased to welcome President dos Santos and his party here to Washington. He's taken some bold steps to move the peace process forward, and we understand this has made possible some changes in our relationship with Angola.

It's obvious that some further things will have to be done in light of the recent cease-fire violations. But we know that President dos Santos is critical to the success of the peace process, and we look forward to a good relationship with a reconciled, peaceful, and stable Angola.

Q. Do you think there can be peace in your country, Mr. President?

President dos Santos. I believe so. But first of all, I would like to thank the—of welcome by President Clinton, to thank also for the kind invitation to visit the United States at this time of year.

I would like to restate our commitment to the peace process. We will do our best for this process to become irreversible, and to—[*inaudible*]—possible. And we are convinced that with assistance from the United States of America and from the international community in general, peace will be consolidated and a new page will be opened in Angola.

We mark our presence here with you to discuss issues regarding bilateral relations. We are convinced that our visit will serve to deepen the friendship between the United States of America and Angola and will set up the basis to establish a trade exchange for more investors to go to Angola in order for them, together with us, to launch into the adventure of economic reconstruction and to consolidate peace and national reconciliation.

U.S. Aid to Angola

Q. Will he be asking for aid for his oil industry during his visit, and how much aid will he be asking for if he is?

President dos Santos. We've come to thank you for the assistance that has been given to us, the assistance that has been given to us to maintain peace. But we also intend to go from this phase of assistance to trade and investment. There are sectors whereby we will be together with the United States of America, and one of those sectors is the oil sector, where the big investments from the United States will be. In other words, we want more investment, not only in the oil sectors but in other sectors of our economy which are open.

Government Shutdown

Q. Do you think there's going to be a Government shutdown again?

President Clinton. I certainly hope not. I have done exactly what I've said I'd do. I vetoed the budget that was passed, and then I made an alternative budget, which I presented yester-

day, that fulfills the criteria of the resolution: It's a 7-year budget; it protects Medicare, Medicaid, education, the environment; it doesn't raise taxes on working people. That's the commitment that I made, and I hope that it will be taken as a good-faith gesture by the Republicans and we'll have some further negotiations.

Now, apparently, they're deciding what they want to do. But I have done what I think I should do, and this budget would be good for America. It will balance the budget and keep our commitments to our future, to our children, to our environment, and to the health care system of this country.

Q. Will you try to keep them in session if they close down the Government?

The President. Well, let's see. I think—that is December 8th? We've got a week, and I think they're waiting for—maybe to do some calibrations of their own on their own numbers. I don't know, but I don't think we should assume that this thing is going to break down. I'm prepared to work as hard as I can to do anything I can to keep working to try to resolve this in a positive way. That's why I presented this budget and why I hope that they will respond in good faith, just as I have.

NOTE: The President spoke at 11:41 a.m. in the Oval Office at the White House. A tape was not available for verification of the content of these remarks.

Message to the Congress on Ordering the Selected Reserve of the Armed Forces to Active Duty
December 8, 1995

To the Congress of the United States:

I have today, pursuant to section 12304 of title 10, United States Code, authorized the Secretary of Defense, and the Secretary of Transportation with respect to the Coast Guard when it is not operating as a service in the Department of the Navy, to order to active duty any units, and any individual members not assigned to a unit organized to serve as a unit, of the Selected Reserve to perform such missions the Secretary of Defense may determine necessary. The deployment of United States forces to con-

duct operational missions in and around former Yugoslavia necessitates this action.

A copy of the Executive order implementing this action is attached.

WILLIAM J. CLINTON

The White House,
December 8, 1995.

NOTE: The Executive order is listed in Appendix D at the end of this volume.

Message to the Congress Reporting on Sanctions Against the Federal Republic of Yugoslavia (Serbia and Montenegro)
December 8, 1995

To the Congress of the United States:

On May 30, 1992, in Executive Order No. 12808, the President declared a national emergency to deal with the threat to the national security, foreign policy, and economy of the United States arising from actions and policies of the Governments of Serbia and Montenegro, acting under the name of the Socialist Federal Republic of Yugoslavia or the Federal Republic of Yugoslavia, in their involvement in and support for groups attempting to seize territory in Croatia and the Republic of Bosnia and Herzegovina by force and violence utilizing, in part, the forces of the so-called Yugoslav National Army (57 *FR* 23299, June 2, 1992). I expanded the national emergency in Executive Order No. 12934 of October 25, 1994, to address the actions and policies of the Bosnian Serb forces and the authorities in the territory of the Republic of Bosnia and Herzegovina that they control.

The present report is submitted pursuant to 50 U.S.C. 1641(c) and 1703(c) and covers the period from May 30, 1995, to November 29, 1995. It discusses Administration actions and expenses directly related to the exercise of powers and authorities conferred by the declaration of a national emergency in Executive Order No. 12808 and Executive Order No. 12934 and to expanded sanctions against the Federal Republic of Yugoslavia (Serbia and Montenegro) (the "FRY (S&M)") and the Bosnian Serbs contained in Executive Order No. 12810 of June 5, 1992 (57 *FR* 24347, June 9, 1992), Executive Order No. 12831 of January 15, 1993 (58 *FR* 5253, January 21, 1993), Executive Order No. 12846 of April 25, 1993 (58 *FR* 25771, April 27, 1993), and Executive Order No. 12934 of October 25, 1994 (59 *FR* 54117, October 27, 1994).

1. Executive Order No. 12808 blocked all property and interests in property of the Governments of Serbia and Montenegro, or held in the name of the former Government of the Socialist Federal Republic of Yugoslavia or the Government of the Federal Republic of Yugoslavia, then or thereafter located in the United States or within the possession or control of United States persons, including their overseas branches.

Subsequently, Executive Order No. 12810 expanded U.S. actions to implement in the United States the United Nations sanctions against the FRY (S&M) adopted in United Nations Security Council (UNSC) Resolution 757 of May 30, 1992. In addition to reaffirming the blocking of FRY (S&M) Government property, this order prohibited transactions with respect to the FRY (S&M) involving imports, exports, dealing in FRY (S&M)-origin property, air and sea transportation, contract performance, funds transfers, activity promoting importation or exportation or dealings in property, and official sports, scientific, technical, or other cultural representation of, or sponsorship by, the FRY (S&M) in the United States.

Executive Order No. 12810 exempted from trade restrictions (1) transshipments through the FRY (S&M), and (2) activities related to the United Nations Protection Force (UNPROFOR), the Conference on Yugoslavia, or the European Community Monitor Mission.

On January 15, 1993, President Bush issued Executive Order No. 12831 to implement new sanctions contained in UNSC Resolution 787 of November 16, 1992. The order revoked the exemption for transshipments through the FRY (S&M) contained in Executive Order No. 12810, prohibited transactions within the United States or by a United States person relating to FRY (S&M) vessels and vessels in which a majority or controlling interest is held by a person or entity in, or operating from, the FRY (S&M), and stated that all such vessels shall be considered as vessels of the FRY (S&M), regardless of the flag under which they sail.

On April 25, 1993, I issued Executive Order No. 12846 to implement in the United States the sanctions adopted in UNSC Resolution 820 of April 17, 1993. That resolution called on the Bosnian Serbs to accept the Vance-Owen peace plan for the Republic of Bosnia and Herzegovina and, if they failed to do so by April 26, 1993, called on member states to take additional measures to tighten the embargo against the FRY (S&M) and Serbian-controlled areas of the Republic of Bosnia and Herzegovina and the United Nations Protected Areas in Croatia. Effective April 26, 1993, the order blocked all property and interests in property of commercial, industrial, or public utility undertakings or entities organized or located in the FRY (S&M), including property and interests in property of entities (wherever organized or located) owned or controlled by such undertakings or entities, that are or thereafter come within the possession or control of United States persons.

On October 25, 1994, in view of UNSC Resolution 942 of September 23, 1994, I issued Executive Order No. 12934 in order to take additional steps with respect to the crisis in the former Yugoslavia (59 *FR* 54117, October 27, 1994). Executive Order No. 12934 expands the scope of the national emergency declared in Executive Order No. 12808 to address the unusual and extraordinary threat to the national security, foreign policy, and economy of the United States posed by the actions and policies of the Bosnian Serb forces and the authorities in the territory in the Republic of Bosnia and Herzegovina that they control, including their refusal to accept the proposed territorial settlement of the conflict in the Republic of Bosnia and Herzegovina.

The Executive order blocks all property and interests in property that are in the United States, that hereafter come within the United States, or that are or hereafter come within the possession or control of United States persons (including their overseas branches) of: (1) the Bosnian Serb military and paramilitary forces and the authorities in areas of the Republic of Bosnia and Herzegovina under the control of those forces; (2) any entity, including any commercial, industrial, or public utility undertaking, organized or located in those areas of the Republic of Bosnia and Herzegovina under the control of Bosnian Serb forces; (3) any entity, wherever organized or located, which is owned or controlled directly or indirectly by any person in, or resident in, those areas of the Republic of Bosnia and Herzegovina under the control of Bosnian Serb forces; and (4) any person acting for or on behalf of any person within the scope of the above definitions.

The Executive order also prohibits the provision or exportation of services to those areas of the Republic of Bosnia and Herzegovina under the control of Bosnian Serb forces, or to any person for the purpose of any business carried on in those areas, either from the United States or by a United States person. The order also prohibits the entry of any U.S.-flagged vessel, other than a U.S. naval vessel, into the riverine ports of those areas of the Republic of Bosnia and Herzegovina under the control of Bosnian Serb forces. Finally, any transaction by any United States person that evades or avoids, or has the purpose of evading or avoiding, or attempts to violate any of the prohibitions set forth in the order is prohibited. Executive order No. 12934 became effective at 11:59 p.m., e.d.t., on October 25, 1994.

2. The declaration of the national emergency on May 30, 1992, was made pursuant to the authority vested in the President by the Constitution and laws of the United States, including the International Emergency Economic Powers Act (50 U.S.C. 1701 *et seq.*), the National Emergencies Act (50 U.S.C. 1601 *et seq.*), and section 301 of title 3 of the United States Code. The emergency declaration was reported to the Congress on May 30, 1992, pursuant to section 204(b) of the International Emergency Economic Powers Act (50 U.S.C. 1703(b)) and the expansion of that national emergency under the same authorities was reported to the Congress on October 25, 1994. The additional sanctions set forth in related Executive orders were imposed pursuant to the authority vested in the President by the Constitution and laws of the United States, including the statutes cited above, section 1114 of the Federal Aviation Act (49 U.S.C. App. 1514), and section 5 of the United Nations Participation Act (22 U.S.C. 287c).

3. Effective June 30, 1995, the Federal Republic of Yugoslavia (Serbia and Montenegro) Sanctions Regulations, 31 C.F.R. Part 585 (the "Regulations"), were amended to implement Executive Order No. 12934 (60 *FR* 34144, June 30, 1995). The name of the Regulations was changed to reflect the expansion of the national emergency to the Bosnian Serbs, and now reads "Federal Republic of Yugoslavia (Serbia & Montenegro) and Bosnian Serb-Controlled Areas of the Republic of Bosnia and Herzegovina Sanctions Regulations." A copy of the amended Regulations is attached.

Treasury's blocking authority as applied to FRY (S&M) subsidiaries and vessels in the United States has been challenged in court. In *Milena Ship Management Company, Ltd. v. Newcomb.*, 804 F. Supp. 846, 855, and 859 (E.D.L.A. 1992) *aff'd*, 995 F. 2d 620 (5th Cir. 1993), *cert. denied*, 114 S. Ct. 877 (1994), involving five ships owned or controlled by FRY (S&M) entities blocked in various U.S. ports, the blocking authority as applied to these vessels was upheld. In *IPT Company, Inc. v. United States Department of the Treasury,* No. 92 CIV 5542 (S.D.N.Y. 1994), the district court also upheld the blocking authority as applied to the property of a Yugoslav subsidiary located in the United States, and the case was subsequently settled.

4. Over the past 6 months, the Departments of State and Treasury have worked closely with European Union (the "EU") member states and other U.N. member nations to coordinate implementation of the U.N. sanctions against the FRY (S&M). This has included continued deployment of Organization for Security and Cooperation in Europe (OSCE) sanctions assistance missions (SAMs) to Albania, Bulgaria, Croatia, the Former Yugoslav Republic of Macedonia, Hungary, Romania, and Ukraine to assist in monitoring land and Danube River traffic; support for the International Conference on the Former Yugoslavia (ICFY) monitoring missions along the Serbia-Montenegro-Bosnia border; bilateral contacts between the United States and other countries for the purpose of tightening financial and trade restrictions on the FRY (S&M); and ongoing multilateral meetings by financial sanctions enforcement authorities from various countries to coordinate enforcement efforts and to exchange technical information.

5. In accordance with licensing policy and the Regulations, the Office of Foreign Assets Control (FAC) has exercised its authority to license certain specific transactions with respect to the FRY (S&M), which are consistent with U.S. foreign policy and the Security Council sanctions. During the reporting period, FAC has issued 90 specific licenses regarding transactions pertaining to the FRY (S&M) or assets it owns or controls, bringing the total specific licenses issued as of October 13, 1995, to 1,020. Specific licenses have been issued: (1) for payment to U.S. or third country secured creditors, under certain narrowly defined circumstances, for preembargo import and export transactions; (2) for legal representation or advice to the Government of the FRY (S&M) or FRY (S&M)-located or controlled entities; (3) for the liquidation or protection of tangible assets of subsidiaries of FRY (S&M)-located or controlled firms located in the United States; (4) for limited transactions related to FRY (S&M) diplomatic representation

in Washington and New York; (5) for patent, trademark, and copyright protection in the FRY (S&M) not involving payment to the FRY (S&M) Government; (6) for certain communications, news media, and travel-related transactions; (7) for the payment of crews' wages, vessel maintenance, and emergency supplies for FRY (S&M)-controlled ships blocked in United States; (8) for the removal from the FRY (S&M), or protection within the FRY (S&M), of certain property owned and controlled by U.S. entities; (9) to assist the United Nations in its relief operations and the activities of the UNPROFOR; and (10) for payment from funds outside the United States where a third country has licensed the transaction in accordance with U.N. sanctions. Pursuant to U.S. regulations implementing UNSC Resolutions, specific licenses have also been issued to authorize exportation of food, medicine, and supplies intended for humanitarian purposes in the FRY (S&M).

During the period, FAC addressed the status of the unallocated debt of the former Yugoslavia by authorizing nonblocked U.S. creditors under the New Financing Agreement for Yugoslavia (Blocked Debt) to exchange a portion of the Blocked Debt for new debt (bonds) issued by the Republic of Slovenia. The completion of this exchange will mark the transfer to Slovenia of sole liability for a portion of the face value of the $4.2 billion unallocated debt of the FRY (S&M) for which Slovenia, prior to the authorized exchange, was jointly and severally liable. The exchange will relieve Slovenia of the joint and several liability for the remaining unallocated FRY (S&M) debt and pave the way for its entry into international capital markets.

During the past 6 months, FAC has continued to oversee the liquidation of tangible assets of the 15 U.S. subsidiaries of entities organized in the FRY (S&M). Subsequent to the issuance of Executive Order No. 12846, all operating licenses issued for these U.S.-located Serbian or Montenegrin subsidiaries or joint ventures were revoked, and the net proceeds of the liquidation of their assets placed in blocked accounts.

In order to reduce the drain on blocked assets caused by continuing to rent commercial space, FAC arranged to have the blocked personalty, files, and records of the two Serbian banking institutions in New York moved to secure storage. The personalty is being liquidated, with the net proceeds placed in blocked accounts.

Following the sale of the M/V Kapetan Martinovic in January 1995, five Yugoslav-owned vessels remain blocked in the United States. Approval of the UNSC's Serbian Sanctions Committee was sought and obtained for the sale of the M/V Kapetan Martinovic (and the M/V Bor, which was sold in June 1994).

With the FAC-licensed sales of the M/V Kapetan Martinovic and the M/V Bor, those vessels were removed from the list of blocked FRY (S&M) entities and merchant vessels maintained by FAC. As of October 12, 1995, five additional vessels have been removed from the list of blocked FRY (S&M) entities and merchant vessels maintained by FAC as a result of sales conditions that effectively extinguished any FRY (S&M) interest: the M/V Blue Star, M/V Budva, M/V Bulk Star, M/V Hanuman, and M/V Sumadija. The new owners of several other formerly Yugoslav-owned vessels, which have been sold in other countries, have petitioned FAC to remove those vessels from the list.

During the past 6 months, U.S. financial institutions have continued to block funds transfers in which there is a possible interest of the Government of the FRY (S&M) or an entity or undertaking located in or controlled from the FRY (S&M), and to stop prohibited transfers to persons in the FRY (S&M). The value of transfers blocked has amounted to $137.5 million since the issuance of Executive Order No. 12808, including some $13.9 million during the past 6 months.

To ensure compliance with the terms of the licenses that have been issued under the program, stringent reporting requirements are imposed. More than 318 submissions have been reviewed by FAC since the last report, and more than 130 compliance cases are currently open.

6. Since the issuance of Executive Order No. 12810, FAC has worked closely with the U.S. Customs Service to ensure both that prohibited imports and exports (including those in which the Government of the FRY (S&M) or Bosnian Serb authorities have an interest) are identified and interdicted, and that permitted imports and exports move to their intended destination without undue delay. Violations and suspected violations of the embargo are being investigated and appropriate enforcement actions are being taken. Numerous investigations carried over from the prior reporting period are continuing. Since the last report, FAC has collected 10 civil penalties totaling more than $27,000. Of these, five were paid by U.S. financial institutions for violative funds transfers involving the Government of the FRY (S&M), persons in the FRY (S&M), or entities located or organized in or controlled from the FRY (S&M). One U.S. company and one air carrier have also paid penalties related to unlicensed payments to the Government of the FRY (S&M) or other violations of the Regulations. Two companies and one law firm have also remitted penalties for their failure to follow the conditions of FAC licenses.

7. The expenses incurred by the Federal Government in the 6-month period from May 30, 1995, through November 29, 1995, that are directly attributable to the declaration of a national emergency with respect to the FRY (S&M) and the Bosnian Serb forces and authorities are estimated at about $3.5 million, most of which represent wage and salary costs for Federal personnel. Personnel costs were largely centered in the Department of the Treasury (particularly in FAC and its Chief Counsel's Office, and the U.S. Customs Service), the Department of State, the National Security Council, the U.S. Coast Guard, and the Department of Commerce.

8. The actions and policies of the Government of the FRY (S&M), in its involvement in and support for groups attempting to seize and hold territory in the Republics of Croatia and Bosnia and Herzegovina by force and violence, and the actions and policies of the Bosnian Serb forces and the authorities in the areas of Bosnia and Herzegovina under their control, continue to pose an unusual and extraordinary threat to the national security, foreign policy, and economy of the United States. The United States remains committed to a multilateral resolution of the conflict through implementation of the United Nations Security Council resolutions.

I shall continue to exercise the powers at my disposal to apply economic sanctions against the FRY (S&M) and the Bosnian Serb forces, civil authorities, and entities, as long as these measures are appropriate, and will continue to report periodically to the Congress on significant developments pursuant to 50 U.S.C. 1703(c).

WILLIAM J. CLINTON

The White House,
December 8, 1995.

The President's Radio Address
December 9, 1995

Good morning. As you all know, we're engaged in a great debate over how best to balance the budget. We must balance the budget. Since I became President, we have cut the terrible deficit we inherited nearly in half. Now we must finish the job.

But let's remember why we want a balanced budget: to strengthen our economy and lift the burden of debt from future generations. To do that, we have to balance the budget in the way that reflects our most fundamental values: increasing opportunity; asking all to assume responsibility; strengthening our families and the economy; recognizing the duty we owe to each other, to our parents, our children, and those who need and deserve our help.

This past week, I took two steps to advance these values. First, I vetoed the Republican budget plan that was sent to me by Congress. I did it because that budget violates our values and would have hurt our economy. I did it because in so doing I vetoed the most massive cuts in Medicare and Medicaid in history, a tax increase on working people, and deep, deep cuts in education and the environment. This effort to balance the budget through wrong-headed cuts and misplaced priorities is now over. Then, I sent to the Congress a plan to balance the budget in 7 years without devastating cuts in these areas. My 7-year balanced budget plan reflects our values and protects our investments in the future. It reflects a good-faith effort to find common ground on the budget. At stake is far more than just numbers and abstract programs and proposals, and far more than the normal political debates in Washington. This debate is about people: the lives they lead, the hopes they have, the desires they have for a better life.

Nowhere is this choice clearer than in our different approaches to Medicaid. For three decades, the Medicaid program has meant that if your child was disabled in an accident or your husband got Alzheimer's or your parent needed nursing home care, you would get the help you need. The Republican budget would cut Medicaid by $163 billion. It would repeal the guarantee of health care for poor children, people with disabilities, pregnant women, and older Americans. Now, this repeal was not an afterthought or an unintended consequence. The congressional Republican majority is actually insisting on it. What would this mean?

Well, in 2002 alone, the year the budget is supposed to be balanced, the Republican budget could deny quality health coverage to nearly 8 million people, deny meaningful health care to over a million people with disabilities, even to 150,000 veterans and to tens of thousands of people with AIDS, many of whom are able to keep working or who can get the help they need without their families being forced into poverty because of the assistance they get from Medicaid.

Today, a poor child who gets sick has access to a family doctor. Under this bill, nearly 4 million poor children could be denied quality medical care. If they got sick, they'd have to pray for charity care at a crowded hospital emergency room. Today, pregnant women know they can get prenatal care for their sake and the sake of their unborn children. But under the Republican plan, hundreds of thousands of pregnant women could be denied regular checkups and other basic services that could lead to an increase in infant mortality or children born with irreversible problems.

Today, elderly women who have devoted themselves to their families know they can count on medical care, even if they don't have much money. But under the Republican plan, as many a 330,000 older Americans could be denied nursing home care.

Today, middle class parents know that in the awful event their child is disabled in an accident and their savings are gone, they'll get help to keep the child at home. Under the Republican plan, hundreds of thousands of disabled children could lose help for home care.

Earlier this week, I had the pleasure of meeting the Striggles family from Forestville, Maryland. Franklin Striggles works hard as a security guard. He and his wife, Denise, have health insurance from his job. But it doesn't begin to pay the cost of caring for their son, Angelo, an energetic 7-year-old who has spina bifida and who's now confined to a wheelchair. That's where Medicaid comes in. With Medicaid, this working family can keep a job, raise and educate their other children, and give little Angelo good care. To see Angelo and his family, it's clear how much love and learning he gets from living at home with his brother and sister. It pains me to think that if the Striggles family lost Medicaid coverage, Angelo could be torn from his family, even forced to be placed in a State institution.

If the Republican cuts in Medicaid take effect, the blunt reality is that as many as 4 million children will simply be denied needed medical care. They'll either be turned away from medical facilities, denied preventive care, or be turned out too soon. That is unacceptable in a country that cares about its children. And I will not permit it to happen.

Yes, the deficit is a burden on future generations, but so is the neglect of our children. And we do not have to sacrifice our children to balance the budget. That's why I vetoed these cuts last week. Now, some Republicans continue to insist on unconscionable cuts in health care for our children as part of a balanced budget. So I'll say once more: If necessary, I'll veto these deep cuts in health care for children again and again and again. I'll do it because they are not

necessary to balance the budget. And they, too, will place an awful burden on future generations.

My 7-year balanced budget plan trims Medicaid and keeps costs down. It cuts Federal spending, lets States be more efficient, targets the money more wisely. But it doesn't end the guarantee of health care for millions of Americans who depend upon it now.

We expect every family to pay its bills and to care for its children. Well, our country can do the same. We don't have to hurt our children to balance the budget.

It's time for men and women of both parties to put aside their narrow interests and extreme ideology and together pursue the national interest. I have reached out to bridge the differences between us so that our country can move forward. If we'll all just work together and keep our eye on the future, we can get this job done.

Thank you for listening.

NOTE: The address was recorded at 5:57 p.m. on December 8 in the Oval Office at the White House for broadcast at 10:06 a.m. on December 9.

Interview With Quinn Buckner of CBS Sports in Fayetteville, Arkansas
December 9, 1995

Mr. Buckner. I'm here with the First Fan. All right, now you're undefeated. Your team is now 33–24. If you had a chance to write out a play, what would you write for Nolan Richards?

The President. I just think they need a chance to get a better shot. Cincinnati is a great defensive team. Looking at these games they're winning and the teams they're beating at very low scores, and our guys are great athletes, but they're freshmen. They're junior college transfers. They're just learning to play together. They have great potential, but Cincinnati is a great defensive team. We've got to figure out a way

to break their defense to get good shots, and then they'll win the game.

Mr. Buckner. Are you having much fun doing this? I mean, how often do you get to watch the Razorbacks?

The President. Wherever they're on television I try to watch them, and then if I'm working at night, I try to have somebody film it so I can watch it later. I try to get down here to see a couple of games a year, and then if they get in the NCAA, of course, I try to see them a time or two.

NOTE: The interview began at 1:10 p.m. at Bud Walton Arena.

Remarks at a Dinner Honoring Senator David Pryor in Little Rock, Arkansas
December 9, 1995

Thank you very much, Jimmie Lou. I will treasure this always. I wish you could have gotten me a ballot of a precinct that I carried. [*Laughter*] You know, I ran in Sebastian County a zillion times, and I started in 1974. It took me until 1990, where I finally carried it. [*Laughter*] But thanks to some of you in this room, it finally happened. I thank you very much. I thank you, Jimmie Lou Fisher, for being my dear friend and for introducing me in October of 1991 on the steps of the Old State Capitol. You seem to bring good luck to me and to everyone else whom you touch.

I thank Maurice Mitchell and Skip Rutherford and everyone else who had anything to do with this dinner tonight. Chairman Gibson; my dear friend Mack McLarty, who came out with me tonight and who has done a wonderful job on all of our behalfs in Washington. I'm so grateful to him for being there with me these last 3 years. To Congresswoman Blanche Lambert Lincoln; if there is a living soul in this country who can change a deer season, it's her. [*Laughter*] I've gotten to where when she starts coming at me, I just say yes before she ever says anything. It saves a lot of time and a lot of energy, always the same result. [*Laughter*]

Senator Bumpers, you do not have to get off the back door tomorrow. [*Laughter*] But however, after a few of those jokes tonight, I hope you won't mind if I ask you to board by the back door. [*Laughter*]

I want to say that I am profoundly grateful to Dale Bumpers for what he's done for our State and what he's done for our Nation and for the kind of voice that he's been in the United States Senate for all of these 18 years or 22 years or however long he's been there— since—it seemed like before I could vote— [*laughter*]—but never more than the last 2 years when he has found that soaring eloquence in the service of views that seemed to be fading from fashion until the last few months. And it's because people like Dale Bumpers speak up in the lean times as well as the good ones that this country stays on the path to progress and keeps its common sense about it, and I'm very grateful to him, and all of you should be as well.

So, Governor Tucker, let me say I hope you pass your bond issue, and I hope you pass a constitution. He was too gracious to say it, but when he was reeling off all of the names of the Governors that tried to get a new constitution, he could have said, had he been less gracious, that we all failed. [*Laughter*] But that doesn't mean we don't need one. And I am especially grateful to you for taking on a lot of tough issues that are often thankless because you know that 10 or 20 or 30 years from now, if we do these things, people will look back and say, "Thank you very much. It might not have been popular at the time and it certainly wasn't easy at the time, but it was the right thing to do." And that's the kind of Governor you've been, and I am very grateful to you for it.

To Senator Pryor and Barbara and all of the Pryor family, let me say I am very honored to be here tonight. Hillary wishes she could be here. She called David; they had a long conversation this morning. Neither one of them would tell me everything they discussed. But she loves you very much, as you know, and wishes that she could be here with you. But our daughter is engaged in an activity tonight that required her presence in Washington, and I know you understand that. But she and I feel a special debt to you and a special bond.

Ladies and gentlemen, I've got to be honest with you: I'm kind of like Dale. This is a night I hoped would never come. I'm glad you showed up, and I thank you for your devotion to the Democratic Party and to Dale Bumpers and to Jim Guy Tucker and to our Congressman and our Congresswoman and especially to Senator Pryor. But I hoped that this night would never come.

You know how there are just things in life you assume would go on forever? I just assumed David Pryor's career in the Senate would go on forever. I thought long after I retired from the White House I would be back here with you, you know, wearing his buttons and having his bumper sticker on my car. [*Laughter*] I figured I would be writing him someday, asking him to help me with my Social Security check. I just thought it would go on forever. [*Laughter*]

So today my whole life has been parading before me. I flew into Fayetteville and went to the ballgame, and then I came down here, and I got to see the Ozarks, and I got to see the river valley that I love so well, and I got to relive my whole life with David Pryor. The first time I ever met David Pryor, I remember it just like it was yesterday, he was walking down the street in some small town in south Arkansas, asking people to vote for him for Congress. And I was not quite 20 years old. And I thought he was really something. It turned out I was right; he was really something.

I remember once when I was a senior in college, and he and Barbara were standing outside a restaurant in Washington, DC, one night, and I was just walking down the street and I ran into them. And he was a Congressman, and I was a college student. They invited me in to sit down and have a bite with them and just talk. And I couldn't believe it. There was nothing in it for them, and it was a night they could be alone and away from politics and away from the pressures of the job. It probably didn't mean much to him, but I've never forgotten it after all of these years.

I remember when he suffered the only defeat he ever endured in 1972, the incredible dignity and grace and generosity with which he bore it. It was a lesson that I had occasion to apply later on—[*laughter*]—more than once, I might add, but one I never forgot.

I remember when he ran for Governor in 1974, as Jimmie Lou said when I ran for Congress, what a tough time it was, how hard it was to keep people focused on the fundamental goodness of our way of doing public business and the need to keep pushing forward because we had such a terrible recession. I remember sitting in the back of the Governor's limousine in 1978, when I was attorney general and he was Governor, and he told me he was going to run for Senator, and he suggested I might run for Governor.

And he said—I never will forget this—he said, "You know, as young as you are, you might even make a career of it. You might survive 10 or 12 years." [*Laughter*] Well, I wanted to be Governor, but I thought he had a screw loose. It turned out he was right about that. That race in 1978 gave him a chance to be

a Senator, gave Jim Guy Tucker a chance to be a Governor and, I might add, a great Governor. It gave Ray Thornton a chance to be the president of both of our great, big universities and go on to—come back to Congress and help us all stand against the floodtide up there. It was an interesting year.

One of my great joys all during the decade of the 1980's was going to these events that David and Dale and I used to go to and tell all of our bad jokes over and over again, to see whether we could still get a laugh, knowing all of the time that we were able to do something here, to keep a certain spirit, a certain sense of togetherness, a certain sense of being willing to make a future that a lot of our fellow Americans were having a hard time holding on to—thanks in no small measure to David Pryor.

But the thing I remember most vividly tonight was in the cold, cold winter of 1991 and 1992 in New Hampshire, when our passion for a new future ran into the politics of personal destruction, and everybody said our campaign was over. David Pryor and Barbara Pryor were there day-in and day-out, walking in the snow, knocking on the doors, talking to people about what this country could be and what it ought to be and what kind of direction we ought to have in Washington. And as long as I live, I will never forget. They did not have to be there, but they were, and it made all the difference.

You know, our whole country's existence has basically had three great strands: our love of liberty, our belief in progress, and our struggle to find common ground amid all of our differences. I can think of no public official in my lifetime I have ever met from any place who better embodied all three of those things and who always knew that unless we could find common ground through decency and standing up for the values that made this country great, it would in the end not be possible to preserve progress or even liberty.

In Washington today we are having the debate of the century about what kind of people we are and what kind of future we're going to have, what our obligations to each other are, and whether we really believe in opportunity for all and responsibility from all, whether we really believe we have an obligation to help families stay together and to take care of our parents when they're sick and our children when they're growing up, whether we really believe that we are, as our motto says, from many one.

David Pryor is the embodiment of what I want our country to keep at and to become and to do. Senator Bumpers quoted de Tocqueville. He said a long time ago that this is a great country. "America is great," he said, "because America is good. And if America ever ceases to be good, she will no longer be great." David Pryor has been a great public servant because he is fundamentally good.

William Wordsworth said the last best hope of a good man's life are the little, unremembered acts of kindness and love. David Pryor, over more than 30 years, every person in this room and every person in our State has been embraced by your kindness and love, and we thank you.

NOTE: The President spoke at 8:25 p.m. in Governor's Hall II at the Statehouse Convention Center. In his remarks, he referred to Jimmie Lou Fisher, Arkansas State treasurer; Maurice Mitchell, attorney in Little Rock; Skip Rutherford, former State Democratic chair; and Bynum Gibson, State Democratic chair.

Teleconference Remarks to the Florida State Democratic Convention
December 10, 1995

The President. Thank you. Thank you for that warm and rousing welcome. I've enjoyed listening through my earphone here to what's going on down there. I see that Senator Dodd has almost lost his voice in the enthusiasm and so has your State party chair, Terry Brady. But I want to thank both of them for their leadership and for what they have done and for stirring everybody up and getting you excited over the election we're about to have and the stakes there.

I want to say hello to attorney general Bob Butterworth. I'd also like to send kind greetings to all of my friends down there, especially to Governor Chiles, Lieutenant Governor MacKay, Senator Bob Graham.

I am very pleased to be able to speak with you today at this very important convention. As we move into the Presidential campaign season, you know, I can't help but recall that it was almost 4 years ago to the day that Florida and the Florida Democrats, at this meeting, put our campaign on the map when you helped me to win a decisive straw poll victory on December 15th, 1991. I remember that day so well, for that victory convinced me that the American people were serious about wanting new leadership in Washington and a new direction for our country.

You know, I have many things I want to say, but the most important thing I can do is to say a simple thank you. Thank you for helping me and Al Gore to the White House, to give us a chance to advance the economy and to honor the values that are critical to moving our country forward into the 21st century. So, even though we have to talk a lot today about the future, let me say one more time: Thank you for your faith in me and in Vice President Gore; thank you for your support for these past 3 years.

Today, my fellow Americans, I come to you with a simple and straightforward message. We live in a great country in a time of very great change. We are moving forward from the industrial age to an age of technology. We are moving away from the cold-war era into the era of the global village. We know that. I ran for President to change things in this country, to take advantage of this time of absolutely enormous, enormous possibility so that we could make the most of the lives of every American and give all Americans back their future and so that we would make sure that our country would still be able to lead the world toward peace and freedom and prosperity. We have done that.

Our country is in better shape today than it was 3 years ago. Our economy is stronger, we are coming back to our basic values, and we are leading the world toward peace. But to continue to be true to those values, we have to have a clear vision of the future, and we have to stick with it. You know that.

When I ran for President in 1992, I was committed to restoring the American dream for all our people and to make absolutely sure that America would go into the next century still the most powerful country in the world, the greatest force for peace and freedom and prosperity the world had ever known. I said we would do it by having an economic policy that produced jobs and growth, that expanded the middle class and shrinks the under class by giving us a modern Government that is smaller and less bureaucratic and more entrepreneurial, and most important of all, by being true to old-fashioned American values at a new time: responsibility from all and opportunity for all; the value of work; the understanding that we have to help families stay strong and stick together; and a sense of community that we're all stronger when we work together and we're all in this fight to the future together; also, the strong sense that we do have obligations to our parents, to our children, to one another, and to those who, through no fault of their own, need some help to make the most of their own lives. Let me say again: This country is in better shape than it was 3 years ago. We still have challenges, and we have to keep going in the right direction. But America is on the move.

We've reduced the deficit in 3 consecutive years of this administration. It's now been cut in half. Over 7 years, that works out to about $15,000 of reduced Federal debt for every family of four in Florida. In the past 3 years, we've also seen more than 7½ million new jobs created, more than 590,000 of them right there in Florida. We've got a record number of new businesses, 2½ million more homeowners. Homebuilding in the State of Florida has increased 6 percent a year after dropping 4 percent a year during the previous 12 years.

And America is safer and stronger today than we were 3 years ago. For the very first time since the dawn of the nuclear age, there is not a single Russian missile pointed at an American child. And American leadership is opening the door to peace and reconciliation all over the world, from Northern Ireland to the Middle East to Haiti and to Bosnia.

The United States is leading the world toward a more peaceful future. We've got a chance to end the misery in Bosnia for good. It was our diplomacy, backed by NATO's resolve, that brought the leaders of the Balkans to the peace table in Dayton, OH. And now they have made a commitment to peace.

Our responsibility truly begins now. If we walk away from their request to us to help them preserve their peace, our allies will do the same,

and the peace will fail. The slaughter will begin again, and that conflict could spread like poison throughout the region, drawing us in, in much greater risk to our own soldiers. NATO, the alliance of democracies that has preserved our security for half a century by working with our strong European allies, would be shaken to its core if we walked away from their request to help preserve the peace in Bosnia. And American leadership, not only in Europe but all around this world, will pay a terrible, terrible price. For all of those reasons, we must help to preserve the peace.

This Bosnian peace mission is clearly defined. It has realistic goals to be reached in a definite period of time. Our force will be strong, and they will have strong rules of engagement so that they can protect themselves and pursue the mission. I am convinced that the risks to our troops have been minimized to the maximum extent possible. After all, we're not going to fight a war but to wage a peace. We do it for the people of Bosnia, for the stability of Europe, for American leadership, and for the values we hold dear.

We also have a special interest in promoting peace and democracy in two nations just off your shore, in Haiti and in Cuba. Just over one year ago, our diplomacy, backed by military muscle, forced a brutal military regime in Haiti to surrender its power. We gave democracy there another chance. You know better than people in any other State that this has been good for America and good for Haiti. The tide of refugees from Haiti, which stood at about 16,000 in the months prior to the intervention, has been dramatically reduced. The people of Haiti, with help from the international community, are slowly building a democracy and a working economy. And President Aristide, as he said he would, has been a force for reconciliation.

Now, all of this takes time, and there may be setbacks along the way. But just a week from now, Haiti will hold Presidential elections which will freely transfer power from one democratically elected President to another for the very first time in the nation's history. This is an extraordinary achievement. America, and particularly Floridians, where so many Haitians live, should be proud that we helped to restore democracy to Haiti.

Cuba, of course, is still a different story. It's now the only country in our hemisphere which continues to resist the powerful trend toward democracy. Our administration is working to encourage its peaceful transition to a free and open society. We will continue to do everything we can to promote peaceful change, protect human rights, and move Cuba into the camp of democracy.

With all of the progress we've made, both here at home and abroad, the thing that I am most proud of, I think, is the tangible evidence that our country is coming back together around our core values. Because we not only have economic progress, we not only have the lowest rates of unemployment and inflation in 27 years, but in almost every State in America and almost every major community, the crime rate is down, the murder rate is down, the food stamp rolls are down, the welfare rolls are down. For 2 years, the teen pregnancy rate has dropped, and the poverty rate is down. We are coming back together, and we're moving forward together.

And as you know, I believe we can only move forward if we do it together. We're moving in the right direction, but now we have to make some decisions that will keep us on that track. That really is what this big budget debate in Washington is all about. It isn't just about dollars and cents, it goes to the heart of who we are as a people, what we believe, what we stand for, what kind of America we want our children and grandchildren to inherit in the 21st century.

Last Wednesday, using the pen that was used to sign Medicare and Medicaid into law in 1965, I vetoed the Republican budget. I did it to preserve our commitment to our parents, to protect opportunity for our children, to defend our public health and environment, and to stop a tax increase that undercuts the value of work for the hardest pressed working families and their children in this country. The very next day, I gave Congress a budget that does balance in 7 years without their devastating cuts in Medicare and Medicaid, in education and the environment, and one that does not raise taxes on working families.

Let me tell you again why I vetoed their budget. Americans have always believed we owe a duty to our parents. The Republican budget that I vetoed would turn Medicare into a second-class system. The Medicare system that has served older Americans so well for 30 years would be over, and I'm not going to let that happen.

My 7-year balanced budget secures the Medicare Trust Fund into the future without imposing new costs on hard-pressed seniors. And it preserves Medicaid's guarantee of quality health care for poor children, pregnant women, disabled Americans, and older Americans.

There are many differences between the Republican budget that I vetoed and the one I presented last week. But perhaps the starkest one of all is the different treatment of Medicaid. As I told Governor Chiles in a White House meeting with Governors on Friday, the Republican budget would be a disaster for States like Florida that depend on Medicaid. Medicaid is a guarantee not only to seniors who might need nursing home care, it's also a guarantee to their families against having their financial security threatened if an older parent falls seriously ill. This Republican plan would change all that. Families tomorrow could find themselves forced to pay large sums for quality nursing home care that Medicaid guarantees today. It would force those working families to choose between quality nursing home care for their parents and quality education and health care for their own children. We shouldn't force our working families to have to make that type of choice.

Now, I want to work with the Republican Congress. I want to work to get a balanced budget. But I will not—I will not permit the repeal of guaranteed medical coverage for senior citizens, for disabled people, for poor children, for pregnant women, for people with AIDS. That would violate our values. It would undermine our families and, therefore, even weaken our economy. And what's more, it's not necessary. So if they continue to make this a part of their budget, I'll veto it again and again and again.

My fellow Democrats, we're going to win this battle; we have to. Nothing less than the heart and soul of our Nation are at stake. That's why I'm asking for your continued support now more than ever. All of us who share the same values, whether we're Democrats, Republicans, or independents, all of us who share the same vision for our country and our future, we have got to stand together now for the American people. We need to stand together on behalf of the elderly, the disabled, the pregnant women, and poor children to protect Medicare and Medicaid. We need to stand together on behalf of the millions and millions of young people in this country who would be denied the chance for a better education if the Republicans are successful in slashing Head Start, slashing the college loan options, slashing the college scholarships.

We need to stand together to reward hardworking families by providing the child care mothers need to move from welfare to work and by refusing to raise taxes on 8 million working families. We have to build on the successes of the last 3 years. But we must not turn back the clock.

Some Republicans in Congress have made clear their strategy of trying to force through harmful health care, education, and environmental cuts, that would be very damaging to Florida, by threatening to shut our Government down once again. They did it a month ago, but the threat failed.

Now, as the holidays approach, I sincerely hope that there will be a spirit in the Congress that will make it possible for us to bring good faith to our negotiations. We are now engaged in negotiations on how best to balance the budget consistent with our values. And I proposed the 7-year balanced budget and even proposed a specific compromise so that we could finish our work on this year's budget and keep the Government open.

We have serious differences on Medicare, Medicaid, education, and the environment, on tax fairness and also on research and technology that I know are critical to our future. But we ought to be able to agree on this: Nobody, nobody, should threaten to shut the Government down right before Christmas.

Let me close by reminding all of you how far we've come and what I hope you will do in the year ahead. Remind your fellow citizens in Florida that America is in better shape than we were 3 years ago and Florida is in better shape than it was 3 years ago. We do have a 27-year low in the combined rates of unemployment and inflation. We do have progress in crime and welfare reform, in reducing many of the social problems that still continue to plague us. We do have progress in making the world a more peaceful place.

And Florida has received the attention it deserved from our administration. The Southern Command is moving to Florida. The Summit of the Americas was held in Florida. The defense budgets of the country have been kept strong in a way that has preserved the military presence in Florida that will help us to be secure in the future. Our trade policies, our technology policies have helped Florida.

But if you look to the future and you think of America and what you want it to be like 10, 20, 30 years from now, you know we still have a long way to go. The answer is to redouble our efforts in the direction we are heading, not to derail this train of America's progress. We have to have a vision, and we have to have policies that prepare our children for the vast challenges and opportunities of the 21st century; vision and policy that promote lifelong learning so our workers can meet the demands of change; a vision and a policy that empowers communities to solve their own problems, that ensures the safety of our citizens on our streets, in our schools, and in our homes, that helps us to come together as a country and as one big American community. That's the vision we all share for America.

America is now in the best position to lead the world into the 21st century as well. And you know, with our common security threats, of the proliferation of dangerous nuclear, chemical and biological weapons, with the problems we have with terrorism and drug-trafficking and organized crime, you know we have to put our values into action around the world and come together in that same spirit.

I want you to promise yourself that when you walk out of this room today and for the next year, you are going to walk up to your fellow Americans in every possible venue, and talk about these fundamental values, these fundamental issues, this shared vision that you and I have for our future and for our children. If we will do that, if we will bring the same enthusiasm I heard from you today into our daily lives, into our daily contacts with the kind of people who never have the opportunity to be in a convention hall, we will prevail. But far, far more important, America will have the future that our children deserve.

Thank you, and God bless you all.

Audience members. Four more years! Four more years! Four more years!

[At this point, the moderator thanked the President and introduced a convention participant who asked how proposed budget cuts would affect Medicare and Medicaid.]

The President. Well, first of all, I thank you for the way you asked the question, because I do think a lot of Americans think that it's just bickering and may be just another political fight. But that isn't right.

There is an argument in Washington over the fundamental responsibility of our National Government in the area of health care and whether we do have an obligation to preserve Medicare as it has worked for our seniors for the last 30 years and to preserve, through the Medicaid program, a guarantee of health care for the elderly, for the disabled, for poor children and pregnant women.

Now, let's talk about the facts on Medicare. On Medicare, we do have to find a way to strengthen the Medicare Trust Fund. I've been saying that for sometime now. But the Republican cuts in Medicare are more than twice as great as are necessary to secure the Medicare Trust Fund well into the next century.

What they're doing is a number of things. Let me try to be as specific as I can so you'll understand. They say they want to encourage more seniors to take their Medicare benefits in managed care plans. I'm all for giving people the incentive to do that. But I am against forcing people into managed care plans.

If you look at their budget, what they do is, they charge elderly people much more, not just in premiums but in copays and deductibles, to stay in Medicare. And they fund the traditional Medicare program at such a lower level that they're going to wind up trying to force seniors to pay more for less medical care in managed care plans. And the way the plan is now drafted, it is actually toughest on the oldest, the poorest, and the sickest seniors in the country. It is unconscionable, and it is wrong.

If you look at the Medicaid program, what they do is to cut the Medicaid program so much and to put the States under so much pressure, especially a State like Florida, that we think it is clear that millions of people will lose Medicaid coverage, hundreds of thousands of seniors who now get Medicaid help to stay in nursing homes would be denied it, millions of poor children will lose their coverage, and we will have, in a State like Florida especially, where you have a lot of poor children needing Medicaid coverage and a lot of seniors who are entitled to it, an unbearable burden placed on the States and a lot of human suffering. And it is unnecessary to balance the budget.

So I guess the facts in short are, number one, we need to save the Medicare Trust Fund, but they're doing too much and it's going to

hurt too much and it's going to really turn Medicare as we know it into a second-class system. Number two, the Medicaid program would be devastated. And number three, and this is the most important thing of all, it is not necessary to do this to balance the budget.

I just want to remind the Democrats there that we cut the deficit in half in 3 years with only Democratic votes. We didn't get a single, solitary Republican vote in the Congress to do it. When we passed our program in 1993, they said it wouldn't reduce the deficit; they said it would bring on a recession. And they were wrong. They were wrong. The Republicans say they're against big Government. I want to remind you of something else. Since I've been in office, we're reduced the size of the Federal Government by 200,000. It's now the smallest it's been since John Kennedy was President, and as a percentage of our civilian work force, it's the smallest it's been since 1933. The Democrats did that. We did it by treating our Federal employees humanely, giving them good retirement and severance packages. We did it by increasing the productivity of the fine Federal employees that are left. We reduced the burden of big Government. We're eliminating 16,000 pages of Federal regulation. Those were Democratic reforms.

This is not about the problems of big Government. They want to strip the National Government of its ability to protect and advance the interests of the elderly and the children and the disabled people of this country. That is what is going on here.

[*Another participant asked what the President had done to give children a better education and a brighter future.*]

The President. To answer your question in the way you posed it, the most important thing we have done is to give this country a comprehensive education policy focused not only on greater educational opportunities but on higher standards and higher quality education. And I'd like to give you some specific examples.

We have increased the number of our young people in Head Start programs by tens of thousands. For the public schools, we have written into law the national education goals and said to every State: We will give you extra help if you will commit to try to reach these goals and if you will commit to a system which holds you accountable so that we can see whether you're making progress toward reaching these goals. We will give you extra help, and we will give special help to districts that are poor or that have a lot of poor children, but we all have to have the same high standards and we all have to be willing to be held accountable.

For young people who aren't going to college, we have launched a national school-to-work program to help every State give young people good training so they can get good jobs even if they don't have 4-year college degrees. Then, for young people who are going to college, we've launched a new direct student loan program that has lower cost college loans available to more kids with better terms of repayment.

One of the most successful things we've done—I've talked about it a lot in Florida— we have dramatically increased the number of student loans and the possibility of earning money through college through our national service program, AmeriCorps. Every single one of those things is at risk in the Republican budget, and I am fighting for every single one of them.

But we have a comprehensive education strategy based on national standards and grassroots reforms and more opportunity. That is what I think we ought to be pushing for. No company in the world and no country in the world would go into the 21st century by cutting its investment in education and technology and research. But this budget cuts our investment in education, technology, and research. It is a prescription for bad economics. That's the other thing I want to say to people: This Republican budget is not just bad in human terms, it's going to be bad for the economy. It will undermine the economic strategy that we have pursued that has given us the world's strongest economy again. And I want you to stick with us on the education issue.

NOTE: The President spoke by satellite at 10:17 a.m. from the Dempsey Thomas Film Studio in Little Rock, AR, to the convention meeting in Miami Beach, FL. In his remarks, he referred to Gov. Lawton Chiles and Lt. Gov. Buddy MacKay of Florida, and President Jean-Bertrand Aristide of Haiti.

Statement on the Nomination of Kweisi Mfume as NAACP President
December 10, 1995

I was delighted to hear about the nomination of Representative Kweisi Mfume to the leadership of the NAACP. In his distinguished career as the Representative of Baltimore's 7th District, Congressman Mfume has been an outspoken advocate for working Americans, an articulate voice on race relations and a tireless fighter against crime. His was a voice in the Congress that sought not to be divisive but to find common ground on a wide spectrum of issues. I am disappointed that I will lose his support in the Congress, but I know that he will continue to provide me with wise counsel in his new role. He is a superb choice to lead the NAACP at this juncture, which for so many years has been an extraordinary champion of civil rights. I wish him all the best.

Remarks at "Christmas in Washington"
December 10, 1995

Thank you. Thank you, Kelsey. I'd like to thank all the cast of "Frazier," Peri and Jane and John and David, for the wonderful job they did tonight; Gloria Estefan; Clint Black; Al Green; Dawn Upshaw; the Naval Academy Glee Club—makes you proud to be Commander in Chief—[*laughter*]—the U.S. Army Band's Herald Trumpets also do; the magnificent Eastern High School Chorus; and of course, Ian Frazier and the "Christmas in Washington" Orchestra, for the magnificent music all of you have given us. Let's give them a great hand. [*Applause*]

Every year, Hillary and Chelsea and I really look forward to this wonderful "Christmas in Washington" evening. Besides getting us into the holiday spirit, it also gives us the opportunity to recognize one of our country's preeminent health care facilities, the Children's National Medical Center right here in Washington.

As always, Christmas is a time for us to reflect on our good fortune in the past year. This Christmas, I have much to be grateful for. But among the things I am most grateful for is the way the people all around the world still look at our beloved land. Recently I returned from Europe, where this was brought home to me ever more than before. People see America as a nation graced by God with peace and prosperity, a land of fundamental fairness and great freedom. And even though it sometimes imposes extra burdens on us, it is wonderful to know that people the world over trust us to work with them to achieve and share the blessings of peace.

So at Christmas, as we celebrate the birth of a homeless child whose only shelter was the straw of a manger but who grew up to become the Prince of Peace, let us remember that He said, "Blessed are the peacemakers." And let us ask the blessings of peace this Christmas for everyone, from the Middle East to Northern Ireland, to Bosnia, and not only for the children there but, of course, for our troops as well. And let us also as Americans resolve, each of us, to do what we can to be peacemakers, not only to bring peace and reconciliation around the world but also to the most difficult neighborhoods of our own Nation, to every child who deserves to be free from violence and full of hope. That is our prayer for this Christmas.

Hillary and Chelsea and I offer this wish of our season to all of you and to all Americans everywhere: Peace on Earth, good will toward men. Merry Christmas, and God bless you all. Thank you.

NOTE: The President's remarks were recorded at 6:20 p.m. at the National Building Museum for broadcast at 10 p.m. on December 13. In his remarks, he referred to Kelsey Grammer, Peri Gilpin, Jane Leeves, John Mahoney, and David Hyde Pierce, cast members of the television show "Frazier;" and entertainers Gloria Estefan, Clint Black, Al Green, Dawn Upshaw, and Ian Frazier.

Exchange With Reporters Prior to Discussions With Prime Minister Shimon Peres of Israel
December 11, 1995

The President. Good morning, everyone. It's a pleasure and an honor to have the Prime Minister here. We're about to start our talks. And as you know, after we have those talks, we will have a press conference, and we'll be available for your questions. But I'm very much looking forward to continuing our work on the peace process and continuing our strong partnership.

Q. Will you, Mr. President, become actively involved in an Israeli-Syrian track?

The President. Well, we're going to—let us have our talk, and I'll be glad to answer the questions after we finish our visit.

Thank you.

[*At this point, one group of reporters left the room, and another group entered.*]

The President. Good morning everyone. I want to welcome the Prime Minister here. It's pleasure to have him here and a privilege to continue our partnership, our search for peace. I'm looking forward to our visit. And of course, after the visit we'll have a press conference and the opportunity to answer your questions.

Prime Minister Peres. May I say the President has changed our hearts and changed our language. He changed our hearts by a very moving appearance at the funeral of the late Yitzhak Rabin. And he changed our language by adding two words that were never in our vocabulary: *Shalom, chaver.* It became a household expression.

NOTE: The President spoke at 10:46 a.m. in the Oval Office at the White House. A tape was not available for verification of the content of these remarks.

The President's News Conference With Prime Minister Shimon Peres of Israel
December 11, 1995

The President. Please be seated.

Good afternoon. It's a pleasure to welcome Prime Minister Peres back to the White House. For as along as there has been a prospect of peace in the Middle East, Shimon Peres has stood at the forefront, striving to bring a new day of security and harmony to the people of Israel and to all the people of the region.

From his early years as one of the architects of Israel's defense, he has devoted himself to ensuring the security of his Nation. And from his first term as Prime Minister in the mid-1980's, through the negotiations that led to the signing here of the Declaration of Principles with the Palestinians, to the peace of the Araba with Jordan, to the interim accord ceremony just 2½ months ago, Shimon Peres has been a visionary for peace. He has seen the way. He has been a leader on the path to peace. And time and again he has been proven right.

One of the very last things Yitzhak Rabin said was that Shimon Peres was his full partner in forging peace. With those words and the memory of my friend in mind, let me renew now the pledge I first made to Prime Minister Rabin at the beginning of my Presidency.

Mr. Prime Minister, as Israel continues to take risks for a lasting and comprehensive peace, the United States will stand with you to minimize those risks and to ensure your success. And I pledge to you personally, Shimon, that I will be your partner in peace.

Until an assassin's bullet cut short his life, Prime Minister Rabin rose time and again to the challenges of peace. The United States knows that, just as he has in the past, Prime Minister Peres will do so as well. It is a measure of how much has changed in the Middle East that on his journey here the Prime Minister met with King Hussein, President Mubarak, and Chairman Arafat, and that on his trip home he will visit with King Hassan of Morocco.

I have been especially encouraged to hear the Prime Minister talk about the progress in redeploying Israeli forces. He reviewed for me his meeting with Chairman Arafat, who reaffirmed his commitment to building upon and implementing the Declaration of Principles and the interim agreement.

The key to a lasting settlement in the Middle East is achieving peace between Israel and Syria, and Israel and Lebanon. Today Prime Minister Peres and I agreed to redouble our efforts to achieve these goals. We agree that to close the circle of peace it will take more intensive and more practical negotiations. Each side will need to make a greater effort to take account of the others' concerns. The United States stands ready to help to bring the parties together and to work with them in the negotiations. Peace is our mission. And the Prime Minister and I are determined that nothing—nothing—will deter us from this task in the weeks and the months ahead.

Today I have also spoken with President Asad of Syria about our talks here in Washington. President Asad told me he was committed to do his best to move the peace process forward and to reach an early agreement between Syria and Israel. He also agreed to my proposal that Secretary Christopher travel to the region next week to consult with him on the next steps we will take together.

We, of course, recognize that the differences will not disappear immediately. Great hurdles must be overcome. But an Israel-Syria settlement is worth our every effort. It would end the Arab-Israeli conflict. It would establish a comprehensive peace. It could transform the face of the entire Middle East and the lives of all its inhabitants.

That was Yitzhak Rabin's dream. Here at the White House, that soldier of peace said, "Enough of blood and tears." The United States is heartened that Shimon Peres will carry on.

And together, we will work to fulfill Yitzhak Rabin's legacy.

Mr. Prime Minister, as you go forward, the United States will go with you and proudly.

Prime Minister Peres. Mr. President, Mr. Vice President, Mr. Secretary of State, ladies and gentlemen. Let me say from my heart that we are so moved by the American participation in our great sadness when Prime Minister Rabin was assassinated. Mr. President, you have led a most unusual delegation that moved our heart. The President himself, two former Presidents, the Secretary of State, two former Secretaries, the leaders of the Senate, of the House of Representatives, an important corps of journalists, of leaders. There was greatness in the sadness, as Prime Minister Rabin was assassinated because he was right, not because he was wrong.

And may I say, ladies and gentlemen, that President Clinton did something most unusual. He has added an expression to the Israeli dictionary: *Shalom, chaver.* It is a very unusual combination. And for ones who don't understand Hebrew, let me say, the Russians are saying "a comrade," which I don't know exactly what it is; the Americans are saying "a friend," which I understand what it is; but the Israelis are saying *"chaver,"* which means "togetherness." And since the President has used this word, we feel more together. We feel that we have an enriched dictionary among ourselves and between the United States of America and us. Believe me, I speak on behalf of all the Israelis: For this enrichment of expression and feelings, thank you very much.

Q. Mr. President——

Prime Minister Peres: No, I—[*laughter*]. Don't discriminate the Israeli part. [*Laughter*]

So I should really start by saying, *Shalom, chaver.* These, your farewell words to Prime Minister Rabin, echoed throughout our land. The people of Israel will never forget your moving demonstration of solidarity in a moment of grief, of shock, of disbelief and determination. For us, you're a leader; you're a friend.

I stand beside you, Mr. President, in the footsteps of my partner, a great captain of peace, Prime Minister Yitzhak Rabin. Together with you—and I know how much he trusted you—we scaled the trail from the depths of hostility to the highlands of promising peace. Indeed, together we shall stay the course and, with firm resolve, reach a destiny of lasting and a secure peace. A peace for the whole of the Middle East—Arabs and Jews, Jews and Arabs—this was Yitzhak Rabin's quest. It is my commitment.

Your leadership and devotion to the cause of peace are manifestly clear to Israel and to its neighbors as well. This is a constant direction, not a point of passing. May I say that as Bosnia reeled in agony, you offered a compass and a lamp to a confused situation, ending blood, offering hope, like in the Middle East. It is time to put an end to the Arab-Israeli conflict. With you, Mr. President, in the forefront, by our side, it may become possible, as it did in the past, bringing thereby peace, security, and prosperity to all people. Prophecy may meet reality again and again.

Since your Presidency and through our partnership, the Middle East has already undergone an unbelievable change. Here at the White House on September 13, 1993, we came to grips with the heart of the problem. The Israeli-Palestinian Declaration of Principles created a roadmap by means of which the Palestinians, alongside Israel, are becoming masters of their destinies. Palestinian elections are a new promise that reflects the interaction between peace and democracy. Nothing is a better guarantee for peace than democracy.

Israel and Jordan are displaying its fruits day-in and day-out. A barren rift valley is pregnant with new prospects. Peace with Egypt remains a cornerstone of the peace process for, by it, regional war is no longer the justification of policies that leaves lands deserted rather than flourishing.

Today we seek an opening of a new, maybe a final chapter: the end of war in the Middle East in its totality. Peace between Syria and between Lebanon and Israel will leave no reason whatsoever for the continuation of belligerency. Syria, together with us, stands in a unique position to contribute to a peaceful Middle East. The conflict between us has been bitter, complicated. The land that gave birth to prophecy can now give birth to yet a new vision.

President Asad and myself can, with the assistance of your leadership, Mr. President, and the assistance of your administration and Congress, build a new equation of genuine peace and security to end terror, to begin a market economy. I speak of boundaries of permanent peace. I speak of lands of new and great opportunity. Peace between us must indeed put an end to the conflict that has mired our region for so long. The President, the Secretary of

State, and their peace team will continue to create with us the architecture for peace in the region. We welcome you.

Today I discussed the possible new opportunity with President Clinton. I find a warmth and an openness in our discussion, and I am very grateful. Mr. President, we are proud to be partners with you in working to make this prospect become a reality. It is my hope that President Asad will join us soon on this historic journey.

To my fellow Israelis, I can say we have in you, Mr. President, a true friend and a true partner. There is no time now for political vacation. We don't intend to rest. We intend to continue the momentum, full speed ahead, in the name of all Israelis. And I think all Israelis, they'll tell you, Mr. President, *toda, chaver,* thank you, *chaver.*

Israel-U.S. Space-Based Experiments

The President. Thank you.

Let me make one brief comment, and then I will take questions, as will the Prime Minister.

As part of our effort to support Israel's advances in science and technology, I have today agreed with Prime Minister Peres to proceed with space-based experiments in sustainable water use and environmental protection. These experiments will take place in unmanned space vehicles, in the shuttle program, and in the international space station. And as a part of this effort, we will also train Israeli astronauts to participate in these programs. We look forward to working out the arrangements for this cooperation, and we are absolutely certain that it will benefit Israel's high-tech development as well as our own.

Middle East Peace Process

Q. Mr. President, countries such as Saudi Arabia, Egypt, and Jordan are critical to the Middle East peace process. Yet none of these are true democracies, and all of them are now showing serious signs of internal dissent, even violent dissent. At what point does the firm U.S. backing of such nondemocratic governments become counterproductive?

The President. Well, first of all, those countries have to work out their internal affairs for themselves. But as long as they are responsible actors on the international stage and as long as they are contributing to the peace process in the Middle East, we will consider them our partners for peace in the Middle East. That's the first and most important thing: How do they conduct themselves, and are they supportive of the peace process?

Q. Mr. President, you have just managed to successfully bring three sides together in Dayton, Ohio. Is it the time to use Camp David II model in the Middle East and bring President Asad and Prime Minister Peres together to this country? And if not, did you hear any new ideas from Prime Minister Shimon Peres? Thank you.

The President. Well, yes, Prime Minister Peres had some very good ideas which we shared together and which I think will form the basis of further action. At some point, I think the leaders of countries that are interested in peace have to meet; leaders have to meet and work together and work their problems out. But I think that will come in time.

Keep in mind, we worked quite a long time on peace in the Middle East—I mean, in Bosnia—before the parties came together at Dayton. So that will come, I think.

Balkan Peace Process

Q. Mr. President, on the Bosnia issue, since the accord, Bosnian Croats have reportedly burned a village, two French pilots are still captive, a number of cease-fire violations have occurred. It remains so unstable there. Why should the American people have any confidence that our troops will be safe there?

The President. First of all, I don't think it remains so unstable there. I think, basically, you—in some ways you made the case. It has not been a perfect observation of the agreement, but basically the agreement they made has been observed. There has not been a resumption of hostilities. There are some rough edges there, which is why NATO and others who are cooperating with us were asked to come in and help to separate the forces—supervise the separation of the forces—the transfer of land, the redeployment of forces out of land which they no longer are responsible for, and then to maintain a secure environment while the agreement is implemented.

And I see no reason to believe, based on the evidence so far, that all the parties who signed the agreement are not fully committed to implementing it. In fact, over the weekend we received some more encouraging comments from some of the Serb leaders about being committed to the end of the war and the implementation of the agreement.

Q. Mr. Prime Minister, do you feel——

Prime Minister Peres. You know, gentlemen, Bosnia is Muslim, and Israel is Jewish. Yet, this is not the right distinction when it comes to politics in my eyes. The distinction is between aggressors and defenders. And I salute the United States of America to try to put an end to aggression and really help the people that were attacked to survive and not to suffer any longer.

Thank you.

Middle East Peace Process

Q. Mr. President, do you feel now that the chances for peace between Israel and Syria are better than they were one month or 2 months ago?

The President. Yes.

Q. And is this the impression that you informed today to Mr. Peres?

The President. That is the impression I have today, yes.

Q. Mr. Prime Minister, did you review to President Clinton your readiness to withdraw from Golan Heights as part of the peace agreement with Syria?

Prime Minister Peres. You cannot pin on a single issue. We are talking about the Syrian-Israeli peace process in its totality, and I have revealed the totality.

Q. Yes, but as one of the——

Prime Minister Peres. I understand what you—the answer you are seeking, and that's the answer I am having. [*Laughter*]

Q. Mr. President, do you know the price that Israel is ready to pay for peace with Syria? Are you going to transfer this information to President Asad? And are you maybe considering a visit in the Middle East, in Damascus and Jerusalem?

The President. Well, first of all, the Secretary of State will communicate to President Asad the essential elements of my meeting with the Prime Minister, as agreed upon between the Prime Minister and myself.

But I would just reiterate something that he said. I think the most important thing is not what any particular issue is, but I think that the atmosphere is better than it was before—as the previous questioner asked—and very frankly, as sad as it is to say, I think the Syrian leader and the Syrian people now see the exceptional price that former Prime Minister Rabin

and Prime Minister Peres have been willing to pay in their search for peace.

I think that is the fundamental new reality here. I don't think any of the details matter nearly as much as that fundamental new reality, because in the end, in any peace agreement, the parties have to have two things. One is a certain level of trust that the people actually, on either side, intend to go forward with the agreements they have made because it's in their interest and because they can be believed. And the second is a certain system of observing the implementation of that trust. That's more important than all the details. So that is, I think, the central new reality.

Balkan Peace Process

Q. Mr. President, you've talked about Bosnia a little bit. You still have not gotten the congressional approval you expect. You are about to head off to Paris to sign a commitment. Are you going to send U.S. troops if you don't get that approval from Congress in regards to the timetable you want for sending the troops over there?

The President. First of all, I believe that we will secure that approval. I believe that Congress will support the troops. I had a good talk yesterday with Senator Dole and with Speaker Gingrich, and I know that we have these congressional delegations that have been to Bosnia that are coming back; I think two more are coming back. And I believe when it is all debated and all said and done in the next few days that the Congress will find a way to express their support for our troops. That's what I believe will happen.

Q. Will you send them anyway, sir?

Middle East Peace Process

Q. Mr. President, if you could tell us, do you see in the context of a peace agreement with Syria the need for a formal defense alliance with Israel, an upgrading of security—of the secure relationship. To follow up on that, also, if something would go wrong on Bosnia, do you see how that could affect this whole idea of U.S. troops on the Golan Heights? Thank you very much.

The President. Well, first let me say that the United States has not been asked in any negotiations by either party to put troops on the Golan as of this time. We have not been asked.

Secondly, if one thing should be clear to the entire world in the history of the last several years, it is that the security of Israel is terribly important to the United States. We have made an explicit policy commitment which has been carried through under Presidents of both parties to maintain the qualitative and technological edge that Israel needs to guarantee its security in an atmosphere that has been far more hostile than it is even today.

And so I think you can, as we go forward here, you can be assured that the security of Israel in going to be one of the main pillars of America's defense commitments and one of the main things we will be concerned about as we move through the peace process.

Balkan Peace Process and Jonathan Pollard Espionage Case

Q. Mr. President, one question directed specifically towards you. Can you update us on the possible release of the two French pilots in, presumably in Serbian control, and whether or not that issue could derail the peace agreement signing on Thursday in Paris? And question to both of you on, unrelated, did you have a chance to discuss the Jonathan Pollard spy case now that he has been granted Israeli citizenship, and did the Prime Minister ask you to release Pollard?

The President. You got a lot in there in a little time. [*Laughter*]

Very briefly, I wish I could tell you more about the French pilots. I can tell you this, that we are in very close touch with the French. They are working very, very hard on this. I have no factual update for you. They are working it very hard, and they expect the peace signing to go forward on time.

With regard to Mr. Pollard, the Prime Minister mentioned it to me and gave me a letter setting forth his position on it. As you know, Mr. Pollard came up once before, I think in early 1994. If he requests executive clemency, I will, of course, review that request, as I would anyone who requested it. But he has to make a request, and it has to come through the ordinary channels before I can do that.

Middle East Peace Process

Q. Mr. President, the Palestinian Authority is holding elections next month. I would like to ask you, how do you assess the performance of the Palestinian Authority and the perform-

ance of Yasser Arafat leading to the Palestinian elections? And when are you planning to visit the Palestinian Authority as well as the rest of the Middle East? I asked you this before; I would like to know if you are going to make another trip?

And for Mr. Prime Minister, I just want to— [*laughter*].

The President. You went to the Wolf Blitzer [Cable News Network] school of journalism, I think. [*Laughter*] No, go ahead, please.

Q. Mr. Prime Minister, I just want to wish you the great success in your performing your duties in this very crucial time in Israel and the Middle East. While I'm wishing you this, I would like very much to ask you, Mr. Prime Minister, to release the Palestinian——

Prime Minister Peres. Be careful with your timing.

Q. ——to release the Palestinian prisoners as soon as possible so they will go back to their families and we will really have peace in the region, especially in the Authority. Thank you.

The President. Let me say, first of all, about the elections, I expect them to go forward; I expect them to be successful; I expect them to be held in a way that is generally applauded for their integrity. And I expect to go back to the Middle East at an appropriate time, but I don't have a trip scheduled. I think I'd like it to be in the context of another advance for the cause of peace. And that's where we are.

Prime Minister Peres. Before Christmas, 450 villages in the West Bank and all the major cities, as well as Gaza and Jericho, will be under the rule of the Palestinians for the first time in history. Israel has implemented one of our greatest moral promises: not to rule another people. Believe me, it makes us content and complete by doing so.

Part of the agreement was to release another 1,000 prisoners before the elections. I hope we shall release a little bit more than that, but for the people that have bloodstains on their hands. Until now, we kept every promise, every word. We were ahead of time. And I thought the assassination of Prime Minister Rabin puts an extra responsibility upon me to really do everything true to the commitment.

The President. Thank you very much. Thank you.

NOTE: The President's 110th news conference began at 1:14 p.m. in Room 450 of the Old Executive Office Building. In his remarks, he referred to King Hussein of Jordan, President Hosni Mubarak of Egypt, Chairman Yasser Arafat of the Palestine Liberation Organization, and President Hafiz al-Asad of Syria..

Statement on Action To Protect Retirement Plan Savings
December 11, 1995

Hard-working Americans are doing their part to save for the future. Americans who work to support their families and save for retirement should not have to worry that the money they earned won't be there when they need it most.

Today my administration is taking action to give the Government the tools necessary to assure American workers they can put their 401(k) savings into a system that is as safe as Fort Knox.

Every American should be encouraged to set aside money for their retirement and make investments in their economic future. Our action will assure millions of Americans that they can put their savings and their trust into a financially sound retirement plan. My administration will continue to do its part to stand guard over Americans' retirement funds.

Letter to Senate Democratic Leader Thomas Daschle on the Plan for Implementation of the Balkan Peace Agreement
December 11, 1995

Dear Mr. Leader:

Just four weeks ago, the leaders of Bosnia, Croatia and Serbia came to Dayton, Ohio, in America's heartland, to negotiate and initial a peace agreement to end the war in Bosnia. There, they made a commitment to peace. They agreed to put down their guns; to preserve Bosnia as a single state; to cooperate with the War Crimes Tribunal and to try to build a peaceful, democratic future for all the people of Bosnia. They asked for NATO and America's help to implement this peace agreement.

On Friday, December 1, the North Atlantic Council approved NATO's operational plan, OPLAN 10405, the Implementation of a Peace Agreement in the Former Yugoslavia. On Saturday, General George Joulwan, Supreme Allied Commander Europe, who will be commanding the NATO operation, briefed me in Germany on the final OPLAN.

Having reviewed the OPLAN, I find the mission is clearly defined with realistic goals that can be achieved in a definite period of time. The risks to our troops have been minimized to the maximum extent possible. American troops will take their orders from the American general who commands NATO. They will be heavily armed and thoroughly trained. In making an overwhelming show of force, they will lessen the need to use force. They will have the authority, as well as the training and the equipment, to respond with decisive force to any threat to their own safety or any violations of the military provisions of the peace agreement. U.S. and NATO commanders believe the military mission can be accomplished in about a year.

A summary of the OPLAN is attached. Of course, members of my staff and the Administration are available to answer your questions and further brief you on the OPLAN as you require.

I consider the Dayton peace agreement to be a serious commitment by the parties to settle this conflict. In light of that agreement and my approval of the final NATO OPLAN, I would welcome a Congressional expression of support for U.S. participation in a NATO-led Implementation Force in Bosnia. I believe Congressional support for U.S. participation is immensely important to the unity of our purpose and the morale of our troops.

I believe there has been a timely opportunity for the Congress to consider and act upon my request for support since the initialing in Dayton on November 21. As you know, the formal signing of the Peace Agreement will take place in Paris on December 14.

As I informed you earlier, I have authorized the participation of a small number of American troops in a NATO advance mission that will lay the groundwork for IFOR, starting this week. They will establish headquarters and set up the sophisticated communications systems that must be in place before NATO can send in its troops, tanks and trucks to Bosnia.

America has a responsibility to help to turn this moment of hope into an enduring reality.

As the leader of NATO—the only institution capable of implementing this peace agreement—the United States has a profound interest in participating in this mission, which will give the people of Bosnia the confidence and support they need to preserve the peace and prevent this dangerous war in the heart of Europe from resuming and spreading. Since taking office, I have refused to send American troops to fight a war in Bosnia, but I believe we must help now to secure this Bosnian peace.

Sincerely,

BILL CLINTON

NOTE: A summary of the operation plan for the implementation of the peace agreement in the former Yugoslavia was attached to the President's letter.

Remarks to Citizens Involved in Humanitarian Relief Efforts for Bosnia and an Exchange With Reporters
December 12, 1995

The President. Well, first of all, let me say that I know I speak for everyone here in thanking the people who have spoken and thanking them, more importantly, for their remarkable efforts. I want to express my appreciation to two of their Representatives who joined us: Congressman Ehlers from Michigan and Congressman Moran from Virginia. To Franklin Graham, thank you, sir, for the remarkable work that you are doing and for giving people like Mary the chance to be remarkable in their own right.

What you have just heard is a series of astonishing human testaments. I don't know that I've ever felt more proud to be an American than I did in the last few minutes just listening to these people talk. And I know all of you feel that way as well.

The purpose of our mission is to take advantage of this remarkable opportunity we have when all of the parties have agreed to make peace, when they have agreed that the madness you have just heard recounted ought to stop.

We saw further evidence of their good-faith intention to do their part this morning, when the French pilots were released. And I just, by pure coincidence, had the French Ambas-

sador in this morning, and I told him to convey to President Chirac the joy of all Americans that these pilots are free because the mission that we all undertook together through NATO had a lot to do with bringing about this peace agreement.

Since I became President, I have said that I thought the United States had an obligation to participate in the enforcement of a peace agreement. Because we have a peace agreement which is enforceable, which can be protected, which can be enhanced by the NATO force, the work that you have just heard about will be able to be multiplied hundreds of times over. And that's the thing I want to emphasize to all of you.

The NATO mission in which the United States will play a leading role by separating the forces, by making sure the territory is the way the peace agreement agreed, by maintaining a secure environment, will permit more of these things to be done, will permit the reconstruction effort to proceed, not only the physical reconstruction effort but the human reconstruction effort.

And I have just told all of the folks whom you heard speak that it is very important that these efforts continue in Bosnia and, in fact, be intensified because there are a lot of lives that have to be put together; there are a lot of communities that have to be rebuilt. But this kind of energy by the American people and by others throughout the world who will join now in helping them can help to turn the worst nightmare in Europe since the end of the Second World War into a story of reconciliation and peace and progress.

And again, let me say, there is nothing I can say to add to what these fine people have said. But when Americans like these folks are willing to do what they have done, I think it is incumbent on the United States, the other NATO powers, the others who are joining with us, to make sure that this peace takes hold and is preserved so that they can do it in an atmosphere free of fear for themselves and help that country come back and help all these little children regain their childhood.

I hope we all live to see the day when the only bombs in the world are "peace bombs."

Thank you very much.

Q. Mr. President, are you going to be able to get this through Congress, win approval?

The President. Well, let me say I'm quite encouraged by two things. Number one, a very large number of Members of Congress, especially House Members, have actually gone to the region in the last few days, and I applaud them for doing it. And some of those with deep reservations about the missions have gone. I have no exact vote count for you, but I can tell you that it's clear to me that there's been a real shift among those who have gone. Those who have gone have come back more favorable than they left America. And so I can't believe that when the time for the counting comes that Congress won't support our troops in this mission. I believe they will.

Thank you.

NOTE: The President spoke at 11:15 a.m. in the Roosevelt Room at the White House. In his remarks, he referred to Franklin Graham, president, Samaritan's Purse; volunteer Mary Damron of Ikes Fork, WV; and President Jacques Chirac of France.

Letter to Senators Robert Dole and John McCain on the Plan for Implementation of the Balkan Peace Agreement
December 12, 1995

Dear Mr. Leader:

I am writing in response to your December 12 letter on equip and train. You raise several questions to which I would like to respond.

First of all, the United States will take a leadership role in coordinating an international effort to ensure that the Bosnian Federation receives the assistance necessary to achieve an adequate military balance when IFOR leaves. As in all things related to our effort to bringing peace to the region, U.S. leadership has been critical.

As I stated in my December 10 letter to you, I want to assure the impartiality of IFOR. In the view of my military advisors, this requires minimizing the involvement of U.S. military personnel. But we expect that some individual military officers, for example, working in OSD, DSAA or other agencies, will be involved in planning this effort. We also will offer the

Bosnians participation in U.S. programs such as IMET. I agree that maintaining flexibility is important to the success of the effort to achieve a stable military balance within Bosnia. But I will do nothing that I believe will endanger the safety of American troops on the ground in Bosnia. I am sure you will agree that is my primary responsibility.

I want to assure you that I am focusing on what the United States can do. That is why I sent an assessment team to the region to properly evaluate the needs of the Federation. Training programs and provision of non-lethal assistance can begin immediately after the peace agreement enters into force; and provision of small arms can begin after three months. We intend to move expeditiously.

I have given you my word that we will make certain that the Bosnian Federation will receive

the assistance necessary to achieve an adequate military balance when IFOR leaves. I intend to keep it.
　　Sincerely,

BILL CLINTON

NOTE: This letter was made available by the Office of the Press Secretary on December 12 but was not issued as a White House press release.

Statement on the First Anniversary of the Summit of the Americas
December 12, 1995

Last December, I joined the other 33 democratically elected leaders from the Western Hemisphere in Miami for the historic Summit of the Americas. Working in a new spirit of cooperation, we set a common agenda to strengthen the advance of democracy in our region, to protect our environment and natural resources, to expand opportunities for our nations and our communities, and to promote a new partnership for hemispheric prosperity.

Over the last year, the hemisphere's leaders have worked hard to realize the ambitious program defined at the summit. We are working together to challenge money-launderers, narcotics traffickers, and others who ignore the rule of law. A new hemispheric Partnership for Pollution Prevention will phase out the use of leaded gasoline and other chemicals that contaminate our air and poison our soil.

In June, we hosted a meeting of regional trade and commerce ministers to discuss measures to facilitate trade liberalization and to begin preparations for the negotiation of a Free Trade Area of the Americas by the year 2005. Already, falling trade barriers have allowed our exports to the hemisphere to grow by 12 percent in the first half of 1995 to $112 billion, generating over 180,000 export-related jobs. Steady progress means more jobs and opportunities for American workers and U.S. businesses as we look toward the next century.

Working together, the democratic nations of this hemisphere have achieved much. I know we can accomplish much more. Despite the challenges faced by our hemisphere this past year, the foundations of the summit remain strong and our nations, including the United States, remain committed to our common goals.

Statement on the Resignation of Lee Brown as Director of the Office of National Drug Control Policy
December 12, 1995

It is with regret that I have accepted the decision of Dr. Lee Brown, Director of the Office of National Drug Control Policy, to return to private life and a teaching position. As Director of the Office of National Drug Control Policy and as a former police officer, Dr. Brown has devoted much of his life and the entirety of the past 2½ years to fighting the scourge of drugs in America.

My administration is strongly committed to the battle against drugs, which will never be over until every child in America knows that drug use is dangerous, illegal, and wrong. We

still have far to go, but under Dr. Brown's stewardship, we have made solid progress: cracking down on the international drug trade by breaking the powerful Cali drug cartel, calling for drug testing of high school athletes, toughening punishment of drug-related violence, and challenging the entertainment industry and sports figures to do their part to speak out about the dangers of drugs.

I am grateful for Dr. Brown's good service and for the groundwork that he has laid. My administration will not rest until every young

American knows the difference between right and wrong when it comes to drug use.

Remarks on the Balkan Peace Process Following a Meeting With Elie Wiesel and an Exchange With Reporters
December 13, 1995

The President. Good morning. I have just had the pleasure of a meeting with Elie Wiesel to discuss our efforts to secure the peace in Bosnia. The citation on the Nobel Peace Prize awarded to Elie Wiesel 9 years ago describes him as a messenger to mankind. He is a passionate witness to humanity's capacity for the worst and a powerful example of humanity's capacity for the best. Throughout his life, he has been an advocate for peace and human dignity and the duty we owe to one another. And I'd like to ask him to say just a few words about the decisions that are before our country and the work of peace in Bosnia.

Mr. Wiesel. Mr. President, it is with a great sense of pride and pleasure that I came to support your decision. I believe it is right; I believe it is honorable. Two years ago or so, when we both spoke at the very important event, the opening of the Holocaust Memorial Museum, I left my prepared remarks and appealed to you, to your humanity, which I know is profound, to do something, anything, to stop the killing, the bloodshed, the violence, the hatred, the massacre in former Yugoslavia.

I know how concerned you were. I know you tried. You tried very hard, trying to influence the European nations, the allies, the United Nations. And what you are doing now will be remembered in history, because it is intervention on the highest level and in its most noble form.

We in the United States represent a certain moral aspect of history. A great nation owes its greatness not only to its military power but also to its moral consciousness, awareness. What would future generations say about us, all of us here in this land, if we do nothing? After all, people were dying; people were killing each other day after day. They stopped, thanks to your leadership. I know of no other world figure today who has done so much in the field for foreign affairs as you have, Mr. President. To send American men and women to preserve the peace is an act of courage and of decency, and I use the word advisedly, it's an act of morality, and that is why I am here with you today, Mr. President.

The President. Thank you very much. I'd like just to make, if I might, one or two other remarks. As all of you know, I will travel to Paris this evening to witness the signing of the peace agreement. After nearly 4 years of terrible destruction, Bosnia is at peace. We must not lose sight of that fact. This is an extraordinary achievement, and the question now is whether the peace will endure.

Ultimately of course, that will have to be decided by the Bosnian people themselves. But they cannot have the opportunity to have peace take hold without American leadership. I believe our Nation has already made the difference between war and peace there. Now, I believe only the United States can make the difference between whether the peace takes hold, because the actions of all of our allies depend upon our working together.

I hope that the Members of Congress will recognize that fundamental truth as they consider support for our troops and for the mission of peace in Bosnia. We have an obligation as we make this decision to remember that Bosnia's war involved a lot of innocent people. Snipers and shells turned schoolyards into graveyards. There were terrified faces of women and girls who were raped as an instrument of war. There were skeletal prisoners behind barbed wire fences in what can only be called concentration camps. There were defenseless men who were shot down into mass graves. Now we have a chance to end all that and to give Bosnia a chance at a better future.

I think we should also not forget that the situation there has not always been hopeless; that's another thing I think that has colored this debate. The fact is that for generations, Bosnia was a place where people of different traditions and faiths could, and did, live side by side in peace. Its people were joined by marriage, by language, by culture. One of the most heartbreaking things to me is to see refugees from Bosnia in our own country who comprise families that have Croatian and Serbian and Muslim roots within one family, being driven out of their country.

We now can give that country a future back again, and I hope the Congress will vote to do it, and I believe America must lead the way in doing it. And I thank you, Elie Wiesel, for being a conscience of this terrible conflict for the last 4 years.

Q. What do you think the chances are of getting support in Congress?

The President. I don't know. We're working hard. We had another—I had another long meeting yesterday with the Members of the Senate. And I understand there's going to be a vote—there are a series of votes there sometime today. Then I think the House will have to determine what to do based on what the Senate does. That's—my instinct is that they have not—it's not clear to me where it's going, but we have worked very hard, and we will continue to work hard. And in the end I just can't believe that Congress won't support our troops in this mission. That's what I think will happen.

Q. Mr. President, when you sit down with the three Balkan leaders tomorrow, you will come to them as the leader of a nation that is divided about whether to support them. What will you tell them?

The President. Well, if they're concerned about that, I will tell them that our people have always had a reluctance to send our young people in uniform overseas—that goes back throughout our entire history—and that on the whole that has been a healthy thing because we have not been—we have not been a country that has sought the gains of empire, we have not been a country that has sought to tell other people how they must live their lives; but that we are fundamentally a good people and when we understand our duty, historically, we nearly always do it. That's what I'll—thank you.

Federal Budget

Q. What do you think of the Republicans thinking you shouldn't go and you should work on the budget?

The President. We will be working on the budget.

NOTE: The President spoke at 10:40 a.m. in the Oval Office at the White House.

Message to the Congress Transmitting the Farmington River Report
December 13, 1995

To the Congress of the United States:

I take pleasure in transmitting the enclosed report for the Farmington River in the States of Massachusetts and Connecticut. The report and my recommendations are in response to the provisions of the Wild and Scenic Rivers Act, Public Law 90–542, as amended. The Farmington River Study was authorized by Public Law 99–590.

The study was conducted by the National Park Service, with invaluable assistance from a congressionally mandated study committee. The National Park Service determined that the 11-mile study segment in Massachusetts and the 14-mile study segment in Connecticut were eligible for designation based upon their free-flow-

ing character and recreational, fish, wildlife and historic values.

The 14-mile Connecticut segment of the river has already been designated as a Wild and Scenic River pursuant to Public Law 103–313, August 26, 1994. The purpose of this transmittal is to inform the Congress that, although eligible for designation, I do not recommend that the Massachusetts segment be designated at this time due to lack of support by the towns adjoining it. If at some future date the towns should change their position and the river has retained its present characteristics, the Congress could reconsider the issue. Also, for 3 years from the date of this transmittal, the Massachusetts segment will remain subject to section 7(b) of the

Wild and Scenic Rivers Act. Section 7(b) prohibits licensing of projects by the Federal Energy Regulatory Commission and Federal or federally assisted water resource development projects that would have a direct and adverse effect on the values for which the river might be designated. Finally, the report includes the Upper Farmington River Management Plan that is referenced in Public Law 103–313 as the plan by which the designated river will be managed.

The plan demonstrated a true partnership effort of the type that we believe will be increasingly necessary if we are to have affordable protection of our environment in the future.

WILLIAM J. CLINTON

The White House,

December 13, 1995.

Remarks Prior to Discussions With Balkan Leaders and an Exchange With Reporters in Paris, France
December 14, 1995

Balkan Peace Process

The President. As you know, we will be having formal ceremonies later today, and more remarks will be made then. I just want to say very briefly, because we want to get on to our meeting, that I applaud these leaders for making the decision to turn from war to peace that they will formalize today. And tomorrow they will begin the hard work of making that peace real.

I am pleased that they have asked the United States, our NATO allies, and a number of other countries, to help them secure this peace. And I am pleased that we will be going forward to do it. I'm convinced that working together in good faith, this effort can be successful.

Q. Are you concerned that there may be some reluctance in parts of the Balkans to implement a peace?

The President. All I can tell you is the ceasefire has been in place for a couple of months. It has basically held. There have been many things that have happened in the last 3 years. I'm sure many people have different feelings, but we believe these leaders have acted in good faith and will continue to do so. And if they do, we think we'll be successful.

Q. Do you think the Congress has given you a whole-hearted vote of support on this, or how do you—how do you rate——

The President. I'll tell you how I read the vote. I think Congress—first of all, both Houses decided not to cut off funds and to support the troops. And the Senate, in what could only be characterized as an overwhelming bipartisan

vote, gave its support to the mission subject to conditions with which the administration agrees. So I was quite pleased with where the Congress came out yesterday compared to where they were just a month ago. And again, I think that is in part due to the fact that these leaders have been willing to meet with the Members of the Congress who have traveled to the area in the last couple of weeks. And I think they have seen the people and their desire for peace. And they have heard from these leaders about their desire for peace and their determination. And I feel that we made a lot of progress. And I think now that the time for debate is over; the time for decision is at hand. And I believe the United States and the United States Congress will rally behind our troops in this mission.

Q. Are you satisfied with the pace of the deployment, Mr. President? Are you satisfied that the deployment is proceeding as fast as it can at this point?

The President. Yes, you know, it's the winter; we have snow. We have first one thing, then another, but I think we're going forward in good faith and in an appropriate way.

NOTE: The President spoke at 9:22 a.m. at the Ambassador's residence, prior to meeting with President Alija Izetbegovic of Bosnia-Herzegovina, President Slobodan Milosevic of Serbia, and President Franjo Tudjman of Croatia. A tape was not available for verification of the content of these remarks.

Remarks at the Signing Ceremony for the Balkan Peace Agreement in Paris
December 14, 1995

President Chirac, President Izetbegovic, President Tudjman, President Milosevic, Secretary-General Boutros-Ghali, Secretary General Solana, High Representative Bildt, Prime Minister Filali, Prime Minister Chernomyrdin, Prime Minister Major, Prime Minister Gonzalez, Chancellor Kohl: Let me begin, on behalf of the people of the United States, by thanking all of those whose labor and wisdom helped to keep hope alive during the long, dark years of war, the humanitarian relief workers, the United Nations forces from Europe and beyond. Had it not been for their dedication and their sacrifice, the toll of the war in Bosnia would have been even greater.

And I thank those whose work helped make this moment of peace possible, beginning with our host, Prime Minister Chirac, for his vigor and determination; Prime Minister Major, who was a full partner in the development of the rapid reaction force and our NATO cooperation; and our friend Chancellor Kohl, who has taken so many of the refugees and who now is sending German troops beyond his border in this historic common endeavor. I thank the leaders of the strong NATO and the determined negotiating team of Russians, Europeans, and Americans.

All of you have brought us to this bright new day, when Bosnia turns from the horror of war to the promise of peace. President Izetbegovic, President Tudjman, President Milosevic, by making peace you have answered the call of your people. You have heard them say, "Stop the war. End the suffering. Give our children the blessings of a normal life."

In this chorus for peace today we also hear the hallowed voices of the victims, the children whose playgrounds were shelled into killing fields, the young girls brutalized by rape, the men shot down in mass graves, those who starved in the camps, those who died in battle, the millions taken from their homes and torn from their families. Even from beyond the grave there are victims singing the song of peace today. May their voices be in our minds and our hearts forever.

In Dayton, these three Balkan leaders made the fateful choice for peace. Today, Mr. Presidents, you have bound yourselves to peace. But tomorrow you must turn the pages of this agreement into a real-life future of hope for those who have survived this horrible war. At your request, the United States and more than 25 other nations will send you our most precious resource, the men and women of our Armed Forces. Their mission, to allow the Bosnian people to emerge from a nightmare of fear into a new day of security, according to terms you have approved, in a manner that is evenhanded and fair to all.

The international community will work with you to change the face of Bosnia: to meet human needs; to repair and to rebuild; to reunite children with their families and refugees with their homes; to oversee democratic elections, advance human rights, and call to account those accused of war crimes.

We can do all these things, but we cannot guarantee the future of Bosnia. No one outside can guarantee that Muslims, Croats, and Serbs in Bosnia will come together and stay together as free citizens in a united country sharing a common destiny. Only the Bosnian people can do that.

I know the losses have been staggering, the scars are deep. We feel even today that the wounds have not healed. But Bosnia must find a way, with God's grace, to lay down the hatreds, to give up the revenge, to go forward together. That is the road—indeed, that is the only road—to the future.

We see from Northern Ireland to the Middle East, from South Africa to Haiti, people turning from hatred to hope. Here in Europe, countries that for centuries fought now work together for peace. Soon the Bosnian people will see for themselves the awesome potential of people to turn from conflict to cooperation. In just a few days troops from all over Europe and North America and elsewhere—troops from Great Britain, France, and Germany, troops from Greece and Turkey, troops from Poland and Lithuania, and troops from the United States and Russia, former enemies, now friends—will answer the same call and share the same responsibilities to achieve the same goal, a lasting peace in Bosnia where enemies can become friends.

Why would they do this? Because their hearts are broken by the suffering and the slaughter; because their minds recoil at the prospect of needless spreading war in the heart of Europe. But they—we—do so in the face of skeptics who say the people of the Balkans cannot escape their bloody past, that Balkan hearts are too hard for peace.

But let us remember this war did violence not only to Bosnia's people but also to Bosnia's history. For Bosnia once found unity in its diversity. Generations of Muslims, Orthodox, Catholics, and Jews lived side by side and enriched the world by their example. They built schools and libraries and wondrous places of worship. Part of the population laid down their tools on Friday, part on Saturday, and part on Sunday. But their lives were woven together by marriage and culture, work, a common language, and a shared pride in a place that then they all called home. Now, if that past is any guide, this peace can take hold. And if the people of Bosnia want a decent future for their children, this peace must take hold.

Here in this City of Light, at this moment of hope, let us recall how this century—marked by so much progress and too much bloodshed, witness to humanity's best and humanity's worst—how this century began in Bosnia. At the dawn of the century, when gunfire in Sarajevo sparked the first of our two World Wars,

the British Foreign Secretary, Sir Edward Gray, said these words: "The lamps are going out all over Europe. We shall not see them lit again in our lifetimes."

But they were lit again, by an extraordinary generation of Europeans and Americans. The torch of freedom they carried now shines more brightly than ever before on every continent. That torch can shine on Bosnia again, but first it must warm the hearts of the Bosnian people.

So I say to all the people of the Balkans on behalf of all of us who would come to see this peace take hold: You have seen what war has wrought. You know what peace can bring. Seize this chance and make it work. You can do nothing to erase the past, but you can do everything to build the future. Do not let your children down.

Thank you.

NOTE: The President spoke at 12:50 p.m. in the Salon des Fetes at the Elysee Palace. In his remarks, he referred to President Jacques Chirac of France, U.N. Secretary-General Boutros Boutros-Ghali, NATO Secretary General Javier Solana, High Representative of the Balkan peace conference Carl Bildt, Prime Minister Abdellatif Filali of Morocco, Prime Minister Viktor Chernomyrdin of Russia, Prime Minister John Major of the United Kingdom, Prime Minister Felipe Gonzalez of Spain, and Chancellor Helmut Kohl of Germany.

Remarks on Presenting the Presidential Citizens Medals
December 15, 1995

The President. Good afternoon. Congressman Davis, Secretary Perry, General Shalikashvili, Deputy Secretary Talbott, distinguished friends: Let me say it is a great honor to welcome the Frasure family, the Kruzel family, the Drew family here today.

Yesterday in Paris I watched the Presidents of Bosnia, Croatia, and Serbia sign an agreement that turns their troubled region from war to peace. Then on behalf of our Nation, I witnessed the agreement.

I witnessed it also in a more personal sense on behalf of three great Americans who could

not be there: Bob Frasure, Joe Kruzel, and Nelson Drew. For without their efforts there would have been no agreement in Dayton, and no signing in Paris. The shells would still be falling in Sarajevo.

When Bob, Joe, and Nelson died on Mount Igman on August 19th, they were serving in the greatest of all missions, working for peace and freedom. How I wish they could know that their efforts were destined to be crowned with success. I think they do.

They knew their mission was dangerous. They talked about the risks the night before they set out for Sarajevo. Just a few days earlier they had tried to get in by helicopter, but were forced back by bad weather. But because of who they were, they never hesitated, and the next morning they set out again.

To the family and friends of these three good and brave men, let me say again, as I have said before, we will never forget them. Their sacrifice reminds us of the tragedy they sought to relieve and reinforces the urgency of the search for a solution. They worked together as a team, but each had unique strengths.

Bob Frasure was a career diplomat who found the most difficult assignments, or perhaps it would be better to say they found him. From Angola to Ethiopia, to Estonia, and of course, to Bosnia, he helped to write some of the most dramatic chapters in the history of modern American foreign policy, yet he never sought the limelight for himself. As Secretary Christopher has said, he was a man of great accomplishment but little visible ego. His ingenuity and skill were matched by exceptional wit. His telegrams were so well written and compelling that they instantly became the talk of the State Department. His warmth touched countless colleagues and his judgment and resourcefulness countless lives.

Joe Kruzel was also a man with an apparently endless sense of humor. Over a three-decade career of service to our Nation, he retained also his idealism about our goals, while leavening it with a healthy dose of realism about the foibles of any large bureaucratic effort. One of his colleagues remarked that while others were focused on day-to-day events, Joe's eyes were always on the horizon. He saw that an undivided democratic Europe was within reach, and he led the Pentagon's efforts in reaching out to the East to make that dream a reality. All of us, including myself and Bill Perry, valued his sage and firm advice. He did not mince words, and we all listened.

Nelson Drew, who served on my own staff, was a rare combination of remarkable soldier, respected scholar, profound strategic thinker, and a fine human being: born to a military family, achieving an exceptional military career, but he made peace his calling. I remember meeting him for the very first time in my office this past July just after I had finished a call with Prime Minister Major. I asked those in the room a question about Bosnia, and Nelson stepped forward to answer it with his usual succinct and clear wisdom. He was always ready to step forward for peace in Bosnia.

Bob, Joe, and Nelson devoted their lives and they gave their lives to achieve that goal. Now we must follow the example they set to make sure this peace takes hold. Nothing we can say or do can bring our friends back again. But by striving to seal the peace in Bosnia for good, we can shape a future worthy of their noble sacrifice.

We honor their memory today and forever with the President's Citizens Medal.

Commander, post the orders.

[*At this point, Lt. Comdr. John M. Richardson, USN, Naval Aide to the President, read the citations, and the President presented the medals.*]

The President. Let me just say in closing that all Americans, whether or not they knew Bob, Joe, and Nelson, have been touched by their service to our country. Yesterday I saw it myself in Paris and just last month in my trip to the United Kingdom, to Ireland, to Germany and Spain. From people on the streets to Presidents and Prime Ministers, the world is looking for our leadership for peace because they know America can be trusted.

The world places that faith in our Nation because of the work of individual American citizens like Bob and Joe and Nelson. They embodied the spirit of service that sets our Nation apart. They stood for something larger than themselves. Like so many of their colleagues, they accepted hardship and the risks that go along with the job they embraced.

Often they were rewarded for their efforts only by more difficult assignments, for our country needs its best people precisely where the challenges are greatest. They answered that call to duty with courage and conviction and grace. They understood that our leadership requires our involvement and our commitment, not from the sidelines but on the ground at the heart of events.

These three exemplify the qualities that make our country strong: a faith that one person can touch the lives of many, a willingness to work hard for something they believed in, a generous heart and spirit. Their wonderful families that you have applauded so warmly today are perhaps the best and finest testament to the lives that they lived.

Without pause or complaint, they took it upon themselves to bring the gift of peace and freedom to others around the world, not for personal ambition but solely because it was the right thing to do.

Ralph Waldo Emerson once wrote, "Let him be great, and love shall follow him." Looking at the faces of Katharina Frasure and Sarah and Virginia, Gail Kruzel and John and Sarah, Sandy Drew and Samantha and Philip, and all the other family members here, we can say that love has truly followed these three great Americans we have honored.

May God bless and protect their memories, their families, and the country they gave everything to serve.

Thank you very much.

NOTE: The President spoke at 3:24 p.m. in Room 450 of the Old Executive Office Building. The medals were awarded posthumously to Robert Frasure, Joseph J. Kruzel, and Samuel Nelson Drew, who died on August 19 when their military vehicle crashed en route to Sarajevo, Bosnia.

Remarks on the Budget Negotiations
December 15, 1995

As all of you know, today the Republicans in Congress broke off our negotiations on how best to balance the budget in 7 years. They said they would not even continue to talk unless we agreed right now to make deep and unconscionable cuts in Medicare and Medicaid. That's unacceptable. The cuts they propose would deprive millions of people of health care: poor children, pregnant women, the disabled, seniors in nursing homes. They would let Medicare wither on the vine into a second-class system. And these things simply are not necessary to balance the budget.

You know, I don't agree with their very large tax cuts for wealthy Americans and for all the special interests that get help in their bill, but I did not require them to drop those provisions as a condition of just talking. But they wanted us to agree to big cuts in Medicare and Medicaid simply to talk.

Last week, before these talks even began, I forwarded to Congress a detailed plan to balance the budget in 7 years without violating our values. That plan contained a large amount of deficit reduction over and above our original proposal. Today we made yet another good-faith effort to resolve our differences. I have sought reasonable discussions and honest compromise to balance the budget.

Now the Republicans in Congress are not only refusing to talk; once again they're threatening to shut the Government down if I do not accept their deep cuts in health care, education, the environment, and their tax increases

on working families. I would not give in to such a threat last month, and I will not give in today.

I would remind you when we signed the last resolution, we said we would work in good faith to balance the budget in 7 years without harmful cuts in Medicare, Medicaid, education, the environment, agriculture, veterans benefits, and without raising taxes on working families.

So let me say again—and all Americans must understand this—the decision by the Republican congressional majority to shut the Government down has nothing, nothing, to do with the discussion over the 7-year balanced budget plan. Congress has simply refused to pass this year's budgets and has forced the Government to operate on a series of temporary approvals so that they can use the threat of a shutdown to pressure me and the congressional Democrats into approving long-term reductions in Medicare, Medicaid, education, and the environment that we believe strongly are not good for America.

It is wrong, it is simply wrong, for the congressional Republicans to insist that I make deep cuts in Medicare and Medicaid or they will not even talk, and furthermore, they will shut the Government down again just before Christmas.

The Congress should simply pass straightforward legislation to keep the Government open. And then our negotiators should return to the table without threats, without ultimatums, to discuss how we can find common ground on balancing the budget. That is what we ought to do. That is what I am willing to do. And the idea that we should abandon the commitment we made and they agreed to just a few days ago in not having unacceptable cuts in Medicare and Medicaid as a condition of talking is wrong, is wrong, and we should not do that.

Thank you very much.

NOTE: The President spoke at 5:39 p.m. in the Oval Office at the White House.

Letter to Congressional Leaders on the Low Income Home Energy Assistance Program
December 15, 1995

Dear Mr. Leader:

I am increasingly concerned that, under the current continuing resolution, the Low Income Home Energy Assistance program (LIHEAP) is not meeting the needs of families requiring heating assistance.

With the onset of winter, low-income families need more help to keep their homes warm. Each year, LIHEAP assistance goes to about six million needy households, many of which have an elderly or disabled member or young children.

Normally, by this time of year, States' energy assistance programs would be adequately funded to help households tackle high energy bills and insulate drafty homes. This year, however, Congress still has not passed a full-year appropriations bill for Labor, Health and Human Services, Education, and Related Agencies—the bill which funds LIHEAP. The House voted to end LIHEAP altogether.

Under the two continuing resolutions that have been enacted this fall, LIHEAP has been funded at only $232 million. Last year, over three times that amount was available to States between September and the end of December.

I strongly urge Congress to pass a full-year appropriation as soon as possible that includes funding for LIHEAP. At a minimum, Congress must enable the Administration to make available a seasonally appropriate share of the previously appropriated funds for LIHEAP.

Congress should act quickly. Since winter is almost upon us, a rising number of low-income Americans, particularly those living in colder regions, will continue to need more help to keep warm at home.

Sincerely,

BILL CLINTON

NOTE: Identical letters were sent to Newt Gingrich, Speaker of the House of Representatives; Robert Dole, Senate majority leader; Richard Gephardt, House Democratic leader; and Thomas Daschle, Senate Democratic leader.

Message on the Observance of Hanukkah
December 15, 1995

Warm greetings to all who are celebrating Hanukkah.

Each year, as the days grow shorter and the nights colder, we welcome the return of this Festival of Lights, and each year we find fresh meaning in its ageless story of the triumph of the Maccabees. We are reminded of God's powerful presence in our lives, strengthening and sustaining us in times of struggle. We are inspired to reflect upon the meaning of courage, commitment, and faith. We are encouraged to acknowledge our blessings—the love of family, the strength of community, the hope of peace. We rediscover the wisdom of pausing, in the rush and hurry of everyday life, to give joyful thanks for these blessings.

This year, especially, we need such reminders, for with the death of Yitzhak Rabin, a great man, a true friend, and a peacemaker was taken from our midst. But as families throughout our nation and around the world gather to rekindle the flames of the menorah, let us renew our faith that God will continue to guide our steps through adversity until we can all rejoice in the light of peace.

Hillary and I extend best wishes for a joyous Hanukkah and a wonderful holiday season.

BILL CLINTON

Statement on the Nomination of General Joseph W. Ralston to be Vice Chairman of the Joint Chiefs of Staff
December 15, 1995

I am pleased to announce that I have nominated Gen. Joseph W. Ralston, U.S. Air Force, for assignment as Vice Chairman of the Joint Chiefs of Staff, succeeding Adm. William A. Owens, who is retiring.

General Ralston currently serves as the Commander, Air Combat Command. In this capacity, he is responsible for training and equipping all active Air Force, Air National Guard, and Air Force Reserve combat wings and squadrons in the United States and Panama. During his distinguished career, General Ralston flew more than 2,500 flying hours, including 147 combat missions over Laos and North Vietnam. He also served as the Air Force's Director for Tactical Programs and its Director for Operational Requirements. In the latter capacity, his championing of the rapid transition of advanced technology to the battlefield was instrumental in determining the shape and force structure of tomorrow's Air Force. General Ralston brings to the job of Vice Chairman a wealth of experience in the development of military requirements and an indepth knowledge of the defense acquisition

process. These and other attributes provide General Ralston the requisite leadership and management necessary for the post of Vice Chairman at a critical time in the history of the Armed Forces.

I will depend upon General Ralston to continue the initiatives of Admiral Owens which are designed to ensure that our Armed Forces best determine their warfighting requirements and capabilities. I commend Admiral Owens for his exemplary service to his Nation. His sound military advice on the use of military power to back U.S. diplomacy, his crucial role in shaping our forces to fight as a joint team, and the superlative leadership he provided in harnessing the information and technological revolution to our current and future defense posture will ensure that our military will remain the best in the world as we enter the 21st century. Admiral Owens will truly be missed in the senior decisionmaking ranks of our national security structure. Hillary and I join in wishing him the very best as he begins a new phase of his life.

The President's Radio Address
December 16, 1995

Good morning. At midnight last night, for the second time in a month, the Republican Congress shut down the Federal Government in an effort to force through their unacceptable cuts in health care, education, and the environment.

For weeks, my administration and the Republicans in Congress have been in serious negotiations over how to reach common ground on balancing the budget. A week ago, I forwarded to them a plan that would protect our principles and balance the budget in 7 years. I had hoped

that this time would be different, that we were past the Republican threats to shut down the Government just to get their way.

But yesterday, they broke off our talks. Unbelievably, they actually said that as a condition for our talks to continue, we had to agree right now to make deep and unconscionable cuts in Medicare and Medicaid. That is unacceptable.

The cuts they propose would deprive millions of people of health care: poor children, pregnant women, the disabled, seniors in nursing homes.

They would let Medicare wither on the vine into a second-class system. Now, these things simply are not necessary to balance the budget.

Let me be clear: As I have said from the beginning, I very much want to work with Congress to get a balanced budget. After all, working with the previous Congress in my first 2 years as President, we cut the deficit I found when I became President in half. We reduced the size of the Federal Government by 200,000. We ought to finish the job. We shouldn't leave a legacy of debt to our children, but neither should we leave the next generation a legacy of neglect.

We've cut the deficit in half while continuing to invest in education, technology, research, the environment, Medicare, and Medicaid and cutting taxes on the most hard-pressed of our working people. That's what we ought to do in this budget plan.

Now as far as shutting the Government down goes, this is not a result of our lack of agreement on a balanced budget plan; the two things have no connection. The facts are plain: The Congress has failed to pass a budget for next year and the bills that would fund the agencies of Government on purpose. They have deliberately done this to force me to accept their long-term agenda of big cuts in Medicare, Medicaid, education, and the environment and a tax increase on working people. That's what's in their balanced budget plan. But it's not necessary to balance the budget. So for them to cause a shutdown, denying Americans the services their tax dollars support, as a tactic in the budget debate is wrong. It's irresponsible. I won't give in to the threat. I didn't last time, and I can't now. Let me tell you why.

I know you've been told that the winners and losers of this budget battle are all in Washington and it's all politics. But that's not true. America's children would bear the most pain from the sharp cuts proposed by the Republican Congress. If the Republican plan becomes law, millions of children would be denied basics they need: health care they now have, schooling they can count on, school lunches, a safe place to live, or air and water we can be sure is safe to breathe and to drink.

Just consider what would happen to Medicaid. For three decades, Medicaid has been a legal guarantee for millions who need medical care. It has been the primary source of health care for nearly one in five American children. And more than half of the children on Medicaid live in families with working parents. It is not a welfare program. But the Republican plan repeals Medicaid's guarantees, and that spells disaster for families in the middle class who are caught unprepared. Medicaid helps millions of children who are disabled or who suffer from chronic illnesses or who have the AIDS virus. But the Republican plan could pull this lifeline from millions of children.

In education, the Republican plan eliminates Head Start for 180,000 preschoolers. It cuts our efforts to keep drugs and violence out of our schools. It undermines our efforts to help schools meet national standards of excellence for the first time. It kills the AmeriCorps national service program. It denies scholarships to more than 350,000 deserving college students and takes away the best student loan program available to young people—it lowers the cost and eases the terms of repayment.

The Republican plan would raise taxes for over 7 million of our hardest pressed working families. Their budget cuts would leave children exposed to hazardous waste. And we know that pollution affects children more than it does adults. We want to clean up these sites, but the Republican cuts would limit what we can do.

The Republican budget cuts are aimed squarely at our children. They will face larger classes and fewer Head Start programs. Ten million will live near toxic waste sites that won't be cleaned. Fewer will be immunized. Millions will be denied adequate medical care. And more than one million will be forced into poverty.

That is no way to treat our children. Let them threaten to shut the Government down. It is not necessary to do this to balance the budget, and so I am not going to let them hurt our children and compromise their future.

Our budget proposal shows these cuts are not necessary. Our plan balances the budget in 7 years, reforms Medicare and Medicaid, keeps costs down. It protects education and gives working families with children a tax break, not a tax increase. It is wrong for the congressional Republicans to insist that I make deep cuts in Medicare and Medicaid just as a condition to talk. It is wrong for them to shut the Government down again just before Christmas. It would be wrong for me to accept that threat. I rejected it last month; I reject it now.

I know this shutdown will affect the lives of millions of Americans, especially at this holiday season. I'll do whatever I can to lessen the impact. Above all, the Republicans should come back to the table. Congress should immediately pass straightforward legislation to reopen the Government. That is the responsible thing to do. And we should be talking again with each other about how to balance the budget in the interest of the American people.

I'll continue to fight for our American principles in this budget battle because that's the only way our children can come out the winners.

Thanks for listening.

NOTE: The President spoke at 10:06 a.m. from the Oval Office at the White House.

Remarks on the Budget
December 16, 1995

Let me, first of all, welcome all of you here. I thank you for being here. I imagine some of you have stayed here in an unplanned way over the weekend.

We are determined, as Democrats, to try to work together and to try to work with the Republicans to achieve a balanced budget but in a way that is consistent with our principles.

As all of you know, yesterday the Republican congressional leaders called the negotiations off unless we would first put much bigger Medicare and Medicaid cuts on the table. I thought that was wrong and unwarranted.

Virtually all of us don't agree with the large portions of their tax package and particularly a lot of the special interest provisions of it. But we didn't ask them to abandon it just to talk and begin negotiations.

So we hope that we can get back to a constructive dialog consistent with our values, our principles, and what's good for this country. And that's what we're going to be working on today.

We don't believe that decimating Medicare and Medicaid and undermining our investments in education and the environment, raising taxes on working families is a good prescription for America's future. And it is not necessary to balance the budget.

So we're going back to work today. We're going to keep working, trying to reach as much agreement among ourselves as possible, and then we'll keep reaching out to the Republicans in Congress in the hope of passing the right kind of balanced budget.

Thank you very much.

NOTE: The President spoke at 11:40 a.m. at Blair House, prior to a meeting with Democratic Members of Congress.

Remarks on Vetoing Appropriations Legislation for the Departments of the Interior, Veterans Affairs, and Housing and Urban Development and an Exchange With Reporters
December 18, 1995

The President. Good morning, everyone. The Republican Congress has shut down the Federal Government because they haven't passed a budget for this year and because they want to make the price of opening the Government up my acceptance of 7 long years of unacceptable cuts in health care, education, and the environment, in research and technology, cuts that are not necessary to balancing the budget and will have an adverse effect on our way of life and on the strength of our economy.

It is wrong for the Congress to shut the Government down just to make a political point the week before Christmas. It is unfair to the American people and unfair to the public employees. This is a season of peace, and it should be a season of cooperation, not rancor or threats. Congress should reopen the Government. I am ready to work with them to balance the budget in a way that reflects our values and that is consistent with the resolution to which we both agreed when the Government was reopened a few weeks ago.

So I call on Congress to reopen the Government, to come back to the negotiating table to resume discussions on finding common ground. We have to balance this budget in a way that reflects our values and our obligations to our children.

The ultimate test of any budget is what kind of world it leaves for future generations. If we balance the budget without investing in our children or protecting their environment, it means we are really borrowing from the next generation without ever paying them back. Protecting the environment is one of the most important ways to uphold this value. We want to pass on to our children the good Earth God gave us. We want to give them the opportunity we enjoy. We want to safeguard their health. Then any budget must ensure strong protection of the environment.

These science students who are with me today from Jefferson Middle School in Virginia have done a lot of work on the environment. They have helped to reduce energy use at their school. They have promoted recycling at home and at school. They know that the decisions that we make today will affect them and our Nation in the future. We owe it to them to put partisanship aside and to work in their interest to balance the budget in a way that protects the environment.

I say again, when I agreed a few weeks ago to work with the Congress to balance the budget in 7 years, Congress committed to a budget that protects the environment. These bills that I have to veto today I do because they do not meet that test. For 25 years, leaders of both parties have recognized that our country is stronger when we control pollution and protect public health. Environmental protection is not, or at least it never has been until now, a partisan issue. It's an American issue. It's an American issue outside Washington. But Republicans in this Congress have attempted to roll back decades of bipartisan environmental protection. It's wrong, and I cannot permit it to happen.

They have sent me legislation that would give our children less clean drinking water, less safe food, dirtier air. If I sign these bills, I would be condemning more than 10 million children under the age of 12 to living near toxic waste sites that might not be cleaned up for years. Therefore, in the interest of our children I am vetoing these measures because they would cripple these kinds of environmental protections.

The bill that funds the Environmental Protection Agency, for example, would cut enforcement by 25 percent and pull the cop from the pollution beat. There would be a 45 percent cut in safe-and-clean-drinking-water aid to local governments. The bill that funds the Department of the Interior would endanger some of our most precious natural resources. It would permit clearcutting in the Tongass National Forest in Alaska, and it would undercut our newest national park, the Mojave National Preserve in California, the largest addition to the park system in the lower 48 States.

I'm vetoing the bills not only because of the impact they have on the environment that we leave our children but also because of other things they do that violate our values. They completely eliminate the national service program, which has been very successful and is broadly supported by people across partisan lines and communities all across America. They cut innovative programs for economic development in our cities, the area which has been left most untouched by the economic recovery of the last 3 years. They drastically, drastically, cut services for Native Americans, and they cut health care for veterans. None of these things are necessary to balance the budget.

Let me be clear: It is time to finish the job of passing a budget for this year, and I am eager to work with the Congress to reach agreement on a balanced budget plan. We should be able quickly to reach agreement on how to fund the Government for the months to come.

I have made a specific compromise offer to finish this year's budget so we can get the Government working for the people. Then we can resolve our larger differences over how best to balance the budget consistent with our values. We owe it to our children and their children to do both these things. We do need to balance the budget, and I am committed to doing it.

I would remind you that we've cut the budget deficit in half since we've been here, and I want to go all the way. But doing things that weaken our environment is not the way to balance the budget and is directly contradictory to the resolution that both the Congress and I agreed upon just a few weeks ago.

So I'm going to sign the veto messages, and then I'll answer a few of your questions.

[At this point, the President signed the veto messages.]

Q. Have you been in touch with the Republican leadership today, and is there a chance of any kind of a meeting and is there any chance of bringing workers back to work?

The President. Well, I expect to talk to them today, and I look forward to that. And I'm going to do what I can to make some suggestions about how we can begin our talks. And I hope that they will agree to put the Government back in business. That, of course, is a decision within their domain. I think it's always a mistake to shut the Government down.

We should go back to the ordinary, constitutional way of dealing with this. I have dealt with them in good faith. I will continue to do so. I worked all weekend—continued to work all weekend on budgetary matters. I have spent an enormous amount of my time as President trying to get rid of the deficit and invest in our future at the same time. We have differences of opinion about how to do it, but there's no doubt that I want to do it. And I think that this shutting the Government down is just wrong. It's not right for the American people, it's not necessary, and it's not part of the ordinary, constitutional way of doing things around here.

Q. Mr. President, do you have a 7-year—a new 7-year proposal that balances the budget using CBO numbers?

The President. Well, I want to talk to the leadership, Mr. Blitzer [Wolf Blitzer, Cable News Network], about what we're going to say today, and then we'll be glad to answer questions after that.

Q. When do you think it will happen that you'll talk to them?

The President. Soon. Pretty soon. I've got to work out the times.

Q. Are they going to come over here, do you think?

The President. I don't know.

Q. Senator Dole says that if he and you and Speaker Gingrich could just sit down together for a few hours you could work this problem out pretty rapidly.

The President. I think that is possible. It requires—all three of us have to want to. But I want to.

Q. Why not do it?

The President. But we've all got to come in, and we've got to be flexible and we've got to look at what we're doing. I mean, you know, you mentioned the CBO—one of the things that the resolution said was that there would be extensive consultation with OMB and with the private sector. This budget of theirs now predicts a recession at 7 years. Now, how in the world they could know there's going to be one in year 6 and 7 is beyond me, but I believe if we were to balance the budget, particularly if we continue to invest in education and research and technology, it would grow the economy. It would get interest rates down; it would grow the economy.

They gave us a new set of assumptions which now has higher unemployment and higher interest rates, even with low inflation. I don't know how you can predict inflation goes down and interest rates go up. So—and, you know, I realize to a lot of Americans this may sound like just haggling or numbers or whatever, but there are people behind these numbers.

In this budget there are Native American children who won't get health care. In this budget there are serious, serious erosions in environmental protection. There are people—there are human interests here. We have to be careful as we do this. We cannot pretend that all these numbers are the same and it's just a political deal. This is not about politics; this is a very, very serious discussion. We are going to make some tough decisions, and we have to do it with a very great level of sensitivity about the impact of our decisions on people.

Q. You've provided us with your problems, some of your problems with the new CBO assumptions. Is it possible to protect your priorities and come up with a 7-year plan, according to their new forecast?

The President. Well, it depends on what kind of control mechanisms we have. It's conceivable. But I need to talk to them about that. And I intend to talk to them about it. I have no—and I'm not playing games with you. I just want to have my conversation with them first. I owe that to them. I don't want to carry on a war in the press over this. I would like it very much if we could just sit down and work through this.

But I sure think—it's Christmas week; they ought to open the Government again. That's the least we can do for the American people that have—you know, this is the only time of the year some people have to come here to Washington. And we've got a lot of Federal employees that don't need to lose a paycheck this week. They've got Christmas shopping to do; they've got things to do. I just think we ought to do it.

Q. Why do they keep saying you're not telling the truth?

The President. I don't know. You'll have to ask them that. I haven't—you know, I've tried to be very careful in this whole debate to deal with the specific facts and not to do characterizations like that. We have very different views, but if you read this—go back and read the resolution we agreed to. We agreed to strive to do our best to reach a 7-year balanced budget that the CBO would certify as balanced after consulting with OMB and with the private sector, that would protect the environment, would protect education, would protect agriculture and other things, and would invest in a way that really protected Medicare and Medicaid. And so we have certain standards to meet.

This is not easy to do; nobody ever pretended it would be easy to do. But I have been working to do it, and often I've felt that I was working only with myself. But over the weekend, we worked hard. We tried to involve more of the Democrats in the effort. We tried to—Mr. Panetta went up to see that bipartisan group of Senators. And I am eager to meet and discuss this with Senator Dole and with the Speaker.

But we ought to open the Government. We owe that to the American people. It's Christmas week; we need to open the Government and then work this out. We can do it.

Q. Is the key their cutting their tax cut proposal and your coming up with additional savings on Medicare and Medicaid?

The President. Well, that may be the key from their point of view. The key from my point of view is that there's got to be—there has to be funds—funds have to go back into the Medicare and Medicaid programs and into education and the environment and research and technology.

You know, I don't want—you can burden—we would burden future generations with the debt if we don't balance the budget. But we also will burden future generations if we don't protect the environment and we don't invest in education, research, and technology. And we just—on pure human terms, we cannot have this level of health care cuts.

So we're going to have to work this out. But I think it can be done, but we don't—they should open the Government, and I will work with them to get this done.

Speaker of the House Newt Gingrich

Q. How do you feel about fellow Time magazine man of the year?

The President. I think he's had a big impact on events. That's the standard. That's it.

Q. Thank you.

The President. Thank you very much.

Q. Thank you. Merry Christmas. Where did you get that tie?

The President. Someone gave it to me. It's one of my Christmas ties. You know, I try to wear one every day for the last 12 days before Christmas.

NOTE: The President spoke at 11:40 a.m. in the Oval Office at the White House.

Message to the House of Representatives Returning Without Approval the Department of the Interior and Related Agencies Appropriations Act, 1996
December 18, 1995

To the House of Representatives:

I am returning herewith without my approval H.R. 1977, the "Department of the Interior and Related Agencies Appropriations Act, 1996."

This bill is unacceptable because it would unduly restrict our ability to protect America's natural resources and cultural heritage, promote the technology we need for long-term energy conservation and economic growth, and provide adequate health, educational, and other services to Native Americans.

First, the bill makes wrong-headed choices with regard to the management and preservation of some of our most precious assets. In the Tongass National Forest in Alaska, it would allow harmful clear-cutting, require the sale of timber at unsustainable levels, and dictate the use of an outdated forest plan for the next 2 fiscal years.

In the Columbia River basin in the Pacific Northwest, the bill would impede implementation of our comprehensive plan for managing public lands—the Columbia River Basin Ecosystem Management Project. It would do this by prohibiting publication of a final Environmental Impact Statement or Record of Decision and requiring the exclusion of information on fisheries and watersheds. The result: a potential return to legal gridlock on timber harvesting, grazing, mining, and other economically important activities.

And in the California desert, the bill undermines our designation of the Mojave National Preserve by cutting funding for the Preserve and shifting responsibility for its management from the National Park Service to the Bureau of Land Management. The Mojave is our newest national park and part of the 1994 California Desert Protection Act—the largest addition to our park system in the lower 48 States. It deserves our support.

Moreover, the bill would impose a misguided moratorium on future listings and critical habitat designations under the Endangered Species Act. And in the case of one endangered species, the marbled murrelet, it would eliminate the normal flexibility for both the Departments of the Interior and Agriculture to use new scientific information in managing our forests.

Second, the bill slashes funding for the Department of Energy's energy conservation pro-grams. This is short-sighted and unwise. Investment in the technology of energy conservation is important for our Nation's long-term economic strength and environmental health. We should be doing all we can to maintain and sharpen our competitive edge, not back off.

Third, this bill fails to honor our historic obligations toward Native Americans. It provides inadequate funding for the Indian Health Service and our Indian Education programs. And the cuts targeted at key programs in the Bureau of Indian Affairs are crippling—including programs that support child welfare; adult vocational training; law enforcement and detention services; community fire protection; and general assistance to low-income Indian individuals and families. Moreover, the bill would unfairly single out certain self-governance tribes in Washington State for punitive treatment. Specifically, it would penalize these tribes financially for using legal remedies in disputes with non-tribal owners of land within reservations.

Finally, the bill represents a dramatic departure from our commitment to support for the arts and the humanities. It cuts funding of the National Endowments for the Arts and Humanities so deeply as to jeopardize their capacity to keep providing the cultural, educational, and artistic programs that enrich America's communities large and small.

For these reasons and others my Administration has conveyed to the Congress in earlier communications, I cannot accept this bill. It does not reflect my priorities or the values of the American people. I urge the Congress to send me a bill that truly serves the interests of our Nation and our citizens.

WILLIAM J. CLINTON

The White House,
December 18, 1995.

Message to the House of Representatives Returning Without Approval the Departments of Veterans Affairs and Housing and Urban Development, and Independent Agencies Appropriations Act, 1996
December 18, 1995

To the House of Representatives:

I am returning herewith without my approval H.R. 2099, the "Departments of Veterans Affairs and Housing and Urban Development, and Independent Agencies Appropriations Act, 1996."

H.R. 2099 would threaten public health and the environment, end programs that are helping communities help themselves, close the door on college for thousands of young people, and leave veterans seeking medical care with fewer treatment options.

The bill includes no funds for the highly successful National Service program. If such funding were eliminated, the bill would cost nearly 50,000 young Americans the opportunity to help their community, through AmeriCorps, to address vital local needs such as health care, crime prevention, and education while earning a monetary award to help them pursue additional education or training. I will not sign any version of this appropriations bill that does not restore funds for this vital program.

This bill includes a 22 percent cut in requested funding for the Environmental Protection Agency (EPA), including a 25 percent cut in enforcement that would cripple EPA efforts to enforce laws against polluters. Particularly objectionable are the bill's 25 percent cut in Superfund, which would continue to expose hundreds of thousands of citizens to dangerous chemicals and cuts, which would hamper efforts to train workers in hazardous waste cleanup.

In addition to severe funding cuts for EPA, the bill also includes legislative riders that were tacked onto the bill without any hearings or adequate public input, including one that would prevent EPA from exercising its authority under the Clean Water Act to prevent wetlands losses.

I am concerned about the bill's $762 million reduction to my request for funds that would go directly to States and needy cities for clean water and drinking water needs, such as assistance to clean up Boston Harbor. I also object to cuts the Congress has made in environmental technology, the climate change action plan, and other environmental programs.

The bill would reduce funding for the Council for Environmental Quality by more than half. Such a reduction would severely hamper the Council's ability to provide me with advice on environmental policy and carry out its responsibilities under the National Environmental Policy Act.

The bill provides no new funding for the Community Development Financial Institutions program, an important initiative for bringing credit and growth to communities long left behind.

While the bill provides spending authority for several important initiatives of the Department of Housing and Urban Development (HUD), including Community Development Block Grants, homeless assistance and the sale of HUD-owned properties, it lacks funding for others. For example, the bill provides no funds to support economic development initiatives; it has insufficient funds for incremental rental vouchers; and it cuts nearly in half my request for tearing down the most severely distressed housing projects. Also, the bill contains harmful riders that would transfer HUD's Fair Housing activities to the Justice Department and eliminate Federal preferences in the section 8, tenant-based program.

The bill provides less than I requested for the medical care of this Nation's veterans. It includes significant restrictions on funding for the Secretary of Veterans Affairs that appear designed to impede him from carrying out his duties as an advocate for veterans. Further, the bill does not provide necessary funding for VA hospital construction.

For these reasons and others my Administration has conveyed to the Congress in earlier communications, I cannot accept this bill. This bill does not reflect the values that Americans hold dear. I urge the Congress to send me an appropriations bill for these important priorities that truly serves the American people.

WILLIAM J. CLINTON

The White House,
December 18, 1995.

Remarks on Signing the Memorandum on Federal Arrestee Drug Testing and an Exchange With Reporters
December 18, 1995

The President. I want to welcome the Attorney General; United States Attorneys Eric Holder of Washington, DC, and Kathryn Landreth of Nevada; the Attorney General of Minnesota, Skip Humphrey; District Attorney Lynne Abraham of Philadelphia; District Attorney Michael Barnes of South Bend, Indiana, who is president of the National District Attorneys Association; and Jeremy Travis of the National Institute of Justice. I thank all of them for joining me here today.

I am about to sign a directive to the Attorney General instructing her to take the next step in our administration's all-out effort to break the cycle of crime and drugs.

The criminal justice systems of our country are overburdened with drug-abusing defendants who cycle through the system while continuing to use drugs. Far too many criminals brought into our system have a substance abuse problem. In fact, a 1993 study by the Justice Department found that more than half of the arrestees tested positive for an illicit substance. Unless we break the cycle of drugs and crime, criminal addicts will end up back on the street committing more crimes and then right back in the criminal justice system still hooked on drugs. That's not fair to the taxpayers, the crime victims, or the American public. The cycle must be broken.

All across our country employers have accepted responsibility to reduce the level of drug use in the workplace. Teachers and coaches have accepted the responsibility to reduce the level of drug use in our schools. Now it is time for agencies in our criminal justice system to use all their power to reduce drug use by Federal arrestees.

With this directive, when you enter the Federal criminal justice system, you will be tested. If you have been taking drugs, you should suffer the consequences. The administration is committed to breaking this link between crime and drugs. Indeed, if we could break it, we could dramatically lower the crime rate.

As a nation, there is only one message we can send: Continued drug use is unacceptable. We can't have a comprehensive crime-fighting effort until we end drug offenders' habits. That's

why it's critical that the criminal justice system put all its power behind cleaning up drug-abusing criminals.

This directive is another example in which the Federal criminal justice system can serve as a model for States. I'm very honored to be joined by the Minnesota Attorney General, Mr. Humphrey, and the district attorneys of Philadelphia and South Bend, Indiana. When they leave here today they're going home to ask their State legislatures to follow our lead in making sure all offenders are drug tested. I call upon every Governor, every State assembly, every State attorney general to do the same.

I'm proud of our antidrug strategy. It combines tough enforcement with a real, comprehensive prevention program and more investment in treatment. This directive is another step in our efforts to eliminate illegal drug use.

We know that reducing drug use will require everyone's effort. That's why today, our drug director, Dr. Lee Brown, is in California urging high school coaches to adopt drug testing of their athletes in order to reduce drug use among our teenagers.

These two actions send a clear and unambiguous message: Drug use and drug abuse are both wrong and illegal. We can't tolerate a revolving door of criminal drug abusers in our system. And if we work together, we can ensure that all the offenders in our country become drug-free and stay drug-free if they're going to stay out of jail.

Just yesterday, the FBI reported that for the first 6 months of this year, violent crime was down by 5 percent and the murder rate was down by 12 percent. Over the last 3 years, we've made "three strikes and you're out" the law of the land, passed the Brady bill, the assault weapons ban. We're well on our way to putting those 100,000 new police officers on the American streets. But there is still one very disturbing and unacceptable finding in the FBI report, the trend of violence being committed by juveniles.

Later this week, I will be sending the Enhanced Prosecution of Dangerous Juvenile Offenders Act to the Congress. This legislation will help to address the critical problem of youth criminals by strengthening Federal laws designed to deal with genuinely violent use. It's an additional tool for prosecutors to deal with violent juvenile criminals by holding dangerous youth criminals accountable for their actions. Once they've been arrested, we must stop them from repeating their crimes.

With these steps that we've announced today, Federal arrestees who are abusing drugs will no longer be out on the streets, and hardened criminals will be dealt with accordingly, even if they're juveniles.

[At this point, the President signed the memorandum.]

Drug Policy

Q. Do you think that's constitutional?

The President. The way it is drawn, I do. The Attorney General might want to explain it, but basically, in the places where this has been tried the people who are arrested are asked to undergo drug testing. As I understand it, about 80 percent of them agree. If they don't agree, instead of being forced it's just reported to the judge in making a determination about how high to set bail and what the conditions of bail should be.

Q. Well, if they are found to have taken drugs, does this mean they're not eligible for bail?

The President. Well, it means it can change the circumstances under which they're tried and what they might have to do as a condition.

Do you want to discuss that?

Attorney General Reno. What it is saying—it is clearly constitutional to condition bail on testing. And what this says is, if you are going to get bail, you may have to agree to testing, you may have to agree to continued testing, to supervision, to certain conduct while you're on bail. Or it may mean that you have got to remain in the jail because the conditions would not ensure that you would be drug-free once you were on the streets.

Q. Wouldn't you be subject to additional charges, though? You know, in other words, you're arrested on some totally unrelated charge and you're found to have had drugs.

Attorney General Reno. What we're trying to do is to prevent the unrelated charge that happens once they've left the courthouse. And if they are using drugs and if drugs are what is fueling so much of crime in this country, to

send them back out without doing something to interrupt that cycle and to let a crime happen that was drug induced doesn't make any sense.

What the President is doing here is saying, look, we're going to try to do everything we can to ensure the safety of our streets based on these offenders and their condition, and we're also going to try to do something to make sure that we interrupt the cycle of drug use on the part of these offenders.

Budget Impasse

Q. Mr. President, what do you hear from the Speaker and Senator Dole on the budget and opening the Government again?

The President. Well, I had talks with both of them this afternoon, and I offered—first, I asked them to open the Government again, and to do it immediately, so that the people who have made plans for Christmas week to be here and elsewhere would not be disappointed and so that the Federal employees would not be basically disoriented during this Christmas week. And I offered some ideas about how we might reopen the Government and how we might resume our budget negotiations. And they agreed to take my ideas under advisement and to speak with each other, perhaps with others as well.

So I don't think I should talk about specifically what I said to them until I hear back from them. I think that would be wrong. I owe it to them to have a chance to consider this in a confidential matter on their own time.

Q. Did you invite them to come over here to sit down with you and try to resolve this?

The President. I talked about how we could get together and my personal willingness to be involved. But I'd rather not talk about the specifics of it until I hear back from them.

Q. Do you think they'll respond tonight?

The President. I just don't know. I hope so. I want the Congress to open the Government again. This is not—this whole action is without precedent. I think we should stop it, and we should go back to the ordinary way of dealing with this.

I have demonstrated, I think, repeatedly, that I am committed to balancing the budget. I have shown that I will put forward a plan in 7 years. I have told them that I will work with them. And I will work with them, and I believe we can do it. But we ought to re-open the Government, the Congress should, for the benefit of the American people, especially this week. We shouldn't—this week the people and the employees should not be subject to this Government closing.

Q. Are you willing to have them over here as early as tonight, Mr. President?

The President. Well, I'd like to give them the chance to get back to me. I think it's important that I not talk anymore about the contents of my conversation until they have a chance to consider it and get back to me.

Q. Are you more encouraged, though, by what you heard in this phone call that the Government can get back to working 100 percent?

The President. I hope so. That's all I can say. I hope so.

NOTE: The President spoke at 4:35 p.m. in the Oval Office at the White House.

Memorandum on Federal Arrestee Drug Testing
December 18, 1995

Memorandum for the Attorney General

Subject: Development of the Administration's Federal Arrestee Drug Testing Policy

Illegal drugs plague our communities, causing despair and illness, and, most importantly, contributing significantly to unacceptable levels of crime and violence. More than half of all individuals brought into the Nation's criminal justice system have substance abuse problems. Too often, the same criminal drug users cycle through the court, corrections, and probation systems still hooked on drugs and still committing crimes to support their habit.

We can and will continue to prosecute and convict these criminal drug users. Yet our criminal justice system must do more to try to reduce drug use. Across the country, employers have accepted their corporate responsibility to reduce the levels of drug use within their workplaces.

So too, the agencies of our criminal justice system must do their part, giving criminal drug users powerful incentives to stay off drugs by putting a high price on continued drug use. These incentives—commonly referred to as "coerced abstinence"—should be applied at the earliest possible stage in a person's interaction with the criminal justice system—following arrest.

To ensure that we are doing all we can to break the cycle of drugs and crime, I am directing you to develop a universal policy providing for drug testing of all Federal arrestees before decisions are made on whether to release them into the community pending trial. I further direct that you establish a policy whereby Federal prosecutors will seek appropriate measures for arrestees who fail pretrial drug tests.

The Federal criminal justice system should serve as a model for State criminal justice systems—where the majority of criminal cases are processed and the cycle of repeat drug-related offenders is most evident. Therefore, I am also directing you to take all appropriate steps to encourage States to adopt and implement the same policies that we are initiating at the Federal level.

You should report to me in writing by March 31, 1996, on the specific steps you will take to implement this policy.

WILLIAM J. CLINTON

Remarks on Signing the Lobbying Disclosure Act of 1995 and an Exchange With Reporters
December 19, 1995

The President. Good morning, ladies and gentlemen. Today, after two decades of gridlock,

I am very proud to be able to sign this legislation to bring lobbying in Washington into the sunlight of public scrutiny.

Last year when lobbying reform legislation was filibustered to death, there were lobbyists crowded outside the Senate Chamber who literally cheered. Today I sign that bill into law. And that's something for the American people to cheer about.

I want to begin by thanking those whose efforts made this possible. And their efforts were constant, longstanding, and carried on, I might add, from time to time under great duress.

First, let me say I believe this new law to bring lobbying into the open would never have happened without the leadership of Senator Carl Levin. The first conversation that he and I had after I was elected President was about this legislation, and therefore in a very real sense this lobby reform law is a monument to the years and years of effort that Carl Levin has made. And I thank you, Senator, for that.

There are many, many other Members of Congress in both parties who played a pivotal role in enacting this needed reform. Many of them are here today, and I want to thank them. I want to thank Senator Cohen and Senator Wellstone. And I want to thank Congressman Bryant, Congressman Canady, Congressman Frank, Congressman Fazio, Congressman McHale, Congressman Chris Shays, Congressman Goss, Congressman Doggett, and Congressman Barrett, who was not able to be here today.

On this matter, Democrats and Republicans acted together to put the public interest before partisanship. And they faced withering pressure to do otherwise. This law is also a testament to the thousands of citizens who were members of groups lobbying for this, members of Common Cause, Public Citizen, and many other groups, who have sought to make real the promise of our democracy. It is also, frankly, a testament to the efforts of thousands of citizens who belong to no particular group but who showed up at town meetings that these Members and others had all across our country. They were Republicans and Democrats and independents, people who wanted this kind of change, real change, for a very, very long time.

Lobbying has its rightful place in our system. I believe every Member here and every Member who voted for this bill understands that and understands what a valuable role lobbying can play in the American system. At one time or another, just about every American citizen has

wanted to be a lobbyist before the Congress on one issue or another.

But ordinary Americans also understand that organized interests too often can hold too much sway in the halls of power. They know that in Washington an influence industry too often operates in secret and gets special privileges not available to most Americans. Lobbyists in the back room secretly rewriting laws and looking for loopholes do not have a place in our democracy. All the people should know what is done by people who affect public decisions.

I ran for President in large measure to renew our democracy, to give ordinary Americans a greater stake in our Government. I strongly called for reform measures, including this bill, from the very beginning. Shortly after I took office, I implemented the toughest ethics code on executive officials in our history, barring senior appointees from lobbying their own agencies for 5 years after leaving office and from ever lobbying for foreign governments. We repealed the tax loophole that let lobbyists deduct the cost of their activities and enacted the motor voter bill which will add millions of new voters to the rolls.

Until today, the rules governing lobbyists, virtually unchanged since 1946, have been more of a loophole than a law. For the first time this new law requires professional lobbyists to disclose publicly who they are, for whom they work, what they're spending, and what bills they're trying to pass, kill, or amend. The bill is tough. It will pull back the curtains from the world of Washington lobbying. It will help to restore the trust of the American people in their Government. It is a good bill for America.

At the outset of this year, I asked the Congress to take four major steps toward political reform. First, I asked them to apply to themselves the laws that they pass governing the rest of America. Congress took this step, thanks to the hard work of many lawmakers here today.

Second, I asked the Congress to give up gifts, meals, and trips from lobbyists. Earlier this year, Congress agreed to that, and I applaud them for that.

Thirdly, I asked Congress to enact strong lobbying disclosure. Shortly, I will sign that bill into law. And I think it is fair to say, thanks to the efforts of these gentlemen and others, that bill is much stronger than most people ever dreamed would pass the United States Congress.

Fourth, I asked the Congress to reduce the influence of money on elections. And though Congress still has not acted, there is sign of hope here as well. Truly bipartisan legislation is now moving forward in both the Senate and the House to limit spending, curb PACs and lobbyists, provide free TV time for candidates, and end the soft money system, proposals virtually identical to the ones I advocated in 1992. They are real reform. And I look forward to working with lawmakers from both parties in the months ahead to quickly enact campaign finance reform as well.

For now, let us recognize and appreciate the significant step being taken today. This law says the days of secret lobbying are over. Throughout our history, the people of our country have fought to make the Government heed their voice. This new law is in the best tradition of America, one articulated by President Andrew Jackson a long time ago, "Equal opportunity for all; special privileges for none."

Thank you very much, all of you.

[At this point, the President signed the legislation.]

Budget Impasse

Q. Do you think you're going to get a CR before Christmas?

The President. I certainly hope so. We're going to have a meeting this afternoon, and I'm looking forward to it. The Speaker and Senator Dole are coming over, and then we'll have some more meetings. And I hope we can work it out.

If you look at this legislation, this is an example of what we can do if we focus on one goal and determine to achieve that goal and bridge our other differences. And I believe that about 80 percent of both Houses in Congress, maybe even more, would like to pass a 7-year balanced budget that has real credibility with the financial markets, that would keep interest rates coming down, keep home mortgages being refinanced, keep investment flowing into the country to keep this economy going.

Q. They won't agree to your conditions.

The President. Well, you don't know that. We'll see. We're going to keep talking. We've worked hard. I've worked hard. I worked all last weekend on this budget to do everything I can to pass a budget that is consistent. I even got—I gave this to all our folks today to make

sure that they would read and reread this—the actual language of the last continuing resolution. And so we're working on it very hard.

Q. You said that in this bill the Democrats and Republicans put partisan considerations aside and worked for the public interest. Do you feel that the White House and the Republicans can do that now on the budget?

The President. Yes. It's more difficult because there are 80 or 90 issues—policy issues that we have some differences on. But if we say what our goal is, our goal is to pass a credible balanced budget plan, recognizing that no one can foresee what will happen in every year of the next 7 years but that a plan that is passed, that is credible, that is ultimately certified by the Congressional Budget Office, that the financial markets and the business community, the ultimate judge of this, say, this is a good plan. This is going to work. That would be a very good thing for America. I think we can do it.

The Economy

Q. You sound concerned, Mr. President, about the financial markets; you brought it up twice this morning. Are you worried about the hit it took yesterday?

The President. Not especially. I don't like to comment on short-term changes in the market. You know, when I ran for President, I said I thought if we could pass a credible deficit reduction plan in 1993, we could create over 8 million jobs and we'd get a stock market of 4,000. I never dreamed it would go to 5. [Laughter] So the American economy is very strong, very vibrant. And in an economy with a free market system with this much activity, there's going to be changes in the market. You know there are, always have been, always will be. I don't think we should comment on that or read too much into it one way or the other.

Securities Litigation Reform

Q. Are you going to sign the securities litigation reform, Mr. President?

The President. For the last week, I have spent several hours on that. I believe that some legislative activity there is warranted, and I'm going to have a final review today. Yesterday I had a long meeting, and I asked one particular question and asked it to be researched at some length. I'll have a meeting later this afternoon; I'll have an announcement sometime today about it.

Thank you.

NOTE: The President spoke at 10:09 a.m. in the Roosevelt Room at the White House. S. 1060, ap-proved December 19, was assigned Public Law No. 104–65.

Statement on Signing the Lobbying Disclosure Act of 1995
December 19, 1995

Today I am pleased to approve S. 1060, the "Lobbying Disclosure Act of 1995." I have strongly supported the purposes and principles embodied in this legislation since the beginning of my Administration. During my first days in office, I barred all top executive branch officials from lobbying their agencies for 5 years after leaving office and from ever lobbying for foreign governments. During the 103rd Congress, my Administration lent its strong support to congressional backers of legislation that served as the model for the Lobbying Disclosure Act of 1995.

As a general matter, S. 1060 provides for the disclosure of efforts by paid lobbyists to influence the decision-making process and actions of Federal legislative and executive branch officials. It replaces the existing patchwork of lobbying disclosure laws with a single, uniform statute that covers the activities of all professional lobbyists. Among other things, the bill streamlines lobbyist disclosure requirements and requires that professional lobbyists register and file regular reports identifying their clients, the issues on which they lobby, and the amount of their compensation. These are important steps in the right direction.

The Department of Justice has identified certain provisions in the Act that raise constitutional concerns—in particular, the role given to the Secretary of the Senate and the Clerk of the House of Representatives and the specific man-ner in which the legislation seeks to protect the exercise of religion. I shall instruct the Attorney General to apply and enforce the Act in a constitutional manner. This will ensure that the Act survives any challenge in court and thereby guarantee that the Act is fully effective in accomplishing its objectives, including the protection of religious expression.

In addition, section 21(b) of the Act would forbid the appointment as United States Trade Representative or Deputy United States Trade Representative, of anyone who had ever "directly represented, aided, or advised a foreign [government or political party] . . . in any trade negotiation, or trade dispute with the United States." The Congress may not, of course, impose broad restrictions on the President's constitutional prerogative to nominate persons of his choosing to the highest executive branch positions, and this is especially so in the area of foreign relations. However, because as a policy matter I agree with the goal of ensuring the undivided loyalty of our representatives in trade negotiations, I intend, as a matter of practice, to act in accordance with this provision.

WILLIAM J. CLINTON

The White House,
December 19, 1995.

NOTE: S. 1060, approved December 19, was assigned Public Law No. 104–65.

Remarks on Vetoing the Departments of Commerce, Justice, and State, the Judiciary, and Related Agencies Appropriations Act, 1996, and an Exchange With Reporters
December 19, 1995

The President. Good afternoon. I'm delighted to be joined by these police officers and by the Attorney General and Secretary Brown and the mayors of Chicago and Philadelphia and representatives of law enforcement who are here today.

For yet another day, the Republican Congress continues to keep our Government closed. Shortly, I will meet with Senator Dole and Speaker Gingrich. I hope we can resolve the situation and give the American people their Government back by Christmas.

We also should give them a balanced budget that reflects our values of opportunity for all, respecting our duty to our parents and our children, building strong communities and a strong America.

There is no value more basic than keeping our children safe. Unfortunately, the bill that the Congress passed to fund the Justice, Commerce, and State Departments failed to fulfill that essential obligation.

Last year, with the support of Members of both parties in Congress, I signed a crime bill into law. The key to that crime bill was our effort to put 100,000 new police officers on the street because we had clear, hard evidence that more police officers in community policing would actually lower the crime rate not only by catching more criminals but by preventing crime. Today we are awarding 5,500 police officers to communities all across America. That brings the grand total in less than 15 months to 31,000 new police officers for America's streets, almost a third of the 5-year total.

Everywhere I go, mayors and police chiefs and sheriffs tell me that community policing is helping them to fight crime and lower the crime rate. And the tide is turning. Yesterday, the FBI reported that the murder rate has dropped 12 percent in the last year. That's the largest decline in the murder rate since the FBI started keeping statistics 35 years ago. Violent crime is down 5 percent overall from last year's rate. We are turning the tide. We are beginning to win the fight against crime. This is no time to turn back the clock.

The crime bill is working because it provides funds for police officers directly to police departments. Unfortunately, this bill replaces this initiative which is guaranteed to put 100,000 police on the street with a block grant that has no guarantees at all. The bill that is before me does not guarantee that even one more police officer will be put on our streets, not one.

I gave my word in 1992 that I would work for 100,000 more police officers on the street. In 1994, when I signed that bill into law, it represented a solemn commitment by the United States Government that we would put 100,000 more police officers on the street. I intend to keep my word.

That is not the only reason I am vetoing this bill. Looking out for our families and our children is essential, and to do that, we have to look out for our future. The dawn of the information age is no time to turn out the lights on our research laboratories and our technology centers. But the Republican budget could cut nondefense research and development by as much as one-third over the next 7 years.

America thrives because we create opportunities for our children to create a better future. In this era of rapid technological change, we will only pass opportunity on to our children if we take advantage of American ingenuity and innovation. No business in the world today facing the pressures of the 21st century would gut its investment in research and technology, and no country should either.

The Japanese are in the midst of a serious recession. Yet their government just announced plans to double the Japanese research budget over the next 5 years. We have the lowest combined rates of unemployment and inflation in 27 years, and I do not intend to preside over a decision by Congress to cut our investment in research and technology by a third.

Look at the people who are winning the Nobel Prizes and see how many of them got Government-funded research. Look at the research that has been funded by our Government agencies over the last several years in new technologies, in new developments, and see the contribution that is made here. America has the strongest economy in the world in large measure because we are leading the race to the technology age. And I don't believe we should drop out of the race on the edge of a new century.

Of course, we have to balance the budget, but we don't need to do it by cutting back on police officers and risking our safety. We don't need to do it by slashing our research in science and technology and risking our future. Remember, balancing the budget is more important to our children than anything else. It's lifting the burden of future debt off our children. We don't want to impose on our children a restricted future by making them less safe today and less secure in terms of economic opportunity tomorrow.

There is one last thing I'd like to say. Eight months ago today, terror visited our children in Oklahoma City. The memory of that awful tragedy will be with us forever. Just yesterday, law enforcement officers found a bomb outside a Federal office building in Reno, Nevada. In the weeks after Oklahoma City, I sent to the Congress a bill to give law enforcement the tools they need to crack down on terrorism and to protect our families—terrorism arising from within the United States, terrorism coming from beyond our borders.

The Senate passed the bill last June with sweeping bipartisan support. But a few people with extreme views have prevented the House of Representatives from even considering the bill. They have held it up long enough. Here in this time of peace for our country, I ask all Americans to remember the victims of Oklahoma City, and I ask the Congress to give law enforcement the tools they need to be truly peace officers.

When they send me a bill that protects our families by keeping our promise to put 100,000 police officers on the street, they should also protect our families by keeping their promise to send us a strong antiterrorism bill.

Thank you.

[*At this point, the President signed the veto message.*]

Q. Mr. President, are your numbers on Medicare and Medicaid savings negotiable?

The President. You know what I said yesterday; I said—I carry this little statement around with me. This is the agreement I made with the Congress when we reopened the Govern-

ment. The agreement says that we will enact legislation to balance the budget in 7 years, protecting Medicare, Medicaid, education, the environment, and other things, and that the agreement we finally make must be scored by the Congressional Budget Office as bringing the budget into balance. What is not negotiable with me is that we must protect these things. I have proposed savings in Medicare and Medicaid that are considerable but that will protect both the integrity of the programs and the interest of the people who depend upon Medicare and Medicaid.

So what I said to the Speaker and to Senator Dole yesterday was if they wanted me to put down a 7-year budget on the front end, I expected them to respond to the second part of this resolution. This is not a resolution about just any old 7-year budget. This 7-year budget has all these things that we all agreed to to protect, and Medicare and Medicaid are at the top of that list.

Q. Can you protect Medicare and Medicaid with——

Q. ——seven years protecting all these things, including the things the Republicans added to it?

The President. Well, it depends on a lot of other variables. That's why—we were negotiating in good faith at the time they called the negotiations off last week, apparently because of the group in the House that has been controlling a lot of the decisions here for the last several months. We have put forward more than twice as many policy changes as they had in a good-faith effort to reach agreement.

The answer to your question is, yes, we could pass a 7-year budget that protects Medicare and Medicaid, education and the environment, and that does not—and our research and technology budget—and does not raise taxes on working families and that has great credibility in the financial markets. We can do that. If that is what the Congress wants to do, we can do it.

If instead the balanced budget is a cover for making war on the ability of the National Government to protect our common interest and to move us ahead, then I can't go along with that. But of course we can do it. And I hope that after this meeting I'm going to have in a few minutes, we'll be closer to doing it.

Q. Do you expect to get an agreement to reopen the Government at this meeting?

The President. I don't know. That's up to the Congress. Only the Congress can shut the Government down, and only the Congress can reopen it. But they can certainly reopen it, and I hope they will, particularly this week. It's just wrong for the Federal employees, and even more for the American people, to have the Government close the week before Christmas. It is a decision they made, and they can undo it and I hope they will.

Q. Do you share the concerns, Mr. President, of the financial markets that lack of a budget agreement may keep interest rates locked in place or even turn them around and head them back upward?

The President. Well, let me say this. I think the action of the Federal Reserve today—although I don't want to comment on the merits of it one way or the other, but there's a general understanding that we have a—first of all, back in '93, we made some very tough decisions without any bipartisan support to bring the deficit down and to increase investment in technology and research and education and the environment, things that would grow the economy. Interest rates came down; billions of dollars were invested; there was a homebuilding boom; we got the economy going again.

The fundamentals of this economy were sound. There is good growth. There is low infla-

tion—I will say again, the lowest combined rates of inflation and unemployment in 27 years. And we have to continue on that track. I think the message ought to be to people who are concerned about that is that this deficit is going to keep coming down, regardless. There is too much determination for that. That is not what this debate is all about. The deficit will keep coming down, regardless. The leadership of both parties favors that.

But we must have a 7-year balanced budget plan that reflects our other values. We are doing well in the world economy because the deficit is coming down and because the other things that are being done in the private sector are good and because the other things the Government is doing are good things. So we have to keep doing all the right things if we want to succeed. That's what the debate over the budget plan is about.

If the markets are worried about whether the deficit is going to keep coming down, they should forget about that. The deficit is going to keep coming down, regardless.

Thank you.

NOTE: The President spoke at 2:34 p.m. in the Oval Office at the White House.

Message to the House of Representatives Returning Without Approval the Departments of Commerce, Justice, and State, the Judiciary, and Related Agencies Appropriations Act, 1996
December 19, 1995

To the House of Representatives:

I am returning herewith without my approval H.R. 2076, the "Departments of Commerce, Justice, and State, the Judiciary, and Related Agencies Appropriations Act, 1996."

This bill does not meet the priorities and needs of our Nation and people. It would undermine our ability to fight the war on crime; decimate technology programs that are critical to building a strong U.S. economy; and weaken our leadership in the world by drastically cutting funding for international organizations, peacekeeping, and other international affairs activities.

First, the bill represents an unacceptable retreat in our fight against crime and drugs. It eliminates my COPS initiative (Community Oriented Policing Services) to put 100,000 more police officers on the street. Already, this initiative has put thousands of police on the street, working hand-in-hand with their communities to fight crime. The block grant that H.R. 2076 would offer instead would not guarantee a single new police officer. That's not what the American people want, and I won't accept it. As I have said, I will not sign any version of this bill that does not fund the COPS initiative as a free-standing, discretionary grant program, as authorized.

The bill also eliminates my "drug courts" initiative. And it unwisely abandons crime prevention efforts such as the Ounce of Prevention Council and the Community Relations Service. I am also disappointed that the funding levels in the bill fall short of my request for the Drug Enforcement Administration, and OCDETF (Organized Crime Drug Enforcement Task Force). This is no time to let down our guard in the fight against drugs.

Second, the bill constitutes a short-sighted assault on the Commerce Department's technology programs that work effectively with business to expand our economy, help Americans compete in the global marketplace, and create high quality jobs. As we approach a new, technology-driven century, it makes no sense to eliminate an industry-driven, highly competitive, cost-shared initiative like our Advanced Technology Program (ATP), which fosters technology development, promotes industrial alliances, and creates jobs. Nor does it make sense to sharply cut funding for measures that will help assure our long-term growth and competitiveness—such as our National Information Infrastructure grants program, which helps connect schools, hospitals, and libraries to the information superhighway; the GLOBE program, which promotes the study of science and the environment in our schools; the Manufacturing Extension Partnership, which helps small manufacturers meet the hi-tech demands of the new marketplace; Defense Conversion; or the Technology Administration. And I oppose the bill's harmful cuts for the Census Bureau and for economic and statistical analysis.

Third, I am deeply concerned that this bill would undermine our global leadership and impair our ability to protect and defend important U.S. interests around the world—both by making unwise cuts in funding for international organizations and peacekeeping activities, and by cutting programs of the State Department, the Arms Control and Disarmament Agency, and the United States Information Agency. These cuts would impair our ability to support important activities such as the nonproliferation of weapons, the promotion of human rights, and the control of infectious disease like the Ebola virus. Moreover, sections of the bill include inappropriate restrictive language, including language limiting the conduct of U.S. diplomatic relations with Vietnam, that I believe infringe on Presidential prerogatives. And I cannot accept the provision that would cut off all funding for these agencies on April 1, 1996, unless the State Department Authorization Act and related legislation had been signed into law.

Fourth, the bill includes three additional provisions that I cannot accept.

It cripples the capacity of the Legal Services Corporation (LSC) to fulfill its historic mission of serving people in need—slashing its overall funding, sharply limiting the administrative funds LSC needs to conduct its business, and imposing excessive restrictions on LSC's operations. LSC should be allowed to carry on its work in an appropriate manner, both in its basic programs and in special initiatives like the migrant legal services program.

Section 103 of the bill would prohibit the use of funds for performing abortions, except in cases involving rape or danger to the life of the mother. The Justice Department has advised that there is a substantial risk that this provision would be held unconstitutional as applied to female prison inmates.

The bill also includes an ill-considered legislative rider that would impose a moratorium on future listings under the Endangered Species Act by the National Oceanic and Atmospheric Administration and other agencies. That rider not only would make bad policy, it also has no place in this bill.

Finally, I would urge the Congress to continue the Associate Attorney General's office.

For these reasons and others my Administration has conveyed to the Congress in earlier communications, I cannot accept this bill. H.R. 2076 does not reflect my priorities or the values of the American people. I urge the Congress to send me an appropriations bill that truly serves this Nation and its people.

WILLIAM J. CLINTON

The White House,
December 19, 1995.

Message to the House of Representatives Returning Without Approval the Private Securities Litigation Reform Act of 1995
December 19, 1995

To the House of Representatives:

I am returning herewith without my approval H.R. 1058, the "Private Securities Litigation Reform Act of 1995." This legislation is designed to reform portions of the Federal securities laws to end frivolous lawsuits and to ensure that investors receive the best possible information by reducing the litigation risk to companies that make forward-looking statements.

I support those goals. Indeed, I made clear my willingness to support the bill passed by the Senate with appropriate "safe harbor" language, even though it did not include certain provisions that I favor—such as enhanced provisions with respect to joint and several liability, aider and abettor liability, and statute of limitations.

I am not, however, willing to sign legislation that will have the effect of closing the courthouse door on investors who have legitimate claims. Those who are the victims of fraud should have recourse in our courts. Unfortunately, changes made in this bill during conference could well prevent that.

This country is blessed by strong and vibrant markets and I believe that they function best when corporations can raise capital by providing investors with their best good-faith assessment of future prospects, without fear of costly, unwarranted litigation. But I also know that our markets are as strong and effective as they are because they operate—and are seen to operate—with integrity. I believe that this bill, as modified in conference, could erode this crucial basis of our markets' strength.

Specifically, I object to the following elements of this bill. First, I believe that the pleading requirements of the Conference Report with regard to a defendant's state of mind impose an unacceptable procedural hurdle to meritorious claims being heard in Federal courts. I am prepared to support the high pleading standard of the U.S. Court of Appeals for the Second Circuit—the highest pleading standard of any Federal circuit court. But the conferees make crystal clear in the Statement of Managers their intent to raise the standard even beyond that level. I am not prepared to accept that.

The conferees deleted an amendment offered by Senator Specter and adopted by the Senate that specifically incorporated Second Circuit case law with respect to pleading a claim of fraud. Then they specifically indicated that they were *not* adopting Second Circuit case law but instead intended to "strengthen" the existing pleading requirements of the Second Circuit. All this shows that the conferees meant to erect a higher barrier to bringing suit than any now existing—one so high that even the most aggrieved investors with the most painful losses may get tossed out of court before they have a chance to prove their case.

Second, while I support the language of the Conference Report providing a "safe harbor" for companies that include meaningful cautionary statements in their projections of earnings, the Statement of Managers—which will be used by courts as a guide to the intent of the Congress with regard to the meaning of the bill—attempts to weaken the cautionary language that the bill itself requires. Once again, the end result may be that investors find their legitimate claims unfairly dismissed.

Third, the Conference Report's Rule 11 provision lacks balance, treating plaintiffs more harshly than defendants in a manner that comes too close to the "loser pays" standard I oppose.

I want to sign a good bill and I am prepared to do exactly that if the Congress will make the following changes to this legislation: first, adopt the Second Circuit pleading standards and reinsert the Specter amendment into the bill. I will support a bill that submits all plaintiffs to the tough pleading standards of the Second Circuit, but I am not prepared to go beyond that. Second, remove the language in the Statement of Managers that waters down the nature of the cautionary language that must be included to make the safe harbor safe. Third, restore the Rule 11 language to that of the Senate bill.

While it is true that innocent companies are hurt by frivolous lawsuits and that valuable information may be withheld from investors when companies fear the risk of such suits, it is also true that there are innocent investors who are defrauded and who are able to recover their losses only because they can go to court. It is appropriate to change the law to ensure that companies can make reasonable statements and future projections without getting sued every time earnings turn out to be lower than expected or stock prices drop. But it is not appropriate to erect procedural barriers that will keep wrongly injured persons from having their day in court.

I ask the Congress to send me a bill promptly that will put an end to litigation abuses while still protecting the legitimate rights of ordinary investors. I will sign such a bill as soon as it reaches my desk.

WILLIAM J. CLINTON

The White House,
December 19, 1995.

NOTE: This message was released by the Office of the Press Secretary on December 20. H.R. 1058, passed December 22 over the President's veto, was assigned Public Law No. 104–67.

The President's News Conference
December 20, 1995

Budget Impasse

The President. Good afternoon. Yesterday, Speaker Gingrich, Senator Dole, and I reached an agreement to work together in good faith to balance the budget and to reopen the Government. Today the most extreme Members of the House of Representatives rejected that agreement.

These Republicans want to force the Government to stay closed until I accept their deep and harmful cuts in Medicare and Medicaid, in education, in the environment, and agree to raise taxes on the hardest pressed working families, all, in part, to pay for their very large tax cut.

I won't yield to these threats. I'm determined to balance the budget. But I won't be forced into signing a budget that violates our values, not today or tomorrow, not ever.

This is a very troubling development. The President and the leaders of the two Chambers of Congress reached an agreement on a matter of great national urgency. But a small minority in the House of Representatives is determined to keep the Government closed until they get exactly their way. Their way is the wrong way for America.

We should reopen the Government now. We should work to balance the budget now. We should start the negotiations without any threats, without more ultimatums, without continuing this shutdown. This shutdown hurts the very people we are duty-bound to serve. If Congress doesn't vote to reopen the Government by to-morrow morning, 3.3 million veterans will not receive their benefits on time. If Congress fails to act by Friday, 8 million children will not receive their benefits on time. Every day of the shutdown, 20,000 college loan and scholarship applications go unprocessed. Air and water pollution goes unstopped because they've taken all the environmental protectors off the job.

Christmas is only days away. I have said before and I will say again, we ought to be guided by the spirit of the season, not the spirit of partisanship. We can balance the budget in a way that reflects our values and is good for our future, but only if we put aside rancor and extremism. I say again, I hope that we can go to work.

Q. Mr. President, what can you do about this? Do you have any recourse to get these benefit checks to these poor people?

The President. Well, I'm hoping that Congress will move on the veterans benefits today. And of course, I hope they will move on the other thing.

Q. Can they do that independently——

The President. Apparently, they can. I have talked to Senator Dole twice today. I just got off the phone with him a few minutes ago, and we have—I don't want to reveal exactly what we said because I think that he's making a good-faith effort here to honor the agreement we made.

Q. Can you clear up the question, Mr. President, about whether you're willing to score your budget on the CBO? There seems to be some dispute about that, and in fact, Republicans are blaming this breakdown on what Vice President Gore said last night just minutes after this apparent agreement was struck.

The President. Well, there's no doubt—there's no difference about what the discussion was and what the agreement was. I have said—if you go back to the agreement in the last continuing resolution, I have said that any budget we agree to would have to be scored by the Congressional Budget Office as being in balance. That's what I said, and I say that again.

What the Vice President said last night was that should not be taken to preclude our ability to discuss in the budget negotiation the specific suggestions we have already made or any discussions we still have about what we think ought to be considered in the ultimate decision of the Congressional Budget Office. That's all we said. We have never disputed the fact that the final agreement, once we make it, would have to be scored by the Congressional Budget Office as being in balance.

Q. [Inaudible]—what the agreement that occurred yesterday apparently had to do with whether any plan, any budget plan that did not meet that standard could be on the table as part of the talks. That seemed to be Mr. Gingrich's understanding. Mr. Gore saw it a different way. And that appears to have been at the root of all this. Did the way the Speaker worded his understanding of this yesterday—did that get it wrong, in your view?

The President. Well, I don't think that is at the root of all this. There was a clear understanding, and I believe our staffs agreed on it, that we would come back with our ideas.

As I said to them, I would actually—I offered them two options. We would either go back and take the other budgets that had been proposed as a starting point and work together to try to get a balanced budget that would be scored as balanced by the CBO, or if they wanted me to put one down right now that would be scored right now as balanced by the CBO, I would do that, but they would have to come to the Medicare and Medicaid investment levels that I had recommended because I've already moved 3 times as much as they have.

Q. Just to follow, Mr. President, Senate Democrats have now come forward with a plan today very much like yours in some important respects. It does get to balance in 7 years using CBO numbers now. They apparently—the Re-

publicans say they're prepared to talk about that one. Are you prepared——

The President. We said we were prepared to talk about——

Q. ——to endorse that one and make that your starting point?

The President. No, but I'm prepared to discuss that in the context of the negotiations. We encouraged everybody who wanted to come out with a plan to come out with it and we would discuss them all and we would see where we are on that.

Q. [Inaudible]—just a small minority. Why are they so powerful? What do you think is behind it?

The President. I think that there has been a decision on every issue except the environment, where some moderate Republicans decided that they could no longer go along with it, to put those people in control of the House of Representatives. And they have varied—the moderate Republicans who have disagreed with them, I think, on many, many issues have broken ranks with them, to the best of my knowledge, only on the environment, and then in a modest way.

Now, sooner or later, they're either going to have to let the Speaker honor his commitments—that group. And if they're not going to do that, because what they really want is to end the role of the Federal Government in our life, which they have, after all, have been very open about. I mean, a lot of them will be happy about this because they don't think we ought to have a Government up here anyway. And the tail will keep wagging the dog over there until those moderate Republicans find a way to do what they did on a couple of the environmental votes or until they decide to let the Speaker honor his commitment.

Q. You're saying that these people control the Speaker of the House; he doesn't control them?

The President. No. First of all, I don't think he ever asserted that he controlled them. I am saying that at the present time, they control what their decisions—the leadership decisions, which are in the hand of this very conservative group, the anti-Government group, control what the shape of the measures that come up for a vote. That's what this is. And there are only two ways to resolve this, I think. We either—over the long run, other options that could get the support of both Democrats and Republicans will have to be permitted to come to the floor of the Congress, or they will have to give the Speaker at least the leeway to do what he said he would do yesterday when we left.

Q. Mr. President, since so much is at stake right now, all these veterans benefits and these other benefits, why don't you simply pick up the phone and call the Speaker, the Senate majority leader and invite them to come back to the White House and rack your brains and not leave until there is an agreement that can be implemented?

The President. First of all, I had an agreement last night. I don't know who I'm supposed to make an agreement with. But what the Vice President said is not the basis on which this agreement came—I will do anything I can to reach an honorable agreement. But the people in the House are misreading their own agreement. They voted for the other continuing resolution. The other continuing resolution has us agreeing, our side agreeing, to work for a balanced budget in 7 years, that the agreement would be scored by the CBO as being in balance. It has them agreeing to work to meet our standards of protecting Medicare and Medicaid, education, and the environment. And ever since that agreement was reached their group has treated this as a one-way street. And I'm hoping that we can find a way out of this.

Let me say, I'm happy to meet with anybody, anytime. But it's hard for me to know—what would happen now is—I mean, we can only conclude that what would happen now is that the three of us could sit down and make an agreement with Senator Daschle and Representative Gephardt and then everybody would be for it, and they'd take it back to the House and the same crowd would say, "No, thank you. We want exactly what we passed."

Q. So what you're saying is there's absolutely nothing else that you can do to meet with them because of this group?

The President. No, no, no. Wait a minute, no, no. I just told you I've already had two conversations with Senator Dole and that we're trying to work this out. We're working at this moment. And I do not—I believe when Speaker

Gingrich left here yesterday he intended to come back today and begin the negotiations with the continuing resolution going on.

But you're asking me why we're not meeting right now. I'm telling you what we have to determine is who we can meet with and expect if we give our word and somebody else gives their word, that whatever we say is going to be done will get done. That's what we've got to determine.

Q. Mr. President, why is it necessary for you to get an agreement from——

Q. Mr. President, does the Government have to be reopened? Because last night there was no talk of that being a precondition when both sides came out. And if you did reach an agreement with the Democratic and Republican leaders, presumably you would have enough votes in Congress to override the Republicans.

The President. Well, that's what we thought. And that might be the case now if such a vote were to be taken. And I think that's one of the things that's being discussed. But I think it's very important that all of you understand here, you've got a group of people that in my judgment do not represent even the majority in the House of Representatives, and certainly not the majority opinion of Republicans in America, who are prepared to shut the entire Government down unless we agree with their priorities. That's what's going on.

And they today made it impossible for an agreement made in good faith between the President, the Speaker of the House, and the leader of the Senate to be implemented.

Now, I am, obviously, willing to do whatever I can to continue whatever constructive talks can be continued. But I showed up today ready to do my part, and the thing that you have in this business that has to work is when you say you're going to do something, it has to be that way.

Thank you.

NOTE: The President's 111th news conference began at 3:47 p.m. in the Briefing Room at the White House.

Message on the Observance of Christmas
December 20, 1995

Warm greetings to everyone celebrating Christmas.

The Christmas story is dear and familiar to us all—shepherds and angels, Wise Men and King Herod, Mary and Joseph, and, at the heart of it all, a Child. This Child was born into poverty in a city too crowded to offer Him shelter. He was sent to a region whose people had endured suffering, tyranny, and exile. And yet this Child brought with Him riches so great that they continue to sustain the human spirit two thousand years later: the assurance of God's love and presence in our lives and the promise of salvation.

Each year at Christmas, we celebrate these gifts with family and friends. We place candles in the window as a sign that there is always room for Christ in our homes. We put angels and stars and twinkling lights on the Christmas tree to remind us of the glory and mystery of Christ's birth. We sing the old and beloved Christmas carols to express the joy filling our hearts, and we share special gifts with those we love, just as God shared His Son with us. And, in contemplating the nativity scene under the tree or in a neighbor's yard, we realize that children hold a special place in God's heart, since He sent His only Son to us as a little Child.

With this simple truth in mind, let us observe Christmas this year by making a solemn commitment to the children of our communities, our nation, and the world. Let us pledge to love and nurture them and promise to give them strong values and a chance to make the most of their God-given talents. Let us resolve that they will grow up in a world that is free and at peace. By cherishing the children God sends us, we express our love and gratitude for the one Child He sent whose coming offers forgiveness and hope to us all.

Hillary and I send best wishes for a blessed and joyous Christmas season and every happiness in the new year.

BILL CLINTON

Statement on Welfare Reform and Budget Negotiations
December 21, 1995

I am disappointed that Republicans are trying to use the words "welfare reform" as cover to advance a budget plan that is at odds with America's values. Americans know that welfare reform is not about playing budget politics; it is about moving people from welfare to work.

I am determined to work with Congress to achieve real, bipartisan welfare reform. But if Congress sends me this conference report, I will veto it and insist that they try again. This welfare bill includes deep cuts that are tough on children and at odds with my central goal of moving people from welfare to work. The Republican budget cuts in Medicaid and the earned-income tax credit would undermine real reform and penalize people who choose work over welfare.

At a time when we are trying to engage in serious negotiations toward a balanced budget that is consistent with our priorities—one of which is to reform welfare, as last month's agreement between Republicans and Democrats made clear—this is a sign of bad faith by the Republican leadership and an affront to those in both parties who genuinely want to enact real reform. My administration remains ready at any moment to sit down in good faith with Democrats and Republicans in Congress to work out a real welfare reform plan.

Letter to Congressional Leaders on the Deployment of United States Military Forces for Implementation of the Balkan Peace Process
December 21, 1995

Dear Mr. Speaker: *(Mr. President:)*

I last reported to the Congress on December 6, 1995, concerning U.S. support for the United Nations and North Atlantic Treaty Organization (NATO) efforts to bring peace to the former Yugoslavia. In that report I noted the success of our diplomatic efforts at Dayton, Ohio, to assist the parties to reach a negotiated settlement to the conflict in the former Yugoslavia and reported the deployment of a NATO "enabling force" and U.S. support forces in order to lay the groundwork for the deployment of the main body of the NATO-led Implementation Force (IFOR). I am now able to report that on December 14, 1995, the peace agreement that was initialed in Dayton was formally signed in Paris.

Following the formal signing of the peace agreement by all the parties, and consistent with our consultations with the Congress, United Nations Security Council Resolution 1031, and the North Atlantic Council (NAC) decision of December 16, 1995, I have ordered the deployment of approximately 20,000 U.S. military personnel to participate in the IFOR in the Republic of Bosnia and Herzegovina, principally in a sector surrounding Tuzla. Approximately 5,000 U.S. military personnel will also deploy as part of the IFOR in other states of the former Yugoslavia, principally Croatia. The IFOR, including U.S. forces assigned to it, will be under NATO operational control and will operate under NATO rules of engagement. In addition, a total of approximately 7,000 U.S. support forces, under U.S. command and control and rules of engagement, will deploy in Hungary, Croatia, Italy, and other states in the region in support of IFOR. These force levels are those stated by U.S. commanders to be appropriate for the missions assigned to them.

The IFOR's mission, as outlined in more detail in the summary of the operation plan (OPLAN), which I sent to the Congress on December 11, 1995, is to monitor and help ensure compliance by all parties with the military aspects of the peace agreement. In particular, IFOR will ensure withdrawal of the forces of the parties to the agreed inter-entity borders

within an agreed period and enforce establishment of agreed zones of separation between forces of the parties. IFOR will also create secure conditions for the safe, orderly, and speedy withdrawal from the Republic of Bosnia and Herzegovina of those elements of the U.N. Protection Force not assigned to NATO. Finally, within the strict limits of its key military tasks, IFOR will endeavor to create secure conditions for the conduct by other agencies and organizations of tasks associated with the peace agreement. NATO and U.S. military commanders believe, and I expect, that the military mission can be accomplished in about a year.

Many of the U.S. forces that will deploy to the Republic of Bosnia and Herzegovina will be drawn from the U.S. Army's 1st Armored Division stationed in Germany, including two mechanized brigades and an aviation brigade. Other participating U.S. forces include special operations forces, airfield operations support forces, naval and air forces previously assigned to support NATO's Operations Sharp Guard and Deny Flight, and an amphibious force in reserve in the Mediterranean Sea. Additionally, a carrier battle group will provide support for IFOR's air operations.

All of our NATO allies are contributing forces as well (except for Iceland, which has no military). Non-NATO nations whose offers to provide forces to IFOR are under consideration include Austria, the Czech Republic, Estonia, Finland, Hungary, Latvia, Lithuania, Pakistan, Poland, Romania, Russia, Slovakia, Sweden, and Ukraine. These forces also will be under NATO operational control and rules of engagement. In total, approximately 60,000 military personnel are expected to be deployed by IFOR to the Republic of Bosnia and Herzegovina. As in the U.S. case, the non-U.S. contingents in Bosnia will in most cases be supported by forces of their respective countries at home and in nearby countries and waters.

I authorized these deployments and U.S. participation in IFOR in conjunction with our NATO allies and other troop contributing nations following the relevant U.N. Security Council resolutions and NAC decisions and as part of our commitment to secure the peace and halt the tragic loss of life in the former Yugoslavia. I have directed the participation of U.S. forces pursuant to my constitutional authority to conduct the foreign relations of the United States and as Commander in Chief and Chief Executive.

I am providing this report as part of my effort to keep the Congress fully informed about developments in the former Yugoslavia, consistent with the War Powers Resolution. I remain committed to consulting closely with the Congress and I will continue to keep the Congress fully informed regarding these important deployments of our forces.

Sincerely,

BILL CLINTON

NOTE: Identical letters were sent to Newt Gingrich, Speaker of the House of Representatives, and Strom Thurmond, President pro tempore of the Senate. This letter was released by the Office of the Press Secretary on December 22.

Message on the Observance of Kwanzaa
December 6, 1995

Warm greetings to everyone who is observing the festival of Kwanzaa.

Across America and around the globe, Kwanzaa is a vibrant celebration of African culture, encouraging us to gain a deeper appreciation of our families and the many blessings we enjoy. Kwanzaa's seven basic principles—unity, self-determination, collective work and responsibility, cooperative economics, purpose, creativity, and faith—stir our imagination, stimulate thought and reflection, and bring new purpose to our daily lives.

Transcending international boundaries and embracing the rich cultural traditions of Africa, this joyous festival links diverse individuals in a unique celebration of a dynamic heritage. Renewing hope and restoring faith, Kwanzaa uplifts the human spirit, helping us to revitalize the bonds of family and the spirit of community.

As millions of my fellow Americans commemorate Kwanzaa, I am delighted to send best wishes for a wonderful festival and a very happy new year.

BILL CLINTON

NOTE: This message was released by the Office of the Press Secretary on December 22.

Exchange With Reporters on Bosnia in Arlington, Virginia
December 22, 1995

The President. Good morning.

Q. Mr. President, do you hope to go to Bosnia in the next month or so?

The President. I want to go when the Secretary of Defense and General Shalikashvili tell me it's an appropriate thing to do. I don't want to interrupt the deployment in any way. You know, we've had a few weather delays, but I'm here to get a briefing on the deployment and what's going on and how we're doing. I've got a few questions I want to ask. If it were solely up to me, I would go tomorrow, literally tomorrow. But I think it's very important that I not do anything which interrupts the deployment. I can go as soon as it's consistent with the military mission, and I will do that.

Q. What have you heard so far, even before this briefing, on how the operation is going in Bosnia?

The President. I think our people are doing a very good job. I think the others in IFOR are doing a good job, and I think the people there, so far, are receiving them well. But I've got some specific questions, and that's why I want this briefing.

Q. Do you think Senator Dole should go if you can't go?

The President. I think that all of us should consult with the military leaders and do what is consistent with the interest of our troops and the mission.

Q. In other words, no.

Q. Mr. President, do you worry about casualties?

The President. Every day I worry about that, but I think they're showing their training and their discipline and the integrity of the plan in the way that they are working to minimize casualties and maximize the effectiveness of the mission.

Q. Do you think the American people understand that, understand the risks that are involved?

The President. Yes.

NOTE: The exchange began at 9:25 a.m. at the Pentagon, prior to a briefing on Bosnia.

Interview With the Armed Forces Media
December 22, 1995

Bosnia

The President. First let me say that I have just come from a briefing here at the Pentagon with our senior military officials who are working on the mission in Bosnia. We've also had a teleconference with General Joulwan, getting the latest up-to-date briefing on the conditions of the deployment. And I would say—I should emphasize to you two things.

One is that, notwithstanding some weather problems and a few delays occasioned by Christmas traffic on the rails in Germany, we're pretty much on schedule. And secondly, and even more important, the attitude toward compliance thus far in Bosnia by all parties has been quite good. Now, it's early in the mission, but so far the attitude toward compliance has been very good, and we're encouraged by that. And we think we can stay on schedule for the separation of the forces and the other elements of it.

And also in this Christmas season, I'd like to remind the people who serve our country that we are doing this essentially for three reasons. First of all, because we can do it, and when we can do something like this, it's consistent with our values to stop suffering and slaughter on the scale we've seen it in Bosnia.

Second, because it's very much in our interest to contain and end this war, to prevent it from spreading in a way that can involve our NATO allies on opposite sides and many other countries that are critical to the stability of Europe. It's also important for us to do what we can to promote a stable and democratic and free Europe. We, after all, have fought two World Wars because we did not have such a Europe; we had a long cold war because we did not have such a Europe. So it's in our interest.

And finally, it is critical to our ability to lead the world for the next 10 or 20 years as we sort out what the security arrangements of the post-cold-war era will be. I can tell you that our leadership of NATO specifically, and in general our ability to lead in the world toward peace and democracy, is very much tied to our willingness to assume a leadership role in this Bosnia mission.

I could see it on my recent trip to Europe, whether it was talking to Prime Ministers in Great Britain or Ireland or Germany or Spain or just to people on the street. It means a lot to them to know that the United States is still there working and leading and being a good partner.

So for all these reasons, I think this is a very, very important mission to our country.

Q. Thank you, sir. Mr. President, I'm Austin Camacho from the AFRTS News Center. After Operation Joint Endeavor, what do you see as the U.S. role in that area formerly known as Yugoslavia? What will be our role there?

The President. Well, I think, first of all, we'll still be there through NATO and whatever role that NATO assumes in the general area beyond our NATO member nations. But more importantly, I would expect, after this mission is over, we will continue to have American citizens, both people who work for and represent our Government and people in the private sector, going in and out of there helping in the reconstruction effort, contributing to that, supporting the political process in whatever way we can.

But I think it is quite important that the NATO force not become an occupying army. We're not dealing with Berlin here. We're not—all we're trying to do is to give this peace agreement a chance to take hold. And we have a very clear and limited mission. In fact, I want to make sure that all of our folks know that, as far as I know, this peace agreement is the first one ever where the military annex to the agreement was actually written by the military commanders who were going to be expected to implement it. That is, the parties actually asked our military people to fashion the military annex to the agreement that was initialed in Dayton so that there would be a limited, defined, strictly military mission.

Q. Mr. President, do you agree with the premise that Bosnia is really the first test of post-cold-war policy?

The President. Well, I think it's been tested in other ways, but it's certainly the most significant military test of our post-cold-war policy. If you accept the premise that what happened in the Gulf at the Gulf war could have occurred during the cold war as well as afterward, that this is literally a post-cold-war problem, then it is the biggest military test.

Q. Does that mean that—what does the success or failure of this then mean to American foreign policy 10, 15 years down the line?

The President. Well, let me just say I think the most important thing here is that the United States was prepared to lead and to work with our NATO allies. If you remember, in the beginning when the Bosnian war broke out, a lot of our European allies said, "Well, we ought to take the leadership role here. We'll do this. We'll do it through the United Nations." And we've played a very strong supporting role through NATO. After all, it's important that the United States never forget that during these last 4 tough years, we led in the conduct of the largest humanitarian airlift in history; we led in enforcing the no-fly zone, keeping the war out of the air, and a lot of other things that were done, including NATO's willingness to use air strikes to, first of all, bring about a relatively peaceful 1994 and then to bring about the conditions in which a peace agreement could be made in 1995.

But what I believe this means, if we make this effort and if we succeed in our military mission, even if, God forbid, after we're all gone the thing should come apart, at least we will be united in doing what we can do to promote stability in Europe and to take a stand for peace in the post-cold-war era.

If you remember when I sent our troops into Haiti with a U.N.-led mission, and then when I left a smaller number there when the United Nations took over on schedule, I always said that we could not guarantee the people of Haiti a future; they would have to do that for themselves. The same is true for the Bosnians. We cannot guarantee for them a future without war. What we can guarantee for them is a year without war, during which they can implement their own agreement and in which time they can have elections, they can begin the economic reconstruction, they can begin to see the benefits of peace, and then some equilibrium within the country can be established from a security point of view.

But I think it would be a mistake for the United States or for NATO to believe that we should be going around anywhere guaranteeing the results of peace agreements which have to be guaranteed in the minds and hearts of the people who are making them.

So this will be a success for our alliance, for our leadership, just by doing the mission. Obviously, it will be a much, much greater success if the humanitarian relief, the refugee relocation, the economic reconstruction all are completely successful and Bosnia has a permanent peace. That is the real measure of success. But the main thing is we have to define together where we must try and where we must stand against chaos. And I think we've done a good job of that here.

Q. Mr. President, Cindy Killion from the European Stars and Stripes. Under what circumstances would you order the U.S. forces to withdraw from Bosnia within the next year, before the one-year mark?

The President. The only circumstance that I can imagine doing that is if the mission no longer existed. That is, keep in mind, we are there not to fight a war. We are there not to stop a war. We are there to implement a peace agreement. We anticipate that there will be violations of this agreement but that the leaders will not abandon it and that the vast bulk of the people will not abandon it. So we have to be prepared for some violations. We even have to be prepared for some casualties, although I think our people have trained and planned as hard against problems for this mission as they ever have for any.

But that would not cause me to withdraw. I believe that NATO would determine, if all the factions decided they wanted to go fight again, that there was no longer a mission to perform.

Defense Authorization Bill

Q. Hi, Bill Matthews with Army Times. Switching a little bit to the defense authorization bill, you have said you are going to veto it. The bill includes a pay raise and a housing allowance increase for military people. Since some of them are headed off to Bosnia, are you concerned that not getting the pay raise, not getting the housing allowance increase would be detrimental to morale? And is there some alternative?

The President. Very much. Yes, there is an alternative. The Congress could send me a separate bill with the pay raise and the allowances in it, and I would sign it in a heartbeat. I think, indeed I hope, that they will do one of two things: I hope they will either do that, or when I veto this bill, assuming my veto would be sustained, which I believe it would because there are some unconstitutional restrictions on the President's authority as Commander in Chief in this bill which compels me to veto it—so they can either send me the pay raise and the allowance increase in a separate bill, or they could delete the offending portions of the defense authorization bill and send it right back to me. They can do either one of those things. And I would hope the Congress would promptly act to do that.

I do not want any erosion of morale and spirit among not only our people in uniform but their family members. I believe that we are completely united in supporting the full pay raise and the allowance increase. And I have done my best to budget for these things over a period of several years.

I have visited a large number of our military facilities, both in the United States and beyond our borders. I have talked to a lot of people in uniform about this. And I think it is a very important issue. If we want to keep the very best people in our military, we're going to have to see to the quality-of-life issues. We've allocated a lot of money for it over the next budget

cycle, and I want to release it, starting with these two issues.

Defense Spending

Q. Mr. President, Jim Wolffe, also from the Army Times. On a slightly longer term budget issue, the Republican 7-year budget plan, while it has more money for defense in the first couple of years, actually targets less money towards defense spending in the out-years 2000 and beyond. Secretary Perry said earlier this week that that would force him into the difficult decision of actually cutting force structure to pay for modernization.

You've talked a lot about social spending in the budget debate, but I haven't heard you talk much about defending defense spending. Is that something you're willing to give away to get a deal?

The President. Well, let me say that I still hope that I can work with Congress in a way that that choice won't be necessary. It is true that they front-loaded more defense spending than we did, which made it very attractive to all the people who wanted it in these years. But what we tried to do was to have a balanced commitment.

I think the worst thing that can happen to the military is to be jerked around with these up and down budgets and unpredictability. What we tried to do is to get our folks together here and to say, "Okay, what do we need over the next 5 years? What do we need over the next 7 years?" The only thing I can say to you, and I would say with some sense of assurance, is that our political system has shown a willingness now to respond if there's a problem created for our forces in uniform and for our national defense.

I mean, I think—one of the things you see that in the last 3 years is we've had a remarkable bipartisan ability to maintain a strong defense as a part of our continuing engagement in the post-cold-war world. And I think that everyone knows that the military went through a significant downsizing with a remarkable maintenance of excellence and morale and that now we have to sustain the system that we have created.

And so I would say to our forces in uniform, I'm going to get the very best budget agreement I can. I hope we can get an agreement. But if there is an alarming tailoff in years 6 and 7, I think it can be corrected in the future. And I believe if we balance the budget, get interest rates down, the economy will grow more quickly. And one of the big differences between me and the Republicans in Congress is that they have now given me an economic plan which says if we do everything they want, at the end of 6 or 7 years interest rates and unemployment will be higher than they are now. I find that very hard to believe. I think that we're going to be better off, not worse off, if we do this, and we'll have more money, therefore, to invest in defense.

So I would not worry too much about the out-years. Whatever happens in this budget agreement, at least as long as I am here—and I can't conceive of anyone else coming into this job or anyone coming into control of the Congress that would not try to sustain a long-term plan for the military, because that's what we've learned—that if the military has a plan they can do nearly anything, but we can't jack around the plan. And we don't want to play games with people's lives or with the national security.

Bosnia and Politics

Q. Mr. President, I'm Dave Gollust from Voice of America. Can I jump back to Bosnia for a second and politics? How important do you consider the success of the Bosnia operation to your own political prospects? Is it a defining moment for you? And secondly, from a tactical point of view, would you mind if Senator Dole was the first senior political presence in Bosnia on Christmas?

The President. Well, let me answer the first question. If you look at recent American history, the evidence is that the success of the Bosnia operation may not have much to do with the election in 1996, but the failure of the Bosnia operation or the sustaining of significant casualties could have a great deal to do with it in a negative way. And that's all. The conventional political wisdom is, "Why would the President do this? There's no upside and tons of downside."

But I have to say, when you take a job, you have to do what you—you have to do the job. And to be President at the edge of the 21st century, in a time of dramatic, dramatic change in the way we work and live and relate to each other, means that you can't predict the future and you just have to do what you think is right. So for me, this was not—once I became convinced we could train for this mission, that we could define the mission in the peace agree-

ment, that we could minimize the risks to our troops, then the decision to me was not so difficult, no matter what the political downside, because I believe, in a time like this, you have to ask yourself which decision would you rather defend 10 years from now when you're not in office, if it goes wrong?

I would much rather explain to my child and my grandchildren why the United States tried to stop slaughter, prevent the spread of the war, maintain NATO instead of destroy it, maintain the leadership of the United States in the world for peace and freedom. I would much rather explain why we tried to do that than why, because of the short-term political problems, we permitted the war to resume, it expanded, NATO's alliance was destroyed, and the influence of the United States was compromised for 10 years.

I think it's obvious if you look at it that way—what do you want to tell your grandchildren 10 years from now—that the United States is doing the right thing. And the political risk is part of the price you pay for being President. Anybody who doesn't want to take any political risk at a time like this should not run for the job.

Now, in terms of who goes to Bosnia when, I don't think we should politicize it. Senator Dole and I worked together to get the support that the Senate gave to this mission. He expressed his reservations about it, but he supported my decision as Commander in Chief. I appreciated that. And obviously, at the appropriate time, I have no objection to either Senator Dole or anyone else for that matter going to Bosnia.

The question is, when is the appropriate time? If I had my way, I would be spending Christmas Eve and Christmas morning there. That's what I wanted to do. But our commanders made it clear that when a President comes into Bosnia, if I fly into that airport at Tuzla, and then I go down to Sarajevo when they're in the middle of this deployment, it would be exceedingly disruptive. So even though I wanted to go there to say to the American people I believe this mission is on the right track and, most importantly, to support the troops and to reassure their families, I'm taking the advice of the military commanders. I do not want to interrupt this mission.

The mission's success is the most important thing. And that's what I believe should guide everyone. I think everyone—there are different levels of disruption that different trips would cause, and I think we ought to try to just keep it nonpolitical. I hope anybody that wants to go there that has a reason to go, including Senator Dole, will be able to go at the appropriate time. And that's the determination that needs to be made.

Q. Mr. President, you mentioned the safety of the troops as being part of your decision a couple times in that last answer. We're sending quite a large force involved in the Bosnia mission. Some might say, awfully large for a peaceful mission. How extensive do you think the danger is to our troops there?

The President. Well, I think there is—let's look at what the sources are. No one can— the extent of the danger depends on factors that we can't fully predict. But I believe that we have minimized the risks. What are the possible problems? First of all, if you look at what the United Nations went through over the last 4 years, I think something over 200 people lost their lives in Bosnia. But more than half of them lost their lives in accidents. So we have really worked hard to train against accidents, to prepare—to look at the roadways, to look at the railways, to look at the airfields. We've worked hard to minimize the loss of life or serious injury due to accidents.

Then we know there are a lot of landmines there. I got a very encouraging report today that the parties themselves in many places are assisting us in removing the mines. But there are a lot of places where there are a lot of mines laid where the land was first in one hand and then another, where we don't have records of the mines, where people don't have memories of them. So we have trained very hard to deal with landmines. I think that's the next biggest danger after accidents.

Then the third problem is people that fought in that war who are either from the country or who came in from without the country who may have either a specific grudge against the United States or, more likely, will just be frustrated because they don't agree with the peace agreement that the leaders made and, therefore, some—and then, fourthly, there is just the possibility of encounters that go wrong. The only casualty we sustained in Haiti had nothing to do with opposition to our being there. It was a man who was literally a common criminal who ran through a barrier, and there was an incident, and he shot one of our soldiers dead.

So I would say that those are the dangers in order.

Q. Mr. President, I think that's all the time we have.

The President. Thank you, and Merry Christmas. I appreciate what you do.

NOTE: The interview began at 10:35 a.m. in the Visual Recording Facility at the National Military Command Center, the Pentagon. The following journalists participated in the interview: Sgt. Austin Camacho, American Forces Radio and Television Service; Jim Garamone, American Forces Information Service; Cindy Killion, Stars and Stripes; Bill Matthews and Jim Wolffe, Army Times; and David Gollust, Voice of America. In his remarks, the President referred to Gen. George A. Joulwan, USA, Supreme Allied Commander, Europe.

Remarks on Budget Negotiations and an Exchange With Reporters
December 22, 1995

The President. I hope—as you see, we're running a little behind today, so I hope you'll forgive us if we don't do a lot of questions; we have a lot of work to do. But let me just say from my point of view, I am pleased that our representatives met yesterday. They did make some progress. Obviously, a lot of the biggest issues remain. But the process seems to be working, and I'm encouraged. And I want to continue to do it until we reach agreement on a balanced budget. That's what I think clearly we all want.

I would say here that 2 days before Christmas I hope some way can be found to get the checks for the 3½ million veterans and the aid to the 8 million children who need it just to exist. And there are almost half a million Federal workers who have been working who won't get their paychecks today that they would otherwise get. So I think those problems need to be addressed.

But on the other issue, I at least believe that we made some good progress yesterday, and I'm looking forward to the report today and continuing this process until we succeed, until we get this job done.

Q. Can we ask the leaders, Mr. President, if they will get the checks out and——

Q. Do you think the Congress should go home when millions are denied subsistence checks over Christmas?

Speaker Gingrich. Well, let me just say, if I could for a second, Mr. President, I think both the House and Senate hope to get those bills down here today so that the—the AFDC and the—as the President mentioned the other day on television.

Q. What are the chances of reopening the Government, Mr. Speaker?

Speaker Gingrich. I think we're going to talk about that now.

Q. Mr. Speaker, do you feel like a dog being wagged by its tail? [*Laughter*]

Speaker Gingrich. It's amazing you guys get paid for some of these questions, on the eve of Christmas. Merry Christmas.

Q. No, it's not my expression; it's the President's analysis.

The President. I never called the Speaker a dog. [*Laughter*]

Q. No, I know you didn't.

Speaker Gingrich. And I'm deeply grateful. [*Laughter*]

Q. Mr. President, do you think you can get a framework of a deal by Christmas?

The President. I'm prepared to—let me just say, I'm prepared to just keep working. I think all of us want to have Christmas with our families, but beyond that, I'm prepared to keep working. And I'm going to do everything I can to succeed, and that's what we're going to talk about.

Q. Mr. Speaker——

The President. Thank you. We really need to go to work.

NOTE: The President spoke at 12:52 p.m. in the Cabinet Room at the White House, prior to a meeting with congressional leaders. A tape was not available for verification of the content of these remarks.

Statement With Congressional Leaders on Budget Negotiations
December 22, 1995

Today we had good meetings which built on the progress made in yesterday's discussions. Staff will prepare further analysis to clarify options for the budget advisory group, which will then advise the principals on outstanding issues. Following the meeting of the budget advisory group, the principals will meet again next Friday afternoon.

NOTE: This statement was announced jointly with Newt Gingrich, Speaker of the House of Representatives, and Bob Dole, Senate majority leader.

Statement on Signing Limited Continuing Appropriations Legislation
December 22, 1995

Today I have signed into law House Joint Resolution 136, which ensures that the Government makes veterans' benefit payments to 3.3 million veterans and their survivors without further delay.

The resolution also provides funding for several vitally important programs for children and families. It continues funding for Aid to Families with Dependent Children (AFDC), ensuring that nearly 9 million children receive benefits vital to their well-being. It funds child care for about 600,000 children whose parents are trying to work their way off welfare. And it continues funding for State child support enforcement agencies to ensure that "deadbeat dads" do not get a reprieve from supporting their children.

In addition, H.J. Res. 136 provides authority for the District of Columbia to continue full operations. The resolution contains an objectionable provision that would single out poor women by prohibiting the use of District funds for providing abortion services. I have opposed including this provision in the regular fiscal year 1996 District of Columbia appropriations bill. Nevertheless, H.J. Res. 136 allows the District government to continue to operate without disruption.

Although I welcome H.J. Res. 136, it is a poor substitute for what the Congress should do immediately—that is, send me an acceptable continuing resolution to reopen the departments and agencies that are at least partially shut down because they lack fiscal year 1996 appropriations. Along with the Departments of Veterans Affairs and Health and Human Services, they include the Departments of Education, Labor, Housing and Urban Development, Commerce, Justice, State, and the Interior; the Environmental Protection Agency; the National Aeronautics and Space Administration, and the Small Business Administration.

To be sure, H.J. Res. 136 prevents the serious impact that the partial shutdown could have had on 3.3 million veterans and their survivors as well as nearly 9 million low-income children. But the shutdown continues to hurt millions of innocent Americans—from the 20,000 parents and students each day who cannot apply for student aid, to the 2,500 moderate- and low-income working families each day who cannot get their Federal Housing Administration (FHA) mortgage loans processed.

The shutdown also has forced the affected departments and agencies to furlough a total of about 280,000 Federal employees, throwing their lives into disruption and raising their fears just as the holidays approach. Federal workers, who are already being asked to do their jobs more efficiently as we downsize the Government, deserve better.

The congressional majority apparently wants to use a partial Government shutdown to force me into accepting their extreme budget plan. It did not work last month, when the majority prompted an earlier shutdown by not sending me an acceptable continuing resolution. And it will not work now.

The Congress should send me an acceptable continuing resolution to reopen the Government, return to work the 280,000 Federal employees who were furloughed through no fault of their own, provide back pay for these workers, and give the American people the services they expect from their Government.

WILLIAM J. CLINTON

The White House,
December 22, 1995.

NOTE: H.J. Res. 136, approved December 22, was assigned Public Law No. 104–69. An original was not available for verification of the content of this statement.

Statement on the Airline Tragedy Near Buga, Colombia
December 22, 1995

Hillary and I offer our profound condolences to the many families whose loved ones perished in the crash December 20 of American Airlines flight 965 near Buga, Colombia. Coming on the eve of the holiday season, this tragic event takes on even greater poignancy. I have dispatched an interagency team to the site which, working alongside Colombian authorities, will pursue the goals of searching for survivors, identifying victims, and determining the cause of the crash.

Our hopes and prayers, along with those of all Americans, are with those whose lives have been so affected by this tragedy.

The President's Radio Address
December 23, 1995

Good morning. As you know, I have spent the last week in intense discussion with congressional leaders over how to balance the budget in 7 years. It's important to balance the budget to lift the burden of debt from future generations.

In the last 3 years, we've cut our deficit in half, and we need to finish the job. But we have to balance the budget in a way that reflects our most fundamental values: increasing opportunity; asking everyone to assume responsibility; strengthening our families and the economy; and recognizing the duty we owe to each other, to our parents, our children, and those who need and deserve our help. That's how we've reduced the deficit since I took office: cutting unnecessary programs; reducing the size of the Federal Government by 200,000; reducing redtape but investing in education, the environment, research and technology; protecting Medicare and Medicaid; reducing taxes on the hardest pressed working families. It's worked. It's given us more jobs, more new businesses, low inflation, and record economic performance in the stock market and in many other places.

Now, that's how I want to finish the job of balancing the budget. But even as we continue talking, I hope Congress will agree to open the Government and open all the agencies that have closed so that we can end the financial and emotional turmoil for more than 280,000 furloughed Federal employees and 460,000 working-but-not-getting-paid Federal employees.

In the spirit of the holidays, we should do everything we can to put these people back to work and to resume critical services the American people need and deserve. Just last night, I signed legislation that Congress passed yesterday to allow 3.3 million veterans and 13 million needy children and their mothers to receive their benefits by January 1st. That's a good start. I hope we can resume all services as we work together to balance the budget.

Our talks are making progress. Yesterday we agreed to resume our negotiations next week with the goal of reaching an agreement as soon as possible. I am confident we can end this impasse and pass a 7-year balanced budget.

As we look back at this year, in this season of hope, I think we ought to take just a little time to reflect on the progress and accomplishment of America. It should give us real optimism that we can finish this budget job and go on to greater things in 1996.

Nineteen ninety-five was a year in which our country had the opportunity and the responsibility to play our role as the world's premier peacemaker. Our efforts opened the door to peace in places where only rancor and war had previously existed. As a peacemaker, not a policeman, we have helped the peace process finally begin to take hold in the Middle East, while we joined the world in mourning the tragic assassination of Israeli Prime Minister Yitzhak Rabin. We have done what Prime Minister Rabin would have wanted us to do: We've kept moving forward. And finally it looks like Israel and Syria will sit together in the United States to seek a way to resolve their differences and live together peacefully.

We're also helping to bring peace to Bosnia. The Dayton agreement and our decision to join in the international effort to secure the peace in Bosnia has given the people of the former Yugoslavia a chance to rebuild their lives. After 4 long years of horrible violence, America now has the opportunity to lead in the effort to bring lasting peace to that war-torn country and to stabilize Central Europe as well.

In Northern Ireland, I saw thousands and thousands of children beginning to celebrate their second Christmas season of peace. And in Haiti, they will soon celebrate the very first peaceful transfer of power from one democratically elected President to another in the history of the country. And American leadership helped to make both those celebrations possible.

The seeds of peace are also sinking deeper roots right here in America. We just learned that last year our murder rate dropped 12 percent, the largest decline in 35 years. Violent crime overall is down 5 percent. Now, we know our work is far from done on too many of our mean streets. Too many of our children still are raising themselves, not being taught right from wrong. There is still too much crime and violence, and it's still rising among teenagers in many parts of the country. But we are beginning to turn the tide. And we do know what works.

Much of the success is due to efforts in communities throughout our country to get guns off our streets and put more police on the streets and to give our young people something to say yes to as well as something to say no to. More importantly, it is due to the outpouring of grassroots community involvement in all these efforts, in the comprehensive fight against crime and violence. People are getting the message that community policing works. And it's up to every citizen to rise up, reach out, and link arms with local police to keep their own neighborhoods safe and their schools safe. Now, the progress we've seen is cause for hope. We just have to keep working on it here at home.

From the Middle East to Northern Ireland, to our troops in Bosnia, to our toughest neighborhoods, America is leading the way to peace and reconciliation. All around the world billions of people look to America as a model of democracy and freedom. And we should see ourselves as others see us. We should finish the job of balancing the budget and reopening the Government in the spirit of cooperation and unity so that we can continue to grow and prosper together and be a force in the world for peace and freedom. That is the spirit of the season and the spirit of America.

Let each of us resolve to do what we can to be peacemakers. Let us bring peace to every child who deserves to be free from violence and full of hope. And as we celebrate the birth of a child whose only shelter was the straw of a manger, let us remember the words of the Prince of Peace who said, "Blessed are the peacemakers." We ask the blessings of this peace for everyone. That is our prayer this Christmas.

Thanks for listening.

NOTE: The President spoke at 10:06 a.m. from the Oval Office at the White House.

Christmas Eve Message to United States Troops in Bosnia-Herzegovina
December 24, 1995

Merry Christmas, and best wishes to all of you on this Christmas Eve. I am honored to speak today to the men and women of Operation Joint Endeavor, in Bosnia, Croatia, Hungary, and Italy, on ships at sea and skies overhead, and those preparing to deploy. I know that all around the world Americans who wear our Nation's uniform are listening, and I want to wish all of them well, just as I know they wish you well as you embark on this historic mission.

With me today are the families of seven Americans serving in and around Bosnia: Lieutenant Colonel Bob Norman of the 621st Air Mobility Control Squadron in Tuzla; Command Master Chief Jim Sirles on the U.S.S. *America* in the Adriatic; Sergeant William LeBright of the 26th Marine Expeditionary Unit on board the U.S.S. *Whidbey Island*; Warrant Officer Willie Wade with the 586th Assault Bridge Company; Lieutenant Colonel O'Malley Smith of the 353d Civil Affairs Group; Sergeant Mark Ackerman with the 114th Public Affairs Detachment; and Linda Carsey, an Army civilian contract specialist on her way to Tuzla.

These families here remind us all of the Americans we're sending to Bosnia. They're leaving their families behind. And many of them are already far from their loved ones this Christmas Eve. I want to extend a special greeting to those families today. I know that when we call on our troops to protect America's interests and values, we also call on their families. Their families' special sacrifice may not make the headlines, but we could not be successful without it, for as our troops stand up on America's behalf, it is their families who stand behind them, who keep them strong with confidence, support, and love.

These thoughts are especially close in our minds this time of year. As Americans come together in this season of peace, we know that you, the men and women of Operation Joint Endeavor, are serving on a mission of peace, the noblest mission of all. The pride your families have in each of you is shared by all your fellow Americans all across our Nation.

Ten days ago in Paris, the Presidents of Bosnia, Croatia, and Serbia signed an agreement that turns their troubled region from war to peace. Our Nation has an important interest in seeing that peace take hold for the people of Bosnia who have suffered so much for so long; for the stability of Europe, which is so crucial to our own stability; and for the safer, stronger world we want to leave for our children.

There is too much at stake in Bosnia today for our Nation to sit on the sidelines, and that's why we've turned to you, our men and women in uniform. You provide us with the power to meet threats to our security. You have the strength to bring hope and stability to people exhausted by war. We know and the people of Bosnia know that you will get the job done and that you will do it right.

Each side there wants NATO to help them safeguard the peace they have agreed to make and to help them live up to their commitments to one another. They trust you to create a secure environment so they can seize this chance to rebuild their lives and their land. They see in you how much can be achieved when people find strength in their diversity. That is the power of America's example.

I know this will be a demanding mission, but I know, too, that you are up to the task. General Joulwan and General Nash have assured me of that. And I have seen it for myself. Earlier this month, I visited with the men and women of Task Force Eagle in Germany. I saw in them the qualities that all of you share, the qualities that have earned our Nation the respect and trust of the entire world. Your training, equipment, and preparation are unequalled. Your reputation precedes you. The most advanced technology protects you. But just as important, you are strong in your character. Time and again, without pause or complaint, you step forward to serve our Nation.

In this new era of challenge and change, America's obligation to lead for peace and human dignity has remained as important as ever. In Bosnia, you, the men and women of our Armed Forces, will bear that charge with great honor. You will make the difference between horror and hope, between a war that resumes and a peace that takes hold.

I am proud to be your Commander in Chief and to thank you on behalf of your nation. Your mission of peace and good will in Bosnia reminds us all what this season is all about for all people everywhere.

Tomorrow, on Christmas Day, and as long as you are there, Hillary and I will have you in our thoughts and prayers. May God bless and protect you and your families and bring you success and a very safe return. And may God bless America, the nation you do so much to serve.

NOTE: The message was recorded at 10:13 a.m. in the Oval Office at the White House for broadcast at 12:15 p.m. In his remarks, the President referred to Maj. Gen. William L. Nash, USA, Commanding General, 1st Armored Division.

Message to the Congress on Suspension of Sanctions Against the Federal Republic of Yugoslavia (Serbia and Montenegro)
December 27, 1995

To the Congress of the United States:

Section 1511 of the National Defense Authorization Act for Fiscal Year 1994 (hereinafter the "Act"), requires that the sanctions imposed on Serbia and Montenegro, as described in that section, shall remain in effect until changed by law. Section 1511(e) of the Act authorizes the President to waive or modify the application of such sanctions upon certification to the Congress that the President has determined that the waiver or modification is necessary to achieve a negotiated settlement of the conflict in Bosnia-Herzegovina that is acceptable to the parties.

In accordance with this provision, I have issued the attached Presidential Determination stating that the suspension of the sanctions described in section 1511(a) (1–5) and (7–8) and in conformity with the provisions of United Nations Security Council Resolutions 1021 and 1022 is necessary to achieve a negotiated settlement of the conflict. As described in the attached Memorandum of Justification, this sanctions relief was an essential factor motivating Serbia and Montenegro's acceptance of the General Framework Agreement for Peace in Bosnia and Herzegovina initialed in Dayton, Ohio, on November 21, 1995 (hereinafter the "Peace Agreement").

I have directed the Secretaries of the Treasury and Transportation to suspend immediately the application of these sanctions on Serbia and Montenegro and have authorized the Secretary of State to suspend the arms embargo at appropriate stages consistent with United Nations Security Council Resolution 1021. The first stage would be 91 days after the United Nations Secretary General reports to the United Nations

Security Council that all parties have formally signed the Peace Agreement.

The measures taken to suspend these sanctions may be revoked if the Implementation Force (IFOR) commander or High Representative determines that Serbia and Montenegro or the Bosnian Serbs are not meeting their obligations under the Peace Agreement.

WILLIAM J. CLINTON

The White House,
December 27, 1995.

NOTE: This message was released by the Office of the Press Secretary on December 28. The Presidential determination of December 27 is listed in Appendix D at the end of this volume.

Message to the House of Representatives Returning Without Approval the National Defense Authorization Act for Fiscal Year 1996
December 28, 1995

To the House of Representatives:

I am returning herewith without my approval H.R. 1530, the "National Defense Authorization Act for Fiscal Year 1996."

H.R. 1530 would unacceptably restrict my ability to carry out this country's national security objectives and substantially interfere with the implementation of key national defense programs. It would also restrict the President's authority in the conduct of foreign affairs and as Commander in Chief, raising serious constitutional concerns.

First, the bill requires deployment by 2003 of a costly missile defense system able to defend all 50 States from a long-range missile threat that our Intelligence Community does not foresee in the coming decade. By forcing such an unwarranted deployment decision now, the bill would waste tens of billions of dollars and force us to commit prematurely to a specific technological option. It would also likely require a multiple-site architecture that cannot be accommodated within the terms of the existing ABM Treaty. By setting U.S. policy on a collision course with the ABM Treaty, the bill would jeopardize continued Russian implementation of the START I Treaty as well as Russian ratification of START II—two treaties that will significantly lower the threat to U.S. national security, reducing the number of U.S. and Russian strategic nuclear warheads by two-thirds from Cold War levels. The missile defense provisions would also jeopardize our current efforts to agree on an ABM/TMD (Theater Missile Defense) demarcation with the Russian Federation.

Second, the bill imposes restrictions on the President's ability to conduct contingency operations essential to national security. Its restrictions on funding of contingency operations and the requirement to submit a supplemental appropriations request within a time certain in order to continue a contingency operation are unwarranted restrictions on a President's national security and foreign policy prerogatives. Moreover, by requiring a Presidential certification to assign U.S. Armed Forces under United Nations operational or tactical control, the bill infringes on the President's constitutional authority as Commander in Chief.

Third, H.R. 1530 contains other objectionable provisions that would adversely affect the ability of the Defense Department to carry out national defense programs or impede the Department's ability to manage its day-to-day operations. For example, the bill includes counterproductive certification requirements for the use of Nunn-

Lugar Co-operative Threat Reduction (CTR) funds and restricts use of funds for individual CTR programs.

Other objectionable provisions eliminate funding for the Defense Enterprise Fund; restrict the retirement of U.S. strategic delivery systems; slow the pace of the Defense Department's environmental cleanup efforts; and restrict Defense's ability to execute disaster relief, demining, and military-to-military contact programs. The bill also directs the procurement of specific submarines at specific shipyards although that is not necessary for our military mission to maintain the Nation's industrial base.

H.R. 1530 also contains two provisions that would unfairly affect certain service members. One requires medically unwarranted discharge procedures for HIV-positive service members. In addition, I remain very concerned about provisions that would restrict service women and female dependents of military personnel from obtaining privately funded abortions in military facilities overseas, except in cases of rape, incest, or danger to the life of the mother. In many countries, these U.S. facilities provide the only accessible, safe source for these medical services. Accordingly, I urge the Congress to repeal a similar provision that became law in the "Department of Defense Appropriations Act, 1996."

In returning H.R. 1530 to the Congress, I recognize that it contains a number of important authorities for the Department of Defense, including authority for Defense's military construction program and the improvement of housing facilities for our military personnel and their families. It also contains provisions that would contribute to the effective and efficient management of the Department, including important changes in Federal acquisition law.

Finally, H.R. 1530 includes the authorization for an annual military pay raise of 2.4 percent, which I strongly support. The Congress should enact this authorization as soon as possible, in separate legislation that I will be sending up immediately. In the meantime, I will today sign an Executive order raising military pay for the full 2.0 percent currently authorized by the Congress and will sign an additional order raising pay by a further 0.4 percent as soon as the Congress authorizes that increase.

I urge the Congress to address the Administration's objections and pass an acceptable National Defense Authorization Act promptly. The Department of Defense must have the full range of authorities that it needs to perform its critical worldwide missions.

WILLIAM J. CLINTON

The White House,
December 28, 1995.

NOTE: The Executive order of December 28 on adjustment of certain rates of pay and allowances is listed in Appendix D at the end of this volume. On February 29, 1996, the President signed an Executive order making further adjustments for the uniformed services (61 FR 8467).

Letter to the Speaker of the House of Representatives on Supplemental Legislation To Increase Military Pay and Housing Allowances
December 28, 1995

Sir:

Today I returned to Congress without my approval H.R. 1530, the National Defense Authorization Act for fiscal year 1996, which includes authority for the annual military pay raise. I consider passage of the annual military pay raise to be of crucial importance. Accordingly, I ask Congress to consider the enclosed FY 1996 supplemental language request that would authorize a 2.4 percent pay raise and other allowance increases.

I vetoed H.R. 1530 Act because it would restrict my Administration's ability to carry out national security policy and would substantially interfere with the implementation of key national defense programs. Moreover, certain provisions in the Act raised serious constitutional issues by restricting my authority to conduct foreign affairs and to act as Commander in Chief.

Nevertheless, I believe that our men and women in uniform should not be harmed as we work to obtain a bill that I can support.

Therefore, I ask the Congress to enact the supplemental language to provide the increases in military pay and housing allowances, effective January 1, 1996, that both Congress and I fully support. If this legislation is not enacted, our military personnel will receive a 2.0 percent raise instead of a needed 2.4 percent raise. The legislation is also required to provide an additional increase in the Basic Allowance for Quarters that will help improve the quality of life of our service members and their families.

Speedy enactment of this legislation is imperative at a time when our military personnel are working under challenging conditions to help implement the peace agreement in Bosnia. I urge Congress to enact this legislation as quickly as possible.

Sincerely,

WILLIAM J. CLINTON

NOTE: This letter was made available by the Office of the Press Secretary but was not issued as a White House press release.

Remarks on the Budget Negotiations and an Exchange With Reporters
December 29, 1995

The President. I want to welcome the congressional leaders back here after Christmas. We're going to have, I think, a good meeting today, based on the work that has already been done this morning. I expect us to make further progress.

We will begin to deal with some of the difficult issues today involving how we can balance the budget and protect things like Medicare and Medicaid and education and the environment, which I think are very important. I believe we're proceeding in good faith, and I think we're making progress.

I do believe that we ought to move to reopen the Government. As you know, I feel very strongly about that. The public services will begin to be significantly curtailed. And of course, I'm concerned about the Federal employees, those that aren't working who want to work, who are going to get paid regardless, and those who are working who haven't gotten paid who are going to run into some very serious financial problems with their mortgages and other things soon. So I hope we can get some agreement to reopen the Government so that these problems can be averted.

Q. Is there some room for compromise now that you've had a little bit of time to think it over over the holidays?

The President. Well, we're—I've gotten a preliminary report. I think we'll have some more progress this afternoon, and then I expect we'll work all day tomorrow. I'm prepared to spend whatever time it takes to move as quickly as we can move. But some of these issues are quite complicated in terms of their impact on the American people. But I'm ready to go, and I think that all of us are.

Q. Mr. Speaker, do you see any way of having an agreement that can reopen the Government without the——

Speaker Gingrich. We'll discuss it this afternoon. And I think that Senator Dole and Congressman Armey and I have been trying to work out a way to both get the currently nonessential employees deemed essential, which Senator Dole began to work on last week after our meeting here, and also to find a way to possibly get everyone paid. We feel strongly that Federal employees ought to be back—all the Federal employees ought to be at work. We know they want to be, and it's not fair to them. And we also feel strongly we ought to try to find some way to get everyone paid. We also have an obligation under the continuing resolution that was adopted about 6 weeks ago to get a balanced budget by next Wednesday morning, at the latest, at the end of the first session of Congress.

So I agree with the President. I think there are reasons to be cautiously optimistic. I wouldn't exaggerate them, but I think we've made some progress over the last few days. And I would hope in the next 2 or 3 days we could basically get this done and then have everything up and running and everyone paid for while the staff work was finished out on the actual technical details.

Q. Let me clarify, though, sir, is there any way to get the people back to work without resolving a balanced budget plan?

Speaker Gingrich. There might be a way, yes.

Senator Dole. Yes.

Speaker Gingrich. We're going to explore today some ways to get that done by unanimous consent over the next 2 days. But I think it takes working it out together, and we haven't done that yet.

Senator Dole. Just let me add that we're sending—we're in recess now in the Senate, subject to call of the Chair, and I hope to be able to give Senator Daschle some language to look at this afternoon. And I want to congratulate Congressman Armey for his leadership on the House side with the Speaker, because if we can work this out it could be done yet today.

Q. And have people back to work?

Senator Dole. Well, it would go down to the President as quickly as we could. It's a Middle East peace facilitation act. It's the same language we passed last Friday in the Senate deeming people essential. And the third element of the package would be expedited procedure, if we get an agreement, so we can get it through the Senate in less than 60 days, I guess. We just take the budget reconciliation language and shorten the time and put that in the resolution.

Speaker Gingrich. We'll try to get that down here by sometime this evening if we can get it all worked out. It's all got to be done—our system is complicated even at best, and it takes a little while, but we hope to get it worked out today.

Q. President Clinton, what's your reaction to that, sir?

The President. I think the people ought to go back to work, and I think they ought to be paid. And I think if we don't do it, we're going to see some very serious consequences that should not—that neither the public nor the public employee should have to endure. And I think we need to keep working at this until we get an agreement. I'm prepared to work until we get an agreement. We've just got to keep working through it.

But these are complex issues. To protect Medicare and Medicaid, education and the environment, the things that are at the core of the resolution we adopted, and get the budget balanced in 7 years is not easy to do. We're going to have to work at it.

Q. [*Inaudible*]—the Republicans rejected last time? You thought you had an agreement on something like this and the House Republicans rejected it?

Q. Why did you change your position, Mr. Gingrich?

The President. Wait, wait, wait. Let's don't ask any more questions like that. We're trying to work this out, and I think—give us a chance to meet today, and give them a chance to do their work. Let's see what happens.

NOTE: The President spoke at 3:40 p.m. in the Cabinet Room at the White House, prior to a meeting with congressional leaders. A tape was not available for verification of the content of these remarks.

Message to the Congress Transmitting a Report on Most-Favored-Nation Trade Status for Russia
December 29, 1995

To the Congress of the United States:

On September 21, 1994, I determined and reported to the Congress that the Russian Federation is in full compliance with the freedom of emigration criteria of sections 402 and 409 of the Trade Act of 1974. This action allowed for the continuation of most-favored-nation (MFN) status for Russia and certain other activities without the requirement of an annual waiver.

As required by law, I am submitting an updated report to the Congress concerning the emigration laws and policies of the Russian Federation. You will find that the report indicates continued Russian compliance with U.S. and international standards in the area of emigration.

WILLIAM J. CLINTON

The White House,
December 29, 1995.

Statement on Signing the ICC Termination Act of 1995
December 29, 1995

I have today signed into law H.R. 2539, the "ICC Termination Act of 1995." In my State of the Union address this year, I called upon the Congress to terminate the Interstate Commerce Commission (ICC). I also called for further reductions in unnecessary regulations. This legislation is consistent with those goals, but it does not go far enough.

The bill eliminates the ICC, transferring many of its functions to a new Surface Transportation Board (STB) located within the Department of Transportation (DOT). The bill reduces some ICC functions, including those that overlap with DOT with regard to overseeing safety and insurance requirements in the trucking industry. With the sunset of the ICC and the consolidation of motor carrier functions at DOT, the bill will produce moderate budget savings.

The bill will also help provide a smooth transition now that appropriations for the ICC have been terminated. And the bill empowers the new STB to promote deregulation administratively on a case-by-case basis. I call upon the Board to use this authority to the fullest extent to benefit consumers and facilitate economic growth.

I am also satisfied that the Congress addressed my Administration's strong objections to earlier versions of this legislation, which would have severely curtailed labor protection for railroad employees adversely affected by certain railroad transactions, including mergers. And I note that the final version of the bill continues intact the important rail reforms of 1980, which have helped improve rail service and bring the railroad industry back to profitability.

Nevertheless, I am disappointed in this bill. While it eliminates the ICC, it creates a new independent agency, the STB, within the Transportation Department. Overall, the bill falls short of my Administration's much bolder proposal for extensive deregulation of transportation industries.

Regulatory reform of the Nation's transportation industries has been an outstanding success. Beginning with air cargo deregulation in 1977 and continuing with sweeping rail and trucking reforms over the past 15 years, much of the stranglehold of government regulation has

been broken. Today, only about 20 percent of all domestic freight transportation is regulated, compared with 75 percent 20 years ago. These reforms have reduced the cost of transporting everything we buy and use. They have also enabled U.S. producers and retailers to employ "just in time" manufacturing and inventory systems to save many billions of dollars in warehousing and distribution costs.

The Congress had an opportunity to build on this success but, instead, provided for only very modest reform. While this legislation eliminates a number of obsolete and unnecessary functions of the ICC, it still exempts transportation industries from many of the disciplines of competition. These exemptions are no longer justified in today's strong and competitive market economy.

For example, the Nation's trucking industry has enjoyed antitrust immunity for collective ratemaking for the last 47 years. Continuation of this immunity reduces potential benefits to consumers and protects inefficient carriers. This bill also maintains special merger standards for railroads. The railroad industry should be subject to the same merger standards as other transportation industries.

The bill vests the Chairman of the Surface Transportation Board with the authority to appoint "officers and employees of the Board." The Appointments Clause of the Constitution, Art. II, sec. 2, cl. 2, permits the Congress to vest the appointment of inferior officers in the head of a department. Because the Board is "established within the Department of Transportation," it is a bureau or component of a department, and cannot be a department unto itself for purposes of the Appointments Clause. Accordingly, it would be unconstitutional for the Chairman to appoint persons to serve as "officers" in the constitutional sense. Therefore, I am signing this bill with the understanding that it does not authorize the Chairman to appoint "officers" in the constitutional sense.

The bill provides for the authorization of appropriations for the Board to expire after 3 years. During this period, my Administration will monitor the regulatory activities of the Board to determine whether it should continue and whether further reforms would be beneficial. My Administration remains committed to continued deregulation of the transportation industry.

WILLIAM J. CLINTON

The White House,

December 29, 1995.

NOTE: H.R. 2539, approved December 29, was assigned Public Law No. 104–88. This statement was released by the Office of the Press Secretary on December 30.

The President's Radio Address
December 30, 1995

Good morning. Tomorrow is New Year's Eve, a time for celebration, friendship, and hope. Nineteen ninety-five has been a good year for our country, and the coming year can be even better.

In Washington, we all know this has been a year of serious differences and profound debate over our Nation's future direction. But if we remain true to our values, we will prove once again that in America we can have serious differences without leaving deep divisions. We know our Nation is strongest when we're true to our fundamental values, giving every American the opportunity to make the most of their lives, remembering the duty we owe to our parents and our children, preserving our families and our communities, keeping America the strongest force for peace and freedom in the world.

In our effort to advance these values, 1995 has been a time of real progress and concrete achievement. The key to our strength is economic opportunity for every American. In 1995, the ingenuity and hard work of our people has kept the economy growing, steady and strong. In the past 12 months the economy created 1¾ million new private sector jobs. In every month the unemployment rate has been below 6 percent. All told, since 1993, we Americans have created nearly 8 million new jobs. The stock market has broken every record. The deficit dropped for the third year in a row, for the first time since Mr. Truman was President. Long-term interest rates continue to fall, bringing lower mortgage payments for working families and more affordable credit for small businesses and consumers. A growing economy and lower interest rates are why a million new Americans became homeowners for the very first time

in 1995. There were more new businesses incorporated this year than in any previous year.

And here in Washington, in spite of all of our differences, we made some real progress on an important issue, political reform. At long last, Congress passed a law which applies to themselves the same laws they impose on the private sector. And at long last, after 3 years of effort, the Congress passed lobby reform legislation, banning gifts to Congressmen and requiring extensive disclosure about the activities of lobbyists.

Most important, our communities all over America are coming together around our values again. In city after city, in State after State, violent crime is down; the welfare and food stamp rolls are down; the poverty rate is down; even the divorce rate is down; and for 2 years in a row now, the teen pregnancy rate has dropped.

It hasn't always been an easy year for America. There have been moments that tested our national community. In the wake of the terrible bombing in Oklahoma City, which took the lives of 169 people, our Nation reached out and recognized the bonds that hold us together. Out of the ashes of that tragedy a new sense of national spirit took hold. We affirmed once again that all Americans are in it together. We recognized once again that we can't love our country and hate our Government.

And a strong America has been the world's strongest force for freedom, peace, and democracy in 1995. Our brave men and women today are in the snows of Bosnia, helping to uphold the peace agreement to end the worst bloodshed in Europe since World War II. And from the cobblestone streets of Northern Ireland to the sands of the Middle East, a strong America has helped to bring peace to regions long torn by strife.

Yes, 1995 has been a good year for America. Our people have accomplished a lot. And it goes without saying, we still have one major task to finish to top off the accomplishment of this year. We have to finish the job of balancing the budget and to do it in the right way.

As you know, for the last 2 weeks the Congress has refused to pass legislation that would keep the Federal Government open to serve the American people. This has never happened before for this length of time in the whole history of the Republic. And it's been very hard on three-quarter of a million public servants who have to pay rent and utilities and mortgage payments and buy food. And they're losing pay at holiday time. And it's also cut off services for millions of Americans who depend upon them.

This Tuesday, if the Government is not open, cleanup efforts will be stopped cold at 32 toxic waste sites in neighborhoods around our country. Next week, Federal funds for unemployment insurance will begin to run out, forcing States to scramble to find ways to keep helping workers who have lost their jobs. And the Meals on Wheels program to our senior citizens won't go forward. Every day, 9 of 10 workplace safety complaints go unanswered. And every day 2,500 people can't get guaranteed home mortgages. Every day, thousands of young people looking for college loans can't apply for them. If ever we needed a reminder that our Government is not our enemy, this is it.

Let me be clear: I am committed to balancing the budget. Our administration already has cut the deficit nearly in half, and I am determined

to finish the job. For weeks I've been working in good faith with Republicans and Democrats in Congress to find common ground, to balance the budget in a way that reflects our values. Yesterday I met well into the evening with Speaker Gingrich and Majority Leader Dole. And in just a few moments I will sit down with them again, along with the Democratic congressional leaders.

We are making real progress. We know that our work is not done. We know we have much to do, so that the American dream will remain alive for every citizen and so that we can come together as a people and so that America can remain the strongest force for peace the world has ever seen.

So on this New Year's, let's resolve that we will balance the budget, but that we'll do it in a way that will keep our country growing and that will be true to our basic values. That is, we'll balance the budget without gutting Medicare and Medicaid, without deeply cutting education or the environment, without raising taxes on working families. Let's resolve to re-open the Government and do it now. And let's resolve to act without rancor or partisan bitterness in the spirit of the new year and in the interests of the American people.

Nineteen ninety-five has been a year when we've been true to the best of America. If we'll just work hard and work together and follow our values, 1996 can be even better. Hillary and I want to wish you and your families a happy and healthy New Year.

Thank you for listening.

NOTE: The address was recorded at 9:44 a.m. in the Oval Office at the White House for broadcast at 10:06 a.m.

Remarks on the Budget Negotiations and an Exchange With Reporters
December 30, 1995

The President. I want to be brief today because we're getting off to a little late start. We've got a lot to do. I have three things to say: I think we made a good start yesterday; we're making progress; and I believe we need to open the Government. I hope we can agree to do all that.

Bosnia

Q. Sir, do you know any more information on the soldier who was wounded in Bosnia?

The President. Our reports are sketchy, and I have tried to get an update, but what I do know is that there were apparently two vehicles and four soldiers involved. Only one was seriously hurt, and he has been med-evac'd to Croatia, in a hospital there, and we understand he's in stable condition.

But mines have always been our biggest concern, and we're working very hard on it, but that's what happened. And we'll continue to monitor it and do the best we can. The mission itself is going very well. The people have received our soldiers very well, and I'm very well satisfied with the progress. And I'm obviously very sorry this happened, but they're making good progress on the mine problem, but it's going to be difficult to get rid of them all.

Budget Negotiations

Q. [*Inaudible*]—the measure to get the workers back that's going to get through Congress?

Senator Dole. Well, it passed the House. We hope we can pass it in the Senate today, so make some progress.

Senator Daschle. We tried to pass a clean CR, one without any conditions. And that was objected to, but I hope we can work something out.

Q. But isn't the fact now that the Democrats are holding things up?

Senator Daschle. Not at all. As a matter of fact, as I said, we passed a continuing resolution—we had no conditions. It sent people back to work, and that was objected to. So we're

not trying to hold anything up here. We hope we can get some sort of an agreement as early as today.

Q. Well, what's it going to take to get a deal?

Speaker Gingrich. Well, let me just say something. I think the President had a right—we're glad to have you all in. We have a lot of work to do. We made, I thought, real progress last night. It is not easy. We have very significant areas we have to work on, but I thought the spirit was very positive. We don't just want to get the Federal workers back, we want to get them paid. And in order to do that, I think we've got to get this whole thing worked out. But I thought we had a great start last night. And with you all's permission, I think we can get a lot more done in the next few hours.

Q. Mr. President, is the message from the Democrats basically that they don't trust you?

The President. We've got to go to work. Thank you very much.

NOTE: The President spoke at 11:35 a.m. in the Cabinet Room at the White House, prior to a meeting with congressional leaders. In his remarks, he referred to Spec. Martin J. Begosh, USA, whose vehicle hit a landmine in Bosnia on December 30. A tape was not available for verification of the content of these remarks.

Exchange With Reporters on the Budget Negotiations
December 31, 1995

Q. Mr. President, are you close to a deal today?

The President. Let me tell you where we are today. We had a very long discussion yesterday. We discussed almost all the issues where we had differences on our plans financially, in terms of the dollars. And this morning we're going to have an extensive discussion of the Medicare policy. And then we're going to give our staffs some instruction. We're going to meet again on Tuesday, and we're going to do our best to work through this and come to an accord.

My New Year's wish is that we'll get this balanced budget plan, and we'll do it in a way that protects the things that we care about, the Medicare, the Medicaid, the education and environment, the other issues. And we've been

working at it. I've been very well pleased, and I think we've been somewhat successful because we haven't said very much about it. We've just got to keep working until we reach an accord.

Q. Mr. President, will you touch on—[*inaudible*]—negotiations——

Q. Will you leave town today without reopening the Government, of the three——

Speaker Gingrich. I'm sure we'll be talking about that, that's one of the things we want to get done and get agreed to. So we're trying to work out how to get the Federal employees back to work. We'd also like to get them paid. I think that's an integral part of getting them back to work. But as the President said, I think, frankly, most of our success so far has been that we've been in this room talking with each other and not getting involved in negotiating in public, and I think we've made a lot of progress.

Q. To follow on that, sir, is it healthy to have the House Speaker talking on CNN yesterday on the——

Speaker Gingrich. Oh, that is nonsense. I told the President on Friday that I was so favorable about him in answering their big question on "Evans & Novak" that I thought he'd want to see it. The fact is we're working very well together. I was asked a question about the campaign next year, and I suspect if you ask Mr. Gephardt or Vice President Gore about how they'll campaign next year, they'll give you similar answers. We're negotiating very well from a Government standpoint in here, and I think we have a lot to be proud of. Our New Year's wish ought to be that we get this done and give the American people a balanced budget and the Government paid for and back to work.

Senator Dole. The Senate is going to meet at noon; we'll try to pass something to help the Federal employees.

Q. Are you closer?

Senator Dole. Oh, we're about 6 feet apart. [*Laughter*]

Senator Daschle. We'll be a lot closer in a couple of hours. [*Laughter*]

The President. We're working at it steady.

Happy New Year, everybody.

NOTE: The exchange began at 9:50 a.m. in the Cabinet Room at the White House, prior to a meeting with congressional leaders. A tape was not available for verification of the content of this exchange.

Appendix A—Digest of Other White House Announcements

The following list includes the President's public schedule and other items of general interest announced by the Office of the Press Secretary and not included elsewhere in this book.

July 1

In the afternoon, the President and Hillary Clinton traveled from Miami, FL, to New Haven, CT. They returned to Washington, DC, late in the evening.

July 3

In the afternoon, the President and Hillary Clinton went to Camp David, MD.

July 5

In the afternoon, the President and Hillary Clinton returned to the White House from Camp David.

The White House announced that the President has invited President Ernesto Perez Balladares of Panama for an official working visit on September 7.

The President announced his intention to nominate John Raymond Garamendi to be Deputy Secretary of the Department of the Interior.

The President announced his intention to nominate Cheryl Halpern as a member of the Broadcasting Board of Governors for the International Broadcasting Bureau, U.S. Information Agency.

The President announced his intention to appoint Irving J. Stolberg to the Commission for the Preservation of America's Heritage Abroad.

July 6

In the afternoon, the President attended a reception in Riggs Library at George Washington University.

The White House announced that the President has accepted the invitations of the British and Irish Governments to visit the United Kingdom and Ireland, November 29–December 2.

The White House announced that the President has invited President Nicephore Soglo of Benin to the White House for an official working visit on July 13.

The President announced his intention to nominate Richard Henry Jones as Ambassador to Lebanon.

The President announced his intention to renominate Ernest W. DuBester to the National Mediation Board.

The President announced his intention to appoint Ruth Ann Minner to the Advisory Committee on the Arts of the John F. Kennedy Center for the Performing Arts, Smithsonian Institution.

July 10

In the morning, the President traveled to Nashville, TN, where he visited the Vice President's mother, Pauline Gore, at the Vanderbilt University Medical Center. In the afternoon, he returned to Washington, DC.

In the evening, the President hosted a dinner for congressional leaders on the State Floor.

The White House announced that the President and Czech President Vaclav Havel exchanged letters celebrating the fulfillment of their agreement of July 1994 to move Radio Free Europe/Radio Liberty from Munich, Germany, to Prague, Czech Republic.

The White House announced that the President has invited Prime Minister P.J. Patterson of Jamaica for a working visit on September 13.

The President announced his intention to nominate Carl Spielvogel as a member of the Broadcasting Board of Governors for the International Broadcasting Bureau, U.S. Information Agency.

July 11

The President announced his intention to nominate Joseph H. Neely to be a member of the Board of Directors of the Federal Deposit Insurance Corporation.

July 12

The President declared a major disaster in West Virginia and ordered Federal funds to supplement State and local recovery efforts in communities struck by severe storms, heavy rain, and flash flooding on June 23–27.

The President announced his intention to nominate James Franklin Collins as Ambassador at Large and Special Adviser to the Secretary of State for the New Independent States of the Former Soviet Union.

The President announced his intention to nominate Joseph A. Presel for the rank of Ambassador during his tenure of service as Special Negotiator for Nagorno-Karabakh.

The President announced his intention to nominate Stanley Tuemler Escudero as Ambassador to Uzbekistan.

The President announced his intention to nominate Darcy E. Bradbury as Assistant Secretary for Financial Markets at the Department of the Treasury.

The President announced his intention to nominate Joe Scroggins, Jr., as a Commissioner of the Federal Maritime Commission.

The President announced his intention to appoint the following individuals to be members of the National Commission on Crime Control and Prevention:

Lee Fisher, Chair;
Dennis Wayne Archer;
Paul Helmke;
Deborah Prothrow-Stith;
Andrew J. Shookhoff; and
Esta Soler.

July 13

In the morning, the President met with President Nicephore Soglo of Benin in the Oval Office. Following their meeting, the President hosted a working lunch for President Soglo in the Old Family Dining Room.

In the late afternoon, the President had a telephone conversation with President Jacques Chirac of France to discuss the situation in Bosnia.

In the evening, the President had a telephone conversation with Chancellor Helmut Kohl of Germany to discuss the situation in Bosnia. Later in the evening, the President and Hillary Clinton attended a fund-raiser at a private residence in Sandy Spring, MD.

The President announced his intention to nominate Michael Paul Dombeck as Director of the Bureau of Land Management at the Department of the Interior.

The President announced his intention to nominate Charles H. Twining as Ambassador to Cameroon.

July 14

In the morning, the President and Hillary Clinton participated in a wreath-laying ceremony at the Central Intelligence Agency in Langley, VA.

In the afternoon, the President had a telephone conversation with Prime Minister John Major of the United Kingdom to discuss the situation in Bosnia.

The President announced his intention to nominate Greta Joy Dicus to serve as a Commissioner of the Nuclear Regulatory Commission.

The President announced his intention to nominate Donald S. Wasserman to the Federal Labor Relations Authority.

July 18

In the morning, the President met with senior foreign policy advisers to discuss the situation in Bosnia and with Members of Congress to discuss affirmative action.

In the evening, the President met with David Daliberti, an American who had been imprisoned in Iraq after crossing the Iraqi border on March 13. Later in the evening, the President and Hillary Clinton hosted a picnic for members of the press on the South Lawn.

The President announced his intention to nominate John A. Knubel to be Chief Financial Officer of the Department of Housing and Urban Development.

The President announced his intention to appoint William F. McSweeny to the Board of Trustees of the John F. Kennedy Center for the Performing Arts, Smithsonian Institution.

July 19

In the morning, the President had telephone conversations with President Jacques Chirac of France and Prime Minister John Major of the United Kingdom.

In the afternoon, the President met with Members of Congress to discuss the situation in Bosnia.

The President announced his intention to appoint Harriett M. Wieder to the Council of the Administrative Conference of the United States.

The President announced his intention to appoint Steven M. Eidelman; John F. Kennedy, Jr.; Barbara Yoshioka Wheeler; and Sheryl White-Scott to the President's Committee on Mental Retardation.

July 20

The White House announced that the President will attend World War II 50th anniversary commemorations in Honolulu, HI, on September 1–3.

The President announced his intention to reappoint Barry M. Goldwater to the U.S. Air Force Academy Board of Visitors.

July 21

The President announced his intention to nominate James A. Joseph as Ambassador to South Africa.

The President announced his intention to nominate Hal C. DeCell III to be Assistant Secretary for Congressional and Intergovernmental Relations at the Department of Housing and Urban Development.

The President announced his intention to nominate Paul M. Homan as Special Trustee for American Indians at the Department of the Interior.

The White House announced that the President made available $100 million in emergency home energy assistance to States that have experienced extremely hot weather.

July 24

In the afternoon, the President had a telephone conversation with President Jacques Chirac of France.

The President announced his intention to appoint Richard D. Klausner as Director of the National Cancer Institute at the Department of Health and Human Services.

July 26

The President announced his intention to nominate Joan M. Plaisted as Ambassador to the Marshall Islands and Kiribati.

The President announced his intention to nominate Don Lee Gevirtz as Ambassador to Fiji, Nauru, Tonga, and Tuvalu.

The President announced his intention to appoint Daniel Lecht to the Advisory Committee on the Arts of the John F. Kennedy Center for the Performing Arts, Smithsonian Institution.

July 27

In the morning, the President participated in a wreath-laying ceremony at the Tomb of the Unknowns at Arlington National Cemetery, VA.

The President announced the nomination of Charles B. Curtis as Deputy Secretary of the Department of Energy.

The President accorded the personal rank of Ambassador to James H. Pipkin, Jr., in his capacity as Special Negotiator for the U.S.-Canada Pacific Salmon Treaty.

The President announced his intention to appoint Raymond W. Smith to the President's Committee on the Arts and Humanities.

July 28

In the morning, the President went jogging with President Kim Yong-sam of South Korea. He then had a telephone conversation with President Boris Yeltsin of Russia.

In the evening, the President and Hillary Clinton attended a reception for White House staff.

The White House announced that the President awarded Maj. Richard J. Meadows, USA (Ret.), the Presidential Citizens Medal for his service in the U.S. Special Forces and for his contributions after retiring from military service.

July 31

In the morning, the President traveled to Burlington, VT. In the evening, he returned to Washington, DC.

August 1

The President announced his intention to nominate Rear Adm. John Carter Albright as a member and National Oceanic and Atmospheric Administration Representative to the Mississippi River Commission.

The President announced his intention to nominate Elizabeth K. Julian to serve as Assistant Secretary for the Office of Fair Housing and Equal Opportunity at the Department of Housing and Urban Development.

August 2

In the evening, the President attended a fundraiser for former Governor of Virginia L. Douglas Wilder at a private residence.

The President announced his intention to nominate J. David Carlin as Assistant Secretary for Congressional Relations at the Department of Agriculture.

The White House announced that Prime Minister Jean-Claude Juncker of Luxembourg has accepted the President's invitation for a working visit in Washington, DC, on August 7.

August 3

The President made available $53 million in emergency funds to fishermen in the Northeast, Northwest, and the Gulf of Mexico due to heavy uninsured losses from the collapse of commercial fish stocks and other

disasters. He also made available funds to support emergency requirements resulting from the bombing of the Federal building in Oklahoma City, OK; enhanced antiterrorism efforts; and other disaster-related needs.

The President declared a major disaster in Oregon and ordered Federal funds to supplement State and local recovery efforts in the area struck by flash flooding on July 8–9.

The White House announced that the President has invited President Sali Berisha of Albania for a working visit in Washington, DC, on September 11.

August 4

In the morning, the President met with Members of Congress.

In the afternoon, the President attended a birthday celebration for journalist Helen Thomas of United Press International in the Briefing Room.

August 5

In the morning, the President met with families who have benefited from the Family and Medical Leave Act at the Children's Inn at the National Institutes of Health in Bethesda, MD.

August 7

In the morning, the President met with Prime Minister Jean-Claude Juncker of Luxembourg.

In the afternoon, the President had telephone conversations with Prime Minister John Major of the United Kingdom, President Jacques Chirac of France, and Chancellor Helmut Kohl of Germany to discuss the situation in Bosnia.

The President announced his intention to appoint Kumiki Gibson to the Council of the Administrative Conference of the United States.

August 8

The White House announced that the President has invited President Ion Iliescu of Romania to Washington for a working visit on September 26.

August 9

In the morning, the President met with foreign policy advisers to discuss the situation in Bosnia. Following the meeting, he traveled to Charlotte, NC. In the afternoon, he returned to Washington, DC.

The President announced his intention to nominate Kevin G. Chavers to serve as President of the Government National Mortgage Association at the Department of Housing and Urban Development.

The President announced his intention to nominate Gail Clements McDonald to be the Administrator of the Saint Lawrence Seaway Development Corporation at the Department of Transportation.

The President announced his intention to nominate Phillip A. Singerman to be the Assistant Secretary of Commerce for Economic Development at the Commerce Department's Economic Development Administration.

The President announced his intention to nominate Isaac C. Hunt, Jr., and Norman S. Johnson to be members of the Securities and Exchange Commission.

The President announced his intention to nominate Gov. Ned R. McWherter to the Board of Governors of the U.S. Postal Service.

The President announced his intention to nominate Gov. Mel Carnahan to serve as a member of the Board of Trustees of the Harry S Truman Scholarship Foundation.

The President announced his intention to appoint Ernest Lofton, Jr., as a member of the Community Adjustment and Investment Program Advisory Committee for the North American Development Bank.

The President announced his intention to appoint Patricia M. Duff to the Library of Congress Trust Fund Board.

The President announced his intention to appoint Richard J. Boxer to the National Cancer Advisory Board.

August 10

The President announced his intention to nominate David C. Williams to be Inspector General of the Social Security Administration.

The President declared a major disaster in Florida and ordered Federal aid to supplement State and local recovery efforts in the area struck by Hurricane Erin on August 2–3.

The White House announced that the President will travel to Japan on November 16–21 to participate in the Asia-Pacific Economic Cooperation leaders meeting and for a state visit.

August 11

The President announced his intention to nominate Linda Colvin Rhodes as Deputy Commissioner of the Social Security Administration.

The President announced his intention to appoint Beth Dozoretz to serve as a member of the U.S. Holocaust Memorial Council.

The President announced his intention to appoint Gregory Lashutka and reappoint Paul Burke to the Advisory Commission on Intergovernmental Relations.

August 14

The White House announced that the President named Donald A. Baer as Assistant to the President and Director of Communications.

The President announced his intention to nominate Patricia J. Beneke to serve as Assistant Secretary for Water and Science at the Department of the Interior.

The President announced his intention to nominate Nancy E. McFadden as General Counsel of the Department of Transportation.

The President announced his intention to appoint Phillip J. Shepherd as Federal Representative to the Ohio River Valley Sanitation Compact Commission.

August 15

In the afternoon, the President and Hillary Clinton traveled to Jackson Hole, WY, for their vacation.

The President announced the renomination of Chester A. Crocker, Theodore M. Hesburgh, and Max M. Kampelman in addition to the nomination of Seymour Martin Lipset to the Board of Directors of the U.S. Institute of Peace.

The President announced his intention to nominate Lowell Junkins as a member of the Board of Directors of the Federal Agricultural Mortgage Corporation.

The President announced his intention to nominate Gov. Zell Miller of Georgia to serve as a member of the James Madison Memorial Fellowship Foundation.

August 16

The President announced his intention to nominate Charles A. Hunnicutt to be Assistant Secretary for Aviation and International Affairs at the Department of Transportation.

The President declared a major disaster in Vermont and ordered Federal aid to supplement State and local recovery efforts in the area struck by excessive rain and flooding on August 4–6.

August 17

The President announced the renomination of David A. Brock and Joseph F. Baca to the Board of Directors of the State Justice Institute.

August 18

The President declared a major disaster in Minnesota and ordered Federal aid to supplement State and local recovery efforts in the area struck by severe storms, straight line winds, and tornadoes on July 9–14.

August 23

In the morning, the President traveled from Jackson Hole, WY, to Washington, DC.

In the afternoon, the President met with members of his foreign policy team and the following newly appointed members of the U.S. negotiating team in Bosnia-Herzegovina: Roberts Owen, Brig. Gen. Donald Kerrick, James Pardew, and Christopher Hill. He then returned to Jackson Hole, WY.

August 24

In the evening, the President had a telephone conversation with Senator Alfonse D'Amato and Gov. George Pataki of New York to discuss emergency efforts to extinguish brush fires on Long Island.

August 25

In the morning, the President traveled to Yellowstone National Park. Later in the day, he returned to Jackson Hole.

The President announced his intention to appoint Ember Reichgott Junge to the Council of the Administrative Conference of the United States.

The President declared a major disaster in Ohio and ordered Federal aid to supplement State and local recovery efforts in the area struck by severe storms and flooding on August 7–18.

August 28
The President announced his intention to appoint Parker Westbrook to the Advisory Council on Historic Preservation.

August 30
In the morning, the President met with ranchers at the Sweetwater Restaurant. Later, he had a luncheon meeting with energy industry representatives at the Acadian Restaurant.

The President announced his intention to nominate Susan King to be Assistant Secretary for Public Affairs at the Department of Labor.

August 31
In the morning, the President and Hillary Clinton traveled from Jackson Hole, WY, to Honolulu, HI.

The President announced his intention to appoint Constantino Y. Amores and Alison H. Deem to the Advisory Committee on the Arts of the John F. Kennedy Center for the Performing Arts, Smithsonian Institution.

September 1
In the morning, the President met with troops outside Hangar 206 at Wheeler Air Force Base. In the afternoon, he had lunch with veterans in the Consolidated Mess.

In the evening, the President had a telephone conversation with NATO Secretary General Willy Claes to discuss NATO operations in Bosnia-Herzegovina.

The President declared a major disaster in Oklahoma and ordered Federal funds to supplement State and local recovery efforts in the area struck by tornadoes, severe storms, and flooding, beginning on July 21 through and including August 6.

The President announced his intention to appoint Elaine B. Griffin to the White House Commission on Presidential Scholars.

The President announced his intention to appoint Ada E. Deer, Joseph D. Duffey, Madeleine M. Kunin, and Shirley Sachi Sagawa to the Board of Trustees of the American Folklife Center.

September 2
In the afternoon, the President and Hillary Clinton had lunch with veterans aboard the U.S.S. *Carl Vinson* in Honolulu, HI. They then participated in a wreath-laying ceremony at the U.S.S. *Arizona* memorial and viewed a veterans parade at Fort DeRussy. Following the parade, the President toured the Okinawan festival at Kapiolani Park.

September 3
In the afternoon, the President traveled from Honolulu, HI, to San Jose, CA. Following his arrival at Moffett Air Force Base in the evening, he traveled to Monterey, CA.

September 4
In the afternoon, the President traveled from Monterey, CA, to Pleasanton, CA. In the evening, he returned to Monterey.

September 5
In the morning, the President traveled from Monterey, CA, to Selma, CA. In the afternoon, he traveled to Fresno, CA, where he met with agricultural leaders in Wofford Executive Hangar at Fresno Airport. Later in the afternoon, the President traveled from Fresno to Washington, DC, arriving after midnight.

September 6
In the morning, the President met with President Ernesto Perez Balladares of Panama.

In the late afternoon, the President and Chelsea Clinton traveled to Baltimore, MD, where they met with Cal Ripken, Jr., at Oriole Park at Camden Yards and attended the shortstop's recordbreaking 2,131st consecutive baseball game. In the late evening, they returned to Washington, DC.

September 7
In the afternoon, the President met with Democratic congressional leaders.

September 8
The President nominated Jeffrey R. Shafer to be Under Secretary of the Treasury for International Affairs.

The President announced his intention to nominate David A. Lipton to be Assistant Secretary of the Treasury for International Affairs.

The President announced his intention to nominate Melissa T. Skolfield to be Assistant Secretary for Public Affairs at the Department of Health and Human Services.

September 11
In the morning, the President traveled to Carbondale, IL.

In the afternoon, the President returned to Washington, DC. He then met with members of the Principals Committee and Assistant Secretary of State Richard Holbrooke to discuss Bosnia-Herzegovina.

The President announced his intention to nominate Donna Dearman Smith to the Board of Trustees of the Barry Goldwater Scholarship and Excellence in Education Foundation.

The President announced his intention to appoint Morris S. Arnold to the Board of Directors of the James Madison Memorial Fellowship Foundation.

The President announced his intention to appoint John J. Pikarski, Jr., to the Commission for the Preservation of America's Heritage Abroad.

The White House announced that the President has invited President Thomas Klestil of Austria to Washington, DC, for a working visit on October 19.

The White House announced that the President will award the Presidential Medal of Freedom to the following individuals in a White House ceremony on September 28:

Peggy Charren;
William T. Coleman, Jr.;
Joan Ganz Cooney;
John Hope Franklin;
A. Leon Higginbotham, Jr.;
Frank M. Johnson, Jr.;
C. Everett Koop;
Gaylord Nelson;
Walter P. Reuther;
James W. Rouse;
Willie Velasquez; and
Lew R. Wasserman.

September 12
In the morning, the President met with President Sali Berisha of Albania.

In an Oval Office ceremony in the afternoon, the President presented the Congressional Gold Medal posthumously to Rabbi Menachem Schneerson.

September 13
In the morning, the President traveled to Elkridge, MD.

Following his return to Washington, DC, in the afternoon, the President met with Prime Minister P.J. Patterson of Jamaica. He then met briefly with His Holiness the Dalai Lama to discuss the preservation of Tibetan religion and culture.

The White House announced that the President has invited President Jacques Chirac of France to Washington, DC, for a state visit on November 3.

September 14
The President announced his intention to appoint Vera C. Rubin, Eric S. Lander, Marcia K. McNutt, and George S. Hammond as members of the President's Committee on the National Medal of Science.

The President announced his intention to appoint R. Scott Warner as a member of the Panama Canal Consultative Committee.

September 15
In a morning ceremony in the Oval Office, the President received diplomatic credentials from Ambassadors Var Huoth of Cambodia, Mustafa S. Nyang'anyi of Tanzania, Pastor Micha Ondo Bile of Equatorial Guinea, Alvaro Diez de Medina of Uruguay, Knud Erik Tygesen of Denmark, John Kerr of the United Kingdom, and Antonio France N'balu of Angola.

In the afternoon, the President met with representatives of the Catholic press.

In the evening, the President and Hillary Clinton hosted a Democratic National Committee trustees dinner on the State Floor.

The President announced his intention to nominate Jane Bobbitt to be Assistant Secretary of Commerce for Legislative and Intergovernmental Affairs.

September 16
The President declared a major disaster in the U.S. Virgin Islands and ordered Federal aid to supplement recovery efforts in areas struck by Hurricane Marilyn beginning on September 15.

The President declared a major disaster in Puerto Rico and ordered Federal aid to supplement Commonwealth and local recovery efforts in the areas struck by Hurricane Marilyn beginning on September 15.

September 18
In the afternoon, the President traveled to Philadelphia, PA. While en route on Air Force One, he had a telephone conversation with NATO Secretary General Willy Claes to congratulate him on NATO's success in Bosnia. Following his arrival, he met with ministers and community leaders in the Mount Carmel Baptist Church.

In the evening, the President traveled to Jacksonville, FL.

The President announced his intention to nominate James C. Riley to be a Commissioner of the Federal Mine Safety and Health Review Commission.

September 19
In the evening, the President traveled to Denver, CO.

The President announced his intention to appoint M. Sharon Cassidy, Teresa Ghilarducci, and Joseph S. Perkins to be members of the Advisory Committee of the Pension Benefit Guaranty Corporation.

September 20
In the evening, the President attended a Clinton/Gore fundraiser at the Marriott City Center. He then traveled to San Francisco, CA.

The White House announced that the President named Stephanie S. Streett and Anne L. Walley as Deputy Assistants to the President and Directors of Scheduling.

The White House announced that the President has appointed Jack Quinn as Assistant to the President and White House Counsel to replace Abner Mikva, who will retire November 1.

September 21
In the morning, the President met with business leaders from the information industry to discuss goals for education technology.

In the afternoon, the President traveled to Culver City, CA, and later to Los Angeles.

In the evening, the President attended a Saxophone Club fundraiser at the House of Blues.

The President announced his intention to nominate Anthony Cecil Eden Quainton to be Director General of the Foreign Service.

The President announced his intention to nominate Eric James Boswell as Assistant Secretary of State for Diplomatic Security.

The President announced his intention to appoint Cecille Pulitzer to the Library of Congress Trust Fund Board.

The President announced his intention to name Ira L. Hobbs to the Committee for Purchase From People Who Are Blind or Severely Disabled.

September 22

In the morning, the President traveled to Santa Ana, CA, and in the afternoon, he traveled to San Diego.

In the evening, the President returned to Washington, DC, arriving after midnight.

The President announced his intention to appoint Peter Lucas to be a member of the Advisory Commission on Intergovernmental Relations.

The President nominated former Tennessee Senator Jim Sasser as Ambassador to the People's Republic of China.

September 24

In the morning, the President and Hillary and Chelsea Clinton traveled to Scranton, PA. In the evening, they returned to Washington, DC.

September 26

In the morning, the President had a working visit with President Ion Iliescu of Romania.

The President announced his intention to nominate John N. Erlenborn to the Board of Directors of the Legal Services Corporation.

The President announced his intention to appoint Jill L. Long Thompson as a Department of Agriculture Federal Representative to the Rural Telephone Bank Board.

September 27

In the morning, the President had a telephone conversation with President Boris Yeltsin of Russia.

The President announced that he has named the following individuals to the President's Oklahoma City Scholarship Fund Advisory Board:

George Nigh, Chair;
Henry Bellmon;
Michael Enoch;
Melvin Hall;
W.R. Howell;
Lou C. Kerr;
Martha King;
Ruth Leebron Levenson;
Ronald J. Norick;
M. Susan Savage;
James Lee Witt; and
Stanton Young.

September 28

The President announced his intention to appoint Burton P. Resnick to the U.S. Holocaust Memorial Council.

September 29

In the late morning, the President had meetings with President Hosni Mubarak of Egypt and King Hussein I of Jordan.

The President announced his intention to nominate Laveeda Morgan Battle as a member of the Board of Directors of the Legal Services Corporation.

The White House announced that the President has invited President Suleyman Demirel of Turkey to Washington, DC, for a working visit on October 18.

The White House announced that the President, at the invitation of King Juan Carlos I of Spain, will visit Madrid to attend the United States-European Union summit on December 3.

October 1

In the morning, the President attended the annual red Mass at St. Matthew's Cathedral with members of the Supreme Court.

October 2

In the morning, the President had a telephone conversation with President Heydar Aliyev of Azerbaijan.

In the afternoon, the President met with NATO Secretary General Willy Claes.

The White House announced that the President has invited President Jiang Zemin of China to attend a bilateral summit meeting in New York City on October 24.

The President announced his intention to appoint the following individuals to the Commission on Dietary Supplement Labels:

Malden Nesheim;
Annette Dickinson;
Shiriki K. Kumanyika;
Norman R. Farnsworth;
Margaret Gilhooley;
Robert S. McCaleb; and
Anthony T. Podesta.

October 4

In the afternoon, the President and Hillary Clinton traveled to Newark, NJ. Later in the afternoon, the President met with Pope John Paul II at Sacred Heart Cathedral.

In the evening, the President and Hillary Clinton attended a vespers prayer service. Following the service, they returned to Washington, DC.

The President announced his intention to nominate David Finn to the National Council on the Humanities.

The President announced his intention to renominate Ernest G. Green as Chairman of the Board of Directors of the African Development Foundation.

The President announced his intention to nominate C.E. (Abe) Abramson and Walter Anderson to serve as members of the National Commission on Libraries and Information Science.

The President announced his intention to appoint Frank Ballesteros, John Litzenberg, Clara Miller, and George Surgeon as members of the Community Development Advisory Board.

The President announced his intention to appoint Joseph Sewall to serve as a member and Kenneth M. Curtis to serve as an alternate member of the Roosevelt Campobello International Park Commission.

The President selected the following delegates to attend the White House Conference on Travel and Tourism on October 30–31:

Peter Armstrong;
Peter A. Bakke;
Sally Begay;
Robert D. Billington;
Hope J. Boonshaft;
Aaron Broussard;
David Van Buskirk;
Romy Cachola;
Stephen J. Cloobeck;
Oshel B. Craigo;
Andrew P. Daly;
Stephen T. Economy;
Robert Giersdorf;
John David Gunner;
Beverly A. Hollingworth;
Sylvan (Sonny) Holtzman;
Geoffrey F. Hurtado;
Jeanne Jacobsen;
Shelley Johnson;
Sandra D. Jones;
Kathy S. Lewand;
Stephen J. Lombardo;
Crit Luallen;
Anthony MacConnell;
Granger Mac-farlane;
Jacqueline B. McNulty;
Montine McNulty;
Melanie Mills;
Agnes Hui-Chun Mu;
Neil W. Ostergren;
Mary Lou Parks;
James L. Pouravelis;
Patrick Sciarratta;
Judy Sidran;
Keith Stokes;
Marilyn J. Tomasi;
Carmen Delia Venticinque;
Craig D. Walter;
Shelby Woods;
Alon Yu;
Nina Zagat; and
Tim Zagat.

October 5

The President and Hillary Clinton recognized the following winners of the National Award for Museum Service for their work in the Nation's communities: the Brooklyn Children's Museum, Brooklyn, NY; the Mexican Fine Arts Center Museum, Chicago, IL; the Montshire Museum of Science, Norwich, VT; and the Wing Lauke Asian Museum, Seattle, WA.

October 6

In the morning, the President addressed the Bilderberg Steering Committee at the Four Seasons Hotel. He then attended a Democratic National Committee luncheon at the Hay Adams Hotel.

In the evening, the President and Hillary Clinton traveled to Martha's Vineyard, MA.

October 8

In the afternoon, the President and Hillary Clinton returned to Washington, DC.

October 10

In the morning, the President met with business leaders in the Cabinet Room.

The President announced his intention to nominate Arthur L. Money to be Assistant Secretary of the Air Force for Acquisition.

October 11

The President announced his intention to nominate William P. Foster to be a member of the National Council on the Arts.

October 12

In the evening, the President attended a Clinton/Gore fundraiser at the Hotel Washington.

The President announced his intention to appoint Maj. Gen. John P. Herrling, USA (Ret.), to serve as Secretary of the American Battle Monuments Commission.

October 13

In the morning, the President met with Weigelt-Wallace Award recipients J. Andy Sullivan and David Tuggle, physicians from Oklahoma City, OK, who were recognized for their medical services following the bombing of the Alfred P. Murrah Federal Building.

In the early evening, the President traveled to Williamsburg, VA, and he returned to Washington, DC, later in the evening.

The President declared a major disaster in Alaska and ordered Federal funds to supplement State and local recovery efforts in the area struck by severe storms and flooding on September 18 and continuing.

The President announced his intention to nominate Gerald Wesley Scott to be Ambassador to Gambia.

The President announced his intention to nominate David P. Rawson to be Ambassador to Mali.

The President announced his intention to nominate Robert E. Gribbin III to be Ambassador to Rwanda.

The President announced his intention to nominate Ralph R. Johnson to be Ambassador to the Slovak Republic.

The President announced his intention to renominate Barry M. Goldwater and Peter S. Knight to the Communications Satellite Corporation (COMSAT) Board of Directors.

The White House announced that the President will attend the dedication of the National Czech and Slovak Museum and Library and will meet with President Vaclav Havel of the Czech Republic and President Michal Kovac of the Slovak Republic on October 21 in Cedar Rapids, IA.

October 15

In the morning, the President traveled to Hartford, CT. Following his arrival at Bradley International Airport, he greeted a group of young people working to combat teenage smoking.

In the evening, the President traveled to Austin, TX.

October 16

In the morning, the President traveled to Dallas, TX, and in the evening, he traveled to Los Angeles, CA.

The President announced his intention to appoint Natalie Cohen to be a member of the Advisory Committee on the Arts of the John F. Kennedy Center for the Performing Arts, Smithsonian Institution.

The White House announced that the President will meet at the White House with President Soeharto of Indonesia on October 27.

The White House announced that the President congratulated Armstrong World Industries' Building Products Operation and Corning Telecommunications Products Division as recipients of the 1995 Malcolm Baldrige National Quality Award.

October 17

In the morning, the President traveled to San Antonio, TX, and in the evening, he traveled to Houston, TX. Later in the evening, he returned to Washington, DC.

The President announced his intention to appoint Cynthia A. Murray-Beliveau to be a member of the Advisory Committee on the Arts of the John F. Kennedy Center for the Performing Arts, Smithsonian Institution.

October 18

In the evening, the President traveled to Baltimore, MD, where he attended a fundraising dinner at a private residence. He then returned to Washington, DC.

The President announced his intention to appoint A. Leon Higginbotham, Jr., to the U.S. Commission on Civil Rights.

The White House announced that the President and President Jacques Chirac of France have agreed to reschedule President Chirac's November 3 state visit at the White House for February 1, 1996.

October 19

In the morning, the President had a working visit with President Thomas Klestil of Austria.

In the evening, the President attended the Africare reception at the Washington Hilton Hotel.

The President announced his intention to renominate Lottie L. Shackelford to be the small business designate on the Overseas Private Investment Corporation Board of Directors.

The President announced his intention to appoint Vigdor L. Teplitz to the Scientific and Policy Advisory Committee of the U.S. Arms Control and Disarmament Agency.

October 20

In the morning, the President traveled to Columbus, OH, and in the afternoon, he traveled to Des Moines, IA.

The President selected the following additional delegates to attend the White House Conference on Travel and Tourism on October 30–31:

Carol Baumgarten;
John Brissenden;
Ray Bryant;
Gregg Carano;
Nancy Patton Conway;
Eduardo Diaz;
Sho Dozono;
Mary Eaddy;
Patricia Gentry Edington;
Marc Fruchter;
Chris Gallant;
Wayne Greenhaw;
Nabil Haddad;
Phyllis Y. Hamilton;
Yolanda Kizer;
A.K. (Kirk) Lanterman;
Don Madden;
Patrick Murphy;
Jerry T. Nagler, Jr.;
Mark Nichols;
Deborah L. Ortega;
Ruth Ann Pastrick;
Clyde V. Prestowitz, Jr.;
Linus Raines;
Randy Randall;
Nancy Reuther;
Y. Sherry Sheng;
Calvin Smyre;
Kathleen Anne Sweeton;
Royette Tarry;
Henry Topel;

J. Kim Tucci;
Arthur Turnbull;
Janet Turner;
Thomas W. Walsh;
Kenneth C. Wilkins; and
Amy Vanderbilt.

October 21

In the morning, the President traveled from Des Moines, IA, to Cedar Rapids, IA.

In the afternoon, the President toured the National Czech and Slovak Museum and Library. Following the tour, he attended a reception for museum supporters and staff members in the Meeting Room and held meetings with President Michal Kovac of the Slovak Republic and President Vaclav Havel of the Czech Republic in the Library. He then returned to Washington, DC.

October 22

In the morning, the President and Hillary Clinton traveled to New York City. Later in the morning, the President met with Prime Minister Janez Drnovsek of Slovenia at the United States Mission to the United Nations.

In the afternoon, the President met with Secretary-General Boutros Boutros-Ghali at United Nations Headquarters. He then met with President Meles Zenawi of Ethiopia at the Waldorf Astoria Hotel.

In the evening, the President and Hillary Clinton hosted a reception for heads of state in the Gottesman Exhibition Hall at the New York Public Library.

October 23

In the morning, the President traveled to Hyde Park, NY, and in the afternoon, he returned to New York City.

The President announced his intention to appoint Yvonne Lee to the U.S. Commission on Civil Rights.

The President made available $125 million in emergency funds for disaster loans to help the States and the U.S. Virgin Islands recover from Hurricanes Marilyn and Opal.

The White House announced that the President and Hillary Clinton will make a state visit to Japan on November 19–21.

October 24

In the evening, the President returned to Washington, DC.

The President announced his intention to appoint Jay Mazur to the Advisory Committee for Trade Policy and Negotiations.

October 25

In the evening, the President met with Prime Minister Yitzhak Rabin of Israel in the Secretary's Sitting Room at the State Department.

October 26

In the morning, the President met with Second Deputy Prime Minister Prince Sultan Bin Abdul Aziz Al-Saud of Saudi Arabia.

October 27

The President announced his intention to appoint James D. Casto and Peter Field to the Advisory Committee on the Arts of the John F. Kennedy Center for the Performing Arts, Smithsonian Institution.

The President announced his intention to appoint Francis B. (Frank) Moore to the United Service Organizations, Inc., Board of Governors.

The President announced his intention to appoint Vance D. Coffman, Paul E. Wright, and Van B. Honeycutt to the National Security Telecommunications Advisory Committee.

The President announced his intention to appoint Deborah G. Groeber, Kenneth J. Oscar, and Maj. Gen. Ray E. McCoy, USA, to the Committee for Purchase From People Who Are Blind or Severely Disabled.

The White House announced that the President will attend the dedication of a memorial cairn at Arlington National Cemetery, VA, on November 3, to commemorate the victims of the terrorist bombing of Pan American Airlines Flight 103.

October 28

In the evening, the President had a telephone conversation with Ted Turner, owner of the Atlanta Braves baseball team, to congratulate the team on winning the 1995 World Series.

October 30

In the evening, the President and Hillary Clinton met with King Harald and Queen Sonja of Norway in the Diplomatic Reception Room.

The President announced his intention to nominate Patricia W. McNeil as Assistant Secretary for Vocational and Adult Education at the Department of Education.

The President selected the following additional delegates to attend the White House Conference on Travel and Tourism on October 30–31:

James D. Andrews;
Dick J. Batchelor;
Charles H.P. Duell;
Donna Ferrara;
Celso Guzman, Jr.;
E. Marie Johnson;
David Milenthal;
Stephanie Neff;
John O'Brien;
Jose M. Perez;
John A. Redhead;
Diana Rosario;
Elisa Maria Sanchez;
Sean J. Shannon; and
Thomas J. Shortell.

October 31

The President selected additional delegates Melanie Benjamin and Helen Cottingham to attend the White House Conference on Travel and Tourism on October 30–31.

November 1

In the morning, the President briefly attended the Vice President's meeting with Ulster Unionist Party leader David Trimble to discuss the Northern Ireland peace process.

In the afternoon, the President met with congressional leaders.

The President accorded the personal rank of Ambassador to Philip Bates Taylor III in his capacity as the head of the U.S. delegation to the Inter-American Council for Education, Science, and Culture and the Inter-American Economic and Social Council.

November 2

In the morning, the President went to the J.W. Marriott Hotel, where he met with the family of Maryland State trooper Edward A. Plank, Jr., who was killed in the line of duty on October 17.

In the evening, the President attended a Clinton/Gore reception and dinner at the Sheraton Carlton Hotel.

The President announced his intention to appoint Jorge L. Bolanos as a member of the Enterprise for the Americas Board.

The White House announced that the President signed S. 227, the Digital Performance Right in Sound Recordings Act of 1995.

November 5

In the afternoon, the President and Hillary Clinton traveled to Tel Aviv, Israel.

November 6

Following their arrival in Tel Aviv in the morning, the President and Hillary Clinton traveled to Jerusalem and visited the grounds of the Knesset, where the body of Prime Minister Yitzhak Rabin lay in state.

In the afternoon, the President and Hillary Clinton visited the Prime Minister's widow, Leah Rabin, at the Prime Minister's Residence.

In the evening, the President had meetings with Acting Prime Minister Shimon Peres of Israel, King Hussein I of Jordan, President Hosni Mubarak of Egypt, and Likud Party leader Binyamin Netanyahu of Israel at the King David Hotel. Following the meetings, the President and Hillary Clinton returned to Washington, DC.

November 7

The White House announced that the President invited President Jose Eduardo dos Santos of Angola to the White House for an official working visit on December 8.

The President announced his intention to appoint Kathryn G. Thompson as a member of the Federal National Mortgage Association Board of Directors.

The President announced his intention to nominate Joshua Gotbaum to be Assistant Secretary of the Treasury for Economic Policy.

The President announced his intention to nominate Norman I. Maldonado to be a member of the Board of Trustees of the Harry S Truman Scholarship Foundation.

The President announced his intention to appoint Connie E. Evans, Jacqueline Lee Johnson, Carol Parry, and John E. Taylor as members of the Community Development Advisory Board.

The President announced his intention to nominate Wallace D. McRae to the National Council on the Arts.

November 8

In the morning, the President had a telephone conversation with Christian Science Monitor reporter David Rohde, who had been released after being held captive by Bosnian Serbs since October 29.

In the afternoon, the President and Hillary Clinton hosted a tea for Queen Beatrix and Prince Claus of The Netherlands.

The President accorded the personal rank of Ambassador to Brian Frederick Fontes in his capacity as chair of the U.S. delegation to the International Telecommunication Union's 1995 World Radio Communications Conference.

November 9

In the morning, the President met with public health and environmental leaders.

In the afternoon, the President met with congressional leaders.

The President announced his intention to nominate Yolanda Townsend Wheat to the National Credit Union Administration Board of Directors.

The President announced his intention to nominate Robert S. Litt to be Assistant Attorney General for the Criminal Division at the Department of Justice.

November 12

In the evening, the President and Hillary Clinton attended the Ford's Theatre Gala at the theater.

November 13

The President announced his intention to appoint Gila Joy Bronner to the U.S. Holocaust Memorial Council.

The President announced the appointment of Marvin F. (Bud) Moss to the National Historical Publications and Records Commission.

November 20

In the evening, the President met with Democratic Members of Congress on Capitol Hill.

The President announced his intention to appoint Kenneth L. Salazar to serve as a member of the Western Water Policy Review Advisory Commission.

November 21

In the morning, the President had telephone conversations with President Lech Walesa and President-elect Aleksander Kwasniewski of Poland.

In the afternoon, the President had lunch with the Vice President. He then had a telephone conversation with President Alija Izetbegovic of Bosnia-Herzegovina, President Franjo Tudjman of Croatia, and President Slobodan Milosevic of Serbia to congratulate them on the Bosnia-Herzegovina peace agreement.

In the evening, the President attended a reception at the Los Angeles Times Washington bureau.

November 22

The President announced his intention to appoint John H. Davidson to serve as a member of the Western Water Policy Review Advisory Commission.

November 23

In the morning, the President and Hillary and Chelsea Clinton went to Camp David, MD, for the Thanksgiving holiday.

November 24

The White House announced that the President will travel to Ramstein, Germany, on December 2 to meet with U.S. forces preparing for deployment to the Balkans.

The White House announced that the President has invited Prime Minister Shimon Peres of Israel for an official visit at the White House on December 11.

November 26

In the afternoon, the President and Hillary and Chelsea Clinton returned to the White House from Camp David.

November 27

In the afternoon, the President had a telephone conversation with Speaker of the House Newt Gingrich on Bosnia. In the evening, he had telephone conversations with former President George Bush and former Chairman of the Joint Chiefs of Staff Colin Powell on Bosnia.

The President announced his intention to nominate H. Martin Lancaster to be the Assistant Secretary of the Army for Civil Works.

The President announced his intention to nominate James E. Johnson to be the Assistant Secretary of the Treasury for Enforcement.

The President announced his intention to nominate LeVar Burton to be a member of the National Commission on Libraries and Information Science.

November 28

In the afternoon, the President attended a luncheon on Capitol Hill with Senate Democratic leaders.

In the evening, the President and Hillary Clinton traveled to London, England.

November 29

In the morning, the President planted a tree at the U.S. Ambassador's residence. Later, the President and Hillary Clinton toured Westminster Abbey, where the President laid a wreath at the Tomb of the Unknown Warrior.

In the afternoon, the President and Hillary Clinton had tea with Queen Elizabeth II and Prince Philip at Buckingham Palace.

The President announced his intention to nominate Luis Rovira to serve as a member of the Board of Trustees to the Harry S Truman Scholarship Foundation.

November 30

In the morning, the President and Hillary Clinton traveled to Belfast, Northern Ireland; in the afternoon, they traveled to Londonderry, Northern Ireland; and in the early evening, they returned to Belfast.

In the evening, the President had meetings with Sinn Fein leader Gerry Adams and Democratic Unionist Party leader Ian Paisley at Queen's University. He then met with Ulster Unionist Party leader David Trimble at the Europa Hotel.

The President announced his intention to appoint J. Robert Beyster to the President's National Security Telecommunications Advisory Committee.

The President announced his intention to reappoint Susan R. Baron as a member of the Board of Directors for the National Corporation for Housing Partnerships.

December 1

In the morning, the President and Hillary Clinton traveled to Dublin, Ireland.

In the late afternoon, the President had meetings with Fiana Fáil party leader Bertie Ahern, Nobel Prize winner Seamus Heaney, and Progressive Democrats Party leader Mary Harney at the U.S. Ambassador's residence.

The President announced his intention to appoint Thomas L. Baldini as the U.S. Commissioner of the U.S.-Canada International Boundary Commission.

The President announced his intention to reappoint Joseph John DiNunno as a member of the Defense Nuclear Facilities Safety Board.

The President announced the appointment of Thomas P. Cross to the Presidential Advisory Committee on Gulf War Veterans' Illnesses.

The President announced the appointment of the following individuals to the Presidential Advisory Council on HIV/AIDS:

Stephen N. Abel;
Tonio Burgos;

Jerry Cade;
B. Thomas Henderson;
Helen M. Miramontes;
Robert Michael Rankin; and
Richard W. Stafford.

December 2
In the morning, the President and Hillary Clinton traveled from Dublin, Ireland, to Ramstein, Germany, and then to Baumholder, Germany. In the afternoon, they had lunch with American troops of the 1st Armored Division at Baumholder Army Base.

In the early evening, the President and Hillary Clinton traveled to Ramstein, Germany, and then to Madrid, Spain. Later in the evening, they toured the Prado Museum.

December 3
In the afternoon, the President and Hillary Clinton returned to Washington, DC.

In the evening, they attended the Kennedy Center Honors at the John F. Kennedy Center for the Performing Arts.

December 5
In the morning, the President met with Bosnian refugee families who had resettled in the United States.

The President announced the release of the second report on Federal agencies' customer service standards issued by the National Performance Review.

December 6
The President announced his intention to nominate Alfred C. DeCotiis to be a Representative to the 50th session of the United Nations General Assembly.

The President announced his intention to nominate Jeanne Moutoussamy-Ashe to be an Alternate Representative to the 50th session of the United Nations General Assembly.

The President announced his intention to nominate Joseph Lane Kirkland to be an Alternate Representative to the 50th session of the United Nations General Assembly.

The President announced his intention to appoint James Hamilton and the reappointment of Anthony S. Harrington and Robert J. Hermann to the President's Foreign Intelligence Advisory Board.

The President announced his intention to nominate Charles H. Twining, currently pending confirmation as Ambassador to Cameroon, to serve concurrently and without additional compensation as Ambassador to Equatorial Guinea.

December 7
In the afternoon, the President attended a Democratic National Committee luncheon at the Hay Adams Hotel.

The President announced his intention to appoint Mack G. Fleming as a member of the World War II Memorial Advisory Board.

December 8
The President announced his intention to appoint Curtis A. Prins to the Board of Trustees of the Christopher Columbus Fellowship Foundation.

The President announced his intention to appoint Andrew A. Rosenberg as a member of the North Atlantic Salmon Conservation Organization.

The President announced his intention to appoint Jim Kelly to the President's Council on Physical Fitness and Sports.

December 9
In the morning, the President traveled to Fayetteville, AR, and in the afternoon, he traveled to Little Rock, AR.

December 10
In the afternoon, the President returned to Washington, DC.

December 11
In the early afternoon, the President had a telephone conversation with President Hafiz al-Asad of Syria.

December 12
In a morning ceremony in the Oval Office, the President received diplomatic credentials from Ambassadors Francois Bujon de l'Estang of France, Cheick Oumar Diarrah of Mali, and Jalbuugiin Choinhor of Mongolia.

In the afternoon, the President had telephone conversations with Senate majority leader Bob Dole and Speaker of the House Newt Gingrich on budget negotiations.

Later, the President met with Democratic and Republican Senators to discuss Bosnia.

The President announced his intention to nominate A.E. Dick Howard to the James Madison Memorial Fellowship Foundation.

The President announced his intention to appoint Thomas L. Baldini as Commissioner of the International Boundary Commission, United States and Canada.

December 13
In the afternoon, the President met with a bipartisan group of Governors to discuss Medicaid.

In the evening, the President traveled to Paris, France.

December 14
In the evening, the President returned to Washington, DC.

The President announced his intention to nominate Princeton Lyman to be Assistant Secretary of State for International Organization Affairs.

The President announced his intention to nominate Patrick Davidson and Townsend D. Wolfe III to the National Council on the Arts.

The President announced his intention to nominate George W. Black, Jr., to be a member of the National Transportation Safety Board.

The President announced his intention to appoint Roslyn A. Mazer to be Chair of the Interagency Security Classification Appeals Panel.

The President announced his intention to appoint Col. Warren L. Freeman to be commanding general of the District of Columbia National Guard.

The President announced his intention to nominate Pascal D. Forgione, Jr., to be Commissioner of the National Center for Education Statistics.

December 15

The President announced that Ugo Fano and Martin Kamen were the recipients of the 1995 Enrico Fermi Award.

The President announced his intention to appoint Thomas J. Scotto and Patrick J. Sullivan, Jr., to the National Commission on Crime Control and Prevention.

The President announced his intention to nominate Speight Jenkins to the National Council on the Arts.

December 18

In the afternoon, the President had telephone conversations with Senate majority leader Bob Dole and Speaker of the House Newt Gingrich on budget negotiations.

The President announced his intention to appoint Robert M. Lyford to the U.S. Military Academy Board of Visitors.

The President announced his intention to nominate Sarah M. Fox to the National Labor Relations Board.

December 19

In the late afternoon, the President had separate meetings with Senate majority leader Bob Dole and Speaker of the House Newt Gingrich and with Senate Democratic leader Thomas A. Daschle and House Democratic leader Richard A. Gephardt to discuss budget negotiations.

In the evening, the President had telephone conversations with Senators Arlen Specter and Christopher J. Dodd on securities legislation.

The President announced his intention to nominate Gaston L. Gianni, Jr., to be Inspector General for the Federal Deposit Insurance Corporation.

December 20

In the afternoon, the President had a telephone conversation with Senate majority leader Bob Dole and Speaker of the House Newt Gingrich on budget negotiations.

The President declared a major disaster in Georgia as a result of severe storms and tornadoes on November 7–8.

December 21

The President announced his intention to appoint Gerard D. DiMarco to the Board of Trustees of the Christopher Columbus Fellowship Foundation.

The President announced his intention to appoint Elmo R. Zumwalt, Jr., and reappoint Ann Caracristi as members, and to reappoint Warren B. Rudman as Vice Chairman and member of the President's Foreign Intelligence Advisory Board.

The President announced his intention to nominate Thomas Paul Grumbly as Under Secretary of the Department of Energy.

The President announced his intention to nominate Rita Derrick Hayes for the rank of Ambassador during her tenure if service as Chief Textile Negotiator.

December 22

In the afternoon, the President hosted a Christmas celebration for children in the East Room.

The White House announced that the President named Victoria L. Radd to be Deputy Assistant to the President and Deputy Director of Communications.

The White House announced that the President named Michael Waldman to be Deputy Assistant to the President and Director of Speechwriting; Carolyn Curiel to be Special Assistant to the President and Senior Presidential Speechwriter; and Terry Edmonds, Jonathan Prince, and David Shipley to be Special Assistants to the President.

The President announced his intention to nominate Peter B. Edelman to be Assistant Secretary for Planning and Evaluation at the Department of Health and Human Services.

December 26

The President had telephone conversations with President Jean-Bertrand Aristide and President-elect Rene Preval of Haiti.

The President also had a telephone conversation with Senate majority leader Bob Dole on the budget negotiations.

The White House announced that the President will pay a state visit to Japan on April 17–18, 1996.

December 27

The President met with Office of Management and Budget Director Alice M. Rivlin to discuss the budget negotiations.

The President announced his intention to nominate Alvin L. Alm as Assistant Secretary of Energy for Environmental Management.

December 31

In the afternoon, the President and Hillary Clinton traveled to Hilton Head, SC, where they attended the 1995 Renaissance Weekend.

Appendix B—Nominations Submitted to the Senate

The following list does not include promotions of members of the Uniformed Services, nominations to the Service Academies, or nominations of Foreign Service officers.

Submitted July 10

Cheryl F. Halpern,
of New Jersey, to be a member of the Broadcasting Board of Governors for a term of one year (new position).

Marc B. Nathanson,
of California, to be a member of the Broadcasting Board of Governors for a term of 3 years (new position).

Stanley A. Riveles,
of Virginia, for the rank of Ambassador during his tenure of service as U.S. Commissioner to the Standing Consultative Commission.

Carl Spielvogel,
of New York, to be a member of the Broadcasting Board of Governors for a term of one year (new position).

John R. Tunheim,
of Minnesota, to be a U.S. District Judge for the District of Minnesota, vice Donald D. Alsop, retired.

Submitted July 12

James Franklin Collins,
of Illinois, a career member of the Senior Foreign Service, class of Minister-Counselor, to be Ambassador at Large and Special Adviser to the Secretary of State on the New Independent States.

Stanley Tuemler Escudero,
of Florida, a career member of the Senior Foreign Service, class of Minister-Counselor, to be Ambassador Extraordinary and Plenipotentiary of the United States of America to the Republic of Uzbekistan.

Joseph A. Presel,
of Rhode Island, a career member of the Senior Foreign Service, class of Minister-Counselor, for the rank of Ambassador during his tenure of service as Special Negotiator for Nagorno-Karabakh.

Stephen D. Potts,
of Maryland, to be Director of the Office of Government Ethics for a term of 5 years (reappointment).

Submitted July 14

Darcy E. Bradbury,
of New York, to be an Assistant Secretary of the Treasury, vice Hollis S. McLoughlin, resigned.

Michael P. Dombeck,
of Wisconsin, to be Director of the Bureau of Land Management, vice Jim Baca.

Jeanne R. Ferst,
of Georgia, to be a member of the National Museum Services Board for a term expiring December 6, 1999, vice Roy L. Shafer, term expired.

Jill L. Long,
of Indiana, to be Under Secretary of Agriculture for Rural Economic and Community Development (new position).

Joseph H. Neely,
of Mississippi, to be a member of the Board of Directors of the Federal Deposit Insurance Corporation for a term of 6 years, vice C.C. Hope, Jr.

Joe Scroggins, Jr.,
of Florida, to be a Federal Maritime Commissioner for the term expiring June 30, 2000 (reappointment).

Charles H. Twining,
of Maryland, a career member of the Senior Foreign Service, class of Minister-Counselor, to be Ambassador Extraordinary and Plenipotentiary of the United States of America to the Republic of Cameroon.

Submitted July 17

Eileen B. Claussen,
of the District of Columbia, to be Assistant Secretary of State for Oceans and International Environmental and Scientific Affairs, vice Elinor G. Constable.

Greta Joy Dicus,
of Arkansas, to be a member of the Nuclear Regulatory Commission for the term of 5 years expiring June 30, 1998, vice James R. Curtiss, term expired.

Lee F. Jackson,
of Massachusetts, to be U.S. Director of the European Bank for Reconstruction and Development, vice James H. Scheuer, resigned.

Eluid Levi Martinez,
of New Mexico, to be Commissioner of Reclamation, vice Daniel P. Beard, resigned.

Ernest J. Moniz,
of Massachusetts, to be an Associate Director of the Office of Science and Technology Policy, vice Mary Rita Cooke Greenwood, resigned.

Donald S. Wasserman,
of the District of Columbia, to be a member of the Federal Labor Relations Authority for a term of 5 years expiring July 1, 2000, vice Pamela Talkin, term expired.

Harris Wofford,
of Pennsylvania, to be Chief Executive Officer of the Corporation for National and Community Service, vice Eli J. Segal.

Withdrawn July 17

Robert M. Sussman,
of the District of Columbia, to be a member of the Nuclear Regulatory Commission for a term of 5 years expiring June 30, 1998, vice James R. Curtiss, term expired, which was sent to the Senate on January 5, 1995.

Submitted July 19

Thomas R. Bloom,
of Virginia, to be Inspector General, Department of Education, vice James Bert Thomas, Jr., resigned.

Jill L. Long,
of Indiana, to be a member of the Board of Directors of the Commodity Credit Corporation, vice Bob J. Nash, resigned.

Sidney R. Thomas,
of Montana, to be U.S. Circuit Judge for the Ninth Circuit, vice Dorothy Wright Nelson, retired.

Submitted July 20

James A. Joseph,
of Virginia, to be Ambassador Extraordinary and Plenipotentiary of the United States of America to the Republic of South Africa.

Submitted July 21

John H. Bingler, Jr.,
of Pennsylvania, to be U.S. District Judge for the Western District of Pennsylvania, vice Maurice B. Cohill, Jr., retired.

Submitted July 25

Paul M. Homan,
of the District of Columbia, to be Special Trustee, Office of Special Trustee for American Indians, Department of the Interior (new position).

Michael R. Murphy,
of Utah, to be U.S. Circuit Judge for the Tenth Circuit, vice Monroe G. McKay, retired.

Submitted August 8

Isaac C. Hunt, Jr.,
of Ohio, to be a member of the Securities and Exchange Commission for the term expiring June 5, 2000, vice Richard Y. Roberts, resigned.

Norman S. Johnson,
of Utah, to be a member of the Securities and Exchange Commission for the term expiring June 5, 1999, vice Mary L. Schapiro.

Ned R. McWherter,
of Tennessee, to be a Governor of the U.S. Postal Service for the term expiring December 8, 2002, vice Robert Setrakian, term expired.

Phillip A. Singerman,
of Pennsylvania, to be an Assistant Secretary of Commerce, vice William W. Ginsberg, resigned.

Submitted August 10

Joseph Francis Baca,
of New Mexico, to be a member of the Board of Directors of the State Justice Institute for a term expiring September 17, 1998 (reappointment).

Bruce D. Black,
of New Mexico, to be U.S. District Judge for the District of New Mexico, vice Juan Guerrero Burciaga, retired.

D.W. Bransom, Jr.,
of Texas, to be U.S. Marshal for the Northern District of Texas for the term of 4 years, vice W. Bruce Beaty.

David Allen Brock,
of New Hampshire, to be a member of the Board of Directors of the State Justice Institute for a term expiring September 17, 1997 (reappointment).

Chester A. Crocker,
of the District of Columbia, to be a member of the Board of Directors of the U.S. Institute of Peace for a term expiring January 19, 1999 (reappointment).

Hal C. DeCell III,
of Mississippi, to be an Assistant Secretary of Housing and Urban Development, vice William J. Gilmartin.

Susan J. Dlott,
of Ohio, to be U.S. District Judge for the Southern District of Ohio, vice S. Arthur Spiegel, retired.

Theodore M. Hesburgh,
of Indiana, to be a member of the Board of Directors of the U.S. Institute of Peace for a term expiring January 19, 1999 (reappointment).

Elizabeth K. Julian,
of Texas, to be an Assistant Secretary of Housing and Urban Development, vice Roberta Achtenberg, resigned.

Max M. Kampelman,
of the District of Columbia, to be a member of the Board of Directors of the U.S. Institute of Peace for a term expiring January 19, 1999 (reappointment).

Hugh Lawson,
of Georgia, to be U.S. District Judge for the Middle District of Georgia, vice Wilbur D. Owens, Jr., retired.

Zell Miller,
of Georgia, to be a member of the Board of Trustees of the James Madison Memorial Fellowship Foundation for a term expiring November 6, 1995, vice Carroll A. Campbell, Jr., term expired.

Zell Miller,
of Georgia, to be a member of the Board of Trustees of the James Madison Memorial Fellowship Foundation for a term expiring November 6, 2001 (reappointment).

Frank Policaro, Jr.,
of Pennsylvania, to be U.S. Marshal for the Western District of Pennsylvania for the term of 4 years, vice Eugene V. Marzullo.

Eli J. Segal,
of Massachusetts, to be a member of the Board of Directors of the Corporation for National and Community Service for the remainder of the term expiring February 8, 1999, vice James A. Joseph.

Hilda G. Tagle,
of Texas, to be U.S. District Judge for the Southern District of Texas (new position).

Kim McLane Wardlaw,
of California, to be U.S. District Judge for the Central District of California, vice David V. Kenyon, retired.

E. Richard Webber,
of Missouri, to be U.S. District Judge for the Eastern District of Missouri, vice Edward L. Filippine, retired.

Submitted September 5

Patricia J. Beneke,
of Iowa, to be an Assistant Secretary of the Interior, vice Elizabeth Ann Rieke.

Merrick B. Garland,
of Maryland, to be U.S. Circuit Judge for the District of Columbia Circuit, vice Abner J. Mikva, retired.

Gail Clements McDonald,
of Maryland, to be Administrator of the Saint Lawrence Seaway Development Corporation for the re-

mainder of the term expiring March 20, 1998, vice Stanford E. Parris, resigned.

Withdrawn September 5

Leland M. Shurin,
of Missouri, to be U.S. District Judge for the Western District of Missouri, vice Scott O. Wright, retired, which was sent to the Senate on April 4, 1995.

John D. Snodgrass,
of Alabama, to be U.S. District Judge for the Northern District of Alabama, vice E.B. Haltom, Jr., retired, which was sent to the Senate on January 11, 1995.

Submitted September 8

Robert Nelson Baldwin,
of Virginia, to be a member of the Board of Directors of the State Justice Institute for a term expiring September 17, 1998 (reappointment).

Jeffrey R. Shafer,
of New Jersey, to be an Under Secretary of the Treasury, vice Lawrence H. Summers.

Melissa T. Skolfield,
of Louisiana, to be an Assistant Secretary of Health and Human Services, vice Avis LaVelle.

Submitted September 11

David A. Lipton,
of Massachusetts, to be a Deputy Under Secretary of the Treasury, vice Jeffrey Richard Shafer.

Florence K. Murray,
of Rhode Island, to be a member of the Board of Directors of the State Justice Institute for a term expiring September 17, 1998 (reappointment).

Submitted September 18

Jane Bobbitt,
of West Virginia, to be an Assistant Secretary of Commerce, vice Loretta L. Dunn, resigned.

Donna Dearman Smith,
of Alabama, to be a member of the Board of Trustees of the Barry Goldwater Scholarship and Excellence in Education Foundation for a term expiring March 3, 1998, vice Howard W. Cannon, term expired.

Hazel Rollins O'Leary,
of Minnesota, to be Representative of the United States of America to the 39th Session of the General Conference of the International Atomic Energy Agency.

Shirley Ann Jackson,
of New Jersey, to be an Alternate Representative of the United States of America to the 39th Session

of the General Conference of the International Atomic Energy Agency.

Nelson F. Sievering, Jr.,
of Maryland, to be an Alternate Representative of the United States of America to the 39th Session of the General Conference of the International Atomic Energy Agency.

John B. Ritch III,
of the District of Columbia, to be an Alternate Representative of the United States of America to the 39th Session of the General Conference of the International Atomic Energy Agency.

Withdrawn September 18

Howard W. Cannon,
of Nevada, to be a member of the Board of Trustees of the Barry Goldwater Scholarship and Excellence in Education Foundation for a term expiring March 3, 1998 (reappointment), which was sent to the Senate on January 5, 1995.

Submitted September 20

James William Blagg,
of Texas, to be U.S. Attorney for the Western District of Texas for the term of 4 years, vice Ronald F. Ederer, resigned.

Susan Robinson King,
of the District of Columbia, to be an Assistant Secretary of Labor, vice Doug Ross, resigned.

Submitted September 22

Eric James Boswell,
of California, a career member of the Senior Foreign Service, class of Minister-Counselor, to be an Assistant Secretary of State, vice Anthony Cecil Eden Quainton.

Anthony Cecil Eden Quainton,
of the District of Columbia, a career member of the Senior Foreign Service, class of Career Minister, to be Director General of the Foreign Service, vice Genta Hawkins Holmes.

Submitted September 27

Michael V. Dunn,
of Iowa, to be an Assistant Secretary of Agriculture, vice Eugene Branstool, resigned.

Michael V. Dunn,
of Iowa, to be a member of the Board of Directors of the Commodity Credit Corporation, vice Eugene Branstool, resigned.

Submitted September 29

Patricia A. Gaughan,
of Ohio, to be U.S. District Judge for the Northern District of Ohio, vice Ann Aldrich, retired.

Joan A. Lenard,
of Florida, to be U.S. District Judge for the Southern District of Florida, vice James Lawrence King, retired.

Clarence J. Sundram,
of New York, to be U.S. District Judge for the Northern District of New York (new position).

Submitted October 10

C.E. Abramson,
of Montana, to be a member of the National Commission on Libraries and Information Science for a term expiring July 19, 2000, vice Barbara J.H. Taylor, term expired.

Walter Anderson,
of New York, to be a member of the National Commission on Libraries and Information Science for a term expiring July 19, 2000, vice Norman Kelinson, term expired.

LaVeeda Morgan Battle,
of Alabama, to be a member of the Board of Directors of the Legal Services Corporation for a term expiring July 13, 1998 (reappointment).

John N. Erlenborn,
of Illinois, to be a member of the Board of Directors of the Legal Services Corporation for a term expiring July 13, 1998, vice John G. Brooks, term expired.

David Finn,
of New York, to be a member of the National Council on the Humanities for a term expiring January 26, 2000, vice Billie Davis Gaines, term expired.

Joseph H. Gale,
of Virginia, to be a Judge of the U.S. Tax Court for a term expiring 15 years after he takes office, vice Edna Gaynell Parker, resigned.

Ernest G. Green,
of the District of Columbia, to be a member of the Board of Directors of the African Development Foundation for a term expiring September 22, 2001 (reappointment).

Submitted October 11

P. Michael Duffy,
of South Carolina, to be U.S. District Judge for the District of South Carolina, vice Matthew J. Perry, Jr., retired.

Sue E. Myerscough,
of Illinois, to be U.S. District Judge for the Central District of Illinois, vice Harold A. Baker, retired.

Jed S. Rakoff,
of New York, to be U.S. District Judge for the Southern District of New York, vice David N. Edelstein, retired.

William P. Foster,
of Florida, to be a member of the National Council on the Arts for a term expiring September 3, 2000, vice Roy M. Goodman, term expired.

Lowell Lee Junkins,
of Iowa, to be a member of the Board of Directors of the Federal Agricultural Mortgage Corporation, vice Edward Charles Williamson.

Submitted October 13

David P. Rawson,
of Michigan, a career member of the Senior Foreign Service, class of Counselor, to be Ambassador Extraordinary and Plenipotentiary of the United States of America to the Republic of Mali.

Gerald Wesley Scott,
of Oklahoma, a career member of the Senior Foreign Service, class of Counselor, to be Ambassador Extraordinary and Plenipotentiary of the United States of America to the Republic of The Gambia.

Robert E. Gribbin III,
of Alabama, a career member of the Senior Foreign Service, class of Counselor, to be Ambassador Extraordinary and Plenipotentiary of the United States of America to the Republic of Rwanda.

Ralph R. Johnson,
of Virginia, a career member of the Senior Foreign Service, class of Minister-Counselor, to be Ambassador Extraordinary and Plenipotentiary of the United States of America to the Slovak Republic.

Submitted October 18

Nina Gershon,
of New York, to be U.S. District Judge for the Eastern District of New York, vice Leonard D. Wexler, retired.

Barbara S. Jones,
of New York, to be U.S. District Judge for the Southern District of New York, vice Kenneth Conboy, resigned.

John Thomas Marten,
of Kansas, to be U.S. District Judge for the District of Kansas, vice Patrick F. Kelly, retired.

Submitted October 19

Arthur L. Money,
of California, to be an Assistant Secretary of the Air Force, vice Clark G. Fiester.

Submitted October 20

Nanette K. Laughrey,
of Missouri, to be U.S. District Judge for the Eastern and Western Districts of Missouri, vice Joseph E. Stevens, Jr., retired.

Lottie Lee Shackelford,
of Arkansas, to be a member of the Board of Directors of the Overseas Private Investment Corporation for a term expiring December 17, 1998 (reappointment).

Submitted October 27

Charles R. Stack,
of Florida, to be U.S. Circuit Judge for the Eleventh Circuit, vice Peter T. Fay, resigned.

Submitted October 31

Patricia Wentworth McNeil,
of Massachusetts, to be Assistant Secretary for Vocational and Adult Education, Department of Education, vice Augusta Souza Kappner, resigned.

Submitted November 3

Joshua Gotbaum,
of New York, to be an Assistant Secretary of the Treasury, vice Alicia Haydock Munnell, resigned.

Anne H. Lewis,
of Maryland, to be an Assistant Secretary of Labor (reappointment).

Submitted November 7

Markos K. Marinakis,
of New York, to be a member of the Board of the Panama Canal Commission, vice John J. Danilovich.

Submitted November 8

Norman I. Maldonado,
of Puerto Rico, to be a member of the Board of Trustees of the Harry S Truman Scholarship Foundation for a term expiring December 10, 1999, vice Margaret Truman Daniel, term expired.

Wallace D. McRae,
of Montana, to be a member of the National Council on the Arts for a term expiring September 3, 1998, vice Robert Garfias, term expired.

Submitted November 9

Robert S. Litt,
of Maryland, to be an Assistant Attorney General,
vice Jo Ann Harris.

Yolanda Townsend Wheat,
of Puerto Rico, to be a member of the National Credit
Union Administration Board for the term of 6 years
expiring August 2, 2001, vice Robert H. Swan, term
expired.

Withdrawn November 9

Dan M. Berkovitz,
of the District of Columbia, to be a member of the
Nuclear Regulatory Commission for the term expiring
June 30, 2000, vice E. Gail de Planque, term expiring,
which was sent to the Senate on January 5, 1995.

Submitted November 27

Ann L. Aiken,
of Oregon, to be U.S. District Judge for the District
of Oregon, vice James H. Redden, retired.

Joseph A. Greenaway,
of New Jersey, to be U.S. District Judge for the District of New Jersey, vice John F. Gerry, retired.

Faith S. Hochberg,
of New Jersey, to be U.S. District Judge for the District of New Jersey, vice H. Lee Sarokin, elevated.

Ann D. Montgomery,
of Minnesota, to be U.S. District Judge for the District
of Minnesota, vice Diana E. Murphy, elevated.

Submitted November 28

LeVar Burton,
of California, to be a member of the National Commission on Libraries and Information Science for a
term expiring July 19, 2000, vice Kay W. Riddle, term
expired.

James E. Johnson,
of New Jersey, to be an Assistant Secretary of the
Treasury, vice Ronald K. Noble.

H. Martin Lancaster,
of North Carolina, to be an Assistant Secretary of
the Army, vice Nancy Patricia Dorn, resigned.

Submitted November 30

John R. Lacey,
of Connecticut, to be a member of the Foreign Claims
Settlement Commission of the United States for a
term expiring September 30, 1998 (reappointment).

Luis D. Rovira,
of Colorado, to be a member of the Board of Trustees
of the Harry S Truman Scholarship Foundation for

a term expiring December 10, 2001, vice Lorraine
Mindy Meiklejohn, term expiring.

Submitted December 4

Susan R. Baron,
of Maryland, to be a member of the National Corporation for Housing Partnerships for the term expiring
October 27, 1997 (reappointment).

Barry M. Goldwater, Sr.,
of Arizona, to be a member of the Board of Directors
of the Communications Satellite Corporation until the
date of the annual meeting of the Corporation in
1998 (reappointment).

Peter S. Knight,
of the District of Columbia, to be a member of the
Board of Directors of the Communications Satellite
Corporation until the date of the annual meeting of
the Corporation in 1999 (reappointment).

Submitted December 7

Charles N. Clevert, Jr.,
of Wisconsin, to be a U.S. District Judge for the
Eastern District of Wisconsin, vice Terence T. Evans,
elevated.

Bernice B. Donald,
of Tennessee, to be U.S. District Judge for the Western District of Tennessee, vice Odell Horton, resigned.

Charles H. Twining,
of Maryland, a career member of the Senior Foreign
Service, class of Minister-Counselor, to be Ambassador
Extraordinary and Plenipotentiary of the United States
of America to the Republic of Equatorial Guinea.

Submitted December 8

C. Lynwood Smith,
of Alabama, to be U.S. District Judge for the Northern
District of Alabama, vice E.B. Haltom, Jr., retired.

Withdrawn December 8

C. Richard Allen,
of Maryland, to be a Managing Director of the Corporation for National and Community Service (new
position), which was sent to the Senate on June 6,
1995.

Submitted December 11

Princeton Nathan Lyman,
of Maryland, a career member of the Senior Foreign
Service, class of Career Minister, to be an Assistant
Secretary of State, vice Douglas Joseph Bennet, Jr.,
resigned.

Alfred C. DeCotiis,
of New Jersey, to be a Representative of the United States of America to the 50th Session of the General Assembly of the United Nations.

Joseph Lane Kirkland,
of the District of Columbia, to be an Alternate Representative of the United States of America to the 50th Session of the General Assembly of the United Nations.

Tom Lantos,
of California, to be an Alternate Representative of the United States of America to the 50th Session of the General Assembly of the United Nations.

Jeanne Moutoussamy-Ashe,
of New York, to be an Alternate Representative of the United States of America to the 50th Session of the General Assembly of the United Nations.

Toby Roth,
of Wisconsin, to be an Alternate Representative of the United States of America to the 50th Session of the General Assembly of the United Nations.

Submitted December 12

A.E. Dick Howard,
of Virginia, to be a member of the Board of Trustees of the James Madison Memorial Fellowship Foundation for a term of 6 years, vice Lance Banning.

James P. Jones,
of Virginia, to be U.S. District Judge for the Western District of Virginia, vice James H. Michael, Jr., retired.

Cheryl B. Wattley,
of Texas, to be U.S. District Judge for the Northern District of Texas (new position).

Submitted December 13

Tom Lantos,
of California, to be a Representative of the United States of America to the 50th Session of the General Assembly of the United Nations.

Toby Roth,
of Wisconsin, to be a Representative of the United States of America to the 50th Session of the General Assembly of the United Nations.

Withdrawn December 13

Tom Lantos,
of California, to be an Alternate Representative of the United States of America to the 50th Session of the General Assembly of the United Nations, which was sent to the Senate on December 11, 1995.

Toby Roth,
of Wisconsin, to be an Alternate Representative of the United States of America to the 50th Session of the General Assembly of the United Nations, which was sent to the Senate on December 11, 1995.

Submitted December 18

George W. Black, Jr.,
of Georgia, to be a member of the National Transportation Safety Board for the remainder of the term expiring December 31, 1996, vice Carl W. Vogt, resigned.

Patrick Davidson,
of California, to be a member of the National Council on the Arts for a term expiring September 3, 2000, vice Mel Harris, term expired.

Pascal D. Forgione, Jr.,
of Delaware, to be Commissioner of Education Statistics for a term expiring June 21, 1999, vice Emerson J. Elliott.

Townsend D. Wolfe III,
of Arkansas, to be a member of the National Council on the Arts for a term expiring September 3, 2000, vice Earl Roger Middle, term expired.

Sarah McCracken Fox,
of New York, to be a member of the National Labor Relations Board for the term of 5 years expiring August 27, 2000, vice James M. Stephens, term expired.

Robert E. Morin,
of the District of Columbia, to be an Associate Judge of the Superior Court of the District of Columbia for the term of 15 years, vice Curtis E. von Kann, retired.

Submitted December 19

Speight Jenkins,
of Washington, to be a member of the National Council on the Arts for a term expiring September 3, 2000, vice Philip Brunelle, term expired.

Mary Ann Vial Lemmon,
of Louisiana, to be U.S. District Judge for the Eastern District of Louisiana, vice Peter Hill Beer, retired.

Michael D. Schattman,
of Texas, to be U.S. District Judge for the Northern District of Texas, vice Harold Barefoot Sanders, Jr., retired.

Submitted December 20

Gaston L. Gianni, Jr.,
of Virginia, to be Inspector General, Federal Deposit Insurance Corporation (new position).

Rita Derrick Hayes,
of Maryland, for the rank of Ambassador during her tenure of service as Chief Textile Negotiator.

Withdrawn December 20

Norwood J. Jackson, Jr.,
of Virginia, to be Inspector General, Federal Deposit Insurance Corporation (new position), which was sent to the Senate on January 5, 1995.

Submitted December 21

Thomas Paul Grumbly,
of Virginia, to be Under Secretary of Energy, vice Charles B. Curtis.

Martin A. Kamarck,
of Massachusetts, to be President of the Export-Import Bank of the U.S. for the remainder of the term expiring January 20, 1997, vice Kenneth D. Brody, resigned.

Donald W. Molloy,
of Montana, to be U.S. District Judge for the District of Montana, vice Paul G. Hatfield, retired.

Susan Oki Mollway,
of Hawaii, to be U.S. District Judge for the District of Hawaii, vice Harold M. Fong, deceased.

Submitted December 22

Alvin L. Alm,
of Virginia, to be an Assistant Secretary of Energy, Environmental Management, vice Thomas P. Grumbly.

Submitted December 29

Charles William Burton,
of Texas, to be a member of the Board of Directors of the U.S. Enrichment Corporation for a term expiring February 24, 2001 (reappointment).

Gerald N. Tirozzi,
of Connecticut, to be Assistant Secretary for Elementary and Secondary Education, Department of Education, vice Thomas W. Payzant, resigned.

Appendix C—Checklist of White House Press Releases

The following list contains releases of the Office of the Press Secretary which are not included in this book.

Released July 5

Statement by Press Secretary Mike McCurry on the upcoming visit of President Ernesto Perez Balladares of Panama on September 7

Statement by Press Secretary Mike McCurry on the President's letter to congressional leaders on AIDS legislation

Released July 6

Statement by Press Secretary Mike McCurry on the President's upcoming visit to the United Kingdom and Ireland

Statement by Press Secretary Mike McCurry on the upcoming visit of President Nicephore Soglo of Benin on July 13

Released July 10

Statement by Press Secretary Mike McCurry on the announcement by Burmese authorities of the release of Aung San Suu Kyi

Statement by Press Secretary Mike McCurry on the upcoming visit of Prime Minister P.J. Patterson of Jamaica

Statement by Press Secretary Mike McCurry on Radio Free Europe/Radio Liberty headquarters in Prague, Czech Republic

Announcement of nomination for U.S. District Judge for the District of Minnesota

Released July 11

Transcript of a press briefing by Press Secretary Mike McCurry

Transcript of a press briefing on the President's decision to normalize diplomatic relations with Vietnam by National Security Adviser Anthony Lake, Deputy Secretary of Veterans Affairs Hershel Gober, and Assistant Secretary of State for East Asian and Pacific Affairs Winston Lord

Transcript of a press briefing on proposed budget legislation by Chief of Staff Leon Panetta, Secretary of Education Richard Riley, Office of Management and Budget Director Alice Rivlin, and Deputy Secretary of Labor Thomas P. Glynn

Press package on the President's announcement on Vietnam, which included:

Fact sheet on progress
Fact sheet on background on POW/MIA accounting
Fact sheet on background on economic relationships
Fact sheet on background on diplomatic relationships

Released July 12

Transcript of a press briefing by Press Secretary Mike McCurry

Transcript of a press briefing by Secretary of Education Richard Riley and Walter Dellinger, Assistant Attorney General, Office of Legal Counsel, on religious expression in public schools

Statement by Press Secretary Mike McCurry on National Security Adviser Anthony Lake's meeting with Ching-lee Chen, wife of human rights activist Harry Wu

Released July 13

Transcript of a press briefing by Press Secretary Mike McCurry

Statement by Press Secretary Mike McCurry on the President's meeting with President Nicephore Soglo of Benin

Statement by Press Secretary Mike McCurry on the President's approval of the Defense Base Closure and Realignment Commission recommendations

Statement by Press Secretary Mike McCurry on the President's telephone conversations with President Jacques Chirac of France and Chancellor Helmut Kohl of Germany on Bosnia

Released July 14

Transcripts of press briefings by Press Secretary Mike McCurry

Released July 17

Transcript of a press briefing by Press Secretary Mike McCurry

Announcement of the President's request for additional funds for antiterrorism initiatives

Announcement of the President's transmittal to the Congress of 1996 budget amendments for the Departments of Defense and Health and Human Services and the Social Security Administration

1961

Released July 18

Transcript of a press briefing by Press Secretary Mike McCurry

Statement by Special Associate Counsel to the President Mark D. Fabiani on the Senate Whitewater hearings

Announcement of nominations for Chief Executive Officer and a member of the Board of Directors of the Corporation for National and Community Service

Announcement of nomination for U.S. Director of the European Bank for Reconstruction and Development

Announcement of nomination for Inspector General of the Department of Education

Released July 19

Transcript of a press briefing by Press Secretary Mike McCurry

Transcript of a press briefing by Senior Adviser for Policy and Strategy George Stephanopoulos and Special Counsel to the President Chris Edley on affirmative action

Announcement of nomination for U.S. Circuit Judge for the Ninth Circuit

Released July 20

Transcript of a press briefing by Press Secretary Mike McCurry

Statement by Press Secretary Mike McCurry on the President's plans to attend World War II 50th anniversary commemorations in Honolulu, HI

Transcript of remarks by National Security Adviser Anthony Lake to the National League of POW/MIA Families

Announcement of nomination for Assistant Secretary of State for Oceans and International Environmental and Scientific Affairs

Released July 21

Transcript of a press briefing by Press Secretary Mike McCurry

Announcement of White House tours for Korean war veterans and their families

Announcement of nomination for U.S. District Judge for the Western District of Pennsylvania

Released July 22

Statement by Counsel to the President Abner Mikva on Independent Counsel interviews with the President and Hillary Clinton

Released July 23

Statement by Press Secretary Mike McCurry on the joint United Kingdom-France-United States message to the Bosnian Serb leadership

Released July 24

Statement by Press Secretary Mike McCurry on the Korean War Veterans Memorial dedication ceremony

Transcript of a press briefing by Press Secretary Mike McCurry

Released July 25

Transcript of a press briefing by Press Secretary Mike McCurry

Statement by Press Secretary Mike McCurry on the Supreme Court decision upholding Megan's Law

Announcement of nomination for U.S. Court of Appeals Judge for the Tenth Circuit

Released July 26

Transcript of a press briefing by Press Secretary Mike McCurry

Transcript of a press briefing by Secretary of Housing and Urban Development Henry Cisneros on empowerment zones

Transcript of a press briefing by National Security Council Senior Director for Asian Affairs Stanley Owen Roth on the visit of President Kim Yong-sam of South Korea

Statement by Press Secretary Mike McCurry on the inquiry into the death of Michael Devine and the disappearance of Efrain Bamaca Velasquez

Fact sheet on proposed foreign relations legislation

Announcement of nomination for U.S. Attorney for the District of the Virgin Islands

Released July 27

Statement by Press Secretary Mike McCurry on the meeting between administration officials and nongovernmental organizations involved in Burundi

Transcript of a press briefing on the nuclear framework with North Korea by Assistant Secretary of State for East Asian and Pacific Affairs Winston Lord, National Security Council Senior Director for Asian Affairs Stanley Owen Roth, and National Security Council Senior Director for Nonproliferation and Export Controls Daniel B. Poneman

Released July 28

Transcript of a press briefing by Press Secretary Mike McCurry

Statement by Press Secretary Mike McCurry on the President's telephone conversation with President Boris Yeltsin of Russia

Statement by Press Secretary Mike McCurry on the award of the Presidential Citizens Medal to Maj. Richard J. Meadows, USA (Ret.)

Statement by Press Secretary Mike McCurry on the participation of former President Gerald Ford and Deputy Secretary of State Strobe Talbott in the upcoming CSCE Helsinki Final Act 20th Anniversary Symposium in Helsinki on August 1

Transcript of a press briefing by Vice President Albert Gore, Jr., and Environmental Protection Agency Administrator Carol Browner on appropriations legislation

Released July 31

Transcript of a press briefing by Office of Management and Budget Director Alice Rivlin and Council of Economic Advisers member Martin Bailey on the midsession review of the Federal budget

Transcript of a press briefing by Deputy Assistant to the President for Domestic Policy Bruce Reed in Burlington, VT, on welfare reform

Statement by Press Secretary Mike McCurry on the President's establishment of Presidential Emergency Board No. 227

Released August 1

Statement by Press Secretary Mike McCurry on House action to lift the arms embargo against Bosnia and Herzegovina

Announcement of nomination for U.S. District Court Judge for the Southern District of Florida

Released August 2

Transcript of a press briefing by Press Secretary Mike McCurry

Statement by Press Secretary Mike McCurry on the upcoming working visit of Prime Minister Jean-Claude Juncker of Luxembourg on August 7

Released August 3

Transcript of a press briefing by Press Secretary Mike McCurry

Statement by Press Secretary Mike McCurry on the upcoming working visit of President Sali Berisha of Albania on September 11

Statement by Press Secretary Mike McCurry on U.S. counterterrorism policy

Fact sheet listing administration accomplishments on terrorism

Announcement of emergency funds for fishermen in the Northwest, Northeast, and the Gulf of Mexico and for Oklahoma

Released August 4

Statement by Press Secretary Mike McCurry on the Executive order on access to classified information

Released August 5

Announcement of amendments to FY 1996 appropriations requests for the Department of Energy

Released August 7

Transcript of a press briefing by Press Secretary Mike McCurry

Statement by Press Secretary Mike McCurry on the President's telephone conversations with Prime Minister John Major of the United Kingdom, President Jacques Chirac of France, and Chancellor Helmut Kohl of Germany

Released August 8

Transcript of a press briefing by Press Secretary Mike McCurry

Transcript of a press briefing by Environmental Protection Agency Administrator Carol Browner on environmental protection

Statement by Press Secretary Mike McCurry on the annual report to Congress on Foreign Economic Collection and Industrial Espionage

Statement by Press Secretary Mike McCurry on the upcoming working visit of President Ion Iliescu of Romania on September 26

Released August 9

Transcript of a press briefing by Press Secretary Mike McCurry

Statement by Press Secretary Mike McCurry on human rights violations committed by Bosnian-Serb forces

Announcement of nomination for U.S. Marshal for the Northern District of Texas

Announcement of nomination for U.S. Marshal for the Western District of Pennsylvania

Released August 10

Statement by Press Secretary Mike McCurry on the President's upcoming visit to Asia on November 16–21 to participate in the APEC leaders meeting

Transcript of a press briefing by Secretary of Health and Human Services Donna Shalala and Commissioner of Food and Drugs David Kessler on proposed regulations on teenage smoking

Released August 11

Transcript of a press briefing by Press Secretary Mike McCurry

Transcript of a press briefing by National Security Council Senior Director for Defense Policy and Arms Control Robert Bell on the comprehensive test ban treaty

Transcript of a press briefing by C.M. (Mick) Kicklighter, Executive Director of the 50th Anniversary of World War II Commemoration Committee, and World War II veterans on ceremonies commemorating V–J Day

Announcement of nomination for six U.S. District Court Judges

Fact sheet on comprehensive test ban treaty safeguards

Fact sheet on arms control and nonproliferation

Released August 14

Transcript of a press briefing by Press Secretary Mike McCurry

Statement by Press Secretary Mike McCurry announcing the appointment of Donald A. Baer as Assistant to the President and Director of Communications

Statement by Press Secretary Mike McCurry on the upcoming meeting of Angolan leaders in Franceville, Gabon, on August 10

Released August 16

Transcript of a press briefing by Deputy Press Secretary Ginny Terzano

Released August 17

Transcript of a press briefing by Deputy Press Secretary Ginny Terzano

Statement by Press Secretary Mike McCurry on the nuclear test by China at the Lop Nur test site

Statement by Special Associate Counsel to the President Mark Fabiani on the Independent Counsel's indictments

Released August 18

Transcript of a press briefing by Deputy Press Secretary Ginny Terzano

Announcement of Secretary of the Interior Bruce Babbitt's appointment of a Special Representative for the Guam commonwealth negotiations

Released August 19

Statement by National Security Adviser Anthony Lake on the death of the American diplomats in Bosnia-Herzegovina

Released August 21

Statement by Press Secretary Mike McCurry on the terrorist attack in Jerusalem

Released August 22

Transcript of a press briefing by Deputy Press Secretary Ginny Terzano

Released August 23

Transcript of a press briefing by Press Secretary Mike McCurry

Statement by Press Secretary Mike McCurry on the decision to award posthumously the Presidential Citizens Medal to Ambassador Robert C. Frasure, Dr. Joseph J. Kruzel, and Col. S. Nelson Drew, USAF

Statement by Press Secretary Mike McCurry on the President's meeting with Assistant Secretary of State for European and Canadian Affairs Richard Holbrooke and the new members of the team which will continue diplomatic efforts in Bosnia-Herzegovina

Released August 24

Statement by Press Secretary Mike McCurry on the expulsion of Harry Wu from China

Released August 25

Statement by Press Secretary Mike McCurry announcing that the First Lady will attend the United Nations World Conference on Women in Beijing, China, September 5–6

Released September 1

Statement by Press Secretary Mike McCurry on the alternative plan for Federal pay adjustment

Released September 3

Transcript of a press briefing by Press Secretary Mike McCurry

Released September 5

Statement by Press Secretary Mike McCurry on the amendment adopted by the Senate in favor of prompt ratification of the START II treaty and the Chemical Weapons Convention

Statement by Press Secretary Mike McCurry on the underground nuclear test by France at the Mururoa test site

Statement by Press Secretary Mike McCurry on the appointment of David T. Johnson as Special Assistant to the President, Deputy White House Press Secretary for Foreign Affairs, and National Security Council Senior Director of Public Affairs

Released September 6

Transcript of a press briefing by Press Secretary Mike McCurry

Statement by Press Secretary Mike McCurry on the appointment of Jill A. Schuker as Special Assistant to the President and Deputy Director for National Security Policy

Announcement of the President's letter to congressional leaders on welfare reform

Announcement of nomination for U.S. Court of Appeals Judge for the District of Columbia Circuit

Released September 7

Transcript of a press briefing by Press Secretary Mike McCurry

Transcript of a press briefing by Senior Policy Adviser to the Vice President Elaine Kamarck and Office of Management and Budget Deputy Director for Management John Koskinen on the National Performance Review

Statement by Press Secretary Mike McCurry on the appointment of Antony J. Blinkin as Special Assistant to the President for National Security Affairs and Senior Director for Speech Writing, National Security Council

Released September 8

Transcript of a press briefing by Press Secretary Mike McCurry

Released September 11

Statement by Press Secretary Mike McCurry announcing the Presidential Medal of Freedom recipients

Statement by Press Secretary Mike McCurry on the President's meeting with Principals Committee members and Assistant Secretary of State Richard Holbrooke on Bosnia-Herzegovina

Statement by Press Secretary Mike McCurry on the upcoming visit of President Thomas Klestil of Austria

Released September 12

Transcript of a press briefing by Press Secretary Mike McCurry

Statement by Press Secretary Mike McCurry on the President's meeting with President Sali Berisha of Albania

White House statement on career transition assistance for Federal employees

Statement by National Economic Adviser Laura D'Andrea Tyson on Republican proposals for medical savings accounts

Transcript of remarks by Secretary of State Warren Christopher and Deputy Prime Minister and Minister of Foreign Affairs Mate Granic of Croatia on the negotiations for peace in Bosnia and Croatia

Released September 13

Transcript of a press briefing by Press Secretary Mike McCurry

Statement by Press Secretary Mike McCurry on the President's meeting with Prime Minister P.J. Patterson of Jamaica

Statement by Press Secretary Mike McCurry on the upcoming visit of President Jacques Chirac of France

Statement by Press Secretary Mike McCurry on the meeting between Vice President Albert Gore, Jr., and His Holiness the Dalai Lama

Statement by Press Secretary Mike McCurry on National Security Adviser Anthony Lake's meeting with Sinn Fein leader Gerry Adams of Ireland

Released September 14

Transcript of a press briefing by Press Secretary Mike McCurry

Released September 15

Transcript of a press briefing by Deputy Press Secretary Mary Ellen Glynn

Transcript of a press briefing by National Security Council Senior Director for European Affairs Alexander Vershbow on the cease-fire agreement in Bosnia

Released September 18

Transcript of a press briefing by Deputy Chief of Staff Harold Ickes on the President's trip to Pennsylvania, Florida, Colorado, and California

Statement by Chief of Staff Leon Panetta on lobby reform legislation

Announcement of nomination for U.S. Marshal for the District of New Jersey

Released September 19

Statement by Press Secretary Mike McCurry on the President's letter to the Chair of the Federal Communications Commission on the Children's Television Act of 1990

Announcement of nomination for U.S. Attorney for the Western District of Texas

Released September 20

Statement by Press Secretary Mike McCurry on the appointment of Stephanie Streett and Anne L. Walley as Deputy Assistants to the President and Directors of Scheduling

Statement by Press Secretary Mike McCurry on the Westinghouse commitment to increase CBS's educational and informational programs for children

Statement by Press Secretary Mike McCurry announcing the retirement of White House Counsel Abner Mikva and the appointment of Jack Quinn

Released September 21

Transcript of a press briefing by Chief of Staff Leon Panetta on his letter to Speaker of the House of Representatives Newt Gingrich and Senate majority leader Bob Dole on the proposal for a continuing resolution

Transcript of a press briefing by Assistant to the Secretary of Commerce and Office of Policy and Strategic Planning Director Jonathan Sallet on the technological initiative in California schools

Statement by Press Secretary Mike McCurry on Chief of Staff Leon Panetta's letter to Speaker of the House of Representatives Newt Gingrich and Senate majority leader Bob Dole on the proposal for a continuing resolution

Statement by Press Secretary Mike McCurry on the results of the meeting on Bosnia between the Principals Committee and the U.S. negotiating team

Statement by Press Secretary Mike McCurry on Office of Management and Budget Director Alice Rivlin's letter to Senator Frank Murkowski on attempts to open the Arctic National Wildlife Refuge to oil drilling

Released September 22

Transcript of a press briefing by Vice President Albert Gore, Jr., and Secretary of the Interior Bruce Babbitt on the Interior Department appropriations bill

Statement by Vice President Albert Gore, Jr., on the Interior Department appropriations bill

Released September 25

Transcript of a press briefing by Press Secretary Mike McCurry

Released September 26

Transcript of a press briefing by Press Secretary Mike McCurry

Statement by Press Secretary Mike McCurry on the President's meeting with President Ion Iliescu of Romania

Statement by Press Secretary Mike McCurry on the first roundtable conference of donors on Angola

Released September 27

Transcript of a press briefing by Press Secretary Mike McCurry

Transcript of a press briefing by Ambassador Dennis Ross, Special Middle East Coordinator, on the Middle East peace process

Statement by Chief of Staff Leon Panetta on the continuing resolution agreement

Transcript of a press briefing by Office of Management and Budget Director Alice Rivlin on Senate action on the VA/HUD appropriations bill

Released September 28

Joint declaration of the Washington summit

Fact sheet on nuclear materials security in the former Soviet Union

Statement by Press Secretary Mike McCurry on action to reduce the risk of illicit transfer of nuclear weapons

Released September 29

Transcript of a press briefing by Press Secretary Mike McCurry

Statement by Press Secretary Mike McCurry on the President's upcoming visit to Madrid, Spain, for the European Union-U.S. summit

Statement by Press Secretary Mike McCurry on the upcoming visit of President Suleyman Demirel of Turkey

White House statement on the Intelligence Oversight Board review of CIA communications to Congress and the Department of Justice

Statement by Press Secretary Mike McCurry on the establishment of a Presidential Emergency Board to resolve the dispute between the Metro-North Commuter Railroad and its workers

Announcement of nomination for three U.S. District Court Judges

Statement by Press Secretary Mike McCurry on the announcement by Director of Central Intelligence John Deutch of disciplinary decisions regarding CIA operations in Guatemala

Released September 30

Statement by Press Secretary Mike McCurry on the meeting between Vice President Albert Gore, Jr., and Deputy Prime Minister and Foreign Minister Richard Spring of Ireland

Statement by Press Secretary Mike McCurry on the U.S. Court of Appeals decision on religious expression in schools

Released October 1

Statement by Chief of Staff Leon Panetta on the Republican Medicaid proposal and spousal impoverishment

Statement by Press Secretary Mike McCurry on the underground nuclear test by France at the Fangataufa test site in the South Pacific

Released October 2

Transcript of a press briefing by Press Secretary Mike McCurry

Statement by Press Secretary Mike McCurry on the President's upcoming summit with President Jiang Zemin of China

Statement by Press Secretary Mike McCurry on the review of the October 1 statement by General Abacha of Nigeria

Announcement of the 1995 National Medal of the Arts recipients and the 1995 Charles Frankel Prize in the Humanities recipients to be honored on October 5

Announcement of nomination for a U.S. Tax Court Judge

Released October 3

Transcript of a press briefing by Press Secretary Mike McCurry

Released October 5

Transcript of a press briefing by Press Secretary Mike McCurry and Deputy Secretary of the Treasury Lawrence Summers on Mexico's economy

Transcript of a press briefing by National Security Council Senior Director for European Affairs Alexander Vershbow on Bosnia

Statement by Press Secretary Mike McCurry on Executive Order 12976—Compensation Practices of Government Corporations

Released October 6

Transcript of a press briefing by Press Secretary Mike McCurry

Fact sheet on export controls on computers

Released October 7

Transcript of a press briefing by Chief of Staff Leon Panetta on the Republican tax increases on working families

Released October 10

Transcript of a press briefing on the President's meeting with President Ernesto Zedillo of Mexico by U.S. Ambassador to Mexico James Jones, Assistant Secretary of State for Inter-American Affairs Alexander Watson, and National Security Council Senior Director for Inter-American Affairs Richard Feinberg

Released October 11

Transcript of a press briefing by Press Secretary Mike McCurry

Statement by Press Secretary Mike McCurry on the Bosnian cease-fire agreement

Announcement of nomination for three U.S. District Court Judges

Released October 12

Transcript of a press briefing by Press Secretary Mike McCurry

Released October 13

Transcript of a press briefing by Press Secretary Mike McCurry

Statement by Press Secretary Mike McCurry on the President's plans to attend the dedication of the National Czech and Slovak Museum and Library in Cedar Rapids, IA, on October 21

Transcript of a press briefing by Office of Management and Budget Director Alice Rivlin and National Economic Adviser Laura D'Andrea Tyson on Republican budget proposals

Released October 16

Transcript of a press briefing by Press Secretary Mike McCurry

Statement by Press Secretary Mike McCurry on the 1995 Malcolm Baldrige National Quality Awards

Statement by Press Secretary Mike McCurry on the upcoming visit of President Soeharto of Indonesia

Statement by Press Secretary Mike McCurry announcing Turkey's postponement of the visit of President Suleyman Demirel

Released October 18

Transcript of a press briefing by Press Secretary Mike McCurry, Assistant to the President for Science and Technology and Office of Science and Technology Policy Director John H. Gibbons, and National Economic Adviser Laura D'Andrea Tyson on the importance of science and technology to economic growth

Statement by Press Secretary Mike McCurry on treatment of prisoners by the Nigerian military regime

Statement by Press Secretary Mike McCurry on the cloture vote on the Helms/Burton legislation on Cuba

Announcement of nomination for three U.S. District Court Judges

Statement by Press Secretary Mike McCurry on the postponement of the state visit of President Jacques Chirac of France

Released October 19

Transcript of a press briefing by Press Secretary Mike McCurry

Transcript of a press briefing by Deputy National Security Adviser Samuel Berger on the President's visit to New York City

Statement by Press Secretary Mike McCurry announcing the President's intention to veto Medicare legislation

Statement by Press Secretary Mike McCurry on the President's letter to Senator Edward M. Kennedy on proposed employment non-discrimination legislation

Released October 20

Statement by Press Secretary Mike McCurry on the postponement of the Senate Foreign Relations Committee business meeting

Statement by Press Secretary Mike McCurry on the resignation of NATO Secretary General Willy Claes

Announcement of nomination for U.S. District Judge for the Eastern and Western Districts of Missouri

Released October 22

Transcript of a press briefing by Press Secretary Mike McCurry

Transcript of a press briefing by National Security Adviser Anthony Lake on the President's meetings and activities at the 50th anniversary of the United Nations

Transcript of a press briefing on sanctions against Cali cartel drug traffickers by Assistant Secretary of State for International Narcotics and Law Enforcement Matters Robert Gelbard; Department of the Treasury Office of Foreign Assets Control Director R. Richard Newcombe; Acting Assistant Secretary of State for International Organization Affairs George Ward; and National Security Council Senior Director for Global Issues and Multilateral Affairs Richard Clarke

Statement by Press Secretary Mike McCurry announcing that the President signed H.R. 1976, the Agriculture, Rural Development, Food and Drug Administration, and Related Agencies Appropriations Act, 1996

Fact sheets on the President's speech at the United Nations 50th anniversary

Released October 23

Transcripts of press briefings by Press Secretary Mike McCurry

Transcript of a roundtable discussion led by Chief of Staff Leon Panetta on the impact of the Republican budget on children

Statement by Press Secretary Mike McCurry announcing the President's and Hillary Clinton's upcoming visit to Japan

Statement by Press Secretary Mike McCurry announcing the relocation of the President's meeting with President Jiang Zemin of China

Fact sheet on nuclear materials security

Released October 24

Transcript of a press briefing by Press Secretary Mike McCurry

Transcript of a press briefing by Assistant Secretary of State for East Asian and Pacific Affairs Winston Lord and National Security Council Director of Asian Affairs Robert Suettinger on the President's meeting with President Jiang Zemin of China

Transcript of a press briefing by National Security Council Senior Director for Public Affairs David Johnson on the President's meeting with President Heydar Aliyev of Azerbaijan

Statement by Press Secretary Mike McCurry on legislation to require the relocation of the U.S. Embassy in Israel to Jerusalem

Released October 25

Transcript of a press briefing by Press Secretary Mike McCurry

Released October 26

Transcript of a press briefing by Press Secretary Mike McCurry

Statement by Chief of Staff Leon Panetta on the budget vote by the House of Representatives

Statement by Press Secretary Mike McCurry on the signing of Saudi Arabian airlines contracts for aircraft purchases

Fact sheet on the Saudi Arabian airlines contracts for aircraft purchases

Released October 27

Transcript of a press briefing by Press Secretary Mike McCurry

Statement by Press Secretary Mike McCurry on the President's meeting with President Soeharto of Indonesia

Statement by Press Secretary Mike McCurry on the meeting between Vice President Albert Gore, Jr., National Security Adviser Anthony Lake, and Northern Ireland Democratic Unionist Party leader Ian Paisley

Statement by Press Secretary Mike McCurry on the dedication of the memorial cairn to the victims of the terrorist bombing of Pan American Flight 103

Announcement of nomination for U.S. Court of Appeals Judge for the Eleventh Circuit

Released October 30

Transcript of a press briefing by Press Secretary Mike McCurry

Released October 31

Transcript of a press briefing by Press Secretary Mike McCurry

Released November 1

Transcripts of press briefings by Press Secretary Mike McCurry

Statement by Press Secretary Mike McCurry on the meeting between Vice President Albert Gore, Jr., and Northern Ireland Ulster Unionist Party leader David Trimble

Released November 24

Statement by Press Secretary Mike McCurry on the President's upcoming visit to Ramstein, Germany, on December 2

Statement by Press Secretary Mike McCurry on the upcoming official visit by Prime Minister Shimon Peres of Israel on December 11

Released November 27

Transcript of a press briefing by Press Secretary Mike McCurry

Announcement of nomination for four U.S. District Court Judges

Released November 28

Transcript of a press briefing by Press Secretary Mike McCurry

Transcript of a press briefing by George Mitchell, Special Adviser to the President and Secretary of State on Economic Initiatives for Ireland, on arms decommissioning

Statement by Press Secretary Mike McCurry announcing that the President signed S. 395, ending the ban on exporting oil from Alaska's North Slope

Statement by Press Secretary Mike McCurry announcing that the President signed H.R. 440, releasing more than $5 billion for transportation projects

Released November 29

Transcript of a press briefing by Press Secretary Mike McCurry

Transcript of remarks by George Mitchell, Special Adviser to the President and Secretary of State on Economic Initiatives for Ireland

Statement by Press Secretary Mike McCurry on House action on the VA/HUD appropriations bill

Released November 30

Transcript of a press briefing by Press Secretary Mike McCurry

Released December 1

Transcript of a press briefing by Press Secretary Mike McCurry

Statement by Press Secretary Mike McCurry on the situation in Burma

Released December 2

Statement by Press Secretary Mike McCurry announcing that former Governor Ann W. Richards of Texas will head the U.S. delegation to the 26th International Conference of the Red Cross and the Red Crescent on December 3–8 in Geneva, Switzerland

Fact sheet on the President's trip to Madrid, Spain

Fact sheet entitled "The U.S.-EU Economic Relationship: Expanding and Enhancing the Transatlantic Marketplace"

Released December 3

Fact sheet entitled "The U.S.-EU Economic Relationship: The New Transatlantic Marketplace"

Released December 5

Transcript of a press briefing by Press Secretary Mike McCurry

Announcement of the release of the second customer service standards report issued by the National Performance Review

Released December 6

Transcript of a press briefing by Press Secretary Mike McCurry

Released December 7

Transcript of a press briefing by Press Secretary Mike McCurry

Announcement of nomination for U.S. District Court Judges for the Eastern District of Wisconsin and the Western District of Tennessee

Released December 8

Transcript of a press briefing by Press Secretary Mike McCurry

Announcement of nomination for U.S. District Court Judge for the Northern District of Alabama

Released December 11

Statement by Press Secretary Mike McCurry on the President's letter to Senate Democratic leader Thomas Daschle on the plan for implementation of the Balkan peace agreement

Released December 12

Transcript of a press briefing by Press Secretary Mike McCurry

Statement by Press Secretary Mike McCurry on National Security Adviser Anthony Lake's meeting with Wei Shanshan, sister of Chinese democracy activist Wei Jingsheng

Announcement of nomination of U.S. District Judges for the Western District of Virginia and the Northern District of Texas

Released December 13

Transcript of a press briefing by Press Secretary Mike McCurry

Statement by Press Secretary Mike McCurry on China's conviction and imprisonment of democracy activist Wei Jingsheng

Statement by Press Secretary Mike McCurry on the apprehension of suspected terrorist Wali Khan

Announcement of nomination of U.S. District Judge for the Western District of Missouri

Released December 14

Transcript of a press briefing by Press Secretary Mike McCurry

Statement by Press Secretary Mike McCurry on the United Nations vote of condemnation on the execution of Ken Saro-Wiwa and eight others by the Nigerian Government

Statement by Press Secretary Mike McCurry announcing the Presidential delegation to observe the Haitian Presidential elections on December 17

Announcement of economic reconstruction and humanitarian assistance for Bosnia

Released December 15

Transcript of press briefings by Press Secretary Mike McCurry

Transcript of a press briefing by National Security Council Senior Director for Nonproliferation and Export Controls Daniel B. Poneman on the Korean Peninsula Energy Development Organization

Announcement on the presentation of Presidential Citizens Medals to the families of the three U.S. diplomats who died in Bosnia on August 19

Released December 18

Transcript of a press briefing by Press Secretary Mike McCurry

Announcement of nomination for District of Columbia Superior Court Judge

Released December 19

Transcripts of press briefings by Press Secretary Mike McCurry

Transcript of a press briefing by Vice President Albert Gore, Jr., Senator Tom Daschle, and Representative Dick Gephardt on the President's meeting with congressional leaders

Announcement of nominations for U.S. District Judges for the Eastern District of Louisiana and the Northern District of Texas

Released December 20

Transcripts of press briefings by Press Secretary Mike McCurry

Released December 21

Transcript of a press briefing by Press Secretary Mike McCurry

Statement by Press Secretary Mike McCurry on the seventh anniversary of the terrorist attack on Pan American Flight 103

Announcement of nominations for U.S. District Judges for the District of Montana and the District of Hawaii

Statement by Press Secretary Mike McCurry on the resumption of the budget advisers' discussions

Released December 22

Transcript of a press briefing by Press Secretary Mike McCurry and Santa Claus

Statement by Press Secretary Mike McCurry on the congressional veto override of the Private Securities Litigation Reform Act of 1995

Statement by Press Secretary Mike McCurry announcing the appointment of Michael Waldman as Deputy Assistant to the President for Speechwriting

Statement by Press Secretary Mike McCurry announcing the appointment of Victoria L. Radd as Deputy Assistant to the President and Deputy Director of Communications

Statement by Press Secretary Mike McCurry on the ongoing violence in Burundi

Statement by Press Secretary Mike McCurry announcing that the President signed legislation designating the Federal Triangle project currently under construction as the Ronald Reagan Building and International Trade Center

Announcement of nomination for U.S. District Judge for the Southern District of Ohio

Announcement of nominations for U.S. Court of Appeals Judges for the Fourth Circuit

Released December 26

Statement by Press Secretary Mike McCurry on the President's upcoming visit to Japan on April 17–18, 1996

Released December 28

Transcript of a press briefing by Press Secretary Mike McCurry

White House announcement on the President's veto of the National Defense Authorization Act for Fiscal Year 1996

Released December 29

Transcripts of press briefings by Press Secretary Mike McCurry

Released December 31

Transcript of a press briefing by Press Secretary Mike McCurry

Appendix D—Presidential Documents Published in the Federal Register

This appendix lists Presidential documents released by the Office of the Press Secretary and published in the Federal Register. The texts of the documents are printed in the Federal Register (F.R.) at the citations listed below. The documents are also printed in title 3 of the Code of Federal Regulations and in the Weekly Compilation of Presidential Documents.

PROCLAMATIONS

PROCLAMATIONS—Continued

EXECUTIVE ORDERS

OTHER PRESIDENTIAL DOCUMENTS

OTHER PRESIDENTIAL DOCUMENTS—Continued

Subject Index

Name Index

Document Categories List